New Society

Sociology for the 21st Century

Fourth Edition

New Society
Sociology for the 21st Century

Robert J. Brym
University of Toronto

THOMSON
NELSON

Australia   Canada   Mexico   Singapore   Spain   United Kingdom   United States

THOMSON

NELSON

New Society: Sociology for the 21st Century
Fourth Edition
by Robert J. Brym

Editorial Director and Publisher:
Evelyn Veitch

Executive Editor:
Joanna Cotton

Acquisitions Editor:
Cara Yarzab

Marketing Manager:
Lenore Taylor

Developmental Editor:
Glen Herbert

Production Editor:
Carrie McGregor

Photo Researcher:
Cindy Howard

Permissions Coordinator:
Cindy Howard

Copy Editor:
Valerie Adams

Proofreader:
Valerie Adams

Indexer:
Belle Wong

Production Coordinator:
Hedy Sellers

Creative Director:
Angela Cluer

Interior Design:
Renata Chubb/Mighty Design Inc.

Interior Design Modifications:
Peter Papayanakis

Cover Design:
Andrew Adams

Cover Image:
© Bill Ross/CORBIS/MAGMA

Compositor:
Carol Magee

Printer:
Transcontinental Printing Inc.

National Library of Canada Cataloguing in Publication Data

Main entry under title:

Brym, Robert J., 1951–
  New society: sociology for the 21st century / Robert J. Brym.—4th ed.

Includes bibliographical references and index.
ISBN 0-17-622467-X

1. Sociology. I. Title.

HM51.B897 2004   301
C2003-903978-1

In memory of Jim Richardson, 1941–2003

PREFACE

The job of figuring out what to do with one's life and how to act in the world is more difficult than ever before. Sociology contributes to the task of clarification; sociologists are in the business of analyzing the pressing social issues of the day, showing how those issues affect all of us, and setting out options for dealing with them. Moreover, as you will learn in the following pages, sociology views social issues from a unique disciplinary perspective. All in all, it is a controversial and exciting business. Social problems are typically complex. The various options for action often involve different benefits and disadvantages for different groups. Sociologists usually see things differently from other social and natural scientists. Not surprisingly, therefore, sociology, like any vibrant academic discipline, involves a lot of heated debate.

Unfortunately, most introductory sociology textbooks don't give one much of a feel for the excitement of the discipline. They usually resemble encyclopedias full of definitions and presumably undeniable facts. They make sociological knowledge resemble the tablets some people say were brought down by Moses from Mount Sinai: abstract principles carved in stone, eternal truths that most people agree with but that tell us little about the way life is actually lived.

In preparing this book, I tried to overcome this deficiency in two ways. First, when I recruited authors to write chapters I asked them to focus on social issues that are likely to be of real, everyday concern to Canadian undergraduates at the beginning of the twenty-first century. Second, I asked the authors to highlight the controversies in the field, not the tired clichés. There is no sense in keeping secret what any good scientist knows: advances in knowledge usually result from intellectual conflict, not consensus.

WHAT'S NEW IN THE FOURTH EDITION

In preparing the fourth edition of *New Society*, I benefited from the recommendations that emerged from Nelson's excellent user survey. Major changes include the following:

- The fourth edition of *New Society* has been thoroughly updated to reflect the results of the latest Census of Canada and the most recent sociological research findings in the various fields covered in the text.
- Four chapters have undergone major revisions or have been replaced outright to better reflect the interests of users and the state of the discipline. These chapters include:
  - Culture (Chapter 3)
  - Socialization (Chapter 4)
  - Inequality among Nations (Chapter 11)
  - Education (Chapter 14)

  We welcome new authors Myrna Dawson, Ian Gomme, and Michael Rosenberg.
- All of the ancillaries (see below) have been thoroughly revised and a sixth volume has been added to the *Nelson Sociology Video Series*.

ORGANIZATION OF THE TEXT

Chapter 1 sets the tone for the rest of the book. Instead of sermonizing on the arid question "What Is Sociology?" as most other textbooks do, I ask "Why Sociology?"—that is, why does an undergraduate in this particular time and place need to know what sociology has to offer? My aim in Chapter 1 is not so much to trace intellectual pedigrees, outline theories, and introduce methods whose relevance to the life of the reader is still unclear. Instead, I focus on showing how sociological thinking can clarify and perhaps even help resolve the real-life social issues that confront all of us here and now. Enticement, not didacticism, is the task I set myself in Chapter 1.

Chapter 2 is a concise presentation of research methods. Neil Guppy's clarity, research experience, and balanced approach add much-needed lustre to a subject that first-year students often find dull and unrewarding. Guppy leaves the reader with the firm sense that, for all the intellectual liveliness and contro-versy displayed in this book, sociology can be and is disciplined by the judicious use of logic and evidence.

The remainder of the book is divided into four parts. Part II could be subtitled "Becoming Human." In Chapter 3, I make a case for the view that ours is an increasingly fragmented and globalized "postmodern" culture that increases our freedom to fashion our identities to suit our individual tastes. I also show that, paradoxically, our increased cultural freedom develops within definite limits beyond which it is more and more difficult to move. In Chapter 4, Jack Haas, William Shaffir, and Michael Rosenberg thoroughly discuss the mechanisms through which we learn beliefs, symbols, values, and self-identities throughout the life cycle and in various institutions, including, most recently, the Internet. Rhonda Lenton then devotes Chapter 5 to an in-depth analysis of what might seem to be the most intimate and biologically determined aspects of our identity—our gender and sexuality—and demonstrates that in fact they have deep roots in culture and society. There follows a comprehensive examination of two of the most important cultural institutions in our society. In Chapter 6, Graham Knight outlines and analyzes the impact of the pervasive and highly influential mass media. In Chapter 7, Reginald Bibby assesses the social origins, consequences, and future of religion, relying heavily on his own fundamentally important survey research to argue his case. In sum, the analyses of Part II will give the reader a solid appreciation of how we become part of society and how society becomes part of us through the transmission of culture from generation to generation.

Part III is about how people become and remain unequal. Harvey Krahn shows in Chapter 8 that, despite recent assertions of the demise of social classes, stratification persists and continues to structure our life-chances in profound ways. In Chapter 9, Monica Boyd convincingly demonstrates that gender is an equally important basis of social inequality, both in the economic and the political sphere. Vic Satzewich devotes Chapter 10 to highlighting the deficiencies of biological and purely cultural approaches to understanding the bases of ethnic and racial inequality. Finally, in Chapter 11, Gordon Laxer incisively criticizes modernization and other theories of economic underdevelopment and global inequality, offering a compelling argument for the analytical benefits of a modified dependency approach to the problem. The reader will complete Part III with a firm understanding that, although we are all human, we are highly differentiated and differently rewarded, depending on our social location.

Part IV shifts the reader's attention to some of society's fundamental institutions. A virtue of Bonnie Fox's analysis of families in Chapter 12 is that she usefully draws on a broad historical and anthropological literature to supplement her sociological overview, providing a clear sense of how families have developed and where they may be headed. Sandy Welsh devotes Chapter 13 to tracing the development and future shape of work, showing, among other things, that steady well-paying jobs may soon be as rare as traditional nuclear families. And in Chapter 14, Ian Gomme dissects our educational system, demonstrating that, paradoxically, it is as much a cause of the persistence of inequality as it is an avenue for upward mobility.

Change and conflict are the subjects of Part V. Here the reader is introduced to the main forces of turbulence in our society. John Hannigan's analysis of urbanization in Chapter 15 is a novel and revealing look at how cities have developed from preindustrial to industrial to postmodern forms. He then devotes Chapter 16 to one of the most pressing issues of the day—the environment—and analyzes such problems as the scope and social roots of the environmental movement and the process by which environmental issues are socially constructed. In Chapter 17, Roderic Beaujot clearly and carefully surveys the sociological study of population, emphasizing the immediacy and significance of such issues as the global population explosion, the aging of the Canadian population, and the attendant health issues. Globalization is the theme of Chapter 18, by Martin Albrow. Culturally, politically, and economically, Albrow shows, the world is becoming a single place and its inhabitants are developing a global consciousness. This does not imply that we are becoming one big happy family. To the contrary, conflict has persisted and even intensified at the end of the twentieth century, as the last two chapters of this section demonstrate. In Chapter 19, Rosemary Gartner and Myrna Dawson elegantly analyze one form of social conflict—deviant and criminal behaviour. They undermine several common misconceptions in the process. Finally, in Chapter 20, I survey the evolution of politics and social movements, showing how various forms of conflict emerge, change our lives, and become institutionalized.

ANCILLARIES

INSTRUCTOR'S MANUAL

This chapter-by-chapter outline helps instructors make the most of *New Society*. It summarizes each chapter in the form of lecture notes, describes how best to integrate each chapter with all of the ancillary products, and provides suggestions on how to create the most effective lectures possible.

STUDENT LEARNING GUIDE

This concise guide helps students to check their progress with sample quizzes. Critical-thinking questions encourage them to use their imaginations to develop a richer sociological perspective.

THINK OUTSIDE THE BOOK: NELSON VIDEOS FOR SOCIOLOGY

Be part of something exciting! Nelson is proud to present our Think Outside the Book: Nelson Video Series for Sociology. This five-volume series, which includes video segments each 5–27 minutes in length, was created to stimulate discussion in your classroom. Many selections are excerpted from national and international award-winning films.

Videos were selected by leading sociologist Robert Brym. His keen eye for finding relevant, powerful, and engaging selections allows students to "think outside the book" and brings sociology concepts to life. A video guide for instructors will include a synopsis of each video, questions for critical analysis, and references to Nelson's innovative and imaginative introductory sociology titles.

INSTRUCTOR'S RESOURCE CD

All testing and presentation software is now available in one place: the *New Society Instructor's Resource CD*. This resource contains both the computerized test bank and a full set of PowerPoint® slides:

Computerized Test Bank

The test bank contains approximately 1000 multiple-choice and true-or-false questions. The computerized format allows instructors to generate a wide variety of customized tests and to edit, delete, or add to the existing bank of test items.

PowerPoint® Slides

Over 400 full-colour slides offer a detailed summary of each chapter of the book along with supplementary graphs, tables, and diagrams to illustrate key points. The slides can be easily output from a computer in several formats. The PowerPoint® Viewer that is packaged with the slides enables them to be (1) viewed on a computer, or (2) projected from a computer to a viewing screen in the classroom. If you have the entire Microsoft PowerPoint® package, the slides can also be (3) printed out as full-colour transparencies for use with an overhead projector, or (4) printed out as black-and-white handouts for students.

NEW SOCIETY ON THE WEB

The *New Society* website contains much more than the standard features you have come to expect from Thomson Nelson Web ancillaries. In addition to chapter-by-chapter links to secondary sources, online quizzes and other self-testing material, it boasts exciting original features, including interactive exercises, online research projects, and a focus on Canada in a global context. Also, visit the online lecture hall to hear lectures delivered in audio by a range of prominent sociologists, including Robert Brym. These features, and others, make the *New Society* website unique and useful to Canadian instructors and students. It allows students to do sociology and better understand their place in the world.

ACKNOWLEDGEMENTS

The fourth edition of *New Society* stills bears the imprint of Heather McWhinney, Dan Brooks, Megan Mueller, and Semareh Al-Hillal of Harcourt Canada, Brad Lambertus, and Camille Isaacs, as well as Cary Heather of Media9 and Gary Marcuse and John Pungente of Face-to-Face Media. They shepherded the book and its ancillaries through its first two editions, helping to make *New Society* distinctive and highly successful.

For the past year I was privileged to work closely with publishing professionals of the highest calibre, all of whom contributed heavily to the successful completion of the fourth edition. In particular, Brad Lambertus and Cara Yarzab worked diligently and with good humour on this complex project, always mindful of the need to balance the diverse needs of instructors, students, and authors. Glen Herbert's energetic and meticulous approach to the project was evident from beginning to end. Visually and linguistically, this book owes much to his exemplary skills as a developmental editor. I would also like to thank Carrie McGregor (production editor) and Valerie Adams (copy editor and proofreader).

But, of course, *New Society* could not become what it is without the authors of the following chapters. They include some of the very best sociologists in Canada. I believe that while concentrating on the exposition of their own subfields they have conveyed to the novice a real sense of the excitement and promise of sociology. I am deeply indebted to them, as tens of thousands of introductory sociology students and their instructors inevitably have been and will be.

I would also like to thank the reviewers whose comments helped shape this edition: Victor Ujimoto, University of Guelph; Graham Johnson, University of British Columbia; Geriant B. Osborne, Augustana University College; Constance de Roche, University College of Cape Breton; Jon Young, University of Manitoba; Lloyd Wong, University of Calgary; Donald S. Swenson, Mount Royal College; Peter Maidstone, Camosun College; Michelle Webber, Brock University.

R.J.B.
Toronto

CONTRIBUTORS

MARTIN ALBROW, UNIVERSITY OF SURREY ROEHAMPTON

RODERIC BEAUJOT, UNIVERSITY OF WESTERN ONTARIO

REGINALD W. BIBBY, UNIVERSITY OF LETHBRIDGE

MONICA BOYD, UNIVERSITY OF TORONTO

ROBERT J. BRYM, UNIVERSITY OF TORONTO

MYRNA DAWSON, UNIVERSITY OF GUELPH

BONNIE FOX, UNIVERSITY OF TORONTO

ROSEMARY GARTNER, UNIVERSITY OF TORONTO

IAN M. GOMME, UNIVERSITY OF SOUTHERN COLORADO, PUEBLO

NEIL GUPPY, UNIVERSITY OF BRITISH COLUMBIA

JACK HAAS, MCMASTER UNIVERSITY

JOHN HANNIGAN, UNIVERSITY OF TORONTO

GRAHAM KNIGHT, MCMASTER UNIVERSITY

HARVEY KRAHN, UNIVERSITY OF ALBERTA

GORDON LAXER, UNIVERSITY OF ALBERTA

RHONDA L. LENTON, YORK UNIVERSITY

MICHAEL ROSENBERG, DAWSON COLLEGE

VIC SATZEWICH, MCMASTER UNIVERSITY

WILLIAM SHAFFIR, MCMASTER UNIVERSITY

SANDY WELSH, UNIVERSITY OF TORONTO

BRIEF CONTENTS

CONTENTS

PART THREE INEQUALITY

INTRODUCTION

PART ONE

CHAPTER ONE

INTRODUCING SOCIOLOGY

In this chapter you will learn that:

- The causes of human behaviour lie partly in the patterns of social relations that surround and penetrate people.

- Sociologists examine the connection between personal troubles and social relations.

- Sociological research is often motivated by the desire to improve the social world. At the same time, sociologists adopt scientific methods to test their ideas.

- Sociology originated at the time of the Industrial Revolution. The founders of sociology diagnosed the massive social transformations of their day. They also suggested ways of overcoming the social problems created by the Industrial Revolution.

- Today's Postindustrial Revolution similarly challenges us. The chief value of sociology is that it can help clarify the scope, direction, and significance of social change. Sociology can also suggest ways of managing change.

ROBERT J. BRYM

UNIVERSITY OF TORONTO

INTRODUCTION

WHY I DECIDED *NOT* TO STUDY SOCIOLOGY

When I started university at the age of 18, I was bewildered by the wide variety of courses I could choose from. Having now taught sociology for more than 20 years, and met a few thousand undergraduates, I am quite sure most students today feel as I did then.

One source of confusion for me was uncertainty about why I was in college in the first place. Like you, I knew higher education could improve one's chance of finding good work. But, like most students, I also had a sense that higher education is supposed to provide something more than just the training necessary to embark on a career that is interesting and pays well. Several high school teachers and guidance counsellors had told me that college was also supposed to "broaden my horizons" and teach me to "think critically." I wasn't sure what they meant, but they made it sound interesting enough to make me want to know more. Thus, I decided in my first year to take mainly "practical" courses that might prepare me for a law degree (economics, political science, and psychology). I also enrolled in a couple of other courses to indulge my "intellectual" side (philosophy, drama). One thing I knew for sure. I didn't want to study sociology.

Sociology, I came to believe, was thin soup with uncertain ingredients. When I asked a second-year student what sociology is, he told me it deals mainly with why people are unequal—why some are rich and others poor, some powerful and others weak. Coming as I did from a poor immigrant family in the Maritimes, an economically depressed region, it appeared that sociology could teach me something about my own life. But it also seemed a lot like what I imagined economics and political science to be about. What, then, was unique about sociology? My growing sense that sociology had nothing special to offer was confirmed when another second-year student told me that sociologists try to describe the ideal society and figure out how to make the world a better place. That description appealed to my youthful sense of the world's injustice. However, it also sounded a lot like philosophy. A third-year student explained that sociology analyzes how and why people assume different roles in their lives. She made sociology appear similar to drama. Finally, one student reported that in her sociology class she was learning why people commit suicide, homicide, and other deviant acts. That seemed like abnormal psychology to me. I concluded that sociology had no distinct flavour all its own. Accordingly, I decided to forego it for tastier courses.

A CHANGE OF MIND

Despite the opinion I'd formed, I found myself taking no fewer than four sociology courses a year after starting university. That revolution in my life was due in part to the pull of an extraordinary professor I happened to meet just before I began my second year. He set me thinking in an altogether new way about what I could and should do with my life. He exploded some of my deepest beliefs. He started me thinking sociologically.

Specifically, he first put Yorick's dilemma to me. Yorick is a character—sort of—in *Hamlet*. Toward the end of the play, Hamlet finds two gravediggers at work. They unearth the remains of the former court jester, Yorick, who used to amuse Hamlet and carry him around on his back when Hamlet was a child. Holding high his old friend's skull, Hamlet reflects on what we must all come to. Even the remains of Alexander the Great, he says, turn to dust.

This incident implies Yorick's dilemma and, indeed, the dilemma of all thinking people. Life is finite. If we wish to make the most of it we must figure out how best to live. That is no easy task. It requires study, reflection, and the selection of values and goals. Ideally, higher education is supposed to supply students with just that opportunity. Finally, I was beginning to understand what I could expect from college apart from job training.

The professor I met also convinced me that sociology in particular could open up a new and superior way of comprehending my world. Specifically, he said, it could clarify my place in society, how I might best manoeuvre through it, and perhaps even how I might contribute to improving it, however modestly. Before beginning my study of sociology, I had always taken for granted that things happen in the world—and to me—because physical and emotional forces cause them. Famine, I thought, is caused by drought, war by territorial greed, economic success by hard work, marriage by love, suicide by bottomless depression, rape by depraved lust. But now, this professor repeatedly threw evidence in my face that contradicted my easy formulas. If drought causes famine, why have so many famines occurred in perfectly normal weather conditions or involved some groups hoarding or destroying food so others would starve? If hard work causes prosperity, why are so many hard workers poor? If love causes marriage, why are so many families sites of violence against women and children? And so the questions multiplied.

As if it were not enough that the professor's sociological evidence upset many of my assumptions about the way the world worked, he also challenged me to understand sociology's unique way of explaining social life. He defined **sociology** as the systematic study of human behaviour in social context. He explained that *social* causes are distinct from physical and emotional causes. Understanding social causes can help clarify otherwise inexplicable features of famine, marriage, and so forth. In public school, my teachers taught me that people are free to do what they want with their lives. However, my new professor taught me that the organization of the social world opens some opportunities and closes others, thus constraining our freedom and helping to make us what we are. By examining the operation of these powerful social forces, he said, sociology can help us to know ourselves, our capabilities and limitations. I was hooked. And so, of course, I hope you will be too.

Life is finite, and if we wish to make the most of it we must figure out how best to live. Sociology offers a useful perspective for understanding our current predicament and seeing possible ways of dealing with it.

SOURCE: M.C. Escher's "Relativity" © 2000 Cordon Art B.V.—Baarn—Holland. All rights reserved.

THE GOALS OF THIS CHAPTER

In this chapter I aim to achieve three goals:

1. I first illustrate the power of sociology to dispel foggy assumptions and help us see the operation of the social world more clearly. To that end, I examine a phenomenon that at first glance appears to be solely the outcome of breakdowns in individual functioning: suicide. You will see that, in fact, *social relations* among people powerfully influence suicide rates. This exercise introduces you to what is unique about the sociological perspective.

2. I show that, from its origins, sociological research has been motivated by a desire to improve the social world. Thus, sociology is not just a dry, academic exercise but a means of charting a better course for society. At the same time, however, sociologists adopt scientific methods to test their ideas, thus increasing their validity. I illustrate these points by briefly analyzing the work of the founders of the discipline.

3. I suggest that sociology can help you come to grips with your century, just as it helped the founders of sociology deal with theirs. Today we are witnessing massive and disorienting social changes. Entire countries are breaking up. Women are demanding equality with men in all spheres of life. New religions are emerging and old ones reviving. People's wants are increasingly governed by the mass media. Computers are radically altering the way people work and entertain themselves. There are proportionately fewer good jobs to go around. Environmental ruin threatens us all. As was the case a hundred years ago, sociologists today try to understand social phenomena and suggest credible ways of improving their societies. By promising to make sociology relevant to you, this chapter should be viewed as an open invitation to participate in sociology's challenge.

But first things first. Before showing how sociology may be able to help us comprehend and better our world, let us briefly examine the problem of suicide. That will help to illustrate how the sociological perspective can clarify and sometimes overturn commonsense beliefs.

THE SOCIOLOGICAL PERSPECTIVE

By analyzing suicide sociologically, you can put to a tough test the claim that sociology takes a unique, surprising, and enlightening perspective on social events. After all, suicide appears to be the supremely antisocial and nonsocial act. It is condemned by nearly everyone in society. It is typically committed in private, far from the public's intrusive glare. It is rare. In 1997, there were 12.3 suicides for every 100 000 Canadians (Statistics Canada, 1999: 122, 168). And when you think about why people commit such acts, you are likely to focus on their individual states of mind rather than on the state of society. In other words, what usually interests us are the aspects of specific individuals' lives that caused them to become depressed or angry enough to do something as awful as killing themselves. We usually do not think about the patterns of social relations that might encourage such actions in general. If sociology can reveal the hidden social causes of such an apparently antisocial and nonsocial phenomenon, there must be something to it!

THE SOCIOLOGICAL EXPLANATION OF SUICIDE

At the end of the nineteenth century, French sociologist Émile Durkheim (1951 [1897]), one of the pioneers of the discipline, demonstrated that suicide is more than just an individual act of desperation resulting from psychological disorder, as was commonly believed at the time. Suicide rates, he showed, are strongly influenced by social forces.

Durkheim made his case by examining the association between rates of suicide and rates of psychological disorder for different groups. The idea that psychological disorder causes suicide is supported, he reasoned, only if suicide rates tend to be high where rates of psychological disorder are high, and low where rates of psychological disorder are low. But his analysis of European government statistics, hospital records, and other sources revealed nothing of the kind. He discovered there were slightly more women than men in insane asylums. Yet there were four male suicides for every female suicide. Jews had the highest rate of psychological disorder among the major religious groups in France. However, they also had the lowest suicide rate. Psychological disorders occurred most frequently when a person reached maturity. Suicide rates, though, increased steadily with age.

Clearly, suicide rates and rates of psychological disorder did not vary directly. What then accounts for variations in suicide rates? Durkheim argued that suicide rates vary due to differences in the degree of **social solidarity** in different groups. According to Durkheim, the more a group's members share beliefs and values, and the more frequently and intensely they interact, the more social solidarity there is in the group. In turn, the more social solidarity there is in a group, the more firmly anchored individuals are to the social world, and the less likely they are to take their own life if adversity strikes. In other words, Durkheim expected groups with a high degree of solidarity to have lower suicide rates than groups with a low degree of solidarity—at least up to a certain point (see Figure 1.1).

To support his argument, Durkheim showed that married adults are half as likely as unmarried adults are to commit suicide. That is because marriage usually creates social ties and a sort of moral cement that bind the individual to society. Similarly, he argued that women are less likely to commit suicide than men are. Why? Women are generally more involved in the intimate social relations of family life. Jews, Durkheim wrote, are less likely to commit suicide than Christians are. The reason? Centuries of persecution have turned them into a group that is more defensive and tightly knit. And the elderly are more prone than the young and the middle-aged to take their own lives in the face of misfortune. That is because they are most likely to live alone, to have lost a spouse, and to lack a job and a wide network of friends. In general, Durkheim wrote, "suicide varies with the degree of integration of the social groups of which the individual forms a part" (Durkheim, 1951 [1897]: 209). Note that his generalization tells us nothing about why any particular individual may take his or her life. That is a question for psychology. But it does tell us that a person's likelihood of committing suicide decreases with the degree to which he or she is anchored in society. And it says something surprising and uniquely sociological about how and why the suicide rate varies from group to group.

SUICIDE IN CANADA TODAY

Durkheim's theory is not just an historical curiosity. It sheds light on the factors that account for variations in suicide rates here and now. Consider Figure 1.2, which shows suicide rates by age and sex in Canada. Comparing rates for men and women, we immediately see that, as in Durkheim's France, men are about four times more likely than women to commit suicide. However, looking at differences between age groups, we see a striking difference between Durkheim's France and contemporary Canada. When Durkheim wrote, youth suicide was extremely rare. In Canada today, it is much more common, having increased substantially since the 1960s. That is why suicide rates do *not* increase steadily with age in Canada today. They increase to comparatively high levels only among people above the age of 79.

Although the rate of youth suicide was low in Durkheim's France, his theory of social solidarity helps us to understand why it has risen so quickly in Canada. In brief, shared moral principles and strong social ties have eroded since the early 1960s, especially for Canada's youth. Consider the following facts:

- Church, synagogue, mosque, and temple attendance is down, particularly for young people.

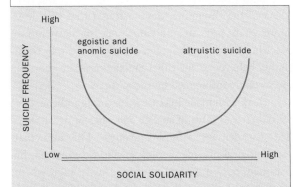

FIGURE 1.1 DURKHEIM'S THEORY OF SUICIDE

Note: Durkheim argued that the suicide rate declines and then rises as social solidarity increases. Durkheim called suicide in high-solidarity settings altruistic. **Altruistic suicide** occurs when norms tightly govern behaviour. Soldiers knowingly giving up their lives to protect comrades commit altruistic suicide. Suicide in low-solidarity settings is egoistic or anomic. **Egoistic suicide** results from poor integration of people into society because of weak social ties to others. Someone who is unemployed is more likely to commit suicide than someone who is employed, because of their weaker social ties. **Anomic suicide** occurs when vague norms govern behaviour. The rate of anomic suicide is likely to be high among people living in a society lacking a widely shared code of morality.

FIGURE 1.2 SUICIDE BY AGE AND SEX, CANADA, 1997   ■ MEN ■ WOMEN

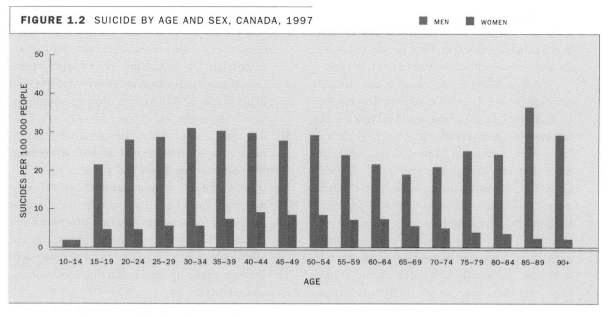

SOURCE: Calculated from Statistics Canada (1999: 122, 123, 168)

Thus, well over half of Canadians attended religious services weekly in the 1960s. Today the figure is below one-third, and it is only 15 percent for people born after 1960.

- Unemployment is up, again especially for youth. Thus, the unemployment rate was in the 3 percent range for most of the 1960s. It rose steadily to the 10 percent range for most of the 1990s and stood at 7.5 percent in mid-2002. Moreover, the unemployment rate is more than twice as high for Canadians under the age of 20 as it is for older Canadians.

- The rate of divorce has increased sixfold since the early 1960s. Out-of-wedlock births are also much more common than they used to be. As a result, children are more often brought up in single-parent families than in the past. This suggests that they enjoy less frequent and intimate social interaction with parents and less adult supervision.

In sum, the figures cited above suggest that the level of social solidarity is now lower than it was just a few decades ago, especially for young people. Less firmly rooted in society, and less likely to share moral standards, young people in Canada today are more likely than they were 40 years ago to take their own lives if they happen to find themselves in the midst of a personal crisis.

FROM PERSONAL TROUBLES TO SOCIAL STRUCTURES

You have known for a long time that you live in a society. Yet until now, you may not have fully appreciated that society also lives in you. That is, patterns of social relations affect your innermost thoughts and feelings, influence your actions, and thus help shape who you are. As we have seen, one such pattern of social relations is the level of social solidarity characteristic of the various groups to which you belong.

Sociologists call relatively stable patterns of social relations **social structures**. One of the sociologist's main tasks is to identify and explain the connection between people's personal troubles and the social structures in which people are embedded. This is harder work than it may at first seem. In everyday life, we usually see things mainly from our own point of view. Our experiences appear unique to each of us. If we think about them at all, social structures may appear remote and impersonal. To see how social structures operate inside us, we require sociological training.

An important step in broadening one's sociological awareness involves recognizing that three levels of social structure surround and penetrate us. Think of these structures as concentric circles radiating out from you:

1. **Microstructures** are patterns of intimate social relations. They are formed during face-to-face interaction. Families, friendship circles, and work associations are all examples of microstructures.

   Understanding the operation of microstructures can be useful. Let us say you are looking for a job. You might think you would do best to ask as many close friends and relatives as possible for leads and contacts. However, sociological research shows that people you know well are likely to know many of the same people. After asking a couple of close connections for help landing a job, you would therefore do best to ask more remote acquaintances for leads and contacts. People to whom you are weakly connected (and who are weakly connected among themselves) are more likely to know different groups of people. Therefore, they will give you more information about job possibilities and ensure that word about your job search spreads farther. You are more likely to find a job faster if you understand "the strength of weak ties" in microstructural settings (Granovetter, 1973).

2. **Macrostructures** are patterns of social relations that lie outside and above your circle of intimates and acquaintances. Macrostructures include class relations, bureaucracies, and **patriarchy**, the traditional system of economic and political inequality between women and men in most societies.

   Understanding the operation of macrostructures can also be useful. Consider, for example, one aspect of patriarchy. Most married women who work full-time in the paid labour force do more housework, child-care, and care for the elderly than their husbands. Governments and businesses support this arrangement insofar as they give little assistance to families in the form of nurseries, after-school programs for children, senior homes, and so forth. Yet the unequal division of work in the household is a major source of dissatisfaction with marriage, especially in families that cannot afford to buy these services privately. Thus, sociological research shows that where spouses share domestic responsibilities equally, they are happier with their marriages and less likely to divorce (Hochschild with Machung, 1989). When a marriage is in danger of dissolving, it is common for partners to blame

themselves and each other for their troubles. However, it should now be clear that forces other than incompatible personalities often put stresses on families. Understanding how the macrostructure of patriarchy crops up in everyday life, and doing something to change that structure, can thus help people lead happier lives.

3. The third level of society that surrounds and permeates us is composed of **global structures.** International organizations, patterns of worldwide travel and communication, and the economic relations between countries are examples of global structures. Global structures are increasingly important as inexpensive travel and communication allow all parts of the world to become interconnected culturally, economically, and politically.

   Understanding the operation of global structures can be useful too. For instance, many people are concerned about the world's poor. They donate money to charities to help with famine relief. Some people also approve of the Canadian government giving foreign aid to poor countries. However, many of these same people do not appreciate that charity and foreign aid alone do not seem able to end world poverty. That is because charity and foreign aid have been unable to overcome the structure of social relations between countries that have created and sustain global inequality.

   Let us linger on this point for a moment. As we will see in Chapter 11 ("Inequality among Nations"), Britain, France, and other imperial powers locked some countries into poverty when they colonized them between the seventeenth and nineteenth centuries. In the twentieth century, the poor (or "developing") countries borrowed money from these same rich countries and Western banks to pay for airports, roads, harbours, sanitation systems, basic health care, and so forth. Today, poor countries pay far more to rich countries and Western banks in interest on those loans than they receive in aid and charity (see Figure 1.3). Thus, it seems that relying exclusively on foreign aid and charity can do little to help solve the problem of world poverty. Understanding how the global structure of international relations created and helps maintain global inequality suggests new policy priorities for helping the world's poor. One such priority might involve campaigning for the cancellation of foreign debt in compensation for past injustices, a cause that former Liberal finance minister Paul Martin has championed.

As these examples illustrate, personal problems are connected to social structures at the micro, macro, and global levels. Whether the personal problem involves finding a job, keeping a marriage intact, or figuring out a way to act justly to end world poverty, social-structural considerations broaden our understanding of the problem and suggest appropriate courses of action.

THE SOCIOLOGICAL IMAGINATION

Half a century ago, the great American sociologist C. Wright Mills (1959) called the ability to see the connection between personal troubles and social structures the **sociological imagination**. He emphasized the difficulty of developing this quality of mind. His language is sexist by today's standards, but his argument is as true and inspiring today as it was in the 1950s:

> When a society becomes industrialized, a peasant becomes a worker; a feudal lord is liquidated or becomes a businessman. When classes rise or fall, a man is employed or unemployed; when the rate of investment goes up or down, a man takes new heart or

goes broke. When war happens, an insurance salesman becomes a rocket launcher; a store clerk, a radar man; a wife lives alone; a child grows up without a father. Neither the life of an individual nor the history of a society can be understood without understanding both.

> Yet men do not usually define the troubles they endure in terms of historical change.... The well-being they enjoy, they do not usually impute to the big ups and downs of the society in which they live. Seldom aware of the intricate connection between the patterns of their own lives and the course of world history, ordinary men do not usually know what this connection means for the kind of men they are becoming and for the kind of history-making in which they might take part. They do not possess the quality of mind essential to grasp the interplay of men and society, of biography and history, of self and world. They cannot cope with their personal troubles in such a way as to control the structural transformations that usually lie behind them.

> What they need ... is a quality of mind that will help them to [see] ... what is going on in the world and ... what may be happening within themselves. It is this quality ... that ... may be called the sociological imagination (Mills, 1959: 3–4).

The sociological imagination is a recent addition to the human repertoire. It is only about 225 years old. True, in ancient and medieval times, some philosophers wrote about society. However, their thinking was not sociological. They believed God and nature controlled society. They spent much of their time sketching blueprints for the ideal society and urging people to follow those blueprints. And they relied on speculation rather than evidence to reach conclusions about how society works.

The sociological imagination was born when three modern revolutions pushed people to think about society in an entirely new way. First, the **Scientific Revolution** began about 1550. It encouraged the view that sound conclusions about the workings of society must be based on solid evidence, not just speculation.

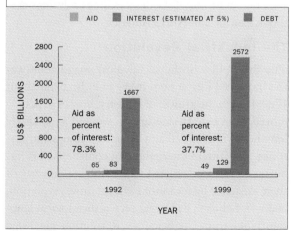

FIGURE 1.3 FOREIGN AID, DEBT, AND INTEREST PAYMENTS OF DEVELOPING COUNTRIES, 1992 AND 1999 (IN US$ BILLIONS)

SOURCES: World Bank (1999a, 1999b, 2001a, 2001b).

Second, the **Democratic Revolution** began about 1750. It suggested that people are responsible for organizing society and that human intervention can therefore solve social problems. Third, the **Industrial Revolution** began about 1780. It created a host of new and serious social problems that attracted the attention of many social thinkers. Let us briefly consider these three sources of the sociological imagination.

ORIGINS OF THE SOCIOLOGICAL IMAGINATION

The Scientific Revolution

It is said that a group of medieval monks once wanted to know how many angels could dance on the head of a pin. They consulted ancient books in Hebrew, Greek, and Latin. They thought long and hard. They employed all their debating skills to argue the issue. They did not, however, resolve the dispute. That is because they never considered inspecting the head of a pin and counting. Any such suggestion would have been considered heresy. We, in contrast, would call it the beginning of a scientific approach to the subject.

People often link the Scientific Revolution to specific ideas, such as Copernicus's theory that the earth revolves around the sun and Newton's laws of motion. However, science is less a collection of ideas than a method of inquiry. For instance, in 1609, Galileo pointed his newly invented telescope at the heavens, made some careful observations, and showed that his observations fit Copernicus's theory. This is the core of the scientific method: using evidence to make a case for a particular point of view. By the mid-1600s, some philosophers, such as Descartes in France and Hobbes in England, were calling for a science of society. When sociology emerged as a distinct discipline in the nineteenth century, commitment to the scientific method was one firm pillar of the sociological imagination.

The Democratic Revolution

The second pillar of the sociological imagination is the realization that people control society and can change it. Four hundred years ago, most Europeans thought otherwise. For them, God ordained the social order.

Consider the English engraving reproduced in Figure 1.4. It shows how most educated Europeans pictured the universe in Shakespeare's time. Note the cloud at the top of the circle. The Hebrew name of God is inscribed on it. God's hand extends from the cloud. It holds a chain, which is attached to a woman representing Nature. Nature also holds a chain in her hand. It is connected to "the ape of Nature," representing humankind. The symbolism is clear: God and his intermediary, Nature, control human action. Note also that the engraving arranges everything in a linked hierarchy. The hierarchy includes the mineral, vegetable, and animal kingdoms, the elements, heavenly objects, angels, and so forth. Each level of the hierarchy corresponds to and controls some aspect of the level below it. For example, people believed Archangels regulate the movements of the planet Mercury and the movements of Mercury affect human commerce. Similarly, in the medieval view, God ordained a hierarchy of people. The richest people were seen as the closest to God and therefore deserving great privilege. Supposedly, kings and queens ruled because God wanted them to (Tillyard, 1943).

The American Revolution (1775–83) and the French Revolution (1789–99) helped to undermine these ideas. These democratic political upheavals showed that society could experience massive change in a short period. They proved that people could replace unsatisfactory rulers. And they suggested that *people* control society. The implications for social thought were profound. For if it were possible to change society by human intervention, then a science of society could play a big role. The new science could help people figure out ways of overcoming various social problems, improving the welfare of all citizens, and finding the most effective way to reach given goals. Much of the justification for sociology as a science arose out of the democratic revolutions that shook Europe and North America.

The Industrial Revolution

The third pillar of the sociological imagination was the Industrial Revolution. It began in England about 1780. Due to the growth of industry, masses of people moved from countryside to city, worked agonizingly long hours in crowded and dangerous mines and factories, lost faith in their religions, confronted faceless bureaucracies, and reacted to the filth and poverty of their existence by means of strikes, crime, revolution, and war. Scholars had never seen a sociological laboratory like this. The Scientific Revolution suggested that a science of society is possible. The Democratic Revolution suggested that people *can* intervene to improve society. The Industrial Revolution now pre-

FIGURE 1.4 THE ELIZABETHAN WORLDVIEW

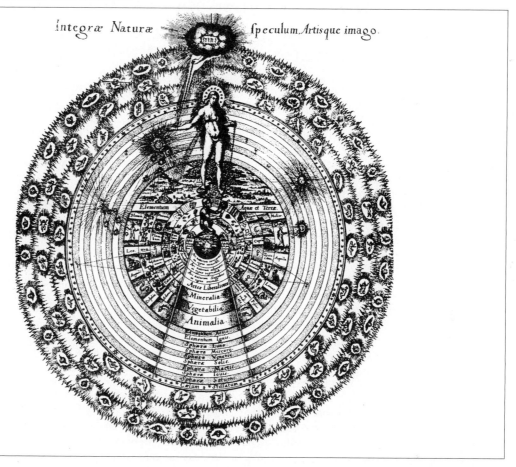

SOURCE: From Robert Fludd's *Utriusque Cosmi Historia* (1617–19). Reprinted with permission of the Harvard College Library.

sented social thinkers with a host of pressing social problems crying out for solutions. They responded by giving birth to the sociological imagination.

SOCIOLOGICAL THEORIES

THE ORIGINS OF SOCIOLOGY

The term *sociology* was coined by the French social thinker Auguste Comte in 1838 (Comte, 1975). Comte tried to place the study of society on scientific foundations. He wanted to understand the social world as it is, not as he or anyone else imagined it should be. This was a highly original approach to the study of society. In ancient and medieval times, philosophers from diverse civilizations had sketched blueprints for the ideal society. We see evidence of this in the work of Confucius in China, Ibn Khaldun in Tunisia, and Plato and Aristotle in Greece, to name

only a few of the best-known figures. But Comte was swept up in the scientific revolution of his time. He was inspired by the astronomers and physicists of the modern era—Copernicus in Poland, Galileo in Italy, Newton in England. He wanted to test the validity of his ideas through careful observation of the real world rather than assuming that "God" or "human nature" determined the shape of society (see Box 1.1).

Yet, despite Comte's breakthrough, there was a tension in his work. For although he was eager to adopt the scientific method in his study of society, he was a conservative thinker, motivated by strong opposition to rapid change in French society. His was a time not only of scientific but also of political and social revolution. Comte witnessed the democratic forces unleashed by the French Revolution, the early industrialization of society, and the rapid growth of cities. And what he saw shocked and angered him because rapid social change was destroying many of

BOX 1.1   SCIENTIFIC VERSUS COMMONSENSE KNOWLEDGE

To better understand how scientific knowledge differs from the nonscientific variety, consider the following statements, each of which represents a commonly accepted basis for knowing that something is "true" in our everyday lives:

1. *"The proper place for women is in the home. That's the way it's always been."* This statement represents knowledge based on *tradition*. While some traditional knowledge is valid (sugar will rot your teeth), some is not (masturbation will not blind you). Science is required to sort out valid from invalid knowledge.

2. *"Apparently, weak magnets can be used to heal many illnesses. I read all about it in the newspaper."* This statement represents knowledge based on *authority*. We often think something is true because we read it in an authoritative source or hear it from an expert. But authoritative sources and experts can be wrong. For example, nineteenth-century Western physicians commonly "bled" their patients with leeches to draw "poisons" from their bodies, often doing more harm than good. As this example suggests, scientists should always question authority in order to arrive at more valid knowledge.

3. *"The car that caused the accident was definitely dark brown. I was driving my bike last night when I saw the car accident."* This statement represents knowledge based on *casual observation*. However, we are usually pretty careless observers. That is why good lawyers can often trip up eyewitnesses in courtrooms; eyewitnesses are rarely certain about what they saw. In general, uncertainty can be reduced by observing in a conscious and deliberate manner and by recording observations. That is just what scientists do.

4. *"If you work hard, you can get ahead. I know because several of my parents' friends started off poor but are now comfortably middle class."* This statement represents knowledge based on *overgeneralization*. For instance, if you know a few people who started off poor, worked hard, and became rich, you may think any poor person may become rich if he or she works hard enough. You may not know about the more numerous poor people who work hard and remain poor. Scientists, however, sample cases that are representative of entire populations. This enables them to avoid overgeneralization. They also avoid overgeneralization by repeating research. This ensures that research findings are not idiosyncratic.

5. *"I'm right because I can't think of any contrary cases."* This statement represents knowledge based on *selective observation*. Sometimes we ignore evidence that challenges our firmly held beliefs. Thus, you may know people who work hard but remain poor. In order to maintain your belief that hard work results in wealth, you will have to ignore those cases. The scientific requirement that evidence be drawn from representative samples of the population minimizes bias arising from selective observation.

6. *"Mr. Smith is poor even though he works hard but that's because he's disabled. Disabled people are the only exception to the rule that if you work hard you can get ahead."* This statement represents knowledge based on *qualification*. Qualifications or "exceptions to the rule" are often made in everyday life—and they are in science too. The difference is that in everyday life qualifications are easily accepted as valid, whereas in scientific inquiry, they are typically treated as hypotheses that must be tested as rigorously as the original hypothesis.

7. *"The Toronto Blue Jays won half their baseball games last month but 80 percent of the games they played on Thursdays. Because it happened so often before, I bet they'll win next Thursday."* This statement represents knowledge based on *illogical reasoning*. In everyday life, we may expect the recurrence of events without reasonable cause, ignoring the fact that rare sequences of events often occur just by chance. For example, it is possible to flip a coin ten times and have it come up heads each time. On average, this will happen once every 1024 times you flip a coin ten times. In the absence of any apparent reason for this happening, it is merely coincidental. It is illogical to believe otherwise. Scientists refrain from such illogical reasoning. They also use statistical techniques to distinguish between events that are probably due to chance and those that are not.

8. *"I just can't be wrong."* This statement represents knowledge based on *ego-defence*. Even scientists may be passionately committed to the conclusions they reach in their research because they have invested much time and energy in them. It is other scientists—more accurately, the whole institution of science, with its commitment to publishing research results and critically scrutinizing findings—that puts strict limits on ego-defence in scientific understanding.

BOX 1.1 (continued)

9. *"The matter is settled once and for all."* This statement represents knowledge based on the *premature closure of inquiry.* This involves deciding all the relevant evidence has been gathered on a particular subject. Science, however, is committed to the idea that all theories are only temporarily true. Matters are never settled.
10. *"There must be supernatural forces at work here."* This statement represents knowledge based on *mystification.* When we can find no rational explanation for a phenomenon, we may attribute the phenomenon to forces that cannot be observed or fully understood. Although such forces may exist, scientists remain skeptical. They are committed to discovering real, observable causes of real, observable effects.

SOURCE: Based on Earl Babbie, *The Practice of Social Research,* 6th ed. (Belmont, CA: Wadsworth, 1992), pp. 19–27. Reprinted with permission of Wadsworth, a division of Thomson Learning: www.thomsonrights.com. Fax 800-730-2215.

the things he valued, especially respect for authority. He therefore urged slow change and the preservation of much that was traditional in social life. Thus, at its very origin, sociological research was motivated by adherence to scientific methods of research *and* a vision of the ideal society.

The same sort of tension is evident in the work of the most important early figures in the history of sociology, Karl Marx, Émile Durkheim, and Max Weber. These three men lived in the period 1820–1920. They witnessed various phases of Europe's wrenching transition to industrial capitalism. They wanted to understand why people were moving from countryside to city, working agonizingly long hours in crowded and dangerous factories, losing faith in their religions, confronting faceless bureaucracies, and reacting to the conditions of their existence by means of strikes, crime, revolution, and war. Like Comte, they were all committed to the scientific method of research. However, they also wanted to chart a better course for their societies. The ideas they developed are therefore not just diagnostic tools from which we can still learn much, but also, like many sociological ideas, prescriptions for combating social ills.

THEORY, RESEARCH, AND VALUES

To clarify the tension in sociology between analysis and ideal, diagnosis and prescription, we can usefully distinguish three terms: theory, research, and values.

Sociological ideas are generally stated in the form of theories. A **theory** is a tentative explanation of some

Before delving into social research, one must first develop hypotheses—testable claims about the social world. Testing hypotheses by means of research helps determine the validity of theories.
SOURCE: Dick Hemingway.

aspect of social life that states how and why certain facts are related. For example, in his theory of suicide, Durkheim showed how facts about suicide rates are related to facts about social solidarity. This enabled him to explain suicide as a function of social solidarity. In this broad definition, even a hunch qualifies as a theory if it suggests how and why certain facts are related.

After theories are formulated, the sociologist can conduct research. **Research** is the process of carefully observing social reality to assess the validity of a theory. It is because research can call the validity of a theory into question that theories are said to be only "tentative" explanations. The research process is discussed in detail in Chapter 2 ("Research Methods").

Before sociologists can formulate a theory, however, they must decide which problems are important enough to study and how the parts of society fit together. If they are going to recommend ways of improving the operation of some aspect of society, they must even have an opinion about what the ideal society ought to look like. As we will soon see, these issues are shaped in large measure by sociologists' values. **Values** are ideas about what is right and wrong. Inevitably, values help sociologists formulate and favour certain theories over others (Edel, 1965; Kuhn, 1970 [1962]). So sociological theories may be modified and even rejected due to research, but they are often motivated by sociologists' values.

Durkheim, Marx, and Weber initiated three of the major paradigms in sociology: the functionalist, conflict, and symbolic interactionist paradigms. A fourth paradigm, feminism, has arisen in recent decades to correct some of the deficiencies of the three long-established traditions. It will become clear as you read this book that there are more sociological theories than just these four. However, because these four traditions have been especially influential in the development of sociology, you will find it useful to read a thumbnail sketch of each one here at the beginning.[1]

FUNCTIONALISM

Durkheim's theory of suicide is an early example of what sociologists now call **functionalism**. Functionalist theories incorporate four features:

1. They stress that human behaviour is governed by relatively stable patterns of social relations, or social structures. For example, Durkheim

emphasized how suicide rates are influenced by patterns of social solidarity. Usually the social structures analyzed by functionalists are macrostructures.

2. Functionalism underlines how social structures maintain or undermine social stability. Typically, Durkheim analyzed how the growth of industries and cities in nineteenth-century Europe lowered the level of social solidarity and contributed to social instability. One aspect of instability, said Durkheim, is a higher suicide rate. Another is frequent strikes by workers.

3. Functionalist theories emphasize that social structures are based mainly on shared values. Thus, when Durkheim wrote about social solidarity he sometimes meant the frequency and intensity of social interaction, but more often he thought of social solidarity as a kind of moral cement that binds people together.

4. Functionalism suggests that re-establishing equilibrium can best solve most social problems. Thus, Durkheim said social stability could be restored in late-nineteenth-century Europe by creating new associations of employers and workers that would lower workers' expectations about what they could expect out of life. If, said Durkheim, more people could agree on wanting less, social solidarity would rise and there would be fewer strikes, less suicide, and so on. Functionalism, then, was a conservative response to widespread social unrest in nineteenth-century France. A more radical response would have been to argue that if people are expressing discontent because they are getting less out of life than they expect, discontent can be lowered by figuring out ways for them to get more out of life.

Although functionalist thinking influenced North American sociology at the end of the nineteenth century, it was only during the continent's greatest economic crisis ever, the Great Depression of 1929–39, that functionalism took deep root here (Russett, 1966). With 30 percent of the paid labour force unemployed and labour unrest reaching unprecedented levels, it is not surprising that sociologists with a conservative frame of mind were attracted to a theory that focused on how social equilibrium could be restored. Functionalist theory remained popular in North America for 30 years. It experienced a minor revival in the early 1990s but never regained the dominance it enjoyed from the 1930s to the early 1960s.

Sociologist Talcott Parsons was the foremost proponent of functionalism. He is best known for identifying how various institutions must work to ensure the smooth operation of society as a whole. For instance, when the family successfully raises new generations, the military successfully defends society against external threats, schools are able to teach students the skills and values they need to function as productive adults, and religions create a shared moral code among the people, then, said Parsons, society is well integrated and in equilibrium (Parsons, 1951).

Parsons was criticized for exaggerating the degree to which members of society share common values and social institutions contribute to social harmony. This led North America's other leading functionalist, Robert Merton, to propose that social structures may have different consequences for different groups of people. Merton noted that some of those consequences might be disruptive or **dysfunctional** (Merton, 1968 [1949]). Moreover, said Merton, while some functions are **manifest** (visible and intended), others are **latent** (invisible and unintended). For instance, a manifest function of schools is to transmit skills from one generation to the next. A latent function of schools is to encourage the development of a separate youth culture that often conflicts with parents' values (Coleman, 1961; Hersch, 1998).

CONFLICT THEORY

The second major paradigm in sociology emphasizes the centrality of conflict in social life. **Conflict theory** incorporates these features:

1. It generally focuses on large, macrolevel structures, such as the relations between classes.
2. Conflict theory shows how major patterns of inequality in society produce social stability in some circumstances and social change in others.
3. Conflict theory stresses how members of privileged groups try to maintain their advantages while subordinate groups struggle to increase theirs. From this point of view, social conditions at a given time are the expression of an ongoing power struggle between privileged and subordinate groups.

4. Conflict theory typically leads to the suggestion that eliminating privilege will lower the level of conflict and increase the sum total of human welfare.

The conflict paradigm originated in the work of Karl Marx. A generation before Durkheim, Marx observed the destitution and discontent produced by the Industrial Revolution and proposed a sweeping argument about the way societies develop (Marx, 1904 [1859]; Marx and Engels, 1972 [1848]). Marx's theory was radically different from Durkheim's. Class conflict lies at the centre of his ideas.

Marx argued that owners of industry are eager to improve the way work is organized and to adopt new tools, machines, and production methods. These innovations allow them to produce more efficiently, earn higher profits, and drive inefficient competitors out of business. However, the drive for profits also causes capitalists to concentrate workers in larger and larger establishments, keep wages as low as possible, and invest as little as possible in improving working conditions. Thus, said Marx, in factory and in mine, a large and growing class of poor workers come to oppose a small and shrinking class of wealthy owners.

Marx felt that workers would ultimately become aware of belonging to the same exploited class. Their sense of "class consciousness," he wrote, would encourage the growth of trade unions and labour parties. These organizations would eventually seek to put an end to private ownership of property, replacing it with a system in which everyone shared property and wealth. This was the "communist" society envisaged by Marx.

Marx's predictions about the inevitable collapse of capitalism are now largely discredited. Max Weber, a German sociologist who wrote his major works a generation after Marx, was among the first to point out some of the flaws in Marx's argument (Weber, 1946). Weber noted the rapid growth of the "service" sector of the economy with its many nonmanual workers and professionals. He argued that many members of these occupational groups would stabilize society because they enjoy higher status and income than manual workers in the manufacturing sector. In addition, Weber showed that class conflict is not the only driving force of history. In his view, politics and religion are also important sources of historical change (see below). Other writers pointed out that investment in technology made it possible for workers to toil fewer hours under less oppressive conditions. This was contrary to Marx's expectations. Nor did Marx expect manual workers to be pacified by higher wages, better working conditions, and welfare state benefits. We see, then, that many of the particulars of Marx's were called into question by Weber and other sociologists. Nonetheless, Marx's insights about the fundamental importance of conflict in social life are still very influential.

SYMBOLIC INTERACTIONISM

Above we noted that Weber criticized Marx's interpretation of the development of capitalism. Among other things, Weber argued that early capitalist development was caused not just by favourable *economic* circumstances. In addition, he said, certain *religious* beliefs facilitated robust capitalist growth. In particular, sixteenth- and seventeenth-century Protestants believed their religious doubts could be reduced, and a state of grace assured, if they worked diligently and lived modestly. Weber called this belief the **Protestant ethic.** He believed it had an unintended effect: people who adhered to the Protestant ethic saved and invested more than others. Thus, according to Weber, capitalism developed most robustly where the Protestant ethic took hold. He concluded that capitalism did not develop due to the operation of economic forces alone, as Marx argued. Instead, it depended partly on the religious meaning individuals attached to their work (Weber, 1958 [1904–05]).

The idea that subjective meanings must be analyzed in any complete sociological analysis was only one of Weber's contributions to early sociological theory. Weber was also an important conflict theorist, as you will learn. At present, however, it is enough to note that his emphasis on subjective meanings found rich soil in North America. For here was an idea that resonated deeply with the individualism of North American culture. A century ago, it was widely believed that individual talent and initiative could achieve just about anything in this continent of opportunity. Small wonder, then, that much of early North American sociology focused on the individual or, more precisely, on the connection between the individual and the larger society. For example, George Herbert Mead at the University of Chicago was the driving force behind the study of how indi-

Max Weber likened the modern era to an "iron cage." Sociology promises to teach us both the dimensions of that cage and the possibilities for release.

SOURCE: Carol Waino, *Untitled* (1985). Acrylic on canvas, 33" x 50". Photograph courtesy of the S.L. Simpson Gallery, Toronto. Reproduced with permission of the artist.

vidual identity is formed in the course of interaction with other people. We discuss his contribution in Chapter 4 ("Socialization"). Here we note only that the work of Mead and his colleagues gave birth to symbolic interactionism, a distinctively North American theoretical tradition that continues to be a major force today.

Functionalists and conflict theorists assume that people's group memberships—whether they are young or old, male or female, rich or poor—determine their behaviour. This can sometimes make people seem like balls on a pool table. They get knocked around and cannot determine their own destinations. We know from our everyday experience, however, that people are not like that. You often make choices, sometimes difficult ones. You sometimes change your mind. Moreover, two people with similar social characteristics may react differently to similar social circumstances because they may interpret those circumstances differently.

Recognizing these issues, some sociologists focus on the subjective side of social life. They work in the symbolic interactionist tradition. **Symbolic interactionism** incorporates these features:

1. It focuses on face-to-face communication, or interaction in microlevel social settings. This distinguishes it from both the functionalist and conflict paradigms.
2. Symbolic interactionism emphasizes that an adequate explanation of social behaviour requires understanding the subjective meanings people attach to their social circumstances.

3. Symbolic interactionism stresses that people help to create their social circumstances and do not merely react to them.[2]

4. By underscoring the subjective meanings people create in small social settings, symbolic interactionists validate unpopular and nonofficial viewpoints, thus increasing our understanding and tolerance of people who may be different from us.

To understand symbolic interactionism better, let us return briefly to the problem of suicide. If a police officer discovers a dead person at the wheel of a car that has run into a tree, it may be difficult to establish with certainty whether the death was accidental or suicidal. Interviewing friends and relatives in order to discover the driver's state of mind just before the crash may help to rule out the possibility of suicide. But, as this example illustrates, understanding the intention or motive of the actor is critical to understanding the meaning of a social action and explaining it. Suicide, then, is not just an objective social fact, but an inferred, and therefore subjective, social fact. A state of mind must be interpreted, usually by a coroner, before the dead body becomes a suicide statistic (Douglas, 1967).

For surviving family and friends, suicide is always painful and sometimes embarrassing. Insurance policies often deny payments to beneficiaries in the case of suicide. As a result, coroners are inclined to classify deaths as accidental whenever such an interpretation is plausible. Being human, they want to minimize the family's pain after such a horrible event. Sociologists believe that, for this reason, official suicide rates are about one-third lower than actual suicide rates.

The study of the subjective side of social life reveals many such inconsistencies, helping us to go beyond the official picture, deepening our understanding of how society works, and supplementing the insights gained from macrolevel analysis. Moreover, by stressing the importance and validity of subjective meanings, symbolic interactionists also increase respect for and tolerance of minority and deviant viewpoints.

FEMINIST THEORY

Few women figured prominently in the early history of sociology. This was largely because the strict demands placed on women by the nineteenth-century household and the lack of opportunity outside the household prevented most of them from obtaining a higher education and finding work that could support sociological research. Not surprisingly, therefore, the women who did make their mark on the discipline in its early years had unusual social backgrounds. These exceptional people introduced into the discipline gender issues that were largely ignored by Marx, Durkheim, and Weber. Appreciation for the sociological contribution of these pioneer women has grown in recent years as concern with gender issues has come to form a substantial part of the modern sociological enterprise.

Harriet Martineau is often called the first woman sociologist. Born in England at the beginning of the nineteenth century to a prosperous family, she never married and was able to support herself comfortably from her journalistic writings. Martineau translated Comte into English. She undertook critical studies of slavery and factory laws. She also wrote about gender inequality and was a leading advocate of voting rights and higher education for women, as well as gender equality in the family. As such, Martineau was one of the first feminists (Martineau, 1985).

Despite its auspicious beginnings, feminist thinking had little impact on sociology until the mid-1960s, when the rise of the modern women's movement drew attention to the many remaining inequalities between women and men. Since then, feminist theory has had such a big influence on sociology it may now fairly be regarded as sociology's fourth major paradigm. There are several variants of modern feminism (see Chapter 9, "Gender Inequality"). However, the various strands of **feminist theory** share the following features:

1. Feminist theory focuses on various aspects of patriarchy, the system of male domination in society. Patriarchy, feminists contend, is at least as important as class inequality in determining a person's opportunities in life, and perhaps more so.

2. The feminist paradigm holds that male domination and female subordination are determined not by biological necessity but by structures of power and social convention. From their point of view, women are subordinate to men only because men enjoy more legal, economic, political, and cultural rights.

3. The feminist paradigm examines the operation of patriarchy in both micro and macro settings.

4. The feminist paradigm contends that existing patterns of gender inequality can and should be changed for the benefit of all members of society. The main sources of gender inequality include differences in the way boys and girls are brought up, barriers to equal opportunity in education, paid work, and politics, and the unequal division of domestic responsibilities between women and men.

The paradigms outlined above are summarized in Table 1.1. As you will see in the following pages, sociologists in Canada and elsewhere have applied them to all of the discipline's branches (see Box 1.2). They have elaborated and refined each of them. Some sociologists work exclusively within one tradition. Others conduct research that borrows from more than one tradition. But all sociologists are deeply indebted to the founders of the discipline.

Standing on the shoulders of giants, we are able to see farther.

THEIR REVOLUTION AND OURS

In the nineteenth century, the founders of the discipline devoted their lives to solving the great sociological puzzle of their time, the causes and consequences of the Industrial Revolution. However, the ideas that stirred them did not spring fully grown from their minds. Rather, their social experiences helped to shape their ideas. There is an important lesson to be learned here. In general, sociological ideas are influenced by the social settings in which they emerge.

This lesson immediately suggests two important questions. First, what are the great sociological puzzles of *our* time? Second, how are today's sociologists responding to the challenges presented by the

TABLE 1.1 THE MAIN SOCIOLOGICAL PARADIGMS

PARADIGM	MAIN LEVEL OF ANALYSIS	MAIN FOCUS	MAIN QUESTION	IMAGE OF IDEAL SOCIETY
functionalism	macro	values	How do the institutions of society contribute to social stability?	A state of equilibrium
symbolic interactionism	micro	meaning	How do individuals communicate so as to make their social settings meaningful?	Respect for the validity of minority views
conflict theory	macro	class inequality	How do privileged groups seek to maintain their advantages and subordinate groups seek to increase theirs, often causing social change in the process?	The elimination of privilege, especially class privilege
feminism	micro and macro	patriarchy	What social structures and interaction processes maintain male dominance and female subordination?	The elimination of gender inequality

BOX 1.2   THE FOUR PARADIGMS IN CANADA

Each of the four major sociological paradigms has influenced research in Canada. This is evident from the following thumbnail sketches of some of Canada's leading sociologists.

S.D. Clark (1910–2003) received his Ph.D. from the University of Toronto. He became the first chair of the Department of Sociology at that institution. Born in Lloydminster, Alberta, he is especially well known for his studies of Canadian social development as a process of disorganization and reorganization on a series of economic frontiers (Clark, 1968 [1962]). The influence of functionalism on his work is apparent in his emphasis on the way society re-establishes equilibrium after experiencing disruptions caused by economic change.

SOURCE: Photo courtesy of Ed Clark.

John Porter (1921–79) was Canada's premier sociologist in the 1960s and 1970s. Born in Vancouver, he received his Ph.D. from the London School of Economics. He spent his academic career at Carleton University in Ottawa. There he served as chair of the Department of Sociology and Anthropology, dean of Arts and Science, and vice-president. His major work, *The Vertical Mosaic* (1965), is a study of class and power in Canada. Firmly rooted in the conflict paradigm, it influenced a generation of Canadian sociologists in their studies on social inequality, elite groups, French–English relations, and Canadian–American relations.

SOURCE: Carleton University Archives.

Erving Goffman (1922–82) was born in Mannville, Alberta. He studied sociology and anthropology as an undergraduate at the University of Toronto and completed his Ph.D. at the University of Chicago. He pursued his academic career at the University of California, Berkeley, and the University of Pennsylvania. Goffman developed an international reputation for his "dramaturgical" approach to symbolic interactionism. This approach highlights the way people present themselves to others, managing their identities in order to create desired impressions on their "audience," in much the same way actors do on stage (Goffman, 1959).

SOURCE: American Sociological Association.

Margrit Eichler (1942–) was born in Berlin, Germany. She did her Ph.D. at Duke University in the United States before beginning her academic career in Canada. She served as chair of the Department of Sociology at the Ontario Institute for Studies in Education and head of the Women's Studies Programme at the University of Toronto. She is internationally known for her work on feminist methodology (Eichler, 1987). Her work on family policy in Canada has influenced students, professional sociologists, and policy makers for nearly two decades (Eichler, 1988 [1983]).

SOURCE: Margrit Eichler.

social settings in which *they* live? We devote the rest of the book to answering these questions in depth. In the remainder of this chapter, we offer an outline of what you can expect to learn. To provide a context for this outline, we first say a few words about how the Industrial Revolution of the nineteenth century was transformed into the Postindustrial Revolution of our day.

THE INDUSTRIAL REVOLUTION

The Industrial Revolution began in Britain in the 1780s. It involved the application of science and technology to industrial processes, the creation of factories, and the formation of a large class of "blue-collar" workers. Within about a century, the Industrial Revolution had taken firm root throughout Western Europe, North America, and Japan. A century after that, industry had begun implanting itself in most of the rest of the world.

As noted in our discussion of Marx, the industrial working class protested long workdays, low pay, and dangerous working conditions. Workers went out on strike, formed unions, and joined political parties. Their protests forced governments to tax citizens in order to provide at least minimal protection against ill health, unemployment, and poverty. Working-class protests also forced employers to limit the length of the workweek to 40 hours, improve working conditions, and raise wages. Employers were still able to increase their profits, however, by making the organization of work more efficient and introducing new technologies.

Collecting taxes, administering social services, and investing heavily in technological change required the growth of government and business offices, hospitals, schools, universities, and research laboratories. Thus, alongside the old manufacturing sector of the economy, the new "service" sector was born. Its employees came to be known as "white-collar" workers. Highly trained professionals stood at the peak of the service sector. Secretaries and clerks were positioned near its base. By 1980, more than half of all people working in Canada's paid labour force were in nonmanual occupations (Ornstein, 1983: 252).

Sociologists call this most recent transformation of human society the **Postindustrial Revolution.** Specifically, the Postindustrial Revolution refers to the technology-driven shift from manufacturing to service industries and the consequences of that shift

on virtually all human activities (Bell, 1976; Toffler, 1990). The causes and consequences of postindustrialism form the great sociological puzzle of our time. Much of this book is devoted to analyzing postindustrialism and its effects. In concluding this chapter, a review of some of the sociological issues raised by the Postindustrial Revolution is therefore in order.

POSTINDUSTRIALISM: OPPORTUNITIES AND PITFALLS

In 1998, *Wired* magazine, the exuberant voice of North American computer culture, published a special fifth-anniversary issue devoted to analyzing the state of the planet. One contributor wrote that "[t]he life of *Wired* coincides with the best five years humanity has ever experienced." Not only is the world free of large-scale conflict, but in addition, "we are squarely in the midst of the most amazing upsurge of knowledge and wealth ever seen on Earth. And that trend is—for the first time in human history—irreversible" (Simon, 1998: 66). A few months earlier, in a special issue of the *New York Times Magazine* devoted to technology, one staff writer gushed:

> Individuals are acquiring more control over their lives, their minds and their bodies, even their genes, thanks to the transformations in medicine, communications, transportation and industry. At the same time, these technologies are providing social benefits and undoing some of the damage of the past. Technology helps to conserve natural resources and diminish pollution.... The Information Revolution, besides enabling us to visit Mars at will, is fostering peaceful cooperation on Earth by decentralizing power. Political tyrants and demagogic warmongers are losing control now that their subjects have tools to communicate directly with one another. People are using the tools to do their jobs without leaving their families. They're forming new communities in cyberspace and forming new bonds with their neighbors in real space. Technology has the potential to increase individual freedom and strengthen community.... (Tierney, 1997: 46–47).

Most sociologists are less starry-eyed than these journalists. Sociologists agree that postindustrialism promises many exciting opportunities to enhance the quality of life. However, they also see many social-structural barriers to the realization of that promise. For most sociologists, the Postindustrial Revolution is so far only half a revolution. And it is uncertain whether the second half will turn out as well as the optimistic writers at *Wired* and the *New York Times Magazine* imagine.

The unresolved social issues that confront us in the postindustrial era fall under three headings. Each issue is addressed in the following chapters:

1. *Autonomy versus constraint.* One of the major themes that emerges from *New Society* is that many people are freer to construct their own identities than ever before. Almost everyone used to retain their religious, ethnic, racial, and sexual identities for a lifetime, even if they were not particularly comfortable with them. In the postindustrial era, however, various social developments and technological advances, ranging from international migration to the World Wide Web to greater acceptance of sexual diversity, free people from traditional constraints. The theme of increasing personal autonomy is taken up in Chapter 3 ("Culture"), Chapter 4 ("Socialization"), Chapter 5 ("Sex, Gender, and Sexuality"), Chapter 6 ("The Mass Media"), and Chapter 7 ("Religion").

   However, some chapters point out that we experience increased freedom only within certain limits. For example, we can choose a far wider variety of consumer products than ever before. But consumerism itself increasingly seems a compulsory way of life (Chapter 3, "Culture"). Moreover, it is a way of life that threatens the natural environment (Chapter 16, "Sociology and the Environment"). Meanwhile, new technologies, such as surveillance cameras, cause us to modify our behaviour and act in more conformist ways (Chapter 19, "Deviance and Crime"). As these examples show, the autonomy promised by postindustrialism is only half the story. The other half is that postindustrialism places new constraints on us.

2. *Prosperity versus inequality.* The second major theme that emerges from *New Society* is that postindustrialism opens up new economic, political, and educational opportunities. It makes work less onerous for many people. It raises the average standard of living. It enables women in particular to make rapid strides in all institutional spheres.

With postindustrial society more tolerant of diversity than any previous form of society, our cities are more socially heterogeneous. At the same time, the globalization of economic, political, and cultural affairs may threaten the survival of distinct national cultures.
SOURCE: © Biddle, Paul/The Image Bank.

Again, however, we must face the less rosy aspects of postindustrialism. Tremendous economic and political inequality persists between women and men (Chapter 9, "Gender Inequality"). So does inequality between Aboriginals and other Canadians (Chapter 10, "Race and Ethnic Relations"). Inequality between rich and poor in Canada has not decreased (Chapter 8, "Social Stratification"). It is maintained partly by the educational system (Chapter 14, "Education"). Inequality between rich and poor nations has increased sharply (Chapter 11, "Inequality among Nations"). There are more good jobs at the top of the occupational structure, but many more bad jobs at the bottom (Chapter 13, "Work and Occupations"). The quality of the Canadian health-care system is threatened at precisely the moment when our population is rapidly aging and most in need of health care (Chapter 17, "Population, Aging, and

Health"). And although elections are regularly held throughout much of the world, it is an illusion to think that democracy has conquered the planet (Chapter 20, "Social Movements and Politics"). Thus, economic and political inequality persists despite growing prosperity and opportunity.

3. *Diversity versus uniformity.* The third major theme that emerges from *New Society* is that postindustrial society is more tolerant of diversity than any previous form of society. Immigration policies no longer stipulate racial, ethnic, or religious criteria for entry into the country. As a result, our cities are more socially heterogeneous than ever before (Chapter 15, "Urbanization"). The traditional nuclear family made up of mother, father, and children has given way to a wide variety of new family forms. Dozens of radio stations, hundreds of TV channels, thousands of newspapers and magazines, hundreds of thousands of CD titles, millions of books, and tens of millions of Web sites are now available to us.

Yet despite growing social diversity, there is a strong push to conformity in many spheres of life. For example, most of our diverse cultural consumption is governed by the tastes and the profit motive of vast media conglomerates, most of them American-owned (Chapter 6, "The Mass Media"). Powerful interests are trying to shore up the traditional nuclear family despite its inappropriateness for many people in postindustrial society (Chapter 12, "Families"). The globalization of economic, political, and cultural affairs may be threatening the survival of distinct national cultures (Chapter 18, "Globalization"). The push to uniformity thus counters the trend toward growing social diversity.

WHY SOCIOLOGY?

The renowned English sociologist Anthony Giddens wrote that we live in an era "suspended between extraordinary opportunity ... and global catastrophe"

(Giddens, 1982: 166). Due to the collapse of the USSR in 1991 and the work of international terrorists, nuclear, chemical, and biological catastrophes are more likely now than they were just a few years ago. A whole range of environmental issues, profound inequalities in the wealth of nations and of classes, racial and ethnic violence, and unsolved problems in the relations between women and men continue to stare us in the face and profoundly affect the quality of our everyday lives.

Despair and apathy is one possible response to these complex issues. But it is not a response that humans have often favoured. If it were our nature to give up hope we would still be sitting around half-naked in the mud outside a cave.

People are more inclined to look for ways of improving their lives, and this period of human history is full of opportunities to do so. We have, for example, advanced to the point where for the first time we have the means to feed and educate everyone in the world. Similarly, it now seems possible to erode some of the inequalities that have always been with us and have always been the major source of human conflict.

Sociology offers no easy solutions as to how these goals may be accomplished. It does, however, promise a useful way of understanding our current predicament and seeing possible ways of dealing with it (see Table 1.2), of leading us a little farther away from the mud outside the cave. You sampled its ability to tie personal troubles to public issues in the discussion of suicide. You reviewed the major theories that enable sociologists to connect the personal with the social-structural. You saw sociology's ability provide an historical and critical understanding of where we are and where we might head when the half-fulfilled promises of postindustrialism were outlined.

The questions raised in this book are tough to answer. Sharp controversy surrounds them all. However, if you try to grapple with them you will enhance your understanding of your society's, and your own, possibilities. That, ultimately, is the purpose of sociology.

TABLE 1.2   JOBS COMMONLY HELD BY CANADIAN SOCIOLOGY GRADUATES

GOVERNMENT
community affairs officer
urban/regional planner
legislative aide
affirmative action worker
foreign service officer
human rights officer
personnel coordinator

RESEARCH
social research specialist
consumer researcher
data analyst
market researcher
survey researcher
census officer/analyst
demographer/population analyst
systems analyst

CORRECTIONS
corrections officer
criminology assistant
police officer
rehabilitation counsellor
criminal investigator
juvenile court worker
parole officer

TEACHING
college placement worker
public health educator
teacher
admissions counsellor

COMMUNITY AFFAIRS
occupational/career counsellor
homeless/housing worker
public health/hospital administrator
child development technician
public administration assistant
social assistance advocate
resident planning aide
group home worker
rehabilitation program worker
rural health outreach worker
housing coordinator
fund-raising director/assistant
caseworker/aide
community organizer
youth outreach worker

BUSINESS
project manager
sales representative
market analyst
real estate agent
journalist
public relations officer
actuary
insurance agent
human resources manager
production manager
labour relations officer
administrative assistant
quality control manager
merchandiser/purchaser
computer analyst
data entry manager
publishing officer
advertising officer
sales manager

Note: A 1988 study found that 70 percent of the 2500 Canadians who received sociology B.A.s in 1986 held full-time jobs, compared to 61 percent of all other social science graduates. (The remainder were still studying in university, employed part-time, or unemployed.) They had median incomes of $23 000 per year, compared to $24 000 for all other social science graduates. About 60 percent of the jobs held by sociology graduates required high qualification levels. These figures all refer to sociology graduates who were in the labour force for only two years; they rise significantly with increased labour-force experience.

SOURCE: Neil Guppy and R. Alan Hedley, *Opportunities in Sociology* (Montreal: Canadian Sociology and Anthropology Association, 1993).

SUMMARY

1. Durkheim showed that even apparently nonsocial and antisocial actions are influenced by social structures. Specifically, he showed how levels of social solidarity affect suicide rates.

2. Due to the rise in youth suicide, the pattern of suicide rates in Canada today is not exactly the same as in Durkheim's France. Nevertheless, Durkheim's theory explains the contemporary Canadian pattern well.

3. Sociologists analyze the connection between personal troubles and social structures.

4. Sociologists analyze the influence of three levels of social structure on human action: microstructures, macrostructures, and global structures.

5. Values and theories suggest which sociological research questions are worth asking and how the parts of society fit together. A theory is a tentative explanation of some aspect of social life. It states how and why specific facts are connected. Research is the process of carefully observing social reality to assess the validity of a theory.

6. There are four major theoretical traditions in sociology. Functionalism analyzes how social order is supported by macrostructures. The conflict paradigm analyzes how social inequality is maintained and challenged. Symbolic interactionism analyzes how meaning is created when people communicate in microlevel settings. Feminism focuses on the social sources of patriarchy in both macro and micro settings.

7. The rise of sociology was stimulated by the scientific, industrial, and democratic revolutions.

8. The Postindustrial Revolution is the technology-driven shift from manufacturing to service industries and the consequences of that shift for virtually all human activities.

9. The causes and consequences of postindustrialism form the great sociological puzzle of our time. The tension between autonomy and constraint, prosperity and inequality, and diversity and uniformity are among the chief interests of sociology today.

QUESTIONS TO CONSIDER

1. Do you think the promise of autonomy, prosperity, and diversity will be realized in the twenty-first century? Why or why not?

2. In this chapter you learned how variations in the level of social solidarity affect the suicide rate. How do you think variations in social solidarity might affect other areas of social life, such as criminal behaviour and political protest?

3. Is a science of society possible? If you agree that such a science is possible, what are its advantages over common sense? What are its limitations?

GLOSSARY

Altruistic suicide occurs in settings that exhibit very high levels of social solidarity, according to Durkheim. In other words, altruistic suicide results from norms very tightly governing behaviour.

Anomic suicide occurs in settings that exhibit low levels of social solidarity, according to Durkheim. In other words, anomic suicide results from vaguely defined norms governing behaviour.

Conflict theory generally focuses on large, macrolevel structures, such as the relations between classes. It shows how major patterns of inequality in society produce social stability in some circumstances and social change in others. It stresses how members of privileged groups try to maintain their advantages while subordinate groups struggle to increase theirs. And it typically leads to the suggestion that eliminating privilege will lower the level of conflict and increase the sum total of human welfare.

Dysfunctions are effects of social structures that create social instability.

Egoistic suicide results from a lack of integration of the individual into society because of weak social ties to others.

Ethnomethodology is the study of how people make sense of what others do and say in terms of norms that exist independently of social actors.

Feminist theory claims that patriarchy is at least as important as class inequality in determining a person's opportunities in life. It holds that male domination and female subordination are determined not by biological necessity but by structures of power and social convention. It examines the operation of patriarchy in both micro and macro settings. And it contends that existing patterns of gender inequality can and should be changed for the benefit of all members of society.

Functionalist theory stresses that human behaviour is governed by relatively stable social structures. It underlines how social structures maintain or undermine social stability. It emphasizes that social structures are based mainly on shared values or preferences. And it suggests that re-establishing equilibrium can best solve most social problems.

Global structures are patterns of social relations that lie outside and above the national level. They include international organizations, patterns of worldwide travel and communication, and the economic relations between countries.

The **Industrial Revolution**, often regarded as the most important event in world history since the development of agriculture and cities, refers to the rapid economic transformation that began in Britain in the 1780s. It involved the large-scale application of science and technology to industrial processes, the creation of factories, and the formation of a working class.

Latent functions are invisible and unintended effects of social structures.

Macrostructures are overarching patterns of social relations that lie outside and above your circle of intimates and acquaintances. Macrostructures include classes, bureaucracies, and power systems such as patriarchy.

Manifest functions are visible and intended effects of social structures.

Microstructures are the patterns of relatively intimate social relations formed during face-to-face interaction. Families, friendship circles, and work associations are all examples of microstructures.

Patriarchy is the traditional system of economic and political inequality between women and men.

The **Postindustrial Revolution** refers to the technology-driven shift from manufacturing to service industries and the consequences of that shift for virtually all human activities

The **Protestant ethic** is the sixteenth- and seventeenth-century Protestant belief that religious doubts can be reduced, and a state of grace assured, if people work diligently and live ascetically. According to Weber, the Protestant ethic had the unintended effect of increasing savings and investment and thus stimulating capitalist growth.

Research is the process of carefully observing reality to assess the validity of a theory.

Social structures are relatively stable patterns of social relations.

The **sociological imagination** is the quality of mind than enables one to see the connection between personal troubles and social structures.

Social solidarity refers to (1) the degree to which group members share beliefs and values and (2) the intensity and frequency of their interaction.

Sociology is the systematic study of human behaviour in social context.

Symbolic interactionism focuses on face-to-face communication, or interaction in microlevel social settings. It emphasizes that an adequate explanation of social behaviour requires understanding the subjective meanings people attach to their social circumstances. It stresses that people help to create their social circumstances and do not merely react to them. And, by underscoring the subjective meanings people create in small social settings, it validates unpopular and nonofficial viewpoints. This increases our understanding and tolerance of people who may be different from us.

A **theory** is a tentative explanation of some aspect of social life that states how and why certain facts are related.

Values are ideas about what is right and wrong.

SUGGESTED READING

On the development of Canadian sociology, including theoretical debates and empirical findings, see the following four readings:

Brym, Robert J., with Bonnie J. Fox. (1989). *From Culture to Power: The Sociology of English Canada.* Toronto: Oxford University Press.

Brym, Robert J., and Céline Saint-Pierre. (1997). "Canadian Sociology," *Contemporary Sociology* 26: 543–46.

Brym, Robert J. (2002). "Canadian Sociology: An Introduction to the Upper Thirteen," *The American Sociologist*, 33: 5–11.

Hiller, Harry, ed. (2001). "Legacy for a New Millennium," Special issue of *The Canadian Journal of Sociology* 26 (3).

Wallerstein, Immanuel, ed. (1998). "The Heritage of Sociology and the Future of the Social Sciences in the 21st Century," *Current Sociology* 46 (2). Offers an international perspective in which leading sociologists from around the world assess the state of the discipline and its future.

NOTES

1. More detailed discussion of these theories will be found in various places throughout the book. For example, on functionalism, see Chapters 7 and 14. On conflict theory, see Chapters 7, 8, 12, and 20. On symbolic interactionism, see Chapter 3. On feminism, see Chapters 5, 9, and 20.

2. By emphasizing how social reality is constructed during interaction, symbolic interactionists downplay the importance of norms and understandings that precede any given interaction. **Ethnomethodology** tries to correct this shortcoming. Ethnomethodologists study how people make sense of what others do and say but stress that norms exist independently of social actors. Indeed, in the ethnomethodological view, everyday interactions could not take place without pre-existing shared norms. Say you pass an acquaintance on the street, who offers a friendly "How are you?" If you proceed to outline in detail your financial situation, your love life, interesting developments at work, and so forth, the acquaintance will quickly become annoyed. Most people expect "How are you?" to be answered with an equally brief reply. Violate the norm, and communication quickly breaks down (Garfinkel, 1967).

CHAPTER TWO

RESEARCH METHODS

In this chapter you will learn that:

- Science is one of several sources of knowledge. Like other sources of knowledge, it can be wrong. However, unlike other ways of knowing, science uses methods of gathering theoretically relevant evidence that are designed to minimize error.

- Research methods are used by sociologists to gather evidence in order to test theories about recurring patterns of human activity. Underlying these techniques is a variety of assumptions about the nature of facts, objectivity, and truth.

- In comparison with the evidence available to natural scientists, an added complexity confronts social scientists: Humans assign meaning to their actions, and interpreting meaningful action is very complicated.

- Sociologists have devised many useful methods of obtaining evidence about the social world, including experiments, interviews, observational techniques, and surveys.

- Good sociological research adds to our knowledge of the social world, expanding opportunities and options by helping to solve social problems.

NEIL GUPPY

UNIVERSITY OF BRITISH COLUMBIA

INTRODUCTION

Social research is all about purposeful, systematic study. The systematic nature of sociological research comes, in part, from the methods sociologists use to study society. Basic to such study is the collection of evidence. However, only evidence relevant to theoretical ideas is useful in social research. And even then, only evidence collected according to established principles is useful. Systematic sociological study integrates sound theory with careful methods.

This chapter introduces you to the principles of research methods. I begin by outlining some basic assumptions involved in social science research, including assumptions about personal values or bias, the nature of facts, and the sources of knowledge. Next I explain how the subject matter of the social sciences, people, differs from the objects of inquiry in the natural sciences (e.g., molecules, plants). People studying people adds complexity to social research. This is especially the case because social behaviour is meaningful. That is, people interpret their own behaviour and the behaviour of others by trying to establish meanings. This complexity has led to the development of various methods of social research, and I review these techniques of research in the final section of the chapter. Methods of observation and questioning lie at the heart of much research, and I review the strengths and weaknesses of each of these approaches.

PERSPECTIVE

Both Guy Paul Morin and David Milgaard were convicted of murder. In January 1995, three years after his conviction, Guy Paul Morin was formally exonerated, through DNA tests, of all charges against him. In July 1997, after 23 years in prison, David Milgaard too was exonerated. Again DNA testing played a prominent role. Judges, juries, and prosecutors had all weighed evidence that they believed demonstrated the guilt of these men. Circumstantial evidence, filtered by expectations and values, had led justice astray. Subjective judgments seriously compromised the men's lives.

An inquiry into Guy Paul Morin's conviction claimed that science helped both to convict and to exonerate him (Kaufman, 1998). But what counts as scientific evidence? Alan D. Gold (1998) claimed that "good science" exonerated Morin, but it was "not science that helped convict him." What makes for "good science"?

Wrongful convictions are rare. The criminal justice system minimizes such error through rules of

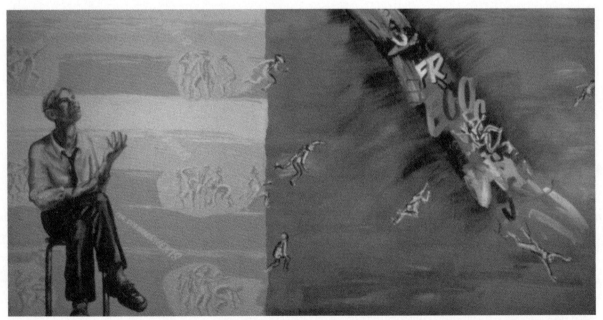

Sociological theories were first proposed in the nineteenth century as secular accounts of rapid social change. By the early twentieth century, systematic methods for empirically testing hypotheses were being introduced.
SOURCE: Carol Wainio, *We Can Be Certain*. Photograph courtesy of the S.L. Simpson Gallery, Toronto.

evidence and presumptions of innocence. Likewise, science is organized to reduce bias. Science is not perfect, however, and it is important not to put scientific practice on a pedestal, somehow immune to human foibles. Like all human activities, the social practice of science is influenced by subjectivity.

SCIENCE AS A SOCIAL PRACTICE

Science needs subjectivity but it cannot be overwhelmed by subjectivity. Subjectivity is important only to certain phases in the practice of science, while detrimental to others. Understanding the complexities of scientific methods requires distinguishing between times when subjectivity is beneficial and times when it is not. But just what is subjectivity? Most people would agree that our personal values and expectations are a core part of subjectivity. Frequently people separate the world into facts and values, the real and objective versus the personal and subjective.

But what appears to us as reality is filtered or screened. Reality exists, certainly—it is no figment of the imagination. However, our values and expectations filter reality. While the saying "what you see is what you get" has an intuitive appeal, we know the claim to be false. It exaggerates. Other things, especially our expectations and values, affect what we see.

Skeptical readers will need convincing of a filtered reality. Okay. Here is an example of filtering. The sun is real. It is no figment of our imagination. We commonly speak about "sunsets" and "sunrises" as though they were real. But these terms deceive. Although we have all watched a "sunset," the sun does not set. Our language conditions us to think of a moving sun, but it is the earth that rotates around the sun. The earth's spin creates the *illusion* of a moving sun.

Being skeptical of my claim about a filtered reality is important. Values and expectations influence our perceptions of reality, but they do not completely determine what we see. This is a critical point. The *extent* to which values and expectations influence what we see is debatable, but that is a secondary point. The key point is that *if* our perceptions of reality can be affected by our values, *then* how can scientists ever know for certain that what they "see" is true? Put another way, if observation cannot be a rock-solid foundation of scientific knowledge, then how is the practice of science to be understood?

An important claim of this chapter is that reality does not exist as some neutral scientific judge. Pure observation does not rule supreme. To think of an individual scientist as a spectator of the physical or social world, making observations to test ideas, is to profoundly misunderstand science. The scientific method is not a mechanical process of collecting facts in order to prove things. Science is a much more complex activity and the methods of scientists are designed in the face of such complexity. Here is an illustration of how values and expectations creep into scientific work.

Recall from your high school biology classes the work of Gregor Mendel. Mendel is the father of genetics. He cross-fertilized varieties of pea plants and noted that inherited traits followed consistent numerical ratios (i.e., the expression of dominant and recessive genes over successive generations). These experiments, demonstrating landmark principles of heredity, remain controversial (see Orel, 1996). R.A. Fisher, while a Cambridge University undergraduate, demonstrated that Mendel's results seemed fabricated. The likelihood that Mendel produced results conforming so closely to his hunches about heredity was, Fisher showed, in the order of one in thirty thousand.

Fisher's contention has itself been hotly disputed. Mendel may have been lucky, producing possible but very unlikely results. Alternatively, Mendel, or his assistant, may have unconsciously misclassified some pea plants. Classifications made by Mendel were not clear-cut, and so his experimental results may have been interpreted as favouring his preconceived ideas. Mendel may not have rigorously checked the experimental results because they proved what he expected. In this vein, Fisher (1936/1966) claimed that Mendel's results were a "carefully planned demonstration of his conclusion" (p. 123).

The concept of "observer bias" (making unconscious mistakes in classifying or selecting observations) is now commonly discussed as a danger to good methodological procedure. Mendel did not clearly and publicly describe his procedures. His data are no longer available for re-examination. While it is impossible to know exactly why his results came out as they did, his ideas about genetics have proven invaluable.

Good research methods are designed to minimize the types of errors that have been attributed to

Mendel's experimental evidence.[1] These methods do not eliminate the biasing effect that values and expectations have on scientific research. They do, however, seek to minimize their impact on scientific conclusions.

MINIMIZING BIAS IN SCIENCE

As a social science, sociology applies scientific practices to the study of human society. These scientific practices incorporate several ways of reducing bias, especially the twin pillars of public (open) scrutiny and skeptical reasoning. Scientific ideas become provisionally accepted only after the scientific community has scrutinized them. It is not enough for an individual scientist to proclaim a link between HIV and AIDS or between a parent's occupation and a child's school success. These links must be demonstrated by presenting research findings at scientific conferences, subjecting findings to peer-review, and ensuring that research results can be replicated. The community of scientists is organized to promote critical scrutiny.

Scrutiny is not enough however. If the scrutiny is not rigorous and probing, then it is of little value. Scientific practice also encourages skeptical reasoning. New ideas are accepted only after others have critically examined them, only after they have withstood a barrage of questions from doubters. Examples of this doubting come from questions like this: Could something other than HIV cause AIDS? If HIV does cause AIDS, exactly how does the causal process work? Does HIV cause AIDS among all people? This process of doubting is built into the way science is conducted.

Scientists are also trained in methods of research designed to minimize the influence of their personal values and expectations on the results of their research work. They work to root out error both in reasoning and in observation. So, for example, scientists learn to collect and analyze information according to rules that reduce the risk that results will be affected by bias. Much of the latter part of this chapter focuses upon these specific research techniques.

Science has prospered because of this healthy skepticism and public scrutiny. Both natural and social science have played a pivotal role in making our world a better place in which to live, by helping to curtail malaria, improving the life chances of children with disabilities, and reducing gender inequity. Scientists are not infallible saints, however. The scientific community is not some sacred haven where only truth and enlightenment reign. Instances of fraud and deceit are part of science (Park, 2000).

It is also important to correct a possible misinterpretation about the role of values and expectations. I have portrayed these as "problems." This is far too one-sided. Science would be substantially weaker, if not impotent, without values and expectations. Science is soaked through with individual judgments. Mendel's brilliance came from his expectation that passive and recessive genes played a fundamental role in explaining inheritance. Mendel provided a new way of seeing the world, a new conceptual map for understanding (see Box 2.1).

Expectations and values are in tension within the scientific enterprise. Without them the spark of creativity and passion would be very low, but with them we can be led to false conclusions (as judges and juries are occasionally misled). Put differently, objectivity and subjectivity each play an important role in science, including sociology. **Objectivity** (the attempt to minimize the effect of personal bias on research results), which is what courtroom judges and jurors strive for, stresses that observations should be free of the distorting effects of a person's values and expectations. Subjectivity is celebrated in the idea that "beauty is in the eye of the beholder." Without people championing their own values, their own perceptions of beauty, we would have little creativity and yet it is creativity that is one of the hallmarks of science. Mendel's was a beautiful solution to the mystery of inheritance, even if he may have been over-exuberant in his experimental research.

Science depends upon both the creativity of new explanations about how things work and the assessment of whether these explanations are plausible. In sociology this dual character resides in a division between theory (explanations of how the world works) and methods (ways of assessing the veracity of explanations).

Most of this chapter is about ways of assessing evidence. It explores how sociologists work within the rules of scientific method. First, however, I contrast scientific knowledge with other forms of knowledge. The discussion moves next to the steps involved in the sociological research process. I then describe

BOX 2.1 SEEING SCIENCE SOCIOLOGICALLY

One of the most influential academic books of the twentieth century was Thomas Kuhn's (1962) *The Structure of Scientific Revolutions*. Before Kuhn, many people held a "brick-building" conception of scientific progress. They thought that individual scientists contributed to building a wall of scientific knowledge, one brick at a time. As scientific knowledge accumulated, the wall became taller and sturdier.

Kuhn challenged this view on several fronts. First, he held that science developed by contributions from a community of scholars who use "paradigms" as guiding tools about how the world is organized (Mendelian genetics is such a paradigm). Paradigms guide questions and answers. Evidence not fitting a paradigm is ignored. However, if anomalous evidence persists, a "scientific revolution" results. Scholars opt for a new guiding paradigm. The transition from Newtonian mechanics to Einsteinian relativity illustrates a paradigm shift, or a scientific revolution (Kleppner and Jackiw, 2000).

Second, Kuhn proposed a discontinuous view of scientific progress. The community of scholars did not keep building the Newtonian wall, but shifted to a new structure defined by the Einstein paradigm. This discontinuous view of scientific progress also influenced debates about truth. The earth as the "third rock from the sun" we now hold as a fundamental truth. But our ancestors were equally convinced that the earth was the central rock in the universe. In the future, will our "third rock" conception seemed equally odd? Kuhn's view suggests that truth is contextual. A new paradigm establishes a new context showing us that beliefs we once held to be true were naïve or misleading.

Finally, the argument about community was sociologically compelling. In Kuhn's hands the practice of science was not understood as individual scientists ruthlessly questioning all ideas. To the contrary, paradigms provided a set of convictions about how the world was ordered. With faith in a paradigm, a community of scholars searched for what they were convinced existed. Paradigms had a disciplining effect, focusing attention on a delimited set of questions and answers. Notice also that Kuhn's view emphasized that scientific change was not gradual, but sudden (revolutionary) and that the change was organized or predictable (structured). While not everyone agrees with Kuhn's argument, his work is one of the most influential social science texts of the last century.

the main methods of gathering sociological data and the decisions that have to be made during the research process. Finally, I return in the conclusion to the role of subjectivity in research.

SCIENTIFIC VERSUS NONSCIENTIFIC THINKING

To differentiate good and bad science, consider what characterizes scientific thinking. Prior to the rise of science during the Enlightenment (an importantly descriptive word) of the 1700s, our ancestors knew many things about how the world worked. Much of this was custom or common sense—when to plant, what to plant, where to plant. Religious knowledge also held centre stage in community life. Stories of our creation, of how we came to be on earth, were powerful tales giving coherence to peoples' lives. Religious doctrine and common sense remain powerful in many societies, but scientific ways of knowing have increasing authority in most industrial nations.

What characterizes this scientific way of knowing? A key contribution came from the Scottish philosopher David Hume (1711–76). He disputed the popular argument of his day that science begins with observation. Hume argued that no matter how many observations you make, you cannot infer that your next observation will be identical. This is known as the **problem of induction**. Put more graphically, no matter how many white swans you see, you cannot infer that all swans are white. However, observing one black swan is sufficient to refute the claim that all swans are white.[2] Hume was railing against Francis Bacon's claim that observation was the bedrock of science. His point was that mere collection of "facts" is useless unless you understand how to interpret them.

In Charles Dickens's *Hard Times*, Mr. Gradgrind demands facts—"What I want is Facts.... Facts alone are wanted in life." Contrary to the popular saying, though, facts do not speak for themselves. Blue mould growing on spoiling food is a fact of life that many people have observed. It was only in 1928, however, that Alexander Fleming recognized this blue mould as a potent medical tool. Blue mould was a fact many people had experienced. Only Fleming understood it as penicillin, a powerful antibiotic drug. Mr. Gradgrind could have collected a lifetime of blue mould, but that would have done him, or anyone else, little good. Science is not a collection of facts. It is, however, among other things, a method of collecting facts.

Facts are bits of evidence, information that you or I can verify using our senses. Since trillions upon trillions of bits of human activity might be taken as facts, how do we select what should count as evidence? How do sociologists avoid random, idiosyncratic, fact gathering? Sociological theory provides guidance for the hunting and gathering of facts. Evidence is gathered to test ideas, hunches, or theories. Only selected bits of human activity are used as evidence. Those selected bits are chosen only because they relate to a sociologist's hunch about how the world works.

In the twentieth century Sir Karl Popper furthered these ideas with his provocative notion of falsification. As he claimed, observations refuting a well-conceived idea are always more important than evidence supporting or proving a theory (e.g., black swans). For Popper, science does not start with the gathering of raw facts. It starts with a question or hunch, or in his words, a well-conceived conjecture.

Two core ideas about distinguishing scientific thinking from other ways of thinking have been presented earlier: public scrutiny and skeptical reasoning. Popper added the principles of testability and uncertainty. Testability is easy to understand. For an idea to be scientific it must have testable implications; it must be falsifiable.

The concept of uncertainty may be more difficult to accept. Many people misunderstand science as a doctrine of certainty. As Park (2000) puts it, "many people are uneasy standing on ... loose soil; they seek a certainty that science cannot offer"(p. 39). As Hume argued centuries before, observations cannot be the bedrock of science because of the problem of induction. Equally, however, science cannot proceed, as Popper correctly argued, without the possibility of observations that could refute a scientific claim. Observations based on well-reasoned methods can ferret out error and misunderstanding, although these same observations cannot guarantee universal truth.

NATURAL VERSUS SOCIAL SCIENCE

The science practised by chemists and the science practised by sociologists share many elements. In both the natural and social sciences, research methods help in understanding and explaining why certain patterns emerge. Furthermore, values are important in this process because these values underlie the creative imagination so central to scientific puzzle solving. Values also have the potential to bias or distort observations, and both the natural and the social sciences must guard against distortion. If the scientific method is defined as a set of practices or procedures for testing knowledge claims, both chemists and sociologists could be seen as doing science.

There is, however, a profound difference between the subject matter of the natural and the social sciences: Bacteria don't blush. This phrase neatly captures a key distinction between the research methods of chemists and those of sociologists. Human beings are conscious and creative; we can think, act, reason, and decide. We are, as Anthony Giddens (1984) phrases it, "knowledgeable actors." As sociologists, we study "ourselves"—that is, our contemporaries and our peers. Bacteria, having no knowledge of social norms, do not blush when exposed to the beam of an electron microscope. Bacteria cannot think, act, reason, and decide; they cannot consciously control their surroundings or reactions in the same way human beings can.[3]

What this difference in subject matter means for sociologists and chemists is a matter of debate. Perhaps the single most important difference is that sociologists study **meaningful action**—that is, activities that are meaningful to the people involved. For example, bacteria may not blush when studied, but people often react self-consciously when they know they are being observed. To study love, friendship, or charm depends on learning something about the meanings people ascribe to their actions. This has advantages and disadvantages for sociologists. Unlike chemists, we can ask questions of the people whom we study (bacteria don't talk either!). But this advantage can also be a disadvantage. Interpreting people's answers is not easy.

Because of this difference in subject matter, sociologists have developed an array of methods to help them understand and explain human activity. Since asking questions has advantages and disadvantages, good sociological research either employs a variety of ways to ask questions or relies on observational techniques to aid in understanding and explanation.

METHODS OF SOCIAL RESEARCH

EXPLANATION

Sociologists have shown repeatedly that the years of schooling people receive is strongly influenced by family background. Children raised in poverty tend not to go as far in school as do children from upper-class families. Although this research demonstrates a link between family background and educational attainment, this link is, as I have reported it, descriptive, not explanatory. I have offered no reason *why* this relationship between family origin and educational destination exists. It is true that I have noted a potential cause (family background) and an effect (years of schooling), but I have failed to provide any mechanisms through which this implied causal process might operate. An **explanation** would be judged adequate only if it could show how family background actually influences educational outcomes.

The mere association or correlation between social origin and educational destination does not prove causality. The relationship between smoking and lung cancer is a good example of the rule that *correlation does not prove* **causation.** Smoking has long been linked to lung cancer, but only in the past two decades have we learned more about the causal mechanisms underlying this correlation. Cigarette companies, especially, have argued that the presumed connection was **spurious**, that something other than smoking caused lung cancer (see Box 2.2). Accumulated evidence and a more precise notion of the underlying modes of transmission have established that the original correlation is causal.

There are several ways that we might try to explain the link between family and schooling (see Davies, 2003). An obvious factor is money. Although public schooling is free, costs are incurred for field trips, tutoring, international tours, postsecondary education, and a host of other events. Children living in poverty may remain in school for fewer years than their upper-class peers because of these costs.

Money seems to be a partial explanation for the link, but other factors may be at work as well. Many skills and values taught in school may be more readily grasped by children from upper-class families, not because these children are smarter than are children living in poverty, but because the home environments of the children may expose them to different skills and values. The classroom climate may be more like the climate of the upper-class home (e.g., abstract word games are valued, reading and music are prized) and these children may therefore be advantaged.

The first explanation is largely about money and material resources. The policy implications of this explanation point to eliminating or reducing the costs of schooling. This has been accomplished in large measure in Canada. However, even when the costs of postsecondary education have also been reduced (e.g., in Quebec and Newfoundland), social-class disparities in educational attainment have remained. The second explanation points to cultural factors in the home (e.g., reading) as a reason for the family–school link. This explanation has influenced policies related to compensatory education, such as Head Start and After Four, educational programs designed to help disadvantaged children by giving them educational enrichment.

We explain something by showing how or why a cause has a certain effect. The mechanisms by which causes have effects are essential for adequate explanation. Perhaps the cardinal lesson regarding explanation is that there is hardly ever a single explanation—*the* explanation—for anything. Because multiple causes are involved in social-scientific explanations, a single, unitary cause or explanation is rarely sufficient. Sociologists search for the multiple factors that can help explain some particular state of affairs. So, in the family–school example, although only two explanations for the link are mentioned here, other explanations may also be tested and refined as sociologists attempt to see how equality of educational opportunity might be attained.

UNDERSTANDING

Sociologists must not be content merely to offer explanations for why a particular relationship exists. These explanations are often sterile unless they also address the meaningfulness of human activity. People make the social world happen, and in doing so they give meaning to their actions and to the actions of others. A failure to address these meanings would leave sociology underdeveloped.

BOX 2.2 CORRELATION AND CAUSATION

Where fires cause much damage, many fire trucks usually gather. This is a correlation; a lot of damage tends to go along with many trucks, while minimal damage tends to draw only a few trucks. This simple illustration makes the point that correlation does not prove causation. Consider Figure 2.1, below. The curved, double-headed arrow depicts the correlation between the amount of damage and the number of trucks on the scene. The single-headed, straight arrows show the direction of causation. The size of the fire is a common prior cause of both other variables.

Causality is controversial because it often involves something we cannot observe directly. For example, no one can see lung cancer being caused by smoking. We infer that conclusion from assembled evidence that fits with theoretical conjecture.

Here is another example. Women living in poverty eat less nutritious meals and consequently are more likely than better-off women to have premature babies. But not all women living in poverty have premature babies. There is a correlation between poverty levels and the incidence of premature births, and nutrition level has been identified as a key causal stimulus. Notice, however, that living in poverty does not guarantee premature births. Living in poverty only raises the probability that a mother will have a premature baby.

In a causal relationship, a change or variation in one thing produces a change or variation in another. If four basic conditions are met, causality may be established. First, two variables must be associated or correlated. Consider two variables—the likelihood of premature births and poverty. Premature births must be more likely to occur among poor women than among women who are not poor if a causal relationship exists. Second, the independent variable (poverty level) must precede the dependent variable (premature births) in time. Establishing that a woman is poor while she is pregnant confirms the causal ordering or temporal sequencing of the variables.

Third, the original association must not disappear once the effects of other variables on the dependent variable are examined. We need to verify that we have not made a false inference. Does the causal process really go from poverty to poor diet to premature babies?

FIGURE 2.1 AN EXAMPLE ILLUSTRATING THAT CORRELATION DOES NOT PROVE CAUSATION

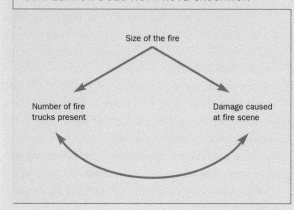

Size of the fire

Number of fire trucks present

Damage caused at fire scene

Could it be that stress, and not poverty, is the causal agent? It may be that poor women are under more stress and that stress, not poverty, increases the likelihood of premature births. The initial causal relation between poverty and premature births would be spurious if stress was determined to be the operative factor (poverty may be correlated with stress, of course, but stress may still be the real causal agent).

Finally, we must offer a theoretical account of how one variable causes another. We must illustrate the mechanism(s) through which causation operates. This theoretical reasoning also enables us to establish which variables are important to examine when we test to see whether a causal relation might be spurious. In the example, we theorize that poverty affects nutrition, which in turn affects the likelihood of premature birth.

It is no simple matter, however, to understand what someone or some group means by their actions or utterances. One way to think about **understanding** is as follows. The first time I saw a traditional Greek dance, I was unable to follow the patterns of movement or appreciate the symbolism of certain motions. Similarly, the first time I watched a cricket match, I could not fathom what was happening. To the extent that I have come to understand either of these complex social activities, I have learned *how to proceed with the activity*. To understand a Greek dance or a cricket match means being able to participate fully in the activity, knowing what others mean by their actions and utterances, and knowing how others will interpret our actions and utterances.

A fundamental social process, called "taking the role of the other," nicely captures this idea of understanding. By imagining yourself in the role of another, you come to appreciate someone else's point of view. You come to understand, to reflect upon, his or her ideas and issues. I do not mean that you must become Caesar to understand him; that would be impossible. Instead, sociologists focus on the web of relations in which people interact, paying attention to how people understand and interpret the views of others. They pay attention to "the definition of the situation," to the meanings of the people involved.

Erving Goffman's work in an "insane" asylum is a good illustration of sociological understanding (Goffman, 1961). Goffman was not interested in getting inside the heads of the mental patients to learn what and how they thought about things. Rather, he was interested in how the patterns of social activity in the asylum were organized. He came to see the mental hospital from the patients' point of view. By dispensing with the medical categories and scientific labels assigned to individual patients, Goffman began to understand the ways in which patients worked cooperatively to produce a coherent social structure. He learned to appreciate how the patients defined the routine activities of the asylum, and how they coped with institutional procedures that denied them privacy and stripped them of their personal identities (e.g., by issuing institutional clothing and removing personal objects).

Goffman (1961: 129) also learned about what he calls the "careers" of mental patients:

> Persons who become mental-hospital patients vary widely in the kind and degree of illness that a psychiatrist would impute to them.... But once [in treatment] they are confronted by some importantly similar circumstances and respond to these in some importantly similar ways. Since these similarities do not come from mental illness, they would seem to occur in spite of it.

Although social life on the "inside" might seem unique or even bizarre at first, Goffman argues that anyone, patient or researcher, would, in time, come to find it much like many other communities in which one has participated, possessing an identifiable social organization and rhythm of activity.

Returning to the education example, explanations of high-school dropout rates that ignore the attitudes and values of dropouts themselves are one-sided. An appreciation of the experiences of dropouts is essential to a more complete account of the schooling process. Especially important here is the resistance of students to authority, often expressed through music and clothing. This resistance is not some idiosyncratic expression of random individuals, but represents part of a youth subculture that must be understood by anyone who wants to alter the schooling process to make it a better environment. How young school resisters define the situation of schooling is important to a full appreciation of dropping out.

Understanding and explanation work together. While explanations of dropping out that ignore student values are deficient, merely reporting the stories of young resisters would be equally vacuous. A full appreciation of dropping out, or of any other social activity, requires both understanding and explanation. Often these activities are pursued by different researchers and their combined results contribute to fruitful research programs leading to social change.

TECHNIQUES OF SOCIAL RESEARCH

Sociologists have developed a variety of techniques to gather evidence. I will review three of the most important: experiments, survey research, and observational studies. As you read my accounts of research procedures, keep asking yourself: How do sociologists go about developing insights about, or knowledge of, the social world? How do they come to know what they claim to know? What methods do they use and how believable are the results generated by these methods?

EXPERIMENTS

Experiments are the hallmark of scientific research and are commonly, though inaccurately, equated with science itself. Experiments are useful because they enable researchers to isolate causes. By no other method can researchers determine causation so precisely. An example is the best way to illustrate the point.

In exploring how ethnicity influences social interaction, Martha Foschi and Shari Buchan (1990) assigned people to one of two experimental conditions. Each person was told that he or she would be working with a partner of the same sex seated on the other side of an opaque partition. Their task was to make judgments about the relative sizes of graphic images. After seeing two contrasting images, but before finally selecting the one they felt contained the most white space, people were told of their partner's choice. Foschi and Buchan wanted to know whether the ethnicity of a partner would affect people's likelihood of sticking with their own selection or switching to their partner's choice. Many people change their mind when they hear what decisions others have made. Foschi and Buchan were keen to see whether the likelihood of a person changing his or her mind depended on the ethnicity of the other person.

In one case ("condition one") the partner was described as East Indian, while in the second case ("condition two") the partner was described as English Canadian.[4] Because the experimenters wanted to examine the effects of ethnicity on personal judgments, they had to ensure that the only difference between conditions one and two was the partner's ethnicity. They could not, for example, let the participants meet their partners because that would expose them to more than just the partner's ethnicity (e.g., the partner's demeanour, clothing, height). All of the participants in the experiment were of European ancestry, but their "partners" were either East Indian or English Canadian. How could the experimenters subtly inform people of their partner's ethnicity, without arousing suspicion?

Foschi and Buchan developed a clever solution. First, they asked the participants to complete a short questionnaire. Then, under the guise of wanting to let the participants know something about their partners, the experimenters gave everyone their partner's completed questionnaire. In fact, each participant received a questionnaire that Foschi and Buchan had previously completed. By design, only two fictitious partners existed and they differed only by surname (Edwards or Sidhu), country of birth (Canada or India), and language (English or English/Punjabi). Apart from those three attributes (i.e., the difference between conditions one and two), participants in the experiment received identical descriptions of their partner (e.g., same age, level of schooling, place of residence).

The experimental results suggested that men were less likely to be influenced by East-Indian than by English-Canadian partners. Women did not systematically change their judgments according to their partner's ethnicity. The common attribute among men who were less influenced by their partner was their partner's ethnicity. The experimenters were confident that ethnicity was the only factor distinguishing the two groups because each person in the experiment was randomly assigned to one of two conditions—an English-Canadian or an East-Indian partner.

Random assignment or **randomization** lies at the heart of experimental design. Using a random procedure (e.g., flipping a coin, rolling a die), people in an experiment are assigned to an experimental condition on the basis of chance. If the flipped coin comes up heads, a person is automatically placed in experimental condition one; if the coin comes up tails, the person is assigned to condition two. Although individual participants will differ with respect to age, sex, weight, and so on, the two experimental groups will contain an approximately equal number of women and men; the average age of the two groups will be similar; and so on. This group similarity is accomplished by random assignment. Foschi and Buchan used random assignment to ensure that the only difference between conditions one and two was the partner's ethnicity.

For women, the partner's ethnicity made no difference. The treatment condition—East-Indian or English-Canadian partner—had no effect on the judgments women made. Exactly why men were influenced by ethnic cues and women were not remains open to debate. Foschi and Buchan suggest that women might be less prejudiced than men, perhaps because women have more frequently themselves been the victims of discrimination. The experimenters were quick to add, however, that there could be other explanations. In particular, they surmised that women may have been more likely than men to believe that ethnicity was of no relevance to a person's ability to make judgments about the visual images.

By dissecting the Foschi and Buchan experiment, we can examine more carefully the key design features of an experiment. The researchers began with a **hypothesis**—an unverified but testable knowledge claim about the social world. In the example, the experimenters hypothesized that ethnicity affects behaviour in social interaction. In more formal terms, Foschi and Buchan (1990: 5) "predicted different perceptions of competence and resulting behaviour for

White subjects performing a task with a partner, depending on whether the partner was White or East-Indian."

To test this hypothesis, Foschi and Buchan examined the relationship between two **variables**. A variable is a measurable concept that can have more than one value. Age is a concept we use in talking about how long someone has lived. For newborns, age is measured in weeks or months, but for everyone else it is measured in years. One variable studied by Foschi and Buchan is ethnicity. They designed the experiment so that ethnicity could have one of two values: East Indian or English Canadian. In this experiment, ethnicity is the **independent variable**, which is presumed to affect other variables. Differences in this variable are hypothesized to affect a second variable, the **dependent variable**. In the experiment by Foschi and Buchan, the dependent variable is the amount of influence a person will accept from his or her partner. It was measured by the frequency with which people changed their initial judgments after learning of their partner's choice.

Nevertheless, how do Foschi and Buchan know that only a partner's ethnicity and not another factor, such as a partner's age or social class, influence judgments? They are confident of their conclusion because, by design, they know that only the ethnicity of the fictitious partner differed between conditions one and two. Apart from ethnicity, partners were identical. Could it not be, however, that the people making the judgments differed? After all, no two people are alike and perhaps this fundamental variation was at work in the experiment. For example, perhaps the people in condition one (East Indian) were older than the people in condition two (English Canadian), and older people may reject their partner's influence more often. Foschi and Buchan eliminated this possibility by randomly assigning people to one or the other treatment condition. Randomization, as I explained earlier, is a procedure used in experiments to assign people to experimental conditions on the basis of chance. Because participants cannot choose which treatment condition to enter (i.e., they cannot self-select), the groups can be made alike.

Sociology experiments of the type conducted by Foschi and Buchan are relatively rare, in large part because many social processes that interest sociologists are not amenable to laboratory testing. Ethical and practical problems limit the use of laboratory

experiments. Furthermore, we must be cautious in generalizing the results of laboratory experiments to non-laboratory situations. This latter concern is technically expressed as a problem of **external validity**, or the degree to which experimental findings remain valid in a non-laboratory situation. External validity is often low; relationships discovered in sociological experiments do not always hold in more "real-life" settings because these settings differ in many ways from the laboratory. Still, the relevance of laboratory findings is an empirical question. There is reason to be cautious about generalization, but often findings from the laboratory apply in other real-life contexts.

As I mentioned earlier, when people know they are being studied, they often become self-conscious. The very fact of being studied may influence their behaviour. This was demonstrated in productivity experiments conducted by Roethlisberger and Dickson (1939) at the Western Electric Company's Hawthorne factory. They found that productivity (the dependent variable) increased when they brightened the lighting, but then also increased when they dimmed the lighting. The researchers realized that people worked harder because the research team was studying them. Productivity increased in response to the researchers' presence rather than because of any other changes they introduced. Social scientists have subsequently used the term **Hawthorne effect** when referring to changes in people's behaviour caused by their awareness of being studied. Bacteria don't blush because the Hawthorne effect does not operate in the natural sciences.

Field experiments have been used in sociology in an attempt to avoid some of the problems of laboratory experiments, especially problems of external validity. A good example of a field experiment is one undertaken in Toronto by Effie Ginsberg and Frances Henry (1985; Henry, 1999). They investigated the extent of job discrimination faced by people of different ethnic backgrounds. In one study, they sent actors, one Black and one white, to apply for advertised job vacancies. The actors were given similar credentials and were trained to make their job-search behaviour as identical as possible. The researchers wanted to test the hypothesis that racial discrimination existed in the Toronto labour market. Their independent variable was the race of the job applicant and their dependent variables—their measures of discrimination—included the number of interviews granted and/or job offers made to each actor. They found evidence supporting the discrimination hypothesis, with whites having a 3-to-1 advantage over Blacks in job offers (for discussion of a similar, more recent test of this hypothesis, see Reitz, 1993: 35).

The field experiment, conducted in a natural as opposed to a laboratory setting, reduces problems of artificiality. However, Ginsberg and Henry could explore only a limited range of jobs and were unable to focus on other urban centres, where discrimination may be more or less of a problem. Sociologists have had to develop other techniques to include larger populations.

SURVEY RESEARCH

The social survey is the primary means of collecting social science evidence. Researchers collect information using surveys by asking identical questions of a sample of people. Political pollsters, market researchers, labour unions, governments, and university researchers all rely heavily on survey-based knowledge. Survey research is so useful because it provides a method of systematically comparing answers to identical questions from a large sample of people, and allows researchers to generalize the results to the larger population from which the sample was chosen. Questions can be posed either on a **self-administered questionnaire** or through a personal **interview**. Increasingly the Internet is used as a way of conducting surveys (Brym and Lenton, 2001).

Rhonda Lenton (1990) used survey research to investigate parents' aggression toward their children. Because of strong taboos against child abuse, asking questions about abusive behaviour is very difficult. The privacy surrounding child discipline makes observation or experiments inappropriate. Furthermore, asking blunt questions about "smacking your child" is unacceptable. Just as many alcoholics deny they have a drinking problem, many child abusers think of themselves as "strict disciplinarians." Parents use different strategies to influence their children, and Lenton wanted to examine the full range of this behaviour. Therefore, she chose to use a survey in which parents could be questioned by experienced and trained interviewers. She included questions covering an array of child–parent interactions, from praising and positive modelling through withholding privileges and love, to spanking, slapping, and hitting.

A key problem facing Lenton was whether her questions about aggression and discipline would really measure child abuse. Child abuse is a theoretical concept. You and I may use the same term to mean different things. What types of maltreatment ought to be considered as child abuse? Lenton (1990: 159) defines child abuse as "any act, excluding sexual mistreatment [which she separated as sexual abuse], carried out by a parent ... that has the intention of, or is perceived as having the intention of, hurting a child." The idea of intention is tricky here. Lenton wanted to include as "abuse" any act that a parent understands may hurt the child. To measure abuse, she asked parents whether they had done any of the following, ever, and in the past year: yell at a child, ridicule a child, withdraw emotionally from a child, hit a child with an object, withhold food from a child, and 24 other actions. Do these items provide an indication of what Lenton defines as child abuse? That is, are these valid indicators? **Validity** refers to accuracy or relevancy. Lenton's measurement of child abuse is valid to the degree that the items she uses as measures of abuse actually measure abuse as she defines it theoretically.

Lenton interviewed each parent and child separately. Each family member was asked to complete a child-discipline questionnaire, on which each of the 29 abuse items was listed. This sheet was completed privately and handed to the interviewer in a sealed envelope. By comparing the responses of all family members, Lenton could determine the consistency with which abuse was reported by different family members. This gave her confidence in the **reliability** of her measure. **Measurements** are reliable if they are consistent or repeatable. If different measures or indicators of the same concept give similar results, the measurements are reliable or, in other words, internally consistent.

Lenton faced another problem when selecting the families to include in her study. She wanted families from across the spectrum of child discipline and, of course, she needed families with children. No publicly available list of such families exists. Lenton selected a random sample of Toronto families from the telephone directory. After first phoning to ensure that children lived in the household, members of the research team visited each eligible address to ask for permission to interview spouses and children.

Surveys always involve the selection of **samples**. Lenton's research team could never have interviewed all Toronto families (a complete enumeration of all families would be a *census*), nor would the expenditure of time and money have been efficient. Although the entire population could not be interviewed, it is this larger population about which Lenton wished to draw conclusions. To use a different example, in doing research on urban household waste, interviewing all city dwellers is both unnecessary and impractical, even though the intention might be to use survey results to help design city policy. Information obtained from a subset of the population, the sample, is used to represent the views and

characteristics of everyone. For this reason, the survey sample must represent the population. Samples selected using rules of chance or probability provide random samples. These random samples give surveys better external validity than experiments.

Samples must represent the larger population from which they are drawn. For example, one or even a few kindergarten classes cannot be taken to represent all kindergarten classes, because not all kindergarten classes are alike. They vary in size, the ratio of boys to girls, and so forth. Therefore, if we wish to generalize about social processes common to all kindergarten classes, we need to select a number of classes for study. Because we cannot afford to study all kindergarten classes, we need a representative sample. Probability samples that rely on random

Researchers collect information using surveys by asking people in a representative sample a set of identical questions. People interviewed on a downtown street corner do not constitute a representative sample of a country's adults. That is because the sample does not include people who live outside the urban core, it underestimates the number of disabled and elderly people, it does not take into account regional diversity, and so on.

SOURCE: Dick Hemingway.

processes for their generation are the most likely to yield samples that represent the population.

Exactly how many kindergarten classes or, more generally, how many units must be included in a sample is a complex question. The precise answer depends mainly on the amount of variation or heterogeneity in the population and the degree of accuracy required in the study's conclusions. If you need very accurate results, you need larger samples. Likewise, if the population is very variable, you need a larger sample to reflect that heterogeneity adequately. In studies of the Canadian electorate, very accurate forecasts of voting can be achieved with a random sample of about 1200 voters. The mathematical laws of probability can be used to generate efficient sample sizes.

Selecting samples is not as easy as it might seem. How would you go about selecting a random sample of students in your faculty? Distributing questionnaires in classes would be one method, but many students do not attend every class. Students who attend regularly are, by definition, different from those who attend infrequently. A sample of students present in classes would therefore be biased. Registration lists give an approximation of the student population, but these lists are never perfect. Some students drop out as the term progresses, while others change their addresses and phone numbers. If you were studying student retention or student financial needs, the people who might be hardest to find might be the very people to whom it is most important to speak. Even with this severe limitation, however, student lists maintained by the registrar might be the best alternative available. The list from which a sample is selected is called the *sampling frame*. This frame must come as close as possible to including everyone in the population.

Recently, market-research firms have been making greater use of telephone interviews in conducting their surveys. These firms usually rely on *random-digit-dialling* procedures to establish random samples. They select "banks" (i.e., lists) of working telephone numbers (e.g., 902-424-79xx), and let the computer randomly dial the last, or the last two, numbers. This method, used by Statistics Canada in some of its surveys, provides a random sample of households, including households with unlisted telephone numbers. Two important refinements are used. First, some households have more than one telephone number, and their chances of inclusion are therefore increased. Statistics Canada asks respondents how many working telephone numbers there are in a house so that it can correct for this small bias. Second, the person who is interviewed in the house must also be randomly selected (because, for example, women are more likely than men to answer the phone even when both are at home). One popular strategy for obtaining a random sample of household members is to interview the person who has had the most recent birthday.

Telephone surveys require that people be interviewed. An alternative to interviewing is the use of self-administered questionnaires, which can be either mailed or delivered to members of the sample. Mailing questionnaires to people and handing them out to groups (e.g., students in a classroom, patients in a clinic) are less expensive than interviewing. However, questionnaires lack the personal touch of interviewing. In an interview, misunderstandings can be clarified and responses can be expanded upon. This cannot be done with self-administered questionnaires. Questionnaires work best with what are called close-ended questions, like those on multiple-choice exams, to which there are a limited number of set answers. Interviews, especially face-to-face as opposed to telephone interviews, allow for more open-ended questions, where respondents can be encouraged to elaborate their responses to ensure that they are properly understood. Lenton, for example, chose to use personal interviews because she thought that the subject matter was best handled with face-to-face interaction. Notice, however, that she incorporated a short questionnaire on disciplinary techniques because she thought the questionnaire would be less threatening to people in that it was more anonymous.

Once Lenton had established her sample and pretested her research strategy to ensure that she would obtain usable information, she set out to gather evidence that would allow her to evaluate the merits of three different hypotheses. A "cycle of violence" hypothesis holds that practices of child abuse are handed down from generation to generation. A "social-situational" hypothesis maintains that abusive parents may be reacting to stress and that stress itself may be linked to a family's socioeconomic status. Finally, a "cultural" hypothesis stresses that it is the attitudes of the family toward corporal punishment that best differentiate between the use of aggressive and nonaggressive behaviour in child discipline. Her research was designed to yield evidence that would help her decide which hypotheses were wrong. No researcher designs the definitive test of alternative explanations. After analyzing the data, Lenton (1990: 176) concluded that "parents are inclined to use the disciplinary repertoires they learned when they were children—but only as long as certain current structural conditions are consonant with these repertoires." In particular, she pointed to structural conditions such as unemployment in the family and low family income. To the extent that these structural conditions can be eliminated or reduced, the "cycle of family violence" can be arrested.

I mentioned earlier that the ability of sociologists to ask questions of people has both advantages and disadvantages. Lenton's work illustrates this. The physical punishment of children in the privacy of the home represents social activity that is not easily studied by any sociological method. Yet, as Lenton argues, child abuse is a public issue, not a private matter. By asking questions of people she was able, first, to describe the extent of physical aggression used to discipline children and, second, to explain why some families were more likely than others to use physical discipline. The disadvantage of asking questions of people, especially questions that people may find threatening, is that people may distort their responses. For example, Lenton found that in over 75 percent of all families, children had been spanked or slapped in the previous year. Given current social norms about child abuse, this estimate of physical discipline is more likely to be an underestimate than an overestimate of such activity. If, however, different social classes subscribe to these norms to different degrees, people's responses to the 29 disciplinary measures might have altered. Lenton herself anticipated this criticism and asked people not just about their behaviour, but also about their attitudes. She was therefore able to examine whether people from different social classes held different norms about child discipline.

This distinction between attitudes and behaviours, or words and deeds, is important. I always intend to give more money to charity than I do. Most people believe that littering is irresponsible, but most people still litter sometimes. When you read research that focuses on people's attitudes, remember that thought is not easily translated into action. This dis-

tinction goes beyond the asking of questions to issues of policy as well. Too often, people think that changing attitudes will solve social problems—if only people knew more, they would act more responsibly. A broken New Year's resolution is but one simple reminder of how often good intentions fail to translate into good deeds, no matter how aware we might be of the consequences.

Interpreting the answers that people give to researchers' questions is complicated by more than this behaviour–attitude distinction. In asking people questions, either in interviews or on questionnaires, we must be careful about making assumptions (Gray and Guppy, 2003):

- *Do not assume that people understand what you are asking.* Language is notorious for its ambiguity. How many friends did you see yesterday? This question may look simple at first, but people will differ in their understanding of "friends" and others will take "see" in the most literal way. The same words may mean different things to different people. Asking about family members requires care because some people will include only immediate family, and others will include extended family members.

- *Do not assume that people know the answer to questions.* Most people do not want to appear ignorant when asked a question. This was illustrated nicely in a study of the prestige of occupations by Peter Pineo and John Porter (1967). They asked people to rate the prestige of two fictitious jobs, archaeopotrist and biologer. Most respondents cooperated and assigned these nonexistent jobs a prestige rating. When asked about their attitude on some issue, many people feel they must respond, even if they have no opinion on the topic or only a weakly formulated view.

- *Do not assume that people will admit the answer to themselves.* Alcoholics frequently claim that they can "quit any time." They refuse to admit that they are addicted. Similarly, child abusers may define themselves as strict disciplinarians. People routinely deceive themselves, sometimes only in minor ways, but "admitting the truth to ourselves" is a problem. Sometimes we will admit these things more freely to strangers than to ourselves or our friends, but sometimes we admit these things to no one, including ourselves.

- *Do not assume that people will give valid answers to others*. People feel better about themselves when they are seen in a favourable light. In asking questions of people, researchers face the potential problem of "social desirability," because respondents may only give answers that reflect well on themselves. "What type of work do you do?"—"Oh, I'm in public relations." Such a response could come from people working as telephone receptionists, tourist guides, or corporate representatives.

Sociologists use many techniques in asking questions to gather valid and reliable evidence. For example, they will ask several questions rather than relying on only a single question; use supplementary questions to expand upon or clarify answers; and test questions before using them to improve any wording that is unclear or misleading. Many more techniques are set out in *Constructing Questions for Interviews and Questionnaires* (Foddy, 1993).

Survey researchers do not focus only on individuals, although it is individuals who respond to survey questions. For example, it is possible to survey organizations, groups, corporations, electoral ridings, or job vacancies. Although people answer survey questions, the questions may apply to a unit or group of which someone is a member. Sandra Burt (1990) studied women's organizations using a survey to gather information about how various women's groups were organized (e.g., their size, authority structure, networks). She mailed questionnaires to each group, asking that a knowledgeable person answer all of the questions. Fiona Maybin (1993), in a study of job-search procedures, interviewed personnel officers about the characteristics of recent job vacancies. Among other questions, she asked how the vacancy was advertised, how many people applied, and how long the vacancy had existed. Several people she spoke with reported on more than one vacancy.

I am making two points here. First, surveys can focus on different units of observation (individuals, corporations, countries, etc.). Second, individuals can act as informants to report information that pertains not to themselves but to some group or unit about which they have information. People can, for example, report on individual events (e.g., job vacancies), family composition, or corporate policy. Although each of these represents different units of observation, individuals are still answering the questions.

OBSERVATIONAL STUDIES

Another method commonly used by sociologists to gather information is observation. Sometimes sociologists act as outside observers, at other times as insiders or **participant observers**. The obvious advantage of observation is that sociologists can see what people actually do, rather than relying on reports of what people say they do. The disadvantage is that gaining access to private actions or events can be difficult. For example, Lenton might have tried to observe parents disciplining their children rather than relying on what parents told her they did. But entering the privacy of people's homes to make such observations would have been difficult. Furthermore, her presence may have influenced the type of discipline parents used (the Hawthorne effect).

In observation studies, examining the intentionality of social action is especially important. Max Weber (1949 [1904, 1905, 1917]) was one of the first sociologists to address the issue of intention as a problem of social research. Weber argued that our interactions with other people draw upon meanings. For example, the clothing we choose to wear speaks to others. All of us are conscious of intentionally dressing in certain ways to impress others. We attribute meaning to bow ties, jackboots, Laura Ashley scarves, and baseball caps. None of this is done innocently, because what we wear helps define who we are. Skateboarders, for example, dress in a particular style; they wear a uniform of sorts. Making social life intelligible is part of what Weber thought sociologists must address. To understand skateboarding, it is essential to see how skateboarders "define the situation." It is important to learn about their culture and to understand their systems of meaning. The aim of such research is not to explain the behaviour of skateboarders from an outside point of view, but to investigate their shared values and beliefs—their "worldview."

Weber maintained that causal logic can be used to accomplish some of what sociologists wish to do. He thought, however, that sociology also had to make intelligible the subjective basis on which social action rested. Weber used the German word *Verstehen*, or understanding, to refer to this mode of sociological analysis. To understand the meaning of social action requires being able, at least in principle, to participate in the social activity of which the action is a part. An example is the best way to illustrate such understanding.

Youth subculture in Canada seems less influential, less prominent than in countries like the United Kingdom or the United States. Sometimes this is expressed in the claim that youth culture in Canada is derivative of trends south of the border or across the Atlantic. However, as skateboarders and squeegee kids have risen in profile, as youth unemployment has grown, and as the plight of young criminal offenders has been debated, understanding youth subcultures has become increasingly important. For that reason, Brian Wilson (2002) undertook a study of the rave subculture in Southern Ontario.

Locking up all youth considered deviant is an all-too-frequent suggestion for social policy. Banishing squeegee kids or skateboarders to some less visible place, be it jail, another neighbourhood, or "just off the streets," is one reaction. Denouncing ravers as irrational, for amphetamine drug use and social disturbance, is another. What these suggestions mainly reflect is a misunderstanding of youth culture and its social context. Gaining an appreciation of the rave subculture was Wilson's intent. Among the issues he pursued were the reasons for people participating in this subculture—put simply, was it the lure of adventure and excitement in the rave scene or was it a push from family and/or school that led to involvement with the rave subculture?

To gain an understanding of this process he chose participant observation as one of his methodological strategies. He attended over a dozen raves, hung out in rave record stores, sat in on rave radio sessions, and attended public meetings focused on the rave phenomena. He observed the rave subculture by participating in it, by being a part of the party. By participating with ravers in rave parties and in rave settings he was able to learn, firsthand, about their lifestyles, their values, and their aspirations.

However, Wilson did more than just participate in the rave scene. He also interviewed 37 young

In participant observation, it is often necessary to "look" the part. Brian Wilson participated in rave parties to study firsthand the rave subculture of Southern Ontario.
SOURCE: Thérèse Joyce Gagnon, *Génération X.* (1994) © SODART (Montreal) 2003.

people who were active participants. He used what he calls "in-depth, open-ended, semi-formal interviews" (Wilson, 2002: 301). An in-depth interview means that he explored specific topics in great detail, often pursuing nuances and tangents. They were open-ended in the sense that he allowed those he interviewed to range widely in the subject matter they discussed. Finally, they were semi-structured in that he had a set of general issues he wanted to discuss, but he did not ask every person he interviewed exactly the same questions in exactly the same order. His goal was to have a meaningful conversation with each person, guided by his interest in the subject but also by their knowledge, willingness, and interest in pursuing specific details.

He also did not interview a representative sample of rave participants. Such a sample would be difficult to define since no one has a listing of regular rave members. Instead Wilson sought to talk with a variety of people and he was careful not to draw all of the people he interviewed from the same place. Diversity was more important to him than was representation.

Finally, Wilson also paid particular attention to written materials that form part of the rave scene. This included magazines (both hard copy and e-zines), flyers promoting specific raves, and rave recordings (complete with commentary by the DJ). These provided another window into how ravers communicated with each other, what they stressed and emphasized.

In essence he used a cluster of methods, with observation being his primary source of data. The participant observation was critical in giving him personal access to the subculture. He supplemented this by reading material and listening to rave productions. Finally, he also interviewed people to check out his interpretations of the rave subculture. In particular, he used the interviews to assess his own impressions of the rave scene.

Ethnographers study people in their own environment or their own natural setting. Although **ethnography** (the detailed description of a particular culture or way of life) includes the researcher being immersed in a group or a subculture, it also typically involves a cluster of methods including both in-depth, unstructured interviewing and the analysis of documents. Speaking with key informants who are central to the group or the subculture is crucial (Creswell, 1998).

In part, Wilson came to understand the rave subculture in generational terms. Youth rebellion against perceived autocratic organizations (school, family, the justice system) leads to a lifestyle of resistance—to escaping authority, flaunting convention, and disregarding conservative norms. But it is a resistance that is not about political change or efforts to alter organizational forms. It is a resistance focused mainly on creating an autonomous space where social identity can be fostered, nourished, and supported. In this sense the subculture has a "magical" quality where the reality of other worlds can be transcended or bracketed. It is a movement based more on personal identity than on political change. Contrast this with, for example, the student-led demonstrations in many countries pushing for stronger democratic gover-

nance (e.g., China, Indonesia, Iran, and Korea) or the resistance to globalization seen at World Trade Organization events.

Wilson was able to gain an understanding of the rave lifestyle by participating in the life of the group. By hanging out with them, he gained an in-depth appreciation of their activity. As a participant observer, he was able to ask many questions of many different group members, gradually drawing a sociological portrait of the rave scene. In particular he was able to contrast various interpretations of the rave scene—was it about resistance, simple pleasure seeking, or simply escapism? As his work progressed, Wilson was able to refine his understanding. He could cross-reference his observations by seeing how other group members reacted to each new insight he gained, thereby increasing both the reliability and validity of his conclusions. In short, he came to "define the situation" as rave participants themselves define it.

As with experiments, the external validity of ethnography can be problematic. How confident can Wilson be that his conclusions are not dependent upon the impressions he formed from a single group of ravers? The intensive, in-depth nature of ethnography makes generalizability problematic. The key tradeoff is between the richly textured, "thick description" of ethnography and the insularity of detailed study of one or a few settings. Unlike survey researchers, ethnographers do not select different sets of random individuals or groups. The groups or settings they investigate are purposively chosen, sometimes because of easy access. For example, Wilson did not randomly choose rave subcultures. He made arrangements to participate with some rave scenes in Southern Ontario, and even then it was only one form of youth subculture.

Wilson's research portrays a culture from its members' points of view. There are potential pitfalls of which Wilson had to be aware. First, how much did his presence influence his findings? Did people act differently when he was not around? In principle, there is no way of answering this question, although ethnographers have tried to account for the effect of their presence in various ways. Some researchers conceal their research role; in effect, they try to be known to the other participants as one of them, rather than as a researcher (the ethics of this are dicey). Other researchers report that, with time, participants' awareness of their presence fades and they are treated as a member. Notice that this problem of presence is the Hawthorne effect in another guise. Whether in survey research, experiments, or observation studies, the researcher's presence can distort the domain of investigation. Researcher presence may undermine validity.

Beyond the potential pitfall of mere presence is the problem that the findings of researchers may be ethnocentric. That is, researchers may impose their own values—their own worldviews—on the subject matter of their study. How do we know, for example, that Wilson is depicting the ravers' point of view and not his own? One method of reducing personal bias is known as the "member test of validity" (Douglas, 1970: 21). For example, if the rave participants Wilson spoke with did not recognize themselves in his account—that is, if they saw Wilson's account as inauthentic—then we would worry about bias or distortion. Wilson was careful to "test" his tentative observations and insights on his informants by asking them questions and checking for observations that would falsify his impressions. Again, this is a research problem that extends well beyond ethnography. In fact, ethnography can be seen as the method that takes most seriously the task of understanding the members of a group from the members' point of view, stressing in particular their definition of the situation.

A third problem beyond presence and ethnocentrism is this: How do researchers know that the "tools" of their inquiry (e.g., questions, instructions, requests) did not in fact "create" or "generate" the resulting "findings"? For example, did Wilson create a finding by focusing attention on the ravers' resistance to dominant culture? Alternatively, did Lenton invent a relationship between social class and child discipline by asking questions that might be interpreted in different ways by the members of different classes? Again, this involves issues of reliability and validity. Lenton can be confident that she did not construct or create a pseudo-relationship between class and discipline to the extent that she shows that the basic pattern of findings is repeated across different questions about the disciplining of children. Wilson distinguished between (1) ravers' comments made in response to his questions and (2) statements his informants volunteered or that he overheard during his fieldwork. In addition, he used information provided to him by others on the margins of the

rave scene, DJs, security guards, and radio station personnel. These alternative sources of information helped him avoid the problem of "creating" meaning. If ravers volunteered information that corroborated Wilson's impressions, and if these impressions were further reinforced by other knowledgeable observers, his faith in the authenticity of his account increased.

Not all observation can involve participation. Rik Scarce (2000) was interested in nature, and especially our human domination of nature. His interest was in whether we could still speak of "wild salmon" or whether, like the cow and the dog, salmon were now domesticated. He argues that the very concept of "resource management," a buzz phrase among fishery specialists for several decades, speaks to the idea of humans improving upon nature, of scientists enhancing nature.

In studying the "domestication of salmon," Scarce used ethnographic methods. He could not participate as a scientist, but he could observe what scientists did, interview them, read their papers, and listen to their testimony at public inquiries. In doing all these things, he wrote an ethnographic account called "Fishy Business: Salmon, Biology, and the Social Construction of Nature."

He was especially interested in how salmon on both the Atlantic and Pacific coasts had been manipulated to serve human ends. In the modern fishery, phrases like fish farming, aquaculture, genetic engineering, fish stocking, and fish hatcheries are commonplace. In British Columbia few natural river systems remain. We have engineered a new breed of salmon, mixing wild stocks and creating farmed salmon.

Scarce learned about this in his ethnographic research by hanging around fish hatcheries and asking questions, by visiting fishery research centres and watching what scientists were doing in their experiments, and by talking with scientists at their conventions and at public inquiries. He learned about the controversies and the angst that existed among scientists, many of whom worried about how we were increasingly controlling nature, but all too often in ways that were unsophisticated and too superficial. He came to see the fish hatchery as a biological factory and to understand how salmon were increasingly "tooled" and "engineered." Observation was his staple method. He immersed himself in the science of salmon to learn about the social practices of fishery biologists.

The believability of Scarce's research is enhanced by the fact that he observed events in their natural settings. He did not create a situation to see how people reacted (e.g., laboratory experiments), nor did he rely on people reporting on their own attitudes or behaviours (as in survey research). He was not a participant in the activity and so his involvement could not have distorted events (as may occur in participant observation). It is true that his presence as an observer may have influenced how people conducted themselves, but he often was one of many observers (e.g., at scientific conferences and public inquiries).

Direct observation is a very good research strategy, one that many people rely on in their own lives—"seeing is believing." The problem in much scientific research, in both the social and the natural sciences, is that we cannot see many things with "our own eyes." Natural scientists routinely use instruments such as electron microscopes and magnetic resonance imaging machines to "see" the natural world (e.g., electrons, cell membranes). Similarly, social scientists use a variety of techniques (e.g., surveys, experiments) to help them "see" the social world.

OTHER METHODS OF RESEARCH

Historical Sociology

Many sociologists study social change. Max Weber, for example, attempted to explain the rise of capitalism by showing how Protestantism invigorated capitalist growth. Émile Durkheim was interested in how moral education helped to socially integrate a rapidly changing society. Both writers sought to answer sociological questions by examining historical change as evidence of significant social processes. Sociologists are more likely than historians to use historical evidence to test theories of social change. Sociologists place less emphasis on history for history's sake.

Gordon Laxer's (1989) work shows how sociologists can also make effective use of comparative, historical methods. Laxer sought to explain why the Canadian economy has remained heavily tied to the production of resources (e.g., wood, oil, grain, minerals) with high levels of capital investment by foreigners. He wanted to test different theories about economic development, such as whether Canada's relatively late industrialization explains our present economic structure. To do this, he systematically compared Canadian economic patterns (e.g., levels of manufacturing activity, levels of foreign investment) with those of other countries, and in particular other late-developing countries such as Japan and Sweden.

Laxer suggests that we can best understand Canada's relative position in the world economy, and especially our greater reliance on exporting raw materials as opposed to the sale of manufactured goods, on the internal politics of early Canadian development—principally, a weak farmers' movement around the turn of the twentieth century. In contrast to countries such as Sweden and Japan, Canada did not have a strong, ethnically united farming class that could push for domestic economic policies (such as the creation of banks willing to lend money for long-term investment) that ultimately facilitated strong industrial development.

The logic of Laxer's analysis is not unlike that of other sociological research. His key dependent variable is foreign investment and he measured how this investment changed historically in several different countries. Among his independent variables is the organizational strength of farmers (the agrarian class). By comparing an admittedly small number of cases, he sought to decide what was both similar and different in the cases. By comparing the historical record using a small number of variables across a set of different countries, he was able to sort out plausible causal factors that influenced Canada's position relative to other countries.

Sociologists like Laxer sometimes rely on other researchers' historical accounts. He relied primarily on economic histories that had already been written about each country he included in his analysis. Other sociologists go back to original sources to reconstruct a historical record pertinent to their focus. For example, Gillian Creese (1988, 1999) examined gender relations in the Vancouver labour force and labour movement early in the twentieth century. Her aim was to improve our understanding of the historical dynamics leading to the segregated work of women and men. Included in the archival material that she used were the full proceedings of the Royal Commission on Labour Conditions in British Columbia, documents on strikes and lockouts between 1907 and 1939, the minutes of local labour unions, and press coverage from newspapers. Any single source could give only partial coverage of the events she wished to examine. By using a variety of sources, she was able to increase the reliability of her findings. Creese also relied on published data from the Canadian censuses for the decades in which she was interested.

Use of Official Statistics

Governments have a long history of collecting statistical data. Government bureaucracies first began to collect statistics to help rulers determine both the size of their taxation base and the number of fighting men they could put on the battlefield. Since then, the scope of government or official statistics has expanded and now includes information on births and deaths, unemployment rates, imports and exports, and so on. Sociologists have made good use of official statistics.

For example, Brym (1986) was interested in how support for social-democratic political parties was related to the resources on which different social classes could draw. His dependent variable, electoral support for leftist political parties, was measured as the percentage of voters casting ballots supporting social-democratic or communist parties in ten capitalist democracies, including Canada. He focused on three key independent variables: a measure of the inequality of income in a country, the type of electoral system in a nation, and the percentage of the labour force that was unionized. His measures of these variables (except the type of electoral system) were derived from official statistics. Brym showed that, contrary to earlier research, class-based political activity was still strong in many countries he studied, especially if there were leftist political parties with the resources necessary to run effective campaigns.

McMullan and Swan (1989) used official statistics in their investigation of arson in Nova Scotia. They relied on police-reported arson for the period 1970–85. The data showed a substantial rise in both the actual number and the rate of reported arson (number of arsons per 1000 fires) between 1973 and 1981, with a modest decline in subsequent years. Arson, of course, is difficult to prove, and McMullan and Swan were careful to check with a second source to verify the pattern they had established. When they used fire-marshal data, as opposed to police-report data, they found similar trends. In accounting for the fluctuating arson rate (their dependent variable), they pointed to interest rates and unemployment rates as

the variables affecting arson rates. On the basis of official reports, and from interviews that they conducted with enforcement and insurance officials, McMullan and Swan concluded that most arson involves the burning of one's own property, even though the criminal definition of arson continues to emphasize vandalism.

The arson example nicely illustrates a central problem with official statistics. These statistics are not objective facts on which everyone can agree. The very definition of arson makes it difficult to prove. Furthermore, different interest groups have a great deal at stake over whether a fire is officially reported as arson. More and more arsonists are property owners themselves, and their interests are typically opposed to those of insurance investigators, who wish to pay no settlements for illegal fires. Again, issues of validity are at stake: Do the official definitions used to generate, say, arrest statistics, arson rates, or strike statistics correspond to the theoretical concepts that sociologists wish to use? In addition, sociologists must be certain that official statistics reflect changes in the behaviours they are examining, rather than changes in the practices of the officials collecting the statistics.

THE ANALYSIS OF NUMERICAL DATA

As these research examples imply, sociological evidence frequently comes in numerical form—that is, as quantifiable evidence (e.g., number of disciplinarians, arsons, or voters). Finding and interpreting patterns in numerical data is complex. To help in summarizing numerical information, social scientists routinely rely on statistical techniques. In this section I briefly illustrate some key aspects of the process. I begin with a simple puzzle: Education affects income. In more formal terms, I begin with a hypothesis: The more education a person has, the more the person earns. Men and women have, on average, very similar levels of schooling. However, as a group, men earn higher wages or salaries in the labour market than do women. So, if education is a good predictor of income, and if women and men have similar amounts of schooling, why do men typically earn more than women?

There is a causal logic to what is being described here. Education is hypothesized to affect income.

However, since women and men earn different wages in the labour market, yet have similar levels of schooling, maybe the causal link between education and income differs by sex. Although I can present only an elementary analysis here, issues of a wage gap between the sexes are part of the continuing debate over pay equity, comparable worth, and employment equity, all important policy questions.

To begin, we need to examine whether the basic facts, as I have just stated them, are accurate. I do this by using data from the 1997 Survey of Consumer Finance, a survey conducted by Statistics Canada of a nationally representative sample of Canadians (69 461 randomly chosen Canadians, to be precise). Does education have a big effect on income? Table 2.1 gives us an answer. This table, called a contingency table or a cross-tabulation, shows the relationship between education and income. Education, the independent variable displayed across the top of the table, has three categories (low—12 or fewer years of schooling; medium—13 or 14 years of schooling; and high—more than 14 years of schooling). For ease of presentation, annual personal income, the dependent variable, has been divided into two categories (low—personal income below $24 000 annually; and high—annual income at or above $24 000). The causal logic of the relationship, which underlies the construction of the table, is that education affects income (see Box 2.2 on page 34 for the basic issues of causality).

Notice first how the table is arranged. The title describes the two variables being related. The independent variable (education) is placed on the top of the table and its values are clearly delineated. Below each value for education is a column of numbers. The dependent variable (income) is arrayed on the side of the table, again with the value labels clearly shown. Beside each value of the dependent variable is a row of numbers. The cross-classification of the two variables then creates a series of cells in the table (six cells in this case). To illustrate, Table 2.1 shows that there are 2131 people in the top left-hand cell, the cell defined by a low level of education and a low income. At the intersection of each column and row is a table cell (there are six cells here because row and column totals are ignored in counting the number of cells in a table).

The concept of a contingency table comes from the idea that the category into which a person falls on the dependent variable is contingent on, or depends on, the category that a person occupies on the independent variable. If that hypothesis were true in this case, we would expect that, as we move across the education categories from low to high, the number of people receiving high incomes ought to rise. Do the data reveal this pattern? For people with low education, 1658 had high incomes. For people with a high level of education, 1188 had high incomes. These figures seem, at first glance, to run counter to our expectation. Notice, however, that because of how education was categorized, 3789 people had what I defined as low education, while only 1837 had high

TABLE 2.1 THE RELATIONSHIP BETWEEN LEVEL OF EDUCATION AND EARNED INCOME FOR PEOPLE AGED 25–34, CANADA, 1997.

	LEVEL OF EDUCATION			
INCOME	Low	Medium	High	**ROW TOTALS**
Low	56% (2131)	48% (1721)	35% (649)	49% (4501)
High	44% (1658)	52% (1868)	65% (1188)	51% (4714)
Column totals	100% (3789)	100% (3589)	100% (1837)	100% (9215)

SOURCE: Data from Statistics Canada, 1997 Survey of Consumer Finance, Cat. No. 13M0001XDB.

education. Comparing the actual number of people in each cell is therefore misleading, because there are different numbers of people in each column.

Rather than focusing on the raw numbers, we get a better understanding of the patterns when we standardize the data. We should ask not how many of the people in the low-education column had high incomes, but what *percentage* had high incomes. By expressing the numbers as percentages—that is, by standardizing the data—it is much easier to see the key patterns. So, 1658 of 3789 people in the low-education column had high incomes, or 44 percent (1658 divided by 3789 and then multiplied by 100). This tells us that for every 100 people with low education, 44 had high incomes. Making the same calculation for the high education column—([1188/1837] × 100)—we find that 65 percent of highly educated people earned high incomes (or 65 of every 100 people).

If you examine Table 2.1, you will see that the percentages are entered in the table. The actual number of people in each cell appears in parentheses. It is important to recognize that the percentages run down (or are calculated down) the columns, producing what are known as column percentages (i.e., 100 percent in each column). It is possible also to calculate row percentages, but these are not as useful in understanding the relationships appearing in contingency tables when the independent variable is placed across the top of the table.

So, do relatively more people with high education receive high income in comparison to people with low

education? Yes. Of every 100 people in the high-education column, 65 receive high income (65 percent), compared with only 44 of every 100 in the low-education column (44 percent). The difference between these two percentages (21 percent) is one measure of the strength of the relationship between education and income. However, with no standard of comparison, it is difficult to say whether 21 percent signals a strong or a weak relationship. In a moment I will turn to a method of comparison that allows us to make such judgments.

In studying this table, some of you may have taken exception to my definitions of high and low incomes. Why should earning over $24 000 be considered a high income? What is defined as low and high income is arbitrary. However, when I define the lows and highs of income and education differently and produce several different tables, the basic patterns in the tables do not change. This replication gives me confidence that my decision about how to categorize the variables does not affect the results. (I chose $24 000 because this is close to the median, the income above and below which half of all the cases fall.)

The evidence in Table 2.1 corroborates the first part of the puzzle about the relationship between education and income that I hypothesized. But how does gender figure into the pattern? Table 2.2 contains two contingency tables. Here the question is how the link between education and income varies for women in comparison with men. Table 2.2 can be usefully thought of as Table 2.1, but with women and men separated into their own tables.

TABLE 2.2 THE RELATIONSHIP BETWEEN LEVEL OF EDUCATION, EARNED INCOME, AND GENDER FOR PEOPLE AGED 25–34, CANADA, 1997

	WOMEN Level of Education				MEN Level of Education			
INCOME	Low	Medium	High	TOTAL	Low	Medium	High	TOTAL
Low	73%	61%	40%	(2722)	44%	34%	30%	(1779)
High	27%	39%	60%	(1782)	56%	66%	70%	(2932)
Totals	100% (1646)	100% (1836)	100% (1022)	(4504)	100% (2143)	100% (1753)	100% (815)	(4711)

Note: Column and row totals are not equal for women due to rounding error.

SOURCE: Data from Statistics Canada, 1997 Survey of Consumer Finance.

For women, the basic pattern of Table 2.1 is repeated in Table 2.2: 60 percent of women with a high level of education are likely to have high income, whereas only 27 percent of women with a low level of education are likely to have a high income. The difference between these two cell percentages is 33 percent.

For men, while the pattern is similar, the percentage difference is smaller. Of men with a high level of education, 70 percent have a high income, whereas for men with a low level of education, 56 percent have a high income. The percentage difference is only 14 percent. This suggests that for young men education level is not as important as it is for young women in earning a high income. Contrasting the percentage differences between the two subtables in Table 2.2 gives us a way of comparing the strength of the link between income and education for women versus men. A more complex method of investigating the causal linkages between gender, education, and income relies on multiple regression—see Box 2.3.

So, what do we learn from this analysis? We learn first, from Table 2.1, that people with more education are likely to earn higher incomes. Second, from Table 2.2 we learn that this is especially true for young women, in that for men education level has less of an impact on earning high incomes than is the case for women (remember only people between 25 and 34 are included in the tables).

Notice what we did not learn. I did not present a table showing the link between gender and income, although it would be easy to create this table. If you were to do so you would learn that men are more likely to earn high incomes than women are. Since I was interested in a hypothesis linking education and income, I did not present the table showing the link between gender and income. Likewise, I did not present the table linking gender and education (this table would show more women with high levels of education).

Why is the link between education and income different for women and men? First, men without university education may still earn high pay in resource and manufacturing jobs where education level is less important. That could account for the difference. Second, the labour force is still at least partially differentiated into "male" and "female" jobs, and education level may be more important for finding work in traditional female jobs than in male jobs. Third, women and men could be working different numbers of hours per week, or weeks per year, and these differences could be related to both education and income. Many other possible explanations exist, and further research is essential to sort them out (Guppy and Davies, 1998; Wannell and Caron, 1995).

THE FUTURE OF SOCIAL RESEARCH

Social research involves the systematic study of the social world. The aim of such research activity is to develop explanations and understandings of social patterns so that we may improve the human condition. As we move through the early years of the twenty-first century, it is becoming increasingly obvious that we need to find innovative ways of organizing and running our human affairs. Starvation, environmental degradation, violence, and social injustice are among the many social problems we must confront. Solutions require adequate explanations and understanding for how these problems arise and persist.

Earlier in the chapter, I outlined several different sources of knowledge: common sense, religious faith, and science. Although these forms of knowledge share certain features (e.g., they are all imperfect), scientific reason encourages a set of practices, open review, and critical skepticism, which together work to reduce error.

Another way of emphasizing what is distinctive about the scientific method is to compare how social research differs from the work of other professionals who concentrate on similar social issues (e.g., the environment, gender relations). For example, what differentiates the work of documentary filmmakers, novelists, or journalists from that of social researchers? I have emphasized three features of scientific research that, in combination, separate it from the work of these other professionals. These three features of scientific work can be summarized as follows:

- research results are confronted by the critical skepticism of other scientists;
- social theory guides, either directly or indirectly, the evidence gathered; and
- evidence is systematically collected and analyzed.

Although some of these features are found in the work of other professionals, such as journalists, all

BOX 2.3   INTRODUCING STATISTICAL IDEAS ABOUT REGRESSION ANALYSIS

In exploring the linkage between gender, education, and income, I introduced a series of alternative explanations. Testing each of these ideas using contingency tables would be extremely difficult because, with so many possible confounding variables, the tables we would have to generate would quickly become huge and unwieldy. An alternative to contingency-table analysis is regression analysis. The basic idea of regression, in summarizing the linkages between variables, can be explained most easily in graphic form.

Below (Figure 2.2) is a graph with years of schooling arrayed along the horizontal axis (*x*-axis) and annual income levels displayed along the vertical axis (*y*-axis). Using these two lines as guides, we can then plot where each person in our sample falls. In other words, we can choose someone from our sample at random and move along the *x*-axis until we come to the level of education attained by our selected person. We can then proceed up from there, now using the *y*-axis as our guide, until we reach the level of the same person's annual income. The point that we reach is the intersection of two perpendicular lines, one drawn vertically from the *x*-axis (at the person's level of education) and the other drawn horizontally from the *y*-axis (at that person's annual income). For each person in our sample, we can locate exactly where these two lines fall in our graph, and place a mark or a dot at the appropriate spot. The result, similar to what I have depicted, is a scatterplot.

Notice that the scatterplot and the contingency table are related in important ways. First, as in the contingency table, the independent variable (education) is arrayed horizontally. Second, note that the cells in the contingency table are analogous to the points on the graph, except, of course, that the cells are cruder categories (e.g., everyone with twelve or fewer years of schooling was in one cell whereas in the graph these people can be at different points). The key question, however, is what is analogous to the percentage difference?

A scatterplot can be summarized statistically using regression techniques. To summarize the relationship between education and income, a straight line can be drawn through the data points in such a way that the distance from each point to the line can be minimized. If all of the points lie exactly on the line, the fit of the line to the data will be perfect. The farther the points are from the best-fitting line, the poorer is our ability to use a straight line to summarize the information and the weaker is the association between the two variables. The strength of association between two variables in a scatterplot is given by the *correlation coefficient* (*r*). The value of *r* can vary from −1 (a perfectly inverse relationship or negative association) to 0 (no association) to +1 (a perfectly proportionate relationship or positive association). The further *r* is from 0, the stronger the association. The correlation coefficient is, then, analogous to the percentage difference in tables.

With the education and income scatterplot, we can capture the central characteristics of our best-fitting line with two numbers. One number captures the slope of the line and tells us how much vertical increase (or decrease) occurs in the line for every unit of horizontal change along the *x*-axis. Using our example, for every additional year of schooling, how much does annual income increase? An easy way to remember this is to think of this number as the rise (income increase) over the run (change in years of schooling). A second number tells us at what point the line intersects the *y*-axis. If we have a perfectly fitting line, the equation for a straight line can be expressed as $y = a + bx$, where *x* and *y* are values on the two axes of the graph, *a* is the point at which the line crosses the *y*-axis, and *b* is the slope of the line.

What I have described here is a statistical technique known as simple linear regression, for one independent and one dependent variable. To explore the alternative interpretations for the link between gender, education, and income that I offered earlier, you would need to use multiple regression, where one dependent variable can be linked to a series of independent variables.

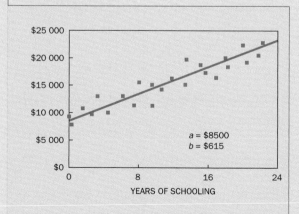

FIGURE 2.2 HYPOTHETICAL RELATIONSHIP BETWEEN EMPLOYMENT INCOME AND YEARS OF SCHOOLING

$a = \$8500$
$b = \$615$

YEARS OF SCHOOLING

three features are found in good social research. Replication and reproducibility have high currency in science as ways of encouraging skepticism. Good research contributes new ideas or evidence to our common stock of social theory. Finally, good research shows the careful collection and analysis of evidence.

These principles are a feature of all good research, but the methods that sociologists use to pursue their goal of explaining and understanding the social world take many forms. This diverse array of methods, including observing, questioning, and experimenting, offers sociologists many ways of inquiring about the social world. Each specific method has different strengths and weaknesses, which makes the choice of research strategy dependent on the sociological question.

Social science research will continue to contribute to our sense of the world around us. Research on the environment, reproductive technology, multiculturalism, violence, and social-support networks all point to practical ways in which our human problems can be influenced by research findings. Effective policy solutions that benefit all people require sound social research.

SUMMARY

1. Research methods are ways of getting evidence to test suppositions about the world around us. Behind the various techniques (e.g., experiments, interviews) we use to obtain evidence and expand our knowledge of the social world, we must recognize important assumptions about such things as facts, objectivity, and truth.

2. Science is one of several sources of knowledge. Like other kinds of knowledge, scientific knowledge can be wrong. However, unlike other ways of knowing, science incorporates explicit methods designed to reduce error in what is currently accepted as scientific knowledge. Evidence must be systematically collected and rigorously evaluated.

3. Good science integrates both good theory and good research. The latter two are inseparable. Theories are ideas about how the world works or claims about how to explain or understand the recurring, patterned nature of human activity.

4. Evidence is crucial to developing, revising, or discarding theoretical claims. In comparison with the evidence available in the natural sciences, the evidence available to social scientists presents added complexity because of the meaningful character of human social action. People, unlike molecules, assign meaning to their actions and to the actions of others.

5. Sociologists have devised many useful methods to obtain evidence about the social world. Observation and questioning are the two principal techniques, although each of them is conducted using a variety of formats, including experiments, surveys, participant observation, and interviews.

6. Good research adds to our knowledge of the world around us. Such knowledge expands our opportunities and options. Sociological knowledge helps either in solving social problems or by sensitizing us to our collective human condition, expanding our social horizons.

QUESTIONS TO CONSIDER

1. The teaching of faculty members in university and college departments could be evaluated in various ways. Suggest some different methods of doing such an evaluation and comment on the strengths and weaknesses of each approach.

2. Lenton chose to examine issues of child abuse by focusing more broadly on child discipline and by surveying parents about their disciplinary techniques. Suggest alternative designs for her study, commenting on the strengths and weaknesses of the various approaches.

3. Policy makers frequently debate raising or lowering age restrictions on activities such as driving a car, drinking alcoholic beverages, or voting. Suggest how you might design a study that could provide evidence about the possible consequences of either raising or lowering one of these age restrictions.

4. Immigration levels remain a contentious issue in Canada. Construct a short series of interview questions designed to assess people's knowledge of current immigration practices. Ask these questions of your friends and/or family. Ask how many immigrants enter Canada and from which countries they originate. Compare your findings with official statistics that are available in government publications at your college or university. How might you explain the patterns you discovered?

5. Discuss the claim that "facts speak for themselves." What problems exist in claiming that facts do "speak for themselves"? Conversely, what problems exist in claiming that facts do not "speak for themselves"? Consider especially the claim that we need firm standards against which to evaluate ideas or theoretical claims. Is it possible to establish such standards?

6. At parties, people are expected to be laid back, relaxed. Parties are times for having fun, for stepping outside the routines of school and work. However, phrases like "party pooper" suggest that parties too have rules and that violators of such rules can be ostracized. Others are glorified as "party animals," implying that some people take to partying better than others. How might you engage in a participant observation study to investigate these hunches systematically? Do categories such as "party animal" or "party pooper" exist, and, if so, how are they understood? Do "rules" exist at a party even though parties are in very important ways "escapist"? How might a sociologist seek to understand party life at your college or university?

GLOSSARY

Causation is a relationship between two variables where change or variation in one variable produces change or variation in a second variable. Four criteria are essential to establishing a causal relation between two variables: association, time ordering, nonspuriousness, and theoretical rationale.

A **dependent variable** is a variable that is assumed to depend on or be caused by one or more other variables (independent variables). It is the variable that is the effect, or outcome, in a cause–effect relationship.

Ethnography is the detailed description of a particular culture or way of life; it is the written results of a participant-observation study.

An **experiment** is a controlled test of the causal effects of a particular variable or set of variables on a dependent or outcome variable.

An **explanation** is an account of the causal logic that shows how and why variables influence one another.

External validity is the generalizability of a particular finding from the study group to a larger population. It also refers to the relevance of conclusions for a larger population and the ability to infer that the results of a study are representative of processes operating for a broader population.

The **Hawthorne effect** is the idea that people involved in a study may be influenced by the very process of being studied; it is the impact of a study on the subjects of the study.

A **hypothesis** is a knowledge claim or hunch about how the world works; it is a testable statement, derived from a theory, about the relationship between two variables.

An **independent variable** is a variable presumed to affect or influence other variables; it is the causal variable.

An **interview** is a method of collecting information by asking people questions, either in person or over the telephone. Interviews range from highly structured (preset questions in a fixed order) to loosely structured (topic guidelines, but no prescribed question wording).

Meaningful action is human action, as distinct from physical behaviour, that occurs with specific intentions or reasons in mind. The uncontrollable tic in a person's eye is physical behaviour, which differs from that of a person who is winking at someone, where intention or purpose is central to understanding what is happening. Most human activity is meaningful action or social action.

Measurement refers to procedures for assigning numbers to observations according to preset rules; it is the act of finding data or information relevant to theoretical concepts.

Objectivity is the attempt to minimize the effect of personal bias on research results; it is the idea of impartiality, of "fair hearings." Objectivity is an ideal enhanced by the work of any single researcher being open to the critical scrutiny of others, but objectivity as complete impartiality is a myth.

Participant observation is the study of social life involving the participation of the researcher, to varying degrees, in the activities of the group under investigation; it is an attempt to give an "insider's" account of a particular way of life or cultural system.

Randomization is a procedure used in experiments to assign test subjects to experimental conditions on the basis of chance.

Reliability refers to consistency of measurements; it is the ability to reproduce the same measurements on repeated occasions.

Sampling is a process of selecting units from a larger population. Random sampling involves the selection of representative units (e.g., people, organizations) from a population (e.g., all Canadians, voluntary organizations in a city). Samples may be selected by probability (where every unit has a nonzero chance of selection) or non-probability (where chance does not enter into the selection of sample units).

A **self-administered questionnaire** A method of collecting information by having people record their own answers to preset questions.

Spuriousness is an incorrect inference about the causal relations between variables.

Understanding is the ability to provide a definition of the situation that members of a culture find authentic and valid.

Validity refers to the relevance or accuracy of measurement in relation to the theoretical concept that it is supposed to measure.

A **variable** is something that varies; it is an attribute or event that can take on more than one value (e.g., unemployment rates, age, sex).

SUGGESTED READING

Babbie, Earl, and Lucia Benaquisto. (2002). *Fundamentals of Social Research.* Toronto: Nelson. Babbie and Benaquisto provide the best general account of research methods available in sociology. This Canadian adaptation covers an array of methodologies and provides many illustrations and examples to emphasize key points.

Becker, Howard. (1998). *Tricks of the Trade: How to Think about Your Research While You're Doing It.* Chicago: University of Chicago Press. Written by one of sociology's strongest qualitative researchers, Becker's book discusses how to think about research and is valuable to both qualitative and quantitative researchers.

Denzin, Norman. (1997). *Interpretative Ethnography: Ethnographic Practices for the 21st Century.* Thousand Oaks, CA: Sage. A good general introduction to the practices and debates of qualitative research.

Gray, George, and Neil Guppy. (2003). *Successful Surveys: Research Methods and Practice*, 3rd ed. Toronto: Nelson. A practical guidebook to developing research designs and using effective survey research techniques. This book covers questionnaires and interviews.

Tashakkori, Abbas, and Charles Teddlie. (1998). *Mixed Methodology: Combining Qualitative and Quantitative Approaches.* Thousand Oaks, CA: Sage. A helpful discussion of how to combine the two primary approaches of contemporary research methods.

NOTES

1. In the event that you worry that Mendel's case is a scientific anomaly, an equally compelling case, just as central to scientific knowledge, relates to the "peppered moth" and Darwinian evolution. Most biology science texts of the last four decades have cited the peppered moth as the definitive proof, the missing link, providing key evidence to support natural selection and evolutionary biology. However, in what is eerily similar to the Mendel tale, the fundamental experimental research is suspect (see especially Hooper, 2002).

2. Black swans, native to Australia, were unknown to Europeans before exploration. The idea that all swans are white is thus similar to the idea that the earth is the central body in the solar system—a claim once understood to be true but now thought to be false.

3. Please do not over-interpret this claim. As a community we have frequently treated humans as exceptional. We have distanced ourselves from nature. Our theories and actions often evince a "control of nature" paradigm. Highlighting differences between the subject matter of the natural and the social sciences is extremely complicated. For example, monkeys make friends with zoologists and, when studied, may react in similar ways to humans. It is important to consider in what ways the studying of people by people may add complexity to research, and how this in turn may stimulate us to think differently about how people study nonhumans. For example, issues of animal rights and environmental ethics raise questions about our traditionally human-centric view of the world. Perhaps bacteria do blush and we are just too ignorant to notice!

4. Foschi and Buchan use the term "White" rather than English Canadian.

PART TWO

CULTURE

CHAPTER THREE

CULTURE

In this chapter you will learn that:

- Culture is the sum of ideas, practices, and material objects that people create in order to adapt to, and thrive in, their environments.

- Humans have been able to thrive in their environments because of their unique ability to think abstractly, cooperate with one another, and make tools.

- We can see the contours of culture most sharply if we are neither too deeply immersed in it nor too much removed from it.

- As societies become more complex, culture becomes more diversified and consensus declines in many areas of life. This increases human freedom.

- As societies become more complex, the limits within which freedom may increase become more rigid. This constrains human freedom.

- Although culture is created to solve human problems, it sometimes has negative consequences that create new problems.

ROBERT J. BRYM

UNIVERSITY OF TORONTO

INTRODUCTION

CULTURE AS PROBLEM SOLVING

Canadian hockey legend Wayne Gretzky refused to get his hair cut while playing on the road because the last time he did, his team lost. He always put his equipment on in the same order: left shin pad, left stocking, right shin pad, right stocking, pants, left skate, right skate, shoulder pads, left elbow pad, right elbow pad, and finally, jersey—with only the right side tucked into his pants. During warm-up, he would always shoot his first puck far to the right of the goal. When he went back to the dressing room, he would drink a Diet Coke, a glass of ice water, a Gatorade, and another Diet Coke—and always in that order

Hockey legend Wayne Gretzky would tuck only the right side of his jersey into his pants. This superstitious practice helped to put his mind at ease before and during play. It is an example of how people create culture to cope with anxiety and other concrete problems they face.

SOURCE: CP Picture Archive/F. Scott Grant.

("Mad About Hockey: Superstitions," 2002). He believed these routines brought him luck.

Nomar Garciaparra, the star shortstop of the Boston Red Sox, can take ten seconds to repeatedly pull up his batting gloves and kick the dirt with the toes of his cleats before he swings the bat. He has other superstitious practices as well. For example, he never changes his cap. And although his name is really Anthony, he adopted "Nomar," his father's name spelled backwards, for good luck. Garciaparra's nervous pre-batting dance, as well as his other superstitious practices, make some people chuckle. But they put Garciaparra at ease. They certainly didn't hurt his .372 batting average in 2000. As Garciaparra says: "I have some superstitions, definitely, and they're always going to be there. I think a lot of people have them in baseball.... [It] definitely helps because it gets you in the mind set" ("Garciaparra Explains His Superstitions," 1999).

Like soldiers going off to battle, college students about to write final exams, and other people in high-stress situations, athletes invent routines to help them stop worrying and focus on the job at hand. Some wear a lucky piece of jewellery or item of clothing. Others say special words or a quick prayer. Still others cross themselves. And then there are those who engage in more elaborate rituals. For example, sociologists Cheryl and Daniel Albas of the University of Manitoba interviewed 300 college students about their magical practices before final exams. One student felt she would do well only if she ate a sausage and two eggs sunny-side up on the morning of each exam. The sausage had to be arranged vertically on the left side of her plate and the eggs placed to the right of the sausage so they formed the "100" percent she was aiming for (Albas and Albas, 1989). Of course, the ritual had more direct influence on her cholesterol level than on her grade. But indirectly it may have had the desired effect. To the degree it helped to relieve her anxiety and relax her, she may have done better in exams.

When some people say culture, they refer to opera, ballet, art, and fine literature. For sociologists, however, this definition is too narrow. Sociologists define **culture** broadly as all the ideas, practices, and material objects that people create to deal with real-life problems. For example, when Gretzky developed his dressing habits and the university student invented the ritual of preparing for exams by eating a sausage and eggs arranged just so, they were creating culture in the sociological sense. These practices helped Gretzky and the student deal with the real-life problem of high anxiety. Similarly, tools help people solve the problem of how to plant crops and build houses. Religion helps people face the problem of death and how to give meaning to life. Tools and religion are also elements of culture because they, too, help people solve real-life problems.

Note, however, that religion, technology, and many other elements of culture differ from the superstitions of athletes and undergraduates in one important respect. Superstitions are often unique to the individuals who create them. In contrast, religion and technology are widely shared. They are even passed on from one generation to the next. How does cultural sharing take place? By means of human interaction, communication, and learning. In other words, culture becomes shared when it is socially transmitted. A society involves people interacting socially and sharing culture.[1] Culture, then, is the sum of the *socially transmitted* ideas, practices, and material objects that enable people to adapt to, and thrive in, their environments.

THE ORIGINS OF CULTURE

You can appreciate the importance of culture for human survival by considering the predicament of early humans about 100 000 years ago. They lived in harsh natural environments. They had poor physical endowments, being slower runners and weaker fighters than many other animals. Yet, despite these disadvantages, they survived. More than that—they prospered and came to dominate nature. This was possible largely because they were the smartest creatures around. Their sophisticated brains enabled them to create cultural survival kits of enormous complexity and flexibility. These cultural survival kits contained three main tools. Each tool was a uniquely human talent. Each gave rise to a different element of culture.

The first tool in the human cultural survival kit was **abstraction**, the capacity to create ideas or ways of thinking. **Symbols**, for example, are one important type of idea. They are things that carry particular meanings. Languages, mathematical notations, and signs are all sets of symbols. Symbols allow us to classify experience and generalize from it. For example, we recognize that we can sit on many objects but that only some of those objects have four legs, a back, and space for one person. We distinguish the latter from other objects by giving them a name: "chairs." By the time a baby reaches the end of her first year, she has heard that word repeatedly and understands that it refers to a certain class of objects. True, a few chimpanzees have been taught how to make some signs with their hands. In this way, they have learned a few dozen words and how to string together some simple phrases. But even these extraordinarily intelligent animals cannot learn any rules of grammar, teach other chimps what they know, or advance much beyond the vocabulary of an 18-month-old human (Pinker, 1994). Abstraction at anything beyond the most rudimentary level is a uniquely human capacity. The ability to abstract enables humans to learn and transmit knowledge in a way no other animal can.

Cooperation is the second main tool in the human cultural survival kit. It is the capacity to create a complex social life by establishing **norms**. Norms are standards of behaviour or generally accepted ways of doing things. When we raise children and build schools, we are cooperating in order to reproduce and advance the human race. When we create communities and industries, we are cooperating by pooling resources and encouraging people to acquire specialized skills, thus enabling them to accomplish things no person could possibly do alone. An enormous variety of social arrangements and institutions, ranging from health-care systems to forms of religious worship to political parties, demonstrate the advanced human capacity to cooperate and adhere to norms. Of course, there is also plenty of war, crime, and revolution in the world. However, even when people engage in conflict they must cooperate and respect norms or fail to achieve their survival aims. The bank robber who is left stranded by his getaway man will be caught; the navy captain whose sailors mutiny will lose the battle.

Production is the third main tool in the human cultural survival kit. It involves devising and using tools and techniques that improve our ability to take what we want from nature. Such tools and techniques are known as material culture. Of course, all animals take from nature in order to subsist, and an ape may sometimes use a rock to break another object. But only humans are sufficiently intelligent and dexterous to *make* tools and use them to produce everything from food to computers. Understood in this sense, production is a uniquely human activity.

Table 3.1 illustrates each of the basic human capacities and their cultural offshoots with respect to three types of human activity: medicine, law, and religion. It shows, for these three types of activity, how abstraction, cooperation, and production give rise to specific kinds of ideas, norms, and elements of material culture. In medicine, theoretical ideas about the way our bodies work are evaluated using norms about how to test theories experimentally. Experimentation, in turn, results in the production of new medicines and therapies, which are parts of material culture. In law, **values**, or shared ideas about what is right and wrong, are embodied in a legal code, or norms defining illegal behaviour and punishments for breaking the law. The application of the law requires the creation of courts and jails, which are also part of material culture. And in religion, **folklore**—traditional ideas about how the universe was created, the meaning of life, and so on—is expressed in **folkways**, or norms regarding how to worship and how to treat fellow human beings. Folklore and folkways can give rise to material culture that includes churches, their associated art and architecture, and so forth. Thus, as these examples show, the capacity for abstraction, cooperation, and production is evident in all spheres of culture.

In concluding this discussion of the origins of culture, it must be noted that people are usually rewarded when they follow cultural guidelines and punished when they do not. Taken together, these rewards and punishments aimed at ensuring conformity are known as **sanctions** or the system of **social control**. Rewards (or positive sanctions) include everything from praise and encouragement to money and power. Punishments (or negative sanc-

tions) range from avoidance and contempt to physical violence and arrest.

Despite efforts to control them, people often reject elements of existing culture and create new elements of culture. The reasons for this are discussed in Chapter 19 ("Deviance and Crime") and Chapter 20 ("Politics and Social Movements"). Here it is enough to say that, just as social control is needed to ensure stable patterns of interaction, so resistance to social control is needed to ensure cultural innovation and social renewal. Stable but vibrant societies are able to find a balance between social control and cultural innovation.

CULTURE FROM THE MARGINS

Martians can never hope to grasp the tacit knowledge of real human beings. On the other hand, they sometimes see things real human beings fail to notice.

—Michael Ignatieff (2000: x).

I was once introduced to an interesting woman at a party and began a conversation with her that started agreeably. Within ten minutes, however, I found myself on the other side of the room, my back pressed hard against the wall, trying to figure out how I could politely end our interaction. I wasn't immediately aware of the reason for my discomfort. Only after I told the woman I had to make an important phone call and had left the room did I realize the source of the problem: she had invaded my culturally defined comfort zone. Research shows the average North American prefers to

TABLE 3.1 THE BUILDING BLOCKS OF CULTURE

HUMAN CAPACITIES	Abstraction	Cooperation	Production
	↓	↓	↓
ELEMENTS OF CULTURE	Ideas	Norms	Material culture
CULTURAL ACTIVITIES			
Medicine	theories	experiments	treatments
Law	values	laws	courts, jails
Religion	religious folklore	religious customs	church art, architecture

SOURCE: Adapted from Robert Bierstedt, *The Social Order* (New York: McGraw-Hill, 1963).

stand 30 to 36 inches (about 75 to 90 cm) away from strangers or acquaintances when they are engaged in face-to-face interaction (Hall, 1959: 158–80). But this woman had recently arrived from her home in a part of the Middle East where the culturally defined comfort zone is generally smaller. She stood only about two feet (60 cm) away from me as we spoke. Without thinking, I retreated half a step. Without thinking, she advanced half a step. And soon we had waltzed across the faculty club lounge, completely unaware of what we were doing, until I had no further room to retreat and had to concoct a means of escape.

As this example shows, culture, despite its central importance in human life, is often invisible to people who are immersed in it. That is, people tend to take their own culture for granted; it usually seems so sensible and natural they rarely think about it. I was unable to understand how my culture was affecting me while I was in its grip. I understood its effect only when I removed myself from the faculty club lounge, the immediate context of its operation, and thought hard about how it was making me behave.

If people often take their own culture for granted, they are often startled when confronted by cultures other than their own. That is, the ideas, norms, and techniques of other cultures frequently seem odd, irrational, and even inferior. Judging another culture exclusively by the standards of one's own is called **ethnocentrism**. Ethnocentrism impairs the sociological understanding of culture quite as much as taking one's own culture for granted.

The negative effect of ethnocentrism on sociological understanding may be illustrated by a practice that seems bizarre to many Westerners: cow worship among Hindu peasants in India. Hindu peasants refuse to slaughter cattle and eat beef because, for them, the cow is a religious symbol of life. Pin-up calendars throughout rural India portray beautiful women with the bodies of fat white cows, milk jetting out of each teat. Cows are permitted to wander the streets, defecate on the sidewalks, and stop to chew their cud in busy intersections and on railroad tracks, causing traffic to come to a complete halt. In Madras, police stations maintain fields where stray cows that have fallen ill can graze and be nursed back to health. The government even runs old age homes for cows where dry and decrepit cattle are kept free of charge. All this seems utterly inscrutable to most Westerners, for it takes place amid poverty and hunger that could presumably be

alleviated if only the peasants would slaughter their "useless" cattle for food instead of squandering scarce resources feeding and protecting them.

The trouble is, ethnocentrism misleads many Western observers (Harris, 1974: 3–32). Cow worship, it turns out, is an economically rational practice in rural India. For one thing, Indian peasants can't afford tractors, so cows are needed to give birth to oxen, which are in high demand for ploughing. For another, the cows produce hundreds of millions of kilograms of recoverable manure, about half of which is used as fertilizer and half as cooking fuel. With oil, coal, and wood in short supply, and with the peasants unable to afford chemical fertilizers, cow dung is, well, a godsend. What is more, cows in India don't cost much to maintain since they eat mostly food that isn't fit for human consumption. And they represent an important source of protein and a livelihood for members of low-ranking castes, who have the right to dispose of the bodies of dead cattle. These "untouchables" eat beef and form the work force of India's large leathercraft industry. Thus, the protection of cows by means of cow worship is in fact a perfectly sensible and highly efficient economic practice. It only seems irrational when judged by the standards of Western agribusiness.

We can draw much the same lesson from the case of cow worship in India as from my hurried exit from the faculty club lounge. Culture is most clearly visible from the margins, as it were. We see its contours most sharply if we are neither too deeply immersed in it (as I was during the faculty club conversation) nor too much removed from it (as most Western observers are when they analyze cow worship in India). Said differently, if you refrain from taking your own culture for granted and judging other cultures by the standards of your own, you will have taken important first steps towards developing a sociological understanding of culture.

THE TWO FACES OF CULTURE

Having defined culture, discussed its origins, and located the ideal vantage point for analyzing it, we can now turn to the chapter's main theme. You will now see that, while some aspects of culture make us freer, others constrain and even endanger us.

When we develop new ideas, practices, and artifacts, we give ourselves more choices and often come closer to realizing our full human potential. For example, you will see below that we are now freer than ever to draw on all cultures in all their variety. This allows us to fashion our identities to suit our individual tastes. The story is much the same whether we consider ethnic identities, religious beliefs, political affiliations, or sexual orientations. We now become who we are less because traditional authority imposes a set of cultural definitions on us, more because we are able to choose who we want to be.

On the other hand, cultural freedom develops within definite limits. Beyond those limits it is more and more difficult to move. In particular, our lives are increasingly governed by the twin forces of rationalization and consumerism:

- **Rationalization** is the application of the most efficient means to achieve given goals and the unintended, negative consequences of doing so. For example, modern bureaucracies exemplify the rationalization process (Weber, 1946 [1922]). The factory, the government office, the military, the system of higher education, and the institutions of science all seek to apply the most efficient means to achieve given goals (see Box 3.1). Yet bureaucracies are composed of unelected officials. Consequently, they concentrate power and threaten democracy. Moreover, bureaucracies discourage officeholders from considering what the goals of their organization ought to be. Bureaucrats are asked only to determine the best way of achieving the goals defined by their superiors. Officeholders thus lose their spontaneity, their inventiveness, and all opportunity to act heroically. Like other aspects of the rationalization process, the growth of bureaucracy thus constrains our freedom.

- **Consumerism** is a lifestyle that involves defining one's self in terms of the goods one purchases. Some sociologists argue that consumerism impoverishes the self and society by drawing resources and attention away from pressing social issues and encouraging environmentally dangerous levels of consumption. From this point of view, culture, which started out as a means of solving real-life problems, has become the biggest real-life problem of all (Postman, 1992).

Let us begin our examination of the two faces of culture by first considering the ways in which culture makes us freer.

CULTURE AS FREEDOM

CULTURAL DIVERSIFICATION AND GLOBALIZATION

Thirty or forty years ago, the Christmas pageant was a fixture of every elementary school in the country. Today, some Canadian public schools have abolished Christmas pageants. Others have put Christmas on a par with the Hindu Diwali, the Jewish Chanukah, and the seasonal festivals of other ethnic and religious groups. In some schools, an ethnically and religiously neutral "winter solstice" forms the basis of celebration in mid- to late December. The reason for this change is plain: According to the most recent census, more than a fifth of Canadians do not identify with Christianity. Moreover, many Christians recognize that using public institutions to promote their religion is an imposition that creates discomfort for many minority students and denies the value of non-Christian cultures. Therefore, particularly in big-city schools, where "minority" students are sometimes in the numerical majority, cultural uniformity has given way to cultural diversity.

Canada used to be composed almost exclusively of northern Europeans and an Aboriginal minority. By eliminating the most overt forms of racism in its immigration policies in the 1960s, Canada began to diversify culturally. In the 1970s, the Canadian government continued the trend by adopting a policy of multiculturalism, which funds the maintenance of cultural diversity (Fleras and Elliott, 2002).

Canada's growing cultural diversification is well illustrated in Table 3.2 on page 65. In 1961, nine of the top ten source countries for Canadian immigrants were in Europe and North America. In 1996, seven of the top ten source countries were in Asia. As a result of the inflow of immigrants from nontraditional sources—not just Asia, but also the Caribbean, Latin America, and Africa—there were 5.7 million non-whites in Canada in 2001, nearly 18 percent of the population. In Montreal, Edmonton, Calgary, and Winnipeg, the figure was closer to one-quarter. In Vancouver, it was nearly 40 percent, while in Toronto nonwhites made up about 45 percent of the population (Henry, Tabor, Mattis, and Rees, 2001: 145–47).

Some critics argue that our immigration and multiculturalist policies weaken Canada's social

In the last quarter of the nineteenth century, it was already clear that turning scientific principles into technological innovations was going to require not just genius but substantial resources, especially money and organization. The first "invention factory" was established by Thomas Edison at Menlo Park, New Jersey, in the late 1870s. Historian of science Robert Pool notes:

> [T]he most important factor in Edison's success—outside of his genius for invention—was the organization he had set up to assist him. By 1878, Edison had assembled at Menlo Park a staff of thirty scientists, metalworkers, glassblowers, draftsmen, and others working under his close direction and supervision. With such support, Edison boasted that he could turn out "a minor invention every ten days and a big thing every six months or so" (Pool, 1997: 22).

The phonograph and the electric light bulb were two such "big things." Both were inspired by Edison. Both, however, were also expensive team efforts, motivated by vast commercial possibilities. (Edison founded General Electric, the most profitable company in the world in 1999 and the second most valuable based on market capitalization; see "Global 1000," 1999.)

By the middle of the twentieth century, the great bulk of technological innovation was organized along industrial lines. Entire armies of experts and vast sums of capital were required to run the new invention factories. Only governments and, increasingly, giant multinational corporations could afford to sustain the research effort of the second half of the twentieth century. In the course of the century, the number of research scientists in the industrialized countries increased a hundredfold. Between 1960 and 2000, research and development spending tripled after taking inflation into account, and the proportion spent by corporations increased from one-third to two-thirds of the total (Hobsbawm, 1994: 522–57; *Statistical Abstract...*, 1998: 609).

In light of these developments, it should come as no surprise that military and profit-making considerations now govern the direction of most research and development. A reporter once asked a bank robber why he robs banks. The robber answered: "Because that's where the money is." This is by no means the only motivation prompting scientists and engineers to research particular topics. Especially in theoretical, as opposed to applied, research, and especially in universities, as opposed to the research institutes of governments and private industry, the direction of inquiry is strongly influenced by personal interests, individual creativity, and the state of a field's intellectual development. It would, however, be naïve to think that practicality doesn't also enter into the scientist's calculation of what he or she ought to study. Even in a more innocent era, Sir Isaac Newton studied astronomy partly because the explorers and mariners of his day needed better navigational cues, just as Michael Faraday was partly motivated to discover the relationship between electricity and magnetism by his society's search for new forms of power (Bronowski, 1965 [1956]: 7–8). The connection between practicality and research is even more evident today, when many researchers—even many of those who do theoretically driven research in colleges—are pulled in particular directions by large research grants, well-paying jobs, access to expensive state-of-the-art equipment, and the possibility of winning patents and achieving commercial success. For example, many of the leading molecular biologists have established genetic engineering companies, serve on their boards of directors, or receive research funding from them. In not a few cases, these companies have been bought out by major pharmaceutical and agrochemical corporations who see their vast profit potential (Rural Advancement Foundation International, 1999; Rifkin, 1998: 56).

Economic lures, increasingly provided by the military and big corporations, have generated moral and political qualms among some researchers. Some scientists and engineers wonder whether research on particular topics achieves optimum benefits for humanity, and some are even troubled by the possibility that some types of research may be harmful to humankind. A growing number of researchers, however, if they are at all preoccupied by these issues, recognize that to do cutting-edge research they must still any residual misgivings, hop on the bandwagon, and adhere to military and industrial requirements and priorities. That, after all, is where the money is.

fabric. Specifically, multiculturalism supposedly encourages immigrants to cling to their past rather than shrug off their old self-conceptions and create a distinctive *Canadian* identity (Bissoondath, 2002 [1994]). There are two problems with this viewpoint. First, it is by no means certain that we lack a distinctive Canadian identity. In fact, as noted below, a defining element of our distinctive Canadian identity

TABLE 3.2 TOP TEN PLACES OF BIRTH OF CANADIAN IMMIGRANTS

IMMIGRATED BEFORE 1961		IMMIGRATED BETWEEN 1 JANUARY 1991 AND 30 APRIL 1996	
Country	% of All Immigrants	Country	% of All Immigrants
1. UK	25.2	1. Hong Kong	10.5
2. Italy	15.3	2. China	8.5
3. Germany	10.2	3. India	6.9
4. Netherlands	8.4	4. Philippines	6.9
5. Poland	5.5	5. Sri Lanka	4.3
6. USA	4.3	6. Poland	4.3
7. Hungary	3.1	7. Taiwan	3.1
8. Ukraine	2.6	8. Vietnam	3.1
9. Greece	2.0	9. USA	2.8
10. China	1.7	10. UK	2.4
Other	21.7	Other	47.2
Total	100.0	Total	100.0

SOURCE: Statistics Canada, "Top Ten Places of Birth for Total Immigrants, Immigrants Arriving Before 1961 and Recent Immigrants for Canada, 1996 Census—20% Sample Data," Cat. No. 93F0023XDB6003. Reprinted by permission of the Minister of Industry, 2000.

is precisely our deep respect for diversity. Second, contrary to the claims of the critics of multiculturalism, survey research shows that support for multiculturalism is *not* correlated with traditional attitudes (such as religiosity) that keep people rooted in the past. Support for multiculturalism *is* correlated with various modern trends, such as support for equality between women and men (Adams, 1997: 173).

From this point of view, Canada's multiculturalist policies are simply the latest stage in a long process of cultural evolution. In general, cultures tend to become more diverse or heterogeneous as societies become more complex, with important consequences for everyday life. Thus, in preliterate or tribal societies, cultural beliefs and practices are virtually the same for all group members. For example, many tribal societies organize puberty ceremonies to mark the end of childhood and the beginning of adulthood, fertility dances to pray for good crops and healthy babies, and other rites. These religious rituals involve elaborate body painting, carefully orchestrated chants and movements, and so forth. They are conducted in public. No variation from prescribed practice is allowed. Culture is homogeneous (Durkheim, 1976 [1915]).

In contrast, preindustrial Western Europe and North America were rocked by artistic, religious, sci-

entific, and political forces that fragmented culture. The Renaissance, the Protestant Reformation, the Scientific Revolution, the French and American Revolutions—between the fourteenth and eighteenth centuries, all of these movements involved people questioning old ways of seeing and doing things. Science placed skepticism about established authority at the very heart of its method. Political revolution proved there was nothing ordained about who should rule and how they should do so. Religious dissent insured that the Catholic Church would no longer be the supreme interpreter of God's will in the eyes of all Christians. Authority and truth became divided as never before.

Cultural fragmentation picked up steam during industrialization, as the variety of occupational roles grew and new political and intellectual movements crystallized. Its pace is quickening again today in the postindustrial era under the impact of a variety of globalizing forces.

The roots of **globalization** are many (see Chapter 18). International trade and investment are expanding. Members of different ethnic and racial groups are migrating and coming into sustained contact with one another. A growing number of people from these diverse groups date, court, and marry across religious, ethnic, and racial lines. Influential "transnational" organizations such as the International Monetary Fund, the European Union, Greenpeace, and Amnesty International are being created. Inexpensive international travel and communication make contacts between people from diverse cultures routine. The mass media make Vin Diesel and *Friends* nearly as well known in Warsaw as in Winnipeg, and MTV brings rock music to the world via MTV Latino, MTV Brazil, MTV Europe, MTV Asia, MTV Japan, MTV Mandarin, MTV India, and MTV Canada (Hanke, 1998). Globalization, in short, destroys political, economic, and cultural isolation, bringing people together in what Canadian communications guru Marshall McLuhan (1964) called a "global village." As result of globalization, people are less obliged to accept the culture into which they are born and freer to combine elements of culture from a wide variety of historical periods and geographical settings. Globalization is a Bombay schoolboy listening to Bob Marley on his CD player as he rushes to slip into his Levis, wolf down a bowl of Kellogg's Basmati Flakes, and say goodbye to his parents in Hindi because he's late for his English-language school.

The spread of English is, in fact, a key marker of the extent of globalization. In 1600, English was the mother tongue of between four and seven million people. Not even all people in England spoke it. Today, 750 million to 1 billion people speak English worldwide, over half as a second language. With the exception of the many varieties of Chinese, English is the most widespread language on earth, and it is by far the most important. Over half the world's technical and scientific periodicals are written in English, as are three-quarters of the world's letters, telexes, and telegrams, and 80 percent of the text stored in the world's computers. English is the official language of the Olympics, of the Miss Universe contest, of navigation in the air and on the seas, and of the World Council of Churches.

English is dominant because Britain and the United States have been the world's most powerful and influential countries—economically, militarily, and culturally—for more than two centuries. (Someone once defined "language" as a dialect backed up by an army.) In recent decades, the global spread of capitalism, the popularity of Hollywood movies and American TV shows, and widespread access to instant communication via telephone and the Internet have increased the reach of the English language. There are now more speakers of excellent English in India than in Britain, and when a construction company jointly owned by German, French, and Italian interests undertakes a building project in Spain, the language of business is English (McCrum, Cran, and MacNeil, 1992).

Even in Japan, where relatively few people speak the language, English words are commonly used and Japanese words that are badly translated into English often become popular. The result is what is commonly known as "Japlish." Sometimes the results are unintelligible to a native English speaker. "Push to my nose! I might be changing to you?" says the catchy sign in a T-shirt store in Tokyo's Ueno district. Certain computer terms are more comprehensible to a native English speaker. For example, when you learn to open a computer file's *ai-kon* (icon) you are told to *daburu-kurikku* (double-click) the *mausu* (mouse) (Kristof, 1997).

In view of the extensive use of English in Japan, *The Japanese Times*, one of Tokyo's four English daily newspapers, ran a story a few years ago noting the pressures of globalization and suggesting it might be time for Japan to switch to English. However, there is an official backlash. To limit the anglicization of Japanese, the Ministry of Health and Welfare banned excessive use of English in its documents a couple of years ago. The Ministry of Education is now replacing many English words in official documents—words such as *sukeemu* (scheme), *eensenchibu* (incentive), *deribatibu* (derivative), and *identyityi* (identity). Whether official pronouncements will have much effect on the way English and Japlish are used in advertising and on the streets is, however, another question entirely. As one Japanese newspaper pointed out, given the popularity of English words, it's doubtful there will be much *foro-uppu* (follow-up).

For Japanese teenagers, English and Japlish are certainly considered the very height of fashion. "Japlish words are easy to pronounce. And English sounds very cool," says 11-year-old Mai Asai (quoted in Delmos, 2002). A 15-year old girl, wearing her trademark *roozu sokusu* (loose socks), might greet a friend sporting new sunglasses with a spirited *chekaraccho* (Check it out, Joe). If she likes the shades, she might say they're *cho beri gu* (ultra-good) and invite her friend *deniru* (to go to a Denny's restaurant) or *hageru* (to go to a Häagen-Dazs ice cream outlet). Of course, the girl might also *disu* (diss, or show disrespect towards) her friend. She might come right out and inform him that the new shades look *cho beri ba* (ultra-bad) or *cho beri bu* (ultra-blue, depressing, or ultra-ugly). If so, the situation that develops could be a little *denjarasu* (dangerous). Terms of affection, such as *wonchu* (I want you), might not be exchanged. The boy might decide that he has made a *misu* (mistake) and that the girl is too *hi mentay* (high maintenance) to justify pursuing. The budding relationship might go nowhere. Nonetheless, we can be pretty sure that Japanese teenagers' use of English slang will intensify under the pressures of globalization.

THE RIGHTS REVOLUTION

Underlying cultural diversification is the **rights revolution**, the process by which socially excluded groups have struggled to win equal rights under the law and in practice. After the outburst of nationalism, racism, and genocidal behaviour among the combatants in World War II, the United Nations proclaimed the Universal Declaration of Human Rights in 1948. Its preamble reads in part:

> Whereas recognition of the inherent dignity and of the equal and inalienable rights of all members of the human family is the foundation of freedom, justice and peace in the world.... Now, therefore The General Assembly proclaims this Universal Declaration of Human Rights as a common standard of achievement for all peoples and all nations, to the end that every individual and every organ of society, keeping this Declaration constantly in mind, shall strive by teaching and education to promote respect for these rights and freedoms and by progressive measures, national and international, to secure their universal and effective recognition and observance ... (United Nations, 1998).

Fanned by such sentiment, the rights revolution was in full swing by the 1960s. Today, women's rights, Aboriginal rights, gay and lesbian rights, the rights of people with special needs, constitutional rights, and language rights are a key part of our political discourse. As a result of the rights revolution, democracy has been widened and deepened (see Chapter 20, "Politics and Social Movements"). The rights revolution is by no means finished—many categories of people are still discriminated against socially, politically, and economically—but in much of the world all categories of people now participate more fully than ever before in the life of their societies (Ignatieff, 2000).

The rights revolution raises some difficult issues. For example, groups that have suffered extraordinarily high levels of discrimination historically, such as Aboriginal Canadians, Jewish Canadians, Chinese Canadians, and Japanese Canadians, have demanded reparations in the form of money, symbolic gestures, and, in the case of Aboriginal Canadians, land and political autonomy.[2] Much controversy surrounds the extent of the obligation of current citizens to compensate past injustices.

Another problem raised by the rights revolution concerns how we can achieve an acceptable balance between the right to be equal and the right to be different. For example, most residents of Quebec expect all Quebeckers to be able to compete on an equal footing for jobs, regardless of whether they are of French, English, or other origin. This is the right to equality. But Quebeckers of French origin have also exercised their right to be different. They have, for instance, passed laws restricting the use of English on public signs. These laws are controversial. Some English Quebeckers accept them as legitimate; others do not. Controversy therefore persists regarding the balance between the right to equality and the right to be different.

These problems notwithstanding, the rights revolution is here to stay and it affects our culture profoundly. Specifically, the rights revolution fragments Canadian culture by legitimizing the grievances of groups that were formerly excluded from full social participation and renewing pride in their identity and heritage. Our history books, our literature, our music, our use of languages, our very sense of what it means to be Canadian have diversified culturally. White male heterosexual property owners of British origin are still disproportionately influential in Canada, but our culture is no longer dominated by them in the way that it was just four decades ago.

POSTMODERNISM

In part due to the rights revolution, so much cultural fragmentation and reconfiguration has taken place in the last few decades that some sociologists think a new term is needed to characterize the culture of our times: **postmodernism**.

Postmodern culture has three main features:

- First, it involves *an eclectic mixing of elements from different times and places*. That is, in the postmodern era it is easier to create individualized belief systems and practices by blending facets of different cultures and historical periods. Consider religion. Surveys conducted by Reginald Bibby of the University of Lethbridge show that Canadians often supplement Judeo-Christian beliefs and practices with less conventional ideas about astrology, psychic powers, communication with the dead, and so forth (Bibby, 1987). People who attend church regularly are just as likely to hold such unconventional beliefs as non-attenders. But despite the widespread acceptance of unconventional beliefs, the overwhelming majority of Canadians still turn to established religions for **rites of passage**, or cultural ceremonies that mark the transition from one stage of life to another (e.g., baptisms, confirmations, weddings) or from life to death (funerals). Individuals thus choose their own mix of unconventional and conventional beliefs and practices. They draw on religions much like consumers shop in a mall; as Bibby says, they practise religion *à la carte*. Meanwhile, the churches in Canada have diversified their menus in order to appeal to the spiritual, leisure, and social needs of religious consumers and retain their loyalties in the competitive market for congregants and parishioners. The mix-and-match approach we see when it comes to religion is evident in virtually all spheres of culture.
- A second important feature of postmodern culture involves *the erosion of authority*. Half a century ago, Canadians were more likely than they are today to defer to authority in the family, schools, politics,

medicine, and religion. In fact, Canadians were often characterized as an especially deferential people, more respectful of authority than, say, their individualistic, revolutionary, violent, and entrepreneurial cousins in the United States. In the second half of the twentieth century, however, Canadians grew skeptical about authority in all social institutions—even more skeptical than Americans in many respects (Brym with Fox, 1989; Nevitte, 1996; see Figure 3.1 and Box 3.2 on page 70). For example, voting and other forms of conventional politics are less popular than they used to be, while nonconventional political action is more popular. In 2000, 30 percent of Canadians said they had participated in nonconventional political actions (joining a boycott, taking part in an unlawful demonstration, joining an unofficial strike, or occupying a building or a factory). That was up from 24 percent in 1980. Meanwhile, just 63 percent of eligible voters cast a ballot in the 2000 federal election, down from 73 percent in the 1980s (see Figure 3.2).

- Finally, postmodern culture is characterized by *the decline of consensus around core values*. Half a century ago, people's values remained quite stable over the course of their adult lives and many values were widely accepted. Today, value shifts are more rapid and consensus has broken down on many issues. For instance, half a century ago, the great majority of adults remained loyal to one political party from one election to the next. Today, people are more likely to vote for different parties in succeeding elections (Clarke, Jenson, LeDuc, and Pammett, 1996 [1984]: 139–46).

The decline of consensus may also be illustrated by considering the fate of Big Historical Projects. For most of the past 200 years, consensus throughout the world was built around Big Historical Projects. Various social movements convinced people they could take history into their own hands and create a glorious future just by signing up. German Nazism was a Big Historical Project. Its followers expected the Reich to enjoy 1000 years of power. Communism was an even bigger Big Historical Project, mobilizing hundreds of millions of people for a future that promised to end

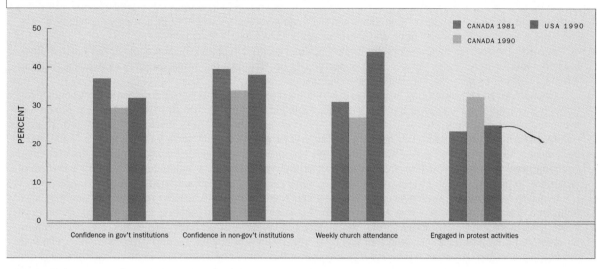

FIGURE 3.1 "CANADIANS GREW SKEPTICAL ABOUT AUTHORITY IN ALL SOCIAL INSTITUTIONS—EVEN MORE SKEPTICAL THAN AMERICANS IN SOME RESPECTS."

SOURCE: Adapted from Nevitte (1996: 56, 60, 80, 210).

inequality and injustice for all time. However, the biggest and most successful Big Historical Project was not so much a social movement as a powerful idea—the belief that progress is inevitable, that life will always improve, due mainly to the spread of democracy and scientific innovation.

The twentieth century was unkind to Big Historical Projects. Russian communism lasted 74 years, German Nazism a mere 12. And the idea of progress fell on hard times as a hundred million soldiers and civilians died in wars; the forward march of democracy took wrong turns into fascism, communism, and regimes based on religious fanaticism; and pollution due to urbanization and industrialization threatened the planet. In the postmodern era, more and more people recognize that apparent progress, including scientific advances, often has negative consequences (Scott, 1998; see Figure 3.3 on page 71).

The aspects of postmodernism listed above—the eclectic mixing of cultural elements from different times and places, the erosion of authority, and the decline of consensus around core values—have many parents, teachers, politicians, religious leaders, and not a few university professors worried. How can we

make binding decisions? How can we govern? How can we teach children and adolescents the difference between right and wrong? How can we transmit accepted literary tastes and artistic standards from one generation to the next? These are the kinds of issues that plague people in positions of authority

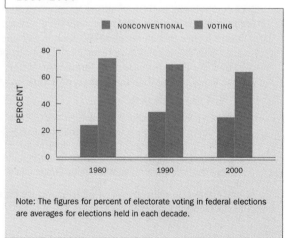

FIGURE 3.2 PERCENT OF ELECTORATE VOTING IN FEDERAL ELECTIONS AND PARTICIPATING IN NONCONVENTIONAL POLITICAL ACTION, CANADA, 1980–2000

Note: The figures for percent of electorate voting in federal elections are averages for elections held in each decade.

SOURCES: "Canada: Parliamentary Elections" (2000); Naumetz (2000); *World Values Survey* (2000).

Until the mid-1960s, the image of Canadians among most sociologists was that of a stodgy people: peaceful, conservative, respectful of authority, and therefore quite unlike our American cousins.

According to conventional wisdom, the United States was born in open rebellion against the British motherland. Its Western frontier was lawless. Vast opportunities for striking it rich bred a spirit of individualism. Thus, American culture became an anti-authoritarian culture.

Canada developed differently according to the conventional view. It became an independent country not through a revolutionary upheaval but in a gradual, evolutionary manner. The Northwest Mounted Police and two hierarchical churches (Roman Catholic and Anglican) established themselves on the Western frontier *before* the era of mass settlement, allowing for the creation of an orderly society rather than a "wild West." Beginning with the Hudson's Bay Company, large corporations quickly came to dominate the Canadian economy, hampering individualism and the entrepreneurial spirit. Thus, Canadian culture became a culture of deference to authority. That, at least, was the common view until the 1960s (Lipset, 1963).

While the contrast between deferential Canadian culture and anti-authoritarian American culture may have had some validity 40 years ago, it is an inaccurate characterization today (Adams, 1997: 62–95). As we have seen, the questioning of authority spread throughout the Western world beginning in the 1960s. Nowhere, however, did it spread as quickly and thoroughly as in Canada. Canadians used to express more confidence in big business than Americans, but surveys now show the opposite. Canadians used to be more religious than Americans, but that is no longer the case. Fewer Canadians (in percentage terms) say they believe in God and fewer attend weekly religious services. Confidence in government has eroded more quickly in Canada than in the United States. Americans are more patriotic than Canadians, according more respect to the state. Finally, they are more likely than Canadians to regard the traditional nuclear family as the ideal family form, and to think of deviations from tradition—same-sex couples, single-parent families, cohabitation without marriage—as the source of a whole range of social problems. Thus, whether sociologists examine attitudes towards the family, the state, government, religion, or big business, they now find that Americans are more deferential to traditional institutional authority than Canadians are.

Because Canadians are less deferential to traditional institutional authority than Americans are, some commentators say that Canadians lack a distinct culture. For example, American patriotism sparks awareness of great national accomplishments in art, war, sports, science, and, indeed, all fields of human endeavour. Anthems, rituals, myths, and celebrations celebrate these accomplishments and give Americans a keen sense of who they are and how they differ from non-Americans. Not surprisingly, therefore, a larger percentage of Americans than Canadians think of themselves in unhyphenated terms—as "Americans" plain and simple rather than, say, Italian-Americans. In Canada, a larger percentage of the population thinks of itself in hyphenated terms; compared to the Americans, our identity is qualified, even tentative.

Does this mean that Canadians lack a distinct national culture? Hardly. It means that, while American culture is characterized by a relatively high degree of deference to dominant institutions, Canadian culture is characterized by a relatively high degree of tolerance and respect for diversity. We are more likely than Americans to favour gender equality, accept gay and lesbian relationships, encourage bilingualism and multiculturalism, and accept the right of Aboriginals to political autonomy. Characteristically, a large international survey by a condom manufacturer found that Americans have sex more often than anyone else, but Canadians are most likely to say that the pleasure of their partner is very important. As public opinion pollster Michael Adams writes:

> Twenty-five years of public-opinion polling in Canada has taught me a seemingly paradoxical truth. Canadians feel *strongly* about their *weak* attachments to Canada, its political institutions and their fellow citizens. In other words, they feel strongly about the right to live in a society that allows its citizens to be detached from ideology and critical of organizations, and not to feel obliged to be jingoistic or sentimentally patriotic. Canadians *lack* of nationalism is, in many ways, a distinguishing feature of the country (Adams, 1997: 171).

In short, Canadian culture *is* distinctive, and its chief distinction may be that it qualifies us as the first thoroughly postmodern society.

FIGURE 3.3 "IN THE LONG RUN, DO YOU THINK THE SCIENTIFIC ADVANCES WE ARE MAKING WILL HELP OR HARM HUMANKIND?"

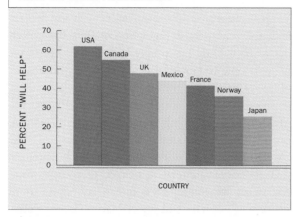

SOURCE: World Values Study Group. World Values Survey, 1981–1984 and 1990–1993 [Computer file]. 2nd ICPSR version. Ann Arbor, MI: Institute for Social Research [producer], 1999. Ann Arbor, MI: Inter-University Consortium for Political and Social Research [distributor], 1999.

today. Although their concerns are legitimate, many of them seem not to have considered the flip side of the coin: The postmodern condition, as described above, empowers ordinary people and makes them more responsible for their own fate. It renders them more tolerant and appreciative of ethnic, racial, religious, and sexual groups other than their own—no small matter in a world torn by group conflict. The postmodern attitude encourages a healthy skepticism about rosy and naïve scientific and political promises. And it frees people to adopt religious, ethnic, and other identities they are comfortable with, as opposed to identities imposed on them by others.

Thus, the news about postmodern culture is not all bad. However, as you will now see, it's not all that good either.

CULTURE AS CONSTRAINT AND AS DANGER

We noted above that culture has two faces. One we labelled "freedom," the other "constraint." Diversity, globalization, and postmodernism are all aspects of the new freedoms that culture allows us today. We now turn to an examination of two contemporary aspects of culture that act as constraining forces on our lives: rationalization and consumerism.

RATIONALIZATION

In fourteenth-century Europe, an upsurge in demand for textiles caused loom owners to look for ways of increasing productivity. To that end, they imposed longer hours on loom workers and installed the first public clocks. The clocks, known as *Werkglocken* ("work clocks") in German, signalled the beginning of the workday, the timing of meals, and quitting time.

Workers were accustomed to enjoying many holidays and a fairly flexible and vague work schedule regulated only approximately by the seasons and the rising and setting of the sun. The regimentation imposed by the work clocks made life harder. So the workers staged uprisings to silence the clocks. But to no avail. City officials sided with the employers and imposed fines for ignoring the *Werkglocken*. Harsher penalties, including death, were imposed on anyone trying to use the clocks' bells to signal a revolt (Thompson, 1967).

Now, more than 600 years later, many people in the world's rich countries—especially big-city couples who are employed full-time in the paid labour force and have pre-teen children—are, in effect, slaves of the *Werkglock*. Life often seems an endless round of waking up at 6:30 A.M., getting everyone washed and dressed, preparing the kids' lunches, getting them out the door in time for the school bus or the car pool, driving to work through rush-hour traffic, facing the speed-up at work that resulted from the recent downsizing, driving back home through rush-hour traffic, preparing dinner, taking the kids to their soccer game, returning home to clean up the dishes and help with homework, getting the kids washed, brushed, and into bed, and (if you haven't brought some office work home) grabbing an hour of TV before collapsing, exhausted, for six-and-a-half hours before the story repeats itself. Life is less hectic for residents of small towns, unmarried people, couples without small children, retirees, and the unemployed. But the lives of most people are so packed with activities that time must be carefully regulated, each moment precisely parcelled out so we may tick off item after item from an ever-growing list of tasks that need to be completed on schedule (Schor, 1992). In 2000, 14 percent of Canadians in the paid labour force worked for pay 50 or more hours a week, up from 11 percent

Taking public transportation often forces us to abandon our culturally defined personal space. However, this abandonment of personal space is itself a cultural norm.

SOURCE: Andrew Benyei, *Commuters*.

in 1976. In 1999, the figure was 38 percent among senior managers, the most overworked job category. Among transport and equipment operators, the second most overworked job category, the figure was 27 percent. Among teachers and professors, the sixth most overworked job category, the figure was 18 percent (Lowe, 2001: 8, 9).

After more than 600 years of conditioning, it is unusual for people to rebel against the clock in the town square anymore. In fact, we now wear a watch on our wrist without giving it a second thought, as it were. This signifies that we have accepted and internalized the regime of the *Werkglock*. Allowing clocks to precisely regulate our activities seems the most natural thing in the world—which is a pretty good sign that the internalized *Werkglock* is, in fact, a product of culture.

Is the precise regulation of time rational? It certainly is rational as a *means* of ensuring efficiency, that is, maximizing how much work you get done in a day. But is it rational as an *end* in itself? For many people, it is not. The precise regulation of time has gotten out of hand. Life has simply become too hectic for many people to enjoy fully. In this sense, rationality of means has led to irrationality of ends.

For American sociologist George Ritzer, the McDonald's fast-food restaurant epitomizes the rationalization process. Ritzer speaks of the "McDonaldization" of the world, by which he means that the organizational principles of the fast-food restaurant are coming to dominate more and more sectors of society and more and more societies (Ritzer, 1993, 1996).

At McDonald's, a set list of carefully weighed food portions with identical ingredients are cooked according to a uniform and precisely timed process. But, says Ritzer, the application of assembly line procedures to meal preparation is dehumanizing for both employees and customers. Thus, the work is done by mainly non-unionized, uniformed, teenage workers who receive minimum wage. To boost sales, they are required to smile as they recite fixed scripts ("Would you like some fries or a drink with your burger?"). Nearly half of all McDonald's employees are so dissatisfied with their work they quit after a year or less. To deal with this problem, McDonald's is now field-testing vending machines that will be used to replace staff and boost sales. Anyone for an e-burger? ("McDonald's Testing E-burgers," 1999). Meanwhile, customers are expected to spend as little time as possible eating the food—hence the drive-through window, chairs designed to be comfortable for only about 20 minutes, and small express outlets in subways and department stores where customers eat standing up or on the run. Customers are also expected to eat unhealthy food. A Big Mac, small fries, medium Coke, and an apple Danish can bring you up to 67 percent of your recommended daily calorie intake and 88 percent of your recommended daily fat intake, which is why doctors and nutritionists regularly decry the popularity of fast food (calculated from McDonald's, 1999). Nonetheless, powerful forces propel its popularity. On the demand side, fast food fits the rushed lifestyles of many individuals and families in the more affluent countries of the world and the growing middle class in the developing countries. (More than half of McDonald's sales are now outside North America). On the supply side, there are big profits to be made from making meal preparation a mass production industry. Motivated by these forces, rationality of means results in irrationality of ends, as it does in other spheres of life.

Taking McDonaldization to a new extreme, one restaurant in Japan has even installed a punch-clock for its customers. The restaurant offers all you can eat for 35 yen per minute. As a result, "the diners rush in, punch the clock, load their trays from the buffet table, and concentrate intensely on efficient chewing and swallowing, trying not to waste time talking to their companions before rushing back to punch out. This version of fast food is so popular that, as the restaurant prepares to open at lunchtime, Tokyo residents *wait in line*" (Gleick, 2000 [1999]: 244; emphasis in the original). Meanwhile, in New York and Los Angeles, some upscale restaurants have got in on the act. An increasingly large number of business clients are so pressed for time they feel the need to pack in *two* half-hour lunches with successive guests. The restaurants oblige, making the resetting of tables "resemble the pit-stop activity at the Indianapolis 500" (Gleick, 2000 [1999]: 155).

As the examples of the *Werkglock* and fast food show, rationalization enables us to do just about everything more efficiently, but at a steep cost. Because it is so widespread, rationalization is one of the most constraining aspects of culture today. In Weber's view, it makes life in the modern world akin to living inside an "iron cage."

The second constraining aspect of culture that we will examine is consumerism, the tendency to define our selves in terms of the goods we purchase.

CONSUMERISM

In 1999, the Gap hired Hollywood talent to create a slick and highly effective series of TV ads for khaki pants. According to the promotional material for the ad campaign, the purpose of the ads was to "reinvent khakis," that is, to stimulate demand for the pants. In *Khakis rock*, "skateboarders and in-line skaters dance, glide, and fly to music by the Crystal Method." In *Khakis groove*, "hip-hop dancers throw radical moves

to the funky beat of Bill Mason." In *Khakis swing*, "two couples break away from a crowd to demonstrate swing techniques to the vintage sounds of Louis Prima" ("Gap," 1999).

About 55 seconds of each ad featured the dancers. During the last five seconds, the words "GAP khakis" appeared on the screen. As the imbalance between stylish come-on and mere information suggests, the people who created the commercials understood well that it was really the appeal of the dancers that would sell the pants. They knew that to stimulate demand for their product, they had to associate the khakis with desirable properties such as youth, good health, coolness, popularity, beauty, and sex. As an advertising executive said in the 1940s: "It's not the steak we sell. It's the sizzle."

Because advertising stimulates sales, there is a tendency for business to spend more on advertising over time. Because advertising is widespread, most people unquestioningly accept it as part of their lives. In fact, many people have *become* ads. Thus, when your father was a child and quickly threw on a shirt, allowing a label to hang out, your grandmother might admonish him to "tuck in that label." Today, in contrast, many people proudly display consumer labels as marks of status and identity. Advertisers teach us to associate the words "Gucci" and "Nike" with different kinds of people, and when people display these labels on their clothes they are telling us something about the kind of people they are. Advertising becomes us.

Since the 1980s, there has been an explosion of advertising directed at children in particular. Here, advertisers recognized, was a vast untapped market; children could be used to nag their parents to buy more products. The manipulation of children by advertisers soon became a sort of quasi-science. One advertising guru said there are seven basic types of nagging tactics that can be unleashed by effective child-directed advertising:

A *pleading* nag is one accompanied by repetitions of words like "please" or "mom, mom, mom." A *persistent* nag involves constant requests for the coveted product and may include the phrase "I'm gonna ask just one more time." *Forceful* nags are extremely pushy and may include subtle threats, like

"Well, then, I'll go and ask Dad." *Demonstrative* nags are the most high-risk, often characterized by full-blown tantrums in public places, breath-holding, tears, a refusal to leave the store. *Sugar-coated* nags promise affection in return for a purchase and may rely on seemingly heartfelt declarations like "You're the best dad in the world." *Threatening* nags are youthful forms of blackmail, vows of eternal hatred and of running away if something isn't bought. *Pity* nags claim the child will be heartbroken, teased, or socially stunted if the parent refuses to buy a certain product (Schlusser, 2002 [2001]: 44).

Note, however, that getting children to nag their parents to buy more products is only one aim of child-directed advertising. In addition, advertisers recognize that ads directed at children can be used to develop brand loyalty that will, in the ideal case, last a lifetime. Executives at one large brewery must have been delighted to read the results of a consumer survey in 1999, which found that while the most popular ad among American children was a Taco Bell commercial featuring a talking chihuahua, their favourite television ad overall was for Budweiser beer.

The rationalization process enables us to produce more efficiently, to have more of just about everything than our parents did. But it is consumerism, the tendency to define our selves in terms of the goods we purchase, which ensures that all the goods that are produced will be bought. Of course, people living in the world's rich countries have lots of choice. We can select from dozens of styles of running shoes, cars, and all the rest. We can also choose to buy items that help to define us as members of a particular **subculture**, adherents of a set of distinctive values, norms, and practices within a larger culture. But, regardless of individual tastes and inclinations, nearly all of us have one thing in common: we tend to be good consumers. We are motivated by advertising, which is based on the accurate insight that people will likely be considered social outcasts if they fail to conform to stylish trends. By creating those trends, advertisers push us to buy. That is why North Americans' "shop-till-you-drop" lifestyle prompted French sociologist Jean

Baudrillard to remark pointedly that even what is best in America is compulsory (Baudrillard, 1988 [1986]).

Consuming Dissent

As is the case for rationalization, consumerism has unintended, negative consequences (Klein, 2000). For example, our culture of excessive consumption causes environmental degradation (see Figure 3.4). We discuss this problem in Chapter 16 ("Sociology and the Environment"). In addition, consumerism is remarkably effective in taming expressions of freedom and individualism, including acts of dissent and rebellion. That is, under the impact of consumerism, deviations from mainstream culture often lose their power to drive change. They get turned simply into means of making money. Some examples from the world of popular music will help illustrate the point:

- Ozzy Osbourne is the godfather of heavy metal. Beginning in the late 1960s, he and his band, Black Sabbath, inspired Metallica, Kiss, Judas Priest, Marilyn Manson, and others to play loud, nihilistic music, reject conventional morality, embrace death and violence, and foment youthful rebellion and parental panic. In 1982, he bit the head off a bat during a performance and urinated on the Alamo. He was given rabies shots for the former and arrested for the latter. Around the same time, Tipper Gore, wife of the future U.S. vice-president, formed the Parental

FIGURE 3.4   RENEWABLE RESOURCES, WORLD, PROJECTED PERCENT CHANGE, 1990–2010

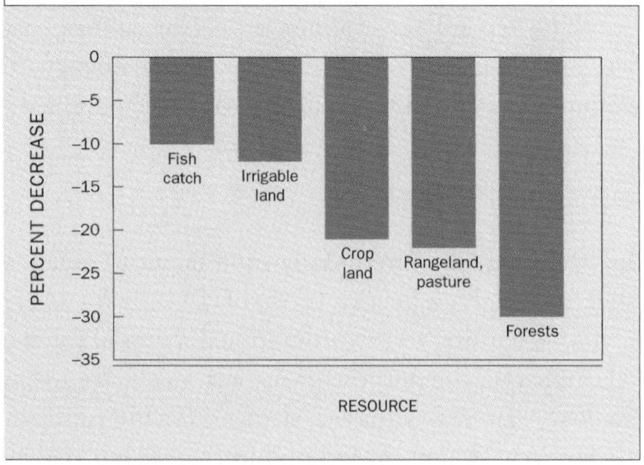

SOURCE: Adapted from Postel (1994: 11)

Music Resource Committee to fight against violence and sex in the lyrics of popular music. Osbourne was one of the committee's principal targets. The "Prince of Darkness," as he was often called, was about as rebellious a figure as one could imagine in 1982. Flash forward 20 years. Osbourne, now in his 50s, has the sixth most popular show on American television among 18- to 34-year-olds, just behind *Survivor* in the ratings. MTV placed a dozen cameras throughout his Beverly Hills mansion, and every Tuesday night viewers get to see everything going on in the Osbourne household for half an hour. According to *USA Today*, it turns out that Osbourne is "a lot like anyone's adorable dad. Shuffles a bit. Forgets things. Worries about the garbage. Snores on the couch while the TV blares. Walks the dog" (Gundersen, Keveney, and Oldenburg: 1A). There is a lot of swearing in the Osbourne family. His 17-year-old daughter sports pink hair and his 16-year-old son wears dark nail polish. But CNN's Greta Van Susteren says she finds the Osbournes "charming," while Rosie O'Donnell says to Ozzy's wife, Sharon: "What I love most about [your show] is not only the relationship you have with Ozzy—and you obviously adore each other—but the honesty with which you relate to your children. The love is so evident between all of you. It's heartwarming" (Gundersen, Keveney, and Oldenburg: 2A). *The Osbournes*, it turns out, is a comfort to many people. It proves that the frightening rejection of mainstream culture in the '70s and '80s was just a passing phase and that things of eternal value—especially the nuclear family and commercialism—remain intact. Ozzy Osbourne has thus been transformed from the epitome of rebellion against society to a family man, a small industry, and a media icon. In April 2002 alone, he appeared on the covers of *Time*, *Entertainment Weekly*, and *Rolling Stone*, and on *The Rosie O'Donnell Show* and *Live! With Regis & Kelly*.

- Punk rock is another genre of musical rebellion from the '70s. In the U.K., the most important early punk rockers were the Sex Pistols and the Clash. Punk rockers tore their clothes, wore dog collars around their necks, cut their hair Mohawk style, tattooed bar codes on their necks, and shoved safety pins through their ears—all to illustrate how society devalued and degraded people. In 1977, when Queen Elizabeth celebrated her Silver Jubilee, the Sex Pistols opened up an anti-monarchist barrage. They released "God Save the Queen," an attack on the monarchy. Because the song was banned from the airwaves and most record stores, they hired a boat to follow the Queen's flotilla down the Thames. According to one account, "[t]heir raggedy fans crowded onto London's bridges and swung from the lampposts, screaming and ecstatically chucking debris onto the boat as it blasted out the vicious lyrics: 'God save the Queen / she ain't no human being / she made you a moron / a potential H-bomb / God save the Queen / we mean it maaan!'" (McClaren, 2002). Flash forward 25 years. The Queen is now celebrating her 50th year on the throne. Punk rocker Vic Garbage, who blasted "God Save the Queen" for eight hours straight from his public housing complex in 1977 and wore a "Stuff the Wedding" T-shirt when Prince Charles and Lady Diana married, is proud of his red, white, and blue haircut and is playing a gig in the conservative northern town of Bolton to honour of the Queen. Punk has been tamed. Remastered classics from the punk "revolution" are available in lovely boxed sets at HMV. A display of desecrated Queen's heads is featured at an East End London art gallery. The Sex Pistols' Johnny Rotten is upset he wasn't asked to play at the official Buckingham Palace concert celebrating the Queen's 50 years on the throne. "I've come to the point of view," says Rotten, "that, bad as it all is, it's my kind of bad, and I have paid for it, and I want to celebrate it somehow" (McClaren, 2002). As is the case for heavy metal, punk has for the most part been commercialized and therefore de-clawed.

- And then there is hip-hop (Brym, 2001). Originating in the squalor of inner-city American ghettoes in the '70s, hip-hop was at first a highly politicized rebellion. Early hip-hop artists glorified the mean streets of the inner city and held the police, the mass media, and other pillars of white society in utter contempt, blaming them for arbitrary arrests, the political suppression of Black activists, and the malicious spreading of lies about African Americans. However, by the time Public Enemy became a hit in the late 1980s, MTV had aired its first regular program devoted to the genre and much of hip-hop's audience was composed of white middle-class youth. Hip-hop artists were quick to see the potential of commercialization. Soon WU-Tang Clan had its own line of clothes, Versace was marketing clothing influenced by ghetto styles, and Puff Daddy (who later had a makeover as P. Diddy) was reminding his audience: "Nigga get money, that's simply the plan" (from his 1999 CD, *Forever*). No less than heavy metal and punk, hip-hop's radicalism gave way to the lures of commercialism.

In sum, the stories of heavy metal, punk, and hip-hop are testimony to the capacity of postmodern culture to constrain expressions of freedom, individualism, dissent, and rebellion (Frank and Weiland, 1997). They are compelling illustrations of postmodern culture's second face.

SUMMARY

1. Humans have been able to adapt to their environments because they are able to create culture. In particular, the ability to create symbols, cooperate, and make tools has enabled humans to thrive.

2. Culture can be invisible if we are too deeply immersed in it. The cultures of others can seem inscrutable if we view them exclusively from the perspective of our own culture. Therefore, the best vantage point for analyzing culture is on the margins, as it were—neither too deeply immersed in it nor too much removed from it.

3. Culture becomes more diversified and consensus declines in many areas of life as societies become more complex. This increases human freedom, giving people more choice in their ethnic, religious, sexual, and other identities.

4. So much cultural diversification and reconfiguration has taken place that some sociologists characterize the culture of our times as postmodern. Postmodernism involves an eclectic mixing of cultural elements from different times and places, the erosion of authority, and the decline of consensus around core values.

5. While the diversification of culture increases human freedom, the growth of complex societies also establishes definite limits within which this diversification may occur. This is illustrated by the process of rationalization, the optimization of means to achieve given ends.

6. Although culture is created to solve human problems, it sometimes has negative consequences that create new problems. This is illustrated by the growth of consumerism, which has resulted in dangerously high levels of consumption.

7. The market (competition) is insufficient to solve the environmental problems that have resulted from our consumer society. In addition, increased cooperation is required.

QUESTIONS TO CONSIDER

1. We imbibe culture but also create it. What elements of culture have you created? Under what conditions were you prompted to do so? Was you cultural contribution strictly personal or was it shared with others? Why?

2. Do you think of yourself in a fundamentally different way from the way your parents (or other close relatives or friends at least 20 years older than you) thought of themselves when they were your age? Are your attitudes towards authority different? Interview your parents, relatives, or friends to find out. Pay particular attention to the way in which the forces of globalization have altered ethnic, racial, and religious self-conceptions and how your attitudes to authority differ from those of your elders.

3. One of the main themes of this chapter is that rationality of means sometimes results in irrationality of ends. Select a sphere of culture (religion, education, the mass media, etc.) and illustrate the point.

GLOSSARY

Abstraction is the human capacity to create complex symbols, including languages, mathematical notations, and signs, in order to classify experience and generalize from it.

Consumerism is a lifestyle involving defining one's self in terms of the goods one purchases.

Cooperation is the human capacity to create a complex social life.

Culture is the sum of practices, languages, symbols, beliefs, values, ideologies, and material objects that people create to deal with real-life problems. Cultures enable people to adapt to, and thrive in, their environments.

Ethnocentrism is the tendency to judge other cultures exclusively by the standards of one's own.

Folklore refers to traditional ideas.

Folkways are norms that follow from traditional ideas.

Globalization is the process by which economic, political, and cultural isolation is destroyed and people are brought together in a "global village."

Norms are standards of behaviour or generally accepted ways of doing things.

Postmodernism is characterized by an eclectic mixing of cultural elements and the erosion of consensus.

Production is the human capacity to make and use tools. It improves our ability to take what we want from nature.

Rationalization is Max Weber's term for the systematic application of standardized means to predetermined ends.

The **rights revolution** is the process by which excluded groups have obtained equal rights under the law and in practice.

A **rite of passage** is a cultural ceremony that marks the transition from one stage of life to another or from life to death.

Sanctions are rewards and punishments intended to ensure conformity to cultural guidelines.

The system of **social control** is the means by which members of society ensure people conform to cultural guidelines.

A **subculture** is a distinctive set of values, norms, and practices within a larger culture.

A **symbol** is anything that carries a particular meaning, including the components of language, mathematical notations, and signs. Symbols allow us to classify experience and generalize from it.

Values are shared ideas about what is right and wrong.

SUGGESTED READING

Adams, Michael. (1997). *Sex in the Snow: Canadian Social Values at the End of the Millennium.* Toronto: Penguin. Adams is a sociologist and Canada's leading public opinion pollster. Here he identifies and analyzes the core values of Canadian culture, highlighting differences by generation, gender, and country (Canada vs. the United States).

Griswold, Wendy. (1992). "The Sociology of Culture: Four Good Arguments (And One Bad One)," *Acta Sociologica* 35: 322–28. Concisely analyzes some of the major issues in the subfield.

Klein, Naomi. (2000). *No Logo: Taking Aim at the Brand Bullies.* Toronto: Vintage Canada. The definitive work on the negative effects of marketing on our culture by the young *Globe and Mail* columnist.

Schlosser, Eric. (2002 [2001]). *Fast Food Nation: The Dark Side of the All-American Meal.* New York: Perennial. You may never eat another fast-food meal after reading this insightful exposé, but you will learn much about the major forces shaping our culture.

NOTES

1. Older definitions emphasize that social interaction and cultural sharing must occur within a specific geographical area for a society to exist. However, new forms of society created on the Internet ("virtual communities") show that physical proximity is not a necessary part of the definition.

2. Many children of Aboriginal Canadians were put into residential schools in the twentieth century, and many of them were physically and sexually abused by the ministers, priests, and nuns who ran these schools. Many Aboriginal Canadians also claim that much land was taken from them illegally. Some 21 000 Japanese Canadians living within 160 km of the Pacific Coast, three-quarters of them Canadian citizens, were forcibly moved to prisoner-of-war, internment, and work camps in 1942. They lost most of their property. Descendants of many Chinese Canadians were forced to pay an exorbitant "head tax" in the late nineteenth and early twentieth centuries, the purpose of which was to encourage them to leave the country. The Nazis enslaved and slaughtered millions of European Jews in World War II and stole their property. Survivors, a considerable number of them residing in Canada, later sought and received reparations from the German and Swiss governments.

CHAPTER FOUR

SOCIALIZATION

In this chapter you will learn that:

- Socialization refers to the active processes whereby people become members of society, develop a sense of self, and learn to participate in social relationships with others.

- Socialization takes place at all stages of the life cycle and in a variety of settings: families, schools, peer groups, the mass media, and occupational groups.

- Among the major contributors to socialization theory are Charles Cooley (who argued that individuals develop a sense of self as they interact with others), George Herbert Mead (who focused on the way we actively create a sense of self by taking the roles of others), and Erving Goffman (who suggested that socialization often involves people competing to control how they are seen by others).

- Socialization continues into adulthood. As people work, marry, divorce, raise children, and retire, they enter new relationships with others, learn new behaviour, and adopt new roles.

- Sometimes our self-concept undergoes abrupt change as we learn new role identities and negotiate a new self-image. Such resocialization occurs when we replace our way of life with a radically different one—it is most evident in jails, mental hospitals, boot camps, and in religious and political conversions.

WILLIAM SHAFFIR, MICHAEL ROSENBERG, AND JACK HAAS

MCMASTER UNIVERSITY/DAWSON COLLEGE/MCMASTER UNIVERSITY

INTRODUCTION

Anyone who has been a parent is probably more familiar than they would like with what is called the "terrible twos." This refers to the stage many children go through at about the age of two known to childhood development experts as "negativism." During negativism a child will often be contrary and obstinate, refusing to cooperate even in simple tasks and saying "no" to everything and everyone. What's worse, the child may often willfully and blatantly break the norms, or generally accepted ways of doing things, in the household—sometimes also breaking valued objects, dishes, or almost anything else that comes to hand. Negativism can be a very difficult stage to live through, not only for the parents but for the child. Yet, childhood socialization, experts insist, is an essential stage in developing a sense of self and becoming an autonomous human being.

An anecdote may illustrate what is meant by negativism. One of the authors of this chapter used to have a large houseplant (a dracaena) in his living room of which he and his wife were very fond. When their first child was still young, they made it very clear to the child that he was not to touch the plant. "Plants are beautiful things that we must cherish, nourish, and allow to grow," they explained. Still, there was always a gleam in their son's eyes when he looked at that plant, and they were careful never to leave him alone when he was near it.

One day, when he was about one-and-a-half, the child walked into the living room while his father was reading a book, walked right up to the plant, looked at it for several seconds and then muttered "no" to himself. He then looked at his father with a big smile on his face. His father, smiling back at him, said, "That's right. No." The child left, but came back a few minutes later and repeated his actions, once again reminding himself with a smile, "No." His father, not yet sensing disaster, smiled back. He left, but a few minutes later returned yet again, walking up close to the plant, looking at it, and saying "No" with a big smile. But this time he grabbed the largest leaf of the plant as he spoke and, crushing it, repeated "No" yet again. The plant was given away to neighbours the next day.

The truth is, of course, that young children are constantly being told "No" by the adults around them: "Don't touch that!" "Don't eat this!" "Don't go there!" If children were always to listen to what their parents said, they would be able to do next to nothing. They would certainly never be able to think for themselves. Negativism is the way a child learns what really can or cannot be done. It is a way of testing the limits to find out which of the many No's they hear are serious and which are only a preference. It is also a form of rebellion whereby the child sets limits for the parents as well. Parents also have to learn how far they can go in restricting and controlling the child. Children are not robots who just follow instructions; they need to develop as autonomous, competent, and self-directed actors if they are to be full-fledged members of a family—and of society (see Box 4.1). The social process whereby they undergo such development through interacting with the people around them is known as **socialization**.

To be socialized means to learn how to act and interact appropriately with others, to transform oneself into a member of society. Yet, paradoxically, sociologists assert that to be socialized is also to develop a **self**, a sense of individual identity that allows us to understand ourselves and differentiate ourselves from others. Each of these processes depends on and implies the other: To have a self one must interact with others; to interact competently one must reflect upon and understand oneself in relation to those others. That is why understanding socialization requires us to examine both people's sense of belonging and their sense of autonomy, both how people are constrained by norms and values (shared ideas about what is right and wrong) and how people are autonomous agents able to make decisions for themselves. Freedom and constraint, we will see, are not opposites but interconnected features of everyone's ordinary, everyday life.

The approach taken in this chapter is that socialization is an active process, one in which those being socialized participate in and contribute to that socialization. It is also an interactive process in which those who are socializing, like the parents in the example above, are themselves undergoing a learning process. Of course, we may learn from others without their knowledge; we learn from role models, from stories about heroes or villains, from the example of our parents and friends, and just by observing the people around us. But the most important learning, the cru-

BOX 4.1 KINDERGARTEN AS ACADEMIC BOOT CAMP

Kindergarten is generally conceived by educators as a year of preparation for school. It is thought of as a year in which small children, five or six years old, are prepared socially and emotionally for the academic learning which will take place over the next twelve years. It is expected that a foundation of behaviour and attitudes will be laid in kindergarten on which the children can acquire the skills and knowledge they will be taught in the grades.... The kindergarten teachers in one ... elementary [school, which] we shall call the Wilbur Wright School, said their goals were to see that the children "grew" in all ways: physically, of course, emotionally, socially, and academically. They said they wanted children to like school as a result of their kindergarten experiences and that they wanted them to learn to get along with others.

None of these goals, however, is unique to kindergarten; each of them is held to some extent by teachers in the other six grades at the Wright School. And growth would occur, but differently, even if the child did not attend school. The children already know how to get along with others, in their families and their play groups. The unique job of the kindergarten in the educational division of labor seems rather to be teaching children the student role. The student role is the repertoire of behavior and attitudes regarded by educators as appropriate to children in school. Observation in the kindergartens of the Wilbur Wright School revealed a great variety of activities through which children are shown and then drilled in the behavior and attitudes defined as appropriate for school and thereby induced to learn the role of student. Observers pointed both to the teaching and learning of classroom routines as the main element of the student role. The teachers expended most of their efforts, for the first half of the year at least, in training the children to follow the routines which teachers created. The children were, in a very real sense, drilled in tasks and activities created by the teachers for their own purposes and beginning and ending quite arbitrarily (from the child's point of view) at the command of the teacher. One teacher remarked that she hated September, because during the first month "everything has to be done rigidly, and repeatedly, until they know exactly what they're supposed to do." However, "by January," she said, "they know exactly what to do [during the day] and I don't have to be after them all the time." Classroom routines were introduced gradually from the beginning of the year in all the kindergartens, and the children were drilled in them as long as was necessary to achieve regular compliance. By the end of the school year, the successful kindergarten teacher has a well-organized group of children. They follow classroom routines automatically, having learned all the command signals and the expected responses to them. They have, in our terms, learned the student role.

The kindergarten has been conceived of here as the year in which children are prepared for their schooling by learning the role of student. In the classrooms of the rest of the school grades, the children will be asked to submit to systems and routines imposed by the teachers and the curriculum. The days will be much like those of kindergarten, except that academic subjects will be substituted for the activities of the kindergarten. Once out of the school system, young adults will more than likely find themselves working in large-scale bureaucratic organizations, perhaps on the assembly line in the factory, perhaps in the paper routines of the white-collar occupations, where they will be required to submit to rigid routines imposed by "the company" which may make little sense to them. Those who can operate well in this situation will be successful bureaucratic functionaries. Kindergarten, therefore, can be seen as preparing children not only for participation in the bureaucratic organization of large modern school systems, but also for the large-scale occupational bureaucracies of modern society.

SOURCE: Harry L. Gracey, "Learning the Student Role: Kindergarten as Academic Boot Camp," in Dennis H. Wrong and Harry L. Gracey, eds. *Readings in Introductory Sociology*, 3rd ed. (New York: Macmillan, 1976), pp. 289, 290, 299. © 1976. Reprinted with permission of the author.

cial learning that transforms us into cultural beings, proceeds through interaction with others who are important to us and—usually—to whom we are also important.

The crucial learning process that occurs in childhood and makes us members of society is called **primary socialization**. Because primary socialization is so important to becoming who and what we are, it is the focus of the first part of this chapter. But because humans are creative, adaptable beings, learning and change continue throughout our lives. Learning to be a student, a husband or wife, or a parent; learning one's job and how to carry it out effectively; making new friends and undertaking new commitments—all of these involve socialization. This kind of learning is called **secondary socialization** because it occurs after people have already undergone primary socialization. It is not secondary in importance, however. We live in a world of constant and dramatic change, and secondary socialization is an ongoing feature of our lives.

As Chapter 3 showed us, culture provides us with the tools to solve the problems of survival. Symbols, norms, values, and everyday practices are examples of such tools. Their use allows us to master nature and build orderly societies. They must, however, be learned. Indeed, insofar as the human being is a cultural being, these tools must become a part of us—internalized through socialization. In a very real sense, then, it is socialization that makes social interaction, social organization, and social order possible.

Think of all the things we do every day involving other people. When we walk on the sidewalk of a busy street, for example, we are able to pass dozens—sometimes hundreds—of other pedestrians heading towards us and do so without colliding with any of them. This is possible because of the norms that regulate sidewalk behaviour without our being aware of them. For example, most of the time each of us will move to the right to avoid colliding with someone walking towards us. We don't even have to think about it, we simply move to the right. If we move to our right when walking towards others and they move to their right (which is our left) when walking towards us, then we will not collide (see Wolff, 1973, for a detailed discussion of other norms and strategies used in walking along sidewalks). Norms such as these make social life orderly and allow us to deal with and interact with hundreds of anonymous strangers daily. It is not only norms that regulate behaviour, however. There are also many conventions, rituals, rules, and even laws, that direct our behaviour both with people whom we know well, such as co-workers, and people who are simply strangers.

How do we know to act on such norms, conventions, or rules? How do we know to move to the right to avoid colliding with a fellow pedestrian? We know through socialization. There is nothing "natural" about moving to the right to avoid a collision. In some societies, people move to the left; in others they don't particularly mind bumping into others. In our society we have learned to move to the right by watching others, and by seeing how others react when, on occasion, we have moved to the left by mistake. In this respect, norms constrain us; they channel and guide our behaviour in everyday life. But consider the alternative. Imagine what it would be like to have to decide separately as we walked along a sidewalk which way we should move in order to avoid colliding with each person we were walking towards. Norms make smooth and orderly interaction possible, freeing us from the need to plan out every step we take or communicate in detail with everyone we meet about all of the possible ways we could interact.

Because the process of becoming socialized occurs in a cultural context, the content of socialization differs greatly from one society to another. People in a particular society learn the norms, values, and lifestyles specific to their social environment. At the same time, however, within every society individuals differ in significant ways from one another. Such individual differences, too, are to some extent the product of socialization. Each person is influenced by distinctive or overlapping subcultures of family and friends, by class and gender. A **subculture** is a group within the larger culture that has distinctive values, norms, and practices. Our unique personal histories permit us not only to share in the larger society, but also to participate in a specific part of it. The socialization process helps to explain both similarities and differences among people in a particular society.

NATURE AND NURTURE

Does that mean that everything we do and know is a product of socialization? Don't we have **instincts**, such as an instinct for survival, or maternal instincts? What about natural differences among people? Aren't there people with charismatic personalities, who have more of an impact on others than ordinary people do? Aren't some brighter than others, some more aggressive than others, some more compliant than others? Aren't there people who simply won't get out of the way when you walk towards them?

While there obviously are natural differences among people, such differences explain very little about social behaviour or how a society is organized. It is very doubtful, for instance, that human beings have either an instinct for survival or a maternal instinct. There are countless examples of people who clearly give little thought to their own survival or who

Most socialization takes place informally, with the participants unaware that they are being socialized. These little girls are unconsciously learning gender roles by playing dress-up.
SOURCE: Photo courtesy of Nurit Bodemann and Shira Brym.

have proven to be indifferent or abusive parents. Still, there is no denying that some human behaviour is the outcome of biological factors, and the debate over whether it is nature (biological inheritance) or nurture (the social environment) that is more important in shaping our beliefs and behaviour is an old one. Most sociologists who participate in this debate emphasize the importance of society and of socialization, suggesting that someone who is aggressive in our society might well have become gentle—or at least less aggressive—had that person been born in some other society or raised in some other set of circumstances.

Sociologists are also suspicious of explanations that emphasize biological inheritance because such explanations often shift from an initial focus on individual differences to an emphasis on group differences. In this way, they often lead to racist or sexist explanations or views (Gould, 1996). An example is the longstanding debate over intelligence: Is our intelligence the outcome of hereditary and genetic factors, or is it a product of social variables such as class and family structure? Phrased that way, the debate is about the sources of individual differences. True to many sociologists' concern, however, this

debate has shifted from a concern with individual differences to one focused on the supposed connection between race and IQ test scores, as in the controversial book *The Bell Curve* (Herrnstein and Murray, 1994), which argues that there are innate racial differences in IQ.

Numerous studies have challenged the racist assumption that individual and group differences are due to genetic differences and have demonstrated the significance of social–cultural influences and contexts. One of the best-known studies of sociocultural influences on IQ focused on the power of teachers to affect IQ test results. Through this research, Rosenthal and Jacobson (1968) demonstrated the power of the **self-fulfilling prophecy**—when an expectation leads to behaviour that causes the expectation to become a reality.

Rosenthal and Jacobson administered a standard IQ test to all children in a school from Grades 1 to 6. Teachers in the school were told that this was a special test able to predict which students were likely to undergo intellectual "blooming." The teachers were then told to expect that certain students—*who had in fact been randomly selected*—would develop into higher achievers. By the end of the year, the researchers found that this randomly selected group of children scored significantly higher on the same intelligence test they had taken at the beginning of the year. Their classmates did not. The test results demonstrated that the children whom the teachers expected to "bloom" actually did score higher.

What accounts for the higher scores of the first group? Rosenthal and Jacobson suggest that teachers treated these students as if they were special, giving them more confidence and more satisfaction from their schoolwork. It was this special treatment that led them to become high academic achievers.

Of course, special treatment or a positive approach cannot overcome all obstacles. Still, it is becoming more and more apparent today that the old debate on nature versus nurture sets up a false opposition. It is clear that nature and nurture are both complementary and inseparable. The human brain provides the physiological apparatus required for interpreting experiences, but unless children have the opportunity to learn, to reason, and to solve problems in early life, the brain itself may not fully develop (Begley, 1995). Attempts at determining the relative importance of nature and nurture in human development are much like trying to establish whether width or height is more significant in determining area.

Indeed, there is strong evidence that human beings have a biologically grounded need for social interaction and intimate relations with others. Evidence suggests that human infants have both a biological and an emotional need to cling to and interact with a warm, sheltering figure. Verbal communication may not be part of this contact, but some form of communication is—whether smiles, laughs, or touch. Without this contact, socialization is impaired and irreversible damage may be done to the person's sense of self.

Convincing evidence comes from studies of children raised in isolation by their families. The case of Anna is the best-known instance of the long-term social isolation of an infant. Anna was an illegitimate child hidden away in a room until she was nearly six years old. Her mother gave her only enough care to keep her alive. When she was discovered, her clothing and bedding were filthy and she was emaciated and unable to walk, talk, feed herself, or respond to others. As she was cared for and began to interact with others, Anna made slow yet steady progress, but years of social isolation left her permanently disabled. By the age of eight, Anna's mental and social development were still less than that of a two-year-old. Not until she was ten did she show the first signs of using language.

The importance of social contact in the development of human infants was demonstrated when R.A. Spitz (1945) compared infants raised in an orphanage with those raised in a women's prison nursery. The infants in the prison nursery interacted with their own mothers for the first year of their lives, whereas infants raised in the orphanage were attended only by nurses and spent their days lying on their backs, seeing and hearing very few people, and lacking social stimulation. Although in the beginning the orphan children were as healthy as those in the nursery, after two years some of the children in the orphanage were "retarded" and all were psychologically and socially underdeveloped for their age. More shockingly, by age four a third of them had died! No such problems were observed among the prison nursery infants. Socialization, we may conclude, is often a matter of life and death.

These examples show that socialization is essential both to the physical well-being and to the social compe-

tence of an infant. Even when, as in the case of Anna, infants survive lack of interaction and caring in early childhood, they are incapable of becoming fully competent, active members of society. This is not just a matter of "intelligence." Rather, they have not had the opportunity to develop a self; they have no sense of social identity in terms of which they understand themselves and others around them. One may view the self as the point of reference for planning and orientation, for sorting and assessing life's situations in terms of their relative importance. As noted earlier, the self refers to one's awareness of ideas and attitudes about one's own personal and social identity. It is through interaction that such a sense of self emerges and the development of the self is a crucial part of socialization.

THE SELF AND SOCIALIZATION

Where does our sense of self come from? Sociologists and psychologists alike have sought to answer that question. They have examined how individuals develop and modify a sense of who they are—their sense of self—and found that self-image greatly depends on social interaction. For instance, the newborn does not differentiate itself from its mother (Piaget, 1950). Such differentiation occurs gradually as the newborn learns to see its mother as a separate person. Through interaction the infant acquires the ability to see himself or herself reflected in the eyes of others and to sense his or her own identity. It is precisely this ability that children who have been reared in isolation lack.

To understand the process of self-growth, we will examine the theories of two early scholars—Charles Horton Cooley (1864–1929) and George Herbert Mead (1863–1931). We will then see how their ideas were used and modified by a more recent theorist, Erving Goffman (1922–1982).

CHARLES HORTON COOLEY

In the early 1900s, few sociologists or psychologists paid much attention to the role of interaction in socialization. In this respect, Cooley's work was groundbreaking. Cooley introduced the idea of the **looking-glass self**. Cooley suggested that the gestures and reactions of others are a mirror or "looking glass" in which we see ourselves. Just as we look in a mirror to see a reflection of our physical body, we look to others to see a reflection of our psychological and social self. And just as we may be pleased or displeased with what we see when we look at ourselves in a mirror, depending on our expectations about ourselves physically, so too our conceptions about ourselves socially—our feelings about who and what we are—are organized around our evaluation of how we believe ourselves judged by others.

This means that without the social mirror there can be no sense of self. For Cooley, self-image emerges as a product of involvement in groups and communication with others. The first images of the self are received from **significant others**—those, such as parents who are of central importance to the individual in the development of the self. Later, other images both complement and supplant those first images, especially as the child's interaction network expands. Particularly important in this regard is the role played by the **primary group**, or that small group characterized by intimate, face-to-face association and cooperation. Through repeated processes of imagination and identification, the self-concept is built and organized. In this way, Cooley suggested, the structure and content of the self are derived from the society that is represented by the groups and significant others surrounding the individual.

GEORGE HERBERT MEAD

For Cooley, society would not exist without interacting individuals and the individual would not develop without society. George Herbert Mead followed this lead, concentrating his analysis on the importance of the interplay between society and the individual. His major contribution was a theory of the relationship between mind, self, and society. It became a foundation of **symbolic interactionism** and has influenced many sociologists using a wide variety of other perspectives.

Unlike Cooley, Mead did not assume that socialization consists largely of learning to conform to the rest of society. Rather, he saw socialization as an active process in which individuals play a crucial role in their own development.

Key to that active process, Mead suggested, is the ability to communicate, especially to make use of symbolic communication. **Symbols** are gestures,

objects, or sounds that stand for something else and whose meaning depends on shared understandings. A dove, for example, is a bird, but when we see a picture of a dove on a poster, we know that it is supposed to represent—be a symbol of—the concept of "peace." The use of symbols enables the child to conceive of itself in relation to others and is at the core of all stages of the socialization process.

Like other animals, human infants first communicate through nonverbal gestures. Unlike animal communication, however, even at this rudimentary level, most human communication is symbolic, as infants and the others around them develop shared understandings about the meaning of the gestures. This also lays the foundation for the development of language, which makes possible the replacement of gestures with ideas.

Suppose, though, that you are not sure how another person understands the meaning of an action, an object, or a word. Because you share a language,

George Herbert Mead (1863–1931) was the driving force behind the study of how individual identity is formed in the course of interaction with other people. The work of Mead and his colleagues gave birth to symbolic interactionism, a distinctively North American theoretical tradition that continues to be a major force in sociology today.
SOURCE: Granger Collection.

you can ask the other person what he or she means and determine whether your understanding and the other person's are the same. Of course that is not always possible nor always desirable. If you are going for a job interview, you would not wear a pair of dirty jeans to the interview and then ask the interviewer whether he or she considers your clothing to be appropriate. Instead you would try to anticipate in advance how others will see you and react to you. You will take the role of the other, that is, attempt to determine or appreciate the perspective of someone else in a particular situation.

What is true for us only sometimes is always true for an infant. The infant does not know how others understand and react to the world around it, and especially to the child itself. **Taking the role of the other**, then, is an essential skill the child must develop to be an effective member of society. Children are not born able to understand other people. Mead made the important contribution of showing how the child, through its interaction with others, comes to develop the ability to take the role of the other. He was able to show that it is this ability that is key both to the child's understanding of others and to its internalization of the values, attitudes, and beliefs of the society. Mead, though, went even farther. He suggested that it is through taking the role of the other that the child also develops a sense of self. That is, conformity and individuality are interconnected; mind, self, and society are the product of interaction.

The ability to take the role of the other, Mead suggested, is acquired in three stages. The first is the **imitative stage**. Children two years and under do not interact with others because they cannot take the role of the other. They lack the verbal and other skills needed to communicate effectively. Much of their behaviour in this stage is imitative play in the world of make-believe. For hours they may play at being mothers or fathers, doctors or firefighters. At this stage of development, however, children have no real conception of themselves as separate social beings or a real understanding of what it is like to be a mother, father, or doctor. They simply act out the behaviour without understanding the meaning of that behaviour. What they are doing is not true role-playing but only imitations of actions.

The second major developmental stage described by Mead is the **play stage** in which children actually begin to adopt social roles. The roles adopted during this stage are those of significant others—a parent, a sports celebrity, a storybook hero—but the child's play shifts from imitative to imaginative. Through play they learn to imagine how people will respond to them without actually having to act out the situation. Having reached a level of verbal organization, the child can manipulate the various roles without physical action. At this stage, the role need not be firmly rooted in reality but can be defined according to the child's own wishes or its desire to please significant others. Children do not yet see role-playing as a social necessity—they merely play at the social roles of life.

The third and final stage in the development of the self is the **game stage**. In this stage the child has developed a generalized impression of the behaviour people expect as well as an awareness of his or her own importance to the group and vice versa. Mead used the metaphor of a game to describe the complex behaviour that is required in this stage. In an organized game such as baseball, a player must continually adjust behaviour to the needs of the team as a whole and to the specific situations that arise in the game. If the batter is running to first base, we do not throw the ball to the second baseman because we like him better than the first baseman. Instead, our actions are oriented to the general rules and practices that make up the game, not to personal preferences or attachments. At this point, Mead contended, children are responding to what he called the **generalized other**, a conception of how people in general—not someone specific in particular—will respond and react in a situation. This generalized other is internalized; it is composed of the values, attitudes, and beliefs that the individual understands to be a part of the society and in terms of which the individual assumes others will react. In effect, taking the role of the generalized other means that we respond to our idea of the organized group or community of which we are a part.

Our ability to communicate not only allows us to interact with others, but also to communicate with ourselves. As we observe the conduct and reactions of other people, learning their expectations and point of view, we anticipate how *we* should react in a particular situation—then plan, rehearse, modify, and perfect our own behaviour. We may debate alternative courses of action, impress ourselves with our own wit, or cringe in remembered embarrassment at some ancient gaffe. In these and many other ways we engage in what Mead called an internal conversation, and it is through such internal conversations that we come to develop an integrated sense of self. To the degree that we experience the generalized other as a unity, our sense of self, too, will be unitary.

In a way, then, we are not only subjects—thinking, knowing, and feeling beings—but also objects to ourselves—social and cultural beings that we can evaluate, respond to, have feelings about, and try to modify. Because we first imagine ourselves from the perspectives of other people, Mead suggested that we are first aware of ourselves as social objects. This objective element of the self he called the *me*. Accompanying the *me* is the subjective or active part of the self, which he called the *I*. It is this subjective component of the self that allows us to react to and assess ourselves, to engage in what Mead described as an internal conversation. All social experience involves an interaction of the *I* and the *me*, with the *I* initiating action and the *me* reflectively taking the role of the other. In other words, the self is both spontaneous (the *I*) and conformist (the *me*); both active (the *I*) and reflective (the *me*); both experiencing (the *I*) and experienced (the *me*). Throughout our life, our sense of self continues to develop, Mead suggested, because our experiences involve the continuing conversation between the *me* and the *I*. Changing contexts and contacts produce new opportunities for learning. But Mead also believed that our decisions and choices about action affect others. In other words, human beings shape their own circumstances and lives, and those of the people around them.

Mead's discussion of childhood socialization remains rather general. Not everyone is socialized in the same way, however, and the self we develop is not purely the result of our own intentions, preferences, or interactions. There are constraints such as class, ethnic, religious, and geographic differences that have a profound impact on how a person is socialized, on his or her sense of self and of worth, and on that person's understanding of others.

ERVING GOFFMAN

Like Cooley and Mead, Erving Goffman was a major figure in the sociological perspective known as symbolic interactionism. His approach, however, differs in some critical ways from theirs. In contrast to Cooley, who emphasized the integration between the individual and society, and Mead, who emphasized the consensus on norms, values, and beliefs that makes up the generalized other, Goffman looked at the ways in which people compete with one another in everyday life as they seek to control the impressions others have of them. In that sense, Goffman was much more aware of the paradoxical ways in which society both constrains and frees us at the same time.

Goffman's perspective is known as the **dramaturgical approach,** which uses the analogy of life as theatre and of people as actors putting on performances for one another. People learn to play the roles called for by society's script, and their performances are judged by an audience alert for slips that might reveal the actors' true characters and intentions (Goffman, 1959, 1963, 1971). Rather than see society as a mirror from which we derive a self, Goffman looks to the way we try to manage the impressions others have of us by controlling the way we present a self to others. Goffman called this "impression management."

Goffman's approach does not assume a unified "generalized other" or a unified self. The self, Goffman suggested, is a dramatic effect we present to others, and the self we present to one set of people may be very different from the self we present in another context. How is this possible? Because, Goffman suggested, the conventions, beliefs, values, and attitudes of everyday life do not determine our behaviour, but rather serve as symbolic resources. We learn to draw on these symbolic resources as needed to express ourselves to others or to try to control their perception of us.

Goffman made significant contributions to our understanding of socialization. He showed, for example, how patients in mental hospitals are able to adjust to their circumstances and make a meaningful life for themselves despite their lack of autonomy and the difficult circumstances in which they find themselves. The practical issues of learning to live in a mental hospital described by Goffman are far removed from the antiseptic and formal discussion of life as a baseball game found in Mead's work. (We might note that "taking the role of the other" in a mental hospital, as Goffman showed, possesses challenges of its own.)

While Goffman often portrayed the individual as free to draw on the symbolic resources provided by society rather than being determined by society, he was also aware that not everyone is free to present a self as they please. Whereas Mead saw the generalized other, and by extension, the community, as unitary, Goffman recognized that we do not all have equal access to a society's symbolic or material resources. Goffman's work also examined how a stigmatized person, such as someone who is deaf, is excluded from or marginalized by the broader community. In another fascinating study, Goffman (1979) examined the expressions of femininity and masculinity found in advertising. These advertisements, Goffman (1979: 84) suggested, "portray an ideal conception of the two sexes and their structural relationship to each other." Such "idealized" representations do not only express people's expectations, however. They also serve to portray how men and women should look and how they should act in relation to each other. They serve, in other words, to socialize us into culturally "appropriate" gender relations.

GENDER

Socialization is not a unitary process. Different categories of people will be socialized in different ways. One of the most important of those differences is that of **gender**. In many societies it makes an enormous difference whether one is socialized male or female, a difference that determines the course of one's life. What about our own society? What does it mean to be male or female in our society? How are we socialized to be male or female? Are gender definitions changing? Are socialization processes with respect to gender changing as well? We now turn to answering these questions.

Marlene Mackie has focused on the process by which gender is incorporated into an individual's sense of self and has defined gender socialization as the "process through which individuals learn to become feminine and masculine according to expectations current in their society" (1991: 75). As Lenton demonstrates in Chapter 5 of this book, gender identity is learned, as opposed to being assigned to us at birth. Still, gender appears as such a natural part of our everyday life that we typically take it for granted. We assume that one is either male or female and we quickly learn how each is expected to behave. Sometimes, though, we find ourselves in situations where someone's behaviour deviates from our expectations. In such a situation, we are unsure how to

relate to another if we cannot be certain of their sexual identity. While gender identity, or conviction of oneself as male or female, ordinarily emerges early in life and remains unchanged, the experiences of transvestites and transsexuals suggest that moderate to radical changes along this line are possible and may even occur more frequently than we think. More accurately, perhaps, we continuously consider and evaluate our sexual and gender identities and make necessary adjustments and modifications.

To the extent that a culture defines gender roles as distinctly different, parents raise boys and girls so that they *will* be different. Moreover, they will grow up *wanting* to be different, believing that these differences in roles are both normal and necessary. Patterns of sex role socialization reveal that, from the earliest days of life, an infant is not simply a child but a boy or a girl. Infant boys are usually addressed differently from infant girls, the blankets in which they are covered are usually different colours, and the rooms in which they sleep are usually decorated to reflect their gender. Indeed, one of the first things that a child learns is whether he or she is a "he" or a "she." And from a very early age, children show marked gender-specific preferences for certain toys, activities, and so forth (Huston, 1983).

A recent report indicates how the construction of femininity relates to consumption and how shopping occupies a pivotal place in shaping this construction. Russell and Tyler (2002) examined Girl Haven, a chain of retail outlets in the United Kingdom designed specifically for three- to 13-year-old girls. These stores stocked not only a range of clothes, but hair styling products, cosmetics, and accessories. The research illustrates how, through cultural definitions of these items as products for "girls," the meaning of becoming a woman is tied to various aspects of consumer culture.

Parents are usually the first source of children's gender learning, and indications are that parents both hold and communicate different expectations for males and females. An early study (Rubin, Provenzano, and Luria, 1974) showed that, within 24 hours of childbirth, first-time parents saw their daughters as softer, finer featured, and more delicate than did those with sons, while first-time parents saw their sons as firmer, stronger, better coordinated, hardier, and more alert. In a study of children's assigned household tasks, White and Brinkerhoff (1981) found a clear division of labour: While the boys were mowing the lawn, shovelling snow, taking out the garbage, and doing other yard work, the girls were cleaning the house, washing dishes, cooking, and babysitting younger children. In a more recent study, Fox (1998, 2001) found that the transition to parenthood remains gendered. While couples today enter parenthood with a stronger commitment to sharing household responsibilities than in the past, most nevertheless develop gendered patterns typical of Canadian families.

We noted earlier the role of the media in presenting "idealized" images and stereotypes of appropriate masculine and feminine characteristics. To the degree that females were portrayed in a narrow and biased way by the media for years, the impact of gender-role stereotypes negatively affected how children perceived themselves (Narahara, 1998). Oversimplified gender-role stereotypes affected children's self-concept and interaction with peers and adults (Kortenhaus and Demarest, 1993). More recently, researchers examined 83 Notable Books for Children from 1995 to 1999 in terms of the gender of the main character, illustrations, and title (Gooden and Gooden, 2001). They found that gender stereotyping has decreased, but that although female representation has greatly improved since the 1970s, gender stereotypes are still prevalent in children's literature.

Eliminating stereotyping is critical because it contributes to the streaming of males and females into traditional careers. More often than not, teachers and guidance counsellors unwittingly encourage boys and girls to pursue occupational goals that are perceived as appropriate to their gender. This becomes a self-fulfilling prophecy: girls develop a self-image consistent with others' perceptions of them. Along this line, one study of 150 Canadian teenagers found a tendency for girls to make traditionally feminine occupational choices and to express less confidence than boys that they would realize their occupational goals (Baker, 1985). About three-quarters of the girls planned to hold paying jobs as adults. However, they tended to see the responsibility for household and child-care as primarily theirs, and to assume that paid work must fit in with these other duties. This expectation about the future fits clearly with the actual division of household tasks (Barber and Allen, 1992; Blau and Ferber, 1992; South and Spitze, 1994). While more and more women are choosing careers that are not traditionally feminine, women still do not have the range of choice available to men. Even today

there are many careers that most of the public does not see as "appropriate" for women.

What the study of gender shows us is that children and adults are socialized to respond to their social world by developing certain potentials and inhibiting others. It is not innate qualities but differences in the socialization of males and females that affect the assumption of "masculine" and "feminine" characteristics.

SOCIALIZATION THROUGH THE LIFE COURSE

Childhood socialization is referred to as primary socialization because it lays a foundation that influences our self-concept and involvement in social life for as long as we live. But there are other points in our lives when socialization plays a crucial role. Pregnancy and childbirth, for example, bring on new circumstances in which we have to change our understanding of who we are as we undergo new experiences and as new demands are made of us. Such secondary socialization typically changes how we think of ourselves and others.

ADOLESCENCE AND YOUTH

Apart from childhood, it is during adolescence that the most dramatic transformations of identity, **status**, and social relationships tend to occur. (While in everyday speech status means prestige, in sociology it refers to the culturally and socially defined position a person occupies in an interaction.) We enter adolescence as children, and are somehow transformed by the end of that period into young adults.

Adolescence, the period between childhood and adulthood, is a crucial period of life in which people undergo new experiences, deal with new demands and responsibilities, and strive to develop an identity that is distinctively their own. Even more than in childhood, socialization during adolescence requires that we find a balance between autonomy and conformity, between freedom and constraint. Unlike children, however, most adolescents are very aware of the demands being placed on them by others as well as of the demands they place on themselves. This makes adolescence a difficult time of life, not only for adolescents, but also for parents, friends, and teachers.

Because adolescence is such a difficult time for many, we generally associate it with emotional and social turmoil. Young people experience conflict with their parents and other adults as they attempt to develop their own identity, act on their own preferences, and form their own relationships. Though much of the social turmoil at this stage is often attributed to physiological changes linked to the onset of puberty, a more sociological way of thinking focuses on inconsistencies in the socialization process. Adolescents, for example, are repeatedly told by adults to "grow up" but are treated as if they were still children. Sexuality is an excellent case in point: Adolescents receive messages of encouragement from the mass media and restraint from parents. While adolescents associate adulthood with freedom, they get the confusing message from adults that in order to "act like an adult" they must not decide for themselves but rather do exactly what adults tell them to do.

This would not be such a problem if most adolescents did not live at home under the authority of adults. But that has not always been so. In premodern societies there was no adolescence as a separate and prolonged stage of life. Young people would often be married by the age of 16 or 17, sometimes even younger. If they did live at home, they had responsibilities of their own.

It is during adolescence that the most dramatic transformations of identity, status, and social relationships tend to occur.
SOURCE: © Catherine Karnow/CORBIS/Magma.

Adolescence as a distinct period of life is a product of industrialization and the extension of education it introduced. Mass education and compulsory school attendance altered the role of the family and helped give rise to adolescence. Because young people were required to remain in school, they were not expected to assume economic responsibility as soon as they reached sexual maturity. Instead they would continue to live at home. Burgess and Richardson (1984) trace the distinctiveness of adolescence to the modern high school, where students became educated in skills and knowledge that the family was not equipped to impart. Paradoxically, while high school may provide skills that eventually allow the adolescent to become independent of the family, it does so in a context where students have little autonomy.

Although many families subscribe to the ideal of democracy, the reality is otherwise (Solomon et al., 2002). Parents and teenagers often claim that openness is the route to intimacy and democracy, but in actual practice young people experience arbitrary rules imposed by parents and an unwillingness to discuss compromise. Parents, seeking to preserve their own identity, continue exercising control and seek to monitor the adolescent's behaviour by obtaining information that they fail to reciprocate. This is a source of resentment among adolescents who realize that reciprocity in communication is generally missing from parent–teenager relationships. As parents demand more and more information, the relationship moves further away from friendship, not toward it.

We should not exaggerate the impact of adults on adolescents. While, on average, the family exerts more of an influence than peer groups regarding such fundamental matters as religious orientation, political preferences, and career aspirations, there are also occasions when young people are less influenced by their families or teachers than by their peers, and this peer influence promotes youthful autonomy. It is not that adults give young people freedom, but that the conflicting and confusing messages they receive from adults, peers, the media, and their own experiences require them to make up their own minds. For those who are unable to reconcile the demands of the new and the old, adolescence may be a time of considerable confusion and turmoil (Hogan and Astone, 1986). Yet, for all the turbulence and rebellion generally associated with adolescence, evidence suggests that most teenagers have good experiences of adolescence and believe they have positive relationships with their parents (Coleman and Hendry, 1990).

Why is this so? The positive experience of adolescence may be because much of it is also exciting and fun. As they must do in other stages of life, adolescents learn to fill new statuses and roles. Much of this learning is exciting. Friendships, for example, take on a different character in adolescence than in childhood. They often become very intense, and people come to feel very close to their friends, developing attachments that often last for a lifetime. Many new interests arise—in music, in art, or in fashion—that are used by adolescents as symbols of group membership and indicators of personal taste and status. This allows for the development of passionate commitments and a sense of satisfaction and achievement when, for example, one's favourite musical group has a number one song on the charts. Then, of course, there is the excitement of dating, the thrill of romance, and the intense involvement in all of the accompanying activities, such as gossiping with friends, showing off a boyfriend or girlfriend, and going places together. Despite all of the difficulties with adults and school, and all of the demands placed on young people, adolescence is generally accompanied by the development of a sense of autonomy and independence as young people prepare for adult responsibilities.

Finally, adolescence is also a period of **anticipatory socialization**, "the process by which aspirants to a particular social role begin to discern what it will be like to function in that position" (Stebbins, 1990: 99). Through interaction with people who act out various roles, and by observing how roles are portrayed in the media, adolescents learn to incorporate the perspectives and expectations of the larger society and imagine what it would be like to enact the roles to which they aspire (Stryker, 1980: 63). Again, many young people experience this kind of anticipatory socialization as fun. Ahead of them, though, lies an uncertain future and the responsibilities of adulthood.

ADULT SOCIALIZATION

Adult socialization is the process by which adults take on new statuses and acquire new and different social identities. Adults frequently find themselves in new situations at work or in private life, meeting new people, and taking on new responsibilities. This means that to participate effectively in their society, adults must continue to undergo socialization (Clausen, 1986; Hogan and Astone, 1986).

Adult socialization differs from adolescent socialization in several important respects (Brim, 1968). Whereas adolescents seek to achieve autonomy, adults generally have control over the content and direction of their socialization. While adolescents often have little choice but to participate in various activities, adults usually engage in socializing activities voluntarily, such as enrolling in evening courses or joining a church. Because adults can often choose roles of their own free will, they can better understand and articulate their motives for new undertakings.

Marriage serves as the most important example, and constitutes one of the most important changes of adult life that involves extensive socialization. Although many of the traditional role expectations of marriage are no longer accepted uncritically, most people still choose to get married. In contrast to an earlier period when tradition largely determined the choices new couples would make, newlyweds and live-in partners now chart their own courses. This independence is highly valued by most people, but it can lead to severe stresses and strains in relationships with friends, with family, and even between the couple. There are no courses on how to adapt to married life. Most socialization consists of a couple learning, through trial and error, how to get along with others (such as in-laws) as a couple, and how to get along with each other.

A significant decision during adulthood is whether to become parents. Becoming a parent involves acquiring new skills and new statuses. While the statuses are conferred automatically, the roles and expectations accompanying them must be learned. As parents inevitably discover, relationships with children require active negotiation and adjustment. Moreover, children grow and change. This means that adults cannot simply adjust to their new role as parents and then relax. They must continually adapt to and accommodate to changing circumstances and situations. No wonder many parents try to take control in rigid and inflexible ways; they are simply trying to achieve some measure of stability in their lives and that of their family.

Socialization during adulthood also may involve the development of a career. As many college and university graduates are discovering, the difficulty of meeting this challenge successfully is increased by an economy in which employment prospects are uncertain. There is a set of "r words" serving as signposts of the changes taking place in the workplace—restructuring, reorganization, rationalizing, and re-engineering—that strike fear into the hearts of employees and postsecondary students (Lawson, 1996). As well, the type of employment offered to graduates is in flux. Many positions are now contractual, making employment less secure and stable (see Chapter 13). People can now expect to have to undergo career changes, with accompanying retraining, several times in their working career.

Although any job may involve an unfamiliar series of tasks, the new employee usually must also fit into a new social context with its own demands. Occupations typically include a subculture of members who share a system of norms and values related to their work and who have developed distinctive ways of perceiving and responding to their social environment. Once such a subculture is formed, new employees who enter the group are confronted with a set of norms and values to which they are expected to conform.

SOCIALIZATION DURING OLD AGE

Some of the most difficult changes in adult attitudes and behaviour occur in the later years of life (Erikson, 1982). It is during this period that the individual is most directly confronted by lowered prestige, decreased physical ability, and the prospects of chronic illness and death. Our society extends little dignity to aging. While medical advances have prolonged lives, they have not added to dignity and self-esteem for the aged. The media especially present the elderly in stereotypical terms. Consequently, many of us see old age as a period of increasing helplessness and dependence. Achieving the status of "senior citizen" is often accompanied by the loss of useful roles and valued statuses such as those of worker and spouse.

While many people spend a good part of their working life looking forward to retirement from the labour force, the realities of retirement may create identity problems for the retiree. Although most Canadians retire at age 65, there is little preparation for retired life. Cut off from work at an arbitrary age,

retirees are forced to assume what has been called a "roleless status" (Shanas et al., 1972; Hooyman and Kiyak, 1993). Hendricks and Hendricks (1986: 332) observe how the transition from work to retirement typically carries negative consequences:

> If the older worker incorporates the negative societal stereotypes, a gradual shift in self-image will occur.... When the negative appraisal summarized in "We see you as a bumbling fool" becomes internalized to "I am a bumbling fool," a downward spiral is set in motion that is difficult to break.

Many older people, particularly women, must also face the loss of a spouse. Widowhood, like retirement, is a roleless status for which there is little preparation and little guidance offered by society. There are few defined norms that govern when "normal" functioning should be resumed or how this should come about. This period also involves stress as the widowed person seeks to accommodate a new status, a new identity, and a new set of problems.

Finally, socialization in old age also involves facing death and dying. Philippe Aries (1981) observed that Western society attempts to deny death and to remove all reference to it in everyday life. We are taught not to talk about death, particularly to the dying. Relatives often attempt to keep the dying person from knowing their condition, and dying people sometimes keep their own prognosis secret (Atchley, 1994; Glaser and Strauss, 1967; Leming and Dickinson, 1990). As Shepard (1993: 153) has said: "The status of a dying person is, like retirement and widowhood, a status almost devoid of roles."

AGENTS OF SOCIALIZATION

Whatever stage of the life course we may be in, socialization, as we have continually stressed, is a *social* process in which we interact with others, are changed by those others, and in turn may have an impact upon them. Who are these others? They can be almost anyone, but as we have already noted there are certain categories of people especially likely to influence us, such as family members or peers. They serve as **agents of socialization**—individuals, groups, and institutions that impart, and from whom we acquire, the range of information required to interact effectively and participate in society. In addition to parents and peers, there are social institutions such as schools and the mass media that have a significant impact upon us and socialize us. We cannot interact with such institutions directly, although we do interact with people, such as classmates, with whom we participate in these institutions. Since they provide a context within which we come to take on new ideas and sometimes new roles, institutions too can serve as agents of socialization.

You may note that some agents of socialization, such as the family and the school, receive a mandate from society to "train" the next generation of members. In contrast, the peer group and the mass media do much of their "teaching" less formally or directly. Nonetheless, they can profoundly influence how individuals perceive and respond to the people and the world around them.

THE FAMILY

For young children in most societies, the family is virtually their entire world for the first few years of life. Through close interaction with parents and a small number of other people, the child learns to think and speak; internalizes norms, beliefs, and values; forms basic attitudes; develops a capacity for intimate and personal relationships; and begins to develop a self-image (Handel, 1990). Later experiences may lead to a modification of what is learned in the family, but it is not unusual for people to bring into adult life habits and expectations that characterized their childhood. Often, young people who rebelled against their parents' way of life and values as adolescents adopt the very same way of life and values when they become parents.

We discussed socialization into gender roles earlier. While various societal institutions, including schools, the mass media, the church, and sports, may contribute substantially to the child's socialization into feminine and masculine norms and activities, the family's role is critical (Fox, 2001). Parents may not deliberately teach boys to be aggressive or girls to be submissive and dependent (Lytton and Romney, 1991), but the family setting is one in which gender-typing prevails in how children play, the toys chosen for them, and even the chores they are expected to do around the house. It is also in the family that children observe their parents in gender-typed roles and behaviour and eventually model themselves after

their parents (Stockard and Johnson, 1992). Family life also teaches about affection, anger management, financial responsibilities, and respect for others (Benokraitis, 1997). Such socialization occurs informally, often offering a tentative model of marriage and parenthood.

In some ways, the family is well suited to the task of socialization. It is a small group in which all of the members can have constant face-to-face contact with one another. This means that the child's progress can be closely observed and individual adjustments made as necessary. Also, parents are usually well motivated. They have a strong emotional tie to their children, and the most meaningful and effective kind of social interaction for the purpose of socialization is that which is fused with emotion.

However, the family is not always an effective or efficient agent of socialization. Parents sometimes have little understanding of parenting; they may be unprepared emotionally and their dedication and commitment to the task may be offset by competing considerations (see Figure 4.1). Some parents neglect, abuse, or even abandon their children. As well, much evidence indicates that parents may reproduce in their children the negative modelling they experienced in their own upbringing.

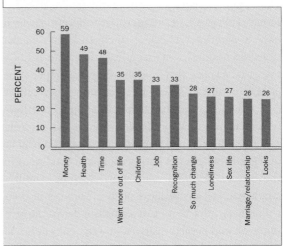

FIGURE 4.1 TOP TWELVE CONCERNS OF CANADIANS (PERCENTAGE CONCERNED "A GREAT DEAL" OR "QUITE A BIT")

SOURCE: Adapted from Reginald W. Bibby, *The Bibby Report: Social Trends Canadian Style* (Toronto: Stoddart, 1995), p. 82. Used with the permission of the author.

At the same time, however, families bestow statuses upon us—such as class statuses—that may significantly affect our lives and sense of self. Class status is very likely to place constraints on the opportunities that we are afforded. Research by Kohn (see Kohn et al., 1990) suggests that middle-class parents tend to rear their children differently from working-class parents. Middle-class families are likely to instill such values as achievement and independent thinking in their children, encouraging their curiosity and initiative. Working-class and poor families, by contrast, stress obedience and authority, punishing their children's transgressions by withholding privileges.

Kohn explained his findings by looking at the different work situations of the two groups. Whereas middle-class parents often work at jobs that permit opportunities for autonomy and creativity, the jobs of working-class parents often involve the repetitive performance of tasks under close supervision. Parents, concluded Kohn, socialize their children in ways that reflect their experiences of autonomy and conformity on the job. However, such differences in socialization patterns have undoubtedly narrowed as families of different social class backgrounds have tuned to similar media sources, including books, television talk shows, and magazines, for advice on rearing children (Luster et al., 1989).

The impact parents have on their children's educational aspirations and occupational success has occupied centre stage in the sociological literature. Here again, research suggests that there are class differences in parents' attitudes toward education, which have a significant effect on their children's educational aspirations. For example, in line with conflict theorists' claims that socialization reproduces the class structure in successive generations, Ballantine (1997) has shown that children in poor and low-income families are socialized to believe that aspiring to lofty ambitions and acquiring an education may be unrealistic in light of existing economic conditions in the family. Middle- and upper-income families emphasize and instill ideas of social success in their children. A culture of professionalism drives the attitudes of middle-class parents toward education. In contrast, working-class people see their chances of upward mobility as slim. For that reason, they resist the educational establishment (Lareau, 1987).

Arlene Skolnick (1991) has described three macrosocial changes over the past century that have strained the institution of the family. First, the shift from an industrial to an information and service economy drew women into the labour force and set the stage for both a feminist revival and an adolescent rebellion. Second, demographic change shortened the active parenting stage and extended old age and living alone as expected parts of the life course. Finally, there has been a growing preoccupation with the quality of intimate relationships, which has contributed to rising divorce rates. Other social changes have also contributed to the reversal of past family trends, including increasing age at marriage, lower rates of marriage, increasing rates of cohabitation outside of marriage, and more single-parent households with "latch-key" children who return home from school before their parents return home from work (Baker, 1989).

Finally, we should mention the ever-increasing diversity of forms taken by the family. It is becoming less and less reasonable to use terms such as the "middle-class" family or the "working-class" family as we did above. Instead families come in all shapes and sizes and the socialization of children and young people in the family can be very different from one household to another. Will the child of two gay men be brought up in the same way as a child living in a "blended" family with multiple half-brothers and sisters? Is it really relevant that in both cases the parents happen to be "middle-class"?

SCHOOLS

Traditionally, schools have been seen as settings within which social learning is just as important as learning such skills as reading, writing, and arithmetic. One of the authors of this chapter used to drive past a high school in an American city that had carved out in large letters above its main entrance the phrase "To Build Character." Building character is what most teachers, school administrators, and parents expect of the school system. Parents send their children to school to be socialized, and schools are deliberately organized to achieve that goal.

School is also usually the first setting in which children are supervised by adults who are not relatives or friends of the family. Moving from an environment of personal and intimate relationships to one that is impersonal is difficult for many children, and something of a shock to almost all of them. Whereas parents may praise their children regardless of the talent they actually display, teachers typically evaluate all students by a common set of standards. As a place where children are taught indirectly to be less emotionally dependent, the school serves as a model of much of the adult world. Although some interpersonal relationships may be based on love and affection, others are impersonal and defined by the society with little regard for the particular individuals who enter them. Of all the functions of the school, adjusting children to its social order—which offers a preview of what will be expected of them as they negotiate their way among the institutions of adult society—may be the most important (Oakes, 1985).

Building character takes time. Accompanying the formal curriculum of the school is a "hidden curriculum"—the informal teaching that helps ensure the student's integration into society (Richer, 1988). Students are exposed to, and rewarded for, the acquisition and display of such desired qualities as good discipline, conformity, respect for authority, and

The student's values are strongly influenced by his or her peer group, which consists of people of similar age and status, regardless of whether they are friends.
SOURCE: © Chuck Savage/CORBIS/Magma.

cooperation. Gender socialization messages, for example, are imparted by teachers who may ask girls to perform "feminine" tasks such as cleaning the blackboard or tidying a shelf, while delegating more "masculine" tasks to boys, such as rearranging desks or carrying sports or audio-visual equipment (Best, 1983; Thorne, 1993). In research on the effects of the teacher's gender, the student's gender, and classroom subject, researchers found that both elementary and high school classroom interactions are related to the gender of teachers and students being taught (Duffy et al., 2001/2002; Hopf and Hatzichristou, 1999). Specifically, female mathematics teachers, male literature/language teachers, and female literature/language teachers directed more interactions towards male students than female ones. Such interactions may well connect to emerging self-concepts among male and female students. As an institution, schools not only affect children's knowledge but also their self-image.

PEER GROUPS

Schools are also the setting where most young people first become acquainted with their peer group. While the family constitutes the most important socializing agent in the early years, peers often begin to be an influence at a very young age. A **peer group** is a set of individuals who are about the same age, share similar interests, and enjoy a similar social status. By the time young people reach their teenage years, the peer group increasingly assumes the role of Mead's significant others. As parents are often annoyed to discover, peer influence in certain areas may override parental influence, as teenagers imitate their friends and as the peer group's norms and values assume a tightening grip over its members.

In childhood, peer groups consist of people of a similar age and of equal social status formed largely by the accident of association. Members of the same peer group are not necessarily friends. For instance, all children in a given classroom may constitute a peer group, but by no means are they necessarily all friends. Later in life, however, one *chooses* peer groups on the basis of such criteria as common interests and activities and similar income level or occupation.

Significantly, the peer group is the only agent of childhood socialization that is not controlled mainly by adults (Corsaro, 1992). While parents typically play the initial leading roles in the inculcation of basic values, peers seem to have the greatest influence in lifestyle issues such as appearance, social activities, and dating (Sebald, 1992). Indeed, research indicates that, especially during adolescence, peers can strongly shape the individual's aspirations and behaviour with respect to both acceptable and criminal behaviour (Giordano et al., 1986). Certainly, the peer group contributes to socialization by enabling children to engage in experiences that may not be provided in the family. Here they can interact in give-and-take relationships—relationships involving exchange, conflict, competition, and cooperation—not always possible at home. In this manner, children are provided with opportunities for self-direction and self-expression (Adler and Adler, 1998). Peer groups allow young people to examine feelings, beliefs, and ideas that are unacceptable to the family. Friends share a vision of the world. They discuss sexual and emotional relationships and developments within their school and friendship circle.

Often, peer group socialization is not very subtle. Peers may pressure one another to conform to a standard deemed appropriate by the group. Little deviation may be tolerated from group norms concerning speech, attitudes, and dress. Adolescents, preoccupied with gaining autonomy from their parents, and anxious about gaining acceptance from others like themselves, may find such pressures difficult to resist (Thorne, 1993). In fact, by the teenage years, the peer group may demand behaviour that conflicts sharply with the norms and values of the parental generation. In this regard, it is understandable why parents often express concern about their children's friends, particularly during the teenage years.

If peer groups often reject the norms and values of their parents, from where does the group get its own norms and values? Chances are, from media sources. Peer groups, and other manifestations of youth subculture, seem to have a fascination with the media and look to forms of media as symbols of identity. One's taste in music, movies, television shows, and fashion not only express a common identity, but a common "style" (Hebdige, 1979) that sets the group apart, both from parents and from other sets of peers.

MEDIA AND TECHNOLOGY

Sociologists agree that the mass media are powerful socializing influences but it is difficult to measure their effects. Most forms of mass media, such as television, radio, newspapers, videos, magazines, movies, CDs, DVDs, and books, are impersonal, transmitting information one-way. This creates an audience conditioned to passively receive what is sometimes called "mass culture," consisting of whatever news, messages, programs, or events that are brought to them. Recently, new, more controversial media have been introduced. Allowing for information to be communicated to a global audience, Internet Web sites provide children with relatively unfettered access to pornography and groups propagating racial strife and violence. Music videos and films, also available on the Internet, contain controversial content that alarms people concerned about their impact on young people.

Recently, television has attracted considerable critical attention in light of several incidents of blatant violence. The killings at Columbine High School in Colorado and W.R. Myers High School in Alberta—and the suspected linkage between the two—are examples (Garbarino, 1999). The American Academy of Pediatrics holds that television viewing can affect the mental, social, and physical health of young people. In studies by the American Medical Association, the American Psychiatric Association, and other agencies, violence in movies and television has been linked to violent behaviour in young people.

Sociological research on violence in the mass media and the real world suggests a weaker connection between the two. As you will learn in Chapter 6, the consensus is that violence in the mass media may push some people *who are already predisposed to aggression* to engage in more violent acts. But it is highly doubtful whether most viewers are similarly incited (Freedman, 2002).

In contrast to television violence, which is passively experienced, video and computer games promote the acting out of violent scenarios. The player not only watches violence, but initiates it, acts it out, and is then rewarded for using it effectively. An example is *Grand Theft Auto: Vice City*, one of the best-selling video games at the time of this writing. According to one reviewer, the game is "... a lush and wild adrenaline-fuelled, shoot-'em-up role-playing game that is surely the most ambitious piece of interactive entertainment ever made" (Fussel, 2003: D16). The player can kill police officers by blowing up their cars, commit drive-by shootings, blow people's heads off with a sniper rifle and watch blood spew from their necks, distribute pornography, and traffic cocaine for organized crime.

Critics of this game have sounded an alarm because it rewards players for criminal behaviour. Whether the game influences anyone to actually commit a crime, the critics suggest, misses the point. Violent video games increase aggressive thoughts and behaviour, thus increasing the likelihood that kids will get into fights in school. Such games, critics say, increasingly desensitize successive generations to violence and ultimately may cause the culture to sustain serious damage.

Apart from the issue of violence, there is no denying that the media have a profound impact upon the public. By selecting and emphasizing certain topics, stressing particular views or interpretations, and concentrating on specific themes, the media create, manage, and control impressions of what is important and real. E-mail and Web pages have clearly enabled outside influences to help shape the direction of socialization, frequently in opposition to values and beliefs conveyed in the family. By displaying role models that the young can imitate, the media may inadvertently perpetuate stereotypes—women, for example, are often characterized as subservient to men, whether in the family setting or in the workplace. As well, media influences are not always apparent; for instance, in our consumer-driven culture they are instrumental in teaching individuals to become obedient consumers.

OTHER SOCIALIZING AGENTS

The family, school, peer group, and media are the main socializing agents, but there are others that may be significant. Religious institutions, for example, may seriously affect the moral outlook of young people even in highly secular societies such as our own. Athletic teams may teach young people to compete, cooperate with others, follow rules, and make friends. Youth groups may be instrumental in teaching young

people about group rules and expectations about conformity, and even about deviance. In complex societies such as ours, conflict among the agencies of socialization is virtually inevitable. Moreover, conflict may also occur in a single socializing agency. For instance, soccer coaches may extol the virtues of cooperation but also insist upon and emphasize the importance of winning at all costs.

IDENTITY AND SOCIAL CHANGE

Are we free to become whoever we want, however we want? The answer is clearly "no." Socialization may be an active process in which we transform our identity as we take on new roles, but not always in conditions of our own choosing. It is important to remember that the social conditions of life powerfully influence identity. Premodern societies formed relatively cohesive communities in which most people could find solidarity and meaning in primary groups such as the family. While primary groups limit the range of personal experience, they confer a strong sense of identity and purpose. Modernity expanded the range of personal choice and permitted a greater diversity of beliefs. Still, while modernization has emancipated people from the tyranny of tradition, it leaves people without the comfort and security of heritage and roots. Modern societies, in general, offer more autonomy but less sense of purpose and fewer enduring social ties than past societies. Not surprisingly, many people have difficulty establishing a stable and coherent sense of who they are.

The result is that some people shuttle from one identity to another, changing their lifestyle in search of an elusive "true self." They may join various social groups in search of purpose and belonging, and even experiment with various religions in the hope of finding a system of beliefs that "fits" them (Wuthnow, 1998). In sociological terms, the difficulty in developing a stable and coherent identity is rooted in the individual's social surroundings. The problem of answering the question "Who am I?" reflects not only a personal crisis but also the complexity and instability of modern society (Berger, 1970).

Understanding the connection between personal development and social conditions calls for a malleable view of human development, one in which there is the constant possibility of change—even radical change. In fact, as many of us are only too aware, not only have we changed but we may know others who have experienced substantial transformations, either forcibly or voluntarily. Some changes are minor or inconsequential, such as wearing different kinds of clothes or dieting for a brief period. But there are also more profound life-altering experiences over which we may exercise relatively little control. A life-threatening illness, incarceration in prison, or a severe depression requiring institutionalization are cases in point. In each of these instances, the individual must learn to adapt to fundamental alterations in daily routines. While these changes may be of a temporary nature, they nevertheless impact forcefully on the individual's identity (see Box 4.2).

Sometimes we are coerced into change, through shame, guilt, or force. But most of us are familiar with individuals who were not coerced into radically modifying their behaviour, but chose this route of their own accord. Shaffir's (1974) research on conversion processes and experiences among Hassidic (ultra-Orthodox) Jews is a case in point.

Hassidic Jews form cohesive religious communities that are under the guidance of a charismatic leader. During his research among one such group of Hassidim, referred to as Lubavitch, Shaffir became aware that significant numbers were not born into this way of life but came from diverse Jewish backgrounds, including those with minimal commitments to Orthodox Judaism. Yet Shaffir found their appearance and behaviour indistinguishable from those whose Hassidic lineage could be traced back several generations. They observed Lubavitch holidays and customs and venerated the Lubavitch charismatic leader. They no longer watched television, went to movies, or participated in secular cultural activities that, prior to their conversion, were important parts of their everyday life. Moreover, their lifestyle change was anything but temporary; their children received a limited secular education and very few of the offspring would attend university, which was perceived by the community as a hotbed of secularism and therefore discouraged.

Why are people willing to change their lives and their identities so dramatically? One explanation, often used to account for religious conversion, is that individuals are "brainwashed," that is, manipulated in some mysterious way (such as being put on a diet of rice or prevented from getting adequate sleep). This manipulation supposedly makes them lose the ability to think rationally. Yet there are other changes of lifestyle and identity just as dramatic as religious conversion. There seems little reason to have a special explanation for why people suddenly become religious as opposed to any other sort of lifestyle or identity change. People who take up martial arts, running, or computer games may exhibit the same degree of fervent commitment as converts to a religious group.

Sociological explanations of conversion emphasize the role of interaction and the development of new social relationships. Lofland's (1966) study of conversion to religious cults shows that conversion usually comes after the potential member has formed a close personal relationship with one or more cult members. During this relationship they learn to value cult members as friends or intimates, and come to feel that they too are valued. At first, the new convert may "go along" with a set of unfamiliar or seemingly peculiar religious beliefs out of a desire not to embarrass their friends or create any conflict. As time passes and they see how seriously these beliefs are taken by people they respect, they begin to wonder what these beliefs have to offer and investigate them more seriously. The more time they spend with members of the religious community, the more plausible the beliefs will seem. The new recruit may soon feel there is "something" to these ideas after all. By this point, they are well along the road to conversion.

Remember, though, that not everyone moves all the way along this path to true belief. Studying only those who convert hides from our view the tentative nature of much of this process. Many choose not to participate. That is why Lofland's study of a religious cult remains a classic of sociological research: Lofland was able to observe and talk with people whose level of commitment to the cult ranged from brief curiosity to total dedication.

RESOCIALIZATION

Conversion is often an example of **resocialization**, the process of discarding former patterns of behaviour and belief and accepting new ones, although at times reluctantly. As part of a transformation in one's life, resocialization is an attempt to correct or instill particular values and behaviours. Sociologists generally restrict

BOX 4.2   THE CLOAK OF COMPETENCE

Medical students during clerkship believe they are expected to act as if they are in the know, not in ways which might put their developing competence into question. The pressure to be seen as competent by faculty, fellow students, hospital personnel, and patients narrows the range of alternative roles students can assume. Students recognize their low status in the hospital hierarchy and on hospital rotations. They realize that the extent of their medical knowledge can easily be called into question by fellow students, tutors, interns, residents, and faculty. To reduce the possibility of embarrassment and humiliation, which, at this stage in their medical career, is easily their fate, students attempt to reduce the unpredictability of their situation by manipulating an impression of themselves as enthusiastic, interested, and eager to learn. At the same time, students seize opportunities which allow them to impress others, particularly faculty and fellow students, with their growing competence and confidence.

... A [strategy] shared by students to manage an appearance of competence is to limit their initiatives to those situations which will be convincing demonstrations of their competence. Some students decide, for example, to ask questions in areas with which they are already familiar, to cultivate an impression of competence.

The general strategy that the students adopt is to mask their uncertainty and anxiety with an image of self-confidence. Image making becomes recognized as being as important as technical competence. As one student remarks: "We have to be good actors, put across the image of self-confidence, that you know it all...."

... Referring to the importance of creating the right impression, [one student said,]

> Dr. Jones, who was my adviser or boss for medicine, he always came and did rounds on Wednesday mornings. Well, he didn't have very many patients on the service, but we always knew that his interest was in endocrinology, and ... if he had an endocrine patient ... we knew ... that he was going to pick that endocrine patient to talk about. And so, of course, ... any dummy can read up Tuesday night like hell on the new American Diabetic Association standards for diabetes or hyperglycemia ... and you can handle general medicine. So the next day you seem fairly knowledgeable.... That afternoon you forget about it because you figure Thursday morning hematology people make their rounds and, of course, you have to read up on hematology....

... Students realize that to be a good student-physician is either to be or appear to be competent. They observe that others react to their role-playing. A student describes the self-fulfilling nature of this process when he says:

> To be a good GP, you've got to be a good actor, you've got to respond to a situation. You have to be quick, pick up the dynamics of what is going on at the time and try to make the person leave the office thinking that you know something. And a lot of people, the way they handle that is by letting the patient know that they know it all, and only letting out a little bit at a time, and as little as possible. I think that they eventually reach a plateau where they start thinking themselves they are really great and they know it all, because they have these people who are worshipping at their feet.

The process of adopting the cloak of competence is justified by students as helpful to the patient. A student summarizes the relationship between acting competently and patients responding to such a performance by getting well when he says:

> You know the patients put pressure on you to act as if you are in the know. If you know anything about the placebo effect, you know that a lot of the healing and curing of patients does not involve doing anything that will really help them, but rather creating confidence in the patient that things are being done and will be done. We know that the placebo effect for example has even cured cancer patients. If they have the confidence in the doctor ... and what treatment they are undergoing, they are much more likely to get well, irrespective of the objective effects of the treatment.

SOURCE: Excerpted from J. Haas and W. Shaffir, "The Cloak of Competence," *Symbolic Interaction*, Vol. 1, No. 1, Fall 1977, pp. 71–88. Copyright © 1991 by Society for the Study of Symbolic Interaction. Reprinted by permission.

the idea of resocialization to those contexts where there are *deliberate* efforts to change the individual or group.

A classic example is Erving Goffman's (1961) research on total institutions. Goffman examined how people may be socialized against their will—for example, in prisons or in mental institutions where they are confined. This is the special world of **total institutions**, settings, such as the military, convents, prisons, boarding schools, and mental hospitals, within which people are isolated from the rest of society for a set period and where all aspects of a person's life are regulated under one authority. According to Goffman, total institutions impose regimented routines with the goal of resocialization into a new identity. The total institution attempts to achieve this objective by completely controlling and manipulating the environment, thus depriving its inmates of contradictory forms of social experience.

Resocialization in total institutions is a two-part process. First, the staff attempts to strip away the new inmate's established identity. This is accompanied by a series of experiences that include humiliations, degradations, and "mortification rituals," which may include physical pain. Second, efforts are made to reconstitute the inmate's sense of self by imposing a new identity and a new way of life upon him or her. In a childlike condition of heightened ambiguity and stress created by degradation and humiliation, the person is ripe for conversion to the expectations of the more powerful group. The desire for security and acceptance often leads to imitation or adoption of the behaviour of authority figures (Light, 1980). The resocialized person often undergoes a symbolic ritual death and rebirth, shedding the old identity and taking on a new one.

An example of resocialization is basic training in the military. Here the primary goal is to modify the recruit's civilian self-image and replace it with a military identity. Recruits are removed from their civilian environment and confined to a military base where they are required to submit to a vast range of stresses, disciplinary measures, and indoctrination to a new set of role expectations. The well-known example in which the new recruit is issued a uniform that does not fit is often presented on television or in the movies as a comic moment, but it has a symbolic significance as well. New recruits are expected to understand that the military is not concerned about them as individuals, only as soldiers. Soldiers follow commands and adapt to the needs of the military, not the other way around.

Identity change in total institutions is often dramatic. Yet even in total institutions, Goffman showed, people interact with, adapt to, and resist others with whom they are in personal contact. Much less dramatic but often anxiety-provoking resocialization occurs outside of total institutions when newcomers are inducted into prestigious professions such as law, the ministry, and medicine. Accounts detail how medical students are resocialized to temper their idealism with the professionally defined realities of medicine (Becker et al., 1961; Haas and Shaffir, 1987).

The control over identity exerted by the total institution stands in contrast to the ways in which people can play with and manipulate their identity using the Internet. Internet users—in 2003 about 600 million strong—are engaged in a wide range of social interactions, from the exchange of e-mail, to conversations in "chat groups," computer-assisted group work, and participation in so-called virtual communities. As such users well know, the Internet allows them to act out roles in their dealings with others that may have little basis in reality. They may cover up who they really are, claiming an age, ethnicity, gender, or expertise that is not their own. Sometimes this is intended maliciously, but often Internet users are very upfront about taking on an identity that they prefer rather than one that's "real." Often they will use a nickname or username that expresses their preferred identity. They may name themselves after a favourite television star, movie character, or comic book hero, or seek a name that they feel expresses their character.

The image of society Goffman presented in his research on total institutions was one in which large, impersonal institutions were gaining more and more control over people—over their actions, their experiences of the world, and their sense of self. Resistance was possible, and often successful, but only in the small events of everyday life, as in forming personal relationships with others or in exchanging gifts and services. Yet today, with the advent of new forms of communication and technology we find that new forms of autonomy have also developed and, some suggest, new sources of freedom. Active, malleable, and innovative, human beings are not content to accept the world as they find it, but look for ways to transform it and adapt it to their social needs and personal desires. Nothing better exemplifies this creative aspect of social life than the process of socialization.

SUMMARY

1. Socialization is an active process through which human beings become members of society, develop a sense of self, and learn to participate in social relationships with others. Through socialization we acquire knowledge, skills, and motivations for participation in society.

2. Each of us is born with a set of human potentials. Nature and nurture interact in contributing to human development.

3. Socialization is lifelong, typically involving relationships with family, school, peer groups, mass media, and occupational groups. Ours is an age-graded society as well, and early childhood, adolescence, adulthood, and old age/retirement are significant stages; different roles and responsibilities are associated with each stage.

4. Several scholars were important in developing the conception of socialization as an active, interactional process. Charles Horton Cooley was noteworthy for his concept of the "looking-glass self," which stressed that we view ourselves as we think others view us. George Herbert Mead emphasized how people assume roles by imagining themselves in the roles of others. Erving Goffman described the intricate ways we try to present ourselves when interacting with others.

5. Gender socialization is the learning of masculine and feminine behaviour and roles. From birth, and in every area of social life, the socialization of the sexes in terms of content and expectations makes the socially constructed gender role more significant than the biological role of male or female. Assumptions about appropriate male and female attributes limit the range of acceptable behaviour and options for both sexes.

6. The most important agent of socialization is the family. As the examples of orphanages and child neglect demonstrate, initial warmth and nurturing are essential to healthy development. The self-concept formed during childhood has lasting consequences.

7. The central function of schools in industrial society is the teaching of skills and knowledge, but they also transmit society's central cultural values and ideologies. Schools expose children to situations in which the same rules, regulations, and authority patterns apply to everyone.

8. Peer groups provide young people with a looking glass unclouded by love or duty, and an opportunity to learn roles and values that adults do not teach.

9. The traditional mass media are impersonal and large-scale socializers. New forms of media are more interactive and allow people to play with and try out different identities.

10. During adulthood, individuals are socialized as they get jobs, marry, divorce, raise children, retire, and prepare for death. These many roles involve new and different relationships with others and guidelines for behaviour.

11. Sometimes there are abrupt changes in our self-concept, and we must learn new role identities and negotiate a new self-image. Resocialization occurs when we abandon or are forced to abandon our way of life and self-concept for a radically different one. This is most efficiently done in total institutions—for example, jails, mental hospitals, and boot camps—or in religious or political conversions.

QUESTIONS TO CONSIDER

1. Consider who the significant others are in your life. Have they changed over time? How have they shaped and influenced your sense of self?

2. Goffman's dramaturgical approach implies that "all the world's a stage" and all of us are merely "players." Do you agree with Goffman? Cite examples of impression management that you rely upon and encounter in everyday life.

3. Prisons and mental hospitals are socialization institutions organized to change, test, or "correct" people. How effective are they and why are they not more successful in meeting their goals?

4. Think of any job you have held and consider the socialization that was required. Distinguish the formal and informal components of the socialization process.

5. What, if any, are the possible effects on personal identity of use of the Internet? Could the consequences be greater separation and alienation from reality, others, and oneself, or might the outcome for the user be a heightened sense of belonging, integration, and shared understandings? Are both extremes possible?

GLOSSARY

Adolescence is the period of life from approximately age 12 to age 20.

Adult socialization is the process by which adults take on new statuses and acquire new and different social identities.

Agents of socialization include individuals, groups, and institutions that impart, and from whom we acquire, the range of information required to interact effectively and participate in society.

Anticipatory socialization is a process by which people hoping to take on a particular role begin to discern what it would be like to function in that role.

The **dramaturgical approach** is Erving Goffman's perspective on social interaction, in which he emphasizes that we are all actors and also audiences for one another.

The **game stage** in Mead's theory of internalization is the period during which a child develops a generalized impression of the behaviour people expect as well as an awareness of his or her own importance to the group.

Gender encompasses the cultural expectations associated with femininity and masculinity.

The **generalized other** is a conception of how people in general are likely to respond and react in a given situation.

The *I* in Mead's theory of internalization is the subjective component of the self that allows us to react to and assess ourselves.

The **imitative stage** in Mead's theory of internalization is a preliminary stage in which children two years old and under imitate role models but do not yet interact with others much because they cannot take the role of the other.

Instincts are inborn patterns of behaviour in animals, such as mating, catching food, and so on.

The **looking-glass self** is the theory developed by Charles Horton Cooley to explain how individuals develop a sense of self through reacting to the impressions others have of them.

The *me* in Mead's theory of internalization is the objective component of the self to which we ourselves react.

A **peer group** is a set of individuals of about the same age, with about the same interests, and with similar social status.

The **play stage** in Mead's theory of internalization is the period in which children begin to experiment with and adopt social roles.

A **primary group** is a relatively small group in which people are emotionally close and interaction is intimate.

Primary socialization is the process by which children are prepared (usually in the family) for the various roles required of members of society.

Resocialization is a deliberate effort to change an individual or group, leading to the acquisition of new values and behaviour.

Secondary socialization involves learning specific institutional roles (such as student, husband or wife, or parent), as well as the attitudes, behaviours, and responsibilities that are a part of these roles.

Self refers to the sense of individual identity whereby we understand ourselves and differentiate ourselves from others.

A **self-fulfilling prophecy** is a circumstance in which an expectation leads to behaviour that causes the expectation to become a reality.

Significant others are those, such as parents, who are of central importance to the individual in the development of the self.

Socialization encompasses the active processes whereby human beings become members of society, develop a sense of self, and learn to participate in social relationships with others.

Status refers to the culturally and socially defined position a person occupies in an interaction.

A **subculture** is a group that has distinctive values, norms, and practices within the larger culture.

Symbolic interactionism is a theoretical approach to the study of social interaction that stresses the symbols and meanings people attach to their own and others' behaviour.

Symbols are gestures, objects, or sounds that stand for something else and whose meaning depends on shared understandings.

Taking the role of the other refers to the attempt to determine or appreciate the perspective of someone else in a particular situation, especially how that person perceives and reacts to us.

Total institutions are Goffman's term for those settings within which people are isolated from the rest of society for a period and where all aspects of a person's life are regulated under one authority.

SUGGESTED READING

Adler, Patricia A., and Peter Adler. (1998). *Peer Power: Preadolescent Culture and Identity.* New Brunswick, NJ: Rutgers University Press. Based on eight years of observation research, this is a first-rate sociological study of the role of peer groups in preadolescent socialization.

Becker, Howard S., Blanche Geer, Everett C. Hughes, and Anselm L. Strauss. (1961). *Boys in White: Student Culture in Medical School.* This is arguably *the* classic study on professional socialization, and it examines how medical students negotiate their transition into the medical profession and are transformed into physicians.

Ebaugh, Helen Rose Fuchs. (1988). *Becoming an Ex: The Process of Role Exit.* Chicago: University of Chicago Press. This excellent study examines the process whereby people learn to disengage themselves from previous roles and claims to identity.

Goffman, Erving. (1961). *Asylums: Essays on the Social Situation of Mental Patients and Other Inmates.* Garden City, NY: Anchor Books. This account analyzes life in total institutions and describes what such institutions make of inmates and how the latter organize their life inside them.

CHAPTER FIVE

SEX, GENDER, AND SEXUALITY

In this chapter, you will learn that:

- Sex refers to biological differences between males and females, while gender refers to the attitudes, beliefs, and behaviours we associate with masculinity and femininity.

- Individuals form a "gender identity" or a sense of biological, psychological, and social belonging to a particular sex. Individuals also learn to play a "gender role," that is, to act in accordance with expectations about how members of their gender are supposed to behave.

- Sexuality refers to activities intended to lead to erotic arousal and produce a genital response. Sexuality is guided by a set of social "scripts" that tell us whom we should find attractive, when and where it is appropriate to be aroused, when it is permissible to have sex, and so forth.

- There are two major perspectives on the relationship among sex, gender, and sexuality. One ("essentialism") holds that gender roles and sexual scripts develop naturally from biological differences between the sexes. The other ("social constructionism") holds that gender roles and sexual scripts emerge in response to the different social positions women and men occupy.

- Because of the way gender and sexuality are structured in our society, intolerance for sexual minorities is widespread and male sexual aggression against women is common.

- A substantial decrease in gender inequality is now possible. The redefinition of sexuality is an important step in that process.

RHONDA L. LENTON

YORK UNIVERSITY

INTRODUCTION

GENDER, SEX, AND THE CASE OF DAVID/BRENDA

In April 1966, identical eight-month-old twin boys were brought to St. Boniface hospital in Winnipeg to be circumcised. They had developed a condition called phimosis, or closing of the foreskin. However, due to mechanical malfunction or doctor error, the electro-cautery needle used for the procedure released a surge of heat. It burnt off the entire penis of one baby. The parents sought expert medical advice but were given little hope. One psychiatrist summarized the baby's future as follows: "[H]e will be unable to consummate marriage or have normal heterosexual relations … he will have to recognize that he is incomplete, physically defective, and that he must live apart…." (quoted in Colapinto, 2001 [2000]: 16). The name of the baby was David Reimer.

Seven months later, now deeply depressed, David Reimer's parents happened to be watching a CBC television program featuring Dr. John Money of Johns Hopkins University in Baltimore. He was discussing how he successfully assigned a male or female identity to children whose external sex organs and internal reproductive system were not clearly male or female. The main criterion he used for deciding the child's sex was expected "erotic functioning" as an adult. He recommended boys born with a penis shorter than 2.5 cm and girls born with a clitoris longer than 1 cm for sex reassignment, preferably within weeks of birth. According to Money, it was imperative, once the child's sex was decided, that doctors and parents never waver in their decision and never tell the child about his or her condition at birth.

Until David Reimer, Dr. Money had never had the opportunity to test his idea on a child born unequivocally a boy or girl. Therefore, when David's mother wrote to him shortly after the television show, he urged her to bring the baby to his office in Baltimore. He considered it a bonus that David was a twin. This would allow him to compare the development of the two siblings. Dr. Money was eager to proceed. He believed that the "gender identity gate"—the time after which a child is "locked" into an identity as a male or a female—closes at two years of age. The parents nevertheless took several months to deliberate and consult with family and friends before giving the go-ahead. On July 3, 1967, David, now 22 months old, underwent surgical castration and reconstructive surgery. He became Brenda Reimer. As the years passed, the parents tried their best to follow Dr. Money's instructions. Brenda was given dresses to wear, skipping ropes and dolls for presents, and regular doses of the female hormone estrogen at puberty.

In 1972, at a meeting of the American Association for the Advancement of Science in Washington, DC, Dr. Money unveiled the story of David/Brenda Reimer. He claimed that the experiment was an unqualified success. In *Sexual Signatures*, a co-authored book intended for the general public, he described David's sex reassignment as "dramatic proof that the gender-identity option is open at birth for normal infants." Money was equally optimistic in a 1978 journal article, where he reported that "[n]ow prepubertal in age, [Brenda Reimer] has … a feminine gender identity and role, distinctly different from that of her brother" (quoted in Colapinto, 1997: 72).

Then, in March 1997, a bombshell: Dr. Money, it emerged, had doctored his reports. A biologist from the University of Hawaii and a psychiatrist from the Canadian Ministry of Health started a scientific scandal when they published an article in the *Archives of Adolescent and Pediatric Medicine* showing that David/Brenda had in fact struggled against his/her imposed girlhood from the start. In December, a long and moving exposé of the case in *Rolling Stone* magazine gave further details.

The authors documented Brenda's resistance to being a girl, including everything from tearing off her first dress to insisting on standing to urinate. According to her brother, Kevin, there was "nothing feminine about Brenda…. She walked like a guy. Sat with her legs apart. She talked about guy things, didn't give a crap about cleaning house, getting married, wearing makeup. We both wanted to play with guys, build forts and have snowball fights and play army" (quoted in Colapinto, 2001 [2000]: 57). By the age of seven, Brenda announced she wanted to be a boy, and she refused to have further vaginal surgery because it would make her look more like a girl. She took estrogen only after being told that failure to do so would result in her limbs being disproportionate to her body. She refused to see Dr. Money after 1978. In 1979, Brenda made the decision to stop living as a girl.

In 1980, her father finally told Brenda what had happened to her. Brenda's first reaction was relief.

David Reimer, February 2001.
SOURCE: © Reuters NewMedia Inc./CORBIS.

She then resolved to become David again. By the age of 16, she started taking male hormone treatments and had her breasts removed and a penis surgically constructed. Subsequent surgeries allowed David to have sex with a woman at the age of 23. He married the woman two years later, in 1990, and adopted her three children. David is now a devoted father who enjoys a happy family life, although he is, understandably, still deeply troubled by his past.

The story of David/Brenda introduces many of the issues raised in this chapter. How do we define *female* and *male*? What is the relationship between biological sex and the attitudes and behaviours that we associate with being male or female? What are the

implications of this relationship for our sexual identity and sexual relations? I will touch on all these questions here. The answers, it will emerge, are not as obvious as they may at first appear.

DEFINING MALE AND FEMALE: SEX AND GENDER

While preparing to write this chapter, I asked my six-year-old the difference between boys and girls. She answered: "Boys have a penis, girls have a vagina." Like most people, she distinguished men and women on the basis of biological **sex**. Your sex depends on whether you were born with distinct male or female genitalia and a genetic program that released either male or female hormones to stimulate the development of your reproductive system. Table 5.1 gives a more complete version of this common view by summarizing four key sex differences.

At the point of conception, a newly formed zygote has 46 chromosomes. If the last chromosome has an XX pattern, the zygote becomes a female. If it has an XY pattern, it becomes a male. About one in 400 children is born with an unusual forty-sixth chromosome pattern caused by the failure of the sperm to divide properly (Berch and Bender, 1987). Most of these combinations are never diagnosed.

Around the sixth or seventh week of gestation, the gonads or sex glands begin to develop—testes in the case of a male, ovaries in the case of a female. The testes and ovaries subsequently produce various hormones in varying amounts. These hormones contribute to the development of the sex organs. Differences between the sex organs are noticeable by

TABLE 5.1 SUMMARY OF BIOLOGICAL SEX DIFFERENCES DURING TYPICAL FETAL DEVELOPMENT

VARIABLE	FEMALE	MALE
Chromosomal pattern	XX	XY
Gonadal	ovaries	testes
Hormonal	more estrogens than androgens	more androgens than estrogens + MIH
Sex organs	uterus, fallopian tubes, vagina, clitoris, labia	epididymis, vas deferens, seminal vesicles, prostate, penis, scrotum

SOURCE: Adapted from E.D. Nelson and Barrie W. Robinson, *Gender in Canada* (Scarborough, ON: Prentice Hall Allyn and Bacon Canada, 1999), p. 48. Reprinted with permission of Pearson Education, Canada.

the fourteenth week after conception. There appears to be only one sex difference in the brain about which the scientific community agrees (Blum, 1997). The part of the brain known as the hypothalamus makes the female brain sensitive to estrogen and is responsible for creating menstrual cycles in women.

There is, however, more to being male or female than biological sex differences, as the case of David/Brenda shows. Recalling his life as Brenda, David said: "[E]veryone is telling you that you're a girl. But you say to yourself, 'I don't *feel* like a girl.' You think girls are supposed to be delicate and *like* girl things—tea parties, things like that. But I like to *do* guy stuff. It doesn't match" (quoted in Colapinto, 1997: 66; my emphasis). As this quotation shows, being male or female involves not just biology but also certain "masculine" and "feminine" feelings, attitudes, and behaviours. Accordingly, biological sex must be distinguished from sociological **gender**. One's gender is composed of the feelings, attitudes, and behaviours associated with being male or female. Furthermore, one's identification with, or sense of belonging to, a particular sex—biologically, psycho-logically, and socially—is known as one's **gender identity**. When one behaves according to widely shared expectations about how males or females are supposed to act, one adopts a **gender role**.

Research shows that North Americans' expectations about how men and women are supposed to act have changed only somewhat over the last 40 years (Broverman et al., 1972; Rosenkrantz et al., 1968; Williams and Bennett, 1975; Williams and Best, 1982; Bergen and Williams, 1991). This is true despite significant changes in women's lives in particular. For example, in the 1960s and 1970s, males were generally expected to act tough and hide their emotions. This is still true today, albeit to a lesser extent. Boys still tend to learn at a young age that crying or displaying their feelings in public is likely to result in taunts and accusations of being a "sissy." As a result, they curb their nurturing abilities, thus fulfilling gender expectations.

Great pressure can be brought to bear on individuals who do not conform to gender expectations. Brenda is a case in point. She was ostracized and tormented by her peers for not acting feminine.

Being male or female involves not just biology but also certain "masculine" or "feminine" feelings, attitudes, and behaviours. One's identification with a particular sex is known as gender identity.
SOURCE: Susan G. Scott, *The Princess.*

Transgendered people report similar experiences of rejection (see Box 5.1). Transgendered people are individuals who want to alter their gender by changing their appearance or resorting to medical intervention. According to Dr. Diane Watson, a psychiatrist who heads the gender-identity clinic at Vancouver Hospital, one in every 5000 to 10 000 Canadians is transgendered (quoted in Nolen, 1999: D1). Moreover, says Dr. Watson, one in 30 000 Canadians is fully **transsexual**. Transsexuals are people who believe they were born with the "wrong" body—that is, they identify with, and want to live fully as, a member of the "opposite" sex. They often take the lengthy and painful path to a sex-change operation. The apparent contradiction between biological sex and gender experienced by these individuals brings us back to the question of how we define males and females.

We typically accept "masculine men" and "feminine women" as normal. That is, we expect individuals to possess unambiguous sex organs and to adopt the gender role that is consistent with their biological sex. In fact, the World Health Organization classifies transgendered individuals as suffering from a psychiatric disorder. As Margrit Eichler points out, however, if our notions of masculinity and femininity were less rigid, sex-change operations would be unnecessary since someone with a "gender identity problem" would not be defined as "sick." From Eichler's point of view, transgendered individuals represent a "problem" for most people only because our society does not recognize the validity of intermediate sexes (Eichler, 1980: 31; emphasis in the original).

In the case of David/Brenda, the rigidity of gender roles probably contributed to the failure of the sex-change operation. David had, after all, been

---

BOX 5.1   THE THIRD WAY: REFUSING TO GENDER IDENTIFY

It's not that Matt Lundie wants to be a man, particularly. He just doesn't want to be a woman.

"Just enough so people won't pick me out as being a freak"—that's his goal for the next year.

He has done two years of engineering at Carleton University in Ottawa, and he is taking the next year off to start another project. Next week, he moves to Winnipeg. In six months, he will begin to take male hormones and, a few months after that, he will have a mastectomy: both of his 38C breasts will be removed and his chest reshaped in a male contour. That will be it for the scalpel, though: "I don't have any need to modify my genitals."

He's having just enough surgery to get him what he wants: not a facsimile of a male body, just a less female one.

Matt was born Fiona, in a small southwestern Ontario town. For 21 years, he lived confused. "Even as a child I knew the expectations placed on me weren't realistic," he says, calm and resolute. "Until puberty, I thought I was a boy. The social messages of my whole childhood, of being told the boy's washroom was down the hall, was that I didn't fit, not in either mould."

Then he arrived at university and began to encounter variations on gender identity in the gay community. Last year, he tried something new: "I didn't gender identify."

He was still Fiona, but offered no other clues. That felt better, better than being a woman, anyway, but it wasn't great. When people couldn't figure him out, they reacted with confusion, awkwardness and often hostility. He got sick of dealing with that every day. So now, at 23, he's starting a new life as Matt.

"I don't believe gender is concrete, and people shouldn't be limited by their biological sex. But I can't really live in between."

Yet if he feels neither concretely male nor female, then why Matt over Fiona? "I like male clothes," he says with a small chuckle, then turns serious. "And the box you put men into has a bit more room."

He tried life in the other box. "Around Grade 11, I made an honest effort to be a traditionally gendered girl. I grew my hair; if you saw my prom picture, you'd think I was my sister or something." It didn't work. "I knew I didn't fit the mould of a woman, but I didn't know I had options. Now I know that neither of those two options fit who I am, so I'm going to stake out a third."

SOURCE: Excerpted from Stephanie Nolen, "The Third Way," *The Globe and Mail*, September 25, 1999, p. D1. Reprinted with permission of *The Globe and Mail*.

raised as a boy for nearly two years. He had seen boys treated differently from girls on television and in storybooks. He had played only with stereotypical boys' toys. After the sex reassignment, however, he got new clothes and new toys. He was also expected to behave differently. The contrast must have been all the more evident because the constant presence of his twin brother reinforced David's early understanding of how boys ought to behave. Evidence suggests that if gender reassignment takes place before the age of 18 months, it tends to be "successful" (Creighton and Mihto, 2001; Lightfoot-Klein et al., 2000).

The rigidity just described fosters the view that gender roles are entirely natural and spring fully formed from human physiology. But there is no one-to-one relationship between sex and gender. The two may be in discord, as transgendered individuals and transsexuals demonstrate. The picture becomes still more complicated when we consider sexual behaviour. Expectations about sexual behaviour are arguably among the most rigid of our gender norms, yet sexual behaviour often departs widely from biological sex and sociological gender.

SEXUALITY

Sexuality refers to activities that are intended "to lead to erotic arousal and produce genital response" (Reiss, 1986: 20). Some people think such activities are idiosyncratic. But, in fact, sexual behaviour is guided by a set of **sexual scripts** that tell us whom we should find attractive, when and where it is appropriate to be aroused, what is permissible, and how to behave sexually. These scripts are linked to gender roles. As the typical Harlequin romance shows, men are usually expected to be the sexual aggressors, typically more experienced and promiscuous than women. Women are expected to desire love before intimacy. They are assumed to be sexually passive, giving only subtle cues to indicate their interest in male overtures. Lacking the urgent sex drive that preoccupies males, women are therefore often held accountable for moral standards and contraception (Jensen, 1984).

For a long time, sexuality was assumed to be heterosexuality. Thus, the term "heterosexuality" was coined only about 30 years after the term "homosexuality" made its appearance in the 1860s. Apparently, before then nobody felt much need to describe what

was felt to be entirely natural. In contrast, homosexuality was considered a serious psychiatric disorder from the mid- to late 1800s until 1974, when it was finally dropped from the *Diagnostic and Statistical Manual of Mental Disorders*, the standard diagnostic tool used by North American psychiatrists (Shorter, 1997: 304). Even today, many people assume that individuals should desire only members of the opposite sex. Sociologists call this assumption **compulsory heterosexuality**.

The assumption of heterosexuality has negative implications for both lesbians and gays. They face discrimination, are denied basic civil rights (such as access to spousal benefits), and risk abuse, including "gay-bashing." In addition, many feminists say that heterosexuality puts *all* women at a disadvantage. That is because heterosexuality is based on unequal economic, political, legal, and social relations between women and men. Adrienne Rich (1996 [1980]: 132–33) thus defines compulsory heterosexuality as "the ideologically and materially enforced insistence that women see themselves entirely as the complements of men and live under male control or risk severe sanctions ranging from social stigma to death." Rich says that the institutionalization of heterosexuality in marriage and the family is a way of ensuring males' rights to physical, economic, and emotional access to women. Some feminists even take the extreme position that women should reject heterosexuality altogether since all such relationships are based on inequality. Below, I present an opposing view—that it is not individual women's heterosexual practices and identities that need to be criticized but rather the institution of heterosexuality as a system of male domination. First, however, let us examine some research on sexual behaviour.

SEXUAL ATTITUDES AND BEHAVIOUR

Traditional sexual scripts expect each of us to meet a member of the opposite sex, fall in love, get married, and then have intercourse with our spouse. However, surveys reveal some departure from tradition and a fair degree of diversity in sexual attitudes and behaviour. For example, premarital sex is widely accepted by the Canadian public. In 1975, 32 percent of Canadians disapproved of premarital sex. The figure fell to 20 percent in 1990. Sociologist Reginald Bibby

(1995: 70) predicts that by about 2010, only a "durable core of some 15 percent will continue to be opposed to such behaviour." In 1995, 78 percent of Canadians approved of an unmarried couple living together (Bibby, 1995: 65–66).

Acceptance of premarital sex extends even to young people. Ninety-four percent of Canadians agree that "birth control information should be available to teenagers who want it" (Bibby, 1995: 65). About 55 percent of 15- to 19-year-olds say they have had sexual intercourse (62 percent of males and 49 percent of females), as do about 75 percent of those of university age, both males and females (Hobart, 1996: 150). However, according to one study, men are more willing than women to participate in unconventional sexual activities (Hatfield, 1995).

A 2001 survey of 18 500 16- to 55-year-olds provides recent information on sexual behaviour in 28 countries, including Canada. Americans have sexual intercourse most often—124 times per year on average. They are followed by Greeks (117) and Croatians and South Africans (116). Japanese have sexual intercourse least often—36 times per year on average. Just above them on the list are residents of Hong Kong (63) and Taiwan (65). Canadians rank fourteenth at 99 times per year; the global average is 97. On average, Canadians become sexually active at the relatively early age of 17.3. Residents of eight countries get started earlier, with the United States topping the list at age 16. Residents of 19 countries become sexually active later, with China in last place at 22 years on average. Canadians also tend to have had many sexual partners—10.6 on average to be exact, placing us fourth on the list of 28 countries in the survey. Americans lead the list at 14.3 partners. At the other extreme are Indians (3.0) and Chinese (2.1). In terms of number of minutes spent having sexual intercourse, Canadians are at the high end according to a comparable 1998 survey of 15 countries. On average we spend 23 minutes having sexual intercourse. Only Americans (at 28 minutes) and Brazilians (at 30 minutes) surpass us. At the low end, Russians spend 12 minutes on average having sexual intercourse, residents of Hong Kong spend 13 minutes, and Thais just 10 minutes (Durex, 2001: 12; Mackay, 2000: 20–21).

Table 5.2 shows the frequency of sexual activity by gender and age in Canada in 1995. Clearly, and not surprisingly, sexual activity declines with age. However, a considerable number of people over the age of 70 say they engage in sexual activity at least once a week. This finding challenges the myth that the elderly are asexual.

Also of interest are male–female differences. For nearly all age groups, men report more frequent intercourse than women, while women more often report abstention than men. For instance, in the 50–59 age group, 13 percent of women say they never

TABLE 5.2   FREQUENCY OF SEXUAL INTERCOURSE AMONG CANADIANS BY AGE AND SEX, CANADA, 1995 (IN PERCENT)

AGE		NEVER	SOMETIMES, BUT LESS OFTEN THAN ONCE A WEEK	ONCE A WEEK OR MORE	TOTAL
18–29	men	4	38	58	100
	women	5	29	66	100
30–39	men	2	20	78	100
	women	4	29	67	100
40–49	men	3	37	60	100
	women	7	35	58	100
50–59	men	1	47	52	100
	women	13	40	47	100
60–69	men	5	65	30	100
	women	41	34	25	100
70+	men	25	53	22	100
	women	58	35	7	100

SOURCE: Adapted from Reginald W. Bibby, *The Bibby Report: Social Trends Canadian Style* (Toronto: Stoddart Publishing Co., Ltd., 1995), p. 67. Reprinted with permission of the author.

have sex compared to only 1 percent of men. And in the 70+ age group, 22 percent of men say they have sex once a week or more, compared to only 7 percent of women. One wonders if these figures reflect a tendency on the part of men to exaggerate their virility in order to conform to gender stereotypes.

Men and women differ in terms of the standards they use to justify sexual activity. Hobart (1996: 148) distinguishes the "love standard," according to which sexual activity is acceptable as long as the partners are in love, from the "fun standard," according to which sexual activity is acceptable as long as both partners want it. He shows that, in Canada, men and francophones are more likely than women and anglophones to endorse the fun standard. For example, almost 52 percent of Canadian francophone men and more than 37 percent of francophone women believe it is appropriate to engage in heterosexual involvement for casual, recreational reasons. The comparable figures for anglophone men and anglophone women are 36 percent and 20 percent, respectively. Hatfield (1995) similarly reports that men are somewhat more concerned than women with sex. Women are somewhat more concerned than men with love. American research shows that women are more likely to cite "affection for partner" as the major reason for their first intercourse experience (48 percent) followed by "curiosity/readiness for sex" (24 percent). Men most often mention "curiosity" (51 percent), followed by "affection" (25 percent). A small percentage of women (3 percent) report having their first sexual experience for physical pleasure. In contrast, 12 percent of men cite this reason (Michael et al., 1994: 93–94).

Canadians are also becoming more tolerant of homosexuality and same-sex marriage and civil union (see Box 5.2). It is sometimes asserted that one in ten North Americans are homosexual. American research shows that this is certainly an oversimplification and probably an exaggeration. (In the absence of comparable Canadian data, we may assume that the situation is little different here.) In the most comprehensive survey on sexuality to date, a group of American sociologists showed that just over 10 percent of men and 8.6 percent of women report *some* same-sex experience *or* desire (Laumann et al., 1994: 299). However, only 5.5 percent of women said they find the thought of sexual activity with another woman appealing, 4 percent reported being sexually

attracted to women, and less than 2 percent reported having a sexual encounter with another woman in the past year. Just over 4 percent said they had had a sexual experience with another woman at some point in their lives. Only 1.4 percent identified themselves as bisexual or homosexual. Among men, about 6 percent said they are sexually attracted to other men, 4.5 percent said they find the idea of sex with another man appealing, and 2 percent reported a sexual encounter with another man in the previous year. Nine percent of men reported a sexual experience with another man at least once since puberty, and 2.8 percent of men identified themselves as homosexual or bisexual. Unfortunately, we do not have comparable Canadian data. However, in a 2000 survey, about 6 percent of Torontonians identified themselves as homosexual or bisexual. This is roughly comparable to the percentage for major American cities, such as New York ("Homosexuality and Bisexuality," 2000).

These findings suggest that estimates of the prevalence of homosexuality depend heavily on how homosexuality is measured. An estimate based on sexual identity results in a lower percentage than an estimate focusing on **sexual orientation**. (One's sexual orientation is the way one derives sexual pleasure, including whether one's desirable partners are of the same or a different sex.) I conclude that it is inaccurate to think about sexuality in terms of a strict dichotomy between heterosexuality and homosexuality. It is more appropriate to conceptualize sexuality as composed of four continua: sexual attraction, sexual desire, sexual behaviour, and sexual identity (Michael et al., 1994: 174–79).

Attitudes about extramarital affairs are more conservative that those about homosexuality, and they are becoming more so. In 1975, 28 percent of Canadian adults felt that sex with someone other than the marriage partner was "almost always wrong" and 50 percent felt it was "always wrong." By 1995, those figures were 25 percent and 60 percent, respectively, suggesting movement in a more conservative direction (Bibby, 1995: 75). As far as actual behaviour is concerned, in a 1998 survey of 13 countries, 30–39 percent of Canadians between the ages of 16 and 45 admitted to sexual infidelity. This puts Canadians in the same league as South Africans, Australians, French, Italians, and Thais. By comparison, 40 percent or more of Americans, Russians, British, and

BOX 5.2 SAME-SEX MARRIAGE AND CIVIL UNION

In 2002, Quebec extended full parental rights to homosexual couples. A year later, the Ontario Court of Appeal redefined marriage as "the voluntary union of two persons." This made Ontario the first Canadian jurisdiction in which homosexuals could marry. The federal government said it would not contest the decision of the Ontario court. In fact, Prime Minister Chrétien announced he would soon introduce legislation allowing the legal union of same-sex couples. Thus, in 2003, Canada seemed ready to follow the lead of the Netherlands and Belgium and become the world's third country to legalize same-sex marriages.

The major world religions officially disapprove of homosexuality for the most part (see Table 5.3), and several Canadian church leaders immediately spoke out against the Ontario court ruling and the prime minister's proposed new law. So did the Progressive Conservative government of Alberta and some federal Members of Parliament in the Liberal, Canadian Alliance, and Progressive Conservative parties. The Alberta

Statistics show Canadians are becoming more tolerant of homosexuality. This couple was united in a commitment ceremony before a United Church minister.
SOURCE: CP Picture Archive/Logan Wallace.

Conservatives threatened to challenge the proposed new law in the courts. Yet Canadian public opinion is divided. A nationwide poll taken in 1996 found that 49 percent of Canadians favoured allowing same-sex marriages while 47 percent were opposed. In a similar poll taken in 1999, 53 percent approved and 44 percent were opposed ("Same-Sex Marriages and Civil Unions," 2002).

Some governments have dealt with such splits in public opinion by distinguishing between marriage and "civil union." A civil union grants *some* of the rights and privileges of marriage to a same-sex couple. Brazil, Denmark, France, Germany, Greenland, Hungary, Iceland, New Zealand, Norway, Sweden, Spain, Slovenia, and two states in the U.S. (Vermont and California) allow homosexual couples to enter civil unions. The new Canadian law will go one step further by making no distinction between heterosexual and same-sex marriage. At the same time, the Canadian law will respect the right of religious organizations to discriminate against homosexuals who wish to marry. No religious organization will be required by law to marry or conduct a civil union ceremony for a homosexual couple.

TABLE 5.3 THE OFFICIAL POSITION OF THE MAJOR WORLD RELIGIONS ON SEXUAL ISSUES, 2001 (NUMBER OF ADHERENTS IN PARENTHESES)

Religion	MASTURBATION	PREMARITAL SEX	EXTRAMARITAL SEX	HOMOSEXUAL SEX
Buddhism (354 mil.)	Acceptable	Mostly acceptable	Unacceptable	Mostly acceptable
Christianity (1.9 bil.)	Generally unacceptable (but no clear position for some Protestant denominations)	Unacceptable	Unacceptable	Unacceptable (but generally tolerated in the United Church of Canada)
Hinduism (762 mil.)	Mostly acceptable	Unacceptable	Unacceptable	Unacceptable
Islam (1.4 bil.)	Unacceptable	Unacceptable	Unacceptable	Unacceptable
Judaism (14 mil.)	No clear position	Mostly acceptable	Unacceptable	Generally unacceptable (but generally tolerated in the Reform and Reconstructionist denominations)

SOURCES: Adherents.com (2001); Mackay (2000: 73).

Germans between the ages of 16 and 45 admitted to sexual infidelity. For Spaniards, Poles, and residents of Hong Kong, the comparable figure was in the 20–29 percent range (Mackay, 2000: 36–37).

Changing attitudes towards extramarital affairs are part of a more general tendency for people to want and have fewer sexual partners. While there are undoubtedly several reasons for this tendency, one of the most important is the spread of sexually transmitted diseases, HIV/AIDS in particular, since about 1980. Sexual attitudes were relatively liberal in the 1960s and 1970s. During those decades, contraception and abortion were legalized. The youth counterculture successfully promoted the idea of "free love." Thus, the culture of the times encouraged people to have multiple sexual partners, while changes in the law minimized the reproductive consequences of doing so. In contrast, once the dangers of HIV/AIDS and other sexually transmitted diseases became widely known in the early 1980s, many people became more cautious in their sexual relations. Sixty-two percent of people interviewed in the 2001 survey of 28 countries mentioned above said they take measures to prevent HIV/AIDS, and the most common method is to stay faithful to one partner (Durex, 2001: 12; see Figure 5.1 and Figure 5.2)

As the foregoing discussion shows, surveys provide evidence of wide variation in attitudes towards sex and sexual conduct over time and place. Therefore, they help to dispel myths about sexuality as natural or "fixed." However, they do not answer questions about the *origins* of sexual scripts or why there are inconsistencies between norms and behaviour. The next section addresses these issues by looking at the relationships among sex, gender, and sexuality.

DOES SEX DETERMINE OUR DESTINY?

ESSENTIALISM

Most arguments about the origins of gender differences in human behaviour adopt one of two perspectives. Some analysts see gender as a reflection of naturally evolved dispositions. Others see gender as a reflection of the different social positions occupied by women and men. Sociologists call these two perspectives, respectively, essentialism and social constructionism. I now summarize and criticize essentialism. I then turn to social constructionism.

Essentialists first observe male–female differences in sexual scripts, the division of labour at home and in the workplace, mate selection, sexual aggression, jealousy, promiscuity, fidelity, and so forth. They then interpret these differences as natural and

FIGURE 5.1 PERCENT TAKING PRECAUTIONS AGAINST HIV/AIDS, 28 COUNTRIES, 2001

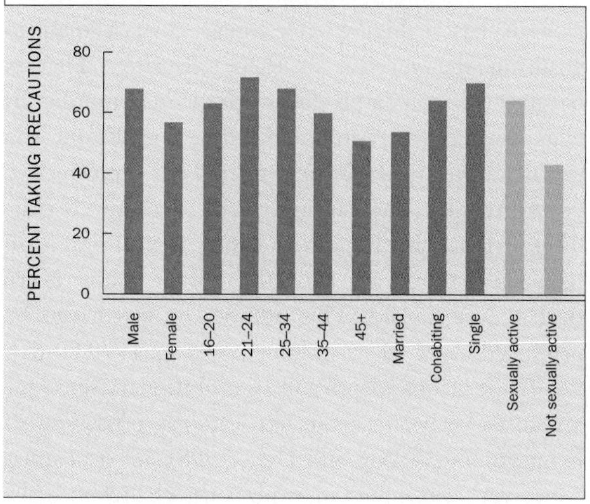

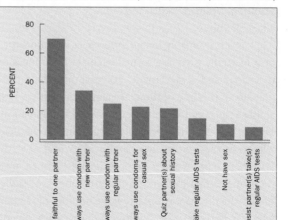

FIGURE 5.2 PREVENTATIVE MEASURES TAKEN BY CANADIANS AGAINST HIV/AIDS, 2001 (IN PERCENT)

SOURCE: Durex (2001: 12).

SOURCE: Durex (2001: 13).

universal. According to essentialists, childrearing may exaggerate differences between men and women but nature is the ultimate force at work in shaping them.

There are many variants of essentialism. Most of them originate in biology and psychology. Here we briefly consider three of the most popular variants: brain studies, sociobiology, and Freudian theory.

Brain Studies

Male–female differences in brain structure are sometimes said to account for male–female differences in behaviour and achievement. The brain is composed of two "hemispheres" of about equal size, connected by a bundle of fibres. The left hemisphere is generally associated with language abilities, the right with non-verbal perception and visual and spatial skills. On this much there is little controversy in the scientific community. However, some brain researchers argue that the two hemispheres develop differently in boys and girls, as do the fibres connecting the hemispheres. Specifically, they claim that when the male fetus starts to secrete testosterone (the hormone responsible for furthering the sexual development of the male), it washes over the brain and briefly inhibits the growth of the left hemisphere. As a result, use of the *right* hemisphere becomes dominant in men. This supposedly allows men to excel in mathematical, artistic, musical, and visual–spatial abilities. Meanwhile (the theory continues), the bundle of fibres connecting the left and right hemispheres is bigger in women. This supposedly allows women to use the hemispheres more symmetrically, giving them an edge in feelings, intuition, language skills, and quick judgments (Bleier, 1984: 92; Blum, 1997: 36–63; Tavris, 1992: 45–46).

Such presumably innate differences in brain structure allegedly give rise to male–female differences in behaviour and achievement. For example, some proponents of this line of thought claim that men are best at jobs requiring logic and visual–spatial manipulation. Hence the disproportionately large number of men who work as scientists, mechanics, pilots, and so forth. For their part, women are presumably best at jobs requiring empathy, intuition, and language skills. Hence the disproportionately large number of women who stay home to raise children and who work outside the home as teachers, secretaries, social workers, and nurses. It follows from this line of reasoning that the gender division of labour is perfectly natural, structured by our brains rather than society.

Sociobiology

Sociobiology is a second variant of essentialism, and E.O. Wilson (1975) is its leading exponent. Wilson argues that all human beings instinctually want to ensure that their genes get passed on to future generations. However, the different reproductive status of men and women means they have had to overcome different adaptive problems and develop different adaptive strategies. This gave rise to patterns of behaviour we now call "masculine" and "feminine." Individuals who possessed the characteristics that best resolved these problems—the most feminine women and the most masculine men—had a better chance of surviving and passing their genes to their offspring. Thus, over time, masculine and feminine behaviours became genetically encoded. According to sociobiology, genetic factors also trigger biochemical processes that further enhance sex differences through varying levels of hormone production in women and men.

David Buss, a well-known evolutionary psychologist, argues that there are four adaptive strategies or "universal features of our evolved selves" that govern the relations between the sexes and contribute to the preservation of the human species (Buss, 1994: 211; see also Buss, 1995a, 1995b, 1998; Dawkins, 1976; Wilson, 1978). First, men want casual sex with women. Second, men treat women's bodies as men's property. Third, men beat or kill women who incite male sexual jealousy. And fourth, women are greedy for money.

Buss bases his argument on the claim that a woman has a bigger investment than a man in ensuring the survival of their offspring. That is because the woman produces only a small number of eggs during her reproductive life. Specifically, she releases fewer than 400 eggs during her reproductive years. At most, she can give birth to about 20 children. Men, on the other hand, typically release between 200 million and 500 million sperm every time they ejaculate. This number of sperm can be produced every 24 to 48 hours (Saxton, 1990 [1968]: 94–95). It is thus adaptive in an evolutionary sense for a man to be promiscuous yet jealously possessive of his partners (Wilson and Daly, 1998), for a promiscuous yet jealous man maximizes the chance that his, and only his, offspring will be produced. Moreover, since men compete with other men for sexual access to women, men evolve competitive and aggressive dispositions that include physical violence. In contrast, Buss says, it is in a woman's best interest to maintain primary responsibility for her genetic child and to look around for the best mate with whom to intermix her genes. He is the man who can best help support the child after birth, hence women's alleged greed for money in contemporary society.

Research certainly supports the view that men and women emphasize different characteristics in selecting a mate. Simon Davis, for example, conducted a content analysis of personal advertisements in the *Vancouver Sun*. He discovered that attractive physical features were the most frequently mentioned desirable characteristic in a partner for both men and women. However, women were more likely than men to list professional status, employment status, financial considerations, intelligence, commitment, and emotion. Men, on the other hand, were more likely to list attractiveness, physique, and sexiness, and to require a picture (Davis, 1991: 43–50). These results do not, however, establish that sex-typed mating preferences are *genetically* determined. As we will see, they are also consistent with differences in how we assign status to masculine and feminine gender roles.

Freud

Freud (1977 [1905]) offered a third influential essentialist explanation of male–female differences. He believed that sexuality is the main human instinct. In his view, it motivates human behaviour and accounts for the development of distinct masculine and feminine gender roles.

According to Freud, children around the age of three to five begin to pay attention to their genitals. As a young boy becomes preoccupied with his penis, he unconsciously develops a fantasy of sexually possessing his mother. He begins to resent his father because only his father is allowed to sexually possess the mother. But because he has seen his mother or another girl naked, the boy also develops anxiety that he will be castrated by his father for desiring his mother.[1] To resolve this fear, the boy represses his feelings for his mother. That is, he stores them in the unconscious part of his personality. In due course, this repression allows him to begin identifying with his father. This leads to the development of a strong, masculine personality.

In contrast, the young girl begins to develop a feminine personality when she realizes she lacks a penis. According to Freud:

> [girls] notice the penis of a brother or playmate, strikingly visible and of large proportions, at once recognize it as the superior counterpart of their own small and inconspicuous organ, and from that time forward fall a victim to envy for the penis.... She has seen it and knows that she is without it and wants to have it. (Quoted in Steinem, 1994: 50)

Due to her "penis envy," the young girl soon develops a sense of inferiority, according to Freud. She also grows angry with her mother, who, she naïvely thinks, is responsible for cutting off the penis she must have once had. She rejects her mother and develops an unconscious sexual desire for her father. Eventually, however, realizing she will never have a penis, the girl comes to identify with her mother. This is a way of vicariously acquiring her father's penis in Freud's view. In the "normal" development of a mature woman, the girl's wish to have a penis is transformed into a desire to have children. However, says Freud, since women are never able to completely resolve their penis envy, the feminine gender identity is normally immature and dependent on men. This dependence is evident from the "fact" that women can be fully sexually satisfied only by vaginally induced orgasm. Thus, a host of gender differences in personality and behaviour follow from the anatomical sex differences that children observe around the age of three.[2]

A Critique of Essentialism

There are six main problems with essentialist arguments, such as those described above:

1. *Essentialists ignore the historical and cultural variability of gender and sexuality.* In some cultures, men are socialized to be nurturing and sensitive. Rape is incomprehensible. For example, anthropologist Margaret Mead reports that the Arapesh, a preliterate people in New Guinea, "know nothing of rape beyond the fact that it is the unpleasant custom of the Nugum people to the southeast of them" (Mead, 1935: 110). More generally, rates of rape vary widely across cultures

(Sanday, 1981). This variability deflates the idea that biological constants account for innate behavioural differences between women and men, such as male aggressiveness and violence. Moreover, societies and cultures often change rapidly without any apparent genetic change taking place. Essentialist arguments have a difficult time explaining, for example, recent changes in child-care arrangements, women's participation in the labour force, and other aspects of women's lives, given the absence of any documented shift in male or female genetic structure that might account for this change.

2. *Essentialists ignore the fact that gender differences are declining rapidly and in some cases have already disappeared* (Caplan and Caplan, 1999 [1994]). Hundreds of studies have shown that women are developing traits that were traditionally considered masculine. For example, psychological research shows that women have become more assertive, competitive, independent, and analytical since the early 1970s. They play more aggressive sports, choose more mathematics and science courses, perform better in standardized tests, take more nontraditional jobs, and earn more money than they used to (Twenge, 1997). In what must be considered a serious blow to brain research on alleged male–female differences, a review of 165 studies of verbal ability representing tests of more than 1.4 million people found no gender differences in verbal skills. A review of 100 studies of mathematics performance representing tests of nearly 4 million students showed small differences favouring *females* in the general population. (Larger differences favouring males were, however, found in samples of precocious individuals.) A review of dozens of studies on spatial ability found that some studies found no gender differences while other studies found only small differences in favour of men (Tavris, 1992: 52). Taken as a whole, this body of research suggests that there are few gender differences in ability left to explain, the few remaining differences are small, and those few small differences are disappearing.

3. *The research evidence employed by essentialists is often deeply flawed.* Consider the sociobiologists' observation that men are more independent than women. Research shows that, in fact, girls are more dependent than boys *only at certain ages*. Thus, while infant girls seem to behave in a more dependent fashion than infant boys, girls at the age of two are more independent than boys (Goldberg and Lewis, 1969; Feiring and Lewis, 1979). Evidence from studies purporting to find a genetic cause of homosexuality is also problematic. Hamer and Copeland (1996), for example, claim to have found a possible genetic marker for homosexuality in 33 of 40 brothers who were both gay. As Peele and De Grandpre (1995) point out, however, the study did not check for the frequency of the supposed marker in *heterosexual* brothers. Nor has anyone been able to replicate the findings. More generally, sociobiologists and evolutionary psychologists have not been able to identify *any* of the genes that, they claim, cause male jealousy, female nurturance, or the unequal division of labour between men and women. Meanwhile, brain researchers have had great difficulty showing how observed physical differences between male and female brains might be related to (nonexistent, small, and shrinking) differences in male and female abilities. That is one reason why several brain theories make contradictory arguments. For example, the theory reviewed above says that men have greater right hemisphere specialization. However, a second theory holds that men have greater *left* hemisphere specialization, which gives them an intellectual advantage over women. Meanwhile, a third theory agrees that men have greater right brain specialization but insists that this gives men superior artistic and musical abilities; yet this contradicts the first theory, which says that women have the edge in musical and artistic skills, which rely on intuition and empathy (Tavris, 1992: 45–49). Lack of hard evidence encourages such unsubstantiated speculation.

4. *Essentialists tend to generalize from the average, ignoring variations within gender groups.* On average, women and men do, of course, differ in some respects. For example, one of the best-documented average differences between women and men concerns aggressiveness. Men are on average more verbally and physically aggressive than women. However, when sociobiologists say men are *inherently* more aggressive than women,

they make it seem as if this is true of all men and all women. As Figure 5.3 shows, however, it is not. When verbal or physical aggressiveness is measured by trained researchers, scores vary widely within gender groups. Aggressiveness is distributed so that there is considerable overlap between men and women. Thus, many women are more aggressive than the average man, and many men are less aggressive than the average woman.

5. *Essentialists exaggerate the degree to which gender differences are unchangeable.* For example, evolutionary psychologist David Buss and colleagues (1990) used data from 37 cultures to show that women consistently prefer older men with high earning capacity as partners. In contrast, men prefer women with good domestic capabilities. Buss claims that this demonstrates a genetic basis for mate selection. But Eagley and Wood (1999) re-examined Buss's data. They show that women's tendency to stress the "good provider" role in selecting male partners and men's tendency to stress women's domestic skills decrease in societies where there is more gender equality. Similarly, women express less preference for older men, and men less preference for younger women, in more gender-egalitarian societies. As this example shows, gender differences vary with social conditions, a fact that essentialists ignore. Another example of how social conditions affect gender differences: The "male" hormone testosterone is associated with greater aggressiveness.

However, Pulitzer prize–winning science writer Deborah Blum (1997: 158–88) notes that social situations involving competition and threat stimulate production of testosterone in *women* and cause them to act more aggressively (compare Caplan and Caplan, 1999 [1994]). For example, when women take jobs that maximize competition and threat—when they become, say, corporate lawyers or police officers—they undergo hormonal and behavioural changes, thus decreasing behavioural differences between men and women.

6. *Essentialists offer explanations for gender differences that ignore the role of power.* Sociobiologists assume that existing behaviour patterns help ensure the survival of the species because they are the patterns that endured as humans evolved. However, their assumption overlooks the fact that some groups (such as men) are in a position of greater power and authority than other groups (such as women). Behavioural differences between men and women may, therefore, result not from any biological imperative but from men's ability to establish their preferences over the interests of women. Indeed, from this point of view, sociobiology may be seen as an example of the exercise of male power, that is, as a rationalization for male domination and sexual aggression. The same may be said of Freud's interpretation. *Must* young girls define themselves in relation to young boys by focusing on their lack of a penis? *Do* they define themselves that way? Freud offers no evidence to support his case. There is no reason why young girls' sexual self-definitions cannot focus positively on their own reproductive organs, including their unique ability to bear children. Freud simply assumes that men are superior to women and then creates a speculative theory that justifies gender differences.

SOCIAL CONSTRUCTIONISM

Social constructionism is the main alternative to essentialism. Social constructionists argue that gender differences are not the product of biological properties, whether chromosomal, gonadal, or hormonal. Instead, gender and sexuality are products of social structure and culture. *Culture* is composed of

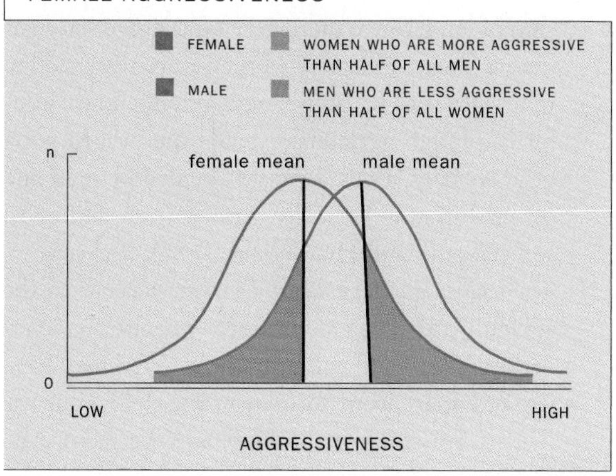

FIGURE 5.3 THE DISTRIBUTION OF MALE AND FEMALE AGGRESSIVENESS

shared systems of meaning. It incorporates people's values and beliefs. While many systems of meaning coexist and compete at any one time, patriarchy, or belief in the validity of male domination, is widely accepted in nearly all societies today. *Social structure* refers to the way major institutions, such as families, the economy, and the political system, are organized. Social structures in most societies today are patriarchal in that they reinforce inequalities between women and men.

Social constructionists stress three main sociohistorical changes that led to the development of gender inequality:

1. *Long-distance warfare and conquest.* Anthropologists have shown that a high level of gender equality existed in foraging or hunting-and-gathering societies, the dominant form of society for 90 percent of human history. Rough equality between women and men was based on the fact that women produced a substantial amount of the band's food, up to 80 percent in some cases (see Chapter 12, "Families."). Archaeological evidence from "Old Europe" tells a similar story. Old Europe is a region stretching roughly from Poland in the north to the Mediterranean island of Crete in the south, and from Switzerland in the west to Bulgaria in the east (see Figure 5.4). Between 7000 and 3500 B.C.E., men and women enjoyed rough equality throughout the region. The religions of the region gave primacy to fertility and creator goddesses. Kinship was traced through the mother's side of the family. Then, sometime between 4300 and 4200 B.C.E., all this began to change. Old Europe was invaded by successive waves of warring peoples from the Asiatic and European northeast (the Kurgans) and the deserts to the south (the Semites). Both the Kurgan and Semitic civilizations were based on a steeply hierarchical and patriarchal social structure. Their religions gave primacy to male warrior gods. They acquired property and slaves by conquering other peoples and imposed their religions on the vanquished. They eliminated, or at least downgraded, goddesses as divine powers. God became a male who willed that women should be ruled by men. Laws reinforced women's sexual, economic, and political subjugation to men. Traditional Judaism, Christianity, and Islam all embody ideas of male

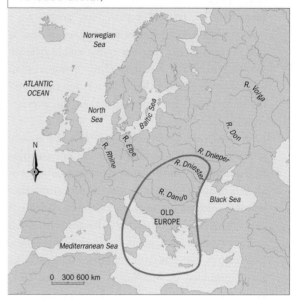

FIGURE 5.4 APPROXIMATE AREA FOR EARLY CIVILIZATION OF OLD EUROPE (CA. 7000 B.C.E. TO 3500 B.C.E.)

SOURCE: Adapted from Marija Gimbutas, *Goddesses and Gods of Old Europe* (Berkeley and Los Angeles: University of California Press, 1982): 16.

dominance and they all derive from the tribes who conquered Old Europe in the fifth millennium B.C.E. (Eisler, 1995 [1987]).

2. *Plough agriculture.* Long-distance warfare and conquest catered to men's strengths and so greatly enhanced male power and authority. Large-scale farming using ploughs harnessed to animals had much the same effect. Plough agriculture originated in the Middle East around 5000 years ago. It required that strong adults remain in the fields all day for much of the year. It also reinforced the principle of private ownership of land. Since men were on average stronger than women, and since women were restricted in their activities by pregnancy, nursing, and childbirth, plough agriculture made men more powerful socially. Thus, land was owned by men and ownership was typically passed from father to son (Coontz and Henderson, 1986).

3. *The separation of public and private spheres.* In the agricultural era, economic production was organized around the household. Men may have worked apart from women in the fields, but the fields were still part of the *family* farm. In con-

trast, during the early phase of industrialization, men's work was moved out of the household and into the factory and the office. Most men became wage or salary workers. Some assumed decision-making roles in economic and political institutions. But while men went public, most women remained in the domestic or private sphere. The idea soon developed that this was a "natural" division of labour. This idea persisted until the second half of the twentieth century, when a variety of social circumstances, ranging from the introduction of the birth control pill to women's demands for entry into university, finally allowed women to enter the public sphere in large numbers.

So we see that, according to social constructionists, gender inequality derives historically from three main circumstances: the advent of long-distance warfare and conquest, the development of plough agriculture, and the assignment of women to the domestic sphere and men to the public sphere during the early industrial era. Although gender inequality is decreasing somewhat in many societies today, it still persists. It is supported by a variety of economic and political arrangements discussed elsewhere in this book (see especially Chapter 9). In what follows, I fill out the social constructionist perspective by outlining just two dimensions of contemporary gender inequality. First, I show how socialization still pushes girls to act in stereotypically feminine ways and boys to act in stereotypically masculine ways. I then discuss eating disorders and male violence against women to show that the social construction of gender has far-reaching implications for women, men, and the relations between them.

CONSTRUCTING GENDER THROUGH SOCIALIZATION

PRIMARY SOCIALIZATION

Research shows that, from the moment of birth, infant boys and girls are treated differently by parents, particularly fathers. Girls are more likely to be characterized as delicate, weak, beautiful, and cute, boys as strong, alert, and well coordinated (Rubin, Provenzano, and Lurra, 1974). Interpretations of behaviour vary by sex. For example, when viewing a videotape of a nine-month-old infant, experimental subjects tend to label startled reactions to a stimulus as "anger" if the baby has been previously identified as a boy, and as "fear" if the baby is identified as a girl, *regardless of the baby's actual sex* (Condry and Condry, 1976). Parents also tend to encourage their sons to engage in boisterous behaviour and competitive play. They tend to encourage their daughters to engage in cooperative play (MacDonald and Parke, 1986). Boys are more likely than girls to be praised for assertiveness, and girls are more likely than boys to be rewarded for compliance (Kerig, Cowan, and Cowan, 1993). Parents reinforce gender-specific behaviour by the design of the child's room, the clothes they buy, and the toys they provide. Boys' toys, for example, are more likely to emphasize aggressive competition and spatial manipulation. Girls' toys tend to be more passive and oriented toward the home (e.g., dolls, kitchen sets, washers and dryers, etc.) (Hughes, 1995 [1991]). Most parents encourage their children to play with gender-stereotyped toys. Preschool boys are just as likely to play with a dish set as a tool set if given a choice—unless they are told that the dish set is a girl's toy and they think their fathers will view playing with it as "bad" (Raag and Rackliff, 1998).

SECONDARY SOCIALIZATION

The process of channelling girls into roles culturally defined as appropriately feminine and boys into roles culturally defined as appropriately masculine continues in school. In most schools, teachers still tend to assume that boys will do better in the sciences and mathematics, girls in languages. Parents reinforce these expectations at home (Eccles, Jacobs, and Harold, 1990). Teachers also praise boys more than girls and give boys more help. They are more likely to agree with boys' comments during class and give boys instructions on how to complete a task rather than do the task for them. This reinforces gender stereotypes and results in a less effective learning experience for girls.

By the age of about 14, interaction with peers becomes an important factor in reinforcing gender-typed attitudes and behaviours. That is because the subcultures of male and female peer groups emphasize gender-stereotypical values. Boys tend to establish less intimate friendships than girls. Moreover, boys' friendships tend to be based on such activities as team sports, which focus on "independence, emotional control and conquest." Girls tend to form less extensive friendship networks than boys and focus on "sociability, popularity and attractiveness" (Udry, 1971: 76, 82; Elkin and Handel, 1989).

THE MASS MEDIA

The symbolic representation of gender in the mass media also creates and reinforces gender stereotypes. The social construction of gender in the mass media begins when small children learn that only a kiss from Snow White's Prince Charming will save her from eternal sleep. It continues in magazines, romance novels, television, advertisements, music, and the Internet. It is big business. For example, Harlequin Enterprises of Toronto dominates the production and sale of romance novels worldwide. The company sells more than 175 million books a year in 23 languages in more than 100 national markets. The average romance reader spends $1200 a year on the genre. Most readers of Harlequin romances consume

Murray Warren, a Port Coquitlam, BC, teacher displays two of three children's books featuring children with same-gender parents at the Supreme Court of Canada in Ottawa, June 2002. The books were banned by the Surrey School Board in which Warren teaches. What gender stereotypes do these kinds of books seek to offset?
SOURCE: CP Picture Archive/Fred Chartrand.

between three and twenty books a month. A central theme in these romances is the transformation of women's bodies into objects for men's pleasure (Grescoe, 1996). As such, romance novels may be seen as a less extreme form of the pornography industry for men.

GENDER SOCIALIZATION AND SEXUALITY

In our society, there is little formal socialization—that is, systematic instruction—regarding sexuality. That is probably because of our rather prudish history and the popular assumption that sexuality is a natural instinct that does not have to be taught. By default, therefore, as adults we tend to express our sexuality in a framework defined by our early, informal gender socialization.

Boys and girls do not always accept informal gender socialization passively. They sometimes resist it. For the most part, however, boys and girls try to develop the skills that will help them perform conventional gender roles (Eagley and Wood, 1999: 412–13). Of course, conventions change. It is important to note in this regard that what children learn about femininity and masculinity today is less sexist than what they learned just a few generations ago. For example, comparing *Cinderella* and *Snow White* with *Mulan*, we see immediately that girls going to Disney movies today are sometimes presented with assertive and heroic female role models rather than the passive and, by today's standards, quite pathetic heroines of the 1930s and 1940s. On the other hand, the amount of change in gender socialization should not be exaggerated, nor its effects on sexuality. *Cinderella* and *Snow White* are still popular movies for girls. Moreover, for every *Mulan* there is a *Little Mermaid*, a movie that simply modernizes old themes about female passivity and male conquest. As we saw above in our discussion of sexual behaviour, survey research shows that men are still more likely than women to adhere to sexual scripts emphasizing fun, conquest, and orgasm rather than love, tenderness, and emotionality. The fact that girls learn that sexuality is something they must fear—think of unwanted pregnancy and sexual assault—also serves to perpetuate passive sexual scripts for women today (Nelson and Robinson, 1999: 351).

The social construction of gender and sexuality has far-reaching implications for men and women. As we have just seen, the social construction of gender during childhood socialization influences the way men and women express their sexuality. You will learn in detail later in this book how the social construction of gender also helps determine the kind of formal education men and women pursue, the kinds of jobs they get, and the way domestic work is divided between men and women. As you will now see, the standards of physical attractiveness that are internalized through gender socialization and sexual scripts have contributed to widespread dieting and eating disorders.

BODY IMAGE AND EATING DISORDERS

The social construction of gender involves defining standards of physical attractiveness for women and men. These standards are reinforced by the mass media.

Physical attractiveness is especially important for women. That is because they are judged on the basis of appearance more often than men. Moreover, unattractive women are described in more negative terms than equally unattractive men (Wolf, 1991). Masculinity is more likely to be assessed in terms of status and power than in terms of physical attractiveness.

Weight has become an increasingly important dimension of body image over the past 40 years. Thus, research shows that *Playboy* centrefold models and Miss America contestants have grown substantially thinner since 1959. A 1997 survey shows that 89 percent of North American women want to lose weight (Garner, 1997). Canadian women list "being overweight" as one of their major health problems (Walters, 1992). Many men are concerned about their body image, too, but among women the emphasis on being thin is especially common. The "cult of thinness" has spawned major industries, including diet and self-help, cosmetic surgery, diet foods, and fitness (Hesse-Biber, 1996).

Standards of breast size pose a special problem for women. Although thin is in, large breasts have been popular since the 1960s (Koff and Benavage, 1998). Breasts, however, are composed mainly of fat; and the amount of breast fat is associated with total body fat. Thus, it is virtually impossible for most women to achieve the ideal standard of beauty.

Many women and men resent the thin models they see in the mass media. Nonetheless, fear of being fat and dieting to lose weight are common in girls as young as nine. One recent study found that half of all teenage girls are on diets (Pipher, 1994: 184–85).

Body image is associated with self-esteem and behaviour. People who are dissatisfied with their bodies are less likely to desire and engage in sexual activity. Conversely, bad sexual experiences contribute to a poor body image. For example, sexual abuse is an important cause of body dissatisfaction. In the 1997 survey cited above, 23 percent of women and 10 percent of men viewed sexual abuse as having been moderately to very important in shaping their body image in childhood or adolescence (Garner, 1997).

At the extreme, concern with body image may result in anorexia nervosa (refusal to eat enough to remain healthy) or bulimia (regular, self-induced vomiting). Estimates of the percentage of young women with such eating disorders range from 2 percent to 20 percent. For young men, estimates are in the 1 to 3 percent range (Averett and Korenman, 1996: 305; Garner, 1997; Lips, 1993: 254; Pipher, 1994: 184–85). Some women and men have changed their body shape by means of surgical procedures such as liposuction and cosmetic surgery. Over 90 percent of cosmetic surgery patients are women (Hesse-Biber, 1996: 51, 53).

There are cultural variations in standards of beauty. For instance, in the United States, Black women are more likely to be above the recommended body weight than non-Black women. At the same time, they are less likely to see themselves as overweight. Obesity also results in fewer social penalties in the case of Black women. Thus, obese white women have smaller family incomes than non-obese white women because they are less likely to be married and more likely to face job discrimination. This is not the case for obese Black women compared to non-obese Black women (Averett and Korenman, 1996).

MALE VIOLENCE AGAINST WOMEN

The way in which gender and sexual scripts are socially constructed also affects the frequency with which men sexually assault and harass women. Let us now consider this issue in detail.

SEXUAL ASSAULT

The sexual assault of women is common. Thus, surveys suggest that one in eight girls growing up in Canada today will be a victim of serious sexual abuse before the age of 16 (Bagley and King, 1990; Gadd, 1997). Perpetrators of child sexual assault are typically male, known to the victim, and in a position of authority over the child. Research demonstrates that, in general, victims of sexual assault are selected less because of sexual desirability than because of their availability and powerlessness (Duffy, 1998). One survey found that 60 percent of high school boys approve of forcing sexual activities on a girl, at least in some circumstances (Davis, Peck, and Stormant, 1993). A survey of Canadian college and university students asked a series of questions about male violence against women during elementary school, during high school, since high school, and in the year preceding the survey (DeKeseredy and Schwartz, 1998). The researchers found that psychological or emotional abuse of women is most common, followed by sexual and then physical abuse. Males consistently reported lower levels of sexual, psychological, and physical violence against women than women reported. However, even the percentages reported by males are disturbingly high. Moreover, the percentages grow as boys turn into men and advance from high school to postsecondary education. For example, 1.5 percent of boys said they forced girls to engage in sexual activities with them in elementary school and 2.3 percent said they forced girls to engage in sexual activities with them in high school. For the year preceding the survey, the percentage was 11 percent. Fully 19.5 percent of men in Canadian colleges and universities said they had forced a woman to engage in sexual activities with them at least once since high school (see also Table 5.4).

Of course, men are the victims of violence too. Like women, they are far more likely to be assaulted

TABLE 5.4 STATISTICS ON VIOLENCE AGAINST WOMEN, CANADA, 1993 (*N* = 12 000)

TYPE OF ASSAULT	NUMBER OF WOMEN (MILLIONS)	PERCENT OF ALL WOMEN
Total women harassed	9.4	87
Harassed by a stranger	9.2	85
Harassed by someone known to victim	5.5	51
Total women assaulted by a stranger	2.5	23
Sexual assault	2.0	19
Unwanted sexual touching	1.6	15
Violent sexual attack	0.7	7
Physical assault	0.8	8
Total women assaulted by a date or boyfriend	1.7	16
Sexual assault	1.3	12
Physical assault	0.8	7
Total women assaulted by a married or common-law partner	2.7	29
Total women forced into sexual activity against their will	0.7	8

SOURCE: Compiled from Statistics Canada, *Violence against Women Survey*, Microdata File, Ottawa, 1994a.

by men than by women. Some studies show that female partners are as likely as male partners to participate in abusive acts—with the exception of sexual assault, which is almost exclusively a male domain (Straus, 1995). Note, however, that women are more likely to use violence as a response to their own powerlessness, attacking partners out of self-defence or lashing out at their children following abuse by their husbands. Men, on the other hand, are more likely to use force to retain control and power over their partners and children. Moreover, abusive men are far more likely to cause serious physical injuries than abusive women, and abused men are therefore far less likely than abused women to report their partners' violent acts to the police (Fitzgerald, 1993; Koss et al., 1994; see Figure 5.5).

The most severe form of sexual assault involves rape. Research shows that some rapists are men who were physically or sexually abused in their youth. They develop a deep-seated need to feel powerful as psychological compensation for their early powerlessness. Other rapists are men who, as children, saw their mothers as potentially hostile figures who needed to be controlled, or as mere objects available for male gratification, and saw their fathers as emotionally cold and distant. Raised in such a family atmosphere, rapists learn not to empathize with women. Instead, they learn to want to dominate them (Lisak, 1992). Significantly, rates of rape are highest in war situa-

tions, when many conquering male soldiers feel justified in wanting to humiliate the vanquished, who are powerless to stop them (Human Rights Watch, 1995). Rape thus involves using sex to establish dominance. The incidence of rape is highest in situations where early socialization experiences predispose men to want to control women, where norms justify the domination of women, and where a large power imbalance between men and women exists.

SEXUAL HARASSMENT

There are two types of sexual harassment in the workplace. **Quid pro quo sexual harassment** takes place when sexual threats or bribery are made a condition of employment decisions. **Hostile environment sexual harassment** involves sexual jokes, comments, and touching that interferes with work or creates an unfriendly work setting. Surveys show that between 23 percent and 51 percent of women have been sexually harassed in the workplace (Gruber, 1997; Welsh and Nierobisz, 1997). When semipublic and public settings are included, up to 87 percent of women report being sexually harassed (see Table 5.4; Lenton et al., 1999). On the basis of available research, it seems clear that relatively powerless women are the most likely to be sexually harassed. Moreover, sexual harassment is most common in work settings that exhibit high levels of gender inequality and a culture justifying male domination of women. Specifically, women who are young, unmarried, and employed in nonprofessional jobs are most likely to become objects of sexual harassment. They are particularly likely to be sexually harassed if they are temporary workers, the ratio of women to men in the workplace is low, and the organizational culture of the workplace tolerates sexual harassment (Welsh, 1999).

As the foregoing discussion makes clear, large power imbalances between men and women and a culture that supports patriarchy are associated with high rates of sexual assault and harassment. Where men are much more powerful than women, and where gender inequality is justified culturally, gender is socially constructed to permit and even encourage violence against women. The research literature is clear on this point. It shows, for example, that men who most enjoy sexist jokes are most likely to report engaging in acts of sexual aggression against women

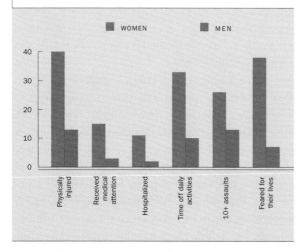

FIGURE 5.5 SPOUSAL VIOLENCE IN CANADA, 1995–1999

SOURCE: Statistics Canada (2002: 15).

(Ryan and Kanjorski, 1998). Men who link sexuality with social dominance are more likely to sexually harass women (Pryor, Giedd, and Williams, 1995). And both men and women who abuse their intimate partners have strong masculine gender orientations that value control and dominance, and weak feminine gender orientations that value harmony in interpersonal relationships (Thompson, 1991).

LOOKING AHEAD: TOWARD A NEW SEXUAL ETHIC

For the past 30 years, most sociologists of gender have criticized the essentialist view that sexual scripts are part of "human nature." Rather than seeing sexuality as natural, they have examined how it is socially constructed. They do not deny the biological basis of sexuality. They simply appreciate that the form sexual expression takes is not inevitable and immutable. In the preceding pages, I illustrated the social constructionist case by examining the historical factors that shaped the emergence of sexual scripts, the relationship between gender socialization and sexuality, the ways in which sexual relations reflect and reinforce power differentials, the privileging of heterosexuality, the marginalization of other sexual identities, and the implications of gender roles for the sexual assault and harassment of women by men.

SEXUAL PLURALISM

Social constructionism has overturned many ideas about sexuality. As a result, more and more people accept that sexuality does not have to be expressed in traditionally feminine or masculine ways. An attitude of **sexual pluralism** is growing (Weeks, 1986). For most people, sexual pluralism does *not* mean "anything goes." Most sexual pluralists recognize that there will always be a need to regulate sexual behaviour. For example, they oppose the abuse of power in sexual relations and see the need for the state to punish, and help prevent, incest, rape, and other forms of sexual abuse. Sexual pluralism *does* mean judging sexual acts only by their meaning for the participants. Are power relations at play? If so, are they harmful to the participants? These are the sorts of questions that sexual pluralists use in evaluating the validity of sexual acts. They do not automatically con-

demn a sexual practice because it is, say, "homosexual" or "heterosexual."

Some feminists are not sexual pluralists. They reject all forms of heterosexuality because, they say, it perpetuates male dominance (Dworkin, 1981; Jeffreys, 1990; Kitzinger, 1994). From a sexual-pluralist perspective, however, heterosexuality is not *inherently* about men dominating women any more than it is inherently about strict adherence to traditional masculine and feminine sexual scripts. The sexual expression of heterosexuality may involve the perpetuation of harmful relations of domination or it may not. Sexual pluralists would judge only the former negatively.

Sexual pluralism, then, fosters a view of sexuality as something more than a form of victimization due to unequal power relations. It also encourages people to see sexuality positively, as a means of achieving greater pleasure, freedom of expression, and self-realization. Consider pornography. From the 1960s to the 1980s, some feminists fought to ban pornography on the grounds that it presents women as powerless sex objects and encourages men to sexually assault women (Dworkin, 1981; MacKinnon, 1987). Most pornography does indeed have that effect. However, must it? Recently, sexual pluralists have argued that pornography does not have to reinforce the domination and degradation of women by men. For example, pornography can be a means for women to create and disseminate their own sexual scripts based on female sexual fantasies, both heterosexual and lesbian. Pornographic art, literature, and movies of this type are now being produced (Matrix, 1996). From the sexual-pluralist point of view, seeing pornography as *necessarily* harmful to women is little more than a new form of essentialism.

Riane Eisler (1995 [1987]) convincingly argues that, for the first time in 7000 years, social conditions now make it possible for humanity to return to the state of rough gender equality that existed before the invasion of Old Europe by conquering hordes from the north, east, and south. At least in the world's rich countries, nothing prevents us from adopting social policies that would create gender equality in the workplace, the home, and other spheres of life (see Chapter 9). As this chapter demonstrates, the examination and redefinition of sexuality is an important step in the process of achieving gender equality.

SUMMARY

1. Sex refers to biological differences between males and females while gender refers to the attitudes, beliefs, and behaviours that we commonly associate with each sex.

2. Although it is popular to trace the origins of masculine and feminine gender roles to biological differences between the sexes, this chapter focuses on the ways in which gender is socially constructed.

3. Three major sociohistorical changes have led to the development of gender inequality: long-distance warfare and conquest, plough agriculture, and the separation of public and private spheres during early industrialization.

4. Conscious sexual learning begins around adolescence in the context of firmly established gender identities.

5. Although there is little formal socialization regarding sexuality, sexual relationships tend to be male-dominated as a result of the character of gender socialization and men's continuing dominant position in society.

6. The social construction of gender and sexual scripts has defined standards of beauty that are nearly impossible for most women to achieve. This contributes to widespread anxiety about body image, leading in some cases to eating disorders.

7. Gender inequality and a sociocultural context that justifies and eroticizes male sexual aggression contribute to the widespread problem of male sexual aggression in our society.

8. The mass media reflect and reinforce the relationship between heterosexuality and male domination.

9. Social constructionism encourages sexual pluralism, which assesses the validity of sexual activities in terms of the meanings of the acts to the participants.

QUESTIONS TO CONSIDER

1. Do you think sexual orientation is genetically programmed or a function of social and psychological experience? On what do you base your opinion? What type of evidence would persuade you one way or the other?

2. Design a study to test whether gender roles are inherent or socially constructed.

3. What policy recommendations would you make to lower the level of sexual assault and sexual harassment? Why do you think these policies would be effective?

GLOSSARY

Compulsory heterosexuality is the assumption that individuals should desire only members of the opposite sex.

Essentialists observe male–female differences in sexual scripts, the division of labour at home and in the workplace, mate selection, sexual aggression, jealousy, promiscuity, fidelity, and so forth. They then interpret these differences as natural and universal.

Gender encompasses a person's feelings, attitudes, and behaviours that are associated with being male or female.

Gender identity refers to a person's identification with, or sense of belonging to, a particular sex, biologically, psychologically, and socially.

Gender role comprises the repertoire of behaviours that match widely shared expectations about how males or females are supposed to act.

Hostile environment sexual harassment involves sexual jokes, comments, and touching that interfere with work or create an unfriendly work setting.

Quid pro quo sexual harassment involves sexual threats or bribery used to extract sexual favours as a condition of employment decisions.

Sex refers to the consequence of being born with distinct male or female genitalia and a genetic program that released either male or female hormones to stimulate the development of one's reproductive system.

Sexual orientation refers to the way one derives sexual pleasure, including whether one's desirable partner(s) are of the same or a different sex.

Sexual pluralism approves of the expression of sexuality in a variety of ways, and not only according to traditionally feminine and masculine gender scripts.

Sexual scripts are assumptions that guide sexual behaviour by telling us whom we should find attractive, when and where it is appropriate to be aroused, what is sexually permissible, and so on.

Sexuality refers to activities that are intended to lead to erotic arousal and produce genital response.

Social constructionism is the main alternative to essentialism. Social constructionists argue that gender differences are not the product of biological properties, whether chromosomal, gonadal, or hormonal. Instead, gender and sexuality are products of social structure and culture.

Sociobiology is the best-known variant of essentialism. It holds that all human beings instinctually want to ensure that their genes get passed on to future generations. However, the different reproductive status of men and women means that they have had to develop different adaptive strategies. This gave rise to "masculine" and "feminine" patterns of behaviour that became genetically encoded because of their adaptive value.

Transgendered people are individuals who want to alter their gender by changing their appearance or resorting to medical intervention.

Transsexuals are people who believe they were born with the "wrong" body—that is, they identify with, and want to live fully as, a member of the "opposite" sex.

SUGGESTED READING

Johnson, Holly. (1996). *Dangerous Domains: Violence against Women in Canada*. Toronto: Nelson. A clear, definitive report by the principal investigator of the 1993 "Violence against Women" survey sponsored by the Canadian Department of Justice.

Eisler, Riane. (1995 [1987]). *The Chalice and the Blade: Our History, Our Future*. New York: HarperCollins. The big picture on gender inequality. Eisler's brilliant examination of the archaeological record uncovers the historical origins of gender inequality and suggests that now, for the first time in 7000 years, we are in a position to put an end to it.

Mackay, Judith. (2000). *The Penguin Atlas of Human Sexual Behaviour*. New York: Penguin. A beautiful presentation of up-to-date global statistics on sexuality, mating, reproduction, sexual health, the business of sex, sexual rites, sex crimes, and the future of sex.

Nelson, E.D., and Barrie W. Robinson. (1999). *Gender in Canada*. Scarborough ON: Prentice Hall Allyn and Bacon Canada. A comprehensive and elegantly written examination of the social construction of gender and sexuality, with a broader, international focus than its title suggests.

Weeks, Jeffrey. (1986). *Sexuality*. London: Routledge. A solid introduction to the sociology of sexuality that discusses its cultural and sociohistorical construction, its relationship to power, and its regulation by the state.

NOTES

1. Freud called this set of emotions the "Oedipus complex" after the ancient Greek legend of Oedipus. Oedipus was abandoned as a child. When he became an adult he accidentally killed his father and unwittingly married his mother. Discovering his true relationship to his mother, he blinded himself and died in exile.

2. Freud called this set of emotions the "Electra complex" after the ancient Greek legend of Electra. Electra persuaded her brother to kill their mother and their mother's lover in order to avenge their father's murder. Incidentally, some sexologists call into question the existence of vaginal orgasm and stress the importance of clitoral stimulation (Masters and Johnson, 1966). This viewpoint emerged around the same time as the modern feminist movement and as more and more people came to view sexuality not just as a means of reproduction but also as a means of erotic enjoyment, including orgasm.

CHAPTER SIX

THE MASS MEDIA

In this chapter you will learn that:
- The mass media may be examined in terms of their economic and political organization, the way they represent ideas, and their effects.
- Newspapers are local monopolies with high levels of ownership concentration; dependency on advertising has an impact on news content because it limits the survival prospects of newspapers with radical views.
- English Canadians watch mostly American television programming, especially prime-time drama and comedies. Advertising dependency, audience preferences, and the lower cost of American programs discourage the production of Canadian television drama. While some analysts view this as a "sellout" of Canadian culture, others regard it as an effect of globalization and argue that it does not undermine the institutional structure of society.
- Some analysts claim that news coverage has a left-liberal political bias while other analysts argue that news coverage is ideologically conservative.
- Many analysts believe that there is a causal link between television violence and violent behaviour, but studies that demonstrate this alleged connection have been criticized on the grounds of flawed methodology; and among those who believe that television violence causes aggressive behaviour, there is disagreement about how it does so.
- Studies on the viewing habits of TV audiences indicate that women and men not only prefer different types of programs, but also watch TV in different ways: men tend to use TV in a more planned way than women, and watch more intently, whereas women are more likely to use TV as a focus for social interaction.
- Access to and use of the Internet reflect broader patterns of social inequality, though these may decline as the technology becomes less costly. Use of the Internet for social interaction creates "virtual" communities that act as a source of identity and social support.

GRAHAM KNIGHT

MCMASTER UNIVERSITY

INTRODUCTION

In the first year of the new millennium, the average Canadian spent just over 20 hours a week listening to radio and slightly more, 21.5 hours a week, watching television (Statistics Canada, 2001b). These amounts vary by social factors such as region, sex, and age, particularly for television. Quebeckers and Maritimers watch more than other Canadians, women more than men, and seniors more than younger adults, adolescents, and children. Seniors, for example, listen to radio and watch television at least twice as much as adolescents. In fact, women over 60 listen to the radio for almost 24 hours a week and watch television for just under 36 hours a week, as compared to 10.5 hours and 14 hours respectively for 12- to 17-year-olds (Statistics Canada, 2001b). This may come as a surprise since we tend to associate radio and television consumption and its effects with teens, not elderly women.

Television watching has actually been declining, while radio listening has remained fairly stable. This points to a number of changes in media technology and use. Since the early 1990s Internet use has grown rapidly, especially home-based use. Between 1997 and 2000 regular home-based use of the Internet grew from 16 percent to 40 percent of Canadian households. The amount of use is also growing rapidly; by 2000 61 percent of home-use households spent at least 20 hours a month online, up from 47 percent just a year earlier (Statistics Canada, 2001a: 11). To some extent television viewing has suffered because of this reality. Television and Internet use tend to be fairly exclusive activities that do not enable the viewer to engage in other concentrated activities at the same time. Radio listening, on the other hand, is frequently done in conjunction with other activities, such as driving or household labour. Because it can be time-shared more easily than television, radio listening has been less affected by new technologies such as the Internet—in fact, almost a quarter of online households use the Internet to listen to the radio (Statistics Canada, 2001a).

Despite the decline in television viewing, the overall picture of media use remains fairly stable. Add movie viewing and newspaper and magazine reading to radio, television, and the Internet and it becomes clear that we spend more time interacting with the media than doing anything else, including working.

The term **media** is the plural of "medium," or middle—hence the idea of media as the means or the channels connecting two or more points. Although the term is sometimes used to refer to any instrument or tool, it is more commonly found in association with the process of communication. **Communication**, whose origin is also Latin, means to bring together or unify by establishing shared meanings and understandings between groups and individuals. This occurs through the transmission of information, knowledge, or beliefs by means of language, visual images, and other sign systems such as music. It used to be common to make a distinction between **mass** media and **interactive** media. With mass media, communication is essentially one-way, from a transmission point such as a television or radio station to a nebulous audience whose members remain anonymous and isolated from one another. With interactive media like the telephone, on the other hand, communication flows back and forth, and people exchange roles with one another in the transmission and reception of communication. This distinction is breaking down, however, with the impact of new media like the Internet (and other forms of computer-mediated communication) that combine aspects of both mass and interactive media.

Given the growing diversity of communications media, some degree of selectivity becomes necessary. In this chapter, therefore, we shall focus primarily on three media: newspapers, television, and the Internet. The chapter will address two main questions about the media. The most obvious is how do the media affect us—how do they influence individuals, groups, and institutions, especially in unconscious ways. The second question is the reverse of this: how do we affect the media—how does society influence and shape the media. To address these questions the chapter is organized into four main sections that deal with political economy, representation and ideology, media effects and audiences, and the Internet. First, however, let us consider the basic theoretical perspectives in media studies. Theories of the media fall into two main types, technological and critical. The principal difference between them concerns the ways in which the structure and role of the media are determined. Technological theories emphasize the ways that different media technologies, such as print versus audio-visual media, determine social perceptions, interactions, and institutional arrangements. Critical theorists, on the other hand, argue for the importance of social values, interests, and conflicts in shaping the technological development, use, and impact of the media.

THE TECHNOLOGICAL PERSPECTIVE

The technological perspective derives primarily from the work of two Canadian scholars, Harold Innis and Marshall McLuhan. From his survey of the history of human communication, Innis (1951) made the distinction between time-biased and space-biased media. **Time-biased media** are modes of communication that endure over time but are not very mobile across space, such as writing on stone or clay tablets. **Space-biased media**, in contrast, can cover much greater areas of space but are much less durable over time—for example, writing on paper or sounds transmitted over the airwaves.

The two types of media foster different arrangements of institutions and cultural values. Time-biased media, for example, are conducive to a strong sense of tradition and custom, and these promote religious forms of power and belief. Space-biased media, in contrast, lead to territorial expansion, empire building, and more secular forms of power and culture as manifested in the dominance of military institutions and the growth of the state. These different forms of power, in turn, create different types of social division and conflict. The elite that controls the means of communication tries to use it to preserve its own privilege and interests. Those excluded from power struggle against elite control, and in the process stimulate the development of new, alternative forms of communication. Historically, such a struggle over the means of communication resulted in the shift from time- to space-biased media.

McLuhan (1964) was influenced by Innis's ideas about the effect of communication on institutions and culture and how this effect changes over time. He argued, however, that the relationship was mediated by the way that forms of communication change our sense perceptions and cognitive processes. The invention of printing, for example, undermined oral communication and its emphasis on hearing, and ushered in a more visually oriented culture. Because print consists of visually separated words strung together in a linear sequence, it encourages us to see the world around us as composed of separate objects, and to interpret that world in a linear, cause-and-effect way. Print removes—it literally abstracts—communication from face-to-face interaction, and so it makes information more abstract. The abstracting effect of print, in turn, fosters individualism, privacy, rationality, and social differentiation. Historically, these further effects of print coincided with the rise of nationalism and the weakening of social ties. Print then served to standardize the national language and became a principal mechanism of social identity.

For McLuhan, the spread of electronic media, particularly television, is spelling an end to the era of print dominance. The impact of TV is crucial for two reasons. First, unlike print, TV does not rely exclusively on one sense (i.e., sight)—it integrates sight and sound and achieves a better *sensory balance*. In fact, for McLuhan the effect of this balance is to make TV a kind of tactile medium in the sense that it "touches" its audience more easily than print. Second, TV allows communication to be *instantaneous*—there is no significant delay between transmission and reception of the message. These differences make TV more socially inclusive than print. This observation has led some of McLuhan's adherents to claim that TV is also more accessible and less hierarchical than print (Znaimer, 1996).

McLuhan's views, however, have proved to be controversial, not least because he tended to see media technologies as something of an autonomous force outside of social control and direction. He has been dismissed as a *technological determinist*, particularly by those who subscribe to the critical perspective.

THE CRITICAL PERSPECTIVE

According to the **critical perspective**, institutions such as the media, and processes such as socialization and social control, cannot be understood from the viewpoint of society as a whole, but only from that of unequal and conflicting groups and classes. In fact, there are really two variants of the critical perspective, one that emphasizes the relationship between media and inequality, and one that emphasizes the relationship between media and social conflict.

The first variant of the critical perspective is derived from the orthodox interpretation of Marxism. In this perspective, the role of the media is defined in terms of how the media serve the economic interests and political power of the dominant class, those who

The invention of the printing press reduced the influence of oral communication as it lessened face-to-face interaction and made information more abstract.

SOURCE: P.J. Crook. *May 2*. Courtesy of Nancy Poole's Studio.

own and control the means of material production. To maintain and consolidate its power and interests, the dominant class also exercises control over the means of cultural and moral production—that is, the production of ideas, beliefs, values, and norms that constitute a society's **dominant ideology**. The media, by disseminating this dominant ideology, are used to create acceptance and legitimization of the status quo.

This view was initially developed by Max Horkheimer and Theodor Adorno (1982 [1947]), who saw the media as part of a broader "culture industry" that functions to create "mass deception" about the exploitive and oppressive character of capi-

talist society. In their view, the role of the media is to distract and pacify people by feeding them standardized images and messages that stifle the capacity for independent, critical thought. Similar to this view of the culture industry is the "propaganda model" of the news media put forward by Edward Herman and Noam Chomsky (1988). They argue that the media serve the interests of the political and economic elites by "filtering" information to reduce or eliminate radical or subversive views. Herman and Chomsky identify five main filters: (1) the media's own orientation to profit-making, (2) their dependency on advertising for revenue and profit, (3) their reliance on powerful institutions and individuals as sources of information,

(4) negative reaction—what they call "flak"—if the media do deviate from elite interests and values, and (5) adherence to anti-communism as an overarching belief system. With the decline of communism, the "war on terrorism" seems to have become the fifth filter, at least for the present.

The second variant of the critical perspective also acknowledges that the capitalist class and other powerful groups use dominant ideology to reinforce their position and maintain the status quo. They do this through **hegemony**—the use of the media and other cultural institutions to represent their interests, values, and understandings as natural and universal. But dominant ideology is not the only ideology. Inequality also engenders resistance and struggle, which result in other, more critical perspectives from which social reality and the dominant ideology can be interpreted. A distinction should be made between **alternative** and **oppositional viewpoints**. Oppositional viewpoints represent the experiences of subordinated groups against those of the powerful; alternative viewpoints occupy an intermediate position, reflecting compromise or "negotiated" understandings, which blend elements of dominant and oppositional viewpoints together (Hall, 1980). Although the media usually promote understandings that conform with dominant ideology, their messages are always at least partially open to the challenge of alternative and oppositional interpretations. To be successful, hegemony has to be flexible enough to accommodate and incorporate a range of different viewpoints (Knight, 1998).

POLITICAL ECONOMY OF THE MEDIA

A strength of the critical perspective is that it draws attention to the ways that the social and cultural role of the media depends on their role as agents of political and economic power and interests. The principal approach sociologists take to analyze this relationship empirically is *political economy*. Political economy focuses on the ownership and control of economic resources, and on the effect of technology and economic power on cultural values, social structure, and political decision-making. Media are organizations that usually are owned and controlled by large corporations or the state, and that function like other bureaucracies. They have to sustain themselves economically through commercial revenue, government funding, subscriber fees and donations, or some mixture of these. What, then, are the primary goals of media organizations—to inform and entertain or to capture market share and make money? And in whose interests do they operate—owners, advertisers, or audiences? These questions are especially pertinent in democratic societies where values such as freedom and diversity of opinion, and the promotion of both minority and national cultural identities are strong.

Ownership and control of the media are generally becoming more concentrated into a smaller number of larger corporate hands. This trend is part of the wider process of economic globalization, and it is leading to the creation of large **multimedia chains**. These are corporations that own a diversified array of media operations and outlets in different fields, such as radio, TV, and publishing, and operate on a worldwide basis. One of the world's best-known multimedia corporations is the Walt Disney Company (see Figure 6.1). The world's largest multimedia chain is AOL Time Warner, which came into existence in 2001 with the merger of AOL and Time Warner. AOL was the largest Internet provider in the United States, with holdings that included Netscape and a partial share of Amazon.com. Time Warner was already the world's largest multimedia company involved a range of ventures including book and magazine publishing, cable and satellite systems, cable networks, music recording, theme parks, film and television production and distribution, and sports team ownership, with brand names ranging from Atlantic music to Warner movies to CNN and *Time* magazine. The company's combined revenue for 2001 stood at US$38.2 billion (See Table 6.1 on page 133). The world's dominant media corporations are primarily American-based. Only two of the top six media giants are headquartered outside the United States—Bertelsmann and Vivendi—and these are located in Western Europe. The developing world accounts for only three of the world's top 50 corporations whose core business is entertainment media. All three are based in Latin America: Globo (Brazil), Clarin (Argentina), and Televisa (Mexico). Two Canadian companies make it into the global top 50, Rogers and CanWest Global.

To secure and enhance their market position, multimedia chains practise both horizontal consolidation and vertical integration. **Horizontal consolidation** refers to the sharing of facilities and resources

FIGURE 6.1 THE WALT DISNEY COMPANY

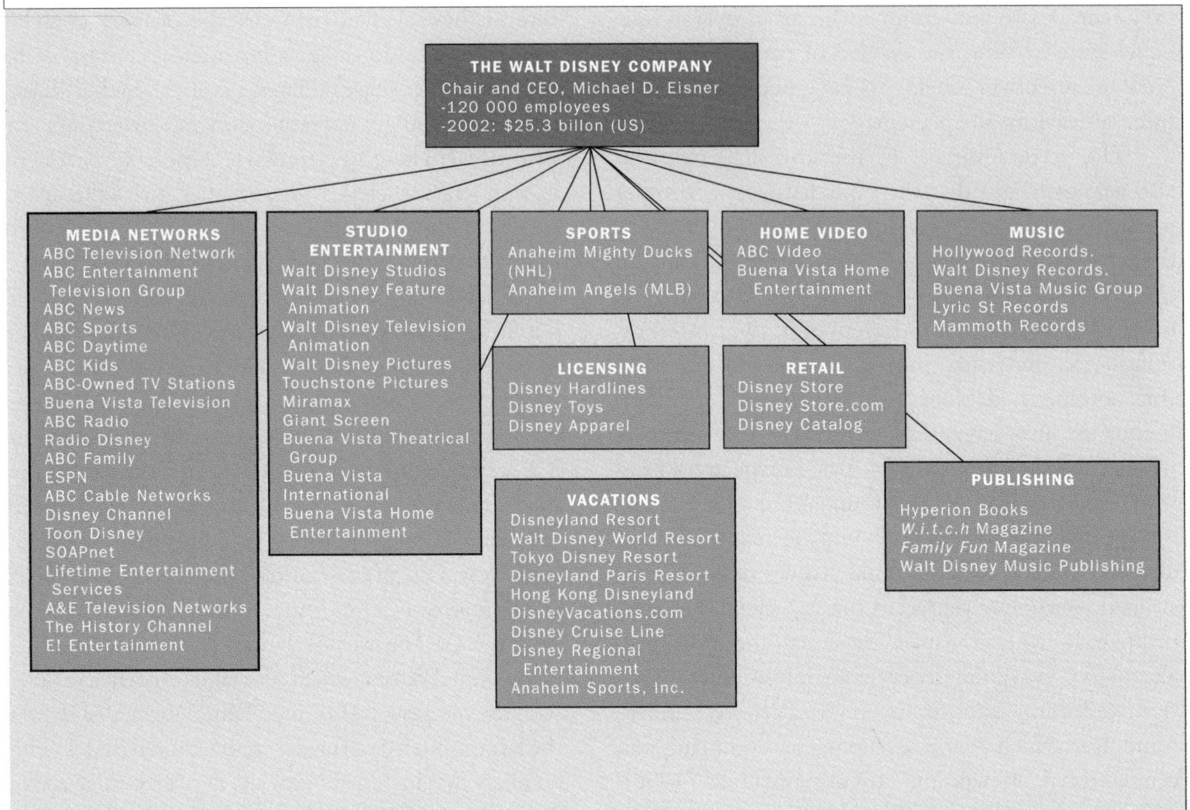

THE WALT DISNEY COMPANY
Chair and CEO, Michael D. Eisner
-120 000 employees
-2002: $25.3 billon (US)

MEDIA NETWORKS
ABC Television Network
ABC Entertainment
 Television Group
ABC News
ABC Sports
ABC Daytime
ABC Kids
ABC-Owned TV Stations
Buena Vista Television
ABC Radio
Radio Disney
ABC Family
ESPN
ABC Cable Networks
Disney Channel
Toon Disney
SOAPnet
Lifetime Entertainment
 Services
A&E Television Networks
The History Channel
E! Entertainment

STUDIO ENTERTAINMENT
Walt Disney Studios
Walt Disney Feature
 Animation
Walt Disney Television
 Animation
Walt Disney Pictures
Touchstone Pictures
Miramax
Giant Screen
Buena Vista Theatrical
 Group
Buena Vista
International
Buena Vista Home
 Entertainment

SPORTS
Anaheim Mighty Ducks
(NHL)
Anaheim Angels (MLB)

LICENSING
Disney Hardlines
Disney Toys
Disney Apparel

VACATIONS
Disneyland Resort
Walt Disney World Resort
Tokyo Disney Resort
Disneyland Paris Resort
Hong Kong Disneyland
DisneyVacations.com
Disney Cruise Line
Disney Regional
 Entertainment
Anaheim Sports, Inc.

HOME VIDEO
ABC Video
Buena Vista Home
 Entertainment

RETAIL
Disney Store
Disney Store.com
Disney Catalog

MUSIC
Hollywood Records.
Walt Disney Records.
Buena Vista Music Group
Lyric St Records
Mammoth Records

PUBLISHING
Hyperion Books
W.i.t.c.h Magazine
Family Fun Magazine
Walt Disney Music Publishing

The Walt Disney Company wants to extend the Disney experience well beyond the theme parks, reaching every form of media delivery, and, in Celebration, Florida, creating environments for people to live within.

between different plants and outlets. **Vertical integration** is the controlling of resources and assets at the different stages of production, such as ownership of a major league sports team along with the stations and cable channels over which the games are televised. The recent development of digital technology has enhanced both horizontal consolidation and vertical integration, and led to a series of corporate mergers, such as AOL Time Warner, that have strengthened the position of multimedia chains as the dominant form of organization. These mergers comprise the union of delivery conduits (cable, satellite, telephony) and content (news, information, and entertainment). In 2000, for example, Canada's leading telecommunications company, Bell Canada Enterprises, gained control the CTV television network as well as *The Globe and Mail* newspaper, and Quebecor Media Inc. acquired the cable company Vidéotron.

The effect of these mergers is that traditional distinctions between print and electronic media is disappearing, at least at the level of corporate organization. At the same time, variations do exist, particularly in the way that the political economy of different media creates different effects and issues. We can see this when we compare newspapers and television.

NEWSPAPERS: CONCENTRATION, MONOPOLY, AND ADVERTISING

In Canada, corporate ownership and control of daily newspapers has undergone rapid change since the 1970s and has become highly concentrated. CanWest Global, Quebecor Media Inc., and Torstar dominate the field. CanWest Global, via its Southam subsidiary, has dailies in major metropolitan areas such as Vancouver, Calgary, Edmonton, Saskatoon, Ottawa, Montreal, and Halifax, as well as control of the Toronto-based *National Post*, one of only two English-language national newspapers. Quebecor Media Inc. controls the Sun chain of tabloids in cities

---

TABLE 6.1 GLOBAL ENTERTAINMENT MEDIA CORPORATIONS

"About six players now own virtually everything, all aspects of the media experience."
—Drew Marcus, Deutsche Bank media sector analyst*

RANK	REVENUE (US$ BILLION)
Top Six (2001)	
1. AOL Time Warner (U.S.)	38.2
2. Disney (U.S.)	25.3
3. Vivendi Universal† (France)	24.6**
4. Viacom (U.S.)	23.2
5. Bertelsmann (Germany)	17.5**
6. News Corp. (U.S./Australia)	13.8
Developing Countries (2001–2002)	
26. Globo (Brazil)	3.2
35. Televisa (Mexico)	2.2
40. Clarin (Argentina)	2.1
Canadian Companies (2001–2002)	
27. Rogers	2.4
43. CanWest	1.4

* SustainAbility, *Good News and Bad: The Media, Corporate Social Responsibility and Sustainable Development*. Downloaded from http://www.sustainability.com, 2002.
** Estimated US$ equivalent; original financial data given in euros.
† Media and communications only.

SOURCES: Top six data taken from *Financial Reports* or other financial data source for each corporation. Downloaded from:
http://www.aoltimewarner.com/investors/annual_reports/pdf/2001ar.pdf;
http://disney.go.com/corporate/investors/financials/annual/2001/pdfs/annual.pdf;
http://finance.vivendiuniversal.com/finance/financials/FY01keydata.cfm;
http://www.viacom.com/pdf/qr01q4.pdf;
http://investor.bertelsmann.de/wms/bertelsmann/fset.php3?ci=2&bereich=facts&language=2; and
http://www.newscorp.com/report2001/pdfs/annual_complete.pdf.
Data for Developing Countries and Canada taken from *Variety*, August 26–September 1, 2002, p. 52.

---

like Toronto and Calgary, as well as French-language tabloids in Quebec City and Montreal. Torstar controls *The Toronto Star*, the largest circulation newspaper in Canada, as well as dailies in Hamilton, Kitchener-Waterloo, and Guelph. CanWest Global and Quebecor Media also have significant interests in other media such as radio, television, and cable, which, in the case of CanWest Global, reach as far as Australia, New Zealand, and Ireland.

The concentration of ownership into the hands of a few multimedia chains has raised serious questions about freedom of the press and the diversity of opinion, both of which are widely regarded as necessary for a democratic society. These concerns came to a head in June 2002 when CanWest Global fired Russell Mills, the long-time publisher of *The Ottawa Citizen*, for running an editorial calling for Prime Minister Chrétien's resignation, without first gaining the approval of corporate head office. Mills's firing came on the heels of a number of changes made by

CanWest Global that tightened corporate control over the editorial content of its Southam newspapers. While there was considerable outcry over CanWest Global's actions—over 3000 people reportedly cancelled their subscriptions to *The Ottawa Citizen*—the ability of newspaper proprietors to dictate news content continues to depend on the need to make a profit. This, in turn, depends on the ability to attract advertisers. Daily newspapers get about three-quarters of their revenue from advertising, and community newspapers get over 90 percent from advertising (Statistics Canada, 1997: 98–99). But to attract advertisers, newspapers must also appeal to readers and subscribers, as these comprise the market that advertisers are trying to reach and persuade.

As newspapers have become more advertising dependent, the scale and costs of operation have grown. The effect of this has been to reduce competition and create local newspaper monopolies in all but the larger urban areas. Even in larger urban areas like

Toronto, where more than one daily newspaper exists, papers have to specialize and appeal to particular market segments in order to survive. The critical perspective sees multimedia chain ownership, local monopolies, and advertising dependency as resulting in the homogenization of news coverage and the decline of diversity in news topics and viewpoints. However, the evidence supporting the link is inconclusive. Studies of the 1980 closure of competing papers in Winnipeg and Ottawa, for example, found that monopolization led to a decline in the volume and length of news stories, especially national and international coverage (Trim et al., 1983; Candussi and Winters, 1988). In contrast, McCombs (1988), in a comparison of Winnipeg and Montreal, claims that monopolization brought about no significant change. If anything, he argues, the quality of the news coverage actually improved somewhat after the closure of competing papers (1988: 136).

TELEVISION: ECONOMY, CULTURE, AND IDENTITY

For television as for newspapers, it is commercialization and advertising dependency that have had the greatest impact on the content and role of the medium. Private television is driven by the profit motive rather than cultural goals such as promoting Canadian content and national identity. Income and profits come largely from advertising, and this means having to cater to large audiences. To attract audiences and advertisers, private Canadian broadcasters, particularly English-language broadcasters, rely heavily on imported, mainly American, programming, especially during prime-time (See Figure 6.2). Even though the cost of licensing American programming has been increasing, it is still less than the cost of producing comparable Canadian programming.

The issue of Canadian content pertains largely to entertainment programming, particularly English-Canadian drama. Audiences have long shown a strong preference for U.S. dramatic programming and, as a result, the audience for domestic programs is not large enough in economic terms to make Canadian drama an attractive proposition, particularly for private broadcasters. Reaction to this situation is split. On the one side are nationalists, who argue that broadcasting should be an instrument of Canadian culture and identity, meaning that it should actively promote Canadian content (Collins, 1990). The nationalists

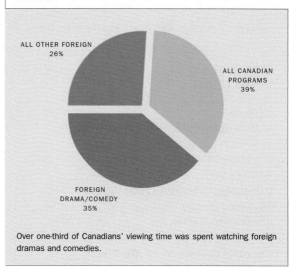

FIGURE 6.2 TELEVISION VIEWING BY PROGRAM SOURCE

ALL OTHER FOREIGN 26%

ALL CANADIAN PROGRAMS 39%

FOREIGN DRAMA/COMEDY 35%

Over one-third of Canadians' viewing time was spent watching foreign dramas and comedies.

SOURCE: Statistics Canada, *Focus on Culture*, Cat. No. 87-004, Spring 1997, p. 3.

single out drama because of its popularity and because of its capacity to promote and reinforce cultural myths and values that solidify a distinct national identity.

Support for the argument about the relationship between TV drama and cultural identity can be found in the case of Quebec, where there is a stronger commitment to francophone drama and other entertainment programming on the part of both public and private TV. This commitment is matched by stronger audience interest and the strengthening of national and cultural identity on the part of francophone Quebeckers. Not only do francophones watch more Canadian programming overall, they also watch proportionately more television drama than anglophones do (see Table 6.2)

The federal government has attempted to address the issue of television drama production by establishing content requirements and offering financial inducements such as production subsidies. While production has been increasing, economic pressure means creating the kind of programming that will attract advertisers and foreign buyers, and this often means that the programming itself lacks a distinctly Canadian character. Canadian television production is increasingly part of a market that is global in scale but still dominated by the American television industry. For critical theorists in particular, this dominance amounts to a situation of **cultural imperialism** in

TABLE 6.2   PERCENT DISTRIBUTION OF TV VIEWING TIME, FALL 1999

	ANGLOPHONE		FRANCOPHONE	
PROGRAM TYPE	Canadian	Foreign	Canadian	Foreign
News and public affairs	14.7	5.8	28.0	1.2
Documentaries	0.7	2.6	1.4	0.9
Instructional	1.1	2.2	0.8	1.3
Religious	0.1	0.1	0.3	—
Sports	5.7	4.0	3.6	1.1
Variety and games	1.2	9.6	12.7	2.1
Music and dance	0.9	0.5	0.5	0.3
Comedy	0.5	12.1	2.2	5.3
Drama	3.4	25.4	14.4	16.4
Other	—	9.3	—	6.2
Total	**28.4**	**71.6**	**65.9**	**34.1**

SOURCE: Compiled from Statistics Canada, "Television Viewing," *The Daily*, January 25, 2001, second and third tables. Downloaded from http://www.statcan.ca/Daily/English/010125/d010125a.htm.

which one society's media exert an overwhelming and unilateral influence over another society's culture (for an overview, see Tomlinson, 1997). As evidence of this, critical theorists point to the uneven flow of television and other cultural products between countries. Canada, for example, is one of the world's largest importers of cultural products and this is growing rapidly, with an increase of 17.2 percent between 1996 and 2000. Over four-fifths of these imports come from the U.S. Although cultural exports are growing faster than imports, Canada still imports almost twice as much from the U.S.—about $4 billion in 2000—than it exports there (Carter and Durand, 2000).

The view that Canadian culture and identity are threatened or undermined by the consumption of American television programs or other cultural products has not gone unchallenged. According to Collins (1990: xii), Canada is becoming a "postnational" society. This is a condition that is becoming increasingly common among Western societies generally, as the association of the nation-state with particular economic, political, and cultural institutions breaks down under the effect of globalization. Canada is a pluralistic society linguistically, ethnically, and subculturally, and so it may not have a strong symbolic culture in the sense of a single, unified system of symbols, representations, and identities. It does, nevertheless, have a strong culture in the anthropological sense of shared institutions and practices (1990: 35). And this culture, Collins argues, is undiminished by the preference of English Canadians for U.S. cop shows and sitcoms.

Collins's argument reminds one of the theory that developed—Western societies are now becoming postmodern. In this view, as the social structure becomes increasingly differentiated, social roles, identities, and experiences are becoming increasingly fragmented and dissociated from one another. Postmodernists believe that **fragmentation** allows groups and individuals greater scope to play with and reconstruct their identities and understandings. It can foster new forms of consciousness, particularly in terms of the popular culture—music, fashion, lifestyle—that is associated with the mass media (Fiske, 1987).

Fragmentation is also occurring at the level of political economy with the proliferation of new TV services such as specialty channels, "superstations," pay-per-view channels, and home-shopping channels, in addition to more conventional broadcast TV stations and networks (Ellis, 1992). As television becomes more differentiated, audiences become more fragmented, a process that is captured by the term *narrowcasting* (as opposed to *broadcasting*). With this development, the role of TV as an agent of common culture is being questioned.

Concomitant with audience fragmentation, a contrary process, **technological convergence**, is also at work. The term refers to the merging and integration of previously separate communications technologies, such as telephony, computers, television, and radio (Ellis, 1992). Convergence has been given a boost by the development of digital technology that has encouraged the spate of media mergers discussed above. Technological convergence is reflected in the growing popularity of the term "home entertainment," which now includes a whole array of social activities such as shopping, banking, and even working ("telecommuting") at home. The implication is that everyday life will become privatized in the household as people find they have less and less need for face-to-face interaction with others. Some evidence to support such a trend can be found in a study of the consequences of the introduction of TV reception to a community in British Columbia (T.M. Williams, 1986). The researchers found that the introduction of TV led to the **displacement** of other activities, such as participation in the community's social and recreational life, as people stayed at home more to watch TV.

REPRESENTATION AND IDEOLOGY: THE MEANING OF THE MESSAGE

Analysis of the media from the perspective of political economy alone is ultimately limited, because it takes for granted the nature of the messages that the media communicate. The emphasis here is on the plural—*messages*. The media communicate on different levels—the pleasurable as well as the meaningful, the entertaining as well as the informative. Such communication entails the process of **representation**—that is, the use of language, visual images, and other symbolic tools to create messages people can understand and find satisfying or enjoyable. Representation, however, is a selective process. It involves countless decisions—only some of which are conscious—about what is to be included and what is to be left out, what is to be emphasized and what is to be downplayed, and about the sequence in which the elements are to be connected into a coherent message. Sociologists use the term **framing** to denote the selective, organized nature of representation (Goffman, 1974; Gitlin, 1980). To frame something (such as a picture or photograph) is to set up boundaries that define where the representation begins and ends, and to organize the contents in a way that distinguishes what is being emphasized (the foreground) from what is treated as secondary (the context or background). The framing of any representation—a news report, an advertisement, a TV drama—has ideological effects inasmuch as it entails a particular inflection or bias. Every frame is only one of several different ways of seeing and interpreting something.

NEWS AND IDEOLOGY

Outside our immediate experience, the news media are one of our principal sources of information about social reality. Conservative and critical writers have disagreed considerably on how news is framed and the ideological effects of news framing. Conservatives argue that the news media have a "left-liberal" bias that runs counter to the views and interests of the mainstream of society. They believe that this bias operates in three related ways. First, the media have an anti-corporate bias (see Box 6.1) and are critical of market-oriented solutions to social problems. Second, the media give greater or more favourable attention to the views of interest groups and constituencies that have liberal or left-wing political views—for example, unions, environmentalists, social welfare organizations, and, in the case of foreign news, left-wing regimes or political movements (Cooper, 1994). Third, the media concentrate on negative events, issues, and news angles, ignoring the positive aspects of social life (National Media Archive, 1993).

In contrast to the conservative perspective, those who employ a critical perspective believe that the news media function chiefly to reproduce dominant ideology. This is not seen as a conscious conspiracy, but as the unconscious effect of the values and practices that journalists employ when they define and gather news. Let us consider the critical perspective in greater detail.

Defining the News

How is news framed? To answer this question we must begin by asking what are the criteria, or **news values**, that the media use to determine what is newsworthy. There are three major criteria: immediacy, personalization, and extraordinariness.

Immediacy By definition, news is about what is new or immediate. Although the media are often unable to capture events as they actually happen, the accent is on reporting them as quickly as possible after they occur. Immediacy has always been a major element in the competition among different media, and the history of media technology is dominated by the goal of making communication faster. Whenever possible, news is written in the present tense to convey the sense that events are still ongoing.

The emphasis on immediacy, however, goes beyond the present to the future. To generate interest and curiosity on the part of the audience, news stories often create some sense of uncertainty about what will happen next. The effect of this approach is that

CANADIAN MEDIA UNCRITICALLY ACCEPT ADVOCACY GROUPS' ASSERTION THAT 1.5 MILLION CANADIAN CHILDREN LIVE IN POVERTY

During the last week in November 1993, Campaign 2000, a 45-group coalition, reported an increase in the number of children living in poverty in Canada. This finding was widely reported in most major Canadian daily newspapers as well as on the national newscasts of the networks.

Each of the reports faithfully conveyed the coalition's findings. All had given the following information as was reported by CTV's Ken Ernhofer: "The child poverty numbers are staggering. A watchdog group, Campaign 2000, says that between 1989 and 1991, an additional 250 000 Canadian children joined the ranks of the impoverished, an increase of 30 percent. In all, 1.2 million children lived in poverty, one child in every five."

Most troubling about the way in which the media reported these stories was that there was no incredulity or question that that many Canadian children were poor. The reporters covered the story in almost exactly the same way, all repeating the information provided to them by the coalition. Despite the unanimity among the reporters, a number of facts presented could have been challenged.

REPORTERS CLAIM CHILDREN LIVE BELOW POVERTY LINE, BUT FAIL TO QUESTION DEFINITION

All reporters covering the child poverty story mentioned the statement that Canadian children were poor or were living under the poverty line. Adrienne Tanner of the *Edmonton Journal*, Alison Bray of the *Winnipeg Free Press*, the Canadian Press report in the *Regina Leader-Post*, Rosemary Spiers of the *Toronto Star* and Carol Goar of the *St. John's Telegram* all provided the definition of the poverty line as being Statistics Canada's Low Income Cutoff (LICO). However, none of the reporters indicated that Statistics Canada does not endorse this as a measurement of poverty: "although LICO are commonly referred to as official poverty lines, they have no officially recognized status nor does Statistics Canada promote their use as poverty lines."*

Only one reporter questioned the measurement in a story: Canadian Press journalist Helen Branswell. In an article printed in the *Winnipeg Free Press*, Branswell writes: "Some contend the low-income cutoffs aren't a good measure of poverty, because they don't assess whether people who live below them can meet their basic needs. Instead the cutoffs assess how those people fared in comparison to those who are better off." While most of the story was also printed in the *Regina Leader-Post*, that section was excluded.

The *Globe and Mail* also noted the LICO figures but referred to them as "the poverty threshold." And while the *Globe and Mail* indicated that former Progressive Conservative MP Barbara Greene had tried to examine a real measure of poverty, her efforts were dismissed by the man who came up with the numbers for Campaign 2000, Clarence Lougheed: "When we talk about poor families there are very few poor families who live at the cutoff, or even close to that level." Contrast this attention to that given to Barbara Greene when she chaired the parliamentary committee on poverty and actually argued that the way in which we count the poor may inflate their numbers. She was vilified in the press and her motives were impugned. For example, Debra O'Connor from the National Anti-poverty Organization said on CTV News on 8 June 1993: "And when Barbara Greene gets up and says 40 to 60 percent of the poor aren't really poor, that just reinforces people's idea that life on welfare is easy and it's too soft, and that couldn't be further from the truth. There's real suffering out there, and Barbara Greene is doing her bit to make that suffering worse."

*Statistics Canada Low Income Cut-offs, 1986, Technical Paper, 1987, p. 1.

SOURCE: National Media Archive, "Canadian Media Uncritically Accept Advocacy Groups' Assertion That 1.5 Million Canadian Children Live in Poverty," *On Balance*, 6 (10) (1993), p. 2. Reprinted by permission.

news tends to be concerned with the consequences of events and issues at the expense of their causes and development (Knight, 1982). Causes belong in the past, and news generally lacks a strong sense of historical perspective and context.

Personalization   When news does deal with causes and explanations, it often reduces them to the level of individual motives and psychology. This is an effect of personalization. To communicate with an anonymous audience, news has to enable the reader or viewer to identify with news events that are often remote from everyday experience by making them more concrete and familiar. This emphasis on personalities has been intensified by the growth of TV news, where the need to be visual makes it more difficult to deal in abstractions, such as unemployment, and easier to deal with people, such as the unemployed. Personalization is especially strong in political news coverage as the media focus on party leaders and other prominent politicians and their respective popularity in the opinion polls. Critics often charge that this detracts from a fuller understanding of the political system and the more substantive aspects of political policy (Taras, 1990).

Extraordinariness Above all else, news concerns events and issues that are *out of the ordinary*, and that entail *conflict, confrontation, deviance*, or *disorder* (Knight, 1982). The implication of this, as conservative critics also point out, is that news is normally about the *negative*. For critical theorists, however, the negative emphasis of news does not undermine mainstream values and beliefs, but in fact reinforces dominant ideology in at least two ways. First, by dwelling on the negative, news invokes and reproduces dominant definitions of what is socially normal and desirable. It identifies events and actors that deviate from this definition—events and actors that are already viewed as dangerous, bizarre, or disruptive—and represents them as a threat to what is socially desirable (Knight, 1982) (see Figure 6.3). Second, news coverage of deviance and conflict tends to focus on the actions of the appropriate social control authorities—the government, the police, the experts—to restore social order and limit disruptive effects. The threat of bad news is offset by reassurance that someone with authority is responding to the problem.

Gathering the News

Initially, newsworthy events come to the attention of the media via news releases, tip-offs, and the routine monitoring of institutional communications like emergency services radio. Further information is then gathered from key sources, usually by means of interviewing. In choosing their sources, news media also take account of a fourth news value: objectivity or fairness (Knight, 1982). In practice objectivity translates into an attempt to achieve a balance of sources representing the different, often antagonistic viewpoints that are involved in the event or issue being reported. These sources include not only authority figures (such as police, politicians, and experts), but also others such as eyewitnesses, victims, and the representatives of groups and organizations ranging from big business to social activist groups that may have a stake in the event or issue.

However, just as news framing tends to focus on the activities of certain social actors rather than others, so it also tends to rely on and privilege certain sources of information over others. Objectivity does not mean absolute parity or neutrality. There is a hierarchy of access to and for the media, and this has important ideological implications as it reflects the general distribution of power in society. The media have easier access to certain sources, and certain sources have easier access to the media. For example, public representatives, such as elected politicians, have a much greater obligation to speak to the media than do private sector officials, such as corporate executives, who can invoke the values of private property as a way to justify their own and their organization's privacy. At the same time, because of their

---

FIGURE 6.3 TORONTO "DAYS OF ACTION" HEADLINES: DISRUPTION-RELATED THEMES IN A LOCAL NEWSPAPER, 1996

These headlines illustrate the way the media emphasize the disruptive or confrontational effects of new events rather than their causes or effects on social solidarity. They also highlight the way labour and other social movements are often portrayed as the source of social disruption and conflict.

Oct. 24:	"Brace yourself for tough tomorrow"
Oct. 25:	"Don't be intimidated by protesters: Harris"
	"Ambulances, police go on high alert" (continuation of previous report)
	"No mail, trash but beer's on. TTC in doubt as protest affects many services"
	"Days of Action hits many services" (continuation of previous report)
	"Parade, rallies expected to jam city tomorrow"
Oct. 26	"Days of Disruption"
	"Day of frustration, frayed nerves" (continuation of previous report)
	"Shut out: Pickets block mayor from city hall"
	"Protest a pain for many StarPhone callers"
	"TTC workers didn't ask for help: Police Chief says heavy police presence kept trouble to a minimum."
	"Barely a blip. The labour protest pretty much failed to disrupt Bay Street. The TSE hummed along nicely."
	"Protestors failed to tarnish Metro's image"
	"Employers cope with disruptions"

power and status, corporate officials can easily gain access to the news media when they choose to do so.

This hierarchy of access is reflected in the division of labour between three broad types of news source—official, ordinary, and alternative (Knight, 1998). **Official sources** are representatives of dominant institutions—for example, politicians, police officers, professionals, experts, and corporate spokespeople. They appear more frequently and prominently than other sources, and are usually treated by the media as authoritative and credible. Official sources normally speak rationally and objectively about an event, issue, or problem, providing information about what is happening and what steps are being taken to respond to the situation. Official sources are offset by **ordinary news sources**. These play a double role in the news as either eyewitnesses or, more importantly, victims of newsworthy events or problems. As victims, ordinary sources personalize the harmful effects (actual and potential) of bad news. They are the ones adversely affected by deviance, conflict, and disruption. They speak more subjectively of personal experiences, feelings, and emotions—anger at what has happened to them, and fear of what may happen next. **Alternative news sources** are the representatives of social movements and social advocacy and activism groups. They stand between official and ordinary voices. Alternative sources address the social problems that underlie the harm that ordinary victims are suffering. In this respect, they compete with official sources over the definition of victimhood: who is a victim, who is responsible, who should act, and what should be done. Alternative sources attempt to reframe the experiences and emotions of victims into a critical, normative, and political perspective of injustice and inequity, and attempt to use the media as a way to publicize their cause, gain legitimacy and social recognition, and pressure dominant institutions to take steps to rectify what is wrong (Carroll and Ratner, 1999).

While all three types of source appear in the media, they do so to varying degrees. Although official sources represent the interests and values of particular institutions or organizations, they are often used to speak on behalf of society as a whole. This gives them an advantage in defining the news frame and establishing what the terms of the event, issue, or problem are. The ideological effect of this is that deviance and disorder tend to be framed from a police perspective, as discrete events that are explained in terms of individual motives, rather than as social phenomena caused by social forces. Ordinary and particularly alternative sources, on the other hand, are used to represent specific points of view. These may often contradict what official sources are saying, but they normally do so on grounds that have already been determined by the news frame. In the case of economic news, for example, the media tend to rely on the representatives of private business (such as economists employed in the banking sector) rather than the labour union movement as their primary source of information and interpretation about the economy as a whole. The views of the union movement, if they are included in the coverage at all, are usually framed as a reaction to this, a reaction that represents only the interests of organized labour.

The effect of this uneven relationship between different types of source can be seen in the media's coverage of Ontario's Bill 40, a 1993 law that prohibited employers from using strikebreakers during legal strikes (Knight and O'Connor, 1995). The news coverage was framed in terms of the strong business opposition to the legislation, but it was represented primarily in terms of potential investment and job loss and harm to workers rather than lost profits and harm to business. Business assumed the role of speaking for everyone. The media gave very little coverage to alternative views of the legislation's potential benefits in promoting equity and workers' rights or in deterring strikes and industrial conflict. The voice of organized labour was restricted mainly to expressing support for the law and criticizing business for being negative.

Alternative sources are often faced with a dilemma in their relationship with the media. On the one hand, they are used simply as a reaction to official sources. In this case, their voice is a negative one of grievances and complaints, rather than a constructive one of analysis and proposals. On the other hand, they can attempt to draw the media's attention to their own framing of an issue or problem. However, to do this they may have to engage in the kind of activity, such as public protests, that associates their views with disruptive behaviour and undermines their legitimacy (Hackett, 1991) (see Figure 6.3). This problem for alternative sources is evident in the news coverage of protest actions by the Ontario Coalition Against Poverty (OCAP) in its recent campaign against homelessness. Although OCAP has succeeded in drawing media attention, its protests have often been framed in

HOMELESS PROTEST TARGETS FILM FEST

Bewildered film-festival fans viewed some unscripted street theatre last night, produced and directed by the Ontario Coalition Against Poverty.

It was showtime for about 50 homelessness protesters outside Roy Thomson Hall during the kickoff for the 24th Toronto International Film Festival.

OCAP leader John Clarke and his cast and crew of anti-poverty activists blew whistles and chanted, "Sure the movie may be nice, but the homeless pay the price."

"When they move poor people out of downtown, big-money interests push that agenda," Clarke said.

Dozens of Toronto Police officers kept demonstrators from the red-carpeted Simcoe St. entrance and a lineup of suit-wearing ticket-holders for the gala premiere of Atom Egoyan's *Felicia's Journey*.

Limos bringing Hollywood superstars were diverted to the back entrance. But director Norman Jewison and former Kid in the Hall Dave Foley slipped in without acknowledging the demo.

The protest spoiled the chances for Margaret Simpson, 50, and her husband Steve of Dorset, England, of seeing some film stars.

"We were surprised there were homeless, but I guess it's like any other big international city," she said.

"It's just a fuss because this is a place to make a fuss," publicist Gino Empry said of the protest. "Most people associated with the festival do things for charity."

SOURCE: Philip Lee-Shanok, "Homeless Protest Targets Film Fest," *The Toronto Sun*, September 10, 1999, http://www.canoe.ca/TorontoSun. Reprinted with permission of *The Toronto Sun*.

a way that implies homelessness is mainly a problem of social control rather than one of social exclusion, political indifference, or economic inequality and deprivation. An example of this is the news report in the *Toronto Sun* on September 10, 1999, about a protest by the homeless at the opening of the Toronto International Film Festival (See Box 6.2). The protest is framed as a piece of "unscripted street theatre" that required police intervention and deprived "fans" of their chance to see "Hollywood superstars." The head of OCAP is quoted briefly on the relationship between social reaction to the homeless and "big-money interests," but he is given no opportunity to elaborate on this relationship or to suggest ways in which the problem should be addressed. The report concludes with two sources, one of them an ordinary eyewitness, whose views imply that there is nothing significant or unusual about either homelessness or protests against it. The "fuss" about homelessness becomes no fuss at all.

Despite the advantage official sources have in defining particular news frames, alternative voices can nonetheless influence and reshape the framing process over the longer term. For example, popular opinion has gradually become more amenable to the views of the environmental movement and more skeptical and critical of governments and big busi-

ness. In their study of the controversy over logging practices in old-growth forests in British Columbia, Doyle and colleagues (1997) show how the forest industry has attempted to control the framing process through publicity campaigns, the use of the world's largest public relations firm (Burson-Marsteller), and sponsorship of the B.C. Forest Alliance, a supposedly independent, nonprofit organization with representatives from the wider community. The strategy of the B.C. Forest Alliance is to try to occupy the middle ground between the industry and the environmental movement by being critical of both. However, it has achieved only "limited success in convincing the media" (Doyle et al., 1997: 263). This is because it continues to frame the issue as a dichotomy—"trees versus jobs"—in which the goals of environmentalists were seen as harmful to the interests of workers. The media reacted skeptically, labelling the Alliance as pro-business and criticizing the "trees versus jobs" frame by noting that job loss in forestry was the result of industry rationalization and downsizing, not environmentalism.

Although critical theorists see the media as generally representative of dominant ideology, they also recognize that relations between journalists and their sources involve an ongoing struggle for control on both sides (Ericson, Baranek, and Chan, 1989). The outcome of this depends chiefly on the status of the sources and the power they can exercise over the flow of information. In the case of crime news, the police enjoy an effective monopoly over the supply of information because there is no alternative, competing source on which the media can rely. With politics, on the other hand, journalists have more leverage over sources by virtue of the adversarial structure of the political process, at least in democratic societies. This does not, however, alter the fact that the government exercises the greatest control over the flow of information because of its political authority and control over policy. What the government does or says is intrinsically newsworthy, and governments attempt to use this fact to manage the media and mobilize popular consent and support for their actions. Governments employ various tactics to try to maximize favourable news coverage and minimize unfavourable coverage, such as providing prepackaged news releases, "freezing out" hostile media by limiting access to information, staging events to attract media attention, timing the release of information to improve positive and limit negative coverage, and leaking information as a way of testing the waters or manipulating public expectations (Taras, 1990).

MEDIA EFFECTS AND AUDIENCES

What is most striking about research in the area of media effects is that the predominant focus has been on the socially problematic aspects of the media's relationship with its audiences. There has been little research on the "prosocial" effects of the media, and this focus on the negative dates back to the earliest days of research in the late 1920s and early 1930s (Forman, 1933). Even in the area of child socialization, research has tended to focus on the way the media reproduce and disseminate negative "stereotypes" of, for example, gender roles, the elderly, or racial and ethnic minorities (Buckingham, 1997: 135–36). Research on television and gender role socialization, however, suggests that the relationship is not one of a direct effect. The relationship is mediated by the child's social context and relationships, and the existing dispositions he or she brings to television viewing. When television images diverge from the information about gender roles that the child has

from other sources, their effect may be undercut. Finally, although television may influence attitudes about gender roles, these do not necessarily translate directly into complementary forms of behaviour (Gunter, 1995: 79–93).

We shall concentrate here on two approaches to the study of media effects. The first is the study of *media violence*, and it deals most directly with the negative aspects of the media's influence. The second approach focuses on the process of *audience interpretation*, and it examines the way viewers make sense of what they see and hear on television.

MEDIA VIOLENCE

The effects of portrayals of crime and violence in the media have been a longstanding matter of social concern and have become a major topic of public policy and debate. What this illustrates is the widespread assumption that media violence is a social problem to be understood in terms of its harmful effects. This may be an obvious point but it is worth emphasizing, because it raises the question of how, why, and when particular social phenomena become defined as problems. It also highlights the fact that concerns about the effects of media violence overshadow concerns about its causes. Focusing on effects suggests the need for social control to resolve the problem by limiting or eliminating the supply of violent imagery, and overlooks the need to understand what creates the demand for it.

Early research on the psychological and behavioural effects of the media swung between two poles of opinion. In the 1930s and 1940s, the effects of the media were generally thought to be harmful, direct, and strong. The metaphor of a "bullet" or "hypodermic needle" was commonly used to describe how the media functioned. By the early 1960s, however, the prevailing view had been revised and the media were seen as more innocuous. Media effects were thought to be minimal, to be mediated by a diversity of intervening social and psychological factors, and to be confined largely to reinforcing existing beliefs and habits (Klapper, 1960). What this shift in views demonstrates is that the issue of media effects is a complex one, and this is especially true in the case of media violence. More recent research on the effects of media violence, particularly on TV, has generated much controversy. There has been extensive debate about what constitutes violence (both on TV and in real life), how to measure its extent and intensity, and how to account for possible intervening factors such as personality differences and social environment.

A strong consensus has not emerged from these debates. Most researchers, however, believe that television violence has some real-life effect. Current research can be broken down into two main approaches. The first examines the effect of TV violence on attitudes. The principal perspective here is known as **cultivation analysis**. It stems from the work of George Gerbner and his associates on the way long-term exposure to television tends to cultivate perceptions that are often at odds with objective reality (Gerbner et al., 1994). One of the main arguments of the cultivation perspective is that people who watch a lot of television, and are exposed to more TV violence, perceive society to be more violent and dangerous than it really is—what Gerbner and colleagues call the "'mean world' syndrome" (1994: 30). The implication here is that heavy television viewers are more likely to be fearful about society than those who watch less.

This argument has stimulated considerable research. Some of this research disputes the view that there is a relationship between the amount of TV viewing and beliefs and emotions. Other research provides qualified support, but argues that the relationship is affected by intervening factors such as the type of programming people watch (for an overview see Wober, 1997). A Canadian study suggests that what may be the central issue in cultivation analysis is the fundamental relationship between perceptions of violence and danger on the one hand, and fear on the other. Gosselin and colleagues (1997) found evidence to support the view that heavy TV viewers believe the world is more dangerous than light viewers, regardless of age and sex. However, while they also found that women who thought the world was dangerous were also more likely to be fearful, they did not find this for men. Moreover, even for women the relationship between perception and fear of danger could not be explained empirically by the influence of television. They conclude that "the influence of television viewing seems restricted to beliefs" and does not extend to the emotions we feel about reality (1997: 155).

The second approach focuses on the effects of television on behaviour, and the predominant view is that television does play some limited role in generating real-life violence (Friedrich-Cofer and Huston, 1986; Geen and Thomas, 1986; Huesmann and Malamuth, 1986; Perse, 2001). Those who accept the majority view claim that there is consistent evidence for a link between TV and real-life violence or aggressiveness, though the strength of the evidence varies according to the methodology used. The strongest support for a causal link comes from laboratory experiments (Friedrich-Coffer and Huston, 1986). These usually compare the responses of two randomly chosen groups who watch TV under the same controlled conditions, with the exception that one group watches violent programming and the other, nonviolent. Various measures of aggressiveness have been used to assess the responses, among them physical and verbal aggressiveness, aggressiveness toward both people and objects, actual and fantasized aggressiveness, and reduced self-discipline (lack of patience and perseverance in trying to accomplish tasks or dealing with others). The lab experiments have shown that television violence has an effect on real-life violence *independent* of the intervening factors that have been shown to affect overall levels of aggressiveness (such as personality, age, gender, and social background).

Studies of the effects of television on behaviour have been subject to a variety of criticisms ranging from ideological bias to imprecise concepts to a misplaced focus on individual psychology at the expense of social processes (Gauntlett, 1997). The most significant criticisms, however, have been methodological. Laboratory experiments have been strongly criticized for their inability to replicate the normal social conditions under which people, particularly children, watch TV (McCormack, 1994). Children, like adults, normally watch a mixture of violent and nonviolent programming that blends together in an ongoing flow (Freedman, 1984). Younger children watch more television than older ones, and they also watch it more intermittently because of their shorter attention spans and because they are easily distracted by their social setting. As a result, although the TV set may be on for long periods, the children are not paying attention to it a large part of the time.

Laboratory experiments have also been criticized for providing research subjects with an artificial social environment. At home, if children act aggressively their parents may punish them, or their siblings or friends may retaliate; in most cases, the possibility of such a response is eliminated in the laboratory. Freedman (1984) also points out that many experimental studies entail some intervention on the experimenter's part to provoke aggressive behaviour after the groups have finished watching TV. This can result in what is known as the **sponsor effect**, as research subjects come to feel the experimenter is expecting or condoning aggressive behaviour simply by showing violent images (Felson, 1996). In addition, Freedman points out that laboratory experiments, primarily for ethical reasons, often measure aggressiveness expressed against surrogate objects such as dolls. Since children generally start to recognize the difference between reality and make-believe at about the age of five (McCormack, 1994), the use of surrogate aggression measures casts some doubt on the results. The evidence from experimental studies, finally, is confined to demonstrating only the short-term link between TV violence and aggressiveness; the evidence for a long-term relationship is weaker and less consistent (Freedman, 1984).

Despite these criticisms, the belief that there is a link between TV and aggression has generated several theories about how the relationship functions. One of the most important findings of studies examining TV viewing in natural social settings is that the relationship between TV and real violence is **bidirectional** (Friedrich-Cofer and Huston, 1986); in other words, watching violent TV fosters aggressiveness, but those who prefer to watch violent TV already have more aggressive tendencies. Consequently, a self-reinforcing cycle is established. Most of the theories, however, have focused on explaining the process whereby viewing violent TV generates aggressive behaviour. Two theories are particularly important because they make opposite assumptions about the relationship between the individual and society.

Disinhibition and Desensitization

Disinhibition refers to the possibility that continued exposure to violent imagery may weaken the mechanisms of self-control that an individual acquires through socialization and that discourage or inhibit the use of violence. Related to this notion is the theory of **desensitization,** which suggests that extended exposure to violent imagery has an emotionally numbing effect that leads to increased tolerance and acceptance of violence by others.

Social Learning

In contrast to disinhibition theory, the social learning perspective does not assume that individuals are intrinsically aggressive but argues that aggression, like any other form of behaviour, is learned through

identification with role models. Aggression is the product of socialization, not of the lack of it. TV acts as a socializing agent by providing children with "scripts" for violence. **Scripts for violence** are packages of information about how, when, and why to use violence. The extent to which a child will learn such scripts and reproduce them in real behaviour depends on the child's overall cognitive development and varies with age. The learning and activation of scripts is also influenced by intervening psychological, social, and cultural factors, such as personality, social environment, family situation, and the broader cultural values to which the child is exposed. The effect of TV on aggressiveness is therefore not uniform but selective and variable, and is cumulative over time (Huesmann and Malamuth, 1986).

Whatever the link between images of violence and real-life violence, the relationship remains complex. TV is a heterogeneous medium, and its imagery is usually open to some interpretative variation. The degree of variation depends partly on the **modality** of the image—that is, the extent to which it approximates real life. Animated cartoons, for example, have a low modality; fictional drama has an intermediary level; and news and other "reality" programming have a high modality. By the end of primary socialization, children have normally learned to distinguish levels of modality and understand the narrative meaning of violence. The paradox of television violence may be that high-modality images have the most disturbing effect (Fiske, 1987), since children can recognize and experience images of violence in news and current affairs programming as representations of real-life aggression and suffering. Yet it is lower-modality programs, especially cartoons and crime shows, that have been the main target of concern about the effects of violence.

AUDIENCE RESEARCH: INTERPRETATION AND MEDIA USE

Theories of disinhibition and cognitive learning focus chiefly on the *unconscious* ways in which children are influenced by television. What this overlooks is the way in which individuals also process *consciously* and *actively* what they see and hear. What may appear as simply the unwitting effect of learning violent scripts may be a more complex interaction between the unconscious influences and conscious uses of TV. For example, TV may provide children with scripts that enable them to make sense of and act back upon their own real-life experiences of subordination, dependency, and aggression in such institutions as the family and the school. Hodge and Tripp (1986), for example, discuss how Australian junior high school students used the characters and plot themes from a TV drama about life in a women's prison to understand and act out their own situation at school; they identified with the ideas of being shut in, coerced to attend, separated from friends, punished for not conforming, deprived of rights, and confronted with arbitrary authority figures and meaningless rules.

As this example illustrates, the effects of TV and other media depend on how they are used, as well as how they are related to the other activities, interests, and involvements of everyday life. We use the media to make sense of everyday life and vice versa. Audiences filter, interpret, and often challenge and resist what they see and hear according to their social context, experiences, and beliefs. But these contexts, experiences, and beliefs are themselves influenced by media use. This is the assumption of recent audience research that has grown out of dissatisfaction with the behaviouristic focus found in media violence research.

Since the 1980s, a growing number of researchers have shifted their approach from treating audience members as isolated individuals, and begun to study television use in its "natural" social settings, especially the home. Much of this research has focused on the ways that the use and interpretation of television is structured by gender relations. British research by Morley (1986), for example, found that men and women differed in the way they watched television and what they preferred to watch. Men were more likely to use TV in a planned way, selecting programs beforehand and watching attentively, whereas women had a "much more take-it-or-leave-it attitude" to program choice, and a generally less attentive way of viewing (1986: 153). Men enjoyed sport and information programming, whereas women found little they liked except soap operas. Women were also much less reluctant than men to admit that they talked about TV with their friends and co-workers, which suggests that television plays a greater role in women's patterns of sociability than men's. Morley attributed this to the fact that women felt guilty about watching TV while "surrounded by their domestic obligations" (1986: 155). Making it a topic of conversation gave it greater legitimacy. The idea of

television as a guilty pleasure also surfaced in research by Hobson (1982), who found that women justified watching TV by engaging in domestic tasks like ironing at the same time.

An American study by Press (1991) found that social class and age also affected the way women watched TV. Working-class women, for example, related to programs in terms of their realism vis-à-vis everyday life. This resulted in a more distanced and critical attitude towards TV, and reduced their ability to identify strongly with the characters and personalities. Yet they claimed to value TV more highly than middle-class women for whom realism was less important, and identification with characters and situations was easier. This paradox, Press argues, illustrates how the reality depicted on TV is essentially a middle-class one from which working-class women are separated. Press also found that older women, who were less likely to have worked full-time outside the home, were more likely to relate to TV in "feminist" terms by stressing how TV had broadened their outlook about women's roles. Among younger, particularly working-class, women, however, TV's portrayal of the ideal nuclear family provoked mixed feelings of skepticism and criticism together with sadness and nostalgia (Press, 1991: 176).

Television has been the primary focus of audience research because it has played a central role in the definition of the private sphere in modern society—family, domesticity, gender relations, consumption, and even suburban living—since World War II. During the 1950s and 1960s, the TV set became a virtual family hearth, the central point of the household around which family members gathered to share a common experience. Television helped define the household's social boundaries, while making those boundaries porous by delivering images from the outside world into the heart of the primary social group (Morley, 2000). This symbolic role has since declined for a number of reasons. The common experience has waned as TV has become more commonplace. It has spread to other social settings such as bars, malls, classrooms, and sports stadiums. TV has also become more dispersed within the household (into the kitchen, bedroom, and even bathroom), not only because it is more affordable but also because having more than one set reduces conflict by allowing household members more autonomy (and privacy) vis-à-vis what they watch. Personalized

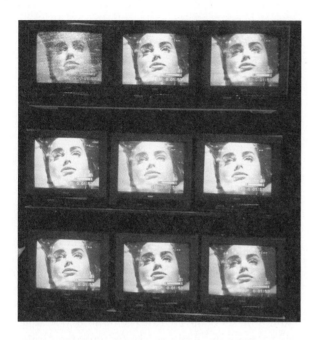

Television dramas generally reproduce gender stratification in occupational roles. Women are more likely to be seen as office workers and in family settings.
SOURCE: Dick Hemingway.

watching has also been encouraged by the proliferation of specialty channels and services catering to particular tastes and interests. And new interactive technologies such as mobile phones and personal computers have also become more accessible, creating a more complex communications environment, which mediates the role and impact that any single medium can have.

These changes have shifted the focus of audience research towards the ways television fits into in this broader media culture and its place in everyday social life. This shift is illustrated by Gillespie's (1995) study of media use by adolescents of Punjabi background in England. The study demonstrates how television is used both to preserve a distinct sense of religious and ethnic customs, identity, and community, and to negotiate individual difference and autonomy in the face of pressures to conform to family expectations. For example, viewing Hindi films on video was a common family practice and was seen as an important way of reinforcing linguistic and cultural identification with India, especially for females, who took on the role of preserving and transmitting cultural traditions more so than males. The young women in Gillespie's study were subject to stronger social control by their families than their brothers were, and this meant that they were

expected to spend more time at home and be more involved in household activities. At the same time, television also exposed these adolescents to the pressures of the wider culture with its emphasis on individualism and consumption. The marketing of products aimed at young consumers, particularly products associated with an American lifestyle such as soft drinks and fast foods, is becoming increasingly globalized. Gillespie found, for example, that TV ads for McDonald's and Coca-Cola as well as the products themselves were consumed as a way of negotiating and accommodating the various identity demands—Punjabi, English, Asian, European, even Anglo-American—these adolescents faced.

THE INTERNET: COMPUTER-MEDIATED COMMUNICATION

The shift in audience research towards an interest in the wider media culture is partly due to the rapid growth and use of the Internet since the early 1990s. The Internet is a term that is now used generically to refer to a variety of different forms of **computer-mediated communication (CMC)** such as e-mail, the World Wide Web, newsgroups, instant messaging, chat forums, MUDs (Multi-User Dungeons or Domains), and MOOs (Multi-User Domains, Object-Oriented). The fact that these have given rise to a host of new terms like *cyberspace*, *life online*, *virtual reality*, *digital culture*, the *electronic highway*, and so on, suggests that the identity of CMC is still uncertain, evolving, and yet to be determined. This uncertainty is compounded by the fact not only that the medium continues to change technologically and socially, but also that research on its structure, use, and effects continues to produce divergent findings and interpretations.

Early research and commentary on the Internet tended to polarize between optimists who saw CMC positively as a vehicle for, among other things, greater democracy, globalism, and identity experimentation, and critics who focused on such negative effects as disengagement from "real" social relations and the spread of offensive images and ideas like pornography and racism. As the Internet has developed, however, research has tended to paint a more mixed and complex picture of its role and how this role may be changing. Macrolevel research has focused mainly on the issue of inequalities in Internet access and differences in overall usage. Microlevel research, on the other hand, has been more concerned with the relationship of reciprocal effects between real and virtual social interaction, that is, with issues of individual and collective identity, community, and social action in situations where people are no longer spatially or even temporally co-present.

THE DIGITAL DIVIDE: CMC AND SOCIAL INEQUALITY

The digital divide is a term that is commonly used to denote the ways in which access to and use of CMC mirror the broader system of social stratification and the class and status divisions it contains. Access to the Internet has grown rapidly since the early 1990s not only in developed nations but also in developing countries. At the same time, there continue to be considerable inequalities in access and differences of use.

Inequalities of Access

As of 2002 about 580 million people are estimated to be online, about 8 percent of the world's population (NUA, 2002). The vast majority of these were located in the affluent, developed world, with Canada, the U.S., and Europe accounting for 63 percent of the total (NUA, 2002). At the same time, the access gap between developed and developing countries was narrowing. In 1997 the U.S. and Canada alone accounted for 63 percent of all online users worldwide; by 2001 this figure had dropped to 35 percent. The biggest proportional increase in users was in Asia and the Pacific, up from 13.5 percent in 1997 to 28 percent in 2001, though the proportion of users in Europe had also grown substantially (Cuneo, 2002, Table 7: 17). The development of online access and use mirrors that of earlier media such as television, originating in developed countries and then spreading to the developing world as the technology becomes more available. In this process a gap also tends to develop between the hardware or technical capacity, and the software or contents of the medium. Just as global television content continues to be dominated by programming produced in the developed world, so the Internet is still dominated by content produced in the developed world. In 2000 the number of Internet hosts based in the top five countries—the U.S., Japan, Canada, Germany, and the U.K.—was 80 percent of all hosts worldwide (Cuneo, 2002: Table 3: 13).

Social class is a strong predictor of who is online. In Canada between 1997 and 1999, Internet access grew for all income levels, but it grew fastest for the top 25 percent, from 53.7 percent to 71.2 percent of households. For the poorest 25 percent of households, on the other hand, access grew much more slowly, from 12.4 percent to 18.8 percent (Dickinson and Ellison, 2000: 7). This means, of course, that the main potential for further growth in access lies in this segment of the population. These inequalities reflect a number of factors. The most obvious one is cost of access, which still acts as a powerful obstacle for poorer Canadians. Occupation is also relevant. Richer households are likely to have adult members who are familiar with CMC because of their work, and this makes home use easier in terms of operating skill. Education, finally, plays an important role. Those with higher levels of education are much more likely to be online, a pattern that holds independently of income and occupation. In 1999 70 percent of Canadian households whose head had a university degree had Internet access, as opposed to less than 12 percent of households whose head had less than high school education (Dickinson and Ellison, 2000: 8). What is also striking is that almost half of the poorest households headed by someone with a university degree had Internet access (Dickinson and Ellison, 2000: 13).

Initial access to the Internet is typically marked by a strong gender bias, with males outnumbering females online by a considerable margin. In 1995, for example, 93 percent of Europeans and 82 percent of Americans online were men (Cuneo, 2002, Table 13: 24). As access and use grow, however, the margin of difference declines. This is particularly evident in Canada and the U.S., the only two countries where women now (slightly) outnumber men online (Cuneo, 2002, Table 14: 25). Similarly, access is also related to race and ethnicity. In the U.S. Internet access is highest in households of Asian and Pacific Island background, followed by whites and African Americans. Access is lowest in Hispanic households, which reflects in part the continuing (though declining) dominance of English as the language of CMC. This pattern of racial and ethnic difference persists when income is taken into account, although the inequality gap does narrow somewhat for higher-income households (Cuneo, 2002, Table 23: 38).

Differences of Use

E-mail is the most commonly used form of CMC among Canadians, but overall use of the Internet is becoming more varied, and increasing for educational, financial, and consumption purposes in particular (see Table 6.3). Like access, use varies by social status and identity. Marketing research, for example, has found that men are more likely to visit "personals" sites than women. Women, on the other hand, are more likely to visit retail and electronic greeting card sites than men (Jupiter Media Metrix, 2002). Research on racial and ethnic differences in Internet use in the U.S. suggests that African and Hispanic Americans are less likely to research or purchase goods online than the general population. In large part this is a result of the fact that at the time of the study these groups had less experience with Internet use; willingness to engage in e-commerce increases with longevity of use. Even when this is taken into account, however, both groups still do less consuming online. On the other hand, African and Hispanic Americans are more likely to use the Internet for purposes of career advancement, family and health information, education, and community and social activities such as participation in chat rooms. Hispanic

Americans are also much more likely to use the Internet to access news, and less inclined to use it for recreational purposes such as hobby information or games (Cultural Access Group, 2001: 18–24).

To a large extent variations in Internet use tend to represent social differences in the real world. The fact that women are more likely to visit retail-oriented Web sites reflects the way that everyday consumption continues to be a greater part of women's family role than men's. Similarly, the greater than average use of the Internet for news by Hispanic Americans can be attributed partly to the fact that a large proportion of the Hispanic population was born outside the U.S. The Internet provides a convenient way to access Spanish-language news from and about "home." Social ties, especially those based on kinship or friendship, are being globalized by CMC. A major reason for the rapid growth of Internet use in Trinidad, for example, is that it has enabled people to keep in frequent and regular contact with family members who have moved abroad (Miller and Slater, 2000). E-mail and instant messaging provide ways in which families can re-create primary social ties in a virtual form. Although differences in Internet use cannot be as easily quantified as variations in access, some researchers believe that they nonetheless represent another dimension of social inequality in CMC—a "second digital divide" (Attewell, 2001).

TABLE 6.3   TYPES OF HOUSEHOLD INTERNET USE, CANADA, 1998 AND 2000

PURPOSE OF USE	2000	1998
E-mail	93.3%	85.6%
General browsing	90.1	78.1
Medical/health information	57.1	42.5
Travel information/arrangements	54.6	N/A*
News	50.8	N/A*
Formal education/training	47.3	29.9
Government information	47.1	36.4
Financial information	46.1	N/A*
Playing games	45.3	34.3
Obtaining/saving music	44.3	N/A*
Electronic banking	36.6	22.9
Chat groups	27.4	25.4
Purchasing goods and services	23.8	10.9

* Not available; category not used in that year's survey.

SOURCE: Adapted from Statistics Canada, *Focus on Culture*, 13 (2), Summer 2001, Table 1, p. 12. Catalogue No. 87-004-XPB.

When, for example, working-class children use the Internet primarily for pleasure, such as playing games, rather than for educational purposes, external class inequalities are reproduced and reinforced. Differences become inequalities inasmuch as they can translate into uneven benefits or advantages in terms of their consequences offline.

VIRTUAL COMMUNITY: THE INTERNET'S IMPACT

As was the case with other media such as radio and TV, the rapid growth of the Internet has created concern that its aggregate social effect would be primarily a negative one. Research, however, has painted a more mixed picture. The negative view was partly borne out by one of the first longitudinal studies of Internet use undertaken in the U.S. between 1995 and 1996 (Kraut et al., 1998). The study discovered that higher Internet use was associated with lower levels of social interaction with family members, a reduction in social ties, and greater feelings of loneliness and depression. The authors dubbed their findings the "Internet Paradox" because they ran counter to expectations. Other studies at that time also arrived at findings that suggest Internet use leads to greater anomie and social disengagement (for a review see DiMaggio et al., 2001).

In a subsequent follow-up study, however, Kraut and colleagues (2002) found that the negative consequences had disappeared. Internet use was positively correlated with social involvement and psychological well-being, but heavy use continued to be associated with higher levels of personal stress and lowered commitment to the local community. Though the study was not designed to account for these changes, the authors suggest that growing familiarity with CMC and changes in the Internet itself are the likeliest explanation for these changes. Again, other research has also found that Internet use can enhance social involvement. Drawing on Wellman's studies of social networks in Toronto, Wellman and Gulia (1999) argue that **virtual communities** are part of a broader shift in modern/postmodern society towards social ties and relationships based on shared interests and aspirations rather than shared locality (neighbourhood) or ancestry (kinship). As such, they can be as socially and emotionally supportive for their members as communities based on face-to-face interac-

tion. Even online forums such as newsgroups that are designed primarily to provide factual or practical information can have socially supportive side effects, as they act as a forum in which participants exchange views and feelings about common concerns. Although virtual communities lack the kind of interpersonal cues available in face-to-face social relationships, this lack can actually promote interaction by removing risks and status or identity barriers that might normally inhibit the successful development of real world ties. In this respect, the Internet can act as an example of what Granovetter (1973) has characterized as the "strength of weak ties," that is, social ties that are not necessarily intimate, intense, or extensive in scope yet function and persist because they can rely on the particular interests and commitment of their members.

The structure of virtual communities has been a topic of particular interest in Internet research. Real communities obviously differ fundamentally from virtual communities inasmuch as people cannot simply log off and walk away from them (Postman, 1992; Watson, 1997). Nonetheless, much of the research has shown the similarities and parallels between the two. We will focus here on two aspects: conflict and social control, and the socialization of newcomers to CMC forums such as newsgroups.

Because online interaction is more anonymous, often asynchronous, and almost entirely based on discursive interaction alone, many of the mechanisms of social control that function in offline communities are weak or absent. It was partly for this reason that the Internet acquired an early reputation for individualistic attitudes and verbal aggression or "flaming," especially in fantasy- or game-oriented forms of CMC, such as adventure MUDs where participants adopt imaginary identities and act out fictitious narratives in which aggression towards others may be acceptable. Despite the emphasis on imagination and fantasy, however, MUDs are usually organized in a stratified way (Reid, 1999). Interaction is structured through a hierarchy of positions with unequal capacities, skills, and knowledge. This gives rise to a virtual "power elite" that can control the domain's programming and the terms on which other users can be involved (Cherny, 1999).

Larger-scale MUDs usually have a more elaborate, formal system of rules and controls, but in smaller-scale ones, where networks of interaction are denser, informal social controls can function effectively when conflict or other disruptions arise. In her study of a MUD community, Cherny (1999), for example, found that gossip distributed through private online conversations acted as a common form of social control by building networks of solidarity, reaffirming shared values and goals, and excluding and ostracizing those seen as a threat to the community. In a similar vein, Baym (2000) discusses how humour, particularly sarcasm, helped to reproduce solidarity among core members of a newsgroup devoted to a TV soap opera. The target of the sarcasm was not other newsgroup participants but the writers of the soap who were mocked for the show's flaws and for underestimating the intelligence of the fans. When disputes arose, those involved tried to minimize personal offence and reaffirm affiliation with one another. Disagreements were usually expressed in a qualified way by, for example, stressing that they were only partial, reframing the terms of the issue, or prefacing critical remarks with an apology. When informal controls are ineffective, however, power-holders usually have to act to limit disruptive effects and sanction offenders through their capacity to structure the terms of participation. Reid (1999) cites one instance of "virtual violence" that led to a policy of having existing users vouch for any new users, and having all users provide the MUD administrator with their legal names and phone numbers. Resorting to offline reality became the way to safeguard online conformity and reassert some degree of group closure.

The extent to which social closure can be achieved in virtual communities is nonetheless problematic. Because involvement is voluntary and based on shared interests rather than other criteria, Internet forums such as MUDs, newsgroups, and chat rooms experience a constant turnover of users. While many of these forums have a core group of regular participants, other users may be involved more sporadically, and, in the case of newsgroups, some may simply browse without posting contributions to the discussions ("lurkers") or participate simply to be disruptive ("trollers"). The increasing number of new users or "newbies" has made socialization into "netiquette"—the norms, expectations, and practices of online interaction—particularly significant. This includes socialization into the specialized terminology and linguistic codes that participants use, just as in any real-world subculture, to conduct their interactions with

one another. In fact because virtual communities lack the material props of offline communities (such as physical objects, spatial surroundings, and bodily gestures) and rely so heavily on language as the means of interaction, knowing the terminology and codes takes on a particular significance as a mark of community membership.

In the case of Baym's (2000) soap opera newsgroup, the influx of new posters and the intensification of flaming gave rise to an institutionalized response in the form of the "Newbie Sponsorship Program" (NSP). The NSP, created by one of the earlier core participants, operates through a Web site that provides information on the newsgroup's conventions and traditions, as well as advice to newbies such as "lurk first" and "attack ideas, not people." Lurking can act as a form of anticipatory socialization by allowing newbies to familiarize themselves with the group's practices and language codes before becoming active posters. Similarly, advising people to criticize ideas rather than their source is a way to prevent disputes from becoming personalized and undermining the friendliness and egalitarian character that members see as an appealing quality of the newsgroup. The Web site also offers to put newbies in contact with a sponsor to act as a personal socializing agent into the group. Many of the group's participants saw the NSP as a positive development that had helped smooth the entry of new users. At the same time, it had not eliminated tensions within the group that had arisen as participation had grown, earlier participants had dropped out, practices had been challenged, and cliques had emerged based on whose posts were deemed worthy of serious response. In virtual communities anyone can have a voice, but not everyone has his or her voice acknowledged and validated to the same extent—if at all. Symbolic resources replace material resources as the mechanism of inequality and influence.

Virtual communities resemble real communities inasmuch as they entail not only shared values and a sense of belonging but also a common project or purpose (Baym, 2000). The shared interests on which these projects are based, however, originate mainly in the offline world even if, as in the case of Baym's soap opera fans, they are situated in media culture more generally. People bring their offline interests, needs, and aspirations to CMC, just as they do to other communications media. By the same token, relationships and knowledge acquired through CMC can spill over into the world of face-to-face reality. The exchanges that occur between the real and virtual worlds is mediated by structures of social relevance, that is, how well experiences in one sphere pertain to interests and concerns in the other (on relevance structures, see Schutz, 1970). This means that virtuality and reality are not so much worlds apart as, to borrow McLuhan's (1964) term, extensions of one another. The Internet is not a radical alternative to—or even escape from—social reality so much as a way of complementing and supplementing it (DiMaggio et al., 2001). And just as social reality has to be constructed and accomplished through ongoing interaction and negotiation, so too does virtuality.

SUMMARY

1. Canadian newspapers have high levels of ownership concentration, are usually part of larger multimedia chains, and function largely as local monopolies. The factor that has the greatest impact on news content, however, is dependency on advertising. In fact, the survival prospects of papers with an alternative or more politically radical view of the news are limited because of it.

2. In the case of television, advertising dependency, the high costs of production, and audience preferences mean that much of the programming Canadians watch is foreign, primarily American. This is especially so for drama and sitcoms, and particularly among anglophones. Nationalists view the situation as a "sellout" of Canadian culture, whereas postmodernists see it as part of the general effect of globalization and do not believe that it undermines the institutional structure of Canadian society.

3. Conservatives claim that news coverage has a left-liberal political bias that is unrepresentative of society's mainstream. Critical theorists argue that news coverage is ideologically conservative, in that it defines reality from the perspective of dominant ideology and views events and issues through the lens of social control. At the same time, some critical theorists argue that the media are not completely closed to alternative voices and viewpoints, and that these can challenge, to some extent, the hegemony of dominant social groups and interests.

4. The majority of observers believe that there is a causal link between television and violent behaviour, but the studies that support this view have been criticized on the grounds of flawed methodology. Moreover, the majority view is split on the issue of how television causes aggression. Some argue that watching TV counteracts the effects of socialization by weakening self-control; others believe that it in fact socializes children in the use of violence.

5. Studies of audiences indicate that TV viewing and the responses to it vary according to gender. Men and women tend to prefer different types of programming. Men are more likely to watch attentively and privately, whereas women watch in a more interactive, social way. Women also tend to be more open about their TV viewing and use TV as a topic of casual social interaction and conversation

6. While early views about the development of computer-mediated communication and the Internet tended to polarize between optimists and pessimists, recent research has yielded a more complex, balanced view. Inequalities of access (especially globally) and differences of use continue to persist; however, the former show signs of declining as the technology becomes less costly. Research on the impact of the Internet shows that virtual communities develop normative structures like real communities, and function as sources of identity and social solidarity. For the most part, however, life online supplements and complements real world social interaction and involvement rather than replacing it.

QUESTIONS TO CONSIDER

1. Why is news mainly bad news? Is this because of a bias on the part of the news media towards issues and events that are negative, or is there an appetite for bad news in society generally?

2. Why, despite the lack of strong, consistent, and unequivocal evidence to confirm a direct link between violence on TV and in real life, are many people convinced that such a link does exist? Television also contains images and messages that are positive (in the normative or ethical sense). Why do we not assume these have just as much effect as images of violence?

3. Critics of media imperialism often point to Canada as an example of a country overwhelmed by American popular culture—movies, magazines, music, and television. What is so appealing about American popular culture, not only in Canada but in other countries as well? In what respects is U.S. popular culture specifically American, and in what respects is it now simply the leading culture in a world moving toward cultural globalization?

4. Do you think that, in the long term, the convergence of communications technologies such as television, telephones, and computers will result in a society where people become increasingly isolated in their homes—working at home, shopping at home, being entertained, informed, and schooled at home—with little reason or desire to interact directly with the outside world? Do you see any factors or developments that might counteract the effects of technological convergence?

5. Alternative news sources often find it difficult to achieve legitimacy because the media represent them as voices of grievance and complaint or as agents of social disruption. What strategies do alternative sources use in the relations with the media to try to offset this and increase their credibility and social impact? To what extent does the social identity of the alternative source make a difference in this respect? Will the growth of the Internet make it easier for alternative viewpoints to reach a wider audience?

GLOSSARY

Alternative news sources are representatives of social movements and social advocacy and activism groups whose viewpoints often diverge from those of dominant social groups and their representatives.

Alternative viewpoints are interpretations that differ from the meanings contained in society's dominant ideology, representing compromises between the latter and the meanings promoted by oppositional viewpoints. See also *oppositional viewpoints.*

The **bidirectional effect** is a self-reinforcing cycle in which television violence contributes to aggressive behaviour, and aggressive tendencies lead to a preference for violent television.

Communication derives from the Latin, meaning "to bring together or unify"; the term is now used to denote the transmission of knowledge, ideas, meanings, and understandings.

Computer-mediated communication (CMC) refers to the social interaction and/or information gathering using computer technology. It's now commonly referred to as the Internet.

The **critical perspective** takes the view that the media reinforce dominant ideology and the position of the dominant class and other powerful groups. The theory has two variants: one sees this process as more open to challenge and resistance than does the other.

Cultivation analysis examines the long-term effects of television viewing on beliefs about social reality. Heavy TV viewers tend to see the world as more violent and dangerous than it really is, and tend to be more fearful.

Cultural imperialism is a situation in which one society's media exert an overwhelming and unilateral influence over another society's culture.

Desensitization refers to the effect of prolonged exposure to television violence that makes people indifferent toward, or tolerant of, real violence by others.

Disinhibition refers to the effect of prolonged exposure to television violence that weakens the mechanisms of self-control acquired through socialization, and thereby contributes to aggressive behaviour.

Displacement is the consequence of devoting time to watching television that involves reducing the amount of time spent on other activities, such as reading or interacting socially.

The **dominant ideology** comprises the interests, perspectives, viewpoints, and understandings of the dominant class and other powerful groups.

Fragmentation, at the level of the individual, refers to the differentiation of social identities and experiences; at the collective level, it refers to the increasing specialization and segmentation of audiences in terms of media tastes and interests.

Framing is the process of defining the boundaries of a representation and the organization of its contents. Framing pertains to the selection of what is included and excluded, what is accentuated and what is played down.

Hegemony is the exercise by the dominant class of cultural leadership by using the media to naturalize and universalize dominant ideology and to absorb the challenge of alternative and oppositional points of view.

Horizontal consolidation is the coordination of different outlets in a media chain for purposes of sharing resources.

Interactive media refers to technologically mediated communication where the flow of messages can be two-way, back and forth between actors who transmit to as well as receive messages from one another (e.g., the telephone).

Mass communication refers to technologically mediated communication in which the flow of messages is largely one-way, from a definite point of transmission to a large, anonymous, dispersed audience of receivers (e.g., radio or television).

Media, which is the plural of medium, comes from the Latin, meaning "middle." The term refers to television, radio, newspapers, magazines, and movies, as means of communication.

Modality is the degree to which a media image approximates real life; for example, an animated cartoon has a low modality, whereas news footage has a high modality.

Multimedia chains are corporations that own and control a string of different media operations or outlets in different fields of mass communication, such as television, radio, and magazines.

News values are criteria such as immediacy, personalization, and extraordinariness, in terms of which news media define and represent events and issues.

Official news sources are authoritative voices that the media use to define the basic meaning of an event or issue—for example, politicians, police officers, and professional experts.

Oppositional viewpoints are used to interpret reality in terms that contradict the meanings of dominant ideology, representing the experiences of subordinated groups against those of the powerful.

Ordinary news sources are news sources that do not have an organizational or group affiliation, such as eyewitnesses or victims of news events and issues.

Representation is the use of language, visual images, or other means of communication to portray something in a coherent and meaningful way that others can understand.

Scripts for violence refer to the packaging of images of violence on television in a way that gives people, particularly children, a model of when, where, and how to use violence in real life.

Space-biased media are media that enable communication over extended distances, such as print, radio, or television. The messages, however, are not long lasting. Space-biased media promote territorial expansion together with secular beliefs and military–political forms of power.

The **sponsor effect** refers to the potential biasing effect of researchers in laboratory experiments on the effects of media violence. By showing violent images, researchers may give the impression to research subjects that they are condoning aggressive or other antisocial responses.

Technological convergence is the integration of different communications technologies, such as television and telephony, into a single system that obliterates the distinction between mass communications and telecommunications.

Time-biased media are media that are durable (the messages last over time), but are relatively immobile, such as stone carvings or inscriptions on clay tablets. Time-biased media promote a sense of tradition as well as religious forms of belief and power.

Vertical integration refers to a media corporation's ownership and control of the means of production at all stages of the production process—for example, from producing newsprint to delivering newspapers.

Virtual communities are long-term forms of social association and interaction based on computer-mediated communication.

SUGGESTED READING

Baum, N.K. (2000). *Tune In, Log On: Soaps, Fandom, and Online Community*. Thousand Oaks, CA: Sage Publications. This study of an Internet newsgroup devoted to discussion of TV soap operas shows how new and old media intersect. Baum illustrates the ways that Internet communication can be used to create a sense of virtual community based on a common interest in TV entertainment. The study also focuses on the threats and challenges to virtual communities, and how these lead to change in the dynamics of online communication.

Collins, R. (1990). *Culture, Communication and National Identity: The Case of Canadian Television*. Toronto: University of Toronto Press. Examines the effect of the Americanization of Canadian television (especially drama) from the perspective of increasing globalization, and argues that the effects are not as harmful to national identity as nationalists assume.

Cooper, B. (1994). *Sins of Omission: Shaping the News at CBC TV*. Toronto: University of Toronto Press. This analysis of CBC TV news, with particular attention to foreign coverage, finds a bias in the reporting that favours left-wing political regimes and movements. The obverse face of this bias is that the violent or repressive actions of these regimes and movements are overlooked or underreported. Cooper is critical of the CBC for being more concerned with promoting "progressive opinion" than with "the provision of reliable information about the world." (p. 221).

Morley, D. (2000). *Home Territories: Media, Mobility and Identity*. London and New York: Routledge. A panoramic survey of (mainly European) theory and research on how different media are used to negotiate identity, social difference, and a sense of "home" in the context of increasing globalization and the emerging conflicts around ethnicity, culture, and politics that globalization is generating.

Taras, D. (1999). *Power and Betrayal in the Canadian Media*. Peterborough, ON: Broadview Press. An analysis of the Canadian media in light of the impact of such factors as corporate concentration, audience fragmentation, and technological convergence on the role of the media in promoting the public interest and fostering democratic debate. The author sounds a critical note, warning that these changes, together with "the growing international commercial culture," are making the media "less open and diverse" despite their continuing expansion (pp. 221, 219).

CHAPTER SEVEN

RELIGION

In this chapter you will learn that:

- Religion is something that can be examined by social scientists, and has been studied from the beginnings of sociology.

- Religion has both individual and social components—people display a wide range of levels of commitment, but groups play a major role in instilling and sustaining personal religiosity.

- Since religious groups are organizations, they can best be understood using organizational concepts and frameworks.

- For the vast majority of people, religious commitment and involvement are rooted in social institutions, particularly the family.

- Religion's influence on individuals tends to be noteworthy but not unique, while its broader influence in most societies supports social structure and culture.

- Despite the numerical problems of some groups, religion's future seems secure, grounded in ongoing spiritual interests and needs.

REGINALD W. BIBBY

UNIVERSITY OF LETHBRIDGE

INTRODUCTION

Religion has been present in virtually every society. Its influence has varied from culture to culture and from century to century. In different places and in different eras, religion has known both dark and golden ages.

The early social scientists were convinced that religion's days were numbered, that it would just be a short time before it was discarded in favour of science. Through the 1960s, the widespread consensus was that religion's influence was declining and that Canadians and people in other technologically advanced countries were leaving religion behind.

Those observers are proving to be wrong. In the first years of the twenty-first century, religion lives on, embraced by significant numbers of people in virtually all cultures. Moreover, there are claims and indications that, if anything, spirituality is on the upswing in many parts of the world, including North America, Russia, and Asia. And events such as the terrorist attacks on September 11, 2001, along with ongoing conflict in a variety of places around the globe that frequently seems to have a religious component, serve to remind us that religion is very much alive, potentially a source of division, yet also something to which millions of people turn when they seek solace, meaning, and hope.

In this chapter, I will examine what some of the early social scientists had to say about religion and then show how sociologists study religion in both its individual and organized forms. I will clarify what sociologists mean by religion and then analyze "how much of it" we have in Canada, what kinds of factors contribute to people being religious, and the influence that religion has on both individuals and societies. I will also reflect on what religious developments can be expected in the foreseeable future.

Although I will take other societies, especially the United States, into account, I will pay particular attention to Canada. Why? Because, until recently, we have known very little about religion in our own society. And, to be honest, I have made religion in Canada my primary research interest now for a number of decades and I am eager to tell you what I've been finding.

Contrary to the opinion of some people, religious belief is not disappearing in Canada. In fact, in urban areas most people have many options for worship.
SOURCE: Dick Hemingway.

SOCIOLOGY AND RELIGION

In using the scientific method of investigation to study social life, sociologists seek to understand social reality by relying on what can be perceived through the senses. Proponents of religion, in contrast, have traditionally asserted that the world we know through the senses is only part of a greater reality that, because of the limitations of perception, can be known only through faith.

Science and religion, then, approach the world and how it is known in different ways. In principle, the two approaches are compatible. Science limits itself to what is perceivable, and religion maintains that reality includes the nonperceivable. Sociologists therefore cannot address such claims as the existence of God or miraculous healing. But, as Émile Durkheim (1965 [1912]: 479) pointed out, religion "can affirm nothing that [science] denies, deny nothing that it affirms." Conflict between science and religion arises only when they invade each other's territory—for example, when scientists refute the plausibility of answered prayer, or "Biblical creationists" want equal time in the science classroom with proponents of evolution.

Although sociology cannot assess the accuracy of supernatural claims, it can explore issues relating to the social aspects of those claims: who believes what; the nature and extent of spiritual needs; involvement in religious groups; why some people tend to be more committed than others; and the consequences, for individuals and societies, of people being religious. "The essence of religion," said Max Weber, is not a concern of sociologists; "we make it our task to study the conditions and effects of a particular type of social behaviour" (1963: 1). For our purposes, whether religious beliefs are true is not as important as whether they are *believed* to be true, and therefore have potential consequences for individual and social life.

THEORETICAL TRADITIONS

The sociology of religion has been strongly influenced by three early theorists: Karl Marx, Émile Durkheim, and Max Weber.

MARX AND CONFLICT

Karl Marx worked from the assumption that religion is a human creation. He maintained, however, that it plays an important role in compensating people who are economically deprived. Its very presence symbolizes the inclination of people to reinterpret rather than change their oppressive conditions. Using the language of the day, Marx (1970 [1843]: 131) wrote: "Man makes religion; religion does not make man." He argued that man has "found only his own reflection in the fantastic reality of heaven, where he sought a supernatural being," and that being religious characterized "the self-consciousness and self-esteem of a man who has either not yet gained himself or has lost himself again."

Central to Marx's thought on religion was the belief that religion serves to hold in check the explosive tensions of a society. Aligned with the interests of the dominant few, religion soothes the exploited majority like an anesthetic—"the opium of the people" (Marx, 1970 [1843]: 131)—blinding them to the inequalities at hand and bottling up their creative energies. Consequently, those who hold power encourage religious belief among the masses as a subtle tool in the process of economic exploitation. So intertwined are society and religion, maintained Marx, that attacks on society are often attacks on religion. Historically, attacks on feudalism were, above

all, attacks on the church, while revolutionary social and political doctrines were simultaneously regarded as theological heresies (Marx and Engels, 1964: 132).

Marx saw religion as an inadequate salve for a sick society. When the sickness is remedied, there will be no need for the salve. Accordingly, he viewed his criticism of religion as an attempt to expose the chain that was binding people, so that it could be removed. Freed from the panacea of religion, individuals would be able "to think, act, and fashion their reality with illusions lost and reason regained" (Marx, 1970 [1843]: 132).

DURKHEIM AND COLLECTIVITY

Émile Durkheim was the son of a rabbi, who was raised in a Catholic educational tradition. He himself was an atheist and an anticleric, who believed that a scientific understanding of society has the potential to raise the quality of social life to utopian heights.

In his classic work *The Elementary Forms of the Religious Life* (1965 [1912]), Durkheim argued that religion's origin is social. People who live in community come to share common sentiments, and as a result a **collective conscience** is formed. It is experienced by each member, yet is greater than the sum of the individual consciences. When individuals have the feeling of being in the presence of a higher power, the experience *is* real. But what they actually are experiencing is the collective conscience. So vivid is the experience that people feel the need to label it. In reality, Durkheim asserted, "God" is the group experiencing itself.

Once proponents of religion experience such an alleged supernatural reality, they proceed to designate some objects as **sacred** and others as **profane**. Christians, for example, have accorded special status to the cross, the Bible, and holy water, in contrast to most everything else. In Durkheim's view, religious beliefs articulate the nature of the sacred and its symbols, and religious rites provide guidelines as to how people should act in the presence of the sacred.

Since all groups feel the need to uphold and reaffirm their collective sentiments, people come together as a church. According to Durkheim (1965 [1912]: 62–63), "the idea of religion is inseparable from that of the Church," since it is "an eminently collective thing." Even when religion seems to be entirely a matter of individual conscience, it still is nourished by social sources. Besides meeting needs at the individual level, he claimed, religion creates and reinforces social solidarity. Collective life is thus both the source and the product of religion. Accordingly, he defined religion as "a unified system of beliefs and practices relative to sacred things ... which unite into one single moral community called a Church, all those who adhere to them" (Durkheim, 1965 [1912]: 62).

Durkheim (1965 [1912]: 475) observed that "we are going through a stage of transition and moral mediocrity." He readily acknowledged the decline of traditional Christianity. However, he did not think that religion would disappear. Although the forms of expression might change, Durkheim predicted that the social sources that give rise to religion will remain and, with them, religion. He also contended that there will always be a place for religious explanations. Science is fragmentary and incomplete, Durkheim wrote, advancing too slowly for impatient people. Religion will therefore continue to have an important "gap-filling" role.

WEBER AND IDEAS

Max Weber's interest in the origin and nature of modern capitalism led him into extensive debate with Marx's ideas, and stimulated much of his work in the sociology of religion. Unlike Marx and Durkheim, Weber was not interested in the question of whether religion is ultimately true or false. Rather, he maintained that religion, in addition to having a supernatural component, is largely oriented toward this world. As a result, religious ideas and behaviour should frequently be evident in everyday conduct. In *The Protestant Ethic and the Spirit of Capitalism* (1958 [1904–1905]), for example, Weber examined the possibility that the moral tone that characterizes capitalism in the Western world—the **Protestant ethic**—can be traced back to the influence of the Protestant Reformation. He hoped that his work would contribute "to the understanding of the manner in which ideas become effective forces in history" (Weber, 1958 [1904–1905]: 90).

Weber maintained that ideas, regardless of whether they are objectively true or false, represent one's definition of reality, and therefore have the potential to influence behaviour. Accordingly, Weber emphasized the need to interpret action by understanding the motives of the actor (a method he called

Verstehen, or understanding). To achieve such awareness, he said, one should place oneself in the roles of those being studied.

Weber understood the need to study diverse societies in order to examine culture's influence on religion. He therefore embarked on a comparative study of religion. In *Sociology of Religion* (1963), Weber noted that god-conceptions are strongly related to the economic, social, and political conditions in which people live. The gods of light and warmth and of rain and earth have been closely related to practical economic needs; heavenly gods that rule the celestial order have been related to the more abstract problems of death and fate. In political conquest, the gods of the conquered are fused with the gods of the conqueror, and reappear with revised characteristics. Furthermore, the growth of **monotheism** (belief in one god) is related to goals of political unification.

Beyond the social sources of the gods, Weber dealt with such major themes as religious organization and the relationship between religion and social class. He reflected on religious leadership and the important process whereby a personal following is transformed into a permanent congregation, which he referred to as "routinization." He noted that different groups in society vary in their inclination to be religious: Peasants are religious when they are threatened; the nobility find religion beneath their honour; the middle class sees religion largely in ethical terms; the working class supplants religion with other ideologies.

To look at Marx, Durkheim, and Weber is to do more than look at the past. As we will see, their influence can be seen in the work of sociologists studying religion right through today.

THE NATURE OF RELIGION

The term "religion" is widely used, but obviously people have different ideas in mind when they use it. In studying religion, it therefore is important to clarify what we mean by the term. A number of years ago, Charles Glock and Rodney Stark (1965) offered some thoughts that continue to be helpful. They pointed out that, in defining religion for social scientific purposes, we should begin by recognizing that humans develop systems of meaning to interpret the world. Some systems—commonly referred to as "religions," including Christianity, Judaism, and Islam—have a supernatural referent. Others, such as a science-based system (scientism) or political "isms" (communism, fascism), do not. These latter systems, they suggested, might be viewed as human-centred or **humanist perspectives**, in contrast to *religious perspectives*, which are succinctly referred to here as **religions**.

The two types of perspectives differ on one critical point: Religion is concerned with discovering life's meaning, and humanist perspectives are concerned with making life meaningful. Humanist Bertrand Russell stated the difference well: "I do not think that life in general has any purpose. It just happened. But individual human beings have purposes" (in Cogley, 1968: 171). Religious perspectives suggest that our existence has meaning, preceding that which we, as humans, decide to give it. In contrast, humanist perspectives assume that life has no "ultimate meaning" and therefore focus on giving it meaning.

PERSONAL RELIGIOSITY

Individuals vary in their levels of religious commitment. Thus, a major issue in the scientific study of religion is how to define and measure **personal religiosity**.

Most of the early religion research used one of three basic indicators to determine the religiosity of a person. All three assumed group involvement: identification, membership, and attendance. People were asked questions such as "What is your religious preference?" "Do you belong to a congregation?" and "How often do you attend worship services?" People who indicated that they had a religious preference, belonged to a local group, or attended services with regularity were regarded as religious.

Simply knowing that someone is a "Protestant," however, tells us very little about the person's actual commitment to the Christian faith. Similarly, mere identification with religious cultural groups such as Jews, Hindus, and Hutterites hardly guarantees that a person takes religion seriously. Likewise, church and temple members may be active or inactive, committed or uncommitted. And service attendance, while measuring participation in a group, excludes people who—by our definition—could be very committed yet not be active in a religious organization.

Since the 1960s, social scientists have responded to the limitations of these three measures by viewing religious commitment as having a variety of dimensions. In one of the more helpful frameworks devised, Stark and Glock (1968) suggested that the religions of the world typically expect their most devoted followers to hold key beliefs, engage in certain practices, have supernatural experiences, and be aware of the central tenets of their faiths. Stark and Glock refer to these belief, practice, experience, and knowledge components of commitment as **dimensions of religiosity**. It is not enough to believe *or* practise *or* experience *or* know; all four traits are expected of the committed.

The ongoing Project Canada national surveys, which were initiated in 1975, have been providing pioneering, comprehensive data on personal religiosity in this country. The surveys have found that Canadians exhibit relatively high levels of religious belief, practice, experience, and knowledge (see Table 7.1). Indeed, some eight in ten say they believe in God, seven in ten maintain there is life after death, six in ten acknowledge that they pray privately at least once a month, and about five in ten think they have experienced the presence of God. About half also exhibit some basic knowledge of Christianity, Judaism, and Islam.

On the surface, then, early twenty-first-century Canadians seem to be a fairly religious people. However, the surveys have also found that while around 50 percent claim to be committed to Christianity or another religion, less than half of the committed demonstrate the belief, practice, experience, and knowledge characteristics that Stark and Glock saw as central to commitment. Among the other 50 percent of Canadians, about three in ten indicate that they are interested in but not committed to any religion, and the remaining two in ten simply say that they are not religious (Bibby, 1993, 2002). According to the 2000 Project Canada survey, only 21 percent of Canadians say that religion is "very important" to them, with most having fairly conventional ideas of religion in mind. Regional variations are striking, with the levels ranging from a high of almost 40 percent in the Atlantic region, through 25 percent in Ontario and the three Prairie provinces, to a low of just under 15 percent in both Quebec and British Columbia. See Box 7.1 on page 160 for a glimpse of how various Canadians view life after death.

In short, isolated religious beliefs and practices known as "religion à la carte" abound. But the majority of Canadians are not strongly committed to

TABLE 7.1   RELIGIOUS COMMITMENT ALONG FOUR DIMENSIONS, CANADA: 2000

DIMENSION	RESPONSE	PERCENTAGE
Believe in God	Yes, I definitely do	49%
	Yes, I think so	32
	No, I don't think so	13
	No, I definitely do not	6
Believe in life after death	Yes, I definitely do	31
	Yes, I think so	37
	No, I don't think so	22
	No, I definitely do not	10
Practise private prayer	Daily	28
	Several times a week	11
	About once a week	8
	About once a month	9
	Hardly ever/never	44
Experience God	Yes, I definitely have	20
	Yes, I think so	27
	No, I don't think I have	31
	No, I definitely have not	22
Knowledge	The first book in the Old Testament? (Genesis)	46
	The name of the sacred book of Islam (Koran)	44
	Who denied Jesus three times? (Peter)	42

SOURCE: Compiled from Reginald W. Bibby, Project Canada 2000 National Survey. Carried out in 2000.

traditional expressions of religion. As we will see, such patterns are hardly unique to Canada.

COLLECTIVE RELIGIOSITY

It is frequently argued that one can be religious without having anything to do with religious organizations such as churches or synagogues. However, most social scientists, beginning with Durkheim, would maintain that personal religiosity is highly dependent on **collective religiosity**, or group support of some kind. Such dependence is not unique to religion. It stems, rather, from a basic fact of life: The ideas we hold tend to come from our interaction with other people. However creative we might like to think we are, the fact is that most of the ideas we have can be traced to the people with whom we have been in contact—family, friends, teachers, authors. Moreover, if we are to retain our ideas, they must continuously be endorsed by at least a few other people. In modern societies where religious ideas compete with

a wide variety of other ideas, it is essential for the maintenance of religion that religious groups exist to transmit and sustain religious ideas.

The Church–Sect Typology

Those who have examined religious groups in predominantly Christian settings have recognized two major kinds of organizations. First, there are numerically dominant groupings—the Roman Catholic Church in medieval Europe, the Church of England, the so-called mainline denominations in Canada and the United States (Anglican, United, Presbyterian, Lutheran), and so on. Second, smaller groups have broken away from the dominant bodies. For example, in the sixteenth century, "protestant" groups including the Church of England broke away from the Roman Catholic Church; but Methodists in turn broke away from the Church of England, and the Salvation Army emerged as a breakaway group from the Methodists. Today, additional "emerging" groups

MAYBE IT'S AN ENERGY THING

"My energy will remain in some way, though I'm not sure in what form. It may dissipate or it may remain intact as a unit waiting for another opportunity to become something living again. Either way my life energy is a part of the ongoing cycle of energy that is life."

—A 31-year-old Ottawa writer, raised Catholic and interested in spirituality, she now is not practising any particular religion.

"What is it that makes a human being go? It is energy. And the physicians tell us that energy never vanishes. So when the body is worn out and dies, where does the energy go? You should never rule out any possibility."

—Robertson Davies in 1994; unsure as to what happens after death, he maintained we need to keep our minds open (Todd, 1996: 138).

SOME ARE COMBINING A NUMBER OF IDEAS

"I like to believe my spirit will go to heaven, and that perhaps spirits become angels, or are re-incarnated. There is something very powerful out there, and I know somehow, we will all be a part of it."

—A Roman Catholic banker, 42; she lives in a small city in Alberta.

"I had a near death experience as a teenager that changed my life. As I burst into the white light I was completely surrounded by a strong, soothing, serene, powerful presence. I felt loved unconditionally, in my true essence, part of the Oneness."

—A 59-year-old Dartmouth court worker; raised Roman Catholic, she hasn't been to church since she was 27.

OTHERS SAY DEATH IS THE END

"Only people who knew me will remember me. I think you are just gone."

—A Vancouver teacher, 34; she says she is United but does not attend church.

"My person shall be gone and my building materials will be recycled."

—A Quebec professor, 64; he describes himself as a practising Catholic.

"Nothing. Worms."

—A 33-year-old urban planner on the west coast who says he is an atheist.

"I certainly don't [believe in an afterlife]. It's just the same as when you squish an ant on the sidewalk. No one thinks ants go to ant heaven. It's sheer hubris that we would have the gall to think there's an afterlife for creatures like us."

—Author W.P. Kinsella, whose works include Shoeless Joe (Todd, 1996: 26).

SOURCE: Drawn from Reginald Bibby, *Restless Gods*, 2002: 132.

include an array of Baptist and Pentecostal denominations and congregations that are found in virtually every North American city.

From this pattern of dominant groups and breakaway groups, sociologists who are trying to make sense of religious groups developed an analytical scheme known as the **church–sect typology**. This framework attempted to describe the central characteristics of these two types of organizations, as well as account for the origin and development of sects.

In perhaps its earliest formulation, Max Weber distinguished between church and sect primarily on the basis of theology (churches emphasize works, sects stress faith) and relationship to society (for churches, accommodation; for sects, separation). Weber noted the irony in the sect's development: Initially a spin-off from an established church, the sect gradually evolves into a church itself (Gerth and Mills, 1958). The sect is at first characterized by spontaneity and enthusiasm. In time, however, these traits give way to routinization and institutionalization.

Although the church–sect typology has been used extensively, alternative ways of understanding religious groups have become increasingly popular.

Organizational Approaches

In sociological terms, religious organizations are no different from other social organizations. Therefore, there has been a growing tendency to analyze religious groups by making use of the same frameworks we use in studying social organizations in general. For example, from an organizational point of view, religious groups in Canada are in effect corporations of different sizes: The Roman Catholic Church is "a multinational corporation," the United Church is a company that is "Canadian-owned and -operated," the Baptist Union of Western Canada is "a regional company" with links to other "regional companies" in central and eastern Canada, and an individual congregation in a given city or town is "a local outlet."

Apart from provocative marketing language and corporate analogies, a general organizational approach to religious groups might lead us to examine them in terms of some basic features, including (1) the nature and the sources of their members, (2) their formal and informal goals, (3) the norms and roles that are established to accomplish their purposes, (4) the sanctions that are used to ensure that norms are followed and roles are played, and (5) the success that groups experience in pursuing their goals.

Membership When one studies the membership of religious groups, what is readily apparent is that the vast majority of those involved are following in parental footsteps. The pattern is true of religious group identification: census data show that when two parents have the same faith, 95 percent of their children are also raised in that faith. The pattern is also true of group membership more specifically (Bibby, 1994, 2000). A 1994 national survey of the United Church of Canada, for example, found that about 70 percent of active members acknowledged that their mother or father had been a United Church member.

Surveys of Anglicans, Roman Catholics, and members of evangelical churches—referred to as conservative Protestant groups by sociologists—have uncovered the same intergenerational pattern. As a result, new additions to almost any given congregation are primarily active members who are on the move geographically. These include people coming to Canada from other countries; for example, during the 1980s and 1990s immigrants contributed to the growth of Hindu, Sikh, Muslim, and Buddhist groups. By the same token, one of the major reasons for a decline in participation is the simple fact that many Canadians who make a residential move don't become involved with a congregation after arriving in their new settings (Bibby, 1997). Research into the growth patterns of 20 conservative Protestant groups in Calgary over 25 years has found that about 70 percent of the new members come from similar evangelical churches, while 20 percent are children of members. Only about 10 percent have roots outside of conservative groups. To the extent that such outsiders are recruited, it is friendship and marriage that draw them in, rather than such highly publicized activities as mass evangelism, religious television programming, and door-to-door visitation (Bibby and Brinkerhoff, 1973, 1983, 1994).

Because most new members come from existing pools of people who view themselves as Roman Catholics, Anglicans, evangelicals, Jews, Hindus, Muslims, and so on, churches and temples frequently compete with each other for members, especially in urban areas where choice abounds. One area of competition is leadership. Smaller, lower-status congregations are usually at a severe disadvantage to larger and more prestigious groups. For decades, ministers within major Canadian and American Protestant denominations have been found to have standards comparable to those of secular managers and executives when it comes to interchurch movement (Mitchell, 1966). But it's not only ministers, priests, and rabbis who equate "large" with "successful"; so do denominations and individual congregations. And "attractive" congregations usually have the resources to search further for their leaders, and hold them longer. It has been widely known for some time in religious circles that the dominant pattern of "successful" clerical movement is from smaller to larger congregations (see, for example, Wimberley, 1971). Yet, in recent years, supply and demand realities in a number of Protestant groups have made employment itself an issue. An oversupply of ministers has forced growing numbers of clergy to find employment in noncongregational ministries (Chang and Bompadre, 1999).

Competition among congregations does not stop with ministers and other workers. A congregation's physical resources and its range of services are also significant. The result is that groups tend to build structures as lavish as their resources will permit. In recent years, a number of Protestant "megachurches" have come into being in both Canada and the United States. They typically have seating for 1000–4000 people, are serviced by multiple full-time staffs, and have annual budgets in the millions of dollars. They are found in major cities such as Toronto, Montreal, Winnipeg, Edmonton, Calgary, and Vancouver. But they also are appearing in smaller communities such as Abbotsford, Red Deer, and St. Catharines. These megachurches make it difficult for other congregations to compete.

Churches, like secular businesses, also expand their services and personnel in keeping with their economic means. Some of the megachurches, for example, offer many of the typical worship and educational opportunities of more traditional, older groups. But they also have extensive programs aimed at children, teenagers, young adults, and seniors. The programs range from small but sophisticated groups studying in homes ("cell groups"), through well-developed music and drama programs, to multimedia education, entertainment, and elaborate Internet sites. A foyer in one British Columbia megachurch is decorated to resemble a 1950s diner—complete with car front, jukeboxes, booths, and stools. As the church's head youth minister told me, "The young people love this room; but, I have to admit, the seniors love it too."

In their pursuit of members, congregations are sensitive to the tension between maintaining their integrity and compromising their "product" in order to attract "consumers." Indeed, competition among groups may be resolved in favour not of the most religious but of the least (Demerath and Hammond, 1969; Bibby, 2002). Then again, there are others who argue that the congregations most likely to "win" are those who place greater, rather than less, demand on their members (Kelley, 1972; Stark and Finke, 2000).

Goals The conscious and unconscious goals of local religious groups vary by congregation and members. Like the goals of other social groupings, these conscious and unconscious goals commonly appear to be in conflict. Formal goals derived from religious doctrine, such as spiritual growth, frequently exist in tension with "survival goals," including numerical growth (Metz, 1967). Glock, Ringer, and Babbie (1967) have suggested that churches have difficulty in reconciling the pastoral or "comfort" function with the prophetical or "challenge" function. Even apart from the goal of offering comfort, efforts to be prophetic can sometimes have unsettling effects. For example, the national leadership of the United Church of Canada has viewed itself as prophetic in its call, since the mid-1980s, for the denomination to allow homosexuals to be eligible for ordination as ministers. In taking such a controversial position, however, the United Church lost a large number of dissenting members and, in some cases, entire congregations (see O'Toole et al., 1993). Prophecy has its organizational price.

Still other observers (Hadden, 1969; Crysdale, 1961; Luidens and Nemeth, 1989) have noted that North American Protestants experience tension in pursuing the goals of individual versus social redemption. Roman Catholics have had difficulty in combining social and individual ministry. Hewitt (1992: 156) concludes that, despite its seemingly high-profile identification with justice, even a group like the Roman Catholic Church in Canada "has largely failed to marry rhetoric to concrete action."

Ironically, there may sometimes be more consensus about goals than religious groups themselves appreciate. In the wake of the divisive homosexual ordination issue in the United Church, many members accused the leadership of having different priorities from those of the laity. Yet the 1994 *Unitrends* national survey of the denomination disclosed that leaders agreed with average members that primary emphases of the church should be worship, spirituality, and ministry to youth. The leaders differed in maintaining that other emphases, notably social and justice issues, should also be given high priority. At the same time, leaders can misjudge the laity—for example, by underestimating their willingness to change. Conrad Kanagy and Leo Driedger (1996) found that among Mennonites—a group widely stereotyped as resistant to change—there have been noteworthy changes in attitudes toward women, political participation, and pacifism since the early 1970s.

Norms, Roles, and Sanctions If groups are to achieve their official or formal goals, they must establish norms for thought and action, and roles for members to play. An examination of who occupies leadership roles, for example, reveals that most religious groups in Canada have been top-heavy with men, a reality that has been variously met with change and resistance (see, for example, Nason-Clark, 1993; Nesbitt, 1997). These norms and roles in turn depend on good communication, and by the use of social controls in the form of rewards and punishments.

Many religious groups, because they typically rely on volunteers, find it very difficult to execute goals in the norms/roles/communication/social control pattern of efficient organizations (Brannon, 1971; Bibby, 1993; Monahan, 1999). Congregations compete for volunteer members and depend on them for attendance, financial support, and general participation. Although groups can establish norms concerning belief and behaviour, and assign organizational roles for members to perform, they have few and weak methods of social control in such a "buyer's market." In short, religious groups are extremely vulnerable organizations. Their paid leaders receive no exemption from such organizational fragility. On the contrary, they are highly dependent on volunteer parishioners. This has important implications for what clergy can do and how they can do it.

Success In their studies of religion in Canada, researchers have tended to emphasize "the numerical bottom lines" of religious groups, and focused on such indicators of success as attendance, membership, and finances.

Through the early 1990s, the research news was not particularly good for organized religion. Overall, attendance and membership were down, with some groups feeling great hardship as a result of inadequate finances. The mainline Protestant groups—the United, Anglican, Presbyterian, and Lutheran churches—were the most severely hit, along with Roman Catholics in Quebec. Despite some attendance and membership losses, the Roman Catholic Church outside of Quebec appeared to be relatively healthy. And while their numbers were not as large as many people think, conservative Protestant groups were at least able to hold their own and grow modestly—a significant accomplishment, given that they have represented only about 8 percent of the population since 1871, and could have readily been absorbed by larger competitors. Other faith groups such as Hindus, Muslims, and Buddhists were having a difficult time growing, primarily because they were having considerable difficulty holding on to their offspring, who frequently were marrying Catholics and Protestants.

As discussed in detail in Chapter 17, the size of a group is largely a function of birth and mortality factors. What was disconcerting for religious leaders in Canada through the early 1990s was that most groups were top-heavy with older people, and many did not seem able to replace them with comparable numbers of younger people. As a result, it was estimated that, by the year 2015, weekly attendance would drop dramatically for mainline Protestants and Quebec Catholics, while remaining stable for conservative Protestants and Roman Catholics elsewhere in Canada. The result? There was a very real possibility that the dominant players on the Canadian religious scene would soon be Roman Catholics and evangelical Protestants.

However, as we will see shortly, there is good reason to believe that this "old story" is being replaced by a "new story." There are signs that Canada's well-established religious groups are beginning to make something of a comeback. Very significantly, such an embryonic renaissance has not taken place by chance, but appears to reflect the explicit efforts of groups to be more effective in addressing the needs and interests of children, teenagers, and young adults. Participation trends clearly are strongly associated with organizational activity.

The Canadian Situation

Affiliation with religious groups has been widespread in Canada since the founding of this country. Close ties have always been apparent between Canadians of British descent and the Church of England, Methodism, and Presbyterianism; between the French and the Roman Catholic Church; and between other ethnic groups and the churches of their homelands. As noted earlier, Islam, Hindu, Sikh, and Buddhist growth in recent years has been directly related to immigration from Asian regions. Such general affiliation continues to be very common in Canada. Indeed, according to the 1991 census (Statistics Canada, 1993), just 13 percent of Canadians indicated that they had no religious preference. Although group preferences differ in various parts of the country, on a national basis Roman Catholics comprise 46 percent of the population and Protestants 36 percent. The remaining 5 percent consist of those with other religious preferences (see Table 7.2). Such data suggest that it is an exaggeration to think of Canada as a highly diversified religious mosaic.

These demographic findings are confirmed by a survey conducted for historian George Rawlyk and released in a cover story by *Maclean's* magazine shortly after the 1991 census (Nemeth, 1993). The poll found that about 75 percent of Canadians defined themselves as Christians, and about 75 percent of those claimed affiliation with a Christian denomination.

The Christian faith also continues to be pervasive in the United States, where surveys show that close to nine in ten Americans identify with Christian groups. However, the numerically dominant groups in the United States are not the same as those in Canada. For example, whereas one in two Canadians are Catholic, the same is true of only one in four Americans. Furthermore, only about one in ten Canadians identify with conservative Protestant (evangelical) groups, in contrast to more than three in ten Americans. Again, beyond cold demographics, there is good reason to believe that to be a Catholic, a mainliner, or a conservative in Canada is not necessarily the same as it is in the United States. A 1996 Angus Reid poll of Canadians and Americans found, for example, a higher proportion of commitment among U.S. Catholics and mainline Protestants than among their Canadian counterparts. Among evangelicals, the proportions exhibiting commitment were about the same (Fledderus, 1997).

When asked about actual *membership* in religious groups, as opposed to mere affiliation or identification, more Canadians—about 30 percent—claim to

TABLE 7.2 RELIGIOUS IDENTIFICATION, CANADA AND THE PROVINCES AND TERRITORIES, 1991 (IN PERCENTAGES)

	CANADA	BC	AB	SK	MB	ON	QC	NB	NS	PEI	NF	YK	NWT
Catholic	**46%**	**19**	**27**	**33**	**30**	**36**	**86**	**54**	**37**	**47**	**37**	**20**	**38**
Roman	45	19	26	31	27	36	86	54	37	47	37	20	38
Ukrainian	1	<1	1	2	3	<1	<1	<1	<1	<1	<1	<1	<1
Protestant	**36**	**44**	**48**	**53**	**51**	**44**	**6**	**40**	**54**	**48**	**61**	**43**	**50**
United	11	13	17	23	19	14	1	11	17	20	17	9	6
Anglican	8	10	7	7	9	10	2	9	14	5	26	15	32
Presbyterian	2	2	2	1	1	4	<1	1	4	9	<1	1	1
Lutheran	2	3	5	8	5	2	<1	<1	1	<1	<1	2	1
Baptist	3	3	2	2	2	3	<1	11	11	4	<1	4	1
Pentecostal	2	2	2	2	2	2	<1	3	1	1	7	2	4
Other	8	11	13	10	13	9	2	5	6	9	10	10	5
Other faiths	**5**	**6**	**5**	**3**	**5**	**7**	**4**	**<1**	**1**	**1**	**<1**	**2**	**1**
Eastern Orthodox	1	1	2	2	2	2	1	<1	<1	<1	<1	<1	<1
Jewish	1	<1	<1	<1	1	2	1	<1	<1	<1	<1	<1	<1
Islam	1	1	1	<1	<1	1	1	<1	<1	<1	<1	<1	<1
Hindu	1	1	<1	<1	<1	1	<1	<1	<1	<1	<1	<1	<1
Buddhist	1	1	1	<1	1	1	1	<1	<1	<1	<1	<1	<1
Sikh	<1	2	1	<1	<1	<1	<1	<1	<1	<1	<1	<1	<1
Other	<1	<1	<1	<1	<1	<1	<1	<1	<1	<1	<1	1	<1
No religion	**13**	**31**	**20**	**11**	**14**	**13**	**4**	**6**	**8**	**4**	**2**	**35**	**11**

SOURCE: Compiled from Statistics Canada, Religions in Canada, 1991 Census of Canada, Cat. No. 93-319 (Ottawa: Industry, Science and Technology Canada). Used by authority of the Minister of Industry, 2000.

belong to churches than to any other single voluntary group. According to various polls, about one in five say they attend services weekly, and roughly the same proportion of people with school-age children expose their children to church schools.

At the same time, however, there has been a considerable decline in church attendance since the 1940s, documented by Gallup poll findings summarized in Figure 7.1. Gallup has been asking Canadians if they have attended a service "in the last seven days"—the phrasing of the inquiry adds sporadic attenders to those who claim they attend every week. Using such a measure, Gallup has found that, since World War II, Protestant attendance dropped from around 60 percent to about 30 percent in the mid-1970s, rebounding to 40 percent by the mid-1990s—led by conservative Protestant groups. The decline in Roman Catholic attendance appears to have started around 1965, dropping from roughly 85 to 40 percent in the 1990s—led by low church-going in Quebec. No such dramatic decline in attendance has taken place in the United States.

The downward pattern of involvement in Canada may, of course, change. Indeed, there is evidence that something of a reversal began to take place during the 1990s. In 1984, 23 percent of the country's 15- to 19-

year-olds were attending services weekly, and by 1992 the figure had dropped to 18 percent. However, by 2000 the weekly figure for this age group rebounded to 22 percent, seemingly reflecting accelerated emphases on youth ministry by a wide array of Protestant, Catholic, and other faith groups. In addition, for the first time in decades, the 1990s saw the proportion of weekly attending 18- to 34-year-olds level off and in some group instances increase, rather than decline. The only notable exception? Quebec. There regular attendance has continued to decline among both teenagers and adults. Nonetheless, overall, there are signs of a possible renaissance of religion in Canada (see Bibby, 2002).

In addition to organizational activity, individual and societal factors play a critically important role in influencing the inclination of people to embrace religion and religious groups.

THE SOURCES OF RELIGION

Much of the early work in the scientific study of religion focused on primitive or simple cultures in which religion was pervasive. Everyone seemed religious. Consequently, it is not surprising that observers sought to understand the origin of religion itself, rather than the sources of individual variations in commitment.

However, individual differences in religion's importance in modern societies have called for explanations as to why some people are religious and others are not. These explanations focus either on individuals or on social structure.

INDIVIDUAL-CENTRED EXPLANATIONS

At least three dominant "person-centred" explanations of religious commitment have emerged.

Reflection

The desire to comprehend reality is widespread among humans. Anthropologist Clifford Geertz (1968: 15) notes:

> it does appear to be a fact that at least some men—in all probability, most men—are unable ... just to look at the stranger features of the world's landscape in dumb astonishment or bland apathy without trying to develop ... some notions as to how such features might be reconciled with the more ordinary deliverances of experience.

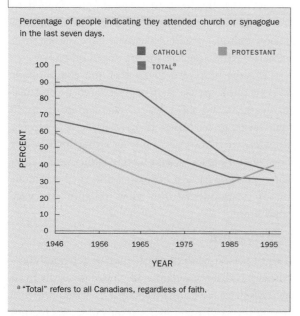

FIGURE 7.1 ATTENDANCE AT RELIGIOUS SERVICES, CANADA, 1946–2000

Percentage of people indicating they attended church or synagogue in the last seven days.

a "Total" refers to all Canadians, regardless of faith.

SOURCE: Gallup Canada, Inc., surveys, 1946–1995.

In the course of reflecting on the meaning of existence, people have commonly concluded that life has a supernatural, "transempirical" dimension. As Weber (1963: 117) put it, religion is the product of an "inner compulsion to understand the world as a meaningful cosmos and take up a position toward it."

There is little doubt that Canadians reflect on life's so-called big questions. Some 80 percent say they think about such issues as the origin and purpose of life, the meaning of suffering, and what happens after we die. Such questions take on particular urgency when people have to come to grips with an event such as "9/11"—or have to deal with the suicide of a friend or the loss of a parent. Still, while such times of reflection may provide religious groups with an opportunity to respond, reflection in itself does not lead to religious commitment and involvement. Fewer than one in three Canadians who often raise these meaningful questions give evidence of being religiously committed.

Socialization

A second person-centred explanation sees religious commitment as the product of learning—socialization factors that were the focus of Chapter 4. Freud (1962 [1928]) went so far as to say that religion is learned pretty much like the multiplication tables. He may not have been exaggerating. In the terms of Durkheim's analysis, personal religiosity depends on collective religiosity, since ideas tend to be instilled through individuals and institutions. Therefore, one would expect that people who are religious have been exposed to social environments that are positive toward religion, whether those environments consist of an entire society, a community, an institution, an ethnic group, or—especially—family and friends.

Accommodation to social pressures, notably those of primary groups, seems to be another source of religious-group involvement. For example, one marital partner may become more active in response to the hopes and expectations of the other; friends in response to friends; and some "baby boomer" parents in response to having young children (see, for example, Roozen, McKinney, and Thompson, 1990; Brady, 1991). In communities where religion is pervasive, accommodation appears to act as an important source of religious involvement.

Research by Bruce Hunsberger (1980; Hunsberger and Brown, 1984) involving students at Wilfrid Laurier University and the University of Manitoba led him to conclude that emphasis on religion in childhood is positively associated with later religiosity. Similarly, the Project Canada surveys have documented a noteworthy relationship between the commitment of respondents and their parents (Bibby, 1993, 1996, 2002). Some 90 percent of Canadians with Protestant parents are Protestants themselves. The same level of identification is also found for children of Roman Catholic parents. Furthermore, about 80 percent of today's weekly attenders were also weekly churchgoers when they were growing up.

It is important to keep in mind that socialization appears to be a *necessary* but not a *sufficient* cause of religiosity. That is, to the extent that Canadians are currently involved in religious groups, most had parents who also were involved. However, the fact that Canadians had parents who were involved does not ensure that they will follow suit. Although about 80 percent of today's weekly attenders had parents who attended weekly, only about one in three Canadians whose fathers or mothers attended services weekly are themselves weekly attenders.

As a result of declining service attendance over the past few decades, a decreasing number of parents are actively involved in religious groups and, therefore, passing the experience of organized religion on to their children. For example, in 1975, some 35 percent of Canadians with school-age children claimed they and their children were attending services on a weekly basis; by 2000, that figure had dropped to around 20 percent (Bibby, 2002: 215). Such a pattern, if not halted, would obviously have devastating numerical consequences for organized religion.

Surveys have also found that the commitment level of one's spouse is strongly related to personal involvement and the valuation of religion. In more than seven in ten cases, if one partner is a weekly attender, so is the other. In fewer than two in ten cases does a person attend weekly if the spouse does not. The same pattern of spousal influence is evident among respondents who view religion as "very important."

Deprivation

A third person-centred explanation of religious commitment is that the religious are drawn primarily from society's deprived or disadvantaged. Religion provides "pie in the sky by and by," a means of compensating

One of the strongest predictors of adult religiosity is childhood religious practice. When parents participate in religious observance with their children, the early socialization experience is often imprinted for life.

SOURCE: Bushnell Soifer/Stone.

for deprivation. The roots of such thinking are found in the work of Karl Marx and Sigmund Freud.

The deprivation argument has been developed more fully by Glock and Stark (1965). They contend that five types of deprivation are predominant in the rise and development of religious and secular movements: economic, social, organismic (that is, physical or mental), psychic, and ethical. The first three types of deprivation are self-explanatory. Psychic deprivation refers to the lack of a meaningful system of values, and ethical deprivation refers to having values that are in conflict with those dominant in a society.

Research suggests that if deprivation is measured using so-called objective indicators such as income, health, and social relationships (which gauge economic, organismic, and social deprivation, respectively), deprivation is not strongly related to religious commitment in either the United States (Roof and Hoge, 1980) or Canada (Hobart, 1974). This is not to say that deprivation is never a significant factor for some individuals and religious groups. But the findings indicate that, as a whole, the religiously committed in North America are not, as a whole, any more or less disadvantaged than others.

STRUCTURE-CENTRED EXPLANATIONS

Thus far, we have been examining what we might call "kinds of people" explanations of religious commitment. What these explanations have in common is their emphasis on individuals, who are said to turn to religion as a result of reflection, socialization, or deprivation. An adequate understanding of commitment, however, must also take into account the influence of the societal context in which people find themselves.

S.D. Clark (1948), for example, has argued that, historically, the emergence of sect-like groups in Canada was tied to the existence of unstable conditions, which were produced by factors such as immigration and economic depression. With industrialization and increased prosperity and stability, sects tended to evolve into denominations—a process referred to as **denominationalism**. A further example of the impact of societal factors on religion can be found in Quebec. Much of the drop-off in Roman Catholic attendance between 1965 and 1980 was related to the accelerated modernization of Quebec, including the church's relinquishing much of its important role in education and social services to the province (see, for example, Rouleau, 1977; Beyer, 1993, 1997).

The climate that contemporary societies provide for religion is a subject of considerable controversy. There are some observers who maintain that increasing industrialization and postindustrialization contribute to a decline in the pervasiveness and influence of religion. This **secularization thesis** can be found in Comte, Durkheim, Marx, and Freud. But there is also a **persistence thesis**. Proponents of this position claim that religion—traditional or otherwise—persists in industrial and postindustrial/postmodern societies, continuing to address questions of meaning and purpose, and responding to widespread interest in spirituality.

In Canada, we can readily explore the relationship between religious commitment and some of the correlates of social and cultural change—such as urbanization, greater education, and work-force participation, along with the passage of time. If the secularization thesis is correct, we would expect commitment to be low, with minor differences by social characteristics such as community size and education. Over time, people in rural areas should come to resemble their urban counterparts in being less religious; the same should also be true of high-school dropouts and college graduates, the elderly, and young adults. The culture should be so secularized that no sector of the population remains untouched. Conversely, if the persistence thesis is correct, we would expect variations, for example, by community size and education: significant numbers of people in

larger communities, including university graduates, would continue to express interest in religion.

What do the findings show? Differences in religious participation and commitment continue to exist by age, reflecting at least in part the different eras in which Canadians were raised. Modest differences also can be observed by community size and work-force participation (see Table 7.3). However, education does not have a sizable negative impact on either participation or commitment. Of considerable importance, the inclination of Canadians to indicate that they have spiritual needs is widespread, regardless of age, community size, education, or employment outside the home. Regional variations consist primarily of people in the Atlantic provinces being the most pro-religious and pro-spiritual, British Columbia residents the least.

TABLE 7.3 SERVICE ATTENDANCE, COMMITMENT, AND SPIRITUAL NEEDS BY SOCIAL CHANGE CORRELATES, CANADA, 2000

	CURRENTLY WEEKLY ATTENDERS	COMMITTED TO CHRISTIANITY OR ANOTHER WORLD FAITH	SEE SELF AS HAVING SPIRITUAL NEEDS
NATIONALLY	21%	55%	73%
Era (date of birth)			
1945 and earlier	38	69	74
1946–65	18	56	74
1966–82	9	43	71
Community Size			
Under 30 000	23	62	75
30 000–400 000	21	53	78
Over 400 000	16	48	70
Education			
High school or less	24	62	72
Some postsecondary	17	51	71
Degree or more	24	55	80
Work-force participation			
Not employed outside the home	28	59	74
Employed outside the home	16	53	72
Region			
Atlantic	32	68	82
Quebec	18	63	73
Ontario	22	52	73
Prairies	22	55	77
British Columbia	16	44	69

SOURCE: Computed from Reginald W. Bibby, Project Canada 2000 National Survey.

While these data suggest some support for secularization, they also reveal that, apart from involvement in organized religion, subjective religious commitment remains widespread. In addition, a majority of Canadians continue to express spiritual needs. Such findings suggest that the pervasiveness of secularization in Canada has been overestimated.

To the extent that Canadians are religiously involved and committed, the key sources are neither institutions such as the media or education, nor the desire for compensation in the face of deprivation. Rather, those who place a high value on religion tend to be those who have been exposed to pro-religious socialization by family, friends, and other significant people. This is not to say that reflection about meaning, felt needs, or a desire for spiritual satisfaction do not play roles. It is, however, to say that social ties are the key links to religious commitment and religious involvement.

THE CONSEQUENCES OF RELIGION

Does religion have an impact on the way individuals live their lives, or is it largely irrelevant? If such an influence exists, does religion tend to contribute to individual and societal well-being, or does it more often produce anxiety and guilt, social indifference, and bigotry? And if religion does have an impact—adding, say, to civility—to what extent is its influence unique?

Those who value faith claim that religion has positive consequences for individuals and, in turn, for societies. Christians, for example, are likely to tell us that, ideally, mature followers are personally influenced by their faith, experiencing emotions like joy, hope, and empowerment. They also aspire to show compassion in their dealings with others, exhibiting qualities such as concern, tolerance, forgiveness, and honesty. At the same time, because religious groups differ considerably on specific norms, such as sexual orientation, gambling, and abortion, the attitudes of the committed would be expected to vary considerably.

Social scientists have explored the effects of religion on personal characteristics and interpersonal relations. Here is what they have been finding.

PERSONAL CONSEQUENCES

Marx and Freud conceded, in essence, that religion contributed to positive personal characteristics such as happiness, contentment, and hope. Their criticism of religion rested in their belief that such qualities were based on illusion rather than reality.

Research findings on religion and what we might refer to generally as "mental health" are contradictory. Highly respected social psychologist Milton Rokeach (1965: 2), summing up a number of his studies, wrote: "We have found that people with formal religious affiliation are more anxious [than others]. Believers, compared with non-believers, complain more often of working under great tension, sleeping fitfully, and similar symptoms."

Yet researchers have consistently found a negative relationship between religious commitment and *anomie* (Lee and Clyde, 1974)—a characteristic of valuelessness and rootlessness that Srole (1956) sees as related to anxiety. Furthermore, involvement in groups such as sects and cults has been shown to provide improved self-images and hope in the face of economic and social deprivation (e.g., Whyte, 1966). Frankel and Hewitt (1994), among others, have found that religious group involvement and mental health are positively related, while research into the Pentecostal-like "Toronto Blessing" congregation has even maintained that physical healing sometimes occurs (Poloma, 1997; Poloma and Hoelter, 1998). What seems apparent is that some forms of religiosity are connected with well-being, while others are not (for overviews, see Bergin, 1983; Gorsuch, 1988).

Canadian analyses suggest that, overall, people who exhibit religious commitment are slightly more inclined than others to claim a high level of happiness, to find life exciting, to express a high level of satisfaction with family, friends, and leisure activities, and to view death with hope rather than with mystery or even fear (Bibby, 1987, 1993, 2002; and see Figure 7.2). However, when controls are introduced, and the impact of other variables such as age, education, community size, and region is taken into account, the apparent modest influence of commitment typically disappears, or at least has to be qualified. For example, Gee and Veevers (1990) found that religious involvement and life satisfaction were positively related nationally, but not in British Columbia.

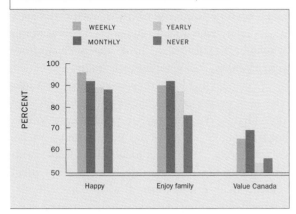

FIGURE 7.2 PERSONAL WELL-BEING AND RELIGIOUS SERVICE ATTENDANCE, 2000

SOURCE: Compiled from Reginald W. Bibby, *The Bibby Report: Social Trends Canadian Style* (Toronto: Stoddart, 1995) p. 136. Used with permission of the author.

In short, religious commitment by itself appears to have a very limited influence on valued personal characteristics. Moreover, it is often less important than such variables as age, education, or employment in predicting personal well-being.

This "no-difference" finding does not mean that faith is not adding something to the lives of people who value faith (see Box 7.2). Rather, in the light of the relatively high levels of happiness and contentment reported by Canadians generally, it suggests that large numbers of other people are finding alternative pathways to personal well-being. Religion is having an impact, but it is not a unique impact.

INTERPERSONAL CONSEQUENCES

One of the first empirical attempts to examine the relationship between religious commitment and compassion was carried out by Clifford Kirkpatrick in Minnesota in 1949. He found that religiously committed people were somewhat less humanitarian in their outlook than others.

Some 20 years later, Rokeach (1969), drawing on American national data, observed that religious commitment was *negatively* related to social compassion; in the case of Roman Catholics, no relationship—positive or negative—existed. Rokeach concluded that "the results seem compatible with the hypothesis that religious values serve more as standards for condemning others ... than as standards to judge oneself by or to guide one's own conduct" (1969: 35).

These findings, however, have not gone unchallenged. Research conducted on specific religious groups and in certain locales has found a positive relationship between commitment and compassion. In a

Among other questions, the sociology of religion asks: Does religion influence the way individuals live? Does religion contribute to individual and societal well-being?

SOURCE: William Kurelek, *Kaszuby Funeral Procession*. Art Gallery of Hamilton, Gift of the Polish Alliance of Canada, and Wintario, 1978.

BOX 7.2   GOD IS GOOD MEDICINE

Health-club memberships: check. Gingko-and-kelp caplets: check. Cigarettes, down; veggies up: check. Religion: che ... what? Yes, health nuts and slugabeds alike, it's time to acknowledge something you may have heard in Sunday school or while perched on Grandma's knee: Like spinach, God is good for you.

Medical science, especially in the West, may still turn up its nose at the mix of health and spirituality, but it's slowly coming around. The research—scads of it—continues to confirm more or less the same thing: people who follow a religious/spiritual path are more likely to enjoy greater longevity and superior overall health than those who do not. And prayer, meditation and other mind-body approaches, whether from the Eastern or Western religious models, appear to be beneficial to the healing process.

That's not to suggest that atheists, agnostics and secular humanists will keel over tomorrow from heart attacks, or that the faithful are immune from alcoholism or obesity. The link between spiritual engagement and health behaviour is, finally, as close to undeniable as it has ever been.

At last count, more than 1,200 studies and 400 reviews, from Canada, Europe and the United States, show that those who regularly attend a house of worship have demonstrably lower rates of illness and death than do infrequent or non-attenders. Actively religious people live longer, on average, than the non-religious. Meditation and prayer have been found to improve patients' overall well-being. High, even moderate, levels of religious faith and/or spiritual awareness are associated with greater resilience to stress, lower levels of anxiety, better coping skills, a greater sense of belonging, and generally, a sunnier, more serene take on life.

SOURCE: Ron Csillag, "God Is Good Medicine," *Globe and Mail*, April 2, 2002, R5.

more immediate relational sense, Wilcox (1998) has found that, although conservative Protestant parents are more likely than others to use corporal punishment in disciplining their children, they also are more likely than other parents to praise and hug their children. Extensive research on religion and racial prejudice, such as Smith's (1999) recent look at anti-Semitism and "the Religious Right," has yielded contradictory results. But Gorsuch and Aleshire (1974) claim to have found the key reason for the discrepancies. Church members often appear to be more prejudiced than those who have never joined a church. But, they say, it is not because of religious involvement. On the contrary, when involvement level is taken into account, the people who turn out to be the most prejudiced are the "marginally involved" members. Gorsuch and Aleshire concluded: "The highly committed religious person is—along with the non-religious person—one of the least prejudiced members of our society" (1974: 287). If this is the case, then, as with personal characteristics, religion may be making a difference interpersonally—but it is not a unique difference.

Ongoing analyses of Project Canada data have found that the religiously committed in this country do not differ significantly from others with respect to their interpersonal relationship attitudes (Bibby,

1995, 2002). They hold a similar view of people, claim a comparable level of compassion, and appear to be no more or less tolerant of deviants, minority groups, and people of other religious faiths than other Canadians. Furthermore, in contrast to the findings of Rokeach and Stark and Glock, no noteworthy differences appear in the interpersonal attitudes held by Roman Catholics and Protestants.

There is, however, one area where religion still appears to speak with a fairly loud if not unique voice—the area of personal morality, notably sexuality. With few exceptions and with varying degrees of explicitness, religious groups tend to function as opponents of "moral innovation." Examples include opposition to the changing of sexual standards, the increased availability of legal abortion, and the legalized distribution of pornographic material. The findings reported in Table 7.4 support this argument.

SOCIETAL CONSEQUENCES

The influence of religion can be examined not only in terms of individuals and social interaction but also with reference to society as a whole.

Peter Berger (1961) has observed that while an adequate sociological theory of religion must be able to account for the possibility of dysfunctions,

TABLE 7.4   PERCENTAGE OF CANADIANS OPPOSED TO SELECTED ISSUES BY ATTENDANCE AT RELIGIOUS SERVICES, 2000

	PREMARITAL SEX	EXTRAMARITAL SEX	HOMO-SEXUALITY	ABORTION: RAPE	ABORTION: CHILD UNWANTED	DISTRIBUTION OF PORNOGRAPHY
Attendance						
Weekly	46%	93%	68%	30%	75%	60%
Less than weekly	7	84	31	4	41	27
Weekly attenders						
Age 50 and over	52	92	70	30	75	69
Under 50	38	99	64	31	81	46

SOURCE: Computed from Reginald W. Bibby, Project Canada 2000 National Survey.

Durkheim's assertion that religion functions primarily to integrate societies seems to offer a good description of religion in America. Religion, or at least the main-line segment of organized Christianity that historically has embraced the largest number of members, has tended to endorse U.S. culture rather than to challenge it, to endorse the status quo rather than call for social transformation. So intense has been the bond between religion and American life that Robert Bellah (1967) and others have described the phenomenon as American **civil religion**. Will Herberg (1960: 75) put it this way:

> Americans, by and large, do have their "common religion" and that "religion" is the system familiarly known as the American Way of Life.... By every realistic criterion the American Way of Life is the operative faith of the American people.... To be a Protestant, a Catholic, or a Jew are today the alternative ways of being an American.

Canada has no such civil religion. As Stahl (1986: 16) colourfully puts it, "Other than a few bands and firecrackers, Confederation was not attended by much emotional outpouring." And religious groups have done little to add fervour to our rather lifeless expressions of nationalism. Still, Fallding (1978) has reminded us that, historically, "Canadian Protestant churches have reflected the British position of legitimizing authority through supporting government, offering prayers, for example, for its success in securing order and justice." The fusion of Catholicism with life in Quebec, Anglicanism with the status quo in southern Ontario, and conservative Protestantism with the political and social life in Alberta are obvious examples.

Nevertheless, religion has, on occasion, challenged North American culture. The civil rights movement in the United States received much of its leadership and impetus from Black evangelical churches. American Catholic bishops and the National Council of Churches have frequently spoken out against perceived injustices, including poverty, racism, and war. Jerry Falwell's "Moral Majority" of the 1980s became a vocal "Christian Right" committed to altering the nature of American life by influencing the country's major institutions. One offshoot, for example, known as "Promise Keepers," attempts to promote spirituality and family responsibility among men.

In this country, Protestant churches have received mixed reviews for their concern about the plight of Jews during World War II; some churches and individuals were silent, while others were not (Davies and Nefsky, 1997). In the 1940s, a radical effort was made by the Roman Catholic Church to support striking workers, a preview of the ongoing inclination of the Canadian Conference of Catholic Bishops to support average Canadians and to be vocal in criticizing the profit orientation of the nation's economy. Protestant groups, usually led by the United Church, along with a growing number of ecumenical consortia and initiatives, and, more recently, evangelical churches, have been making concerted efforts to bring about social change (see, e.g., Crysdale, 1961; Stiller, 1997). Coalitions of churches, among others, are criticizing the cutbacks to social programs in general and in Ontario in particular. They also are being increasingly outspoken with respect to Aboriginal issues (see Lewis, 1993).

Some may decry such a pattern, but religion's inclination to mirror culture rather than to stand apart from it may be unavoidable. If Durkheim is right in his assertion that humans, however unintentionally, tend to create religion in their own image, it is not surprising to find that religion tends to endorse what most of us value, both personally and socially.

It is important to note that locally, nationally, and globally religion clearly has the potential both to bring people together and to tear them apart. Religion's role in contributing to conflict is well known both historically and in the world today. In Canada and the United States there has been much concern in recent years about the sexual abuse of children by clergy, with mistreatment of children in residential schools a particular issue in Canada. Globally, what seems like never-ending conflict in the Middle East, Pakistan, and Ireland provide further contemporary examples of religion playing a role in contributing to divisiveness. Yet, as the aftermath of September 11, 2001, attacks revealed, significant numbers of people who are committed to the very faiths that seem to contribute to conflict and division are also among the first to decry violence and bloodshed, to turn to their faiths for sustenance, and call on people worldwide to find peaceful means of resolving differences. The consequences of religion are far from clear-cut.

THE FUTURE OF RELIGION

You have already been introduced to the controversy over whether religious involvement in the modern and postmodern world is likely to persist or decline, both earlier in this chapter as well as in Chapter 3 ("Culture"). In concluding, I return to this debate in order to place it in the context of a broader question: "What is the future of religion in the world in general and in Canada in particular?"

Proponents of the secularization thesis, you will recall, maintain that religion is bound to be replaced by science and reason as society modernizes. Belgian sociologist Karel Dobbelaere (1981, 2002) argues

that this process has three aspects. *Institutionally*, secularization involves a reduction in the number of areas of life over which religion has authority and meaning. *Personally*, individuals increasingly use the observable world rather than religion as a frame of reference for interpreting and giving meaning to life. *Organizationally*, religious groups become increasingly conformist and routine rather than radical and spontaneous.

Opponents of the secularization thesis counter that humans have needs, such as the need to come to grips with death, that only religion can satisfy. Thus, even if secularization leads to the demise of some religious groups, new expressions of religiosity are bound to appear. New religious forms include sects, or groups that break away from established religions, and **cults**, or groups with origins outside of older religions. Given the emergence of such new groups, secularization may actually stimulate the growth of religion (Stark and Bainbridge, 1985). Moreover, it has been predicted that such growth will be most evident in places where the "religious marketplace" is robust. In the United States, for example, when established religions fail to meet human needs, new religious "firms" move in to increase their "market share." From this point of view, shifts in the overall "religious economy" over time involve "the rising and falling fortunes of religious firms, not the rise and fall of religion per se" (Finke and Stark, 1992: 275).

Much anecdotal evidence can be mustered to support either side of this debate, but systematic and representative observations are preferable. Consider Campbell and Curtis's (1994) data on religious involvement, beliefs, and religious self-image in 21 countries in the period 1981–1983. Although they found that there was a decline in religious involvement overall, they noted that the United States and the United Kingdom were exceptions to this trend. Moreover, the six countries that exhibited the highest levels of involvement differed considerably in terms of their levels of industrialization and urbanization, along with their Catholic versus non-Catholic mix. Thus, there is no consistent pattern between industrialization or postindustrialization and religiosity (see Table 7.5). Campbell and Curtis also considered the merits of the argument that religiosity will be highest in countries characterized by pluralistic and competitive marketplaces. They concluded, on the basis of their research, that such interpretations were roughly consistent with the comparative data, but that there were exceptions, notably Australia and Japan. In those countries, pluralism is high and regulation is low, but involvement levels are weak.

Viewed in an international context, Canada presents us with a paradox. Personal beliefs and practices are high, yet involvement in religious groups is well below that in such countries as Mexico and the United States, and shows signs of dropping to levels found in countries such as England, France, and Germany.

Research has failed to support the idea that large numbers of Canadians are actually deserting the churches in favour of other religions, old or new. Few Canadians are interested in such alternatives as New Age, Transcendental Meditation (TM), Hare Krishna, Eckankar, Scientology, Mormonism, or the Jehovah's Witnesses, and such interest as exists is often fleeting (Bibby, 2002). Furthermore, few "dropouts" from mainline Protestantism and Roman Catholicism are ending up in conservative Protestant groups such as Pentecostals and Baptists. At present, conservative Protestant groups comprise about 7 per-

cent of the population, compared with 8 percent in 1871. Evangelical groups rely heavily on retention of their members and their members' children to maintain their numbers.

Nor is it the case that many Canadians are substituting TV's "electronic churches" for attendance at religious services. Fewer than 5 percent of Canadians say they regularly watch religious services on TV—a decline from 29 percent who were watching such programs on television or listening to them on the radio in 1958. Eight out of ten regular TV viewers also attend services weekly, suggesting that the TV programs are largely a supplement for those involved in religious groups, rather than a substitute for the uninvolved.

If Canadians are not flocking to new religions or to evangelical services and TV programs, then neither is their religion taking a less visible, more private form. At least 50 percent of Canadians do not claim to be religiously committed, privately or otherwise. Can we then conclude that the number of religious Canadians is declining and that the future of religion in Canada is that it has no future? It is true that the

TABLE 7.5   PRACTICES, BELIEFS, AND RELIGIOUS SELF-IMAGE FOR SELECTED COUNTRIES

	PRACTICES				BELIEFS				SELF-IMAGE
	Attend weekly	Attend weekly+	Church role	Pray	God	Life after death	Hell	Rein-carnation	A religious person
Ireland	82%	88%	7%	80%	95%	75%	54%	27%	63%
Mexico	54	75	9	83	97	76	50	46	74
South Africa	43	61	21	85	95	70	40	26	69
United States	42	59	21	85	96	71	68	23	81
Spain	40	53	10	69	86	55	33	25	62
Italy	32	48	5	70	82	46	28	21	80
Canada	**31**	**45**	**15**	**73**	**91**	**61**	**38**	**29**	**74**
Germany	18	34	6	55	68	29	13	18	54
Australia	17	23	11	34	80	49	35	25	58
Britain	14	23	6	49	73	54	26	26	53
France	11	16	3	41	59	35	14	22	48
Hungary	11	16	—	45	44	13	9	7	42
Sweden	5	14	9	33	52	27	10	14	32
Japan	3	12	4	41	39	21	16	30	24
Iceland	2	10	5	42	77	55	12	27	67

SOURCE: Compiled from the World Values Survey as reported in Robert A. Campbell and James E. Curtis, "Religious Involvement across Societies," *Journal for the Scientific Study of Religion*, *33* (1994), pp. 215–29. Used with permission.

number of Canadians who told the census takers that they had no religion rose from 4 percent in 1971 to 12 percent in 1991, and were anticipated to be as high as 20 percent by 2001. However, most of these people are single and young. As they marry and have children, many leave the "no-religion" category and affiliate with the Catholic or Protestant churches. And the group with which they identify is usually the same one as their parents. Most of them appear to re-affiliate, not out of spiritual urgency, but because of the desire for rites of passage pertaining to marriage, the birth of children, and death.

In short, the search for religious dropouts in Canada yields an intriguing result: Few have actually left home. Almost nine in ten Canadians are continuing to identify with fairly established, predominantly Christian groups. A nucleus of only about 20 percent attend services weekly, but another 60 percent attend at least occasionally. Most of the casual attenders expect to receive rites of passage from their identification groups when they are needed. Of particular importance, very few indicate that they have any inclination to turn elsewhere (Bibby, 2002).

It is clear that religious group identification is valued in this country. But it is equally clear that Canadians differ considerably in the role they want religion to play in their lives. Some embrace it wholeheartedly, seemingly as a meaning system that informs much of their lives. Others want some beliefs, some practices, some specialized services. Still others—a small minority—want nothing from religion or religious organizations.

It seems, therefore, that the significant religious development associated with industrialization and postindustrialization in Canada has not been the abandonment of religion but the tendency of Canadians to reject Christianity as an authoritative system of meaning. Instead, they draw on Judeo-Christian "fragments"—certain beliefs, practices, and organizational offerings—in a highly specialized, consumer-like fashion. In a similar manner, Canadians select fragments of other non-naturalistic systems—astrology, ESP, New Age, and so on—without adopting them as substitutes for Christianity. As Stark and Bainbridge (1985) suggest, these other systems function as "consumer cults," providing "add-ons" to their Christian main courses.

Although religious groups might decry such selective consumption, over time they have adapted to this consumer mentality. In the face of consumer demand, Canada's main established groups—the Roman Catholics, United Church, Anglicans, and conservative Protestants—have been offering increasingly varied "religious menus." The diversification of functions by Canada's religious establishment has made it extremely difficult for new rivals to penetrate the country's religion market. Churches have also been patient with individuals who want minimal involvement, seldom withholding from them basic rites of passage, denying them admission to services, or removing them from membership rolls.

The stability of the religious scene in Canada, along with its prevalent "fragment" style, has been further documented by national surveys of teenagers between the ages of 15 and 19 (Bibby 2001). The surveys have found that the country's "emerging generation" differs negligibly from adults when it comes to religion. About 90 percent of teenagers claim the same group affiliation as their parents, and only about 2 percent indicate any strong interest in the new religions. Their belief, practice, experience, and knowledge levels are similar to those of adults. Their interest in other supernatural phenomena is also very high, as is the acknowledgment of spiritual needs (see Table 7.6).

When it comes to commitment and involvement, teen levels closely mirror those of adults. Some 50 percent say that religion is "very important" to them and just over one in five attend religious services regularly—with 21 percent of teens saying that they receive a high level of enjoyment from church or synagogue life, compared to 22 percent of adults. However, young people are inclined to attend services less as they move into their late teens and early 20s: when they are 15 years of age, 19 percent are going to services frequently; by the time they are 19, that figure drops to about 13 percent, similar to the level of attendance of adults in the 18–29 age range.

Like their parents, however, young people are not particularly angry with religious groups. About 40 percent indicate that they have a high level of confidence in religious leaders, which places the clergy behind educational leaders (63 percent) but on a par with politicians. Moreover, teenagers seldom make religion a target of humour. But the dominant tendency is to draw selectively from religion, rather than allowing it to become an all-embracing system of meaning. Like their parents, young Canadians appear

TABLE 7.6   A PROFILE OF RELIGION AND SPIRITUALITY IN CANADA: TEENAGERS AND ADULTS

		ADULTS	TEENAGERS
Beliefs	God	81%	73%
	Divinity of Jesus	72	65
	Life after death	68	78
	Spirit world contact	45	43
Practice (weekly)	Pray privately	47	33
	Attend religious services	21	22
	Read the Bible/other scriptures	16	13
Experience	Have experienced God	47	36
Salience	High religious commitment	55	48
Spirituality	Have spiritual needs	73	48

SOURCE: Reginald W. Bibby, The Project Canada Survey Series.

to be highly selective consumers who approach the nation's religious groups with a "pick and choose" attitude.

It may well be that the structural and cultural changes associated with Canada's entry into the postindustrial "information age" have made meaning systems that encompass all of an individual's life incongruent with the varied roles people must play. In other words, fragments may be more functional than all-encompassing religions in a society that requires people to compartmentalize their experiences in order to play diverse roles. Religious systems may also seem frequently at odds with dominant cultural values such as rationalism, consumption, and enjoyment.

If that is the state of religion in postmodern society, then we do not choose belief, practice, and service fragments over systems because there are no system options. Rather, we choose fragments because they are more conducive to present-day life. As Bryan Wilson (1975: 80) has put it, modern societies offer "a supermarket of faiths; received, jazzed-up, homespun, restored, imported and exotic. But all of them co-exist because the wider society is so secular, because they are relatively unimportant consumer items."

In assessing the Canadian situation, Peter Beyer (1997: 25) speculates that, in at least the immediate future, "most religious consumers, with a relatively

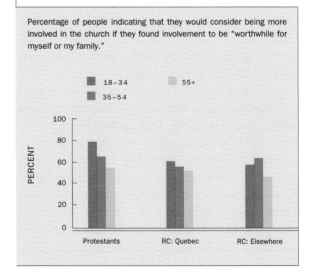

FIGURE 7.3   RECEPTIVITY TO GREATER INVOLVEMENT IN THE CHURCH BY AGE AMONG PROTESTANTS AND CATHOLICS ATTENDING LESS THAN ONCE A MONTH: 2000

Percentage of people indicating that they would consider being more involved in the church if they found involvement to be "worthwhile for myself or my family."

SOURCE: Bibby, *Restless Gods*, 2002: 51.

modest demand for purely religious product, will consume eclectically, with perhaps a fair degree of 'brand' loyalty, but more often than not without membership and the sort of commitment that produced regular participation." Respected religious observer Wade Clark Roof (1999: 9–10) similarly sees Americans as being in an "open, questing mood" as they draw on "an expanded spiritual marketplace," maintaining that "the boundaries of popular religious communities are being redrawn." Peter Emberly (2002) similarly sees Canadians as being on "a spiritual walkabout," embarking on spiritual searches with unprecedented urgency, yet doing with limited regard for churches, synagogues, and temples. There might be some truth to such observations.

Then again, what bears watching is the extent to which religious groups can more adeptly respond to the apparent widespread and persistent interests and needs relating to meaning, the supernatural realm, and spirituality. In 2000, no less than 55 percent of Canadian adults who attend services less than once a month indicated that they would consider being more involved in religious groups if they found it to be worthwhile for themselves or their families. That figure included 64 percent of people who currently are attending on a yearly basis, and 42 percent who say that they never attend. Equally interesting is the finding (Bibby, 2002) that those who express openness to greater involvement included 72 percent of Canadians between the ages of 18 and 34 (see Figure 7.3).

Whether fragments will become meaning systems, and religion more significant personally and socially, will depend, it seems, not only on changing structural and cultural conditions, but also on the ability of religious groups to function far more effectively than they have in recent decades—beginning with young people.

SUMMARY

1. Sociology uses the scientific method to study religion, in contrast to religion, which explores reality beyond what can be known empirically.

2. The sociology of religion has been strongly influenced by the theoretical contributions of Marx, who stressed the compensatory role of religion in the face of economic deprivation; Durkheim, who emphasized both the social origin of religion and its important social cohesive function; and Weber, who gave considerable attention to the relationship between ideas and behaviour.

3. Religion can be defined as a system of meaning with a supernatural referent used to interpret the world. Humanist perspectives make no such use of the supernatural realm, attempting instead to make life meaningful.

4. Personal religious commitment has come increasingly to be seen as having many facets or dimensions. Four such dimensions are commonly noted: belief, practice, experience, and knowledge. Personal commitment is created and sustained by collective religiosity. In Canada, organized religion has experienced a considerable decline in participation in recent years, a trend that has had critical implications for commitment at the individual level.

5. The variations in the levels of individual commitment that characterize complex societies have led to explanations that emphasize individual and structural factors. Reflection, socialization, and deprivation have been prominent among the individual explanations, while the dominant structural assertion has been the secularization thesis.

6. At the individual level, religion appears to be, at best, one of many paths leading to valued characteristics such as personal happiness and compassion. Although religion can be socially disruptive, it more commonly seems to contribute to social solidarity, frequently mirroring the characteristics of groups and societies.

7. Historically, observers of religion have been divided on its future, asserting both secularization and persistence theses. Internationally, there is growing qualitative and quantitative support for the persistence thesis.

8. The search for alleged religious dropouts in Canada reveals that few have turned to new religions, conservative Protestant groups, privatized expressions, or the "no-religion" category. Most still identify with the established groups.

9. The apparent paradox of widespread beliefs and practices existing at the same time as relatively low commitment suggests that many people in Canada find it useful to draw selectively on religion, rather than embracing it as an all-encompassing system of meaning. Such a pattern seems to be common to highly advanced societies more generally.

10. Religion's future will depend not only on social and individual issues, but also on the extent to which religious groups are effective as organizations in responding to widespread interest and need among people of all ages.

QUESTIONS TO CONSIDER

1. Which of the three key theorists do you find to be the most helpful in understanding religion—Durkheim, Marx, or Freud?

2. What does it mean to be religious?

3. To what extent are people in Canada today interested in (a) spirituality and (b) organized religion? What do you mean by the term *spirituality*?

4. What kinds of people do you find are interested in (a) spirituality and (b) organized religion? Do you see any signs of increased interest on the part of young people?

5. Does religion make any difference in the lives of the people you know? Would Canadian society be any different if organized religion disappeared next weekend?

6. Are Canadians interested in the supernatural? What is the evidence?

7. Do you think it is true that secularization stimulates religious innovation—that the decline of old groups provides the opportunity for new groups to surface and prosper?

8. Imagine that you are serving as a consultant to a major Canadian religious group. What might you suggest it consider doing in order to (a) keep the young people it has, and (b) gain the interest of Canadians who are not actively involved?

GLOSSARY

The **church–sect typology** is a framework, originating with Weber, in which religious organizations are studied in terms of ideal-type, church, and sect characteristics.

Civil religion refers to the tendency for nationalistic emphases to be nurtured by a society's religions, so that a culture takes on many religious-like characteristics. The term is most often used with respect to the United States.

Collective conscience is Durkheim's term that refers to the awareness of the group being more than the sum of its individual members, and believing that what is being experienced is the supernatural.

Collective religiosity is religious commitment as manifested in and through religious groups; it is key to the creation and sustenance of personal religiosity.

Cults are religious groups that have their origins outside of older religions; sects, in contrast, are groups that have broken away from established religions.

Denominationalism refers to the tendency for a wide variety of Protestant religious groups to come into being, seemingly reflecting variations not only in theology but also—and perhaps primarily—in social characteristics.

Dimensions of religiosity are the various facets of religious commitment; Glock and Stark, for example, identify four: belief, experience, practice, and knowledge.

Humanist perspectives are systems of meaning used to interpret the world that do not have a supernatural referent (e.g., communism, scientism).

Monotheism refers to belief in one god.

The persistence thesis is the assertion that religion will continue to have a significant place in the modern world, because it never has actually declined, or because people continue to have interests and needs that only religion can satisfy.

Personal religiosity refers to the level of religious commitment characterizing an individual.

Profane See *sacred and profane*.

The **Protestant ethic** is the sixteenth- and seventeenth-century Protestant belief that religious doubts can be reduced and a state of grace assured if people work diligently and live ascetically. According to Weber, the Protestant work ethic had the unintended effect of increasing savings and investment and thus stimulating capitalist growth.

Religions are systems of meaning for interpreting the world that have a supernatural referent (e.g., Christianity, Hinduism).

Sacred and **profane** are the two categories by which Durkheim claimed all things are classified; the sacred represents those things that are deemed to warrant profound respect, and the profane encompasses essentially everything else.

The **secularization thesis** is the assertion that religion as it has been traditionally known is continuously declining, resulting in a loss of religious authority, societally and individually, as well as changes in religious organizations themselves.

SUGGESTED READING

Berger, Peter L., ed. (1999). *The Desecularization of the World: Resurgent Religion and World Politics.* Washington: Ethics and Public Policy Center. A brief and readable book featuring Berger and six contributions from prominent observers who maintain new life is evident in Roman Catholicism, Evangelical Protestantism, Judaism, and Islam. Two additional articles deal with developments in Europe and China.

Bibby, Reginald W. (2002). *Restless Gods: The Renaissance of Religion in Canada.* Toronto: Stoddart. This book draws on the extensive national adult and youth surveys of the author and the work of others in examining religious trends in Canada since the mid-twentieth century, giving attention to developments both inside and outside of religious groups that suggest a religious renaissance may be taking place in Canada.

Christiano, Kevin J., William H. Swatos, Jr., and Peter Kivisto (2002). *Sociology of Religion: Contemporary Developments*. Walnut Creek, CA: AltaMira Press. An excellent introduction to the field that provides a thorough overview of theory, methods, and up-to-date findings on religion and society.

Clark, S.D. (1948). *Church and Sect in Canada*. Toronto: University of Toronto Press. A Canadian classic that examines the social factors contributing to the rise of different types of religious groups in this country.

Dawson, Lorne L. (1998). *Comprehending Cults: The Sociology of New Religious Movements*. Toronto: Oxford University Press. This is a succinct overview of cults that have emerged from the 1970s onward, dealing with such issues as why cults emerge, who joins, and their social significance.

Hewitt, W.E., ed. (1993). *Sociology of Religion: A Canadian Focus*. Toronto: Harcourt Brace. Leading Canadian social scientists provide students with a good introduction both to the work being carried out in the country and to some of the scholars who are most active in this area of research. One of few such works available.

Niebuhr, H. Richard. (1929). *The Social Sources of Denominationalism*. New York: Henry Holt and Company. A classic attempt to probe the role social factors (e.g., economics, nationality, race, and region) had in creating denominationalism in Europe and America. In the process, the author sensitizes students to the social sources of religion more generally.

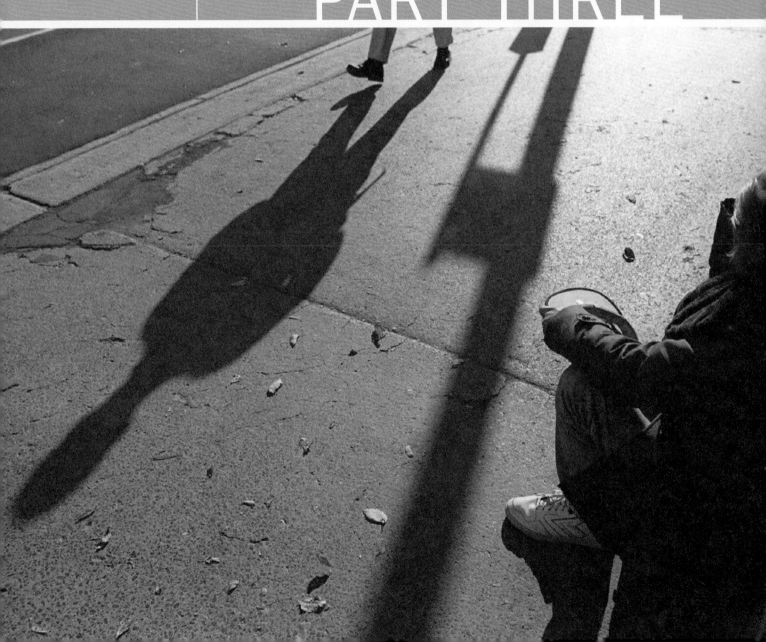

INEQUALITY

PART THREE

CHAPTER EIGHT

SOCIAL STRATIFICATION

In this chapter you will learn that:

- Persistent patterns of social inequality are based on statuses assigned to individuals at birth and on how well individuals perform certain roles. Societies vary in the degree to which mobility up and down the stratification system is possible.

- Explanations of the origins and impact of social stratification include the theory of Karl Marx, which emphasizes the exploitation of the working class by owners of land and industry as the main source of inequality and change; the theory of Max Weber, which emphasizes the power that derives from property ownership, prestige, and politics; structural-functionalist theory, which holds that stratification is both inevitable and necessary; and several revisions of Marx's and Weber's ideas that render them more relevant to today's society.

- Although there has been considerable opportunity for upward occupational mobility in Canada, wealth and property are concentrated in relatively few hands, and one-sixth of Canadians live in poverty. Because of labour-market changes, income inequality has been increasing; thus, the stratification structure we see in the future will probably not resemble the pattern that emerged in the affluent middle of the twentieth century.

- One's position in society's stratification system has important consequences, both for lifestyle and the quality of life. Those who are situated higher in the economic hierarchy tend to live better and live longer.

HARVEY KRAHN

UNIVERSITY OF ALBERTA

INTRODUCTION

While bundling up old newspapers for recycling, I flip through them quickly. Although the news writers don't use the term, I find myself reading about **social stratification**—that is, persistent patterns of social inequality within society. A story with a photo of a grinning young boy sporting a new parka describes how, as part of the annual United Way Coats for Kids and Families campaign, an inner-city social services agency is giving away 5300 winter coats to needy Edmonton families (*Edmonton Journal*, October 19, 2002). A total of 14 500 coats have been distributed in the Edmonton capital region. One of the women choosing coats for her two sons explains that she would normally buy clothes for her family. But she has been living on social assistance, since going on sick leave from her job, and her boyfriend has just been laid off. "I just hope I don't have to depend on this all they time," she explains to the reporter.

Another news item, from the previous day's paper, headlines that "More people [are] homeless in high-rent economy" (*Edmonton Journal*, October 25, 2002). The article explains how a coalition of low-income housing advocacy groups is setting out to conduct its biannual tally of Edmonton's homeless. Two years earlier, a 24-hour search through shelters, drop-in centres, and other places where the homeless might spend the night turned up 1160 people, including 146 children under the age of 15. The coalition expects to count more homeless people this year, because rising rents and very low vacancy rates, both a product of a robust economy, have been leaving more city residents without a roof over their head. A homeless person interviewed at an inner-city mission comments that: "Sometimes life is difficult. I try to go to work all the time. I do odd jobs here and there, and then my life starts falling apart."

While Edmonton's strong economy has left some citizens by the wayside, others have clearly benefited. A local restaurant announces that it has purchased a $22 000 bottle of Scotch whiskey, and will be selling one-ounce drinks to those who can afford them for $1500 each. A local businessman, interviewed for the

Canadian fishers have a history of making do on low incomes. Quotas on certain stocks of fish have made the situation worse.
SOURCE: Lois Dierlam OSA.

article, announces that he plans to sample the 65-year-old whiskey because "I believe that I deserve to reward myself" (*The Globe and Mail*, October 25, 2002).

A pair of short articles, one above the other in the international business section of one of the papers, note that "Wendy's earnings [are] up 16 per cent" and that "Kodak [will] crop up to 1,700 jobs after slump" (*Edmonton Journal*, October 25, 2002). Interestingly, both companies reported that their earnings had risen in the previous three-month period. Wendy's had turned a profit of US$61 million while Kodak reported earnings of US$334 million. But while Wendy's had improved its financial record by streamlining restaurant operations and buying other fast-food chains or, in other words, by continuing to rely on low-wage workers, much of Kodak's profit resulted from the lay-off of much-better-paid workers. The 1700 Kodak employees around the world about to lose their jobs would join the 7000 already cut in the previous year.

Back in Canada, in northern British Columbia, leaders of the Gitksan Nation continue to try to negotiate a treaty with the federal government, a process they began 25 years ago in 1977 (*The Globe and Mail*, October 21, 2002). Over the past quarter-century, they have taken their case all the way to the Supreme Court, but they still have not convinced the federal government to begin treaty talks about the land their ancestors lost without any compensation or any treaty being signed. Their dispute is one of almost 30 outstanding Native land claims and self-government negotiations facing the federal government.

And south of the border, the 2002 mid-term Senate elections are underway. A *Globe and Mail* article (October 24, 2002) comments on the possibility that a Black Democrat from Texas may become the only Black U.S. Senator, and only the third Black Senator since the Civil War. However, experts doubt whether this popular former mayor of Dallas will win the election, even though 47 percent of Texans are of Black or Hispanic origin. Ron Kirk may have lost some of the middle-class white voters he needed when he publicly questioned the wisdom of George Bush starting a war with Iraq to bring down Saddam Hussein. Noting that it is usually the poor and disadvantaged who become the casualties in wars, Mr. Kirk wondered whether there would be as much support for this particular war if "the first 500,000 kids have to come from families that earn $1-million or more?"

The common theme in these quite different stories is the existence of groups—welfare recipients, the homeless, nonwhites, Aboriginal Canadians, the unemployed, and ordinary citizens stuck in low-wage jobs—that are ranked lower than others in the social stratification system. A low position in this ranking typically means having little power, little wealth, and little prestige, whereas a higher position generally implies the opposite. In this chapter, we begin by discussing some of the ways in which sociologists study social stratification. We then examine a variety of theories of social stratification that attempt to explain its origins and impacts. The last section of the chapter focuses on occupational and class structures and material inequality in Canada, and concludes by asking whether inequality has been increasing in the recent past.

STRATIFICATION: A CORNERSTONE OF SOCIOLOGY

Standing back and looking at the whole discipline of sociology, we see four basic areas of inquiry. Sociologists study *social structure*, or the way in which society is organized, both formally and informally. We also ask questions about *social order*. What is it that holds together a society composed of individuals with different interests, and when and why does social order break down? Inquiries about *social change* form a third key area within the discipline. How and why do societies, the institutions and power structures within them, and the values and beliefs held by individual members change? Finally, sociologists spend a lot of time studying *social stratification*, the manner in which valued resources—that is, wealth, power, and prestige—are distributed, and the way in which advantages of wealth, power, and prestige are passed from generation to generation.

In fact, it could easily be argued that social stratification is the cornerstone of sociology. Descriptions of social structure that ignore the stratification system are clearly inadequate. For example, imagine describing Canadian society to someone from another country without referring to some features of stratification. Would the listener really have an adequate understanding of our society if he or she did not know that most large corporations are run by men, that Aboriginal Canadians are much more likely than most others to be living in poverty, that disagreements about the relative power of the English-speaking majority and the French-speaking minority have dominated federal politics for decades, and that the colour of Canadian society is slowly changing, since the majority of immigrants today are members of visible minority groups?

Furthermore, inequalities in wealth can threaten social stability (the poor resenting the wealthy, for example, and demanding more equality), and inequalities in power can be used to maintain social order. For example, powerful corporations might lobby provincial governments for changes in the labour laws that would make it more difficult for unions to organize company employees. In less democratic countries, direct control of the police and military by a powerful minority can lead to the quick and violent suppression of any unrest among the masses.

An understanding of social stratification is also essential for studying social change, since, frequently, it is the stratification system that is undergoing change. For example, changing gender roles and the slow movement of women into positions of power and authority in North America in the past few decades are really features of a changing stratification system. The massive social, economic, and political changes that began in the former Soviet Union in the late 1980s and that continue today are, among other things, changes in stratification systems, as the main source of power shifts from control of the political system to include control of the emerging free-market economy.

SOCIAL HIERARCHIES IN STRATIFIED SOCIETIES

Imagine a society in which stratification did not exist, in which all things of value were distributed equally. Even if you picture a very small group, perhaps a preindustrial society with only a few hundred members, living on some isolated island where the necessities of life are easily obtained, it is still difficult to imagine a nonstratified society. A social hierarchy might emerge as a result of skill differences in fishing, in nursing the ill back to health, or in communicating with the spirits, for example. Inequalities in wealth might develop simply because some families were fortunate enough to have a larger number of chil-

dren, providing more of the labour needed to accumulate valued possessions. And once accumulations of wealth began to be passed from generation to generation, a structured and relatively permanent pattern of inequality would emerge.

Perhaps you imagined some contemporary society composed of adults who, believing strongly in equality, decided to live and work together in some kind of urban or rural commune, sharing all their possessions. Again, it is easy to imagine how a social hierarchy could emerge, as those with more useful skills found themselves playing a more central role in the society. No doubt, when important decisions needed to be made, these individuals would be more likely to influence the outcome.

We do not need to repeat this mental exercise too many times before we see that social stratification in one form or another exists in all societies. But our hypothetical examples are far from typical. In most societies, stratification is much more pronounced, and basic skills are seldom the foundation of primary social hierarchies. Nevertheless, there are cross-cultural variations in the criteria by which individuals and groups are ranked, the degree to which they can move from one position to another within the hierarchy, and the extent of inequality in wealth and power that exists within the hierarchy.

ASCRIBED AND ACHIEVED STATUS

Let's begin by defining the rank or position that one has within a social hierarchy as one's **status**. We can further distinguish between an **ascribed status** and an **achieved status**. The former is assigned to individuals, typically at birth. An ascribed status can be connected with race, gender, age, and other factors that are not chosen or earned, and that cannot be changed. (A few people do choose their gender status, but they are rare exceptions.) In contrast, an achieved status is precisely that—a position in a hierarchy that has been achieved by virtue of how well one performs in some role. The most obvious example is that of occupational status—for instance, individuals who have performed well in law school are entitled to become lawyers, and high-performance athletes strive to achieve the status of "professional athlete." By the same logic, one could achieve the status of "bum" by performing poorly in educational, employment, family, and other social roles.

Although we may accept that a completely non-stratified society is impossible, most of us would probably agree that a stratification system in which higher positions were achieved, not ascribed, would be preferable. In a **meritocracy**, everyone would have equal opportunities to compete for higher-status positions and, presumably, those most capable would be awarded the highest rank. Such a society would exhibit a considerable degree of **social mobility**, as those who were more qualified moved up the social hierarchy to replace those who were less competent and who were consequently compelled to move down.

OPEN AND CLOSED STRATIFICATION SYSTEMS

When we compare Canada with some other societies, or look back at our history, we find that this country has had what appears to be a fairly **open stratification system**, in which merit, rather than inheritance (or ascribed characteristics), determines social rank, and in which social change is therefore possible. For example, dramatic changes in the status of various groups have occurred in this country over time. Although the practice was not nearly as widespread in Canada as in the United States, slaves (most of them Aboriginal people) were bought and sold in Canada during the 1600s and 1700s (Pentland, 1981: 1). Chinese labourers, brought into the country to help build the railways, were kept out of most "white" jobs by law until well into the twentieth century (Li, 1982). Similarly, it was not until the 1960s that Black Canadians were allowed to compete for anything but the lowest-level positions in the Canadian railway industry (Calliste, 1987). By the early 1800s, slavery had disappeared in Canada, and we now have laws against discrimination on the basis of race.

Comparing ourselves with other contemporary societies, we note that Canada does not have an aristocracy such as the one that exists in Britain, where children of wealthy and powerful families of long standing inherit positions and titles. The degree to which Canadians compete for higher-status occupations (in the education system and, later, within the workplace) stands in clear contrast to the situation in India, for example, where the caste into which an individual is born largely determines the type of work that he or she will be allowed to do. Although discrimination on the basis of caste membership has been illegal in India for many decades, the **caste system** continues to underpin an almost totally

closed stratification system. Compared with India, then, Canada offers many more opportunities for upward social mobility, an indication of a more open stratification system.

It is all too easy, however, to overlook the extent to which ascribed statuses continue to limit opportunities for many Canadians as well. Discrimination against members of First Nations and visible-minority groups continues to occur in Canada today. So too does discrimination against members of the gay community, against the disabled and the elderly, and against women. These people are in their lower-status positions not because they competed poorly for some higher ranking in the social hierarchy, but because they are old, disabled, gay, or female.

These are fairly obvious examples of the ways in which ascribed statuses continue to play a prominent role in Canada's social stratification system. But what about the child from a wealthy family who graduates from an excellent high school in an affluent neighbourhood, completes a degree or two in a prestigious and costly university, and then begins a career in a high-status, well-paying profession? Is this simply an example of someone achieving a deserved high-status position, or did the advantages of birth (ascribed status) play some part in this success story? Similarly, when we hear of large companies laying off hundreds or thousands of workers, does their sudden downward mobility reflect their failure to compete in an open, merit-based stratification system, or were they simply unfortunate enough to be employed in a corporation that was being downsized?

As these examples illustrate, the social stratification system consists of a number of different hierarchies, some based on ascribed characteristics, others on achievement. If you flip through this textbook, you will see chapters devoted to dimensions of stratification and inequality such as gender, race, and ethnicity. Other chapters address activities (e.g., work) and institutions (e.g., education) in which stratification processes are extremely important, and still others focus on inequalities between regions and countries. Once you have read all these chapters, you will, no doubt, be convinced of the central importance of social stratification to the discipline of sociology.

CLASS AND CLASS STRUCTURE

You will also notice that, even though studies of gender, race, ethnicity, and work take you in quite different directions, all frequently share an emphasis on inequalities in income and wealth or property, and on resulting inequalities in power. On average, women earn about 70 percent of what men earn. Older women are much more likely than older men to be living in poverty. Members of visible minorities and, particularly, Aboriginal groups are more likely to be unemployed and, if they are employed, to be in low-paying jobs. Owners of large workplaces (employers, in other words) are wealthier than most other members of society, and employees in professional and managerial occupations typically earn a great deal more than lower-level employees. Owners, self-employed professionals, and managers typically have more job security than do nonmanagerial employees who are either paid by the hour or salaried. Recognizing, then, the extent to which such material inequality (i.e., differences in income and wealth or property) parallels and overlaps other social hierarchies, the rest of this chapter will focus primarily on material inequality or, after we define the terms, on *class* and *class structure*.

Although the concept of **class** is seldom absent from discussions of social stratification, the definitions attached to it vary considerably. We will examine some of these definitions in the next section, which outlines several different theories of stratification. My own preference is to use the term in a fairly general sense, to indicate the position of an individual or a family within an economic hierarchy, along with others who have roughly the same amount of control over or access to economic or material resources. Thus, an individual can be said to be a member of a particular class, whether this is a class of large landowners, a class of wage-labourers and salaried workers (i.e., the "working class"), or a "professional/managerial class." It is their similar economic situation and opportunities, a result of their shared position within a society's system of economic production, that makes these individuals members of the same class. In turn, we can use the term **class structure** to refer to the overall economic hierarchy composed of all such classes, choosing the word *structure* deliberately to indicate the relative stability and prominence of this social ranking.

Do you think of yourself as a member of a specific social class? Probably not very often, if at all. Like most North Americans, you probably have a reasonably good idea of how well off you are com-

pared with others in your community. You probably have some sense of where your education, occupation, and income, or the education, occupation, and income of adult members of your household, fit in some general hierarchy of **socioeconomic status**. "Class," however, is unlikely to be part of your everyday vocabulary. Nor is it typically part of the media's vocabulary. The newspaper stories we examined earlier, for example, identified a number of different dimensions of stratification, but class was not among them.

Does this make "class" a useless concept? I argue the opposite. As I have already suggested, and as you will see in this and other chapters, pronounced patterns of material inequality exist in our society, and overlap with most other dimensions of social stratification. The economic hierarchy is obviously not completely closed, but it is relatively stable and permanent, and is composed of some fairly distinct categories of individuals with similar amounts of control over material resources. Hence, it is useful to try to identify the "classes" that make up the stratification system (or class structure), to seek to understand their origin, and to examine the effects of membership in them on individuals and families. Rather than discarding the concept of "class" because few people think in these terms, we can ask why few people think about classes despite their prominence. In fact, we will see that some of the major theories of social stratification address this issue directly, inquiring about the conditions under which members of an economic class begin to recognize their shared interests, and perhaps begin to act accordingly as a group.

In the following section, we begin with a detailed look at the ideas of the nineteenth-century social and political philosopher Karl Marx, who put class at the very centre of his discussions of social structure and his theory of social change. In turn, some of the theories of social stratification developed in the twentieth century downplay the role of class or even ignore it completely, because the theorists appear to believe that material inequalities are decreasing. Summing up this line of reasoning, Terry Nichols Clark and Seymour Martin Lipset (1991: 397) write that

> class is an increasingly outmoded concept, although it is sometimes appropriate to earlier historical periods.... Class analysis has grown increasingly inadequate in recent

decades as traditional hierarchies have declined and new social differences have emerged. The cumulative impact of these changes is fundamentally altering the nature of social stratification—placing past theories in need of substantial modification.

As you read about the various theories of social stratification in the next section, and as you examine the data on material inequalities in Canada in the section after that, keep in mind Clark and Lipset's question: "Are social classes dying?"

EXPLANATIONS OF SOCIAL STRATIFICATION

So far, we have considered some examples of social stratification and its effects, and have added to our vocabulary a number of useful concepts that allow us to discuss the phenomenon and to compare our society with others. But we have not really tried to explain social stratification, to account for its origins and its impacts. In this section, we will briefly examine the theories (or explanations) of social stratification elaborated by a number of important social theorists, including some who were analyzing society decades ago and others who have written about it more recently. As we will see, it is important to take into account the time and place in which a social theory was developed, since theorists construct their social explanations on the basis of what they see around them and expect to see in the future.

KARL MARX: CAPITALISM, EXPLOITATION, AND CLASS CONFLICT

Karl Marx had an immense impact on how we think about social stratification. He was born in Germany in 1818 but lived in England from 1849 until he died in 1883. His writings about the social and economic forces that brought about economic change look back over history, but focus particularly on the rapidly changing European world that he observed during his lifetime. This was a time when industrial capitalism was transforming the economy and society. Large, mechanized, factory-based systems of production were emerging; cities were growing rapidly as rural peasants were being forced off the land or, perhaps, were attracted to the city by the possibility of jobs in factories; and material inequality was extreme, as fac-

tory owners and merchants made huge profits while labourers lived in poverty. Trade unions, labour laws, and other arrangements that came to offer some protection to workers did not yet exist. Thus, as Marx observed, the Industrial Revolution was a time when both the level of economic production and the degree of inequality in society increased tremendously.

Modes of Production and Social Classes

Marx called the overall system of economic activity in a society its **mode of production**. In turn, its major components were the **means of production** (technology, capital investments, and raw materials) and the **social relations of production** (the relationships between the main classes involved in production). Slavery had been the primary mode of production in some societies in earlier times, and feudalism, an economic system in which peasants worked for landowners, not for a wage but for some share of the produce, was the mode of production that gave way to industrial capitalism in Europe.

Within industrial capitalism, Marx identified two major classes—the capitalist class, or **bourgeoisie**, which owned the means of production, and the **proletariat**, or working class, which exchanged its labour for wages. He also described a middle class—the **petite bourgeoisie**—comprising independent owners/producers (farmers, for example) and small-business owners. Marx expected this middle class largely to disappear as capitalism matured and drew some of its members up into the bourgeoisie but most down into the proletariat. Of much greater importance in his theory of class inequality and social change was the relationship between workers and owners.

Marx reasoned that the value of a product sold was directly proportional to the average amount of labour needed to produce it. Thus, for example, an elegant piece of furniture was more valuable than its component pieces mainly because of the labour invested in it by the worker(s) who built it. Marx argued that the value of goods produced by wage-labourers far exceeded the amount needed to pay their wages and the cost of raw materials, technology, and other components of the means of production. Marx referred to this excess as **surplus value**. According to Marx, when commodities were sold, their surplus value was turned into profits for the owner. Marx viewed this as an exploitive relationship, but one that differed from the exploitive relationships that characterized slavery or feudalism. After all, factory workers were paid a wage for their labour and were not legally forced to stay with the job. However, because most workers had few other options for making a living, and because owners controlled all aspects of the work, the legal freedom of wage-labourers to change jobs was, in practical terms, an illusion.

Class Conflict and Class Consciousness

The idea of **class conflict** between the major classes in a society was the driving force behind Marx's theory of social change. Marx noted that previous modes of production had collapsed and been replaced because of class conflict. Feudalism in Europe, for example, had given way to capitalism as a result of the growing power of the merchant class relative to the traditional alliance of landowners and the aristocracy, and the deteriorating relationship between landowners and peasants. Furthermore, Marx argued, capitalism would eventually be replaced by a socialist mode of production, in which private ownership of property would disappear, along with the exploitation and inequality it produced. The impetus for this massive change would again be widespread class conflict, this time between wage-labourers and the owners of the means of production, as inequality between these two classes became more pronounced.

Marx held that this revolution would take place only when members of the working class began to recognize that they were being exploited. In other words, Marx did not take it for granted that members of a class would see how their interests were similar. Whereas capitalists might be conscious of their group interests, wage-labourers needed to become aware of their common enemy. They needed to be transformed from a "class in itself" to a "class for itself." Thus, **class consciousness** was an important social-psychological component of Marx's theory of social inequality and social change. His vision of the future was that of a revolutionary upheaval in which the oppressed working class would recognize its enemy, destroy the institutions of capitalism, and replace them with a classless socialist society based on collective ownership of the means of production.

Responses to Marx

Over the years, many critics of Marx's ideas pointed to the communist countries, with their apparently socialist system of government and absence of private property, and noted that inequality had not disappeared there. Instead, a new hierarchy had emerged, in which control of the political and bureaucratic apparatus was the main basis of power. These observations were largely correct. (According to a Russian joke from the 1970s, under capitalism man exploits man, but under communism it is the other way around.) In fact, one wonders just how critical Marx himself would have been of the Soviet communist system, given the degree to which individual citizens were exploited and harshly treated by a powerful minority. However, it is slowly becoming apparent that the emergence of a capitalist economy in Eastern Europe is not eliminating material inequalities so much as changing their source. Today, individuals with control over some form of production or access to some marketing system are accumulating wealth while the majority of citizens appear to be no better off than before—indeed, many are worse off. In other words, while Marx's predictions about the inevitable emergence of a classless society have not been borne out, his type of class analysis still has considerable relevance for understanding the changing stratification system in Eastern Europe.

Most theories of social stratification developed after Marx were essentially a "debate with Marx's ghost" (Zeitlin with Brym, 1991: 117). Some social philosophers and sociologists elaborated on Marx's ideas, while others attempted to refute them. Among the critics, some focused on the absence of widespread class conflict, the growth of the middle class, and the relative decline in material inequality in Western Europe and North America in the twentieth century. We will examine some of these theories below, along with others that tried to develop more complex models of the contemporary class structure while basically following Marx's form of class-based analysis.

MAX WEBER: CLASS AND OTHER DIMENSIONS OF INEQUALITY

Max Weber was born in Germany half a century later than Marx—in 1864. Like Marx, he built his analysis of social stratification on a careful reading of history as well as a thorough analysis of the economic and political events of his day. But because he was only beginning his university studies about the time Marx died, Weber had the advantage of seeing the direction in which a more mature industrial capitalism was taking European society. He continued to write about many aspects of social stratification and social change until his death in 1920.

Class, Status, and Party

Weber shared with Marx a belief that economic inequalities were central to the social stratification system, and that the ownership of property was a primary determinant of power, or the ability to impose one's wishes on others, to get them to do what one wants them to do. However, he argued that power could lie in controlling other types of resources as well (Weber, 1948 [1922]). Specifically, he proposed that structures of social stratification could be better understood by looking at economic inequalities, hierarchies of prestige (or social honour), and political inequalities (control of power blocs such as political parties or other organizations)—or, in his words, at "class, status, and party." Although these different hierarchies often overlap, they need not do so. For example, suddenly wealthy individuals might not receive the prestige they desire, being rejected in "high society" by those with "old money." Similarly, a politician might have considerable power through control of government resources, but might not be very wealthy or, for that matter, have much prestige.

Since Weber lived to see the emergence of white-collar workers, the growth of large private- and public-sector bureaucracies, and the growing power of trade unions, he was able to write about these alternative sources of power in a stratified capitalist society. He provided an insightful analysis of how power resided in the control of top positions in large bureaucratic organizations, even if the officeholder was not an owner of the organization. He recognized that well-educated wage-labourers might not be as powerless as were the factory workers of an earlier era. He also saw that a new class of middle-level, educated workers might not necessarily align themselves with blue-collar workers, and was less inclined to conclude, as had Marx, that the middle class would disappear (Zeitlin with Brym, 1991: 118–19). In fact, he expected that the number of educated technical and professional workers in bureaucratic capitalist society would increase.

What Weber saw, then, compared with Marx, was considerably more complexity in the social stratification system because of the growing complexity of the occupational structure and of capitalist enterprises.

And although Weber was sometimes pessimistic in his writings about the future of democracy in a bureaucratic capitalist society, he did not link inequality and class conflict to the ultimate demise of capitalism itself, as did Marx. Similarly, although Weber, like Marx, commented on how members of a class might or might not recognize their shared interests, he did not conclude that it was the inevitable destiny of the working class to become a "class for itself."

Social Class and Life-Chances

Despite the above-noted divergences in their thinking, Weber, like Marx, placed primary emphasis on the economic underpinnings of social stratification. However, he defined "class" more broadly. Rather than insisting that a limited number of class positions were based on an individual's relationship to the means of production, Weber saw a larger variety of class positions based both on ownership of property and on other labour-market statuses, such as occupation and education. Furthermore, he tended to emphasize the **life-chances** that class position offered. In other words, a higher position in the economic hierarchy, however obtained, provided more power and allowed an individual and his or her family to enjoy more of the good things in life.

It should be apparent, then, that the general approach to studying stratification that I outlined earlier, one that recognizes the central importance of class while acknowledging that gender, race, and other dimensions of social inequality can also be very important, is in the Weberian tradition. Similarly, my general definition of "class" as a relatively stable position within an economic hierarchy held by an individual or family, along with others with roughly the same amount of control over or access to material resources, follows Weber's use of the term.

DAVIS AND MOORE: A FUNCTIONAL THEORY OF STRATIFICATION

Twentieth-Century Affluence and Structural-Functionalist Theory

Although a number of other social theorists in Europe and North America wrote about social stratification in the early decades of the twentieth century, we will skip ahead in our overview to 1945, when Kingsley Davis and Wilbert Moore published their short but much-debated statement on "some principles of social stratification." In other chapters in this text, you will read about the **structural-functionalist theory** in sociology, an approach that emphasizes consensus over conflict and that seeks to explain the function, for society as a whole, of social institutions and various aspects of social structure. Davis and Moore were part of this intellectual tradition, which arose in reaction to the conflict-oriented and socially radical theories of Marx (and, to a lesser extent, of Weber).

The emergence of structural-functionalism as an alternative theoretical approach can be better understood if we view it as reflecting the optimistic view in postwar North America that affluence was increasing, social conflict was decreasing, and a harmonious future for society was dawning. For example, Arthur Schlesinger, Jr., an American historian writing in 1956, suggested that Americans should start thinking about the "miseries of an age of abundance." Rather than worrying about economic growth, employment, and improving the standard of living, it was time to concentrate on "the bettering of our mass media and the elevation of our popular culture, in short, with the quality of civilization to which our nation aspires in an age of ever-increasing abundance and leisure" (as quoted in Longman, 1985: 75). Thus, during the several decades following World War II, many social scientists were attracted to theories that downplayed conflict and emphasized the benefits, to all, of an apparently ever-expanding economy.

The Functional Necessity of Stratification

Davis and Moore (1945) argued that, because inequality exists in all societies, it must be a necessary part of society. All societies, they noted, have a variety of occupational roles that need to be filled, some requiring much more training than others, some having more functional importance, and some being less pleasant and more difficult to perform. In order to get people to fill important roles and to perform these critical tasks well, and to spend time training for high-skill occupations, societies must ensure that the rewards for performance (money, prestige, and other intangibles) are greater. Thus, for example, doctors and schoolteachers need to be paid more than factory workers and truck drivers, and also must rank higher than the latter in terms of social honour and prestige.

In short, according to Davis and Moore, social inequality is both inevitable and functionally necessary for society. But theirs was not a class-based and conflict-prone stratification system. Rather, Davis and Moore described a much more fluid socioeconomic hierarchy, with many different occupational statuses into which individuals are slotted on the basis of their effort and ability. The system is held together by consensus and shared values (not torn apart by conflict, as Marx theorized), because members of society generally agree that the hierarchy is fair and just. It also follows from this line of reasoning that efforts to reduce social inequality will be ineffective, and might even be harmful to society.

Criticisms of Davis and Moore

Various criticisms have been levelled against Davis and Moore's theory. For example, although some differences in pay might be justified to reimburse those who spend more years in school preparing for an occupation, are the huge income inequalities we see in our society really necessary (see Box 8.1)? Why do women often earn less than men, even if they are doing the same type of work? Are movie stars, professional athletes, and chief executive officers with million-dollar-plus annual incomes really so much more important to society than nurses, day-care workers, prison guards, and most other low-paid workers? And how does a theory like this account for inherited wealth, for the fact that wealth leads to power and the ability to accumulate more wealth?

Given these criticisms, what accounts for the appeal of this theory? Perhaps it is the kernel of truth at its core that is so attractive—namely, the recognition that, *to some extent*, differences in income and prestige are based on different amounts of effort and ability. After all, we can easily think of examples of better-paying occupations that require long years of education and training. Nevertheless, this is far from the complete story about inequality in our society, which is much more pronounced than what such differences in effort and ability might lead us to expect. In fact, the theory's appeal probably lies more in its apparent justification of these large inequalities. You might test this hypothesis by explaining the theory, first to someone with a high income or inherited wealth, and then to someone who is unemployed or earning very little. The odds are that the functionalist explanation of stratification would sound much more plausible to the wealthier person.

GERHARD LENSKI: TECHNOLOGY AND STRATIFICATION SYSTEMS

Writing in the 1960s, a time of economic expansion and growing prosperity in North America, Gerhard Lenski (1966) developed a theory of "power and privilege" that attempted to explain the extent of material inequality in both contemporary and past societies. Lenski's explanation recognized power and conflict much more explicitly than had the Davis and Moore functionalist explanation of stratification. And, like Weber, he identified a number of different dimensions of social stratification, such as education and ethnicity, while emphasizing the centrality of economic inequalities. Although he used the term *class*, he did not define it precisely, choosing instead to talk about the ruling elites in society in general terms, and about how they managed to maintain their wealth and power at the expense of the masses.

Lenski reasoned that a society's technological base largely determines the degree of inequality within it. In simple hunting-and-gathering societies, he argued, the few resources of the society were distributed primarily on the basis of need. But as societies became more technologically complex, resources in excess of those required to fulfill basic needs were produced. Control of those surplus resources, or **privilege**, came to be based on power, allowing ruling elites to take a much larger share of these resources for themselves. Thus, the more com-

plex agricultural societies, such as that of precolonial India, developed highly structured governing and tax-collecting systems, through which the privileged ruling elites accumulated immense amounts of wealth, while the masses lived in poverty.

As a result of industrialization and the complexity of modern technology, this "age-old evolutionary trend toward ever-increasing inequality" (Lenski, 1966: 308) was reversed. Owners of the means of production could no longer control the production process directly and had to rely instead on well-educated managerial and technical workers to keep the complex system operating. Education broadened the horizons of these middle-level employees, introducing them to ideas of democracy, encouraging them to demand a larger share of the profits they were helping to produce, and making them more articulate in their demands for equality.

Thus, Lenski's theory proposed a causal link between complex industrial technology, the higher education of workers, and workers' insistence on sharing the growing wealth of an industrial society. But why would employers give in to such demands? Because, argued Lenski, the industrial elite needed educated workers—they could not produce without them. Equally important, the much greater productivity of industrial societies compared with preindustrial societies meant that the elite could "make economic concessions in relative terms without necessarily suffering any loss in absolute terms" (Lenski,

While high technology has created many new jobs, it has also eliminated many. For the chronically unemployed, the closest they may get to high technology is a computer at the local unemployment office.

SOURCE: Dick Hemingway.

1966: 314). Because the economic "pie" was so much bigger, everyone could have a larger slice.

In one obvious sense, Lenski's theory resembled the functionalist theory of stratification—both noted that better-educated and more highly skilled workers are paid more. However, unlike the functionalist approach, Lenski's theory clearly took power differences into account, emphasizing how the extent of accumulation of wealth by elites, or the degree of material inequality, depends on the power and bargaining ability of middle-level workers. In fact, Lenski placed material inequality at the centre of his theory of stratification. But in contrast to Marx's nineteenth-century predictions of growing inequality as industrial capitalism matured, Lenski, writing in the middle of the twentieth century, saw a movement toward a more equal distribution of society's wealth.

ERIK OLIN WRIGHT: A NEO-MARXIST APPROACH

In reaction against functionalism, Lenski brought power and conflict back into his explanation of social inequality. He placed material inequalities resulting from one group's domination of another at the centre of his model, thus coming closer to the approach taken by Marx and Weber. But he did not carry through with a traditional Marxist analysis built around the relationships of different classes to the means of production. In contrast, a number of neo-Marxist scholars, writing in the 1970s and 1980s, attempted to update the original Marxist model so that it could be applied to the late-twentieth century. We will discuss only one theorist from the neo-Marxist camp, Erik Olin Wright.

Although Marx acknowledged the existence of a middle class composed of several distinct groups, including independent producers and small-business owners, he predicted that the class would disappear, and so spent much more time writing about the relationship between the two primary classes (capitalists and workers). Wright's contribution lies in recognizing that, as industrial capitalism matured, the middle class had grown and become more diverse, and in trying to understand the class dynamics of our more complex capitalist system of production. Of particular importance in Wright's theory is the emphasis on **contradictory class locations**—that is, on occupational groupings that have divided loyalties within a class structure. For example, although managers work for capitalists, supervising lower-level employees and trying to get them to produce as much as possible, managers are themselves employees, potentially exploited by owners. Considering the substantial numbers of people in such contradictory locations, one can begin to understand why the widespread class conflict envisioned by Marx has seldom emerged.

In a more recent reformulation of his ideas, Wright (1985) argued that exploitation of one class by another can occur through control of property or the means of production (as Marx had insisted), as well as through ownership of skill or credential assets and control of high positions within organizations. Thus, he identified three classes of owners (the bourgeoisie, small employers, and the petite bourgeoisie with no employees), and nine classes of wage-labourers (nonowners), differentiated on two dimensions, the possession of organizational assets and of skill/credential assets (Wright, 1985: 88). For example, "expert managers" (e.g., engineers or lawyers in senior management positions within large companies) fill a class location characterized by extensive organizational assets and high skill/credential assets, in contrast to basic "proletarians," who have no specific skill/credential assets and no management or supervisory responsibilities (see Figure 8.1).

Despite his intention of developing a neo-Marxist theoretical model updated to the late twentieth century, Wright's theory is similar to Weber's view of class structure in some ways (Grabb, 2002). Specifically, the different class locations created by the intersection of organizational and skill/credential assets remind us of the different classes Weber described as he commented on how similar educational and occupational statuses resulted in similar control over and access to material resources. Even so, Wright's theory of class structure and his observations about contradictory locations within it are useful because he deliberately attempts to incorporate the complexities of modern capitalist society into his explanation of social inequality.

FRANK PARKIN: A NEO-WEBERIAN APPROACH

While Wright attempted to bring Marx's class analysis back into the discussion of contemporary forms of social stratification, Frank Parkin (1972, 1979) was equally explicit in stating his intellectual debts to Max Weber's discussions of power, class, and social stratification (Grabb, 2002). In fact, Parkin went so far as to argue that neo-Marxist scholars, espousing what he calls "professorial Marxism" (1979: x), were merely putting forth dressed-up Weberian arguments. As a neo-Weberian, Parkin criticized traditional Marxist and contemporary neo-Marxist class-focused analyses for failing to take into account gender, race, religious, and other forms of social stratification that do not grow out of the relations of production in capitalist society but clearly have an origin and permanency all of their own (1979: 4–5). Nevertheless, like both Weber and Marx

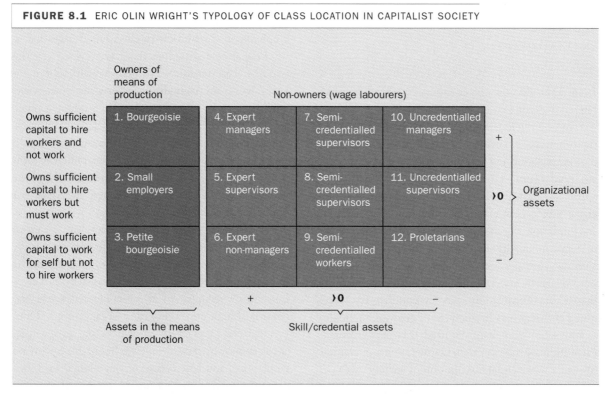

FIGURE 8.1 ERIC OLIN WRIGHT'S TYPOLOGY OF CLASS LOCATION IN CAPITALIST SOCIETY

SOURCE: Erik Olin Wright, *Classes* (London: Verso, 1985), p. 88.

before him, Parkin continued to emphasize the importance of property relations in contemporary stratification systems (Grabb, 2002).

Among Parkin's most useful contributions to stratification theory is his explanation of how patterns of structured inequality, whether based on class, gender, race, or some other ascribed or achieved status, are maintained or changed. To do so, Parkin returned to a concept introduced by Weber, that of **social closure**. Parkin defines this term as "the process by which social collectivities seek to maximize rewards by restricting access to resources and opportunities to a limited circle of eligibles" (1979: 44). He then goes on to elaborate two types of closure strategies that help us understand how patterns of social inequality are maintained, but also sometimes altered.

Exclusion refers to the organized efforts of privileged, more powerful groups to maintain their advantaged position. Processes of exclusion can range from centuries-old caste systems in closed societies to the use, in contemporary open societies, of educational credentials to maintain power and privilege. For example, lawyers and other professional groups have managed to ensure, via legal restrictions, that only they can perform certain types of work in our society. By excluding others from engaging in such work, it is possible to maintain high incomes, enjoy a high standard of living, and exercise a great deal of power. Similarly, members of trade unions can also use legal sanctions to keep nonmembers, who might have the same skills, from taking on some well-paying jobs.

In contrast, **usurpation** refers to the efforts of excluded groups within a stratification system to gain some advantages and power. As Parkin puts it, all usurpation actions have as their goal "biting into the resources and benefits accruing to dominant groups in society" (1979: 74). As with exclusionary practices, usurpation efforts range across a continuum, from lobbying and voting for social change to outright revolt against groups in power. Thus, over the past several decades, we have seen successful efforts by women's groups, First Nations groups, and other disadvantaged groups to change the balance of power and privilege in Canada. Going back further, labour unions took even stronger, sometimes illegal, actions to gain new powers and a more equitable distribution of resources for their members.

Thus, like Lenski, Parkin took a keen interest in the power struggles within society between groups with more and less power (Grabb, 2002). However, Parkin's neo-Weberian theory does not contain a premise of inevitability, either one of increased inequality and eventual social revolution as Marx predicted, or one of reduced inequality resulting from technological change and economic growth, as Lenski predicted. But Parkin did see a clear trend with respect to processes of social closure. With the growing emphasis on education in modern society, the use of educational credentials to maintain power and privilege has become more widespread. As a result, well-educated professionals have become a powerful class grouping, sometimes almost as powerful as wealthy capitalists who control the means of production (Grabb, 2002). Beneath these two powerful groups are a range of other groups with varying amounts of power, trying, when possible, to usurp more power from those above.

EXPLANATIONS OF SOCIAL STRATIFICATION: SUMMING UP

There are other theories of social inequality in addition to those reviewed above (Grabb, 2002). However, having been introduced to Marx and Weber, the functionalist theory of stratification, and a number of more recent approaches, you will now have some sense of the range of existing explanations. Davis and Moore's functionalist approach stressed that inequality was inevitable and useful, and downplayed social conflict resulting from inequality. In contrast to this *consensus* approach to stratification, a variety of *conflict* approaches highlighted differences in power resulting from and contributing to material inequality, the exploitation of some groups by others, and the social conflict that could result. Marx was the most explicit in this regard, arguing that class conflict would eventually transform capitalist society itself.

The theories we have reviewed differ in the assumptions they make and the conclusions they draw about the future of material inequality. Marx clearly saw inequality and exploitation of the working class increasing, and predicted that class conflict would lead to the death of capitalism. Although Weber was not convinced that a socialist society would eventually emerge, neither did he argue that inequalities would gradually decrease (Grabb, 2002). As a neo-Weberian, Parkin takes a similar stance. Wright's emphasis on the growing number of middle-class locations (Wright and Martin, 1987) also does not suggest an increasing level of material inequality, but neither does it imply the opposite. However, the functionalists and Lenski, writing in an era of economic growth and widespread optimism about the ability of capitalism to raise the overall standard of living, clearly felt that material inequalities were shrinking in Western industrial societies.

The various explanations also differ in the degree to which they emphasize class differences in access to and control of material resources. For Marx, class was the primary determining factor in this regard. Weber, using the term *class* somewhat more broadly, emphasized its central role but recognized other important dimensions of social stratification. So, too, did Parkin, who explicitly discussed the independent effects of gender, race, and religion. Davis and Moore basically ignored the concept of class. Although Lenski again focused more directly on economic inequality, he did not really describe society in terms of distinct classes, as Wright, in his neo-Marxist approach, did. Thus, if we view these theories in chronological order, it appears that class, at least as defined in the Weberian sense, has made a comeback as an explanatory concept.

Furthermore, we see that those who felt that the level of material inequality was remaining high or increasing viewed society from a class-based perspective. In other words, they focused on the distinctly different life-chances of individuals and families with similar amounts of access to and control over material resources. In contrast, theorists who thought economic inequalities were declining preferred a model of society composed of many different overlapping strata that reflected a variety of equally important dimensions of social stratification.

Clark and Lipset, whose question "Are social classes dying?" introduced this section, make the latter point explicitly when they state that "one simple, powerful change has affected the economy: growth. And economic growth undermines hierarchical class stratification" (1991: 405). As you turn to the next section of the chapter—an overview of statistics on occupational and class structures and material inequality in Canada today—keep this argument

in mind, because the statistics allow us to assess its validity.

OCCUPATIONS, SOCIAL CLASS, AND INEQUALITY IN CANADA

OCCUPATIONAL SHIFTS OVER TIME

As noted above, explanations of social stratification differ in the extent to which they emphasize social class compared with other bases of social inequality. Some theories focus more on how occupational patterns have changed as industrial capitalism matured. But even theorists such as Erik Olin Wright, who place social class at the centre of their explanations, rely to a considerable extent on occupational data. So it would be useful to begin this section by examining occupational shifts in Canada over the past century.

Table 8.1 displays the types of occupations most common at the beginning (1911) and in the middle (1951) of the last century, and also at the very beginning of the twenty-first century (2001). The most prominent occupational shift over the course of the century is the decline in agricultural occupations, from one-third of all labour force participants in 1911 to only 3 percent in 2001. We also observe a decline, albeit not as steep, in other natural resource–based occupations (forestry, fishing, mining). Manufacturing occupations increased in relative terms (from 14 to 17 percent) between the beginning and middle of the last century, but by 2001 had dropped to only 8 percent of the total labour force.

Manufacturing, construction, transportation, and resource-based occupations are typically called *blue-collar occupations*, in contrast to *white-collar occupations* in the managerial, professional, clerical (office jobs), sales, and service categories. It is apparent from Table 8.1 that white-collar occupations have come to greatly outnumber blue-collar occupations as industrial capitalism has matured. In 2001, 13 percent of Canadian labour-force participants were identified as having managerial occupations, up from only 5 percent in 1911. Professional occupations had multiplied by more than five times in relative terms, from 4 to 21 percent. Clerical, sales, and service occupations also had become more common, although Table 8.1 shows a small relative decline in clerical jobs in the

TABLE 8.1 OCCUPATIONAL DISTRIBUTION OF LABOUR-FORCE PARTICIPANTS,[a] CANADA, 1911, 1951, 2001

OCCUPATION TYPE	1911	1951	2001
Managerial/administrative	5%	8%	13%
Professional	4	7	21
Clerical	4	11	10
Sales	5	7	10
Service	8	10	18
Manufacturing	14	17	8
Transportation	6	8	8
Construction	5	6	6
Agriculture	34	16	3
Forestry/fishing/mining	5	4	1
Other occupations	10	6	2
Total	**100**	**100**	**100**

[a]Labour-force participants include both the employed (paid employees and the self-employed) and the unemployed (those who want a paid job but who are unable to find one); based on the population aged 15 and older.

SOURCE: 1911 and 1951 data: adapted from 1911 and 1951 Census results, presented by Jeff O'Neill, "Changing Occupational Structure," *Canadian Social Trends*, Winter 1991, p. 10; 2001 data: adapted from 2001 Labour Force Survey annual averages, Statistics Canada, CANSIM II, Table 282-0010.

last half-century, perhaps due to the widespread introduction of computer technologies in the past few decades. In contrast, however, service occupations had increased to represent 18 percent of the total labour force by 2001.

What do these occupational changes tell us, with respect to our previous discussions of the bases of social stratification? First, as various theories have indicated, the proportion of occupations requiring higher education has increased, while the proportion of traditional blue-collar, "working-class" occupations has declined. With the expansion in white-collar occupations, average incomes rose, at least until the early 1980s. Thus, to the extent that occupational data can inform us about class structure in the Weberian sense, occupational shifts over the past 90 years suggest greater class diversity, rather than a polarization of classes, as a strict reading of Marx's theory would predict, and a rising standard of living for Canadian workers, rather than increasing poverty and exploitation.

And what do the numbers in Table 8.1 fail to tell us? First, they do not distinguish between the occupations typically held by women and those typically held by men. Since the middle of the last century, a rising proportion of women have been entering the labour force. But, as we will see (Chapter 9), women have been more likely to find employment in the clerical, sales, and service occupations (what might be called a "pink-collar sector") than in blue-collar occupations or in higher-status and better-paying managerial and professional occupations, even though there has been some movement by women into higher-level white-collar occupations in the past decade (Hughes, 1995). Thus, gender-based labour market stratification continues to exist, intersecting with class-based stratification.

Second, even though we might draw some conclusions about social class from the occupational data in Table 8.1, the data do not directly describe workers' relationships to the means of production, in Marx's terms. However, research conducted in the early 1980s does provide us with one picture of the Canadian class structure. Based on a nationwide survey and using an early version of Erik Olin Wright's class framework, Black and Myles (1986) demonstrated that only 1 percent of the labour force could be considered large employers (the bourgeoisie), 3 percent were small employers, and 12 percent fit into the petite bourgeoisie category. In contrast, 44 percent of the labour force fit into the traditional "worker" category (the proletariat), while the remainder were in contradictory class locations. Thus, we can see why Wright felt compelled to revise Marx's more simplistic three-class model.

Third, neither Table 8.1 (which displays occupational change over time) nor the Black and Myles (1986) study (which used "class" data from only one point in time) can give us a sense of how the Canadian class structure might be changing. But we can get one indication of this from other data on self-employment. Over the course of the century, particularly with the decline in the number of people employed in agriculture, the proportion of self-employed Canadians dropped dramatically. By 1971, only 11 percent of the Canadian labour force was self-employed. However, beginning in the 1980s, we began to see a slow reversal in the trend in Canada, the United States, and other Western industrialized countries. By 1998, 12 percent of employed

Many women were able to make important inroads into the labour force during World War II, as this painting illustrates. To this day, women are more likely to find work in the pink-collar sector than in higher-status, better-paying occupations.

SOURCE: Paraskeva Clark, *Parachute Riggers*. Courtesy Canadian War Museum. Reproduced with permission of Clive and Ben Clark, Toronto.

Canadians were own-account self-employed (without any employees) and 5 percent employed others (Krahn and Lowe, 2002: 68–69). Researchers still have not determined whether more Canadians are voluntarily choosing self-employment, or are being pushed into it as a result of higher levels of unemployment and growing corporate and public-sector "downsizing." Nevertheless, this reversal of the decline in self-employment—this increase in the size of the petit bourgeois class—is something that theorists are trying to explain as they attempt to further update Marx's ideas of class-based stratification (Myles and Turegun, 1994; Breen and Rottman, 1995: 87–88).

Finally, the data in Table 8.1 do not reflect some of the dramatic changes in employment opportunities and outcomes that have been occurring in the past three decades. I will return to this topic later, but for now I will simply note that unemployment rates have risen, part-time and temporary work has become much more common, and income growth appears to have stopped, while income and wealth inequality has increased. Consequently, the higher standard of living that accompanied occupational changes in the second half of the twentieth century is no longer guaranteed for all those in middle-status occupations. Thus, it is essential that we look carefully at the distributional side of the occupation and class structures, at "who gets what" in return for their employment, as well as at the occupational and class positions that people hold (Westergaard, 1995). But before beginning our examination of changing patterns of material inequality in Canada, we will first discuss another important feature of stratification systems in modern societies—opportunities for occupational mobility.

OCCUPATIONAL MOBILITY

Many people move up the occupational and income ladders over the course of their careers, frequently after investing in higher education of some kind. And some move down, often because of economic circumstances beyond their control. Sociologists have conducted a great deal of research on such **intragenerational occupational mobility** (mobility within an individual's lifetime), as well as on **intergenerational occupational mobility**, the process of reaching an occupational location higher or lower than the location one's parents held. Research of this type is interesting in itself, since we all like to compare how well we have done relative to others. However, such research is also theoretically important, since it tests hypotheses derived from theories of inequality (the functionalist perspective, for example) that propose that higher positions in society are generally filled by those most qualified, not by those who inherit them.

Canadian researchers Creese, Guppy, and Meissner (1991) used data from Statistics Canada's 1986 General Social Survey, a large random sample of more than 16 000 adults, to examine the factors that influence occupational mobility opportunities or, in other words, the process of **occupational status attainment**. They demonstrated, not surprisingly, that the most important influence on the status of an individual's current job is the status of that person's first job. Individuals who enter the labour market as articling lawyers, for example, typically make their way higher up the occupational ladder than do those who began as unskilled labourers. In turn, the status of that first job is heavily influenced by the amount of education completed.

These findings obviously lend some support to theories that suggest that more qualified people, as indicated by higher education, end up in higher-status and better-paying occupations. However, the researchers also traced the education–job linkages back to the previous generation, showing that those who obtained more education and hence better jobs were more likely to come from families with well-educated fathers in high-status occupations. (Comparisons were not made with the occupations of sample members' mothers since relatively few women in the previous generation held paying jobs.) In other words, for a variety of reasons (e.g., more money for higher education, more well-educated role models), children from more advantaged backgrounds can build on their initial advantages. The same study also revealed that, on average, men experienced slightly more upward mobility than did women, even though women had completed more years of schooling. Similarly, francophones were disadvantaged compared with anglophones, and immigrants did not fare as well as native-born Canadians, even if they had equivalent educational credentials.

In brief, this study of occupational status attainment by Creese, Guppy, and Meissner demonstrates that the Canadian stratification system is relatively open. There are opportunities for upward mobility

within the occupational hierarchy, and education plays a critical role in determining who gets ahead. In fact, comparisons with similar studies in other countries, such as Australia, France, Sweden, and the United Kingdom, suggest that Canada is a somewhat more open society in terms of mobility opportunities (Wanner, 1993: 174). Nevertheless, the 1986 General Social Survey also revealed considerable status inheritance, suggesting that the issue of who gets better jobs (with more status and higher income) is also class-based, and not just a matter of achievement based on merit. Furthermore, the research shows how other dimensions of social stratification, such as gender, ethnicity, and immigrant status, intersect with class-based inequalities.

Overall, the 1986 General Social Survey revealed more upward than downward mobility. Among women, 48 percent reported upward mobility relative to their father's occupation, 12 percent stayed at the same level, and 40 percent had moved down to some extent. The comparable statistics for men were 39 percent upwardly mobile, 25 percent stable, and 36 percent downwardly mobile (Creese, Guppy, and Meissner, 1991: 45–46). If the only intergenerational occupational mobility we were seeing was a result of better-qualified people moving up to replace those who were less qualified, we should also see an equivalent amount of downward mobility. Such a situation of "musical jobs" or, to use the technical term, **circulatory mobility** is not evident, however, because of the simultaneous presence of **structural mobility**, which results from a change in the shape of the overall occupational structure. As noted earlier, over the past half-century, industrial societies have experienced a great deal of growth in white-collar occupations (clerical, managerial, and professional positions) as traditional agricultural and blue-collar industrial jobs declined in relative importance. With an increase in the number of higher-status jobs, each generation had more chances than the preceding one to improve the status of their jobs.

Way back in 1968, John Porter, a Canadian sociologist, observed this phenomenon and predicted that, in the future, the demand for people to fill highly skilled positions would exceed the supply of well-educated workers (Porter, 1968). Porter's fear seems ironic today, when almost one in four employed Canadians state that they are overqualified for their job (Kelly, Howatson-Leo, and Clark, 1997).

With many more well-educated labour-force participants in a labour market in which relatively low-skill, part-time positions are increasing more quickly than high-skill full-time positions, underemployment has become a serious problem (Krahn and Lowe, 1999). Expansion in the middle of the occupational structure appears to have slowed down, or perhaps even stopped, resulting in fewer opportunities for upward (structural) mobility.

THE DISTRIBUTION OF WEALTH

Evidence from various sources demonstrates that a limited number of people continue to own or control a very large portion of the wealth in Canada. Antoniou and Rowley (1986), for example, showed that single owners held a majority of shares in more than one-third of the largest Canadian-owned corporations in 1979. Recognizing that control of a corporation can still be maintained with only a small minority of shares, so long as other shares are held in smaller blocks, Antoniou and Rowley also demonstrated that more than two-thirds of the largest Canadian-owned corporations were controlled by a single owner (holding 20 percent or more of the shares). At least half, if not more, of these owners were families, as opposed to financial corporations, government bodies, or other types of owners.

Richardson (1990) compared 1978 and 1985 data to make the same point about the pronounced and increasing concentration of corporate ownership in Canada. He showed that 76 percent of the assets of the 170 largest Canadian nonfinancial corporations were controlled in 1985 by only 17 large business enterprises (an enterprise consists of one or more corporations under common control), up from 64 percent seven years earlier. Two-thirds (11) of these 17 enterprises were controlled by a single owner. More recently, Yakabuski (2001) documented how, in 2000, one-quarter of the companies listed on the Toronto Stock Exchange 300 Index were controlled by a single owner holding more than 50 percent of the voting shares. These studies and others like them highlight the immense wealth held by families such as the Bronfmans, the Reichmanns, the Irvings, and the Westons, with business holdings spread around the globe as well as in Canada. Together with highly paid chief executive officers and corporate directors, these wealthy families clearly form a distinct upper class, the haute (or high) bourgeoisie in Marx's terms.

At the other end of this ownership scale are the 11 percent of Canadian families who reported no *net worth* in 1999, net worth being defined as the difference between total assets (shares, bonds, savings, property, businesses, and possessions, but excluding future pension income) and total debt (Morissette, 2002). Almost one in five families (19 percent) reported no *net wealth*, defined as net worth minus the value of property that could not be disposed of quickly if necessary (i.e., a home and furnishings and/or a business). In fact, the poorest 10 percent of Canadian families in 1999 reported a median net worth of –$5700, indicating that, on average, their debts outstripped the value of all their assets. Young families, particularly lone-parent families, were most likely to report little or no net worth.

Over the long term, the economic growth experienced in Western industrialized countries, along with some income redistribution efforts by governments, has had an equalizing effect on the distribution of household wealth. Wolff (1991), for example, showed that inequality in household wealth decreased between 1920 and the 1970s in Sweden, Britain, and the United States. Although comparable data are not available for Canada for the same period, it is likely that a similar decline occurred here as well. However, Wolff also noted that, in the mid-1970s, wealth inequality began to increase again in the United States and Sweden (it remained constant in Britain). What about in Canada?

A recent study shows that, between 1984 and 1999, median wealth for the total Canadian population grew by about 10 percent in real terms (i.e., adjusted for inflation). But this growth in wealth was distributed unequally. Over the 15-year period ending in 1999, real median wealth declined for the poorest 30 percent of Canadian families while increasing substantially for the richest 30 percent (Morissette et al., 2002). In other words, wealth inequality has been slowly increasing over the past two decades in Canada.

INCOME DISTRIBUTION

High-Paying and Low-Paying Occupations

Although most of us have virtually no contact with the wealthiest 1 percent of families in Canada, we are much more aware of, or perhaps are even members of, a larger, not quite as wealthy, but still very affluent group of households containing one or more individuals in high-paying occupations. Table 8.2 profiles average weekly wage rates in 2001 across a range of occupational groups. Before discussing the large variations in weekly wage rates within this table, several caveats should be noted. First, self-employed workers are omitted, which means that some of the highest-paid Canadians are omitted (e.g., self-employed lawyers, doctors, and dentists), as are some of the lowest-paid (e.g., self-employed salespersons). Second, there are very large variations within some of these groups, particularly those reporting higher wage rates. For example, the category of "professionals in health/nursing" contains both highly paid brain surgeons as well as moderately well-paid ward nurses. Third, the number of weeks worked per year varies across occupational groups. In particular, employees in construction and in some primary industries often work less in the winter, which means

that their annual incomes would not be as high as one might expect based on these weekly wage rates.

Using the term *class* in the Weberian sense, we would be justified in labelling individuals in managerial and professional occupations as members of an upper-middle class, given their high incomes and their access to and control of material resources through their employment positions. In contrast, retail workers and those employed in some service occupations (e.g., food and beverage services, child-care and home support services) work in the low-paying, insecure occupations that we might describe as the lower working class.

It is noteworthy that the average weekly wage rate for senior managers (women and men combined) was $1250 in 2002, five times as high as the average weekly wage rate for retail sales workers ($252). But as already noted, these are broad occupational categories, and we cannot assume that all Canadian

TABLE 8.2   MEDIAN WEEKLY WAGE RATE OF EMPLOYEES[1] BY SELECTED OCCUPATION[2] BY GENDER, CANADA, 2001

	MEDIAN WEEKLY WAGE RATE[3]		
	Total ($)	Men ($)	Women ($)
All Occupations	**577**	**692**	**473**
Senior management	1250	1374	950
Professionals in business/finance	846	962	750
Clerical occupations	519	577	500
Natural and applied sciences and related occupations	910	961	790
Professionals in health/nursing	795	896	784
Technical and assisting occupations in health	511	620	489
Professionals in social science, government, and religion	715	808	674
Professionals in education (teachers and professors)	846	962	769
Occupations in art, culture, recreation and sport	525	608	462
Retail sales	252	370	223
Service occupations (food and beverage)	280	315	252
Service occupations (protective services)	680	731	475
Service occupations (child-care and home support)	338	432	333
Construction trades (contractors and supervisors excluded)	700	704	400
Transport and equipment operators	676	692	343
Primary sector (agriculture, forestry, mining, fishing)	528	600	346
Manufacturing occupations	570	645	412

[1] Self-employed labour-force participants excluded.

[2] Occupation refers to the kind of work persons (age 15 and older) were doing at the time the information was collected. If the person was unemployed, information about the most recent period of employment was requested. Not all occupational categories are shown.

[3] Wages or salary before taxes and deductions, at main job only. Calculations based on usual paid work hours per week. Number of weeks worked per year varies considerably by occupation.

SOURCE: Adapted from Statistics Canada, CANSIM II, Table 282-0070, http://cansim2.statcan.ca/cgi-win/CNSMCGI.EXE.

employed workers have year-round jobs. Hence, inequality in earned income in Canada is much greater than the data in Table 8.2 would indicate. For example, in 1995, full-time, full-year specialist physicians earned an average of $123 976, ten times more than full-time, full-year baby-sitters and nannies who reported average earnings of only $12 713 (Statistics Canada, 1998: 13).

Table 8.2 also shows that, across all occupations, women's average weekly wage rate was only 68 percent of the average for male employees, demonstrating the extent to which gender inequalities cut across occupational inequalities. In fact, in every occupational category in Table 8.2, women earn considerably less than men. The categories in which the female–male gap is not as large are those occupations where pay is generally very low and where very few men are typically employed (e.g., child-care and home support services, and food and beverage services).

Income Inequality

The data in Table 8.2, based on 2001 Labour Force Survey estimates, give us some indication of the current distribution of employment earnings, the largest component of total income. If we were to look back to the middle of the last century, we would see that the distribution of total income (from employment, investments, government assistance, and all other sources) across households (families and individuals living alone) in Canada has changed relatively little. In 1951, the most advantaged 20 percent of households (the top quintile) received 43 percent of total Canadian income, whereas the bottom quintile (the 20 percent with the lowest incomes) received only 4 percent of all income (Statistics Canada, 1984: 6). In 1999, the distribution still looked quite similar, with the top quintile receiving 45 percent of all income, and the bottom quintile taking home 4 percent (Statistics Canada, 2001: 79).

But while the proportion of total income received by each population quintile shows us how equally or unequally income is being distributed, it tells us little about the standard of living of individuals and families within each quintile. For example, if total income doubled but the percentage received by each quintile stayed the same, the bottom 20 percent with their 4 percent of total income would now have twice as much income as before (of course, the same would apply to the top quintile, who would also have

twice as much). In fact, when we look back over the past five decades, we find that average family income has increased by more than 150 percent, after taking inflation into account. In other words, the Canadian standard of living increased substantially in the decades following World War II. But most of this increase took place in the 1950s and 1960s. By the 1980s, inflation was typically as high as, or higher than, the income gains of Canadian families (Love and Poulin, 1991). In the 1990s, inflation declined but incomes did not really increase. Unemployment rates remained high, and deficit-cutting efforts by the provincial and federal governments led to reductions in income-support payments to both the poorly paid employed and the unemployed. Thus, in constant (1997) dollars (that is, in terms of purchasing power), Canadian family incomes were lower, on average, than they were in 1989 (Statistics Canada, 1999: 17).

If we look more carefully at the income distribution data for the past two decades, we begin to see some evidence of increasing income inequality (Yalnizyan, 1998). Despite four decades of relative stability in income distribution, the top quintile of households increased its share of total income from around 42 percent to about 44 percent between 1981 and the mid-1990s. By 1999, the top quintile was receiving 45.3 percent of total income (Statistics Canada, 2001: 79). But this increase did not come at the expense of the bottom quintile. Instead, the share of total income received by the three middle quintiles declined.

Why did this particular pattern of income redistribution, a reduction in the share of total income received by middle-income households, take place? Only 26 percent of the income received by the lowest quintile of households comes from earnings or self-employment, compared with 48 percent of the income of the second quintile, 72 percent of the third, 83 percent of the fourth, and 89 percent of the top quintile (Statistics Canada, 1999: 162). The three middle quintiles would therefore likely be most affected by a changing labour market in which unemployment remains relatively high and some well-paying jobs are being replaced by jobs that pay less.

In contrast, two-thirds (66 percent) of the income received by the lowest quintile of households comes from government transfer payments. Further reductions in such transfer payments, as governments continue to restrict welfare funding, could lead to shrinking of the already tiny share of total income

(4.4 percent in 1999) received by the bottom quintile of Canadian households.

THE POOR

Defining and Measuring Poverty

Poverty can be defined in different ways. We could talk about **absolute poverty**, arguing that the poor are those who have barely enough to stay alive, like many of the inhabitants of developing countries. Or we could concede, as most Canadians do, that **relative poverty** is really what matters. If your neighbours own their homes, drive cars, eat out at nice restaurants, put money into pension plans, and take vacations outside the country, while you rent a small apartment, ride the bus, look forward to a meal at McDonald's, have no savings, and read about foreign countries in the public library, you probably consider yourself poor. According to this definition, Canada does have a considerable number of poor people.

Most discussions of poverty in Canada rely on the **low-income cutoff line** (commonly known as the "poverty line"), estimated by Statistics Canada on the basis of data obtained from its longitudinal Survey of Labour and Income Dynamics. According to this survey, the average Canadian spends about 35 percent of (pre-tax) income on the basic necessities (food, shelter, and clothing); to establish the low-income cut-off line, Statistics Canada adds 20 percent to this figure. Hence, anyone spending more than 55 percent of gross income on the basic necessities is considered poor (see Box 8.2). Obviously, some people budget better than others, so these are average cost estimates. However, there is no denying that the cost of living is higher in larger urban centres, and that it takes more money to feed and clothe additional people, so different low-income lines are calculated for communities of various sizes and for families of various sizes within those communities (National Council of Welfare, 2002b). For example, based on 2000 income data, Statistics Canada set the (pre-tax) low-income cutoff line for a single person living in a city with more than half a million residents at $18 371, compared with $12 696 for a single person living in a rural area (Canadian Council on Social Development, 2002). The low-income line for a family of three in a large city was $28 560, substantially higher than that for a similar-sized family in a rural area ($19 738).

Who Are the Poor?

Rising unemployment causes the number and proportion of people living below the poverty line to increase. In 1980, for example, 16 percent of all Canadians were below the poverty line, but, with the recession of the early 1980s, that figure climbed to 18.7 percent by 1984. As the economy recovered, the proportion of poor Canadians dropped to 14.0 percent in 1989, but then rose again to 18.0 percent in 1993 (National Council of Welfare, 2002b). Four years later, in 1997, little had changed—18.2 percent of all Canadians were still living below the low-income line. But by 1999, the proportion of poor Canadians had again dropped to 1980 levels of 16.2 percent (Canadian Council on Social Development, 2003).

While poverty rates tend to follow unemployment rates, only a minority of Canada's poor are unemployed or out of the labour force. In 1999, for example, in "low-income" families whose major earners were under 65 years old, 25 percent of these major earners were working full-time and 33 percent had either part-year or part-time jobs. Less than half (42 percent) were not employed, including 10 percent who were unable to work. In short, the **working poor**, those employed in low-wage jobs, make up a sizable proportion of the poor in Canada (National Council of Welfare, 2002b). Hence, not only rising unemployment but also any decline in real wages will lead to an increase in the number of people below the poverty line.

Nevertheless, the unemployed and the working poor are not the only Canadians living below the poverty line. In 1999, 52 percent of single-parent families headed by a female were below the poverty line, compared to only 10 percent of two-adult families with children (see Figure 8.2 on page 205). The incidence of low income has risen only marginally since 1980 for two-adult families with children, while the equivalent statistic has dropped a bit more for female-headed single-parent families. Many of the latter family units are completely dependent on social assistance, since the mother cannot seek paid work while looking after the children.

In 1999, 44 percent of elderly Canadians (65 and older) living alone had incomes below Statistics Canada's "low income" line, compared to less than 5 percent of senior couples. It is clear that shared incomes among the elderly (or anyone else, for that matter) typically keep people above the poverty line,

BOX 8.2   HOW DO WE MEASURE POVERTY?

Whenever a Canadian news outlet uses Statistics Canada numbers to say a certain percentage of Canadians are "below the poverty line," Statistics Canada makes it clear that its numbers say no such thing. The agency sends off letters stating that its low-income cut-off (LICO) figures are not a measure of poverty, but of income inequality. Despite this, many media companies and poverty activists use Statistics Canada's LICOs as Canada's "unofficial" poverty line.

The LICO counts the number of Canadians who spend 20 per cent more of their gross income on food, shelter and clothing than the average Canadian. So, if a family spends more than 55 per cent of its gross income on these necessities, it's below the LICO. About 17 per cent of Canadians are below the low-income cut-off.

Critics of the use of the LICO as a benchmark for poverty say the 55 per cent level is arbitrary and doesn't translate to a state of destitute poverty. A 2000 *National Post* editorial put it this way: "Say 54 per cent of a family's income goes to food, shelter and clothing, it still has 46 per cent to spend elsewhere. That's not poverty."

[A] feature of the LICO that causes controversy is that it's a relative measure of poverty. That is, as the economy grows and people make more money on average, the LICO moves up with it. "Using the LICO to measure the poor means poverty can never be eliminated since there will always be a range of incomes in Canada—unless we adopt a unless a Soviet-style command economy," the *National Post* said in 2000.

Poverty activists argue that it's possible to reduce relative poverty without moving to a completely communist system. "In reality, relative poverty will not be reduced by economic growth unless there is redistribution to the poor," [Richard] Shillington wrote.

Another way to measure poverty is in absolute terms: how many people make less than what is needed to survive or lead a decent life? Human Resources and Development Canada is developing such a measurement, called the Market Basket Measure, based on the costs of goods and services needed for people to eat a nutritious diet, buy clothing for work and social occasions, house themselves in their community and pay for necessary expenditures, such as furniture, public transportation and entertainment. By that measure, most of the country's poverty is in Ontario and British Columbia, where the living costs are highest.

Nipissing University economics professor Christopher Sarlo developed another absolute measure of poverty for the 1992 study "Poverty in Canada." Sarlo defines poverty as lacking the means for the basic necessities of life, such as food, shelter and clothing. The first version of his Basic Needs Index put the poverty rate at just four per cent. It was criticized for its frugality, though: Sarlo's weekly food budget for an elderly woman was $25. A revised version of the index was released in 2001, including such things as out-of-pocket medical expenses. That study put the poverty rate at eight per cent.

SOURCE: "How Do We Measure Poverty" by Martin O'Malley and John Bowman, *CBC News Online,* 7 May, 2002, Updated 4 November, 2002 (http://cbc.ca/news/features/ poverty_line.html).

whereas the experience of losing a spouse and her or his income can push many seniors below the poverty line. Also, because women are less likely to be employed outside the home, and since women typically earn less than men, older women living alone are less likely to have the pensions and savings that men in a similar position might have. Hence, in 1999, 48.5 percent of single elderly women were in the "low income" category, compared to only 31.8 percent of single elderly men (National Council of Welfare, 2002b).

Figure 8.2 demonstrates that relative poverty among the elderly has declined since 1980. Increased government transfer payments to the elderly and an increase in the number of people retiring with per-

sonal pension plans and RRSPs are a large part of the explanation. In contrast, the poverty rate has risen, particularly since 1990, for childless couples (under age 65), two-parent families with children, and non-elderly single individuals. In short, over the past decade, as labour market conditions have deteriorated and as governments have cut back on transfer payments, the working poor and the unemployed have come to make up a larger proportion of Canada's poor (Yalnizyan, 1998).

Although the low-income cutoff line is a useful measurement tool, it can leave us with an oversimplified picture of poverty in Canada, one that separates those who are poor and needy from those who are well off without recognizing the large variations within

FIGURE 8.2 INCIDENCE OF LOW INCOME FOR SELECTED FAMILY UNIT TYPES, CANADA, 1980, 1990, 1999

■ 1980 ■ 1990 □ 1999

INCIDENCE OF LOW INCOME (%)

Family Unit Type	1980	1990	1999
Elderly (65+) Families	17.5	7.5	4.7
Elderly (65+) Singles	66.4	47.8	44
Couple, no Children	6.7	8.1	8.6
Two Parents & Children	9.2	9.4	10.4
Female Single Parent	57.3	58.2	51.8
Male Single Parent	25.4	25	18
Single (under 65)	33.5	32	37

SOURCE: National Council of Welfare, 2002, *Poverty Profile 1999*. Tables 1-16 to 1-22. Cat. no. H67-1/4-1999E. (Ottawa: Minister of Public Works and Government Services Canada).

each group. Using 1992 data, the Economic Council of Canada (1992: 14) filled in some of the detail, suggesting that about 5 percent of working-age Canadians were "destitute" (no market income at all), about 6 percent were "marginally employed" (incomes up to 50 percent of the low-income line), about 8 percent were "working poor" (incomes between 50 percent and 100 percent of the low-income line), and about 11 percent were "hovering poor" (incomes up to 150 percent of the low-income line). The labour-market changes we have witnessed in the past two decades suggest that the number of working poor and hovering poor has increased since then.

Social Assistance for the Poor

Recognizing, then, that not all of the poor are equally poor, where would people dependent on social assistance be located in this hierarchy of low income? There is a fairly common belief in our society that "welfare" and unemployment insurance are much too easy to obtain and that the amount of money received is enough to encourage people to avoid seeking work (Swanson, 2001). Is this true? Because welfare regulations vary across provinces, we will examine data from Ontario, the largest province and among the provinces with the highest welfare incomes in 2000.

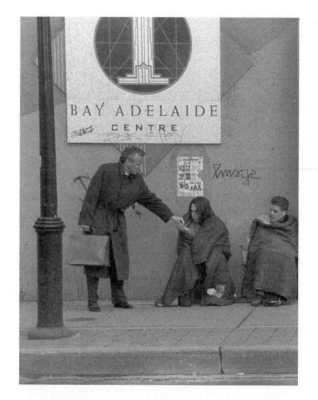

In 1999, Statistics Canada estimated that 17.5 percent of all Canadians were living below the low-income line. Living on the streets is a dangerous alternative to a more socially acceptable struggle for survival.
SOURCE: Dick Hemingway.

Figure 8.3 shows that a single "employable" adult (i.e., an adult who was not disabled, elderly, or considered unable to seek work because of family responsibilities) who was eligible for Ontario social assistance received $6829 in 2000, an amount that was hardly more than one-third (37 percent) of the poverty line and less than one-quarter (22 percent) of the average income for single adults in the province (National Council of Welfare, 2002b). Disabled welfare recipients received a larger total annual transfer payment ($11 763), putting them two-thirds (64 percent) of the way between no income and the low-income line, but at only 37 percent of the average income for single adults. Relative to other welfare recipients, single parents fared the best, with their total income set at 60 percent of the poverty line for one-adult households. Their incomes seem relatively high compared with the average income (39 percent), but only because the average income for all single parents is very low. In contrast, the level of welfare assistance provided to a couple with two children was only 21 percent of the much higher average income of two-adult, two-child households in Ontario in 2000.

In short, in Ontario and the rest of the provinces, the amount of welfare assistance provided is very low, particularly since the mid-1990s, when many provinces cut their welfare rates. Consequently, it is difficult to accept the argument that overly generous welfare systems discourage people from looking for work. Many of those who receive assistance cannot work outside the home, and the money that is provided seldom pushes the poor who receive it anywhere even close to the poverty line.

Moving in and out of Poverty

Discussions of poverty such as this one can leave the impression that the poor and the nonpoor are basically separate groups, and that there is little mobility from one status to the other. In fact, according to the Economic Council of Canada (1992: 22), the annual turnover rate in and out of poverty (as defined by the low-income line) was about 27 percent between 1982 and 1986. In other words, about one in four Canadians (roughly 400 000 in total) who had been poor in a given year rose above the poverty line the next year, and were replaced among the ranks of the poor by about the same number of downwardly mobile individuals. However, many of those moving up would not have made it beyond the "hovering poor" category and, depending on the circumstances, might again find themselves categorized as "poor" in the subsequent year.

More recent Statistics Canada LICO data show that, between 1993 and 1998, one in four Canadians

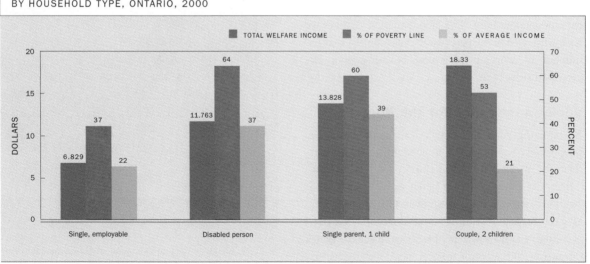

FIGURE 8.3 TOTAL WELFARE INCOME AS PERCENTAGE OF POVERTY LINE AND OF AVERAGE INCOME, BY HOUSEHOLD TYPE, ONTARIO, 2000

SOURCE: National Council of Welfare, 2002, Welfare Incomes, 2000 and 2001. Tables 4 and 6. Cat. no. H68-27/2001E. (Ottawa: Minister of Public Works and Government Services Canada).

(24 percent) lived in a low-income ("poor") family at least one year between 1993 and 1998 (Morisette and Zhang, 2001). Just over 8 percent of the total population experienced poverty (were in the low-income group) for four or more years out of a possible six years. However, among Canadians living in lone-parent families, 38 percent had experienced poverty for at least four years between 1993 and 1998. Thus, as the earlier Economic Council of Canada (1992) report indicated, poverty is not a static status. A sizeable number of Canadians move in and out of poverty each year. Nevertheless, a small minority remain stuck in poverty year after year. As we noted above, losing a job, becoming a single parent, or being widowed can drastically increase the chances of falling into, and remaining stuck, in poverty.

MATERIAL INEQUALITY IN CANADA: SUMMING UP

Is Inequality Increasing in Canada?

Compared with some other countries, and compared with the situation in Canada a century ago, the level of material inequality in this country today is relatively low. Even so, we have seen evidence of a great deal of inequality in wealth and income. Furthermore, there are indications that, for at least a decade and perhaps two, the level of inequality has been slowly rising. Corporate concentration has been increasing as a small number of huge business enterprises, many of them family-owned or -controlled, have gained control over a larger share of the assets of Canada's largest corporations. Wealth inequality in general appears to be increasing, income inequality has risen, and the number of working poor in Canada has increased.

Looking more closely at the labour market, we see that unemployment rates have been rising steadily for several decades. Although these rates have gone up and down a number of times, the long-term trend since the mid-twentieth century has been upward. Hence, in 2001, the average annual unemployment rate was 7.2 percent, representing 1.2 million unemployed Canadians, a number roughly equal to the total adult population of the provinces of Manitoba and Prince Edward Island combined. Similarly, the part-time employment rate has been rising. Forty years ago, fewer than 4 percent of employed

Canadians worked part-time. Today, almost one in five are in part-time jobs; of these workers, one-third would prefer full-time jobs but cannot find them. Since the 1980s, we have also seen a significant increase in temporary jobs, as employers have begun to cut long-term wage costs by offering more limited-term contract positions (Krahn, 1995). Real wages are no longer increasing, inequality in earnings has risen as a result of polarization in hours worked (Morissette et al., 1994), and opportunities for upward mobility have declined.

A More Polarized Society?

It is difficult to avoid the conclusion that, in Canada, the gap between the advantaged (those with full-time, permanent jobs) and the disadvantaged (those with part-time, temporary, or no jobs) is slowly increasing (Myles, 1996; Yalnizyan, 1998; see Box 8.3). A similar pattern has been observed in Britain (Westergaard, 1995) and in the United States (Ryscavage, 1995). This is not to suggest that a new era of massive inequalities is dawning. However, the evidence is clear enough that material inequalities are rising, not declining, and that society is becoming more polarized in terms of access to and control over economic resources. Using Weber's definition of the term *class*, we could conclude that class differences in Canada and the United States (and in other countries like Britain) are becoming more pronounced.

There are obviously many interrelated factors contributing to this growth in material inequality, this increased polarization of North American society (Krahn and Lowe, 2002: 144–48). Although some new high-skill and well-paying jobs have emerged with the introduction of automated production technologies, the overall outcome still appears to have been a reduction in employment opportunities. Globalization, the process whereby goods and services are produced by business enterprises operating in many different countries, has led to a much more competitive economic environment. Business enterprises have responded by shifting some of their activities to countries in which lower wages and less rigorous environmental and labour laws allow higher profits to be made. In North America, layoffs have been a frequent response, along with the replacement of full-time permanent jobs with part-time and temporary positions. Labour unions, which traditionally resisted attempts to cut wages and jobs, have lost some of their power. At the political

BOX 8.3 MORE MONEY, MORE SURFING

Internet use by Canadians continues to increase, although the rate of increase has been slowing down a bit, according to Statistics Canada. In 2001, 49 percent of Canadian households contained at least one person who regularly used the Internet at home. This figure had risen from only 16 percent in 1997, to 23 percent in 1998, 29 percent in 1999, and 40 percent in 2000. However, household income plays a huge part in determining whether or not household members have the opportunity to "surf the net" from home (see Figure 8.4).

In 2001, three-quarters (76 percent) of Canadian households in the highest quartile (the 25 percent of households with the highest income) contained someone who regularly used the Internet at home. This was more than three times the rate for households in the lowest quartile (22 percent). Four years earlier, Internet access was occurring in one-third of the highest-income households, compared to only 5.5 percent of the poorest households.

Access to the "information highway" is critical for success in all levels of the formal education system. It is also of great importance for career success. The fact that individuals living in poorer households are much less likely to have access from home to the Internet does not bode well for the reduction of material inequalities in Canada.

FIGURE 8.4 INTERNET USE IN THE HOME (1997–2001): HIGH-INCOME HOUSEHOLDS HAVE AN ADVANTAGE

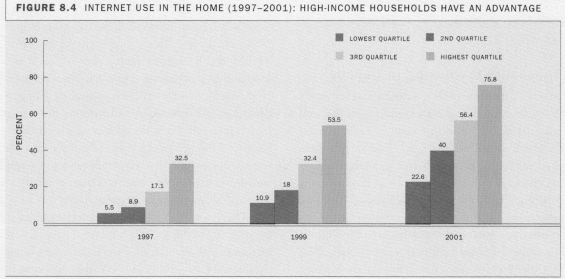

SOURCE: Data from Statistics Canada, 2002. *The Daily.* 25 July 2002.

level, a belief system or ideology emphasizing that "the market knows best" and that we need less rather than more government intervention in the economy and labour market has led to fewer government efforts to reduce material inequalities (Myles, 1996).

We will leave it to other chapters in this text to examine the relevant economic, labour-market, political, and ideological trends in more detail, since this is a chapter on social stratification. Early in this chapter, we invited you to examine the evidence on changing patterns of social stratification in Canada and, while doing so, to keep in mind Clark and Lipset's (1991) question: "Are social classes dying?" Clark and Lipset (1991) answered yes, but given the empirical evidence reviewed in this chapter, it would appear that they were wrong.

CONSEQUENCES OF MATERIAL INEQUALITY

Other chapters in this textbook will go into more detail about some of the many consequences of material inequality for individuals and families. You will see that position in the class structure has an effect on belief systems, behaviours, and lifestyles; that the poor, the middle classes, and the very wealthy frequently hold different opinions on various subjects, may vote differently, and certainly enjoy different lifestyles. But, much more important, people in different positions in society's economic hierarchy experience different life-chances, to use the term introduced by Max Weber.

Consequences for Individuals and Families

Children from poorer families typically do not do as well as more affluent children in school, are more likely to drop out before completing high school (Tanner et al., 1995), and are less likely to go on to higher education (Corak, 1998). As we noted above in our discussion of occupational mobility, such effects of poverty are largely responsible for the perpetuation of class inequalities from one generation to the next.

For a variety of reasons, including better nutrition, access to better health care, and less hazardous working conditions, those who are situated higher in the economic hierarchy are typically healthier than the poor (Townson, 1999). On average, the poor do not live as long as those who are better off (Wilkinson, 1992). Similarly, when dealing with the criminal-justice system, those with greater access to and control over economic resources tend to fare better (National Council of Welfare, 2001–2002). The poor are consequently overrepresented in jails. I could go on, but these examples are probably sufficient to make the point that life-chances are a function of position in the class structure, and that those higher up in the economic hierarchy enjoy a better quality of life.

Consequences for Society

In addition to these substantial consequences of material inequality for individuals and families, can material inequality have other social outcomes? Specifically, given the relatively high and increasing level of inequality in Canada, can we expect to see more social unrest? Will conflict between the "haves" and the "have-nots" increase? Those committed to a classical Marxist theory of social change might welcome such conflict; for them, it would indicate that capitalism was finally beginning to give way to a socialist society. Others might view such conflict much more negatively. Whatever our response to such a possibility, it is clear that our values and beliefs directly influence the way we respond to evidence of inequality and its consequences.

But returning to our question, can we expect to see an increase in social unrest and conflict as a result of higher levels of inequality? During the early 1980s, for example, the solidarity movement in British Columbia brought together members of trade unions, social-welfare organizations, and various community-based groups in opposition to the Social Credit government's cutbacks in government programs and attempts to change labour legislation. Bryan Palmer (1986) described the protests and rallies that took place as evidence of growing class conflict. However, these events were exceptional. Much more often, the poor and the near-poor put up with their less-advantaged position because they have few of the resources (e.g., money, education, organizations) that make it possible to fight for social change (Brym, 1979). In fact, in the past few years, we have seen more opposition from a better-organized middle class, in response to government cutbacks in health and education, than from the poor in response to welfare cutbacks. And we have seen intensified negative stereotyping of the poor and those on welfare, a process that Jean Swanson (2001) calls "poor-bashing."

Thus, it is by no means clear that a higher level of inequality and fewer opportunities for upward mobility will translate into greater social unrest in Canada. Nevertheless, greater inequality means greater hardship and more limited life-chances for more Canadians. While this chapter has documented growing social inequality in Canada, other chapters in this text describe similar processes globally. The long-term consequences for global peace and security as a result of a growing gap between rich and poor countries is difficult to predict. Even so, as Paul Krugman, the influential American economist, has noted: "The ultimate effects of growing economic disparities on our social and political health may be hard to predict, but they are unlikely to be pleasant" (Krugman, 1994: F9).

RESPONDING TO INEQUALITY

Some of us believe that more equal distribution of society's resources would be preferable to the current level of inequality. We believe that the existing differences in life-chances are unjust, and look for ways in which social institutions, laws, and tax systems might be changed in order to reduce material inequality. Others, equally offended by inequality and its consequences, reject this reformist approach in favour of a more radical position, advocating the replacement of capitalist society by some kind of socialist alternative. Still others respond to evidence of extensive inequality with little ambition to change it, believing, simply, that this is "the way things are." Although perhaps bothered by its consequences, members of this group might still conclude that the existing level of inequality is inevitable, and that well-intentioned efforts to reduce it will, in the long run, have little effect. They might even conclude that inequality is functional, as Davis and Moore argued half a century ago, and that efforts to reduce it will be counterproductive. In short, our reactions to the fact of inequality, and our recommendations about what, if anything, should be done about it, directly reflect our values and our political orientation.

Assuming that a lower level of inequality *is* a goal worth striving for, it is clear that the government has a role to play in trying to reach that goal. The Canadian state has an impact on the distribution of wealth and income through tax systems that redistribute wealth from the rich to the poor, through minimum-wage and other types of legislation, and through transfer payments such as pensions for the elderly and the disabled, social assistance for low-income individuals and families, and unemployment insurance (now renamed employment insurance). Even so, compared with a number of other industrialized countries, Canada spends considerably less on attempts to reduce poverty (Economic Council of Canada, 1992: 9–10; Yalnizyan, 1998).

Canada's "liberal" welfare policies place much more faith in the power of a "free market," unregulated by government legislation and policies, to produce wealth and jobs that should, it is expected, trickle down to the poor (Esping-Andersen, 1990). Unfortunately, as our review of labour-market trends indicates, there is little evidence that the "free market" has performed successfully in this regard (Myles, 1996). Instead, unemployment rates have risen and inequality has increased. Furthermore, during the past decade or so, the political mood has changed, and concerns about reducing government deficits, streamlining government, and making Canada more competitive in the global marketplace appear to have been influencing government policy much more than concerns about reducing inequality. In fact, some deficit-reducing initiatives (e.g., reductions in social-assistance payments) have led to increases in material inequality in Canada. But there are other approaches to government spending that do not necessarily involve this trade-off. For example, job-creation strategies may be as useful in the long run as some budget-cutting efforts, and tax alternatives that would raise corporate income taxes or eliminate some of the tax write-offs enjoyed by the upper and middle classes (such as tax deductions for pension plans and RRSPs) might also be appropriate.

A large part of the problem lies, of course, in the fact that any serious effort to redistribute the wealth and income from the well-off to the poor would probably be opposed by the former, by many of us. If we really want to do something about material inequality in Canada, and globally, if we want a different kind of society and a different kind of world, many of us have to be willing to accept less so that others can have more.

SUMMARY

1. Persistent patterns of social inequality within a society are referred to as a structure of social stratification. Some social hierarchies within a society are based on ascribed statuses such as gender, race, or age, which are typically assigned to an individual at birth. Other social hierarchies are based on achieved statuses, which index how well an individual has performed within some role. A society in which considerable social mobility between statuses is possible is said to have an open stratification system.

2. Social theorists have proposed a variety of different explanations of the origins and effects of social-stratification systems. In his class-based theory of social stratification, Karl Marx emphasized the exploitation of the working class by the owners of the means of production and the capacity of class conflict to generate social change. Max Weber also put considerable emphasis on the power that resides in ownership of property, but argued that other hierarchies, those of prestige and political power, are influential as well.

3. The structural-functionalist theory of social stratification suggests that inequality is both inevitable and functionally necessary for a society, ensuring that the most qualified individuals are selected to fill the most important (and most rewarding) roles. Power differences are downplayed in this theory, as is conflict between different social classes. A number of more recent theories of social stratification, including those put forward by Gerhard Lenski, Frank Parkin, and Erik Olin Wright, have placed much more emphasis on power and conflict. While Wright developed a class-based theory of stratification that adapts many of Marx's ideas to contemporary circumstances, Parkin's approach follows in the footsteps of Weber.

4. Examination of occupational shifts in Canada over the course of the past century reveals some of the changing features of Canada's stratification system. However, we can get only partial glimpses of the class structure of our society. Studies of occupational mobility reveal that Canada is a relatively open society. Even so, there is considerable evidence that class-based advantages are passed from one generation to the next.

5. A detailed analysis of material inequality in Canada reveals that ownership of wealth and property is highly concentrated, and that income inequality is relatively high. Using a relative measure of poverty, we observe that about one in six Canadians are living below the "poverty line." There is considerable evidence that the poor and others near the bottom of the social hierarchies in our society enjoy fewer life-chances than do the well-off. For example, they are less likely to do well in school and to continue on to higher education, they are less healthy and have a shorter life expectancy, and they do not fare as well when dealing with the criminal-justice system. But because of their more limited access to social and material resources, the poor have seldom become an active force for social change.

6. Some theories of social stratification developed in the middle of the twentieth century suggested that material inequality was declining as the North American economy expanded. However, the period of rapid economic growth and relative affluence that characterized the middle decades of the century appears to have ended. And, as unemployment rates rise, as part-time and temporary work becomes more common, and as governments cut back on social-assistance programs, evidence accumulates that material inequality is also slowly increasing in Canada.

QUESTIONS TO CONSIDER

1. Does social class play a more or less significant role than do ascribed statuses (such as race and gender) in determining patterns of inequality within Canadian society?

2. How are social and material advantages passed from one generation to the next, resulting in persistent patterns of social inequality?

3. What role, if any, should governments play in addressing persistent patterns of social inequality? How successful have such attempts been in the past?

4. What does "poverty" really mean, and how should we measure it? Does Christopher Sarlo's "absolute poverty" approach (see Box 8.2 on page 204) make more sense than the "relative poverty" approach underlying Statistics Canada's "low-income cut-off lines"?

5. Do wealthy countries have a moral obligation to respond to Third World poverty? Are there other social or economic reasons for trying to reduce global inequality?

GLOSSARY

Absolute poverty is the state of existence of those who have so little income that they can barely stay alive.

Achieved status is a changeable status that is achieved on the basis of how well an individual performs in a particular role.

Ascribed status is a status such as age, gender, or race that is assigned to an individual, typically at birth, not chosen by the individual.

The **bourgeoisie**, according to Marx, is one of the two main classes within a capitalist mode of production. It comprises the owners of the means of production.

A **caste system** is a closed stratification system, most common in India, with strict rules regarding the type of work that members of different castes (the strata of society into which people are born) can do.

Circulatory mobility is the occupational mobility that occurs within a society when better-qualified individuals move upward to replace those who are less qualified and who must consequently move downward.

Class is the position of an individual or a family within an economic hierarchy, along with others who have similar amounts of access to or control over material resources.

Class conflict, according to Marx, is conflict between major classes within a mode of production, which eventually leads to the evolution of a new mode of production.

Class consciousness, according to Marx, is the phenomenon whereby members of a class recognize their shared interests in opposition to members of another class.

Class structure is the relatively permanent economic hierarchy composed of different social classes.

A **closed stratification system** is a stratification system in which little or no social mobility occurs, because most or all statuses are ascribed.

Contradictory class locations, according to Erik Olin Wright, are the locations within a class structure populated by occupational groupings with divided loyalties (e.g, managers who both supervise others and report to owners).

Exclusion, according to Frank Parkin, is the organized efforts of privileged, more powerful groups to maintain their advantaged position.

Intergenerational occupational mobility refers to an individual's occupational mobility, either upward or downward, in relation to her or his parents' (typical) occupational status.

Intragenerational occupational mobility refers to an individual's occupational mobility, either upward or downward, within his or her own lifetime.

Life-chances, according to Weber, are the opportunities (or lack thereof) for a higher standard of living and a better quality of life that are available to members of a given class.

The **low-income cutoff line**, also known as the "poverty line," is an estimate of the income level below which one might be considered to be living in (relative) poverty. It is defined by Statistics Canada as the level of income at which more than 55 percent of income is spent on basic necessities.

The **means of production**, according to Marx, is one of the main components of a mode of production, consisting of the technology, capital investments, and raw materials used in production.

A **meritocracy** is a society in which most or all statuses are achieved on the basis of merit (how well one performs in a given role).

The **mode of production**, according to Marx, is the overall system of economic activity within a society, comprising the means of production and the social relations of production.

Occupational status attainment refers to the process whereby an individual obtains a particular occupational status, and the factors that influence this process.

An **open stratification system** is a stratification system in which merit, rather than inheritance (or ascribed characteristics), determines social rank.

The **petite bourgeoisie**, According to Marx, is a secondary class within the capitalist mode of production, including independent owners/producers (e.g., farmers) and small-business owners.

Privilege refers to the control of a society's surplus resources.

The **proletariat**, according to Marx, is one of the two main classes within a capitalist mode of production, comprising workers who exchange their labour for a wage.

Relative poverty is the state of existence in which individuals have significantly less income than most others in their society, causing their lifestyle to be much more restricted and their life-chances substantially curtailed.

Social closure, according to Max Weber and Frank Parkin, refers to the methods used by more powerful groups to maintain their unequal access to status and resources and to exclude others from such access.

Social mobility is the process whereby individuals, families, or other groups move up or down a status hierarchy.

Social relations of production, according to Marx, are one of the main components of a given mode of production—specifically, the relationships between the main classes involved in production.

Social stratification refers to persistent patterns of social inequality perpetuated by the way wealth, power, and prestige are distributed and passed on from one generation to the next.

Socioeconomic status refers to one's general status within an economic hierarchy, based on income, education, and occupation.

Status is a culturally and socially defined position that a person occupies in a group.

Structural-functionalist theory is a school of thought that views social organization as analogous to a biological organism or system, in which the parts (or organs) exist because of the functions they perform in maintaining the whole. Thus, stratification exists because of vital functions it performs in maintaining social equilibrium.

Structural mobility refers to the occupational mobility within a society resulting from changes in the occupational structure (e.g., the upward mobility of many individuals resulting from the creation of more middle- and upper-level jobs in the economy).

Surplus value, according to Marx, is the value added to a product through a worker's labour (i.e., the profit taken by the owners).

Usurpation, according to Frank Parkin, is the efforts of excluded groups within a stratification system to gain some advantages and power at the expense of more powerful groups.

The **working poor** are individuals who work but whose income leaves them below a designated low-income, or "poverty," line.

SUGGESTED READING

Curtis, James E., Edward Grabb, and Neil Guppy, eds. (1999). *Social Inequality in Canada: Patterns, Problems, Policies*, 3rd ed. Scarborough, ON: Prentice Hall. An interesting and useful collection of readings on the various dimensions of stratification in Canada.

Forcese, Dennis. (1997). *The Canadian Class Structure*, 4th ed. Toronto: McGraw-Hill Ryerson Ltd. A useful overview of class-based inequality in Canada, with additional emphasis on class conflict and class action.

Grabb, Edward G. (2002). *Theories of Social Inequality,* 4th ed. Toronto: Harcourt Canada. This advanced but very readable book discusses various theories of social inequality, some of which were summarized in this chapter.

Marquardt, Richard. (1998). *Enter at Your Own Risk: Canadian Youth and the Labour Market.* Toronto: Between the Lines. The author describes how a changing labour market has created new risks and uncertainties for youth, and discusses how the state might intervene to reduce age-based inequalities.

Swanson, Jean. (2001). *Poor-Bashing: The Politics of Exclusion.* Toronto: Between the Lines. A social activist takes a critical look at how the poor and welfare recipients in Canada are stereotyped and mistreated by the media and government, and offers some useful suggestions for social change.

CHAPTER NINE

GENDER INEQUALITY: ECONOMIC AND POLITICAL ASPECTS

In this chapter you will learn that:

- A main source of inequality between women and men is the greater exclusion of women from public economic and political activity. The persistent tendency of many women to be relegated to domestic affairs leads to less income, prestige, and power for women.

- Although women have entered politics and the paid labour force in increasing numbers in the course of the past century, they still tend to be chiefly responsible for meal preparation, cleaning, laundry, and child-care.

- In the paid labour force, women and men still tend to be segregated in different kinds of jobs; "women's jobs" typically pay less, carry less prestige, offer less security, and bestow less authority.

- Although women make up over half the Canadian population, only one in five of the Members of Parliament are women.

- In recent years, employment equity policies and policies requiring equal pay for work of equal value have been implemented to help lessen gender inequalities, but much research and political action are still required before gender equality is achieved.

MONICA BOYD

UNIVERSITY OF TORONTO

INTRODUCTION

As we look back on the twentieth century, one fact is inescapable—enormous change has occurred in the attitudes, expectations, and behaviours of women and men in Canada. One way to see this change vividly is to compare the likely lifestyle of a man and a woman born in 1925 with that of another man and woman born in 1950, and of a third man and woman born in 1975. The pair born in 1925 would have been 25 years old in 1950, and 35 in 1960. During that ten-year period in the 1950s, they would almost certainly have married and had children. In the 1950s, women were expected to work exclusively in the home and take complete responsibility for domestic tasks and behaviours. Sociologists use the term **social roles** to refer to the behaviours that are expected of people occupying particular social positions. In the 1950s, the attitudes and activities expected of women—that is, their social roles—were those of wives and mothers. In contrast, men were expected to have paying jobs, and their responsibilities were to meet their family's needs for food, clothing, and shelter. Their social roles were those captured by the terms *provider* and *head of household*.

For a woman and a man born in 1950, this idealized "script" would be less rigid than it had been for the couple from the previous generation. Both pairs would have been raised at a time when mothers were expected to stay in the home and fathers were expected to be away for most of the day earning a living. But by the time the pair born in 1950 turned 25 in 1975, the belief that women should marry and work exclusively in the home was rapidly eroding. The average age at marriage had increased, indicating that many women and men were postponing legal marriage. After the divorce laws were revised in 1969, divorce rates also rose, giving a clear signal that fewer women and men would have a spouse for the duration of their adult lives. Other changes were blurring the line between work in the home and work in the labour force. Men were starting to become more involved in household maintenance and childrearing, and more and more women were joining the paid labour force.

The scenario for the pair born in 1975 and turning 25 in the year 2000 is different again. Most of those born during the mid-1970s, both men and women, probably continue to see themselves as even-tually having spouses or partners and raising children. Unlike the generation born in the 1920s, they probably also see themselves as sharing domestic responsibilities with their spouse or partner and as both holding paid jobs in either the private or the public sector.

However, a changed world does not necessarily mean an equal world. Although the term *revolution* is often used in reference to the changes in the direction of gender equality that have been made to date, those changes can hardly be said to constitute a finished revolution. Think, for example, of the low wages often paid to women, the need for affordable child-care, and the importance of paid work for economic security. As I will show in this chapter, gender inequality still exists in Canada, and is likely to persist in the twenty-first century. This means that, throughout your lifetime, you have probably seen and are likely yet to see at least some of the gender inequalities discussed here. At the same time, you are also likely to witness a variety of interventions aimed at reducing these inequalities.

The chapter begins with a definition of gender inequality, then explores the major dimensions of the phenomenon and the three main arenas in Canadian society in which it is evident: the home, the labour force, and politics. The chapter ends with a review of the actions, policies, and legislation that could reduce gender inequality in the future.

UNDERSTANDING GENDER INEQUALITY

GENDER INEQUALITY DEFINED

We frequently use the term *inequality* in reference to differences between groups of people that can be described by phrases such as "less than" or "greater than," or "more/less important." Social scientists usually refer to inequalities between men and women as "gender inequalities" rather than as "sex inequalities." The term *gender* is favoured because it refers to the *social* meanings associated with being a man or a woman, whereas the term *sex* refers to the *biological* characteristics of men and women. For sociologists, social meanings are constructed from social relations. For example, heterosexual marriage is a relationship in which one person becomes the husband and the other person becomes the wife. Although the terms *husband* and *wife* are inherently neutral, we quickly realize that, in our society, they carry expectations about people's obligations to each other, about their behaviour, and about the sex of the partner labelled "husband" and the partner labelled "wife." If you were to write down all the thoughts that occur to you when you think of the terms *husband* and *wife*, you would probably include such phrases as "provider" or "decision-maker" versus "homemaker" or "caregiver."

Gender Stereotypes

Phrases such as "provider" and "caregiver" do more than describe the expected behaviour associated with being a partner in a marriage. They also cause us to evaluate types of behaviour as "masculine" or "feminine." Once in place, these images of masculinity and femininity influence how people see themselves and how they experience the world. For example, the observation "it's a boy" often causes North American parents to decorate the child's room in bold colours, or at least in pale blue as opposed to pink. A male child is likely to receive stuffed animals, trucks, and play tool-kits rather than the dolls, play dishes, and play make-up that are likely to be given a girl. Through parental behaviour, television, movies, and print media (including schoolbooks), children learn to define certain social behaviours as inherent in being chromosomally male or female, even when such traits are probably learned rather than an inevitable consequence of an XY or XX chromosomal structure. By the time children have grown into adults, they have adopted and identified with many of these "masculine" or "feminine" personality traits and related behaviours. In turn, they are likely to treat others

around them through the lenses of their own identities and understandings of masculinity and femininity. In many instances, these conceptualizations are **gender stereotypes**—that is, oversimplified beliefs that men and women, by virtue of their physical sex, possess different personality traits and, as a result, may behave differently and experience the world in different ways. The cartoon below illustrates a gender stereotype, namely that because of DNA differences, women "shop" while men "hunt." This, of course, is not true—no shopping or hunting gene exists. Instead, gender-related identities and behaviours are socially constructed. They are outcomes created as individuals interact with others and encounter taken-for-granted rules and ways of doing things in families, schools, the legal system, politics, and the paid workplace (West and Fenstermaker, 1993).

The fact that gender is learned and that its content is continually renewed and altered through social interaction has three implications. First, gender identities and behaviours are not stable and fixed (see Chapter 5). What is taken to be masculine or feminine varies across societies and across the lifetimes of individuals. Second, gender identities—the internalized sense of being a man or a woman—and gender-specific behaviours need not be congruent with the sex assigned to individuals at birth. And third, along with sexuality and sex, gender identities and behaviours are not binary and polar opposites (Gange and Tewksbury, 1998; Segal, 1998). Yet, images of masculinity and femininity often emphasize opposites.

The fixation on polarizing characteristics of men and women is evident in phrases such as "opposite sex" or "vive la différence." The polarized approach is also evident in psychological studies of gender stereo-

SOURCE: Reprinted with special permission of King Features Syndicate.

types. In one famous study, several U.S. psychologists asked respondents to indicate which traits, from a checklist of 122 adjectives, characterized average men and women. They found that men were described as very aggressive, very independent, very active, very competitive, very logical, able to make decisions easily, and almost always acting as leaders. Women were described as not at all aggressive, not at all independent, very emotional, very passive, not at all competitive, very illogical, able to make decisions only with difficulty, and almost never acting as leaders (Broverman et al., 1972).

These results were obtained from respondents in the late 1960s; a study today would almost certainly have some different results. However, a Canadian sociologist, Marlene Mackie (1980), still found evidence of polarized gender stereotypes in research conducted about a decade later. The persistence of stereotypical thinking of feminine and masculine characteristics as polar opposites should sensitize us to two things. First, the idea of difference is apparently a powerful one, and hard to dispel even when it is contradicted by research. Second, in these polar depictions, feminine traits are viewed as less desirable than masculine ones. You need only reread the lists in the preceding paragraph to see that this is true.

Dimensions of Inequality

Gender stereotypes shape our attitudes about girls and boys, men and women, and they are often important factors in determining the ideologies that perpetuate gender inequalities. Sociologists usually define **gender inequalities** as hierarchical asymmetries between men and women with respect to the distribution of power, material well-being, and prestige (as recognized through deference or honour). This definition does not imply that men as individuals always have greater prestige, wealth, and power than do individual women. It does imply that, in general, compared with women, men have more wealth and greater power, and positions that are accorded higher prestige.

Power refers to the capacity to impose one's will on others, regardless of any resistance they might offer. It thus refers to the capacity to influence, manipulate, and control others. Power is exercised not only in the overt imposition of the will of one individual on others, but also in the control or support by groups or organizations of agendas that either uphold or challenge existing conditions (Duffy, 1986).

Material well-being refers to the ability to obtain the economic resources necessary to pay for adequate food, clothing, housing, and possessions. Two important sources of material well-being are work-related earnings and wealth.

Prestige refers to the social evaluation or ranking, by general consensus, of occupational activities and positions in a hierarchical order that reflects the degree of respect, honour, or deference the person engaged in the activity or occupying the position is to be accorded. Not everyone has to agree with the evaluation. For example, university professors are usually highly respected by the Canadian public, yet you may have no use for a particular professor. (One clear signal of the high general regard for professors is the regulation that Canadian passport applications can be witnessed by them.) Commonly, two or more differently evaluated positions are described as having higher or lower prestige, or "status."

The three dimensions of inequality just defined—power, material well-being, and prestige—are found in discussions of **social stratification**, which is the unequal ranking of groups in a society and the unequal and asymmetrical distribution of prestige, material possessions, and power among those groups. Stratification is the result, achieved over time, of routine and frequently recurring practices and often-unstated rules. From this broader perspective, gender inequality can be seen as a particular type of social inequality.

What explains gender inequalities in prestige, material well-being, and power? And what form do these inequalities take? Let us now examine these issues in turn.

EXPLAINING GENDER INEQUALITY

As sociology developed as a discipline during the twentieth century, the earlier neglect of gender by the fathers of sociology ceased. New theories emerged that explained gender inequality and its persistence. Women often developed these theories, and they frequently included insights taken not just from sociology but also from other disciplines (Chafetz, 1999; Lengermann and Niebrugge, 1996; Lorber, 1998). **Feminism** refers to the body of thought on the cause and nature of women's disadvantages and subordinate position in society and to efforts to minimize or eliminate that subordination.

However, because many different perspectives exist on the sources of gender inequality, we can speak of feminisms, or feminist theories.

Of the many feminist theories that exist, liberal feminism and Marxist-socialist feminism are two popular explanations for gender inequalities in Canada's economy and polity. Liberal feminism is rooted in the traditional liberalism of the 1700s, and it assumes that human beings are rational and will correct inequalities when known. A good society is believed to be one where men and women have equal rights and opportunities. According to liberal feminism, gender inequalities are caused and perpetuated by gender stereotyping and the division of work into "women's jobs" and "men's jobs." Two main ways of achieving gender equality are (1) by fighting and removing gender stereotyping and discrimination in education and at paid work and (2) by changing laws so that men and women have equal opportunities in the labour force and in politics (Lorber, 1998).

Very different perspectives on gender inequality derive from the writing of Karl Marx, who lived in the 1800s. According to Marxist feminists, women's unpaid work in the home maintains and reproduces the labour force. Capitalists benefit because they obtain refreshed workers at the beginning of each day and because children will become future labourers. At the same time, women's paid work also benefits capitalists because women, like men, produce surplus value and because they act as a "reserve army of labour," which can be hired and fired as labour demands change. Marxist feminists believe that gender equality is possible once capitalism as an economic system is replaced by socialism.

Socialist feminists build on Marxist feminism. They agree that gender inequality is caused by the gendered division of labour and its exploitation by capitalism. However, they argue that class relations constitute one system that oppresses women; a second system is that of **patriarchy** in which men rule over women. Patriarchy predates capitalism and the forms it takes vary across time and within societies. But generally, childbearing and the sexual activities of women are the foundation of gender inequalities. Because domestic and public spheres intersect, inequalities in one site can create disadvantages for women in other sites and vice versa. For socialist feminists, specific steps to remove gender inequality include government-subsidized maternal benefits and child-care, and comparable worth programs. However, removing inequality altogether requires the eradication of male dominance expressed through the legal system, the educational system, the family, and in the economy (Chafetz, 1999; Lorber, 1998; Jaggar, 1983).

Many other feminist theories also exist. Multiracial feminism emphasizes the importance of race in understanding gender inequality. This approach modifies the socialist feminist perspective by observing that hierarchical systems of domination incorporate race. For sociologist Patricia Hill Collins, race, class, and gender combine to form a "matrix of domination." All three intersect with the result that how people experience gender inequality depends on their location within class and racially defined structures (Chafetz, 1999; Lorber, 1999; Zinn and Dill, 1997). A wealthy white woman may experience inequality differently from a poor white woman, who in turn may experience inequality differently from a poor Black woman. In this scenario, how gender inequality is experienced reflects both class location and race. Multiracial feminism contributes to our understanding of gender inequality in three ways. First, it highlights differences among women in terms of gender inequality. Second, it points out that women of specific races and in certain class locations are in positions of power and domination over other groups of women. Third, it emphasizes that solutions to gender inequality vary according to the location of groups of women in the matrix of domination.

EXERCISING POWER

For many analysts of gender inequality, the asymmetry of power whereby men influence and control women is a very important aspect of the phenomenon. Since the ability to control and influence—to use power—indicates the twin processes of domination and subordination, most sociologists describe the power relations between men and women as those of male domination and female subordination.

Male influence and control over women is not narrowly defined. It does not, for example, refer just to the predominance of men rather than women in political positions or in the military. Instead, the concern with power is broadly based, including all social relations, routine behaviours, and commonly accepted practices. For example, denying women the right to vote clearly denied them a voice in choosing who would govern them and, equally important, denied them direct input into the formulation of laws that affect them, bestowing that right on men instead. Similarly, a workplace regulation that encouraged or compelled women to quit work upon marriage, such as the one that existed in the federal public service until 1955, made it difficult for married women to earn income and forced many of them to be dependent on their husbands for money. Power is also evident in day-to-day situations, such as when a young woman becomes the object of sexual innuendo or leering by her male classmates, co-workers, or even strangers. In our society, such behaviour on the part of males is often considered "normal"; it draws on conceptualizations of "femininity" and "masculinity" that define women as "sexy" or "available," and men as sexual aggressors. If she protests such leering attention, a young woman may discover that she is the object of further derision, and that no rules or formal appeal mechanisms exist to stop or penalize the offenders. In short, she cannot prevent or protest unwanted attention that arises from the social meanings attached to her biological sex.

Sexual harassment is essentially a display of power in which one person attempts to control, and often succeeds in controlling, another through sexual overtures. Although isolated cases of women harassing men have received attention from a prurient press, in most cases of sexual harassment, it is the man who makes the sexual overtures. When the capacity or incapacity to control and influence becomes routine and patterned, we can speak of power as a *system* of dominance and exploitation.

Sexual harassment is the result of the general belief that men are superior to women and may impose their will on women. It is also the outcome of patterned ways of behaving that are based on this belief and that serve to reinforce it. For example, because of our society's higher evaluation of men (and its corresponding devaluation of women), men are more likely to be employed in positions in which they are the bosses and women are supervised by them. Women are consequently less likely to have the means to contest unwanted advances. This situation was illustrated in the popular movie *Nine to Five*, in which a capable female manager (played by Lily Tomlin) is repeatedly passed over for promotion, while her inept boss constantly leers at and attempts to fondle his female staff. In the movie, the staff is

able to fight back, and they emerge as the winners. But how likely is this outcome in real life?

SEPARATE SPHERES

Power relations are important for understanding inequality simply because power, prestige, and material well-being are often interrelated. For example, although the ability to control others is not necessarily predicated on having a higher income or being wealthy, wealth normally does bestow power, just as power normally enhances the capacity to be wealthy. In seeking to understand gender inequalities, researchers point out that, historically, women have been excluded from certain types of activities that create opportunities for acquiring power, prestige, and wealth. During the late 1800s and for much of the 1900s, the "proper place" of Canadian women was thought to be in the home, where they would be responsible for producing and raising the next generation (Ursel, 1992). They were not expected to participate in politics, to enact legislation, or to be employed. Indeed, the denial of voting rights for women until the end of World War I and the presence of protective legislation that limited the hours and times when women could be employed were major deterrents to their participation in the "public sphere" of Canadian life—that is, in the economy and the political system. The public sphere was viewed as the domain of men, who were expected to be the breadwinners and heads of households.

What have been the consequences of this separation, in which women's place is in the private sphere of the home and men's is in the public sphere of economics, politics, the military, organized religion, and so on? In answering this question, it is helpful to consider what is implied by work in the home. For family members, work in the home is unpaid, and, all too frequently, the amount of skill, effort, and energy expended is invisible because housework is usually done outside the presence of others. Similarly, the socializing results of child-care are usually not apparent for years. Adding to the general devaluation of work in the home is the tendency to view nurturing and care-giving activities as biologically determined traits, rather than as acquired skills.

As a result, the long-time segregation of women into the private sphere of the home has reduced their access to power, prestige, and material well-being.

Participation in the private sphere does not provide direct access to material well-being. Although a woman who works only in the home may receive part of the income of another household member, she is dependent on the person who hands over the money. Economic dependency, in turn, is likely to produce asymmetries in power between the woman and the income earner, who, after all, can withhold money for the purposes of control or influence. Similarly, if all her activities are limited to the private sphere, a woman cannot obtain direct access to power outside that sphere—that is, influence or control through political representation, political office, or legislation.

Finally, because material well-being and power are so closely connected to deference and respect, the societal evaluation of work done in the home is not high. One classic indication of the devaluation of housework is the phrase "just a housewife." Sociological research shows that many activities done in the home, such as cooking, cleaning, and babysitting, are not high in prestige (Armstrong and Armstrong, 1994: Table 16). The low regard for housework is also evident from interviews conducted in 1989 with 1200 17-year-olds in Hamilton, Halifax, and rural Nova Scotia. Sociologists Dianne Looker and Victor Thiessen found that young people view housework as women's work. They consider it tiring, involving as it does long hours, high pressure, and much boredom. It generates few financial rewards. It is unimportant for the community. And young men consider housework—especially if it is full-time—as a job at the bottom of the occupational hierarchy (Looker and Thiessen, 1999).

In short, the belief that a woman's place is in the home disadvantages women relative to men in the distribution of prestige, power, and economic resources. Recognition of these disadvantages has elicited two main responses. First, some people have tried to eliminate the devaluation of domestic labour by (1) having women's unpaid work recognized symbolically and (2) having a dollar value assigned to it. The first objective was achieved in the 1996 census. After intense lobbying, questions on unpaid child-care, unpaid home maintenance, and unpaid elder care were included in the Canadian census (Luxton and Vosko, 1998). The second objective was raised in feminist discussions of "pay for housework" in the 1970s. Today, there is interest in measuring the value of unpaid work in the home. Chris Jackson, a Statistics Canada economist, estimates that unpaid work, if done in the market for wages, would have been worth about $235 billion in 1992, or about one-third of the gross national product (the total value of market-produced goods and services). He also finds that women did about two-thirds of all unpaid work in 1992 (Jackson, 1996).

The second response emphasizes the entry of women into the public sphere. Women's growing labour-force participation and their political activities are often viewed optimistically. That is, many people think these developments generate more money and power for women. Liberal feminists are especially likely to hold this view. However, the fact that women are now part of the public sphere of paid work and politics does not mean that gender equality exists. First, women's labour-force participation rates are still lower than men's, and women are still less likely to become elected politicians. Second, paid work does not mean liberation from unpaid work, and women are likely to engage in unpaid care-giving much more than men. Third, gender inequalities exist in the labour force and in the political sphere. In the remainder of this chapter, we will look at the movement of women into the public sphere, the continued provision of unpaid work in the home, and at the inequalities that still exist today in the public sphere.

SITES OF WORK

FEMALE LABOUR-FORCE PARTICIPATION

> It has become fashionable these days to refer to the "working woman" as if it were a recent phenomenon. But what is new about women working? Women have always worked. (Phillips and Phillips, 1983: 1)

Through the efforts of historians and sociologists, we now recognize that women, like men, have always laboured. In the past, much of this work was unpaid and performed in the home. In the early days of Canadian settlement by Europeans, women processed food, wove fabric, sewed clothing, tended the sick, and reproduced the next generation of labourers. Then, and in the years following Confederation, women took in boarders, did laundry, and prepared meals for others in their homes (Phillips and Phillips, 1983).

Canadian women continue to work in the home. But in the last half-century, they have increasingly done work that is paid and usually performed outside the home. As a measure of economic activity in the public sphere, the **labour-force participation** rate, over time, reveals the changing sites of women's work. At the beginning of the twentieth century, only one in seven women (14 percent) were economically active in the labour force. By the late 1990s, four in seven (nearly 60 percent) were in the labour force, compared with five in seven men (see Table 9.1). The growing labour-force participation of women has changed the composition of the Canadian labour force. At the beginning of the twentieth century, women represented one in seven workers (nearly 15 percent) in the labour force; by the last decade of the century, they constituted nearly half (45 percent) of the labour force.

The marital status of the female labour force also changed dramatically during this century. Until the 1960s, the modal, or typical, female labour-force worker was a never-married (single) woman. In 1941, for example, fewer than one in 20 married women (less than 5 percent) were in the labour force, and eight in ten women in the labour force (80 percent) were single. By 1996, 63 percent of all married women were in the labour force. In the female labour force today, it is married women who make up the majority of the workers (63 percent), with single women representing only one-quarter (25 percent) of female workers (Canada, 1958: Tables 10 and 11; tabulations for 1996 produced by the author from the 1996 Census Public Use Microdata File, Individuals). Also, the labour-force participation rate of women with very young children has increased substantially since the 1970s (Ghalam, 1993). By 2000, six out of ten women with the youngest child under age three were employed (Statistics Canada, 2001: Table 5).

Explaining the Increase

What caused these changes in the labour-force participation rate of Canadian women? Three factors are important: changes in Canada's economy that increased the demand for workers in service jobs, decreases in the number of children born, and increased financial pressures on families. These factors

TABLE 9.1 LABOUR-FORCE PARTICIPATION RATES AND SIZE OF LABOUR-FORCE POPULATION, FOR FEMALES AND MALES IN CANADA, BY DECADES 1901–1998

Year	LABOUR-FORCE PARTICIPATION RATES (PERCENT)		SIZE OF LABOUR FORCE (THOUSANDS)		FEMALES AS A PERCENTAGE OF THE TOTAL LABOUR-FORCE POPULATION
	Females	Males	Females	Males	
1901	14.4	78.3	281	1618	14.8
1911	16.6	82.0	419	2390	14.9
1921[a]	17.2	80.3	563	2750	17.0
1931[a]	19.4	78.4	752	3296	18.6
1941	22.9	85.6	939	3713	20.2
1951	24.4	84.4	1171	4079	22.3
1961	29.3	81.1	1749	4872	26.4
1971	39.4	77.3	2972	5667	34.4
1981	51.8	78.2	4899	7155	40.6
1991	59.9	76.4	6517	7958	45.0
1996	58.6	72.7	6805	8008	45.9
1998	58.1	72.4	7102	8530	45.4

[a] includes persons 10–13 years of age

SOURCE: 1901–61: FH Leacy./Statistics Canada, *Historical Statistics of Canada*, 2nd ed., Series D107-122, Cat. No. 11-516E (Ottawa: Supply and Services Canada, 1983); 1971: Statistics Canada, *Women in Canada*, 2nd ed., Cat. No. 89-503E (Ottawa: Industry, Science and Technology Canada, 1990), Table 1; 1981, 1991, 1996: *http://www.statcan.ca/english/census96/mar17/labour/lab.htm*; 1998: personal communication, Statistics Canada, Labour Statistics Division, October 8, 1999.

altered attitudes toward the paid employment of women and helped remove barriers to such employment during the twentieth century. Let us review each of these factors in turn.

Canada's Changing Economy   In the early 1900s, most Canadian jobs were in agriculture or manufacturing. Starting in the 1920s, more and more jobs became available in firms that provided services. Some of these services, such as trucking goods, mail delivery, telephone communication, and financial assistance, were consumed by other firms as well as by individuals. Other services, such as medical care and educational instruction, were directed primarily at individuals. All services, however, required workers, and the growth in services meant a corresponding increase in the demand for service workers. For example, before computers were used on a large scale, the growth of financial services brought about an increased need for manual record-keeping to track loans and other financial transactions. Similarly, the expansion of retail trade enlarged the volume of paperwork associated with placing orders, sending and receiving shipments, and taking inventory. Demand for workers in teaching and health care also rose as Canadian federal, provincial, and municipal governments assumed responsibility for these activities.

Women were often considered suitable employees for the newly emerging service jobs. By the early twentieth century, women—albeit young and single, in accordance with the prevailing belief that married women belonged in the home—had already supplanted men as office workers (Lowe, 1987) and as teachers (Prentice, 1977). With respect to office work, this development was made possible by the introduction of the typewriter, which was thought to lower the skill requirements of the occupation, and, with respect to both occupations, by the attractiveness to employers of paying lower wages to women, a practice premised on the belief that women were economically supported by the men in their household.

Fertility Decline and Labour Supply   Declining fertility also facilitated women's entry into the paid labour force, since it created an imbalance between the labour demands of the expanding service economy after World War II and the available labour supply. Canada's fertility rates dropped substantially during the 1930s and early 1940s as a result of the Depression and World War II. Consequently, the supply of new workers was relatively small when the postwar Canadian economy boomed. There were too few men and young single women—the traditionally "preferred" source of labour—to meet the growing demands for labour in Canada's new service-based economy. In response to labour scarcity and the desire to minimize wage costs (Connelly, 1978), employers began loosening restrictions against the hiring of married women. The fact that married women were not averse to working for wages—indeed, that they were eager to do so—had been proved by the experience of their employment during World War II (Pierson, 1977). As Table 9.1 shows, female labour-force participation rates increased rapidly in the postwar years.

Family Finances   Family finances also influenced the rise in female labour-force participation. Despite the ideal that a woman's place was in the home, women's employment had always been an important source of income for low-income families. To meet economic needs, many working-class women were employed as domestics and in factories during the late 1800s and early 1900s. After World War II, women's paid employment became an important source of family income for single-parent and two-adult families alike. Today, 14.5 percent of all families are headed by single parents, most of whom are in the labour force. Census data on 1995 incomes show that when single-parent mothers are employed, average family incomes are over 2.5 times that reported by families without earnings from the mother ($33 960 versus $12 765). Similarly, single-parent families headed by men had 1995 incomes, on average, of $45 668, compared to $15 008 for single-parent families without employment earnings from the fathers (Statistics Canada, 1998b: 15). In husband–wife families, wives' earnings not only increase Canadian family incomes but also help to keep many families out of poverty, particularly when the husbands' earnings are low or absent altogether. This was evident in the recession of the early 1990s. Between 1989 and 1993, the percentages of dual-earner families where the wife earned more than the husband rose from 19 percent to 25 percent. This suggests that many women were placed in the position of the primary breadwinner as a result of the losses by men of full-year, full-time jobs during the 1990–92 recession. In only 7 percent of families where the wife earned more than the husband did incomes fall below the low-income cutoff lines. Without the wife's earnings, however, the figure would have risen to 45 percent (Crompton and Geran, 1995). Today, two-earner husband–wife families report average family incomes of over $65 000, or approximately 1.4 times the incomes of families where only the husband has employment earnings (Statistics Canada, 1998b: 15).

DOMESTIC LABOUR

> Though she may toil from sun to sun, a woman's work is never done.

The exclusion of women from the public sphere was part of a more general predicament in which women were almost solely responsible for unpaid domestic production and for work associated with reproduction (bearing and rearing children). Canadian women cooked, cleaned, and took care of children, and men provided the money necessary to sustain the family.

Women normally shoulder the burden of dual responsibility—for child-care as well as for wage earning. Women also spend more time than their male counterparts on housework and child-care.
SOURCE: Photo courtesy of Rhonda Lenton and Talia Lenton-Brym.

Has this structure changed with the rising labour-force participation of women?

Data from the 1996 census show that women are still more likely than men to do unpaid work involving home maintenance and child-care (Statistics Canada, 1998a: 16–19). Women also spend longer hours than men on these activities. For example, in 1996, 25 percent of all women were spending 30 hours or more on housework, compared to 7 percent of all men. Seventeen percent of all women worked 30 or more hours on child-care, compared to 6 percent of men. To date, women and men are less likely to be caring for seniors than to be doing home maintenance or child-care, although even here women more than men are caregivers to seniors.

Even when they are in the paid labour force, married women continue to spend more time than their counterparts—married men—on housework and child-care. Figure 9.1 shows that, compared to men, higher percentages of women spend 15 hours or more on housework and on child-care among those who are married (including common-law marriages) and who also are working full-time (30 hours or more per week) and who have at least one child under age 15 at home (see Chapter 12 for additional discussion of housework).

Not surprisingly, women report spending less time than men watching television, pursuing hobbies,

FIGURE 9.1 PERCENT SPENDING 15 HOURS OR MORE A WEEK ON UNPAID HOUSEWORK AND ON CHILD-CARE, MARRIED WOMEN AND MEN, EMPLOYED 30 OR MORE HOURS A WEEK AND WITH AT LEAST ONE CHILD UNDER AGE 15 AT HOME, CANADA, 1996

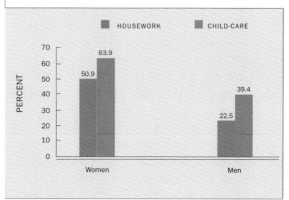

SOURCE: Statistics Canada, *The Daily*, March 17, 1998, Cat. No. 11-001E. Reprinted with permission.

and playing sports and games (Devereaux, 1993). Also, women are more likely than men to report feeling stressed due to lack of time; this is especially true for women who are working full-time and who have young children. In dual-earner families in which both partners were working full-time in the paid labour force and at least one child was living at home, 38 percent of women and 26 percent of men were "severely time stressed" in 1998 (Statistics Canada, 1999: 2).

The greater amounts of time spent by women on unpaid work illustrates the phrase "the double day." Entering the labour force may mean fewer hours spent on work in the home, but it increases the hours of total work, paid and unpaid, performed by women. In fact, the demands on women to provide unpaid care work likely will increase in the early twenty-first century for two reasons. First, during the 1990s, government policy shifts emphasized family-based care-giving instead of state-funded care-giving (Armstrong, et. al., 2002). Second, the aging of a large cohort of baby boomers, born between 1948 and 1962, and longer life expectancies mean that the numbers of elderly in need of care will likely increase. Past care-giving patterns suggest future providers of care are most likely to be women. In 1996, women were nearly two-thirds (61 percent) of informal care-givers of seniors and they spent more time than men on senior care–related tasks (Frederick and Fast, 1999). As offspring of the baby boomers, you may find yourself in the future assisting older parents, perhaps during the time when you are raising children of your own. The term "sandwich generation" refers to this caregiver situation where assistance is given simultaneously to the older and younger generations.

In addition to increasing the hours of unpaid work, care-giving responsibilities alter the way women and men lead their lives. Women who provided informal care to persons with long-term health problems were more likely than men caregivers to modify social activities, move closer to the person(s) needing care, change holiday plans, and experience altered sleep patterns. Over one-quarter of these women reported that helping others affected their heath, compared to 12 percent of men caregivers. The strongest impact, however, is on paid work. Of the employed caregivers, 55 percent of women and 45 percent of men reported that their care-giving activities affected their paid work, causing them to arrive late or leave early or to miss at least one day of work (Cranswick, 1999). This finding, along with the "double day" metaphor, illustrates that the domestic sphere and the "productive" sphere are not separate but intersect. What women, and to a lesser extent men, do in one sphere affects their activities in the other.

LABOUR-FORCE INEQUALITIES

OCCUPATIONAL SEGREGATION AND SEX TYPING

Women rather than men are likely to be unpaid care-givers. Liberal feminists explain this in terms of gender stereotypes and gender roles. Gender stereotypes imply women are thought to be more caring, and therefore better caregivers. Gender roles emphasize that "good" daughters, wives, or mothers are women who care for their parents, partners, or offspring. Social feminists note that such care-giving is consistent with other activities that maintain male wage workers and benefit men. Other sociologists view care-giving as "doing gender" in that the meaning of gender is constituted from and reaffirmed through everyday activities, including those of care-giving.

The equating of women and "care-giving" also is found in paid work. Although more and more Canadian women are now paid workers, they are frequently in jobs that involve care-giving, nurturing, and the sort of management functions typically found in the home. Women tend to be secretaries (the "office wife"), nurses, social workers, teachers, seamstresses, and waitresses. In contrast, men tend to be managers, doctors, professors, and factory and construction workers. This concentration of men in some occupations and women in others is often called the **sex segregation of occupations**, and the notion that a given occupation is appropriate for one sex versus the other is referred to as **sex typing (or sex labelling) of occupations**.

Occupational Segregation

Men and women can be compared across occupations in a designated place (a firm, a city, or a country). If men and women are concentrated in different occupations, the occupational structure is considered sex-segregated. Figures 9.2 and 9.3 show that, according to the 1996 census, sex segregation does exist in Canada. The occupations in which men and women concentrate are very different. For women, the ten most frequent jobs include secretary, registered nurse, elementary school teacher, baby-sitter, and receptionist. For men, the ten most frequent jobs include truck driver, janitor, retail trade manager, farmer, carpenter, and so on. The only occupation that both men and women occupy in large numbers is retail salesperson.

The figures show only the top ten occupations. The census collects information on more than 500 different occupational titles. These longer lists confirm that women and men often are concentrated in different occupations. The degree of occupational segregation has, however, declined somewhat since the 1960s. This decline is attributable mainly to the movement of women into previously male-dominated occupations rather than that of men into female-dominated occupations. However, the persistently large percentages of women employed in clerical occupations, creating a so-called female ghetto, are an important source of continued high levels of occupational segregation between women and men.

Sex labelling of occupations usually accompanies occupational segregation. Certain occupations are seen as jobs for women. Other occupations are seen as jobs for men. Often these views are so ingrained in our thinking that we recognize sex labelling (or "sex typing") only when we contradict unstated expectations. Consider the terms *woman doctor* and *male baby-sitter*. We frequently use these terms to indicate a departure from the implied norm—that men are physicians and women are baby-sitters. We rarely say "female baby-sitter." Or consider the list of the ten most frequent occupations for men and women. What gender comes to mind for "secretary," "nurse," or "receptionist"? What gender comes to mind for "truck driver," "farmer," or "carpenter"? These occupations are strongly sex-typed both in imagery and in reality. Data from the 1996 census indicate that 98 percent of carpenters are men, as are 98 percent of truck drivers and 77 percent of farmers and farm managers. Not all occupations are so skewed in their sex composition. The fact that women comprise

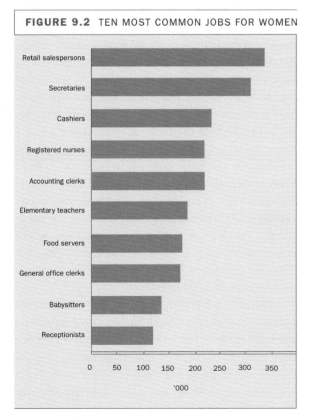

FIGURE 9.2 TEN MOST COMMON JOBS FOR WOMEN

SOURCE: Statistics Canada, "Perspectives on Labour and Income," Cat. No. 75-001, Winter 2000, Vol 1, No. 4. Reprinted by authority of the Minister of Industry, 2000.

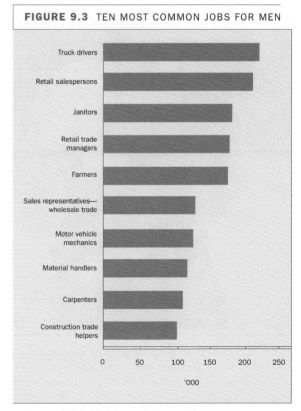

FIGURE 9.3 TEN MOST COMMON JOBS FOR MEN

SOURCE: Statistics Canada, "Perspectives on Labour and Income," Cat. No. 75-001, Winter 2000, Vol 1, No. 4. Reprinted by authority of the Minister of Industry, 2000.

about 45 percent of the labour force is a yardstick for which occupations are female sex-typed or male sex-typed. In occupations such as secondary school teacher, journalist, dry cleaning and laundry supervisor, computer operator, ticket and cargo agent, dispatcher and radio operator, optometrist, actor, and veterinarian, about 40 to 50 percent of the incumbents are women. Thus we can say that these occupations are not sex-typed (percentages calculated by the author from http://www.statcan.ca/english/census96/mar17/occupa/table1/t1p00t.htm).

Why Care?

Why should you be concerned about sex typing and sex segregation? Because the occupations in which women are concentrated are often lower than those held predominantly by men in terms of authority, responsibility, skill requirements, mobility opportunities, and earnings. We will discuss many of these

Sex typing or sex labelling is the designation of an occupation as "female" or "male" depending on the sex for whom it is considered appropriate. Many hockey teams would not hire Hayley Wickenheiser irrespective of her demonstrated skill as a player—proven in part by her performance at the 2002 Olympics. She was hired to play on a men's team in Finland.
SOURCE: CP Picture Archive/Tom Hanson.

inequalities later. The important point for now is that these inequalities indicate male advantages in the labour force. Furthermore, the nature of the sex typing in our society implies that the work traditionally performed by women in the home has created sex stereotypes about the work that women should do in the paid labour force.

POWER AT WORK

Male power over women is evident in the labour market and in public arenas such as law, politics, the military, and the media. We have seen that substantial occupational segregation exists, and that it hints at greater male power, in that men are more likely than women to be managers. But in order to document gender asymmetry in the ability to influence and control others, we must find out whether men are indeed able to make more decisions and exercise authority over women.

In analyzing the 1994 Statistics Canada general social survey, my colleagues and I found that men were more likely than women to describe their jobs as managerial and/or as supervising others. For example, 25.3 percent of women, but 40.4 percent of men, described themselves as supervisors. We also found that male supervisors had more employees to supervise than did female supervisors. As well, male managers were more likely than female managers to hold positions in the top rungs and to plan the activities of all parts of the business. Women were in the lower managerial rungs. They were less likely to be involved in planning business activities and more likely to be only partly involved (Boyd, Hughes, and Miller, 1997). This pattern illustrates the **glass-ceiling** effect: Women face invisible barriers in penetrating the highest levels of organizations where power is concentrated and exercised. Box 9.1 describes the outcomes for women in Canadian business organizations in 2000.

Our research (Boyd, Mulvihill, and Myles, 1991) indicates that men are more likely to hold jobs characterized by the ability to control people and influence outcomes. However, demonstrating gender inequalities in the distribution of power is not quite the same as showing that men have power over women. Studies of specific firms do indicate that men, as managers, foremen, or union organizers, often have control and influence over women

---

BOX 9.1   GLASS CEILING IS FIRMLY IN PLACE AT CANADA'S BIGGEST COMPANIES

When Pat Smith took her first job, a female executive took her aside and gave her some advice.

"She told me to be successful you have to think like a man, act like a lady and work like a dog," remembers Ms. Smith, now a senior vice-president at Maritime Life Assurance Co.

Ms. Smith, 47, says that's exactly what she did, seeking out the "projects from hell," in order to get noticed and opting not to have children so that she could give more time to her career. It paid off and she became one of a small group of women to break into the senior executive ranks at Canada's largest companies.

Yesterday, a benchmark study on Canadian corporate officers—the executives who make up a company's senior management team—made it vividly clear for the first time just how small that group of women is.

The count, conducted by a New York–based non-profit group called Catalyst, found that while women make up 45 per cent of the work force, they hold just 12 per cent of the corporate-officer posts at Canada's 560 largest corporations. In raw numbers, that's 690 of 5,746 jobs.

Further up the ranks, the numbers are even slimmer, with women filling just 3.4 per cent of what Catalyst calls "clout" positions, such as chief operating officer, executive vice-president, or chief executive officer. That means there are just 49 women in those posts, compared with 1,374 men.

CANADIAN WOMEN IN BUSINESS, 2000: BY THE NUMBERS

- 45% of Canadian labour force
- 32% of managers
- 14% of senior managers in private sector
- 12% of corporate officers
- 7.5% of board seats
- 3.4% of titles with clout
- 2% of CEOs

SOURCE: Elizabeth Church, *Globe and Mail*, February 9, 2000. Reprinted by permission of the *Globe and Mail*.

---

workers. Our analysis of a 1982 Canadian survey found that it is common for women to be supervised by men; when women supervise, they usually exercise authority over other women. Only rarely do men have a female superior (Boyd, Mulvihill, and Myles, 1991: 424). In the labour force, men have power over both men and women, whereas women have power primarily over other women.

GENDER AND SKILL

The jobs that women often hold are characterized not only by being less powerful, but also by having lower skill requirements than jobs held by men (Boyd, 1990; Myles and Fawcett, 1990). Since higher-skilled jobs usually differ from lower-skilled jobs in pay and security, employment in lower-skilled jobs implies economic and quality-of-work inequalities between men and women.

Why are women less likely than men to be employed in high-skilled jobs? One possible answer is that there is gender bias in the definition of **skill**. Sex

typing and a general devaluation of work done by women influence commonsense evaluations of what is or is not "skilled" work. For example, nursing occupations may require a high level of interpersonal skill—for example, in dealing with relatives of dying patients—but because this ability to handle a diversity of distraught and upset people is considered "natural" in a woman, it is not recognized as a professional "skill" in a nursing occupation. In contrast, plumbing jobs (usually performed by men) require knowledge of toilets and sinks, soldering, and pipe fitting—so-called technical skills. Bias in the evaluation of skills occurs when such technical knowledge is considered more valuable than knowledge about personal interactions and care-giving.

This example indicates that our definitions of skill are socially constructed. That is, what we define as "skill" reflects other social evaluations and hierarchies—in this case, hierarchies based on gender (Gaskell, 1986; Steinberg, 1990). If we think of women as being worth less than men, we are likely to let this attitude influence how we define the skill requirements of jobs held primarily by women or primarily by men. Jane Gaskell (1986) suggests that women are disadvantaged in the skill definitions assigned to jobs sex-typed as female because, historically, women have not been represented by strong unions that have lobbied in their interest. Furthermore, women are less likely to be trained on the shop floor as apprentices. Instead, the training required for "female" jobs is often incorporated into high-school curricula, with the result that the skill-training component is less visible than it is in occupations in which training is provided on the job.

Skill undervaluation of female sex-typed occupations is a concern for two reasons. First, wage levels are associated with skill requirements. Thus, if the skill requirements of jobs in which women predominate are undervalued, the pay rates in those jobs are likely to be lower. Second, current pay-equity policies often ask whether men and women are receiving equal pay for performing jobs of comparable worth. The "worth" of a job, however, includes its skill requirements. If the skill requirements of jobs employing predominantly women are already devalued, then fair comparisons between appropriate sets of jobs may not be made (Gaskell, 1991; Steinberg, 1990).

NONSTANDARD WORK

As another example of gender inequality, let us now examine gender differences in **standard** and **nonstandard work**. What do these terms mean? If asked to describe a typical job in the labour market, most of you would probably mention full-time, full-year employment with job-related benefits. This is usually what we mean by standard work. In contrast, nonstandard work includes **part-time work**, part-year employment, limited-term contract employment, employment through temporary-help agencies, self-employment, and multiple job holding (Economic Council of Canada, 1991: 71; Krahn, 1995).

Women and Part-Time Work

Compared with men at every age, women in the labour force are much more likely to be part-time workers. In 2000, for example, employed women were three times more likely than men to be part-time workers (27.3 percent of women compared to 10.3 percent of men) (Statistics Canada, 2001: Table

7). Gender differences remain when the definition of "part-time" is extended beyond hours worked per week to include weeks per year. In my analysis of the 1996 Canadian census, I found that 45 percent of all women aged 25–64 in the 1995 labour force were *not* working full-time, full-year, whereas only 33 percent of all men fell into this category ("full-time, full-year" refers to work that is 30 hours or more a week and 49 or more weeks a year. The data analyzed are from the 1996 Public Use Microdata File of Individuals).

As a share of all employment, part-time work has been increasing. The restructuring of the economy is a primary explanation for this increase. Many workers now take part-time employment because they cannot find full-time employment.

Women and Nonstandard Work

During the past two decades, women have consistently made up around 70 percent of the part-time labour force. Part-time work can thus be seen as an employment ghetto for women. Women are also overrepresented in nonstandard work defined more broadly. Using a definition of nonstandard employment that includes self-employment, temporary work, part-time work, part-year work, and multiple job holding, a 1994 Canadian study found that 40 percent of all currently employed women, compared with 27 percent of men, were working in nonstandard employment. Percentages were extremely high for young men and women. Among those aged 15–24, 62 percent of young women and 52 percent of young men had nonstandard employment (Krahn, 1995: Table 3).

Concerns about Nonstandard Work

Employment in nonstandard work is of concern for two reasons. First, it is becoming more and more common, especially among young people. Second, compared with full-year, full-time jobs, nonstandard jobs generally provide less job security, lower pay, and fewer fringe benefits. Part-time workers, for example, are often excluded from employer fringe benefits, including pension plans (Duffy and Pupo, 1992). Thus, nonstandard employment, in general, and part-time work, in particular, imply a marginal work force—marginal in terms of earnings, benefits, and job security. Statistics indicate that more women than men are employed in this marginal work world.

EARNINGS

In addition to gender inequalities in terms of occupations, power, skill, and type of work, women in Canada, on average, earn less than men. In 1997, women employees earned $13.93 per hour or 81 cents for every dollar earned by men ($17.10) (Statistics Canada, 1998c: 10). Shocking as it may be, this ratio represents an improvement over the situation in earlier times. In the late 1960s and early 1970s, the average earnings of women were roughly 46 percent of the average earnings of men (Ghalam, 1993: Table 3.1). Education helps narrow the gap, and during the 1960s and 1970s the numbers and percentages of women with post-secondary education rose. In 1997, for example, hourly wages of women with less than nine years of education were 71 percent of the wages of men with less than nine years of education. However, women with bachelor's degrees earned on average $22.38 per hour or 85 percent of the $26.26 hourly wage of men with bachelor's degrees (Statistics Canada, 1998c: Table 2). These wage rates reflect the earnings of all age groups, so they may differ from what you will be earning when you have your bachelor's degree.

Explanations of Women's Lower Pay

Observers have offered four sets of explanations for the pay gap between women and men: (1) gender differences in the characteristics that influence pay rates; (2) gender differences in the type of work performed; (3) discrimination; and (4) societal devaluation of women's work. All four explanations have strong advocates, and all have critics (England, 1993; Phillips and Phillips, 1983).

Explanations of the first type usually assume that earnings reflect the productivity of workers and that productivity is increased by factors such as higher education, longer labour-force experience, and length of time on the job. Advocates of this explanation argue that the lower wages of women are caused by lower productivity levels resulting from women's lower or different educational achievements and from labour-force interruptions attributable to women's family responsibilities.

The second type of explanation argues that the gender gap in pay reflects the concentration of women in certain occupations and industries characterized by lower wages, and their concentration in nonstandard work, particularly part-time work.

The third type of explanation focuses on discrimination, identified here as differential pay being assigned to women on the basis of their gender. Such discrimination can be personal and deliberate, but it is often impersonal, produced by the standard, unquestioned practices of assigning women to certain jobs and men to others, and of paying men and women different wages even when they hold the same jobs. Much of this impersonal discrimination is called **statistical discrimination**, the process whereby employers make decisions about whether to hire and how much to pay any given woman on the basis of the employers' perceptions of the average characteristics of *all* women. For example, if an employer believes that women typically leave the labour force for long periods to raise children, or will not travel extensively or work overtime because of family responsibilities, the employer may impose those generalized beliefs on particular women. Thus, a single woman with no children might find herself being paid less than a man because of the employer's belief that women, in general, are less productive than men. Alternatively, she might find herself denied opportunities for job training or advancement because of her employer's belief that women, in general, will leave their jobs to have families or will not perform certain tasks, such as long-distance travelling, because of family obligations.

The fourth explanation holds that the lower earnings of women reflect a general devaluation of "women's work"—that is, of tasks initially performed in the home—and the incorporation of that devaluation into pay practices. As we have seen, the work women perform in the home can be invisible and often is not viewed as "work." People who do domestic work for money receive low wages. The devaluation of women's labour is rooted in the historical image of every woman having a male breadwinner to provide for her and not "needing" to be paid the same wage as a man who, after all, has a family to support! Once in place, pay practices persist and fuel a faulty logic that not only sustains pay differences between men and women in the same jobs but also provides a rationale for the lower wage rates paid in sex-typed occupations and jobs. Research by Paula England, a U.S. sociologist, has shown that the wages paid in occupations decline as the percentage of workers in those occupations who are female rises (England, 1993: Chap. 3).

Assessing the Explanations

Most sociologists emphasize discrimination and the devaluation of work performed by women as the main explanations for gender inequalities in earnings. Sociologists point to the absence of proof that women are less productive than men or that they expend less effort (England, 1993: 27). They also observe that earnings gaps persist even when women and men have comparable levels of education; are in full-time, full-year jobs; and/or are in the same occupations (Best, 1995). For example, among those working full-time in managerial occupations, the average weekly wage of women in 1997 was $708, or 72.5 percent that of men (Statistics Canada, 1998c: 19). We also see from Box 9.2 that women are entering the legal profession more and more, and there is no initial earnings gap. However, older women lawyers earn substantially less than their male counterparts. Four factors may explain the lower average earnings for older women in law. First, statistical discrimination may be at work. Second, devaluation of the work done by women may have occurred. Third, if older women were absent from the labour force for long periods of time associated with child-rearing, lower productivity might be a factor. Fourth, concentration by women in less-well-paying areas of law such as family versus corporate law might explain some of the gender gap in earnings. We will have to wait to see what happens to the earnings of young women today as they move through their legal careers.

BIRTHPLACE AND COLOUR MATTER

So far, my discussion of gender inequality in work has proceeded as if all women were alike and all men were alike. In fact, as other chapters in this book show, this is not the case. Some women and men are young; some are old. Some are married or living with a partner; others are not. Some women are born in Canada; others are born elsewhere. In addition, women differ in their colour and ancestral origins, as do men.

The intersection of gender inequality with inequalities stemming from birthplace and colour is of interest to many Canadians. That interest is fuelled by the changing ethnic and colour composition of Canada's population, initiated by changes in Canada's immigration policies starting in 1962. It has become evident since that time that foreign-born women and women of colour experience not only gender inequality but also the inequalities that arise in a society that allocates privileges to certain groups and not to others on the basis of their colour, ethnicity, birthplace, and class.

Figures 9.4 and 9.5 give us an idea of labour-force inequalities among women by birthplace and colour. In these figures, most of the groups are members of "visible-minority" groups. In popular usage and government parlance, the term **visible minority** is used to identify those Canadian residents who are not recognized as part of the white mainstream population (of European and U.S. origin) and who thus may experience discrimination. However, the term is

---

BOX 9.2   MORE WOMEN THAN MEN CALLED TO BAR, BUT MALES STILL EARN MORE ON AVERAGE

After centuries of being outnumbered by men, women aren't simply making inroads into the legal profession. In sheer numbers, they're starting to dominate.

The majority of law graduates admitted into the profession in Ontario yesterday and today—53 percent to be precise—are women. The Law Society of Upper Canada hasn't seen anything like it in its 205 years.

Until 1999, there were still more men being called to the bar than women. In 2000, the sexes tied. Last year [2001], women inched ahead for the first time and made up 51 percent of new lawyers. Overall, they now account for about a third of the profession.

In some cases men still have the upper hand when it comes to partnerships and pay. At the beginning of their careers, male and female lawyers earn about the same, but between ages 30 and 34, men earn about $7,900 per year more on average. That rises to $16,000 more for male lawyers between 35 and 39, according to a report prepared for the law society last year.

Between ages 40 and 49 men make about $35,000 more a year on average, about $65,000 more between 50 and 54.

SOURCE: Tracey Tyler, "More women than men called to bar. But males still earn more than average." Reprinted with permission of Torstar Syndication Services. Excerpted from an article originally appearing in *The Toronto Star* February 22, 2002, p. A18.

an umbrella label for diverse groups. In government statistics, Canada's Aboriginal peoples are not included in the "visible-minority" category. They appear as a separate group. It should be noted that Figures 9.4 and 9.5 refer only to persons living in Montreal, Toronto, and Vancouver, where most of Canada's foreign-born and visible-minority groups reside. This restriction distorts the overall situation of the Aboriginal population, many of whom live either on reserves or in other Canadian cities.

These figures generate at least four conclusions. First, foreign-born women who are permanent residents of Canada are more likely than Canadian-born women to be in occupations that are characterized as "low skill," using the census classification of occupations. They also earn less on average than their Canadian-born counterparts. While a difference of $63 a week may not seem much, it amounts to close to $3300 a year. My research (Boyd, 1999) shows that earnings differentials increase between Canadian-born women and foreign-born women especially when foreign-born women are women of colour and have no knowledge of English or French.

Second, women who are members of Aboriginal or visible-minority groups are more likely than non–visible-minority (i.e., white) women to be employed in low-skill occupations. Such occupations include cleaning hotel rooms or offices and manufacturing jobs in food-processing plants and the textile industry. Many workers in Canada's garment firms are immigrant women of colour, and often their jobs are characterized by irregular employment, deadlines, bad lighting, poor ventilation, and low pay (Das Gupta, 1996; Yanz et al., 1999).

Third, women who are members of Aboriginal or visible-minority groups have lower weekly earnings than non–visible-minority women. Again, while the weekly differences seem small, they grow substantially when cumulated over long periods in the labour force. My own research and that of others (Pendakur and Pendakur, 1998) show that earnings differentials persist between visible-minority women and non–visible-minority women even when we take into account the fact that differences between groups can exist with respect to age, education, and other factors that influence the levels of earnings. This means we cannot rule out discrimination as a factor, and that at least part of the lower earnings of visible-minority and Aboriginal women may be caused by employers not hiring these women for certain jobs, promoting them slowly, or paying them less.

FIGURE 9.4 PERCENTAGES OF WOMEN AGE 25–64 WHO ARE IN THE LOWEST SKILL LEVEL OF OCCUPATIONS, BY BIRTHPLACE AND VISIBLE MINORITY GROUP, CANADA, 1996

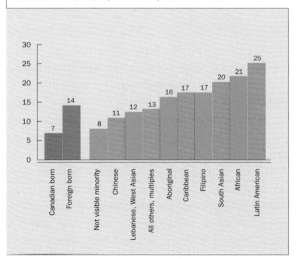

SOURCE: Compiled from Census Public Use Microdata File of Individuals, 1996.

FIGURE 9.5 AVERAGE WEEKLY 1995 EARNINGS FOR WOMEN AGE 25–64 BY BIRTHPLACE AND VISIBLE MINORITY GROUP, CANADA, 1996

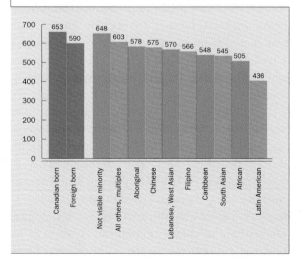

SOURCE: Compiled from Census Public Use Microdata Files of Individuals, 1996.

The fourth and final conclusion to be drawn from Figures 9.4 and 9.5 is that considerable diversity exists among women in their labour-force characteristics. Thus we should not be thinking of women as a homogeneous group. To give a few examples, employment in low-skill occupations is most likely for South Asian, African, and Latin American visible-minority women. These women also have the lowest weekly earnings of the various groups appearing in Figure 9.4. Conversely, among visible-minority groups in Montreal, Toronto, and Vancouver, Chinese, Lebanese, and West Asian women are the least likely to be in low-skill occupations, and they have the highest weekly earnings.

These findings reaffirm the criticisms voiced by minority and foreign-born women—namely, that, for them, inequality issues are not restricted to gender, but also include race and immigrant status, and that each group is unique in the kinds of disadvantages and subordinations it experiences. These criticisms are consistent with multiracial feminism.

WOMEN'S GROUPS: ORGANIZING FOR CHANGE

So far, I have discussed the increasing movement of women out of the home and into the labour force. The economy, however, is only one of several arenas in the public sphere from which women have historically been excluded, and in which their participation remains very limited. Politics is another important arena, one that initially excluded women, but that women have now begun to penetrate. The political arena includes more than acts of formal political engagement, such as voting or running for political office. It can be broadly defined to include any activity that mobilizes people to make their views known, to press for change, and to achieve objectives.

Collective actions aimed at change are called **social movements**. The term *women's movement* is the most general term used to describe the varied actions that have been and are being taken by women's groups on behalf of women. The **women's movement** is a social movement that takes action to improve the status of women. Feminism is an important part of the women's movement. However, as we observed earlier in the chapter, many different forms of feminism exist, each with a different understanding of the causes of gender inequality and subordination and of the actions required to improve the situation.

Over time, as the arenas in which women participate have broadened to include the public sphere, changes have occurred in feminist thought and in the nature of the women's movement. Both before and after women were legally granted the right to vote, early efforts focused on improving the quality of life in the home for women and their families (Brodie, 1996). The large-scale entry of women into the labour force during the 1960s and 1970s elicited a different set of concerns. Based on a model of equal rights between men and women, women pressed for gender equality in employment opportunities and in earnings. A protocol for change emerged in which advocacy groups, some closely affiliated with the federal government, such as the Advisory Council for the Status of Women, and others receiving substantial government funding, would present agendas for change to parliamentarians, ministers, or key persons in government departments. This direct interaction with the formal agencies and members of the state achieved some successes depending on the party in power and how robust the economy was. For example, through the lobbying efforts of various groups, women's rights are now enshrined in the 1982 Canadian Charter of Rights and Freedoms, and legislative changes ensure a fairer division of assets in divorce cases. However, the efforts of women's groups have been limited by at least three factors (Burt, 1993). First, because many women's groups rely on governments for funding, their roles as critics of government policy can be easily compromised. They may change their agenda or adopt a conciliatory style of confrontation in order not to bite the hand that feeds them. The consensus-building approach found within many women's organizations constitutes a second constraint on their effectiveness. This decision-making style can be very time-consuming, and it can place groups at a disadvantage given that political interventions often require quick reactions. The heterogeneity of women's groups is a third factor limiting their impact. There are many different women's groups, and not all of them agree on what should be done for women. For example, diverse opinions exist among women's associations on child-care issues and on access to abortion, and it is often impossible to create a coalition among groups to lobby for one clear policy.

Women's groups still lobby governments for change. However, during the 1980s and 1990s, three factors changed the interaction between women's groups and governments: the electoral success of more conservative parties; the federal government's calls for economic restraint and increased provincial and private-sector responsibility; and the dissatisfaction within women's advocacy groups on agendas reflecting the concerns of white, largely middle-class women (see Tremblay and Andrew, 1998). By the mid-1990s, political representatives and departments of federal and provincial governments (which in the case of Quebec and Ontario had also taken leadership on certain issues such as pay equity) were no longer as responsive to lobby efforts by women's groups. They reduced funding to women's groups. In 1995 the federal government reorganized their units dealing with women's issues and disbanded the Canadian Advisory Council on the Status of Women, which was mandated to inform the public and the Canadian federal government on issues of concern to women. Alongside all these changes, a different model of advocacy emerged in which women's groups operated in coalition with other social-movement–based groups, often rejecting networking and direct contact with political parties (Erickson, 1998; Young, 1998).

Recently, associations that represent the interests of women of colour, immigrant women, and lesbians have been important additions to the landscape of women's associations in Canada. The attention they have directed to issues of racism, sexual identity, and class has forced mainstream groups representing primarily white, heterosexual, and often middle-class women to become more inclusive in their membership base and their agendas. Women of colour have argued that these groups fail to acknowledge concerns other than those of white middle-class women. The mainstream argument that gender subordination reflects the restriction of women to the private sphere fails to recognize that many women of colour have always engaged in paid work and that issues of racism in employment are of equal importance for them. Furthermore, to the extent that women of colour work as domestics, it is white women who have power over them as their employers, and the important issues are both gender oppression and racial oppression. Immigrant women also have their own concerns, which include language training, job-skill training, culturally sensitive child-care, and culturally sensitive assistance in situations of domestic violence. For lesbians, areas of interest are gay rights and related issues, such as the inclusion of sexual orientation in human rights codes, the prohibition of employment discrimination on the basis of sexual orientation, and the extension of married-equivalent benefits to same-sex couples.

GENDER IN POLITICS

> The voice of government, as the Royal Commission on the Status of Women observed [almost 30] years ago, is still a man's voice. Women remain governed rather than governors, legislated rather than legislators. (Brodie, 1991: 9)

Formal politics is an important area of gender inequality for three reasons: It is here that the exercise of power is most obvious, that laws determining rights and entitlements are formulated, and that public policies are set. As political scientist Janine Brodie observes (1991: 9), politics and political representation are the mechanisms whereby the interests of groups are translated into political demands and actions. If groups are politically disenfranchised or face barriers to the representation of their interests, two consequences follow: The needs of the groups may not be met through policies and legislation; and the premise that democratic governments represent all the people is false.

For the first 50 years after Confederation, the notion that the private sphere was the appropriate place for women went hand in hand with the exclusion of women from politics. In the course of the twentieth century, however, women did move into the political arena. The effects of their entry are threefold: (1) they obtained and exercise the right to vote; (2) they participate in political parties and can be elected to political office; and (3) they have created and use associations to represent the special interests of women. Such interests include, but are not limited to, access to abortion, child-care, equality in the labour force, family violence (including spousal violence and child abuse), prostitution, rape, pensions, and participation in politics.

VOTING RIGHTS

Throughout the early part of the twentieth century, Canadian women did not have the right to vote; without that right, they could not elect candidates to represent their interests in government. Between 1916 and 1925, however, all provinces except Quebec enfranchised women. Quebec granted women the vote in 1940. The federal government granted voting rights in 1917 to women who were British subjects and who had served with the military or had a close relative in the military; it extended those rights to women unconnected with the military in 1918. But voting rights were not given to women or men of Chinese, East Indian, or Japanese ancestry until the late 1940s, or to male or female Inuit until 1950, or to registered Indians living on reserves until 1960 (Maille, 1990: 1).

The suffrage movement in English Canada was a factor in obtaining the vote for women (Bashevkin, 1993: Chap. 1). However, Sandra Burt (1993: 216) observes that the vote was granted on the premise that women would use it only to improve the quality of home life, and that enfranchisement would not divert women from their "natural and sacred" duties in the domestic sphere.

Such sex stereotyping of women also led to the expectation that women would not be interested in the realm of politics. Male legislators in the early 1900s believed that women would not vote at the same rate as men. Men also believed that women would vote in a politically naïve and parochial way as a result of being isolated at home. But these stereotypes proved to be false. In Canada today, voting rates—that is, the percentages of eligible voters who cast a ballot—are similar for women and men. The political agendas of men and women do differ, but not because women's views are parochial. Research in the late 1980s showed that women were more likely than men to oppose free trade, foreign investment, cruise missile testing, and military spending and to be more concerned with social-welfare policies (Bashevkin, 1993: Chap. 2). In dispatching the notion that women vote in a conservative or parochial way, Thelma McCormack suggests that female–male differences in voting interests result because women and men operate in different political cultures (which have been moulded by gender differences in political socialization) and have different opportunities to participate in politics. Again and again, women hear that "politics is a man's world." Excluded from political life, women are more likely to be concerned with moral and community-based political issues than with issues pertaining to the acquisition or exercise of power (McCormack, 1975: 25–26). However, there is no evidence that women act as a cohesive voting bloc on all issues (Brodie, 1991).

PARTICIPATING IN THE WORLD OF POLITICS

McCormack's description of women as excluded from political life was written when fewer than 4 percent of Canada's Members of Parliament (MPs) were women. The situation has changed since then. Table 9.2 shows that in the fall of 2002, two in ten elected federal MPs (21 percent) were women, as were three in ten appointed senators. However, enthusiasm over the change in the past 25 years should be tempered by the recognition that women represent over half of Canada's electorate. Table 9.2 also shows variations by party in the percentages of federal MPs who are women, with the highest percentage (35 percent) in the New Democratic Party (NDP). These differences reflect factors such as the recruiting strategies of parties and barriers to women in politics, both of which are discussed later in this chapter. Other variations exist. My analysis of women sitting in the House of Commons in late 2002 shows that nine of the 63 women were foreign-born, which is below the percentage in the female Canadian population as a whole (November, 2002: http://www.parl.gc.ca). Also, visible minorities in general, and visible-minority women in particular, are underrepresented in politics (Ship, 1998).

When elected, women are also seldom found in the upper ranks of political parties. To be sure, Margaret Thatcher was elected prime minister of Great Britain, and Kim Campbell served briefly as prime minister of Canada until the 1993 election. In selecting his cabinet shortly after that election, Jean Chrétien appointed Sheila Copps as deputy prime minister. However, the presence of these women in the upper echelons of power is rare enough to be newsworthy. If gender made no difference, why would the cover of *Maclean's* run a photo of Kim Campbell over the caption "When the Boss Is a Woman" (Oct. 4, 1993) and picture Sheila Copps under the title "Rebel with a Cause," accompanied by a text portraying Copps as "the latest national lightning rod for the prevailing ambivalence about women in power" (Apr. 4, 1994)?

Table 9.2 illustrates the truth of the saying "the higher, the fewer" with respect to the participation of

TABLE 9.2 NUMBERS AND PERCENTAGES OF FEDERAL POLITICAL REPRESENTATIVES WHO ARE WOMEN, CANADA, OCTOBER 2002

| | NUMBERS | | PERCENT |
	Women (1)	Total (2)	Women (3)
House of Commons	**63**	**301**	**21**
Liberal	40	169	24
Bloc Québécois	10	35	29
Canadian Alliance	7	63	20
New Democratic Party	5	14	35
Progressive Conservative	1	14	7
Independent	—	3	—
Vacant	—	3	
Senate	**31**	**105**	**30**
Liberal	23	55	42
Progressive Conservative	8	42	19
Independent	0	5	0
Vacant	—	9	—

SOURCE: Compiled from Parliamentary Internet at http://www.parl.gc.ca (November 7, 2002).

women in Canadian political parties. Sylvia Bashevkin (1993: Chap. 3) found that women are more likely to be local riding secretaries (as opposed to presidents) and that they do the necessary clerical work, paralleling the "pink ghetto" of female-typed clerical work found in the labour force. In the almost 80 years since most women gained the vote federally, only three women have been elected as party leaders, all within the last two decades. Audrey McLaughlin served as leader of the NDP between 1989 and 1995; Kim Campbell was leader of the Progressive Conservatives (PCs) between June and December 1993; and Alexa McDonough was elected leader of the NDP in October 1995 (Young, 1997: 82). Campbell was prime minister briefly, but the PCs failed to retain power in the subsequent 1993 election.

EXPLAINING THE POLITICAL PARTICIPATION OF WOMEN

Four major explanations exist for the underrepresentation of women in Canadian politics. The first relies on sex-role stereotypes. It argues that certain characteristics of women keep them from participating in politics. According to this argument, women are less assertive than men, more oriented to family than to politics, and conditioned, through childhood socialization, to view politics as an inappropriate activity

(Brodie, 1991). For two reasons, this explanation is currently far less popular than it was in the past. First, it stereotypes all women and fails to acknowledge that the traits of men and women often overlap and that women themselves are very diverse, just as men are. Second, it invokes the behaviour of men as the standard, implying that women are "deficient," and that the problem is to be found in women rather than in the characteristics of political life.

The second explanation reverses the emphasis by arguing that the culture of politics is both "male" and hostile to the participation of women. Descriptions of political life as "gladiatorial" create the image of a highly combative blood sport in which the stakes are the acquisition and display of power (Bashevkin, 1991). This is a highly masculine image that reinforces the notion of politics as "a man's world." It creates a chilly climate for female participants, who may have interests beyond those of domination and who may prefer to resolve conflicts in nonconfrontational ways.

Few observers of Canadian political life doubt that politics is still very much a male domain. As we have seen, at the federal level, women are underrepresented as MPs relative to their share of Canada's electorate. And, recently, the success of Sheila Copps was partly attributed to the fact that she "knows how to fight like a man" (McDonald, 1994: 19). The emphasis on male traits in the world of politics also means that women in politics are sex-stereotyped. They are given attention because they are "deviant" or "different" from the "normal" politician, rather than for their competency as politicians. In their research on the media coverage of women politicians, Gertrude Robinson, Armande Saint-Jean, and Christine Rioux (1991) found that, before the 1970s, the portrayal of women MPs emphasized themes such as that of the spinster or the club woman, or focused on the politician's relationship to significant family members, including her husband. According to these researchers, all the labels that were used emphasized a woman's gender and looks or affiliation rather than her competence. Between the 1970s and 1990s, new labels and stereotypes came to be used, but they still failed to evaluate women's political competence. Robinson, Saint-Jean, and Rioux (1991: 142–46) describe these new labels and stereotypes as follows:

- *Superwoman:* A young, intelligent, active, and ambitious woman who succeeds on all levels and has it all.
- *Champion:* Similar to "superwoman," but tends to be used in reference to older women politicians who have led a more traditional life.
- *One of the boys:* A female politician who "adopts a masculine stance, which means either that she does not resort to what are called feminine wiles to achieve her goals (charm, coquetry, wheedling) or that she accepts and operates by the conventional rules of the game."
- *Wife of ...:* Invoked whenever the interests and activities of the female politician are linked by the media to those of her spouse.

Robinson and her co-authors conclude that the media continue to emphasize the personal characteristics (e.g., looks, hair, and dress) of female politicians. The authors also note three additional characteristics of media descriptions of female politicians: (1) they fail to recognize the prior political activities of female politicians, with the result that the women's histories of acquiring competency remain unknown; (2) they suggest that female politicians are responsible for women's issues, when, in fact, gender interests may or may not be on the agenda of any politician, male or female; and (3) they use the term *feminism* or *feminist* to denote negative personal characteristics.

The third reason for women's underrepresentation as politicians is gate-keeping. By controlling the nomination of candidates for elected office, political parties influence the gender composition of their electoral slate and the ridings that the nominees represent. In the past, women candidates were often "sacrificial lambs," allowed to run primarily in ridings in which the chances of winning were small. Janine Brodie (1991: 6) observes that, in today's climate of striving for gender equality, few parties can afford to provide a slate of candidates with few or no women. But parties can and still do assign women to ridings in which their chances of winning are poor. According to Brodie, many of the representational gains that women have made are attributable to a volatile electorate and last-minute voter shifts that carry ridings in which female candidates were not expected to win.

Insufficient resources are the fourth reason for the lack of gender parity in Canadian politics. Money is a very important resource for winning nominations and mounting publicity campaigns. In the late 1980s, for example, the cost of contesting a nomination in a winnable urban riding was in excess of $50 000 (Brodie, 1991: 40). Women may be at a fiscal disadvantage to the extent that they earn less than male candidates and consequently have less to put into a campaign. Bashevkin (1991) notes that, whereas men who enter politics tend to come from law and business, women candidates tend to come from social work, journalism, and education, where earnings are lower. Social networks are also important among the resources needed for contesting nominations and elections. Networks are useful for obtaining financial contributions and generating the volunteers who lobby voters. Yet, to the extent that politics is "an old boys' club," women may not have access to insider or "old boy" networks.

Finally, although this is not a major reason for the lower representation of women in politics, the clash between political life and family life is a factor influencing the participation of some women. The culture that emphasizes politics as a man's world or as a man's sport fails to recognize that politicians also have personal lives and family responsibilities. Indeed, the lifestyle that is part of this culture is almost anti-family. (This has been cited as one reason for the efforts of the Canadian Alliance to establish a "code of conduct" for its MPs.) Ignoring the family needs and responsibilities of politicians affects both men and women. However, because women more than men are designated as the primary child-care providers, their participation in politics can require greater personal and child-care costs.

REPRESENTATION BY WOMEN; REPRESENTATION FOR WOMEN

Until recently, most research on women in politics focused on the question of how many women held party positions or were elected legislators. However, representation by women is not always the same as representation for women. Although both men and women may use their legislative roles to place women's issues on the political agenda and to support party policies and legislation that reflect women's situations and concerns, they may not.

Jane Arscott and Linda Trimble (1997) summarize the views of a number of social scientists and women's groups when they call for "representation by women as if women mattered"—that is, the election of women who will act in the interests of women. However, it also raises another issue: How are differences of class and race among women to be represented? Specifically, can women legislators and party officers understand and speak for women who are different from them and who may have different experiences and concerns? As Arscott and Trimble (1997: 4–5) note, the vast majority of Canadian female legislators are white, middle-class, publicly heterosexual, and well educated. Do they understand, stand for, and speak for other women, including Aboriginal women, women of colour, immigrant women, elderly women, poor women, homeless women, lesbians, and women who are victims of spousal abuse (see also Vickers, 1997: 28)? Furthermore, if mainstream women cannot speak for all women, then should targets or quotas be set for women of colour, poor women, lesbians, and so on? Currently, the answers to these questions are under debate. However, Canadian governments at all levels now appear less willing to exercise the political will, spend the money, and change the electoral laws and party practices that would accommodate such differences.

ELIMINATING GENDER INEQUALITY

Although the magnitude of the change in women's participation in Canada's economic and political life during the twentieth century has been great, gender inequality still exists. In this section, I consider the mechanisms that can be used to lessen the degree of gender inequality in the future, starting with a review of the general approaches, then looking at specific interventions designed to reduce inequalities in the labour force and in political representation.

MODELS OF CHANGE

One's choice of mechanism for bringing about change will depend very much on how one explains gender inequality. If we see gender inequality as arising out of personality differences between men and women, we are likely to prefer a mechanism that influences personality traits—for example, we may seek ways of altering the messages that boys and girls and men and women receive about masculinity and femininity. And if we see inequalities as resulting from organizational rules and practices governing recruitment and promotion, we are likely to emphasize changing those rules and practices.

Starting in the 1970s, North American research on inequality began to shift away from perspectives that attributed unequal outcomes to individual differences in talent, educational achievement, and opportunity. That viewpoint, still prevalent in Canada in the early 1970s, resulted in social programs and public policies oriented to individuals, such as efforts to increase access to education and training for members of less privileged groups (Agocs and Boyd, 1993).

By the 1980s, people were becoming more aware of power relations and the influence of workplace cultures and practices as sources of gender inequality. This awareness was partly fuelled by feminism, with its twin emphases on the undervaluation of women and on the presence of men's influence over women in diverse areas—from family law to hiring practices in the labour force, to the nomination of candidates in political ridings. Accompanying such changing intellectual perspectives was a growing impatience with waiting for organizations to change their practices voluntarily. Increased pressure was also put on governments to develop public policies that lessened or eliminated gender inequalities.

Public policy refers to the statements made and the actions taken—or not taken—by governments with respect to a given problem or set of problems (Pal, 1989: 4). State intervention influences the magnitude of gender inequality, and sustains or minimizes male relations of power over women, in three areas: reproduction, family, and the labour force. In the category of reproduction are government actions pertaining to medical care, new reproductive technologies (such as *in vitro* fertilization), contraception, and abortion. In the category of the family are government policies regarding family law (including regulations governing divorce and property division) and child-care. Government intervention in the labour force affects gender inequality through employment insurance policies, maternity- and parental-leave policies, job-training programs, employment policies, and pay policies. So far, there is no government policy targeted explicitly at gender inequality in politics.

PUBLIC POLICY AND GENDER INEQUALITY IN THE LABOUR FORCE

Two areas of policy development that bear specifically on gender inequality in the labour force are **employment equity**, including **affirmative action**, and pay equity, as expressed in the principle of **equal pay for work of equal value** (or "work of comparable worth"). Policies in both areas seek to correct inequalities in the realm of paid work by removing barriers that handicap certain groups, including women. Many of these barriers are seen as systemic. Rather than reflecting deliberate and conscious decisions to discriminate, systemic barriers (also called systemic discrimination) refer to organizational practices such as informal methods of recruitment or weight and height requirements for designated jobs. These practices often privilege members of one group while handicapping others. However, these policies differ in the populations they cover, the mechanisms they employ to determine and eliminate inequalities, and the aspects of labour-force inequality that they address (i.e., terms, conditions, and systems of employment versus pay).

Assessing the Impact

Numerous publications have outlined the specifics of the various Canadian employment-equity and equal-pay policies (Agocs, Burr, and Somerset, 1992; Weiner and Gunderson, 1990). Do such policies work? Have related programs succeeded in moving women into jobs from which they were previously excluded? Is the real monetary worth of women's work in female job ghettos being acknowledged?

In answer to these questions, there is some "good news" and some "bad news." The good news is that cases do exist in which inequalities have elicited legally mandated action. In the mid-1980s, for example, litigation forced CN Rail to hire women in the St. Lawrence region. At the time of the complaint, women held less than 1 percent of the blue-collar jobs in the company, and a pattern of discriminatory hiring practices was revealed (Agocs, Burr, and Somerset, 1992: 104). The company was ordered to discontinue a number of these practices (including that of testing women's but not men's capacity to lift heavy objects) and to adopt new recruiting and hiring practices. Similarly, equal-pay-for-work-of-equal-value legislation has resulted in pay adjustments in a number of cases. For example, nurses' pay has been raised to match that of orderlies. Recently the federal court upheld the right of pay equity for federally employed women in selected female-dominated occupations. As is true for most cases involving redress of past inequities, this ruling elicited criticism over its high cost (see Box 9.3).

Nevertheless, a few isolated victories do not amount to winning the war. Critics of employment-equity policies note three types of "bad news." First, the legislation is limited in its jurisdiction, and does not apply to a large part of the population. For example, the federal Employment Equity Act of 1995, which replaced the Employment Equity Act of 1986, covers only the public service, federally regulated employers, and portions of the public sector specified by orders-in-council, such as contractors doing business with the government who have 100 or more employees. Second, failure to comply with the legislation is penalized only lightly. Although the federal Employment Equity Act of 1995 imposes fines on employers who do not report the required data or who knowingly provide false or misleading information, the amount cannot exceed $10 000 for a single violation and $50 000 for repeated or continued violations (Canada, 1995: Section 36[2]).

Numerous criticisms have been voiced about equal-pay-for-work-of-equal-value policies. First, many of the policies exclude small firms. Second, they compare men and women within the same firms, with the result that they do not apply to women employed in firms in which the labour force is all female. Third, the method of establishing the comparable worth of two jobs is based on existing job descriptions. Jobs that are considered similar by virtue of pay or classification are evaluated on the basis of knowledge and skills, effort, responsibility, and working conditions (England, 1993; Steinberg, 1990). But such evaluation does not correct for the a priori undervaluation

VIEW 1: CIVIL SERVANTS WIN ON PAY EQUITY

The Federal Court ruled unequivocally yesterday against the Chrétien government in a long-running pay-equity dispute that could cost Ottawa $5-billion, half its estimated surplus next year....

"The federal government thought that because we are women, we'd roll over and be quiet," said Colette Gervais, who expects $40,000 compensation for being underpaid as a payment clerk for 40 years. "I hope they've learned that we are more than second-class citizens."...

Yesterday's ruling was Ottawa's second major defeat in this dispute. Last July, the [Canadian Human Rights] tribunal awarded a multibillion-dollar settlement to about 200,000 clerks, librarians, secretaries and other federal employees in female-dominated positions.

The tribunal ruled that these employees were underpaid for up to 13 years in comparison with employees in male-dominated jobs and deserved an average of about $25,000 each from Ottawa....

Experts said that the decision sends a clear message to employers: Stop using narrow legal arguments to avoid catch-up raises to women staff.

VIEW 2: THE POLITICS OF REDRESS

Helpless taxpayers can only weep. As of this morning, you/we owe probably $4-billion to $5-billion—yes, you read that correctly—to a group of largely female public servants, many of them retired....

No public policy analyst, let alone government, would ever decide to spend $4-billion to $5-billion this way. A hundred other priorities from better roads to daycare centres would make more sense than spending the money as ordered by the tribunal and, now, the Federal Court....

The lucky federal employees can crack open the champagne. The rest of us can only weep.

SOURCE: Dan Leblanc, "Civil Servants Win on Pay Equity," *The Globe and Mail*, October 20, 1999, pp. A1 & A6; Excerpted from Jeffrey Simpson, "The Politics of Redress," *The Globe and Mail*, October 20, 1999, p. A15. Reprinted with permission of the Globe and Mail.

of certain skills (see the discussion of gender and skill on page 227).

For many feminists, these and other criticisms suggest that limited change can be expected from employment-equity and pay-equity policies in their current forms. Supporters are likely to press for stronger policies and broader coverage in the decades to come. However, government and business support for such changes is not assured. Business owners may argue that such equity is unaffordable in times of economic downturn. In Quebec, protests by business leaders caused amendments to the provincial bill on pay equity in the private sector, effective January 1, 1997. As a result of these changes, pay-equity legislation will not be fully implemented until the year 2006 (Séguin, 1996).

CORRECTING THE BALANCE: WOMEN IN POLITICS

As noted above, there is no federal policy aimed at reducing gender inequality among elected politicians. Political parties are sensitive to the issue of increasing the number of women representing them. However,

there are at least six other types of actions that, if undertaken, could increase the numbers and percentages of women in Canadian politics in the years to come. All have to do with reducing barriers erected as a result of social roles and with changing organizational aspects of political recruitment and elections.

The first, and probably the least effective, action can be described as "displaying good intentions." It is commonly manifested in the form of party statements indicating commitment to the principle of gender parity. Compared with other mechanisms, however, party commitments tend to be limited and to have a limited impact. In the 1980s, for example, the only guaranteed commitments written into the constitutions of the Liberal and Conservative parties were to ensure fair representation of women at national party conventions, and fair representation of the national parties' women's groups on governing bodies such as the parties' national executives (Brodie, 1991: 30).

A second way to increase women's participation in politics is to reduce the economic constraints they face in connection with winning nominations and running for office. Reducing the financial burden facing women and some men can be achieved by introducing legislation that would allow candidates the right to take unpaid leave from employment to contest party nominations and elections; setting spending limits for nomination contests and party leadership campaigns; making contributions for nomination contests tax-deductible; reimbursing money spent on nomination contests if the candidate gets a minimum level of support (say, 15 percent of the vote); using centralized party funds for nomination battles; and treating child-care and housekeeping costs as part of the overall campaign costs, thereby making them subject to reimbursement (Brodie, 1991: 49–50; Erickson, 1991).

Although the recommendation to recognize child-care and housekeeping costs is a financial one, it may also be considered part of the third set of actions, which are designed to recognize family needs and responsibilities and the social roles of women. Lynda Erickson (1991) suggests that a fixed term for governments would increase the predictability of politicians' lives rather than leaving them at the mercy of a vote of nonconfidence or a leader's prerogative to call an election. Changing the rules of elections might indirectly help politicians to better anticipate their futures, taking into account the needs of their families.

Eliminating or weakening the gate-keeping tradition is the fourth potentially useful action. It could be accomplished by basing the amount of the government subsidy paid to political parties for their campaign expenses on an upward sliding scale according to the proportion of their elected candidates who are women (Brodie, 1991: 50). Under this system, the amount of the subsidy would vary with the number of women elected.

To the extent that it rewards parties for having women elected and may increase the number of women in politics, such an action can also be seen as a form of affirmative action. Other affirmative action measures include setting quotas to ensure that women are on riding nomination lists and establishing guarantees that a certain percentage of women are nominated for and are present in the party organization.

Research suggests that affirmative action measures can be difficult to implement in a single-member electoral system. Under the single-member system in Canada, a person running for office in a riding wins by getting the most votes. This approach is conducive to the control of nominations by local party organizations. However, attempts to increase the numbers of women holding office are most effective in electoral systems that place decision making about nominations and party representation at levels higher than the local ridings. A more centralized decision-making structure gives party elites more control over the representation of women and other minority groups. Modifying Canada's single-member system is thus the sixth area in which action could be taken to increase the percentage of women politicians (Erickson, 1991).

Which, if any, of these possible changes will be adopted remains to be seen. Many of the recommendations were made as part of research conducted for the Royal Commission on Electoral Reform, and most would require changes in existing legislation governing how political expenses are handled and how elections are run. In the course of the next decade, you will be able to monitor whether any of the above-described changes are implemented.

SUMMARY

1. Many sociologists view the segregation of women and men into the private and public spheres as a very important source of gender inequality. Exclusion from the economic and political arenas of Canadian life can mean disadvantages in access to income, economic well-being, prestige, and power. Restricted in the past to the domestic sphere, women have been economically disadvantaged and have had little or no opportunity to influence legislation directly. In addition, their unpaid work in the home has been considered low in prestige, or at least lower in value than their spouses' paid work.

2. During the twentieth century, women have entered the labour force and the political arena in ever-increasing numbers. Today, more than half of all women are in the labour force. Politically enfranchised, women have also entered the political arena, either as politicians or in connection with groups associated with the women's movement. Many of these changes have occurred—or, at least, have accelerated—since the time most of you were born. Between the 1970s and the early 1990s, the labour-force participation rate of women more than doubled, and the number of elected women MPs quadrupled.

3. If the glass is half full, it also is half empty. Although they do paid work, many women are still responsible for most of the meal preparation, cleaning, and laundry needs of their families. Women still tend to be considered the primary caregivers of children and of the elderly. In short, women are more likely than men to work a double or triple "shift" every day.

4. In the labour force, women and men are occupationally segregated, with women concentrated in jobs stereotyped as "women's jobs." Women are more likely than men to be employed in jobs that are part-time or otherwise nonstandard. They earn less than men, on average, and their skills tend not to be fully recognized or fairly evaluated. To be sure, these issues affect women to varying degrees, depending on their birthplace, race, and ethnicity. Nevertheless, the overall picture is one of gender inequality in the labour force, with women disadvantaged relative to men.

5. There is still evidence of a gender gap in politics as well. Women represent more than half of Canada's adult population, but only 20 percent of federally elected legislators. This imbalance notwithstanding, substantial gains have been made in recent elections. And, as agents pressing for improvements in their own status, Canadian women have left a considerable legacy of influence and change.

6. Many of the challenges that remain are documented in this chapter. Future generations will have to combat not only gender-role stereotypes, but ideologies and structures that privilege men and handicap women as well. In recent years, employment-equity and equal-pay-for-work-of-equal-value policies have been developed to remedy some of the inequalities in the labour force. Analysts have also documented the various ways in which women's participation and influence in the political arena can be enhanced. As you finish your schooling, live with a spouse or partner, hold a paying job, and become politically involved, you will experience or witness some of the gender inequalities discussed in this chapter. However, you may also witness and work toward remedying the gender inequalities that currently exist.

QUESTIONS TO CONSIDER

1. If you grew up in a two-parent household, describe the types of activities that each parent did around the house. Were they different? Did the amount of time each spent on activities in the home vary? Why?

2. Think back to jobs you have held in the past three years that involved working with other people. Reflecting on the type of work you did compared with the work of others, would you say that sex segregation or sex typing existed? Why or why not?

3. In some of the occupational skill assessments that have been conducted in recent years, the job of dog-catcher was deemed more skilled than the job of child-care worker. Why do you think such an evaluation was made? Do you agree with the ranking? Why or why not?

4. This chapter discussed the principles of political "representation by women," "representation for women," and "representation of difference." Should women legislators be elected only if they champion women's causes? Should electoral rules be changed to allow for the proportionate or even disproportionate election of women of colour and other disadvantaged women in order to represent their interests and experiences?

GLOSSARY

Affirmative action comprises the policies and programs designed to create opportunities for, and to further the achievements of, historically disadvantaged groups in the labour force. One form of action to correct past inequalities involves setting targets and quotas for the hiring and promotion of members of groups that have faced barriers and discrimination in the past. The term is often used interchangeably with employment equity; strictly speaking, it is one aspect of employment equity.

Employment equity is the principle of equal treatment of all groups in the labour force. Employment-equity policies and programs seek to dismantle barriers and alter workplace cultures in order to create opportunities for and to further the advancement of historically disadvantaged groups.

Equal pay for work of equal value, which is also known as "equal pay for work of comparable worth," is a principle supported by policies and programs that seek to equalize the wage rates offered for different jobs that are of comparable worth or value in terms of factors such as knowledge, complexity, responsibility, and skill.

Feminism refers both to the body of knowledge about the causes and nature of women's subordination to men in society, and the various agendas, often involving political action, for removing that subordination.

Gender inequalities are inequalities between men and women in the distribution of prestige, material well-being, and/or power. They are also relational inequalities manifested in men's power over women or in relations of male domination and female subordination.

Gender stereotypes are a set of prejudicial generalizations about men and women based on the oversimplified belief that physical sex determines distinct personality traits and, as a result, causes men and women to experience the world and behave in different ways.

The **glass ceiling** is the level in an organization above which women and minorities are seldom found.

Labour-force participation rate is the percentage of the population, age 15 and older, that is in the labour force.

Material well-being refers to the ability to obtain the economic resources necessary to pay for adequate food, clothing, housing, and possessions.

Nonstandard work refers to one or a combination of the following types of employment: part-week employment (reduced hours per week), part-year employment, limited-term contract employment, employment through temporary-help agencies, self-employment, and multiple job holding.

Part-time work refers to jobs with reduced hours of work.

Patriarchy is the situation in which men rule over or dominate women.

Power is the capacity to influence and control others, regardless of any resistance they might offer.

Prestige is the social evaluation or ranking, by general consensus, of occupational activities and positions in a hierarchical order that reflects the degree of respect, honour, or deference the person engaged in the activity or occupying the position is to be accorded.

Public policy refers to the government's stance on issues and problems, as expressed through its statements and actions, or its inaction.

Sex segregation of occupations refers to the concentration of women and men in different occupations.

Sex typing (or sex labelling) of occupations is the designation of an occupation as "female" or "male," depending on the sex for whom it is considered appropriate.

Skill is an ability or expertise in performing a given technique or task. Researchers describe tasks as requiring more or less skill on the basis of their complexity and the degree of autonomy required to perform them. Existing rankings, incomes, and levels of education associated with various occupations are often accepted by researchers as proxy measures of skill.

A **social movement** is an enduring collective attempt to change part or all of society by means of rioting, petitioning, striking, demonstrating, or establishing pressure groups, unions, and political parties.

Social roles are the expectations and behaviours associated with particular positions in society.

Social stratification refers to persistent patterns of social inequality, perpetuated by the way wealth, power, and prestige are distributed and passed on from one generation to the next.

Standard work is full-time, full-year employment, usually accompanied by job-related benefits, such as vacation leave, sick leave, and parental leave, as well as health and pension benefits.

Statistical discrimination is the discrimination that occurs when negative decisions concerning the hiring or promotion of a given individual are made on the basis of the average characteristics of the group to which the individual belongs. Thus, an employer may not hire a particular woman because of a belief that women, in general, are likely to take time off work to have children, even though the woman in question may intend not to have children.

A **visible minority** is a group of people (other than Native people) who are nonwhite and who, because of their race, may face discrimination in hiring and promotion.

The **women's movement** is a social movement that takes action to improve the conditions of women.

SUGGESTED READING

Brodie, Janine, ed. (1996). *Women and Canadian Public Policy*. Toronto: Harcourt Brace and Company, Canada. Focuses on a wide range of public-policy issues that have an impact on women.

Das Gupta, Tania. (1996). *Racism and Paid Work*. Toronto: Garamond Press. Examines discrimination in paid employment as it affects immigrant women and women of colour.

Gaskell, Jane. (1991). "What Counts as Skill? Reflections on Pay Equity." In Judy Fudge and Patricia McDermott, eds., *Just Wages: A Feminist Assessment of Pay Equity* (pp. 141–59). Toronto: University of Toronto Press. An overview that explains how our notions of "skill" are socially constructed and how socially determined definitions of skill can influence equal-pay-for-work-of-equal-value settlements.

Tremblay, Manon, and Caroline Andrew. (1998). *Women and Political Representation in Canada*. Women's Studies Series. Ottawa: University of Ottawa Press. An excellent collection of essays on various aspects of the women's movement in Canada and women's involvement in politics. A chapter by Julia O'Conner looks at women in paid employment.

CHAPTER TEN

RACE AND ETHNIC RELATIONS

In this chapter you will learn that:

- The study of race and ethnic relations involves the analysis of the unequal distribution of power and resources, and involves a number of sociological approaches; frustration-aggression, sociobiology, socialization, and power-conflict approaches are among the most important.

- Ethnicity and race are terms used to categorize groups on the basis of cultural and physical criteria. Although the concept of race has no basis in biology, and although ethnic identities and boundaries are situational, variable, and flexible, race and ethnicity are important parts of social reality.

- Aboriginal people in Canada are made up of Indians, Métis, and Inuit. There are two main sociological interpretations of Aboriginal people's socioeconomic status in Canada—the culture of poverty thesis and the internal colonial model.

- The nationalist movement in Quebec has deep historical roots. The contemporary nationalist movement is united around the goal of maintaining the French character of Quebec. One of the main problems facing the nationalist movement in Quebec is exactly how to define the boundaries of the nation.

- Immigration played a central role in both the early and later phases of Canadian capitalist development. Canada accepts refugees, family class, and independent immigrants, each of which are subject to different selection criteria.

- John Porter's description of Canada as a vertical mosaic is no longer an accurate way of describing the structure of Canadian society.

VIC SATZEWICH

MCMASTER UNIVERSITY

INTRODUCTION

Leo LaChance did not know that the Northern Gun and Pawn Shop he walked into the night of January 28, 1991, was owned by a white supremacist. LaChance, a Cree trapper from northern Saskatchewan, needed a few dollars and thought he would sell his hunting rifle in Prince Albert. Carney Nerland, the shop's owner, did not want to buy the gun. As LaChance left the shop, a bullet from an M-56 assault rifle hit him in the back, puncturing his spleen, pancreas, gall bladder, and liver. Six hours later, LaChance was dead (Cannon, 1995).

Twenty-nine-year-old Carney Nerland was well known in Prince Albert. He liked to strut around town with a brush cut and polished jackboots. As a teenager, he had painted swastikas anywhere he could. He had a picture of Adolf Hitler pinned to a wall in his shop. He had fired shots at Natives in the city before. At the time of the shooting, Nerland was under investigation for distributing anti-Jewish and anti-Native literature. He was a member of the Aryan Nation, a violent white supremacist group, and liked to call himself the future "Führer of Saskatchewan." He once told a group of journalists that his hunting rifle was his form of "Native birth control." When he turned himself in after shooting Leo LaChance, he told the arresting officer, "If I'm convicted of killing that Indian, I should get a medal and you should pin it on me" (Cannon, 1995).

At his trial in December 1991, Nerland said he didn't know that there was a bullet in the chamber of the M-56 when he pointed it at LaChance; "it was just a joke," he said, "an accident." In his ruling, the judge recognized that Nerland was a racist, but he did not believe that racism played a role in LaChance's death. The judge accepted Nerland's version of events and sentenced him to four years in prison for manslaughter. As it turned out, Nerland was an ideal prisoner. He was paroled after serving just over a year of his sentence (Cannon, 1995).

Few Canadians hold the same racist ideas as Carney Nerland. Even fewer are prepared to translate their hatred of certain ethnic and racial groups into acts of physical violence. But other kinds of ethnic and racial problems exist. In British Columbia, 75 percent of the land is currently under 19 different Aboriginal land claims disputes (Frideres and Gadacz, 2001: 223). Non-Aboriginals in the Maritimes are willing to resort to violence to stop Aboriginals from catching lobster out of season. Black parents in Toronto argue that they need to establish Black-focused schools that cater to the specific educational needs of their children. Others holler that this is racism in reverse. A group of former RCMP officers in Lethbridge, Alberta, claim that they have several thousand signatures on a petition demanding that the force change its policy allowing Sikh officers to wear turbans. Less than ten years ago, the country was on the verge of collapse after nearly half the voters in the province of Quebec voted in favour of separation. In the mid-1990s, writer Neil Bissoondath (1994) set off a firestorm of controversy when he argued that the government's policy of multiculturalism is undermining the unity of our country.

These examples all touch in some way on the issue of what different ethnic and racial groups are allowed, and able, to do in our society, and how they are treated. In other words, they all say something about the distribution of power and resources in Canada. The sociology of ethnic and racial relations concerns primarily the study of how power and resources are unequally distributed among ethnic and racial groups. Sociologists who are interested in race and ethnic relations ask a number of interrelated questions: What are the conditions under which ethnic and racial groups come into contact? Which ethnic and racial groups hold power in a society? How do they exercise power? Are there social and economic advantages associated with having a particular ethnic or racial background? What are the social consequences of the unequal distribution of power and resources? How have ethnic and racial groups challenged inequality and power imbalances? How have governments tried to manage and contain ethnic and racial conflict?

My aim in this chapter is to provide some sociological answers to these questions. I begin by examining what sociologists mean by the terms *ethnicity*, *race*, and *racism*, and then discuss various theoretical approaches to the study of ethnic and racial relations. Next, I examine the three main forms of ethnic and racial relations in Canada: Aboriginal–non-Aboriginal relations; French–English relations; and immigrant–non-immigrant relations. In each of these cases, you will see how power and resource imbalances play important roles in structuring relationships among groups.

ETHNICITY AND RACE: THE SOCIAL CONSTRUCTION OF DIFFERENCE

We use the terms *race*, *racial*, *ethnic*, and *ethnicity* in a variety of ways in our everyday lives. Some students in my classes talk about how they are under pressure from their parents to marry someone of the same "race" or "ethnicity." Others are concerned that "race relations" in Canada seem to be getting worse. Yet others describe the joys of living in a "multiethnic" country, of eating meals in a variety of "ethnic" restaurants, and of observing and participating in the rituals and festivals of "ethnic" groups from around the world.

The assumption underlying our commonsense understandings of these terms is that race and ethnicity are *ascribed* characteristics. That is, we assume that we are born with a certain race or ethnicity and that that fact cannot be changed. Sociologists, on the other hand, recognize that, while we cannot change our birth parents, and generally cannot change our skin colour, we do not necessarily have fixed and unalterable ethnic and racial characteristics or identities. Instead, sociologists believe it is more useful to see race and ethnicity as certain kinds of *achieved* statuses—statuses that are acquired by virtue of social definition. Box 10.1 shows how Statistics Canada used ascribed characteristics for its measurement of ethnicity and race in the 2001 census.

BOX 10.1   THE ETHNICITY AND "RACE" QUESTIONS IN THE 2001 CENSUS

ETHNIC ORIGIN

17. To which ethnic or cultural group(s) did this person's **ancestors** belong?

For example, Canadian, French, English, Chinese, Italian, German, Scottish, Irish, Cree, Micmac, Métis, Inuit (Eskimo), East Indian, Ukrainian, Dutch, Polish, Portuguese, Filipino, Jewish, Greek, Jamaican, Vietnamese, Lebanese, Chilean, Somali, etc.

Specify as many groups as applicable

☐
☐
☐
☐

RACIAL ORIGIN

19. Is this person:

Mark or specify more than one, if applicable
Note: This information is collected to support programs which promote equal opportunity for everyone to share in the social, cultural and economic life of Canada.

○ White
○ Chinese
○ South Asian (e.g., East Indian, Pakistani, Sri Lankan, etc.)
○ Black
○ Filipino
○ Latin American
○ Southeast Asian (e.g., Cambodian, Indonesian, Laotian, Vietanemese, etc.)
○ Arab
○ West Asian (e.g., Afghan, Iranian, etc.)
○ Japanese
○ Korean
○ Other—specify

Note: This information is collected to support programs which promote equal opportunity for everyone to share in the social, cultural and economic life of Canada.

SOURCE: Statistics Canada, *1996 Census Handbook*, 1996 Census of Canada, Cat. No. 92-352-XPE (Ottawa: Supply and Services Canada, 1996), pp. 8, 9. Reproduced by authority of the Minister of Industry, 2000.

ETHNICITY AND RACE

Ethnicity

Sociologists do not agree on how to define and measure ethnicity. *Objective definitions of ethnicity* assume that ethnic groups exist because of people's social attachments (Isajiw, 1999). From this point of view, ethnicity is something that people possess because of differences in language, culture, customs, national origin, and ancestry. *Subjective approaches to ethnicity* focus on the process of ethnic identification. Sociologists who emphasize the socially constructed nature of perceived reality insist that ethnicity is a "transactional" process. Ethnic groups are made up of people who identify themselves, or who are identified by others, as belonging to the same ancestral or cultural group. Whether they actually display any of the cultural characteristics of the group with which they identify, or whether they are merely born into that group, is largely irrelevant. When subjective definitions are used, then, "ethnicity" is self-defined and reflects "a shared 'we-feeling' within a collectivity (groupness) whose symbolic components can vary from time and place" (Fleras and Elliot, 1996). From this perspective, ethnic identities and boundaries are situational, variable, and flexible.

Most of the ethnic categories that we now take for granted are actually recent historical creations. The ethnic category "English" would have been unthinkable to the person who lived in the British Isles 800 years ago. People defined themselves, and were defined by others, as Celts, Saxons, Normans, and so on. Only some of those people came to be known as "the English" (Lieberson, 1991). Similarly, the people whom we now think of as "Germans" did not exist 150 years ago. As these examples suggest, the way in which people define themselves, and are defined by others, is in constant flux (Lieberson, 1991: 444). If we take a long view, it is common for ethnic categories and identities to be recast and created anew.

This is what seems to be happening in Canada now. There has crystallized a feeling of commonality that is the basis for a common ethnic identification. In preparing for the 1991 census, Statistics Canada held meetings, organized focus groups, and tested different ways of posing questions that tried to measure the ethnicity of our population. One of the things that Statistics Canada found was that there "was a strong tendency [for respondents] to report Canadian as their ethnic origin and as their ethnic

identity" (White, 1992: 166). Largely because of political pressure, "Canadian" was included as a response category in the ethnicity question for the 1996 census. "Canadians" are now the numerically largest ethnic group in Canada (see Table 10.1).

Why do some of us define our ethnic roots or ethnic identity as "Canadian"? Some of us may simply be unaware of or uninterested in our so-called roots and, hence, by default define ourselves as Canadian. For others, defining ourselves as Canadian is a political act used to express our dissatisfaction with the government's policy of multiculturalism (White, 1992: 168–69). At the same time, though, there are many of us who insist that we are Canadian because that is simply the group with whom we identify, and with whom we share a sense of belonging (Angus Reid Group, 1991; Howard, 1998). According to Rhoda Howard-Hassmann (1999: 528), the emergence of this sense of community means that "the ethnic English-Canadian is a new social creation."

Race

For much of the twentieth century, there was little difference between commonsense understandings of **race** and the way that race was analyzed in the social and natural sciences. Most scientists believed that races were real and objective subdivisions of *Homo sapiens*. These divisions were supposedly based on a combination of unalterable physical and genetic characteristics. Characteristics such as skin colour, hair texture, body and facial shape, genetic diseases, metabolic rates, and distribution of blood groups were used to construct various racial typologies. The most common typology was the division of humanity into "caucasoid," "mongoloid," and "negroid" races (Montagu, 1972).

During the 1930s, scientists began to raise serious doubts about the scientific validity of the concept of race (Barkan, 1992). Since the 1950s, the scientific consensus is that racial classifications of humanity are arbitrary, that genetic differences between groups are small, and that genetic differences are behaviourally insignificant (Montagu, 1972). Racial classifications based on a characteristic, such as skin colour, are as illogical as racial classifications based on the length of index fingers (Miles, 1982). Moreover, only 0.24 percent of all human genes are necessarily shared by members of the same race, genetically defined. Thus, from a strictly genetic point of view, Jean Chrétien may have much more in common with Oscar Peterson than with Lucien Bouchard.

TABLE 10.1   TOP 25 ETHNIC ORIGINS IN CANADA

ETHNIC ORIGIN	SINGLE AND MULTIPLE RESPONSES	SINGLE RESPONSES	MULTIPLE RESPONSES	INDEX OF ASSIMILATION[1]
Canadian	8 806 275	5 326 995	3 479 285	n.a.
English	6 832 095	2 048 275	4 783 820	70.0
French	5 597 845	2 665 250	2 932 595	52.4
Scottish	4 260 840	642 970	3 617 870	84.9
Irish	3 767 610	504 030	3 263 580	86.6
German	2 757 140	726 145	2 030 990	73.7
Italian	1 207 475	729 455	478 025	39.6
Aboriginal	1 101 955	477 630	624 330	56.7
Ukrainian	1 026 475	331 680	694 790	67.7
Chinese	921 585	800 470	121 115	13.1
Dutch	916 215	313 880	602 335	65.7
Polish	786 735	265 930	520 805	66.2
South Asian	723 345	590 145	133 200	18.4
Jewish	351 705	195 810	155 900	44.3
Norwegian	346 310	47 805	298 500	86.2
Welsh	338 905	27 915	310 990	91.8
Portuguese	335 110	252 640	82 470	24.6
Swedish	278 975	31 200	247 775	88.8
Russian	272 335	46 885	225 450	82.8
Hungarian	250 525	94 185	156 340	62.4
Filipino	242 880	198 420	44 460	18.3
American	211 790	22 085	189 705	89.6
Spanish	204 360	72 470	313 895	64.5
Greek	203 345	144 940	58 405	28.7
Jamaican	188 770	128 570	60 200	31.9

[1]Multiple responses expressed as a percent of single plus multiple responses.

SOURCE: Robert Brym, *Canadian Society and the 1996 Census* (Toronto: Harcourt Canada, 1999), p. 9.

In sum, differences between races are arbitrary, extremely small, and without behavioural consequences. Ethnic boundaries and identities are flexible, negotiated, and historically variable. We should not conclude, however, that race and ethnicity are unimportant aspects of modern society. According to W.I. Thomas's famous sociological dictum, if people define situations as real, they are real in their consequences (Thomas and Znaniecki, 1918: 79). Even though race is a hollow biological concept, and even though ethnic identities and boundaries are neither fixed nor unchanging, many people believe in the existence of ethnicity and race, and organize their relationships with others on the basis of those beliefs.

Therefore, race and ethnicity are important parts of our social reality.

Racism

If race is a biological myth, what is racism? Is a school racist if it puts on hot dog days but not chow mein days? Are Black people in Toronto subject to racist policing? Is Don Cherry a racist because he denigrates European hockey players who compete in the National Hockey League? Is Professor Philippe Rushton of the University of Western Ontario a racist because he believes that Black people have smaller brains than whites and Asians? Is a Black woman racist if she wants to marry only a Black man?

Is a white man racist if he wants to marry only a white woman?

Before we can begin to answer these questions, we need to define racism. Sociologists define racism as both a certain kind of idea and a certain kind of institutional practice. I will consider each of these definitions in turn.

Racist Ideas Traditionally, sociologists defined racism as "the belief that humans are subdivided into distinct hereditary groups that are innately different in their social behaviour and mental capacities and that can therefore be ranked as superior or inferior" (Marger, 1997: 27). By this definition, only a small minority of Canadians could be called racist. A survey conducted in 1990 by Decima Research Ltd. (cited in Reitz and Breton, 1994: 68) showed that 90 percent of Canadians agreed with the statement, "All races are created equal." It might be argued, then, that the 10 percent who either disagreed or did not know are racist. How can we reconcile the fact, on the one hand, that so few Canadians believe in the inherent superiority of some races over others with the fact, on the other hand, that people and institutions are so often called racist?

One answer is that, because ideas about the inherent superiority and inferiority of groups have been so thoroughly discredited, racism has taken new forms (Omi and Winant, 1986). Biological versions of racism may very well be "dead," but researchers have developed the concepts of **new racism** and democratic racism as ways of analyzing its changing manifestations.

The concept of new racism was developed by Martin Barker (1981) to analyze the way that racist ideas were being expressed in the 1970s by British Members of Parliament (MPs) when they were speaking out against British immigration policy. That policy permitted people from former British colonies in Asia, Africa, and the Caribbean unrestricted entry to the country. In their speeches, the MPs did not make references to British *biological* superiority or to Indian, African, or Caribbean *biological* inferiority. Instead, they regarded immigrants from these areas as *culturally* different from British people, and alleged that the ability of British people to advance the moral level of humanity was being undermined by immigration policy. The MPs' statements could not be considered "racist" by the traditional definition of racism. However, the statements had the real conse-

quence of helping to stop almost all nonwhite immigration from those countries.

These events suggested that the definition of racism had to be broadened. Accordingly, Barker (1981: 21) argued that the new racism involves the beliefs that, although races of people cannot be ranked biologically, with some being inferior and some superior, they are naturally different from each other, and that social problems are created when different groups try to live together. These beliefs should be considered racist because of their underlying intent: to socially exclude, marginalize, and denigrate certain groups of people, but to do so without reference to unalterable biology.

Democratic racism, according to Frances Henry and colleagues (2000: 19), is an ideology "in which two conflicting sets of values are made congruent to each other." Canadians are committed to the values of equality, justice, and fairness, but at the same time hold negative values about, and engage in discriminatory behaviour toward, minority groups. Democratic racism is made up of mixtures of myths, explanations, and rationalizations that have the effect of reinforcing racial inequality.

One indication of the scope of democratic racism in Canada is given in Table 10.2. It presents selected results from a 1991 national survey conducted by the Angus Reid Group about Canadians' limits to tolerance. In a survey conducted in January 2000, a national sample of Canadians was asked the question: "forgetting about the overall number of immigrants coming to Canada, of those who come would you say there are too many, too few or the right amount who are members of visible minorities?" The survey revealed that 27 percent of respondents indicated that there were "too many" visible minority immigrants. This was up from 25 percent who said so in 1999 and 22 percent who said so in 1998 (Li, 2001: 86–87).

Institutional Racism The concept of **institutional racism** refers to "discriminatory racial practices built into such prominent structures as the political, economic and education systems" (Doob, 1996: 6). Institutional racism can take three forms. First, there are circumstances where institutional practices are based on explicitly racist ideas. There are plenty of examples of this form of institutional racism in Canadian history (Bolaria and Li, 1988). Chinese people were excluded from certain jobs and

TABLE 10.2 CANADIANS AND THE LIMITS TO TOLERANCE, ANGUS REID POLL, 1991

	GENERAL AGREEMENT	GENERAL DISAGREEMENT	NEITHER AGREE NOR DISAGREE
1. It is best for Canada if all people forget their different ethnic and cultural backgrounds as soon as possible.	46%	30%	24%
2. The unity of this country is weakened by Canadians of different ethnic and cultural backgrounds sticking to their old ways.	33	39	28
3. It is a bad idea for people of different races to marry.	65	25	10
4. If employers only want to hire certain groups of people, that's their business.	47	32	21
5. Nonwhites living here should not push themselves where they are not wanted.	57	31	12
6. It makes me angry when I see recent immigrants on television demanding the same rights as Canadians.	41	36	23
7. Recent immigrants should have as much say about the future of Canada as people who were born here.	23	38	39
8. People who come to Canada should change their behaviour to be more like us.	24	48	28
9. Ethnic groups are mainly made up of persons who are born outside Canada.	35	45	20
10. Whites in Canada discriminate against nonwhites.	12	51	37
11. Nonwhites in Canada tend to discriminate against whites.	14	57	29

SOURCE: Canadian Heritage—Multiculturalism Program, Angus Reid Group, *Multiculturalism and Canadians: National Attitude Study 1991* (Ottawa: Multiculturalism and Citizenship Canada, 1991), pp. 9–12. Reproduced with the permission of the Minister of Public Works and Government Services Canada, 2003 and the Minister of Canadian Heritage.

were denied the right to vote in federal elections until 1947. Japanese Canadians were denied their basic civil rights, were forcibly expelled from the west coast of British Columbia, and had their property confiscated during World War II (Bolaria and Li, 1988). Status Indians were denied the right to vote in federal elections until 1960. Residential segregation was widespread for Black people living in Canada. Restrictive covenants in wills, deeds, and leases were used to ensure that property was not sold or leased to Blacks or to Jews. Blacks were frequently refused service in restaurants, theatres, and recreational facilities (Henry et al., 2000: 72, 80). Canada had the worst record of all Allied countries in allowing Jewish immigration during World War II, when mil-

lions of Jews were being gassed in Europe (Abella and Troper, 1982). In each case, ideas about the alleged inferiority of certain groups underpinned institutional practices.

Second, there are circumstances where institutional practices arose from but are no longer sustained by racist ideas (Miles, 1989). For example, in 1966, the federal government admitted a handful of Black workers from the Caribbean to work on Canadian farms. Now, over 10 000 migrant workers from the Caribbean and Mexico enter Canada each year to harvest fruits, vegetables, and tobacco in southern Ontario and other agricultural areas in Canada during the summer months. Canadian government officials originally justified this practice, in part, by arguing that Black workers were racially suited to back-breaking labour under the hot sun, but racially unsuited to the cold Canadian winters (Satzewich, 1991). The present migrant-labour policy had its origins in racist thinking, but racist ideas are no longer used to justify this migration stream.

Third, there are circumstances where institutions unintentionally restrict the life-chances of certain groups through a variety of seemingly neutral rules, regulations, and procedures. This is sometimes referred to as *systemic discrimination*. For example, height and weight requirements for jobs with police forces and fire departments did not necessarily originate in racist ideas, but these requirements meant that, for many years, certain Asian groups could not get jobs as police officers or firefighters. Word-of-mouth recruiting in organizations and inflated educational requirements for nontechnical jobs are also forms of systemic discrimination, because they unintentionally put minority groups at a disadvantage in the distribution of scarce resources like jobs (Special Committee on the Participation of Visible Minorities in Canadian Society, 1984).

THEORIES OF RACE AND ETHNIC RELATIONS

There are a number of sociological approaches to the interpretation of race and ethnic relations (Rex and Mason, 1986). In this section, I will discuss four approaches that seek to explain various forms of ethnic and racial hostility. Such hostility is multifaceted and, depending on the circumstances, is described as racism, prejudice, ethnocentrism, and/or xenophobia.

Social Psychology

Social-psychological approaches to the interpretation of race and ethnic relations focus on how **prejudice**—an unfavourable, generalized, and *rigid belief* applied to all members of a group—and racism satisfy the psychic needs of certain people. *Frustration-aggression* is a popular variant of social-psychological theory. It explains prejudice and racism as forms of hostility that arise from frustration. The theory suggests that people who are frustrated in their efforts to achieve a desired goal—a better-paying job, for example, or entry to a university—respond with aggression (Marger, 1997). Since the real source of frustration is usually too powerful to confront directly, or may not in fact be known, people

take out their frustrations on the less powerful. From this perspective, minority ethnic and racial groups are convenient and safe targets of displaced aggression. This displacement is also referred to as scapegoating. The concept of scapegoating is sometimes used to explain *anti-Semitism*—negative attitudes and everyday discrimination directed against Jews (Brym and Lenton, 1993).

There is a seductive, almost commonsense, appeal to this kind of explanation. We all have bad days at work or at school, and when we get home we sometimes lash out at the people close to us. However, the theory has limitations. First, people respond to frustrating circumstances in a variety of ways. Displaced aggression does not always follow frustration. We sometimes internalize our frustrations and end up giving ourselves an ulcer, or we may direct our frustrations at the real source of our problems. The theory does not say why we respond to frustrating circumstances in different ways. Second, the theory does not explain why some groups, and not others, are chosen as scapegoats.

Primordialism

The **primordialist thesis** suggests that ethnic and racial attachments reflect an innate tendency for people to seek out, and associate with, others who are similar in terms of language, culture, beliefs, ancestry, and appearance (Scott, 1990). From this point of view, ethnic prejudice and racism are ways of maintaining social boundaries. *Sociobiologists* offer a popular form of primordial theory. They suggest that prejudice and **discrimination**—practices that deny members of particular groups equal access to societal rewards—stem from our supposedly biologically grounded tendency to be nepotistic. Sociobiologists argue that the process of natural selection does not operate at the level of individuals, but rather at the level of kin-related groups. Clusters of genes are assumed to be passed on through kin selection (Wilson, 1978). Ethnic and racial groups are seen to be nothing more than very large extended families. Since there is a "natural" tendency for people to want to pass on their genes, they favour their own "families." Thus, people are inherently altruistic (prepared to sacrifice their own individual interests for the sake of the group) and **ethnocentric** because they want to pass on their genes to their own group. Humans, therefore, naturally favour members of their own ethnic or racial group—their "relatives"—and have a natural distrust and dislike of "non-family" members (van den Berghe, 1986: 255).

Are racism, prejudice, and discrimination programmed by our genes? It seems unlikely. The first problem with sociobiology is that shared ethnicity or race does not prevent conflict from erupting. In the history of the United States, white workers have struck against white-owned factories, and Americans have killed members of their own ethnic or racial group without concern for common ethnicity or race (Bonacich, 1980). Second, sociobiology is not able to explain how and why we frequently break out of our supposed genetically programmed nepotism. For example, Canadians of diverse ethnic and racial origins participate together in various kinds of anti-racist social movements (Henry et al., 2000). Ethnic and racial relations, therefore, are not necessarily zero-sum games in which one group wins at the expense of another.

Normative Theories

Normative theories of ethnic and racial prejudices concentrate on the way in which prejudices are transmitted through socialization and the social circumstances that compel discriminatory behaviour (Marger, 1997). For example, the *socialization approach* focuses on how we are taught ethnic and racial stereotypes, prejudices, and attitudes by our families, peer groups, and the mass media. For instance, as a teenager in Saskatchewan in the 1970s, I remember watching the TV show *All in the Family*. People in Saskatchewan at the time held many prejudicial attitudes, particularly toward Aboriginal people. However, the television program *All in the Family* exposed my generation to a repertoire of ethnic and racial slang and stereotypes that we had not heard before. Archie Bunker, the show's central character, was supposed to be a caricature of an American "bigot." He taught us terms like "wop," "dago," "spic," and "nigger," and the corresponding stereotypes.

As Box 10.2 shows, there are subtle ways in which the English language places different values on the colours black and white. Our language, in turn, shapes how we perceive and socially evaluate different racial groups.

Socialization approaches are superior to the first two approaches because they emphasize the way in which ethnic and racial prejudices and attitudes are learned through social interaction. The limitation of socialization theories is that they are unable to explain how prejudicial ideas, attitudes, and practices arise in the first place. This is where power-conflict theories come into play.

Power-Conflict Theories

Karl Marx (1967 [1867]: 751) said that "the turning of Africa into a warren for the commercial hunting of black-skins signaled the rosy dawn of the era of capitalist production." Marx did not take his analysis of slavery and racism much farther than this. Later generations of Marxist scholars, however, have sought to link racism to the overall structure of capitalist societies.

Orthodox Marxists argue that racism is an *ideology*—a set of statements shaped by one's economic interests about the way the social world "really works." Racism is ideological insofar as it is used by capitalists to mystify social reality and justify the exploitation and the unequal treatment of groups of people.

This justification can take many forms. For example, in the seventeenth century, American and Caribbean plantation owners justified the use of Africans as slaves by denying the humanity of Africans (Williams, 1964). In Marxist terms, the existence of racist ideas did not "cause" slavery; rather, slavery was a particular system of labour control that was justified by racist ideology.

In the case of advanced capitalism, racism is viewed by Marxists as an ideology that justifies the especially intense exploitation of racial minority and immigrant workers (Castles and Kosack, 1984; Bolaria and Li, 1988). From this point of view, racist ideas are used by employers as a means of creating artificial divisions in the working class so as to prevent the formation of a class consciousness that would threaten the social and economic order (Bolaria and Li, 1988; Castles and Kosack, 1984; Nikolinakos, 1973). Also, racist ideas help to justify the allocation of certain groups to low-wage, socially marginal jobs.

Race and the Split Labour Market Split labour-market theory was developed by Edna Bonacich (1972, 1979) because of the limitations of orthodox Marxism in analyzing racism. She argues that orthodox Marxism tends to assume that the capitalist class is all-powerful, and that other classes play no role in the development of racist thinking. This is inaccurate; racism may be found in all classes to varying degrees. Second, orthodox Marxism portrays

Language is an integral part of our culture. Language not only expresses ideas but shapes our thought. Our childhood socialization involves, in part, the ability to use language. In the following "Short Play on 'Black' and 'White' Words," Robert Moore shows how aspects of our language help unwittingly to reproduce both negative and positive racial imagery.

Some may blackly (angrily) accuse me of trying to blacken (defame) the English language, to give it a black eye (a mark of shame) by writing such black words (hostile). They may denigrate (to cast aspersions; to darken) me by accusing me of being blackhearted (malevolent), of having a black outlook (pessimistic, dismal) on life, of being a blackguard (scoundrel)—which would certainly be a black mark (detrimental fact) against me. Some may black-brow (scowl at) me and hope that a black cat crosses in front of me because of this black deed. I may become a black sheep (one who causes shame or embarrassment because of deviation from the accepted standards), who will be blackballed (ostracized) by being placed on a blacklist (list of undesirables) in an attempt to blackmail (to force or coerce into a particular action) me to retract my words. But attempts to blackjack (to compel by threat) me will have a Chinaman's chance of success, for I am not a yellow-bellied Indian-giver of words, who will whitewash (cover up or gloss over vices or crimes) a black lie (harmful, inexcusable). I challenge the purity and innocence (white) of the English language. I don't see things in black and white (entirely bad or entirely good) terms, for I am a white man (marked by upright firmness) if there ever was one. However, it would be a black day when I would not "call a spade a spade," even though some will suggest a white man calling the English language racist is like the pot calling the kettle black. While many may be niggardly (grudging, scanty) in their support, others will be honest and decent—and to them I say, that's very white of you (honest, decent).

The preceding is of course a white lie (not intended to cause harm), meant only to illustrate some examples of racist terminology in the English language.

SOURCE: "Racist Stereotyping in the English Language" by Robert B. Moore. (pp. 269–297). Reprinted from *Racism in the English Language* by Robert B. Moore, Council on Interracial Books for Children, 1976.

racism in overly conspiratorial terms. There is little evidence to demonstrate that capitalists sit around plotting new and devious ways of using racism to stop workers from developing a class consciousness. Third, orthodox Marxism has trouble explaining why racialized conflict so often results in *exclusionary practices*—practices that deny employers access to cheaper, more exploitable labour. In 1885, for example, the Canadian government instituted a "head tax" on new immigrants from China. Chinese immigrants had to pay $50 to the federal government. In 1900, the tax was raised to $100, and in 1903 to $500 (Li, 1988: 30). The Chinese Immigration Act of 1923 completely barred Chinese immigration until 1947 (Li, 1988: 30). If racism is developed by capitalists to justify exploitation, then why does it so often result in efforts to *block* the entry of new immigrants, and limit the job opportunities of those already in the country? Bonacich feels that more attention has to be paid to the way in which the competition for jobs and other scarce resources among the working class creates and sustains racism.

Split labour-market theory suggests that racial and ethnic conflict is rooted in differences in the price of labour. For historical reasons—mainly involving military conquest—nonwhite workers have often received low wages and white workers high wages. Employers try to replace high-paid white workers with low-paid nonwhite workers. Meanwhile, high-paid workers, faced with displacement or the threat of displacement, try to protect their own interests by limiting capitalists' access to cheaper nonwhite workers. Thus, cheaper nonwhite workers are the victims of a complicated process of class struggle between expensive labour, cheap labour, and capitalists.

The theory applies well to Canada. During the late nineteenth and early twentieth centuries, the presence of Chinese workers and merchants in British Columbia provoked a negative response on the part of various segments of the white working class and shop owners. As split labour-market theory would predict, the hostility of whites was rooted in differences in the price of labour. According to evidence presented at the Royal Commission on Chinese and Japanese Immigration in 1903, Chinese workers earned about one-half of the wages that white workers earned in the same jobs (Li, 1988: 44). A number of racist organizations emerged whose aim was to limit the places where Chinese people could work and which helped stop additional Chinese immigration (Roy, 1989).

Split labour-market theory makes three other points that are relevant to the analysis of ethnic and race relations in general. First, it argues that individual racism, ethnic prejudice, and institutional racism emerge from intergroup conflict. Second, the theory maintains that prejudicial ideas and discriminatory behaviour are ways of socially marginalizing minority groups whom the dominant group sees as threats to their position of power and privilege. Third, the theory suggests that, in order to understand ethnic and racial relations, we need to look beyond individual personalities and sociobiological processes and analyze processes of economic, social, and political competition between groups (Marger, 1997: 98).

Keeping these three observations in mind will help you understand the three main patterns of ethnic and racial relations in Canada: Aboriginal–non-Aboriginal relations, French–English relations, and immigrant–non-immigrant relations. These are the topics that we turn to next.

ABORIGINAL PEOPLES

Have you ever fumbled trying to find the right way to refer to someone who is ethnically or racially different from yourself? Are we supposed to say that a person is a "Native," an "Indian," an "Aboriginal," or a member of the "First Nations"? Are you sensitive about how you want others to refer to your own ethnic or racial origins? In contrast, you may think that this sensitivity is yet another indication that political correctness has run amok. If so, you should not dismiss the issue of labels and names so easily.

Ethnic and racial labels are about power. Take the term *Indian*. A hopelessly lost Christopher Columbus thought he found a sea route to India when he was discovered in 1492 by people indigenous to this part of the world. He mislabelled the people he met "Indians." Britain's military, political, and economic domination of North America in the 1700s meant that it had the power to ignore the linguistic

and cultural differences between indigenous groups and define them in any way they saw fit. They chose the term *Indian*.

As indigenous people have acquired more power, they have begun to challenge externally imposed labels. In the 1980s, for example, the National Indian Brotherhood renamed itself the Assembly of First Nations, and people in Alberta who were defined by Europeans as Sarcee Indians for most of the twentieth century renamed themselves the Siksika nation. Groups have rejected externally imposed labels as part of a search for forms of consciousness, identity, and culture that are untainted by the colonizing power's definition of the situation (Jenson, 1993).

One, albeit imperfect, way to make our way through the complex issue of naming is to use the definition of "Aboriginal peoples" that is contained in the 1982 Canadian Charter of Rights and Freedoms. In the Charter, the "Aboriginal peoples" of Canada include Indians, Inuit, and Métis. According to the 1996 census, there were 529 040 Indians, 204 115 Métis, and 40 220 Inuit people in Canada, who made up 3 percent of the total population (Brym, 1999).

At its simplest level, the term *Indian* (or *status* or *registered Indian*) refers to people who are recognized as "Indians" by virtue of the federal government's Indian Act. Many people now use the term "First Nations" to refer to Indians. But deciding who is an Indian under the Indian Act is a much more complicated question. Until 1985, Indian women who married non-Indian men, along with their children, lost their federally recognized Indian status; they became *non-status Indians*. In 1985, Bill C-31 was passed. It allowed these women and their dependent children to regain their Indian status. Indian bands, however, now have the power to develop their own membership codes. This means that not all individuals who have had their Indian status reinstated are members of an Indian band (Frideres and Gadacz, 2001: 35).

There are two different definitions of *Métis*. Métis organizations in Western Canada tend to focus on a person's objective "roots" as the condition for being considered Métis. Thus, the Métis National Council defines "the Métis" as "descendants of the historic Métis who evolved in what is now Western Canada as a people with a common political will" (Métis National Council, 1983). Métis organizations in Eastern Canada, such as the Native Council of Canada, argue that the Métis should include descendants of the historic Métis in Western Canada *and* anyone of mixed European–Indian ancestry who defines himself or herself as Métis, and is accepted by other Métis people as such. Thus, subjective definitions of ethnic group membership are more important for groups like the Native Council of Canada.

Finally, *Inuit* people are part of a diverse group of people who have lived for many centuries north of the tree line. In Canada, the name *Inuit* has replaced the earlier name *Eskimo*. The language of the Inuit is Inuktitut (McMillan, 1988: 240).

EXPLANATIONS OF ABORIGINAL CONDITIONS

The socioeconomic conditions of Canada's Aboriginal people amount to a national tragedy (Royal Commission on Aboriginal Peoples, 1996). Canada has made admirable efforts to condemn social inequality and the denial of human rights in other countries, such as South Africa when apartheid—its policy of legalized ethnic separation and inequality—was still in force. Ironically, though, the commitment to social justice for Aboriginal peoples in our own country has not been as strong. In the 1980s, the South African government routinely defended itself against our criticisms of apartheid by saying that we should first clean up our own back yard (Bourgeault, 1988; York, 1989).

Statistical evidence shows that Aboriginal peoples are the most socially and economically disadvantaged groups in the country. About three-quarters of all existing housing for status Indians who live on reserves fails to meet some of the basic standards for safe and healthy living, such as running water, central heating, sewer connections or septic tanks, and electricity (Frideres and Gadacz, 2001: 75). On average, Aboriginal people have much lower family incomes, lower rates of labour-force participation, and higher rates of unemployment than non-Aboriginal Canadians (Frideres and Gadacz, 2001: 90–99). The age-standardized death rate for Aboriginal people in Canada was 9.2 per 1000 in 1991, compared with a rate of 6 per 1000 for Canada as a whole. In 1991, the life expectancy of status Indian men was 68 years, 6 years lower than the Canadian average. Life expectancy for status Indian women was higher than that for Indian men, but was still below life expectancy for other Canadian women: 73.1 com-

pared with 80 years. In 1992, the infant mortality rate (the number of deaths of children under one year old per 1000 people) for status Indians was 17.5, which was more than double the national rate of 7.9. Tuberculosis, which is widely regarded as a disease of poverty, is on the rise in Indian communities; the tuberculosis rate for status Indians is 43 times higher than the rate for non-Aboriginal Canadians (Frideres and Gadacz, 2001: 72).

For many years, Canadian politicians, bureaucrats, and social scientists have puzzled over where these differences and inequalities come from, how and why they persist, and what can be done about them. Indeed, when the federal government announced in 1991 the establishment of the Royal Commission on Aboriginal Peoples, Ovide Mercredi, the chief of the Assembly of First Nations, caustically commented that "Indians have been studied to death." I want first to consider the federal government's historical explanation of these conditions and then examine two sociological accounts of them: the culture of poverty thesis and the conflict theory.

The Government's View

Throughout the first half of the twentieth century, government Indian policy was premised on the belief that Aboriginal culture was both different from and inferior to European culture. Armed with this ethnocentric attitude, the federal government sought to assimilate Aboriginal people into mainstream Canadian society (Gibbins and Ponting, 1986). In 1920, this approach was summed up in the following terms by Duncan Campbell Scott, the deputy minister of the federal government's Department of Indian Affairs: "[O]ur object is to continue until there is not a single Indian ... that has not been absorbed into the body politic and there is no [longer an] Indian question" (quoted in Titley, 1986).

The government, therefore, forcibly tried to Europeanize Aboriginal people and culture. Traditional cultural practices like the potlatch, a winter exchange of gifts and property on the British Columbia coast, and the sun dance, a summer solstice religious ceremony on the Prairies, were outlawed. Such practices were regarded as pagan, anti-capitalist rituals that inhibited the development of both Christianity and a capitalistic work ethic (Cole and Chaikin, 1990; Pettipas, 1995). The federal government also tried to assimilate and Christianize

Aboriginal children by establishing a series of residential schools. These boarding schools were located far from the children's families and home communities. While in school, the children were forbidden to speak in their mother tongue, were forbidden to speak with siblings of the opposite sex, and had their hair shorn. Boys were given extensive training in manual labour and girls were taught domestic labour skills. The goal of this schooling was to resocialize Aboriginal children and to instill in them a new European identity (Titley, 1986). The government's legislative, regulatory, and educational approach to Aboriginal people reflected the view that inequality, poverty, and poor social conditions were rooted in Aboriginal cultural and racial inferiority.

The Culture of Poverty Thesis

In the 1960s and 1970s, many sociologists also saw Aboriginal culture as the source of the "Indian problem." To account for the origins and persistence of the problem, some sociologists proposed a variant of the **culture of poverty thesis**. The concept of a culture of poverty was first developed by Oscar Lewis (1961), an American anthropologist interested in explaining the slow pace at which Mexican Americans and Puerto Ricans were being assimilated into U.S. society. He suggested that some ethnic groups do not readily assimilate, and hence are poor, because their culture does not value economic success, hard work, and achievement.

Kazemipur and Halli (2000) have applied Lewis's framework to the issue of ethnic poverty in Canada, and Nagler (1972) has applied it to the conditions of Aboriginal people. In his view, Indian culture displayed the following characteristics: a present rather than a future time-orientation; a high value on mutual aid without the expectation of return; a lack of emphasis on the possession of material goods; a lack of appreciation for the monetary value of time; and the absence of a capitalist work ethic. These cultural characteristics meant that "a large segment of the Indian population refuse or find themselves unable to partake in full time economic pursuits" (Nagler, 1972: 131).

Sociologists like Steven Steinberg (1981) criticize culture of poverty explanations by arguing that groups generally do not get ahead or lag behind because of their cultural values. Instead, they are born into certain stations in life and adopt the values and attitudes that are consistent with their life-chances. If Aboriginal people have low aspirations, it is likely the result of a realistic assessment of their dismal job prospects and a resignation born out of bitter personal experience. For Steinberg, the *culture* of poverty is the consequence, not the cause, of poverty.

Conflict Theory

Since the 1970s, sociologists have focused on blocked opportunities rather than culture as the explanation for inequalities between Aboriginal and non-Aboriginal people. The *internal colonial model* is the most popular variant of the conflict approach (Frideres and Gadacz, 2001). The internal colonial model analyzes the problem of inequality in terms of power imbalances and the exploitation of Aboriginal people and lands by white society.

Theorists of internal colonialism argue that the Indian Act, which outlines the federal government's policies and procedures for dealing with Indian issues, is a paternalistic document that disempowers Indian people (Frideres and Gadacz, 2001). It places real limits on the actions of both individual Indians and their band councils. When Indians from Brantford, Ontario, wanted to sue the federal government over unfulfilled treaty promises in the 1920s, the government passed a law making it illegal for them to use band funds to hire lawyers to pursue their claims (Titley, 1986). Indians did not get much help from federal or provincial politicians either. Since Indians could not vote in either federal or provincial elections until the 1960s, politicians had no need to stand up for the interests of Indians who lived in their constituency. Chiefs who failed to cooperate with the government's designs were routinely removed from their positions (Satzewich and Mahood, 1994). Band councils are still required to have their decisions approved by the federal minister of Indian Affairs. Thus, rather than helping to create the social conditions that would afford Indian people greater autonomy over their lives, government policy has fostered social marginality and dependence. This is why many Indian leaders have called for the abolition of the Indian Act.

Furthermore, most of the present-day conflicts between Aboriginal people and various levels of government originated in the past misuse of power by government officials. Present-day land-claims disputes sometimes go back 100 years, when government officials could arbitrarily lop off chunks of Indian reserve land and sell it to white interests (Frideres and Gadacz, 2001). The Canadian government and private business have derived tremendous economic benefits from the exploitation of land appropriated from Aboriginal communities. According to internal colonial theorists, the time has come for Canadians to pay the rent. In Alberta, Aboriginal people are suing the federal government over the nonpayment of royalties on the extraction of resources from their land. As Frideres and Gadacz (2001: 7) note, with long-term profits estimated at $1–2 billion, the government and private enterprise "are not about to give up easily."

CLASS AND GENDER DIVERSITY

Criticisms of the internal colonial model have focused on its tendency to overgeneralize about the conditions of Aboriginal people in Canada. As significant as the inequalities between Aboriginal and non-Aboriginal people are, conflict and feminist sociologists argue that it is worth remembering that there is also socioeconomic diversity within Aboriginal communities. These sociologists analyze class and gender differentiation within Aboriginal communities and the implications of such differences for both individual life-chances and wider community life (Satzewich and Wotherspoon, 2001).

Feminist sociologists have been interested in the role of gender in recent debates about the inclusion of the right to self-government in the Canadian Constitution. During the debate over the Charlottetown Accord in 1992, many Aboriginal women were concerned that the proposal for self-government, which was advanced by the predominantly male leadership of Aboriginal organizations, did not contain any guarantees of sexual equality between Aboriginal women and men (Krosenbrink-Gelissen, 1994: 357–60; Fiske, 1996). The Native Women's Association of Canada, therefore, fought against the accord in the months leading up to the referendum.

Other conflict theorists are interested in the political and economic implications of socioeconomic differentiation within Aboriginal communities. Researchers challenge the stereotype that all Aboriginal people are either poor, unemployed, living on welfare, or working in low-skill, dead-end jobs. In fact, a small but nevertheless significant proportion of Aboriginal men and women work in highly skilled professional and technical occupations, and others are owners and managers of both small and large businesses (Gerber, 1990). Menno Boldt (1993: 124)

A significant proportion of Aboriginal men and women are owners and managers of both small and large businesses. John Kim Bell, for example, put his musical career on hold to set up the Canadian Native Arts Foundation.
SOURCE: CP Picture Archive/Colin McConnell.

argues that most Indian reserves are characterized by a two-class social order. The first class consists of "a small, virtually closed élite class comprising influential landowners, politicians, bureaucrats, and a few entrepreneurs," while the second consists of "a large lower class comprising destitute, dependent, powerless [and wage-earning] people" (Boldt, 1993: 124). Boldt argues (1993: 125) that this two-class structure has important consequences for community life and community politics:

> With the élite class controlling the political agenda, lower-class interests get neglected. Elite class interests tend to be primarily "power" not "problem" oriented; that is, such interests are related to expanding their jurisdiction and control over band/tribal

political and administrative structures....
[These] are given preference over the problems that afflict the Indian lower class: high unemployment; excessive rates of family disintegration; alcohol and substance abuse; extraordinary levels of violence, suicide, incarceration, and so on.

Researchers are also studying the formation of a capitalist class within Aboriginal communities. Land-claim settlements, although ostensibly earmarked for the benefit of all community members, are frequently controlled by small ruling elites. In the case of the Inuit, Marybelle Mitchell (1996: 449) argues:

The state's acknowledgment in 1973 of its responsibility to negotiate land settlements with Native people led to the formation of an Inuit ruling class. Created by the state to facilitate access by the multinationals to the Arctic's natural resources, these leaders, a wholly new kind of talking chief, are signing away the land and aboriginal rights of their fellow Inuit in return for limited entitlement to land, some managerial powers and varying amounts of cash channeled through development corporations.

This new capitalist class is different from other Canadian capitalists, in that they do not personally own all the wealth and capital that is at their disposal. They do, however, control the compensation that communities receive from land-claims settlements. They establish development corporations, hire and fire employees, make capital-planning and investment decisions, and decide what and how much to produce. The unanswered sociological question is whether this capitalist class will make decisions about the future that are in their own material interests or in the interests of the community as a whole.

QUEBEC: NATIONALISM AND IDENTITY

On the evening of October 30, 1995, most adult Canadians were tuned to TV or radio coverage of the Quebec referendum on separation. I followed the results that night with mixed emotions. On the one hand, as a second-generation Canadian with no ethnic roots in the old British Empire, I could

empathize with people in Quebec. On the other hand, as a child of the Trudeau years, I was socialized to believe in a vision of Canadian unity. Many on the "No" side believed that a lot of Quebeckers were just bluffing in the pre-referendum rhetoric; when it came to the crunch, they would vote in favour of staying in Canada. Then the results came in. In some parts of Quebec, 90 percent of voters were in favour of separation. As the results from around Montreal were tabulated, the "No" side gained ground. When the final count was tallied, 49.6 percent of Quebeckers voted for, and 50.4 percent voted against, separation. Across Canada, people were both exhilarated and downcast because Canada had "won."

Is the issue of separation going to go away? Despite the ebbs and flows in support for separation, the answer is clearly no. As with other areas of ethnic relations in Canada, an understanding of the contemporary scene must begin with an appreciation of history and of power relations. In this section, I examine three main sociological questions: (1) What is the historical basis for the emergence of Québécois nationalism? (2) Who is a Québécois? (3) What does the close vote mean for ethnic relations in the province and the country?

THE SOCIAL BASIS OF QUÉBÉCOIS NATIONALISM

Even though the 1867 British North America Act asserted that there were two founding peoples of Canada, the English and the French, and that they had equal places in Canadian Confederation, *les Québécois* are one of the oldest colonized peoples in the world (Milner and Milner, 1973). The French government controlled the colony of New France from the early 1600s to 1763. The inhabitants of New France were expected to serve the interests of France. The colony was established in part to pursue the fur trade and to transfer economic resources to the mother country. Much of the French commercial and political elite left the colony following the British victory over France in 1763. When New France was transferred to British control—what the Québécois refer to as "The Conquest"—a new colonizing power came to dominate the society.

An anglophone—a unilingual, English-speaking—elite gradually took over the economic and political affairs of the province. Most French-

Canadian peasants (*habitants*) remained subsistence farmers. During the nineteenth century, some of them emigrated to the northeastern United States to work in the expanding cotton and linen mills; others moved to other provinces in Canada; and still others became part of the urban industrial working class in the province (Ramirez, 1991). By the late nineteenth century, Quebec was a province where "capital speaks English and labour speaks French" (Whitaker, 1993: 22)—a telling description of the way in which linguistic and class structures overlapped. The French Canadians in Quebec, who formed a numerical majority, were worse off than the anglophone minority in virtually every material way (Whitaker, 1993: 22).

The Catholic Church occupied a unique position as a social, political, and religious intermediary between the two groups. In addition to attending to the religious needs of its French-speaking parishioners, the Catholic Church acted as an agent of social control over French-Canadian workers and farmers. The church promoted social ideologies that were conservative and anti-modern. It devalued the importance of formal education for the masses, discouraged workers from forming and joining secular trade unions, encouraged married couples to have large families, and vigorously discouraged French Canadians from taking up professions or establishing businesses of their own. These ideas were not in the best material interests of French-Canadian workers and farmers, but they helped ensure the survival of French-Canadian culture (Latouche, 1993).

This social structure began to change significantly during the rapid industrialization stimulated by World War I, as the industrial working class became a significant player on the political scene. One of the biggest changes in the 1940s and 1950s was the rise of a new francophone middle class of technical workers and professionals. The upper echelons of the corporate world, still under the control of anglophones, remained hostile to the advancement of francophones, even if they were bilingual. The new francophone middle class, therefore, faced a situation of blocked social mobility, which was partly responsible for the Quiet Revolution in Quebec.

The term **Quiet Revolution** describes the social, political, and cultural changes that occurred in Quebec in the 1960s, in part because of the initiatives of this new middle class. These changes included the

secularization of the educational system, the reform of the civil service, growth in the provincially controlled public sector, greater involvement of the Quebec provincial government in the economic affairs of the province, and a questioning of the Catholic Church's authority in all areas of life. Facing blocked mobility in the corporate world, francophones created their own economic opportunities by expanding the power of the provincial government.

Social scientists and political pundits have pored over referendum and federal and provincial election results over the last 30 years in an effort to determine which social forces are responsible for sustaining the push for sovereignty. Some see the present-day sovereignty movement as an expression of *middle-class nationalism* that is a continuation of the Quiet Revolution. From this perspective, separation is being promoted by middle-class professionals as a way of continuing to further their own material interests. Emboldened by the success at expanding the activities of the provincial government during the Quiet Revolution, they desire even more control over their affairs (Whitaker, 1993).

However, likening the sovereignty movement to a massive job-creation project is too simplistic. First, francophone professionals are no longer shut out of the corporate sector in Quebec. Over the past 30 years, middle-class francophones have achieved upward mobility in both the private and the public sectors. Second, there is a diversity of class interests within the sovereignty movement. Many francophone professionals support sovereignty, but there is also a social democratic tradition within the movement that is trying to mobilize working people against foreign (anglophone and U.S.) capitalist domination. Their vision of a sovereign Quebec involves a reorganization of power relations between francophones and non-francophones, and between workers and capitalists. Some francophone capitalists also support the sovereignty movement (Whitaker, 1993).

Clearly, the contemporary sovereignty movement is not based on the support of only one social class. According to Fleras and Elliot (1996), the nationalist movement is sustained by a broadly based desire among most francophone Quebeckers to achieve a common goal—to create the political and economic conditions that will allow them to preserve their French language and culture. Fleras and Elliot argue that, rather than defining support for the sovereignty movement in class terms, it is more useful to conceptualize the movement as made up of groups who have differing views about how best to maintain their language and culture. Thus, the present-day sovereignty movement consists in part of moderates who want to strengthen Quebec's position within the federal system. This involves a new constitutional division of powers that has yet to be settled. Radical supporters, on the other hand, argue that the best way for the French language and culture to survive is for the people of Quebec to have their own state. They argue that they will always be a minority if they stay in Canada and that they will always be subject to the tyranny of the majority. As Louise Beaudoin of the Parti Québécois put it, "I want to be a majority in my own country" (Fleras and Elliot, 1996: 270).

WHO IS QUÉBÉCOIS?

The population of Quebec is ethnically heterogeneous—19.4 percent of the population of Quebec is made up of people whose mother tongue is not French: Jews, anglophones, allophones (people whose mother tongue is neither French nor English), visible-minority immigrants, and Aboriginal people (Fournier, Rosenberg, and White, 1997: 282). One of the central issues facing the nationalist movement in Quebec is the definition of a Québécois. This question cuts to the heart of ethnic relations in the province.

Benedict Anderson (1983) regards nations as "imagined communities." They are imagined in the sense that, even though members of the smallest nation can never know everyone in the community, there is still a common feeling of fellowship with others in the nation. People in Shawinigan do not personally know all other Quebeckers; nevertheless, they have a comradeship that extends beyond personal relationships. Nations also possess physical and symbolic boundaries that define who is a member and who is not. Sociologists interested in nationalism want to identify the symbolic boundaries of the nation. In the case of the nationalist movement in Quebec, this issue is translated into the question of who is "in" and who is "outside" the imagined community. And if some groups are "out," will they ever be accepted as Québécois?

A majority of nationalists, on the one hand, define the imagined community as all those people who now live in the province of Quebec. For them, the social and symbolic boundaries of the nation correspond with the present-day provincial boundaries. Sociologists call this a form of **civic nationalism** (Balthazar, 1993). A minority of nationalists, on the other hand, reject civic nationalism in favour of cultural and linguistic criteria for membership in the nation. *Ethnic nationalists* define the Québécois as people who possess a particular history, culture, ancestry, and/or language. This is where the concept of *pure laine* ("pure wool") Québécois becomes important. Some nationalists regard the true Québécois as only those who are the direct descendants of the French people who settled in the colony of New France before the conquest of 1763. Other groups in the province are defined as "cultural communities" (GRES, 1997: 107). According to the province's policy of interculturalism, these cultural communities must learn to accommodate themselves to the dominant francophone culture and language.

The debate about how to define a nation is not academic hairsplitting. Premier Jacques Parizeau commented on referendum night that the pro-sovereignty forces were defeated by "money and the ethnic vote." After his resignation, Parizeau commented further that it was the first time in Canadian history that the majority (60 percent) of francophone Quebeckers voted in favour of sovereignty. These statements implied that ethnic minorities were not really part of the nation and that *pure laine* votes should be worth more than the votes of others. Parizeau's remarks also confirmed the worst fears of ethnic minorities—namely, that sovereigntists are not civic nationalists but rather ethnic nationalists at heart, and that ethnic minorities will never be considered full and equal citizens in a sovereign Quebec (Ha, 1995). Many people within the sovereignty movement distanced themselves from Parizeau's comments, and the movement is still trying to repair the damage that they caused to ethnic relations. Clearly, the challenge for sovereigntists is to find a place for non-francophones in the imagined community (GRES, 1997: 109).

IMMIGRATION: STATE FORMATION AND ECONOMIC DEVELOPMENT

The third aspect of ethnic and racial relations in Canada that I consider is immigrant–non-immigrant relations. In 1996, there were nearly 5 million immigrants living in Canada, representing 17.2 percent of our population. In large cities, the impact of immigration is even greater. In 1996, immigrants made up 17.8 percent of the population of Montreal, 34.6 percent of the population of Vancouver, and 47.1 percent of the population of Toronto (Badets, 1993). Canada accepts more immigrants and refugees in proportion to our population than virtually any other country in the world (Citizenship and Immigration Canada, 1996).

Migration has been a feature of our history for well over 300 years. However, the nature, sources, determinants, and consequences of immigration have varied through history. In the nineteenth century, immigrants contributed to the processes of capitalist state formation—the process of creating a capitalist system of production and governance. They did this in a number of ways. The early working class in Canada was made up largely of immigrants (Pentland, 1981; Avery, 1995). Immigrant workers helped build the canals, railways, and roads that became part of our economic infrastructure. Many nineteenth-century immigrants were also farmers. Their crops were used to feed Canadian workers and, as productivity increased, were exported to feed people in other countries. Those same farmers, in turn, helped stimulate capitalist industry through their role as consumers of goods. A significant proportion of the corporate elite in nineteenth-century Canada was made up of immigrants (Macmillan, 1985; Clement, 1975), as was a large segment of the early political elite. Canada's first prime minister, Sir John A. Macdonald, was an immigrant from Glasgow, Scotland.

Immigrants continue to make important contributions to the social reproduction of Canadian society. Demographers predict that, in the absence of new immigrants, the population of Canada would begin to decline by 2015. Without new immigrants to replenish our population, the next generation of taxpayers would have to pay far more in taxes and Canada Pension Plan contributions. Retiring at the age of 55, or even 65, would become a pipe dream for many older workers, as employers and governments would need to take steps to retain enough workers. Employers would face serious shortages of workers, and manufacturers would face a much smaller consumer market in which to sell their goods (Economic Council of Canada, 1991).

FACTORS THAT SHAPE CANADIAN IMMIGRATION

There is no single variable that can explain the complex pattern of immigration to Canada. Over the past 100 years, six main variables have influenced which groups of people have been let into the country as immigrants.

The first variable is social class. Most immigrants are admitted to Canada because they fill jobs in the Canadian economy or because they create jobs for other Canadians. As such, the flow of immigrants to Canada has been very closely linked to the overall structure of the Canadian economy. Between 1947 and the early 1960s, for example, immigrants were regarded by the Canadian government as what Australian economist Jock Collins (1988) calls "factory fodder." Immigrants were recruited in order to fill unskilled and semiskilled manual jobs in agriculture, construction, mining, logging, the garment industry, and heavy manufacturing. During this time, it was common for individual employers to demand that the government recruit as many as 300 immigrant workers at a time in order to fill job openings (Avery, 1995).

In the early 1960s, immigration policy began to place more emphasis on the recruitment of highly skilled professional and technical workers, and on immigrants with large amounts of investment capital. As a result, by 1996, immigrants made up 17.2 percent of the population but 18.8 percent of the total Canadian labour force, 20.5 percent of people in managerial occupations, and 20.3 percent of people in professional and technical occupations (Li, 1996).

The second determinant of immigration is ethnic and racial **stereotypes**—exaggerated, oversimplified images of the characteristics of social groups. Before 1962, there was a racialized hierarchy of desirability in Canadian immigration policy. Immigration policy was based on the assumption that European immigrants were racially and culturally superior to all other potential immigrants. Non-Europeans were stereotyped as racially and culturally inferior and, therefore, were not welcome. In the 1950s, for example, immigration officials could bar groups from entering Canada on the grounds that the groups were "unsuited to climatic and economic conditions" or that they were "unable to assimilate" (Bolaria and Li, 1988). These phrases were thinly veiled masks for racial preferences in the selection of immigrants.

Since 1962, ethnic and racial stereotyping in selecting new immigrants has become less important. Canadian immigration policy is now more open in terms of the ethnic and racial origins of immigrants. Before 1961, Europeans made up over 90 percent of total immigrants to Canada. In 2001, immigrants from Europe made up 17.26 percent of the total flow of immigrants to Canada (see Table 10.3).

The third variable that shapes immigrant selection consists of a variety of geopolitical considerations stemming from Canada's relationships with other countries. Racist selection criteria were taken out of immigration regulations in the 1960s, in part because they interfered with Canadian international diplomacy. In the early 1960s, Canada began to assert itself as a middle power in world politics that could mediate social conflicts in and between other countries. Outside of Europe, though, our diplomats did not have much credibility because our immigration policy implied that certain groups were inferior and therefore not suited to life in Canada (Hawkins, 1989).

In the 1980s, the Cold War also played a role in shaping who was let in. According to Whitaker (1987), there was a double standard at work in the admittance of refugees. People who managed to escape from the Soviet Union or other Eastern Bloc countries were routinely granted refugee status in Canada. In 1985, for example, it took a day for the brother of a Czech hockey star who played for the Toronto Maple Leafs to be granted refugee status in Canada. Canadian immigration bureaucrats were much more cautious, however, about admitting "socialist" refugees who were fleeing right-wing dictatorships in various Central American countries.

The fourth variable affecting immigrant selection is humanitarianism. Canada accepts immigrants and refugees partly on humanitarian and compassionate grounds. In 1986, Canada was the first country ever to be awarded the Nansen Medal by the United Nations for its generosity and commitment to international refugee programs (Fleras and Elliot, 1996).

The influence of the fifth variable, public opinion, is more difficult to determine, in part because Canadians do not speak with one voice regarding immigration. A 1991 poll found five distinct segments of opinion regarding immigration. Twenty-three percent were "protagonists" who supported increased levels of immigration and believed that immigrants made important contributions to the betterment of Canadian society; 22 percent were "concerned supporters" who approved of current levels of immigration but who were concerned that immigration had certain negative effects on Canadian

TABLE 10.3   TOP 10 SOURCE COUNTRIES OF IMMIGRANTS TO CANADA, 1968, 2001

TOP 10 SOURCE COUNTRIES OF IMMIGRANTS (PRINCIPAL APPLICANTS AND DEPENDANTS), 1968		TOP 10 SOURCE COUNTRIES OF IMMIGRANTS (PRINCIPAL APPLICANTS AND DEPENDANTS), 2001	
Country of Origin	**Number**	**Country of Origin**	**Number**
United Kingdom	63 291	China	40 296
Italy	31 625	India	27 812
United States	17 514	Pakistan	15 339
Germany	9 263	Philippines	12 903
Portugal	7 930	Korea, Republic of	9 604
France	7 872	United States	5 894
Greece	7 174	Iran	5 736
The Netherlands	3 749	Romania	5 585
Australia	3 329	Sri Lanka	5 514
Switzerland	2 982	United Kingdom	5 345

SOURCE: Manpower and Immigration, *Immigration Statistics, 1966*, Ottawa: Queen's Printer, 1967, p. 5; Citizenship and Immigration Canada, *Facts and Figures 2001*, Ottawa: Minister of Public Works and Government Services Canada, 2002 (Cat. no. MP43-333/2002E), p. 8.

institutions; 21 percent were "indifferent" in their attitudes toward immigration and ambivalent about the contributions that immigrants make; 19 percent were "reactionaries" who felt that the government has lost control over immigration and that immigration was largely negative for Canada. The size of this segment seems to rise when cases of people who appear to be abusing the immigration system come to light. This happened during the summer of 1999 when four boatloads of what appeared to be economic migrants from China were dumped on the Vancouver Island coastline. The remaining 15 percent had no opinion on immigration (Holton and Lanphier, 1994). Holton and Lanphier (1994; see also Zong, 1994) suggest that these findings point to a hardening of Canadian attitudes toward immigration.

The sixth variable, security considerations, has become more important since the terrorist attacks on the United States on September 11, 2001. In the aftermath of the attacks, Canada introduced a new Permanent Resident Card and a number of new measures to increase security of Canadian borders. In addition, Canada and the United States are increasingly discussing the harmonization of immigration policies, particularly in the area of security screening of immigrants and refugees. Some commentators refer to this harmonization as a move towards a "Fortress North America" (Satzewich and Wong, 2002).

THE CONTEMPORARY IMMIGRATION CATEGORIES

There are three main categories of immigrants in Canada: refugees, family class, and independent immigrants. Altogether, there were 250 346 immigrants to Canada in 2001.

Refugees

About 28 000 refugees were admitted to Canada in 2001. There are three categories of refugees that Canada accepts through its immigration program. *Convention refugees* are people who are defined as refugees by the 1951 Geneva Convention Relating to the Status of Refugees and its 1967 protocol. They are people who, by reason of their race, religion, nationality, membership in a particular social group, or political opinion, live outside of their country of nationality or their country of habitual residence, and who are unable or unwilling, because of fear of persecution, to return to their country of origin (Citizenship and Immigration Canada, 1996: 28).

Country of Asylum Class refugees are people who are outside their country of citizenship or residence who are seriously and personally affected by civil war, armed conflict, or massive violations of human rights. Finally, *Source Country Class* refugees include people who would meet the definition of a Convention refugee but who are still in their country of citizenship or residence. This category also includes people who have been detained or imprisoned and are suffering serious deprivations of the right of freedom of expression, the right of dissent, or the right to engage in trade union activity.

Family Class Immigrants

About 67 000 *family class immigrants* arrived in Canada in 2001. Family class immigrants have close family members already living in Canada who are willing and able to support them. A sponsor must be a Canadian citizen or a permanent resident who is over 18 years of age and who is living in Canada. Depending on the specific circumstances, a sponsor must be able to provide for the lodging, care, maintenance, and normal settlement needs of the family member(s) for between three and ten years (Citizenship and Immigration Canada, 2002).

Economic/Independent Immigrants

Economic immigrants numbered about 153 000 in 2001. The federal government has increased the size of this category in total immigration flows, and has decreased the number of family class immigrants, because it believes that the former are of greater economic benefit to Canada. There are four subcategories of independent immigrants. *Skilled workers* are selected by the federal government on the basis of their ability to meet certain minimum work experience requirements, to prove that they have enough funds to support themselves and their family members in Canada, and merit as measured by the **points system**. As Table 10.4 shows, applicants are awarded points for various attributes that the Canadian government deems important in determining an immigrant's economic and settlement prospects. An applicant has to earn a minimum of 75 out of 100 points to "pass" and potentially gain admission to Canada as a skilled worker. The amount of money immigrants need to have when they arrive in Canada

TABLE 10.4   THE POINTS SYSTEM FOR THE SELECTION OF INDEPENDENT IMMIGRANTS, CANADA, 2002

CRITERIA	UNITS OF ASSESSMENT (MAXIMUM)
Education	25 points
Experience	21 points
Age	10 points
Knowledge of French and/or English	24 points
Adaptability	10 points
Arranged employment in Canada	10 points
Pass Mark	**75 points**

SOURCE: Citizenship and Immigration Canada, *Policy and Regulations* (http:www.cic.gc.ca/skilled/qual-5.html, pp. 1–4).

depends on the number of family members they have. For example, an immigrant who brings four family members to Canada needs to have $17 286.

Immigrant entrepreneurs are people who will own and actively manage a business that will contribute to the economy and create jobs. They have to have business experience and a minimum net worth of $300 000. *Immigrant investors* are capitalists who have a personal net worth of at least $800 000 and who plan to invest at least $400 000 in a business in Canada. *Self-employed immigrants* must have the intention and ability to create their own employment. They are expected to contribute to the cultural or artistic life of the country. They can also qualify under this program if they purchase and manage a farm in Canada. In 1999, the net worth of these three categories of immigrants was $4.1 billion (Satzewich and Wong, 2002).

ETHNIC INEQUALITY AND THE CANADIAN LABOUR MARKET

JOHN PORTER AND THE VERTICAL MOSAIC

What happens to immigrants after they come to Canada? How are they sorted and placed in the socioeconomic structure? John Porter's answers to these questions in *The Vertical Mosaic* have had a profound impact on Canadian sociology. Since its publication in 1965, Canadian sociologists have been interested in whether ethnicity and race affect the operation of the labour market, social mobility, and the composition of elites.

Porter argued that Canada is a **vertical mosaic**, a society in which ethnic groups tend to occupy different and unequal positions in the stratification system. He suggested that the first ethnic group to take control of a previously unoccupied or newly conquered territory is the *charter group* of that society. One of the prerogatives that go to a charter group is the ability to decide "what other groups are to be let in and what they will be permitted to do" (Porter, 1965: 62). Canada has two charter groups, the English and the French. Although their power was, and is, unequal, Porter argued that the two charter groups have been able to set the terms by which other immigrants are admitted to Canada. These charter groups reserved for themselves the top positions in the occupational hierarchy. They also made up the upper ranks of the labour, political, bureaucratic, religious, and media elites.

Immigrants who arrived after these charter groups were assigned to less-preferred positions. Non-English and non-French immigrants were assigned an *entrance status* that was linked in part to the social evaluation of their cultural and racial capacities. Groups from northern and western Europe were considered more racially and culturally like the English and French, and were accorded a higher entrance status than southern and eastern European immigrants. The latter were regarded as culturally, if not racially, inferior to the charter groups and were therefore placed in lower levels of the occupational hierarchy and excluded from elite positions. Non-

Europeans were defined as unassimilable and were virtually barred from entry (Woodsworth, 1972).

Porter argued that once the vertical mosaic was established, it took on a life of its own. Immigrants and their descendants who were initially allocated a subordinate entrance status faced limited prospects for upward social mobility. He thought two factors accounted for the rigidity of the vertical mosaic. One was blatant prejudice and discrimination by charter groups. The other was the retention by ethnic groups of cultural practices that were incompatible with economic success in modern, industrialized societies. In other words, certain immigrants and their descendants were caught in an *ethnic mobility trap* because of their continued identification with a subordinated and marginalized ethnic group (Wiley, 1967).

Taken in the context of its time, Porter's analysis was both powerful and insightful. As we have seen, before 1962, the selection of new immigrants was based on ethnic and racial stereotypes. These stereotypes also shaped charter group perceptions of what kinds of jobs other immigrants were fit to do. In the 1950s, for example, Italian immigrant men were regarded by immigration

bureaucrats and members of the economic elite as culturally willing and able to "tolerate irregular employment, low wages and physically demanding work." They were recruited specifically for work in agriculture, mining, domestic service, the metal trades, and logging (Iacovetta, 1992: 28). Black women from the Caribbean, on the other hand, were recruited specifically as housekeepers and nannies for middle-class families in the 1950s and 1960s, in part because they were believed to be nurturing and passive (Daenzer, 1993).

THE DECLINING SIGNIFICANCE OF THE VERTICAL MOSAIC

Does the vertical mosaic still exist? Is the distribution of economic rewards still based on ethnicity? Over the past two decades, debates have raged among Canadian sociologists about whether race and ethnicity continue to shape our stratification system (Brym with Fox, 1989). Gordon Darroch (1979) and Edward Herberg (1990) argue that the vertical mosaic is no longer a useful way of describing our society. Later in his life, John Porter also had doubts

The storefront of a downtown Toronto drugstore reflects the ethnic diversity of most large Canadian cities.
SOURCE: Dick Hemingway.

about its continued existence (Pineo and Porter, 1985). Others argue that, while we may be moving in the direction of greater equality, the vertical mosaic is still a useful metaphor to describe our society. They suggest that the vertical mosaic has been recast along racial lines (Fleras and Elliot, 1996).

There are three main empirical findings that are relevant to the debate about the vertical mosaic in present-day Canada. First, Canadian society is much more open than it once was in terms of the social evaluation of European immigrants and their descendants. The European groups that Porter identified in the mid-1960s as occupying subordinate entrance statuses—particularly Ukrainians, Poles, and Italians—have been able to move up the socioeconomic hierarchy (Hou and Balakrishnan, 1996). This mobility has occurred both within and between generations—that is, it has been both intra- and inter-generational. Long-settled European immigrants and their descendants have attained income and occupation levels that are comparable to those of the charter groups. They have also begun to occupy positions in various elites. For example, it is now common for members of these communities to be elected to federal and provincial legislatures (Iacovetta, 1992).

Second, the earnings and occupational distributions of visible-minority men and women who are born in Canada are, broadly speaking, comparable to those of the charter groups and of other Europeans. Boyd (1992) and Reitz and Breton (1994) demonstrate this by statistically controlling for variations in earning due to factors such as occupation, age, language abilities, years of experience, education, and number of weeks worked per year (see also Geschwender, 1994). Using these methods, they show that, on average, Canadian-born visible-minority women tend to earn about the same, or more, income as non–visible-minority women in Canada (Li, 2000).

On the other hand, there seems to be more inequality between Canadian-born visible-minority and non–visible-minority men. In cities of less than 500 000 people, men earn about the same, but in cities larger than 500 000 visible-minority men tend to earn about 85 percent of what non–visible-minority men earn (see Table 10.5).

Third, the pattern of gender visible-minority differences in earnings is even more evident where immigrants are concerned. That is, the vertical mosaic exists in modified form for male immigrants.

Although immigrants from Europe have been able to make their way up the occupational and income hierarchies, more recent male visible-minority immigrants have been less successful. Despite having education levels that are, on average, higher than the Canadian population as a whole (Lian and Matthews, 1995), visible-minority male immigrants earn less than both European immigrants and those who were born in Canada (Boyd, 1992). According to Table 10.5, with the exception of immigrants who do not live in large cities, when differences in earnings due to a number of other background variables are controlled for, visible-minority male immigrants earn between 62 and 75 percent of what their non–visible-minority Canadian-born counterparts earn; non–visible-minority immigrant men, on the other hand, do better than their visible-minority counterparts, but still do not match Canadian-born men; their earnings are between 82 and 89 percent of those for Canadian-born non–visible-minority men. In all locations, visible-minority female immigrants earn more than non–visible-minority immigrant women.

There is, therefore, not a single, clear-cut pattern of ethnic or racial economic disadvantage in Canada. Studies suggest that, in certain circumstances, ethnic attachments may be a resource that groups of people use to get ahead. Professionals in law, business, and medicine may achieve levels of upward mobility and economic security by offering services in their mother tongue and in ways that are sensitive to the culture of their ethnic group (Brym with Fox, 1989).

But ethnicity is not an advantage for all. There are two interrelated explanations for the lower earnings of visible-minority male immigrants. First, the education credentials of visible-minority immigrants are devalued in the labour market and by certification authorities. In one celebrated case, an evaluation officer of the Ontario Ministry of Education wrote to a Jamaican immigrant that his honours degree from Harvard University and his Ph.D. from Stanford were equivalent to "at least Grade Thirteen in the Ontario school system" (Special Committee on the Participation of Visible Minorities in Canadian Society, 1984). Although this may have been a bureaucratic error, there is evidence showing that many immigrant teachers, doctors, nurses, and engineers find that their non-Western university degrees and diplomas are of little value in Canada (Henry et al., 2000; Basran and Zong, 1998).

TABLE 10.5   NET EARNINGS OF IMMIGRANTS AND NATIVE-BORN CANADIANS AS PERCENT OF EARNINGS FOR NATIVE-BORN, NON–VISIBLE-MINORITY MEN FOR FOUR CMA LEVELS, 1996

		NET EARNINGS, AFTER ADJUSTING FOR INDIVIDUAL AND MARKET CHARACTERISTICS*	
Not CMA		**Native-Born Canadian**	**Immigrant**
Non–visible minority	Male	$31 657	88%
	Female	75%	56%
Not CMA			
Visible minority	Male	99%	89%
	Female	85%	66%
Small CMA (<500 000)			
Non–visible minority	Male	$32 565	89%
	Female	71%	52%
Visible minority	Male	96%	75%
	Female	77%	56%
Medium CMA (500 000–999 999)			
Non–visible minority	Male	$31 657	88%
	Female	72%	50%
Visible minority	Male	84%	64%
	Female	79%	53%
Large CMA (1 000 000+)			
Non–visible minority	Male	$31 913	82%
	Female	72%	51%
Visible minority	Male	85%	62%
	Female	75%	51%

*Net earnings are adjusted earnings after differences in individual characteristics and differences in market characteristics have been taken into account. Individual characteristics include industry of work, occupation, full-time or part-time work, years of schooling, years of work experience, experience squared, number of weeks worked, official languages ability, and number of years since immigrated to Canada for immigrants (native-born = 0); market characteristics include the level of unemployment in the person's region of residence, and the size of immigrants' population as a percent of the region's total population.

SOURCE: Peter Li, 2000. "Earning Disparities Between Immigrants and Native-Born Canadians," *Canadian Review of Sociology and Anthropology, 37*(3): 303.

Second, research on employers' hiring practices has documented the influence of racial discrimination in employment. Henry and Ginsberg (1985) organized a study in Toronto where they sent two actors with virtually identical résumés to apply for various jobs. The only difference between the two was the colour of their skin and/or their accent: One group consisted of actors who were white and who had Anglo-Canadian accents, and the other group of actors were members of visible minorities, some of whom had other accents. The study found that, in both face-to-face interviews and approaches over the telephone, whites received three job offers for every job offered to visible-minority applicants. Visible-minority applicants were five times more likely to be told that the job had been filled when a subsequent white applicant was invited for an interview (Henry and Ginsberg, 1985).

A follow-up study conducted in 1989 showed there was no racial discrimination in job offers following face-to-face contacts between applicants and employers. Blacks and whites received equal numbers of job offers. When it came to approaches over the telephone, however, callers with foreign accents were less likely to be invited for an interview, and more likely to be told that the job was filled when in fact it was not, than callers with North American accents (Henry, 1989).

SUMMARY

1. Ethnic categories and identities are not fixed and unchanging; they evolve socially and historically. Canadians may now be considered an ethnic group, as they display a strong desire to define their ethnicity as "Canadian."

2. Racism refers to certain kinds of ideas and to certain kinds of institutional practices. Institutional racism refers to circumstances where social institutions operate, or once operated, on the basis of racist ideas. There are three forms of institutional racism.

3. Racism, prejudice, and discrimination have been analyzed from different sociological perspectives. Social-psychological theories, primordialism, normative theories, and power-conflict theories each offer different interpretations of ethnic and racial hostility.

4. The term "Aboriginal people" includes people who are defined in the Constitution as "Indian," "Métis," and "Inuit." The terms used to describe Aboriginal people are socially negotiated and change because of shifts in power relations among groups.

5. The culture of poverty thesis was used in the 1970s as a way of explaining the poor socioeconomic conditions of Aboriginal people. Problems with the culture of poverty thesis led to the development of the internal colonial model, a variant of conflict theory. Conflict and feminist sociologists are beginning to be more interested in class and gender diversity within the Aboriginal population.

6. French–English relations in Canada are about power relations. Material inequalities between French and English in Quebec provided the historical basis for the emergence of nationalism in Quebec. The contemporary nationalist movement has a diverse class base.

7. There are debates in the nationalist movement about who is Québécois. Tensions exist between ethnic and civic nationalists. Minorities in Quebec fear that they will not be included in the definition of a sovereign Quebec nation.

8. Immigration has played different roles in Canadian history. During the nineteenth century, immigrants contributed to capitalist state formation. Now, immigrants contribute to the social and economic reproduction of Canadian society.

9. There are six main variables that have shaped immigrant selection in Canada: social class, ethnic and racial stereotypes, geopolitical considerations, humanitarianism, public opinion, and security considerations. Immigrants are categorized as refugees, family class, or independents. Independent immigrants are selected on the basis of the points system.

10. John Porter argued that Canada was a vertical mosaic, a social structure where ethnic groups occupy different, and unequal, positions within the stratification system. Evidence suggests that the vertical mosaic is declining in importance, at least for European immigrants and people born in Canada. Discrimination against visible-minority immigrants is still a problem.

QUESTIONS TO CONSIDER

1. What are the strengths and weaknesses of different sociological approaches to the study of the social significance of race and ethnicity?

2. To what extent do racist attitudes and behaviour affect the life-chances of people in Canada?

3. How do you think the nationalist movement in Quebec will resolve the question of who is part of the imagined community of the nation?

4. Do you think that the importance of class and gender diversity within Aboriginal communities will increase or decrease in the future?

5. Are Canadians an ethnic group? Why or why not?

GLOSSARY

Civic nationalism is a form of nationalism where the social boundaries of the nation are defined in territorial and geographic terms.

The **culture of poverty thesis** is the theory that some ethnic groups do not readily assimilate, and hence are poor, because their culture does not value economic success, hard work, and achievement.

Discrimination refers to practices that deny members of particular groups equal access to societal rewards.

Ethnocentrism is the tendency to judge other cultures by the standards of one's own.

Institutional racism refers to discriminatory racial practices built into such prominent structures as the political, economic, and education systems.

New racism is a theory of human nature that suggests that it is natural for groups to form bounded communities. One group is neither better nor worse than another, but feelings of antagonism will be aroused if outsiders are admitted.

The **points system** is a system used by the Canadian government to select independent immigrants. Applicants are awarded "points" for various attributes that the Canadian government deems important in determining an immigrant's economic contribution to Canada.

Prejudice is an unfavourable, generalized, and rigid belief applied to all members of a group.

The **primordialist thesis** is the theory that ethnic attachments reflect a basic tendency of people to seek out, and associate with, their "own kind."

The **Quiet Revolution** refers to the social, political, and cultural changes that occurred in Quebec in the 1960s, due in part to the emergence of a francophone middle class.

Race is a socially constructed label that has been used to describe certain kinds of physical and genetic differences between people.

The **split labour-market theory** is the theory that racial and ethnic conflict are rooted in differences in the price of labour.

Stereotypes are exaggerated, oversimplified images of the characteristics of social categories.

The **vertical mosaic** is a social structure where ethnic groups occupy different, and unequal, positions within the stratification system.

SUGGESTED READING

Frideres, James, and René Gadacz. (2001). *Aboriginal People in Canada: Contemporary Conflicts*. Toronto: Prentice-Hall. A thorough overview of Aboriginal–non-Aboriginal relations in Canada.

Isajiw, Wsevolod. (1999). *Understanding Diversity: Ethnicity and Race in the Canadian Context*. Toronto: Thompson Educational Publishing. An outstanding introduction to the field of ethnic and racial relations in Canada.

Miles, Robert. (1989). *Racism*. London: Routledge. One of the best theoretical discussions of the meaning of race and racism in modern Western societies. Miles argues strongly for a social constructionist approach to race and racism.

Reitz, Jeffrey, and Raymond Breton. (1994). *The Illusion of Difference: Realities of Ethnicity in Canada and the United States*. Toronto: C.D. Howe Institute. A good discussion of how Canada compares with the United States in terms of how cultural minorities fit into the two societies. Reitz and Breton show that there are fewer differences between the two countries than Canadians often think.

Satzewich, Vic. (1998). *Racism and Social Inequality in Canada: Concepts, Controversies and Strategies of Resistance*. Toronto: Thompson Educational Publishing. This text discusses the continuing significance of racism in Canada.

CHAPTER ELEVEN

INEQUALITY AMONG NATIONS: PERSPECTIVES ON DEVELOPMENT

In this chapter you will learn that:

- Transnational corporations are prepared to shift the site of work in order to maximize profits; this has massive implications for peoples' employment and well-being.

- Two hundred and fifty years ago there were only small gaps in living standards and levels of productivity between countries; now the gaps are huge.

- The poor countries today are mainly those that were colonized by the West.

- Liberal development theory argues that if markets are allowed to function without state interference, prosperity follows; but although liberal theory has been adopted by the U.S., the International Monetary Fund, and transnational corporations, it has not led to policies that improve the well-being of most Third World citizens.

- Dependency theory suggests that underdevelopment results from foreign economic and political control. The spectacular development breakthroughs of Japan, South Korea, and Sweden illustrate that domestic control of corporations and activist governments can be the keys to economic success.

- More democratic and egalitarian development policies, such as those of the Indian state of Kerala, will benefit all countries.

GORDON LAXER

UNIVERSITY OF ALBERTA

INTRODUCTION

In the Philippines, young women sleep in bunks, stacked in fives, in the semiconductor factories where they work. They labour most of their waking hours and sleep in shifts. Two bathrooms serve 150 people. The Philippines is hot, yet the young women have no air conditioning, which is reserved for the upkeep of the machines (Angeles, 1993).

The **globalization** of production has brought working conditions like this to many areas in the Southern hemisphere. In the Philippines they are called **export-processing zones (EPZs)**, in Mexico *Maquiladoras*. These zones are set up for **transnational corporations**, corporations that have subsidiaries in more than one country. Transnational corporations are owned and controlled in the North to exploit cheap Southern labour. Young women are recruited from villages because they are considered "obedient and disciplined workers, willing to do tedious, high-precision work and to submit themselves to working conditions that would not be tolerated in highly developed countries" (Sassen, 1998: 42–43). In a few years, the young women typically suffer from headaches, deteriorating eyesight, and often reproductive problems. They are used up, and replaced by younger, healthier, and more compliant women. A steady stream of new recruits is created by the destitution of tenant farm families, forced off the land by policies known as the "Washington consensus" and promoted by the United States, the **International Monetary Fund (IMF),** and the **World Bank**.

Alan Greenspan, chair of the U.S. Federal Reserve (the U.S. central bank), observes that the Western form of capitalism is now the consensus model of how each country should run its economy (Wade, 1999: 4). Lawrence Summers, President of Harvard University and former U.S. Secretary of the Treasury, argues that "our ideology, capitalism, is in ascendance everywhere" (1996: 3). "Globalist economic policy ... is the forward defense of America's deepest security interest." Anyone critical of the "Washington consensus" is a "separatist," he contends (1996: 3).

Reactions to the tragedy of the September 11, 2001, attacks on the World Trade Center and the Pentagon have made the principles underlying Summers's comments into a new doctrine. This doc-

trine, the Bush doctrine, moves the United States, some critics argue, towards formal **colonialism** from its previous informal colonialism. On September 20, 2002, *The National Security Strategy* (U.S., 2002) declared that the United States has the right to make "pre-emptive strikes" not only against countries that pose an immediate risk, but also against any country that poses a potential risk. Amongst the United States' "non-negotiable demands" is that all other countries must have "respect for private property"— in other words, for U.S. transnational corporations abroad. Critics ask whether the doctrine of pre-emptive war sweeps away diplomacy and the self-determination and sovereignty rights of other countries.

The globalist Washington consensus mandates every country to remove domestic control over their own economies by adopting neoliberal policies. Under neoliberalism, they must dismantle controls over foreign ownership, investment, and exchange; privatize public enterprises (Crown corporations); deregulate businesses (e.g., electrical power); and cut public expenditures (e.g., on health care and education). They must also reduce corporate taxes, balance budgets, and set currencies (e.g., the Canadian dollar) at low levels to encourage exports (Williamson, 1994: 18).

The Washington consensus is the American model. It challenges democratic assumptions about the sovereignty of countries and citizens. Under globalism, states are oriented more to the rights of transnational corporations than to the demands of voters, and are locked into neoliberal principles by **structural adjustment programs (SAPs)** in the "South" (i.e., the poor countries) and international agreements (e.g., NAFTA) and international institutions (e.g., the World Trade Organization) in the "North" (i.e., the rich countries).

If the Washington model leads to working conditions such as those experienced by young Filipino women, is the spread of this model a stepping-stone to economic advancement in the South? Or is it a new way for northern corporations to exploit the South? To answer these questions we explore competing perspectives on why there are rich and poor countries and what can be done to enable everyone to fully develop his or her unique capacities. This exploration may seem oriented toward economics. But sociology's founders such as Karl Marx and Max Weber showed that social, political, and cultural issues must be understood in relation to economics.

SOURCE: Ajit Ninan/India. Reprinted with permission from IPS—Inter Press Service.

WHY ARE THERE RICH AND POOR COUNTRIES?

Why are some countries rich and others poor? Will the global reach of transnational corporations equalize countries or accentuate disparities in economic, social, and political development? If development were spread more evenly to the global South, would the benefits reach everyone?

The experts do not agree on these and other questions. Opinion is divided among four perspectives, which we examine in detail. To begin, we group the major perspectives into two broad approaches: "Western-centric" and "anti-imperialist." Each contains valuable insights, but each ignores important factors. Their assumptions are presented in simplified form.

The Washington consensus is a version of Western-centric approaches and is dominant in Canada and other advanced capitalist countries. We hear it so often that we unconsciously absorb it as objective. It goes like this: *Most countries in the world are poor because Western capitalist institutions and values have not penetrated them deeply enough.* Poor countries will better themselves if they become like "us"—by adopting Western values like capitalism, political democracy, adequate schooling, secularism and science, honesty, and a strong work ethic. Countries that

follow our ancestors' path will soon become as affluent as us. Poor countries failed to become rich because of ignorance, laziness, and corrupt elites, who deny the people "civilization's" benefits. Western-centric perspectives may ease the consciences of affluent Westerners disturbed by Third World hunger, in contrast to our own waste and riches. But we need not feel guilt if we can say those people are poor because it's their fault they are poor.

Anti-imperialist perspectives are mirror images of Western-centric ones. Proponents argue that *most countries are poor because Western capitalism and imperialism have penetrated them too deeply.* Rich countries are rich because they have exploited poor countries. Poor countries cannot follow the neoliberal capitalist path trodden earlier by rich countries because many obstacles now block that path—for one, the entrenched position of the 300 largest transnationals, 97 percent of which are controlled in the North (Dunning, 1993: 15, 17). The world's 63 000 transnational corporations drive foreign ownership and account for about two-thirds of all world trade (UNCTAD, 2001). Their right to enter countries and be treated as "citizens" is backed by rich countries' power. Thus, according to anti-imperialist proponents, power differentials and the persistent advantages of being ahead explain the vast economic disparities among countries.

Rich countries and dominant corporations have an interest, the argument continues, to keep poor countries **underdeveloped** so they will remain sources of cheap labour and resources. Elites in rich countries fear that real democracy and independence in the Third World would be in the interests of most citizens there. By allying with large landholders and military leaders, Western powers maintain exploitation and underdevelopment. Adherents of anti-imperialist approaches blame underdevelopment on external forces and internal **comprador elites**, who would lose power without external support. In their view, poor countries can develop only by weakening ties to rich countries, abandoning capitalism, and developing their own economic, political, and cultural resources.

Although anti-imperialist perspectives have greater merit than Western-centric ones, they are overly deterministic. They cannot explain how South Korea, Taiwan, and Hong Kong broke out of Third World status, for example.

persuade underdeveloped countries to follow liberal principles (see Box 11.1).

Third World Debt[4]

Third World countries receive liberal doctrine not as textbook ideas, but as policies they must follow to resolve balance-of-payments and debt crises. Many developing countries, especially in Africa and Latin America, faced such problems in the 1980s and 1990s. In most cases, the debts were incurred by local corrupt officials, military dictators, and wealthy businessmen. This raises several questions: Should citizens be held responsible for debts incurred by undemocratic elites? Did the national economy and most citizens benefit from the loans? Have the structural adjustment programs (SAPs) imposed by dominant countries and agencies helped resolve these crises?

In the period 1970–82, two major oil price hikes, the internationalization of banking, and slower growth in the rich North led to much lending to the

---

BOX 11.1   WORLD BANK FIRES ITS CHIEF

In 1999 the World Bank fired Joseph Stiglitz, the Bank's chief economist. The cause? He expressed doubts about World Bank and IMF neoliberal policies. The World Bank and the IMF, though separate institutions, are linked by "triggers." For example, taking a World Bank loan to build a school "triggers" a requirement to accept every conditionality—on average 111 per nation—laid down by both the World Bank and the IMF. IMF loans often depend on a package of policies, which used to be called Structural Adjustment Programs (SAPs), recently renamed "Poverty Reduction Programs." The substance is the same. Loans and assistance packages to countries in economic trouble are, says the World Bank, designed after careful in-country investigation. Joseph Stiglitz disagrees. The "investigation" consists of close inspection of a country's five-star hotels, he says. Stiglitz told investigative journalist Greg Palast that World Bank officials analyze each country's economy, and then hand every country's government the exact same four-step program.

- *Step One: Privatization.* Stiglitz says the more accurate name for this step is "briberization." State-owned enterprises and industries are sold to private interests. National leaders, he said, happily flogged their electricity and water companies. "You could see their eyes widen" at the prospect of 10% commissions paid to Swiss bank accounts for simply shaving a few billion off the sale price of national assets.
- *Step Two: Capital Market Liberalization.* In theory, deregulation of financial markets allows capital to flow in and out. Unfortunately, often the money just flows out, leading Stiglitz to call this the "hot money" cycle. "The result was predictable," for example, financial crises in Asia and Latin America in the 1990s.
- *Step Three: Market-Based Pricing.* This means removal of subsidies on basics such as food, cooking gas and water. Predictably this leads to the next step.
- *Step Three-and-a-Half: "The IMF Riot."* Elimination of subsidies on basic needs particularly hits the poor hard. In 1998 riots exploded in Indonesia over the elimination of food and fuel subsidies; Bolivians took to the streets in 2002 over increased water prices; and, in February 2003, the rise in cooking gas prices in Ecuador—imposed by the World Bank—led to widespread demonstrations, met by bullets, tanks and teargas. It's part of the plan: World Bank documents predict that their plans will cause "social unrest."
- *Step Four: Free Trade.* Countries must remove their tariffs and any other barriers to trade and the entry of foreign corporations and play by the rules of the World Trade Organization. Stiglitz is particularly concerned about the WTO's intellectual property rights treaty (TRIPS). Intellectual property rights, says Stiglitz, "condemns people to death" by imposing tariffs and tributes to pay to pharmaceutical companies for branded medicines. "They don't care if people live or die."

The World Bank and IMF's policies are driven by an absolutist ideology, designed in secret and not open to discussion or dissent. That, says the World Bank's former chief economist, is the greatest concern.

SOURCE: Based on Palast, Greg. 2002. "The Globalizer Who Came in from the Cold: The IMF's Four Steps to Economic Damnation." In: *The Best Democracy Money Can Buy,* pp. 50–54. London: Pluto Press.

South. By borrowing from Northern banks, poor countries bought more imports. For their part, banks acted out of self-interest in making loans. US$15 billion per year flowed into Latin America alone between 1978 and 1981 (Pastor and Dymski, 1991: 203). The lending boom ended when world oil prices fell in 1982 and Mexico, a major oil-exporter, declared it could no longer pay debt charges.

After Mexico's debt crisis, little new foreign capital came to Latin America or other Third World states. Indeed, for the rest of the 1980s, the flow of capital reversed direction. Under a deal brokered by the U.S., the IMF, the World Bank, and private bankers, much capital, in the form of debt charges, flowed from poor to rich countries. In 1999, Latin American and Caribbean countries spent 8.1 percent of GDP (US$158 billion) on debt servicing to repay debts that were made especially onerous by very high interest rates (United Nations, 2001a). To export capital on this scale, most Latin American countries had to cut imports and, hence, living standards. They also had to raise exports to earn enough to repay debts. Diversifying their economies had to be postponed.

The debt crisis led the IMF and World Bank to impose SAPs on indebted countries. Liberal doctrine assumed that debt resulted from the "excessive demand" of living beyond their means, importing too much, and exporting too little. This created imbalances in **international transactions**, they argued. The IMF's solution was simple: follow liberal principles and the difficulties will self-correct under the guidance of Adam Smith's "invisible hand." These programs were designed to maximize payments to Northern banks and prevent their financial collapse. They had nothing to do with development concerns.

According to the United Nations Conference on Trade and Development (UNCTAD) and the United Nations Economic Commission for Africa (ECA), the SAPs have not worked. The ECA found that, under SAPs in the 1980s in 15 sub-Saharan countries, the following occurred: on average, consumption per capita dropped, investment fell, economic growth slowed, and deficits rose. The only bright sign—**current**-**account** deficits fell a little (Ecumenical Coalition for Economic Justice, 1990: 14).

The United Nations International Children's Emergency Fund (UNICEF) estimated in a 1989 report, that "at least half a million young children have died in the last twelve months as a result of the slowing down or the reversal of progress in the developing world." UNICEF blamed the unfair debt burden. "It is hardly too brutal an oversimplification to say that the rich got the loans and the poor got the debts" (cited in Adams, 1991: 160).

Why did SAPs fail? World markets do not work according to textbook formulas. Real markets are dominated by a few giant companies that use monopoly positions to capture excess profits. Currency devaluations in developing countries make exports cheaper and imports more costly. Theoretically, this should lead to more exports, fewer imports, and more buying of local goods and services. In practice, however, devaluation did little to raise exports; although devaluation lowered the prices at which giant foreign corporations bought their resources, it did not often lead to greater purchases. Demand is finite. Suppliers are many. Thus, devaluation often led to the opposite of market expectations—fewer U.S. dollars earned for the same export levels.

Controlled by dominant capitalist countries, the IMF and World Bank determine the policies of Third World governments. Instead of allowing governments to develop their own repayment policies, the IMF imposes rigid prescriptions that benefit Northern bankers and local, often corrupt, elites. This approach inhibits democracy by supporting the imposition of unpopular policies by authoritarian governments. Many observers, such as the Institute for African Alternatives, see structural adjustment lending as *Western recolonization* (cited in Ecumenical Coalition for Economic Justice, 1990: 12):

> Under structural adjustment [the IMF and the World Bank] ... manage each country entirely. They have to approve annual national [and] foreign exchange budgets ... approve monetary, trade, and fiscal policies and give clearance certificates before countries can negotiate with other foreign lending agencies.

The effects of SAPs were unevenly distributed. Generally, middle classes lost ground and the poor suffered greatly, sparking hunger riots in Zambia in 1987 (Nelson, 1990: 269), in Venezuela in 1989, and elsewhere. In the 1990s, guerrilla activities rose in Mexico, Colombia, and other Latin American countries, in all cases targeting neoliberalism (see Box 11.2).

In Mexico, liberal policies replaced nationalist economic policies. Income gaps grew. From 1984 to 1995, the richest 10 percent of Mexicans increased their share of national income from 33 to 43 percent, whereas the bottom 40 percent's share fell from 14 to 7 percent. Over four in ten lived on less than US$2 per day, while price levels approached those in the United States

(World Bank, 2000; Castaneda, 1993: 71). Economic and political disasters struck Mexicans in 1994–95. A devaluation crisis and the opening of Mexico's markets because of NAFTA led to plummeting living standards and the Zapatista uprising of dispossessed natives. Meanwhile, 30 leading Mexican businessmen had enough spare cash to contribute US$25 million *each* to attend a fundraising dinner for Mexico's president (Castaneda, 1993: 69). Each contribution was larger than the total expenditure of the British Conservative Party in the 1992 general election.

BOX 11.2 "WASHINGTON CONSENSUS" GIVEN LAST RITES IN LATIN AMERICA

After a decade of promises that capitalism, foreign investment, and free trade would spread prosperity to the people of Latin America, the economies of South America are in trouble again and voters are turning against policy advice from Washington.

The economy of Argentina, once South America's most developed country, fell into shambles in 2001–2002. Two governments fell in 10 days—not in military coups, but as a result of massive public protests. Argentina had been the International Monetary Fund's model student. It did it all in the 1990s: flung open its economy, massively privatized state enterprises, and adopted the American dollar. The result was economic disaster, with more than half the people falling below the poverty line. Tens of thousands of citizens began meeting in neighbourhood assemblies, discussing how to restart local industries and renationalize Argentina's recently privatized assets.

The Washington consensus was declared dead in Rio de Janiero, Brazil, in November 2002 at the World Economic Forum's Latin American business meeting. "I say if it's dead, let's bury it," Juan Manuel Santos, the finance minister of Columbia until 2002, said in an interview. "We are seeing a backlash throughout Latin America against the Washington consensus. Populists who want to return to the past are growing."

According to Henrique de Campos Meirelles, "There is consensus that you can no longer postpone the attack on the social question while waiting for the economy to stabilize." Campos was, until recently, chief executive officer of U.S. banking giant BankBoston.

South American voters began electing left-wing leaders, the critics of Washington consensus policies. The new heads of state advocate addressing the deep problems of poverty, inequality, poor health, and education services. Hugo Chavez was elected and re-elected as president of oil-rich Venezuela on a nationalist platform supporting the poor: land reform, increased education, health and housing spending, and making the rich pay taxes. Chavez survived a Washington-supported coup attempt led by Pedro Carmona, head of Venezuela's Chamber of Commerce, in April 2002 and a two-month long general strike led by upper-income Venezuelans in December 2002 and January 2003.

Luis Ignacio da Silva, affectionately known as "Lula," won a landslide victory in 2002 to become president of Brazil, Latin America's most populous country. Forced by poverty to drop out of school as a teenager, Lula had worked 12-hour shifts in factories. Head of the Workers Party, Lula is Brazil's first working-class president. Before coming to office, he was a leader of the anti-corporate globalization movement and opposed the Washington consensus and the Free Trade Agreement of the Americas. Lula likes to say that the revolution he wants is to guarantee each Brazilian one plate of food a day.

SOURCES: Naomi Klein, "Revolt of the Wronged," *Guardian Weekly*, April 4–10, 2002, p. 11; Kevin G. Hall, "'Consensus' given last rites," *Edmonton Journal*, Nov. 30, 2002, p. A17; Larry Rohter, "Brazil set to get its first working-class president," *Edmonton Journal*, Oct. 10, 2002, p. A17; Julian Borger and Alex Bellos, "US 'gave the nod' to Venezuelan coup," *Guardian Unlimited* (http://www.guardian.co.uk/internaational/story/0,3604,685531.00html).

Critique of Liberalism

Liberalism is an elegant doctrine that appeals to universalism and impartiality and promises equal opportunity for all. Does the record support its claims? Not well. Countries adopting liberal doctrines have entrenched economic elites, whose rise to the top usually owes more to inheritance than merit. By not limiting capital accumulation and by dispossessing the many, liberalism cannot fulfill its promise of equal opportunity.

Liberalism has trouble explaining why today's 20 or so developed countries are virtually the same ones as those of a century ago. Very few countries or cities have gone from Third World to First World status since then. Those that did so—South Korea, Hong Kong, Taiwan, Singapore—did not follow liberal doctrine. Middle Eastern oil-producing countries limited production and drove up oil prices in the 1970s. By using a cartel to distort market mechanisms, these countries made major economic gains. Nor did Britain or the United States, during their early development, follow liberal free trade doctrines—doctrines they now insist other states follow. As we saw earlier in this chapter, Britain's cotton industry grew behind barriers and from looting capital from India. The United States maintained high tariffs from the 1830s, when it started to industrialize, until World War II, when it became the dominant world power.

Liberalism is blind to power inequalities and how they affect equality of opportunity. Its principles are drawn from idealized models of perfect markets. The model of equal buyers and sellers may occur in a farmers' market, but it does not apply to corporate power as ordinary people and even governments deal with the likes of the United Brands Company (formerly United Fruit). United Brands had a reputation for calling in the U.S. Marines or CIA when its monopoly in several Central American countries was challenged (Barnet and Muller, 1974: 57). By embracing the world of economic models and ignoring the real world of vastly unequal power, liberalism justifies the privileges of the already powerful.

THE MODERNIZATION APPROACH

In October 1981, 22 heads of state met at Cancun, Mexico, to discuss North–South development. U.S. President Ronald Reagan advised Third World leaders not to talk about altering power structures in the World Bank or the IMF, or reallocating resources from North to South. Setting aside his text, Reagan gave Third World leaders homespun advice: If you want to develop, copy the example of American pioneers. They were poor, worked hard, saved their money, and believed in private ownership. You can achieve what they did if you *change your attitudes and values and become like Americans*. This was a folksy version of the modernization approach.

By the 1960s, Third World states emerged from European colonialism and adopted economists' liberal prescriptions. However, rosy predictions of growth failed to materialize in most cases.[5] Largely emerging from economics, liberalism explains development by reference to narrow economic factors.

Scholars from other disciplines attempted to rescue liberal explanation and prescriptions by including noneconomic factors. Several prominent sociologists and economic historians developed what came to be called **modernization theory**. They argued that, although liberal institutions were *necessary* for Third World development, they were *not sufficient*. The Third World needed to adopt "modern"—that is, Western—values *before* people would take advantage of capitalism.

Modernization theory has its roots in the evolutionary thinking of Adam Smith in the 1750s. In this view, societies pass through stages, from the most primitive ("hunting and gathering" stage) to the most advanced ("commercial"—that is, capitalist—stage) (Meek, 1976). Even before Darwin's theory of evolution challenged the idea of a predetermined, God-given order, many sociologists accepted Smith's idea that societies inevitably progress to higher stages. Although Marx disagreed fundamentally with these sociologists, he shared their belief that all societies would progress, lose their distinctiveness, and eventually adopt the final, most modern, Western, socioeconomic form (i.e., socialism).

Modernization theorists described sociocultural changes in Western Europe from the 1300s and isolated ones they believed were necessary before capitalism could succeed. As Gerschenkron (1962: 32–33)

put it, "with a slight twist of the pen, all [the] basic traits of a modern economy [were] declared to be 'prerequisites' of industrial development." Third World countries were urged to become Western, more economically differentiated, and more rational. Private property, individual rights, urbanization, universal literacy, modern health care, secularization, bureaucratization, and the shift to nuclear families were considered necessary for progress. So, too, was liberal-democracy: a large unified territory, political participation, elections, an independent mass media, and a merit-based civil service. Culturally, people were encouraged to value choice, objectivity, future-orientation, and achievement over ascription. People had to believe that individual action is effective and reject fatalism. With all these elements present, the stage would be set for the emergence of capital investment, technological knowledge, and an entrepreneurial group willing to calculate and innovate (Gerschenkron, 1962: 32; Goldthorpe, 1984 [1975]: 4–12; Armer and Katsillis, 1992).

Modernization theory was so influential in the 1950s and 1960s that the World Bank told Third World governments that, to qualify for aid, they had to follow modernization prescriptions (Hoogvelt, 1982: 118). In the 1970s, the approach fell into disfavour when it became apparent that a few countries were advancing, while most were not. Economic success was apparently not dependent on modernization.

Critique of Modernization

Modernization theory made advances over classical liberalism. First, it acknowledged that development occurs in cultural, social, and historical contexts and is not automatic. Second, mass education was seen as crucial. Where modernization theory failed was in its ethnocentric, evolutionary assumption that all countries must develop exactly the same way as Western countries. It was naïve and false to explain economic stagnation as a result of failing to become Westernized.

Japan's case discredits modernization theory. Lifetime employment, loyalty to the collective, pronounced status differences, and extended kinship ties—characteristics retained from Japan's precapitalist days—did not fit modernization theorists' vision of necessary development conditions. Clearly, not all the characteristics of Western societies were necessary for the emergence of advanced capitalism.

THE "ECONOMIC BACKWARDNESS" APPROACH

A more sophisticated perspective was developed by Alexander Gerschenkron. A student of Eastern European history, Gerschenkron knew that economically backward countries did not follow in the footsteps of advanced countries. We must recognize, he argued, that "in several important respects, the development of the backward country may, by the very virtue of its backwardness, tend to differ fundamentally from that of an advanced country" (Gerschenkron, 1962: 7). Gerschenkron thought that the experiences of overcoming backwardness in Europe provided lessons for contemporary Third World countries.

According to Gerschenkron, "backward" countries had to discover "substitutions" for British and American liberal markets. The more backward, the more substitutions were necessary. Conservative commercial, English-style banks would not lend money to new, technologically innovative entrepreneurs in mildly backward countries until they proved they could succeed on their own. But they did not have the quantity of capital to start industry to catch up to England, because they could not get credit. It was a "Catch-22" situation. The *industrial investment bank* emerged in Germany and other mildly backward European countries in the 1800s as a major substitution. Such banks developed close relations with local industry. Instead of withholding credit from new industries, investment banks supported (and controlled) them from the beginning. Investment banking helped the then-developing countries in Europe to overcome capital shortages and technological gaps.

In still more backward Eastern and Southern Europe, Gerschenkron argued, the main problem was finding enough workers. This was ironic because these countries had large, semi-idle populations. States intent on creating capitalism faced two questions. Why were people unwilling to become workers? How could they be persuaded or forced to do so?

Gerschenkron accepted Marx's insight that capitalism's innovation was not the creation of markets, which had existed for millennia, but the emergence of wage-earners who had to work for employers who owned the means to create wealth. As long as most people had independent means to make a living by farming, fishing, shopkeeping, or as artisans, why

would they risk working for someone who could fire them at will? The elites' answer was to dispossess them. Remove their property and their ties to the land and now there was a class who, to survive, had to work for a capitalist.

Emancipating peasants from serfdom was, for Gerschenkron, a prerequisite for capitalist industrialization. In backward countries, the state needed to free the peasants, often with the urging of, or direct action by, peasants. To create capitalist inequalities, the state also had to break workers' power, which through guilds, had rules to control the ways work was done. Capitalists did not want those rules to block profits or innovations.

As well, according to Gerschenkron, the state in more backward countries had to fund industrialization. Embryonic banks in the truly backward countries of Europe were too weak. The state became a "substitute" for banks. If Gerschenkron were writing today about Third World debt, he would surely criticize the IMF for reducing the role of activist states in early phases of industrialization.

Gerschenkron observed that, once they broke down traditions and began to develop modern industry and infrastructure across a broad front, backward countries grew faster than had the leading countries in their early development phases. There were advantages to being "backward" countries. They could borrow technologies, capital, and cultural know-how from modern economies.

Applying Gerschenkron's perspective today, we see that the advantages of "following the leader" once breakthrough had been achieved could well explain Japan's rapid economic progress from the 1960s to the 1980s and the extremely rapid growth rates in South Korea, Taiwan, and China in the 1980s and 1990s. It might also help explain Japan's stagnation since 1989, once it had caught up to the U.S. and had to pioneer new technologies, markets, and ways to organize work.

Critique of the "Economic Backwardness" Approach

Gerschenkron's economic "backwardness" perspective had the advantage of emerging from actual history, rather than deductively, from theory or ideology, as in liberal and modernization perspectives. His theory retains the optimism of those perspectives about countries' breaking out of underdevelopment, but rejects their simplistic assumptions of uniform progress.

In the long run, however, Gerschenkron's approach converges with that of liberalism. The institutional arrangements in backward countries that led to "investment banking" and "active states" were substitutions for aspects of the liberal model. Gerschenkron thought that, as these countries developed, the substitutions would gradually recede, and the "crutches" would be discarded. The previously backward economies would then adopt the industrial pioneers' liberalism. Thus, Gerschenkron accepted the liberal, modernist assumptions of progress and convergence, albeit at a later point.

The weakness of Gerschenkron's perspective is that it ignores the power and motivation of the advanced states and leading transnationals to maintain the advantages they already possess, even if this means keeping down the majority of countries. The term *backwardness* implies that the problem is one of leader and laggard, not one of imperialism or unequal power. In contrast, dependency theory places unequal power at the centre of its vision.

DEPENDENCY THEORY

Dependency theory was formulated in the 1940s and 1950s when the Third World failed to meet the expectations of liberals, modernization theorists, and some classical Marxists. Dependency theory was the intellectual response to that failure. Its initial focus was Latin America, which had been free of formal empires since the 1800s, but had yet to experience extensive development. The dependency school had two major sources. The first stream originated from the work of Raúl Prebisch and the United Nations Economic Commission for Latin America (ECLA). A second stream evolved from the work of Paul Baran (1957), an American Marxist who reassessed the classical Marxist proposition that capitalism would spread everywhere, if unevenly. Together, these two streams created the dependency approach, which became influential in the Third World, at the United Nations, and in several academic disciplines during the 1960s and 1970s. Although adherence to the approach declined sharply in the 1980s because it was too deterministic, its rich legacy has been carried on by scholars working within historical-structural approaches and in what some call the "new political economy." Successors to the dependency approach—I count myself among their adherents—criticize some of its assumptions. But most have also been influenced by its research agenda and many of its explanations (Evans, 1987: 321).

ECLA's perspective on development was the opposite of the modernization approach. Instead of assuming that underdeveloped countries are much like what the developed countries had been in an earlier period, ECLA argued that Third World economies were fundamentally different. Because of these structural differences, the liberal assumptions that emerged from the industrial "core" (developed countries) did not apply well to the agrarian "periphery" (underdeveloped countries) (Love, 1980).

ECLA economists analyzed the global conditions that prevailed from 1940 to 1980, and argued that core economies were *homogeneous and diversified*, whereas those in the periphery were *heterogeneous and specialized* (Palma, 1981: 51). "Unequal exchange" between core and periphery led to "unequal development."

The "homogeneity" of the **core countries** referred to the presence of high levels of productivity in all sectors: industry, agriculture, and services. This accounted for the overall high standard of living in these countries. In contrast, peripheral economies showed no such consistency in performance from sector to sector (i.e., they are "heterogeneous"). Their only high-productivity sector was in modern export enclaves, whose products are exported to core countries. These enclaves were dominated by foreign-owned transnationals. **Peripheral countries'** exports consisted almost entirely of raw materials.

Contrary to liberal assumptions, continued Prebisch, modern export enclaves do not benefit peripheral economies. Their effects do not spread to the local economy. The enclaves are tied largely to the core economies. The transnationals purchase their machinery and do their planning, research, and marketing in their core bases. In addition, they process and transform the periphery's resources into finished products in the core (Palma, 1981: 51–52). It might be expected that tax and resource revenues from export enclaves would enable peripheral countries to develop modern education and communications systems. However, revenues are usually very low. For most primary commodities, transnationals have many sources of supply, and demand relief from taxes and resource rents in what are now called "free-trade" or "export-processing zones" (EPZs).[6] If peripheral country A raises taxes, transnationals can usually move to country B.

The major benefit of export enclaves, ECLA argued, comes as jobs for local labour. Wages are usually higher there than elsewhere in the periphery, although they do not rise to core levels because surpluses of workers are continually generated by the country's low-productivity sectors (particularly subsistence-agriculture). Because they lack alternatives, such workers accept extremely low wages. Thus, the "heterogeneity" of productivity in modern and traditional sectors of peripheral economies impedes development and the creation of mass markets for local goods.

Peripheral economies are structurally different from core economies. They are "specialized," not "diversified." Whole countries or regions are dependent on the export of one or two resources, such as coffee, sugar, copper, oil, beef, or wheat. (Canada outside southern Ontario and Quebec is extremely dependent on just a few commodities too.) If there is a world glut of these products, their price falls, sometimes catastrophically. Because the economy is not diversified, it must continue to import most of what it consumes, even when its exports collapse. When that happens, the country no longer earns the revenue with which to import what it needs. In contrast, core economies are diversified, industrial, and monopolistic. If demand declines, their monopoly corporations allow them to cut production and maintain price levels. This cannot usually be done in agriculture, because the thousands of producers lack economic and political coordination. As well, the nature of farming often precludes shutting down output to meet falling demand (Love, 1980: 52). Small farmers usually put in years of work and care before reaping benefits. A coffee bush takes five years to mature, rubber trees and coconut palms eight years, and cocoa fifteen years (Harrison, 1993: 353–54). They cannot reduce production the way transnationals do to maintain world prices. Thus, prices fall for all farmers.

The structural differences between core and periphery, ECLA argued, lead to "unequal exchange," in which the "terms of trade" between the periphery's resources and the core's finished goods worsen. This means that, over time, peripheral countries must export more and more resources to import a given number of finished products, such as cars or computers. Unequal exchange thus stacks the deck against Third World development.

Peripheral countries have to run faster to stay in the same place. If they falter because of falling commodity prices or natural disasters, they have to incur high debts to import necessities. Subsequent debt-servicing charges put them further behind. For most countries in the 1900s, being behind seemed to lack Gerschenkron's "advantages of backwardness."

Can the disadvantages of the periphery be surmounted? Prebisch and ECLA believed they could, calling the means to do so "inwardly-directed development." To overcome having to import so much from the core under worsening terms of trade, peripheral economies must produce domestically as many imported goods as possible. Tariffs must be erected and control wrested from the transnationals. The "import substitution" strategy, or diversification, was followed by many governments in Latin America and elsewhere in the 1960s and 1970s. But by the 1980s and 1990s, it was attacked relentlessly on neoliberal grounds by the United States, transnationals, and agencies responsible for the SAPs. In the end, "free-trade" agreements undermined the approach in Latin America. That is why many consider neoliberalism to be a vehicle for neo-imperialism.

A **Marxist** stream added a rich body of insight to dependency theory. For Marx, capitalist expansionism combines contradictions as the most brutal and dehumanizing economic system ever, with beneficial and inevitable long-run consequences (it establishes socialism's preconditions). Capitalism contains the seeds of its own destruction, wrote Marx. As capitalism replaces less efficient modes of production, such as feudalism, and displaces classes, such as serfs, it creates, in ever-larger numbers, communities of wage-earners who have to sell their labour power as a commodity to enrich capitalists. Marx thought workers would eventually take control on behalf of the propertyless majority (Marx and Engels, 1986 [1848]). Marx also assumed that socialism would come first to advanced capitalist countries.

Confronted by evidence that capitalist development was problematic in the Third World and that communism was more successful there than in advanced countries, Marx's followers changed their minds. Paul Baran (1957) was the Marxist who contributed most to dependency theory.

Baran (1957: 12) argued that, despite the fine talk,

> economic development in underdeveloped countries is profoundly inimical to the dominant interests in the advanced capitalist countries. Supplying many important raw materials ... providing their corporations with vast profits ... the backward world has always represented the indispensable hinterland of the highly developed capitalist West.

Major capitalist powers oppose industrialization in Third World countries, especially those where governments oppose the domination of foreign transnationals, argued Baran.

In Baran's view, the state and corporations of advanced countries form alliances with traditional, precapitalist elites in the underdeveloped countries. Called the "oligarchy" (rule by the few), Third World elites of wealthy landowners, army officers, corrupt state officials and their allies oppose capitalism's spread in their countries because their power and wealth are based on precapitalist modes of exploitation and domination. Much of these countries' surpluses is squandered on luxuries for the oligarchy or is expropriated by foreign capital. Thus, it is in the economic interests of external (Western) and internal (domestic) elites to keep Third World countries underdeveloped (Palma, 1981: 43). The only way out of this trap is to break close ties with the capitalist West. In the 1960s and 1970s, Fernando Cardoso and Enzo Faletto (1979) did influential historical case studies in the dependency tradition. They criticized overly structural and deterministic versions of dependency theory and believed that development could occur despite dependency. (Cardoso served as President of Brazil from 1994 to 2002.)

Many historical cases substantiate dependency theory. Since 1945, the U.S. consistently supported Third World dictatorships based on traditional oligarchies and opposed governments democratically elected to take control of their own economies by nationalizing U.S.-based transnationals (Herman and Chomsky, 1988). An example was the 1973 overthrow of the democratically elected socialist government of Salvador Allende in Chile. General Pinochet's military dictatorship was aided by the United States and U.S. corporations such as ITT. Testifying before Congress, CIA director William Colby said the coup in Chile was a "prototype or laboratory experiment to test the techniques of heavy financial investment in an effort to discredit and bring down a government" (O'Brien, 1976: 229). U.S. Senate testimony showed a connection between ITT and the CIA in plotting against Allende. John McCone, an ex-director of the CIA, was a director of ITT when it attempted to stop Allende's election (Sampson, 1973: 259).

Chile became the first country in the world to experiment with "free-market" neoliberalism. The U.S.-inspired dictatorship hired the "Chicago boys" (Chicago-trained, Chilean right-wing economists) to deregulate and privatize the economy, five years before Margaret Thatcher, prime minister of Britain, and Ronald Reagan, president of the United States, implemented similar changes that favoured the rich and hurt the poor. Thus, neoliberalism began in a brutal Third World dictatorship backed by the U.S. to replace a democratically elected government.

Critique of Dependency Theory

Dependency theory was a great advance over the ahistorical liberal and modernization approaches. Unfortunately, its pessimism about development prospects for the Third World in the 1900s was largely confirmed. Only a few countries, most with relatively small populations, have gone from Third to First World status. Development has been hampered by structural differences in Third World economies in which huge populations are involved in traditional sectors. These conditions keep down wages, hinder the creation of mass markets, and remove much of the incentive for technological advance. Authoritarian regimes are all too frequently erected by landed elites and tiny classes of the superrich, who can hold power against the demands of the masses only by armed force in alliance with the IMF, transnationals, and the United States.

The dependency approach holds many insights, but, like the liberal and modernization approaches, it was too rigidly drawn by some of its leading theorists. Just as it is too simple to argue that nothing prevents any Third World country from developing like the United States or Japan, it is also too simple to argue that Third World countries can never develop under capitalism. A few have done so.

Furthermore, the Third World is becoming more differentiated. On the one hand, there are declining economies that rely on exporting primary products or low-wage mass-production. Most are in Latin America and Africa. On the other hand, there are the developing economies that are branching into "new products," including automatic data-processing equipment, parts, and accessories, telecommunications equipment and parts, semiconductor devices, and electronic microcircuits. Of the 30 top high-tech exporters, 11 are in developing countries, including Korea, Malaysia, and Mexico (United Nations, 2001a: 42).

The worst of the dependency literature simply turned the simplistic liberal and modernization propositions on their heads. There was too much theory and not enough history. Although not true of the best dependency theorists, it was true of so many that the approach became partially discredited (Evans, 1985; Seers, 1981).

We now turn away from overly deterministic theories to actual cases where countries succeeded in transforming themselves from poor to rich countries.

DIVERGENCE IN THE THIRD WORLD

The Third World is becoming more differentiated. Hoogvelt (1997) has identified four groupings, as discussed below.

AFRICA: EXCLUSION

As we saw above, the 1980s debt crisis led to SAPs imposed by the IMF and World Bank. African conditions worsened. Per capita incomes declined by 30 percent in the 1980s and kept falling in the 1990s. But the SAPs worked wonders for rich Northern lenders by more effectively extracting African economic surpluses (Hoogvelt, 1997: 163, 170). Worsening economies accentuated existing social cohesion problems in countries of great tribal diversity and borders that made sense only to the Western empires that created them. With 10 percent of the world's people, Africa had 90 percent of the world's wars in the 1990s (see Figure 11.2).

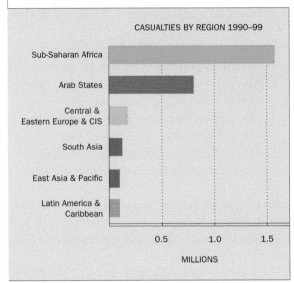

FIGURE 11.2 THE POOREST HAVE SUFFERED THE MOST FROM CONFLICT

SOURCE: From *Human Development Report 2002* by United Nations Development Programme. Copyright © United Nations Development Programme, 2002. Used by permission of Oxford University Press, Inc.

ISLAMIC IDENTITY AND ANTIDEVELOPMENTALIST REVOLT

Twenty-eight countries with a total population of 836 million (almost one-sixth of humanity) have Muslim majorities. They are characterized by dependent incorporation into global capitalism and static development. Attempts to unify oil-rich Arab states with resource-poor ones failed. Everywhere the state became chiefly responsible for extracting surpluses from workers. This led to corrupt state–business relations and lack of democracy (Hoogvelt, 1997: 182–200).

EAST ASIA: DEVELOPMENTAL STATES

Singapore, Hong Kong, South Korea, and Taiwan (known the four "Tigers") have had the world's highest growth rates since 1960. Per capita incomes in Hong Kong and Singapore reached rich country levels. Taiwan and South Korea are nearly there. South Korea was caught in the severe "Asian financial crisis" in 1997–98, but the other three Tigers escaped major damage.

Why did the Tigers grow while most Third World countries failed? Some attribute the Tigers' success to "Confucian" cultures of ethical–moral legitimation, obedience, meritocracy, and harmony. But the more compelling explanation is that these states followed variants of Japan's model of state capitalism, export-led growth, and domestic economic control. To stop the spread of communism beyond China after 1949, the United States poured billions into South Korea and Taiwan to showcase the superiority of capitalism. Hong Kong found a niche as Communist China's gateway for exchanges with the capitalist world. Singapore profited from supplying

oil and repairing American forces' ships during the Vietnam War. Because of their strategic and propaganda value, the Americans tolerated deviance from the liberal model in these cases, whereas they squelched deviance in other Third World countries. But after the Cold War was won, the U.S. and Washington-based institutions insisted on neoliberalism (Bello, 2002: 44–50).

Several Southeast Asian countries tried to copy the four Tigers. None has yet succeeded (see Figure 11.3). Rather than follow the state-centred,

FIGURE 11.3 GLOBAL DISPARITIES IN INCOME: ARE REGIONS CLOSING THE GAP?

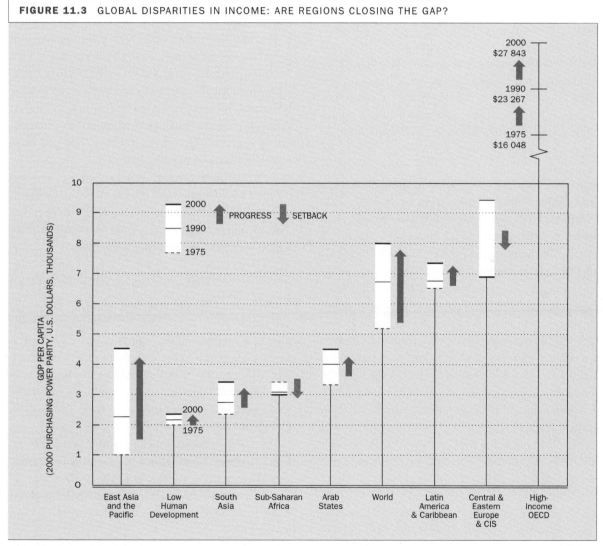

SOURCE: From *Human Development Report 2002* by United Nations Development Programme. Copyright © United Nations Development Programme, 2002. Used by permission of Oxford University Press, Inc.

domestic ownership model of the four Tigers, Indonesia and Thailand invited in foreign transnationals and adopted the Washington model's financial liberalization. Huge foreign capital inflows led to feverish growth in the mid-1990s, only to be followed by even more rapid capital flight when their currencies were about to fall (MacLean et al., 1998: 24–25). Social and economic devastation resulted. It is no coincidence that China and Taiwan controlled capital inflows and outflows and best avoided Asia's financial crisis.

LATIN AMERICA

Latin America was the home of dependency theory, import-substitution industrialization, and economic nationalism. After the 1980s debt crisis, it became home to neoliberal experiments and economic devastation, but not economic breakthroughs, as in East Asia.

In the 1970s, Latin American dictators ran up huge debts to benefit themselves and their corporate allies. "Spectacular waste and corruption fed a spiral of inflation and a frenzy of capital flight in which much of the money being borrowed from abroad was funnelled straight out again" (Hoogvelt, 1997: 227). Northern bankers lent eagerly. When the debt crisis struck in 1982, dictators and their cronies could not repay Northern bankers. How could the bankers recover their money?

Green and Hoogvelt argue that a political revolution, toward the forms—but not the substance—of democracy, was needed. In running up mainly private debts, there was little need for democratic legitimacy. But when dictators and their cronies could not repay the debts, Northern lenders, led by the IMF and the United States, decided to socialize the debts. Governments and all citizens had to sacrifice to repay foreign lenders. It was a cruel twist of history, wrote Green, that made the debt crisis and SAPs coincide with the return (more or less) of democratic rule (Hoogvelt, 1997: 229).

Hoogvelt argues that the World Bank, the IMF, and U.S. bankers were shrewdly aware of needing popular legitimacy to get sacrifices from everyone to pay the debts. To make the poor sacrifice, although only the rich had benefited, required democracy. This is why human rights and electoral democracy suddenly appeared on the U.S. administration's agenda,

she argues. Latin America is still struggling with the debt crisis's aftermath and neoliberalism's imposition. They are thus hindered from following past economic nationalist policies or the path of the East Asian Tigers.

DOMESTIC CONTROL: THE KEY TO ECONOMIC BREAKTHROUGH

The countries that developed most spectacularly in the past century did not follow simple models. South Korea and Sweden, the cases we will examine, are global exporters of highly sophisticated products today, but they were once very poor, agricultural countries. In each case, their transformations were complex, contradictory, and somewhat idiosyncratic. They involved all aspects of society, class and gender structures, resource endowments, cultural traditions, relations with external powers, political and economic unity or disunity, and others. The processes occurred over several generations.

Despite their diverse histories, South Korea and Sweden shared several characteristics. Breaking orthodox liberal rules, they emphasized national rather than foreign corporate control, activist economic roles for the state, and strong national identities.

SOUTH KOREA

South Korea followed a version of Japan's economic nationalist route to development. South Korea (population: 47 million) is the biggest of the Asian Tigers. Since 1960, South Korea went from an impoverished, war-torn country with few natural resources to a sophisticated exporter of automobiles and electronics. Living standards are getting close to Canadian levels.

A status-conscious society with a powerful collective identity, South Korea moved away from military dictatorships in the late 1980s. But just as democracy was strengthening, the IMF imposed harsh conditions that undermined Korea's model and sovereignty.

South Korea's case is contradictory. Its development paralleled Japan's half a century earlier, yet many Koreans dislike Japan, which occupied their country from 1910 to 1945. South Korea was a frontline state in America's war against communism, and the U.S. maintained military bases and provided aid after the bitter civil war of the early 1950s. Yet South Korea refused to become a showcase of American liberal capitalism. It shut out U.S. and other transnationals, and resisted becoming an American economic dependency.

South Korea's elites adopted strong economic nationalist policies to build up industrial capacity. Foreign ownership, except minority shareholding, was forbidden until the 1990s (Mardon, 1990). Unlike Canada, with its foreign-owned auto industry, South Korea developed three successful, independent, export-oriented automobile companies.

South Korea's history contradicts the assumptions of both liberalism and dependency theory. Contrary to liberal doctrine, "the state virtually created South Korea's giant conglomerates" through credit control and import substitution policies (Foster-Carter, 1989: 46). On the other hand, the aggressive exporting of sophisticated goods and the far-reaching land reform in the early 1950s, contradicts dependency theory. South Korea successfully combined industrial exporting with import substitution.

South Korea suffered a short, severe economic shock in the 1997–98 Asian financial crisis, and neoliberalism replaced its development model. Its failings were not government deficits or public foreign debt, but domestic speculation in real estate and a requirement that Korea dismantle economic nationalism to join the prestigious Organisation for Economic Cooperation and Development (OECD). Fearing the emergence of another Japan, a massive American trade blitz in the early 1990s forced Korea to upwardly revalue its currency, so Koreans would import more American goods and export less. Monopoly Korean companies became highly indebted. Foreign investors panicked in 1997. This was an opportunity for the IMF, the United States, and Japan to impose Washington consensus policies, removing remaining barriers to foreign ownership and control (Bullard et al., 1998: 101–106). Demanding the firing of workers, the IMF was dubbed "I am fired" by labour and student movements (Crotty and Dymski, 1999: 194). The IMF package lowered the value of Korea's currency to new depths. Despite the turmoil, South Korea is one of the few countries to escape Third World status.

South Korea did it by not following the Washington consensus (contrast with the situation described in Box 11.3).

SWEDEN

Sweden shared characteristics with South Korea, including independent development, export niches of sophisticated goods, and violation of several liberal rules. But Sweden was an exemplar of democracy and equality. In the mid-1800s, Sweden was poor, overwhelmingly rural, and still subject to famines and epidemics. While industrialization progressed in much of Europe, Sweden remained a backwater. Widespread rural poverty was eased only by massive emigration to America.

In 1870, Sweden, like Canada, was a staple exporter of resources to more advanced economies. Today, it exports engineering goods—ball bearings, telephones, electrical equipment, precision machines, cars, trucks, and aircraft—which comprise half of Sweden's total exports. Raw materials fell to 11 percent of total exports (Swedish Institute, 1992). Sweden now has one of the world's highest living standards and most egalitarian income distributions.

How did Sweden transform itself? As in South Korea, a strong national identity led to a desire to develop independently. Swedes found export niches and prohibited majority foreign ownership without permission (Nordlund, 1989: 298). Prohibiting foreign ownership, in effect from 1916 until 1982, ensured the dominance of domestic corporations. Also, Swedish investment banks made risky investments in innovative firms early in Sweden's development (Gasslander, 1962).

With its long tradition of competence, independence, and integrity, Sweden's state was less economically directive than South Korea's. Powerful unions, local communities, and businesses played a bigger role. There was widespread agreement in Sweden on the goals of equality and jobs for all. The state, usually controlled by a Social Democratic government, encouraged investment, especially during recessions, and ran an active labour-market policy that retrained and quickly re-employed laid-off workers. Influential unions supported rapid technological change through policies of reinvestment, "wage solidarity" (relative wage equality), and

Cochabamba is a city of 800 000 situated high in the Andes Mountains in Bolivia, the poorest country in South America. Seventy percent of its people live below the poverty line and the local minimum wage is US$60 per month. Nearly one child in ten dies before the age of five. In 2000, the city erupted in riots, hundreds were injured, and a 17-year-old boy was shot dead. The issue was water. The spark? The IMF and the World Bank dictated that the city privatize its water supply. In 1999, in a closed-door process with just one bidder, Bechtel (the U.S.-based engineering giant) was granted a 40-year lease to take over Cochabamba's water, through a subsidiary, Aguas del Tunari, formed for that purpose. Bechtel was guaranteed a 16 percent annual rate of profit under the contract.

Within weeks of taking over the water system, Bechtel imposed huge rate hikes on local water users, increasing minimum wage earners' water bills to as much as 25 percent of their income. In response, people took to the streets, with waves of protests from January to April of 2000. Protesters blamed Bechtel for trying to "lease the rain." Deeply indebted, Bolivia has been trying to follow the dictates of the IMF and World Bank since the late 1980s. The country sold its airline, railroad, mining, and electric companies to private, mostly foreign, corporations. The strategy tamed inflation, but led to severe recession and massive unemployment.

James Wolfensohn, then the president of the World Bank, responded to the Cochabamba protests by saying that people in Bolivia and elsewhere would just waste water unless there was a "proper system of charging ... It's just a fact that if you give public services away, I think everyone would agree that that does lead to certain waste." In Cochabamba, water enters most people's homes for an hour every day or two.

Cochabamba residents claimed victory in April 2000, when they reached an agreement with their government that guaranteed the withdrawal of Aguas del Tunari, and granted control over water to a grassroots coalition. The coalition vowed to run the water system as a human right, not a commodity. But without new investment they have been unable to improve or expand service. The government and the World Bank appear unwilling to help.

In November 2001 Bechtel filed legal action against Bolivia, claiming US$25 million in damages for lost future profits. The company filed the case in an arbitration court run by the World Bank under a bilateral treaty between the Netherlands and Bolivia. Bechtel opened a P.O. box in the Netherlands to make use of the treaty.

SOURCES: William Finnegan, June 2002, PBS, Frontline/NOW (wysiwig://8/http://www.pbs.org/frontlineworld/stories/bolivia/thestory.htm and wysiwig://6/http://www.pbs.org/frontlineworld/stories/bolivia/timeline.htm); Earth Justice, August 2002, "Solidarity with Cochabamba Water Uprising: Call for Transparency in ICSID Case Aguas del Tunari vs Bolivia" (http://www.xs4all.nl/~arenaria/water/petition0802.htm); Democracy Centre, June 2000, "Water Privatization in Bolivia" (http://www.democracyctr.org/water/html).

workers' co-determination of corporate decision making (Esping-Andersen, 1985). In the 1990s, Sweden lost some of its distinctiveness as Swedish corporations emigrated *en masse*, and governments adopted many neoliberal policies to join the European Union. But Sweden remains one of the most egalitarian societies on earth.

KERALA

Kerala is a different case from South Korea and Sweden. It was not a matter of domestic economic control leading to breakthrough. As a poor state in India, Kerala does not have the jurisdiction to prevent foreign ownership. Kerala's population is about the same as Canada's. But, while most Keralans are extremely poor materially, they are quite rich in human development terms.

With a per capita income just over 1 percent that of the United States (Frank and Chasin, 2000), life expectancy is 72.5 years, ten years higher than the Indian average and only four years below American levels (Govindan, 1996: 994; United Nations, 1999: 134–36). At 13 deaths per thousand, Kerala's infant mortality rate is only 20 percent that of India as a whole (65 per 1000). Amazingly, Kerala has almost full literacy, in contrast to the Indian average of only 65 percent (Frank and Chasin, 2000).

What accounts for Kerala's remarkable achievements in such a poor state? The state government supports nutrition, fair land distribution, education, and women's equality. Kerala publicly distributes basic food at controlled prices through fair-price shops to most households. School lunches and feeding programs at nurseries for infants and pregnant and lactating women ensure good nutrition of young children. Education reaches even the poorest. Its citizens boast the highest newspaper readership in India. Birth rates have fallen to 18 per 1000, a level almost as low as in rich countries and achieved entirely through voluntary means in contrast to China's coercive birth control policy (Govindan, 1996: 943).

These human development gains occurred because of Kerala's long history of mass mobilization among peasants, workers, and low-caste people demanding their rights and working for change. Since 1957, most Keralan governments have been left-wing coalitions that favour the poor majority (Franke and Chasin, 1991). Recently, Kerala's egalitarian policies and defiance of neoliberal commands have led to economic growth. Between 1988 and 1994, Kerala's annual growth rate was 6.4 percent, compared to 5 percent for India (Frank and Chasin, 2000). Kerala shows that radical reform can lead to remarkable human development gains, even in very poor areas.

The cases of South Korea and Sweden suggest that divergence from liberalism led to successful development. They combined active state roles with aggressive exporting, and, until pressured into adopting neoliberal policies, insisted on domestic control over their economies. Washington consensus policies close these kinds of options for other countries wanting to follow these successful models. In Kerala, active state action and a mobilized people promoted human development and equality in a context of poverty. These policies were the opposite of the SAPs imposed on many countries.

THE CHALLENGE AHEAD

There has to be something fundamentally wrong with a world that can create wondrous new technologies, life-enhancing breakthroughs, and brilliant works of literature and music, but hasn't found ways to spread these benefits to most people. War, hunger, disease, exploitation of workers, forced child labour, illiteracy, homelessness, and ecological disasters are very much with us. Their burden is borne disproportionately by the poor everywhere, who outnumber the rich many times over.

We continually hear about the benefits of free trade, international investment agreements, private enterprise, and new technologies. The profit motive is supposed to provide the spark for continual improvement. But who benefits? A few transnationals control most new technologies. Take health care. Pharmaceutical companies spend billions on research if they anticipate big profits and are protected by extended patents that give them monopolies. But what will motivate health improvements if the keys are dietary and lifestyle changes, environmental protection, and an end to poverty and illiteracy, from which corporations do not profit? More than two million children a year die of easily preventable diseases because no one pays for their immunizations during the first year of life (World Health Organization, 2002).

Transnationals want the freedom to roam the world in search of the lowest wages, the laxest environmental protections, and lowest corporate taxes. Their right to do these things is encoded in international investment agreements. But few people want to follow transnationals from country to country in search of a job. Most prefer to stay put and build families and communities. For most, "home" is a definite place. Transnationals, however, have no location commitment or sense of responsibility to the communities where they make profits.

The Western capitalist model is not sustainable in the long run. A child born in the United States or Canada will consume, on average, 10 times the resources and produce 10 times the pollution of a child born in Bangladesh or Bolivia (Stern, et al., 1997: vii). "We need to recognize," writes Stuart Walker (1993: 46), "that the pattern of excessive consumption epitomized in North America—and envied around the world—is fundamentally unsustainable and unachievable for most of the world's population."

Markets, international cooperation, and new technologies are good if they serve humanity and the environment. However, if their control remains in the hands of a few transnationals who are guided by greed, even at the expense of the many, humanity is not served. The challenge is to ensure that development spreads to all people, conforms to human values, and sustains the environment. Deep democracy, equality, respect for all, and the spirit of community support must be the core of development policies.

SUMMARY

1. The search by transnational corporations for profits leads to shifts between rich and poor countries and in the location of work, and has massive implications for citizens' well-being.

2. Ways of measuring material and nonmaterial well-being show great disparities between rich and poor countries, as well as between classes and genders within all countries.

3. In 1750, there were no substantial gaps in living standards and levels of productivity among countries. Today's poor countries are primarily those once colonized by the West.

4. The assumptions of liberalism and modernization theory about free markets and capitalist development are adopted by the International Monetary Fund, transnational corporations, and the U.S. government, but do not live up to their promises for improving the well-being of most citizens of the Third World.

5. Dependency theory emphasizes the economic and political obstacles to development in the Third World that derive from foreign control.

6. Domestic control of corporations and activist governments were the keys to success in the spectacular development breakthroughs that mark the histories of South Korea and Sweden.

7. More democratic, egalitarian, and supportive policies for development will benefit all countries. Kerala is a good example of this. Those in the rich North may have to sacrifice some material wealth to share more around the world and ensure ecological sustainability.

QUESTIONS TO CONSIDER

1. What are the major obstacles to development in the Third World today? How can they be overcome?

2. Can development be made more democratic and more equal across countries, classes, genders, and races? If so, how?

3. What are the consequences for development of a world where transnational corporations and capital can move wherever the conditions are most favourable, but people (labour) cannot? How does this affect democracy?

GLOSSARY

Balance of payments refers to the summary of all economic transactions between a country's residents and residents (including foreign corporations) elsewhere. Transactions include imports and exports, tourist spending, payments to corporate head offices for management services and research and development, and inflow and outflow of ownership capital (foreign direct investment) and loan (portfolio) capital. If a country runs a persistent balance-of-payments deficit, it must reduce imports, increase exports, or increase foreign indebtedness or foreign ownership of its economy. If these actions fail, it can request an IMF loan. It will lose financial sovereignty if it does so.

Capitalism is a socioeconomic system in which private owners of the means of production hire free, property-less workers. Production is geared toward private profit for the owners.

Colonialism is a synonym for imperialism. In formal colonialism, country A takes over country B by force of arms and rules it without the consent of the people of country B. In informal colonialism, country A decides that all other countries play by its rules, which it enforces by diplomatic means, offering economic benefits or making economic threats, and in the last resort threatening or carrying out "regime change" by military might.

Comprador elites are state and economic elites whose rule in a country depends on alliances with external forces, such as transnationals, and who would be unable to remain in power on the basis of local popular support.

Core countries are the same as developed countries.

Current accounts are part of a country's the balance of payments. They include imports and exports but do not include the movement of capital.

Development is traditionally understood as a society's achievement of high living standards and high productivity levels. More recently, definitions of development have incorporated nonmaterial aspects of well-being, such as opportunities in education, modern health care, access to employment, democracy, civil rights, and a healthy environment.

The **European Union (EU)** is the economic and political union of most Western Europe countries. The EU began with six countries in 1957 (as the European Economic Community, or EEC), expanded to 12 in 1994, and has expansion pending to several Eastern European countries.

Export-processing zones (EPZs) are zones created for transnational corporations to operate under conditions that free them from domestic laws, such as tariffs, corporate taxes, safety and environmental protections, minimum-wage laws, and other labour standards. Unions are often prohibited.

Globalization comprises the processes leading towards greater world integration economically, politically, socially, culturally, in government policies, in communications, and in consciousness. It is a contested term that almost always means a weakening of nations and states. For some it means inevitable integration. Others see ebbs and flows in globalization and discuss "deglobalization" as processes whereby the world is coming apart.

Gross national product (GNP) refers to a nation's total output of goods and services in a year as measured officially in the money economy.

The **G-7** is an organization that seeks to coordinate economic policies among the world's seven richest countries—the United States, Japan, Germany, France, Italy, the United Kingdom, and Canada.

Industrialization is the process of technological development by which machines replace human and animal power. It is usually characterized by large-scale production, large work groups, and increased division of labour.

Infrastructure refers to the underlying foundation for a modern, efficient economy. It broadly includes a modern transportation and communications system, universal education, an efficient and honest government bureaucracy, and a good health-care system.

The **International Monetary Fund (IMF)** is a UN agency that attempts to minimize currency fluctuations among countries by providing credit to countries with balance-of-payments and international-debt problems. The IMF is controlled by the rich countries.

International transactions, which are also referred to as "balance of payments," are the net inflow and outflow of money between one country and the rest of the world.

Liberalism is a political economic doctrine that equates capitalism with freedom and distrusts the power of governments. Liberalism emphasizes market freedom, a minimal state redistributive role, and unrestricted rights for privately owned corporations.

The term **market economy** is used as a synonym for capitalism. See *capitalism*.

Marxism is the economic and political philosophy originating in the works of Karl Marx and Friedrich Engels. It characterizes capitalism as inherently exploitive of wage-earners, and predicts its inevitable demise and replacement by a classless society.

Modernization theory is a theory of development, originating in U.S. sociology, that stresses the importance of attitudinal changes in the transition to a "modern" capitalist society.

The **North American Free Trade Agreement (NAFTA)** is an agreement along neoliberal principles among the United States, Mexico, and Canada for greater economic integration. It includes the removal of tariffs and the right of entry of foreign corporations from member states, and it curtails the power of governments.

Neoliberalism is a resurgence of classical liberalism since the 1970s, but in the new context of the economic preponderance of a few hundred giant transnational corporations. See also *liberalism*.

Peripheral countries refer to the underdeveloped countries, or the Third World.

Structural adjustment programs (SAPs) are programs initiated by the IMF and the World Bank involving stabilization and structural change. Stabilization involves reducing negative balance of payments, government deficits, inflation, and aggregate demand. Structural change is designed to encourage foreign-exchange earnings through exports, and savings through government spending cuts on social services and food subsidies.

Supranational describes anything extending beyond national borders. The term is used in reference to institutions such as transnational corporations and financial institutions, the United Nations, the European Union, the IMF, and the World Bank.

The **Third World** refers to the majority of countries in Africa, Asia, and Latin America. These countries are considered neither advanced capitalist nor communist-industrial. Many other, similar terms are used interchangeably: the majority world, underdeveloped, less developed, developing, backward, the South, periphery, non-industrialized. None of these terms is entirely satisfactory; all fail to capture the wide variations among these countries.

Transnational corporations are corporations that have subsidiaries in more than one country. Most of the biggest are owned and controlled in the six industrial countries of the North—the United States, Japan, Britain, Germany, France, and Italy.

Underdeveloped is a contested term. For liberals, it refers to a precapitalist society. For dependency theorists, it has a colonial or dependent relationship with a major capitalist power, and is to be distinguished from an undeveloped or precapitalist society.

The **World Bank**, formally known as the International Bank for Reconstruction and Development (IBRD), is an affiliate of the United Nations. It provides commercial and low-interest loans to less developed countries on the condition that they follow neoliberal prescriptions. The World Bank is dominated by the major capitalist powers, whose voting shares are commensurate with the amount of their investment in the bank.

SUGGESTED READING

Bello, Walden. (2002). *Deglobalization: Ideas for a New World Economy.* London: Zed Books.

Chomsky, Noam. (1999). *Profit over People: Neoliberalism and the Global Order.* New York: Seven Stories Press.

Chossudovsky, Michel. (1997). *The Globalization of Poverty: Impacts of IMF and World Bank Reforms.* London: Zed Books.

Hoogvelt, Ankie. (1997). *Globalization and the Postcolonial World: The New Political Economy of Development.* Baltimore: Johns Hopkins University Press.

Khor, Martin. (2001). *Rethinking Globalization: Critical Issues and Policy Choices.* London: Zed Books.

NOTES

1. Derived from *Forbes*, February 2002 and UNCTAD, 2001, *Issues Notes for the Third United Nations Conference on the Least Developed Countries.*

2. Derived from *Forbes*, February 2002 and World Bank, *Selected World Development Indicators, 2000.*

3. In the 1920s and 1930s, Argentina and Uruguay developed standards of living comparable to those of Western Europe (Ehrensaft and Armstrong, 1981). However, they were largely agricultural exporters, had little manufacturing, and their living standards fell after 1945 to those prevailing in the rest of South America.

4. Much of the material in this section was drawn from the excellent study produced by the Ecumenical Coalition for Economic Justice (ECEJ), *Recolonization or Liberation* (1990).

5. For example, W.W. Rostow (1965: 38) predicted that, with a sufficient rise in the rate of productive investment, India's and China's economies would "take off" in 1952. They didn't.

6. In these zones, states give sovereignty over domestic laws, regulations, and protections to the transnationals. The first zone was established in Ireland in 1958, but the model for Third World countries was established in Taiwan in 1965 (Marchak, 1991: 139–41).

PART FOUR

INSTITUTIONS

CHAPTER TWELVE

FAMILIES

In this chapter you will learn that:

- While common sense suggests that current dilemmas in family life are private problems, sociology helps uncover their public sources and solutions.

- The family does not take a universal form and its structure is therefore not a product of some biological imperative: Families vary widely in the way they are organized across different cultures and through history, and family organization is loosely related to the way material production is organized.

- Our society is organized around a gendered division of labour and the heterosexual nuclear family; this is the main reason why families that assume a different form—especially lone-parent families—have a particularly hard time meeting the needs of their members.

- As women have increasingly assumed part of the financial support of their families, men have not come to share the work that must be done in the home, nor has society changed in ways that accommodate this changed reality for families.

- The gendered division of labour that makes it possible for nuclear families to care for young children involves sizable liabilities for women and children. The social isolation of full-time mothers and the stress attached to their high-demand, low-control situation reduces the quality of child-care.

- The chief negative effect of divorce for women and children is the loss of income that follows. The most effective solution to this problem—government support of all children—has not been adopted by the Canadian government, although most advanced industrial societies do have such a policy objective.

BONNIE FOX

UNIVERSITY OF TORONTO

INTRODUCTION

Contemporary life presents difficult choices for those of us who live in or plan to live in families. The constraints on these choices affect our lives profoundly. I begin this chapter by reviewing dilemmas in family life in the light of popular myths. Because family life is so familiar to us, we all too easily accept commonsense understandings that portray family problems as personal, private, and attributable to "human nature." Commonsense solutions prescribe individual change and ignore the social context. In contrast, sociology uncovers the social origins of family patterns and the problems they entail.

As a way of challenging the commonsense perspective, the second section of this chapter examines two patterns of family life that are different from our own. In these cases, it is clear that the family patterns people have created are a response to the problems posed by the needs of daily survival. Next, I review the history that produced our own family arrangements.

In the chapter's fourth section, I explore some of the main features of family life today: sexuality, marriage, parenthood, housework, and the **gendered division of labour** (i.e., the difference in the work men and women do). My aim is to analyze how these activities are organized in order to give you an idea of the sources of problems that often plague modern families. I then discuss divorce and its aftermath, lone-parent and reconstituted families. I finish with a brief discussion of government policies to support families.

EXPLORING THE FAMILIAR: FAMILIES IN WESTERN SOCIETY TODAY

DILEMMAS OF CONTEMPORARY FAMILY LIFE

When you imagine yourself at age 39, you probably think of yourself as married, with a child or two. You probably also assume—or at least hope—that your children will enjoy full-time mothering for their early years. You are not unusual if you envision your adulthood in family terms. Moreover, when you think of family, you probably think of the conventional nuclear family, in which the man is the main breadwinner and the woman has primary responsibility for the children.

At the same time, you probably have nagging concerns about your future. Full-time mothering seems a luxury few women can afford these days. Most married women—even those with young children—now have to assume some of the responsibility of breadwinning. Indeed, women attending university anticipate building a career, which involves far more commitment and time than does simply holding a job. Building a career virtually precludes taking time out for children, because the necessary commitment is at odds with the demands of motherhood. These realities lead to obvious questions: Women wonder when there will be time to have children and how they will care for them once they arrive.

Whereas women's concerns about family tend to focus on the difficulties of combining employment and child-care, men's concerns probably centre on the growing elusiveness of the breadwinner role in this uncertain economy. At the same time, men are increasingly pressured by the women they live with to change in ways for which they are unprepared. Manhood was once equated with occupational success, but such success is now both harder to achieve and insufficient for a happy marriage. Today, many women expect men to be emotionally open in ways that women tend to find easy, in addition to aggressively pursuing occupational success *and* sharing the housework.

Although conventional patterns are in decline, our society still seems to be organized around nuclear families and 1950s gender roles. For instance, whether or not the nuclear family is the best unit for raising children, our society offers almost no support for any alternative. Aside from the flurry of gift giving and visiting that occurs when a baby is born, few friends help a new mother with her child-care responsibilities. Whatever support grandparents are inclined to offer is inhibited by the fact that they live in another house, if not another city, as well as by the demands of their employment. In the end, new parents (usually mothers) typically face the dirty diapers and dishes on their own. Moreover, we equate loving, supportive relationships with family. Consequently, when we find ourselves in personal crisis or in need of money, few of us can turn to people outside our immediate families for help.

Conventional gender roles also seem central to the organization of our society. It is difficult to keep a family going with no one at home to buy groceries, plan and make meals, organize doctors' appointments, and meet repairpersons. The dearth of good, affordable daycare means that having children is difficult unless the mother becomes a full-time homemaker. And men have depended on the emotional support and caring work provided by their wives to keep them sane and productive. Thus, for much of the twentieth century, a division of labour by gender sustained families in an economy in which employers bear no direct responsibility for the welfare of their employees' families.

Clearly, the future poses various dilemmas. How will we earn enough money to support a family and raise our children at the same time? How will we sustain loving relationships with our partners while coping with the problems outlined above? Indeed, are our ideals about family sustainable? And if the conventional nuclear family is an unlikely prospect for most of us, how will we live in a society that still assumes it to be an essential part of life?

MYTHS ABOUT FAMILY

Thinking through these dilemmas is especially difficult because myths about family pervade our culture. Measured against the idealized image of family life that emerged during the 1950s and was beamed into homes across the country by television, the problems in family life today assume crisis proportions. "The family" seems to be disintegrating. Actually, real families in the 1950s bore little resemblance to those depicted in *Leave It to Beaver* and *Father Knows Best*. Nevertheless, the 1950s was an unusually "familistic" decade: People married earlier, had more children, and were less likely to divorce than the generations that preceded and followed them (E. May, 1988). The 1950s are thus an odd benchmark. Moreover, when the mental and physical health costs that women pay

While some people still consider the nuclear family to be the norm, full-time mothering is a luxury most women cannot afford. Combining employment and child-care is an act that requires women to wear two masks.

SOURCE: Mimi Matte, *Family Outing*. Photo courtesy Bau-Xi Gallery, Toronto. Collection of Granite Club, Toronto.

for doing full-time homemaking are considered, idealizing the 1950s must be questioned (Coontz, 1992).

Also mythical is the popular view that the traditional European family consisted of three generations of family living harmoniously under one roof, caring for all its members. In fact, **extended-family households**—consisting of three generations—were rare in preindustrial Europe. Moreover, children spent much of their childhood in the care of people other than their parents; and the elderly did not expect to be cared for lovingly by their children. Where large extended families were common—for instance, among the wealthy in ancient China—the lives of all but the male patriarch were wholly circumscribed by his authority over life and limb.

"FAMILY VALUES"

Some politicians have taken advantage of the popular belief that the family is in crisis. The call for a return to "family values" has been especially pronounced in the U.S. political arena. Although it is not clear exactly what "family values" are, the phrase evokes an undefined past, free of today's social problems, a time when the values we associate with family—community, decency, and morality—were dominant. The family in political rhetoric is the symbol of all that is good and decent, and the bedrock on which society rests. Of course, the family in question is the heterosexual breadwinner/homemaker family, and deviations from this ideal are held responsible for myriad social problems.

In practice, family-values advocates call for policies that punish deviations from the nuclear-family ideal. They want to outlaw abortion, prohibit gay and lesbian marriages and parenthood, and encourage women to stay home with their children rather than provide funding for daycare facilities. It seems obvious that what family-values politicians seek to promote is the continued assumption of responsibility for people's welfare by families, with services provided largely by women—at little or no cost to the state. Adopting an ideology of "less government," these politicians seldom promote policies that actually support families of any kind.

Aside from the political implications of family-values arguments, there are a number of problems with the assumptions and logic of the arguments themselves. Highlighting these problems will raise some of the issues addressed in this chapter. First, the idea that the family is in crisis is problematic because it assumes that there is only one kind of family—the heterosexual, nuclear, breadwinner/homemaker family. Closely related is the assumption that children are always best raised at home by full-time mothers. The third flawed assumption—one that is subtler, and of special concern to sociologists—is that "society" is simply the sum of individuals who live in it. This assumption is convenient for the family-values proponents because it suggests that the "good old days" could be restored if only large numbers of individuals adopted "family values."

The idea that society is simply the sum of the people who live in it is worth examining. This idea ignores social structure, and, by doing so, misses what is arguably the most important insight of sociology—namely, that the organization of various aspects of society puts constraints on, and creates opportunities for, individuals. In other words, social structure generates powerful social forces that cannot be reduced to individual motivation. Market forces, for example, rather than the greed of individual capitalists, explain much of what occurs in the marketplace.

What constitutes a family? Should homosexual couples be allowed to adopt children? The decline of the nuclear family has been accompanied by the rise of other family forms. The Alberta couple shown above recently won the right to be legal parents of their child.
SOURCE: CP Picture Archive/Jim Wells.

Consider the following example: A footnote in *Das Kapital*, Karl Marx's groundbreaking analysis and critique of capitalism, tells the story of the efforts of nineteenth-century potter and factory owner Josiah Wedgwood (whose products are still available) to fight the brutal practice of child labour, which was common during early industrial capitalism. Although he was disturbed by the practice, Wedgwood was forced to use children in his own factory in order to keep up with his competition. He therefore wrote to the government to request legislation prohibiting the practice. He explained that market forces made it impossible for him not to use cheap child labour, and he wanted the state to intervene, to curb those forces. He was not alone. Eventually, after campaigns by organized labour along with a general public outcry, the government passed child-labour laws.

Market forces are perhaps the most obvious and easily understood example of influences that arise from the way society is organized. They are not reducible to individual behaviour. In the Wedgwood example, although it is true that individual capitalists themselves had made the decision to hire children as young as seven to work in their factories, they had been pressured to do so by the dynamics of a capitalist economy, which generates competition around the prices of products and thus pressures participants to minimize costs. Consequently, once one producer opted to use child labour, all the others had to follow suit—or find some other way to drastically reduce labour costs. At that point, the situation was out of the hands of individuals.

Systems of class, gender, and racial inequality are also structural. Although sexism, racism, and other such phenomena are partly a matter of individual attitudes, they are also built into the structure of our society—most fundamentally, as divisions of labour. Indeed, a variety of social forces influence family patterns. Although individuals make choices about whether to marry, have children, and so on, the social forces guiding them toward those decisions are so powerful that most individuals end up making the same choices. The regularities or patterns that result attest to the power of social structure, and are what allow the development of "social science." They also are what make the family an institution—that is, a relatively stable set of roles and practices. Family-values advocates ignore the social forces that shape family

patterns; instead, they define family problems and solutions as individual and private.

In sum, the family-values argument represents a popular ideology that confuses attempts to think clearly about family. Sociology offers a more fruitful approach to a subject that is important for us to understand, because we count on family relations to meet our most fundamental needs for love and support. This chapter develops a sociological analysis of family, after debunking what has become a very popular myth.

THE MYTH OF THE NATURAL FAMILY

There is a strong ideology in our culture holding that families should be heterosexual and nuclear—that is, composed of a man, who is the primary breadwinner; a woman, who functions primarily as mother and homemaker; and their children. Because only about 15 percent of Canadian families in 1991 consisted of a married couple in which the man was the exclusive breadwinner, the woman was a full-time mother, and there were unmarried children living at home (Statistics Canada, 1992a, 1993b), concern about families has escalated.

One reason for the popular fixation on the nuclear, breadwinner family is that it seems to derive from the biology of reproduction. Common sense suggests that biology produces the family. Heralded by the news media, arguments based on **biological determinism** are immensely popular these days. One common variant of this approach, known as **sociobiology**, attempts to apply the laws of biological evolution to social behaviour. Sociobiologists hold that, as with physical traits, social behaviour is inherited biologically—in other words, that behaviour can be linked to specific genetic configurations. Typically, sociobiologists construct a story about the history of human evolution that assumes genetic encoding of behaviour—a problematic assumption since there is no evidence to support it (Lewontin, Rose, and Kamin, 1984).

The sociobiological argument about family is that, over the course of human history, certain behaviours were adaptive because they contributed to "reproductive success." Specifically, males who were more aggressive and females who were more nurturant had more offspring. Thus, these behaviours were "naturally selected," and turned up in more and more individuals over the generations. According to this perspective, today's behaviour is the product of human evolution—and thus inevitable. Yet research by psychologists shows that women are no more empathic or sensitive to others than men are. Nor is there a natural maternal instinct that tells mothers how to care for their newborn baby.

The family, consisting of the biological mother and father and their offspring, is also a product of evolution, according to sociobiologists. Because children represent people's genetic investment, they argue, evolutionary forces have selected a pattern that is most likely to ensure the survival of offspring—namely, the union of two biological parents in a lasting relationship.

Although sociobiology accords with common sense, its claims do not accord with observable evidence. Evidence on family patterns across various cultures indicates that, although the nuclear family is common in many cultures, it is often embedded in a larger household that constitutes the unit of production, consumption, and child-care. For example, in Europe in the Middle Ages, the wealthier a married couple was, the larger the household. Spouses and their children lived amidst an array of additional, unrelated people—from children and teens sent "into service" by their parents to adults providing necessary labour to the household. Preindustrial European households also provide evidence that mothers do not always raise, or even live with, their biological children. In many parts of Europe until the twentieth century the babies of women who could afford it were given to "wet nurses," who were paid to nurse and care for them, and young teens were sent into service or apprenticeship in other households. According to ethnographic evidence, in many non-Western cultures, mothers are the primary caregivers for babies but not for older children. Siblings often take on the bulk of the care of children, although in some cultures (like Tahiti or parts of the Caribbean) the children of a young woman are given to her parents or close kin to be raised, and in others (throughout Melanesia and Polynesia) they are adopted after weaning (Edholm, 1982). Moreover, because the biology of reproduction—which we take as "given"—is interpreted in different ways across different cultures, the role of the father in conception is not always recognized. Often the social father is different

from the biological father. Even the role of the mother in conception is interpreted in varying ways: for instance, women have been seen (in European history) merely as the containers of fetuses. Finally, incest rules, which we take to reflect a kind of natural avoidance of inbreeding, have sometimes allowed brother–sister marriage to ensure the "purity" of the royal line (e.g., in Egypt and Hawaii).

Indeed, many of the things we often assume to be natural and universal are neither. There is a diversity of family patterns across history and cultures. The ways in which people organize to ensure their survival, and that of their children, vary.

CONCEPTUALIZING AND DEFINING FAMILY

Structural Functionalism

It is widely believed that the best unit in which to raise children is the nuclear family. This common-sense notion was promoted by Talcott Parsons (Parsons and Bales, 1955), whose writings on family constituted the dominant perspective in post–World War II sociology. In arguing that an institution (in this case, the heterosexual nuclear family) exists because of the useful functions it performs for the larger society, Parsons was making an argument reflecting the school of thought called **structural functionalism**.

Although structural functionalism dominated the study of families until recently, there are obvious problems with this perspective. First, just because an institution performs a social function, there is no reason to assume that some other institution might not perform that function equally well. Whether exclusive care by the biological mother and father is best for children is an empirical question.

The other key problem with the functionalist perspective is its focus on how institutions create social *order*, and its consequent failure to analyze the tensions in family life that can generate social *change*. Moreover, the functions that are emphasized allegedly meet the needs of society, not necessarily of the individuals in it. So, for instance, while Parsons recognized the problems faced by full-time housewives, it was not until feminists analyzed family life that the power dynamics and conflicts common to heterosexual nuclear families were highlighted.

Definitions

How one defines family has practical, as well as methodological, consequences. Rights and responsibilities follow from definitions. For instance, state-regulated institutions such as schools and hospitals often use legal definitions of marriage and family to determine which people will be informed and consulted about the status of someone in the institution. Accordingly, critically ill patients may find that family members with whom they have had little recent contact are admitted to their rooms and entitled to make important medical decisions on their behalf, whereas the friends who have been constant companions and who know them best are excluded. Government entitlements such as widows' pensions and tax deductions for the support of dependants apply only to family relations as defined by the government. A wife of a few years may be entitled to a widow's pension, whereas a same-sex lover of 20 years is not. A woman supporting an elderly and disabled friend cannot take the same tax deduction as a father supporting a child.

Similarly, when social scientists define *family*, some of them still assume the nuclear unit. This tendency has often resulted in a focus on the frequency with which nuclear-family patterns appear across history and cultures. Conceptualizing family in a way that focuses on common properties does not serve the interests of good empirical inquiry, however. Focusing on diversity in social patterns can, in contrast, help us acquire a better understanding of the nature of families. By studying diversity, and by noting the social circumstances that vary with family patterns, we can derive some idea of the social forces and factors that influence those patterns.

Accordingly, I define *family* as the sets of relationships people create to share resources daily in order to ensure their own and any dependants' welfare. What this definition offers is a focus on what is of critical importance to both individual survival and generational reproduction across many cultures. At the same time, it does not exclude groupings of people who are in essence functioning as family, though they may lack formal recognition as such (e.g., lesbian or gay partners with children, or female relatives who live separately but cooperate daily to care for their children).

This definition holds family to be the unit of **social reproduction.** As opposed to biological reproduction, social reproduction refers to a wide range of activities that "maintain existing life and ... reproduce the next generation" (Laslett and Brenner, 1989: 381–403). In other words, social reproduction refers to feeding, clothing, and otherwise looking after people's subsistence needs, as well as nurturing and socializing children and emotionally supporting adults. In short, "family" refers to the sets of relationships that work to reproduce life on a daily and a generational basis.

A LOOK AT OTHER FAMILY PATTERNS

In order to gain some perspective on family life, it is useful to examine family patterns that are significantly different from our own. When we do, one of the things we notice is that family patterns vary with the way people organize themselves to acquire their subsistence. To illustrate this point, I describe two interesting configurations: the communal households characteristic of many foraging (or hunting-and-gathering) societies, and the household economies typical of agricultural societies in preindustrial Europe.

FORAGING SOCIETIES: THE COMMUNAL HOUSEHOLD

In **foraging societies**, people acquire subsistence by gathering edibles and hunting live game. Foragers live in fairly small camps, or bands, comprising people who are compatible and not necessarily related by marriage or blood (as sociobiologists would predict). Because they live off the resources available to them in the local area, foragers are nomadic. Their ability to move when necessary is critical to survival, so they cannot accumulate possessions and they must keep the ratio of dependents (children and the aged) to active foragers low (Lee, 1979).

While foragers meet their subsistence needs by doing relatively little work, their inability to accumulate any surplus means that survival depends upon reciprocity and cooperation among the people living together. Thus, for example, successful hunters distribute game to all members of the camp. Doing so is economically rational for an individual living in an economy based on reciprocity because giving establishes obligations to reciprocate. Hunting is an especially uncertain occupation, so sharing the product is a sort of personal insurance. For the group, sharing ensures that a valuable source of protein is distributed widely.

In addition to sharing, a division of labour by gender and age organizes the acquisition of subsistence in foraging societies. Women typically gather and men typically hunt, although men also gather after an unsuccessful day of hunting and women hunt in some societies. Among the !Kung San of the Kalahari Desert in Botswana, as among many foragers, the food that women gather provides the bulk of subsistence—about 60 to 80 percent (Lee, 1979). In foraging societies, children and older adults typically do not forage for food.

The reciprocity that is the basis of foragers' daily subsistence no doubt generally influences the organization of their societies. Living has a communal character. Responsibilities that are assumed by families in our society—that is, responsibilities that are **privatized**—are held collectively in foraging societies. Thus, while marriage establishes the mother/father/child (i.e., nuclear) unit, the group of cooperating adults that is crucial for survival—the unit of social reproduction—is the camp. That is, all the members of the camp decide together when and where to move, and share food (game meat) and the responsibility for children. Moreover, perhaps because individual cooperation is central to daily living, and because these societies are without authority figures who might enforce such cooperation, individuals are allowed considerable freedom.

Just as subsistence is shared, so too is responsibility for children (Turnbull, 1961; Leacock, 1981). Although women do most of the child-care—which is considerable, when children are carried constantly, as they are among the !Kung—they do not bear the burden alone. Women care for one another's children; they even breastfeed one another's babies. Men also often tend babies and children.

Life in foraging societies seems to produce an absence of possessiveness toward children and spouses. This attitude is clear in the comment of a seventeenth-century Montagnais-Naskapi (Innu) man in response to a Jesuit missionary's attempt to shame him for his non-monogamy: "Thou hast no sense. You French people love only your own children; but we all love all the children of our tribe" (Leacock, 1981: 50). With respect to spouses, anthropologist Colin Turnbull (1961: 125) writes of the Pygmies of Congo:

They think of responsibility as communal. If you ask a father, or a husband, why he allows his son to flirt with a married girl, or his wife to flirt with other men, he will answer, "It is not my affair," and he is right. It is their affair and the affair of the other men and women, and of their brothers and sisters. He will try to settle it himself ... but if this fails he brings everyone else into the dispute.

In addition to a minimized sense of personal life as private, another consequence of communal living is that quarrelling and especially violence between spouses are seen, and treated, as community problems rather than private problems. Whatever disrupts the peace of the community is likely to be stopped—whether it is a beating or an extramarital relationship that takes an adult away from his or her responsibilities.

At the same time, the members of these communal societies have considerable autonomy. On consideration, the reasons are clear: Every adult has access to what is necessary for subsistence, so no person is in a position of dependency on some other, more powerful, person. Moreover, because individual cooperation is essential for the survival of the collective, every person's happiness matters. For these and other reasons, relations between women and men are egalitarian: men have no more power or privilege than women (Leacock, 1981).

Individual autonomy is evident in many aspects of family life. Although a girl's first marriage is typically arranged by her parents, a divorce is fairly easy to obtain (Lee, 1979). Similarly, although women typically have babies only about every four years (largely because they breastfeed each infant for several years and because they have low body fat), they can also decide not to keep every child. Women can choose infanticide if a child is born before other children are able to fend for themselves (thereby overburdening the mother), or if a child is born who requires too much special care (thereby jeopardizing the lives of others). Sexuality is also quite unconstrained. Although monogamy is usually expected in marriage, women and men are typically able to enter into extramarital sexual relations as long as they do not interfere with the performance of their duties.

As this brief sketch demonstrates, the unit of social reproduction among foragers is larger than the nuclear family. Because foragers' survival depends on cooperation and reciprocity, the larger community assumes responsibilities that belong to nuclear families in our society. In turn, the communal basis of life and the absence of private households in foraging societies have far-reaching implications, including collective responsibility for people's welfare, individual autonomy, and gender egalitarianism.

PREINDUSTRIAL AGRICULTURAL SOCIETIES: HOUSEHOLD ECONOMIES

Our family patterns developed out of the patterns that were typical of precapitalist agricultural societies. In those societies, the household itself was the productive unit; producing subsistence was its main objective. This was true of craftsmen's households as well as those of the peasants and nobility who lived directly off the land. Thus, the social relations of family life in precapitalist households—that is, relations between spouses, between parents and children, and among residents of the same household—were also the relations of production. The chief economic relationship was that between husband and wife. Wives did necessary work that was complementary to that of their husbands, so an able-bodied wife was quite indispensable to the survival of the household (Tilly and Scott, 1978).

Land, which was the key means of production, was privately owned in preindustrial Europe. That meant that marriage—and thus adulthood—was predicated on acquiring land, or some other means of livelihood. Consequently, people often married late—and chose their mates according to practical considerations rather than feelings (Mitterauer and Sieder, 1982). Typically, one son waited to inherit the land, his brothers were apprenticed to learn a skilled trade, and his sisters were given dowries. In the interim, children's dependence on their father to set them up for adulthood gave him considerable authority over them (Greven, 1973).

Land scarcity, and the fact that landlords extracted a substantial portion of the year's produce from the peasantry, meant that the struggle to survive was the chief household dynamic in these societies. It was constantly necessary to balance the number of productive adults against the number of dependants and the available economic resources (Tilly and Scott, 1978). Accordingly, household composition varied with changing economic requirements, especially labour requirements. In fact, much of the nature of household and family life was governed by economic considerations. So, in contrast with foragers, the interests of individuals in precapitalist agricultural societies were subordinated to those of the larger kin group and of the land from which they derived subsistence.

Labour requirements dictated household membership. Various types of labourers were taken into households as they were needed. Wives who died were quickly replaced. In peasant households, children were kept home only if their labour was needed. Otherwise, they were sent to wealthier households to be raised, or into neighbouring households that could use extra labour. For this reason, and because of extra adult workers, wealthy households were often huge, consisting of 15 to 30 people (Flandrin, 1979).

It was not only poor children who were sent away, however; few children from any economic background were raised exclusively at home by their mothers. Raising a child usually involved several households. Babies were often sent to "wet nurses," peasant women who were paid to care for them. About one in two children survived and returned home after several years, to be looked after, in most cases, by an older sibling. In their early teens, children were then sent off to be trained for adulthood in yet another household. They were either apprenticed to learn a skilled trade or simply sent to another household to learn basic domestic skills (Mitterauer and Sieder, 1982). Women's critical economic role precluded their spending much time on child-care or being distracted by the needs of loved ones.

Although parents no doubt loved their children and missed those who were living in other households, in many marriages sentiment and emotional connection probably took a distant back seat to practical imperatives (Mitterauer and Sieder, 1982). Similarly, the privacy that we take for granted at home was absent in preindustrial households. Because the household was a place of work, business and family life were not distinguished. Moreover, rooms were not reserved for special purposes like sleeping. In peasant hovels, entire families often slept in the same bed (Flandrin, 1979). In wealthier households, servants often slept with members of the family. Even sexuality was not entirely a private matter. This is clear from evidence of the community's intervention to regulate behaviour—whether to humiliate newlyweds it deemed inappropriate matches, to punish women suspected of adultery, or to force men to stop beating their wives. The interests of the collective—whether the household or the peasant community—seems to have taken precedence over individual autonomy.

Moreover, these were truly patriarchal households: Married women owed their husbands absolute obedience and, according to British common law, could not hold property, enter into contractual arrangements, or, in the rare event of divorce, get custody of the children. Many historians conclude that most married women were entirely subordinate to their husbands.

Nevertheless, women's work was vital to the ongoing survival of the household. The married couple was the chief labour force in every household. Whereas men did the heavy farm work (or supervised those who did), women were typically in charge of the dairy, the poultry, and the garden, as well as household management—mostly supervising the full range of household chores (Tilly and Scott, 1978). Evidence from men's wills testifies to the trust, respect, and love that developed between some spouses (Hanawalt, 1986). Accordingly, some historians argue that a rough equality often developed between husbands and wives.

Instances of near equality notwithstanding, women's and children's interests were generally subordinated to the needs of the household far more than were men's. For example, women had little control over their sexual and reproductive lives; at a time when childbirth was life-threatening, they were subject to pressure to have children, given the value of child labour in an agricultural context.

Finally, it is a myth that preindustrial agricultural households involved extended families, with three generations living under the same roof (Gottlieb, 1993). Short life spans tended to preclude the co-residence of three generations of family. Equally, however, the establishment of the next generation's family was often delayed because male property owners avoided turning the land over to their sons—on whom they would then become dependent—for as long as possible (Mitterauer and Sieder, 1982). In fact, elderly men typically retired only after carefully specifying (in writing) how they were to be provided for by their heirs; feelings between the generations were ambiva-lent enough that the elderly had to protect themselves against possible neglect by their children.

In sum, the nuclear unit was embedded in a larger household in preindustrial Europe. Unlike today, families were not sustained by sentimental or romantic feelings. Family and household relations were primarily relations of work, and individual needs were subordinated to those of the household, to ensure its survival. Whereas the absence of privatized family life empowered individuals in foraging societies, private ownership of the means of production and a considerable struggle to survive meant that, in agricultural societies, all individuals were subordinated to the household enterprise, women were subordinated to men, and children were subordinated to parents.

THE ORIGINS OF CONTEMPORARY FAMILY PATTERNS IN WESTERN SOCIETIES

Given how different family life today is from what I have just described, how did contemporary family patterns develop? Actually, it is only recently in Western history that the family characteristics we take for granted coalesced—namely, the gendered division of labour in which women are primarily responsible for child-care and housework and men for financial provision, motherhood as women's primary vocation, and emotional intensity as the foundation of family relations.

Before the nineteenth century, "family" generally referred to all the people who lived under the same roof, many of whom (as we have just seen) were not related by blood or marriage (Flandrin, 1979). Only when household economies eroded and an economy developed outside the household did our concept of family develop. As we shall see, the concept of family and many of its defining features are products of the separation of public and private spheres that accompanied industrialization. As people grappled with the problems of survival in a new social order, patterns of family life changed.

THE MIDDLE CLASS

Modern ideas about family developed largely out of changes brought about by the development of an industrial capitalist economy. In both England and North America, a "cult of domesticity" developed in reaction to, and as a critique of, an unfolding capitalist economy that people experienced as cruel, immoral, and beyond human control (Cott, 1977). It was an economy in which impersonal forces of supply and demand were replacing face-to-face negotiations and customs such as those reflected in the phrases "an honest price" and "a fair wage." It was an economy in which one could be rich one day and penniless the next. In contrast, the domestic sphere came to be defined as a moral abode characterized by peace, virtuous behaviour, and the selfless care of loved ones—a "haven in a heartless world" (Lasch, 1977).

Domesticity as an ideology and, for those who could afford it, a practice was a way of coping with a rapidly changing social order. For the business and professional class, men's work was increasingly moving out of the household. Home and business were separating as the scale of business increased. The middle-class home became a retreat, where the concerns and evils of the world of business were banished.

Mirroring the separation of men's and women's work, a new conception of gender emerged in the nineteenth century. Probably in an attempt to make sense of the new social order, people came to believe that men and women had fundamentally different natures. Women were assumed to belong naturally in the domestic sphere, as its guardian, and to be naturally nurturing. Men were believed to be suited to the competitive world of business, although their objective there was to provide for their families. Thus, an ideology of gender difference made sense of the unfolding social order, and in the middle class an evolving gendered division of labour developed with the physical separation of public and private spheres.

More than reflecting changes in social organization, these domestic and gender ideologies were developed by the middle class, which emerged in the nineteenth century. In England, this was a class struggling to assert its social identity and establish its right to political power by claiming a moral superiority over the aristocracy and the labouring masses. Borrowing religious imagery common in the Evangelical movements to which they were drawn, members of the middle class on both sides of the Atlantic shaped a domestic ideology that juxtaposed the home and the economy just as religious imagery juxtaposed heaven and earth. Dissociating themselves from a world seen as devoid of morality, the middle class wore their ideology of domesticity as a social badge—a symbol of their moral distance from the business world they inhabited (Davidoff and Hall, 1987).

In practice, these ideas provided more than an identity for the middle class. They also reflect the strategy this class was devising to deal with the fact that in the new capitalist economy fathers could no longer ensure their children's futures by passing on skills or property. That strategy involved educating children in ways that would equip them to adapt to the changing demands of the new economy. It involved instilling proper work habits and attitudes, and keeping them home through their teens so they might attend school rather than go to work. Central to this strategy was a role for mothers. And women themselves seem to have had a hand in fashioning the role of mother as socializer of her children, as they responded to the withdrawal of productive work from the household and the demise of their role as husbands' economic partners (Ryan, 1981). Of course, full-time motherhood—which was equated with womanhood for the middle class in the nineteenth century—entailed women's economic dependence on men.

Finally, the turn toward domesticity brought about a change in the emotional texture of family relations. When the need to produce subsistence was no longer the driving dynamic in daily household life, time and space became available for attending to emotional needs. By the end of the nineteenth century, children were the sentimental focus of middle-class family life (Davidoff and Hall, 1987).

Ironically, although nineteenth-century marriage entailed an ideal of love and companionship, the separation of men's and women's daily work undermined emotional closeness between them. In the increasingly gender-segregated world, women's emotional energy seems, in many cases, to have been directed largely toward other women—family and friends—in addition to children, rather than toward their husbands (Smith-Rosenberg, 1975).

THE WORKING CLASS

While family life was becoming a sentimental focus for the middle class, it was nearly endangered for the working class. Men's wages were so low in the nineteenth century that their children were often forced to work for pay—at long shifts, in horrible factory conditions, for cruel bosses, and risking illness and early death. Although working-class wives attempted to feed and clothe their families, in the tradition of peasant or farm wives, they lacked vital means of production, especially land. In turn, women's dependency on men—who had access to higher wages in the labour market—resulted in strained relations between men and women, marital tensions that focused on money, and probably frequent violence against women (Stansell, 1987). Their ability to cope was so fragile that many working-class families were forced to place their children in orphanages when unemployment, illness, or death occurred (Bradbury, 1982).

As they had in preindustrial times, families developed collective survival strategies to cope with the ravages of developing capitalism. Accordingly, individual needs were often sacrificed to the imperatives of family survival. Teenagers in the labour force gave their parents most of their earnings, and young adults postponed marriage until their parents could withstand the withdrawal of their earnings (Hareven, 1982). Married women did whatever they could, over and above child-care and homemaking, to contribute to household provisions—from doing mending and

laundering for neighbours to hawking goods on the street and taking in boarders (Stansell, 1987). Moreover, families doubled up to save on rent; in England, there were more extended-family households during the Industrial Revolution than before or after it (Anderson, 1971). Neighbours also helped each other out, in urban environments where housing afforded few amenities and little privacy.

Meanwhile, the trade-union movement responded to the straits of working-class life with a campaign for a **family wage**—that is, a wage paid to a man sufficient to support a wife and children (M. May, 1985). Social historians continue to debate the reasons why the goal of the labour movement was a family wage rather than simply decent wages for all. Whatever the reasons, defining the struggle in these terms undoubtedly had the effect of reinforcing a working-class conception of family that was not unlike the middle-class ideal—with women defined as mothers and homemakers, dependent on men as breadwinners.

Forty years after the idealized mother and children photo, we have this harrowing photo of a migrant mother and children. This striking juxtaposition illustrates the difference between middle-class and working-class lives.
SOURCE: Dorothea Lange, *Migrant Mother, Nipomo, California* (1936). The Museum of Modern Art, New York.

By the late nineteenth century, mothers and children were idealized. This image depicts a well-to-do mother and her children in 1894.
SOURCE: The Schlesinger Library, Radcliffe Institute, Harvard University.

To conclude, the breadwinner/homemaker division of labour that has characterized many families in the twentieth century arose out of people's struggles to survive or succeed materially, to care for their children, and to hold on to a sense of identity during times of massive social change. In turn, the patterns that emerged during the course of the twentieth century are clearly connected to the problems and possibilities men and women face in an industrial capitalist society.

SOCIAL RELATIONS IN FAMILIES TODAY

MAIN FEATURES

We have seen how the development of an economy characterized by competition among people led to a mistrust of the public sphere and a turn toward domesticity. The family became the location identified with caring relationships. At the same time, relations between many husbands and wives were hardly romantic. Only in the twentieth century did people begin to assume that romantic love, sex for the sake of pleasure, and marriage should be intimately bound together (Rapp and Ross, 1986).

An emotionally intense relationship between a man and a woman became key to marriage in the twentieth century. In the 1950s, amidst a booming postwar economy, and no doubt in reaction to years of insecurity caused by the Depression and World War II and sustained by the Cold War, adults plunged into marriage and family as never before. Social historian Stephanie Coontz (1992) argues that the 1950s represented the beginning of adult expectations that marriage and family would meet all of their needs. Women's and men's responsibilities in marriage were, of course, different: Women assumed responsibility for household and children, while men assumed responsibility for earning the money. Unfortunately, while some people who married in the 1950s found family life and gender roles to be fulfilling, many women felt constrained ("trapped" according to writers at the time) and stressed by being home all day and, while their husbands fared better, they too often felt less than fulfilled (Coontz, 1992; E. May, 1988). Research indicated that men benefited far more from marriage than women did: Married men's mental and physical health was better than that of single men, while married women fared worse than single women (Bernard, 1972). In the worse cases, conventional gender roles—which place women in the position of meeting husbands' needs—contributed to men's violence against women, as they do today. Women are still more likely to be seriously hurt by husbands, lovers, and especially ex-partners than by anyone else (Gartner, Dawson, and Crawford, 1998–99).

An intense mother–child relationship is also typical of modern families. As we have seen, raising children has not always been a privatized parental responsibility. Although capitalist employers bear no responsibility for the next generation of employees, feudal master craftsmen housed and fed their young apprentices as they trained them and used their labour. In precapitalist times, several households usually contributed to the rearing of a child. Community responsibility for children extended to more recent centuries as well: In the British colonies in North America, community leaders sometimes exercised the power to order households to take in orphans and raise them to adulthood.

In recent years, the state has avoided the assumption of responsibility for the welfare of children, except for their schooling, and instead has enforced fathers' responsibility for the financial support of their children and mothers' responsibility for child-care. When "mothers' allowances" were started early in the twentieth century in Canada, they were paid only to widows—women clearly without men—even though other types of lone mothers were equally in need of assistance (Baker, 1995). Newer forms of social assistance have involved "man-in-the-house" rules, which disqualify any woman who appears to have a man in her life. Moreover, one of the key government responses to growing concerns about child poverty is to strengthen attempts to force fathers who are separated from their wives to meet their child-support obligations. This strategy turns attention away from governmental and community responsibility for children's welfare. Similarly, aside from wartime emergencies, governments have failed to provide affordable daycare sufficient to meet the need for it. Child abuse sometimes results from the heavy responsibilities carried by parents, especially mothers.

In the 1950s, 1960s, and 1970s, when many men earned a "family wage," a majority of married women stayed home and assumed full-time domestic responsibilities. A gendered division of responsibility and labour was the way most families met the daily needs of adults and children. Because wages and salaries have eroded since the 1970s and most women (even those with preschool children) must work outside the home, the issue of who cares for the children is now a social problem. Compounding the problem are government cuts to education, health care, and other social services, which increase the work that must be done in the home. The ongoing assumption that child-care is a private responsibility is increasingly problematic.

The majority of Canadian women are faced with the need to juggle the fundamentally incompatible demands of employment and family every day. The stress of their "double day" of work generates considerable tension between women and their male partners, as men typically have failed to assume an equal share of housework, child-care, and care for the elderly (Marshall, 1994). In many cases, that tension contributes to divorce (Kurz, 1995). Nevertheless, men are doing more housework and child-care now than they did decades ago. And while women who are employed full-time juggle a heavy load, and lose sleep in the process, they also are significantly healthier (mentally and physically) than other women (Barnett and Rivers 1996).

The change in women's lives, coupled with the lack of significant accommodating change in many areas of society, has prompted increased diversity in household patterns (see Table 12.1). More people live alone—and only partly because of population aging. As life-long employment has become more common for women, people are marrying at a later age, and more people are never marrying. Between 1981 and 1991, the percent of people under 50 who never married increased; even the percent of people who were neither married nor cohabiting increased (Beaujot et al., 1995). While many Canadians who live by themselves likely have family relations, living alone raises concerns in a society where people often find support, loving care, and intense emotional connection only in their families.

In terms of family diversity, cohabiting men and women constitute the fastest-growing type of family in Canada. They more than doubled in number between 1981 and 1991; in 1996, 12 percent of Canadian families consisted of a "common-law" couple, and in 2001 almost 14 percent involved a common-law couple (Statistics Canada, 1999, 2002). The popularity of this kind of relationship probably reflects peoples' assessment of the personal costs involved in marriage. The sacrifices that women make after they marry, and especially when they become mothers, are emotionally and financially risky, given current rates of divorce. The interdependence that is characteristic of marriage may be less attractive to younger generations than to older ones who married when women were less able to support themselves without a man and sexual activity outside marriage was frowned upon. Research on how couples handle their money indicates that independence may be an objective of people who cohabit: Common-law couples are more likely to keep their money separate than married couples, who often create joint accounts (Singh and Lindsay, 1996). These relations are also more unstable than those involving marriage; that is, people feel freer to leave them (Marcil-Gratton, 1993).

The growing number of gay and lesbian families reflects some of the same social changes that produce common-law unions—most obviously, increased social acceptance of sexual expression, but also women's decreased economic dependence on men. The 2001 census produced our first estimate of families headed by same-sex common-law couples: 34 200 Canadians declared themselves to be living in same-sex relationships; the number represents 0.5 percent of all couples (Statistics Canada, 2002). About 15 percent of lesbian couples are raising children, and about 3 percent of gay male couples are living with children; in the vast majority of cases, these families have no additional people living with them.

Same-sex couples have faced an uphill battle for acceptance as families. For decades, the courts denied child custody to lesbian mothers leaving their husbands. Same-sex partners were also denied spousal benefits and the right to adopt nonbiological children they were raising. After years of protracted court battles, however, same-sex couples now have the same rights and responsibilities as heterosexual common-law couples. As of 2003, Canada became the third country in the world (after the Netherlands and Belgium) to allow same-sex marriage—in some provinces. Whether federal marriage law will be changed, however, remains a question in 2003, as politicians are divided on the issue.

Heterosexuality and procreative sex may be central to some people's definition of marriage, but

TABLE 12.1 DISTRIBUTION OF CANADIAN FAMILIES AND NEVER-MARRIED CHILDREN, SHOWING PERCENTAGES AND NUMBERS, BY FAMILY STRUCTURE AND EMPLOYMENT STATUS OF ADULTS—1996 AND 2001 CENSUS DATA

FAMILY STRUCTURE AND EMPLOYMENT STATUS OF ADULTS	1996		2001
	FAMILIES	NEVER-MARRIED SONS AND DAUGHTERS AT HOME	FAMILIES
Married couples	74%	73%	70.5%
With children	45		41
Both adults employed	27		
Husband sole breadwinner	10.5		
Wife sole breadwinner	2.5		
Without children	29		29
Both adults employed	10		
Husband sole breadwinner	4		
Wife sole breadwinner	2		
Common-law couples	12	8	13.8
With children	6		6.3
Both adults employed	3		
Husband sole breadwinner	1		
Wife sole breadwinner	4		
Without children	6		7.5
Both adults employed	4		
Husband sole breadwinner	1		
Wife sole breadwinner	6		
Lone-parent families	14.5	19	15.7
Male parent	2		
Employed	1.6		
Female parent	12		
Employed	6		
Total (percentages)	100%	100%	100%
Numbers	7 837 865	9 369 750	8 371 020

SOURCES: Statistics Canada, "Census Families in Private Households by Family Structure, Presence of Children and Labour Force Activity of Husband/Male Common-Law Partner, Showing Labour Force Activity of Wife/Female Common-Law Partner or Lone Parent, for Canada, 1996 Census (20% Sample Data)," Cat. No. 93F0030XDB96004, (downloaded from http://www.statcan.ca/english/census96/june9/f3can.htm, June 9, 1999); Statistics Canada, "Census Families in Private Households by Family Structure, Showing Number of Families, Average Family Size and Number of Never-Married Sons and Daughters at Home, for Canada, Provinces and Territories, 1991 and 1996 Censuses—20% Sample Data," Cat. No. 93F0022XDB96008 (downloaded from http://www.statcan.ca/english/census96/oct14/fam1.htm, October 14, 1999); Used by authority of the Minister of Labour. Statistics Canada, "Profile of Canadian Families and Households: Diversification Continues," *The Daily*. Cat. No. 11-001-XIE. Oct, 2002

same-sex couples display characteristics that approximate family ideals. Their relationships are more likely to break up than heterosexual marriages, but they are no more likely to do so than cohabiting heterosexual couples (Stacey and Biblarz, 2001). The stability of same-sex relationships is, in fact, impressive given the higher standards of emotional intimacy they typically have relative to heterosexual couples, the weaker institutional pressures to stay together, and the fewer social supports to their relationships (Stacey and Biblarz, 2001). They are more likely to have egalitarian housework and child-care arrangements than heterosexual married and cohabiting couples (Blumenstein and Schwartz, 1983). Moreover, given the obstacles they face, the families of same-sex couples can be seen to be the products of *choice* to a greater degree than other families (Weston, 1991). Certainly, while married women often allow "fate" to decide whether or not they have children, lesbians must choose to get pregnant. In turn, the children they raise, despite the stigma they may face, show levels of well-being similar to children who grow up in other families (Stacey and Biblarz, 2001).

Still more family diversity is indicated by the growing precedence of lone-parent families. Families headed by only one adult are not new in Canada, but their numbers have increased in recent decades. In 2001, 15.7 percent of families consisted of one parent—usually a mother—and her dependent children (Statistics Canada, 2002). Early in the twentieth century, when they were as common as today, such families typically involved a widow and her children. Since the early 1990s more than half of them involve separated or divorced women, and in 1991 about 20 percent involved never-married women (Statistics Canada, 1992b: 5). In 2001, 19 percent of Canadian children lived with only one parent (Statistics Canada, 2002) (see Figure 12.1). Considerably more children will live with only one parent over the course of their childhood. Over half of these families were poor in the late 1990s (National Council of Welfare, 1998). The changes many governments are making to social assistance ("welfare") programs, which tie assistance to employment ("workfare") and thus require that one adult both support the household financially and take care of children, increases the problems faced by lone-parent families.

There are other trends that indicate increasing diversity of families. Decades of fairly high rates of divorce have produced large numbers of "reconstituted" families. It is estimated that in 2001 almost 12 percent of couples with children involved a step-parent, compared to 10 percent in 1995 (Statistics Canada, 2002). Children whose parents have remarried after divorce have a fairly complicated network of family relations. Also involving children is an important life-cycle change: More and more young adults are continuing to live with their parents, or returning to their parents' home after leaving it. In 2001, 41 percent of adults 20 to 29 years of age lived with their parents, compared to 27.5 percent in 1981 (Statistics Canada, 2002).

There are racial, ethnic, and class differences in family patterns in Canada as well, although our knowledge of these is limited. Approximately 18 percent of Black women and 15 percent of Aboriginal women in Canada were lone parents, compared to 7 percent of all non-Aboriginal women, in 1991 (Statistics Canada, 1992b: 14, 19). The fact that Black families in Canada are less likely to contain a married couple, or a common-law couple, is related to the lower likelihood that Black men can earn a stable, sizeable income. Rates of marriage increase significantly with income among Black Canadians (Calliste, 2001). We do not know if Black lone mothers regularly compensate for low incomes and absence of a partner by relying on personal support networks of relatives and friends. In the early 1970s, poor African Americans were found to create women-centred

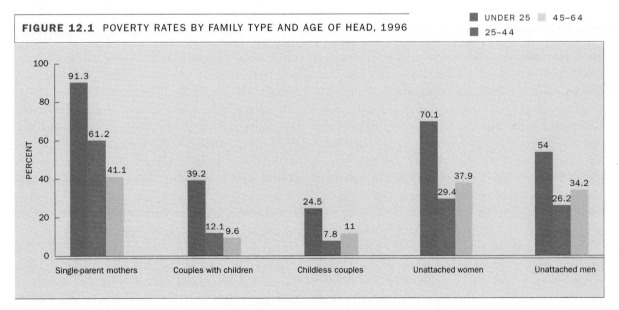

FIGURE 12.1 POVERTY RATES BY FAMILY TYPE AND AGE OF HEAD, 1996

■ UNDER 25   ▨ 45–64
■ 25–44

SOURCE: Human Resources Development Canada, National Council of Welfare, *Poverty Profile 1996* (Ottawa: Minister of Public Works and Government Services, 1998) p. 36. Reprinted with permission of the Minister of Public Works and Government Services, 2000.

networks whose members shared scarce resources and cooperated in child-care (Stack, 1974). Certainly, a pattern of cooperation among kin, across nuclear families—including living together in extended-family households—has been typical of many working-class and immigrant Canadians and Americans (Iacovetta, 1992; Kibria, 1993).

In what follows I discuss the practices and social relationships that are central to family life. Emotional intimacy and sexual expression are so important to the creation of committed relations that I examine them first. Because family life is typically organized around a gendered division of labour, I next discuss the sources of gender differences. Then I review changes in the institutional basis of many families—marriage. Parenthood, child-care, and housework "make family," and I discuss them before considering both divorce and social policies.

SEXUALITY AND FAMILIES

While historically families were largely arrangements for perpetuating wealth or ensuring economic survival, now it is love and the promise of ongoing intimacy and caring that propel people into long-term commitment. Increasingly, we have come to expect lasting sexual, emotional, and social happiness in a relationship. This is an ambitious expectation in a society where we also expect to grow and change as we mature, and where our hours of paid work have risen consistently since the mid-twentieth century.

We also live in a society where images of sexuality surround us, and specifically where non-committed, or recreational, sex is eroticized: Sex in marriage is not a common erotic image. While we think of our sexuality as a very personal matter, our desires are clearly subject to the influence of film, TV, and advertising. Even governments historically have attempted to exert control over their citizens' sexuality. The most obvious reason sexuality has been the object of state control is that the family is the unit of social reproduction. Society depends on families to produce and care for the next generation. Accordingly, with the aim of tying sexuality to reproduction, most Western governments in the nineteenth century passed laws banning the use of all forms of contraception. In Canada, section 179c of the 1892 Criminal Code made the selling or advertising of any contraceptive or device for performing abortion an indictable offence. This legislation was not only a form of **pronatalism** (a policy aimed at increasing the population), it was also the product of the fear that white, middle-class Canadians of northern European descent were not reproducing in large enough numbers, while immigrants of darker skin were doing just that. Not until 1969 was the Criminal Code amended to make contraceptives legal. Abortion remained a criminal offence until 1988, after Dr. Henry Morgentaler's repeated challenges of the law.

Since the "sexual revolution" of the 1960s, women and men typically are sexually active before they marry or begin to cohabit (see Chapter 5). In other words, people enter committed relationships with more knowledge of each other and a better sense of their compatibility on a number of important dimensions. At the same time, sexuality is affected by the social context in which it occurs, and the fact that it occurs between people who are products of gender socialization. Consequently, certain patterns are extremely common over the course of relationships, which present couples with challenges about ensuring the vitality, and even the endurance, of long-term relationships.

The first pattern that presents challenges to couples who love each other and commit to a lasting relationship has to do with the fact that social context, or situation, strongly affects people's sexual behaviour. Because opportunity is a major determinant of the frequency of sexuality, people who live together are on average more active sexually (despite TV images of the singles lifestyle). Married and cohabiting men and women have sex more often than men and women who are single (Schwartz and Rutter, 1998). However, people who are married are significantly less active sexually than people who are cohabiting (comparing people of the same age and who are together the same length of time) (Schwartz and Rutter, 1998). Moreover, for all types of relationship—married, common-law, gay, and lesbian—sexual activity decreases considerably over the course of a relationship, dropping especially after the first two years or so (Schwartz and Rutter, 1998). The decline over time is due not only to the reduced excitement attached to familiarity but also the effects of having children and growing responsibilities. With an infant or a toddler in the house, sleep becomes more valuable than sexuality. Long hours of employment, worries over money, anxieties about children and other issues common to long-term relationships also inhibit sexual desire.

Gender differences also affect sexuality, as well as intimacy. The "sexual revolution" was limited in a number of ways. For instance, there remain different norms for men and women with respect to sexuality. Men are still expected to initiate sexual activity. Although they want women to initiate sex more than they used to, women can still cross a line—they can be too aggressive. Couples have to continually negotiate around this set of expectations. Nonmonogamy is usually seen as the major sexual threat to the stability of marriage. Yet, according to the largest survey of sexual behaviour in North America, the National Health and Social Life Survey of Americans, the vast majority of married men (79 percent) and married women (89 percent) report being monogamous all of their married years (Schwartz and Rutter, 1998:148). Couples who are not married are much less likely to be monogamous, so clearly the expectations around marriage, as well as the reduced opportunities that married people face, affect behaviour.

Sexual behaviour in same-sex couples reflects gender differences. Typically, gay male couples have more frequent sex, and lesbian couples have less sex, than heterosexual couples (Schwartz and Rutter, 1998). That men find recreational sex appealing, and that women are socialized not to initiate sex, present a variety of issues for same-sex couples. Ongoing social stigma attached to these relationships compounds the obstacles to lasting relationships—making their durability all the more impressive.

Aside from sexuality, intimacy must also be negotiated amidst gender differences. While men typically experience sex as the route to intimacy, women need intimacy—and expressions of it—before sex (Rubin 1990). Intimacy is also made more difficult by gender differences in the expression of love and caring. Women typically seem to be better at discussing their feelings (as well as accessing them)—something central to our culture's definition of intimacy—while men may be more likely to express intimacy through caring activities, which may not be recognized as such. These gender differences are neither innate nor necessarily a product of socialization, since there is no evidence that women are more empathic than men. The differences are probably due to gendered experiences and family responsibilities; most obviously,

women need to learn to nurture, given the responsibilities for children's well-being that they take on with motherhood (Tavris, 1992). Overall, it seems there are obstacles to long-term heterosexual relationships in large part due to gender differences in individuals' orientation and norms about gender. Yet the majority of Canadians who marry stay together, so we can only assume that they find their relationships satisfying in a number of respects.

GENDER AND FAMILIES

We go to great lengths to try to ensure that children develop into heterosexual beings. We also spend much time and effort—often unconsciously—making sure that girls and boys develop different orientations. The differences that are promoted are directly related to the gendered division of labour that organizes nuclear families. Accordingly, surveys of Canadian high-school students consistently find that girls plan to take time out of their adult employment to devote to family while boys do not.

There is plenty of evidence that girls and boys are socialized differently as they are growing up, probably in part because of a pervasive conviction that boys and girls are naturally different. Relying on the concept of socialization to explain gender differences is not very useful, however. Some researchers have studied the choices that adults make in their lives about whether to prioritize work or family. They find that childhood socialization has less effect on such choice than adult experiences in paid work and intimate relations (Gerson, 1985). Thus, a better explanation of girls' tendency to focus on domesticity emphasizes that they make decisions in the light of the opportunities and constraints they face. American sociologist Arlie Hochschild (1989) has argued that adults face life with **gender strategies** that involve a prioritization of either career/job or family relationships. That prioritization then guides their life decisions. According to Hochschild, people's gender strategies result from a combination of ideas about gender in the culture, emotionally charged reactions to childhood (especially parents' gender roles), and the opportunities and constraints that they faced as they became adults.

A good illustration of gender strategy can be found in Jane Gaskell's study of the expectations of young people graduating from three high schools in working-class areas of Vancouver. Most of the girls judged paid work to be more satisfying than the domestic roles of mother, wife, and housewife: Their socialization had not produced a desire for domestic roles. At the same time, they overwhelmingly agreed that they would eventually assume primary responsibility for housework and child-care. They saw their futures as bound up with domesticity for a number of reasons. First, they assumed that they would have a male partner and that he would be unwilling and unable to share the household work. Second, they predicted that their future earnings, relative to their spouse's, would be low, and that it would therefore make economic sense for them to assume household responsibility rather than paid employment. Third, they felt that babies were better off at home with their mothers. The boys in the study concurred with the girls about who should take on housework and child-care duties (Gaskell, 1983). Gaskell's findings indicate that girls prioritize domestic responsibilities largely because of the lack of opportunities facing them, from good jobs to good daycare to egalitarian men.

Similarly, a U.S. study of the decisions that women make about whether to prioritize family or paid work found that women who ended up prioritizing family and the care of loved ones often did so because of a negative experience of paid work (Gerson, 1985). Thus, gender inequality in the labour force promotes the gendered division of labour in the home. It also pushes women toward marriage. Women's relatively weaker market position and the growing need for two incomes when there are dependants to support means that if women want children and a decent standard of living, marriage is a wise "choice."

At the same time, labour-market inequality forces impossible choices. Employers still define jobs, especially professional jobs, in terms of employees who are unencumbered by family responsibilities and are able to work after 5 P.M., at night, on weekends, and so on. Job sharing, part-time work with good benefits, workplace daycare facilities, and paid leave for tending sick children are still uncommon in Canada. Careers and family responsibilities are still incompatible for women. Thus, many successful career women are single. In the face of little change in the workplace, dual-earner couples with children are left to design their own ways to balance conflicting responsibilities. One person—usually the woman—cuts back on paid work, works nonstandard hours, and so forth. Meanwhile, the ages of marriage and childbearing are rising as women postpone the balancing act that combining family and paid work entails.

MARRIAGE AND DIVORCE

Today, because relatively few men earn enough to support a family, and women need to do paid work, the conventional gendered division of work and responsibility is no longer viable. Old patterns die hard, however. And the contradictory nature of old family patterns existing in new circumstances has generated an increase in divorce, pressures on men to assume new family roles, and a need for new social policies.

Family law has changed to reflect the new circumstances. Before the late 1970s, the marriage contract stipulated a simple but unequal exchange between a woman and a man: He was responsible for his and her maintenance, and she owed him domestic and sexual services. Meg Luxton (1980) explored the personal consequences of the conventional gendered division of labour in her study of working-class, breadwinner/homemaker families living in Flin Flon, Manitoba, in the late 1970s. Her clearest finding was that breadwinning translated into privilege. Because men's families depended on them, their needs assumed priority—meals prepared according to their taste, children kept quiet for the sake of their need for peace, and so on. Conversely, housewives' economic dependence typically meant an inability to get their own needs met in the relationship.

That these inequalities were typical in a conventional marriage is suggested by statistics on physical and mental health. Comparisons of men's and women's physical and mental health in the 1960s and 1970s show that men benefited from the care they received in marriage, while the work of personal care took a toll on women. Married men were significantly better off physically and mentally than single men, whereas the opposite was true for women (Bernard, 1972).

Divorce has gradually become more common over the course of the last century, and more rapidly since 1968, when federal law was liberalized. Recently, the divorce rate has levelled off. According to popular opinion (and some sociologists), the rise in the divorce rate testifies to increased selfishness, unwillingness to make the compromises required by a relationship, and laziness when it comes to "working out" interpersonal problems. This explanation denies the rights of individuals to happiness and emphasizes instead the importance of maintaining the institution of marriage. It ignores the fact that there have tended to be two experiences of marriage—"his" and "hers"—and that women are typically the ones called on to overcome selfishness, make compromises, and work to create happy homes. In the worst marriages, women are the ones subject to severe violence (Gartner, Dawson, and Crawford, 1998–99). Thus, women are more likely than men to initiate separation and divorce—and do so for reasons often having to do with gender inequities in their marriage (Kurz, 1995).

In view of the fact that women have entered the labour market in increasing numbers—and thus gained the possibility of self-support—and have been exposed to the climate of change brought about by the women's liberation movement, it is not surprising that divorce rates have risen. It is estimated that about 30 percent of marriages in Canada will end in divorce, which is considerably below rates in the United States and Sweden, but high when the consequences for children are considered. (The aftermath of divorce is considered below.) Although the majority of adults who divorce later remarry, marriage is now no longer the only basis of family formation. By the late 1980s, one in five Canadian babies were born out of wedlock; in 1990, 38 percent of Quebec newborns' parents were not married, though most were cohabiting (Marcil-Gratton, 1993).

Meanwhile, marriage as an institution has changed. In the late 1970s, with the explicit aim of recognizing the work that women do in the home, provinces across Canada reformed their family laws to omit any mention of gender-specific obligations and exchanges. Replacing the old model of a "community" of interdependent men and women was one assuming the spousal relationship to be a partnership of equal individuals, both of whom contribute to the marriage and are responsible for themselves. Under the old laws, a woman had no right to "family assets," including property that resulted from her own work over the years (because she owed her husband her labour). Now, "family assets," which include some of the fruits of advanced educational degrees and pensions, are to be divided equally upon divorce (Morton, 1988). The new laws encourage people leaving a marriage to become independent as quickly as possible; women are not entitled to continued support, as they were under the old laws.

Ironically, because the new laws treat women and men equally, the results are inequitable. The assumption that women can support themselves as men do is simply incorrect, given the gender inequality that continues to characterize the labour market. For many working-class women, there is the additional problem that sharing "family assets" simply means sharing the poverty. Not surprisingly, the chief result of divorce is a significantly lowered standard of living for women and the children who usually live with them (Finnie, 1993).

HOUSEWORK AND MOTHERWORK

Although the new family laws stipulate equality, a gendered division of labour still predominates in households. Women may have assumed part of the responsibility of breadwinning—in 1991 they contributed an average of 26 percent of family income (Statistics Canada, 1993a)—but they remain largely responsible for the housework (Marshall, 1994; Presser, 1994). Men do more when their partners are employed, and more housework than they used to, but women continue to bear most of the responsibility and do a majority of the necessary daily chores. Consequently, employed women generally work longer hours than their partners every week, and have less time for sleep, leisure, friends, and children than do full-time homemakers and men. As Chapter 9 argues, this gender difference is both a manifestation and cause of the inequality between women and men in Canada today.

Why does this gender inequity persist? Some men translate higher earnings into privilege at home. Marriage involves negotiations—if not daily, then at least periodically, and especially early in the relationship. Women's bargaining power in those negotiations is undermined by the following factors: women's disadvantage in the labour market; women's perceived disadvantage on the remarriage market (which weakens their courage to push for change in the relationship); a cultural devaluation of caring work; and ideals of gender, especially of masculinity (Hochschild, 1989).

Meanwhile, surveys show that couples who share housework are significantly happier than others. Among couples who do not share housework, the resulting tension in the relationship affects the men and the children as well as the women (Hochschild, 1989). Research also shows that equality in the labour market and at home go hand in hand: Couples who do similar work, especially dual-career couples, seem to be more likely to share household work (Hertz, 1986). Given that gender inequality is still present in the labour market, the unequal division of housework is likely to persist for some time.

Having children also contributes to the division of labour between women and men. Although becoming a parent typically means that a woman is wholly absorbed in the responsibility of caring for the baby, at least for the first six months, fathers usually become much more devoted to making money, often increasing their hours at work (Fox, 1997).

There is a growing conviction that full-time mothering is bad for women and, consequently, for their children, and that men's physical absence from the home also can be detrimental to the social development of children, if men's absence leads to emotional distance from children. For women, the privatized nature of parenting causes problems. Because full-time mothers are home alone much of the day, many suffer from social isolation. Alone with the responsibility, most women find the full-time care of young children stressful because it combines high demands and low control over time (Rosenberg, 1987). A Canadian study likened the work of full-time mothers with young children to that of "front-line" workers servicing people with pressing needs, among whom "burnout" is a common problem. At work and on call 24 hours a day, full-time mothers have no "down time" and often only minimal sleep (Rosenberg, 1987). For single mothers, of course, all these problems are intensified.

These problems are the result of the social organization of child-care in this society. The responsibility for child-care is privatized, which means that it rests with the parents alone. Neither the health-care system nor the educational system provides many services for the early years of children's lives. Drop-in facilities, frequent home visiting, and good-quality daycare have yet to be considered a basic part of our social infrastructure.

At the same time, most of us are certain it is best for babies and toddlers to be at home with their mothers. On dispassionate and careful consideration, however, the more logical conclusion is that toddlers and even infants fare better when they are cared for by several adults and when they spend at least part of the time outside the home. A single, isolated caregiver inevitably loses some inspiration, enthusiasm, and even warmth over the course of 24 hours a day, seven days a week. Moreover, the home is not designed for toddlers; it is both more dangerous and less stimulating than it should be. Indeed, adult needs for order compete with toddler needs to explore and manipulate their environment: Housework and child-care conflict. Moreover, there is considerable evidence that children who are in good-quality daycare from early ages are significantly advantaged in terms of cognitive and social development over those who stay at home (Clarke-Stewart, 1982).

The majority of mothers of young children today are working outside the home, unable to afford full-time motherhood even if they prefer it. The problem they confront is having to handle a stressful balancing act (juggling responsibilities at home and the workplace) every weekday. Although attention to this problem has typically focused on increasing men's contribution, perhaps there is just not enough time in the day to do the work that many couples face. Solutions require a collective response; however, the Canadian government's main response to the problem has been to recruit foreign domestic workers, obliging them to provide domestic service for several years before they can obtain permanent-resident status. Using nannies to solve the child-care problem involves the continued privatization of domestic labour, which, in effect, allows the community to avoid solving the problem. It allows wealthy professionals, who might otherwise combine forces to put political pressure on the government for a solution that would help everyone, to solve the problem privately. This solution also means having child-care and housework done by workers who are highly vulnerable to exploitation, given their long hours of work, their low pay, their social isolation, their lack of citizenship rights, and the private nature of their relationship with the employer (Arat-Koc, 1993). The arrangement puts Third World women in the position of subsidizing the dual careers and comfortable lifestyles of middle-class Canadians.

BECOMING PARENTS

Aside from the work it entails, parenthood changes people's lives profoundly. We have already discussed the difficulties of motherhood due to its privatized nature. Even giving birth in our society indicates that women stand on their own as mothers. Medicalized childbirth offers women very limited assistance—aimed at relieving pain, minimizing physical danger, and delivering the baby.

In the past, in our culture and others, women giving birth were assisted by other women, who continued to care for them and instruct them about mothering in the weeks following the birth. Because women giving birth in hospital today are usually without this kind of support, most experience at least one bout of postpartum depression (which is falsely attributed to hormones) and many begin motherhood upset or angry because of their experience of childbirth (Fox and Worts, 1999). Many new mothers are also overwhelmed by the responsibility they have taken on; most find themselves totally unprepared to care for a new baby. Because midwives are now being licensed and their services are publicly funded in Ontario, Quebec, British Columbia, and Manitoba, many Canadian women can receive their trained assistance and support from before the birth to months afterwards, and still give birth in hospital, as well as at home.[1]

Following a baby's birth, parents go through a challenging time of adjustment, which leads to significant changes in their lives. As we saw, the division of work and responsibility usually becomes more conventional for most heterosexual couples, though usually not for same-sex couples (Fox, 1997; Patterson, 1995). Ties with friends also tend to weaken, as new parents typically spend more time with extended kin (Fox, 1997). These changes obviously are not inevitable. Couples negotiate them, and some resist the various forces moving them in this direction.

Having children entails another, more important change in most parents' lives. Women typically feel that motherhood completely changes their lives. Men who become involved in the care of their children seem to have the same reaction. Most research has found that having children brings profound meaning to people's lives. One study suggested that becoming a mother was not only to "fall in love" with a child but also to experience a transformation in one's sense of self. Women tend to feel more loving and caring, and thus more closely identified with femininity, when they care for their children (McMahon, 1995).

DIVORCE AND ITS AFTERMATH

When people live together as a couple and a family, the dissolution of that unit brings them turmoil for some time. People divorce largely because at least one spouse feels that something central to the marriage no longer exists—something such as a sharing of responsibility or mutual caring. Women are more likely to initiate separation and divorce than men. Another of the chief reasons women do so is violence (Kurz, 1995).

Research indicates that serious violence committed against a woman is likely to involve a pattern of control by a man (Gartner, Dawson, and Crawford, 1998–99). That some men need to be in control is a product of social forces as well as psychological characteristics. In this culture, ideals of masculinity hold men to an expectation of some kind of dominance over women—an ideal often achieved through superior earnings. Poverty and unemployment can, then, be factors in men's violence against women, since they pose threats to men's identity. Moreover, conventional gender roles place women living with men in the position of meeting their needs—whether that involves meeting emotional needs or ensuring that meals are prepared. A woman's failure to do so may trigger violence from a man who feels entitled to her services. Given how central men's control is to violence against women, separation and divorce are times when women are especially vulnerable to further violence (Gartner, Dawson, and Crawford, 1998–99).

Fortunately, violence occurs in only a minority of marriages and common-law relationships. When these relationships break up, people face considerable adjustment. Probably the most important consequence of divorce for women and the children who live with them is a significant decline in family income. This decline is often so great that many fall out of the middle class, lose their family home, move, and thus change schools (Finnie, 1993). A majority of single-parent mothers with dependent children—61.4 percent in 1996—are living in poverty (National Council of Welfare, 1998: 18). Low income is especially significant because it reduces mothers' ability to provide what researchers find to be most important for children's adjustment after divorce—additional emotional support and a predictable daily schedule (Furstenberg and Cherlin, 1991).

The conflict between spouses that precedes and accompanies divorce (and persists for some couples who do not divorce) is certainly damaging for children. Yet, in the vast majority of cases, children return to normal development about two years after divorce. Nevertheless, some research indicates that women whose parents divorced are more likely to marry and have children early, to give birth before marriage, and to have their own marriages break up (McLanahan and Bumpass, 1988: 147). The reasons are not clear, but it is possible that the children of divorce carry emotional baggage from their childhood. As for the adults who divorce, the vast majority feel after a while that their divorce improved their lives. Even women struggling with poverty can feel relieved at least to be in control of the money (Graham, 1987).

Lone Parents

In the last two decades, in addition to an increase in the divorce rate, there has been an increase in the proportion of mothers who are unmarried. In 2001, 15.7 percent of all Canadian families were lone-parent families, and 19 percent of children lived in one-parent families (Statistics Canada, 2002). There are also racial and ethnic differences in the likelihood that children will be raised by one parent. In 1986, 23 percent of Aboriginal families living off reserves were headed by one parent, nearly twice the rate for all Canadians (McKie, 1993: 59).

The chief problem facing lone-parent families is poverty. Most are headed by women, and the majority are poor. The reasons for the poverty are clear. A woman—someone already disadvantaged in the labour market—is expected both to earn money and to care for children, since support from the former spouse (if there is one) and the state is generally meagre. Thus, the tension between employment and family is acute in these families. The evidence is that children who grow up in female-headed families are less likely to complete high school than those living in two-parent families because of the financial stress that lone parents face, and not because of the absence of a father figure (McLanahan, 1985).

Reconstituted Families

Adults who divorce usually remarry, so they and their children establish new families. Although these reconstituted families find themselves in a much better financial situation than lone-parent families, they face their own problems. Stepparents are in a difficult position with respect to their spouses' chil-

A homeless mother holds her sleeping baby.
SOURCE: Copyright © David Urbina/Photo Edit.

dren; stepmothers especially face considerable challenges. According to the research, the outcomes of these new situations are uncertain. In many reconstituted families, both stepparents and stepchildren establish very close relationships; in a sizable number of such families, though, the tensions continue (Furstenberg and Cherlin, 1991). Many reconstituted families do not survive the early years of adjustment: Divorce rates are higher for second marriages, especially if children are present. Children in reconstituted families—like those in lone-parent families—face a small risk of experiencing developmental and social problems, but one that is greater than that for children living in two-parent families that have not experienced divorce.

POLICIES TO SUPPORT FAMILIES

The chief problem for families today seems to be the difficulty of caring for children while earning enough money to support a family. The problem assumes crisis proportions for many lone-parent families, but is also of major importance in dual-earner families. The policies that most industrial countries have developed to address this problem include direct family subsidies, significant paid parental leave following birth, and good-quality, subsidized child-care facilities—especially preschool for children over two-and-a-half years of age (Eyer, 1996). Such policies are predicated both on the assumption of the community's responsibility for all its children and on state actions to support women as mothers *and* wage earners. In some cases, they are based on goals of universality and equity. In Canada, in contrast, children are assumed to be a private responsibility, as is the problem women face in juggling family and employment (see Box 12.1).

While most European countries provide more generous state support of families than Canada, Sweden has especially good policies. There, it is assumed that children are a collective responsibility, and it is an official policy objective to promote gender equality in the home and the labour force. Behind this orientation lies a role of the Swedish state that is very different from that of the Canadian state: The state in Sweden directly acts to control the effects of market forces in order to pursue the goals of social equity and meeting human needs.

The Swedish government very effectively redistributes income from families with high incomes and without children to those with lower incomes and children. Its universal family allowances were four-and-a-half times the amount paid in Canada in 1991. Lone parents receive supplemental child support. Consequently, under 5 percent of lone-parent families in Sweden are poor (Baker, 1995: 72, 126–27).

In Sweden, all new parents can take 18 months of parental leave (i.e., for either a mother or father)—12 months at 80 percent of their previous wage or salary, the next three months at a low flat rate, and the last three months without pay (Eyer, 1996). Most families take 12 months of maternity leave. In addition to parental leave, new parents can reduce their working hours to 30 per week and retain their job until their child is eight years of age. And all employees are entitled to leave from employment to care for a sick child (at 90 percent of their wage or salary) (Eyer, 1996).

Although Swedish babies are cared for at home by their parents, from age six months to seven years (when they enter school) all Swedish children are eligible for daycare services. Since 1988, over 70 percent of children under six years of age have been enrolled in daycare, usually in a daycare centre, but also in family daycare (where a woman takes up to four children in her home and is regularly supervised) (Baker, 1995). Before-school and after-school care is also available for children up to the age of 12. Because of such support, about 90 percent of Swedish women are employed.

English Canada stands in sharp contrast to the situation in Sweden. In a political climate that prioritizes fiscal restraint, both Conservative and Liberal governments have avoided commitment to universal child-care, focusing instead on assistance targeted at low-income families and social-assistance recipients. The Canada Child Tax Benefit only applies to families with incomes up to just slightly above the poverty level. While there has been much talk about creating a high-quality, affordable, regulated child-care system on a national scale, no progress has been made in that direction (Mahon and Phillips, 2002). Consequently, while about half of Canadian children under the age of 12 and with parents in paid work or full-time studies are in some form of nonparental care, most are in unregulated care, provided by unlicensed caregivers outside the home, or nannies (Beach et. al.,

BOX 12.1   IT'S TIME TO ACT ON CHILD-CARE

You can park your children in front of *Sesame Street* and they will learn. But there is not nearly the same impact as if you stay with them and watch.

—Dr. Fraser Mustard, quoted in *Maclean's* magazine, March 1, 1999

A nice mental prod, those words, to thinking about what today's Speech from the Throne is going to say about the long-awaited, much-trumpeted national children's agenda. Are we going to get something real or are we going to get suckered?

Like a lot of quotes from Dr. Mustard, the famed student of child-brain development, this one is layered and rather enigmatic. At one level, his words will guilt-out working parents across the country. At another level, they will be ammunition for advocates of quality child care and early childhood education.

At still a third level, they'll assault all those of us who do not make it home from work until 7 at night; who are too busy working weekends; who have jobs that provide miserly parental leave and time off for family needs; who are under financial pressure to take jobs that mean leaving the children with a neighbour or an untrained teenager down the hall.

Most important, Dr. Mustard's words generically disturb us. For just a moment, a day or two, they focus our minds on how important the children are to our society.

Those who argue that a national children's agenda should be just about tax measures and fiscal transfers to the provinces or just about a national child-care program or just about peripheral nips and tucks to existing programs and a lot of warm statements for the future about federal-provincial co-operation—those people are missing the point.

Here is the point:

By conservative estimate—from a number of scholars and research institutions—the physical health, mental health, competence and future productivity of at least one in four Canadian children is being compromised by psychiatric disorders, school failure and antisocial and violent behaviour.

We know that what aggravates those phenomena are poverty, parental depression and other mental illnesses and financial and workplace stresses on the family. A national children's agenda means addressing the issues of family stress, of what happens to the family when it conflicts with the demands of the workplace.

Here is the point:

McMaster University's System Linked Research Unit studied what happened to 100 mothers on social assistance who were offered a complete range of medical and social services for themselves over two years, along with free access to high-quality child care for the youngsters who required it and well-supervised recreation programs for all children from birth to age 18.

Twenty-five per cent of those mothers left social assistance. In comparison, only 10 per cent of mothers offered no extra services—and, specifically, no licensed quality child care—and only 10 per cent of mothers on the province's workfare program left social assistance in the same time period.

The savings to government calculated by the McMaster researchers was $500,000 over and above the cost of providing the comprehensive services. The McMaster researchers estimated that if the full-service model were to be adopted throughout Ontario, the savings would be $12-million over two years.

The point is this:

A national children's agenda means addressing the requirements of the whole child.

It means a new national standard of longer work-leaves for parents of newborns.

It means firmly cemented national standards on health determinants for children and youth.

It means more federally funded research and demonstration projects on child abuse, on innovative school-based programs for troubled children, on physical and mental-health programs for poor children and immigrant and refugee children. It means addressing homelessness.

The point is this:

A national children's agenda means that the dividend of budget balancing is high-quality, affordable, accessible child care available to Canadian parents who need it. There can't be any more political blather on whether this is necessary.

SOURCE: Michael Valpy, "It's time to act on child care," *The Globe and Mail*, October 12, 1999. Reprinted with permission of *The Globe and Mail*.

1998). Spaces for babies and toddlers in daycare centres are limited and usually expensive. In lieu of commitment to daycare, the Liberal government recently extended parental leave following childbirth to 52 weeks (with considerable limits on earnings and eligibility). The move reinforces parents' responsibility to care for their children full-time, and reduces demand for child-care services.

Since the late 1990s, Quebec has moved in the opposite direction—toward creating a broad set of family policies that feature universal, affordable child-care (Jenson, 2002). After eliminating a long-standing tax deduction for child-care of all kinds, the Parti Quebecois used the savings to support and create child-care facilities featuring programs with an educational emphasis, run by professionals (Jenson, 2002). Parents pay $5 per day for child-care, which is expected to be available to every child who needs it in the near future. Additionally, the Quebec government pays family allowances that are targeted to low-income parents, with additional money going to lone-parent families. So, at present, two very different policy approaches coexist in Canada.

CONCLUSION

Nuclear families centred on the emotional fulfillment of adults and the nurturing of children are relatively new in human history. Fundamental to their existence is women's assumption of domestic responsibilities and men's assumption of financial responsibilities. The fact that most men no longer earn enough to support their families and that the majority of women are essential breadwinners has created strains in nuclear families. The stress is greatest for women, who must daily juggle the conflicting demands of family and paid work. In turn, divorce rates are high, and the numbers of lone-parent families are increasing.

Because the Canadian government provides little support to people raising children, families without two adult income earners are especially likely to struggle financially. Thus, family diversity exacerbates income inequality. And government cutbacks of social services have meant a greater burden on most Canadian families, however they are organized.

Because women deal with the strain between family and employment every day, there is likely to be growing pressure on governments to provide family support, such as good-quality, affordable daycare. There is also likely to be increasing pressure on employers to build flexibility into the workweek and career structures. Thus, just as recent economic change has promoted change in family patterns, we may expect people's family concerns to cause a variety of other social changes.

SUMMARY

1. Commonsense arguments hold that current dilemmas in family life, such as how women can balance the responsibilities of family and paid work and how men can succeed at breadwinning and also do their share of the housework, are private, individual problems. Similarly, family-values advocates argue that change by individuals is the solution to family problems. In the absence of a sociological analysis, the public sources of these problems—and of their potential solutions—remain unclear and unrecognized.

2. Biology does not produce the family, which varies in its organization considerably across different cultures and through history. Although the nuclear family unit is common, it is not always responsible for child-care; often, the family is embedded in a larger household or community that collectively assumes responsibility for all the children of the group.

3. Family organization can be seen as loosely related to the organization of production, especially if family is defined as the sets of relationships that people create to meet the daily needs of adults and children.

4. In foraging societies, the nuclear family is embedded in a larger group that cooperates with respect to subsistence, consumption, and child-care. Paradoxically, the communal nature of these societies grants considerable autonomy to the individuals living in them.

5. In the agricultural societies of preindustrial Europe, households were primarily units of production in which the need to survive took precedence over all else. Household composition, even the texture of emotional life, reflected economic pressures.

6. Contemporary family patterns are the product of a particular history. Our history is marked by the development of an economy outside the household, in which the relations of paid employment are separated from the relations that provide for daily personal needs and the needs of children. A gendered division of labour corresponds to this separation.

7. As women have increasingly come to share the burden of family financial support, men have not proportionally increased the work they do in the home. That jobs are usually geared to people who lack family responsibilities is partly what prevents men from taking on more housework—their time is too limited. However, ideas about gender also make men reluctant to do "women's work."

8. The gendered division of labour that makes it possible for nuclear families to care for young children involves significant liabilities for women, and even for children. The social isolation that full-time mothers experience, combined with the stress attached to their high-demand, low-control situation, reduces the quality of child-care they are able to provide. Now that so many mothers are working outside the home, however, the problems associated with privatized responsibility for child-care may prove too burdensome, and government supports are likely to provide the only viable solution.

9. Because of fairly high rates of divorce, and an increasing incidence of births to unmarried women, many Canadian children will spend some part of their lives in lone-parent families. Most problematic about this type of family is its typically low income and the attendant stress on the parent.

10. The policies of the Canadian state pertaining to families are premised on the assumption that the welfare of family members—even children—is not the responsibility of the government or of the community. Accordingly, family law in Canada now views marriage as the union of two individuals who are responsible for their own support, even in the case of a divorcing woman who was a full-time homemaker.

QUESTIONS TO CONSIDER

1. Common sense holds that, if everyone embraced family values, problems in family life today would disappear. Explain why this perspective is naïve, and describe some of the barriers in the way of solving problems such as child-care, the difficult balance between the responsibilities of family and paid employment, and the unequal allocation of housework.

2. Explain how family patterns are related to the ways that people acquire their subsistence in foraging societies. Do the same for our society.

3. It has been argued that the concept of family takes its meaning from the separation of private and public spheres in some societies. In fact, the term itself was not in popular use in Europe until the eighteenth century, when an economy was beginning to develop outside the household. Explain why the idea of family would make little sense in foraging societies and in preindustrial agricultural Europe, and why it does have meaning in our society.

4. Explain how the development of capitalism influenced family ideals in the nineteenth century. Then sketch how the marketplace today influences family life—even aspects of it as basic as conceiving and having children.

5. Describe some of the "crises" typical of family life today, and speculate on possible solutions.

GLOSSARY

Biological determinism is the argument that individual behaviour or social organization is directly caused by biology or biological processes.

Extended-family households are residential units of people who are blood relatives but consist of more than the members of a nuclear family (e.g., an extended family may consist of children, their parents, and a set of grandparents living together).

A **family wage** is an ideal of the trade-union movement in the nineteenth century; it refers to a wage that is paid to a man and is sufficient to support him, his wife, and his children.

Foraging societies, also known as hunting-and-gathering societies, are societies in which people acquire their subsistence from the resources around them, without cultivating the earth.

A **gender strategy** is an individual's "plan of action" or, more generally, orientation to life based on (1) cultural notions of gender, (2) emotional reactions to gender roles as played out by parents and other important people, and (3) choices made about one's life, given the opportunities one faces and an assessment of one's abilities.

Gendered division of labour refers to the separation of the tasks men and women regularly do.

Privatization is the assumption of responsibility by the individual, the household, or the family; it is the opposite of collectivization.

Pronatalism refers to inducements by government to encourage women to have children.

Social reproduction, as opposed to biological reproduction, refers to all that is necessary to meet the needs of adults and children, from feeding them and clothing them to meeting their emotional needs and socializing them. It is "the activities and attitudes, behaviors and emotions, responsibilities and relations directly involved in the maintenance of life on a daily basis, and intergenerationally" (Laslett and Brenner, 1989: 382).

Sociobiology is a type of biological determinism that views human behaviour as the product of human evolution.

Structural functionalism is a school of thought that views social organization as analogous to a biological organism, or system, in which the parts (or organs) exist because of the functions they perform in maintaining the whole. Thus, institutions such as the family exist because of vital functions they perform in maintaining societal equilibrium.

SUGGESTED READING

Coontz, Stephanie. (1992). *The Way We Never Were: American Families and the Nostalgia Trap.* New York: Basic Books. Fascinating to read, provocative, and very well researched, this book thoroughly reviews and criticizes "family-values" arguments by analyzing family life, past and present.

Gottlieb, Beatrice. (1993). *The Family in the Western World: From the Black Death to the Industrial Age.* New York: Oxford University Press. A fascinating social history of preindustrial family life. The description is so rich and the writing is so good that it reads like a novel.

Hochschild, Arlie. (1989). *The Second Shift: Working Parents and the Revolution at Home.* New York: Viking. This unsettling study addresses the question of why men are so slow to take on household responsibilities as their wives take over some of the responsibilities of breadwinning. On the basis of in-depth interviews, Hochschild offers some important insights about relations between women and men.

Luxton, Meg. (1980). *More Than a Labour of Love: Three Generations of Women's Work in the Home.* Toronto: Women's Press. Now a Canadian classic, this is a study of three generations of housewives in Flin Flon, Manitoba. It shows the changes that have occurred in women's household work over time and also how the capitalist economy shapes women's work and gender relations.

Stack, Carol. (1974). *All Our Kin: Strategies for Survival in a Black Community.* New York: Harper and Row. An American classic, this anthropological study of a poor Black community makes sense of a family pattern that is very different from the pattern common among middle-class North Americans, whether Black or white.

NOTE

1. Based on personal communication with Ivy Bourgeault, one of Canada's leading experts on midwifery.

CHAPTER THIRTEEN

WORK AND OCCUPATIONS

In this chapter you will learn that:

- Work in Canada is dominated by the service economy: Jobs are becoming polarized into good and bad jobs, and nonstandard or part-time jobs are becoming more prevalent.

- The labour market is segmented into areas of good and bad jobs: Job ghettos in the labour market trap certain groups of workers, such as women and visible minorities; labour-market shelters help some workers protect their access to better jobs in the economy.

- The degree to which technology enhances or degrades jobs is contingent on the goals of management, what type of technology is used, and how workers react to the technology.

- Debate has emerged over whether computers increase productivity.

- Management uses a variety of strategies to organize work: From scientific management to Japanese management, these strategies attempt to help management reduce costs and increase the productivity of workers.

- Working in organizations presents specific challenges to women and minorities: Women managers may be perceived as less effective than their male counterparts.

- Job satisfaction measures how workers feel about their jobs, and the characteristics of organizations and jobs are the primary determinants of satisfaction: If employers provide workers with challenging jobs, opportunities for advancement, and adequate pay, workers are more likely to be satisfied.

- Alienation is a structural condition reflecting workers' lack of power over their work and lives: Several types of workplace behaviour, such as sabotage, playing games, and strikes, are typical reactions to alienating conditions.

SANDY WELSH

UNIVERSITY OF TORONTO

INTRODUCTION

WORKING IN RETAIL

Debora De Angelis started working at Suzy Shier, a retail clothing store, in Toronto when she was 17 years old. She had just left a job at McDonald's where she made $4.60 an hour. When she started at Suzy Shier, she made $4.25 and was promised she would get a wage review and a wage increase in six months. As Debora said, "You think retail, you think smiling clerks, you think you're moving up in the world" (Boase, 1998: J2). Yet by 1997, when she had worked there for five years and was now a 22-year-old University of Toronto student, she had never received the wage review or the increase. In fact, the only time her wages went up was when the government raised the minimum wage level.

Over the course of her time there, Debora became troubled by the changes to her working conditions. She was still treated and paid as a part-timer, but she worked full-time hours with full-time responsibilities, including keeping track of the payroll and merchandising. And, if the manager wasn't in, she was responsible for keeping the store in proper order. But for Debora, it wasn't just about the money. One day, a manager told her that she needed to change her appearance and wear make-up on the job so she would look more professional. Yet Debora was already a top-seller in the store without make-up (Eaton, 1998: 24). Debora also had to put up with other rules such as "the one-metre rule: You weren't allowed to be closer than one metre to your co-worker, because [the manager] didn't want us talking. Of course, the employees started getting upset, and whenever she wasn't in the store we used to get in a clump and talk, or yell across the store. So she started having meetings about our attitude problems" (Eaton, 1998: 24).

After these and other unfair treatments, Debora decided enough was enough. She contacted the Union of Needletrades, Industrial and Textile Employees (UNITE) and started organizing a union at her store. The plan was to organize three stores simultaneously. When Suzy Shier management found out about the organizing drive, three top managers from Montreal came to Toronto. Each employee, except Debora, was taken out for one to three hours at a time. The managers "bawled and cried that we are a family here at Suzy Shier, that they were so sorry they had forgotten about us" (Eaton, 1998: 25). Management blamed the local managers for the problems and promised these managers were on their way out.

Management strategies paid off for two of the stores—they voted down the union. But the store where Debora worked voted for the union. Whatever your opinion of unions may be, I think you'll agree that Debora's response to her working conditions went beyond the ordinary. Most of us who find ourselves in jobs that we don't like would probably quit or quietly cope. Or we might throw ourselves into our life outside of work, knowing that at least we were getting a paycheque from our job. What Debora did, though, was engage in a century-old practice used by workers to change their workplace conditions. And Suzy Shier responded in the way that management has for the past century, by fighting back to keep the balance of control firmly in management's hands.

Debora's work experience mirrors a lot of the issues facing all of us who are current and potential employees. She is part of the rising legion of service workers. Her concerns are ours: How can we have a job that pays a decent wage, treats us with respect, and offers some satisfaction? This chapter will take you through many of the key issues facing workers today. We'll discuss what the service economy means for our working lives, how employees and employers battle to gain the upper hand in determining what jobs will be like, what factors lead to "good jobs" or "bad jobs," and if these jobs will be satisfying to workers. Whether we look at a 22-year-old retail worker asking for respect, or doctors across Canada fighting their provincial governments for the right to choose where they practice, the study of work and occupations is a study of both the constraints and the struggles that happen every day in Canadian workplaces.

INDUSTRIAL REVOLUTIONS: A LOOK BACK AT WORK IN CANADA

THE FIRST AND SECOND INDUSTRIAL REVOLUTIONS

Debora De Angelis working at Suzy Shier represents the most recent phase in our economic development.

To understand how we reached this phase, we need to look back to the various shifts in the Canadian economy.

Most researchers speak about changes in the economy and the world of work as revolutions. First in importance is the Industrial Revolution. Starting in England in the late eighteenth century, the economic and social structure began to shift from feudalism to capitalism. Under feudalism, most people worked as peasant farmers, and a few skilled artisans created the necessary tools and goods. As a result of a combination of factors, including the growth of the textile industry and nonlocal markets for wool, landowners started to use their land for sheep grazing and other cash crops. Displaced by this shift in land use and in need of work,

peasant farmers migrated to urban areas, looking for jobs in the emerging factories and artisan shops.

The organization of work dramatically shifted during the Industrial Revolution. Under feudalism, most farmers produced enough to meet their own needs. Work and leisure were not clearly separated. And agricultural labour also had its own work rhythm, connected to the seasons. The transition to capitalism, however, transformed peasant farmers into wage-earning factory workers. Now individuals worked for others and no longer controlled their own work schedules. It was during this time that the division of labour expanded. Work that had been done by skilled craftsmen was broken down into smaller components, so that semiskilled workers, who were paid less than

The second industrial revolution started in the early twentieth century. Henry Ford's assembly line and other mass-production technologies transformed the workplace.

SOURCE: Ellen Griesedieck, *Rouge Assembly Line*. Courtesy Gallery Henoch.

the skilled craftsmen, could perform the jobs in factories. This whole process—a "great transformation" in social and labour organization—led to the rise of an urban capitalist class and working class (Polanyi, 1957).

Canada also went through its own industrial revolution, though it occurred later here than in Europe or the United States (Laxer, 1989). As recently as the early twentieth century, 40 percent of the Canadian population worked in agricultural pursuits (Campbell, 1996). When industrialization did begin, activity centred on Canada's vast natural resources, such as lumber and minerals.

In the early twentieth century, the second industrial revolution started. This revolution included the rise of consolidated companies, where large companies bought up smaller companies engaged in similar types of production, in such industries as steel and railroads. Henry Ford's assembly line and other mass-production technologies contributed to this expansion, as company owners increased their ability to dominate the market and control the activities of workers. Simultaneously, an "administrative revolution" transformed office work (Lowe, 1987). Because of the vast amounts of information produced by companies, such as personnel and transaction records, management needed efficient systems to organize their offices. This led to the creation of a white-collar job sector and the growth of bureaucratic organizations, and with all these changes came an increasing division of labour. Now, there was management to manage, clerical workers to handle paperwork, and production workers to do smaller and smaller parts of the production process.

What this brief background tells us is that work as we know it in Canada and other capitalist economies is a relatively new phenomenon. A hundred and fifty years ago, most of us would not have been living in cities and going to work for an employer in a large bureaucratic organization. Although we still see vestiges of the first and second industrial revolutions in our working lives, many things have changed. Most prominent is the movement away from a manufacturing-based economy toward a service economy.

WORK IN THE SERVICE ECONOMY

Many researchers argue that, in the years since World War II, Canadians have been witnessing—and living through—a third industrial revolution (Toffler, 1980). Our economy has shifted from its early industrial base of primary production (mining and logging) and secondary production (manufacturing) to tertiary production (service industries). As Table 13.1 shows, from 1980 to 2001, the number of Canadians employed in service industries grew from 67 percent to 74 percent. Increased global competitiveness contributed to the lowering of labour costs as companies tried to maintain their market position. Global markets also facilitated the movement of some goods production to low-wage areas. These factors have helped pushed many manufacturing jobs out of Canada. Free-trade agreements with the United States and Mexico and the drive to reduce labour costs have also played a role in the decline of the goods sector (Canadian Labour Congress, 1993). Fewer jobs in the goods sector means that most new jobs will be in the service sector.

Much debate has ensued about the rise of the service, or "postindustrial," economy. Writing in the

TABLE 13.1   CANADIAN LABOUR-FORCE CHARACTERISTICS, 1980 AND 2001

LABOUR-FORCE CHARACTERISTICS	1980	2001
Total number employed (thousands)	10 708	15 077
Percent in goods sector	33	26
Percent in service sector	67	74
Unionization rate (out of all paid workers) (percent)	32	32

SOURCE: Compiled from Statistics Canada, "Social Indicators," Canadian Social Trends, Cat. No. 11-008, Winter 1988, p. 31; Statistics Canada, "Employment by Industry and Sex" (downloaded from http://www.statcan.ca/english/Pgdb/labor10a.htm, October 17, 2002); Statistics Canada, "Key Labour and Income Facts," Perspectives on Labour and Income, Cat. No. 75-001, Spring 2002, p. 72. Used by authority of the Minister of Industry, 2000.

early 1970s when this trend began, Daniel Bell (1973) presented an optimistic picture of the rise of the "postindustrial" economy. In his view, work would be transformed from repetitive, low-skilled production work to highly skilled, knowledge-based work. Today, however, more pessimistic analyses of the postindustrial economy are prevalent. We are witnessing an increase in low-skilled, low-paying service jobs and a steady rise in the level of unemployment. It may be too early to tell whether the optimistic or pessimistic scenario will eventually prevail. As stated by sociologist John Myles (1991: 128), "the issue for the future is not whether we will have a service economy but what kind of service economy" we will have.

GOOD JOBS OR BAD JOBS?

One way to discover what kind of service economy we will have in Canada is to look at the mix of good and bad jobs available for workers. At minimum, good jobs are those that provide **extrinsic rewards**, such as good wages, benefits, employment security, and opportunities for advancement. Good jobs should also provide **intrinsic rewards**, such as decision-making opportunities, challenging nonrepetitive work, and autonomy that allows for self-direction and responsibility over work tasks.

A misconception about the service economy is that the service sector creates only bad jobs and that the goods sector is the source of good jobs. This scenario assumes that all service jobs are alike and ignores important divisions within the service sector. Instead, we should think of the service sector as having a lower tier made up of traditional services, such as retail trade, food, and personal services, and an upper tier consisting of other services, such as finance and business, utilities, health, education, and public administration. Whether you find yourself in a lower- or upper-tier service job has implications for your wages, job security, and the skill content required in your work (Krahn, 1992; Economic Council of Canada, 1991).

Debates also revolve around changes in the skill level of jobs in the service economy. Conventional wisdom suggests that skill requirements are increasing as a result of technology (Spenner, 1983). As Daniel Bell and other postindustrialists propose, we should experience an upgrading of jobs in the economy as skill requirements increase within specific occupations. This group also predicts that job growth will occur in the higher-skilled occupations. In contrast, Harry Braverman (1974) and other postindustrial critics believe that skill levels are being downgraded. In this view, although some highly skilled professional and technical jobs will be created, the majority of jobs will be lower-skilled industrial and service jobs.

So which is it? Are we moving to the postindustrial world of Bell or the downgraded world of Braverman? When we examine the shifts in the Canadian occupational structure, a more complex picture than the ones sketched by Bell and Braverman emerges: Blue-collar jobs in the middle are declining, and job growth is occurring at the top and the bottom of the occupational structure (Myles, 1988; Economic Council of Canada, 1991). Thus, we see an increasing polarization of jobs in the service sector—higher-skilled knowledge jobs on the one hand and lower-skilled "hamburger" jobs on the other (Myles, 1988).

What do recent statistics tell us about these trends? Figure 13.1 shows that four of the top five growth industries in Canada in 2001 were in the service sector while goods-producing occupations in manufacturing declined. Some of the upper-tier service industries grew (e.g., health and educational services) as did lower-tier services such as accommodation, food, and beverage services. Thus, we see a mixed picture with growth in some higher-skilled and lower-skilled jobs.

However, these statistics are partly misleading. Statistics Canada points out that driving the growth in business services is an increase in part-time work and self-employment. So while business service has the potential to create good jobs, some of those jobs may not be full-time. We'll explore the issue of part-time work in the following section.

Finally, let's take a quick look at the ten most common jobs for women and men. The 1996 census shows that retail service jobs dominate for both sexes (see Figures 9.2 and 9.3 on page 225). Missing from the list for women are any non–service-industry jobs. For the men, we see a mix of lower-tier service jobs (retail salesperson, janitor) and blue-collar jobs (material handler, carpenter, and construction trade helper). Missing from the male list are any of the higher-skilled "knowledge" jobs.

FIGURE 13.1 FOUR OF THE TOP FIVE GROWTH INDUSTRIES IN 2001 WERE IN THE SERVICE SECTOR

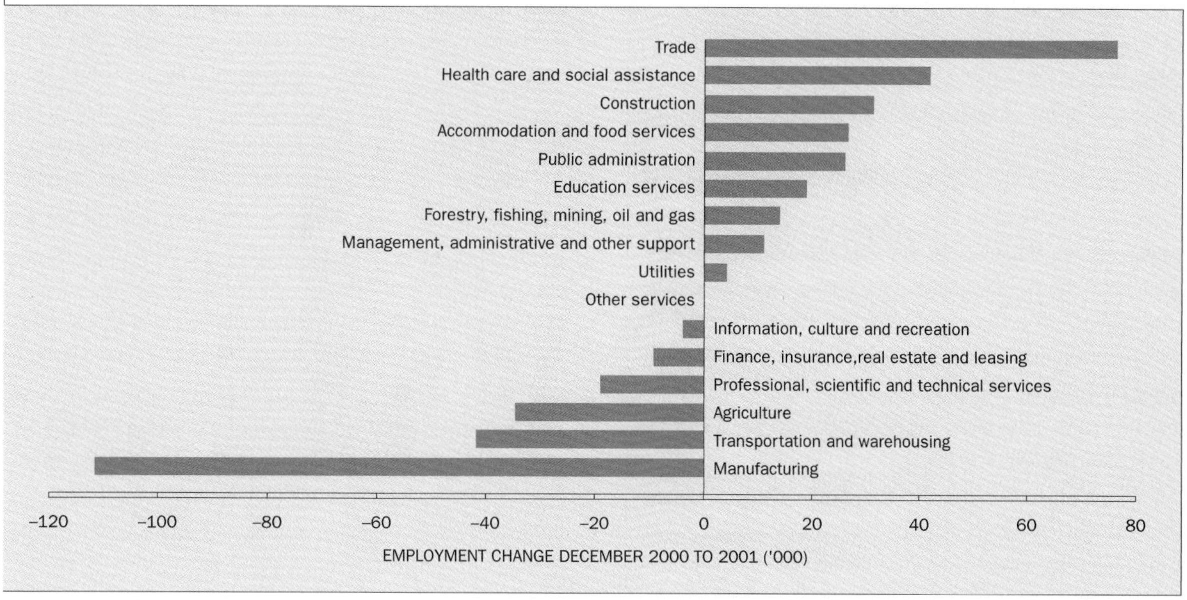

EMPLOYMENT CHANGE DECEMBER 2000 TO 2001 ('000)

SOURCE: Statistics Canada, "Key Labour and income facts," Perspectives on Labour and Income, Cat. no. 75-001-XPE, Spring 2002, p. 61

As the service industry grows, we should be concerned about those who minimize the significance of the goods or manufacturing sector for our economic well-being. Such a view is shortsighted: It is increasingly clear that the goods and services sectors are interdependent and that manufacturing is important for the creation of good jobs (Economic Council of Canada, 1991). For example, the production of telecommunications technology drives the development of telecommunications services in Canada (Myles, 1991). We need both sectors to fuel our economic growth. This is why trade agreements that threaten Canadian manufacturing may be detrimental to our overall economy. The movement of goods-producing industries to other countries could ultimately hurt the ability of the service economy to generate good jobs.

NONSTANDARD JOBS

One crucial outcome of the shift to a service-based global economy is the rise of **nonstandard jobs**. These are jobs that provide temporary, part-time, or part-year employment. For employers, nonstandard jobs can reduce labour costs since part-time and temporary workers receive less in pay and benefits (Economic Council of Canada, 1991; Krahn, 1992).

According to the 1996 Canadian census, 8 percent of Canadians worked in part-time jobs for the full year. Another 15 percent worked in part-time jobs for part of the year (less than 48 weeks). Figure 13.2 also shows that part-time employment is highest in the lower tier of the service sector, with 41 percent of sales and service employees working part-time.

In order to respond to changes in demand for their products and services, some employers now rely on temporary workers, ranging from clerical help to computer programmers, hired through temporary-employment agencies. In 2001, almost 13 percent of Canadian workers were employed in temporary or contract positions. Like part-time workers, temporaries tend to be young and/or women (Economic Council of Canada, 1991). Figure 13.3 shows that youth (age 15–27) are twice as likely to be temporary workers compared to other workers. These temporary workers are usually hired for short-term contracts to fill in for absent full-time workers, or as part of a "just-in-time" labour force called in to fill production or service demands. Although some workers are drawn to temporary work for its perceived flexibility in scheduling, the reality for most workers is that such jobs are often inflexible. As a result of work shortages, many temporary workers find themselves

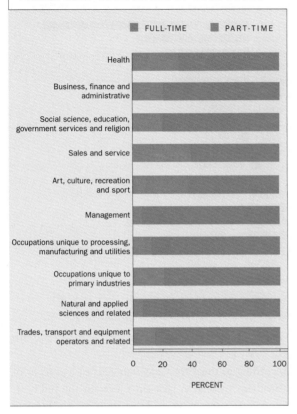

FIGURE 13.2 OCCUPATIONS BY WORK STATUS

SOURCE: Statistics Canada, "Perspectives on Labour and Income," Summer 1998, Cat. No. 75-001, p. 60. Used by the authority of the Minister of Industry, 2000.

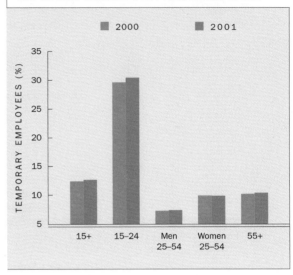

FIGURE 13.3 ABOUT 13 PERCENT OF ALL EMPLOYEES WORKED ON A TEMPORARY BASIS

SOURCE: Statistics Canada, "Key Labour and Income Facts," *Perspectives on Labour and Income*, Cat. no. 75-001-XPE, Spring 2002, p. 72.

taking whatever work is available, even if it means putting up with inappropriate work, such as cleaning offices while on a clerical assignment (Henson, 1996).

Some employees, particularly women and young workers between the ages of 15 and 24, prefer the flexibility of nonstandard work. They voluntarily choose part-time work because it allows time for school attendance and family responsibilities or because they do not want to work full-time. Most disturbing, though, is the growing number of involuntary part-time workers—part-time workers who would prefer full-time work (Noreau, 1994). In most industrial countries, including Canada, one-quarter to one-third of all jobs are now nonstandard (Economic Council of Canada, 1991).

The movement to a service economy, or the third industrial revolution, has affected the type of jobs available in the Canadian economy. Some good jobs are created in financial services and health services, while bad jobs with nonstandard hours are also created, primarily in sales and service. In the following section on labour-market segmentation, we'll continue to explore Canadians' access to good and bad jobs.

LABOUR-MARKET SEGMENTATION

All of us hope to have an equal chance of getting a good job. But do we really have an equal chance, especially given the polarization trends in the service industry? As you know from your study of stratification and inequality (see Chapter 8), some groups of workers, such as individuals from upper-class families or more educated workers, are more likely than less-advantaged workers to end up in good jobs. Another factor that affects your chances is the structure of the labour market. Although some economists, especially human-capital theorists, conceive of the labour market as a single and open competition in which people are rewarded in proportion to their education and skills (Becker, 1975), **labour-market segmentation** theory offers a different perspective. Instead of assuming that we all have an equal chance of getting good jobs, labour-market segmentation theory shows that where you enter the labour market may limit your chances of getting a different, better job.

Labour-market segmentation theory emphasizes that jobs are divided according to their location in the "core" or "periphery" of the economy. A core industry is a group of companies in a relatively non-competitive market, such as the automobile industry. Core industries tend to be capital-intensive, large, and unionized, and they tend to exert control over their environment (e.g., by influencing governments to limit foreign competition). For a variety of reasons, such as the need to maintain skilled workers who can operate expensive capital equipment, and in response to the presence of unions, jobs in core industries tend to be stable and to offer good wages and access to benefits (Morissette, 1991).

The periphery, in contrast, is characterized by lower-tier service jobs and jobs in highly competitive markets. Firms in this sector tend to be smaller, labour-intensive, and non-unionized, and the employment they offer lacks security and pays low wages. Work is also characterized by high turnover rates, owing to product-demand fluctuations and seasonal work cycles, such as in the fisheries on the east and west coasts of Canada.

Your chances of finding a good job are determined not only by the sector of the economy you enter, but also by the existence of **primary labour markets**, both external and internal to firms. Internal labour markets provide opportunities for advancement by providing the chance to climb up the job ladder as you gain skills and knowledge (Althauser, 1989). Secondary labour-market jobs do not offer much of a job ladder. These jobs are sometimes referred to as "dead-end jobs" because of their lack of upward mobility. Workers at McDonald's may be able to move from being on the crew to assistant manager, but unless they buy their own franchise (which is rare), that is the extent of their mobility.

Employers often create primary labour markets for some employees but not for others. In a single firm, managers can have access to mobility through an internal labour market while their clerical, production, and maintenance staff may have little room to move up. In today's service economy, employers' increasing use of temporary and part-time workers is another way in which secondary labour markets are created within companies. Increasingly, these types of secondary markets are found outside the lower-tier

service industries. At the university where I work, and in all other Canadian universities, departments have full-time professors to do research and teach. In addition, "sessional" instructors are hired to teach one or two classes each. Substantial differences exist between these two groups in terms of pay, job security, and mobility opportunities. As a full-time professor, I have a multiyear contract and may be promoted if I fulfill my job duties. My colleague, who is a part-time instructor, has no access to promotions or job security. Instead, she receives year-to-year contracts only if the department needs her to teach a specific course. Although having secondary labour-market positions gives organizations the "flexibility" to unload employees when they are not needed, it increases the insecurity of these employees and decreases their chances of getting ahead, both in their jobs and in life.

Geography also plays a role in our chances of ending up in the primary or secondary labour market. Even if you are a highly skilled and motivated worker, you will have trouble finding a good job in Newfoundland, where the cod fisheries have fallen on hard times (Krahn and Lowe, 1998: 135). Those of us who live in the major urban and industrial areas of Canada are more likely to end up in a better job simply because there are more of these jobs in our regional labour markets.

Geography affects one's chance of finding work. For example, it is more difficult to find a good job in Atlantic Canada than in Alberta.

SOURCE: David Blackwood, *For Edgar Glover: The Splitting Table* Etching 1999. Courtesy The Edward Day Gallery.

We may conclude that whether you end up in a good job or a bad job is the result of more than your individual characteristics or the occupation you choose. Your chances of landing a rewarding job depend on what sector of the economy your job is in and whether your job has an internal labour market associated with it. In the next section, I develop this idea by showing how some groups of workers find themselves stuck in job ghettos.

JOB GHETTOS AND DISADVANTAGED GROUPS

Job ghettos are parts of the labour market that trap certain groups of workers. Structural barriers based on stereotypes work to keep some individuals from entering the primary labour market and the best jobs. The labelling of occupations as "female" or "male" jobs is one such example. In the health-care industry, women are still more likely to become nurses than doctors, and, as doctors, women are more likely to be found in pediatric and family medicine than the higher-paying specialties of neurology and cardiology. Chapter 9 discusses how female job ghettos are formed through occupational sex segregation, sex typing, and other forms of discrimination.

Ethnic job ghettos are a pervasive component of past and current labour markets throughout the world. In Canada, between 1860 and 1960, Black railway workers were restricted to sleeping-car porter jobs and were not allowed to compete for the higher-paid jobs of sleeping-car conductor and dining-car steward (Calliste, 1993). Today, employer prejudice can keep qualified minorities from being hired. Since most visible minorities are also recent immigrants, their ability to move into better jobs is constrained by this dual status, unless they are entrepreneurs. Often, employers will request "Canadian work experience" before hiring white-collar workers. And some professional occupations, like doctor and veterinarian, require additional training for professionals emigrating from certain countries. Highly educated visible minorities in these situations may find themselves forced to take low-level service jobs, such as taxi driver or restaurant worker. For more on this topic, see Chapter 10.

People with disabilities face barriers to good jobs because of the inaccessibility of education and workplaces. Lack of financial resources to attend school,

inflexible workplace schedules, and lack of employers' commitment to hiring disabled workers are some of the reasons people with disabilities have trouble getting good jobs. Jamie Hunter, a 29-year-old with minimal control over his limbs as a result of a diving accident, experiences these barriers first-hand. Speaking about looking for work, he states (quoted in McKay, 1993: 170):

> I recall one fellow, from the personnel department of a major corporation, who was so uncomfortable he couldn't even bring himself to take me to his office. So we sat in the lobby and he read me back my resume. "You're Jamie Hunter? You graduated from York University? You worked for a summer at Ontario Hydro?" Then he said thanks and

Although most Canadian women in the paid labour force are segregated in jobs traditionally dominated by women, they are making advances in traditionally male-dominated jobs.
SOURCE: Dick Hemingway.

left. That was it. The interview was over and I never heard from him again.

Hiring disabled workers is not as costly as some employers believe. Recent studies show that only 20 percent of people with disabilities require changes to the physical accommodations of workplaces in order to work (Shain, 1995). Until more employers make the effort to hire people with disabilities, disabled workers will continue to face barriers to good jobs.

Aboriginal people face formidable barriers in their search for employment. Living in remote areas limits both their job opportunities and their access to education and work training. Even when Aboriginals move to areas where jobs are more readily available, they often lack crucial work experience. Aboriginal workers are especially vulnerable to the "bad-work syndrome" (Krahn and Lowe, 1998). Having access only to low-skill and part-time work gives individuals a spotty work history. They are then caught in a cycle where one low-skill job leads to another. For many, the "bad-work syndrome" makes it impossible to get better jobs.

Finally, *young and old workers* may find themselves trapped in job ghettos that are based on age. Some employers view younger workers as less serious and less interested in full-time jobs. In many ways, trying to improve the jobs in the teenage-student job ghetto was the motivation behind Debora De Angelis's union drive at Suzy Shier in Toronto. Older workers, who are defined as those over 45, also face employment limitations. As a result of downsizing and early-retirement incentives, older workers may find themselves out of a job before they are ready to stop working. Access to better jobs is also limited by the prejudices of employers, who tend to view older workers as less productive and more resistant to new work methods. As the population of older Canadians grows, it is increasingly difficult to ignore the effects of age discrimination.

Labour-market segmentation creates areas of better and worse jobs in the labour market. Although we would like to think that we all have an equal chance of getting the better jobs, the research on job ghettos shows that some groups of workers may get trapped in the worse jobs. And, as I show in the next sections, some workers are able to protect their good jobs through the labour-market shelters of professional occupations and unions.

PROFESSIONS

The occupations of doctor, lawyer, and other professions are some of the most desirable jobs in the labour market. High pay, autonomy, and respect from the outside community are some of the advantages bestowed on members of professional occupations. Many of us consider these occupations to be different from other occupations. This special status has caught the attention of sociologists.

Early studies of professions attempted to delineate their general characteristics or hallmarks. First, all professional occupations control a special body of abstract knowledge, held only by members of that profession. Second, professional occupations are autonomous. Third, professionals generally have authority over their clients and subordinates because of the special knowledge they possess. Finally, professional occupations are supposed to be altruistic because of their focus on helping clients.

But are these four characteristics all there are to professions? Many sociologists believe that the hallmark model is really an "idealized model that imperfectly describes reality" (Hodson and Sullivan, 1990: 266), and that it provides only a checklist for determining which occupations are more or less a profession. Overlooked by this approach is how these occupations became "professions" in the first place. To address this issue, we need to consider power and the contested nature of professions. Doing this will uncover how professions act as **labour-market shelters**, protecting their members' access to good jobs.

Were doctors, dentists or lawyers always considered professional occupations? The answer to this is no because professions are not static categories. What occupations are viewed as legitimate professions changes over time and is part of a historical process. For example, in Ontario in the nineteenth century, there were few dentists as we know them today. Instead many different occupations provided dental services. Most people were served by itinerant "tramp dentists" that travelled from town to town. If citizens needed teeth pulled or false teeth constructed, they could go to their local blacksmith and gunsmith. In terms of the dental services provided, when a patient came to visit, the blacksmith would "leave the forge, wipe his hands on his apron, get the old turnkey wrench, and his brawny arm would soon draw not only the sufferer's tooth, but often the screaming patient himself from the old kitchen chair" (Wood, 1989: 266, quoted in Adams, 2000: 22). This example is far removed from our twenty-first century understanding of dentists.

In order to get to where they are today, dentists, like other occupations, engaged in a professionalization process. This process includes the establishment of "professional dominance" and securing legitimacy from the public (Friedson, 1970; Pescosolido, Tuch, and Martin, 2001: 3). Professional dominance occurs when the government acknowledges an occupation's knowledge claims and expertise and then grants an occupation the right to be the only (or one of a few) practitioners of this knowledge. Professions, though, also need the public's approval to be fully professionalized. This is where securing legitimacy comes into the picture. If the public will not follow the directions of members of the profession or views the profession as not being legitimate experts (or the sole legitimate expert), then professions will have difficulty establishing their authority.

You can see these issues more clearly when you think about the relationships or "battles" between professional occupations over who can claim expertise in a certain body of professional knowledge (e.g., Friedson, 1970). For example, until recently, only doctors had the authority to deliver babies in Ontario. Doctors maintained their authority because of their monopoly over the relevant knowledge and used their national associations to lobby provincial and federal governments to deny others the right to practise. This is how professional dominance helped doctors maintain their position. Yet, doctors' legitimacy as the only deliverers of babies was called into question by the public and other health-care practitioners. As a result of current public demands for access to midwives and the development of professional midwifery schools, doctors have lost some control over the birthing process and have lost their monopoly over this body of professional knowledge.

Some occupations are continually striving for professional status. Semiprofessions are occupations that have some professional characteristics, but to a lesser degree than full-fledged professions (Hodson and Sullivan, 1990). Examples of semiprofessions are nurses, engineers, accountants, pharmacists, and teachers. Although we may call these occupations "professions" in our everyday use of the term, the sociological definition of professions requires us to view these occupations as "not quite" or "semi" professions. Often semiprofessions do not have full control over their body of knowledge, or their autonomy may be constrained by a more powerful profession, as is the case with nurses. Furthermore, female-dominated semiprofessions, such as teachers or librarians, face additional barriers to professionalization because of occupational sex segregation.

Third parties, such as the government, can threaten professional power by intervening in the decisions of professional organizations. We become most aware of this when the government pays for part or all of the services received by a client, as is the case for the Canadian health-care system. During the summer and fall of 1996, doctors in Ontario fought the provincial government over who has the right to decide where doctors work. Doctors wanted to maintain their professional autonomy to work and live where they choose, while the Ministry of Health believed it had the right to force doctors to work in underserviced areas. Some doctors did not accept new patients to protest what they saw as government interference with their autonomy. As it stands now, these protests appear to have helped the cause of the doctors. They made some gains in terms of their salaries and partially satisfied the government's demand for more doctors to work in northern areas of the province. And how this "battle" continues to play out will determine who is the legitimate authority over doctors—their own profession or the provincial government of Ontario.

UNIONS

Unions, like professions and their associations, also attempt to attain or maintain good jobs for their members. Workers have organized unions to gain respect, increase wages, reduce working hours, and gain more control over their working day. In fact, the presence of unions has helped all of us. Without union efforts, we would not have such things as the eight-hour workday, child-labour laws, and occupational health and safety standards. I return to the state of unions in Canada and the role they play in the Canadian labour market when I discuss alienation later in this chapter.

In sum, unions and professional associations, like the Canadian Medical Association, are alike in a number of respects. They both act as labour-market shelters from loss of jobs, pay cuts, and other employment-related risks. Legislation that mandates the hiring of union workers, such as may be found on some construction sites, protects the jobs of union members. Likewise, when the professional association of lawyers restricts access to law school and the number of new lawyers, they too are protecting the jobs and incomes of existing members. Groups of workers who organize—whether it is a local union for flight attendants or a national association of doctors—may increase their ability to maintain their position in good jobs.

TECHNOLOGY AND THE SERVICE INDUSTRY

The use of technology has long been a part of the relationship between employees and employers. One of the most famous pieces of technology, the assembly line, was used to control the pace of work (Edwards, 1979). In today's service economy, managers are more likely to invest in computers and information technology than other forms of work reorganization to improve their firms' productivity and efficiency (Osterman, 1995). Computerizing office systems can reduce the time-consuming work of filing. In some instances, robots can be used to do heavy and dangerous work. Technological changes such as advanced telecommunications systems make the globalization of work possible. Today, it is not surprising to find companies, such as Nike, with factories in Asia and product-development labs in the United States. Technology brings added flexibility to companies. No longer does geography limit the search for inexpensive labour or market expansion.

Even though technology is changing the face of work, it does not mean that we have no control over what happens. Although some technological determinists might have us believe that the implementation of technology in our workplaces is an inevitable process, most sociologists (e.g., Wallace, 1989) view the effects of technology as contingent on various social and technological factors. We now understand that whether technology will have positive or negative effects on work depends on such factors as the outcomes desired by management, the type of technology that companies can afford, and whether workers have a say in the technological changes.

According to Shoshana Zuboff (1988), management can design computer-based jobs to either increase or decrease the need for workers to use knowledge and judgment on the job. She provides examples of jobs being enhanced, on the one hand, when workers were given the opportunity to use computers in complex ways. On the other hand, she also found that, if management is interested only in productivity and efficiency, technology can have detrimental effects on the quality of work. For example, one office used computers to automate and speed up the work of clerks. Any decisions that clerks formerly made about their work were now programmed into the computer. Box 13.1 describes some of the experiences of these workers. The stick-figure drawings represent the drastic change in workers' views of their jobs. What makes these pictures compelling is knowing that a consultant recommended further automation of the clerks' jobs. But management held back. As one manager acknowledged, the company realized it couldn't remove all variety from tasks because "there's a limit to how boring you can make a job if you want even reasonably capable people" (Zuboff, 1988: 134). This example shows us, then, that management can choose to implement technology in a way that either enhances work or downgrades it.

From video cameras to computer programs, workers are finding themselves increasingly monitored by technology. In one high-tech firm, management used scanners to detect motion in rooms that were not supposed to be used (Wallace, 1989). Air Canada uses electronic surveillance to make the job of telephone airline reservation agents more visible and easily controlled (Robertson and Wareham, 1990). Detailed information can be collected about how many phone calls an agent handles, the duration of each phone call, and how long each agent is "out of the system" or unavailable for calls. This information is then used to determine who is working up to speed. Reservation agents complain that these computer measures do not adequately capture all components of their job, such as providing friendly and useful service to customers. As the use of computers and high-technology systems becomes more common, more of us may find ourselves monitored electronically. How far monitoring will go in the name of increasing employee productivity will hinge on the ability of workers and unions to participate in decisions about the implementation of technology.

What can computer technology do to the quality of work life? In her study of technological changes, Shoshana Zuboff asked office workers to draw pictures that "represented their 'felt sense' about their job experience before and after the conversion to the new computer system" that automated and standardized work. Below are two workers' views of how their work experience changed. Note the shifts in facial expressions and the loss of mobility. Even the flower on the benefit analyst's desk has wilted. As one office manager said about work after the conversion: "The system controls the transfer assistants in some ways because it ties them to the desk. It forces them to do the input and to really be tied to the machine. That forces control in terms of physically having to just be there."

TRANSFER ASSISTANT

Before

BENEFIT ANALYST

Before

After

After

"Before I was able to get up and hand things to people without having someone say, what are you doing? Now, I feel like I am with my head down, doing my work."

"My supervisor is frowning because we shouldn't be talking. I have on the stripes of a convict. It's all true. It feels like a prison in here."

SOURCE: Adapted from Shoshana Zuboff, *In the Age of the Smart Machine: The Future of Work and Power* (New York: Basic Books, 1988), pp. 138–41. Copyright © 1988 by Basic Books, a member of Perseus Books, L.L.C. Used by permission of Basic Books.

Computers also affect unemployment and job creation. At Dofasco in Hamilton, computer technology is partly responsible for reducing the work force from 12 500 to 7000 over the past ten years (Campbell, 1996). Automated banking machines have already reduced the number of teller positions in banks (McLaughlin, 1983) while creating a small number of jobs for those who repair and maintain these machines. These examples show technology's initial effect on employment. Although some skilled jobs directly connected to the technology are created, a greater number of lower-skilled jobs are lost. And, more often now, workers facing technological unemployment can find only lower-tier service jobs to replace their previous jobs (Wallace, 1989).

COMPUTERS AND PRODUCTIVITY

Since the 1970s, companies' investment in computers has grown. This increased investment is motivated by the expectation that computers will increase workers' productivity. Yet, if we look at official figures, since 1973 there has been a slowdown in productivity (Triplett, 1999). Therefore, it appears that computers have not made the economy more productive or efficient ("Productivity: Lost in Cyberspace," 1997; David, 1990). Some social scientists believe we are experiencing a "productivity paradox." It's called a paradox because the introduction of computers and new technology has not led to the expected boost in productivity. As Robert Solow, a Nobel–prize-winning economist stated, "You can see computers everywhere but in the productivity statistics" (1987). And as an old Dilbert cartoon once mentioned, the "total time that humans have waited for Web pages to load ... cancels out all the productivity gains of the information age" (quoted in Triplett, 1999).

Much speculation exists as to why the productivity paradox is occurring. The most pessimistic view is that the supposed computer revolution is not in the same league as earlier technological advances. In other words, the computer revolution has only a marginal effect on the average person's life. For example, Paul Krugman, an economist at MIT, states that "computerised ticketing is a great thing, but a cross-country flight still takes five hours; bar codes and laser scanners are nifty, but a shopper still has to queue at the checkout" ("Paradox Lost," 1996: 13).

A second explanation of the productivity paradox looks to history for the answer. Looking at past rela-

tionships between technological implementation and productivity, we see that it often takes several decades before technological breakthroughs increase productivity. The classic example of this is the electric dynamo, which made the commercial use of electricity possible (David, 1990). It took 40 years for the electric dynamo to yield significant productivity gains. Factories slowly adopted electricity, and even then it took time to learn how to organize factories around electric power. Prior to this, machines had to be located near water wheels or steam engines. But electric power allowed for the placement of machines along production lines that maximized the efficiency of the work process. Considering that computers didn't start making their way into offices until the 1970s, we may still be a decade or more away from realizing productivity gains. It is not the *invention* of new technology that increases productivity, but the *identification* of the most efficient uses of technology.

Some economists believe the productivity paradox is the result of "measurement error" or problems in how we assess productivity. When we look at national or industry-wide statistics on productivity, we don't see any increase in productivity. But when we look at productivity for individual firms, there is some increase in productivity in the 1973–1997

New technologies require job retraining, even for middle-aged and elderly workers.
SOURCE: David Pollack/First Light.

period (Lehr and Lichtenberg, 1999). Complicating matters is the fact that computers are used most extensively in the service industry—and it's harder to measure productivity in the service industry than in the goods-producing industry.

There is still a fourth explanation for the productivity paradox that brings in the social or human element (Martinsons and Chong, 1999). The choices that managers make about how to implement technology are part of the equation. Also, some scholars say there is a relatively short "window of opportunity" in which organizations can adopt technology in its most productive and useful form (Tyre and Orlikowski, 1994). When a company brings in computers or a new computer program, employees may circumvent some of the new features that may increase productivity but are difficult to learn. For example, when I first used WordPerfect for Windows, I changed all the commands back to DOS commands because that was what I knew. In the short term it saved time, but in the long term I could not take advantage of any of the new features that could help speed up my work. So do we have a productivity paradox? The answer at this stage is yes and no. It depends on how you measure productivity and whether you look at national or firm-level productivity statistics. As social scientists develop a better understanding of what productivity means in the service industry, we may find that the paradox disappears.

BUREAUCRACIES AND WORK ORGANIZATION

We live and work in a bureaucratic society. According to Max Weber, bureaucracies are the most efficient and rational organizational form for reaching the goals of capitalism. In bureaucracies, written rules provide guidelines for handling routine situations. A complex division of labour ensures that workers know what is required of them and helps to identify who is responsible when something goes wrong. Weber also saw bureaucracies as a way to overcome arbitrary decisions and corruption in nonbureaucratic organizations. For example, by having written rules about how decisions must be made and having a hierarchy of authority that clarifies who makes decisions, it is less likely that organizational decision makers can

decide to hire someone out of loyalty or obligation. Yet, Weber was the first to admit that bureaucracies are not without their problems. Referring to bureaucracies as "the iron cage of the future," Weber was concerned about the potential for bureaucracies to limit creativity and initiative (Hodson and Sullivan, 1990: 184). Bureaucracies also can be rigid, full of "red tape," and lead to communication problems between managers and workers (Jones, 1996).

Weber believed that increased bureaucratization was the fate of modern society. If you look around at the organizations that touch your life, you will see that Weber was correct. But bureaucratic structure alone is not enough to ensure the work of organizations gets done. As the following section discusses, management has been developing strategies to organize how work is done by their employees.

MANAGERIAL STRATEGIES FOR ORGANIZING WORK

In the past 100 years, several approaches to organizing work in bureaucracies have come and gone. Some, like Taylorism and human relations, have endured the test of time (Braverman, 1974). As we'll discuss, many of these strategies emerged in earlier revolutions, but are now integral parts of the service economy. While Taylorism was geared toward removing the need for workers to think on the job, more recent strategies have paid more attention to the ability and desire of workers to participate in workplace decisions. Whether these strategies offer real participation is a question to keep in mind as you read the following sections.

Taylorism

Frederick Taylor, an American industrial engineer, was the founder of scientific management or **Taylorism**. Originating in the 1890s, scientific management was an attempt by management to regain direct control of the labour process. Based on his own experience in factories, Taylor discovered that workers knew more than their managers about the work processes. As long as this was the case, workers could control how fast they worked and how much they produced. To shift control back to management, Taylor recommended a detailed division of labour that broke complex tasks into several subtasks. To do this, management needed to learn how workers did their jobs and then convert this knowledge into formal procedures. Using time and motion studies, managers documented the exact movements of workers and the length of time required to complete the task. Taylor also believed that conceptual work should be separated from the execution of tasks. It was management's job to design work procedures, and the workers' job to follow those procedures. By breaking jobs into their smallest components and removing the need for workers to think, Taylorism opened the door for management to reduce their reliance on skilled labour. Cheaper, unskilled workers could now be hired to perform simplified tasks. Managers and intellectuals worldwide, including the Russian communist leader Lenin, hailed Taylor as a pioneer in the rationalization of work.

Taylorism is not limited to factory work. Lowe (1987) shows how Taylorist principles rationalized office work in early twentieth-century Canada. And Taylorism is still around in many service industry jobs. Making hamburgers in a fast-food restaurant is broken down into minute tasks, and telephone reservation agents for airlines are given scripts to follow when dealing with clients. But today, as in the past, workers complain about the limited opportunities for creativity and self-fulfillment when working under scientific management.

Human Relations

One shortcoming of Taylorism is its assumption that workers are wage-pursuing machines, motivated only by desire for their paycheque (Jones, 1996; Bendix, 1974). In reaction to this simplistic view, the **human relations school of management** pushed management to rethink the Taylorist image of workers by showing the importance of the social aspects of work. Based on a series of experiments at the Western Electric Company's Hawthorne plant in Chicago, Elton Mayo and others found that friendly supervision and attention to the social environment increased workers' cooperation and productivity. These "Hawthorne studies" started the movement to consider how employers can fulfill employees' social needs, increase their satisfaction, and make them feel better about their jobs.

Although the validity of the Hawthorne studies has been called into question (Carey, 1967), most researchers agree that management strategies today still incorporate and build on elements of the human relations school. From suggestion boxes to workplace participation programs, organizations are trying to find the right "human touch" to decrease worker resistance and increase productivity.

Recent "Humanization" of Work and Worker Participation

During the 1970s, management efforts to "humanize" workplaces gave rise to quality-control circles, quality-of-work-life programs, and other forms of workplace participation. At minimum, management introduced some of these newer strategies in order to diminish worker resistance and boost profits (Rinehart, 1996). Unlike worker cooperatives and worker ownership, though, participation schemes implemented by management are not true examples of workplace democracy.

As their name implies, quality-control (QC) circles emphasize the need to improve production quality. QC circles involve a small number of employees working with a team leader or supervisor. Together, these labour–management teams brainstorm about how to solve production problems. Quality-of-work-life (QWL) programs are broader in scope than QC circles. Management promotes QWL programs as democratizing the workplace, by giving workers more responsibility and control over their work through self-regulating work teams and by providing more complex jobs for workers. Although both QC circles and QWL programs make reference to worker participation, the decision-making authority of workers is usually limited to improving individual work tasks or improving the atmosphere at work. Workers are left out of decisions about "what is to be produced, investments, distribution of profits, technology, size of the work force or plant closings" (Rinehart, 1996: 169).

Recently, concepts such as total quality management (TQM), Japanese management, lean production, and "just-in-time" production have been promoted as the panacea for productivity and quality "problems" of management. These programs emphasize quality control through communication and teamwork between management and workers. And the rhetoric surrounding these programs continues to promote the potential for democratizing workplaces and increasing the participation of workers. Because of the attention it has received in North America, I now consider the trend toward Japanese management and lean production in North American plants.

Japanese Management: Lean Production or Mean Production?

Many of you have probably seen the television commercial about the Saturn automobile employee and "the day he stopped the line." While doing his job, this worker noticed a problem with the cars going past him, so he reached up, pulled the cord that stopped the line, and received the help he needed to solve the problem. As part of their marketing campaign, Saturn uses this commercial to show how the commitment to quality production runs throughout the plant. When I first saw this commercial, I remember thinking that this looked like a change from the old forms of production, where workers were told to leave their brains at the door, to a new form of production, where workers were encouraged to use their mental skills. And, to confirm my initial impression, I found out at the end of the commercial that Saturn is a "different kind of company" producing "a different kind of car."

What is Saturn promoting with this commercial? What does this commercial signify about potential changes to the way that work is organized? Saturn, like CAMI in Ingersoll, Ontario, and Subaru-Isuzu in Lafayette, Indiana, is part of the movement to **Japanese production techniques (JPT)**. Initial reactions to these Japanese transplants and joint operations were positive. "Just-in-time" production cut costs as companies reduced their parts inventories and the need for warehouses. And the use of participatory work teams led some academics and industry experts to consider JPT a new way of organizing work (Womack, Jones, and Roos, 1990). They see Japanese production as an alternative to Taylorism and Fordism. (Fordism is a combination of assembly-line technology and bureaucratic organization.) JPT is seen as enhancing workers' skills and their participation at work and, in general, promoting the use of workers' mental capacities in conjunction with their physical labour. In addition, many believe these companies represent a new era in labour–management relations.

But does the Saturn dream of a different kind of company really hold true? A growing body of research from both the United States and Canada suggests that JPT is really a direct extension of Taylorism and assembly-line production (Dassbach, 1996; Robertson et al., 1993). Even though work is subdivided into teams, scientific management is apparent insofar as jobs are still broken down into small tasks. For example, instructions for the first few tasks of a welding shop job at the CAMI plant read as follows: "A) Press the cycle stop button to release the locking pin from the tray; B) Remove empty parts tray and roll over to parts bin; C) Load parts from bin into tray, using 2 hands, lifting approximately 10 parts at a time" (Robertson et al., 1993). This is followed by six or seven more detailed instructions. When the list is completed, another car has moved in front of the worker and the cycle starts all over again. Although JPT does involve some job rotation, it is usually between two similar jobs or it is instituted simply to reduce repetitive strain injuries. Also, as in traditional plants, managers and the computerized assembly-line technology, not the workers, set the speed of the line and the pace of work.

Just as the service industry incorporated Taylorism (e.g., how McDonald's makes hamburgers), we are now seeing the use of JPT and total quality management in service industries. Hotel chains, grocery stores, and airlines now utilize JPT strategies. Often these programs come with names like "Service Excellence." Most of these programs focus on improving customer service and may allow employees some discretion in dealing with customer complaints. For example, as part of a program to increase sensitivity to individual customers, one grocery store in England encourages staff to accompany customers to products rather than just give directions and to send flowers to customers in the event of a service lapse (Rosenthal, Hill, and Peccei, 1997). Employees are given greater discretion in the hope that this will lead to improved service. How successful these programs are for improving service and increasing employee empowerment remains to be seen.

Workers are beginning to question whether lean production represents a new type of worker participation. In 1990, 56 percent of workers at CAMI said they viewed the company as democratic. A little over a year later, only 26 percent viewed CAMI in the same light (Robertson et al., 1993). And when asked whether workers needed a union at CAMI, those who strongly agreed a union was needed increased from 57 percent to 81 percent between 1990 and 1991. A statement by a local union official at the Ingersoll, Ontario, CAMI plant sums things up nicely (quoted in Rinehart et al., 1994: 166):

> This empowerment, when it's cost saving or quality problem, okay, but when it's human problems, a comfort issue, whatever, there's no empowerment. It's one-sided. That's the bottom line.

Results from the service industry are also mixed. There is some new evidence that employee empowerment schemes can increase the development of workers' interpersonal and problem-solving skills because employees have to deal with customers' problems and requests (Smith, 2001). As one employee of a copier service states, "[before the employee involvement program] I used to say [to customers] 'Here's your copies, now get out of here.' Now I have to make sure I'm communicating, *to understand their needs* ... I'm trying to have more sensitivity to their needs" (Smith, 2001: 44). Whether or not these strategies will lead to increased empowerment from workers depends on management's attitude. Just as we saw in the section on technology (e.g., Zuboff, 1988), how management implements these strategies affects their outcomes. As long as these programs continue to be linked solely to management's desire for productivity increases and the "bottom line," their participatory potential will be limited. Alternatives, such as worker-owned companies like Algoma Steel in Sault Ste. Marie, Ontario, may bring us closer to real worker participation (Livingstone, 1993).

DIVERSITY IN ORGANIZATIONS

We previously discussed problems of race, ethnicity, disability, and age in the section on job ghettos. Recently, sociologists have started to focus on issues of diversity in organizations. Organizations now talk about **managing diversity** within their boundaries. This is the catchphrase for programs designed to reduce barriers for women, visible minorities, Aboriginal people, and people with disabilities. Managing diversity can include providing sexual harassment awareness seminars, actively hiring and promoting visible minorities, or establishing mentorship relationships. Most of these diversity programs aim to make the formal structures of organizations discrimination-free and tolerable for all members. Some argue that the term *managing diversity* is problematic (Prasad and Mills, 1997). It places the focus on managing rather than understanding diversity. In this section, I discuss some of the ways we can understand the effect of diversity on organizational life. To begin, we need to understand why women, ethnic and racial minorities, people with disabilities, and others may have trouble adjusting to life in organizations.

A complicating factor in the potential of these programs is the informal structure or *organizational culture* of organizations. Members have shared meanings about what life is like in their organizations. Organizational culture comprises, among other things, implicit understandings of how to complete work and shared assumptions about how to interact and how to treat co-workers. Some sociologists show the image of organizations is one in which race, gender, sexuality, and age are absent or reflect dominant white heterosexual culture (e.g., Mills and Simmons, 1999; and see Chapter 10 for a more detailed discussion of ethnicity and race). In Canada, visible-minority immigrant women speak of experiencing "triple jeopardy" and of having difficulties fitting into organizational life (Mighty, 1997). When the majority of workers are white and heterosexual, the organizational culture may implicitly discount the experiences of minority employees. One lesbian employee was distressed by her own self-betrayal as she attempted to fit into her organizational culture: "I'd just come back from a gay rights march ... and yet in that situation with those people I worked with, I couldn't say anything ... it was extremely upsetting" (quoted in Hall, 1993: 133). To understand diversity, we must do more than change the formal structures of organizations. We must also look at how the informal culture of organizations constrains members of minority groups.

WOMEN IN MANAGEMENT

Much of the research concerning women working in organizations has focused on the movement of women into management. In Canada between 1971 and 1991, the number of women managers increased from 6 percent to 38 percent of all managers (Andrew, Coderre, and Denis, 1994). However, since only 21 percent of senior managers in Canada are women (Andrew, Coderre, and Denis, 1994), the "glass ceiling" for women has by no means disappeared. Research suggests that it is not easy for women to move into the male-dominated world of management.

Do Women and Men Manage Differently?

One barrier that women have to overcome in moving up the managerial ladder is the perception that they are ineffective managers. On the one hand, one stereotype is that of the bossy and overly controlling female manager. Current research points to an image of women as more effective and participatory managers than men. So what are we to conclude? Are women managers authoritarian or consensus-oriented? Are they different from men managers?

In her classic study of a large, white-collar organization she called "Indsco," Rosabeth Moss Kanter (1977) demonstrates that whether women managers are participatory or authoritarian often depends on their position in the organization. Kanter found that women managers at Indsco tend to be in powerless positions in the lower managerial ranks. These positions offer little room for risk taking and limited authority over organizational decisions. These powerless positions also breed rule-mindedness and territoriality on the part of managers. Knowing the rules and being able to force subordinates to follow the rules represents one of the few areas of power for "powerless" managers. Kanter concludes that, regardless of gender, if managers find themselves in a powerless position, they will likely be narrow-minded and overly controlling. So we now have a partial answer to our question. To understand why some managers—male or female—are authoritarian, we need to know whether they are in relatively powerful or powerless positions.

Judy Rosener (1990) offers a different perspective by arguing that some female managers are more interactive and people-oriented than male managers. The women interviewed by Rosener see themselves as encouraging participation, sharing power and information, enhancing the self-worth of others, and energizing co-workers and subordinates. Indicative of this style is the decision-making approach of one female CEO, who stated: "When I face a tough decision, I always ask my employees, 'What would you do if you were me?' This approach generates good ideas and

introduces my employees to the complexity of management decisions" (quoted in Rosener, 1990: 122).

At first glance, Rosener seems to be supporting the view that women and men make essentially different managers. This would lead us to believe that there is something about women—biology, socialization, or life experiences—that turns them into interactive, participatory managers. Yet Rosener also acknowledges that management style is determined by organizational context, such as the location of managers in the organization hierarchy, the degree of bureaucratization and rigidity in the organization structure, and the presence—or absence—of a culture that allows for innovation. In addition, the way in which a woman's managerial style is perceived may lead to the development of different styles. In her study of Canadian managers, Sheppard (1993) found that, while both men and women managers made "gut-level" decisions, men's quick decision making was viewed as more credible than women's. Sheppard argues that the way in which male and female decision makers are perceived may lead women to develop a slower, more participatory style of management.

The answer to the question about gender differences in managerial style, then, is not entirely clear. In some instances, we see differences, but just as often we do not. The consensus that seems to be growing among researchers, however, is that no real differences exist between male and female managerial behaviour and effectiveness (Powell, 1990). This body of research suggests that, rather than defining certain managerial styles as male and female, we should develop a contextualized understanding of managerial styles.

"WILL I LIKE MY JOB?" JOB SATISFACTION AND ALIENATION

The service revolution has changed the structure of work in Canada and across the world. There are more part-time jobs and increased use of computer surveillance, as well as some increases in knowledge-based jobs. Given these changes, how do Canadians feel about their jobs? According to a 2001 survey, 93 percent of Canadians reported they were satisfied with their jobs (McKenzie, 2001). Earlier surveys revealed that getting respect from their bosses and feeling in control of their job mattered most to Canadian workers (Chamberlain, 1996). Less important was the amount of money they made. This finding reflects much of what we know about job satisfaction. To be satisfied at work, intrinsic rewards, such as autonomy and challenging work, are as important as extrinsic or material rewards.

Are 93 percent of Canadians really satisfied with their jobs? What do sociologists mean by **job satisfaction**? These are important questions. Job satisfaction is usually determined by a survey question, such as "How satisfied are you with your job?" In many ways the responses to job satisfaction questions are similar to replies to the question "How are you today?" (Krahn and Lowe, 1998: 408). Most of us would answer "fine" to such a general question. Similarly, many workers respond that they like their jobs when asked how satisfied they are. Some analysts believe, however, that most workers do not want to admit that they do not like their jobs.

One solution to this problem is to use more specific job satisfaction measures, especially measures that refer to behaviours or behavioural intentions (e.g., Rinehart, 1978; Hodson, 1991). For example, the 2001 survey found that 22 percent of Canadians interviewed said they planned on changing their job in the near future (Canadian Press/Leger Marketing, 2001). When we discuss alienation (see page 350), we will look more closely at workers' behaviours to understand their negative reactions to their job. For now, we'll spend a bit more time on job satisfaction. Even though it is a problematic measure, it is still used by management to gauge how happy and how productive their workers are.

WHAT DETERMINES JOB SATISFACTION?

A multitude of factors affect how we feel about our jobs, ranging from our individual characteristics to the size of the firm we work in. To give you an idea of this range, I'll discuss some of the major predictors of job satisfaction.

Individual Characteristics

Based on what we know about job ghettos, it might be a safe assumption to predict that women, older workers, and younger workers will be some of the least satisfied groups of workers. Although it is true

that younger workers are some of the most dissatisfied workers (see Table 13.2), older workers—at least those who have stable jobs—are actually a relatively happy group (Krahn, 1992). The higher job satisfaction reported by older employed workers may be the result of reduced expectations about work, more meaningful lives outside of work, or past advancement in their jobs (Krahn and Lowe, 1998).

When you consider occupational sex segregation and the differences in jobs held by women and men, you might expect women to be less satisfied than men. In a majority of studies, though, women and men report similar levels of job satisfaction (see Table 13.2 and, e.g., Krahn, 1992). However, when evaluating their feelings about their work, women tend to compare themselves with other women (Hodson and

TABLE 13.2   JOB SATISFACTION OF CANADIANS, 1996

EMPLOYEE CHARACTERISTICS	PERCENT WHO ARE "VERY SATISFIED" WITH THEIR JOB
All Canadians	45
Level in company	
Senior manager	57
Middle level	44
Junior level	34
Size of company	
Very small	48
Small	43
Medium	46
Large	41
Age	
18–29	37
30–39	48
40+	46
Gender	
Women	5
Men	44
Employment status	
Full-time	44
Part-time	38
Self-employed	55
Union status	
Union member	41
Non-union member	43

SOURCE: Compiled from an Angus Reid survey reported in "The Happy Gang," *The Toronto Sun*, October 8, 1996, p. B1.

Sullivan, 1990). If women compared themselves with men, their reported level of satisfaction might be lower.

Job and Organizational Characteristics

Opportunities for autonomous and complex work are important predictors of job satisfaction: Satisfaction increases with autonomy and decreases with repetitive or automated work. For example, fast-food workers who repeat the same phrases every day and autoworkers who must do the same task repeatedly are less likely to be satisfied than other workers. Opportunities for participation can increase satisfaction. Workers at the CAMI plant in Ingersoll, Ontario, initially were excited about Japanese management. But when the promise of participation faded, workers' negative feelings increased (Robertson et al., 1993).

Organizational structure, such as technology and firm size, affect how happy we are at work. Blauner's (1964) classic study, *Alienation and Freedom*, shows how workers' alienation increased as technology shifted from craft work to machine tending and assembly-line work. In contrast, technology that requires the use of conceptual skills increases job satisfaction. Employees in small companies experience higher levels of satisfaction. In 1996, 48 percent of Canadians who worked in very small companies were very satisfied, compared with 41 percent who worked in large companies (see Table 13.2). As company size increases, so do workers' feelings of isolation and powerlessness. Thus, workers in small, locally owned companies are more likely to be satisfied than those working in regional and national corporations (Hodson and Sullivan, 1985).

When I consider all the individual, job, and organizational factors that influence job satisfaction, I am struck by the realization that much of our satisfaction at work is determined by things over which we have little or no control. Our employers determine how much we are paid and how challenging and autonomous our jobs will be. And the chance to work in a small, locally owned company has much to do with the employment opportunities where we live.

ALIENATION

If job satisfaction focuses on the individual worker's feelings about his or her job, alienation is linked to the lack of control or powerlessness an individual experiences in relation to his or her job. Originating in the work of Karl Marx, the concept of **alienation** examines how the structural conditions of work lead to workers' lack of power over their work and lives (Rinehart, 1996). For Marx, alienation is an "objective condition" that stems from capitalism. Marx argues that capitalism robs workers of control over the means of production and the products of their labour and puts this control in the hands of owners.

According to Marx, there are four sources of alienation existing for workers under capitalism. First, workers are alienated from the product that they produce. They do not own the products they are producing, they have no say over how the product will be disposed, and they are not producing something that may be useful to themselves. Rather, under capitalism, work is now a *means to an end*—work provides a paycheque so workers can buy the things they need, but workers no longer directly produce what they need. Second, workers do not have control over the process of production. The high division of labour of much work is indicative of this condition. Decisions about how fast to work, the order in which to complete tasks, and the use of equipment are made by someone other than workers. Workers lose control over their daily work activity, like the CAMI workers discussed earlier who have their job tasks broken down in great detail. Third, workers are alienated from themselves or from engaging in creative activity. And fourth, workers are alienated from others as there are fewer opportunities to talk and connect with co-workers. Work is also not a collective process that can help the whole community. Overall, the division of labour under capitalism physically and emotionally isolates workers from one another.

Recently, some sociologists have conceptualized alienation as a way to think about how workers' psychological and emotional states are linked to the organization of work (Rogers, 1995). For example, when work is repetitive and does not allow for interaction between co-workers, workers may experience a high level of alienation. Some sociologists conceptualize alienation as a subjective state that arises from the reality of capitalist working conditions. Here the emphasis is on workers' feelings of powerlessness and lack of control or connection to their work and fellow employees. Box 13.2 provides more details on alienation in the workplace, particularly in the case of temporary clerical workers.

BOX 13.2   ALIENATION FROM WORK

In the classical Marxist depiction, alienation from work has at least two components. Workers are alienated not just from the product of their work, but from the work process as well: "alienation shows itself not only in the result, but also in the act of production, inside productive activity itself" (McLellan, 1977: 80). With temporary work, labor is twice alienated from its product. The worker's labor belongs not only to the company for whom she works, but also to the temporary agency that receives a fee for her services. For example, the company that hires a temporary may pay the agency $10 an hour for her services; however, the temporary worker may only receive $7 an hour. Thus, the alienation Marx depicted is taken one step further through the subcontracting relationship that exists in temporary employment.

More important for this analysis is the fact that temporary workers also are alienated from the labor process. This type of alienation is characterized by temporaries' lack of control over their work, their lack of control over the conditions of their work, and their lack of understanding of the purpose of their work....

Clerical temporaries are seldom provided with enough information for them to understand the purpose of the work that they perform. Little time is invested in instruction regarding the task to be performed, particularly for short-term assignments. When asked about their tasks, the temporaries I interviewed were seldom able to describe the purpose of their work. One woman who was doing temporary work after losing her "permanent" job stated:

> I still don't know what it was that I was doing. I just sat there and entered, I think they were coordinates or something. It's some kind of program that builds a building. They just gave me the coordinates to punch in. (Julie Grovers, 30-year-old White woman)

Another temporary described the purpose of her filing "hundreds of boxes" over a period of 3 to 4 weeks:

> For some reason they were redoing all their files because they changed something, they changed the districts or something like that. Whatever, I don't really know. (Irene Pedersen, 24-year-old White woman)

SOURCE: Jackie Krasas Rogers, "Just a Temp: Experience and Structure of Alienation in Temporary Clerical Employment," *Work and Occupations*, Vol. 22, No. 2, pp. 145, 146. Reprinted with permission.

Fighting Alienation: Individual and Collective Responses to Work

To understand alienation, we also need to look at how workers resist it (Schmitt and Moody, 1994). This can shed light on their negative feelings toward work. When a worker engages in sabotage or repeatedly skips work, management may define the worker as destructive or lazy. Yet, in the minds of workers, these seemingly insubordinate behaviours may actually be an attempt to gain control over their job or reduce the amount of alienation they experience. To overcome a boring job where she was not assigned enough work, one temporary clerical worker stated, "I used to sleep there. Yes there's nothing to do. I always bring my book. When I get sick and tired of reading, I sleep. Sometimes, OK, you're not supposed to make phone calls, but what am I going to do with 8 hours?" (Rogers, 1995: 157). If management had provided enough work, this temporary worker might have exhibited good work habits. When viewed as potential resistance to alienating conditions, the "misbehaviour" of workers

appears in a different light. Some researchers argue that the alienating conditions of work lead some workers to "fight back" or react to these conditions (Edwards and Scullion, 1982; Rinehart, 1996). You may have had similar reactions to work, such as slacking off if you believed your supervisor required you to work too hard, or turning your work into a game to make the time go faster. Engaging in these behaviours does not mean you are lazy or incompetent. Rather, they are typical reactions to alienating work.

To cope with poor working conditions, some workers quit their jobs. Those who cannot quit may respond passively by socializing with co-workers, playing games, or reducing their productivity (see, e.g., Burawoy, 1979). Management often devises strategies to prevent these types of behaviours. For example, Taylorism was motivated in part by management's desire to reduce opportunities for workers to restrict their output.

For management, theft and destruction of company property are particularly bothersome behaviours.

But these criminal acts may be motivated by poor working conditions. A few years ago, an undergraduate student in my class confessed that, while working in a small T-shirt design factory, she purposely poked holes in some shirts. Because management had a policy of giving damaged T-shirts to employees, one might think she did this only to take advantage of her situation. As it turns out, though, employees were paid low wages and worked under conditions of extreme heat. This student saw her behaviour as a protest against the inadequate pay and difficult working conditions. Other workers engage in sabotage to gain concessions from management or to gain control over the work process. Factory workers may damage the assembly line to slow down the pace of work, or clerical workers may hide files to reduce their workload (Hodson and Sullivan, 1990; Rinehart, 1996).

Workers often resist alienating work conditions. Forms of resistance include striking, absenteeism, quitting, slacking off, and industrial sabotage.

SOURCE: Juan Manuel Sanchez. Courtesy Simon Patrich Gallery

Do these individual acts of resistance behaviours change the amount of alienation workers experience? The answer to this question is complex. Many sociologists, beginning with Marx, illustrate how alienation is a condition of objective powerlessness that exists regardless of whether workers themselves consciously recognize it (e.g., Rinehart 1996). Some workers become aware or conscious of the alienating conditions they experience at work. As predicted by Marx, these workers may respond to these conditions by forming unions, going on strikes, or engaging in revolutionary behaviours focused on overthrowing capitalism. However, many workers do not develop a "class consciousness." Sociologists Harvey Krahn and Graham Lowe (1998: 419) state:

> In the absence of a well-defined alternative to the current economic system, we would not expect most workers to be able to clearly articulate their alienation and act on it. Apathy, or an attempt to forget about work as soon as one leaves it behind, are the common responses of many workers to a situation to which there were no viable alternatives.

This means that hiding files or poking holes in a shirt may make the worker feel better and thus make it possible to get through the day. These types of activities may reduce the subjective feelings of alienation: workers may feel less powerless or may feel they have more control over their working conditions. But these types of individual strategies do not necessarily change the structural conditions of work. Collective responses to workplace conditions are more likely to lead to lasting changes in how work is organized. These collective responses, such as forming a union, may not "overthrow" the economic system but they can improve working conditions. Debora De Angelis's co-workers that voted to form a union put themselves in a position to bargain collectively for improved pay, job security, and working conditions. Although playing games and stealing may momentarily increase workers' feelings of control over their jobs, most researchers agree that, for lasting change to occur, collective responses are needed. For example, wildcat strikes, where workers spontaneously walk off the job, are effective ways to protest poor working conditions and arbitrary treatment (Rinehart, 1996). Chapter 20 provides more details about the role of strikes in the Canadian labour movement's struggle for economic and social rights.

Unions play an important role in facilitating collective action by workers. Today, 32 percent of the non-agricultural paid labour force are in unions (see Table 13.1 on page 333). Compared with the experience in some other countries, such as the United States and Australia, *union density*, or the percentage of paid workers who are unionized, has not significantly declined in Canada over the past 30 years (Krahn and Lowe, 1998: 246). Over the past 150 years, the characteristics of unionized workers have shifted. During the late 1800s, craft workers organized; during the 1930s and 1940s, workers in the goods-producing sectors followed suit. Public-sector workers began to organize in the 1960s and 1970s. Figure 13.4 shows that in 2000 public-sector industries had the highest rates of unionization. Some

union supporters warn that union density will stagnate if union organizing does not expand to cover new groups of workers, particularly young workers in service industries (White, 1993). From McDonald's workers in Ontario to Starbucks' employees in British Columbia, we should expect to see more union drives in the service industries.

Service workers are not the only area of potential growth for unions. Over the past 20 years, the number of women in unions has increased; in 1990, women accounted for 43 percent of all union membership (Galarneau, 1996). Unions still face difficulties in organizing women. First, women are more likely to be in lower-tier service and part-time jobs—jobs that are difficult to unionize, in part because of job insecurity. Second, unions must demonstrate their commitment to women's issues, such as daycare, family leave, and sexual harassment, if they are to attract more female members.

FIGURE 13.4 THE HIGHEST UNION RATES WERE IN PUBLIC SECTOR–DOMINATED INDUSTRIES   ■ 2000 ■ 1999

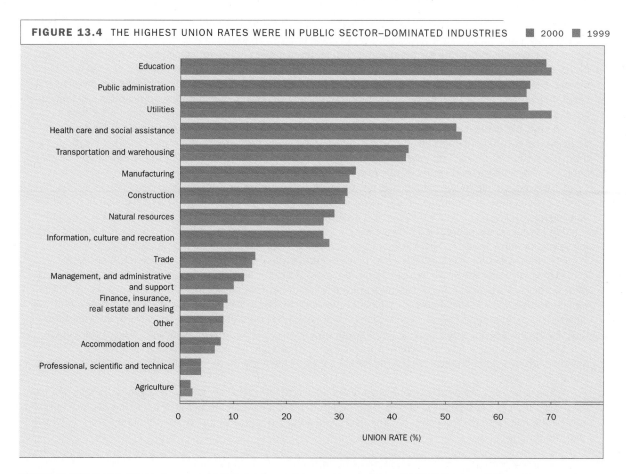

SOURCE: Statistics Canada, "Unionization—an update," *Perspectives on Labour and Income*, Cat. no. 75–001-XPE, Autumn, 2000, p. 40

Whether the number of unionized workers in Canada will grow or decline depends on how unions deal with changes in the labour market and the economy. The rise of nonstandard work and the ease with which companies can move their businesses to other countries raise serious challenges to unions. Box 13.3 provides a young union organizer's views about why youth should be more involved with unions. His views highlight how unions are one of the few ways to bring about real and lasting changes to the objective conditions of work.

THE FUTURE OF WORK

Good and bad jobs, nonstandard jobs, alienating work—what will the future of work hold? Although sociologists don't usually try to predict the future, we can look at some of the current trends to see where we are going.

In the immediate future, we can expect employers to continue looking for ways to reduce operating costs. As in the past, the focus will be on reducing the cost of labour. Employers continue to move factories to countries with the lowest labour costs. This, along with labour-reducing uses of technology, may further the trend of downsizing and company restructuring. As a result, fewer employees will spend their lifetime with the same employer. As the head of production for the PowerPC microchip said in 1994, "I'm here for the duration, five years or so" (quoted in Osterman, 1995: 72).

Some researchers and futurists debate what jobs will look like. As in the debates over the service economy, the debate divides along pessimistic and

---

BOX 13.3   YOUNG PEOPLE AND UNIONS

I'm 21, and I live in Calgary. I work at Garden Market IGA, which is organized by UFCW Canada Local 401. An average day in my life usually involves getting up, going to work, coming home from work, and going out. I also do some volunteer organizing for the union.... I think the biggest challenge facing workers today, in Canada, is the right-wing, corporate agenda, which focuses solely on the bottom line. It's all about money, money, money, and not about the people. For instance, right now they're closing a Catelli pasta-production plant that Local 401 represents in Lethbridge. An American company wanted to eliminate the competition, so they just came in, bought the company, and closed it. Now there are 71 unionized, well-paid workers out of work.

Another big challenge is people's lack of education about their rights. People don't know their rights because the governments don't want them to know. Our system pretty much brainwashes kids at a young age that, "Hey, you can make it on your own, everybody can do it themselves, you don't need any help from anybody." Which is just a lie. Everybody needs a hand up.

I think educating young people has got to be priority number one for unions, because we're the new people coming into the workforce. Plus, labour itself has started to age. You go to a convention now and you hear people saying, "I've seen that same guy at the convention for the last 20 years." That's a problem. If you don't bring in new people and new ideas, you'll never change—and change has to happen. It has to occur for unions to move forward, become more productive, and represent their members better.

I think the best thing unions do is look after the concerns of working people. The worst thing we do is we don't blow our own horn or pat ourselves on the back. We don't let people—even our own members—know what we do. Say we go out and we settle a grievance about pay that our members should have received. Like, we just settled one—I think it was for $34,000. But nobody knows about it because we didn't publicize it. We didn't go running around saying, "Look what we did! Look what we did!" I believe we have to do a lot more of that, so people see the good that we actually do, and they don't just believe what they read in the papers.

Unions need to get young workers involved. We have to organize new workplaces, and we have to make unions a stronger force in the country. Right now, we don't have the power to walk up to government and say, "Change the laws."

We have to educate people about why unions are important, and why labour laws are important: to stop the exploitation by big business, and to stop the growing gap between the rich and poor. The country will fall apart if the rich keep getting richer and the poor keep getting poorer. With more workers unionized, we'll have more power.

continued

BOX 13.3 YOUNG PEOPLE AND UNIONS *(continued)*

The unions have to go into the high schools and talk to kids who are just joining the workforce. You've got to point out things like, in Alberta—depending on how much money you make—it's illegal to be charged for a uniform, but companies are doing it because the people don't know. The government hasn't provided the information to them. Nobody's been there to tell them. I think telling people how the companies are stealing from them would help them realize the need for unions, and to organize and stand up for their rights. It would help them stop being exploited just because they're young.

I think we have to move into more non-traditional union settings, like the fast food industry, and try non-traditional ways of organizing. You can't just walk into a place and say, "Hey, join the union. Look what we've done." You have to give people a reason. Young workers, older workers, and people of ethnic minorities all have different reasons for joining the union. They all have different beliefs and different ideas which we have to take into account. A young person's going to have a completely different idea of what they want at work than somebody who's 45 and married, with two kids. Somebody who's 17 is liable to want a raise more than anything else, while somebody older is liable to want a benefit plan. So, we have to look at the workplaces we're organizing, and go in the direction the members want, not just do what we've traditionally done in the past.

We also have to get governments to change the laws so we can organize temporary workers. There's a huge new Wal-Mart warehouse in Calgary, and every person working there is hired through a temp agency, so we can't organize them. You walk in there and try to apply for a job, and they send you to a temp agency. Every employee is charged by the temp agency, they're all getting barely over minimum wage, and the working conditions are disgusting ...

Some say young people don't care about unionizing. It's not that they don't care. It's that young people don't care about the same things as somebody who's older than them. Somebody who's 45 doesn't have the same outlook as a 17-year-old person: their lives are completely different. So, we have to change the way we organize and represent young people.

Young people can no longer look forward to getting a good job working in a plant someplace, and providing for their family. Now you have to work two part-time jobs. You can't get a full-time job because companies sit there and go, "Well, if I make you full-time, I have to give you benefits. I don't want to do that." So everybody ends up in a dead-end, part-time job.

We have to get into using young people to organize young people. In my store, the younger people mostly talk to me, and the older people mostly talk to the older shop steward. You're more comfortable talking to somebody your own age, they'll have the same experiences and the same ideas as you. It's why we use Spanish-speaking people to organize Spanish-speaking people. It's somebody they can understand and relate to, someone who has faced the same discrimination.

How can workers in different countries develop solidarity with each other? That's the million dollar question. Globalization and free trade are the most destructive forces out there right now. Look at the Catelli plant in Lethbridge. It's being closed because they can produce pasta cheaper in a right-to-work state in the United States. I think globalization has made us stand up and see that the rich are getting richer and the poor are getting poorer no matter where you are, whether you're in India, Brazil or Canada. I think globalization opened our eyes in North America to the plight of everybody else, and that it's not just them, it's us, too, who are being affected ...

I think there are two things unions have to do. We have to educate the members we already have: show them why it is we do stuff, so we don't have members out there who look at unions as simply a deduction off their paycheque. And we have to also organize new members. As companies get bigger, they're going to downsize to make more money, and if we don't keep organizing new members, we aren't going to be able to fight the fight as well as we can now. We're not going to be able to move forward and pressure governments and companies to treat people fairly.

Chris O'Halloran is vice-president of the Alberta Federation of Labour, representing youth and youth issues. He is a member of UFCW Canada Local 401.

SOURCE: Chris O'Halloran, 2001. "Young People and Unions: Making the Connection." *Our Times* 20(5): 19–23.

optimistic lines. Optimists emphasize the "end of the job" as we know it (Bridges, 1994) and the rise of self-employed, autonomous entrepreneurs. Part of the optimistic scenario is based on the hope that the service industry will continue to create good jobs, such as in finance and medicine. Pessimists like Jeremy Rifkin (1995) predict the "end of work." Based on an analysis of jobs in the United States, Rifkin believes that as many as three out of four white-collar and blue-collar jobs could be automated. This will push people out of work with no jobs to replace the ones lost to automation. In Rifkin's view, unemployment levels will continue to rise and more of us will scramble for the few remaining jobs. By the middle of the twenty-first century, millions of workers could be left permanently idle. These optimistic and pessimistic scenarios are linked to trends we've discussed in this chapter: Will technology increase or decrease productivity? Will the service industry create more good jobs than bad jobs? Will the number of workers in job ghettos increase or decrease? Both optimists and pessimists agree, however, that the days of work in large corporations may be coming to an end. But it's too early to tell which scenario, if either, will emerge.

As you've learned in this chapter, employers and employees do have some control over whether technology creates good jobs or bad jobs or reduces alienating conditions. An important issue for the future of work is whether employers or employees will set the terms by which such changes will be judged. It is clear that the century-old battle between workers and management will probably continue. And it is workers like Debora De Angelis who will attempt to organize their co-workers, so that employees improve their chances of having a say in what work will look like in the future.

SUMMARY

1. In the first industrial revolution, large segments of the population moved from being peasant farmers to being wage-earning factory workers living in urban areas. During the second revolution, companies increased in size and developed administrative offices with a complex division of labour.

2. The rise of the service economy is changing the types of jobs available in the labour market. The types of jobs available in the service economy are being polarized into good jobs in upper-tier industries and bad jobs in lower-tier industries.

3. The proportion of Canadians employed in nonstandard jobs is growing. Much of this job growth is fuelled by the expansion of the lower-tier service sector.

4. Labour-market segmentation shows that different segments exist in the labour market. Good jobs are located in core industries and firms with primary labour markets, while bad jobs may be found in peripheral industries and firms with secondary labour markets. Job ghettos are areas of the labour market that trap disadvantaged groups of workers. Labour-market shelters, such as professional associations and unions, help their members maintain access to good jobs.

5. From Taylorism to Japanese management, various management strategies are used to control workers and increase their productivity. Most strategies fall short on their claims to be participatory.

6. Research does not show a difference in men's and women's management styles. Differences are due to the position of managers or their organizational context.

7. Job satisfaction measures how workers feel about their jobs. Work and organizational characteristics are the primary predictors of how satisfied workers are.

8. Alienation is a structural condition of powerlessness that arises from the organization of work in the capitalist economy. Workers respond to alienating conditions in various ways, such as engaging in sabotage or quitting their jobs. Strikes and other collective forms of resistance may have some success in changing the conditions of work.

QUESTIONS TO CONSIDER

1. Thinking about your own work experience, do you see evidence of the service economy creating good jobs or bad jobs?

2. Do Japanese production techniques (JPTs) represent a different way of organizing work from Taylorism? If yes, how are JPTs different? Do JPTs offer new forms of participation for workers?

3. How is technology changing the world of work? Do you believe that we are experiencing a productivity paradox? What evidence would you use to support your argument?

4. What is the difference between the concepts of job satisfaction and alienation? Is Marx's concept of alienation relevant for understanding work today? Why or why not? Have you ever engaged in workplace behaviour that could be interpreted as a reaction to alienating conditions? Did these behaviours change the alienating conditions? Why or why not?

GLOSSARY

Alienation, in Marxist theory, refers to a structural condition of "objective powerlessness." Workers do not have power or control over their work situation and are separated from the means of production. This situation is indicative of work in a capitalist economy.

Extrinsic rewards are the material benefits of working. Adequate pay, benefits, and opportunities for advancement are examples.

The **human relations school of management** is a theory of management that emphasizes the importance of the social aspects of work. Proponents argue that more satisfied workers are more productive workers.

Intrinsic rewards are the social-psychological benefits of working. They are derived from challenging work, nonrepetitive work, autonomy, and decision-making opportunities.

Japanese production techniques (JPT) refer to a management strategy that combines teamwork with assembly-line work to improve efficiency and productivity of workers.

Job ghettos are parts of the labour market that trap certain groups of workers.

Job satisfaction is a measure of how workers feel about their jobs. It is determined by asking workers in a survey, "How satisfied are you with your job as a whole?"

Labour-market segmentation refers to the separation of the labour market into sectors of good and bad jobs.

Labour-market shelters are organizations that protect the jobs of certain groups of workers. Professional associations and unions are examples.

Managing diversity refers to a management strategy to help women and minorities succeed in the workplace. This strategy consists of anti-racism and sexual harassment policies and awareness classes, mentorship programs, and other nondiscriminatory procedures.

Nonstandard jobs include the following types of employment: part-week employment (reduced hours per week), part-year employment, limited-term contract employment, employment through temporary-help agencies, self-employment, and multiple-job holding.

Primary labour markets are the source of most good jobs. They usually provide a job ladder and the opportunity for upward mobility.

Taylorism is a style of management that breaks job tasks into their smallest components. Work is also separated into conceptual and manual tasks, removing the need for workers to make decisions about their work. It is named after its developer, Frederick Taylor, and is also known as scientific management.

SUGGESTED READING

Betcherman, Gordon, Kathryn McMullen, Norm Leckie, and Christina Caron. (1994). *The Canadian Workplace in Transition.* Kingston, ON: Industrial Relations Centre Press. Using current survey information, this text provides an empirical overview of changes occurring in Canadian organizations.

Duffy, Ann, Daniel Glenday, and Norene Pupo. (1997). *Good Jobs, Bad Jobs, No Jobs: The Transformation of Work in the 21st Century.* Toronto: Harcourt Brace. Chapters deal with contemporary labour force issues in Canada, including technology, restructuring, work and family, unemployment, and training.

Krahn, Harvey J., and Graham S. Lowe. (1998). *Work, Industry and Canadian Society,* 3rd ed. Scarborough, ON: Nelson. This text provides an overview of major topics and research in the study of work and occupations in Canada.

Myles, John. (1988). "The Expanding Middle: Some Canadian Evidence on the Deskilling Debate." *Canadian Review of Sociology and Anthropology, 25* (3), 335–64. A key assessment of the polarization of the Canadian labour market into good and bad jobs.

Rinehart, James W. (1996). *The Tyranny of Work: Alienation and the Labour Process,* 3rd ed. Toronto: Harcourt Brace. A compelling look at the history and sociology of alienation and work.

CHAPTER FOURTEEN

EDUCATION

In this chapter you will learn that:

- Education is an enormous enterprise that affects life-chances and quality of life, and is widely believed to help solve many social problems and maintain democratic ideals, equality, social justice, and productivity.

- Major approaches to the sociological study of education include structural-functionalism, which emphasizes the contribution education makes to maintaining social equilibrium; conflict theories, which emphasize the power struggles that take place in educational contexts along the lines of class, gender, and race; and symbolic interactionism or interpretive theories, which emphasize the importance of meaning and the interpretation of conditions and circumstances in everyday social interaction.

- Doing well in school is not just a matter of intelligence; students' social characteristics such as gender, ethnicity, and socio-economic status affect educational attainment.

- The school experience involves exposure to structured sorting mechanisms, such as tracking, and to teacher expectations, language, cultural capital, and informal curricula, all of which influence students' experience of the school climate and their performance.

IAN M. GOMME

UNIVERSITY OF SOUTHERN COLORADO, PUEBLO

INTRODUCTION

The Canadian school system confronts a host of problems initiated by massive funding cuts during the 1990s. Governments have translated budget constraints into expectations that educators have to be more efficient; they must "do more with less." With that sentiment has come frequent and intense labour unrest as evidenced by three strikes in three years for the Toronto Board of Education. Not only are demoralized teachers and support staff exiting the system at every turn, but we are told that significant teacher shortages are looming. Provinces' rigid funding formulas have forced school boards to shut schools; chop "unnecessary" subjects such as art, music, and physical education; and cut back many special-ed programs. With schools starved for cash, parents and teachers are left to take up the slack paying out of their own pockets for essential textbooks and supplies.

Maclean's magazine cites two polls conducted in 2001 suggesting that public confidence in Canada's school system is middling at best. In a Gallup poll, less than half the respondents claimed satisfaction with the education of Canadian children. In an Ontario Institute for Studies in Education survey, the percentage who believe public education is improving dropped from more than 35 percent in 1979 to less than 20 percent in 2001. In part, the public's response has been to abandon the public system entirely and pursue alternatives; an estimated 80 000 families across Canada home-schooled their children in 2001 and, in the previous decade, the number of students enrolling in private schools grew 23 percent to nearly 300 000.

The response of provincial governments has been to adopt market-oriented bureaucratic solutions. *Maclean's* highlights the case of Ontario where, between 1995 and 2001, Mike Harris's Conservative government introduced measures aimed at increasing accountability and tightening bureaucratic control. The government's initiatives called for a common curriculum, standardized testing, and uniform report cards for students, as well as compulsory testing and professional upgrading for teachers. The Ontario government also increased the instructional workload and made possible mandatory teacher supervision of extracurricular activities, more school choice for parents, and expansion of the postsecondary sector by private organizations. Box 14.1 examines one recent and popular market-oriented reform—school choice.

In this chapter, we explore how sociological theory and research can shed light on the operation of schools in a modern industrial society such as Canada. We begin by noting the critical importance of education both to individuals and to society. We examine three major sociological perspectives on education and discuss the insights that these explanatory frameworks have provided historically and contemporarily. We also examine what research based on these perspectives reveals about the operation of schools and the effectiveness of Canadian education.

THE IMPORTANCE OF EDUCATION TO INDIVIDUALS AND SOCIETY

On the individual level, education largely determines a person's social status and quality of life through its impact on occupation, income, and prestige. More years in school generally translate into greater labour-force participation, higher income, and lower unemployment. Education is also associated with receiving respect and deference, living longer and healthier, being more tolerant of group differences, participating politically, and doing volunteer work (Guppy and Davies, 1998).

College graduates in 1997 earned around $25 700, whereas those with bachelor's degrees earned more—around $32 000. The median salaries of those with master's degrees and doctorates, while identical, were even higher—$47 000 (Taillon and Paju, 1999). Using the bachelor's degree as a base reference and comparing people in the same sex, age cohort, region, and industry, Guppy and Davies (1998) examined salaries by education level. They calculated that someone with a bachelor's degree earned a yearly salary almost $10 000 higher than a high school dropout. Compared to those with bachelor's degrees, high school and community college graduates earned about $7000 and $5000 less respectively. Those with professional degrees such as the M.D. or LL.B. earned $24 000 more. Individual investment in education clearly pays dividends.

A national survey of 1995 graduates provides evidence that increased education lowers the risk of unemployment (Taillon and Paju, 1999). Figure 14.1 on page 362 shows unemployment rates by educational attainment for 25- to 29-year-olds in 1997, the year of data collection for the 1995 graduates. Also, in an examination of the population more generally,

BOX 14.1   REFORMING EDUCATION THROUGH MARKET PRINCIPLES

Market critics of contemporary schooling point out that education is both an essential service and a monopoly. Essential and without competitors, critics argue that the system is overly autonomous, unresponsive, and resistant to change. Lacking any real accountability, educational administrators shun hard-nosed decision making and permit systemic inefficiencies to fester and grow.

School choice for parents is presently severely circumscribed since a child's assignment to a school is based primarily on residential location, especially where space is at a premium. Parents may elect to move to another neighbourhood in search of a better school. They may send their children to private or alternative schools for "at-risk" students, or in some provinces, to charter schools. Or they may opt for "home-schooling." Options are limited.

Advocates of market-based reform strategies maintain that school choice would breed competition, greatly improve responsiveness and accountability, and thereby enhance the quality of education. Lacking guaranteed resources from government, schools would market themselves to parents and students on some combination of excellence, curriculum, standards, innovative programs, and specialized instruction. In turn, they would be funded on some combination of the number of students attracted and their specific program needs. Schools with high numbers and needier students would receive more financial support. Good schools would survive and prosper while poor schools would falter and eventually go out of business. With only efficient schools remaining in operation, educational quality overall would rise.

The market approach has several points of emphasis worth noting. First, parents know their children best and can make the most appropriate program selections on their behalf. Second, parents seeking to meet their children's unique needs require more choice in certain content areas of the curriculum. Third, students will be strongly motivated to achieve in order to secure and maintain their places in the best schools. Fourth, the market system promotes equity by ensuring more choice for poorer families. Finally, society benefits because schools will be forced to adapt quickly to economic and labour market changes or risk going out of business.

The provincial governments of Ontario, Alberta, and British Columbia have been willing to experiment with greater school choice. School choice resonates with governments and the electorate because it meshes with popular sentiment that business and privatized public organizations are more efficient and flexible because they are subject to competition. Moreover, it is widely believed that they provide the highest quality at the lowest cost and can turn on a dime to meet society's rapidly changing skill requirements. The fit survive and the unfit perish.

Resonance aside, the market approach is not without its detractors. First, opponents of market principles in education express concern that schools will market themselves on quality and then create that quality through selection rather than training. The admission of only high-performing students virtually ensures the continuing high performance of schools; what comes in one end, goes out the other. Critics also argue that affluent and involved parents may exercise choice to select schools that enrol children exclusively from backgrounds like their own. Parents find it difficult to remain objective and fair when it comes to their own chid's welfare. Furthermore, critics warn that, to maintain their reputations for high performance, elite schools may exclude students who might be assessment liabilities. Students who are intellectually challenged, disruptive, or have special needs may be denied access in an effort to keep results on standardized tests and graduation rates respectable. Since poorer performing students must be instructed somewhere, the school system might become stratified with elite institutions at one end of the continuum and "ghetto-like" schools, with concentrations of low achievers, on the other.

Second, opponents of market principles argue that fulfilling the desired diversification of curriculum recognizes and gives voice to special interest groups. It also flies in the face of current trends toward standardization. In this view, the creation of enclaves of like-minded clients, be they parents or students, especially if it were to occur along racial or religious lines, would undermine democratic ideals and the promotion of tolerance in a multicultural society. In addition to dilemmas posed by ethnic stratification, allocating equal time to subjects such as evolution and creationism, teaching Eurocentric versions of history, and eliminating controversial subjects such as sex and drug education would be hotly debated and divisive.

Third, critics speculate that open school choice would create practical problems. For example, the amount of travel to and from freely chosen schools would very likely increase substantially. Whether borne by taxpayers supporting bussing or by parents using their own cars, transport costs would escalate markedly. Also, critics worry that schools in competition for students would find themselves compelled to divert a considerable part of their financial resources from education to advertising.

SOURCE: Based mainly on N. Guppy, S. Davies, and A. Ludditt (1999) "A New Twist in Education Reform: Bringing the Market to Schools" in James Curtis, Edward Grabb, and Neil Guppy, eds., *Social Inequality in Canada: Patterns, Problems, and Policies*, 3rd ed. (Toronto: Prentice Hall), pp. 151–158.

Schools socialize students by fostering the development of attitudes, knowledge, and skills that are necessary in adult society.

SOURCE: William Kurelek, *One-Room School at Kaszuby*. Art Gallery of Hamilton, Gift of the Polish Alliance of Canada, and Wintario, 1978.

Statistics Canada reports that the **labour-force participation rate**, the percentage of adults with jobs, is 82.1 percent for those with a university degree, compared to only 25.8 percent for those with less than eight years of schooling. Viewed from the opposite direction, the unemployment rate for university graduates is only 4 percent, while for those with only eight years or less of schooling it is 13 percent (Statistics Canada, 2001b).

On the societal level, Canadians view large-scale or "mass" education as a national priority. They see it as essential for ensuring both social justice and economic productivity. For social justice, education first serves as the cornerstone of democracy; only a literate and knowledgeable citizenry can make the sensible, rational, and fair decisions that presumably underpin a democratic society. This is particularly true in a world of increasing complexity in which ethical, eco-

nomic, political, and moral dilemmas abound. Second, Canadians believe that everyone, regardless of social origin or economic background, should be afforded an **equal opportunity** to achieve success. Only through an open and free system of mass education, the thinking goes, can equality of opportunity be assured for all.

A nation's economic productivity in an age of industrialization and technological development requires a highly skilled and knowledgeable labour force to compete, survive, and prosper in the new eras of information transfer and global economic competition. A highly effective education system is indispensable to the creation of the "**human capital**" that will facilitate and stimulate economic productivity as Canada competes with other developed nations for increasingly mobile investment dollars (Guppy and Davies, 1998).

Education is also vital because Canada, like other industrialized nations, faces its share of pressing social problems. Believing there is a connection between education, progress, and social betterment, people look to educational processes and institutions as means of curing a wide variety of social and eco-

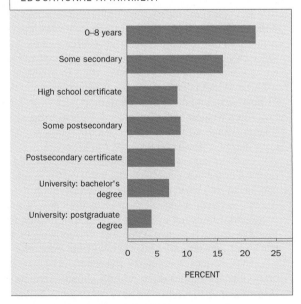

FIGURE 14.1 UNEMPLOYMENT RATES OF YOUNG ADULTS AGED 25 TO 29 YEARS OF AGE, BY EDUCATIONAL ATTAINMENT

SOURCE: J. Taillon and M. Paju (1999), *The Class of '95: The Report of the 1997 National Survey of 1995 Graduates* (Ottawa: Minister of Public Works and Government Service of Canada), p. 3.

nomic ills. Among these maladies are economic recession, environmental degradation, violence against women and children, drug and alcohol abuse, the spread of AIDS, functional illiteracy, youth unemployment, teenage pregnancy, racism, and juvenile delinquency.

We turn our attention in the sections that follow to the explanatory frameworks and empirical insights that sociology provides for understanding the workings of education systems and appreciating the controversies inherent in their operation. Of particular interest are issues of inequality of access and benefit.

SOCIOLOGICAL PERSPECTIVES ON EDUCATION

Functionalism and **conflict theory** are macrolevel perspectives. They focus on the big picture, explaining large-scale structures and patterns. **Symbolic interactionism** is a microlevel framework that focuses on understanding the processes involved in social learning. As an interpretive perspective, it explores how people develop identities and self-concepts and how these in turn affect behaviour.

FUNCTIONALISM

Functionalists think of society as a system, with parts that work together to maintain the whole. The functionalist perspective generally emphasizes interdependence and cooperation, order and stability, value consensus and integration, and gradual and evolutionary social change (Parsons, 1951). Functionalists argue that education, like other social institutions, operates to satisfy several different needs that must be met if society is to survive and prosper. For example, the growth of mass education is held to be a direct response to the skill and knowledge requirements of industrial society (Collins, 1977).

Manifest and Latent Functions of Education

According to functionalists, **manifest functions** are the intended and formally articulated goals of the education system. **Latent functions** of schooling are outcomes that, while unintended and informal, nonetheless contribute to society's maintenance. The manifest functions of education include personal development, cultural reproduction, social integration, selection and screening, and the creation, preservation, and dissemination of knowledge.

Education offers personal growth by providing a rich environment for intellectual activity, artistic refinement, and emotional maturation. Education is also an important means of preserving culture and transmitting it from one generation to the next. Schools teach values, beliefs, norms, language, and traditions both formally and informally. Students learn, for example, to view their nation with pride, to see the law of the land as fundamentally just, to appreciate the good sense of majority rule, and to believe that democracy is the only sensible form of government (Travers, 1983; Washburn, 1985). The school is second only to the family as an agent of socialization. By fostering a common cultural identity, education promotes conformity, integration, and social control.

An economically vibrant industrial and technological society committed to equal opportunity requires the optimal use of its finest minds. According to functionalists, because they identify talent and aptitudes, schools serve as important instruments of selection and screening. They ensure that the brightest and the most industrious are chosen and trained for the most important and challenging jobs. Able students learn literacy, numeracy, and technical skills. They also acquire good work habits, such as cooperation, punctuality, and deference to authority. Finally, universities in particular are an important means of creating knowledge. Professors routinely expose university students to recent research findings and innovative thinking in a wide variety of fields. By creating knowledge, fostering creativity, and nurturing criticism, universities serve as vital agents of social change.

Schooling also has some very important unintended and unarticulated consequences for the operation of society. First, schools rationalize and legitimize social and economic inequality. Their message emphasizes that free and open competition among individuals results both in the success of the talented and industrious and in the failure of the inept and lazy. We learn that unequal rewards are an appropriate consequence of differences in ability and effort. The conviction that all inequality is earned, and therefore fair, contributes to the maintenance and reinforcement of social and economic stratification;

losers and winners alike willingly and peacefully accept their lot.

Schools also support family and work in unintended ways. Colleges and universities serve as marriage markets of unparalleled size. They bring together enormous numbers of eligible partners of all descriptions. Moreover, for eight hours a day, five days a week, nine months a year, schools provide vital daycare. They keep children and youth off the streets, out of harm's way, and out of trouble. Finally, schools contribute to the economic well-being of employed adults by keeping hundreds of thousands of youth out of the labour market. Their exclusion restricts competition for jobs and helps keep wages high.

CONFLICT THEORY

Conflict theory differs from functionalism, with its emphasis on social harmony, order, and gradual social change. Conflict theory stresses discord among social groups and classes. Conflict theory asserts that, to the extent that they exist, value consensus and integration are products of power and coercion exercised by the strong over the weak. Conflict theorists predict that social change will be more revolutionary than evolutionary. They highlight the school as an arena of social conflict and emphasize the role of education in reproducing the social and economic order of capitalism (Collins, 1977).

Education as a Capitalist Tool

There are several versions of conflict theory. One version draws on the ideas of Karl Marx. It holds that mass education developed alongside industrialization to benefit the interests of the capitalist elite. The **formal curriculum**, the knowledge and skills pupils were expected to acquire through the course of their official studies, provided the literate work force necessary to meet the growing needs of business and industry as the capitalist economy expanded.

In addition, proponents of this perspective argue that the school's informal curriculum also has a profound impact on students through its reinforcement of certain values and norms. The informal curriculum is embodied in the form of schooling and in the messages transmitted through institutional organization and practice. The **hidden curriculum** encourages students' acceptance of authority and social control. Today's informal curriculum teaches tomorrow's

workers to line up, follow directions, and respect authority. Life in school, with its set rules, established routines, hierarchical authority structure, and generous dose of tedium, prepares people for more of the same in the workplace. Such school–workplace equivalents produce labourers who have learned to accept as fair both the capitalist system and their place in it. Learning orderly conduct, punctuality, obedience, and loyalty to the prevailing political and economic system helps young people fit their future roles as employees in industry and commerce (Bowles and Gintis, 1976).

Resistance Theory

A second version of conflict theory, known as **resistance theory**, attributes lower-class students' modest achievement or failing grades not to their inability but to their unwillingness to perform. It notes that, in general, lower-class youth do not embrace the middle-class enthusiasm for status striving. Rather, they commit themselves to sharing norms of defiance built upon the historical struggle of the working class with their capitalist employers. This commitment manifests itself in showing a preference for solidarity over competition, taking pride in manual labour, and expressing antagonism to institutional authority (Willis, 1977).

Resistance theory has two fundamental premises. First, many, if not most, working-class youth are indifferent to school and put little effort into their education. They also participate actively in school deviance as means of securing a measure of self-esteem and dignity. Second, the anti-school subculture of the working class is fundamentally proletarian. As such, the closely knit lower-class teen peer group of the school mirrors the factory culture of the shop floor. Extolling the virtues of manual as opposed to cerebral work, lower-class students disparage "pencil pushing" and its associated tasks and rewards. Moreover, they firmly resent the way teachers and the curriculum demean manual work. Working-class youth's antagonism to teachers finds its parallel in the factory in worker antipathy to supervisors and bosses (Davies, 1999; Hallinan, 2001).

Resistance culminates in the rejection of schooling for the real world of employment, marriage, and family. A large number of working-class youth acquire working-class jobs as a result of their resistance and rebellion. Opposition in school condemns them to academic failure in a world where education is their only realistic means of upward mobility.

Credentialism

In a third version of conflict theory, known as **credentialism**, Collins (1979) builds on Max Weber's ideas about credentials and their relation to the way people acquire status. He argues that it is not education per se and the knowledge and skills it confers that people seek out. Rather, it is the degree, diploma, or certificate that is the desired commodity. The credential symbolizes that the person holding it is intelligent, knowledgeable, and industrious. People want the credentials because they know that entry into good jobs with superior incomes, higher levels of prestige, and greater degrees of autonomy requires appropriate certification. Occupational groups professionalize and elevate their status expressly to eliminate competition. In the process, they overstate the significance of individual merit and technical competence and seek to control entry to their ranks through certification and licensing requirements. Professional schools and faculties develop in universities where the professions control them. Such is the case for medicine and law. By excluding competitors, professionalized occupations tighten their collective grip on scarce social and economic rewards.

Jobs that once called for only an elementary or secondary school diploma now require a university degree, and jobs that once required an undergraduate degree now call for a graduate or professional degree. There are two fundamental reasons why employers demand these additional qualifications despite the fact that the actual content of many lines of work has remained much the same over time. First, selection on the basis of certification represents a solution to the problems posed by an oversupply of capable workers; it narrows the field considerably. Second, despite the lack of solid evidence, it is widely believed that workers with more education are more productive. To support their argument, credentialists point to studies indicating that better-educated workers, who have obviously spent more years in school, do not perform measurably better than their less educated colleagues in the same field. They cite studies showing that professors with Ph.D.s teach no more effectively than those with M.A.s, that nurses trained in four-year baccalaureate programs provide no

better health care than those with abbreviated training in colleges or hospitals, and that police officers with university degrees solve no more crime than those with high school graduation (Ritzer and Walczak, 1986).

According to the credentialist framework, it is not the need for increased knowledge and skill, as functionalists argue, that drives the increase in educational requirements for higher-status occupations. Rather, it is the promotion of vested interests—in income, prestige, autonomy, and power—that motivates occupational groups. Although the sons and daughters of lower-class families are going farther in school than they have in the past, they usually remain relegated to the bottom rungs of the occupational ladder, say proponents of credentialism. The children of the higher classes themselves continue to raise their own educational qualifications to even higher levels to retain their grip on society's top jobs. Because everyone, advantaged and disadvantaged alike, moves up the ladder together, there is no sustained change in rank. Because the ranks stay the same, the benefits of higher education continue to go to those from privileged backgrounds (Collins, 1979).

EQUALITY OF OPPORTUNITY AND OUTCOME

Much of the research informed by macrolevel perspectives has focused on issues of inequality, especially along socioeconomic lines. Indeed, examining the degree to which **ascribed statuses** such as sex, ethnicity, and socioeconomic background affect student experiences and performance outcomes is central to sociological inquiry. It is to these concerns that we now turn.

True equality in education implies that schools are able to produce the same beneficial results for females, disadvantaged minority group members, and lower-class people as they do for those who are male, white, English-speaking, and middle class. Functionalist theory sees schools as doing just that. They provide equal opportunities for learning and certification. Once students gain access, ability and effort are the prime determinants of their success. To the extent that students' backgrounds affect their achievement, the system is dysfunctional. It is inefficient, unbeneficial, and even harmful for society to exclude talented women, minorities, and members of the lower classes from the competition for status. Exclusion of talented and motivated people lowers their contribution to society and undermines its viability.

In contrast, conflict theories predict that inherited, ascribed characteristics significantly affect potential and performance. Given this inequality, the rewards ultimately attached to school achievement are hard to justify. Competition in school is unfair and injustice is not overcome by the provision of equal opportunity alone, according to conflict theorists. Even where schools provide equal opportunity, problems remain. Contestants with different backgrounds are not equally prepared for the competition. Equality of access and **equality of benefit** are not the same thing (Richer, 1988).

While functionalism acknowledges the existence of inequality based on sex, race, and background, it sees the gaps as small and diminishing. Functionalists recommend changes within the existing system to overcome inequities based on students' backgrounds. Conflict theory, on the other hand, views inequality as an outcome of power struggles in pursuit of vested interests. Because inequality is structural and more deeply entrenched, its eradication requires more radical systemic change.

Let us now assess these competing viewpoints by turning our attention to evidence regarding inequality in Canadian education along the lines of sex, ethnicity, and socioeconomic status.

Sex

Historically, Canadian research has shown little difference between males and females when it comes to quantitative measures of educational aspirations and high-school completion rates. This pattern has held regardless of students' socioeconomic backgrounds. At the secondary level, however, census data indicate that females between the ages of 16 and 18 are somewhat more likely than males to stay in school and to be enrolled full-time. Another difference is that from kindergarten through high school, females have consistently outperformed males. Research has also shown that in the past females were overrepresented in certain high school programs (e.g., commercial) while males were overrepresented in others (e.g., technical) (Breton, 1972; Porter, Porter, and Blishen, 1982, Guppy and Davies, 1998; Council of Ministers of Education, 1999).

Women's **participation rates** in postsecondary education, as a whole, overtook those of men in 1987. At the community college level, for career programs, women have been obtaining more diplomas than men for some time—60 percent as far back as 1975–76. Women's dominance in diploma attainment at the college level continued though the 1980s, and the gap separating male and female college graduation continues to widen (Guppy and Davies, 1998). Female graduates, however, are concentrated in particular college programs such as health sciences (83 percent), social sciences and services (76 percent), and business and commerce (67 percent). Women are most underrepresented as graduates in engineering and applied science (20 percent) and natural science and primary industries (42 percent) (Statistics Canada, 2001b).

With respect to university graduation, times have definitely changed. In 1951, men were 2.5 times more likely than women to graduate from university. By 1995, the situation had reversed with the odds of men compared to women completing a degree dropping to 0.75 (Guppy and Davies, 1998). Nonetheless, men and women tend to register in and graduate from different university programs. Women university graduates are concentrated in health care (86 percent), fine art (80 percent), education (72 percent), humanities (69 percent), and social sciences (64 percent). They are significantly underrepresented in engineering and applied sciences (21 percent) and mathematics and physical sciences (32 percent) (Statistics Canada, 2001b).

Segregation by sex in college and university program participation and graduation is of considerable significance for several reasons. First, some programs offer greater certainty of labour-force entry opportunities. Social sciences, fine art, and humanities, fields in which women are overrepresented, are less directly marketable than others such as engineering and applied science where men predominate. Second, training in some fields leads to jobs with higher levels of remuneration. Engineering and computer science, where women are underrepresented, are examples. Third, sex segregation in the world of work means there is a narrower range of jobs for which women can compete in practice. Women heavily dominate the competition for certain jobs such as teaching and nursing. Heightened competition in any occupational domain acts to depress wages. Thus, sex segregation in education helps produce and reinforce a sex-segregated labour market and its associated social and economic disadvantages for women (Guppy and Davies, 1998).

Ethnicity

Education is a vital concern to ethnic groups in three ways. First, it can offer access to better-paying jobs and upward social and economic mobility. Second, education can be a means of providing or strengthening a collective sense of self and group identity. French-language education in various provinces, for example, has done much to reinforce French-Canadian culture and distinctiveness. Finally, education can be an effective means of reducing prejudice and discrimination. Tolerance increases particularly with postsecondary education.

The early educational experience of Canada's Aboriginal peoples represents a stark and unequivocal example of racism. Efforts to "civilize" and Christianize Native people through a system of residential schools for children and youth began in the 1880s and extended to the 1970s. The federal government separated children from their families in northern communities and sent them south to be taught by church officials in schools especially designated for this purpose. With links to their families and communities severed, authorities immersed these children in an English-speaking European cultural environment. It was their hope that cultural immersion, rigorous training, and strict discipline would effectively usher Canadian Aboriginals into the modern world (Davies and Guppy, 1999). The real effect, as is now evident, was to increase the marginalization and exclusion of the Aboriginal peoples through cultural annihilation and the physical and sexual abuse of their children (Gomme, 2002).

A similar fate befell Aboriginals and Blacks south of the border. In the United States, state governments historically denied Blacks any access at all to education; teaching a slave to read and write was a crime. From the end of the American Civil War through the first half of the twentieth century, Black education was both separate and distinctly unequal. Even in the recent era of desegregated schools, from the 1950s to the present, there are substantial gaps separating Black from white attainment. The gap narrowed between 1970 and 1990 but now shows signs of widening. The average Black student still scores below 75 percent of whites on most standardized tests. In the last decade, a 17-year-old Black demonstrated an average proficiency in reading, writing, science, and math roughly equivalent to a 13-year-old white (Hallinan, 2001).

But what of other ethnic groups in Canada and what of the present? Does Canada's education system exhibit **institutional racism** by inhibiting minority access and promoting white European culture to the exclusion of other cultures? In the absence of discrimination, access and attainment should be proportional to a group's distribution in the population. In other words, if Aboriginal people represent 3 percent of the population, they should represent 3 percent of all dropouts and grade retentions and 3 percent of all high school and postsecondary graduates. Under-representation is widely taken as evidence of institutional racism and discrimination.

In his pioneering study of class and ethnicity in the 1950s, John Porter constructed an image of Canadian society as a "vertical mosaic" in which ethnic groups were both separate and unequal. Those who were of British ancestry and white enjoyed easy access to educational opportunity. The same was true for those of Northern European lineage; Scandinavians and Germans, after all, were also white. Many other ethnic groups, especially visible minorities and Aboriginals, experienced blocked access and the inability to benefit from education. Later research by Porter on the 1971 census, however, challenged this image by demonstrating, among other things, that people of British descent did not demonstrate the highest level of educational attainment.

More recent studies concur with Porter's revised assessment. Based on data from the 1981 census, Herberg (1990) examined the educational attainment, measured by years of schooling completed, of foreign- and Canadian-born ethnic group members. Five of the top six groups were visible minorities and the other one was Jewish. Li (1988) conducted a similar analysis but included only the Canadian-born. He reasoned that people born outside the country might have attained their educations not in Canada but in their countries of origin. Li found that the Canadian-born ethnic group members with the highest educational attainments were, in order, Jewish, Chinese, Croat, Czech, Slovak, Greek, and Italian. The British ranked

12th out of 17 and their attainment was below the national average.

Guppy and Davies (1998) used 1991 census data to explore the same question. They measured educational attainment in terms of (1) acquiring high school certification and (2) holding a university degree. Table 14-1 shows, among foreign-born and Canadian-born males and females, fully 10 out of 11 visible minorities had high school graduation rates higher than their non–visible-minority counterparts. Also worth noting is the fact that Blacks, both foreign and Canadian born, had above-average graduation rates. Moreover, those belonging to more than one visible minority (the "Multiple Visible Minorities" category) experienced similar success.

Examining foreign- and Canadian-born Canadians, Guppy and Davies (1998) also found that the British did not occupy a top spot for university degree completion. In Table 14-2, visible minorities' rankings are mixed. Both male and female Chinese and Filipinos, especially in the 25–34 age range, are

the most likely to possess a university degree. Alternatively, some non–visible-minority groups fall under the national average in all categories, among them French, Scandinavian, and notably, English. Blacks were below the average in all age and sex groups except for men 55–64 years of age. Dramatically below the average in each age and sex category were persons of Aboriginal descent. There is some evidence of a similar picture in the United States. Research indicates that several groups of Asian descent, notably Japanese, Chinese, Filipinos, and Koreans, outperform Latinos, African Americans, and whites (Blair and Legazpi, 1999; Schmid, 2001).

Figure 14.2 on page 370 illustrates years of school completed for Canadian-born men and women 30–39 years of age, the youngest age group for whom schooling is likely to be completed. Three patterns are discernable for both sexes. First, visible minorities are less likely than non–visible minorities to drop out of school before completing 12 years. Second, visible minorities are less likely than

TABLE 14.1 PERCENTAGE OF CANADIANS 20 YEARS OF AGE AND ABOVE WITH SECONDARY SCHOOL GRADUATION CERTIFICATE BY VISIBLE-MINORITY STATUS, BY IMMIGRATION STATUS, AND SEX, 1991

	WOMEN		MEN	
	Native-Born	Foreign-Born	Native-Born	Foreign-Born
All Canadians	**54.5**	**50.7**	**51.5**	**54.2**
Visible-minority population	69.6	57.7	68.6	64.5
Non–visible-minority population	54.3	46.9	51.3	48.7
Korean	83.3	75.0	92.5	86.1
Chinese	80.4	53.5	79.4	61.5
Filipino	78.1	77.7	73.3	79.6
South Asian	75.5	57.3	72.6	66.3
West Asian and Arab	73.2	62.5	70.8	72.3
Latin American	71.4	55.9	64.1	60.6
Japanese	69.2	69.8	69.1	72.3
Other Pacific Islanders	61.3	58.4	54.2	59.8
Blacks	57.6	55.2	55.4	60.1
South East Asian	53.3	39.5	50.0	48.6
Multiple Visible Minorities	73.2	65.2	70.7	66.0

Notes: Visible-minority status is coded in accordance with the federal government's Employment Equity Act (1986). No 1991 Census question asked about race or colour. Visible-minority status was derived by Statistics Canada, from responses to ethnic origin, language, place of birth, and religion questions. Ethnic categories have been collapsed so that, for example, Black includes people of African, Caribbean, American, and Canadian descent, while South East Asian includes people of Vietnamese, Thai, Laotian, Cambodian, and Indonesian descent. Black was explicitly identified on the 1991 Census questionnaire, while South East Asian responses required people to write in information in a "Please specify" section.

SOURCE: N. Guppy and S. Davies (1998), *Education in Canada: Recent Trends and Future Challenges* (Ottawa: Statistics Canada), Catalogue 96–321, p. 106.

TABLE 14.2 PERCENTAGE OF CANADIANS WITH A UNIVERSITY DEGREE BY AGE, SEX, AND ETHNIC GROUP

	WOMEN		MEN	
ETHNIC GROUP	**25–34**	**55–64**	**25–34**	**55–64**
Jewish	49.6	5.0	55.0	34.1
Chinese	28.9	5.9	37.6	14.3
Filipino	28.8	23.7	20.8	30.5
Greek	21.4	1.8	24.0	3.5
Polish	19.8	4.8	18.3	10.9
Italian	18.6	1.0	18.8	2.3
Hungarian	18.6	7.0	17.2	11.2
Ukrainian	17.1	3.1	16.2	9.1
Scottish	16.3	6.3	15.7	11.8
Irish	15.4	5.4	14.8	10.1
Dutch	14.9	3.1	12.9	7.8
Scandinavian	14.4	4.6	12.5	8.1
French	12.6	3.4	13.0	7.2
Spanish	11.7	6.3	11.5	13.8
English	11.0	4.3	11.7	9.3
Black	9.8	3.7	12.9	13.9
Portuguese	6.4	0.5	4.5	1.2
Aboriginal	2.6	0.7	1.9	1.1
All Canadians	15.7	5.0	15.9	10.1

Notes: Ethnicity is measured by self-report. Only individuals listing a single ethnic origin are included in the table. The smallest number in any specific cell of the table used in calculating the percentages is for Portuguese women between 55 and 64 with university degrees (*N* = 55; out of a total 10 330 such women). NB: Both foreign-born and native-born people are included.

SOURCE: N. Guppy and S. Davies (1998) *Education in Canada: Recent Trends and Future Challenges* (Ottawa: Statistics Canada), Catalogue 96–321, pp. 103–04.

non–visible minorities to end their schooling having completed only 12 years. Finally, visible minorities are more likely than non–visible minorities to continue their education beyond 12 years (Davies and Guppy, 1999).

Regardless of the measure of attainment used, data from the 1991 census do not support claims of restricted educational access to visible minorities as a consequence of institutional racism in Canadian schools. The performance of some ethnic groups, some of them visible minorities, is superior to the performance of some non–visible minorities, notably the English. Nonetheless, Aboriginals continue to fall far below other groups as they have done historically.

Socioeconomic Status

While Canadian research does not provide evidence of significant educational detriment due to sex and ethnicity, the same cannot be said of socioeconomic status. Studies over the years have repeatedly demonstrated strong and enduring disadvantage on the basis of socioeconomic background. This remains the case despite the expansion of education begun in the 1960s in part to produce greater equality of opportunity.

Recent evidence of a relationship between socioeconomic status and access to education comes from the national Survey of Labour and Income Dynamics and is presented in Table 14.3. The analysis first divided the 18- to 21-year-old population into four equal quartiles (25 percent groups) on the basis of family income when subjects were 16 years old. Research then compared postsecondary participation across these four groups. The study shows that 71 percent of young people from the top 25 percent of families had participated in some form of postsecondary education by 1998. By comparison,

FIGURE 14.2a YEARS OF SCHOOLING BY VISIBLE MINORITY STATUS FOR CANADIAN-BORN MEN AGED 30–39

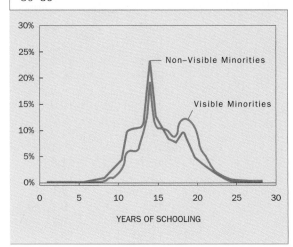

FIGURE 14.2b YEARS OF SCHOOLING BY VISIBLE MINORITY STATUS FOR CANADIAN-BORN WOMEN AGED 30–39

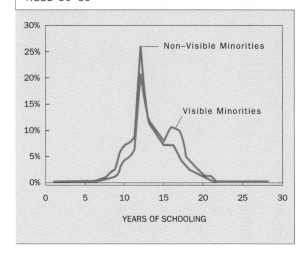

SOURCE: Adapted from N. Guppy and S. Davies (1998) *Education in Canada: Recent Trends and Future Challenges.* Ottawa: Statistics Canada. Catalogue 96–321, pp. 107–08.

fewer than 49 percent of youth from the bottom 25 percent had done so. Among young people 18 to 21 years old from low-income families who had pursued postsecondary education, the majority went to college. Among those from high-income families who had pursued postsecondary education, the majority went to university (Statistics Canada, 2001b).

While the data suggest that there were no significant differences in college participation across income groups, the same is not true for university participation. Youth from top-quartile families were 2.5 times more likely than those from bottom-quartile families to have attended university. Among those from the most affluent quartile, about 40 percent had

attended university. For those from the lowest quartile, the proportion was only 16 percent.

In their analyses of the 1994 General Social Survey, Guppy and Davies (1998) echo these findings as illustrated in Figure 14.3. Those young men and women whose fathers were in the professional-managerial group were likely to have studied at the university level (about six in ten). By comparison, those whose fathers were farmers (about one in ten) or worked as unskilled labourers (roughly two in ten) were much less likely to have done so.

In sum, a student's sex affects program selection much more than it affects the likelihood of program completion. Visible-minority status does not

TABLE 14.3 POSTSECONDARY EDUCATION PARTICIPATION AND FAMILY INCOME, 18- TO 21-YEAR-OLDS, 1998

| | FAMILY INCOME AT AGE 16 | | | |
HIGHEST LEVEL OF EDUCATION PARTICIPATED	Lowest Quartile	Middle Half	Highest Quartile	Average
All postsecondary	48.8	61.4	71.0	60.7
University	16.3	26.1	39.6	27.0
College	26.7	29.5	28.2	28.5

SOURCE: *The Daily.* (2001) "Participation in postsecondary education and family income." Friday, December 7. Ottawa: Statistics Canada http://statcan.ca/Daily/English/011207/td011207c.htm.

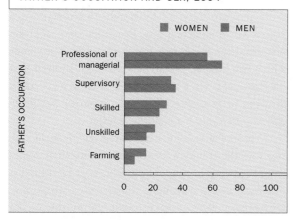

FIGURE 14.3 PERCENTAGE OF 25- TO 34-YEAR-OLDS WITH UNIVERSITY-LEVEL EDUCATION, BY FATHER'S OCCUPATION AND SEX, 1994

SOURCE: N. Guppy and S. Davies (1998) *Education in Canada: Recent Trends and Future Challenges.* Ottawa: Statistics Canada. p. 120. Catalogue 96-321, December 1998.

adversely impact on academic performance in a systematic way, but Canadian Aboriginals are in a league of their own when it comes to disadvantage. In this case, historical precedent remains sharply reflected in contemporary reality. The clearest and most consistent evidence of systematic disadvantage in access and attainment occurs along socioeconomic lines.

But what precisely are the mechanisms that produce these patterns? Sociologists working in the interactionist and interpretive tradition have sought to answer these questions by taking a close look at individual experiences in home and school settings relevant to educational attainment.

SYMBOLIC INTERACTIONISM

Symbolic interaction is an interpretive framework with two components. First, people use nonverbal and verbal symbols to communicate. Second, communication requires interaction. A central focus of symbolic interactionism is the development of self-image, self-concept, or identity. Interactionists view a person's self-concept as the product of the manipulation and interpretation of symbols in long-term social interaction. Over time, people develop positive or negative senses of self in response to the perceived reactions of others who surround and are important to them.

Symbolic interactionism stresses the importance of social meaning. Humans act toward things on the basis of the meanings those things have for them and they interpret things differently. Some see growing up in poverty, sleeping three to a room, or having an abusive parent as unbearably stressful. Others see the same circumstances as the stuff of personal challenge. Behaviour is not determined directly by conditions but is influenced by the meanings that a condition has for a specific individual in a particular context.

Symbolic interactionists contend that the meaning of things originates in social interaction with others. Neither the thing itself nor the person alone provides meaning. Rather, it is the observation and interpretation of verbal and nonverbal symbols manipulated by others that communicates the meanings of objects (e.g., desk, blackboard, stars, checkmarks), conditions (e.g., poverty, "broken" homes, unemployment), and acts (e.g., taking a test, being expelled). In the process of observation and interpretation, people acquire and internalize much of the meaning attached to things, to circumstances, and to behaviours.

Finally, symbolic interactionists note that people take an active part in creating meaning. People handle and modify meanings through an active interpretive process as they deal with the things they encounter. Because people actively interpret symbols, they may see slightly or even radically different meanings from what others would see under the same circumstances. People are partly passive receivers of meaning and partly its active creators.

Out of the meanings arising from interaction, people construct three important definitions that greatly affect their current and future actions—self, society, and situation. Each of these definitions significantly influences subsequent behaviour.

In the definition of self, the reactions of others supply symbolic information that, once interpreted, provides the individual with crucial details about the nature of his or her personal identity. For example, our conceptions of ourselves as smart, attractive, incompetent, or failing arise from our interpretations of the symbolic reactions directed to us by those in our social environment. Our positive and negative evaluations of ourselves originate in our interpretations of the ways in which others react to us. In the long term, the positive and negative meanings we attach to our sense of self affect how we act toward ourselves and others.

An individual's definition of society as either full of opportunity or inhospitable develops in interaction with various agents of socialization, including family members, teachers, peers, and the mass media. Once this perception is created, it subsequently affects the way people behave. Perceiving social and economic opportunities as plentiful, whether or not they are, results in the person happily working hard to get ahead. Conversely, the perception of restricted opportunities may produce unhappiness, disenchantment, and withdrawal despite the reality of economic well-being.

People also define situations according to how the interaction process unfolds. Once the situation is defined a certain way, its meaning influences people's actions. Consider how differences in the definition of the same situation can produce conforming behaviour in some people and rule-breaking behaviour in others. Some children respond to discipline by behaving themselves while others rebel more.

One prominent area of social science research that uses an interactionist perspective is the study of teacher expectations and their ultimate impact on student performance. Other studies in which interpretive perspectives have informed educational research include examinations of tracking, language use, cultural capital, and the informal or hidden curriculum. To these we now turn.

Teacher Expectations

Researchers have noted that teachers' expectations of students' academic performance and behaviour can create anticipated outcomes (Rosenthal and Jacobson, 1986). In other words, **self-fulfilling prophecies** operate when initial expectations based on false definitions of the situation lead to behaviour that causes the expectations to come true. Evaluations of students as dull rather than gifted, disruptive as opposed to well behaved, and lazy versus hard-working have a negative effect on students' self-concept and self-esteem. The resulting low self-concept in turn adversely affects academic achievement and behaviour (Boocock, 1980).

The most famous study of the self-fulfilling prophecy in the field of education was conducted by Rosenthal and Jacobson in San Francisco during the 1960s. The researchers set out to test the hypothesis that children whose teachers expected them to grow intellectually would do so at a faster rate than comparable children whose teachers held no expectation of a sudden I.Q. gain. Rosenthal and Jacobson con-

structed a natural experiment that involved pupils in Grades 1 through 6. They began by testing students with an instrument that could supposedly identify those about to "bloom." In fact, the instrument was a nonverbal intelligence test. Rosenthal and Jacobson identified for teachers a group of "gifted" students. Their test results, researchers claimed, showed that these students were primed for a spurt in intellectual growth. In fact, the identified bloomers had been chosen randomly from all those tested.

Months later, all the students were given an **I.Q. test** and the results were compared with their scores from the previous year. Those who were identified as bloomers outperformed those who were not. Differences were most pronounced in the earlier grades. Identified bloomers in Grades 1 and 2 increased their performance scores over the previous year by 27 points and 16.5 points, respectively. For those not identified as potential bloomers, the increases were much smaller—12 points for Grade 1s and 7 points for Grade 2s. Despite difficulties in replicating these results, it is widely believed that teachers' expectations affect students' academic attainment (Braun, 1976).

Tracking

Tracking, streaming, or ability grouping is a long-standing practice by which schools sort students into groups on the basis of ability and achievement. Once educators group students in sections, they present lessons geared to the capabilities and motivations of each group. Grouping ostensibly makes teaching easier and more effective, thereby increasing efficiency. In theory, when instruction is aimed at the correct ability level, high performers are neither slowed down nor bored and the less gifted are neither confused nor left behind (Kerckhoff, 1986, 2001).

Traditional forms of streaming divided students into three tracks at an early stage in their educational career. The academic track included those bound for postsecondary education. The vocational track was composed of students destined for the skilled labour force. Educators reserved the terminal track for those whose dismal academic performance marked them for unskilled jobs or unemployment (Hallinan, 2001). In countries where tracking is highly formalized, occurs early, and is firmly entrenched, such as Germany and the United Kingdom, allocation to a particular stream at an early age directly and unequivocally determines occupational status as an adult (Kerckhoff, 2001).

Although streaming is less rigid in Canada, it still exists, particularly at the high school level. At the elementary level, rather than being separated into different classes, schools often group students into different segments within the same classroom. Ability grouping occurs very early and continues for the duration of the student's career in school. When students are divided within a single classroom, classroom organization and layout, class size, and available materials determine the number of groups. Research indicates that the typical number of groups in any one class is three and that these groups tend to be roughly equal in size (Hallinan and Sorensen, 1986; Barr and Dreeben, 1983).

Tracking, streaming, or ability grouping has been a hotly debated practice for decades. Are "ability groups" determined solely by ability or do nonacademic criteria such as sex, class, and ethnicity affect placement in a track? Do students change tracks as time passes? Does ability grouping produce the best results for all students?

Student records, demeanour, test scores, dress, appearance, parental background, sex, and ethnicity combine in complex ways to affect teacher expectations and evaluations of student potential and performance. It is perhaps not surprising then that much research challenges the efficacy of streaming and points to its discriminatory nature. First, some researchers have found that socioeconomic status and ethnicity influence teachers' placement of students in ability groups regardless of their past achievement or I.Q. scores (Schafer, Olexa, and Polk, 1970; Oakes, 1985; Oakes and Guiton, 1999). Therefore, lower-class students and those from some minorities disproportionately populate lower tracks. Second, few students assigned to the bottom stream later change to a higher one (Finlay, 1984). Third, students in lower streams are more likely to drop out of school than those in the higher tracks. Finally, in the U.S. at least, streaming appears particularly detrimental to the educational experiences of Blacks (Dimaggio, 1982).

Some investigations indicate that talented students in the advanced streams do somewhat better than their equally gifted counterparts in nonstreamed or mixed-ability classrooms. Other research, however, shows no significant differences between talented children in grouped and nongrouped environments.

Interpretive studies in the sociology of education examine the everyday interactions and understandings that constitute schooling.
SOURCE: © Network Productions/Index Stock Imagery.

For children in the lower tracks, however, the picture is less rosy. Students in low streams learn less and what they do learn is absorbed at a slower pace (Dar and Resh, 1986; Kerckhoff, 1986, 2000; Rowan and Mirade, 1983; Shavit and Featherman, 1988; Hallinan and Sorenson, 1986; Shavit, 1984; Oakes, 1985). Students in low-ability groups are also more alienated by school, more punitive in their dealings with others, and more negative about themselves (Oakes, 1982; Eder, 1981; Felmlee and Eder, 1983).

Researchers account for these findings by contrasting the low- and high-track learning environments. Students in high tracks receive better instruction, suffer less distraction, and spend more time "on task." They are surrounded by high achievers as role models since their peers are talented students and their teachers tend to be the cream of the crop. Teacher and peer expectations are higher and the learning environment in these classrooms is more serious (Davies, 1999; Hallinan, 2001). Conversely, their students' apparent lack of effort and commitment, more disruptive behaviours, and comparative lack of achievement combine to discourage low-track teachers. They become less and less motivated and lower their expectations for their students' performance. Poor achievement becomes a self-fulfilling prophecy; teachers expect and demand less of students, who, in response, give less (Ballantine, 2001). Evidence also suggests that nonstreamed environments enhance the demonstrated proficiencies of academically challenged lower-class and minority students (Davies, 1999; Hallinan, 2001; Ballantine, 2001).

While research argues for the elimination of tracking, politics dictate otherwise. Davies (1999) reports, for example, that the NDP government in Ontario destreamed Grade 9 in the early 1990s with the intention of eventually phasing out the practice in higher grades as well. With teachers and the public in opposition, the experiment ended with the election of Mike Harris's Conservatives in 1995. Livingstone and colleagues (2001) note that support for streamed classrooms continues. More than 90 percent of parents and teachers in Ontario support some form of streaming, and a third of both groups support tracking at or before Grade 9.

In a similar vein, Wells and Oakes (1996) found that detracking is resisted by higher-class parents who lobby hard to reinstitute different curricula for different tracks. Even where destreaming has occurred,

studies suggest that students in formally open grades self-select into informal track-like study and friendship groups. These clusters maintain their structure over their members' high school careers and have effects similar to formal streaming. Furthermore, student differences in academic attainment grow wider from Grade 9 to Grade 12 (Kerckhoff, 2001).

To solve the attainment deficits inherent in lower-track assignment, researchers recommend mixing students of differing abilities. If that is not possible, they advocate lowering the numbers of youth assigned to lower streams and reinforcing among teachers the necessity of holding high expectations for lower-track students. Researchers also advocate providing more resources to facilitate learning in these environments (Hallinan, 2001; Ballantine, 2001). Box 14.2 discusses the historical context of "reforms" in education that have at one time or another championed or decried such strategies as tracking.

Language

Based on his research in east London, England, in the 1960s and 1970s, Bernstein (1977) developed the argument that parents teach their children to communicate using two fundamental language codes—restricted and elaborated. According to Bernstein, language constructions in the **restricted code** focus on the immediate and concrete in terms of both circumstance and time. Words are basic. Grammar is simple. Sentences are short. Themes are personal and descriptive. In contrast, the elaborated code involves the expression, in symbolic form, of complex, impersonal, and abstract ideas, sentiments, and feelings. Explicit diction and complicated constructions make the **elaborated code** more suitable for the discussions, ideas, and abstractions typically explored and evaluated in schools. Although children from both lower- and higher-class families learn to utilize each of these linguistic codes, the predominant code in the lower-class home is restricted. For the middle and upper classes, the language of the home is more often elaborated.

Bernstein maintained that language places lower-class students at a disadvantage in school in two ways. First, their greater reliance on the restricted code makes it more difficult for them to think about and communicate abstract concepts. Second, since educators value elaborated code more highly than

BOX 14.2   THE LIBERAL–CONSERVATIVE PENDULUM OF CANADIAN EDUCATION

Observers of long-term trends in education liken the conservative–liberal continuum to a pendulum. Educational themes and strategies come and go in cycles of reform. Electorates, governments, and educators institute conservative approaches that, in turn, inevitably fail to work perfectly. The defects spur development of liberal alternatives. Liberal initiatives subsequently suffer the same fate. They do not work perfectly and the remedies are found in conservative reforms. The attractiveness of these "new" alternatives, of course, is enhanced with the passage of time. Politicians, educators, and the public alike have forgotten the shortcomings of the conservative measures that drove the liberal reforms in the first place. History, with some fine-tuning, repeats itself. Recent manifestations of this cycle of reform are apparent in the Canadian context.

OPEN SCHOOLS

Open education maximizes student-centred approaches while minimizing relationships based on authority. It relaxes rules and diversifies the curriculum in nontraditional areas. Students set their own goals, learn at their own pace, and are evaluated without the use of grades.

Open education on a large scale had its origins in the social protest of the 1960s. During that turbulent decade, the United States and, to a lesser degree, Canada were profoundly affected by the civil rights movement, the peace movement, and the women's liberation movement. The central participants in these revolutions were university students, whose challenges to the status quo spilled over into the realm of education. University students called into question, challenged, and won changes in grading practices, course requirements, teacher–student power differentials, and the content and relevance of programs. In a short time, democratization worked its way down into the public schools. Everything from student evaluation and curriculum to dress codes and rules of daily conduct became less restrictive. In some instances, schools were constructed without walls separating classrooms in an effort to promote openness and flexibility (Ballantine, 2001).

Research comparing the outcomes of open and traditional schooling during the 1970s generally produced mixed results. In terms of academic achievement, neither the open nor the closed approach proved unequivocally superior. In terms of other criteria, such as independence, cooperation, curiosity, attitude to school, creativity, and self-concept, there was some evidence that more flexible approaches produced better results (Horwitz, 1979). Nonetheless, criticism of open education was intense, and commentators have agreed that, overall, the educational reforms of the 1960s ended in failure.

THE "BACK TO THE BASICS" MOVEMENT

A "back to the basics" movement followed. It had several sources. First, a general air of political conservatism swept both Canada and the United States during the early 1980s, as evidenced by the landslide election victories of Brian Mulroney (1984) and Ronald Reagan (1980). Second, considerable negative publicity and intense public criticism surrounded several key indicators of the performance of the education system. Conservative critics on both sides of the border claimed that schooling had turned soft, if not entirely rotten. Despite massive expenditures on public education, standardized test scores had dropped and were low in comparison with those of Japan, Germany, and other countries. The public was told that the quality of many North American high school, college, and university graduates was low. The rate of functional illiteracy—the inability to read a newspaper, fill out basic forms, and follow written instructions—was alarmingly high. These criticisms were even more stinging in the context of North America's economic malaise and the rhetoric of globalization. Influential reports, such as that of the U.S. National Commission on Excellence in Education, pinned hopes for economic recovery in North America on the revitalization of education and, in effect, on the rejuvenation of the human capital thesis (Gardner, 1983) that investing resources in people's education and training will contribute substantially to economic growth. Recommended remedies included returning to the fundamentals of reading, writing, math, and science; increasing homework; implementing standardized testing; elevating graduation requirements; and beefing up discipline.

Critics pointed out that little research supports the view that returning to the basics improves school performance. In fact, doing so may prove harmful. Reminiscent of their predecessors from the 1960s, they caution that rigidity and standardization lowers students' self-esteem and enthusiasm for school, thereby increasing dropout rates. The "back to the basics" movement also discriminates against students from the lower class and from disadvantaged racial and ethnic groups.

restricted code, the language of the school is to some extent foreign. Its use calls on lower-class children to leave their familiar language at the door—in effect to abandon temporarily their cultural heritage. Similar accommodations are not demanded of middle- and upper-class children. While intriguing, Bernstein's research has proven difficult to replicate, calling into question its generalizability beyond the site and time of his observations (Davies, 1999).

Cultural Capital

High-status or elite families provide their children with a lot of what Bourdieu (1973) calls "**cultural capital**." Cultural capital accumulates through exposure in the home to fine art, classical music, ballet, opera, and the great books. This exposure encourages people to define themselves as "cultured" and this definition fosters in children strong self-concepts that are valuable assets in the educational process (Dimaggio and Mohr, 1985). Children of privilege experience academic success because schools and teachers are more likely to see them as intelligent and gifted. They reward students' elite cultural practices with more attention and assistance (Kingston, 2001).

While interesting theoretically, research has qualified the significance of cultural capital. First, studies show a weak link between cultural capital and educational attainment when other related resources such as family income, parental encouragement, and parental involvement in schooling are considered in the equation. Second, research also shows a feeble connection between elite background and cultural capital. Many in the elite, it seems, have forsaken ballet for Saturday night hockey and abandoned opera for Willie Nelson and the Rolling Stones. Finally, observers point out that teachers are a weak link as well in that many avoid high cultural forms (Kingston, 2001).

The Informal, or Hidden, Curriculum

The school through its "hidden curriculum" operates as an important agency of informal socialization (Jackson, 1968). Research on processes embedded in the hidden curriculum shows that it often operates to the disadvantage of females, certain ethnic minorities, and the lower classes.

Teachers present role models based on their own middle-class backgrounds. What they say and what they do promote the middle-class virtues of self-discipline, orderly conduct, deference to and cooper-

ation with authority, punctuality, and, above all, conformity. In his study of the hidden curriculum in Ottawa schools, Richer (1988) observes how experience in the early grades encourages students to be competitive and to hold material possessions and private property in high regard. Primary grade experience also encourages pupils to value work over play and to show deference to authority.

The hidden curriculum has two aspects—the cognitive and the social. The cognitive dimension involves a message about the nature of knowledge. This message emphasizes the importance of schedules and the demarcation of subject matter into discrete blocks. Schools encourage children to develop a style of thinking that takes account of the world as fragmented rather than interconnected. On the social dimension, the playing of classroom games, the awarding of stars and animal stamps for successful performance, and the emphasis on order and control teach children the value and rightness of competition, materialism, hard work (as opposed to play), and submission to authority.

Richer (1988) argues that the hidden curriculum favours middle- over lower-class children. Research indicates that students from lower-class backgrounds are less motivated, especially when the rewards for effort are symbolic rather than material, and that lower-class culture places more emphasis on the present than on the future. Children coming out of lower-class backgrounds are disadvantaged in school, whereas middle-class youngsters are not. The culture of the middle class socializes children to act competitively, defer gratification, and pursue symbolic rewards. It also promotes verbal over physical skill. Mastery of the values and behaviours championed by the school means that middle-class students receive a disproportionate amount of praise, support, and positive attention in the classroom. By contrast, teachers more often subject lower-class children to discipline and authority.

While certain features of the hidden curriculum are changing with the times, remnants of past themes persist. For example, the role models provided in school offer important informal lessons regarding the appropriate distribution of power and authority in society. Women comprise 64 percent of elementary and secondary teachers in Canada. They transmit basic knowledge to children and youth, nurture their personal development, and keep them safe. The "child care" aspect of the work diminishes its stature.

On the other hand, college instructors and particularly university professors enjoy higher status, more prestige, and more power for several reasons. First, they have more advanced educational qualifications. Second, they produce knowledge as well as transmit it. Third, their teaching activity involves presenting sophisticated arguments and original analyses to a clientele comprised of adults. College and university educators are predominantly male—61 percent and 74 percent respectively (Statistics Canada, 2001b).

Historically, research has unearthed biases in teachers' lessons and the information presented in instructional materials. There is evidence of some change but both teachers and texts, especially at the elementary and secondary levels, present the ideals rather than the realities of everyday living. When these perspectives on the world are presented early and intensely, children rapidly internalize them and accept them with little question.

Some examples: Representations of the family presented in schools tend to exclude mothers working outside the home, apartment living, divorce and single parenting, poverty and poor housing, or sibling fights and illegitimate pregnancies. Discussions of politics seldom centre on abuses of power, acceptance of bribes, or the misuse of government resources. Stories typically portray boys as taking initiative and showing independence, and girls, when they depict them at all, as passive and meek. When stories do involve female heroines, they place them in domestic or school settings. Male heroes, on the other hand, range over a wide variety of strange and exciting terrains (Statham, 1986). Textual and pictorial depictions of men flying planes and women cooking meals—or, for that matter, of Aboriginal people worshipping the land and Newfoundlanders catching fish—may not be the main point of the story. Nonetheless, they promote stereotypes. While the most recently published texts are the least biased, they are by no means the ones most likely to be used in class. Texts are very expensive and budgets have been cut; it is not at all unusual to find dated material used widely in classrooms today (Ballantine, 2001).

Research also reveals informal sex role socialization in both public schools and institutions of higher learning. Adler, Kless, and Adler (1992) investigated the dynamics of popularity for boys and girls in elementary school peer groups. For boys, popularity in school means conforming to the traditional "male ethos"—the demonstration of physicality, autonomy, and "coolness." For females, being at the centre of the action means demonstrating the ability to buy things, exuding quality and style in personal apparel, and living in the "right" area of town.

Similar informal peer processes have been observed in the university. Holland and Eisenhart (1990) document how female peer groups nurture a culture of romance on campus that values young women for their ability to attract men rather than for their academic prowess and career potential.

Once again at the postsecondary level, Gilbert and Pomfret (1991) explore how aspects of the hidden curriculum figure prominently in explaining why so few women study mathematics and science at the postsecondary level. At the elementary and secondary levels, males and females are enrolled in roughly equal numbers. Females are better readers, communicate more effectively, get higher grades, fail fewer subjects, and are less likely to drop out. Despite these successes, however, there is a distinct lack of participation by females in math and science programs.

Computers are now widely available in Canadian schools, raising both computer literacy and access, and in time will affect demographics within the technology industry.
SOURCE: Dick Hemmingway.

There appear to be several reasons for their dramatic underrepresentation. First, math and science have traditionally been male domains and discrimination against women has been common in these pursuits. There is evidence that teachers and guidance counsellors encourage and reward females for making educational and occupational choices consistent with their gender roles. Second, the pursuit of degrees in these disciplines requires a time investment that intensifies the double burden of school and family obligations. This double burden tends to confront females more than males because social expectations dictate that women more than men clean houses, cook meals, and care for dependents. Finally, there is evidence that women's self-concept causes them to prefer learning that allows for the expression of qualities such as caring for others and reciprocity. Success in science, by contrast, has traditionally involved the expression of masculine qualities of autonomy and limited cooperative learning. According to this view, science satisfies neither women's emotional nor ethical preferences and, as such, represents a discomforting educational environment that women tend to avoid (Gilbert and Pomfret, 1991). As in many areas of the education system, subtle discrimination operates just beneath the surface of things.

SUMMARY

1. Sociologists study education for several reasons. Educational attainment is linked to entry into the labour force, and affects both life-chances and quality of life. Effective mass education in Canada is a national priority. It is widely believed to play an important role in maintaining democratic ideals, equality, social justice, and economic productivity. Schooling is broadly considered to be an appropriate means of solving a wide variety of social problems, including poverty, discrimination, crime, and illness.

2. Structural-functionalism presents education as part of, and contributing to, a larger social system. It emphasizes equilibrium, value consensus, and gradual social change.

3. Manifest, or intended, functions include personal development, cultural transmission, and the creation, preservation, and dissemination of knowledge. Latent, or unintended, functions include providing a marriage market, legitimizing social inequality, and restricting competition for jobs.

4. Conflict theories of education are based on the work of Max Weber and Karl Marx. They emphasize disagreements and power struggles in educational contexts, particularly along the lines of class, ethnicity, and gender.

5. Marxist conflict theory analyzes schooling as a tool of the capitalist elite and as a generator of working-class resistance.

6. Weberian conflict theory presents the argument that schooling is a means of bestowing credentials.

7. Symbolic interaction is an interpretive framework that focuses on the development of self-image, self-concept, or identity. Interactionists view a person's self-concept as the product of the manipulation and interpretation of symbols in long-term social interaction. Over time, people develop positive or negative senses of self in response to the perceived reactions of significant others who surround them.

8. Out of the meanings arising from interaction, people construct three important definitions that greatly affect their current and future actions—self, society, and situation. Each of these definitions significantly influences subsequent behaviour, including behaviour in school and educational outcomes.

9. Evidence suggests that student characteristics are correlated with educational outcomes and that equality of opportunity is not the same as equality in results. Students from lower-class and some ethnic backgrounds (e.g., Aboriginal) do not do as well in school as students from higher-class and other ethnic backgrounds (e.g., Jewish and Asian).

10. Female students perform as well or better than male students. Although differences between male and female participation rates in postsecondary education have disappeared in recent years, important differences remain with respect to particular programs.

11. Student outcomes are affected by the interaction of personal traits, home environment, and school experiences. Key elements of the home that affect schooling are language use and access to cultural capital. Important elements of the school experience include teacher expectations, tracking, and the informal (or hidden) curriculum.

QUESTIONS TO CONSIDER

1. Discuss the ways in which the hidden curriculum prepares children and youth for adult work roles in bureaucratic settings. How do functional and conflict theories explain the connections between school and work? Do different theories place different emphases on the importance of formal and informal curricula?

2. What does it mean to think critically? Do diverse segments of society have different conceptions of thinking critically? Why might this be the case? Think back to your own experience in school. Do schools encourage critical thinking?

3. Some observers are concerned that placing greater emphasis on basics, increasing curriculum content levels, and raising standards may escalate dropout rates. Why might this be the case? If standards are raised, what groups will be most likely to drop out? How is leaving school prematurely likely to affect their life-chances?

4. Schools in Canada are organized bureaucratically in the name of fairness and efficiency. Identify the problems and outcomes associated with organizing the delivery of education services in this way. What changes would you advocate and why?

5. Some commentators argue that rising tuition, tighter loan regulations, and increased competition for placement are threatening accessibility to university. What implications for social mobility do you see arising in the long term? What measures would you advocate to equalize opportunity more evenly across the class structure?

GLOSSARY

Ascribed status is based on traits acquired at birth, such as sex and ethnicity, or automatically through the aging process. Ascription differs from achieved status that is based on individual ability and effort.

Conflict theory stresses discord among social groups, segments, and classes, and points to the contradictions inherent in the social system. It predicts that social change will be more revolutionary than evolutionary.

Credentialism is a conflict theory that holds that it is not education per se that people seek out but the degree, diploma, or certificate that is the end product.

Cultural capital refers to wealth in the form of knowledge or ideas, the possession of which legitimizes the maintenance of status and power.

Elaborated code is a language code that involves the expression, in symbolic form, of complex, impersonal, and abstract ideas, sentiments, and feelings. Explicit diction and complicated constructions make it more suitable for the discussions, ideas, and abstractions typically explored and evaluated in schools.

Equality of opportunity exists when all members of a society have an equal chance to compete for social and economic rewards such as income, prestige, and power.

Equality of benefit exists when all members of a society have equal capacities and resources to benefit from the experience of schooling and enjoy outcomes of success.

Formal curriculum refers to the knowledge and skills students acquire through the course of their official studies.

Functionalism is a theory that views society as a system, with parts that work together to maintain the whole. It generally emphasizes interdependence and cooperation, order and stability, value consensus and integration, and gradual and evolutionary social change.

The **hidden curriculum** refers to the set of values, attitudes, and knowledge that is embedded in the organization and processes of schooling and that is implicitly conveyed to students.

Human capital theory is the theory that investing resources in people's education and training, as opposed to simply pumping money into plants and machinery, will contribute substantially to economic growth.

Institutional racism refers to seemingly objective and neutral structures and unbiased policies that confer advantage on one group at the expense of another.

I.Q. tests are standardized tests with items designed to test specific mental abilities. These tests purport to assess innate ability, controlling for environmental and cultural factors.

Labour-force participation rate refers to the percentage of adults with jobs.

Latent functions are outcomes that, while unintended and informal, nonetheless contribute to society's maintenance.

Manifest functions are the intended and formally articulated goals of the education system.

Participation rates, with respect to education, are the percentages of those in eligible age groups who are in school.

Resistance theory is a conflict theory attributing lower-class students' failure at school to their unwillingness to perform. They show defiance built upon the historical struggle of the working class with their capitalist employers and consequently express antagonism to institutional authority.

Restricted code is a language code that focuses on the immediate and concrete in terms of both circumstance and time. Words are basic, grammar is simple, sentences are short, and themes are personal and descriptive.

A **self-fulfilling prophecy** is an event that occurs as a consequence of having been expected to occur.

Symbolic interactionsim is an interpretive framework examining how nonverbal and verbal symbols operate in interactive communication to promote the development of self-image, self-concept, or identity.

SUGGESTED READING

Ballantine, Jeanne H. (2001). *The Sociology of Education: A Systematic Analysis*, 5th ed. Englewood Cliffs, NJ: Prentice-Hall. This American textbook provides a good introduction to the field. It emphasizes an open-systems approach and provides a good account of classroom interaction and its effects on students, while taking into consideration the larger picture and the conflicts inherent in the teaching and learning enterprise.

Demaine, Jack. (2001). *Sociology of Education Today*. New York: Palgrave. This book provides a thorough examination of key issues in contemporary education including class, gender, family, social justice, and globalization. It offers a section containing a comparison of different education systems from around the world.

Guppy, Neil, and Scott Davies. (1998). *Education in Canada: Recent Trends and Future Challenges*. Ottawa: Statistics Canada. A detailed analysis of education in Canada based on the 1991 census, this monograph discusses trends in Canadian education and provides a thoughtful assessment of their implications for Canadian society in the future. The authors provide a solid discussion of links between education and work.

Porter, John, Marion Porter, and Bernard Blishen. (1982). *Stations and Callings: Making It through the School System*. Toronto: Methuen. In this classic work, the authors report findings from a large-scale survey of Ontario students. The study examines the degree to which education based on a meritocratic, equality-of-opportunity model that meets the needs of students from a variety of backgrounds. The book provides an excellent example of skilfully executed and theoretically informed research.

Sociology of Education: Extra Issue. (2001). A journal of the American Sociological Association, *Sociology of Education* is the leading outlet for research articles in the field. The journal offers an excellent resource for keeping abreast of the latest developments in the sociology of education. This special issue includes a series of "state of the art" literature reviews on contemporary education, including the article "Currents of Thought: Sociology of Education at the Dawn of the 21st Century." The coverage of race and class issues is particularly strong.

PART FIVE

CHAPTER FIFTEEN

URBANIZATION

In this chapter you will learn that:

- The choice of opportunities, experiences, and lifestyles available to urban residents is shaped and constrained by two sets of factors: those related to the physical environment and those dictated by the changing structure of the wider economy.

- Contrary to the theory that the core of Canadian cities is hollowing out like the hole in a doughnut, recent evidence suggests that city centres are remaining relatively stable economically and demographically; in contrast, the ring of older suburbs around the city core is stagnating, losing jobs and population to a constellation of edge cities in the surrounding region.

- The fastest-growing middle-class neighbourhoods today are private communities, where control over local government, public services, and security rests in the hands of non-elected, professional managers; one popular form of such neighbourhoods is the gated community, where nonresidents are considered intruders and are monitored and kept out by guards, alarm systems, and surveillance cameras.

- Downtown areas of Canadian and U.S. cities are being transformed into urban theme parks, whose planning and design reflect the requirements of a rapidly growing symbolic economy rooted in popular culture and entertainment.

JOHN HANNIGAN

UNIVERSITY OF TORONTO

INTRODUCTION

Several years ago, *The Globe and Mail* published an opinion piece by Elinor Florence, a British Columbia woman who, with her husband and three teenage children, had moved from Richmond, a rapidly developing suburb on the southern boundary of Vancouver, to Invermere, an alpine town of 3000 near the Alberta border. Leaving behind a mushrooming population, the stresses of urban driving, and "a junk culture that undeniably rears its head everywhere but snarls louder in cities" (Florence, 1997), the Florence family appears to have found happiness in the shadow of the Rockies. Among the benefits that she cites are a slower pace of life, more leisure time, a greater sense of personal security, no fast-food restaurants, and the ability to walk everywhere.

Elinor Florence's profile of small-town life highlights a theme that has resounded through the discipline of sociology since its founding in the late nineteenth century. Urban life, it is said, is qualitatively different from a rural or small-town existence: meaner, more stressful, more alienating. Obsessed as they are with efficiency and making money, urbanites are said to have no time for relating to others in a more holistic and humane way. Increasing population size and density, such as that which is beginning to plague Richmond, bring with them a host of urban problems, from traffic gridlock and pollution to family breakdown and crime.

The tale of the Florences illustrates one of the most influential ways of looking at residential settings. Termed **environmental-opportunity theory** (Michelson, 1973), it posits that people actively choose where they want to live depending on the extent to which a particular place either meshes with or constrains their preferred lifestyle. Not all of us, of course, get to choose our community freely, but people will always strive to match their choices with their needs. This is well illustrated in the case of "Prairie Edge," a small Alberta municipality where residents perceived the "rural advantage" as being directly linked to the reduced parental anxiety that comes from a "safe" everyday environment (see Box 15.1).

There is another approach that asserts that the urban experience is constrained not just by the nature of the physical environment, but also by the changing configuration of international, national, and local economic arrangements. In recent years, the emergence of a globalized economy has had profound implications for North American cities, changing both their physical form and their social-class patterns. In particular, it has resulted in an increasing polarization between rich and poor, affecting the homeless person sleeping in the park, the highly paid professional eating in the chic urban restaurant, and the suburban homeowner shopping in a "big-box" megastore on the fringes of the city (Kleniewski, 1997: 135).

Similarly, resource towns and farming communities have been hard hit by international trade agreements and a harsher rural–urban division of labour in the global economy. In this changing climate, the countryside comes to serve two new and very different purposes—vacation playground and toxic dumping ground. Thus, while towns in the British Columbia interior and the Alberta foothills are transformed into ski and golfing resorts linked to global tourism, other communities are forced to "grasp at environmentally dubious schemes like hazardous waste treatment, strawboard manufacture, tire incineration and mega-hog barns" (Epp and Whitson, 2001: xv).

In this chapter, we will look at this dual influence of environment and structure on city life over the course of the twentieth century. In the course of our discussion, you will encounter three main types of cities: the industrial city, the corporate city, and the postmodern city. The industrial city originated in the nineteenth century and reached its zenith in the 1920s and 1930s; the corporate city arose after World War II and dominated during the 1950s and 1960s; and the postmodern city dates from the 1970s up to the present.

EARLY CITIES

Cities are defined as "relatively large, dense, permanent settlements in which the majority of the residents do not produce their own food" (McGahan, 1995: 1). By most accounts, the city as a distinct form dates back five or six thousand years to 3000–4000 B.C.E., when it first appeared in Mesopotamia (now southern Iraq) and Egypt. Initially, these ancient cities were established largely as centres of religious worship and were not much larger than most single-industry towns in Canada today. For example, Memphis, at the head of the Nile River delta, had an estimated population of

40 000 in 3000 B.C.E. Cities later swelled: Babylon had a population of 200 000 during the reign of Nebuchadnezzar in the seventh century B.C.E.; Alexandria, Egypt, surpassed 300 000 three centuries later; and Rome reached 800 000 at its peak in the second century C.E. (Chandler and Fox, 1974).

Calgary, shown above, is the fastest-growing city in Canada.
SOURCE: CP Picture Archive/Adrian Wyld

Three elements of prime importance characterized these preindustrial cities: the existence of a food surplus in fertile valleys, which permitted the specialization of labour in zones of dense settlement; the achievement of literacy among scribes, priests, and other elite members of society, which allowed for the keeping of financial and other records; and technological innovations, notably metallurgy, agricultural irrigation, and the harnessing of wind and water power for sailing and grain milling.

After the fall of Rome to Germanic tribes in the fifth century C.E., cities stagnated and declined over large parts of Europe. They continued to flourish, though, in the rising Islamic empire, which, at its zenith, stretched from Spain to India. More decentralized than the Roman world, the Islamic empire contained a number of cities that reached impressive levels of size and sophistication. For example, more than 500 000 people lived in Cairo in the fourteenth century, when Egypt held a trade monopoly on the east–west spice route (Abu-Lughod, 1991: 38).

From the eleventh century onward, a number of city-states along the Mediterranean—Florence, Genoa, Venice, Pisa—succeeded in re-establishing trade routes to Asia and the Middle East by means of the Crusades. The commercial revival that followed was felt even in the merchant towns of the North Sea and the Baltic, which themselves had begun to develop a brisk trade in wool and cloth. From this renaissance there developed a distinct class of professional merchants who established their own municipal laws and institutions distinct from those in the surrounding feudal society, and there also emerged a market for housing and a variety of other goods and services, which generated further urban growth (Golden, 1981: 120–22).

Although preindustrial cities were important as centres of commerce, knowledge, and art, they never contained much more than a small fraction of the overall population. Even at their height, ancient and medieval cities were incapable of supporting urban populations of more than 5 or 10 percent of society, primarily because they could not generate a sufficiently large agricultural surplus to feed a huge urban populace. When the cities did begin to swell, periodic outbreaks of the bubonic plague (the notorious "Black Death"), spread by fleas from infected rats, killed as many as half the people in Europe's cities. Thus, by 1800, of the roughly 900 million people in the world, only about 3 percent lived in urban places of 5000 or more inhabitants (Hauser, 1965: 7). And, despite significant changes in architectural styles and building materials, the physical layout of the communities in which they lived had not changed all that much from antiquity to the eighteenth century—they were still built up within protective walls and organized around a central market square and places of worship, such as cathedrals, temples, or mosques (Abu-Lughod, 1991: 49–50).

THE INDUSTRIAL CITY

By the end of the eighteenth century, a brand-new type of city had begun to emerge, first in England and later in continental Europe and America. This industrial city was larger, more complex, and more dynamic than any urban settlement that had preceded it. At century's end, more than 50 percent of the population of England and Wales was found to be residing in places with 20 000 or more people, compared with only 17 percent a century earlier (Weber, 1963 [1899]: 47). Global urbanization trends from 1800 to 2000 are shown in Figure 15.1.

What contributed to the growth of industrial cities? One popular theory emphasizes advances in

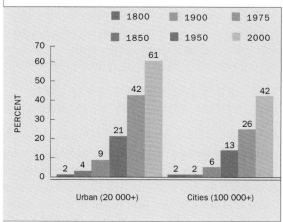

FIGURE 15.1 PERCENT OF WORLD POPULATION LIVING IN URBAN AREAS AND IN LARGE CITIES, 1800–2000

SOURCE: Adapted from Kingsley Davis, "The Origin and Growth of Urbanization in the World," *American Journal of Sociology*, 60 (1955) p. 430.

transportation and agricultural technology, inasmuch as these factors contributed to the production and movement of agricultural surpluses from farm to city. Among the innovations were better methods of land drainage, the use of fertilizers, methods of seed selection, techniques of animal breeding, toll-road building, and the application of steam power to farm machinery and rail transport. Other scholars emphasize a boom in trade and commerce, which provided a powerful inducement to greater investment, technological improvements, and, ultimately, increased agricultural productivity.

Another key factor appears to have been a shift in the sources of capital accumulation—that is, how factory owners raised the investment money needed to build and improve their manufacturing facilities. In England after 1850, capital investment was facilitated by the creation of the joint stock company, a business structure that pooled the capital of many investors and that had limited liability (i.e., the shareholders could not be held personally responsible for enterprises that failed).

Finally, urban growth has been linked to the invention of the factory. Previously, under the "putting-out" system, piecework was done in village or rural cottages and collected at regular intervals by the agents of merchant entrepreneurs. With the advent of the factory system, workers were required to work in a central location. Initially, factories had to be located next to rivers, in order to run directly on water power. Then, as steam-powered machines became the standard, factories concentrated in cities because steam power could not be distributed economically over a wide grid, as electrical systems can today.

THE DEVELOPMENT OF AN URBAN-INDUSTRIAL ECONOMY IN CANADA

At the time of Confederation in 1867, Canada lagged significantly behind both Britain and the United States in the development of an urban-industrial economy. The British North American colonies, both inside and outside the new political union, traded very little with each other, looking instead to the United States or Great Britain. According to the first manufacturing census in 1870, such localized activities as sawmilling, flour milling, shoemaking, and clothing manufacture accounted for almost half the value of the manufactured goods produced in Canada (Nader, 1975: 207). At the same time, only a tiny minority of Canadians lived in urban areas: In 1871, fewer than one in five (18 percent) lived in a town or a city (Stone, 1967: 29).

By century's end, industrial cities had finally begun to emerge. While Toronto and Montreal were the largest industrial centres, factory towns also grew up elsewhere in Ontario, chief among them Windsor, because of its proximity to industry and markets in Detroit, and Hamilton, because of its port and strategic location on the Great Lakes. In addition to strategic location, the availability of investment capital played a significant role in directing where industry was established. The Canada Bank Act of 1871 was instrumental in concentrating economic power in a few national metropolitan centres, notably Toronto and Montreal. The act adopted the British model of a branch-banking system wherein a handful of major banks each established a network of branches. In contrast, under the U.S. unit-banking system, many more banks are independent. Investment capital was thus concentrated in a handful of urban centres rather than being widely dispersed across the country (Nader, 1975: 215).

Through various interventions by the federal government—the building of the transcontinental railroad, the imposition of a protective tariff system to encourage domestic manufacturing, a vigorous immigration policy that encouraged agriculture on the Prairies—a system of national economic markets was eventually established. In particular, at the turn of the century, these interventions found form in the expansion of wheat production for export. With cash from wheat sales jingling in their pockets, Prairie grain farmers were able to purchase manufactured goods from the factories of Ontario and Quebec, thus stimulating a marked upsurge in Canadian urbanization in the two decades from 1891 to 1911 (Stone, 1967: 20–21). By 1911, four cities had populations exceeding 100 000: Montreal (470 480), Toronto (376 538), Winnipeg (136 035), and Vancouver (100 401). However, the formation of a national market led to the deindustrialization of the Maritime provinces (see Brym, 1986).

As the twentieth century progressed, the proportion of the Canadian population that was classified as "urban" increased dramatically, crossing the 50 percent mark before 1931 and reaching 70 percent in 1951. By 1991, 77 percent of the Canadian population was living in towns and cities (see Table 15.1). Toronto, Montreal, and Vancouver continued to hold the largest number of Canadians, but, as can be seen in Figure 15.2, the sharpest growth rates after 1951 were in the western cities of Calgary and Edmonton.

Over the last decade of the twentieth century, Toronto and Vancouver (together with Calgary) made a major comeback as growth centres. As can be seen in Box 15.2 (page 390), these three Canadian cities added new residents in different ways. Immigration has bol-

---

TABLE 15.1   URBAN–RURAL POPULATION, CANADA, 1931–1996

	1931	1951	1991	1996
Rural farm	31%	11%	3%	3%
Rural non-farm	15	19	20	19
Urban	54	70	77	78
Total	100	100	100	100

SOURCE: Adapted from Statistics Canada, "Urban vs. Rural Population," http://www.statcan.ca (September 20, 1996). Used by permission of the Minister of Industry, 2000.

FIGURE 15.2 POPULATION OF CANADA'S NINE BIGGEST METROPOLITAN AREAS, 1951–1996 (IN 000s)

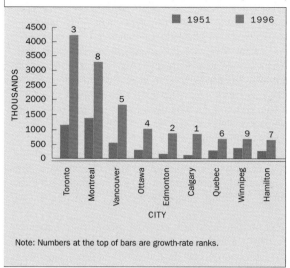

Note: Numbers at the top of bars are growth-rate ranks.

SOURCE: Adapted from Brian Biggs and Ray Bollman, "Urbanization in Canada," *Canadian Social Trends*, vol. 2 (Toronto: Thompson Educational Publishers, 1994), pp. 67–72 at p. 69; and Robert J. Brym, *Canadian Society and the 1996 Census* (Toronto: Harcourt Brace Canada, 1999).

---

stered Vancouver and Toronto, but this growth has been partially offset by the loss of residents to other parts of their respective provinces. While migrants from other provinces flocked to Calgary and Vancouver, few were attracted to Toronto. Natural increase has been more of a factor in Calgary and Toronto than in Vancouver (Little, 1999).

RESEARCHING THE INDUSTRIAL CITY: THE CHICAGO SCHOOL

By the final quarter of the nineteenth century, U.S. cities were seeing jumps in population that rivalled and even surpassed those in Britain. Nowhere was this more dramatic than in Chicago, which mushroomed from 122 000 people in 1860 to 1.7 million in 1900 and 3.4 million in 1930. Such rapid growth left in its wake social dislocation and human misery. Among those who sought to address these problems was the chairman of the Sociology Department of the University of Chicago, Robert E. Park.

Park and his colleagues believed that they could improve conditions for the disadvantaged by discovering what made the city "tick" and then using this knowledge to help solve its "social pathologies"—

crime, juvenile delinquency, family breakdown, and mental illness. To carry out this task, they employed an assortment of methods and models. On the one hand, Park argued that researchers should consider themselves urban anthropologists who would venture out into the field and study the natives, their customs, beliefs, and practices. This inspired a rich ethnographic tradition of urban research in which Park's colleagues and students rendered richly detailed, firsthand accounts of such things as homeless men, gangs, and "taxi-dance" halls. At the same time, Park also urged his students to consider the city of Chicago as a kind of social laboratory in which various natural processes took place. One way of documenting these processes was through the development of urban-growth models (discussed in the next section) by which the changing social and spatial structure of the city could be depicted visually. Another was to use "ecological spot maps" in which differences in the rate of various deviant behaviours, such as juvenile delinquency and schizophrenia, could be plotted geographically in order to discover underlying patterns.

Some of the most memorable work to come out of the Chicago School tradition drew upon personal documents and other biographical materials. For example, Harvey Zorbaugh (1929) made use of a huge cache of letters, life histories, school essays, social-service agency records, and a school census. To contrast the experience of Polish peasants in the old country with that of urban migrants to America, William I. Thomas and Florian Znaniecki (1918–20) employed court and agency records, an in-depth autobiography, and thousands of letters exchanged between newcomers to Chicago and their relatives in Poland.

To put this mountain of data into some kind of theoretical order, Park and his colleagues used several approaches. First, they tapped into a long tradition of exploring the contrast between rural and urban life. In the latter part of the nineteenth century, the German social philosopher Ferdinand Tönnies (1957 [1887]) had attempted to depict the difference between traditional and modern societies by introducing a distinction between a *Gemeinschaft*—the "community of feeling" that exists in villages, tribes, and small communities—and the *Gesellschaft*—the characteristic feature of social relations in the city. Tönnies favoured *Gemeinschaft* and saw its decline as

BOX 15.2 THREE CANADIAN CITIES: WHAT MAKES THEM GROW SO BIG

In a decade of modest population growth, three of Canada's big cities—Toronto, Vancouver and Calgary—stand out. Not only has their performance been sizzling, they have been adding people in very different ways.

Between 1991 and 1998, the national population grew 8.1 per cent, which is moderate by historical standards. But in the three hottest-growth cities, the rates of expansion were much faster—21.2 per cent in Vancouver, 18.4 per cent in Calgary and 14 per cent in Toronto. [In 1998, 24.7 per cent of Canadians lived in those three centres as compared to 23 per cent in 1991.] By size they are Canada's first-, third- and fifth-largest centres. The Toronto CMA (Census Metropolitan Area), which goes well beyond the boundaries of the city proper, had 4.6 million people in 1998, Vancouver had two million and Calgary 907,000.

What is most striking about the fast-growth cities is the way they grew.

From 1991 to 1997, Vancouver added about 53,000 people a year. Its single biggest source—about 68 per cent of the total—was net international immigration [immigrants minus emigrants]. Those were the years when immigration from Asia was especially strong, particularly from Hong Kong, where many residents were worried about the 1997 handover of the British colony to China. Migrants from the rest of Canada accounted for another 29 per cent.

Now move east to Calgary, which added almost 18,000 people a year on average. Here the newcomers were largely home-grown. Natural increase [births minus deaths] was responsible for 43 per cent of the growth [as against 20 per cent for Vancouver]. Other countries accounted for 31 per cent and other provinces 22 per cent. Calgary, in effect, was firing on all cylinders, adding people by every way possible.

In Toronto, the population grew by an average of 79,000 people a year from 1991 to 1997. Net international immigration was an even bigger source of growth—85 per cent of the total—than it was in Vancouver. And natural increase supplied another 45 per cent, roughly the same as Calgary. But unlike its western counterparts, Toronto lost people to other provinces (2 per cent of the total). And like Vancouver, but not Calgary, it lost people to the rest of its own province—a number equal to 24 per cent of its population growth.

So, while the three hot cities all have a rapidly growing population, when it comes to what's making them grow, they part company.

SOURCE: Excerpted from Bruce Little, "Tale of Three Cities: What Makes Them Grow So Big," *The Globe and Mail*, September 20, 1999, p. A2. Reprinted with permission.

---

a loss of all that is natural and satisfying about small-town life. In contrast, he wrote, *Gesellschaft* denotes a lifestyle based on money, commercial contracts, individual interest, and class antagonism. Although he was more positive about the possibilities for individual freedom in modern urban life, the German sociologist Georg Simmel (1950) used the same rural–urban contrast as a central method of dealing with the meaning of the shift to an urban society.

This rural–urban dichotomy runs through much of Chicago School theorizing. Thomas and Znaniecki, for example, depict the city as being responsible for destroying the traditional institutions of Polish peasant life—family, neighbourhood, church—and substituting nothing but an empty well of social disorganization. Freed from the ties that formerly bound the community together, marriages

German philosopher Ferdinand Tönnies coined the term *Gemeinschaft* to describe the community of feeling that exists in villages and small communities.
SOURCE: Sheila Maloney, *Zephyr Ontario*. Courtesy Nancy Poole's Studio.

dissolve, teenagers run wild, and even murder is not uncommon. In his modification of Simmel's social-psychological profile of urban life, Louis Wirth (1938) proposed that the city is characterized by the concurrent trends of increasing size, density, and heterogeneity. In his view, the city creates a distinct way of life—"urbanism"—that is economically efficient but socially destructive. Wirth's shortlist of urban characteristics includes the decline of the family, the disappearance of the neighbourhood, and the undermining of traditional bases of social solidarity. Urbanites are said to be superficial, unable to step outside their narrow occupational roles to relate to people in a holistic and meaningful way, and guided by an all-consuming drive for success and money.

ECOLOGY OF THE INDUSTRIAL CITY

Industrial cities were also unique in their ecology—that is, their spatial layout, physical structure, and distribution of population. In order to depict the spatial or ecological patterns of the city, a group of sociologists and geographers from the University of Chicago devised a set of urban-growth models in the 1920s and 1930s.

Burgess's **concentric-zone model** conceptualized the expansion of cities as a succession of concentric rings, each of which contained a distinct resident population and type of land use (Burgess, 1961). This concentric model of urban growth identified five zones (see Figure 15.3).

Zone 1, the central business district (CBD), is the commercial pulse of the city. It is the site of the major department stores, live theatres, hotels, banks, and office space. The land here is the most valuable in the city, which means that residential and low-rent commercial uses are inevitably displaced in favour of big-money commercial enterprises.

Zone 2 is called the zone in transition. In the 1920s, large parcels of land in Chicago's transitional zone were being held by speculators who fully expected that the CBD would push outward, making them millionaires. In the meantime, zone 2 stood as an area of cheap housing that became the initial resting point for each new wave of immigrants who took jobs in the nearby factories. Also located here were a variety of marginal businesses—pawn shops, tattoo parlours, second-hand stores—that could not

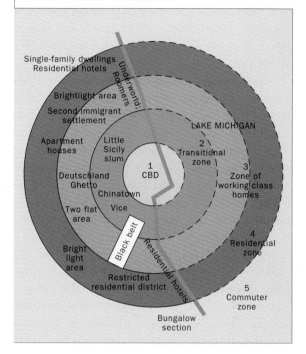

FIGURE 15.3 BURGESS'S CONCENTRIC ZONE MODEL APPLIED TO CHICAGO

SOURCE: Redrawn from Ernest W. Burgess, "The Growth of the City: An Introduction to a Research Project," in George A. Theodorson, ed., *Studies in Human Ecology* (Evanston, IL: Row, Peterson, 1961), p. 41.

afford the high rents of the city centre. The transitional zone also attracted a raft of illegal commercial activities—gambling, prostitution, drug dealing—that needed to be accessible to clientele in the CBD but that were considered socially unacceptable in the high-profile heart of the downtown area.

Zone 3, the zone of working-class homes, denotes the area settled by second-generation immigrants and rural migrants. In Burgess's time, zone 3 was a neighbourhood of semidetached, two-family homes where fathers still worked in inner-city factories but from which the upwardly mobile children aspired to escape, into the middle-class suburban zones.

Zone 4, the zone of better residences, was where the bulk of the middle class could be found: small-business people, professionals, sales personnel, and office employees. Initially, it was an area of single-family detached houses, but, by the mid-1920s, it was increasingly characterized by apartment buildings and residential hotels.

Finally, zone 5, the commuter zone, was an area beyond the political boundaries of the city composed of satellite towns and suburbs. With the growth of commuter railroads and automobile travel, zone 5 was a precursor of the suburbs that boomed after World War II.

Burgess's concentric-zone model made three interrelated assumptions. First, all commercial growth was said to emanate from the dominant city-centre nucleus and proceed outward in an orderly and predictable manner. Second, residential growth took place at the periphery, where it was easier and cheaper to obtain open land for development purchases. New housing was added here, but it was intended primarily for the middle and upper classes, who were increasingly able to take advantage of newly constructed commuter rail lines and, later, expressways. Third, the model was dynamic in that it assumed a sort of filtering-down process. As housing aged, it deteriorated, became less desirable, and was abandoned by better-off citizens, who moved into newer housing farther away from the city centre. The homes they left behind, some of them mansions, were subdivided into rooming houses, flats, and dormitories for artists and students. In recent years, many of these have been restored to a measure of their former glory, either by residential "gentrifiers" or by commercial users such as restaurateurs or hairstylists. Furthermore, Burgess assumed that, as immigrant newcomers to the industrial city found their balance and began to prosper, they would want to upgrade their housing. For example, the second generation of "white ethnics"—the acculturated sons and daughters of those who had come as part of the Polish, Italian, German, and other European immigration around the turn of the last century—could be expected to settle in the zone of working-class homes, which possessed housing superior to that occupied by their parents in the transitional zone.

Burgess's urban-growth model appears to have fit Chicago in the 1920s reasonably well, but, as a scheme for understanding all cities in different places and times, it does not do as well. First, the notion of a single growth nucleus has not held up very firmly. Cities such as Calgary and Edmonton, which developed later in the century and which were shaped largely by the automobile, are more likely to possess more than one nucleus or growth centre. Similarly, Los Angeles is widely known as "the city without a downtown." This was first recognized in the 1940s by

geographers Chauncey Harris and Edward Ullman (1945), who proposed a **multiple-nuclei model** of urban growth in which were located a series of growth centres—retail, wholesale, residential—each representing the concentration of a specific function or activity within the urban economy.

Second, Burgess seems to have underestimated the importance of transportation corridors as magnets for urban growth. Geographer Homer Hoyt (1939) developed a **sector model** of urban growth after studying 142 U.S. cities during the Depression years. He argued that cities grew not in concentric circles but in sectors or wedges along major transportation arteries, extending like the tentacles of an octopus from the CBD. Within each sector, the social character of the residential housing would remain constant. For example, upper-income groups would follow a northward progression, and working-class groups a southward path, thereby producing a distinct sectoral pattern to the developing city. Montreal and Vancouver seem to fit this sector model, because their populations tended to spread out along the natural shorelines of the bodies of water on which they are located (Driedger, 1991: 90).

Third, Burgess failed to appreciate that some resident groups would develop strong residential attachments to their neighbourhoods and refuse to move on, even in the face of an aging housing stock. This was first pointed out by Walter Firey (1947) in his study of Boston. Firey gives several examples that span the socioeconomic spectrum, from Beacon Hill, an elite area near the city centre, to the North End, a blue-collar Italian area where the residents chose to remain in their old neighbourhoods because the places were cherished as symbols of the residents' family connections, traditions, and culture.

THIRD WORLD URBANIZATION

A century ago, most urban growth was concentrated in the rapidly industrializing countries of Europe and North America. Today, nearly two-thirds of the world's urban population resides in the less developed regions of Asia, Oceania, Africa, Latin America, and the Caribbean (Gugler, 1996: vii). While urbanization in the "South" has followed sundry paths, it has displayed some common features.

To a greater extent than with Northern cities, cities of the South are characterized by a high degree of **urban primacy**. This describes a situation where one metropolitan centre, usually the capital city, is considerably larger and more dominant than any of the others. In Mexico, for example, this primacy is indicated by roadside markers throughout the country that indicate the distance to Mexico City, which is six times the size of its nearest rival, Guadalajara (Flanagan, 1995: 154). Primacy is most evident on the African continent, where 11 out of the 20 most extreme examples of primate systems occur (Clark, 1996: 27). In many cases, primate cities are located on the geographic margins along the sea coast, a legacy of colonial times when they operated as transhipment points for raw materials on their way to Spain, France, England, and other imperial powers. Much the same pattern has persisted in modern times where resource-producing regions funnel export commodities to primate cities from which the goods are subsequently shipped overseas. This is said to contribute to the underdevelopment of the interior, where provincial towns and cities tend to stagnate, unable to sustain a robust local industrial and commercial base. In recent years, however, cities with populations between 100 000 and 500 000 have experienced remarkable growth, especially in some Latin American countries. In Argentina, for example, intermediate cities have grown faster than Buenos Aires, while in Mexico, interior cities that have plugged into the international economy have outstripped the growth rate of Mexico City (De Oliveira and Roberts, 1996).

Cities of the South are often described as victims of **overurbanization**. This means that the population of urban areas, especially primate cities, is growing faster than the urban economy, services, and resources can absorb it. This creates an underclass of residents who live in illegal squatter settlements and employ themselves in marginal trades such as selling food and lottery tickets on street corners (Flanagan, 1995: 153). Canadian cities have recently had a taste of this in the form of growing numbers of panhandlers, "squeegee kids," and other homeless urban people, but the numbers in Southern cities are much larger. With public housing scarce, squatter settlements are common. In such settlements, people occupy urban land without legal title, frequently organizing "invasions" at set times and places. Once they have staked out their plots, the squatters put up makeshift shelters and establish basic public services such as water supply and sewage disposal. Some

squatter settlements remain poor, but others significantly upgrade their housing and eventually persuade municipal governments to extend utilities and health and sanitary services into the area.

The concept of overurbanization has provoked considerable debate among social scientists. Some claim that overurbanization is the single most important factor leading to the generation and intensification of serious social problems in southern cities: grinding poverty, mass unemployment, inadequate services, social unrest, increasing crime, and political instability (D. Smith, 1996: 148). Others claim that it is misleading to isolate the mismatch between demographic growth and employment opportunities, arguing that it makes more sense to look to larger structural factors such as undue reliance on foreign multinational corporations and continued deep inequality between an urban-based elite and the urban and rural masses.

Some countries in Asia, Africa, and Latin America have exhibited distinctive patterns of **peri-urbanization**, whereby the rural and the urban have become blurred in unplanned settlements on the outskirts of large cities. The motivation for this pattern is mostly economic: land in these peri-urban zones is cheaper and more easily obtained; shelter can be constructed economically using locally available materials; and families can keep farm animals and cultivate subsistence crops without violating any of the restrictions of the formal planning system (Stren and Halfani, 2001: 478). In contemporary Asian cities, for example, urbanization is increasingly characterized by the *desakota* (from the Indonesian words for village and city). Here, most people continue to live in village settings and almost all the land is under cultivation; but, most family income comes from nonagricultural sources. Some family members may even commute to work in the city, or live in the city and remit portions of their salaries to the family (Ginsburg et al., 1991). The linked processes of peri-urbanization and desakota challenge the conventional paradigm of the urban transition derived from the case of Western Europe and North America in the nineteenth and early twentieth centuries. Rather than remain strictly separated, the rural and the urban coexist in densely populated areas on the fringe of large mega-urban regions (McGee, 1991: 4–5).

Finally, sociologists who study urbanization in the South have been much concerned with **urban**

bias, that is, uneven investment and development that favour urban over rural areas. Despite the problems generated by overurbanization, landless migrants continue to flow into cities, which they see as their best chance to improve their lot in life. Economic growth strategies focus primarily on these rapidly growing cities, while the rural hinterland is overlooked. Thus, for the two decades following independence (the 1960s and 1970s) many of Africa's first-generation political leaders penalized agriculture through their monetary and tax policies in order to obtain resources to finance industrial development in the cities. In addition, public services were concentrated in the large cities, especially national capitals (Lofchie, 1997: 24–25). While poverty statistics are not always reliable, recent figures from the United Nations and the World Bank suggest that absolute poverty in rural areas continues to overshadow that found in the cities. For example, in Brazil, where there are notoriously poor slums in Rio de Janeiro and São Paulo, 65.9 percent of the population in rural areas continues to live below the poverty line, compared to 37.7 percent in the cities. In Mexico, the figures follow the same pattern. Much the same holds true for most African nations. India, by contrast, shows more or less comparable levels of poverty in urban and rural areas (Drakakis-Smith, 1988).

THE CORPORATE CITY

Although the industrial city continued to exist in North America into the 1970s, it began to lose ground after 1945 to a new urban form. Simply defined, the **corporate city** denotes the perception and organization of the city as a vehicle for capital accumulation—that is, as a money-making machine.

The corporate city is composed of five major elements (Lorimer, 1978; Reid, 1991). First are *corporate suburbs,* which are designed on the assumption that every family owns one or more cars. They incorporate a housing design that emphasizes large lots, single-family use, multi-car parking, and huge fenced back yards. They also entail a new land development process by which a single developer assembles a large tract of land plus services such as sewers, lights, roads, and so on; finances the new subdivision; and sells the lots and houses to homeowners at a price that includes the cost of servicing.

Second are *high-rise apartment buildings,* which are built at high densities in both older downtown neighbourhoods and on the fringe of the new suburbs. They offer minimum-standard housing at affordable rents on sites isolated from the surrounding urban fabric.

Third are *suburban industrial parks,* large tracts of land owned by a single developer and planned to accommodate one-storey factories and warehouses. Sprawling over acres of land, these areas have changed the geography of postwar cities by shifting industries out of the central city to the suburban fringe.

Concentrated in the central business district are *downtown office towers,* the fourth element of the corporate city. These are large-scale buildings rising to 60 storeys or more. The developers are the owners; businesses are the tenants. Office towers also combine office space with other profitable uses, notably ground-level or subterranean retail-shopping space.

Finally, *shopping centres* or *malls* are usually found in suburban or exurban areas. They are served primarily by cars and major roads, and typically remain inaccessible to public transit. They are located off the street, and the stores open internally into a central pedestrian passageway and courtyard. Most malls depend on large retail chains, especially department stores and supermarket "anchors," and often exclude small, independent retailers. The developers of malls control competition among retail tenants.

Each of these five elements of the corporate city has evolved over the years. Some of their central features have recently changed. Facing the spectre of shopper boredom and increased competition from both revitalized downtown retail districts and exurban "big-box" stores (e.g., Home Depot, Costco, Wal-Mart), shopping centres have been undergoing a redesign that includes a more diverse mix of retail tenants. In the face of changing demographics, suburban developments have also been forced to include a greater variety of housing types, including more townhouses and row houses and such innovations as "granny flats" (separate quarters for aged parents). After years of being half-empty, some downtown office buildings have begun to convert to condominiums. Nevertheless, the process by which the corporate city has been assembled and maintained remains much the same, and stands in marked contrast to that which undergirds the building of the industrial city. Nowhere has this been more evident than in the case of the corporate suburb.

THE CORPORATE SUBURB

Before World War II, North American cities such as Toronto were configured in a grid system, with residential avenues crossing long commercial streets at right angles. Since most urban residents lived within a few blocks of neighbourhood stores and services, there was constant pedestrian traffic up and down the streets. This spawned a lively "front-yard culture" in which passers-by regularly interacted with porch sitters, since front yards and families faced the street rather than the house itself (Fowler, 1992: 205).

When cities expanded, they did so incrementally, often a dozen houses at a time. The cost of extending sewers, water lines, and other city services was assumed by the municipality and paid for over 20 or 30 years through tax increases or special bonds. Lots were narrow and houses were two or three storeys high. Parking space was mostly on the street and, as auto ownership spread rapidly, increasingly scarce.

In the early 1950s, all this changed with the building of Don Mills, Canada's first mass suburb, on the northern fringe of Toronto. Don Mills emphasized a system of short curving roads in the form of circles and crescents. Initially, this layout was probably meant to convey a sense of privileged exclusivity, although over time it also came to reflect a desire to shield children from the perceived danger of through-traffic. In any case, it made public transit difficult, consigning buses to main arterial roads on the perimeter of the housing subdivision. Don Mills houses were placed on wider lots with larger setbacks from the streets. With no sidewalks, small front porches, and minimal pedestrian traffic (most residents drove to the nearby Don Mills Plaza to shop), the social action shifted to the fenced-in back yards, which were, in any case, favoured by parents, who appreciated being able to keep an eye on their toddlers from the kitchen window. Don Mills was one of the first residential areas in Canada to be planned completely from scratch and built all at once. In contrast to the development pattern in the central city, almost all the servicing costs, including that of a sewage treatment plant along the Don River, were

assumed by the developer, E.P. Taylor. By doing so, Taylor changed the rules of urban development, relegating the municipality to a more passive role and introducing corporate success as a major planning consideration (Sewell, 1993: 95).

With the triumph of Don Mills, the corporate suburb spread rapidly across Canada and the United States. (The United States had already introduced its own early prototype of a planned, mass-produced suburb in Levittown, Long Island, about 30 kilometres from New York City.) Although there were local differences, these first-generation postwar suburbs shared five main characteristics: a peripheral location, relatively low population densities, architectural similarity, a relatively low purchase price for houses, and a fairly high degree of economic and racial homogeneity (Jackson, 1985: 238–43).

"SUBURBANISM AS A WAY OF LIFE"

In the 1950s, the suburbs were routinely disparaged as being sterile social and cultural wastelands where conformity ruled and individual taste and thought were stifled. This notion was given wide exposure in the 1956 bestseller *The Organization Man*, a study of Park Forest, Illinois, about 50 kilometres south of Chicago, by *Fortune* magazine writer William H. Whyte. Suburban dwellers were invariably depicted as living in mass-produced housing that was uniform in design and decoration. This image is bitingly evoked in folk singer Malvina Reynolds's 1950s ditty "Little Boxes" (Reynolds, 1964: 28):

> Little Boxes on the hillside
> Little Boxes made of ticky tacky,
> Little Boxes on the hillside,
> Little Boxes all the same.

Not only was the physical appearance of suburban areas said to be homogeneous, but life there was said to revolve around a "dry-martini culture." During the workweek, fathers commuted in car pools or by rail to jobs at IBM, General Motors, and other corporate giants, while mothers ferried the children around in the family station wagon and socialized at coffee parties. On the weekend, the husbands washed the cars and tended to well-manicured lawns, while the wives shopped for groceries at nearby plazas. At night, couples socialized in one another's homes, around the pool or the barbecue pit.

For sociological researchers, suburbanism represented an important trend. In a much-quoted 1956 article, "Suburbanism as a Way of Life," Sylvia Fava did a take on Louis Wirth's classic 1938 essay. Fava claimed that suburbanites were far more likely than their counterparts in the central city to be both sociable and socially active. Similarly, in a much-cited before–after study of middle-class couples in Toronto who chose to relocate during the early 1970s, Michelson (1973) found that suburban movers increased their involvement with neighbours, while city relocators increased interactions with friends and relatives.

Another key feature of the suburban lifestyle was its emphasis on children and the family. Perhaps the most influential study with regard to the importance of children in suburban communities was that by Seeley and Loosley (1956) in *Crestwood Heights*, a profile of the affluent community of Forest Hill Village in 1950s Toronto. Although Crestwood Heights was more a neighbourhood on the northern edge of the city, its organization around the needs of its children (schools, camps, counselling) was said to be typical of the developing suburbs of the time.

Suburbanism was further depicted as a lifestyle choice rather than strictly an economic decision. City dwellers who packed up and left the central city were said to be embracing a new, family-oriented way of life, seduced by advertisements in the real-estate section of the Saturday newspaper promising "bourgeois utopias" (Fishman, 1987). Not all residents, however, embraced this lifestyle with equal enthusiasm. Women in the suburbs frequently felt cut off from the social and cultural stimulation of the central city with its theatres, art galleries, restaurants, and shopping streets. Sociability in the corporate suburb was restricted to private gatherings in the home or the back yard with one's neighbours. Not surprisingly, a number of researchers found that women were less satisfied than their husbands with their choice of residence, often having a sense of stagnation and isolation despite relatively frequent visiting and entertaining (Michelson, 1973).

Significantly, this lifestyle did not appear to be replicated in working-class suburbs, where people's values and social behaviours remained firmly anchored in blue-collar culture. Berger (1960) refers to the **myth of suburbia**, by which he means a standardized and stereotyped view of the suburbs as uniformly middle-class, homogeneous, conformist, child-centred, female-dominated, and hotbeds of sociability.

It is possible to discern three alternative interpretations of the relationship between suburban residence and lifestyle patterns (McGahan, 1995: 232–36). According to the *structural* interpretation, the environmental and demographic characteristics of the suburb encourage a distinct style of life. For example, by excluding stores and services such as restaurants, bars, and movie theatres from residential neighbourhoods and by discouraging public transit, the Don Mills model promoted a greater reliance on private sociability, as evidenced by the weekday morning coffee klatches and weekend pool parties that came to be identified with suburban life in the 1950s and 1960s.

In contrast, the *selective migration* interpretation denies that the suburban environment exercises any independent effect on behaviour patterns. Rather, it is suggested that those who chose to move to the corporate suburbs after World War II were already primed to embrace **familism**—a lifestyle that places a high value on family living, marriage at a young age, a brief period of childlessness after marriage, and child-centredness of the type that Seeley and his colleagues observed in Crestwood Heights (Bell, 1968: 147).

Finally, the *class and life-cycle* interpretation proposes that what Berger had branded the "suburban myth" was nothing more than a snapshot of middle-class life at mid-century. Today, many of the same characteristics—child-centredness, commuting, backyard culture—can be observed in the second wave of gentrification in the central city. As the corporate suburb matured, it changed appreciably, with a new set of social activities replacing those that had prevailed at an earlier stage in the life cycle of both the suburb and the families who settled there.

Whether it was the Don Mills–style suburb or downtown office towers, the corporate city did not just happen: It was the deliberate product of an alliance between government and business interests. Logan and Molotch (1987) have termed this alliance an **urban-growth machine**, a loosely structured coalition of local economic and political interest groups with a commitment to sustained growth and development. Urban-growth machines can include an extensive cast of players: businesses, property owners, investors and developers, politicians and planners, the media, utilities, cultural institutions (museums, theatres), professional sports teams, labour unions, and even universities. Growth machines pursue a narrow band of interests, sacrificing the sentimental and symbolic value of places—which is associated with jobs, neighbourhood, hometown, and community—in favour of a strict emphasis on land use as an investment and commodity to be bought and sold (Palen, 1995: 20). Although government and business may honestly believe that local communities thrive only if they continue to expand economically, it could also be said that the structure that growth machines impose on urban living gives people a minimum of freedom to live their lives in the corporate city as they would choose (Lorimer, 1978: 220).

THE POSTMODERN CITY

In recent years, a new kind of urban form has appeared on the landscape: the postmodern city. Although there is some debate over what exactly is meant by this term, several aspects do seem clear.

First, the postmodern city is powerfully shaped by the globalization of consumption. In contrast to the industrial city, the areas of which reflected the local content of the neighbourhoods in which they were situated, today's urban landscapes are more likely to embody global tastes, especially those influenced by the entertainment industry. For example, the typical restaurant in the industrial city was small, ethnic, and neighbourhood-based, but the typical restaurant in the postmodern city has an entertainment theme that is recognizable worldwide.

Second, the postmodern city is characteristically fragmented, even chaotic. Elizabeth Wilson (1991: 136) describes it as resembling "a split screen flickering with competing beliefs, cultures and 'stories.'" Geographically and socially split, the postmodern city does not have a single "way of life" of the sort identified by Wirth for the industrial city and Fava for the corporate suburb.

Finally, the postmodern city is characterized by the privatization of public space. Privatization occurs across a wide spectrum of settings, from downtown malls and festival marketplaces to private, "gated" communities on the fringes of the city. Although suburban dwellers have always put a premium on private space, from the enclosed back yard to the drive-in theatre, this value is now washing over the city as a whole, and, in the process, drastically reducing the number of public places where people can come together to shop or socialize (Goldberger, 1996: 139).

In this section, we will examine three overlapping components of the postmodern city: the edge city, the dual city, and the fantasy city. Although each component has a real-life spatial component, none exists in pure form. Instead, they are constructions, formulated by academic researchers or journalists, that help us visualize an important dimension of the globalized, privatized, and fragmented postmodern city.

THE EDGE CITY

Although they differed significantly in their patterns of housing, transportation, and shopping, the industrial city and the corporate city displayed more or less the same spatial configuration: an urban core containing the bulk of the office space, cultural institutions, and factories, and a ring of suburbs where much of the more affluent middle class resided. Even with the growth of shopping centres and industrial parks in the 1950s and 1960s, the lion's share of jobs and services remained within the city itself, and suburbanites were, by definition, daily commuters.

During the past quarter-century, however, this traditional pattern has been turned inside out with the rapid growth of **edge cities** (Garreau, 1991). Situated in exurbia—the rural residential area around the suburbs within commuting range of the city—these edge cities have no dominant single core or definable set of boundaries; they are typically "clusters of malls, office developments and entertainment complexes that rise where major highways cross or converge" (Fishman, 1990: 18). Some edge cities are expansions of existing satellite cities, but others sprout up in unincorporated townships, lacking clearly definable borders and legal status as places (Palen, 1995: 187).

What has led to the growth of edge cities? Leinberger and Lockwood (1986) offer five reasons for their recent emergence. First, there has been a major shift in North American economies from manufacturing to a service and knowledge base. One result of this shift is that middle-class employees are now more willing to live near where they work than they used to be when jobs were located in factories that were dirty, noisy, and unattractive. An example of the older pattern can be found in Ontario's steel industry, where the managers and executives at Stelco and Dofasco traditionally settled on the other side of the Skyway Bridge in Burlington, while the mill workers remained in Hamilton. In contrast, Kanata, the outer suburban location of Ottawa's microchip computer industry, is solidly middle class.

Second, there have been significant changes in transportation patterns that favour trucks and cars over fixed-line carriers—subways, streetcars, and trains. As a result, urban facilities have scattered over the exurban landscape, unfettered by the requirement of locating along established transportation corridors.

Third, recent advances in telecommunications technology have reduced the necessity for offices to locate downtown in close physical proximity. Some types of businesses—such as stock brokerages and banks—still prefer to be close to one another and to central city services. But the tremendous growth of technology, such as fax machines, cellular phones, and e-mail, has geographically freed many employees whose linkages to the workplace are now activated on the road or from home offices.

Fourth, as it has become increasingly expensive to operate in the city, offices, industries, and professional practitioners (lawyers, accountants, etc.) have pulled up their roots and moved to cheaper locations in exurbia. Among other things, parking is more plentiful and less expensive out of the city.

Fifth, the coming of age of dual-income, "baby-boom" families with one or two children has meant that people's lives are increasingly governed by considerations of time, convenience, and efficiency. The clustering of offices, shopping centres, and recreational facilities at the juncture of exurban highways meets the needs of this subpopulation, the members of which have little time left in their lives to commute downtown to shop, eat, or be entertained.

Edge cities have been of particular interest to urban sociologists because they are neither suburbs nor centralized cities but a hybrid that incorporates elements of each. Unlike the typical suburb, which is primarily residential, edge cities contain many of the functions of the traditional city—shopping, office space, housing, and entertainment facilities. Also, in contrast to suburbanites, who commute to work in the central city by rail or car, edge-city residents are inclined to live and work in the same geographic area. Commuting now means driving to an adjoining suburb or exurb, rather than heading downtown.

This can be seen in the "905 belt" surrounding Metro Toronto, where a number of areas now function as "magnets." That is, more people travel to jobs there each day than journey out of the community to jobs elsewhere in the greater Toronto area. Finally, in contrast to the typical suburb, which lacks a well-developed infrastructure of sports, entertainment, and cultural facilities, the edge city is increasingly the site of a burgeoning number of performing arts centres, sports palaces, and entertainment complexes.

Nevertheless, it would be wrong to think that there are no real differences between edge cities and the older cities. Unlike the industrial city, the edge city lacks a single centre. In the former, it was always possible to start downtown and eventually reach the outer boundaries of the city. In contrast, the spatial logic of the edge city dictates that centres and boundaries are not needed. Instead, the edge city is made up of three overlapping types of socioeconomic networks: household networks, networks of consumption, and networks of production. Each of these runs on the guiding principle of convenience. Two-income families with children, who make up the largest demographic segment of the edge-city population, are increasingly pressed for time and, as a result, frequently create their own "personal cities" out of the destinations they can reach within a manageable time (Fishman, 1990).

THE DUAL CITY

With the edge city increasingly becoming the occupational, residential, and commercial centre for the middle classes, what has become of urban downtowns? The central city, some analysts suggest, has become balkanized between two starkly different realities that are spatially discrete and that have only the name of the city and some public places in common. Situated just blocks or streets away from one another, the "city of despair and squalor" and the "city of hope and splendour" are light years apart. This split reality has been called the "dual city."

The term **dual city** has come to refer to the urban expression of two increasingly divergent streams in the global economy. On the one hand, there is an information-based, formal economy rooted in financial services, telecommunications, and the microchip. Typically, those who are part of this upper-tier informational city live in a world of computer software, fax machines, mobile telephones, and Internet surfing. Residentially, they can be found in "gentrified" niches of the inner city (gentrification is discussed below) or in exclusive suburbs, where they isolate themselves both socially and geographically from the rest of the city. In Castells's (1989) description, these spaces constitute a microsociety with their own separate circuit of leisure, lifestyle, and services.

On the other hand, juxtaposed to the informational city, there is an "informal economy" that has been excluded from the main loop. Residents here rely not on high-technology communications, but on face-to-face social networks, usually established on the basis of shared race and ethnicity. People are engaged in a wide range of activities, from labouring in immigrant sweatshops in the clothing trade to offering such services as furniture making, home renovation, and auto repairs (Gordon and Sassen, 1992). Although this informal economy cannot be equated with urban poverty per se, its participants stand relatively little chance of ever penetrating the upper-tier informational economy.

Gentrification

In the 1970s and 1980s, considerable attention was paid by urban researchers to the phenomenon of **gentrification** in the dual city. By gentrification, we mean the transformation of working-class housing into fashionable downtown neighbourhoods by middle- and upper-income newcomers. Gentrification is neither anticipated nor accounted for by the

ecological growth models discussed earlier. Similarly, it runs counter to predictions about the mass flight to the suburbs that dominated urban sociology in the 1950s and 1960s. A comparison of the suburban lifestyle and the postmodern urban lifestyle as typified by gentrification is set out in Table 15.2.

Four primary explanations for gentrification have been advanced (Ley, 1991: 182–85). First, demographic changes led to gentrification in the 1970s and 1980s. At this time, the baby boomers who were born and raised in the suburbs began to look for housing of their own. Facing high demand levels and a shortage of supply, they turned to inner-city housing, which was cheap but in dire need of rehabilitation. They opposed demolition, favoured by urban-renewal advocates. Unlike suburban settlers in the previous period, these urban migrants were childless and career-oriented. This meant that schools, playgrounds, and parks were not their major concerns and they were happy with smaller housing units without the big back yards and basement recreation rooms that were characteristic of Don Mills–type housing. Since many of these young professionals worked downtown, they were willing to trade off space for proximity to their places of employment and to downtown cultural and entertainment facilities.

Second, gentrification may be accounted for by economic changes related to the flow of capital in and out of the housing market. In this view, gentrification functions as a "back to the city movement by capital not people" (Smith, 1979). As we have seen, in the

TABLE 15.2   COMPARISON OF SUBURBAN AND POSTMODERN URBAN LIFESTYLES

	SUBURBAN	POSTMODERN URBAN (AS PER GENTRIFICATION)
Neighbourhood social involvement	Deliberate and sustained	Incidental
Lifestyle focus	Family	Consumerism
Typical activities	Home activities (gardening, entertaining)	Dining out, shopping
Typical occupation of resident	Middle manager	Architect, designer
Housing type	Split-level, detached	Victorian, semidetached
Social composition	Class-exclusive	Socially and culturally diverse
Ideology	Anti-urban	Pro-urban

SOURCE: John A. Hannigan, "The Postmodern City: A New Urbanization?" *Current Sociology, 43* (1) (1995), p. 180.

1950s and 1960s, financial capital flowed into the building of the suburbs under the guidance of governments that viewed the construction of large-scale projects by development companies as the fastest, most efficient way of coping with the pressures created by the baby boom. Developers were encouraged by an array of incentives: tax breaks, government-backed mortgages, guarantees, and insurance with low down payments. By the 1970s, the profit levels in suburban building had begun to shrink, and capital flow switched back to the urban centre to take advantage of the **rent gap**—that is, the difference between the current value of land in its "depressed" state and the value that could be charged given a higher or better land use (Smith and LeFaivre, 1984).

Third, middle-class newcomers to the central city arrived in search of a lifestyle that was more distinctive and cosmopolitan than that available within the constraints of suburban conformity. In the central city, they could express a distinctive aesthetic and style of consumption, characterized by a dislike of mass-produced goods and a penchant for objects and buildings from a bygone era, notably the Victorian age (Filion, 1991: 554). This new lifestyle also extended to the surrounding neighbourhood, which filled up with wine bars, California-style restaurants, franchise coffee outlets, and trendy boutiques.

A fourth explanation of gentrification looks to the kind of changes in the urban economy that were described at the beginning of the section on the dual city. With the tremendous boom in jobs in advanced service industries, such as those connected to the "globalized information economy," there has been a dramatic increase in the number of well-paying occupations located downtown. This growth has, in turn, produced a pool of middle-class workers interested in trying the experience of inner-city living.

It should be emphasized, however, that the image of gentrifiers as returning from the suburbs is false; gentrification is, in fact, a "stay in the city" rather than a "back to the city" movement (Wittberg, 1992: 27). Ley (1991: 186) cites data from Canadian cities that indicate that only 2–3 percent of a sample of households moving into Toronto's Don Vale neighbourhood between 1966 and 1976 originated in the suburbs. Similarly, a high percentage of those in Ottawa's Centretown (55 percent), Vancouver's False Creek (78 percent), and Montreal's Milton-Parc, Plateau Mont-Royal, and Papineau (79 percent)

neighbourhoods had previous addresses in the central city. This research suggests that gentrifiers are devoted to an inner-city lifestyle, even when they have reached a stage in the life cycle where one might have predicted that they would move to the suburbs.

Among those most likely to settle in gentrified areas of the inner city are women. Summarizing the empirical evidence available from these studies, Warde (1991: 228) lists the following as typical of gentrified enclaves:

> a female population increasing faster than the male population; an unusually high proportion of young and single women; very high proportions of women in professional and technical occupations; high levels of academic credentials; a high proportion of dual-earner households, but few families; presence of young professional women; and the postponement of marriage and childbearing.

Why do gentrified neighbourhoods appeal to these groups of women cited by Warde? One explanation is that inner-city communities help relieve some of the pressures of women's dual roles as both members of the work force and as mothers of young children. The advantages include relatively cheap housing, public transit, and readily available child-care and social-support systems. Travel time is an especially important consideration. Female gentrifiers tend to have jobs in downtown office buildings, so inner-city housing allows them to lead their lives on a tight schedule, with services such as shopping, schools, daycare, and medical clinics located nearby. In contrast, suburban residence requires long daily commutes, especially when the weather is bad, as well as the devotion of a good share of one's leisure time travelling to widely scattered stores and services. Gentrification thus represents an environmental solution to a potential set of social problems (Rose, 1984: 66).

Private Communities

In recent years, another phenomenon—the rise of private communities—has embraced an even greater number of middle-class homeowners than has gentrification. Located in the newer suburbs and in edge cities, private communities compete with central cities for residents, offering as incentives a homogeneous middle-class population, physical security, stable housing values, local control, and freedom from exposure to the social problems of the inner city (McKenzie, 1989: 257).

In the United States, nearly 4 million residents are estimated to live in closed-off, gated communities, and another 28 million in areas governed by private community associations. This makes private communities the fastest-growing residential communities in that country (Egan, 1995). Of all the new housing developments in California, as many as one-third are thought to be gated communities (Kleniewski, 1997: 207). Growth has been less rapid in Canada, but private communities have begun to multiply in some areas, notably around Toronto and in the Okanagan Valley in British Columbia. Typical of these are Northtown Casitas, a gated condominium community built on the site of a failed indoor shopping centre, and Swan Lake Village, an "adult-lifestyle village" in Markham. The latter, a retirement community, employs a round-the-clock security guard at the controlled-entry front gate and a second guard who roams throughout the settlement looking for intruders. Northtown Casitas is no less security-oriented, with a gatehouse complete with smoked windows, surveillance cameras, and a personally encoded suite-intrusion alarm system to register any incursion by "outside elements" (Lorinc, 1996).

The Fortress City

At the same time as middle-class home-owners are barricading themselves in private gated communities, the public–private partnerships that increasingly dictate what happens to postmodern cities are said to be systematically privatizing and militarizing public space in order to secure it against the homeless and the poor. Emerging from such alliances is the "fortress city" in which the urban disadvantaged are isolated socially and spatially from office workers, tourists, and suburban day-trippers.

The fortress city has been described in *City of Quartz*, Mike Davis's (1990) sweeping examination of present-day Los Angeles. LA, Davis notes, is a city obsessed with urban security. What passes for a downtown, a series of billion-dollar, block-square megastructures around Bunker Hill, has been insulated by removing almost all pedestrian linkages to the poor immigrant neighbourhoods that surround it

on every side. To make public facilities and spaces as unlivable as possible for the homeless and the poor, the city is engaged in a virtual war against them. Tactics and defences include the establishment of barrel-shaped, "bum-proof" bus benches that make sleep impossible, the random deployment of outdoor overhead sprinklers in Skid Row Park to discourage overnight camping, and the removal of public toilets and washrooms in areas patronized by vagrants. To secure its garbage, one popular seafood restaurant has spent $12 000 to build a "bag-lady-proof trash cage" out of three-quarter-inch steel rods with alloy locks and vicious curved spikes. To cope with a burgeoning inmate population, law-enforcement agencies are venturing into carceral development, building downtown jails and prisons designed by celebrity architects to look like hotel-convention centres or office buildings, thus camouflaging their real purpose.

Nor is the fortress city restricted to Los Angeles. In the late 1970s, Henry Ford II persuaded the heads of 50 large corporations in Detroit to put equity capital into the Renaissance Center, a $357 million megaproject along the Detroit River opposite Windsor, Ontario. Poorly planned, the hotel-office venture resembled a castle with virtually invisible pedestrian entrances. It was cut off from downtown Detroit by a wide road and railroad tracks. It stands, Frieden and Sagalyn (1989: 222) observe, as a "symbol of isolation: an extreme case of a self-contained, inward-facing complex, surrounded by fortress-like two-story walls covering the heating and ventilating equipment."

The clash between the guardians of the fortress city and the urban poor was recently highlighted in the "Tent City Eviction" in Toronto. Tent City refers to a five-acre plot of polluted, abandoned industrial land near the shore of Lake Ontario. For five years, as many as 110 residents had been squatting on the waterfront property (owned by big-box building-supplies store Home Depot), making it Canada's largest homeless community. After a high profile story in the *New York Times* described the site, which seemed to be increasingly hosting prostitution and drug-dealing activities, Home Depot abandoned any further pursuit of plans to erect, safe affordable housing and sent in private security guards accompanied by police to evict the squatters. Guards were posted and the former residents given 72 hours to retrieve their belongings.

A homeless person carrying her cat is evicted from her dwelling in the shantytown on Toronto's waterfront on Tuesday, September 24, 2002. Home Depot, the company that owns the land, requested that police remove the squatters.
SOURCE: CP Picture Archive/Frank Gunn.

THE FANTASY CITY

The third and final component of the postmodern city is called the **fantasy city**. Its planning, design, and identity reflect the influence of the exurban theme park, most notably Disney World in Orlando, Florida. Theme-park cities are both a product and a part of a rapidly developing **symbolic economy**— that is, an economy based not on manufacturing and selling tangible goods, such as cars and refrigerators, but on the marketing of images and representations that derive from popular culture and entertainment.

Symbolic economies and their keenest promoters—large retail and entertainment giants, such as Disney, Universal Studios, Warner Bros., Sony, and Nike—have become so important to the future of contemporary cities because they are regarded as the best and, in some cases, the only chance for reversing the economic decline associated with de-industrialization. That is, cities are having to cope with the consequences of declining automotive, steel, textile, and other manufacturing industries, as a result of shrinking markets, increased foreign com-petition, or relocation of existing factories to regions of the world in which wages are low, unions are weak, and environmental regulations are lax. Local growth machines that once engaged in "smokestack chasing"—offering tax holidays and other incentives in order to attract industry—today seek out "mega-events" (Olympic Games, Expos, the Super Bowl), tourist attractions, and professional sports teams. By doing so, they hope to lure out-of-town visitors, especially those attending conventions and trade shows.

Another important part of the planning process of fantasy cities is the creation of "place images" by which cities become known worldwide. Although some cities have distinctive images of considerable vintage (e.g., New Orleans, Paris), many of today's urban centres have found it necessary to invent a new set of attributes and then market them aggressively. Among the best known of these are Manchester, England, and Glasgow, Scotland, both of which have attempted with some degree of success to discard their images as dirty, industrial cities and substitute a new identity as centres of European culture.

The first large amusement park in this country was Canada's Wonderland (now called Paramount Canada's Wonderland). Its centrepiece is a 50-metre artificial mountain. It is surrounded by several areas, each with a different fantasy theme.
SOURCE: Image reproduced by permission of Paramount Canada's Wonderland.

"Comeback cities" in Canada and the United States have been especially attracted by the possibilities of sports and themed entertainment as identity enhancers. Two leading examples are Baltimore and Cleveland, both of which have built highly acclaimed neotraditional baseball stadiums on the edge of inner-city neighbourhoods, as well as an ever-expanding infrastructure of other attractions, such as Harborplace, a waterfront festival market (Baltimore), and the Rock and Roll Hall of Fame (Cleveland). Other cities have looked to casino gambling, hoping to reinvent themselves as mini-versions of Las Vegas, which still has one of the fastest-growing economies in the United States.

As they did the corporate suburbs of the 1950s, many urban commentators, critics, and researchers regard fantasy cities with some alarm. Sorkin (1992: xiii), for example, cites three characteristics that give them a "sinister" twist.

First, the fantasy city is characterized by despatialization—that is, the severing of all natural ties between the city and local and physical geography. Whereas a community used to be unique because of its indigenous landscape, urban place images today are both generic and modular, capable of being inserted anywhere and everywhere. For example, the *Wall Street Journal* recently profiled the Irish Pub Co., a design and construction business that has exported 1000 "genuine" new Irish pubs to 35 countries. Each completely finished pub is delivered with everything from beer taps to old whisky bottles for decoration, and comes in a choice of five models: Victorian Dublin, Gaelic, Irish Brewery Pub, Irish Pub Shop, and Irish Country Cottage (Goldsmith, 1996). As such products spread globally, local space is departicularized—that is, stripped of its unique qualities that make it both distinctive and human (Hannigan, 1995: 160).

A second sinister aspect of the fantasy city is pervasive surveillance and security. Festival marketplaces, for example, may appear to be open to all, but in fact are meant only for affluent tourists and suburban visitors. To insulate them from surrounding neighbourhoods that are considered unsafe, developers have put in place a sophisticated security system, modelled in part on that used in Disney World.

And, finally, the fantasy city is a city of simulations. That is, urban cityscapes are deliberately constructed so as to replicate reality, but without any of the warts to be found in the original. A good illustration of this is City Walk, an urban entertainment centre at the Universal City complex in California. A "pseudo-city" street of shops and entertainment, City Walk thoroughly fuses—or confuses—the urban "real" and the entertainment "ideal." One is left asking, as Goldberger (1996: 141) does: Is it a city street masquerading as a theme park, or a theme park masquerading as a city street?

The various features that distinguish the industrial city, the corporate city, and the postmodern city are compared in Table 15.3.

TABLE 15.3 INDUSTRIAL CITY, CORPORATE CITY, AND POSTMODERN CITY COMPARED			
	INDUSTRIAL CITY	**CORPORATE CITY**	**POSTMODERN CITY**
Urban economy depends on	Manufacturing	Financial and retail	Information; leisure services; entertainment
Key retailing institution	Department store	Shopping centre	Urban entertainment centre
Class distance maintained by	Cost of real estate	Physical separation of suburb and central city	Privatization of urban space
Where the middle class lives	Central city (outer edge)	Suburbs	Edge cities
Urban critics concerned with	Overcrowding; social disorganization	Mass confirmity (suburbs); decline of downtowns	"Disneyfication" of the metropolis

SUMMARY

1. Cities are defined as relatively large, dense, permanent settlements in which the majority of the residents do not produce their own food.

2. Until the Industrial Revolution, cities were incapable of supporting more than about 5 percent of the total societal population, largely because of the absence of agricultural surpluses great enough to feed a huge urban population.

3. The best-known urban-growth model in the social sciences is Ernest Burgess's concentric-zone scheme in which the expansion of cities is conceptualized as a successive series of rings and circles, each of which segregates a distinct resident population and type of land use. Other more recent explanations favour patterns of urban growth resembling pie-shaped wedges that develop along transportation routes or multiple nodes of economic activity, each with its own nucleus.

4. In contrast to the rise of the city in Western Europe and North America, cities of the South have grown at a much faster rate than the industrial economy. The resulting "overurbanization" has accelerated problems of poverty and unemployment, which are rooted in basic structural inequalities and uneven development.

5. The corporate city of the 1950s and 1960s was the product of an urban-growth machine in which a coalition of politicians, planners, real-estate developers, business people, and other interest groups joined forces in order to engineer economic development and progress. The main products of this alliance were (a) the corporate suburbs, (b) shopping centres, (c) suburban industrial parks, (d) downtown office towers, and (e) high-rise apartment buildings.

6. Three alternative theories—structural, selective migration, and class and life-cycle stage—have been proposed to explain the relationship between suburban residence and lifestyle patterns. Although all these theories have merit, the suburban way of life observed by many researchers in the 1950s and 1960s appears to have been a unique product of a particular time and place.

7. In recent decades, the contemporary city has mirrored and incorporated a bifurcated global economy. On the one hand, there is an upper-tier informational city whose members work in jobs related to financial services, telecommunications, and high technology and live either in gentrified downtown neighbourhoods or in private communities on the edge of the city. On the other hand, there is an informal economy whose members are excluded from the informational city and who live in ethnic or racial ghettos that are often, but not necessarily, located in the inner city. Together, the informational city and the informal economy constitute the dual city whose residents have little in common with each other.

8. One of the defining characteristics of the postmodern city is the increasing privatization of public spaces. This is manifested in three ways: (a) the growth of private enclosed places, such as malls, festival marketplaces, and themed entertainment complexes, that offer pale imitations of urbanity; (b) the booming growth of gated communities and other private residential enclaves where outsiders are not welcome; and (c) the construction of fortress cities where tourists and other affluent consumers are kept in while the homeless and the urban poor are kept out.

QUESTIONS TO CONSIDER

1. Are edge cities real cities? Support your answer by including examples from both Canadian and U.S. urban areas.

2. Map out your own "personal city" by keeping a record for a full week of all the trips you take to work, school, shopping, medical and dental appointments, friends' houses, restaurants and night clubs, and so on. What proportion of these trips occur within your neighbourhood? Within the community in which you live? Across the wider metropolitan area?

3. To what extent does the big city in which you live or which you live closest to constitute a dual city?

4. How has suburban life been depicted in the mass media? Think, for example, of popular television series, such as *Clueless* and *The Simpsons*. To what extent do these depictions support the "myth of suburbia"?

5. Locate the Statistics Canada Web site (http://www.statcan.ca) on the Internet. What kinds of questions about cities could you answer from this data source?

GLOSSARY

A **city** is a relatively large, dense, permanent settlement in which the majority of the residents do not produce their own food.

The **concentric-zone model** is the classic urban-growth model proposed by Ernest Burgess in which the expansion of cities is visualized as a successive series of concentric rings or circles, each of which contains a distinct resident population and type of land use. As social groups become more established and prosperous, they move farther away from the city centre.

The **corporate city** refers to the perception and organization of the city as a vehicle for capital accumulation. The corporate city contains five major elements: the corporate suburb, high-rise apartments, suburban industrial parks, downtown office towers, and shopping malls.

The **dual city** refers to the juxtaposition and mutual isolation of an upper-tier information city and a lower-tier city. Members of the upper tier work in jobs related to financial services, telecommunications, and high technology and live in gentrified neighbourhoods and private communities on the edge of the city. A lower tier of people work in low-technology jobs and live in ethnic or racial ghettos.

Edge cities are self-contained entertainment, shopping, and office areas that have emerged in formerly suburban areas or just beyond the fringe of suburbia.

Environmental-opportunity theory is the idea that people actively choose where they want to live depending on the extent to which a particular place either meshes with or constrains their preferred lifestyle.

Familism is a lifestyle that places a high value on family living, marriage at a young age, a brief period of childlessness after marriage, and child-centredness.

The **fantasy city** is a new form of urban development based on the marketing of sports and entertainment brands and images and modelled after Las Vegas and the Disney theme parks.

Gentrification refers to the transformation of working-class housing to fashionable downtown neighbourhoods by middle- and upper-income migrants.

The **multiple-nuclei model** is a model of urban growth characterized by a series of growth centres—retail, wholesale, residential—each representing the concentration of a specific function or activity within the urban economy.

The **myth of suburbia** is a standardized and stereotyped view of the suburbs as uniformly middle-class, homogeneous, child-centred and female-dominated, conformist, and a hotbed of sociability and local participation.

Overurbanization is the process whereby the population of urban areas is growing faster than the urban economy, services, and resources can absorb. This is especially evident in primate cities of the South.

Peri-urbanization is a process of urbanization observed in Asia, Africa, and Latin America whereby the rural and the urban have become blurred in unplanned settlements on the outskirts of large cities. One instance of this is the *desakota* in Indonesia.

Rent gap refers to the difference between the current value of land in its "depressed" state and the value that could be charged given a higher or better land use.

The **sector model** is a model of urban growth that proposes that the city expands outward from the centre in a series of sectors or wedges along major transportation arteries, such as highways and railroad lines.

The **symbolic economy** is an economy based on images and representations derived from popular culture and entertainment.

Urban bias refers to uneven investment and development that favour urban over rural areas.

The **urban-growth machine** is a loosely structured coalition of local economic and political interest groups that hold in common a commitment to sustained growth and development.

Urban primacy is a situation in which one metropolitan centre, usually the capital city, is considerably larger and more economically dominant than any of the others.

SUGGESTED READING

Drew, Bettina. (1998). *Crossing the Expendable Landscape*. Saint Paul, MN: Graywolf Press. A thoughtful travelogue through the postmodern mallified American landscape by a noted essayist. Includes stops at

Celebration, Disney's "new urbanist" community in Florida, and Branson, Missouri, a town whose economy depends completely on country music and entertainment.

Hannigan, John. (1998). *Fantasy City: Pleasure and Profit in the Postmodern City*. London and New York: Routledge. A thoroughly researched and comprehensive account of the rise of the city as theme park in the 1980s and 1990s. Hannigan argues that megaplex cinemas, themed restaurants, casinos, and other large-scale entertainment spaces allow leisure and conviviality without real social interaction.

McGahan, Peter. (1995). *Urban Sociology in Canada*, 3rd ed. Toronto: Harcourt Brace. Still the best urban-sociology text on the Canadian market. Note especially the discussions of urban migration, immigration, and ethnic residential segregation.

Palen, John J. (1995). *The Suburbs*. New York: McGraw Hill. A concise, information-packed, and up-to-date overview of the suburban experience, by the author of *The Urban World*. It includes a useful discussion of edge cities and private communities.

Sewell, John. (1993). *The Shape of the City: Toronto Struggles with Modern Planning*. Toronto: University of Toronto Press. A generously illustrated history of urban growth and planning in Canada's largest city, by a well-known activist, author, and former mayor of Toronto.

CHAPTER SIXTEEN

SOCIOLOGY AND THE ENVIRONMENT

In this chapter you will learn that:

- A major focus of the sociology of the environment is the conflict between environmentalists and their opponents in industry and science.

- Support for environmentalism has remained constant for nearly two decades, with a majority of people generally supportive of environmental values and a young, well-educated, urban, liberal group leading the movement for environmental change.

- In order to mobilize the reluctant majority, organizers of the environmental movement develop and spread interpretations of events that play up the possibility of environmental crises.

- The goals of conserving resources, reducing pollution, and restricting population increase are especially difficult to achieve in the Third World.

- At the community level, willingness to act on environmental problems rises as trust in authority figures declines.

- Environmental problems are often contested on the basis of acceptable risk; the definition of what is acceptable risk is strongly influenced by the distribution of power in society, with more powerful individuals and groups better able to determine what is and what is not risky.

JOHN HANNIGAN

UNIVERSITY OF TORONTO

INTRODUCTION

During the winter of 1994, hundreds of millions of television viewers worldwide watched the Winter Olympic Games in Lillehammer, Norway. The Lillehammer Olympics will be remembered not only for the media blitz that accompanied the figure-skating rivalry between Nancy Kerrigan and Tonya Harding, but also because they were the first "Green Games," at which the issue of environmental protection was placed front and centre. Among other measures, private cars were banned from routes into the Olympic area, the cutlery and plates at Olympic sites were made from biodegradable potato starch, and a special fuel was developed for the Olympic flame to reduce the amount of pollution from the symbolic fire (*The Globe and Mail*, Feb. 11, 1994: A1).

In this chapter, I examine how sociology has dealt with the rising global crescendo of environmental awareness, concern, and action that was symbolized by Norway's Green Olympics. After briefly discussing the traditional lack of concern with the environment in sociological theory and research, I outline the basic value conflict in contemporary societies between those who favour unlimited economic expansion and technological solutions to human problems and those who embrace a new "ecological" view of the world, in which nature is accorded a central place. Next, I review theory and research in the four principal areas of sociological inquiry relating to the environment (Buttel, 1987): (1) environmental attitudes, concern, and behaviour; (2) the environmental movement; (3) the political economy of the environment; and (4) environmental risk and risk assessment. I conclude by arguing that it is important to deal with the environment from a "social-constructionist" perspective in order to bring more sociology into the sociological study of the environment.

TOWARD ENVIRONMENTAL SOCIOLOGY

In contrast to some other social sciences, notably anthropology and geography, sociology's interest in the environment is of relatively recent vintage, stretching back only about three decades. There are several reasons for this neglect (Dunlap and Catton, 1983).

First, for the early-twentieth-century pioneers of sociology, the term *environment* came to mean some-

One focus of environmental sociology is the conflict between environmentalist and mainstream views. According to the mainstream view, people have the unalienable right to dominate nature, even if that involves polluting the environment, as this McDonnell Douglas plant does.
SOURCE: Dick Hemingway.

thing quite different from our physical surroundings. In order to carve out a distinctive place for sociology as a new academic discipline, Émile Durkheim and the other founders of the field downplayed the role of biological and physical factors in influencing human affairs while at the same time elevating the importance of "social facts," such as norms, groups, and institutions. In accounting for the emergence of a wide range of behaviours, from juvenile delinquency to racism, sociologists opted for explanations that framed these behaviours in terms of "nurture" rather than "nature."

A second explanation for sociology's reluctance to embrace the study of the environment concerns sociologists' own view of technology, natural resources, and human progress. In the past, most sociologists shared the assumption of the general public that the world would see steady gains in material progress, fuelled by an apparently unlimited availability of natural resources such as coal, lumber, and water. From this perspective, technology functioned as the linchpin of economic development, allowing humans to overcome the challenges presented by hostile habitats such as jungles, swamps, and deserts. This **human-exceptionalism paradigm** featured the ideals of steadily evolving social progress, increasing prosperity and material comfort, and class mobility for all segments of society. There was little room in this worldview for sociological attention to the environmental "costs" of growth—pollution, health hazards in the workplace, and the loss of diversity in plant and animal species. Nor was there much consideration given to the constraints that might be imposed on further economic expansion by declining resources, the exhaustion of nutrients in the soil, and the destruction of natural ecosystems.

By the early 1970s, stimulated by increased societal attention to urban decay, pollution, overpopulation, resource shortages, and so on, a number of sociologists began at last to study environmental issues. In the first comprehensive review of the emergence of environmental sociology as a distinct area of inquiry, Dunlap and Catton (1979) distinguished between a "sociology of environmental issues" and "environmental sociology." The former, they observed, was concerned primarily with environmentally related phenomena, such as resource-management problems in wildland recreation areas or the origins, membership, and beliefs of the environmental movement. The latter focused on "the physical environment as a factor that may influence (or be influenced by) social behavior" (Dunlap and Catton, 1979: 255). This suggests that the environment can function as a contextual, an independent, or a dependent variable—that is, as background, cause, or effect.

Today, "environmental sociology" has become a catchall for the study of all social aspects of the environment. This has both advantages and disadvantages. On the plus side, it has propelled sociological inquiry into a number of important new areas—for example, studying public opposition to, and mobilization against, toxic wastes. At the same time, the very breadth of the field today has made it difficult to assemble a cohesive body of work built on strong theoretical foundations. Rather than emerging from a central core, the sociological study of the environment has developed from multiple nuclei, each reflecting a different philosophical position and a corresponding research agenda. This tendency has been exacerbated by the decision of some authors, journals, and organizations to consider both the natural and

"Say, we must be nearer civilization than we thought. This is oil!"

the human-built environments under the same umbrella. Furthermore, some terms—notably, *social ecology*—have come to acquire several very different meanings, depending on the branch of environmental sociology to which the researcher claims allegiance. One unifying element, however, is the widely shared recognition of the existence of a key value conflict in contemporary society between those who hold an "environmentalist" view of the world and those who do not.

ENVIRONMENTAL VALUE CONFLICT

Values, the most abstract level of culture, are guideposts that help us to sort out the choices we make in life. Although the vast majority of the Canadian population may be in agreement on some values (freedom, humanitarianism), other values are more controversial.

A central focus for many sociologists interested in the environment is the value cleavage between environmentalists and their opponents. At the core of this disagreement is the long-accepted notion that the environment is something to be actively used and exploited. Many of the key values that have governed North American life—activism, achievement, progress, pursuit of the good life, materialism—permit this orientation toward the environment (Turner, 1981: 87). Environmentalists, in contrast, support a different value orientation, one that advocates a more passive, less manipulative approach to nature.

How environmentalists differ from the mainstream population has been most explicitly set out by British sociologist Stephen Cotgrove (1982). Cotgrove lays out two conflicting paradigms (a *paradigm* is a type of social lens through which we view the world)—the **dominant paradigm** and the **alternative environmental paradigm** (see Table 16.1).

The dominant paradigm is anchored by two core values: the moral imperative of material-wealth creation and the moral conviction that humans have the inalienable right to dominate nature and harness the environment to that end. All of our major institutions reflect the widespread acceptance of this paradigm. Governments at all levels operate ministries, consulates, and trade offices that have a mandate to promote commerce and attract foreign investment.

University business schools run programs in "entrepreneurship." The media act as cheerleaders, linking political competence and achievement with an expanding economy and job creation. Economic growth carries with it a number of supplementary values: the view that society is best organized on a large-scale, centralized basis; respect for authority; the ascendancy of law and order; and confidence in science and technology.

Allied with this moral imperative of material wealth is the conviction that humans have a right and even a responsibility to dominate nature. Progress is interpreted as the increasing encroachment of civilization on jungles, deserts, frozen tundra, and other "wild" geographic environments. History, as it has been taught in our schools, is an account of how the explorers, missionaries, traders, and industrialists rolled back the frontier, "tamed" nature, and brought prosperity to "virgin" lands. Typically, one popular Hollywood epic of the 1960s was titled *How the West Was Won*. The great achievements of the last two centuries, including the opening of the Panama Canal, the completion of the Canadian transcontinental railway, and the landing of astronauts on the moon, all represent a triumph by science and industry over natural hazards and barriers.

The alternative environmental paradigm categorically rejects both of the pillars of enterprise culture (Cotgrove, 1982: 28–29):

> Not only do [environmentalists] challenge the importance attached to material and economic goals, they by contrast give much higher priority to the realization of nonmaterial values—to social relationships and community, to the exercise of human skills and capacities and to increased participation in decisions that affect our daily lives.... They have little confidence in science and technology to come up with a technological fix to solve the problems of material and energy shortages. And this is in part rooted in a different view of nature, which stresses the delicate balance of ecological systems and possible irreversible damage which may result from the interventions of high technology.

Adherents of the alternative environmental paradigm value the natural environment for its own sake,

TABLE 16.1   COUNTER-PARADIGMS OF THE ENVIRONMENT

	DOMINANT PARADIGM	ALTERNATIVE ENVIRONMENTAL PARADIGM
CORE VALUES	Material (economic growth) Natural environment valued as resource Domination over nature	Nonmaterial (self-actualization) Natural environment intrinsically valued Harmony with nature
ECONOMY	Market forces Risk and reward Rewards for achievement Differentials Individual self-help	Public interest Safety Income related to need Egalitarian Collective/social provision
POLITY	Authoritative structure 　(experts influential) Hierarchical Law and order	Participative structure (citizen/ 　worker involvement) Nonhierarchical Liberation
SOCIETY	Centralized Large-scale Associational Ordered	Decentralized Small-scale Communal Flexible
NATURE	Ample reserves Nature hostile/neutral Environment controllable	Earth's resources limited Nature benign Nature delicately balanced
KNOWLEDGE	Confidence in science and technology Rationality of means Separation of fact/value, thought/feeling	Limits to science Rationality of ends Integration of fact/value, thought/feeling

SOURCE: S.F. Cotgrove, *Catastrophe or Cornucopia: The Environment, Politics, and the Future* (Chichester, UK: John Wiley & Sons, 1982). Copyright John Wiley & Sons Limited. Reproduced with permission.

thus questioning the human right to domination. The earth's resources, they claim, are limited and must therefore be conserved. Drawing on the insights of the economist E.F. Schumacher (1973), they believe that "small is beautiful." In this view, society should adopt small-scale, decentralized economic and political structures that are in harmony with nature.

The value conflict just described arches over a wide spectrum of issues and problems related to sociology and the environment. It is, for example, at the core of the dispute over commercial logging of the old-growth forests of Vancouver Island and the Lake Temagami region of northern Ontario. It infuses the continuing debate over world population growth as a primary factor contributing to environmental degradation. It helps account for the rise of the "Greens"

in Western Europe and of other political ecology parties whose vision closely parallels the alternative environmental paradigm.

A major attempt to bridge the differences between the dominant and alternative environmental outlooks can be found in the idea of **sustainable development**. This concept achieved global currency in 1987 as a result of its use in the report of the United Nations World Commission on Environment and Development, more commonly known as the Brundtland report (after the chair of the commission, Norwegian prime minister Gro Harlem Brundtland). The Brundtland report defined *sustainable development* as "development that meets the needs of the present without compromising the ability of future generations to meet their own needs" (World Commission on Environment and Development, 1987: 43). It foresaw a new form of economic growth, especially for Third World nations, that would be both environmentally aware and egalitarian, integrating objectives for social development with the demands of science. In short, the Brundtland report suggested that it is possible to have the best of both worlds: continued economic growth, but not at the expense of the environment.

However, many environmentalists have been critical of the concept of sustainable development. They argue that, in real life, it is not very easy to balance economic growth and natural-resource use with environmental protection. For example, they would argue that situating a jetport in the middle of an environmentally sensitive natural area would be ecologically destructive no matter what measures were taken to reduce noise pollution or catch the run-off of aviation fuel. In fact, environmentalists such as David Suzuki insist that the environmental dangers we face today are so extensive that we can survive as a species only by totally dismantling the "buzz saw of progress" in the industrial nations of the North, and by halting its advance in the less-developed countries of the Third World.

Furthermore, critics of the Brundtland report point out that sustainable development requires an extraordinary degree of mutual cooperation and a deep commitment to reform. This is difficult to achieve, especially in the nations of the Southern Hemisphere, where rural economies are still controlled by wealthy landowners, and the poor are forced to engage in ecologically damaging practices, such as stripping the rapidly dwindling forests for cooking fuel, in order to survive.

ENVIRONMENTAL ATTITUDES, CONCERNS, AND BEHAVIOURS

The existence of a distinct set of environmental attitudes and concerns in our society has been documented by a large number of polls conducted over the last quarter-century. One of the first and most important efforts to develop a research tool with which to measure an environmental view of the world was Dunlap and Van Liere's (1978) new environmental paradigm (NEP) scale. Using survey data from two samples of Washington state residents and from the membership of a statewide environmental organization, Dunlap and Van Liere developed a 12-item scale that measures the extent of agreement with such statements as "the balance of nature is very delicate and easily upset" and "humans need not adapt to the natural environment, because they can remake it to suit their own needs" (see Table 16.2). The researchers found that the general public moderately accepted the content of the emerging environmental paradigm, whereas environmentalists strongly endorsed it.

In addition to this "measured agreement" method favoured by Dunlap and his co-researchers, two other techniques have been used to measure environmental concern. One simple and straightforward approach is to ask people how worried or upset they are about a series of environmental problems. A second strategy, which strives for greater concreteness, is to ask respondents to weigh trade-offs between, for example, environmental protection and jobs (Freudenburg, 1991).

Has public concern with environmental quality changed since the first survey results were carried out in the early 1970s? Two complementary hypotheses address this question (Jones and Dunlap, 1992). Grossman and Potter (1977) formulated the **broadening-base hypothesis**, which predicts that environmental concern will eventually diffuse throughout all groups in the nation. Buttel (1975) promoted the **economic-contingency hypothesis**, which suggests that the broadening of the social bases of environmental concern depends on prevailing economic conditions. Buttel argued that when economic conditions worsen or are perceived to be getting worse, those who are least well off will be the first to shift their focus from the environment to the economy. However, other researchers, using U.S. data for the years 1973–90, found little support for either hypothesis (Jones and Dunlap, 1992); they found instead that the level and social location of support for environmental protection have remained remarkably stable for nearly 20 years.

What are the social bases of environmental concern? It was originally thought that support for environmentalism was limited to the affluent. However, most surveys in the 1970s and 1980s found that income and occupational prestige were only weakly related to environmental concern (Buttel, 1987; Van

TABLE 16.2 AVERAGE SCORES ON THE NEW ENVIRONMENTAL PARADIGM (NEP) SCALE BY THE GENERAL PUBLIC SAMPLE (GPS) AND THE ENVIRONMENTAL ORGANIZATION SAMPLE (EOS)[a]

	GPS	EOS
1. We are approaching the limit of the number of people the earth can support.	3.00	3.63
2. The balance of nature is very delicate and easily upset.	3.18	3.68
3. Humans have the right to modify the natural environment to suit their needs.	2.76	3.30
4. Humankind was created to rule over the rest of nature.	2.63	3.67
5. When humans interfere with nature, it often produces disastrous consequences.	3.03	3.49
6. Plants and animals exist primarily to be used by humans.	2.81	3.61
7. To maintain a healthy economy, we will have to develop a "steady-state" economy in which industrial growth is controlled.	2.85	3.48
8. Humans must live in harmony with nature in order to survive.	3.52	3.86
9. The earth is like a spaceship with only limited room and resources.	3.21	3.85
10. Humans need not adapt to the natural environment, because they can remake it to suit their own needs.	3.25	3.74
11. There are limits to growth beyond which our industrialized society cannot expand.	2.94	3.64
12. Humankind is severely abusing the environment.	3.11	3.81

[a]High scores indicate strong agreement with the pro-NEP position. Range = 1.0–4.0. Eight of the items are worded such that agreement reflects acceptance of the NEP, while for the other four (3, 4, 6, 10) disagreement reflects acceptance of the NEP. Respondents were assigned scores of 4 for "strongly agree," 3 for "mildly agree," 2 for "mildly disagree," and 1 for "strongly disagree" for the eight non-NEP items; scoring for the four anti-NEP items was reversed.

SOURCE: Adapted from Riley E. Dunlap and Kenneth D. Van Liere, "The New Environmental Paradigm: A Proposed Measuring Instrument and Preliminary Results," *Journal of Environmental Education*, 9 (1978), pp. 10–19.

Liere and Dunlap, 1980). Instead, higher levels of education, youth, political liberalism, and urban residence were found to be the best predictors of concern with environmental quality (Dunlap and Catton, 1979). The social bases of environmental concern have remained more or less the same from 1973 to 1990, as have levels of support (Jones and Dunlap, 1992). Greenbaum (1995) has characterized the social bases of environmental concern as "complex and subtle." That is because environmental concern spans a wide variety of subject matters, from species extinction and the thinning of the ozone layer to the contamination of local drinking waters by toxic chemicals. Although it may be possible to isolate general clusters of environmental concern, as have Dunlap and Van Liere in their NEP scale (see Table 16.2), people may not be very consistent across various issues. Part of the reason for inconsistency is that individual environmental problems may affect us in very different ways. How concerned we will be about a particular environmental problem, or whether we even perceive it as a "problem," will depend on how the activity in question affects our "interests"—that

is, how we will be affected by its benefits, costs, and risks (Greenbaum, 1995: 127; and see Box 16.1).

Do these pro-environmental attitudes convert directly into environmentally friendly behaviour? Most studies have failed to confirm these linkages. As Maloney and Ward (1973: 585) have noted, "most people say they are willing to do a great deal to help curb pollution problems and are fairly emotional about it, but in fact they actually do very little and know even less." In a study carried out in Pennsylvania in the 1990s, Theodori and Luloff (2002) found that those who indicated in a survey that they were "proactive" in their positions on environmental issues (5.5 percent of the total) were significantly more likely to report engaging in pro-environmental behaviours than were those who described themselves as being "sympathetic" (62.2 percent). In particular, they were more inclined to attend a public hearing and meeting about the environment and to contact a government agency to get information or complain about an environmental problem. For the most part, however, those who score positively in environmental-concern polls do not show any particular willingness to go beyond

BOX 16.1   WISE ADVICE FROM FOUR "ECO-PATHFINDERS"

COLLEEN MCCRORY: NEVER GIVE UP

Colleen McCrory, executive director of the Valhalla Wilderness Society, can claim numerous victories. Her tenacity helped bring a stop to clear-cutting on British Columbia's South Moresby Island and establish the Valhalla Wilderness Park. "Not everyone has to join an organization," she says. "It's more important that the environment is an important part of your everyday life. If you're working on an issue, never give up and never let go. Even if you lose, what you've done will help the next person continue the battle."

BRUCE WALKER: DON'T SACRIFICE CREDIBILITY

In the fall of 1972, Bruce Walker was a 20-year-old college dropout living in Montreal. Now, 27 years later, Walker is research director for the Society to Overcome Pollution. The organization has played a large role in introducing curbside blue box recycling to the Montreal region, getting an island-wide sewage-treatment system installed, and establishing air-quality monitoring, as well as educating the public....

If you want to make an impact, [Walker] advises, don't wait for an issue to hit you over the head.... [And] never assume every issue is being taken care of by other organizations. "You'll need loads of patience, persistence, and a sense of humour," he says. "Be vigilant, and use your five senses, plus a sixth—common sense—to detect environmental threats. And lastly, never sacrifice credibility for visibility; state the facts without exaggeration."

LINDA MANZER: FOCUS YOUR ANGER

For Linda Manzer, Toronto-based guitar maker for the stars, the journey down the activist road began with a chance television viewing of an elephant hunt. She was among the first guitar artisans to stop using ivory, and soon others followed suit. "I started asking questions about where products came from," she says. "Some suppliers had good answers, others squirmed." She then focused her attention on the old-growth spruce required to make top-grade instruments. She now ensures that only trees downed by the wind serve as her medium....

Manzer urges people to volunteer. "It's easier than you think," she says. "Jump in where your heart tells you. Focus your anger; use it as a tailwind and a positive force."

SHEILA WATT CLOUTIER: RESPECT THE CIRCLE

A head of the Inuit Circumpolar Conference, Sheila Watt Cloutier spends much of her time convincing southern Canadians of the importance of traditional foods. Caribou, whale, and seal have sustained her people for thousands of years, and the suggestion that Inuit should switch to imported beef, pork, and chicken angers her.

Cloutier advises those who want to make the world a better place to remember the connectedness of all living things. "I can't imagine, with all the challenges we face as a people, that we now have to worry about breast-feeding our children," she says, referring to the presence of persistent organic pollutants in arctic wildlife. "People must realize that a poisoned Inuk child is a poisoned Arctic is a poisoned planet."

SOURCE: Martin Silverstone and Kendra Toby, "Pathfinder Talk," *Equinox* (August/September 1998), p. 90.

low-cost, personal actions (recycling, buying "green" products) to make deep-cutting sacrifices for the environment. Uusitalo (1990), for example, found that support for measures to help the environment declined when they required any change of personal habits.

From this evidence, it appears that most people are willing to pay lip service to protecting the environment and will behave responsibly as long as it is not appreciably more expensive or inconvenient to do so. After studying recycling behaviour across the province of Alberta, Derksen and Gartrell (1993) concluded that the key factor accounting for partici-

pation in recycling programs was the easy availability of curbside pickups rather than positive attitudes toward the environment. In fact, those who were environmentally concerned were no more likely to recycle than those who were unconcerned.

THE ENVIRONMENTAL MOVEMENT

Although environmental concern exists across a wide cross-section of the population, it has been most intensely concentrated in the environmental movement. One study from the 1990s of 733 residents of Cornwall, Ontario, found that only one in ten could be labelled an "activist" willing to invest time and energy in behaviours aimed at preserving or improving the quality of the environment. And even here, there was a big difference between easy-to-perform actions such as voting for a government proposing environmentally conscious policies and more demanding behaviours such as participating in protests against current environmental conditions and writing letters to firms that manufacture harmful products (Seguin et al., 1998). Movement activists have waged environmental battles with loggers, utility companies, whalers, agri-corporations, developers, and other defenders of the dominant paradigm. Although the environmental movement has not always represented a "vanguard for a new society" (Milbrath, 1984), it does directly incorporate many of the elements of the alternative environmental paradigm in its philosophies and actions.

SOCIAL BASE AND COMPOSITION

In its early manifestations in the nineteenth century, the environmental movement was largely the creation of an elite. For example, the leadership and much of the membership of American wildlife-preservation organizations such as the Sierra Club, the Save the Redwoods League, and the Boone and Crockett Club were drawn almost exclusively from a tightly knit network of lawyers, educators, and wealthy businessmen. Similarly, in England, preservationist causes were pursued primarily by members of the clergy and the aristocracy. Occasionally, these elite organizations would enlist the support of the general public in specific campaigns. In the fight to save Niagara Falls (1906–10), for example, a national publicity campaign waged in the pages of American popular magazines such as *Ladies' Home Journal* resulted in more than 6500 letters written in support of the preservation of the falls (Cylke, 1993: 22).

In Canada, the conservation movement developed in a different fashion. Environmental initiatives, such as the establishment of national parks and the protection of wildlife, were more likely to be developed by small groups of dedicated civil servants who were able to convince the federal government to take action (Foster, 1978). Two of the most significant events in early Canadian conservation history, the

establishment of the first national park in Banff in 1887 and the signing of the Canada–U.S. Migratory Bird Convention in 1917, followed this pattern.

When the modern environmental movement emerged in the late 1960s and early 1970s, it was largely a creature of the upper middle classes. The dominant social groups in environmental organizations were well-educated professionals from urban and suburban backgrounds and college students from white-collar backgrounds (Gale, 1983). Mainstream EMOs (environmental movement organizations) consequently favoured issues related to "saving" nature over those relating to urban environments. For example, few EMOs in the 1970s showed much interest in pursuing problems related to high concentrations of lead in the soil of inner-city properties, despite the fact that lead levels detected in the blood of local children were way above normal. These organizations only took up the issue when it became evident that lead emissions from motor vehicles were unacceptably high.

More recently, environmentalists have been identified as members of a "new middle class" drawn primarily from social and cultural specialists—teachers, social workers, journalists, artists, and pro-

The environmental movement has grown tremendously since the 1960s. Some members of the middle class in particular are now more personally involved in the environmental movement and raise environmentally conscious children.
SOURCE: Dick Hemingway.

fessors—who work in creative and/or public-service-oriented jobs. This new middle class is on the firing line in the day-to-day conflicts between the engineers and technocrats who tend to ignore the human costs of progress and the ordinary citizens who are victimized by them.

There are two kinds of explanations for why members of the new middle class tend to be more radical as a group than the population as a whole. On the one hand, they are more likely to seek out jobs in the public sector, away from the pressures of a business environment that is hostile to their values. At the same time, they tend to become personally involved in the problems faced by their clients, even to the point of becoming advocates for their interests (Kriesi, 1989: 1084). For example, a doctor working in a community health centre whose patients suffer an unusually high incidence of asthma might recognize that the source of the illness is a local incinerator and may campaign to have the polluting facility closed.

Evidence for this new class theory of social movements comes from a number of different nations. Cotgrove and Duff (1981) found that nearly half (43.4 percent) of their sample of environmentalists in England (compared with only about 12 percent of the general public) were employed in service, welfare, and creative occupations. Kriesi (1989) found that 23 percent of those who reported having participated in the Dutch ecology movement (compared with 12 percent of the population as a whole) were social and cultural specialists. And Tindall (1994) showed that people who had higher levels of income and education and/or were employed in the public sector were more likely to join the Vancouver Island wilderness-preservation movement, although these factors did not affect their level of participation after joining.

ENVIRONMENTAL MOBILIZATION

In addition to researching the social composition of the environmental movement, sociologists have also been interested in learning how environmentalists mobilize people to their cause.

Much of the research on this topic has focused on community-based, grassroots environmental organizations. Formed in opposition to the pollution problems caused by local industries and utilities, these citizens' groups differ somewhat from the rest of the environmental movement insofar as they draw their members from blue-collar as well as white-collar neighbourhoods. The prototype of the grassroots, locally based environmental group is the Love Canal Homeowners Association, formed in the 1970s by some Niagara Falls, New York, homeowners whose properties had been contaminated by toxic waste buried 30 years earlier by a local chemical company.

It is by no means a simple matter to mobilize one's neighbours in the face of an environmental threat. In fact, most people want to avoid trouble and must be actively convinced that their present situation is both unjust and intolerable before they will consider taking action. Capek (1993: 11) describes the initial reluctance of homeowners in Carver Terrace, a contaminated residential subdivision in the U.S. South, to recognize the dangers facing them:

> Residents knew at some level about bad-smelling air, mysterious illness or deaths among people with no prior history of medical problems, plants that would not grow or grew strangely, animals becoming ill or [being] born deformed, and a variety of other experiences that lacked explanation. The amorphous and invisible nature of chemical exposure, however, and the difficulty of diagnosing its consequences either at a popular or professional level worked against the integration of this knowledge.

Caught up in the demands of everyday life, respectful of the voices of authority who downplay the problem, and blinded by the pride of home ownership, people tend to accept the status quo and must be persuaded to redefine their situation in such a way that they can see it as a violation of their basic rights. This is easier to do when citizens are ideologically primed to question the image of progress as continuous economic development (Ladd and Laska, 1991), but even those who lack this attitudinal underpinning can be brought around.

There are four stages through which local communities pass in the process of challenging polluters (Cable and Benson, 1993). In the first phase, residents come to see themselves as "victims" of corporate environmental crime. In phase two, they make individual appeals to government regulatory agencies to take action to force an end to the toxic dumping or other problem situation. In the third phase, the complainants become disillusioned with the slow pace or absence of official action and begin to seek environmental justice. In the final phase, increased democratic pressure has either convinced government regulators to enforce environmental standards or proven insufficient, in which case the problem continues unchecked.

Like other social movements, the environmental movement aims to convince as wide a segment of the public as possible that its interpretation of the world is correct and should, therefore, be acted upon. To that end, members of the movement develop "frames"—that is, interpretations of events and their meanings. Successful framing has three elements: diagnostic, prognostic, and motivational. Diagnostic framing involves identifying a problem and fixing the blame for it. Prognostic framing offers a proposed solution to the diagnosed problem. Motivational framing is a call to arms to potential recruits to take specific corrective action. The better these three frames are integrated, the greater their capacity for mobilizing people (Gerhards and Rucht, 1992: 583).

Contemporary environmental frames are frequently constructed around the image of an impending global collapse. In the early 1970s, this approach was typified by the best-selling book *The Limits to Growth* (Meadows et al., 1972), in which the authors forecast that earth's **carrying capacity**—that is, the optimum population size that the planet can support under present environmental conditions—would eventually be exceeded. With the aid of a computer model, they estimated how five interrelated factors—population growth, industrial output, food production, pollution, and nonrenewable natural resources—would interact over time. They predicted that, within a century, we would face a major crisis brought on by uncontrolled population growth and rising levels of pollution.

In the 1980s, the threat shifted to that of "biosphere crisis," generated by global climatic changes resulting from increased emissions of "greenhouse" gases, such as carbon dioxide, chlorofluorocarbons, methane, and nitrous oxide, into the atmosphere. Such changes in global weather patterns have the potential to trigger major environmental changes, including rising sea levels, hotter summers, more frequent and more severe droughts, dust storms, forest

"So *that's* where it goes! Well, I'd like to thank you fellows for bringing this to my attention."

fires, and the rapid extinction of thousands of species of plants and animals.

The solution, environmentalists claim, is to embrace wholeheartedly the alternative environmental paradigm. In *Beyond the Limits* (1992), the sequel to *The Limits to Growth*, Meadows, Meadows, and Randers caution that we must draw back and ease down: conserve resources, reduce pollution, and adopt deliberate social constraints on population and industrial growth. In the less-developed nations, this means both controlling family size and finding new, more sustainable avenues of economic expansion. In the industrialized world, a new value system is said to be necessary so that people will stop trying to use material growth to satisfy what are in fact nonmaterial needs—for acceptance, self-importance, and community identity (Fields, 1993: 40).

More research is needed on the relationship between grassroots mobilizations protesting toxic dumps, incinerators, nuclear power plants, and other pollution sources and these wider ecological worldviews. Although we might assume that environmentalists, in accordance with the popular slogan "think globally, act locally," first become imbued with the alternative environmental paradigm and then put it to practical use in their own neighbourhoods and communities, another possibility is that ecological values arise directly out of firsthand experience. In the latter view, it is the process of dealing with recalcitrant polluters, bureaucratic cover-ups, and overly cautious scientists that eventually causes the penny to drop for local environmentalists who previously had not given much thought to broad environmental philosophies. Members of community-based, grassroots environmental organizations thus engage in a form of social learning as they go about researching their case against polluters. This social learning is further facilitated by the assembly of a widening net of environmental contacts. Irene Paparo-Stein, a Winnipeg woman who formed a citizens' lobby group to fight chemical spraying in her city, describes the environmental networking process this way (Stein, 1988: 52):

> One thing I had discovered, there was quite a network in the U.S. And the Americans, once I explained the situation and the need for information, were ready with their help. They understood the enormity of the problem, of the lay persons up against the governments, bureaucracy, and industry, and knew what to do. They were generous with their aid. We had soon compiled a list of contacts from all over the U.S.

Inevitably, someone in the network introduces the community activist to an "ecological" perspective.

IDEOLOGICAL DIVISIONS

Although we often speak of the environmental movement as a single entity, there has in fact long been a basic philosophical split between "value-oriented environmentalists," whose main concern is to change the way we view the world, and "success-oriented environmentalists," whose chief goal is to stop pollution and other activities that damage the physical environment (Eyerman and Jamison, 1989). These two factions differ significantly in their perceptions of the root causes of environmental problems, their preferences among strategies for coping, and their visions of an ecologically sound society (Cylke, 1993: 69).

This division became evident at the beginning of the twentieth century in the differing ideological approaches to the environment taken by the two main wings of the U.S. conservation movement—the "resource conservationists" and the "preservationists." The former wished to "manage" natural resources by applying modern engineering and administrative techniques, whereas the latter, guided by aesthetic and even spiritual ideals, believed it was necessary for the government to intervene in order to preserve areas of natural beauty and scientific importance. For example, in a difference of opinion that has carried over to the present day, resource conservationists wanted to "harvest" public forests in a "scientific" manner, whereas preservationists advocated setting these lands aside as natural parks, in which logging would be prohibited.

On Canada's West Coast where logging is still a major industry and source of employment, the heirs to the resource conservation wing of the early twentieth century are the 300 organizations who belong to the Forest Alliance of British Columbia. An industry-sponsored coalition of corporations, community associations, and municipalities, the Forest Alliance "aims to find ways to balance environmental, social and economic values in forest-use decisions" ("End War in Woods …," 2000: 5). In recent years, much of the strategic action undertaken by this coalition has centred on efforts to counter claims of environmental opponents and establish public confidence in the industry's environmental performance through "certification" schemes. Operated through organizations such as the Canadian Standards Association and the Forest Stewardship Council, forest certification is a voluntary tool directed toward lumber retailers, homebuilders and other big customers designed to re-assure them (and their customers) that their purchases are derived from "well-managed" forests. The Forest Alliance's promotional literature especially favours the notion of "sustainable development" (the title of its newsletter is *Sustainability Update*).

Furthermore, value differences over the true meaning of environmentalism have become the basis for the emergence of various alternative ecophilosophies, the best known of which are "deep ecology" and "ecofeminism." Whereas success-oriented environmentalists are primarily concerned with the direct effects of industrial pollution on individuals and communities, value-oriented environmentalists stress the survival of all living and nonliving things as components of healthy ecosystems. In doing so, they come closest to any segment of the environmental movement to popularizing the alternative environmental paradigm.

Deep Ecology

The **deep-ecology** argument was set out in the early 1970s by Norwegian philosopher Arne Naess (1973), and was elaborated by U.S. ecological thinkers Bill Devall and George Sessions (1985). In contrast to the **anthropocentrism** that characterizes much of the environmental movement, deep ecologists believe in a "biocentric" approach, which emphasizes that humans are one species among many on earth and have no special rights or privileges. This **biocentric egalitarianism** states that all things on the earth have an equal right to live and blossom and reach their own forms of self-realization.

Although the intellectual roots of this principle are varied, it owes much to the thinking of John Muir, the leading preservationist in the early American conservation movement. A second touchstone for deep ecology is the "land ethic" of Aldo Leopold, an American naturalist. Formulated in 1949, Leopold's land ethic affirms the right of soils, waters, plants, and animals to coexist in their natural state with humans, whose role is viewed not as conqueror of the land but as member and citizen of it.

Deep ecologists believe that the relation of the individual to nature cannot be fully grasped intellectually but must ultimately be experienced directly. This quite clearly sets deep ecology in opposition to mainstream environmentalism, which is primarily concerned with gathering "facts" about nature and our despoiling of it. Indeed, deep ecologists regard science and scientists with a fair degree of suspicion, depicting them as being a part of the problem as much as a part of its solution. An exception to this is the "**Gaia hypothesis**," formulated in the late 1960s by British scientist James Lovelock (1987) and American microbiologist Lynn Margulis, which holds that the earth is a living superorganism with its own internal system of regulation. From this perspective, it is possible to see ourselves as having a moral obligation not just to plants, animals, and other human beings but to the planet itself (Yearley, 1991: 145).

Ecofeminism

A second alternative ecophilosophy is **ecofeminism**. The term was first coined in 1974 by the French writer Françoise d'Eaubonne, who believes that the oppression and exploitation of women and the domination of the natural environment are part of the same phenomenon. Ecofeminists identify a distinctly "feminine" way of thinking and being that is more nurturing, more cooperative, and more communal than the mainstream, paternalistic culture. *Mother Nature*, a long-accepted term in the English language, is given a new meaning and significance by the ecofeminists, who celebrate the ancient pagan tradition of Goddess worship and nature cults; the Goddess is seen as the symbol of ecological wisdom.

Both deep ecologists and ecofeminists express the need for developing a new human consciousness and vision. However, there is also a certain degree of tension between these two ecophilosophies, centred on differing conceptions of the central cause of the current environmental crisis: Deep ecologists point

Greenpeace activists put a banner on the statue of Christ the Redeemer in Rio De Janeiro, Brazil, September 5, 2002. The protest was held to draw attention to lack of focus on renewable energy at the World Summit on Sustainable Development. The banner read, "Rio + 10 = A SECOND CHANCE, Greenpeace."
SOURCE: © Reuters New Media Inc./CORBIS/Magma.

to a gender-neutral anthropocentrism, whereas ecofeminists claim that "androcentrism" (male-centredness) is the real culprit. Furthermore, deep ecologists have trouble accepting the ecofeminist claims that women are more innately and more sensitively attuned to nature than men are and, therefore, have the unique capacity to construct a new, more enlightened approach to the environment (Warren, 1990).

In a recent transnational study, Perrin and colleagues (2001) identified three types of "green" orientations among leaders of environmental NGOs that they surveyed in Quebec and Costa Rica: ecologists (n = 30), mainstream environmentalists (n = 107), and market environmentalists (n = 83). Both of the latter perceived science and technology more positively than did ecologists; however, market environmentalists were less likely to accept economic sacrifices for the sake of the environment than were mainstreamers. This typology, Perrin and his colleagues (2001: 849) claim, is "consistent with studies using the NEP scale of Dunlap and Van Liere (1978), but, instead of differentiating between those who support the NEP and those who do not, it reveals differences within the NEP."

POLITICAL ECONOMY OF THE ENVIRONMENT

A third major area of inquiry within environmental sociology is the study of the political economy of the environment.

A starting point for many studies undertaken from a political-economy perspective is Alan Schnaiberg's *The Environment: From Surplus to Scarcity* (1980). Schnaiberg distinguishes between production and consumption activities in society and points the finger of blame for the environmental crisis at production activities. Rather than looking to irresponsible consumers who insist on embracing an extravagant, wasteful lifestyle despite its harmful environmental effects, Schnaiberg identifies the real villain as the relentless process of economic development that is controlled by industrial capitalists and buttressed by the state.

According to Schnaiberg, the political economy of environmental problems and policies is shaped by modern industrial society's **treadmill of production**. This term refers to the inherent need of our economic system to continually yield profits by creating consumer demand for new products, even where this means expanding the ecosystem to its furthest limits. Corporate producers create this demand primarily through the medium of advertising. For example, in a recent issue of a leading Canadian urban-living magazine, readers are advised that a Porsche will stir the "power of passion" in its owner, a Jenn-Air cooktop system is "the sign of a great cook," and a Kohler spray-and-brush attachment will "turn your shower into a personal luxury spa." Consumers are thus persuaded from early childhood to become part of a dominant materialistic culture in which personal identity depends on material possessions.

The state is said to buttress this treadmill of production by providing a variety of economic incentives to new industries, from tax breaks to worker-training programs. Traditionally, the state has also encouraged untrammelled economic growth by ensuring a continuous flow of natural resources to industrial producers. For example, in the latter years of the nineteenth century, the "gospel of efficiency" (Hays, 1959) in U.S. politics dictated that the growing power of the federal government be used to regulate competition and ensure a steady supply of lumber and other resources to industry. The idea was that only government measures could ensure that resources be set aside and, then, be exploited in a controlled fashion, rather than squandered in the cutthroat competition of the unregulated marketplace (Koppes, 1988: 234). In Canada, the prevailing view has been that nature can be privately requisitioned virtually without limit (Williams, 1992), as evidenced by our exportation of oil, natural gas, minerals, lumber, and, more recently, water, to industrial centres in the United States, often despite negative environmental consequences.

One far-reaching example of this approach to natural resources is the Great Whale hydro-electric project, initiated by former Quebec premier Robert Bourassa and Hydro Quebec. Great Whale is the second phase of the massive James Bay hydro-electric project, which calls for the diversion or alteration of 20 northern rivers through the construction of 36 dams and more than 1000 dikes. The project is now on hold due to Cree objections and other expert opinion, but if it is ever completed, the development will flood "23 000 square kilometres of land the size of Newfoundland island and Labrador combined and [shatter] two cultures that have flourished there—surviving both natural disaster and foreign intrusion—for 5000 years" (Dwyer, 1992: 30).

Of course, the despoiling of the environment is not limited to countries that have functioned under a capitalist system: Soviet-style societies devastated the environment to an even greater degree. Two of the most memorable photographic images to come out of Eastern Europe in the early 1990s were of the Romanian town of Copsa Mica totally blackened by carbon dust from the local carbosin plant and of schoolchildren from the Czechoslovakian town of Most who had to wear face masks on "sulphur dioxide alert" days to filter the pollution-laden air. There are also indications that recent economic expansion in China has produced its own environmental nightmares. In 1988, for example, Benxi, a city covering 43 square kilometres, vanished from satellite photographs beneath a cloud of smog (Silvertown, 1989: 550). Thus, the accusing finger should be pointed not at the capitalist system, but at unbridled industrialism, with its accompanying lack of environmental responsibility.

Schnaiberg has described a pervasive conflict in advanced industrial societies between the treadmill of production and the rising public demand for protecting the environment. That is, governments are increasingly torn between a commitment to promote economic development and job creation and the goal of environmental preservation. The bitter conflict over the future of old-growth forests on Vancouver Island is a dramatic illustration of the conflict (see Box 16.2). Environmentalists argue that the temperate rain forests of Clayoquot Sound and other parts of the province have nearly disappeared and must be declared out of bounds to further logging, particularly if it employs "clear-cutting" methods. The forestry industry replies that this solution would cripple one of British Columbia's major industries, throwing tens of thousands of loggers out of work.

In such situations, governments search for a viable compromise. That search is typically complicated by the fact that the civil service is rarely of one mind, with various departments and diverse personnel defending conflicting positions. One approach to resolving these contradictions involves the adoption of "environmental-management" techniques. **Environmental management** refers to moderate government interventions that afford some limited protection to the environment without seriously curtailing economic development.

The continuing conflict between economic development and environmental preservation is illustrated in Novek and Kampen's (1992) comparative case study of two proposed pulp-and-paper megaprojects: the Japanese-owned Alberta-Pacific mill to be built on the Athabasca River in northern Alberta, and the proposed expansion of the Repap mill in The Pas in northern Manitoba. They found that the provincial governments attempted to resolve their contradictory commitments to economic development and environmental protection primarily by implementing the *environmental-assessment process*. This is a formal legal mechanism whereby the environmental impacts of proposed developments, such as these pulp-and-paper mills, are subjected to scientific and technical scrutiny. Novek and Kampen also found that this public review process failed to quell opposition from northern Aboriginal groups and other opponents of the two projects, because it excluded consideration of broader social and environmental concerns, including, in particular, the terms under which the forestry companies were granted access to the land.

The treadmill of production exerts a major influence on the developing nations as well, where many people want access to the consumer culture that we enjoy. The unsustainable development that some industrializing countries have consequently espoused has led to considerable friction with environmentalists from northern countries, who fear that it will lead to serious worldwide environmental problems (e.g., increased destruction of tropical rain forests can lead to accelerated global warming). Third World leaders reply that, having enjoyed the benefits of a century of industrial growth, environmental activists from Europe and America cannot in fairness now deny developing countries the fruits of economic expansion on ecological grounds. (For an attempt to reconcile development with environmental integrity in the Third World, see Adams, 1990.) At the same time, Third World planners and politicians have not always learned from the mistakes of their counterparts in the North. For example, urban planners in São Paulo, Brazil's largest and most heavily polluted city, evidently modelled their transportation system on that

Ucluelet sits on the southern tip of a peninsula on Vancouver Island, which is the site of one of the most prized wilderness tourism destinations in Canada as well as some of the country's most valuable timber and aquatic life. A community of 1800, Ucluelet is home to the loggers who used to work the old-growth forests of Clayoquot Sound, as well as several seafood-processing plants. In the mid-1990s, Clayoquot became the focus of a world-wide environmental campaign against clear-cutting, a logging method where every tree is cut down, leaving fields of stumps. By 1998, forestry giant MacMillan Bloedel closed its logging camp in the Sound. The closure was followed shortly by the collapse of the local salmon-fishing and fish-processing industries.

With 17 percent unemployment, one of the highest rates in the province of British Columbia, Ucluelet has set its sights on a new economic future as proposed by the federal and provincial governments and the local Chamber of Commerce. Inspired by the success of Tofino, a town just to the north, which specializes in eco-tours, high-end resorts, and hemp clothing, it was decided that Ucluelet would become a "tourist destination," shifting from an economy based on resource extraction to one with jobs in hotels and restaurants. The centre-piece of this new tourism-based economic revival is "Reef Point," a $60-million resort planned for the out-skirts of Ucluelet that will offer adventure sports and "experiential vacations." Anchoring Reef Point is "Roots Lodge," a project undertaken by Canada's most marketing-savvy clothing company.

Ucluelet is being buffeted by two conflicting visions. Many in the town, especially the growing contingent of migrants from cities, want to create a "fantasy of the wild" complete with whale-watching trips, kayak eco-tours, and backwoods hiking trails. Ex-loggers have been offered provincial subsidies and loans to develop "forestry tourism initiatives" such as day trips on the logging roads around Clayoquot Sound. The federal fishing authorities have urged salmon fishermen to sell their licences back to the government and convert their trawlers into whale-watching and sport-fishing boats. Tourism British Columbia has developed a "Super Host" course to teach local hospitality workers to provide "The West-Coast Wow," a uniformly high level of enthusiastic service. While many in Ucluelet are embracing this tourism-and-development vision, others are resisting the idea. They do not believe that, in order to attract more tourists, the town needs to discard its work boots along with the resource-based industries that once built the local economy. Robert Lee, a sociol-ogist at the University of Washington in Seattle who has studied economic transitions in resource towns in the Pacific Northwest, cautions that Ucluelet faces impending "Whistlerization," whereby locals become part of a new marginal service class which cannot afford to compete with vacation renters for a limited supply of housing. This, then, is the paradox of Ucluelet's transition: a working-class town that was earning upper-middle-class salaries is about to become a yuppie town built around the romance of the rain forest where most of the citizens earn half of their former wages.

SOURCE: Adapted from Naomi Klein, "The Tourist Trap," *Saturday Night* (September 1999), pp. 50–64.

of Los Angeles without taking into account the grid-locked traffic and persistent smog that characterize that city.

A second source of environmental degradation in the lower-income countries is that associated with "unsustainable impoverishment." In other words, the poor engage in ecologically damaging practices just to survive from day to day (Gallopin, Gutman, and Maletta, 1989). For example, rural dwellers are often forced to strip the rapidly dwindling forests in order to obtain fuel for cooking. As the Brundtland com-mission recognized, it is futile to attempt to deal with environmental problems in the Third World without addressing broader issues of poverty and inequality. These problems in turn are rooted in a variety of social arrangements, from the continuing dominance of wealthy elites in the developing nations to eco-nomic dependency on the industrialized countries, associated with massive debts.

Nevertheless, it is important to note that environ-mental violations in the high-income countries of the North are directly tied to potential ecological catastro-phes in the poorer nations of the South. Roberts (2001) has shown how global warming, which is linked to emissions of greenhouse gases in rich nations (20 per-cent of the world's population is responsible for 60 per-cent of current emissions of greenhouse gases), threatens poor nations with devastating disasters—hurricanes, draughts, floods, heat waves. At the same time, global warming contributes to the "pollution of poverty," whereby the world's poor are forced to use renewable energy sources for their basic fuel needs. As

Roberts (2001: 508) stresses, "equity and ecology must be dealt with together" through aggressive efforts to support national advancement in the South, if a healthy planet is to be maintained.

RISK AND RISK ASSESSMENT

Risk refers to the probability that a particular hazard will actually occur. Everyday life is full of risks, from slipping on the ice on our front steps to being hit by a bolt of lightning on the golf course. Normally, we base our decision on whether to take a particular course of action that carries with it a degree of risk on a series of individual factors: past experience, confidence in our own abilities, and our assessment of the apparent safety of a situation. In the present-day world, however, it is increasingly difficult to make such judgments, especially with regard to new technologies and environmental conditions. For example, a summer afternoon spent sunning on the beach may seem innocent, but it may in fact contribute to the onset of skin cancer unless a sun-block lotion is applied to counteract the ultraviolet rays coming through the thinned-out ozone layer. Many of today's environmental hazards (chemicals, radiation, electromagnetic currents) are, in fact, invisible to the naked eye.

In order to cope with such risks, we have increasingly come to rely on the judgment of medical and scientific experts, who appear to be best qualified to decide what is safe. We avoid high-fat foods, buckle our seat belts, and buy bottled spring water because risk professionals tell us that it may be risky not to do so.

Each week seems to bring some newly discovered risk to our attention. Increasingly, such risks are environmentally related—from dioxins and heavy metals in our drinking water to radiation leaks from nuclear power plants, to urban smog that can cause respiratory problems. Toxic hazards are particularly devastating because they render many of the seemingly innocuous or even beneficial things that we depend on—the air we breathe, the water we drink, the sea and soil that nourish the food we eat—quite dangerous (Clarke and Short, 1993).

Sociologists have taken a particular interest in three aspects of risk and risk assessment: the organizational basis of risk, the community perception of risk, and the social distribution of risk.

ORGANIZATIONAL BASIS OF RISK

One consequence of the increasing size and complexity of modern industrial systems is that the source of risk has shifted to large-scale organizations that are all but beyond individual control. When environmentally threatening accidents happen, they are attributable to more than human error; they reflect a set of structural arrangements that make breakdowns inevitable. For example, the gigantic 1989 oil spill that occurred after the supertanker *Exxon Valdez* ran aground in Prince Edward Sound, Alaska, was attributable to cutbacks in maritime safety standards as much as to personal lapses by the captain (Smith, 1992).

Indeed, **normal accidents**—the inevitable failures in nuclear power facilities, petrochemical plants, air-traffic control nets, and other high-risk technologies—are common. Sometimes these flaws are identified during the construction process, but, on other occasions, design flaws manifest themselves only years later, in the form of disasters such as the Three Mile Island nuclear accident. Rather than being anomalies, such technological accidents are the normal consequences of profit-driven, high-risk systems (Perrow, 1984).

Organizations are not only the source of accidents, but are responsible for responding to them as well. The ways in which they do so often amplify the risk (Clarke and Short, 1993: 392). For example, in the wake of the 1984 gas leak at a Union Carbide pesticide plant in Bhopal, India, in which 8000 people were killed and an estimated 300 000 were injured, neither the company, which lacked the necessary support structure and contingency plans for dealing with major accidents, nor the immense government bureaucracy, which took a long time to mobilize, was able to move quickly enough to cope with the catastrophe (Shrivastava, 1987).

COMMUNITY PERCEPTION OF RISK

Contrary to expectations, it is not possible to predict the public perception of risk accurately on the basis of the standard set of demographic and sociological variables (age, gender, political affiliation, etc.). Instead, the best predictor of whether people are likely to perceive risk is the degree to which they trust the ability of expert institutions, including local industries themselves, to manage danger (Freudenburg, 1993; Wynne, 1992). For example, during the Windscale inquiry into the establishment of a nuclear reprocessing facility on the east coast of England, the nuclear experts and the judge who chaired the inquiry approached the issue from a completely different vantage point from local citizens. Whereas the former restricted the scope of the inquiry to technical risk considerations, the latter wished to deal with larger questions, such as how adequate the past performance of the nuclear plant had been and what should be the future of nuclear power. As a result, public trust in both the project and the inquiry was undermined and the perception of risk magnified (Wynne, 1992).

Trust in institutions varies among the members of a community. Those who trust institutions least are most likely to define environmental conditions as risky and therefore actionable. In the Love Canal case, the residents of the neighbourhood that was affected by toxic seepage could be divided into two types: "minimalists," who denied that there was a problem at all or acknowledged a problem of only minor significance, and "maximalists," who believed that the risks were substantial and that the chemical contamination might be more widespread than officially acknowledged. Minimalists were generally found to be social isolates in their neighbourhoods, without children at home, with occupational links to the chemical industry, and with strong attachments to their homes, which they viewed as their principal economic resource in old age. In contrast, the maximalists were typically young parents who shared common interests, placed greater emphasis on health than on property issues, and were active in seeking out risk information, especially from nonofficial sources (Fowlkes and Miller, 1987). In other cases, too, researchers have confirmed that a major motivation for families to become involved in neighbourhood action against toxic wastes is concern about the quality of the community for raising children (Hallman and Wandersman, 1992). Environmental-risk perception, then, is not only a product of how much trust citizens put in the explanations and assurances offered by those in authority positions, but is also linked to people's participation in family life, neighbourhood social networks, and community affairs.

SOCIAL DISTRIBUTION OF RISK

Finally, recent research in the sociology of environmental risk has documented how marginal groups in society bear a disproportionate burden of the risk associated with oil refineries, chemical plants, toxic dumps, garbage and sewage incinerators, and other sources of hazardous exposure. Racial and ethnic minorities, women, low-income urban dwellers, and residents of poor, isolated rural regions are particularly affected. After analyzing the distribution of toxic "Superfund" hazardous waste site locations in Texas and Louisiana, Denq and colleagues (2000) concluded that the three dimensions of class, status, and power are all important in explaining why toxic dumps are disproportionately located in communities with higher percentages of minorities and poor people. Rather than "environmental racism," they argue that the environmental justice issues involved here are better conceptualized as "environmental classism." Disadvantaged communities are overrepresented as risk sites because corporate polluters view them as constituting the path of least resistance, since their inhabitants are generally both economically poor and politically powerless. In many cases, existing patterns of discrimination are closely linked with inequalities in the distribution of environmental hazards.

Disadvantaged people are the primary victims of pollution (most of it generated by or on behalf of the middle and upper classes) because they live closest to the sources of pollution—power plants, industrial installations, and, in central cities, heavy vehicle traffic. Usually, they have no choice as to where they live. Discrimination created the situation, and those with wealth and influence have the political power needed to keep polluting facilities away from their homes. Living in a poor area is bad enough; high levels of pollution make it worse (Bullard, 1990).

Although the scale of environmental-risk inequality is smaller in Canada than in the United States, there are some striking parallels. For example, in July 1993, a Micmac band in Pictou Landing, Nova Scotia, was reported to have accepted a federal government package worth an estimated $35 million as compensation for the pollution of Boat Harbour, the body of water adjoining the band's reserve. At one time, Boat Harbour had clear beaches and was a source of fish and lobster for the Micmac, but in the mid-1960s, almost half the harbour was purchased for $60 000 to treat waste water from a kraft mill operated by Scott Maritimes, Ltd., a subsidiary of Scott Paper Company. The harbour subsequently became one of the most polluted spots in the province, with

Frederick Street in Sydney, Nova Scotia, runs alongside the Sydney tar ponds, the worst toxic waste site in Canada and arguably the worst in North America. With a legacy of 100 years of steelmaking, the tar ponds contain 35 times more toxic sludge than New York's infamous Love Canal. As a result, Sydney has the highest cancer rate in Canada—19 percent for men and 14 percent for women, more than double the national averages. After 12 years of trying to clean up the mess, the clean-up project was declared a failure and the residents of Frederick Street were relocated in 1999. The toxic waste remains.

SOURCE: Warren Gordon/*Frederick Street: Life and Death in Canada's Love Canal.*

87 million litres of a coffee-coloured effluent being processed each day by the provincial treatment lagoon (*The Globe and Mail*, July 6, 1993: A7).

A similar case occurred two decades earlier in northern Ontario, when the Reed pulp-and-paper plant at Dryden was found to be responsible for dumping nine tonnes of mercury into the English Wabigoon river system between 1962 and 1970 (Macdonald, 1991: 106). The Ojibwa who lived in the area suffered serious health and economic problems. Not only were they penalized by a commercial fishing ban, but they were found to be suffering from "Minimata disease"—mercury poisoning from fish—

a toxic syndrome named after a fishing village in Japan, where victims took court action against Chisso Corporation, a large chemical firm.

Environmentally risky activities are also more likely to be located in peripheral communities, areas that are out of the mainstream by virtue of their relative geographic remoteness, their economic marginality, their political powerlessness, or their social isolation. For example, Sellafield, a town in northwest England on the Irish Sea, became a major repository for nuclear waste reprocessing. Sellafield was the archetype of a peripheral community, accessible only by twisting road and branch railway, situated in an area of high unemployment, and economically dependent on the local nuclear power plant (Blowers, Lowry, and Solomon, 1991). Cases such as this are often found in regions that Gidengil (1990) has termed the "vulnerable periphery" and the "depressed periphery," regions with chronic economic problems and dependencies and a high susceptibility to boom-and-bust industries.

Research on the social distribution of risk not only is important for humanitarian reasons, but also influences how we think about power, decision making, and institutional analyses of environmental risk (Clarke and Short, 1993: 394). Among other things, it suggests that risk decisions are not based entirely on "objective" technical and scientific criteria, but are also influenced by sociological factors related to inequality and power. This represents an important addition to public-policy debates on the dynamics of risk, which have tended to treat risk allocation as something that takes place outside of the normal workings of society.

SOCIAL CONSTRUCTION OF ENVIRONMENTAL PROBLEMS

Among the most promising new areas of research in environmental sociology is the "social-constructionist" approach. According to this perspective, environmental issues rarely arise spontaneously; rather, they must be discovered, presented, promoted, and kept alive. Furthermore, environmental problems, like social problems in general, are not free-floating but are owned and managed by policy entrepreneurs in science, environmental-movement organizations, and the media. These "environmental claims-makers" invest considerable time and resources in attempting to elevate problems such as acid rain, global warming, and ozone depletion onto national and international agendas for action.

Consider, for example, the issue of indoor air pollution from radon gas. In the United States, policy entrepreneurs in Congress aggressively pressed the Environmental Protection Agency to take action to publicize the problem. Citizen groups were influential in making the public aware of the dangers of radon, especially when these were first discovered in the state of Pennsylvania. In contrast, a lack of comparable environmental claims-makers in Canada meant that the problem never really "caught on" here beyond a few investigative stories in *The Globe and Mail* (Harrison and Hoberg, 1991).

Hannigan (1995) notes that there are three central tasks in the construction of environmental claims—assembling, presenting, and contesting—each of which involves its own activities, opportunities, and pitfalls. To secure public attention and support, prospective problems must surmount a series of hurdles. They have to be considered newsworthy; they must acquire a measure of scientific credibility; and they have to be skillfully navigated across the shoals of political interest and policy relevance. Finding a way around these roadblocks is more likely if several conditions are met. First, it helps to have onside one or more scientific "popularizers" like David Suzuki who can bridge the gap between environmentalism and science, packaging claims so that they appeal to editors, journalists, political leaders, and other opinion-makers. Second, success is more likely if there are positive incentives for taking action. Moral appeals can effectively direct attention toward an environmental problem, but, unless there are stakeholders in undertaking a concerted program of action, the issue may fizzle out. Protecting endangered species and conserving biodiversity in the tropical rain forest, for example, are made more attractive by the possibility that failure to do so would mean losing a wealth of as-yet-undiscovered pharmaceuticals that may be hidden there. Finally, it is crucial to recruit the support of institutional sponsors, such as the Rockefeller Foundation and the United Nations, to ensure both continuity and legitimacy, as well as financial support.

Social constructionists depict environmental problems as passing through a series of stages, from initial discovery to the waning of public interest. Earlier work in political science characterized environmental concern as inevitably proceeding through the five stages of a fixed **issue-attention cycle** (Downs, 1972). In the pre-problem stage, some highly undesir-

able social or environmental condition exists but has not yet captured much public attention, even though experts or interest groups may have identified it. In the second stage—"alarmed discovery and euphoric enthusiasm"—the public becomes aware of, and frightened by, the problem and is convinced that it can be solved if action is taken immediately. By the third stage, the public begins to realize the cost of significant progress and to perceive that solving the problem will not be as easy as it seemed; solutions require money, sacrifice, and loss of benefits for some. In the fourth stage, intense public interest gradually declines as the growing realization of how difficult any solutions will be sinks in. In the final, post-problem stage, the issue moves off the public-policy agenda, although it may recapture public interest at some point in the future.

More recent research has suggested that environmental issues rise and fall in the public eye in response to a number of different factors, including the clarity and viability of scientific evidence, the ability of environmental claims-makers to sustain a sense of dramatic crisis, and the rise of competing new environmental problems (Ungar, 1992).

A basic assumption of the social-constructionist perspective is that neither the appearance of collective values, such as those described by the alternative environmental paradigm, nor the documented existence of an actual environmental threat is sufficient, by itself, to create an environmental problem that ranks on the public agenda. For example, although tropical rain forest destruction in Malaysia is every bit as serious as its counterpart in Brazil, the latter has received extensive worldwide publicity whereas the former is rarely discussed. Rather, what is significant is the process through which environmental claims-makers pressure those who hold the reins of power to recognize definitions of environmental problems, to implement them, and to accept responsibility for solving them.

It is important to note that the social construction of environmental problems does not occur in isolation. Rather, just as socioeconomic structures influence the social distribution of risk, so the powerful in society have the ability to determine what is and what is not relevant with respect to the environment. It is this synergy between social definition and power inequality that makes social constructionism a distinctively sociological route to studying environmentalism and the environment.

SUMMARY

1. Sociological interest in the natural environment is quite recent, having first developed in the early 1970s. Sociology's reluctance to embrace the study of the environment reflects its heritage, wherein biology and nature were banished from the discipline in favour of socially based theories of behaviour.

2. A central focus for much of the sociological examination of the environment has been the deep-seated value cleavage between environmentalists and their opponents in industry and science. The latter support a dominant social paradigm that stresses materialism, economic growth, and the human right to dominate nature. In contrast, environmentalists propose an alternative environmental paradigm that emphasizes the need to adopt small-scale, decentralized economic and political structures that are in harmony with nature. This value-oriented environmentalism has found its fullest expression in a number of "ecophilosophies"— deep ecology and ecofeminism—that have recently flourished on the margins of the environmental movement.

3. Support for environmentalism has remained remarkably constant for nearly 20 years. Although the majority of the population is generally supportive of environmental values, a young, well-educated, urban, liberal core has taken the lead in working for environmental change. Most other Canadians will recycle, purchase "green" products, and act positively toward the environment, but only to the extent that such action does not require any real sacrifice in terms of time and money.

4. In order to mobilize the reluctant majority, environmental-movement organizers develop frames (interpretations of events) that play up the possibility of an impending global collapse as a result of uncontrolled population growth and continued industrial growth. Global warming, expanding holes in the ozone layer, and the worldwide loss of biodiversity are the most recently identified symptoms of the impending crisis. The only solution, it is claimed, is to draw back and ease down, conserving resources, reducing pollution, and restricting population increase. However, these goals are especially difficult to achieve in the expanding economies of the Third World, where the environment is threatened by both unsustainable development and unsustainable impoverishment.

5. At the level of the local community, willingness to act on environmental problems rises as trust in expert institutions declines. This loss of trust is characteristic of neighbourhood-based environmental conflicts, in which citizens typically find the explanations and assurances offered by scientists and other authority figures to be faulty. Environmental-risk perception and action are also linked to people's participation in local social networks and community affairs.

6. The role of environmental entrepreneurs or claims-makers is vital in moving environmental issues from free-floating concerns to problems that are recognized and acted upon by those in power. These promoters, situated in science, environmental organizations, and the media, define problems such as acid rain, global warming, and ozone depletion; package them; and elevate them to action agendas.

7. The social construction of environmental problems does not occur in a vacuum but is shaped by political and economic factors, to the extent that the powerful in society have the ability to act as gatekeepers, determining what is and what is not relevant with respect to the environment. Environmental problems, then, are actively contested, often on the basis of acceptable or unacceptable risk. Social constructionism in the context of power inequality represents a promising sociological route to understanding the environment–society relationship.

QUESTIONS TO CONSIDER

1. What types of environmental hazards do you and members of your community routinely face? Who do you think determines what is an acceptable level of risk in these situations? Scientists? The government? The media?

2. Analyze the environmental content of your local newspapers and/or television news programs over the course of several weeks. Is environmental coverage balanced or does it favour a specific point of view? What types of media frames (interpretations of events) are used to organize information relating to environmental issues?

3. Keep a diary of all your consumer activities (shopping, transportation, leisure) for a week. Which of the products you buy and services you use are most likely to contribute to the deterioration of the environment? Which show signs of a "green" attitude among manufacturers, merchants, and service providers?

4. In the 1970s, Downs (1972) estimated that concern over the environment was about midway through the issue-attention cycle. Where in the cycle do you think it is now? What factors do you think have influenced its progression over the last three decades?

5. What is meant by the term *environmental management*? Think of some specific examples from Canadian political life in which governments have sought to use this strategy in order to distance themselves from environmental controversies.

GLOSSARY

The **alternative environmental paradigm** comprises a set of beliefs that challenge the centrality of economic growth, technological progress, and the human domination of nature as pillars of our society. This paradigm stresses the need to adopt small-scale, decentralized economic and political structures that are in harmony with nature.

Anthropocentrism refers to human-centredness. It's an ideology that assumes that humans are separate from and superior to all other natural things, and judges human actions in the natural environment accordingly.

Biocentric egalitarianism is the principle, held by deep ecologists, that all things on earth have an equal right to exist. In this view, humans have no special rights or privileges that allow them to subdue and destroy their natural surroundings.

The **broadening-base hypothesis** says that environmental concern will eventually spread beyond its present social base—that is, of young, well-educated, urban, politically liberal citizens—to all of society.

Carrying capacity refers to the optimum population size that the planet can support under present environmental conditions.

Deep ecology is an environmental ethic emphasizing that all species in nature are of equal value. Our experience of nature, deep ecologists claim, should be the foundation for an energetic environmentalism that opposes the present domination by rational science.

The **dominant paradigm** is a widely accepted view of the world that emphasizes the moral imperative of material-wealth creation and the moral conviction that humans have the inalienable right to dominate nature and harness the environment to that end.

Ecofeminism is an environmental ethic that sees androcentrism (male-centredness) as the root of ecological destruction. Ecofeminists identify a distinctly feminine way of thinking and acting that is nurturing, cooperative, communal, and sensitive to nature.

The **economic-contingency hypothesis** says that the broadening of the social base of environmental concern is contingent on prevailing economic conditions. When economic conditions worsen or are perceived as worsening, those who are least well off will be the first to shift their focus away from the environment to the economy.

Environmental management refers to moderate government intervention in environmental conflicts that accords some limited protection to the environment without seriously curtailing economic development.

The **Gaia hypothesis** is a controversial idea that proposes that the earth is a living organism that adjusts and regulates itself in the same manner as does the human body. It was first proposed by British atmospheric scientist James Lovelock and American microbiologist Lynn Margulis in the late 1960s.

The **human-exceptionalism paradigm** is a worldview that features the ideals of steadily evolving social progress, increasing prosperity and material comfort, and class mobility for all segments of society, while ignoring the environmental costs of economic growth.

The **issue-attention cycle** is a five-stage sequence through which the "career" of most social problems is said to pass.

Normal accidents are inevitable failures in nuclear power stations, petrochemical plants, air-traffic control nets, and other high-risk technological systems. Such accidents are regarded by corporate organizations as an inevitable consequence of operating a hazardous facility.

Risk refers to the relative probability that a particular hazard will actually occur.

Sustainable development is economic development that meets the needs of the present without compromising the ability of future generations to meet their own needs.

The **treadmill of production** is the inherent need of our economic system to continually yield profits by creating consumer demand for new products, even when this means expanding the ecosystem to its furthest limits.

SUGGESTED READING

Barlow, Maude, and Elizabeth May. (2000). *Frederick Street: Life and Death on Canada's Love Canal*. Toronto: HarperCollins. Compelling dramatic account by two well-known social activists detailing the struggle by residents of a Cape Breton neighbourhood to force politicians and bureaucrats to clean up what could be Canada's single worst toxic site. The final chapter provides a useful survey of other toxic hot spots across the country.

Bullard, Robert D. (1990). *Dumping in Dixie: Race, Class and Environmental Quality*. Boulder, CO: Westview Press. A pioneering study of the environmental impact on poor Black communities in the U.S. South as a result of the locating of petrochemical factories, oil refineries, hazardous waste facilities, and other sources of industrial pollution.

Carson, Rachel. (1962). *Silent Spring*. Boston: Houghton Mifflin. The book that launched the modern environmental movement. Still a profound and relevant statement of the dangers posed by agricultural chemicals to the natural world and the human food chain.

Davis, Susan G. (1997). *Spectacular Nature: Corporate Culture and the Sea World Experience*. Berkeley and Los Angeles: University of California Press. The product of nearly a decade of archival, observational, and interview research at San Diego's marine "nature park," Davis's book presents a penetrating analysis of how corporations package and sell nature and the environment in contemporary America.

Hannigan, John A. (1995). *Environmental Sociology: A Social Constructionist Perspective*. London and New York: Routledge. The essential ingredients of environmental sociology, Hannigan contends, are questions of risk, media, science, nature, regulation, postmodernity, and social movements. In this highly readable overview of the field, students are provided with a social-constructionist model for analyzing environmental issues that can form the basis for their own research projects.

Harrison, Kathryn, and George Hoberg. (1994). *Risk, Science and Politics: Regulating Toxic Substances in Canada and the United States*. Montreal and Kingston, ON: McGill-Queen's University Press. A comparative study of government regulation of toxic substances in two neighbouring countries. The authors present case studies of six controversial substances suspected of causing cancer in humans: the pesticides Alar and alachlor, urea-formaldehyde foam insulation, radon gas, saccharin, and asbestos.

World Commission on Environment and Development [The Brundtland Commission]. (1987). *Our Common Future: Report to the United Nations General Assembly*. New York: Oxford University Press. A much-cited examination of the relationship between economic development, Third World poverty, and global environmental problems.

CHAPTER SEVENTEEN

POPULATION, AGING, AND HEALTH

In this chapter you will learn that:

- Demography involves the study of population size, growth, distribution, composition, fertility, mortality, and migration.
- Demography distinguishes between population states (size, distribution over space, and composition by various characteristics) and population processes (fertility, mortality, and migration); it analyzes how processes influence states and vice versa.
- Malthus argued that populations have a tendency to grow more rapidly than other resources and that people can control the growth of population by reducing births. In contrast, Marx argued that economic and social conditions determine the rate of population growth and that proper social arrangements should be able to accommodate population growth.
- The demographic-transition theory summarizes the history of population growth through three stages as birth and death rates decline.
- Since Confederation, life expectancy in Canada has increased from 42 to 79 years because of increased standards of living, improvements in sanitation, and medical improvements; average births have declined from 7 to 1.5 per woman, and the net balance between immigration and emigration accounted for close to a quarter of population growth in Canada during the twentieth century.
- Societal aging first occurred due to a decline in the numbers of children (aging through fewer persons at the bottom of the age pyramid), while now the baby boom is moving to older ages (aging at the middle), and there is higher survivorship at older ages (aging at the top).
- The health status of the population can be analyzed in terms of risk factors for poor health and the extent to which the health system can alleviate the ensuing problems. With an older population, there is a larger number of persons at ages where health problems are more likely to occur, presenting difficult decisions regarding the allocation of increasingly expensive health technology.
- We now face challenges in education, employment, health care, and pensions due to Canada's slower growing and aging population.

RODERIC BEAUJOT
UNIVERSITY OF WESTERN ONTARIO

INTRODUCTION

One of the most important features of any society is the number of people and the relative size of the various subgroups. When populations grow or shrink, and when subgroups change in relative size, serious repercussions follow.

Consider English–French relations in Canada. For a long time, the French constituted about a third of the population. In response to heavy English immigration, French-Canadian society emphasized the importance of births for maintaining the relative power of the French element in the country. A Catholic priest called for *La revanche du berceau* ("the revenge of the cradles)"—that is, for maintaining a high French birth rate as a means of securing the status of the French in the country. When Quebec fertility fell in the 1960s and the French-speaking population of Canada dropped to nearly a quarter of the total, the long-term accommodation of the country's two charter groups was threatened.

Particularly problematic for Quebec was the eagerness of various immigrant groups to associate with the English minority of the province. In the early 1970s, there was even concern that French would no longer be the working language in the province of Quebec. Various accommodations have been made to this demographic change, such as the Official Languages Act, the policy on multiculturalism, the recognition of a distinct role for Quebec in immigrant selection, and the Quebec Charter of the French Language (Bill 101). The constitutional crises since the 1990s, particularly as they pertain to the concept of Quebec as a distinct society, indicate that Canada is still looking for ways to accommodate the changing demographics.

Aging is another key feature of the changing relative size of various subgroups of the population. This time it is the age groups that are changing, and this affects the society in a variety of ways. While aging is a long-term phenomenon that has been taking place for more than a century, there are different stages, which have different consequences. At first, aging largely involved fewer numbers of children. For instance, over the period 1966 to 1981 the population grew by 22 percent but the number of persons under age 15 declined by 17 percent. These earlier stages of aging were relatively easy to accommodate. While changing sizes of age groups implied

difficult accommodations in the school system, in a broad sense adults were freer, given that they had fewer children to care for. These changes both maximized the proportion of the population that was at an employable age and freed women from family preoccupations, encouraging them to participate in the labour force. These trends permitted an expansion of the social programs that depend on revenues from the taxation of employed persons (particularly health, education, social security, and pension programs).

However, at later stages of aging it is no longer the relative size of the population of labour-force age that is growing, but rather the numbers of seniors. Already over the period 1986 to 2001, the population grew by 19 percent but the number of persons aged 65 and over increased by 45 percent. The population aged 65 and over represented 10.7 percent of the total in 1986, compared to 13.0 percent in 2001, and will probably comprise a quarter of the population by 2036 when the baby boom is completely retired. In effect, our social programs were put into place when the demographic and economic contexts were rather different. When the population at labour-force ages is growing, and real incomes are increasing, it is not hard to enrich social programs, including those, such as health and pensions, that benefit the elderly. Policy debates surrounding taxation and social programs indicate that the accommodations in the later stages of aging may not be as easy as in the earlier stages. Some observers have come to question whether we will be able to afford all our social programs. Others call for different forms of accommodation, such as greater individual responsibility for personal health, greater repayment for the economic benefits of government-subsidized education, a longer work life, lower pension benefits, and even the promotion of higher birth rates and increased immigration.

Health status is another phenomenon that can be studied from the point of view of population change. In effect, well-being in society is often analyzed through income and its distribution (see Chapters 8 and 9), or through conflict, crime, and victimization (see Chapter 19), but we can also look at well-being through population health. The comparison of the relative health status of various sectors of the population permits an analysis of the differences across groups, and this points to the dynamics of well-being. For instance, men have a lower life expectancy, but women's advantage has shrunk from seven to five years. Besides the purely biological factors in this difference, there are important differences in risk factors, including smoking as well as drinking and driving. Although the gender differences in smoking for young persons have largely disappeared, the mortality of older persons is still affected by past differences in behaviour. But smoking also needs to be analyzed in relation to social expectations for fitting into groups, for physical appearance, and as a means of relieving tension in categories of persons who are under stress. Similarly, the higher life expectancy of married persons can be analyzed in terms of the "protective role of marriage." Married persons benefit from having someone who can help in times of illness, and married men, in particular, benefit from having better diets and lower levels of risk behaviour than unmarried men (Trovato, 1998).

We can also look at the consequences of population change at the level of the total human population. Some scholars have proposed that the rapid growth of the human species represents in biological terms a catastrophic event for the planet, comparable to an ice age or a major meteoric collision. Biologists measure change over millions of years and, in this context, the human presence, which was once insignificant, can be seen as changing the very environment of the planet. Many call for sustainable development, and various world meetings sponsored by the United Nations are attempting to find ways to ensure that the sheer size of the human population does not endanger our viability on the planet.

These few examples illustrate the importance of studying population dynamics along with the associated phenomena of aging and health. This chapter will first consider the ways in which populations are studied. After looking at the growth of the world population, various theoretical perspectives will be considered for analyzing the causes and consequences of population change. We will then take a closer look at Canadian trends, especially the dynamics of mortality/health, fertility, and immigration, and their implications for the size, aging, and geographic distribution of the population.

THE STUDY OF POPULATION

People are born, they move around, and they die. When these events are added up for a number of people, demographers call them *fertility*, *migration*, and *mortality*. These events mark a person's life-course: Any short biography would certainly include when the person was born, where he or she lived, and when he or she died.

Although these events are clearly experienced by individuals, added together they also demarcate the development of societies over time. At the group

Between 1986 and 2001 the number of people aged 65 or over increased by nearly 45 percent. This increase puts a strain on social programs, such as health care and pensions.
SOURCE: Ilse Hughes, *In the Corridor.*

level, fertility and immigration are the basic mechanisms through which populations, countries, societies, and communities are regenerated. These regenerative processes not only add numbers to the population, ensuring demographic continuity in the face of departures through death and emigration, they also change the character of the population and, consequently, of the society. The character of the population is changed in terms of age and sex structure, socioeconomic composition, cultural make-up, and regional distribution.

An understanding of society needs to take into account the nature of the population: How many people are there? How are they distributed over space? How many children are there? How many older people? How many have university degrees? How many have low incomes? How many have disabilities or poor health? And so on.

We also want to know something about these basic numbers for the purpose of *comparing* societies. For instance, at the time of Confederation in 1867, Canada's population was relatively small. At 3.5 million, it was about one-tenth the size of each of France and the United Kingdom; at an estimated 31.1 million in 2001, Canada is now half the size of each of those countries. If Canada had remained a relatively very small country, it probably would not have become part of the Group of Seven (G-7), the seven major Western industrial countries.

The other side of the coin is this: It is by means of understanding the society that we are able to interpret trends in the vital events of births, deaths, and geographic movement. What makes people want to have children? Why do people have fewer children now than they did in the 1950s? Why have abortions become more acceptable? What kinds of people find abortions acceptable, and under what circumstances? Why are there fewer deaths resulting from infectious diseases, and more from cancer? Why does migration in Canada tend to be to the west and to the south? Who tends to move and why? Why is Canada more open to immigration than most other industrialized countries? Why do people leave Canada? The analysis of these questions brings us to analyze important aspects of our society.

Putting this discussion in the language of sociological methodology and statistics, population phenomena can be treated as independent or dependent variables. If we were to analyze the effect of age structure on health-care needs, we would be treating population composition by age as an independent variable whose consequences we wanted to understand relative to the consequences of the other independent variables such as risk behaviour, health practices, and health services. Alternatively, if we were to analyze the impact of income, education, and attitudes on the number of births, we would be treating fertility as a dependent variable, the causes of which we were seeking to understand.

POPULATION AND POLICY

Given that demographic processes are fundamental to societies and their regeneration, society has a vested interest in ensuring that population dynamics operate to produce an overall net benefit (Demeny, 1988). All societies attempt to shape the decision-making framework of individuals in such a way as to promote this common benefit. With respect to fertility, behaviour that promotes reproduction will sometimes be encouraged and sometimes constrained. With respect to mortality, behaviour that will prolong a person's life in the society will be encouraged, and the society will often take some responsibility for the health and safety of its citizens. With respect to immigration, the society as a whole will typically establish structures, policies, and rules through which entry (and sometimes exit) are controlled in order to produce a social benefit.

There are a number of questions that interest the society as a whole. How many new members are to be added and by what means (through births or immigration)? How are the costs of these additions to be paid, and who receives the benefits? How should the costs and benefits of children be absorbed by the families to which they are born, the larger extended family, the community, and the society as a whole? How are the costs and benefits of immigration to be distributed between, on the one hand, the immigrants themselves and their sponsoring families and, on the other hand, the receiving country, province, city, and community? To what extent are health and safety the responsibility of the individual or the surrounding society? How does the society accommodate itself to an aging population, in terms of regenerating the labour force, pensions, and health care, while ensuring that intergenerational equity does not disadvantage the young? These are among the policy questions that all societies must address. Policy orientations to changing demographics can take two forms: that of attempting to influence the course of demographic events or that of ensuring that the society makes the adjustments necessary to accommodate the population change.

Such policy considerations underline the importance of gathering accurate information. Censuses were first taken to enable rulers to tax their citizens and to determine the number of men available for military service. With the advent of the welfare state, it is particularly important for governments to have accurate and up-to-date information on the population whose welfare they are trying to enhance. It is crucial to know how given groups would benefit or suffer from given policies.

POPULATION STATES AND PROCESSES

Demography is the study of populations—their size, distribution, and composition—and the immediate factors causing population change (births, deaths, and migration). We are interested in the stock and the flow of population. The **population stock**, or the state of the population, is a picture of the population at one time, including its size, its distribution over geography, and its composition in terms of a variety of characteristics, such as age, sex, marital status, education, language spoken at home, occupation, income, and health status. The *flow*, or the **population processes**, involves changes in population from one time to another as a function of births, deaths, and movements of people. As noted earlier, in demography these processes are called, respectively, fertility, mortality, and migration.

LINKS BETWEEN POPULATION STATES AND PROCESSES

Population states and processes are dynamically interrelated. For instance, lower birth rates (a process) produce an older population (a state); conversely, an older population tends to have a lower birth rate.

Let us explore further the links between population processes and states, beginning with the impact of processes *on* states. A change in population *size*— that is, a change from one state to a second state—is

clearly a function of intervening births, deaths, **immigration**, and **emigration**. Births minus deaths is called **natural increase** (or decrease), and immigration minus emigration is called **net migration**. Thus, the basic equation for population at a given time is as follows:

$$P2 = P1 + B - D + I - E,$$

where $P2$ represents the population at a given time; $P1$, the population at an earlier time (normally, the time at which a census is taken); B, the number of births in the interval; D, the number of deaths in the interval; I, the number of immigrants who arrived in the interval; and E, the number of emigrants who departed in the interval.

For example, over the first nine decades of the twentieth century, net migration (more people coming than leaving) comprised some 22 percent of Canadian **population growth**, with natural increase (more births than deaths) comprising the other 78 percent. However, in the period 1991–2001, slightly more than half of population growth was attributable to net migration. Were it not for migration, Canada's population growth during this period would have been well under 1 percent per year.

In considering the *distribution* of the population over space, the analysis becomes more complex. For one thing, international immigrants tend to settle in certain parts of the country more than in others. For another, **internal migration**, in terms of both places departed and destinations, is not evenly distributed throughout the country. Finally, regions may differ in fertility and mortality rates. For example, over the period 1931–61 in particular, higher birth rates in Quebec helped to maintain its relative size among the provinces of Canada. Today, differences in natural increase have little impact on the relative growth of regions, but trends in international and internal migration tend to increase the relative size of Ontario, British Columbia, and Alberta, and to reduce the relative size of the Atlantic provinces, Manitoba, and Saskatchewan.

Changes in a society's *age structure* can also be related to births, deaths, and migration. The age structure of a population is often depicted as a pyramid, with the youngest age groups at the base; males are represented on one side and females on the other. (See Figures 17.1 and 17.6 on pages 439 and 455 for examples of age pyramids.) All births occur at what demographers call "age zero" of the age structure, whereas deaths can occur at various ages, as can migrations. It is often thought that the increase in the proportion of older people in the population is attributable to the fact that people are living longer, making for more people at the top of the pyramid. However, it is births and the way they change over time, rather than deaths, that are most responsible for determining the basic shape of an age-structure pyramid. Deaths, being spread out over a range of ages, do not have as great an impact on the shape of the pyramid.

Other analyses of changes in population states follow the same pattern. Recall that a population stock, or state, is the picture of a given population at one point in time in terms of size, distribution, or composition. For instance, we could analyze the change in composition by marital status, educational attainment, or labour-force status. Health status may be studied in terms of the transitions from states of good to poor health, and vice versa, along with the factors that help predict these transitions.

We have been considering how the population processes of fertility, mortality, and migration affect the population states of size, distribution, and composition. We could also consider how population states affect population processes. For instance, one of the reasons for the decrease in the number of births in Canada is that the composition of the population by marital status is currently characterized by a reduced proportion of young adults living in marital or cohabiting unions. As another example, the number of deaths in Canada is increasing not because death rates in given age groups are increasing, but because there is now a greater predominance of people at ages at which deaths are more common—that is, we have an older population. Might it also be that the growing size of the world population, along with increased level of consumption, are having consequences on the quality of our physical environment, or the health of our planet's ecosystem?

Box 17.1 provides further examples of the importance of looking at the age structure of the population when considering changes in Canadian society. Economist David Foot emphasizes how an individual's opportunity structure is related to that person's place in the age pyramid, especially the relative size of the generation into which he or she was born. At the societal level, Foot shows that demographics help to predict various phenomena.

POPULATION GROWTH AT THE WORLD LEVEL

Although necessarily vague, estimates suggest that the population of the world 12 000 years ago was in the range of 5 to 10 million people. The estimated number for 2002 is 6.2 billion (see Table 17.1).

TABLE 17.1 ESTIMATES AND PROJECTIONS OF WORLD POPULATION, 10 000 B.C.E. TO 2100 C.E. (IN MILLIONS)

YEAR	WORLD POPULATION	REGIONS OF EUROPEAN ORIGIN PLUS JAPAN[a]	LESS-DEVELOPED REGIONS[b]
10 000 B.C.E.	6	–	–
0	252	–	–
1750 C.E.	760	191 (25.1%)	569 (74.9%)
1950	2516	835 (33.2%)	1681 (66.8%)
2000	6055	1188 (19.6%)	4867 (80.4%)
2025	7824	1215 (15.5%)	6609 (84.5%)
2050	8909	1155 (13.0%)	7754 (87.0%)

[a] includes Europe, the former U.S.S.R., Japan, Australia, New Zealand, the United States, and Canada.
[b] includes Africa, Asia (minus Japan and parts of the former U.S.S.R.), and South America.

SOURCE: Massimo Livi-Bacci, *A Concise History of World Population* (Cambridge, MA: Blackwell, 1992), p. 31; Thomas W. Merrick, with PRB Staff, "World Population in Transition," *Population Bulletin 41*, no. 2 (Washington, DC: Population Reference Bureau, 1986), p. 12; United Nations, *World Population Prospects: The 1998 Revision*, UN ST/ESA/Ser A/177 (New York: United Nations, 1999).

BOX 17.1   BOOM, BUST & ECHO 2000

Demography, the study of human populations, is the most powerful—and most underutilized—tool we have to understand the past and to foretell the future. Demographics affect every one of us as individuals, far more than most of us have ever imagined. They also play a pivotal role in the economic and social life of our country....

Demographics tell you, as an individual, a great deal about who you are, where you've been, and where you're going. If, for example, you were lucky enough to be born in 1937 and you've been successful, it wouldn't hurt to learn a little humility. You haven't had much competition, because few people were born in Canada in 1937. That demographic good fortune probably had as much to do with your success as you did.

On the other hand, perhaps you had the misfortune to enter the world in 1961, one of the worst years in [the twentieth] century to be born. You're one of a huge crowd of late boomers, also known as Generation X. The mass of older boomers who preceded you occupied most of the best jobs and pushed the price of real estate way up, possibly out of your reach until recently. Chances are that life has been a struggle for you. And your parents, the lucky people who were born in 1937 or thereabouts, probably don't understand how tough that struggle has been. For your own peace of mind, you need to understand that some of the setbacks you have experienced may relate more to demographics than to any personal failings....

The baby-busters [born between 1967 and 1979] have done pretty well so far, especially the younger ones. They have been able to get into just about any school or summer camp they wanted. They had no difficulty finding babysitting, lawn-mowing, and other part-time jobs in high school, unlike their older brothers and sisters, who had less opportunity to earn money while in high school because they had so many competitors. During the 1990s, university entry standards fell, making it easier for busters to get into the school of their choice.

There is good reason for people in their 20s at the millennium to be both more realistic and more idealistic than those in their 30s. In fact, the baby-busters resemble the front-end boomers, who could espouse idealistic causes during the 1960s safe in the knowledge that a good job and a prosperous lifestyle would be there for the taking once they were ready for those bourgeois things....

[At the societal level, the two key questions are] the number of people in each age group and the probability that each person will participate in a given behaviour. Express the number of people doing a certain thing as a percentage of the number of people in the population and you get the activity participation rate for the society as a whole. Probability and participation rate are the same thing, except that probability applies to an individual while participation rate applied to a whole society. Multiply the participation rate by the population, and you get the actual number of people who are bowling or buying houses or having heart attacks or whatever else you may want to measure....

In fact, age is a proxy for many of the socioeconomic variables that differentiate human beings. A 30-year-old, for example, is more likely to be married than a 20-year-old. A 40-year-old probably has a higher income than a 30-year-old. For this reason, focussing on age captures many other factors and simplifies the analytical process.

Analyzing human behaviour according to age has the great advantage of allowing us to know what is actually going on instead of living in a fog of misconception. Most journalists look at the total participation in an activity—crime, for example—and then exclaim in print, "It's going up!" or "It's going down!" But these changes, if based on the population as a whole, may be misleading, reflecting only the changing age composition of society. In an aging society, the number of crimes goes down because older people don't commit as many crimes as younger ones. A drop in the overall crime rate, therefore, may have no connection to any change in behaviour, the economy, social attitudes, or law enforcement techniques. It may be unrelated to anything at all except a decline in the number of people in the crime-prone youth age groups. On the other hand, the appearance of a higher crime rate among a particular age group would signify genuine change.

SOURCE: *Boom Bust & Echo: Profiting From the Demographic Shift in the 21st Century.* Copyright © 1998 by David K. Foot. Reprinted by permission of the author.

Where there was once one person, there are now a thousand. Growth has escalated dramatically over the past two centuries. It is estimated that world population reached its first billion around 1800, its second in 1930, its third in 1960, its fourth in 1975, its fifth in 1987, and its sixth billion in 1999.

Human history can usefully be divided into segments characterized by different population-growth

SOURCE: Cam/*Ottawa Citizen*. Used with permission.

dynamics. Ten thousand years ago, people lived in *hunting-and-gathering* societies. It appears that the long-term growth dynamics in those societies were minimal. There were probably periods of growth, but there were other times of high mortality due to conquest, famine, or disease. Fertility was also considerably less than the biological maximum because births needed to be spaced to ensure the survival of infants. Evidence from societies that until recently lived as hunters and gatherers suggests that the difficulty of finding soft food for children and the consequent need for long periods of lactation kept average births per woman in the range of five or six (Howell, 1979).

The Agricultural Revolution, which began 10 000 to 12 000 years ago, involved the emergence of agriculture and the domestication of animals, allowing more people to be supported by the environment. The more secure food supply would have reduced deaths, but famines associated with climatic conditions were still prevalent, and increased population density fostered the spread of communicable diseases. It would appear that the agricultural revolution brought more deaths from all causes except inadequate nutrition (Muhsam, 1979: 50). The number of births probably increased as the availability of softer foods made shorter lactation periods possible.

The next period was that of European population expansion over the two centuries from 1750 to 1950. This period of rapid population growth in countries of European settlement occurred largely because of a reduction in death rates, which was in turn attributable to the nutritional improvements

afforded by agricultural innovations. Improvements in public sanitation followed, and the practice of medicine also started to have an effect. After about 1870, birth rates started to decline, and this ultimately slowed down European population growth.

The last period, which started around 1950 and will probably continue into the first two decades of the twenty-first century, might be called the period of Third World population expansion. Here again, death rates declined, in fact more rapidly than they had in the case of the European populations. This was also a function of improved living conditions, better sanitation, and improved medicine. It was largely after 1970 that birth rates started to decline in the developing countries, and there remains much variability. However, as an average for all developing countries, it is estimated that 57 percent of women of childbearing age are using contraception and the average family size is 3.2 births per woman. As we will see in the next section, the demographic transition involves average births per woman declining from six to two. In that context, more than half of the transition has been achieved.

It is useful to see the rapid population growth of the less-developed countries in a historical context. First, it is important to appreciate that this growth has been caused by reductions in mortality rather than increases in fertility. More precisely, in both the European and Third World expansions, growth has occurred because death rates fell sooner and faster than did birth rates. Second, it is noteworthy that, in some regards, the two population expansions have compensated for each other. It is estimated that, in 1750, 25 percent of the world population lived in Europe, North America, Oceania, and Japan (now called the more-developed countries), whereas 75 percent lived in the remaining parts of Asia as well as in South America and Africa (that is, in the less-developed countries). By 1950, the population of the more-developed countries had risen to 33 percent of the world population, but today, it is back to 20 percent.

However, the future is likely to witness a continuation of the relative expansion of the population of the less-developed countries, which will intensify the demographic contrasts. According to the projections of the United Nations (1999), the European/Japanese population will drop to roughly 15 percent of the world population by 2025, and to only 13 percent by the year 2050.

As Figure 17.1 further illustrates, the population of the less-developed countries is young and growing rapidly, whereas that of the more-developed countries is aging and growing much more slowly. It is significant to note that the larger, more rapidly growing population has a significantly smaller share of the world's economic product; moreover, it is the wealthy, smaller population that wields power in the world (see Chapter 10). From the perspective of such inequalities, demographic trends can be considered explosive. John Maynard Keynes, the father of modern economics, thought that big historical events are often caused by slow demographic processes. The differences in demographic dynamics between the less-developed and the more-developed countries are likely to bring about changes in international relations: It seems inevitable that the larger countries and regions will eventually come to have more power in defining our destiny.

Concerns about population growth led the United Nations to organize three World Population conferences (in 1974, 1984, and 1994), bringing together government representatives from countries around the world to deliberate on the action that needs to be taken to forestall potential disaster. The 1974 conference was characterized by heated debates between those who wanted all countries to commit themselves to lower birth rates and those who argued that birth rates would fall only as a consequence of economic development. As we will see in the next section, the debate was effectively between Malthusian and Marxist views. Malthusians argued that, in order to reduce poverty, we must promote the use of contraception worldwide and work to reduce fertility. Marxists countered with the slogan "Development is the best contraceptive." In other words, they argued that it was only through development that fertility would decline significantly.

By 1984, there was greater consensus among nations, on both the importance of the problem of population growth and the approach that should be adopted to deal with it. It was generally agreed that improvements in health and standards of living (through economic development) and a greater availability of contraception were both necessary, as mutually reinforcing strategies.

The 1994 conference faced strong pressures on four fronts in particular. Environmentalists, while recognizing that overconsumption and high standards of living are partly responsible for the growing

FIGURE 17.1 POPULATION AGE PYRAMIDS FOR LESS-DEVELOPED AND MORE-DEVELOPED COUNTRIES, 2000 AND 2050

■ 2000
□ 2050

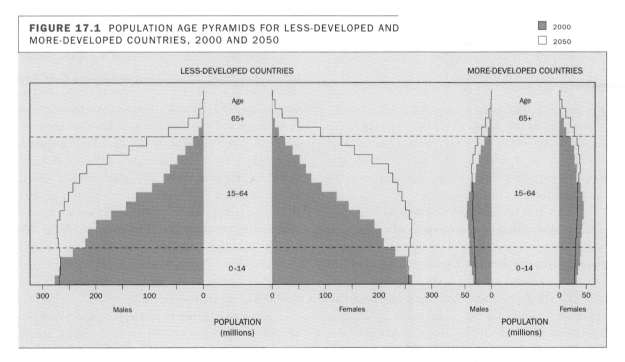

SOURCE: United Nations, *Sex and Age Distribution of the World Population: The 2000 Revision*, 2001 United Nations ST/ESA/Ser. A/199.

stress on the environment, emphasized the dangers of population growth in this regard. Civil-rights activists argued against the coercive family planning that some governments have been imposing on their populations, and argued that family size should be a matter of individual choice. European countries in particular expressed concerns about massive international migration as a consequence of population pressures. Finally, media attention at the conference focused on the abortion controversy. There were, however, strong elements of consensus in the final 1994 conference document. Population problems were recognized as part of the difficulty of sustainable development, in terms of providing access to education, health, and clean water. The conference suggested various actions "to ensure the basic right of all couples and individuals to decide freely and responsibly the number and spacing of their children and to have the information, education and means to do so" (United Nations, 1995: 30). Regarding international migration, the document speaks of enacting policies that would make migration a positive phenomenon for both sending and receiving countries, as well as for migrants themselves. For abortion, the document first says that "in no case should abortion be promoted as a method of family planning," and, later, that "in circumstances where abortion is not against the law, such abortion should be safe" (United Nations, 1995: 44).

In effect, the conference recognized population as an issue at the societal or macro level, but emphasized individual or microlevel policy for addressing the problem. For instance, it argued against constraints from the broader society, such as those imposed by China's one-child policy. It focused on satisfying the unmet need for contraception and empowering individual women, enabling them to control their reproductive destiny.

The world attention to these population issues, along with the impact of many other social and economic changes, have clearly brought reductions in the rate of world population growth, from a peak of just over 2 percent per year in the 1960s, to 1.3 percent in 2001. Some people have even suggested that the world population will soon decline. Eberstadt (2001) has talked about "population implosion," and Ibbitson (2002) wrote under the title "The Long, Slow Exit of the Human Race." In effect, some populations are on the verge of decline, due either to long

periods of low birth rates, or to the HIV/AIDS epidemic. However, for the population of the whole world, it is important not to confuse slower growth and decline. Even the lowest assumptions in the United Nations (2001: 38) projections anticipate a world population that reaches the peak of 7.9 billion only in 2045. In this low projection there is still a 30 percent growth between 2000 and 2050. The growth to 2050 is 54 percent in the medium projection, and 80 percent in the high projection.

THEORETICAL PERSPECTIVES ON THE CAUSES AND CONSEQUENCES OF POPULATION CHANGE

This section reviews various theoretical perspectives on population change, focusing on those that explore the causes and consequences of change.

THOMAS MALTHUS

The political economist Thomas Malthus (1766–1834) was the first to develop a systematic theory of population change and its relation to economic conditions (Malthus, 1798). He considered the causes of population growth to be grounded in human nature. On the one hand, because of the natural attraction between the sexes, along with what he called an "urge to reproduce," he thought there was a natural tendency for the population to grow—and to do so at such a rapid rate as to outgrow the available food supply. On the other hand, he saw two checks on population growth. One, which he called "positive," occurred through mortality, from causes such as famine, epidemics, wars, and plagues. The other, which he called "preventive," occurred through fertility, and could take the form of "moral restraint," that is the postponement of marriage or abstinence within marriage, or the form of "vice," which included the prevention of births in marriage through abortion, infanticide, and other unacceptable methods of contraception.

Today, infanticide is condemned and there are serious disagreements about abortion. Some people disagree with specific methods of contraception, such as the "morning-after pill," on ethical grounds, and others are concerned about the health risks associated with certain methods. It is perhaps not surprising, then, that Malthus, an Anglican clergyman, argued for the delay of marriage until a young person was sufficiently established to have children, and for abstinence.

While we may disagree with some of Malthus's moral values, the debate goes on regarding what are acceptable and unacceptable means of reducing births. The dominant view at the 1994 United Nations Conference on Population and Development was that the unacceptable means include "population control" while the acceptable means are called "reproductive health" (United Nations, 1995).

Malthus also had a clear view of the basis for population change. Populations grow if births outnumber deaths. If this growth strains the available resources, there are likely to be more deaths and/or fewer births. If births take place mostly in the context of marriage, the postponement of marriage or the use of contraception by married couples could be relied upon to produce fewer births.

Malthus thought that the consequences of population growth were fairly serious. He argued that, left unchecked, population growth would proceed in a geometric progression (2, 4, 8, 16), whereas resources would grow arithmetically (2, 4, 6, 8). What is key here is not whether there is precisely a geometric versus an arithmetic progression, but the basic conclusion that population has a tendency to grow more rapidly than do available resources, particularly the supply of food. As a consequence, population growth could be expected to produce poverty and misery.

Particularly in his early writings, Malthus did not hold out much hope for finding a solution to this problem. If for some reason the food supply increased more than the population did, people would probably get married earlier and have more children, so there would eventually be even more people living in poverty. He feared that if the conditions of the poor were improved (for instance, through a more equitable distribution of income), there would be even more population growth and thus a larger problem in the long term. He felt strongly that people had to absorb the consequences of their own actions, and he preached "responsible procreation" or "moral restraint" as a way of avoiding excessive growth.

Today, we often refer to Malthus's theory as the "Malthusian trap." Population is limited by the means of subsistence; continuous growth is not pos-

sible in a limited world. The "Malthusian solution" is to encourage a reduction of births, both through later marriage and, especially, through the use of contraception, in order to avoid an increase in deaths. Malthus's contribution thus lay in his view of population growth as a serious problem that causes poverty, strains resources, and undermines efforts to improve society.

Present-day neo-Malthusian thinking is less concerned with questions of food supply because it is possible to produce more food; it is a question of access to food. The main concerns have shifted to the environment as a "sink" for the byproducts of our affluent society: polluted water and air, the concentration of carbon dioxide in the atmosphere and its impact on climate change, and ozone depletion with its consequences for exposure to ultraviolet light. In effect, the concerns are less with the number of people who can be fed, and more with the health and mortality consequences of a changing environment.

Ehrlich and Ehrlich (1990) have advanced this thinking by observing that the impact on the environment is a function of population size, level of affluence, and technology. This is known as the "PAT" equation:

$$I = P \times A \times T$$

where I represents the impact on the environment; P, the population size; A, the level of affluence or consumption; and T, the technology used to obtain that affluence. This equation makes it clear that stress is associated not only with the population size, but also with the level of consumption and the extent to which the technology used is hard on the environment. These variables do not always act independently. There can also be interaction effects. For instance, a declining and aging population may not be well placed to change the technology in an environmentally friendly direction.

KARL MARX

Karl Marx (1818–83) wrote extensively on economic, political, and social relations in society, but his writing on population was mostly in opposition to Malthus (Meek, 1971). Marx thought that there were several stages in human history (slavery, feudalism, capitalism, and socialism) and that each stage was different in terms of the vested interests of given groups in society. Each stage had a unique "mode of production," or a way in which economic production was organized, and specific "relations of production," or relations among classes of people with different stakes in the production process. He also thought that each stage of human history had its own "laws of population." Stated differently, Marx considered that the dynamics of population growth derived from the "mode of production" and the "relations of production," as these worked themselves out in specific stages of human history.

Although Marx did not specify the "laws of population" for each stage of history, he did write about the population dynamics under capitalism. Specifically, he argued that the capitalist class had a tendency not only to become more powerful as it came to exercise increasing control over the means of production, but also to become smaller in size. In contrast, the working class, as it lost control over the product of its labour, had a tendency to get larger. He argued that workers were not paid the full value of their labour and that the "surplus value" they generated was appropriated by the capitalist class, who would often invest this surplus in technologies that displaced labour.

Marx observed that the capitalist economy tends to experience periods of strong growth and periods of recession. More workers are needed during growth periods; during recession periods, those who are not needed are let go. Besides, surplus labour ensures that wages can be kept low in order to maximize the amount of "surplus value" that is extracted Thus, the capitalist system depends on a "reserve army of labour."

Because the capitalist system has become a world economic system, some of these dynamics have become evident at the global level. In particular, the richer countries are becoming smaller in relative size, and the system is becoming more dependent on cheap labour and raw materials from the rapidly growing populations of the Third World.

Marx concluded that problems of excess population were specific to the capitalist system. According to him, the problem was not that there were too many people, but that there were too many poor people, and they were impoverished as a result of the exploitation of workers. He proposed that, in a more equitable society, the problem would disappear. Contrary to Malthus, Marx felt that, with the proper economic and social arrangement—which he called "socialism"

and "communism"—we would be able to produce all the food and other resources necessary to accommodate population growth. More people, he reasoned, should be able to create more wealth and more food.

Even if we do not agree with the specific "stages of human history" that Marx elaborated, and even if we question some of his conclusions regarding the "laws of population under capitalism," we may still be impressed by his view that, given certain economic and social arrangements, particular population dynamics will follow. In other words, if population dynamics are to be changed, it is first necessary to change basic economic and social arrangements. In Marx's view, rapid population growth is not a cause of social problems, as Malthus argued, but a consequence of specific socioeconomic conditions.

Marxist thinking regarding current population problems places these issues in the broader context of development. It argues that development in the poor countries would reduce the numbers of poor people and, consequently, reduce population pressure. Social development (i.e., improvements in health, education, security, and equity) is more important than economic development in reducing fertility. However, these forms of development are dependent on establishing a new economic order with significant redistribution of wealth from the richer to the poorer countries. In that sense, they require a revolution (see Chapter 20).

THE MALTHUSIAN–MARXIST DEBATE

The debate between advocates of Malthusian and Marxist thought on population has taken various forms. On the one hand, Ehrlich and Ehrlich (1990) argue that, given limited resources, rapid population growth will tear our world apart. On the other hand, Simon (1990) argues that people constitute the ultimate resource that stimulates economic growth. Clearly, Ehrlich and Ehrlich were inspired by Malthus's thinking, and Simon by that of Marx. Ehrlich and Ehrlich propose that rapid population growth, particularly at the world level and in poorer countries, is creating misery and poverty. Simon proposes that human capital is mainly what promotes economic growth and, consequently, that population growth increases our ability to solve the problems of hunger and poverty.

The Malthusian–Marxist debate has also been evident in Canada. Some scholars have argued that the dangers of population growth involve not only the strain it places on limited resources, but also its deleterious effects on the environment, including the possibility of global climatic change. Others have argued that population growth is good for Canada, because its population is small and a larger population would create more markets and more economic development. In short, some arguments point to the disadvantages of population size and growth, whereas others point to their advantages.

From Malthus, we learn that society needs to be concerned about its population, whether because growth is too rapid or because it is not rapid enough. In other words, questions of population are important to the welfare of societies, and it makes sense to implement policies that promote the evolution of the population in a direction that corresponds to the social benefit. From Marx, we learn that population dynamics are largely a function of socioeconomic arrangements, particularly of broadly defined economic structures. As the society changes, population dynamics also change. In order to understand population trends, it is essential to understand the underlying economic and social dynamics.

HUMAN ECOLOGY

Human ecology is a broad perspective that embraces the subject of the causes and consequences of population processes. The study of ecology is basically the study of categories of organisms, or *populations*, in their environment—of how those populations gain their sustenance from the environment and, in so doing, how they introduce certain changes to that environment. Thus, the term *population* can be used for species other than humans. This reminds us of the similarity of the human species to other species, each of which needs to find its sustenance and niche in the environment.

In considering human ecology, however, we must take into account two major factors that do not apply to other species: In gaining their sustenance from the environment, human populations employ *organization* and *technology*. The ways in which humans organize themselves, and the technologies they develop, are central to understanding how they adapt to and influence the environment.

The dynamic interplay of these four basic considerations (population, organization, environment,

and technology—POET for short) presents an over-arching picture of population dynamics (see Figure 17.2). Each factor influences the others. For instance, historically, more rapid population growth has tended to follow the introduction of new forms of organization or new developments in technology. The urban revolution involved a new way of organizing human settlements that permitted considerable growth in population. Similarly, the Industrial Revolution involved major changes in technology that fostered population growth; particularly important in this regard were developments that allowed resources to be extracted more efficiently from the environment.

Changes in the environment, such as climatic changes, can also produce opportunities or hazards with respect to population. Some observers have argued that population pressure on the environment and technological developments can bring about environmental changes (as, for example, has the intensive use of fossil fuels) and, thus, changes in the potential for sustenance. Conversely, difficulties imposed by the environment can induce a population to find new forms of organization and technology that will enable it to survive and prosper—a process commonly known as "adaptation."

The human-ecology perspective highlights the fact that both benefits and problems can be associated with large numbers of people. Population growth can be seen as reducing average well-being because resources have to be shared with more people. In this view, larger numbers simply mean more competition for scarce resources. If there are more people, will there be enough jobs? If there are more old people, will there be enough services for them? With higher numbers come various forms of "crowding," which typically place people at a relative disadvantage in the

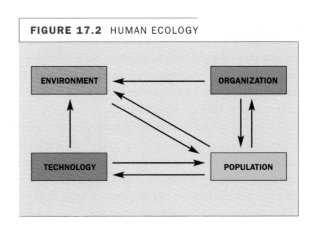

FIGURE 17.2 HUMAN ECOLOGY

competition for resources. In another sense, however, larger numbers mean greater strength, in that there are more people to deal with the existing problems. For instance, with more scientists, better and more efficient technologies might be developed to compensate for scarcities in natural resources. Crowding can also reinforce positive factors—larger cities, for example, offer more amenities of various kinds. Especially in a democracy, larger numbers can mean more political weight. The "grey power" groups certainly realize that their numbers give them the strength they need to change social arrangements to their benefit. As another example, Quebec has been concerned that the decline in its relative share of the Canadian population reduced its relative weight in national decision making. In effect, these alternative assessments mirror the contrast between the Malthusian view (that with more people, there are more problems) and the Marxist view (that with the proper social arrangements, more people can bring more resources to solve the problems as they arise).

THE DEMOGRAPHIC TRANSITION

One of the main demographic theories is that of the **demographic transition**. This theory has been used to summarize the historical demographic experience of societies of European origin over the past two centuries, as well as the more recent experience of Third World societies. The basic elements of the theory are presented in Figure 17.3. Births and deaths per 1000 population are represented on the vertical axis; time is shown along the horizontal axis. Although the rates and dates vary by country, the basic pattern is a movement from an equilibrium of high birth rates and high death rates, through a transitional disequilibrium in which death rates decline more than birth rates, to a second equilibrium of low birth rates and low death rates. In the pre-transition and post-transition states of equilibrium, there is little change in population size. The transition period, however, is characterized by a large increase in population size—sometimes as large as sevenfold.

Stage 1 of the demographic transition is one of high but fluctuating mortality and high fertility. Mortality is high because of poor nutrition, low standards of living, poor sanitation, and poor control over disease. Several reasons can be given for high fertility. The demographic argument proposes that, under

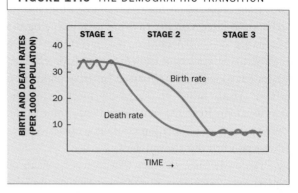

FIGURE 17.3 THE DEMOGRAPHIC TRANSITION

conditions of high mortality (among infants and children, in particular), fertility needs to be high in order for the group to survive. The economic argument suggests that, because the family was the main economic unit in preindustrial society, children were important to parents both as producers and as a source of security for the future. The cultural argument focuses on ideas and values, suggesting that preindustrial societies did not consider deliberate family limitation to be appropriate behaviour.

In stage 2, mortality declines as a result of various agricultural, industrial, sanitation, and health innovations. Again, it is the interpretation of the fertility decline that has received the most attention.

There are two interpretations of the fertility decline, one economic, the other cultural. The economic argument notes that the economic and industrial transformation of society in the Industrial Revolution changed the role of the family—that is, most economic production came to be organized outside the family context. As a consequence, children became less valuable in family production, and the costs of raising them increased as they came to spend a larger portion of their lives in school. Stated differently, the economic role of children changed from that of producer to that of dependant. Later, social security replaced the family as the basic welfare net in the face of economic hardship, incapacity, and old age. With the expansion of the role of the state, the economic rationale for having children was reduced; family and kin groups became less important as guarantees of economic security.

The cultural explanation suggests that the idea of limiting births within marriage, along with the use of contraception, gained legitimacy over time. From this perspective, fertility changed as new models of the family and of appropriate behaviour became prevalent. The deliberate regulation of births within marriage was a new model of behaviour that spread across societies through cultural contact, first in Europe and eventually around the world.

Cultural barriers sometimes impeded the spread of the new models of behaviour. In Belgium, for instance, fertility declined faster in the French-speaking population than in the Flemish population. Similarly, for a long time, fertility remained higher among French Canadians than among English Canadians. Certain minorities, such as the Native peoples, resisted the penetration of different forms of behaviour, including the adoption of changed modes of fertility. In support of this cultural explanation, Van de Walle and Knodel (1980) note that the beginning of the fertility decline has occurred in a variety of different socioeconomic conditions, and that, once the decline starts, the process appears to be irreversible.

Stage 3, as shown in Figure 17.3, involves persistent low mortality with low but fluctuating fertility. Mortality is now under control, with fertility varying slightly with economic and cultural conditions. Depending on the economic and social climate, it may be considered more or less feasible (economically) and more or less appropriate (culturally) to have children.

The essence of the demographic-transition model is that decreases in mortality precede reductions in fertility and that populations move from relatively high and stable vital rates to relatively low and stable vital rates. In the process of the transition, the gap between births and deaths causes the population to expand considerably.

However, there are various debates regarding this model. For instance, some scholars have noted that fertility reductions can occur when standards of living are threatened. The early fertility declines in France may not have been a function of economic improvements and mortality decline, but rather of economic stagnation in a rural society. There are also cases in the Third World in which economic reversals appear to have accelerated fertility decline (Sinding, 1993).

Other discussions focus on the third stage, suggesting that a number of rich countries may have gone beyond stable low birth and death rates to a fourth stage, characterized by more deaths than births. The latter stage involves considerable population aging and the threat of eventual population decline in the absence of substantial immigration

(Van de Kaa, 1987). Some have called this fourth stage a second demographic transition, where there is much change in family behaviour (Lesthaeghe, 1995). In particular, there is flexibility in entry into and exit from relationships, as represented by cohabitation and divorce, along with delays in childbearing, and fewer births (Beaujot and Bélanger, 2001).

The liveliest debate about the demographic-transition model pertains to the relative importance of economic versus cultural considerations. This discussion can be traced back to the Malthusian–Marxist debate. In some ways, however, the demographic-transition model brings into question both the Malthusian and the Marxist perspectives. Malthus would have to admit that, historically, improvements in standards of living and increases in the food supply did not induce people to have more children; on the contrary, fertility declined. Marx, for his part, would have to admit that demographic dynamics changed without a movement from capitalism to a new socialist stage of human history.

Focusing on different aspects of the demographic transition, however, both Marx and Malthus could argue that history also supports their perspectives. Marx would note in particular that fertility declined as a function of major economic and industrial transformations. Although it was not a revolution from capitalism to socialism, industrialization involved a significant change in the economic structure of society. Thus, as the economic context of people's lives changed, fertility declined. Malthus, on the other hand, might argue that his focus on ideas such as "moral restraint" and "responsible parenthood" helped to instigate new moral values, prompting people to take control of their reproduction and to deliberately limit family size. He would probably have less objection to specific methods of contraception. In other words, Malthus would subscribe to the cultural argument, noting that the diffusion of modern contraception has not only given people the means to limit their families but also promoted new values. According to these new values, it is appropriate to control conception, and small families are best.

The experience of various countries suggests that the fertility transition requires that people be ready, willing, and able to control their family size (Coale, 1973; Lesthaeghe and Vanderhoeft, 1997). The changed economic climate makes people ready to have fewer children because they do not need the children from an economic point of view, the prevalent norms make them willing to use contraception, and the effective access to family-planning services enables them to control their births.

COMPONENTS OF POPULATION CHANGE IN CANADA

MORTALITY AND HEALTH

In the case of the Canadian demographic transition, we have witnessed remarkable changes in longevity and health care over the course of Canadian history. At the time of Confederation, the average **life expectancy** was 42 years. As an average, this takes into account the many infant and child deaths and the not-infrequent deaths in early adult years that characterized the latter half of the nineteenth century; a relatively small number of people lived into their 60s, 70s, or later at that time. A life expectancy of 42 is very low by today's standards. Only eight African countries had such low life expectancy in 1999 (Population Reference Bureau, 1999). The Canadian data for 1999 indicate life expectancies of 76.3 for men and 81.7 for women. Only a few countries had higher life expectancy than Canada: Japan, Sweden, and Switzerland for men and women; France, Spain, and Italy for women; and Iceland for men (Bélanger, 2002: 31). These countries largely do not have the problem of providing health services over an area at all like the size of Canada.

Between 1851 and 1931, life expectancy in Canada rose from 41 to 61. This improvement was largely a function of reductions in the prevalence of infectious diseases such as tuberculosis, pneumonia, diphtheria, scarlet fever, enteritis, and diarrhea. Although diseases struck at all ages, the very young were particularly vulnerable. In fact, the declining **infant mortality rate** was the most important factor contributing to the improvement in life expectancy. In 1831, 1 in 6 children did not survive their first year; in 1931 it was 1 in 14, and by 1999 only 1 in 190 children did not survive their first year.

The question of why infectious diseases have declined brings us to consider standards of living as well as medical knowledge. As a component of the standard of living, improved nutrition appears to have played an important role (McKeown, Brown, and Record, 1972). Poor nutrition not only makes us more susceptible to infection, but also increases the likelihood that infection will be fatal. Medical improvements in the treatment of infectious diseases have included preventive medicine, from knowledge about the importance of sanitation and improvements in the care and feeding of infants, to the development of effective vaccines.

Improvements over the period 1931–99 have also been impressive, raising life expectancy from 61 to 79 years. Today, the leading causes of death are degenerative diseases that affect individuals predominantly in the later decades of life.

The epidemiological transition involves four stages (Bah and Fernando, 1991). The first three stages, which we have talked about, included that of (1) pestilence, (2) decline of infectious diseases as the primary causes of death, and (3) replacement by degenerative diseases associated with cardiovascular disease and cancer. The fourth stage includes delayed degenerative diseases and "hubristic" behaviour. The main causes of death remain those associated with heart disease and cancer, but these occur at an older age. It is remarkable how much progress has been made in the age-specific incidence of these causes of death. Heart disease was first affected, due both to improvements in risk factors such as diet and exercise, and to the medical treatment of heart-disease victims. For instance, over the period 1979–95 the age-adjusted death rates due to cardiovascular disease declined by almost 40 percent (Nault, 1997: 38). Since about 1985, cancer mortality has been declining for several forms of cancer (Belliveau and Gaudette, 1995). Once again, medical interventions are playing a role, but risk factors associated with lifestyle are also important. For instance, men's lung cancer has declined following their lower rates of smoking, but the opposite is true for women. The mortality rate for lung cancer among women now exceeds that of breast cancer.

The fourth phase is also characterized by "hubristic" behaviour or excessive self-confidence, which may involve reckless driving and sexual activity, for example. For persons under age 45, accidents of all kinds are the most important cause of death. However, here again there are improvements as a function both of safety measures (use of seat belts and safety helmets, controls on drinking and driving,

At Confederation, average life expectancy in Canada was 42 years. In 1999, it was 79 years. The number of people 65 years and older has increased because of improved hygiene, sanitation, and nutrition, as well as medical advances.
SOURCE: Dick Hemingway.

safer highway design) and the medical treatment of accident victims. Sexual activity is another concern in the fourth phase, with the danger of sexually transmitted diseases, and AIDS in particular. For instance, there are 29 countries in sub-Saharan Africa where the average life expectancy is 47 years. Life expectancy would have been 54 years without the AIDS epidemic (United Nations, 1999: 4).

Regardless of the phase of the epidemiological transition, it is clear that a variety of factors influence the mortality and health of a population. While everyone dies of something, there are various risk factors associated with given causes, and the health system can cope with different health problems to varying degrees. Clearly, our health is not just a function of the quality of the medical system, but is related to environmental quality and individual behaviour with respect to diet, lifestyle, and risk-taking. These behaviours can in turn be analyzed in terms of broader issues such as opportunities and social support by social class. For instance, the higher mortality of lower-class men due especially to heart disease can be related to the stresses associated with their precarious economic situation, along with lack of social support for a healthy lifestyle, which can promote detrimental behaviour such as smoking, poor diet, and excessive drinking (Nathanson and Lopez, 1987; Chen and Millar, 1998; Millar and Stephens, 1992).

In many areas of public policy, when a social problem is alleviated, the need to allocate resources

to the problem declines. However, in the area of health and longevity, the opposite appears to be true: The higher the life expectancy of the population and the more successful the prevention of disease, the greater the need for services and resources to cope with the health problems of those who survive. Although people live longer, their additional years of life are not necessarily spent in good health. With longer life come longer average periods of poor health and disability. Not surprisingly, therefore, there is currently much discussion about health budgets, the proper form of the health system in terms of things like hospitals and home care, and the extent of individual and social responsibility for health (see Box 17.2).

FERTILITY

There has also been a substantial long-term change in fertility, from about seven births per woman in the 1850s to fewer than two births in the 1980s and 1990s. Changes in fertility, however, have not been as uniform as changes in mortality. The baby boom of the period 1946–66 presented a major exception to the long-term trend. The analysis of fertility is also more complex than that of mortality: Whereas everyone dies (and dies just once), typically of an identifiable cause, some people have no children while others have several.

Figure 17.4 on page 449 depicts changes in fertility through the **total fertility rate**. This is called a "period" measure because it takes the rates of childbearing of women at the various childbearing ages in a given year and adds them up over all the childbearing years. The result is a measure of what would be the average births per woman if the rates for one period or year represented the actual lifetime experiences of women. The **cohort completed fertility** rate follows women who were born into a given **cohort** and observes how many children they have in their lifetime. The disadvantage of this measure is that it cannot be calculated for a given cohort of women until childbearing is completed. The fluctuations are similar but not as extreme as those depicted in Figure 17.4. For instance, the cohort of women born in 1931 had the highest fertility this century, with an average of 3.4 births per woman, while those born in the early 1960s had an average of 1.75 (Ford and Nault, 1996: 44; Beaujot and Bélanger, 2001).

BOX 17.2   WE CAN'T LET OLD AGE CRIPPLE HEALTH CARE

As a percentage of GDP, total health costs increased from 7 percent in the later 1970s, to somewhat above 8 percent in the mid-1980s, to reach 10 percent in 1992 and about 9.5 percent in 2001. Private expenditure on health amounts to slightly less than 25 percent of these total expenditures. The total government expenditure for health in 1999 was $86.0 billion, which amounts to $2800 per capita or $5700 per employed person. Since 1986 the total government expenditure for health in Canada has been higher than the expenditure for education.

In the excerpt below from his report to the Romanow Commission on the Future of Health Care in Canada, Réjean Hébert of the Institute of Aging of the Canadian Institutes of Health Research makes the case that we need to be willing to increase health funding to accommodate an aging population.

The population is undergoing an age transformation that will have profound consequences on individuals, communities and the nation as a whole. Can Canada's health-care system handle the needs of our aging population in the future without bankrupting taxpayers? Let's examine this question based on solid science.

People's lifestyles have over time become healthier. Developments in therapies, practices, programs and policies have also improved heath. Does this mean that everything is fine for older Canadians, and that our younger population doesn't need to worry about future health-care needs? Not quite.

Indicators suggest that baby boomers in their later years will be in better health than today's seniors. However, they are likely to expect and require different things from the health-care system. Compared to other health issues, research on aging-related ailments, such as Alzheimer's or general mental and biological decline, is underdeveloped. Cognitive decline, such as Alzheimer's and other dementia, currently affects one in four Canadians over the age of 65. With the dramatic increase of that age group by 2026, the number of cases is expected to reach epidemic stages.

While research on aging is being carried out, current scientific findings, if implemented, can help the health-care system handle the needs of our aging population. The following findings are among those I recently pointed out to the Romanow commission.

- *Better social conditions for seniors:* These decrease their demand for health-care services. Among others, initiatives related to income, transportation and housing will improve the health of seniors.
- *Home care and other community services:* Such services provided to frail seniors are always less costly to the system than care and services given in institutions.
- *Adequate investment:* No scientific data shows a need to entrust the private sector with the financing, management and delivery of care and services. Studies prove that despite the fact that the United States spends more of its money on its health care than countries with public systems, the quality of care is not superior; life expectancy is lower and infant mortality is higher. In Canada, many of the current problems with the health-care system are attributable to the steady decline of public health expenditures per capita since 1992. It is time to reinvest in our health-care system.

With adequate spending, the safety and efficiency of Canada's health-care system will improve to the point where it will be able to handle the needs of future older Canadians. Then baby-boomers, including myself, can take comfort in the realization that there will be no health-care apocalypse on the horizon.

SOURCE: Excerpted from Réjean Hébert, "We Can't Let Old Age Cripple Health Care" (*The Globe and Mail*, 2 August 2002, p. A15).

The rate of 2.1 births per woman has been viewed as the level of **replacement fertility**—that is, the level of fertility at which one generation will be fully replaced by the next. Two births are needed to replace the parents and about 0.1 to compensate for the small number of deaths that occur before the next generation reaches reproductive age. Demographers speak of **population momentum**, whereby a population continues to grow for some time after fertility declines. Births continue to outnumber deaths because the demographic bulge in the population age structure is at reproductive ages. Thus, even though the generation constituting the demographic bulge is having fewer births than are needed for replacement, this generation is sufficiently numerous to ensure more births than deaths. In Canada, the current population momentum will continue for some time. Even with fertility remaining constant at 1.5 births per woman, births will continue to outnumber deaths until 2025.

For the period 1976–2001, there are two important observations concerning fertility: (1) The rates have been relatively constant but have declined over the period from 1.78 to 1.51 births per woman; and

FIGURE 17.4 PERIOD TOTAL FERTILITY RATE FOR 1871–2001, CANADA

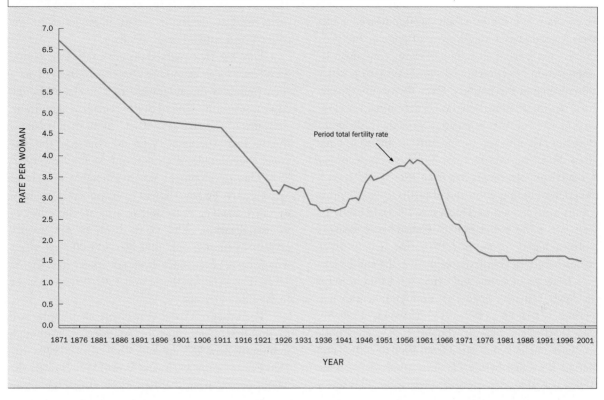

SOURCE: Anatole Romaniuc, *Current Demographic Analysis: Fertility in Canada: From Baby-boom to Baby-bust* (Ottawa: Minister of Supply and Services, 1984), pp. 121–22; Statistics Canada, 1993, Selected Birth and Fertility Statistics, Canada, 1921–1990. Cat. No. 82-553 and Special Tabulations.

(2) the average age at childbearing has moved to older ages, with 46.9 percent of births occurring after age 30 in 2001 compared to 19.6 percent in 1976. The explanation of these trends brings us to consider proximate factors, and more distant factors at both the micro and macro levels (Beaujot, 2000):

- *Proximate* or immediate factors involve delay in the formation of long-term unions between women and men, lower proportions of people getting married, more cohabitation, more divorce, and widespread use of modern contraception techniques.
- *Micro* factors involve the value and cost of children in both economic and cultural terms. It is clear that children are expensive to raise, but there are also other noneconomic costs involved in childrearing, such as the limitation of individual freedom and the heavy associated responsibilities. Children no longer represent an economic value to parents. They do, however, represent cultural values; children are seen as a source of joy, of unique experiences, and also of secure relationships when other interpersonal relationships are less secure.
- *Macro* factors involve especially the structure of production and reproduction. In particular, both women and men play productive roles, and it is difficult to fit into life the reproductive activities associated with caring for children. Since work roles are crucial, the orientation of young people is often to complete their education and establish themselves before having children. That is, they invest in their productive abilities before investing in reproduction. Given this predominant model, persons who start relationships and have children early are often at a disadvantage, especially if the relationships do not last. For instance, in 1991 at ages 15–29, 68.8 percent of formerly married women had children, compared to 48.5 percent of married or cohabiting women and 7.2 percent of never-married women (Ravanera, 1995: 18).

IMMIGRATION

In contrast to many other advanced industrial countries, Canada has a long history of policies and programs that encouraged immigration; consequently, immigration has contributed significantly to population change in this country. Over the twentieth century, net international migration accounted for close to a quarter of total population growth. This figure does not take into account the further impact of children born to immigrants. Fully 41 percent of Canada's population growth from 1966 to 1991 was a function of immigration and of births to these immigrants over the period (Duchesne, 1993). In 2001, 18 percent of the population of Canada was foreign-born, a higher proportion than that in any other major industrial country, except Australia and Israel.

In terms of trends and dynamics, I find it useful to divide Canada's history of immigration into five periods: 1861–96, 1897–1913, 1914–45, 1946–89, and 1990 to the present. (Figure 17.5 depicts both immigration and emigration from 1900 to 2001.) The period from just before Confederation to the mid-1890s saw more departures than arrivals. This was a time of depression in international trade, which undermined markets for Canadian raw materials.

The earlier industrialization of the U.S. economy offered employment prospects that attracted residents of Canada, both recent immigrants to the country and native-born Canadians.

The year 1896 marked the end of the long period of international economic depression, as well as a turnaround in net migration to Canada. Although departures to the United States remained significant, the gains of the decade 1901–11 more than balanced the net loss experienced over the course of the previous four decades (Beaujot and McQuillan, 1982: 83). This development was attributable in part to active efforts by government to encourage settlement of the Canadian West and in part to the onset of industrialization. The years 1911–13 saw record arrivals of immigrants (300 000–400 000 per year), which have never since been surpassed (see Figure 17.5). The total for the period 1897–1913 was close to 3 million arrivals.

The onset of World War I marked an abrupt end to this first major wave of immigration. Although immigration picked up somewhat in the 1920s, the Depression of the 1930s and World War II made the whole period from 1914 to 1945 something of an interlude in immigration, with total arrivals numbering roughly 1.3 million.

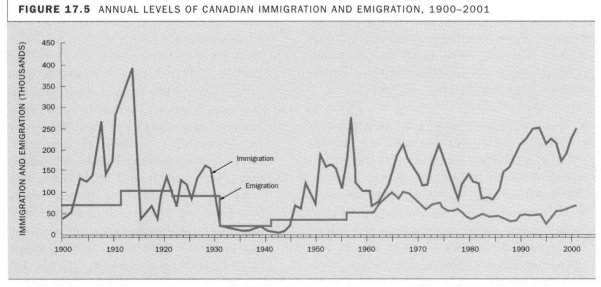

FIGURE 17.5 ANNUAL LEVELS OF CANADIAN IMMIGRATION AND EMIGRATION, 1900–2001

SOURCE: Alain Bélanger, *Report on the Demographic Situation in Canada, 2001*, Cat. no, 91-209 (Ottawa: Supply and Services Canada, 2002), p. 10; Roderic Beaujot, K.G. Basavarajappa, and Ravi B.P. Verma, *Current Demographic Analysis: Income of Immigrants in Canada*, Statistics Canada, Cat. No. 91-527 (Ottawa: Supply and Services Canada, 1988), p. 7. From R. Beaujot, *Population Change in Canada* (Toronto: Oxford University Press, 1991), with updates.

The post–World War II period can be viewed as a second major immigration wave. Total arrivals between 1946 and 1989 amounted to 5.8 million. In 1962, there was a major change in immigration policy, in that the racial components of immigrant selection criteria were removed. Subsequently, the places of origin of immigrants to Canada became much more diverse. The increase from a low point in the mid-1980s was the outcome of a deliberate government program of "moderate controlled growth" in immigration levels.

With the sustained higher levels of the 1990s, this can be viewed as a new phase of immigration. These higher levels were maintained through the recession of the early 1990s, bringing the total for the period 1990–2000 to 2.4 million or an average of 220 000 per year. While the period before World War I remains unique, only the four consecutive years 1910–13 had levels above 200 000, while there have now been eight consecutive years (1990–97) with these levels. There are other indicators of the uniqueness of this most recent period. In the period 1946–89, net migration accounted for about a quarter of population growth, but in the 1990s it comprised about half of population growth. The *Report on the Demographic Situation in Canada 2001* speaks of three concentrations of immigration at the beginning of the new century: a higher proportion are from Asia, greater proportions are going to Ontario, and a higher proportion are from the economic class selected on the basis of skills and other qualifications (Bélanger, 2002: 49).

As noted earlier, immigration has become highly diversified by ethnic origin since the 1960s. Whereas three-quarters of the immigrants to Canada came from Europe and the United States in the period 1946–67, in the period 1976–96 the proportion from Asia, Latin America, and Africa rose to 80 percent of the total. Three-quarters of the 1991–96 immigrants were classified as being from *visible minorities* (Chard and Renaud, 1999).

The Impact of Immigration

From a demographic point of view, immigration clearly contributes to population growth. However, it has only a small impact on a population's age structure, because immigrants arrive at a variety of ages and, in any given year, they represent only a small proportion of the total population. Since immigrants concentrate in Toronto, Vancouver, and Montreal, immigration reinforces the growth trends of the largest cities.

Although the demographic side of immigration is relatively easy to assess, the economic implications are harder to delineate. The Economic Council of Canada (1991) concluded that the overall economic impact of immigration in terms of per capita GNP, unemployment, productivity, and tax and dependency burdens is small but positive over the long term. This positive impact is largely a result of the fact that immigrants tend to arrive at ages of high economic productivity—that is, at the beginning of their work life. The main costs associated with immigration are encountered in the shorter term, specifically in relation to initial settlement and adjustment.

Other summaries of the economic impact of immigration are less optimistic. Richmond (1988) finds that immigrants from Europe and their descendants have done well in Canada, but doubts that the trends will be as favourable for the more recent arrivals from the less-developed countries. Based on analyses of the 1986, 1991, and 1996 censuses, Reitz (2001) finds a trend toward lower rates of employment and earnings relative to the Canadian-born population. Looking at successive cohorts of immigrants, he finds in particular that the increased education of the Canadian-born population has reduced the relative advantage of immigrants. In addition, over time, the increased returns to education have become stronger for Canadian-born people than for immigrants. For instance, among persons aged 20–64 who are employed, immigrant men who had been in Canada less than 25 years, and women who had been in Canada less than 15 years, had average 1995 incomes that were below those of their Canadian-born counterparts of the corresponding gender (Reitz, 2001: 35). Reitz discusses three possible sources of changes in immigrant socioeconomic status: changes in the skills that immigrants bring, changes in the treatment received by immigrants within the labour market, and changes in the structure of the labour market itself. Compared to the 1960s, the skills of immigrants have increasingly been defined by academic degrees rather than technical training. Racial discrimination could be the reason for the increased discounting of immigrant skills, but this explanation seems inadequate since white immigrants are also affected, although to a lesser degree.

The changed structure of the labour market toward a service economy may undermine the value of educational credentials obtained abroad, and may accentuate the negatives associated with lack of "Canadian experience" and Canadian references. Box 17.3 discusses the human resource side of both immigration and emigration.

Refugees

Refugees are one component of immigration. These arrivals started with the United Empire Loyalists, around 1776, and continued through to World War I with various groups including the Quakers, Mennonites, Blacks, Doukhobors, Hutterites, Mormons, and Jews (Ziegler, 1988).

Some of the harshest controls on refugee arrivals were set in the 1930s and 1940s. Avery (1979) appropriately entitled his book *Dangerous Foreigners* to give a sense of the attitudes toward immigrants that prevailed at that time. A well-known case in point was Canada's refusal to allow Jews entry into the country just before World War II. In 1939, for example, the *St. Louis*, an ocean liner carrying 907 desperate German Jews, was refused entry into Canada and was forced to return to Europe. Abella and Troper (1982) reveal the extent of Canadian prejudice against Jewish immigration, to the point of obvious persecution.

In the period immediately following World War II, Canada opened its doors to refugees from war-torn Europe. They were known as "displaced persons," and the tag "DPs" soon took on a negative connotation. Subsequently, the major refugee movements included Hungarians, Czechoslovakians, U.S. draft dodgers and deserters (though they were not admitted as refugees), Tibetans, Ugandan expellees, Chileans, and Indo-Chinese. Since 1978, the planning of immigration levels has taken anticipated refugees into account, and the source countries of immigrants have consequently become considerably more diversified. Over the period 1978–98, refugees have represented 16 percent of total immigration.

In the 1980s, Canada encountered the problem of people claiming refugee status after they had arrived in the country. (The standard procedure involves applying for refugee status from abroad.) As a signatory to the International Convention on Refugees, Canada is obliged to give safe haven to people who have left their country because of persecution. The problem thus became one of determining whether claims of refugee status were legitimate. Although the public is generally supportive of accommodating refugees, there is also a sense that the system should not be abused. The pressure on Canada is particularly strong because it allows refugees to settle permanently.

The Future of Immigration

The importance of immigration to Canada is emphasized by the fact that legislation requires the minister of immigration to make an annual "statement to Parliament" that outlines the government policy on immigration, including the anticipated level of admission.

The determination of an appropriate immigration level and its composition are clearly matters of values and politics. Research can shed some light on the past, but it is for the political community to decide what is best for the future and how immigration is to figure into that social vision. Weinfeld (1988) suggests that there are two predominant visions that apply to immigration. One view, which in its extreme version might be called "Fortress Canada," sees the country as well established and needing to protect its resources and its inheritance against destabilizing external forces. This perspective is apprehensive about a multi-ethnic society. In this view, tradition is preferable to change, and immigration policy should be cautious. As the total number of Third World immigrants and their descendants increases, Canadian society will continue to face significant challenges in seeking ways to avoid conflict between racial, linguistic, and cultural groups. A solution is simply to reduce the intake of immigrants. In opinion surveys, as many respondents say there are "too many" immigrants as say the level is "about right." Fewer than 10 percent think there are "too few" immigrants (Palmer, 1997).

The alternative perspective, according to Weinfeld (1988), views Canada as a country that is young, rich, and, as yet, not fully developed. From this perspective, immigration is part of a process of nation building; ethnic variety and demographic growth are interpreted positively. As stewards of this large land and its resources, we might be seen as managing our endowment for the greater benefit of humanity and less for our narrow self-interest. An openness to the cultures of the world may be taken as a sociocultural and demographic challenge that would bring Canada into the modern international world, in which

BOX 17.3 THE "BRAIN DRAIN" FROM CANADA

This study considers emigration of skilled persons from Canada, along with immigration to Canada. Knowledge workers, defined as persons in professional or managerial occupations, have various opportunities, and they are thus more likely to be "on the move" to take advantage of these opportunities. Their departure is often called a "brain drain," but this is balanced by the numbers arriving from other countries. This article brings together the empirical evidence on Canada's brain drain to the United States, in relation to the acquisition of knowledge workers from the rest of the world.

It is difficult to have accurate data on emigration, since there is not a systematic requirement to register one's departure. The data used here are taken from tax filers who declare that they are no longer Canadian residents for purposes of taxation. Other data are taken from work visas registered in the United States, and from surveys of recent graduates from Canadian educational institutions.

The departures in any one year involve a very small proportion of tax filers, representing only 1 per 1000 persons with employment income, and less than 1 percent of the stock of workers in any given occupation of knowledge workers. However, there is evidence that the higher the income, the higher the likelihood of departure, with the departure rate of 9 per 1000 in 1996 for persons with incomes over $150 000 compared to 1 per 1000 persons with employment income. The departures in 1996–1997 represent 0.7 per 1000 workers, but almost 8 per 1000 physicians. Stated differently, in 1996–1997, the departures of both physicians and nurses represented the equivalent of a quarter of one year's graduating class in these professions. While only 1.5 percent of 1995 postsecondary graduates from Canadian schools were in the United States in 1997, the likelihood was higher for those with higher qualifications, as indicated by awards received or higher degrees. For instance, 12 percent of persons obtaining Ph.D. degrees were in the United States. Some of these departures are of short duration; 18 percent of the 1995 postsecondary graduates who were in the United States in 1997 had moved back to Canada by 1999.

Canada clearly receives more university graduates from elsewhere than it loses to the United States. For every university graduate migrating from Canada to the United States, four degree holders migrate from the rest of the world to Canada. In particular, immigrants of the 1990s accounted for about one-third of the increase in employment among computer engineers, systems analysts, and computer programmers. According to the 1996 census, immigrants who had arrived in Canada before 1990 were more strongly represented than Canadian-born persons in the occupational category of entrepreneurs, investors, executives, managers, and administrators. Adjusting for age, recent immigrants are close to twice as likely as people born in Canada to have a university education, and about four times as likely to have a Ph.D. degree. For the occupation of computer scientist, especially at ages under 30, there were similar 1995 employment incomes for the 1985–1994 immigrants as for the Canadian born.

The article does not consider other fields where employment incomes of recent immigrants with university degrees are sometimes significantly lower than those of comparable Canadian-born persons. We might observe that while Canada receives more than it loses, there are differences between those arriving and leaving. As indicated, there are higher departure rates for those with the highest qualifications, while those arriving sometimes have difficulty achieving incomes comparable to their levels of education. That is, while "knowledge workers are on the move," and Canada profits more than it loses from this movement, it remains difficult to completely assess the associated human resource implications.

SOURCE: "Knowledge Workers on the Move" by John Zhao, Doug Drew, and T. Scott Murray, 2000. *Perspectives on Labour and Income* 12(2): 32–46, Catalogue 75–001.

European-based societies are a declining component. Tepper (1987) proposes that societies that find ways to manage ethnicity and pluralism may well be in a stronger position to face future challenges in the interdependent world of nations.

Pressure from the Outside

Although we can debate the relative advantages of these alternatives, it is also important to recognize that international movements of population are not totally under Canada's control. It is estimated that there are some 125 million international migrants in the world, seeking to establish themselves in a favourable country, including some 19 million refugees (United Nations, 1995: 51, 55). It is clear that migration pressure at the global level will continue to be greater than the numbers that can be accommodated in receiving countries (Pacini, 1992).

These population displacements follow on various circumstances, including global economic restructuring and the break-up of the former Soviet Union. In addition, the very process of development brings with it various economic disruptions, uprooting people, especially in subsistence rural economies. Note that it was precisely when Europe was industrializing that large numbers of Europeans left the continent. Until World War II, the net movement was in fact from the North to the South—that is, from Europe to Africa, Latin America, and Asia. This migration obviously went hand in hand with political and economic domination, including the colonization of much of the South.

Now the tables are turned, and the countries of Western Europe are trying to set up various legal fortifications against migration from Eastern Europe, Africa, Asia, and even Turkey, while the United States tries to control arrivals from Mexico and places south. Compared with European countries, Canada has a longer history of immigration policies and of building a multiethnic society. However, there is also a felt need to control a process that is very difficult to manage and regulate, let alone control.

CANADIAN POPULATION CHANGE: PAST, PRESENT, AND FUTURE

Having analyzed mortality, fertility, and migration, we can now sketch the overall picture of population change in Canada. We will consider past growth patterns and prospects for the future, along with some of the broader implications of existing trends.

GROWTH AND POPULATION

In 1851, the population of Canada was 2.4 million; by 2001, it had grown to 31.1 million. This rate of growth is considerably faster than that of many other countries, including England and France, and that of the world as a whole.

The main components of Canada's shifting demographic situation today are low fertility, low growth, and population aging. These trends are setting parameters that differ in many respects from those that prevailed in the past. In the 50-year period between 1951 and 2001, Canada's population more than doubled from 14.0 to 31.1 million. Most would

interpret this change positively, noting that the baby boom and the immigration boom of the post–World War II period have permitted Canada to flourish. Projections made in 1946 did not foresee these fertility and immigration changes, and estimated that the population would reach a maximum of only about 15 million. It is arguable that the actual, strong growth of Canada's population has ensured more domestic control over resources, elevated the country's status among the nations of the world, and contributed to economic growth and social development.

Projections indicate that, unless there is a substantial increase in fertility, population growth will slow and may even come to a halt during the 50-year period from 2001 to 2051. The highest projection from Statistics Canada (2001b) gives a 2051 figure of 43.0 million, or a growth of only 38 percent after 2001. In the low projection, the population reaches a peak of 34.2 million in 2030, and in the medium projection this peak is 37.1 million in 2040. There will also be other changes, including more deaths than births after about 2025, and population renewal occurring through immigration much more than through fertility. At the same time, it is important not to exaggerate the trends. When the 2001 census data were first released, the opening sentence in the lead article in *The Globe and Mail* read that "Canada is facing a population decline ... beginning as early as nine years from now" (Armstrong, 2002). This population decline was based projections that assumed zero immigration since 1991! It is important to appreciate that slower growth is not the same as decline, and that even the lowest projections do not anticipate a population decline for Canada as a whole until after the third decade of the century.

POPULATION AGING

The way age cohorts are distributed has important consequences for the society (see Figure 17.6). In 1951, the age distribution was shaped like a pyramid, with large numbers of young persons at the base and small numbers of old persons at the top. Eventually, the shape will be more like that of an inverted vase, with about the same number of people in all age cohorts except the oldest, which will contain fewer people. This change is known as population aging.

It is useful to divide population aging into three phases. The first phase dates back to the beginning

FIGURE 17.6 AGE PYRAMIDS OF THE POPULATION OF CANADA, 1951, 1981, 2001, 2036

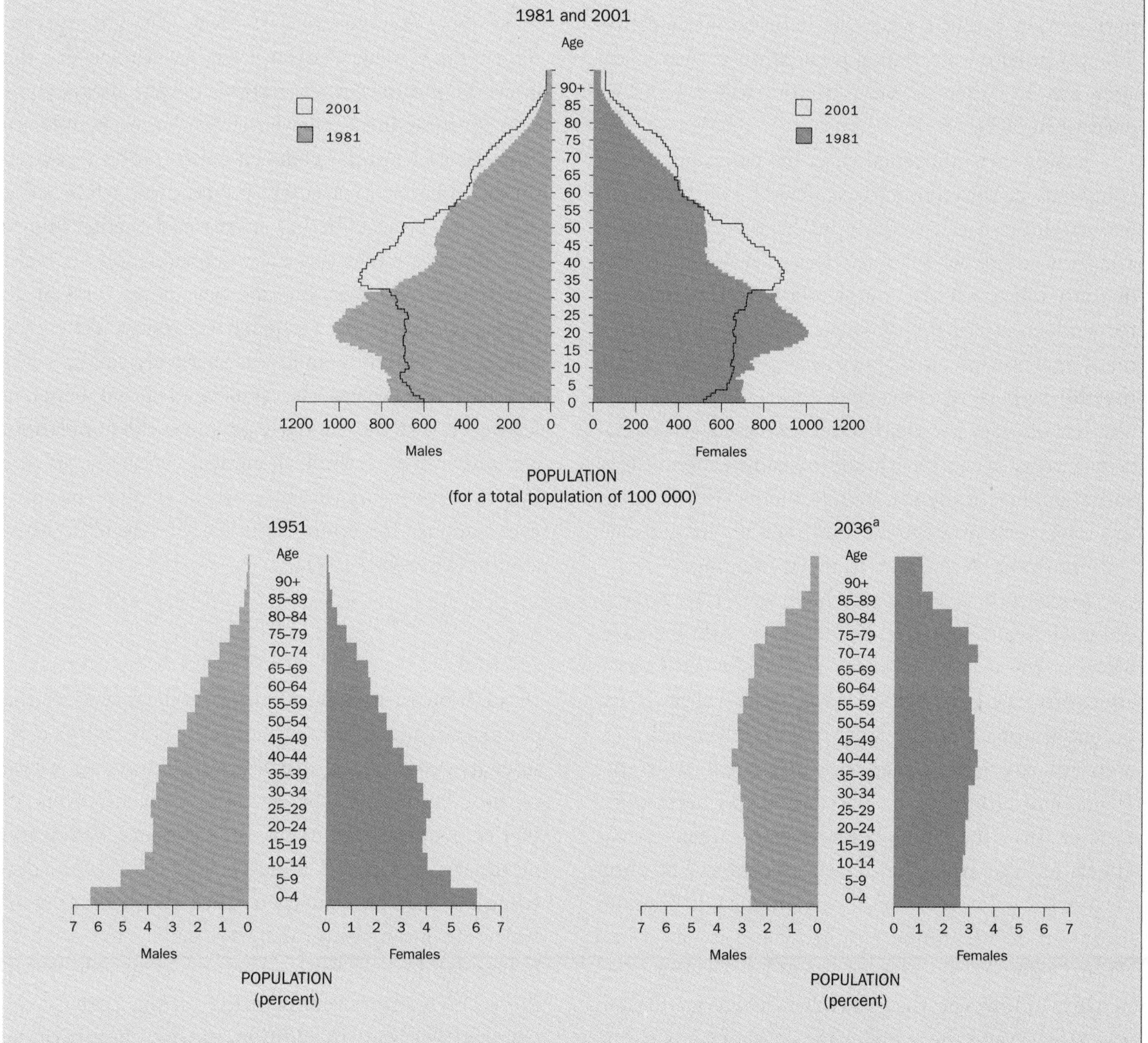

aProjections for 2036 are based on fertility of 1.8, life expectancy of 80.6, immigration of 200 000 per year, and emigration of 25 per 1000.

SOURCE: Statistics Canada, 2002, *Annual Demographic Statistics 2001*, Ottawa: Statistics Canada, Cat. No. 91-213, p. 11; Desjardins, Bertrand, 1993, *Population Aging and the Elderly*, Ottawa: Statistics Canada, Cat. No. 91-533, p. 18.

of fertility decline in the last quarter of the nineteenth century. This was a period of slow aging because fewer births were compensated for by more young survivors. The second phase started around 1961, and it was largely due to reductions in fertility. We might call this the phase of "aging at the bottom," because the increased average age was largely a function of fewer births and young people. The third phase started around 1976, and it is a func-

tion of both low fertility and increased longevity. The lower mortality of adults, or "aging at the top," is responsible for a quarter of the aging. In the Canadian case, the year-by-year upward movement of the baby-boom cohort is now causing "aging in the middle." Since both fertility and mortality are contributing to aging in the third phase, the pace has increased. For instance, the median age of the population was 26.3 years in 1961, and 29.5 in 1981, but

37.6 in 2001 (Desjardins, 1993: 16; Statistics Canada, 2002). Measured in terms of the proportion aged 65 and over, aging will be particularly rapid in the period 2011 to 2031 when the baby boomers retire. The proportion of the total population at retirement ages was 13.0 percent in 2001 and will reach 23.6 percent in 2031.

Besides the quickened pace, the consequences of aging may be different in these phases. When aging is overwhelmingly due to fewer births, this can be liberating for adults, who can pay less attention to reproduction and can more completely devote themselves to production. In this context, there is a maximum number of people at labour-force ages. However, in the third phase of aging it is especially the relative number of older people that has increased, with associated pressure on health and pension expenditures, and changing residential requirements. While aging is a long-term process, we know less about the societal implications of the third phase of aging.

Some things are clear, however. The relative costs of health and public pensions will increase, whereas there may be some decline in the cost of education (Fellegi, 1988). What is less clear is the potential impact on the labour force. Although population growth has been slowing down since the 1950s, and although the population has been aging for a century, the labour force was not subject to the effects of these trends until more recently. The entry of the baby boomers and women into the labour force caused its numbers to grow and resulted in a slight decline in the average age of labour-force participants. However, the growth of the labour force is now slower, and the average age of workers is rising. Once again, it is important not to exaggerate the trends. Some observers have interpreted slower labour-force growth as implying a labour shortage. Yet, in 2001 there were 40 percent more people at ages (15–24) of labour force entry than at ages (55–64) of labour force exit (Statistics Canada, 2002: 30). An older labour force might mean less unemployment and less need for new investments, but it might also mean less flexibility and lower productivity relative to labour costs.

Box 17.1 (see page 437) illustrates how population composition and the relative size of cohorts influence individual and social issues. At the individual level, the baby-bust cohort, born after the mid-1960s, has the advantage of being a relatively small cohort: Its members experience less competition for jobs. However, the disadvantage is that they follow a large cohort whose members have taken most of the good jobs. At the societal level, the attempts to reform the Canada Pension Plan have shown that the interests of different generations do not always coincide (Beaujot and Richards, 1997). Young people are more likely to prefer reduced contributions, or even the elimination of a costly public plan, while older people prefer sustained or increased benefits. Figure 17.7 illustrates that there are dependencies on social programs at all ages, but the per capita costs of an older population are particularly striking. When the number of elderly people was relatively small, it was not hard to expand the associated social benefits. However, with more elderly people in the population, we must now rethink benefits, especially in the interest of ensuring that the costs of aging do not prevent support for young families who want to have children (Beaujot, 1991).

POPULATION DISTRIBUTION

In addition to looking at the overall growth of the population and its age structure, it is useful to consider its geographical distribution. Before the arrival of the Europeans, the greatest concentrations of Native peoples were in the St. Lawrence Valley and on the Pacific Coast (Careless, 1963: 18–21). The distribution that has emerged since the beginning of European immigration is quite similar. The analysis of population distribution is an important indicator of the relative attractiveness of the various parts of the country over time. In addition, the distribution of the population plays an important role in the regional dynamics of the country. (Figure 17.8 shows population growth for the provinces and the country during the period 1951–2001).

The Atlantic provinces have declined in relative size with the diminishing importance of wood and fish as export commodities and with the establishment of the St. Lawrence Seaway, which allowed the Atlantic provinces to be bypassed as a transportation route. The region has received few immigrants and has tended to be an area of net **out-migration**. As a consequence, the population is ethnically relatively homogeneous and has long-established roots in the region.

Quebec has received a considerable number of immigrants over the years. Montreal was a favourite

FIGURE 17.7 EXPENDITURES PER CAPITA ON HEALTH, EDUCATION, AND SOCIAL SECURITY, BY GENDER AND AGE GROUP, CANADA, 1985

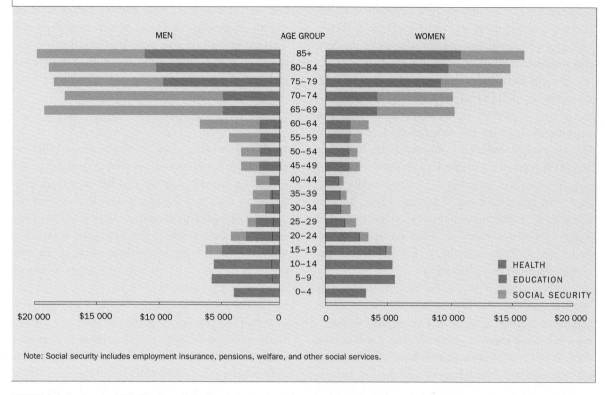

Note: Social security includes employment insurance, pensions, welfare, and other social services.

SOURCE: Industry Canada, 1991, *New Faces in the Crowd: Economic and Social Impacts of Immigration*, Ottawa: Economic Council of Canada, 22–171, p. 12. Reproduced with the permission of the Minister of Public Works and Government Services Canada, 2003.

FIGURE 17.8 POPULATION GROWTH, 1951–2001, CANADA AND THE PROVINCES

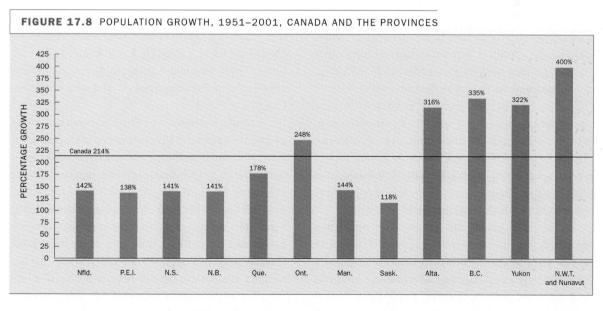

SOURCE: Statistics Canada, *A Profile of the Canadian Population: Where We Live,* Cat. no. 96F0030. (Ottawa: Industry, Science and Technology Canada, 2003), p. 16. Reproduced by authority of the Minister of Industry, 2000.

destination, especially when it was viewed as Canada's major metropolis (see Chapter 14). However, the province has not always managed to retain its immigrants (especially those who were not French); it even lost some of its nonimmigrant population to the general westward movement in North America.

Ontario has made population gains through both immigration and internal migration. With its link to the Atlantic Ocean via the St. Lawrence Seaway and with its proximity to the rich farmland of southern Ontario and the mineral resources of the Canadian Shield, Toronto has become Canada's major metropolis. In 1951, Toronto was 18 percent smaller than Montreal; by 2001, it was 37 percent larger. Nine of Canada's 27 census metropolitan areas are located in southern Ontario, between Windsor and Ottawa. Since the 1970s, immigration has diversified the ethnic origins of this population.

The population of the Prairies has declined in relative size with the decreasing importance of its agricultural base. Alberta's oil resources, however, have provided growth potential. The harsh winter climate and lack of precipitation limit both the agricultural potential of the Prairies and their attractiveness for population settlement. The ethnic origins of the population are largely European, but nearly half are neither British nor French.

British Columbia has made continuous population gains because of the enduring importance of wood and mineral resources and the province's agreeable climate. Next to Ontario and Quebec, British Columbia has become the largest magnet of immigration. As a result of numerous arrivals from other parts of Canada and other countries, close to half the population was born outside the province.

The North represents a large part of the Canadian land mass but a very small part of the population. Defined as including the Northwest Territories, the Yukon, and Nunavut, the region had a population of only 93 000 in 2001, or 0.3 percent of the Canadian total. It is a relatively young population, 48 percent of which is of Aboriginal ancestry.

The 2001 census has shown that population growth is very uneven over the country. Four major urban regions have shown considerable growth: Ontario's extended Golden Horseshoe, Montreal and adjacent region, British Columbia's Lower Mainland and southern Vancouver Island, and the Calgary–Edmonton corridor. While the population of the country as a whole grew by 4 percent between 1996 and 2001, those provinces that did not include one of these major urban regions either declined slightly or grew by less than 1 percent over five years. This should not be a surprise knowing that international migration comprises about half of the growth and that immigrants go to the largest cities.

HEALTH STATUS

Health status is one of the many phenomena that can be studied in relation to population groups. In the section on mortality, we saw that life expectancy continues to rise, and Canada is among the countries with the highest life expectancy. However, longer life means added years of both good and poor health. The stage of delayed degenerative diseases can mean large numbers of frail elderly people who suffer from various debilitating diseases.

For the entire population aged 15 and over, just over half (55 percent) reported at least one chronic health problem in 1994, and 77 percent used at least one prescription or over-the-counter drug in the month before the survey (Millar and Beaudet, 1996). The most common chronic conditions were allergies, back problems, arthritis, rheumatism, and high blood pressure. Chronic pain is reported by 17 percent of adults, and 21 percent have a long-term limitation that restricts the kind or amount of activity that they can perform at home, at work, at school, or during their leisure time. In 1998–99, 79 percent of the population aged 12 and over had consulted a physician and 11 percent had ten or more consultations. These frequent consultations rise to 21 percent in the population aged 65 and over (Statistics Canada, 2001a: 33).

Calculations show that at age 45, men can expect to live 10.7 years, or 32.5 percent of their remaining lives, with some disability, and the same would apply to women for 15.1 years, or 40.1 percent of their remaining lives (Martel et al., 2001: 127). Part of women's longer life is lived in a state of dependence. For instance, beyond age 85 there are more women in health-care institutions than in private households (Martel and Bélanger, 1999: 173). Using various weights to adjust for periods of poor health, it is estimated that the **health-adjusted life expectancy** is some eight years less than total life expectancy (Wolfson, 1996: 43).

At ages 15–64, 7–8 percent of people have disabilities that affect their ability to work. Consequently, they may be subject to the provisions of employment equity (Michaud et al., 1996: 17, 27). The figure is under 5 percent for people aged 15–19, but reaches 15 percent for people in their mid-60s.

While 7 percent of people aged 65 and over live in institutions, the majority of seniors living at home (73 percent) report that their overall health is relatively good. Nonetheless, most do have some kind of chronic health condition, such as heart trouble, diabetes, rheumatism, or arthritis, and 39 percent said their activity was somewhat restricted by their condition (Lindsay, 1999). Although the elderly are in relatively good health, 34 percent of people aged 65 and over have some need for health-related personal assistance, such as grocery shopping, meal preparation, and housework, including 11 percent who need help for personal activities such as eating and bathing (Chen and Wilkins, 1998). At ages 85 and over, these rates rise to 75 percent and 43 percent respectively. Dementia is another problem that rises sharply with age, affecting 37.1 percent of women and 28.7 percent of men aged 85 and over (Hill et al., 1996: 8).

The present and future health status of young persons is partly a function of risk behaviours associated with smoking, drinking, and sexual activity. The 1994–95 Population Health Survey determined that about a third of people aged 15–24 were daily or occasional smokers, over half had engaged in binge drinking (five or more drinks on one occasion in the 12 months preceding the survey), a fifth had had two or more sex partners in the past year, and a quarter had been sexually active but never or seldom used a condom (see Table 17.2). While a third had not engaged in any of these risk behaviours, 40 percent had engaged in two or more of the activities. Engaging in multiple-risk behaviour was found to be more common for those who were never married, but less common for students and for those living with parents, suggesting that family relationships act as a deterrent (Galambos and Tilton-Weaver, 1998). Other research on smoking indicates that the likelihood of having quit smoking after 15 to 17 years is lower for persons who started smoking before age 18 (Chen and Millar, 1998: 43). Accidents are another important form of health problem for young people. At ages 15–19, 30 percent reported at least one injury

in the past year that was severe enough to limit their daily activity (Millar and Beaudet, 1996).

These are only a few of the observations on health status that can be made with the help of surveys of the health conditions of the population. The 1994–95 survey will follow the same respondents over time. It will therefore enable subsequent analysis of the consequences of various detrimental behaviours. This kind of analysis is important because people may change their behaviour based on good research regarding the impact of smoking, excessive drinking, unsafe sex, poor diet, inactive lifestyles, and obesity. The research on the predominance of various conditions also helps establish priorities, both for promoting healthy behaviour and for treating the victims of various debilitating conditions. This research also points to the disadvantages faced by certain sectors of the population, especially those with lower socioeconomic status, along with the need to reduce social inequities and, in particular, to ensure equitable access to health facilities.

OVERVIEW

The study of population starts with the processes of fertility, mortality, and migration; analyzes the

---

TABLE 17.2 RISK BEHAVIOUR OF ADOLESCENTS AND YOUNG ADULTS, CANADA, 1994–95

	15–19		20–24	
	M	**F**	**M**	**F**
	%	%	%	%
Daily or occasional smoking	28	30	33	40
Binge drinking[a]	52	35	73	51
Sexually active in past year	44	43	78	81
At least two sex partners in past year	21	13	27	16
Sexually active and never or seldom used a condom[b]	22	12	41	36

Notes:
a. Drinking five or more alcoholic beverages on one occasion
b. Excludes those who were married, cohabiting, or formerly married

SOURCE: Nancy Galambos and Lauree Tilton-Weaver, "Multiple-Risk Behaviour in Adolescents and Young Adults," *Health Reports*, Catalogue 82-003, Vol. 10, No. 2, 1998, pp. 9–20. Reprinted with permission of Statistics Canada.

SOURCE: Graham Harrop, *Vancouver Sun*, September 20, 2001, and the Simon Fraser University Editorial Cartoons Collection (http://edocs.lib. sfu.ca/ projects/Cartoons/). © Graham Harrop.

immediate impact of those processes on population size, composition, and distribution; and, finally, considers the broader causes and consequences of demographic change.

At the level of the total world population, where we can ignore migration, we are currently observing very significant changes in mortality and fertility. Particularly impressive has been the change in mortality: In 1950, average life expectancy globally was 46.5 years; by 1995–2000, it had risen to 65.4 years. Fertility has also declined, from an average of 5.0 births per woman to an average of 2.7 over the same period. The faster change in mortality than in fertility, as interpreted by the demographic-transition model, is the reason for the rapid growth in world population. Although the rate of growth reached a peak of 2.04 percent per year in the period 1965–70,

it remains very high by historical standards, at 1.3 percent per year in 2001. What is more, the net additions amount to 78 million persons annually (United Nations, 1999: 1).

A number of consequences and implications arise from these trends at the global level. Concerns persist about the high level of mortality in many countries (particularly the high level of infant mortality) and the variability in maternal mortality from country to country. According to the World Health Organization, the lifetime risk of dying from pregnancy or childbirth-related causes is 1 in 20 in some developing countries, compared with 1 in 10 000 in some developed countries (United Nations, 1995: 42). More generally, there is widespread concern for all people to have access to basic health care—a goal that can easily be undermined when a society supports expensive technological facilities that benefit the few and deplete resources that could subsidize basic care for the many. With respect to fertility, there has been much progress, with more than half of all women of childbearing age now using contraception. However, in some countries, the demand for contraception is higher than the supply, and in other places there is a need to encourage people to have smaller families.

More broadly, the rapid change in world population is accompanied by various concerns, ranging from the difficulty of enhancing standards of living in rapidly growing populations, to the stress that large populations place on the environment. As noted earlier, such concerns brought the United Nations to sponsor several international conferences to consider how the world is to deal with population questions. It has generally been agreed that development is key to bringing down the rate of population growth. Inspired in part by Marxist thinking, the World Population Plan of Action concludes that lack of development, as manifested by "widespread poverty, unemployment, malnutrition, illiteracy, low status of women, exposure to environmental risks and limited access to social and health services ... contribute[s] to high levels of fertility" (United Nations, 1995: 13). However, there is also a need to supply contraception and to promote the idea of smaller families. Recalling the concerns of Malthus, many international agencies and governments have come to conclude that it is essential to slow down population growth by deliberately promoting birth control. The closing address at a 1992 conference organized by the International Planned Parenthood Federation stated that "contraception is the best development."

Canadian trends also involve significant changes. Over the period 1951–99, life expectancy rose from 69 to 79 years, and average births per woman dropped from 3.5 to 1.5. Here, the fertility change is more rapid, and the reduction in the relative number of young people has brought about a considerable increase in the average age of the population. Earlier changes in mortality benefited mostly children and young adults, but, since 1971, older adults are also among those living longer. With longer life, however, come longer average periods of poor health, which can drain health-care funds. Surveys of the health status of the population indicate that many people suffer health problems.

Canada's fertility change is particularly significant since it implies that, over the long term, there will be more deaths than births. There are currently more births simply because of the large numbers of people who are still at reproductive ages. Low fertility is a function of effective contraception, but, more broadly, it is a function of the high cost of children (especially the opportunity cost in terms of parents' careers). Since most people want children, this points to the importance of enabling parents to have both productive and reproductive roles—that is, both to work and to raise children.

Given decreasing levels of natural increase, immigration has come to play a larger role in population change. Over the period 1991–2001, 55 percent of population growth in Canada was a function of net international migration (the other 45 percent was the result of natural increase). Indeed, many people think of immigration as a way of compensating for declining fertility. Although immigration does support population growth, it can change the ethnic composition of the population dramatically and requires various forms of adaptation on the part of both immigrants and the receiving society (see Chapter 10). Canada must ensure that its immigrant groups do not become an economic underclass. Fortunately, compared with many other countries, Canada has a long history of public policies concerning the selection of immigrants and their integration into a changing society.

Besides slower growth and the greater role of immigration, aging represents the most significant aspect of population change. The age structure is particularly relevant given the patterns of health status over different age cohorts, but it affects the society in a variety of ways, including the possibility of a less flexible labour force and difficulties in achieving intergenerational equity. That is, while paying attention to the larger number of elderly people, it is also important to ensure benefits for younger people who want to have children.

Clearly, population dynamics present both Canadian society and the world community with numerous serious challenges.

SUMMARY

1. The consideration of demographics—population size, growth, distribution, composition, fertility, mortality, and migration—is important to the study of societies as they change over time. Conversely, studies of changes or differences in fertility, mortality, and migration require sociological analysis.

2. Demography analyzes population states (size, geographical distribution, and composition by various characteristics) and population processes (fertility, mortality, and migration), their reciprocal influences, and their various determinants and consequences.

3. Malthus concluded that populations have a tendency to grow more rapidly than other resources and that it is important to control the growth of population by reducing births. Marx concluded that economic and social conditions determine the rate of population growth and that proper social arrangements should be able to accommodate population growth. Both of these perspectives are useful.

4. The demographic-transition model summarizes the historical tendency of populations to move from an equilibrium of high birth rates and high death rates to one of low birth rates and low death rates. Because death rates decline sooner and faster than birth rates, there is considerable population expansion during the course of the transition. In the European populations, the demographic transition occurred mostly over the period 1750 to 1970, whereas in Asia, Latin America, and Africa, it started only in the 1950s.

5. Since Confederation, life expectancy in Canada has increased from 42 to 79 years as a result of higher standards of living, improvements in sanitation, and advances in medicine. Degenerative diseases have replaced infectious diseases as the major causes of death. In the same period, average births declined from seven to 1.5 births per woman, though the decline in fertility was not as uniform as the decline in mortality (the baby boom of the period 1946–66 represented a major exception to the downward trend). Average births are now fewer than would be needed for the long-term replacement of the population.

6. Immigration has contributed considerably to Canadian population growth. The net balance between immigration and emigration is responsible for close to a quarter of the population growth over the past century, and 18 percent of the current population is foreign-born. Net migration in the period 1991–2001 accounted for 55 percent of the country's population growth. Immigration has brought significant ethnic diversity to Canada's population, including, since the mid-1960s, large numbers of arrivals from Asia, Latin America, and Africa. Controlling the level of immigration, particularly refugee arrivals, poses challenges in the context of demographic pressures at the world level.

7. Canada's population has grown rapidly since Confederation—twice as rapidly as the population of the world as a whole. Today, however, fertility is low, growth is less rapid, and the population is aging—a process that poses various challenges of adaptation, particularly in the areas of education, the labour force, health care, and pensions. At the same time, population distribution has tended to be very uneven, with different growth dynamics in the various regions. Movement has tended to be toward the western and southern parts of the country. In addition, immigrants have tended to concentrate in the three largest cities (Toronto, Montreal, and Vancouver). With the exception of Montreal, immigrants do not contribute to the relative size of the population of Quebec and the Atlantic provinces.

8. In terms of its population characteristics, Canada displays some unique features. Only 2.1 percent of the world population live in countries with a higher life expectancy than Canada's, and only 10.3 percent in countries with lower fertility. In other ways, Canada shares in the slower population growth and consequent population aging that typically characterize the more-developed countries and distinguish them from the younger and faster-growing populations of the developing world. Canada's relatively high and diversified immigration promotes a cultural mosaic that may help us to retain a common sense of destiny with the three-quarters of humanity that populate the less-developed countries.

QUESTIONS TO CONSIDER

1. Using the frameworks of Malthusian and Marxist theory, discuss the relationship between population and development.

2. In the case of the Canadian demographic transition, do you think that economic or cultural arguments were more relevant?

3. What advantages and disadvantages do you face as a result of your position in Canada's age distribution?

4. Poorer countries typically have higher fertility than richer countries, and poorer people within any given country have more children than richer people, but the main reason middle-class people give for not wanting more children is that they cannot afford more. Moreover, the baby boom occurred during a period of economic expansion. Is the relationship between income and fertility positive or negative? What qualifications must be introduced in order to understand this relationship?

5. As minister responsible for immigration, what kind of a statement to Parliament would you make regarding the level and composition of immigration for the short-term future? Why?

GLOSSARY

A **cohort** is a group of people, observed through time, who share a common temporal demographic experience. For example, the birth cohort of 1960 is the people born in that year. There can also be marriage cohorts, university-admission-year cohorts, and so on.

Cohort completed fertility refers to the number of births per 1000 women for women of given birth cohorts who have completed their childbearing years.

Demographic transition is the theory that the rate of population growth passes through three stages—stable, rapid, and stable—as fertility and mortality rates decline.

Demography is the study of populations, their size, distribution, and composition, and the immediate factors causing population change (births, deaths, and migration).

Emigration is the number of people leaving a country over a given period of time.

Health-adjusted life expectancy is an estimate that combines total life expectancy with the incidence of disabling conditions. To calculate this life expectancy, a series of categories of less-than-optimal health are first assigned values based on a survey that asks respondents to rank their preferences for various health conditions. For instance, the state of near-sightedness but being fully healthy on all other attributes receives a score of 95 percent, while completely disabling pain might be evaluated as a life not worth living. These scores are then multiplied by the years of life that someone would be expected to live under various conditions, to obtain a life expectancy that is adjusted for the health status of the population.

Human ecology is the study of how human populations interact with their sustaining environments.

Immigration refers to the number of people moving into a country over a given period of time.

The **infant mortality rate** is the number of deaths of infants under one year of age per 1000 live births in a given year.

Internal migration is the movement of people within a given country. Generally, only movement across municipal boundaries is counted as internal migration; interprovincial migration is one kind of internal migration.

Life expectancy is an estimate of the average number of additional years a person can expect to live, based on the age-specific death rates of a given year. Unless otherwise indicated, the term refers to life expectancy at birth.

Natural increase is the difference between the number of births and the number of deaths in a population over a given period. Natural increase can be given in absolute numbers or as a percentage of the mid-year population.

Net migration is the difference between the number of immigrants and the number of emigrants in a population over a given period. Net migration can also refer to the net balance of internal migration (in-migration minus out-migration to a particular area).

Out-migration is the process of leaving an administrative subdivision of a country to take up residence in another subdivision of the same country.

Population growth refers to the change in population size over a specific period of time. For a given country, population growth is a function of natural increase (births minus deaths) plus net migration (immigration minus emigration).

Population momentum is the tendency of a population to experience natural increase even when the total fertility rate involves below 2.1 births per woman, as a function of the high proportion of persons of childbearing age in the population.

Population processes are the three ways in which populations change from one time to another, through births, deaths, and migration.

Population stock refers to the size, distribution, and composition of the population at a given point in time.

Replacement fertility is a level of fertility that, if continued over a long period of time, would ensure the replacement of one generation of women by another generation of daughters who are themselves able to reach reproductive ages. Given that some deaths occur before women reach reproductive age, the total fertility rate of 2.1 is generally used as an indicator of replacement fertility.

Total fertility rate refers to the average number of children that would be born to a woman during her lifetime if she were to pass through all her childbearing years conforming to the age-specific fertility rates of a given year. It is an indicator of the level of childbearing in a population, measured in terms of births per woman.

SUGGESTED READING

Beaujot, Roderic. (1991). *Population Change in Canada: The Challenges of Policy Adaptation*. Toronto: Oxford University Press. An interpretation of population change in Canada, with suggestions of policy issues for discussion. Policy issues are raised in terms of either influencing population change or adapting to population change.

Bélanger, Alain. (Annual). *Report on the Demographic Situation in Canada*. Statistics Canada, Cat. No. 91-209. Ottawa: Industry, Science and Technology Canada. This annual publication gives data on the changing demographic situation in Canada and provides an analysis of some of the major observations. Each issue also focuses on a topic of special interest.

Charbonneau, Hubert. (1987). *Naissance d'une population*. Montreal: Les Presses de l'Université de Montréal. The beginnings of the French population in Canada are explored through an analysis of records of people who settled in this country in the seventeenth century.

Foot, David K., and Daniel Stoffman. (1998). *Boom, Bust and Echo 2000*. Toronto: Macfarlane Walter and Ross. This bestseller reflects on how the age structure affects individual opportunities and how population change is transforming Canada's social and economic life.

Haines, Michael, and Richard Steckel. (2000). *A Population History of North America*. Cambridge: Cambridge University Press. This large edited collection includes two chapters on the history of the Aboriginal populations, a chapter on Quebec population history, and two chapters covering Canada in the nineteenth and twentieth centuries.

Livi-Bacci, Massimo. (1992). *A Concise History of World Population*. Cambridge, MA: Blackwell. This book considers population throughout human history, and reviews the issues that faced the world population in the late twentieth century. Questions of population and resources are addressed throughout.

Population Reference Bureau. (1991). *Population Handbook*. Washington, DC: Population Reference Bureau. A quick guide to population dynamics, focusing on definitions, methods of calculating various rates, and interpretive examples.

Wargon, Sylvia T. (2002). *Demography in Canada in the Twentieth Century*. Vancouver: University of British Columbia Press. This history of the discipline of demography in Canada focuses on the different developments in French and English parts of the country. It makes the case that demography has been central to establishing social statistics in Canada.

CHAPTER EIGHTEEN

GLOBAL SOCIETY

In this chapter you will learn that:

- World society is not just an international system of nation-states. It is a worldwide network of people and agencies oriented to the fate of the globe.

- The global age may be seen as a new historical period or a level of social organization above and beyond the nation-state.

- The world economy has become a single transnational system. However, globalization may promote local economic activity rather than concentrate it in one or a few locations.

- People travel and communicate across national borders so frequently that social relations have been lifted out of local contexts.

- Global images and information from the mass media enhance global consciousness and encourage the growth of new globalist social movements, such as the environmental movement.

- Global economic, political, and cultural forces impinge on people's everyday lives and can generate insecurity.

- Homogenization and fragmentation of social groups and individual consciousness are equally possible outcomes of globalization.

- Sociologists face a major challenge in correcting the overemphasis in public policy on economic globalization and contributing to the construction of a global society.

MARTIN ALBROW

UNIVERSITY OF SURREY ROEHAMPTON

INTRODUCTION

The facts are plain. In many ways, people throughout the world are linked together as never before. For example, in 1980 just 3.5 percent of the world's population travelled internationally as tourists. By 2001, that figure had more than tripled to 11.3 percent. There were about 14 000 international organizations in the world in 1980. By 1999, there were three-and-a-half times as many. The Internet did not exist in 1980 but by 2002 it was composed of 165 million servers connecting people from around the world through e-mail, file transfers, Web sites, videoconferencing, and so forth. These and other indicators point unmistakably to the **globalization** of the planet, the growing interdependence and mutual awareness among individuals and economic, political, and social institutions (Guillén, 2000). Sociologists have taken note; the number of published sociology articles on globalization increased eleven-fold between 1980 and 1998 (see Table 18.1).

Globalization is a set of contradictory processes that focuses our attention on the prospects for a global society and culture. It causes us to revisit the theme of the unity of humankind, which was long obscured while sociology was dominated by the concerns of the nation-state.

Global forces change people's lives, including your own. Globalization works through practices that cross national boundaries and tie everyday life to worldwide processes. It may have begun with Western expansion, but globalization now has no single point of origin or direction. Any place in the world now exhibits a bewildering variety of lifestyles that compete for space and attention.

It's a confusion that extends to international affairs. Capitalist democracy now dominates the world. There is a unified global capital market. But the suddenness of outbreaks of war and global financial crises show that no one is in charge of the globe, however much national public figures talk about globalization. Lack of direction and control as well as worldwide injustice provoke widespread public concern represented in movements for human rights, women, children, indigenous peoples, political prisoners, environmental protection, endangered species, and the rain forests.

Globalization creates controversy among sociologists, as well as provoking public and political concern. Is it a process that can be stopped? Should sociology be seriously revised in view of globalization? Whatever the answers, globalization has put the construction of global society on the agenda for both citizens and sociologists.

GLOBALIZATION, NETWORKS, AND IDENTITY

Some analysts have called globalization the process that makes the world a single place (Robertson, 1992: 64) or that binds the population of the world into a single society (Albrow, 1993: 248). These definitions highlight the inclusiveness of globalization but they leave open the question of whether there is anything new in it. After all, the idea that human

---

TABLE 18.1 INDICATORS OF GLOBALIZATION, EARLY 1980S TO CIRCA 2002

	1980–81	1998–2002	% CHANGE
Foreign direct investment as % of GDP	4.6[1]	8.8[5]	91.3
International tourist arrivals as % of world population	3.5[1]	11.3[6]	222.9
Internet hosts	0[1]	165 000 000[7]	undefined
Number of international organizations	14 273[2]	50 373[4]	252.9
Annual entries on globalization, *Sociological Abstracts*	89[1]	1 009[3]	1 033.7

Notes: 1. 1980; 2. 1981; 3. 1998; 4. 1999; 5. 2000; 6. 2001; 7. 2002.

SOURCES: Guillén (2001); Internet Software Consortium (2002); United States Census Bureau (2002); World Bank (2002); World Tourism Organization (2002); "International organizations by year and type (Table 2)" (2001).

beings belong to a single species and their relations with each other bind them into a single humankind is as old as written history.

Sociologists have considered the unity of humankind as axiomatic. We accept the findings of other sciences that biological differences between individuals are only minor variations in a common genetic pool (see Chapter 10 for the insignificance of genetic differences between groups). The unity of humankind is not, however, just biological. It extends to culture too. Every human culture is accessible to every other. We acknowledge no limits to human understanding that prevent a person from interacting meaningfully with a person from another culture.

Travel has always been the way in which bonds are established across group boundaries. Travellers in foreign lands have always found ways to communicate with local inhabitants even before learning their language. The stranger is a universal category and in this sense there has never been a culture isolated from outside influence. The group that sends visitors to another in turn receives visitors from a third and a network of links fans out to cover the face of the earth. There is a longstanding theory in sociology that even in a world of more than 6 billion people there are never more than six acquaintanceship links between any two people in the world. Columbia University researchers have recently aimed to test this "Small World" phenomenon on a global scale by requesting help from interested people (to participate, see Department of Sociology, Columbia University, 2002).

All this suggests that even the most distinct cultures and civilizations have only enjoyed *relative* seclusion from others. None has succeeded in permanent separation from the rest of humanity. In this sense human society has always been a unity. World society has always existed behind the façade of conflicting groups, peoples, and civilizations.

Awareness of world society took many forms in the past. The ancient Greeks and Chinese knew about the world outside their own but they called it "barbarian" or "uncivilized." Socrates declared himself a citizen of the world, rather than merely of Athens, but his was a minority view. In fact, the view that humankind forms a single world society has been an intellectual dream until recently. Only with the spread of Western ideas of nationhood did it take a concrete shape sufficient to affect relations between peoples. As Western imperialism extended its reach, the idea of a world order took on a new meaning. We will see that much of what has become known as globalization arises out of that extension.

In the past we thought of the world as composed of nation-states. Today we increasingly imagine a global society. We think about the common fate of humankind, the fact that the planet is in danger from the immense destructive and productive forces we have released and struggle to control. This shift in focus has been made possible by extraordinary forms of communication that permit worldwide instantaneous conversation between individuals and corporations and worldwide economic activity that is integrated into a global economy, managed (albeit with difficulty) by international financial institutions.

Consciousness of the globe and efforts by a myriad of groups and individuals to work towards a better future for it and the whole of humankind now influence the policies of nations and corporations. Global society has in the last six decades emerged as a new kind of world society, crossing national boundaries—open, contested, stratified, hugely unequal, with little democratic legitimacy. Global requirements influence choices in household consumption and local community policies. The activities of self-declared global citizens, the mobilization of transnational movements, the exercise of global strategic power by the officials of international agencies, all unfold in a global space. Global society provides for the work and play of a global corporate elite, for individual participation at one extreme and the exercise of immense power and influence by the few at the other. The contending political forces in the new society have polarized around globalization, but both the pro- and the anti- sides agree that the agenda is global. For the first time in human history, a society has arisen where the fate of the species depends on the shape and direction of the global agenda.

Manuel Castells (1996–98) has made the idea of a network the key to understanding the new era. Networks—that is, complexes of linked relations—can hold any content, convey any messages, and take innumerable shapes, irrespective of national boundaries. They also govern our lives, threatening and liberating at the same time. This is as true for individuals as for countries. For once the boundaries of countries are crossed, so the certainties of fixed national identity come into question. Now people can be seen much more as embarking on a personal odyssey to find self-identity in a fluid world. They confront the difficulty of choosing who they are (Giddens, 1991), when national identity is only one and often a minor factor in their sense of self.

Nova Scotia writer and social development worker Kingsley Brown captures this quest for identity in Box 18.1 in an obituary of his friend Albertha Francis. Gender and professional identities are woven into her movement between countries and cultures. We can see history etched into her life, especially slavery and the needs of the welfare state, but at the end she finds that home is with friends and, in keeping with her disdain for documents, we never learn her nationality.

How do we best consider individuals in relation to society? Should we consider them as members of one society among many, with their lives bounded by that membership? Or should we consider them part of an all-inclusive human society to which the whole population of the world belongs? Albertha Francis's story prompts those questions. Globalization as the story of the contemporary world makes us question the very idea of society. For those who have seen it as essentially linked to the nation-state, society as such has declined as globalization has gathered strength.

For those who have regarded the nation-state's dominance over society as excessive, globalization marks the re-emergence of society as an independent factor. Either way, politically or intellectually, society is on the agenda, and this is what makes globalization so challenging for sociologists.

FROM THE MODERN TO THE GLOBAL AGE

HISTORY AND THEORY

If you ask when globalization began, answers will vary, in part because of different ways of defining it, in part because of disagreement about facts. These are not superficial difficulties. They arise for any concept that deals with change in the real world. Sociology makes a craft of seeking to answer such a question without dismissing the difficulties.

At its simplest, the problem is that if you define globalization one way, then a particular set of facts becomes relevant to deciding when it began. If you define it another way, then a different set of facts is involved. Bearing this in mind, let us look at three broad types of definition:

BOX 18.1 IDENTITY IN A GLOBAL SOCIETY

Albertha Francis died November 1, 1999, of a stroke in Antigonish, Nova Scotia, aged 85. Descended from the proud and strong Coromantee tribe of Africa's Gold Coast brought as slaves to Jamaica in the 16th century, she was born on January 28, 1914, in Salem, Jamaica. Her father was a planter who disappeared to the cane fields of Cuba. Encouraged by a woman employer, she entered the United States in 1940 and saved enough from garment factory work in New York to get a boat to England. "She wanted a profession," said Eileen White, her closest friend in St. Petersburg, Florida. "She had a passion for education." She entered training as a nurse at St. Luke's Hospital at Bradford, Yorkshire. As a midwife, she delivered nearly 300 babies in the industrial cities of the Midlands. Being a registered nurse and certified midwife gave her freedom and independence. She felt no need of a man. She had come from a matriarchal society where a legacy of slavery still made a man's place in the family less than secure. Unexpectedly, she found a home and a job as a public-health nurse in 1968 among the Acadians in the village of Monk's Head on the Northumberland Strait, not far from Antigonish, Nova Scotia. To pay for her little house she worked with the sick from the hard streets of New York in the psychiatric wards of famed Bellevue Hospital. She lived in a residence nearby and corresponded with friends from her travels all over the world. She came home every summer. "Albertha was never happier than she was at Monk's Head," said Miss White. "She died among the people who loved her." She went to Florida for the winters and flew north early each spring. Miss Francis left no official papers, certificates, citations, or diplomas. Found one day cutting them up with scissors, she told Miss White: "They're no good to me now, dear."

SOURCE: Adapted from Kingsley Brown, "Albertha Francis: Obituary," *The Globe and Mail*, November 22, 1999. Reprinted with permission.

1. The first we can call "analytical." Here is an example: "Globalization as I shall conceive it in what follows … is not only, or even primarily, about economic interdependence, but about the transformation of time and space in our lives" (Giddens, 1998: 30–31). Anthony Giddens talks here about time and space, but doesn't specify any particular date or place. In principle, then, we could talk of globalization wherever there are people whose time and space is transformed. We could use the concept in archaeology to discuss the impact of the sail or the wheel, or in history with reference to the invention of printing or to the European voyages of discovery.

   Analytical concepts are helpful for making comparisons between different times and places and for highlighting factors that are universal. For any account of society whatsoever, it must be possible to discuss the frame of time and space in which people conduct their lives and come to some judgement about changes in it. This definition suggests that one of the reasons we talk so much about globalization today is because changes in this time/space frame have been so rapid.

2. The second main type of definition is historical. For example: "The slow, stable, chopped up Cold War system that had dominated international affairs since 1945 had been firmly replaced by a new, very greased, interconnected system called globalization" (Friedman, 1999: xiii). Note here how dates enter in, with a reference to a specific power conflict and a suggestion that this is a unique period of history. In fact, Thomas Friedman alludes to a previous period that bore similarities to the period after 1945, one between the mid-1800s and 1920. Then, too, there was a single world marketplace. But there are other differences that make the later period unique—in particular, telecommunications. With this historical definition there is no special weight attached to the term *globalization*. It does not belong to an attempt to theorize social relations for any period or place. It just happens to be the term that captures what is going on in the world today.

3. Note that the authors of our two examples are, respectively, a social theorist and a journalist. They set out with different aims. The first bases his argument on a general theory of how society works. The second aims to describe the trends of our time. They both agree, however, that the globalization that began in the second half of the twentieth century was something special. Now suppose we try to merge the two kinds of accounts, the analytical and the story of our time. Since the first provides a way of looking at any period and the latter describes a sequence of events, a merger of the two results in a general theory of history—globalization as a process through all historical time, with the present as its culmination.

   The best example of such a combined approach is in the work of Roland Robertson, the first scholar to make globalization a sociological theme. Note how in the following quotation he combines analytical elements—"compression" and "intensification"—with a time perspective—"over many centuries": "Globalization as a concept refers both to the compression of the world and the intensification of consciousness of the world as a whole. The processes and actions to which the concept of globalization now refers have been proceeding with some interruptions for many centuries but the main focus of discussion of globalization is on relatively recent times" (Robertson, 1992: 8). Robertson suggests that the world has become one place, but our awareness of it as one place, while also intensified, is a distinct issue. By referring to "interruptions," he makes it clear that globalization is not some irresistible force. Indeed, it also depends on human actions. Finally, he implies that the focus on recent globalization is itself new.

The careful nature of Robertson's formulation illustrates why we cannot expect a simple answer to our initial question: "When did globalization begin?" It raises at least three distinct but related issues: Were there periods of greater or lesser globalization? How were these periods related to consciousness? What led to the new focus of discussion? In sociology these issues have all been bound up with intensive debate about the nature and course of **modernity** and the expansion of the Western world (with modernity being understood as the complex of features that has distinguished Western cultures and societies over the last 300 or 400 years, including rationality, individualism, and the quest for improvements and novelty).

MODERNITY AND ITS OUTCOMES

Three forces impelled the expansion of the West. First, *universalism* views and values the world from a single set of concepts, as in scientific measurement or ideas of human rights and representative democracy (Tomlinson, 1991). Second, *imperialism* imposes supposedly universalistic ideas on others by means of Bible and sword, Koran and scimitar, Communist Manifesto and tanks. Third, *capitalism* has helped to ensure the domination of the world by the West.

The expansion of the West could not have happened without ideas in combination with military force, but the motives behind it were often the quest for wealth, resources, and trade (J.A. Hall, 1985; Mann, 1986). From prehistoric times, the search for opportunities to exchange goods to mutual advantage has stimulated exploration and expansion. Indeed, the economic dynamism of the West arose out of a combination of trade and an expansionary state, with science and religion serving those ends (Wallerstein, 1974). The West developed the distinctive form of systematic production, consumption, means of exchange, and wealth accumulation known as capitalism. Like its partners, universalism and imperialism, capitalism is inherently expansionist, always requiring new markets simply to survive, always seeking to develop new ways of generating profit. At the beginning of the 1990s, with the collapse of state socialism in Eastern Europe, capitalism finally became the unrivalled world economic system.

The expansion of the West over the last 500 years coincides with what is called the "modern age." But the term *modern* is more than just the name of a time period. It is used to convey the quality of living that results when the new, the technically advanced, and the rational push traditional ways of doing things into the background. We refer in this sense to "modern culture" as well as "modern society."

The culture of the modern age, with its emphasis on rationality, science, and technology, appears to bring the world into a single frame of reference. The internal-combustion engine and the computer work the same way in Tokyo as they do in New York and they bring with them similar consequences for ways of living. This phenomenon has been called the "logic of industrialism," and has been cited in evidence of what has come to be known as convergence theory—the idea that all societies are taking on the same characteristics (Kerr et al., 1960).

It seems that even the modern personality is a Western product (Elias, 1978, 1982; Inkeles, 1983). This impression is strengthened by the activities of Western states, which export their forms of administration to developing countries and make their aid dependent on the adoption of Western practices of management, education, and even family life. *Modernization* was the term used to describe efforts by the United States in particular, but by other advanced states as well, to bring Third World countries into the capitalist economic system.

These features of the modern age led Giddens (1990: 63) to say that "modernity is inherently globalizing." However, this raises the prospect of a world without variety, of a uniform way of doing things from which there is no escape. From this point of view, it would seem that Max Weber's threatening vision of an advancing technical and economic machine trapping everyone in an "iron cage" has indeed become a reality (Weber, 1976 [1904–1905]: 181). However, the plain fact is that old industries have declined rapidly over the past several decades. New service occupations have emerged, especially in the area of information technology. As a result, new theories of postindustrial society have been formulated, according to which manufacturing industry no longer plays a dominant role in shaping social structure (Bell, 1976; Touraine, 1971). In addition, theories of **postmodernity** argue that, contrary to modernist claims, society is culturally fragmented rather than homogeneous, lacking direction toward "progress" or any other single goal (Lyotard, 1984; Jameson, 1991). One analyst has even claimed that cultural homogeneity and unanimity of purpose never existed and that modernity was therefore *always* a myth (Latour, 1993).

Not everyone has had so gloomy a view of the direction of modernity. The passage from Henry David Thoreau (1927 [1854]) in Box 18.2 shows how it was his sense of the huge variety in kind and place of origin of the world's products that made him feel like a world citizen. The "extent of the globe" inspired him to find unity in diversity.

Globalization has added another dimension to this debate (Waters, 1995). Should we regard global-

Commerce is unexpectedly confident and serene, alert, adventurous, and unwearied. It is very natural in its methods, withal, far more so than many fantastic enterprises and sentimental experiments, and hence its singular success. I am refreshed and expanded when the freight train rattles past me, and I smell the stores which go dispensing their odours all the way from Long Wharf to Lake Champlain, reminding me of foreign parts, of coral reefs, and Indian Oceans, and tropical climes, and the extent of the globe. I feel more like a citizen of the world at the sight of a palm-leaf, which will cover so many flaxen New England heads the next summer, the Manilla hemp and coconut husks, the old junk, gunny bags, scrap iron, and rusty nails.

SOURCE: Henry David Thoreau, *Walden, or Life in the Woods* (London: Chapman and Hall, 1927 [1854]), p. 103.

ization as a late stage of modern society? Or is it an aspect of postmodernity and of the general fragmentation of society, as many postmodern writers declare? Or should we really be talking about a new historical epoch, beyond the modern, but not postmodern either—a "global age" (Laszlo, 1989: 48)? These questions belong to sociological theory conceived as the broadest possible inquiry into the history and development of human society.

Two of the most important contributors to the emerging sociological theory of globalization are Roland Robertson and Anthony Giddens. Both suggest that, as big structures change at the global level, so do people's daily lives. Robertson (1992: 27) speaks of "relativization," the process by which the relationships between selves and societies shift in the context of a changing world system. Giddens (1990: 21–29) emphasizes the idea of **disembedding**: People increasingly put their faith in abstract systems that were organized over the course of decades, span thousands of kilometres, and involve millions of people. A good example is that of lending and exchange in worldwide economic relations.

A central difference between Robertson and Giddens lies in their causal ordering of events. Giddens considers modernity to be a cause of globalization. He thus focuses on how new technologies of communication have helped globalize the world. For Robertson, however, the causal sequence is the other way around: Modernity, he says, is the result of globalization. Thus, focusing on institutions of social order at the global level and values that focus on globality, Robertson traces their origins back at least 2000 years, long before the modern era.

My own way out of this disagreement (Albrow, 1997) is simply to define the global age as the time when the global entered our lives as never before. From this point of view, the global age has replaced the modern age only in the last few decades. The transition has taken place not simply because people everywhere relate their lives to global forces and issues, but because they have generally lost confidence in the core feature of modernity—the idea that people's rational control of nature and society is increasing all the time. Knowledge societies (Stehr, 1994) are also risk or "non-knowledge" societies (Beck, 1992). The nuclear bombs dropped on Hiroshima and Nagasaki in 1945 brought this realization as never before: Great scientific achievement can destroy the world. We can now see the repercussions of this event as the beginning of the end for the modern age. These various causal arguments are summarized graphically in Figure 18.1, where arrows indicate the direction of causality.

FIGURE 18.1 INTERPRETATIONS OF GLOBALIZATION

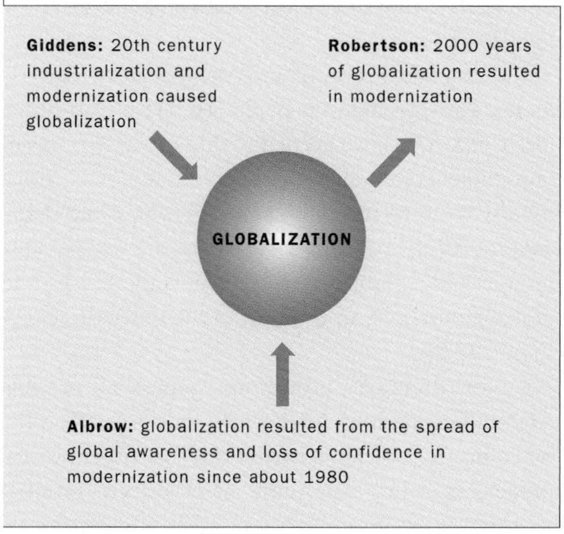

Giddens: 20th century industrialization and modernization caused globalization

Robertson: 2000 years of globalization resulted in modernization

GLOBALIZATION

Albrow: globalization resulted from the spread of global awareness and loss of confidence in modernization since about 1980

The outcome of the global age is in the unknown future, but the idea has been criticized by Held and colleagues (1999: 3–10) as "hyperglobalizing" and overemphasizing the unity of world society. For them, "globalization may be thought of initially as the widening, deepening and speeding up of worldwide interconnectedness" (Held et al., 1999: 2) and as such can be identified in premodern times as well as early modern, modern, and contemporary. But then we have to ask: What is different about contemporary globalization, or is it just more of the same?

THE GLOBAL SHIFT

Let us consider the changes in the recent past that have made the global level more important in our lives and begin by considering relations between people in terms of **levels of analysis**. We can think of social life as made up of people interacting at three levels: households, communities, and nation-states. Each level depends on the others. For instance, the organization of household routines depends in part on how communities organize and schedule schools. Similarly, the state enters into relations between marriage partners in a household—for example, through property law and debates on sexual rights. In practice, all three levels of analysis exist only in and through the lives of individual people.

Now add a fourth level of analysis: global social organization. The inclusion of the global level is evident in discussions of the global becoming local, of worldwide organizations operating locally—for example, McDonald's and the Green Movement, each in its own way a global concern operating at the local level.

If you add a level of analysis, it is clear that you increase the complexity of theory. With only three levels of analysis, we needed to think only in terms of household–community, household–state, and community–state relations—that is, three possible interactions. With a fourth level, there are six possible interactions: global–state, global–community, and global–household, in addition to the other three (see Figure 18.2).

Now think of a project to complete all possible communication links worldwide. That is in effect the outcome of "the modern project." In other words, modernity, the expansion of Western rational

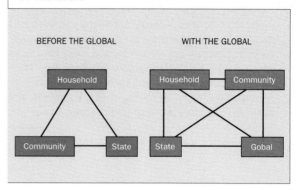

FIGURE 18.2 INTRODUCING THE GLOBAL LEVEL OF ANALYSIS

methods and technology, reached its culmination when communication with all became open to all. When Canadian communications scholar Marshall McLuhan (1962: 31) announced that the "new electronic interdependence recreates the world in the image of a **global village**," he used the term *global* in a new way to highlight the worldwide direct communication, transmission, and reception of speech and images. The world, or many worlds, now entered one's own locality.

Globalization released the potential of each individual to think, act, and feel as a global citizen. In one's own locality, it suddenly made sense to relate directly to events in other parts of the world. Settled comfortably in one's downtown apartment, one could telephone a family member living in another country or watch a hockey game on television that was being played in Moscow. One could campaign for the rights of indigenous peoples in the Amazon or make an investment in the Hong Kong stock exchange.

When formerly independent human activities are linked to a global frame of reference, their nature changes. Thus, the woman in a Bangladesh village who made baskets for her family now makes baskets for money, and a trader sells them in Vancouver. The state, supported by international agencies, gave her start-up capital and free contraceptive products to discourage her from having more children. Even her daily personal and intimate life has apparently become part of a global framework.

It is not only the market forces of capitalism that transform lives. Agencies and movements work together to promote values that take the globe as their point of reference. For example, people who devote their careers to spreading the gospel of family planning are driven by the idea that there is a limit to the population size that the world can sustain. **Globalism** refers to values that make the fate of humanity and the earth the centre of their concern.

Increasingly, globalist values are replacing older universalist values and the political ideologies of industrial societies. The quest for equality and liberty, the secularized heaven on earth that inspired the revolutions of the eighteenth century and the Russian Revolution of 1917, has given way to a focus on improving the quality and conditions of life as lived.

One of the major elements of globalist consciousness now is the vivid realization of the limits in time and space of living on a planet with finite resources. Moreover, once the world came to be seen as one place, it also came to be treated as a common and shared territory. Not far behind was the recognition that it was the *collective* products of human activity globally that were endangering the atmosphere, destroying the forests, and poisoning the oceans.

The global physical environment is now seen as a potent condition and casualty of any lifestyle. Ecology as a global concern focuses on the idea of sustainable development and the management of the world's resources (Sachs, 1993). Sociologists have correspondingly sought to adapt their thinking to take account of this changed social reality. For Ulrich Beck (1992), this has meant thinking of society in terms of response to risk rather than in terms of the distribution of wealth.

This change of outlook has been prompted by world events with far-reaching consequences. The oil price rises of the early 1970s led Ralf Dahrendorf (1975) to reflect that modern expansion was over and the best we could look forward to was survival with justice. The idea of limits to growth (Meadows et al., 1972) is diametrically opposed to the assumptions of the modern project, which valued expansion above all else. For many people, events like the dropping of the nuclear bombs in 1945 and the dismantling of the Berlin Wall in 1989 signalled the end of old directions and the beginning of something new.

We should recognize the interconnectedness of these changes. Market forces, environmental impacts, communication technology, international politics, and social movements have become interdependent and have all globalized. We can call this a global shift

(Dicken, 1992; Burbach and Robinson, 1999) since the globe seems to enter into each sector and into everyone's lives.

Let us now review different aspects of world social organization, including politics, the economy, social relations, and the media. We will find that globalization has not resulted in a predictable world order. On the contrary, it is taking us into an unknowable future.

ONE-WORLD POLITICS

NATION-STATES AND GLOBAL GOVERNANCE

The event that shook the world more than any other since the end of World War II was the 1989 dismantling of the Berlin Wall. The Berlin Wall represented the division of Germany and the rest of the world into two power blocs led by the United States and the Soviet Union. The latter disintegrated in 1991 and its subject Eastern European regimes turned away from communism.

Many people hoped that a consensual and predictable "new world order" would soon emerge. It did not. For one thing, without an enemy, many democratic states no longer sought a leader and the United States began to question its role in the world. For another, first Japan and then China became potential economic threats to the United States, putting into question its ability to maintain its leadership role for long. Globalization became a central theme for state policy makers worldwide, and people began to question the relationships among state, nation, and society as never before.

Until the late-twentieth century, nation-states that had not assimilated their peoples into one nation were regarded as, in some sense, less than fully modern. So, for instance, John Porter's (1965) classic account of Canada's social structure treated its "mosaic" of ethnicities as a residue of past culture that is dysfunctional in modern society. Yet subsequent research showed that ethnicity could be useful at any time (Brym with Fox, 1989: 117). Events in the 1990s and the early years of the twenty-first century reinforced the point.

In fact, the Canadian ethnic mosaic is now promoted as a positive feature by the Canadian government and can be seen more as a precursor of developments elsewhere than as a relic from the past. In the United States, with Spanish the first language of the majority in many parts of the country, assimilation of immigrants is no longer taken for granted. The United Kingdom has recognized the claims of the Celtic nations to their own governments. Above all, the break-up of the Soviet Empire has demonstrated that the relation of state to nation is always a contested issue. The multiethnic state and peoples without statehood are normal, not exceptional states of affairs. There is no ethnically homogeneous state in the world (see Figure 18.3).

For many commentators, rising nationalism is both a response to, and promoted by, globalization. With the new communication technology, ethnic and other groups are able to organize across state boundaries more effectively than ever before and to command world attention through the media. Nation-states themselves may also assert their independence against forces of globalization, as, for instance, Malaysia has done by proclaiming specifically Asian values.

The counterpart to claims to ethnic identity and national independence has been the growing interdependence of nation-states within supranational structures such as the security alliance NATO (North Atlantic Treaty Organization) and the economic pact NAFTA (North American Free Trade Agreement). In some cases federal structures have developed, such as the European Union (EU) with its 15 member countries and 13 "candidate countries" soon hoping to join. The EU has its own central bureaucracy in Brussels and has been accorded many state functions by its members.

These organizations, coupled with the major international bodies that were created at the end of World War II, such as the International Monetary Fund, the World Bank, and the United Nations with its many agencies, have developed an interlocking framework of institutions. These institutions bind member states together and, in effect, manage the globe in what they deem to be the collective interests of humankind. Nation-states are inextricably bound up now in a global system of state governance. As

---

FIGURE 18.3 MAJOR ETHNIC GROUP (AS PERCENTAGE OF POPULATION)

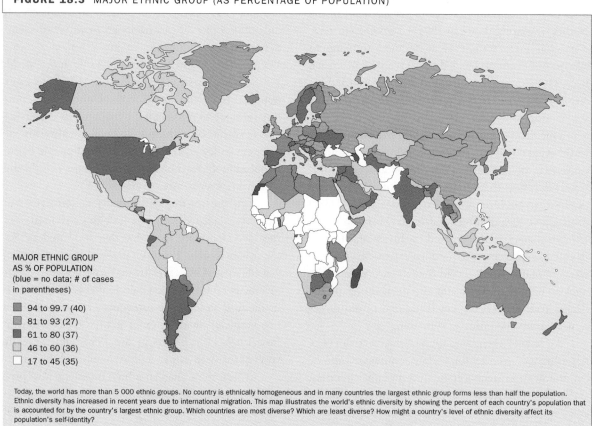

MAJOR ETHNIC GROUP
AS % OF POPULATION
(blue = no data; # of cases
in parentheses)

- 94 to 99.7 (40)
- 81 to 93 (27)
- 61 to 80 (37)
- 46 to 60 (36)
- 17 to 45 (35)

Today, the world has more than 5 000 ethnic groups. No country is ethnically homogeneous and in many countries the largest ethnic group forms less than half the population. Ethnic diversity has increased in recent years due to international migration. This map illustrates the world's ethnic diversity by showing the percent of each country's population that is accounted for by the country's largest ethnic group. Which countries are most diverse? Which are least diverse? How might a country's level of ethnic diversity affect its population's self-identity?

SOURCES: "Ethnic Groups in the World," *Scientific American.* On the World Wide Web at http://www.sciam.com/1998/0998issue/0998numbers.html (December 4, 2001); *CIA World Factbook 2001,* on the World Wide Web at http://www.cia.gov/cia/publications/factbook/ (January 10, 2002).

they have combined for common purposes, they have effectively ceded some of their sovereignty even if they don't always acknowledge it.

Some commentators link the decline of the nation-state to the process of globalization, often deploring the loss of national control. National politicians may even campaign on the issue. But there is no reason, historically or theoretically, to assume that states are coterminous with nation-states (Burbach and Robinson, 1999: 16). What is happening is that state functions are being taken over by bodies operating at a different level. It is becoming obsolete to think of the "state" as represented by nation-states and their organs; we must start thinking of state functions as being distributed among various organizations and agencies, from the United Nations at one extreme, to the local community council at the other.

As a result, at the beginning of the twenty-first century, there is no nation-state that does not take a stance on global issues. If you want to take a typical case you need go no further than the Web site of the Policy Research Initiative of the Canadian government (Policy Research Initiative, 2002). The Initiative accepts globalization as a fact of life and the need to adapt public policy to it as an overriding necessity. At the same time it acknowledges the pressures resulting from globalization on the social and cultural fabric of the country.

Those pressures in turn become the focus of attention for groups that wish to promote alternative policy agendas. The Council of Canadians is such a group, claiming 100 000 members, and "safeguarding our social programs, promoting economic justice, renewing our democracy, asserting Canadian sovereignty, advancing alternatives to corporate-style free trade, and preserving our environment." (Council of Canadians, 2002). Its Chair, Maude Barlow, has argued that Canadian capital has gone global and that globalization is dismantling Canadian democracy (Barlow, 1996).

Globalization, then, has entered into the heart of political debate. In the United States and the United Kingdom, the governments of Bill Clinton and Tony Blair have promoted the idea of a Third Way that claims to go beyond old divisions between Left and Right. The acceptance of globalization is the premise of an argument that links social democracy to a policy of accepting technological advance, promoting lifelong learning, and initiating "welfare to work" programs. The redistribution of wealth and the expansion of the welfare state, long-held goals of socialist parties, have been replaced by the goal of "reinventing government," which aims to restrain state expenditure, make state agencies more efficient, and foster public–private partnerships in the interests of an expanding economy.

If these developments assume the separation of nation and state, they also promote the distinctness of society from state. It is no coincidence that the leading sociologist of globalization, Anthony Giddens, is a close adviser to British Prime Minister Blair. In his book *The Third Way* (1998), he calls for a renewal of civil society as a partner of the state, not subordinate to it. He hopes that communal energies can be harnessed to, but also act as a check on, state aims.

HUMAN RIGHTS AND GLOBAL MOVEMENTS

Corresponding to the move from domestic to global premises for national public policies, oppositional movements have shifted their attention to global agencies. So, for instance, when the World Trade Organization met in Seattle from November 30 to December 3, 1999, a consortium of campaigning groups long used to working on a global scale, including Friends of the Earth and Greenpeace, took out a series of full-page advertisements in the *New York Times* attacking WTO policies and organized well-publicized demonstrations. They effectively turned the world's attention away from free trade, as such, to its consequences for the environment, national culture, and employment. The Council of Canadians is also a member of this consortium, seeking to influence a global body that in turn influences Canadian policy makers (see Box 18.3).

Classic theories of representative democracy have seen the nation-state as the natural arena for the exercise of citizenship. But without a vote as a world citizen, the individual has to find other ways of influencing global agencies. This has led David Held (1995) to propose a new order of cosmopolitan democracy and Ulrich Beck (2000) to advocate new transnational community ties to underpin transnational sovereignties. In practice, individuals have long assumed the role of world citizen by acting on the values enshrined in the founding documents drawn up for the United Nations.

Individuals may not have a vote as world citizens, but they can influence the agencies whose functions now embrace the world. The United Nations was formed by nation-states "to maintain international

BOX 18.3   THE ANTI-GLOBALIZATION MOVEMENT: A REPORT FROM THE CANADIAN SECURITY INTELLIGENCE SERVICE (CSIS)

Shock and surprise were widespread in the wake of the disruptive protests and associated violence that characterized the Seattle World Trade Organization (WTO) Ministerial Conference, 29 November–3 December, 1999. Yet the demonstrations were not something new, nor was the principal target—multinational corporate power—an unexpected focus. Opposition to corporate globalization has been growing for several years, a trend underscored by increasing media attention since 1995. Security agencies at Seattle, however, were caught off-guard by the large number of demonstrators and scope of representation, combined with the use of sophisticated methods and technology that effectively shut down the Conference....

Meetings of international monetary, trade and environmental organizations, which in the past incited little or no protest interest, are now drawing the attention of thousands of anti-globalization activists. Representing a broad spectrum of groups, lobbyists, and overlapping networks, including some violent extremists whose presence raises security concerns, they share a mutual antipathy—that of multinational corporate power. Often described as more influential and stronger than government, some corporations boast budgets larger than the gross domestic product (GDP) of many nations: "... of the top hundred economies, fifty-one are multinationals and only forty-nine are countries."

Alleged abuse of corporate power by multinationals is the basic focus of protest activity. Large corporations with international undertakings stand accused of social injustice, unfair labour practices—including slave labour wages, living and working conditions—as well as a lack of concern for the environment, mismanagement of natural resources, and ecological damage. Anti-globalization demonstrations have achieved worldwide support partly because the target, per se, its representatives, and its effects are global in nature. Major brand names, among them Nike, Starbucks, McDonald's, and Shell Oil, are principal targets, ironically because their massive advertising campaigns designed to engender public prominence have been successful—and that status is being used to highlight the charges brought against them.

Protest objectives extend beyond the claimed corporate impropriety, however. Multinational economic institutions, such as the World Trade Organization (WTO), the World Bank (WB), and the International Monetary Fund (IMF), are seen as establishing, monitoring, and rendering judgements on global trade practices, and are viewed as the spearheads of economic globalization. These institutions, considered to be the servants of corporate interests, exercising more power than elected governments and interested only in the profit motive, have increasingly become principal demonstration targets. Underlying the anti-globalization theme is criticism of the capitalist philosophy, a stance promoted once again by left-of-centre activists and militant anarchists....

In her book, *No Logo*, Canadian Naomi Klein claims

> ... corporate investment in the Third World was seen ... as a key to alleviating poverty and misery. By 1996, however, that concept was being openly questioned, and it was recognized that many governments in the developing world were protecting lucrative investments—mines, dams, oil fields, power plants and export processing zones—by deliberately turning a blind eye to egregious rights violations by foreign corporations against their people.

> ... Diversity is a major characteristic of anti-globalization protests and demonstrations, which are often described as "multi-generational, multi-class, and multi-issue." Participants represent a variety of issues and not all are pursuing globalization as their primary target. For some protesters, anti-globalization is a principal concern, but for others it is merely a shared goal, with the demonstrations simply a means to an end. That is, the combination of groups and participants coming together creates a powerful impression and an impact out of all proportion with their individual strengths....

> The Internet will continue to play a large role in the success or failure of globalization protests and demonstrations. Groups will use the Internet to identify and publicize targets, solicit and encourage support, organize and communicate information and instructions, recruit, raise funds, and as a means of promoting their various individual and collective aims.

SOURCE: Canadian Security Intelligence Service (CSIS), *Perspective* 2000/08, "Anti-Globalization—A Spreading Phenomenon." G. Davidson (Tim) Smith, Ph.D. Reproduced with the permission of the Minister of Public Works and Government Services, 2003.

peace and security," according to the first article of the UN Charter. But the charter also reaffirmed "faith in fundamental human rights, in the dignity and worth of the human person, in the equal rights of men and women and nations large and small" (Sieghart, 1985: 170).

The charter was followed by the Universal Declaration of Human Rights, which begins: "All human beings are born free in equal dignity and rights." This statement represents the culmination of centuries of philosophy and struggle to assert universal reason in human affairs. The United Nations also issued a series of more detailed agreements covering genocide, the status of refugees, discrimination against women, the right to unionize, and so forth.

Declarations of good intentions carry no guarantee that they will come into effect. They do, however, provide hope and justification for the aspirations of people in all parts of the world. They serve as a common reference point for movements that spring up in different countries and that might otherwise remain isolated. This is what has been called "globalization from below," opening the possibility of a one-world community with global citizenship (Falk, 1992). In effect, globalization from below involves citizens working toward a new global state, a reversal of the older order where it was assumed that the state turned people into citizens.

The United Nations has, in turn, found ways to respond to such movements. For example, it declared 1975 as International Women's Year, and the 1980s as the United Nations Decade for Women. In the name of the latter it organized an international conference in Mexico City. Delegates from women's organizations worldwide returned from that conference with new ideas for action in their own countries. They built their own groups in liaison with their sisters overseas. *Sisterhood Is Global* (Morgan, 1984) was the apt title for an anthology of writings by people involved in the international women's movement.

Worldwide grassroots movements for political rights, disarmament, environmental protection, and poverty relief operate in the same way, establishing their own networks and responding to and stimulating the activities of international agencies (Willetts, 1982). Together, they amount to a "new world order" for dealing with crises of unprecedented magnitude (Ekins, 1992). The new technical possibilities for instant communication (telephone, fax, and the Internet) reinforce the importance of the global framework for local initiatives (Janelle, 1991). A transnational political mobilization that focuses individual energies on global issues rather than on the nation-state is well under way.

So we see that the world political system has developed neither as the empire of a super-state (often feared as the likely outcome of the superpower

struggle) nor as a single world state. Instead, it has become a forum for global consciousness, where opinions are formed and conflicts resolved by hammering out common global interests. No single agency controls this process. The process creates agencies. The globalized world is "decentred."

THE GLOBAL ECONOMY

Applying the idea of globalization leads to a change in thinking about economic activity: Instead of thinking of the world as divided among different national economies, begin by thinking of the world economic system and the way it influences regions and localities. Initially, the idea of economic globalization was stimulated by the lowering of trade barriers between nations and the transnational activities of multinational corporations. The recognition that the spread of new technologies and changes in management practices were features of a change in the total world economy came later.

The global economy involves the following elements:

- international economic institutions such as the International Monetary Fund;
- transnational corporations such as IBM, Glaxo, and Nissan;
- world financial markets in New York, London, Tokyo, and elsewhere;
- the global spread of new production practices and consumption patterns;
- competitive economic nationalism, as governments seek to improve the performance of their own country in the world; and
- a worldwide division of labour and class system.

These elements cannot be considered in isolation from one another. Taken together, their development amounts to a change in the total world economic system.

THE GLOBAL MARKET

Our understanding of the way the global economic system works still depends on insights from earlier periods of capitalist expansion. After Adam Smith (1910 [1776]) in the eighteenth century argued that the expansion of free trade helped the development of specialized occupations for the benefit of all, Karl Marx (1970 [1867]) rejected both Smith's theory and the system on which it was based by arguing that the expansion of markets resulted in the concentration of capital in a few hands and the impoverishment of the working masses. For us the important point is that both Marx and Smith acknowledged the international character of capitalist activity.

Scholars have since examined the theme of capitalism's international scope in the context of the economic impact of modern Western states on the rest of the world. Frank (1967) argued that underdevelopment in one part of the world is a product of development in another. Cardoso and Faletto (1979) view the internal political dynamics of Latin American states as the outcome of dependency on foreign capital. Wallerstein (1974, 1980, 1989) has made the development of the world economy the theme of his world-system theory, which considers economic relations only from the perspective of the world as a whole, with states representing merely one force among many.

However the past of the world economic system is interpreted, since 1945 the most powerful nation-states have deliberately sought to secure the system's stability through institutions such as the International Monetary Fund and the World Bank. They see in stable economic growth the basis for satisfying both popular demand for improved standards of living and the demand of business for profits. The several international agreements that have been negotiated since World War II by the member countries of the World Trade Organization have reduced national barriers to free trade worldwide and have thereby made states increasingly interdependent.

The advance of capitalism does not stop when all the world's territory has come under its influence. It then looks to new sources of labour—in the family, for instance. The participation of women in the paid labour force has increased dramatically in advanced economies, in part because women have traditionally worked for no wages in the patriarchal family and their labour has been inexpensive relative to that of men. Capitalism transforms the position of women and thereby transforms the family by bringing women into the labour market. It accordingly prompts feminist demands for equal rights, which, as we saw earlier, have grown parallel to capitalism on a global scale.

Capitalism unsettles all kinds of traditional relations and global capitalism unsettles nation-states as well. Thus, even as the great economic powers work to make the world a single market, they are apprehensive about the consequences. The United States fears Japanese competition. Newly industrializing countries threaten the industrialized countries. The fears of the latter have been prompted in part by studies that forecast growing unemployment in industrialized countries resulting from the new international division of labour (Fröbel, Heinrichs, and Kreye, 1980). This theme continued into the 1990s. U.S. President Clinton convened a conference of the seven countries with the most powerful economies (the G-7) in Detroit on March 14 and 15, 1994, to address the conventional wisdom that globalization destroys jobs. The conference heard that the global spread of new production practices could have quite different consequences.

GLOBAL PRODUCTION AND CONSUMPTION

The expansion of markets has been associated with the growth of huge transnational corporations (TNCs) whose operations span the globe (Sklair, 1991). TNCs seek both to diversify their activities into every area of the market and to develop goods that will sell everywhere in the world. These are not necessarily compatible objectives, and there is no sure way for a TNC to achieve world dominance. But for the largest TNCs, that has become the aim.

The idea of globalization first gained prominence in marketing strategies in the 1970s. In the 1980s, companies like Coca-Cola and Kellogg's expanded into non-Western countries. McDonald's opened its first store in China in 1991.

Source: © Wally McNamee/Corbis/Magma.

The idea of globalization first gained prominence in the marketing strategies of the TNCs. In the 1970s, Coca-Cola was the most prominent global product. In the 1980s, McDonald's became equated with the globalization process itself—as evidenced in phrases such as the "McDonaldization of everything" and in the use of the prefix "Mc" to denote any standardized activity that can be repeated anywhere (Ritzer, 1992). All TNCs had to develop global strategies for a world market.

Interestingly, the consequences have been twofold: Globalization does not work in only one direction, toward standardization. It may also lead to deliberate local adaptations. From the 1970s onward, firms have sought the right combination of a product standardized the world over yet marketed to appeal to different tastes in different cultures (Yip, 1993). Those cultures in turn respond in their own way to worldwide marketing.

Globalization produces all kinds of contradictory pressures for traditional societies. To succeed economically, they must attempt to capture world markets. At the same time, they are under pressure to impose global standards in areas such as environmental conservation. Ancient cultures find themselves trying to resist Western penetration even as they try to develop an image that will help them sell goods worldwide.

The world economy now has a very different shape from either Adam Smith's vision of a world of merchants and tradesmen or Marx's grim spectacle of a factory-based urban proletariat. Revolutions in the technology of production replaced the machine worker with the worker on the assembly line, who in turn is giving way to the robot. Developed methods of transportation and communication make it possible for finished products to be assembled anywhere in the world by firms whose offices and plants may be dispersed worldwide. Ownership of firms has lost national identity. Decision-making can be conducted with the aid of fax and video-link technology by people located in different countries (Carnoy et al., 1993).

Such developments suggest that globalization does not mean a simple transfer of jobs to areas of low wages (Best, 1990; Oman, 1994). Flexibility has become a watchword in both management practices and production. Old methods associated with assembly-line production and strict hierarchies of managers and workers have given way to a "lean production" approach and new information links between customers, firms, and component suppliers that now permit local production for local preferences. The globalization of the new information technology has thus encouraged the localization of production, and by reducing direct labour costs it has prevented the dramatic outflow of jobs from the West to the East that was predicted in the early 1980s. "Post-Fordism," as this general organizational change is often called, also obscures the old divide between managers and workers. It does not, however, reduce power inequalities.

GLOBAL MONEY AND POWER

International Capital

As with politics, economic activity, in becoming global, has also lost its centre. No longer is there a clearly dominant area of production in the world. There are now many important areas. Even if Japan is the most prominent new manufacturing nation, it is threatened by competition from the developing Asian economies of Korea, Taiwan, Singapore, Thailand, and, in the longer run, China. Moreover, Japanese corporations themselves have established plants that employ Japanese methods in North America and Europe. Everywhere, governments feel bound to encourage foreign direct investment. This is bringing Asian wage levels closer to North American and Western European levels (see Figure 18.4.)

Nowhere is the loss of independence of national economies better demonstrated than in the sphere of financial capital. At one time, money for investment in a given national economy came mainly from within that country and stock exchanges traded in stocks and shares of companies based in that country. Now, more than half the value of shares traded in London, for instance, is for overseas stocks. Furthermore, the major investors are no longer individuals. Banks, insurance companies, and pension funds now conduct more than half the trading in all the major investment centres. These organizations are prepared to invest anywhere in the world.

Governments themselves, having promoted the freeing of financial markets, now find that they have to follow the dictates of those markets. Increasingly, they find themselves limited in their taxation policies because capital can move to countries with favourable

FIGURE 18.4 WAGE CHANGES ADJUSTED FOR PRICE CHANGES, BY REGION, 1995–2005

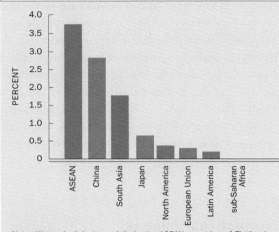

Note: Wages in Asia (especially in the ASEAN countries of Thailand, Singapore, Philippines, Indonesia, and Brunei) will converge with those in North America and the European Union over the next decade, but wages in Latin America and sub-Saharan Africa will diverge from North American and Western European wage levels.

SOURCE: Adapted from United Nations Development Program, *World Development Report 1995: Workers in an Integrated World* by World Bank, copyright © 1995 by The International Bank for Reconstruction and Development/The World Bank (New York: Oxford University Press, 1995), p. 57.

tax regimes and rich people can move easily to escape high personal tax bills.

Global Cities

The great financial centres are global in terms of both the activities they finance and the people who do the financing (King, 1990; Sassen, 1991). Although these centres are located within nation-states, their operations are largely independent of national control and the transactions conducted in them are part of the global economic system.

Thus, although London is the capital city of a state whose economy is relatively minor in today's world league, it is the world's largest foreign-exchange transaction centre, as well as being second only to Tokyo as a banking centre. But the banking conducted in this centre is not predominantly British. It is dominated by Japanese and U.S. banks.

Cities such as London, New York, and Tokyo are not simply centres for financial transactions. They are places people live in and visit (Budd and Whimster, 1992). But more and more of the people

who stay there look to the rest of the world for both their personal ties and their business interests. Similarly, these cities hold a strong attraction for people from the rest of the world. For these reasons, they have come to be called **global cities**.

An International Elite

The globalization of capital is not simply a matter of large organizations gaining ever-increasing control over the world's economy. With globalization, the chances for people to accumulate vast personal fortunes have also increased. For example, in 1992, the American financier George Soros earned more than US$1 billion speculating on the devaluation of the British pound.

Financiers and executives of multinational enterprises think of the world as their market. They are also prepared to place and spend their personal fortunes anywhere in the world. They may divide their time among several residences in different countries, and they enjoy a lavish, "jet-set" lifestyle. It should be noted that, today, it is not only capitalists who live in this style. The senior employees of international organizations have also become used to a lifestyle in which they may be posted anywhere in the world and are rewarded in a way that sets them apart from the local population.

Globalization has also affected the lives of sports and media stars. Their fame is directly dependent on catering to a world audience, and they must travel widely to cultivate their markets. They take part in global tournaments and concert tours, and may maintain residences in several places around the world.

In the 1950s, American sociologist C. Wright Mills (1956) made an enormous impact with his book *The Power Elite*, in which he explored the connections among money, politics, and fame in the United States. Mills's work has been replicated for many other countries since then. National elites have not been superseded. Now, however, a new issue has emerged. To what degree are these national elites integrated into an elite that exists beyond national boundaries? One study comparing Canadian and Australian corporate elites shows that the Canadian corporate elite is more centralized and national while the Australian network is more entwined with foreign interests (Carroll and Alexander, 1999).

Members of the international elite speak English as their primary language but are often bilingual or multilingual. They spend leisure time together, intermarry, send their children to international schools, and often have more than one nationality (Van der Pijl, 1989). They have also begun to exhibit the signs of a self-conscious elite by promoting collective philanthropy for the global masses. Billionaire Ted Turner established the United Nations Foundation in 1997 to donate US$1 billion to the United Nations over a ten-year period. Bill Gates has established a fund to support AIDS victims in India and many other causes. George Soros, one of the world's richest men, has founded a global network of foundations devoted to promoting an open society (Soros, 2002).

SOCIAL RELATIONS WITHOUT FRONTIERS

TIME, SPACE, AND TRAVEL

Members of the international elite can cross the boundaries of nations and cultures with ease. Distance is not a major obstacle to their social relations. But they are not alone in being able to overcome what used to be insuperable barriers of time and space. Modern means of transportation allow people and goods to travel once-unthinkable distances. Telephones make it possible to talk to someone on the other side of the world. Satellites beam images worldwide. Recording technology enables us to preserve the voices and images of people from the past. All this amounts to what has been called **time–space compression** (Harvey, 1989: 241), which has led us to perceive the world very differently from the way our predecessors perceived it. Places that were once remote have come within our reach. The past has become familiar to us.

The possibilities of travel and communication over long distances increased throughout the modern period. Improvements in navigation made possible the sea voyages that led to the expansion of Europe at the beginning of the modern era. Later, trains, automobiles, and planes appeared in quick succession, opening up travel in previously unimaginable ways for millions of people (see Figure 18.5).

These changes have had consequences for the economy and culture. Possibilities for the transportation of goods have revolutionized world trade. The possibility of separating home and workplace has

changed both production methods and the shape of human settlement. Finally, what now claims to be the world's largest industry, tourism, has developed on the basis of inexpensive means of transportation for the masses.

These developments in transportation must be related to the development of distance communications. In the nineteenth century, a worldwide postal system made it possible to send a letter from New York to London and get a reply within a month. Facsimile machines now make it possible to send a letter in seconds. There is now an international telephone network that allows direct dialling between individual numbers in most of the countries of the world at a cost accessible to the mass of telephone subscribers. And hundreds of millions of Internet users are now able to send each other text, images, and sounds—all virtually instantly.

Taken together, developments in travel and telecommunications have transformed personal relationships as well as business practices and leisure activities. Consider, for example, the effects of modern-day travel. If we travel to another country, we are free to return home whenever we please. The Quaker Pilgrims, in contrast, had to assume that they would never again see the families they had left behind. Today, we can stay in close contact with our families by telephone. In fact, we can have family and friends in several countries, and remain "close" nonetheless. That may be important for financial as

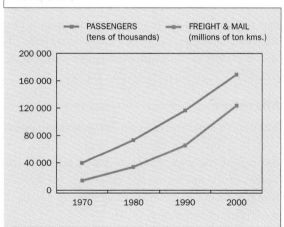

FIGURE 18.5 VOLUME OF AIR TRANSPORT, 1970–2000

SOURCE: International Civil Aviation Organization (2002).

well as emotional reasons. People are freer to travel because it is so easy to stay in contact.

Thus, the personal interactions that once had to be conducted within a relatively small territory can now span the globe. Because of the dramatic reduction in the time it takes to communicate across space, relationships can be maintained irrespective of physical distances between people.

The consequences of the communications revolution for interpersonal relationships have not yet been fully documented. People have certainly been freed from many of the territorial and nation-state constraints that had previously been taken for granted. In that sense, the effects of the new technologies are political as well, constituting another element in the loosening of nation-state control. But, in yet another paradox of globalization, advanced communications technology simultaneously facilitates surveillance of people by the state.

The results of time–space compression can be contradictory. Although we have greater access to more people and places, familiar things tend to disappear more quickly. The faster pace of life is linked to the speed with which things pass away: Our contacts with people and things have become more ephemeral. Although opportunities to find the best of everything may have increased, the best, by definition, can be found in just one place in the world. Both worldwide fame and ease of travelling promote the development of unique world centres such as Hollywood for films, Silicon Valley for computers, and the Parisian Left Bank for philosophy. This is known as the "Mecca effect," Mecca being the place revered above all other places by Muslims. Although ease of travel may make location immaterial, it may also cause physical space to be guarded more jealously than ever. We will encounter similar paradoxes in the following discussion of migration and tourism.

Migration

The ease of travel and of maintaining communication over long distances has made migration less harrowing. At the same time, the globalization of the world's economy has opened up greater possibilities to move from one country to another in search of work (Castles and Miller, 1993).

The stresses that have arisen from the globalization of politics have caused growing numbers of people to try to flee their countries. The availability of advanced means of travel has facilitated these attempts. Consequently, the number of refugees throughout the world has increased steadily in recent years. For example, 13 years of war in Afghanistan resulted in about 6 million people leaving that country, and in 1991 turmoil in Eastern Europe following the dissolution of Soviet power led 28 000 Albanians to try to enter Italy in one weekend (Brown, Kane, and Ayres, 1993: 100).

The twin impact of growing numbers of immigrants and refugees is especially evident in Germany. At the end of 1999 there were 7.3 million foreign residents in the federal republic, constituting 8.9 percent of the total population (German Embassy, Washington DC, 2002). They were made up of both long-resident immigrant workers, primarily from Turkey, and refugees from the collapsing Eastern European regimes. Throughout the 1990s, there were numerous outbreaks of violence against immigrants and refugees alike.

Whether searching for work or fleeing political oppression, foreigners in a new country look to people of similar origin for mutual support. In doing so, they create the circumstances that allow them to bring up families in their own cultural traditions. This pattern can pose a problem for nation-states, which usually set state education standards, marriage laws, and health and employment requirements.

States have increasingly been pursuing policies of multiculturalism in an attempt to reduce tensions among the various ethnic groups within their borders. This trend, coupled with the relative ease with which members of immigrant groups can maintain contact with their countries of origin, has meant that ethnic identity can more easily be maintained abroad and that it can be separated from territory.

Various minorities in different countries belong to transnational ethnic or racial communities and, increasingly, do not expect to return to a homeland. For instance, Poles living outside of Poland make up what they call "Polonia" and are almost as numerous as Poles in Poland, to which few expect to return to live. But, as an ethnic group, they maintain close contact with one another through social networks and organizations throughout the world.

Immigration always reflects the situation in the wider world. Two factors determine the composition of an immigrant population—who the host country will accept and who seek to enter. Canada's inflow of immigrants reflects as much the increasing diversity of the world flow of migrants as it does immigration policy. In 1969, 80 percent of arrivals in Canada came from 22 countries. In 1988, 80 percent came from 37 countries (Basavarajappa, Beaujot, and Samuel, 1993). Figure 18.6 shows how the distribution of immigrants in Canada is increasingly coming to reflect the population proportions of the world as a whole. The mosaic is becoming global.

Tourism

Travel for noneconomic reasons has deep roots in history. The political envoy figures in the earliest historical accounts. In the premodern period, pilgrims often travelled hundreds of kilometres, inspired by hope of salvation. The medieval wandering scholar was the forerunner of the modern scientific conference. The Grand Tour of the eighteenth century was designed to educate the young men of the European aristocracy.

To a large extent, these early forms of travel attested to the supranational nature of cultural and political ties. Often, their purpose was to seek historical relics of common culture. Early travel was undertaken in full awareness of the wider community of human beings. In short, it was an early intimation of the possibility of world society.

Modern tourism is an industry that mass-produces hints of the possibility of access to historic roots and cultural diversity (MacCannell, 1976). It promotes fantasies of personal fulfillment against the backdrop of images of exotic places. At the same time,

it reproduces the comforts of modern furnishings, sanitation, and cuisine, which make the experience predictable in any setting. Tourism thus operates at two levels. To varying degrees, it brings disparate cultures into contact and promises the experience of otherness, while producing a standard tourist environment recognizable anywhere in the world. The search for difference generates global sameness (see Figure 18.7).

THE GLOBAL VILLAGE

News and Risk

The interdependence of the world combines with the scientific knowledge of the modern period to produce what Ulrich Beck (1992) has called "global risk." Science has not only produced innovations that have worldwide application, it has also become aware of the consequences of their use for the world. For example, one product of nuclear physics is the nuclear reactor, which provides energy for industrial and everyday uses. Scientists are able to predict the likelihood of an accident involving a reactor, the amount of radioactive fallout that could be expected from it, and the consequences it would have for the health of both the current population and future generations. Safety measures are in place to prevent such accidents or, if they occur, to minimize their consequences.

Globalized conditions of life involve becoming attuned to global risk. Awareness of global risk was sustained during the Cold War by the rhetoric of the opponents and the activities of the peace movement, which sought the destruction of nuclear weapons. A worldwide interest in peace then transcended boundaries and patriotic commitments. News items about nuclear tests and the protests organized against them gained worldwide interest.

People became less preoccupied with the threat of nuclear holocaust following the end of the Cold War (although the threat of global terrorism since September 11, 2001, has revived some of the old fears). The destruction of the ozone layer and the danger of global warming have attracted more attention in recent years. The world's ecology has become a matter of concern to individuals. Many who were involved in the peace movement have since transferred their commitment to the ecological movement, a current worldwide focus of concern.

Viewing risk globally takes place at both the individual and the organizational level. Individuals may

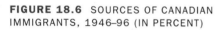

FIGURE 18.6 SOURCES OF CANADIAN IMMIGRANTS, 1946–96 (IN PERCENT)

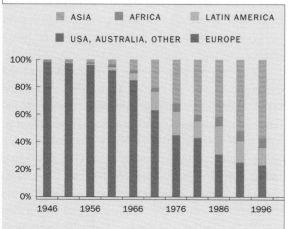

SOURCE: Basavarajappa, Beaujot, and Samuel (1993: 44); Statistics Canada (2002).

FIGURE 18.7 FOREIGN VISITORS, 1998 (PER 100 POPULATION)

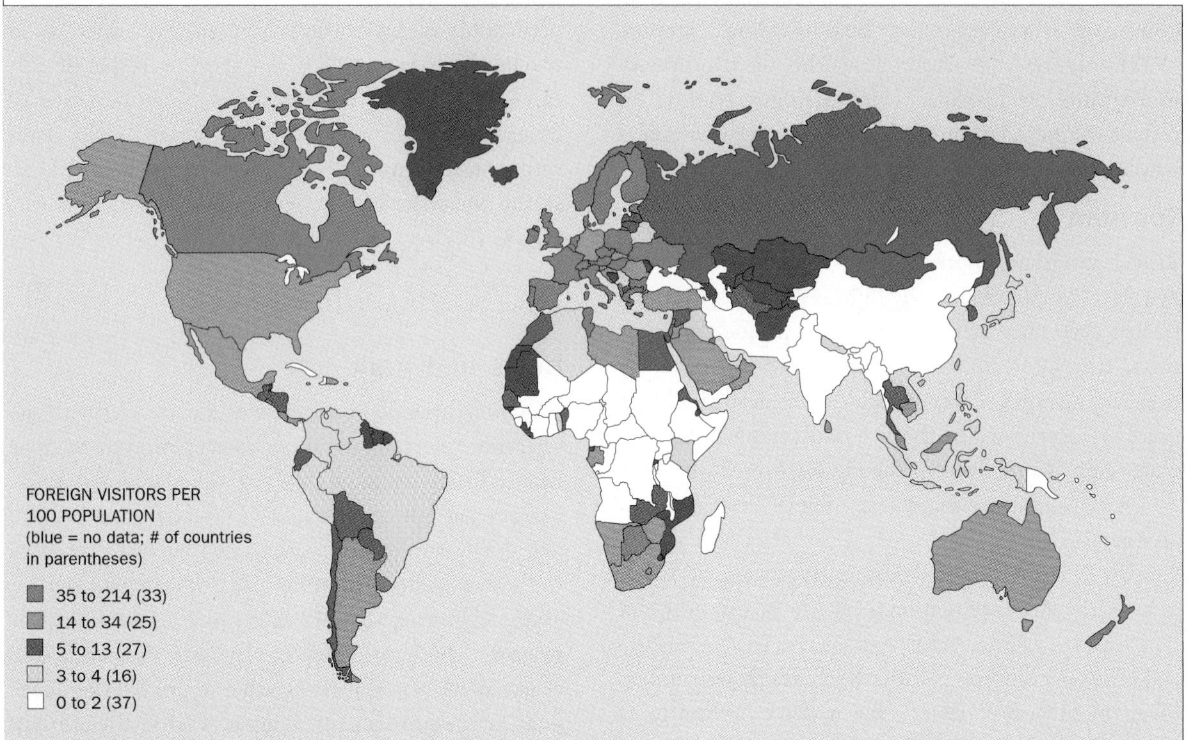

FOREIGN VISITORS PER
100 POPULATION
(blue = no data; # of countries
in parentheses)

- 35 to 214 (33)
- 14 to 34 (25)
- 5 to 13 (27)
- 3 to 4 (16)
- 0 to 2 (37)

International tourism leads to the sense that the world forms one society. However, exposure to international tourism is higher in some countries than others. This map shows the number of foreign visitors who travelled to each country per 100 members of the local population in 1998. Which countries are most exposed to international tourism? Which countries are least exposed? What consequences might differential exposure have for people's self-identity?

SOURCE: United Nations Educational, Scientific and Cultural Organization, "World Culture Report 2000—Cultural Trade and Communications Trends: International Tourism." On the World Wide Web at http://www.unesco.org/culture/worldreport/html_eng/stat2/table18.pdf (December 5, 2001).

accord great weight to the future of the planet even if the risks during their own lifetime are minuscule. Their commitment is a matter of values. Large organizations think in terms of global risk for several reasons. The attitudes of millions of individuals are important to the extent that they create a vast market for new products. Corporations thus take both individuals' values and the objective global risks into account in conceiving and selling such new lines as "green" products. Other kinds of corporations consider the chances that global warming will alter objective conditions. Thus, the largest reinsurance company in the world, Munich-Re, has increased its premiums for customers with property in low-lying regions due to the likelihood of rising sea levels as polar ice caps melt.

In recent years, there has been increasing news coverage of global risks. A big hurricane, such as Hurricane Floyd on the East coast of the United States in 1999, produces dramatic images, which it is now technically feasible to transmit worldwide on channels such as CNN. In addition, natural disasters have major consequences for the world insurance market, because the risks are so extensive that they have been distributed among insurance providers worldwide. Thus, such events are news at many levels.

The current global scope of the media and the correspondingly vast market to which they extend make them attractive commercial prizes. Consequently, worldwide multimedia conglomerates, such as Rupert Murdoch's News Corporation, are being built up, incorporating a mix of television, radio, film, and publishing companies. Those who fear that globalization implies homogenization see the threat of worldwide cultural domination in this growth of global media giants. They take no comfort in the fact that Microsoft president Bill Gates has lately turned his attention to buying large blocs of shares in major North American cable companies and that AOL and Time-Warner have merged. The capacity of media conglomerates to influence opinion worldwide is now greater than ever, while it is beyond the scope of political leaders working within the confines of nation-states.

Paradoxically, the global reach of news coverage today provides the means and the opportunity for attacks on global power structures. Terrorism relies for its impact on the immediate global broadcasting of images of its destructive power. This is what made the destruction of the twin towers of the World Trade Center on September 11, 2001, the most dramatic media event of all time. You could be in the air space over New York at the time, as I was, without knowing what was happening, and then land in Baltimore to watch the horror unfolding on the airport television screens and take frantic cell phone calls from friends in Australia watching the same events.

Yet the power of such events can reinforce rather than undermine global connectedness. At a memorial service five days after September 11, 2001, sociologist Marta Tienda declared "that the word 'United' in our name ['United States'] stands for the strength of our character to become and act as one for greater global purpose." She added: "[W]e can and we will lead by example and action to make world security a global priority" (American Sociological Association, 2001). The unresolved issue that has dominated global politics since September 11 is the shape of the global security order. Can the U.S. act unilaterally in asserting a global purpose, or should it work multilaterally through the United Nations? The fate of the world may depend on the answer.

Fame and Fashion

Global media enhance the possibility of global fame. In the 1920s, the movies made Rudolph Valentino a household name, as they did Marilyn Monroe in the 1950s. In the 1960s, the vinyl sound-recording disc gave the world Elvis Presley and the Beatles. In the 1980s, the video-recording tape gave us Madonna and Michael Jackson.

Music and film appear to obey the same laws of concentration of production that hold for material goods. The massive size of the English-speaking market, ownership of advanced technology, and access to the capital needed to launch a product on the world market combine to facilitate U.S. domina-

tion of a mass culture that threatens the survival of distinct national cultures. Even if the political domination of the United States no longer seems assured, the American superstar appears to exercise a firm grip on the world.

However, homogeneity is not a necessary outcome of advances in media technology. A visitor to Eastern Europe or China in the 1970s would have heard completely homogenized—indeed, identical—messages broadcast into houses, streets, and fields by means of quite primitive radio communication. The content of those broadcasts was under tight political control. Conversely, governments today can actively promote national culture to counteract homogenization (usually Americanization). The Canadian government, for example, set up Telefilm Canada to produce television programs that have local appeal but that are also able to attract international sales. Although financial constraints have often put the survival of such efforts in doubt, new computerized production technologies hold out the hope for inexpensive local production that will enable local programming to compete successfully for audiences (Perlmutter, 1993).

New technology even makes it possible for individuals to generate their own media products. People make video recordings of their own activities, create their own travel films and Web pages, take part in interactive television programs from their own homes, and perform popular songs with full instrumental backup before audiences. The technology that facilitates the latter, called karaoke, allows for a form of individual participation in mass culture that bears the stamp of Japanese culture—namely, that culture's predilection for customized products. One might argue, however, that, despite allowing for a kind of individual expression, karaoke simply standardizes tastes around commercially promoted world (largely American) music. After all, Japanese karaoke singers delight in singing in English.

There is a more substantial criticism of the homogenization thesis that focuses on the contemporary fragmentation and diversification of cultural expression. When Filipinos sing American popular songs they are not returning to an earlier America but creating a yearning for something they never had. It's what Arjun Appadurai (1996: 29) calls "nostalgia without memory." This is not Americanization, since the United States has no control over these imaginings and the communities they inspire have no local site. The collective representations of community are deterritorialized. The global media, far from creating a global village, have spawned multiple imagined worlds without territorial boundaries. In this sense, rather than Americanization, we have the diversification of a global culture distinct from the cultures of the United States or of any other nation-state (Hannerz, 1996). These visions are the opposite of those that see globalization as involving the projection of the United States around the world—whether as a benign social system (Friedman, 1999) or a ruthless standardizing "McDonaldizing" machine (Ritzer, 1992).

Clothes and hairstyles permit a blending of ethnic themes and individual choice. So does food. Not only is it possible to choose from Indian, Italian, Chinese, French, Mexican, Caribbean, Middle Eastern, and many other ethnic foods in most major cities today, but the food people prepare for themselves at home is increasingly characterized by a mix of recipes and ingredients from different culinary traditions. As this example illustrates, the intensification of communication worldwide, the enhancement of possibilities for travel, and the globalization of the economy actually permit individuals to make an increasingly personalized choice from among the diverse cultural resources available to them. The fragmentation of culture leaves people free to make up their own minds, choose their own style, and find their own identity. As a result, old identities are replaced by new hybrids (S. Hall, 1992: 310–14). We can therefore set against homogenization the apparently equal and opposite tendency of **hybridization**. Each is directly related to the overall process of globalization, and both seem to be in equal evidence in the world today. Which one we choose to deplore and which to applaud depends more on personal values than on the objective predominance of the one over the other. In other words, globalization does not present us with a case of building a "world nation" on the historical model of the building of nation-states.

New Styles: New Concepts

We can contrast the current situation with that of earlier times, when the building of Canada was an example of creating national identity. Canadian identity was created in a "new" territory and in the context of an outside environment of existing nation-states. Today, we are witnessing the multiplication of new identities *within* existing nation-states.

Consequently, there is no reason to think the outcome will be the same.

Indeed, Giddens (1991: 5) suggests that globalization forces individuals into a process of self-inquiry because the fundamental indeterminacy of the world creates anxiety and insecurity: "The more tradition loses its hold, and the more daily life is reconstituted in terms of the dialectical interplay of the local and the global, the more individuals are forced to negotiate lifestyle choices among a diversity of options."

Thus, globalization engenders choice and uncertainty quite as much as it promotes sameness. The traditional idea of home as a private place bounded in material and nonmaterial ways from outside influences gives way to an image of it as a cultural site, an arena of discretionary consumption, wired to receive global messages (Putnam, 1993). In this respect, the idea of globalization easily merges with the notion of a postmodern culture (Harvey, 1989; Jameson, 1991). No single style dominates. A confusion of images from different parts of the globe comes together in one place.

TOWARD GLOBAL SOCIETY?

Even if globalization does not signal a new age, its main theorists view it at least as a fundamental transformation of the old one. If that is the case, we can expect sociological concepts to undergo a fundamental change as well—a discomfiting prospect for those who have become accustomed to them. Sociology originates in the modern age; if the modern changes, so must the discipline.

Take an idea such as community. It has long held a key position in sociological theory. In the late nineteenth century, the small rural community in which everyone knows everyone else was regarded as a point of departure against which the cities and associations that developed later, in industrial society, could be compared. Then it was recognized that cities could also contain within them familiar localities, neighbourhoods, and milieux in which people also felt at home with one another. The notion of "belonging" was thus removed from the rural. But if one takes into account the attachments that people feel to those who are distant from them—particularly the attachment migrants feel for family and compatriots in their homeland—one recognizes that "belonging" does not depend on being in the same place. For this reason, Benedict Anderson (1991) suggests that we recognize

Interracial and interethnic marriages have increased dramatically in recent years. In order to dramatize this phenomenon, the editors of *Time* magazine used computer "morphing" to illustrate the various combinations of offspring that might result from the mating of seven men and women of various ethnic and racial backgrounds. *Time* suggests that this chart is a preview of the faces of the multicultural society that is likely to emerge in this century.

SOURCE: Ted Thai/Kin Wah Lam—Time Magazine.

nations as "imagined communities" that are not essentially linked to a territorially based nation-state. The nation is not the only concept that has to be revised when we separate place from social unit. Since globalization involves this separation, it has consequences for a whole range of sociological concepts (Albrow et al., 1994).

Suppose we find the lifestyles of a group of people congenial and we join with them for that reason. People who relate to each other out of shared private interests and consumption patterns form what Robert Bellah and his colleagues (1985: 71–75) call a "life-style enclave." Young people, in particular, group together on the basis of lifestyle. A recurrent theme in Douglas Coupland's *Generation X* (1991) is the quest for a new style in a globalized world (see Box 18.4). Older people also seek out lifestyle companions, as exemplified by the large numbers of people who migrate to Florida on retirement. They gather together in one place, but on a quite different basis from traditional communities.

The other side of the coin is that people living in a locality may have little to do with each other. This is just what gives rise to the lament for lost community (Etzioni, 1994). However, if people find their meaningful ties at a distance, loss of local community may matter little to them. Indeed, John Eade (1997) has identified new local social processes as global in extent. We find new "socioscapes" in the city, people coexisting in a single place but engaged in social relations at a distance, familiar milieux that extend far beyond the locality to the ends of the earth (Dürrschmidt, 2000).

Now consider the kind of belonging that brings people together on a computer network. People who share an interest today can communicate instantly worldwide over the Internet. They can use the Internet to discuss business, scientific research, political views, sex, or rare birds. Indeed, there is no limit to the number of people or topics that can be involved. This new form of community is known as a **virtual community**.

In sum, globalization involves the transformation of our lives and the way we talk about them. It is up to the discipline to consider also whether globalization transforms the very idea of society, the most gen-

---

BOX 18.4   GLOBAL LIFESTYLES

In his acclaimed first novel, *Generation X*, Canadian author Douglas Coupland finds many ways of depicting the confusions and uncertainties of living in a globalized culture. Coupland has one of his three central characters, Andy, mock a younger brother who lives at home, wants to work in a big corporation, and spends all his money on clothes:

> How cliquish are these Global Teens? It really boggles. Not one of them can go to Waikiki for a simple one-week holiday, for example, without several enormous gift-laden send-off parties in one of three classic sophomoric themes: Tacky Tourist, Favourite Dead Celebrity, or Toga. And once they arrive there, nostalgic phone calls soon start: sentimental and complicated volleys of elaborately structured trans-Pacific conference calls flowing every other day, as though the jolly vacationers had just hurtled toward Jupiter on a three-year mission rather than six days of over-priced Mai Tais on Kuhio Street.
>
> They're nice kids. None of their folks can complain. They're *perky*. They embrace and believe the pseudoglobalism and ersatz racial harmony of ad campaigns engineered by the makers of soft drinks and computer inventoried sweaters. (p. 106)

But Andy has his own problems with the global. He lives adrift with Claire and Dag in the California desert, looking for a different kind of life, but remaining dependent on the casual "Mcjobs" that the global economy supplies. When he leaves for Mexico, his Volkswagen, containing its two dozen bottles of Evian water, is surrounded by locals in their Hyundais. He is caught in what Coupland calls "terminal wanderlust":

> A condition common to people of transient middle-class upbringings. Unable to feel rooted in any one environment, they move continually in the hopes of finding an idealized sense of community in the next location. (p. 171)

SOURCE: Excerpts taken from Douglas Coupland, *Generation X: Tales for an Accelerated Culture* (New York: St. Martin's Press, 1991), pp. 106, 171. Copyright © 1991 by Douglas Coupland. Reprinted by permission of St. Martin's Press, Incorporated.

eral concept on which sociology has traditionally been centred.

On the basis of the foregoing discussion, three views of the future of society are possible. One is that the fragmentation of modern life and the transformation of the nation-state that goes with it involve the disintegration of society itself. This is a radical view that often inspires strenuous political and religious debate (Polanyi, 1944). The second alternative suggests that the new forms of life and relationships developing in a globalized world make the idea of society, which has been so closely associated with the nation-state, obsolete and in need of replacement (Mann, 1986; Bauman, 1991). The third possible view is to accept that the relationships that connect people can now crisscross the globe and that the institutions we depend on are worldwide in scope. This view allows us to argue that we can retain the idea of society if we revise it to take account of its global dimension—that is, the development of institutions for the management of global problems and the new consciousness of the globe among actors and agencies across the planet. The third view proposes that the fate of the human species depends on the outcome of the struggle to shape emerging global society (Albrow, 1990; Archer, 1991).

There is nothing inevitable about the outcome of that struggle. After all, much of the world has suffered more than it has gained from globalization (see Chapter 10). Literally billions of people therefore deeply resent universalism, imperialism, and capitalism, the driving forces of globalization. Their resentment has given rise to particularism, anti-imperialism, and anti-capitalism, which have in turn led to mass violence that may undermine hopes for the birth

of a truly global society. This is surely one of the most troubling consequences of the events of September 11, 2001.

Much now seems to depend on whether pressure will continue to be placed on world leaders to ensure that the benefits of globalization are distributed more justly. Much also depends on whether world leaders have the vision and the resolve to carry out such a global redistribution of benefits, even in the face of powerful resistance. There are some encouraging signs. For example, in anticipation of the first anti-globalization riots that broke out in Seattle in 1999, U.S. President Clinton adopted one of the planks of the protesters—sanctions against poor employment standards in the less-developed countries. Shortly afterwards, Josef Stiglitz resigned as chief economist of the World Bank, declaring that the practice of imposing conditions on countries seeking economic aid had failed and may have undermined democracy in many less-developed countries. The winner of the 2001 Nobel Prize in Economics, Stiglitz went on to argue that the World Bank's efforts to liberalize the world economy shows "fundamental misunderstandings" of the social and political institutions on which markets are based (Stiglitz, 2002: 73). Meanwhile, Paul Martin, the former finance minister and likely the next Canadian prime minister, has been at the forefront of the movement to cancel the enormous debt the less developed countries owe to Western banks and governments. Debt cancellation would serve as partial compensation for the damage done to less-developed economies by Western imperialism and colonialism. It seems clear that only if these and many similar initiatives are undertaken will global society be able to realize its promise.

SUMMARY

1. Western expansion and consciousness of threats to the globe as a whole have added the new idea of a global society to the old one of world society.

2. Globalization may be seen as ushering in a new historical period and creating a level of social organization beyond that of the nation-state.

3. The end of the Cold War has resulted not in a unitary power centre for the world but in a new sense of interdependence and a perceived weakness of the nation-state.

4. Although the world economy has become a single transnational system, globalization may nonetheless promote local production.

5. The people of the world travel and communicate across national borders as never before, lifting social relations out of their local contexts.

6. Global images and information from the mass media enhance global consciousness and facilitate the development of new globalist social movements.

7. Globalization can impinge on people's everyday lives in ways that create anxiety and insecurity, and cause them to re-evaluate their identity and lifestyle.

8. Homogenization and hybridization are equally possible outcomes of globalization.

9. Because of reactions against globalization, there is no guarantee that a global society will realize its full promise. Much depends on whether the benefits of globalization can be distributed more justly throughout the world.

QUESTIONS TO CONSIDER

1. What do you consider to be the forces underlying globalization? Will they continue to have an impact in the future, and are they more likely to produce order or disorder in the world?

2. What are the effects of globalization on democratic participation? Do people have more or less control over their national governments as a result of globalization?

3. Think of the different ways in which globalization could affect employment in Canada. Are your job prospects better or worse as a result?

4. Why do Canadians choose to watch American and other foreign television programs and to take holidays abroad? Do these and similar choices undermine our national culture?

5. In what ways can sociologists contribute to the shaping of global society?

GLOSSARY

Disembedding is the act of lifting social relationships out of local settings and maintaining them over indefinite times and distances.

Global cities are cities, such as London, New York, and Tokyo, that are centres of activity for the global economy, with an importance extending far beyond the boundaries of the nation-states in which they are located.

The **global village** refers to the immediate experience of sights and sounds from anywhere in the world when transmitted by electronic media.

Globalism is an orientation to values that identifies the world as the focal point of concern.

Globalization refers to the growing interdependence and mutual awareness among the world's individuals and economic, political, and social institutions.

Hybridization is the combination of two or more different influences or types in a single entity.

Levels of analysis are differing degrees of scale and scope in social organization.

Modernity refers to the complex of features that has distinguished Western cultures and societies over the last 300 or 400 years, including rationality, individualism, and the quest for improvements and novelty.

Postmodernity, in contrast to modernity, involves cultural fragmentation and lacks direction toward "progress" or any other single goal.

Time–space compression refers to the effect of processes that speed up the pace of life and seem to shrink the space that surrounds us.

A **virtual community** is a community in which relationships are maintained at a distance through telecommunications.

SUGGESTED READING

Brecher, J., T. Costello, and B. Smith. (2000). *Globalization from Below: The Power of Solidarity.* Boston: South End Press. This text is described as a "resource and strategy project for globalization from below" challenging globalization from above and thus changing the conditions for human action.

Coupland, D. (1991). *Generation X: Tales for an Accelerated Culture.* New York: St. Martin's Press. This is a first novel by a Canadian author in which three characters in their 20s experiment in their lives and imaginations with the paradoxes of contemporary culture. Look for the global themes and symbols in it.

Giddens, A. (1999). *Runaway World: How Globalization Is Reshaping Our Lives.* London: Profile Books. Five lectures broadcast on the BBC World Service by the sociologist who is director of the London School of Economics and also an adviser to British Prime Minister Tony Blair.

Robertson, R. (1992). *Globalization: Social Theory and Global Culture.* Newbury Park, CA: Sage. Based on a series of essays and commentaries dating from 1985 by the scholar who first argued that the concept of globalization should occupy a key place in general sociological theory.

Watson, W.G. (1998). *Globalization and the Meaning of Canadian Life.* Toronto: University of Toronto Press. This is a vigorous assertion by an anthropologist of the view that globalization is neither new nor poses a threat to Canadian life, and that misunderstanding globalization has prompted a number of mistaken policies.

CHAPTER NINETEEN

DEVIANCE AND CRIME

In this chapter you will learn that:

- What becomes defined as deviant or criminal depends on the circumstances of time and place because definitions of deviance
and crime are subject to conflict and change. These definitions
are the outcome of political processes and power relations in
which different groups compete to define right and wrong.

- There are many consequences of defining deviance. Reacting to
deviance can increase a group's social solidarity and clarify its
moral boundaries. But these reactions are also an important
source of deviance and may lead to more serious and organized
forms of deviance.

- Sociological explanations of deviance can be grouped into two
types: Those that emphasize the social factors that motivate or
allow people to engage in deviance, and those that emphasize
the political processes and power relations that result in some
individuals and behaviours being defined and treated as deviant
while others are not.

- Crime rates have been declining in Canada during the past
decade; however, rates of serious crime are still higher in
Canada than in many other industrialized countries and are distributed unequally among various groups.

- Legal reactions to crime in Canada balance two goals: Protecting
society and protecting the rights of those accused of crime.
Traditionally, the protection of society has received greater
emphasis in the legal process. Canada incarcerates more
people per capita than most industrialized countries, but is
increasingly relying on alternatives to incarceration for less
serious criminal offences.

ROSEMARY GARTNER AND MYRNA DAWSON

UNIVERSITY OF TORONTO/UNIVERSITY OF GUELPH

INTRODUCTION

If Thomas Haythe had been born 25 years earlier, he would probably still have his job, his reputation, and his name on the law firm. Tory Haythe was the eighth-largest law firm in Canada. It was created in October 1999 by the merger of Haythe's New York firm and the Toronto-based firm of Tory, Tory, DesLauriers and Binnington. However, during a November celebration of the merger at a Toronto bar, Haythe apparently got drunk and groped several female lawyers and bar employees. Within four days, the new firm put Haythe on permanent medical leave and arranged to have his name removed from its masthead. At the age of 60, Haythe, a graduate of Harvard Law School and one of North America's most successful lawyers, had run up against a corporate culture and legal climate different from that of a generation ago when such behaviour would certainly not have had public repercussions. A generation ago, employers could not be held liable for sexual harassment in the workplace as they can be today.

If Harold Samuel Fine had been born 25 years later, he would not have ended up with a criminal record for violating Section 207 of the Canadian Criminal Code, which prohibited dissemination of information about birth control. In April 1961, Fine, president of Prestige Drug Products, was convicted of advertising and selling condoms through the mail. In his testimony to the court, Fine argued that he mailed his products only to married couples with children, and that he was serving the public by providing them with family-planning information. Noting that the facts of the case were not in dispute, Toronto magistrate Thomas Wolfe imposed a fine of $100 or one month in jail on the charges against Fine. It was not until 1969 that the Criminal Code was amended to allow Canadians unregulated access to contraceptive information and birth control technology.

Both of these cases attracted widespread controversy, though for very different reasons. Some observers of the Haythe case, including several lawyers, expressed both surprise and disapproval over his dismissal. A corporate lawyer from Manhattan said that "taking his name off is a pretty Draconian thing to do," and another likened the move to capital punishment (Fine and Milner, 1999). Others wondered whether Haythe's behaviour would have received the same censure had he not made his unwanted advances to relatively powerful female lawyers.

Fine's conviction also generated public debate and an organized effort to change the law. Two days after his trial, *The Globe and Mail* ran an editorial which criticized those who had informed on Fine as well as the "archaic law which compelled a magistrate" to convict him. Later the same year, a Toronto couple founded the Planned Parenthood Association of Toronto and launched what would become a nationwide campaign to legalize the dissemination of birth control information and technology.

What makes these cases interesting to a sociologist of deviance is not whether the decisions to publicly label and punish Haythe and Fine as deviant were right or wrong, misplaced or appropriate. They are sociologically interesting because they illustrate how definitions and perceptions of deviance change over time, and how disagreements often arise over those definitions. Common sense may tell us that

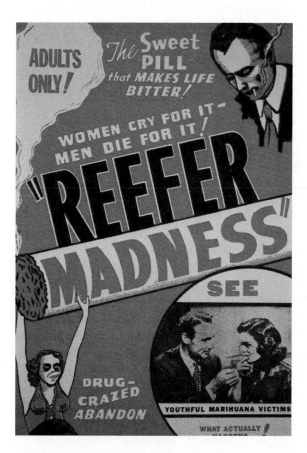

This 1936 movie poster illustrates how relative deviance is. The movie suggests that people go insane from smoking marijuana.
SOURCE: *Reefer Madness*, 1936. Directed by Louis Gasnier.

deviance involves breaking rules. However, sociologists who study deviance remind us that rules change and that people often disagree with the rules. Moreover, breaking rules does not always get one labelled as deviant, and sometimes people are labelled deviant without breaking any rules. So understanding deviant behaviour requires that we look at the people and the organizations that define and react to deviance—the rule makers and the rule enforcers—as well as at those who break the rules.

In this chapter, we discuss the different ways in which sociologists have thought about deviance. Some are interested primarily in where rules about deviance come from, how and why these rules change, and the consequences of labelling people or behaviours as deviant. Others focus on why some people become rule-breakers. We also look at recent crime trends in Canada as well as changes in crime and social control around the world. A central theme of this chapter is that deviance is not simply about marginal people and odd behaviours. Studying how deviance is defined and how people react to it tells us about how a society is organized; how power, privilege, and resources are distributed; and how social order is achieved. Deviance and crime, then, are at the heart of the struggles every society goes through to organize its social life.

DEVIANCE AND CRIME AS OUTCOMES OF SOCIAL CONTROL

Deviance does not always mean nonconformity; nor is deviance synonymous with rule violation. All of us are nonconformists at one time or another in our lives, but few of us are labelled deviant or formally punished. Nonconformity becomes deviance when it produces a negative social reaction and when there are concerted public efforts to change the behaviour or punish the person. These efforts are what sociologists call **social control** and it takes many forms. Informal social control occurs through interactions among individuals and includes expressions of disapproval, avoidance, and the many other ways that we try to communicate and enforce what we feel are standards of appropriate behaviour in our everyday lives. All of us have been stopped from doing something by an internal voice asking, "What would

others think?" This voice represents self-control—one type of informal social control and the most effective at preventing rule violations.

Formal social control is that practised by the state through official organizations and agents, primarily within the criminal justice system. In contrast to informal social control, formal social control relies largely on the external control of people after they have been defined as deviants. Between informal, interpersonal control and the more punitive controls of the criminal justice system lies a network of social controls based in different organizations, agencies, and institutions, such as social welfare organizations, psychiatric agencies, public health clinics, and so on. These "softer" forms of control—some of them the focus of the work of Michel Foucault (1979)—seek to regulate behaviour through reason, persuasion, and scientific authority, but can also be repressive and coercive. Many organizations and agents of social control do much more than react to deviance, however. We will see that they are also actively involved in influencing which people and what type of behaviours are classified as deviant, and how different types of deviance are dealt with. As some sociologists point out, these decisions may depend more on the interests of those seeking to shape definitions of deviance than they do on the particular acts that are targeted for control.

Although deviance is defined by negative social reactions, it can have positive consequences for some social groups. This notion was an important theme of Émile Durkheim's work. Since deviance and crime occur in all societies, Durkheim (1938) reasoned, they must serve some positive social function. One benefit a group can gain from rule breaking by its members is increased social solidarity or integration. Serious violations of a group's rules typically bring people together in collective expressions of outrage and loss, reminding them of their common values. For instance, the killing of 14 female engineering students at the University of Montreal in 1989 was a tragedy felt throughout Canada. Both the immediate response and the continuing commemoration of the killings have brought together Canadians of all sorts in a common condemnation of violence against women.

Another potential benefit of deviance, according to Durkheim, is the clarification of a group's moral boundaries. In defining and confronting deviance, a group highlights its standards of right and wrong to its members. The "No Means No" campaign sent a message to both women and men that sex without consent is rape. As in other cases of defining deviance, this campaign drew a distinction between acceptable and unacceptable behaviour in an area of conduct that was prone to interpretational disagreement. When, as is inevitable, someone ignores the message that "no means no" and is charged with sexual assault, the public definition of his or her behaviour as deviant serves another function. It allows those who follow the rules to feel virtuous and reinforces their conformity by reminding them of the costs of rule breaking.

Durkheim stressed another social benefit of deviance. Societies need deviance, he said, to keep them flexible and to allow them to adapt to a changing world. When people test society's rules by challenging them, they provide an opportunity to consider whether the rules should be changed. For example, in the 1980s, Dr. Henry Morgentaler regularly performed abortions in Quebec abortion clinics, not hospitals, and performed them on demand—without the approval of a therapeutic abortion committee, as required by law. He was prosecuted for doing so, but twice acquitted by juries, even though he admitted breaking the law and there was no legal defence available to him. After the second acquittal, the government gave up prosecuting him. This effectively permitted abortion on demand at specialized clinics.

With these functions of deviance in mind, you can see why Durkheim and others have argued that deviance and crime are not only inevitable but may also be integral and useful for social order. Yet deviance has clear costs or dysfunctions for society. Too much of it, as Durkheim argued, can lead to chaos and conflict, undermining the stability of society. No society can afford to spend too much of its time, energy, and resources on defining and punishing deviance. Efforts to define and punish deviance have other costs as well. In his examination of the ironies of social control, Gary Marx (1981) identifies a number of ways in which these efforts actually produce more deviance. For example, high-speed chases by police have resulted in serious injuries and deaths of bystanders, often leading to manslaughter charges against people who otherwise would have faced less serious charges. Stepped-up enforcement actions, such as those aimed at traffickers in illegal drugs or illegal immigration, drive away amateur criminals and

encourage the development of more sophisticated organized crime groups that open new markets, drive prices up, and are more adept at avoiding prosecution. Efforts to control deviance, then, can have unintended and harmful consequences for individuals and for society as a whole, as we discuss in more depth below.

Deviance is created through social control—in other words, through reactions to behaviours—and is not simply a characteristic of behaviours. The same act—adultery, for example—can be treated as merely an indiscretion in some societies and as a capital crime in others. Being gossiped about and shunned by friends signals that adultery is considered by many Canadians to be somewhere between improper and immoral behaviour. But, in other times and other places, adultery is a crime. For example, in August 2002, a woman in Nigeria received a sentence of death by stoning, a punishment prescribed for adultery under some versions of Islamic law. The sentence is to be carried out in 2004 after she has finished weaning the baby who was used as proof of her adultery at trial. Deviance, then, is not simply a characteristic of behaviours, but exists in the territory between behaviours and reactions to them.

Crime is a special case of deviance. It is defined by social norms that are formalized in criminal law. There is often—but not always—greater consensus about the wrongfulness of crimes than other forms of behaviour defined as deviant. For example, people consistently rate criminal acts as more deserving of harsh punishment than noncriminal acts that violate norms (Wolfgang et al., 1985). On the surface, the consensus surrounding crimes such as murder may seem obvious and natural. But, as with other forms of deviance, crime—even in its most serious forms—is also relative. Virtually all Canadians would say that the intentional killing of one person by another should be treated as a serious crime. But how many would say that euthanasia, the death penalty, killing by soldiers during times of war, or fatal shootings by police—all of them instances of intentional killing—should be treated as serious crimes? Conversely, many people feel that the criminal law on homicide should apply to a wider array of acts, such as abortion or deaths caused by the negligence of corporations. The controversy over Saskatchewan farmer Robert Latimer's second-degree murder conviction and life sentence illustrates the debates that can take place over what types of killings should be punished (see Box 19.1).

BOX 19.1 THE MERCY-KILLING DEBATE

More than 60,000 people have signed a petition seeking clemency for Robert Latimer, a Saskatchewan farmer serving a life sentence for killing his severely disabled daughter. He says he did it to ease her suffering; critics say murder is murder. Latimer, 48, has been locked up since Jan. 18 [2001], when the Supreme Court of Canada ruled he could not be exempt from the mandatory minimum punishment for second-degree murder—a life sentence with no chance of parole for 10 years. Latimer's only hope to avoid or reduce his sentence is under the Royal Prerogative of Mercy, which can only be granted by the Governor General or cabinet.

Groups for the disabled have fought to see that Latimer serves his full term. Anything less would devalue the lives of society's most vulnerable and signal that they deserve lesser justice, said Diane Richler of the Canadian Association of Community Living. Richler attributed the strong levels of public support for Latimer to the fact that most people don't have close contact with someone with a severe disability.

Latimer killed Tracy, 12, in 1993 by putting her in the cab of his pickup truck and pumping in exhaust. He has always said he did it to spare her further torture from chronic pain brought on by surgeries to ease her cerebral palsy. She could not walk, talk or feed herself. The Supreme Court ruled that Latimer could have opted for medically supervised pain management but he decided against it. He is eligible for day parole on Dec. 8, 2007.

SOURCE: Excerpted from Lisa Schmidt, "Latimer Petition Draws 60,000 Signatures," Canadian Press, Dec. 13, 2001.

Acts ranging from adultery to intentional killing, then, are subject to conflicting opinions and dramatically different social reactions. Because it is social reactions and social controls that define deviance, many sociologists contend that understanding the political processes and power relations that create definitions of deviance and determine to whom those definitions are applied is the key to explaining deviance. These sociologists, who are sometimes called critical theorists, ask questions about the relationships among power struggles over defining deviance, the organization of social control, and the consequences for those defined as deviant. As such, they study deviance as a socially constructed concept.

THE SOCIAL CONSTRUCTION OF DEVIANCE AND ITS CONSEQUENCES

Understanding where definitions of deviance come from, and why they are often fluid and subject to conflict, requires that we look at the processes through which they are created—or what is called the social construction of deviance. These processes involve different groups and institutions sometimes cooperating and sometimes competing to articulate norms and expectations for behaviour for the rest of society. Some efforts to define deviance—called **moral crusades**—

are initiated by individuals or grassroots organizations acting as moral crusaders or claims makers. In this role, they push for the creation of deviance definitions by making claims that certain behaviours or conditions violate fundamental moral standards and, therefore, require formal recognition as wrong, and perhaps criminal, as well as appropriate intervention.

One example of a moral crusade is the campaign by Mothers Against Drunk Driving (MADD) to educate the public about the costs of drunk driving, to stigmatize those who drink and drive, and to increase criminal penalties for drunk driving. The success of MADD's campaign, like that of many other moral crusades, reflects the group's ability to gain the support of the media and various politicians, through which both legal and popular definitions of drunk driving were changed. More recently, various groups have come together to educate the public about the health and social costs of cigarette smoking, emphasizing the consequences of secondhand smoke. This has resulted in the implementation of no-smoking bylaws in many municipalities and cities throughout North America. These bylaws prohibit people from lighting up in public places such as restaurants and bars and, in some cities, on sidewalk space directly outside business entrances. Moral crusades are not always successful, however. Anti-abortion groups, for example, have failed to garner sufficient support to have abortion redefined as a crime. The success of a moral crusade depends on the extent to which claims makers can enlist the support of groups with substantial political and economic power, especially the state's official rule makers (e.g., legislatures) and rule enforcers (e.g., courts).

Some moral crusades are launched by groups holding or vying for political power. For example, in their 1999 campaign for re-election, the Ontario Tories publicized their determination to criminalize any "behaviour that jeopardizes the safe use of the streets" (Ontario Legislature, 1999), arguing that squeegee people and beggars had made Toronto unsafe and unattractive for tourists, commuters, and city dwellers. True to their word, in January 2000 the Tory government passed the Safe Streets Act, "the first time a modern provincial government [had] enacted a provincial statute against begging conduct in public space" (Hermer and Mosher, 2002: 12). The act and the first criminal charges laid under it were the topic of considerable debate; lawyers for 13 defendants charged under the act—called "squeegee workers" by opponents of the act and "squeegee kids" by its supporters—questioned the act's constitutionality and argued that it both infringed on the right to freedom of expression and criminalized subsistence activities of the poor. Nevertheless, in August 2001 the 13 were convicted, affirming the Ontario government's claim that the act was a legitimate response to concerns over public safety and security.

Why do such moral crusades occur? A commonsense response is that claims makers recognize the

Should squeegee kids' actions be considered criminal, a nuisance, or a form of subsistence work?

SOURCE: CP Picture Archive/Fred Thornhill.

harm in the behaviours or conditions they seek to define as deviant and take it upon themselves to educate the rest of society. However, this answer fails to recognize that some behaviours defined as deviant are of questionable or limited harm (e.g., begging) and that some harmful behaviours are not widely viewed as deviant (e.g., unsafe sex). The commonsense response is also not very good at explaining why moral crusades often meet with resistance and why the process of defining deviance is, therefore, often fraught with conflict. What explains this conflict?

STATUS CONFLICT AND THE SOCIAL CONSTRUCTION OF DEVIANCE

A number of sociological perspectives on deviance see conflict at the root of deviance defining. For Marxist theorists, conflict between different classes, and the desire of the capitalist class to control the working class results in some behaviours (such as burglary) being targeted for control more than other behaviours (such as corporate crime). For critical perspectives based on Foucault's work, fundamental but often-disguised conflicts in modern society emerge over knowledge and the ways it is produced and legitimated through the media, technology, and scientific expertise. Knowledge and the languages that express it are intimately linked to power, especially the power to construct definitions of right and wrong, good and evil.

A related answer to the question of why defining deviance is often characterized by conflict can be found in the **status-conflict perspective** that has its roots in the work of Max Weber and was further developed by critical theorists Vold (1958), Turk (1969), and Quinney (1970). According to this perspective, the various social, economic, political, ethnic, religious, and professional groups that characterize modern societies continually compete with each other for status and influence. Among the outcomes they compete for is control over definitions of right and wrong—deviance and conformity. The law, especially the criminal law, is an important target of these struggles because of its power to define and punish deviance. The rewards of being a winner in these struggles are many. Winning groups can advance their interests over losing groups, gaining greater access to power, resources, and authority. By controlling definitions of deviance, winning groups accomplish at least two goals. First, they legitimate their moral standards and, hence, their claims to moral authority over losing groups. Second, they can determine the types of social controls applied to deviance—and, in turn, affect the demand for different professions and occupations, such as social workers, physicians, or criminologists, and for different social control bureaucracies. These struggles over defining deviance and social control are ultimately about symbolic politics and the social construction of perceived reality.

The central themes of the status-conflict perspective can be seen in Erickson's (1996) analysis of the criminalization of psychoactive drugs in Canada during the last century. At the beginning of the twentieth century, psychoactive drugs, such as opium, heroin, and cocaine, were widely available in Canada and commonly used, most often in the form of patent medicines. Users were rarely stigmatized, perhaps not surprisingly since many were middle-class women and men. However, within two decades, use of many psychoactive drugs was criminalized and subject to severe penalties, including long prison terms with hard labour and whipping. This dramatic change was the result of a concerted campaign by various interest groups and politicians, especially Prime Minister William Lyon Mackenzie King. To justify the crackdown on some psychoactive drugs, moral crusaders cited the dangers they posed to physical health. But, as Erickson notes, these definitions of dangerousness were socially constructed by the moral crusaders, rather than based on scientific evidence. The true motivations behind the campaign included cultural and economic antagonism toward Asian immigrants, *some* of whom brought a new form of drug use—opium smoking—to Canada. Because these immigrants were willing to work for lower wages than working-class whites, they were strongly resented by white workers. In addition, certain occupational groups supported the campaign, partly out of a desire to strengthen the power base of government bureaucrats. The ultimate consequences of the campaign were the control and criminalization of less powerful cultural groups in the interests of more powerful groups.

Organized interest groups also engage in similar kinds of campaigns in order to *challenge* existing definitions of deviance. The gay and lesbian rights movement in Canada is an example of such a "deviance-defying" campaign. In the mid-1960s, sodomy was a crime in Canada and RCMP investigations into the background of federal employees led to the dismissal of gays from the civil service, the CBC, and the National Film Board. By 1970, however, gay rights' groups were actively challenging legal and medical definitions of homosexuality as deviance and pushing for an end to discrimination against gays in immigration, employment, housing, family policy, and the military. However, as Adam's (1995) history of the gay and lesbian movement recounts, conservative groups mobilized a counter-campaign in the late 1970s that encouraged police raids on gay bars and bathhouses in Montreal and Toronto. The effort to get human rights coverage extended to gay men and lesbians was first successful in Quebec in 1977. Active opposition meant that almost 20 years passed before the federal government added sexual orientation to the list of protected categories in its human rights legislation in 1996. Same-sex marriage became legal in Canada in 2003, but only after decades of political and legal battles.

THE CONSEQUENCES OF DEVIANCE DEFINING

An important contribution of critical perspectives on deviance is their focus on the consequences for the people and the groups who are targets of the deviance defining process. The **labelling perspective** is organized around the idea that societal reactions to deviance are an important *cause* of deviance. Rather than looking at the events and conditions in people's lives before they are defined as deviants, the labelling perspective directs attention to what happens after someone has been singled out and labelled deviant (Becker, 1973; Lemert, 1967). It is the people who react to deviance and the character and consequences of their reactions, then, that are the focus of the labelling perspective. The reactors include agents of social control (such as police or psychiatrists), significant others in the labelled person's life (such as family members and friends), and members of society at large, whose disapproval of the deviant act is typically known to the labelled person.

As we already noted, all of us engage in behaviour that others strongly disapprove of at one time or another in our lives, sometimes behaviours serious enough to get us in trouble with the law. Typically, these acts—which are caused by accident, by pressure or encouragement from others, by lapses in conscience or judgment, and so on—are hidden or occasional so they can be ignored, explained away, or justified by ourselves and others. This **primary deviance** (Lemert, 1967), however, can turn into **secondary deviance** if it becomes public and the person becomes the target of a strong and enduring negative reaction by others. Public disapproval can take many forms. Family and friends may avoid you, your employer may fire you, and social control agents may treat you as if your deviance is key to who you really are—eventually becoming your **master status.** In other words, your status as a university student, a son, a brother, and a musician will matter little in comparison to your status, for example, as a regular heroin user. When, as a consequence of the social reaction, you come to define yourself as essentially and indelibly a drug addict, secondary deviance has occurred. In the final stage of this process, you have become what you were defined as: Your commitment to your deviance increases as your claims to conventionality are lost or denied. As "Ken," a young man convicted of passing a bad cheque, said: "What the hell—if I'm going to be named a criminal I might as well be one" (Frazier, 1976: 136). This is the self-fulfilling prophecy of the labelling process and it demonstrates how reactions to deviance are one of its important causes.

The process by which reactions to deviance can stabilize and reinforce such behaviours has been described in studies of mental patients, homosexuals "outed" in the early 1960s, adolescent "troublemakers," the physically handicapped, and, more recently, young, Black males (Becker, 1964; Chambliss, 1973; Scott, 1969; Anderson, 1990). But, as some of these studies show, it would be a mistake to see those defined as deviants as simply passive, compliant subjects. Faced with the stigma and rejection caused by a deviant label, some fight back by denying the deviance of their actions or questioning the motivations of reactors. In 2002, Mark Hall, an Ontario high school student, a Roman Catholic, and a homosexual, won the right to take his boyfriend to the school prom by challenging the Durham District Catholic School Board. The school board had banned the gay couple from the dance, but a Superior Court found that this violated Hall's rights to freedom from discrimination on the basis of sexual orientation.

The shared experience of being labelled deviant can also bring people together in collective responses. Sometimes these responses are efforts to resist the labels and change the definition of deviance, as we saw earlier in our discussion of the activities of gay rights groups. Other groups of stigmatized people have formed voluntary organizations to provide support and positive recognition for their nonconformity, to educate the public, and to challenge discriminatory policies. For example, organizations like the National Association to Advance Fat Acceptance, the Living Large Club, and the Ample Opportunity Group urge their members and the public to question the social intolerance of obesity (Findlay, 1996). Similarly, in response to their increasingly deviant identity, some smokers are aggressively contesting their stigmatization. For instance, they have set up a Smokers' Home Page on the World Wide Web that includes a series of articles denouncing smoking restrictions and urging block voting by smokers, who have more numerical clout than many other lobbying groups.

At other times, collective responses may lead to the development of a **subculture**, in which those labelled deviant embrace their identity and reject their labellers or express disdain for the values of conventional society. Outlaw biker gangs, skinheads, and cyberpunks can be considered deviant subcultures. Their members typically share an argot (or insider language), distinctive clothing and body language, networks of mutual support, and a set of beliefs and norms some of which contrast with those of mainstream society. These attributes are also characteristic of many youth subcultures, of course. Whether these subcultures are *deviant* is often a source of much debate, particularly among parents, educators, police, and the youths involved. The Straight Edge subculture, for example, is highly critical of many aspects of mainstream society—especially the use of animals for food and clothing—and is opposed to tobacco, alcohol, and drug use, but its adherents disavow the label of deviant (Irwin, 1999). Similarly, youths who identify with the rave culture object to how it has been portrayed by the media and politicians

Collective responses by those labelled deviant can have positive consequences. For instance, the recognition of shared experiences of rejection can bring otherwise isolated, and perhaps self-blaming, people together. Whether or not such groups are able

Social diversions are variations in lifestyle that help make our lives more interesting and, at times, more exciting: the fads and fashions of speech, appearance, and play.
SOURCE: Dick Hemingway.

to alter how the wider public perceives their members, they at least can counter some of the more damaging consequences of social condemnation. As with other moral crusades to define deviance, campaigns by groups to eliminate deviant definitions will succeed to the extent that they marshal political support and favourable media attention. Both constructing and repudiating definitions of deviance, then, involve power struggles and symbolic politics, and these struggles have been the focus of research by many sociologists.

For other sociologists, however, understanding deviance and crime requires more than understanding conflicts over definitions. Arguing that some behaviours—particularly many criminal acts—have serious individual and social costs, these sociologists have devoted considerable attention to the question of why people engage in such acts.

WHY DO PEOPLE ENGAGE IN CRIMINAL BEHAVIOUR?

On April 20, 1999, two teenage friends in Littleton, Colorado, walked into their high school during lunch break carrying an assault rifle, a semi-automatic pistol, two sawed-off shotguns, and about three-dozen homemade bombs. Over the next 90 minutes, they wandered through the school laughing and shooting teachers and students who cowered behind desks or dashed through hallways. After killing 13 people and wounding 23 others, they shot and killed themselves in the school library. Eight days later, a 14-year-old boy in Taber, Alberta, entered W.R. Myers High School with a .22-calibre semi-automatic rifle and shot two students on their way to class after lunch break. He then pointed the gun at several others before a Grade 9 student convinced him to put down the weapon. One of the wounded students, Jason Lang, died shortly after he was taken to hospital.

How can we explain these and other types of serious criminal acts? Dozens of sociological explanations of crime have been proposed, but they can be distinguished by the different assumptions they make about the sources of human behaviour. One set of explanations asks, "Why do people engage in crime?" and answers by identifying social factors that motivate or push people toward crime. These are **motivational theories**. The other set of explanations asks, "Why doesn't everyone engage in crime?" and answers by identifying social factors that control or prevent people's criminal behaviour. These are **control theories** and **opportunity theories**. Let's consider how these theories account for criminal behaviour and what they might tell us about high school shootings.

MOTIVATIONAL THEORIES

Strain Theories

Motivational theories argue that most criminal behaviour occurs because a social context exists that encourages or pushes a person toward crime. One of the best-known examples is Robert Merton's **strain theory** (Merton, 1938). For Merton, the motivation to crime lies in society, not in individuals: "Social structures exert a definite pressure upon certain persons in the society to engage in non-conforming rather than conforming conduct" (Merton, 1957: 32). Some societies have higher rates of crime than others because their cultures value certain achievements, but their social structures fail to provide many people with legitimate ways to attain these valued goals. For example, in North America, children learn at home, at school, and from the media to value economic achievement and the status that comes with it. From an early age, we see others evaluated on the basis of what they own and what they can buy. At the same time, the structure of North American society limits available opportunities for economic success. Therefore, a college education and a high-paying job may not be realistic nor attainable goals for many people.

The lack of fit between cultural goals and social structural opportunities—or what Merton, following Durkheim, called **anomie**—means that many people feel strained because they are not able to achieve what they have been taught to value or desire. In response to this strain, people react in a variety of ways. Most continue to conform to societal norms despite the strain they feel. Others choose deviance. They may drop out of conventional society and withdraw from the competition over cultural goals. They may abandon the goal of success but follow other cultural goals in a ritualistic manner. They may rebel against convention and support alternative goals and means. Or, finally, they may find alternative but illegitimate ways to achieve cultural goals. This last deviant adaptation—Merton called it **innovation**—is the one that will most likely lead people to commit economic crimes, such as burglary, forgery, or selling drugs. For Merton, each of these adaptations is a normal reaction to the lack of fit between cultural goals and approved means. Criminals, then, are not sick, evil, or stupid. They are simply responding unconventionally to a contradiction that exists in conventional society.

But how can strain theory help us understand what happened in Littleton or Taber? There is no evidence that the young killers lacked legitimate opportunities or were economically deprived. Indeed, the Littleton killers came from comfortable middle-class families. They usually drove to school together in a used BMW that one of them owned. But commentators on the killers noted that they felt like outcasts, were sometimes the target of ridicule, and resented the student hierarchy that valued athletic and other "preppie" accomplishments (Phillips, 1999; Bergman, 1999). Thus, the killers may have experienced a different type of strain—status frustration—because they

were unable or unwilling to achieve goals within the dominant student culture (Cohen, 1955). They may have expressed this frustration by dramatizing their strong rejection of that culture through the shootings.

This account, while plausible, illustrates some of the shortcomings of strain theory. Many teenagers feel rejected by their peers or their teachers, yet they do not react by killing them. So strain may be a necessary, but not a sufficient, condition for many types of criminal behaviour. Strain theory also does not tell us whether someone experiencing strain will choose to drop out, rebel, innovate, or conform. Another motivational theory, however, provides some insights into how strain might give rise to particular types of deviant actions.

Learning Theories

A second variant of motivational theories contends that, just as we learn to play hockey or appreciate hip-hop, we learn to engage in criminal behaviour. Like strain theory, **learning theories** see crime as a socially formed response to one's environment. Like strain theory, learning theories also assert that one's environment provides the motivation to engage in crime. The best-known version of learning theory is Edwin Sutherland's theory of **differential association** (Sutherland, 1939). Sutherland pointed out that Merton's strain theory could not predict with any precision how people under strain would respond. Would they conform or deviate? And if they deviated, would they become wife beaters, crack users, or terrorists? To understand how and why people choose any particular criminal activity, Sutherland directed his attention to people's learning histories and environments.

Throughout our lives, each of us interacts with people whose attitudes, values, and behaviour patterns sometimes encourage, and sometimes discourage, crime. Whether you engage in any particular type of crime depends on the mix of pro-criminal and anti-criminal influences in your environment. Crime occurs, said Sutherland, because one has experienced more pro-criminal influences. If you choose to become a car thief, then, it is because you have learned from others that it is acceptable to steal cars; and you have learned which cars are easiest to steal, how to break into them, how to avoid the police, and how to justify your activities to others.

A distinctive feature of differential association theory is its ability to account for crime at all levels of society. Thus, Sutherland (1949) applied the theory in his landmark study of **white-collar crime**. White-collar criminals, according to Sutherland, are like street criminals in that they often express contempt for the law, share an organizational or business culture that rewards rule breaking, and associate with others from whom they can learn both the skills and the rationalizations needed to carry out their crimes. Despite Sutherland's early, path-breaking work, sociologists have continued to focus on street crime more than "suite" crime, although a recent rash of well-publicized corporate misdeeds has attracted the attention of scholars, as well as the criminal justice system, as we discuss below.

What can learning theories tell us about the high school shootings? There are at least three ways in which learning theories can be applied to these events. The Littleton killers were said to be avid consumers of death-cult music, the movie *Natural Born Killers*, and violent video games. Some learning theories argue that long exposure to violent images desensitizes young people to violence and conveys the message that violence is an acceptable way to respond to frustration (Eron, 1986). Other evidence suggests that the Littleton killers learned how to make the bombs they took to school from various Web sites. As Sutherland's differential association theory notes, many types of crime require opportunities to learn specific techniques and procedures. Finally, the copycat nature of the Taber shootings suggests that, as some learning theories argue, much crime is imitation or modelling of others' behaviours.

A common theme uniting strain and learning theories is that for crime to occur some kind of motivating influence must be present. Motivational theories assume that, in the absence of such influences, people will rarely misbehave. Hence, their question, "Why do people engage in crime?" Moreover, both strain and learning theories assume an underlying consensus over definitions of crime, an assumption shared by control and opportunity theories, as discussed next. Here the similarity ends, however, as the next group of theories assumes that all people are capable of crime if the rewards are sufficient; given the lack of controls or increased opportunities, these theories argue, most of us would break the law.

CONTROL AND OPPORTUNITY THEORIES

Control and opportunity theories find it easy to explain crime: It's rewarding. Stealing is a fast way to make money. Getting high on drugs can be an easy way to feel good. Trashing a subway platform is risky fun. The question then, for control and opportunity theorists, is not "Why do people commit crime?" but "Why do most of us play by the rules most of the time?" In answering this question, control and opportunity theories look to somewhat different processes.

Control Theories

For control theories, crime occurs because of the absence of controls. In one of the most influential versions of control theory, Hirschi (1969) argued that juvenile delinquency results from the lack of strong bonds to conventional social institutions. Adolescents with few attachments to their parents, teachers, or other conventional role models; with little commitment to family, school, or other conventional institutions; with weak beliefs in conventional values; and with little involvement in conventional activities are free to act on their deviant impulses. Adolescents with strong bonds to conventionality, on the other hand, will not want to risk breaking the rules. Ask yourself, have you ever stopped short of cheating, stealing, or driving under the influence because you did not want to hurt your parents or your chances of getting into university or college? If so, your deviant impulses were controlled or contained by your social bonds.

In a later version of control theory, Gottfredson and Hirschi (1990) identify self-control as the key to conformity. People with low self-control will try to get what they want quickly, easily, and without thinking about others and, if doing so involves excitement and risk, so much the better. As you might expect, behaving in this way often means breaking rules or failing to fulfill conventional responsibilities—in other words, being deviant. Weak self-control, then, frees people to gamble, to drink and drive, to bribe officials, or to do anything else that provides quick and relatively effortless gratification. Hagan and colleagues (1987) have used concepts from control theory to explain gender differences in delinquency. Families exert greater control over girls than boys by socializing girls to avoid risks and by supervising them more closely. In contrast, boys are encouraged by their families to take risks and be independent. As a result, boys are freer to engage in delinquent acts. Families, then, are the major source of controls that prevent deviance, according to control theories. Early childhood socialization—the ways in which parents reward and discipline children's behaviour and the extent to which they develop affectionate bonds with them—is critical to all control theories. If those controls are developed early in life, children will not be as susceptible to the deviant influences of peers, nor will they respond to strain with deviant actions.

Several observers of the high school shootings described earlier saw evidence of control theory's predictions at work. The Littleton teens spent many hours alone together, unsupervised by their parents, who claimed not to know that their children had acquired several guns, built dozens of explosive devices, and developed a Web site that advertised their violent inclinations. In diaries and other writing, the teens indicated their disdain for school and other conventional institutions and pursuits. A Canadian researcher on teen violence, Alan Leschied of the University of Western Ontario, characterized the boys in the language of control theory when he said they had "a lessening of ties to conventional supports" (Chisholm, 1999: 22). But control theories, like strain theories, do not tell us what *type* of deviance the person who lacks bonds to conventional others will turn to, or why some people who lack bonds to society do not engage in deviance. Opportunity theories have tried to answer these questions.

Opportunity Theories

Proponents of opportunity theories, like control theorists, assume that in the absence of inner controls, such as a conscience, or external controls, such as a police officer on the corner or a lock on the door, most of us would engage in crime. The type of crime we choose, according to these theories, would depend on the opportunities available to us. Opportunities are structured by everything from other people's routine daily activities (is the house down the street empty during the day?), to one's access to the tools to carry out the crime (do you have a computer, a car, a gun?), to the availability of easy and attractive targets (CDs are easy to steal, big-screen televisions less so).

According to one version of opportunity theory, the large increase in property and violent crimes that occurred in North America beginning in the late 1960s can be explained, in part, by the fact that people were spending less time at home and many consumer goods were becoming more durable and more portable (Cohen and Felson, 1979). With more women in the work force, more people living in single-family homes, and more people spending evening hours at the movies and in bars, empty houses became more attractive targets for burglars during the day and entertainment seekers became more available as targets for muggers at night. As televisions, radios, and music systems became smaller, more lightweight, and more durable, they became more attractive targets for shoplifters and snatch-and-grab artists.

Opportunity theories do not try to explain why people decide to commit crime. They simply assume that many people lack the controls to stop them. When these people encounter criminal opportunities, they will act, but the type of crimes they commit will depend on the opportunities they encounter. Opportunity theories, thus, connect the potential offender described by control theories to particular offences.

The high school shootings described earlier occurred, according to opportunity theories, not only because the teens lacked bonds to society, but also because they had access to the tools necessary to kill people easily—that is, guns. The widespread availability of guns in North America, and especially in the United States, is linked not only to its high homicide rates, but also to its high suicide rates, especially rates of suicide by teens. Canadian males aged 15–24 kill themselves three times more often than 15–24-year-old males in Italy, England, or Hong Kong (World Health Organization, 1998); and 85 percent of these suicides in Canada are committed with guns. As Dr. Katherine Leonard, an expert in adolescent depression, points out: "Teenagers who don't have a firearm available are less likely to kill themselves. You might think 'Oh, they'll just jump off a bridge or something.' That's simply not the case" (Phillips, 1999: 24).

Where lethal weapons are more available, then, the opportunities for lethal violence are much greater.

Table 19.1 summarizes the major sociological theories of crime and deviance.

PATTERNS OF DEVIANCE AND CRIME

MEASURING DEVIANCE AND CRIME

Our discussion of where definitions of deviance and crime come from and why people behave in ways that get them defined as criminal suggests that rates of deviance and crime should vary among social groups as well as among societies. Documenting such variation with any accuracy is not easy, however, because of the hidden nature of much deviance and the political nature of defining it. If deviance becomes the target of formal control, it can be documented through statistics produced by official social control agents and organizations. However, these statistics are affected by more than just deviant behaviour. Control agents and the wider public make decisions about which deviant acts or persons to report and which to ignore. So, for example, if public intolerance of young "troublemakers" increases—think of the expansion of zero-tolerance policies in schools in the last few years—official statistics on youth crime may indicate an increase, not because there is more of it, but because more of it is reported to police (Tanner, 1996).

Sociologists of crime and deviance, aware of the limitations of official statistics, often rely on other information sources. Surveys that ask people to report on their own involvement in deviance or on their victimization experiences produce results closer to actual behaviours and so avoid many of the problems associated with official statistics. However, survey data, like official statistics, are affected by people's willingness and ability to reveal their own or others' deviance. Indirect measures of deviance can avoid many of these problems. Examples include statistics on deaths due to

---

TABLE 19.1   SOCIOLOGICAL THEORIES OF CRIME AND DEVIANCE

THEORY	KEY NAMES	ELEMENTS
Status conflict	Weber; Vold; Turk; Quinney	Focuses on how groups compete to control definitions of right and wrong.
Labelling	Becker; Lemert	Focuses on how societal reactions to crime and deviance are an important cause of such behaviour.
Strain	Merton; Cohen	Focuses on the motivations for crime and deviance that arise as a result of disjuncture between culturally prescribed goals and culturally approved means to achieve those goals.
Differential association	Sutherland	Emphasizes the way in which individual learning histories and environments may contribute more pro-criminal than pro-conformity influences.
Control	Hirschi; Gottfredson and Hirschi; Hagan, Simpson, and Gillis	Explains crime and deviance by focusing on the absence of controls (i.e., lack of strong bonds, lack of self-control, differential controls).
Opportunity	Cohen and Felson	Focuses on the role played by available opportunities in the production of crime.

cirrhosis of the liver as a measure of alcohol abuse, or statistics on sales of medical syringes as a measure of intravenous drug use.

How we count deviance and what we know about it, then, is the outcome of social and political processes. While it is important to keep in mind that all sources of information on deviance are imperfect, combining information from many sources permits greater confidence in our depiction of deviance. This means that we have a better idea of the extent and nature of some kinds of deviance than others because some kinds of deviance can be documented through a variety of sources. Let's turn to what we know about one of the most well-documented types of deviant behaviour: crime.

CRIMINAL BEHAVIOUR IN CANADA

Recent Crime Trends

Contrary to what many Canadians believe, the crime rate in 2001 was about the same level as in 1979 (Savoie 2002), and the homicide rate was 41 percent lower than in 1975 (see Figure 19.1). Paralleling these declines in crime is an increasing number of Canadians who indicate that they feel safe in their neighbourhoods. In 1999, three out of four Canadians reported that they walked alone after dark

and 88 percent said that they felt safe doing so (Besserer and Trainor, 2000). Nevertheless, close to 30 percent of the population said they thought crime levels had increased in their area during the past five years and another 54 percent believed crime had remained stable.

Why does a substantial minority of Canadians think crime has increased when the evidence suggests otherwise? To answer this question, we need to know about the factors that shape people's perceptions about crime. One of the most important factors is the media. Most people get the bulk of their information about crime from watching television and reading newspapers and, in recent years, media coverage of crime has increased greatly (Committee of Concerned Journalists, 1998). Crime stories lead off the nightly news and appear "above the fold" in the daily newspapers more often now than in the past. As we hear more about crime, we perceive it to be more prevalent. People's fears about crime also increase as they age, and the Canadian population is aging (see Chapter 17). In the late 1990s, crime also became a popular topic in many Canadian political campaigns in which the need for increased law and order was emphasized. Like increased media coverage, this reflects and reinforces people's fears about crime.

Another question raised by the crime statistics cited above is "Why did crime decrease during the 1990s in Canada?" Politicians, criminal justice officials, and sociologists have all offered views on the decline in crime. Some claim it is a consequence of more effective forms of community policing. Others argue that "get tough" crime policies are working, and still others point to the recent upswing of the economy. None of these explanations is sufficient, however, because crime rates decreased not only in Canada, but also in the United States and England; in cities without community policing; in provinces that have reduced their incarceration rates; and in regions with bleak economic conditions. A trend common across all these settings can help explain some of the decline in crime: A decrease in the proportion of the population in the most crime-prone age group— people between 15 and 24 years of age. So, just as the aging of the population may be associated with rising concerns about crime, it is also associated with reduced crime rates. Demographics cannot fully explain the drop in crime, however, because the crime rate is dropping faster than the population is aging.

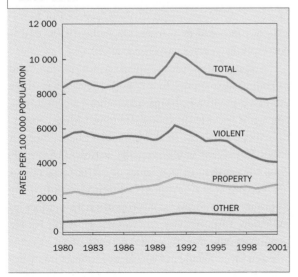

FIGURE 19.1 CRIME RATES IN CANADA, 1980–2001

SOURCE: Compiled from *Juristat 22*, 6, Rates of Criminal Code Incidents.

Improved employment opportunities and changes in collective values also may have played a role in the falling crime rate (Ouimet, 2002).

Although Canadians do not appear to be at greater risk of criminal victimization now than they were in the 1970s or 1980s, they continue to be at greater risk than citizens of some other industrialized nations. Victimization surveys indicate that rates of violent offences, theft, and burglary are higher in Canada than in several European countries (Canadian Centre for Justice Statistics, 1996). The risk of being a victim of homicide is also greater in Canada than in several other developed nations, though substantially less than the risk in Russia and the United States (see Table 19.2). Crime in Canada, therefore, remains distinct from crime in the United States in an important respect. While Canadians are more likely than Americans to be the victims of burglaries and car thefts, they are much less likely than Americans to be the victims of serious violent crime, such as aggravated assault, robbery, and homicide (see Table 19.3).

The Risks of Victimization and Offending: Sex, Age, and Ethnicity

Crime is unequally distributed within and among societies. In Canada, crime rates have historically been lower in the Atlantic provinces and Quebec than in the western provinces and highest in the territories

TABLE 19.2   HOMICIDE RATES FOR SELECTED COUNTRIES, 2001

COUNTRY	HOMICIDE RATE PER 100 000 POPULATION
Russia	21.13
United States	5.64
Finland	2.98
Hungary	2.48
Austria	1.93
Sweden	1.87
France	1.78
Canada	**1.78**
England and Wales	1.66
Ireland	1.60
Germany	1.05
Norway	0.81

SOURCE: Adapted from Statistics Canada publication, "Homicide in Canada, 2001," Catalogue 85-002, September 2002.

TABLE 19.3 CRIME RATES (PER 100 000 POPULATION) FOR CANADA AND THE UNITED STATES

	CANADA, 2001	UNITED STATES, 2001
Murder and non-negligent manslaughter	1.8	5.6
Robbery	88	149
Aggravated assault	147	319
Burglary	909	741
Larceny	2211	2485
Motor vehicle theft	548	431

SOURCE: Complied from Josee Savoie, "Crime Statistics in Canada, 2001," *Juristat*, vol. 22, no. 6. Ottawa: Statistics Canada, Canadian Centre for Justice Statistics; and Federal Bureau of Investigation, Uniform Crime Reports, 2000 (http://www.fbi.gov/ucr/00cius.htm).

(see Figure 19.2). Urban dwellers, young Canadians, those who are single, separated, or divorced, and those with lower household incomes report higher rates of personal victimization than do rural dwellers, older Canadians, married couples, and those with higher household incomes (Besserer and Trainor, 2000). There is very little difference in the overall risk of personal victimization for women and men. Males, however, commit a disproportionate number of violent and property offences. Criminal offenders also tend to be younger than the general population. Contrary to public perceptions about youth violence, however, the average age of those accused of homicide has *increased* in Canada since the 1970s, and is currently 29 years (Dauvergne, 2002).

Some types of criminal victimization and offending also appear to be more prevalent in some ethnic and cultural groups than others. For example, Aboriginal people (including Inuit and Métis) constitute about 3 percent of the Canadian population, but about 15 percent of all homicide victims (Dauvergne, 2002). Because most homicides are intra-racial (about 85 percent of Aboriginal victims are killed by Aboriginal offenders), a disproportionate number of homicide suspects are Aboriginal as well. Native people account for about 25 percent of all persons arrested for homicide in Canada, according to statistics compiled by the Canadian Centre for Justice Statistics. Police agencies in Canada do not publish or analyze data on the ethnic and cultural backgrounds of those arrested, and so it has been difficult for researchers to determine whether other groups are overrepresented among arrestees. However, due to public concern over Black-on-Black violence in Toronto, the *Toronto Star* newspaper compiled information on arrestees from police reports for the period 1996 through early 2002. It found that Blacks accounted for about 27 percent of all arrests for violent crimes in Toronto whereas they constitute only about 8 percent of Toronto's population (Rankin et al., 2002).

Black and Aboriginal people are also overrepresented among those serving time in Canada's jails and prisons. In 1999–2000, Aboriginal people accounted for 17 percent of persons admitted to provincial, territorial, and federal institutions (Lonmo, 2001). Their admissions to provincial and territorial institutions have remained relatively stable during the past two decades, whereas their representation among those sentenced to federal institutions has increased steadily from 8 percent to 17 percent. Blacks make up about 2 percent of the Canadian population, but they represent 6 percent of prisoners under federal juris-

diction; and their incarceration rate is about five times greater than that of whites (Wortley and McCalla, 2003).

There are at least two ways to explain these patterns. First, Aboriginals and Blacks may be at higher risk of incarceration because they engage in the kinds of behaviours that put them in conflict with the law. Although official crime statistics by race are currently not published for crimes other than homicide, the data cited above lend some support to this explanation, at least with regard to violent crimes. In addition, other evidence suggests that Aboriginals and Blacks are exposed to many of the correlates of criminal behaviour—such as poverty, family disruption, and unemployment—at much higher rates than other Canadians (Frideres, 1996; Satzewich, 1998). These and other indicators of strain and weak social bonds—such as high rates of suicide and depression among Aboriginal people—would predict greater involvement in crime.

The second explanation for the overrepresentation of Aboriginals and Blacks in the criminal justice

FIGURE 19.2 CRIME RATES TEND TO INCREASE FROM EAST TO WEST AND ARE HIGHEST IN THE NORTH

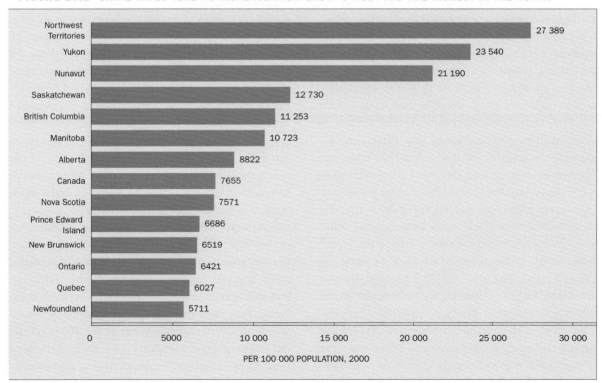

SOURCE: Adapted from the Statistics Canada publication, "Juristat: Canadian Crime Statistics, 2000," Catalogue 85-002, July 2001, Vol. 21, No. 8, page 16.

system is that there may be discrimination in the creation and application of criminal definitions (Roberts and Doob, 1997). This possibility has been investigated in a series of federal and provincial inquiries which have concluded that "systemic" or "institutional" racism is responsible for at least part of the overrepresentation of Aboriginals and Blacks in the criminal justice system (Cawsey, 1991; Province of Manitoba, 1991; Commission on Systemic Racism in the Ontario Criminal Justice System, 1995). Discrimination and disparity can occur at various stages in the criminal justice process. For example, Aboriginal people and members of some other visible minority groups appear to be policed more closely than whites, and relations between these groups and the police are often hostile and distrustful, which can lead to a higher likelihood of arrest. Once arrested, Blacks and Aboriginals also are significantly more likely than members of other ethnic groups to be denied pre-trial release on bail and to spend longer periods in pre-trial detention, both of which increase their likelihood of conviction and incarceration (Hamilton and Sinclair, 1991; Roberts and Doob, 1997).

The possibility that "racial profiling" by police could lead to an overrepresentation of certain ethnic and cultural groups in the criminal justice system has recently become a topic of considerable controversy. In Canada, police forces are not required to record the race or ethnicity of those they stop and search, and so police statistics cannot be used to determine whether racial profiling exists. Recent surveys in Toronto, however, have found that Black people—especially young, Black males—report having had involuntary contact with the police more often than whites or Asians, and these higher rates of police contact are not explained away by greater involvement in deviant activity by Black youth. In fact, racial differences in police contact are *greatest* among youth with little or no involvement in deviance or drug use (Wortley and McCalla, 2003). This suggests that racial profiling is responsible for at least part of the overrepresentation of Blacks, and perhaps Aboriginal Canadians, in the criminal justice system. It may also explain why many members of these ethnic and racial groups have negative perceptions of the Canadian criminal justice system (Foster, 1996; Wortley, 1996).

CRIME AND SOCIAL CHANGE

If the explanations for criminal behaviour discussed earlier are valid, we would expect to see changes in crime rates accompanying social changes that might affect criminal motivations, social control, and criminal opportunities. For example, new and changing technologies have created opportunities for committing old crimes in new ways and have led to new types of crime. An important tool in the commission of these new technological crimes is the Internet. Much media attention has been devoted to teenage "cybercriminals," such as Mafiaboy, or to other individuals who use the Internet for illicit purposes. But these new technologies have probably had their greatest impact on corporate and organized criminal activities and their control, because the global and decentralized nature of this technology and the instantaneous movement of data over national boundaries create profound problems for law enforcement.

Corporate Crime, Organized Crime, and Globalization

Globalization is affecting all arenas of human behaviour, including criminal behaviour (see Chapter 18). As the economies of nation-states become more integrated and interdependent—a move encouraged by the proliferation of electronic technology—both the motivations and opportunities for global economic crime have increased enormously, as have the difficulties in controlling it. As a result, corporate crime and organized crime are moving beyond national boundaries, just like the pursuit of profit through legitimate activities. "Crime is now as much a feature of the emergent globalized culture as is every other aspect of its consumerism," according to Michael Findlay in his book, *The Globalization of Crime* (1999: 2).

A large portion of global crime is corporate crime, that is, crime committed by legitimate business organizations. It includes violations of antitrust, environmental, food and drug, tax, health and safety, and corruption laws. The economic costs of these crimes have been estimated at 50 times those associated with street crimes (Rosoff et al., 1998). While the profits of global corporate crime are impossible to estimate precisely, some sense of them is suggested by the kinds of fines that have been levied against corporations that have been successfully prosecuted. For example, in the spring of 1999, the Swiss pharmaceutical giant F. Hoffmann–La-Roche Ltd., pled guilty in a U.S. court and agreed to pay a US$500 million criminal fine for its role in a ten-year, worldwide conspiracy to raise and fix prices of vitamins. Archer-Daniels-Midland, on whose board of directors former prime minister Brian Mulroney served, paid a fine of US$140 million in the United States in 1996 and a fine of $16 million in Canada in 1997 for its role in a global price-fixing conspiracy. More recently, multi-billion-dollar scandals involving energy giant Enron, cable TV company Adelphia, the Tyco conglomerate, and WorldCom (owner of the second-biggest long-distance phone company in the United States and headed by Canadian-born Bernie Ebbers) have led to convictions of corporate executives on charges of conspiracy and securities fraud, and there are been several major lawsuits involving Canadian corporations. In 2002 the Canadian Imperial Bank of Commerce, for example, was named in a class-action suit filed against several top Enron executives and its lenders, including the CIBC.

Controlling corporate crime that spans national boundaries remains exceedingly difficult, in part, because of the limited resources controllers have to work with and also because of national differences in how corporate misconduct is defined. Globalization has made it easier for corporations to move their factories to countries with lax occupational health and safety laws. It has also made it easier for corporations to sell products that developed countries have banned as health hazards to countries with less restrictive food and drug laws. Due to massive foreign debts and other economic pressures, less-developed countries have become the largest, but not sole, market for these corporate activities. In the 1980s, the United States exported most of its hazardous wastes to Canada because Canadian laws regulating the disposal of these wastes were less stringent than U.S. laws (Rosoff et al., 1998).

Criminal organizations are also benefiting from new opportunities for crime spawned by globalization. Previously local or nationally based criminal organizations, such as the American Mafia, the Chinese Triads, the Japanese Yakuza, the Russian Mafia, and the Colombian drug cartels, have formed global alliances

to gain access to new markets and take advantage of each other's special skills. These alliances have been fostered by a number of events, including the creation of free-trade blocks such as the European Union, the development of the World Wide Web, the collapse of the Soviet Union, and the commercialization of China (Richards, 1999). The illegal activities engaged in by global organized crime are highly diverse and include trafficking in drugs, arms, and human beings; contraband smuggling; money laundering; telecommunications piracy; and the sexual exploitation of children. A recent U.N. report on worldwide organized crime groups notes that as a result of their increasingly sophisticated strategies and diverse modes of operation "they are able to infiltrate the financial, economic and political systems of countries all over the world" (United Nations, 1999: 4).

Money laundering—the process by which proceeds from criminal activities are disguised as legitimate income—is key to the health of global organized crime groups. The Financial Crimes Enforcement Network estimates that money laundering could now be the world's third-largest business, with more than US$750 billion a year in illicit funds being laundered worldwide (Richards, 1999). Canada has become an increasingly popular site for money-laundering rings because of its proximity to the United States, its stable economy and sophisticated financial sector, as well as its lack of both mandatory reporting requirements and controls on currency crossing the Canada–U.S. border. An estimated $15 billion is laundered in or through Canada and Canadian financial institutions each year (Criminal Intelligence Service Canada, 1996).

Crime and Changing Gender Stratification

As noted in Chapter 9, one of the most influential social changes of the last generation has been the growing awareness and abatement of many forms of gender inequality. In the 1970s, some criminologists expected this change to reduce the longstanding gender gap in crime: Men have historically been much more likely than women to engage in criminal acts. This expectation was rekindled in the 1990s by some high-profile cases of violent crime by teenage girls, such as the killing of 14-year-old Rena Virk in

Victoria in 1997. Put simply, some analysts believed that decreasing gender stratification might mean that females would catch up to males in their criminal behaviour as their access to less traditional roles expanded, the stresses associated with new roles increased, and controls over their activities decreased. The evidence has not backed up this expectation, however. A large gender gap persists in most crimes, especially the kinds of serious violent crimes traditionally dominated by men. In Canada, for example, the ratio of males to females charged with murder has remained at about 7 to 1 for at least the last 25 years. And the homicide rate among teenage girls was lower in 2001 than it was in 1991 (see Figure 19.3).

Changes in gender stratification are, however, related to one aspect of women's involvement in crime—as victims, not offenders. In developed nations since World War II, as women have moved into the labour force in unprecedented numbers, they have also taken on less traditional domestic roles by having more children out of wedlock, marrying later, and divorcing more often. This shift toward less traditional gender roles for women has affected their risks of homicide victimization in complex ways (Gartner, Baker, and Pampel, 1990). In countries where women's status is relatively low, women's risks of being homicide victims have increased with these changes. However, in countries where women's status is relatively high—such as Canada—women's risks have not increased relative to men's risks as women have assumed less traditional roles. In fact, in Canada, the gender gap in homicide victimization has grown

substantially since the early 1970s. Males are currently more than twice as likely as females to be victims of homicide (Dauvergne, 2002).

Major social, economic, and political transformations can have profound and complex effects on patterns of crime and deviance, as we have seen. It is not surprising, then, that these transformations also affect patterns of social control.

PATTERNS OF SOCIAL CONTROL

For most of human history, families, communities, and the church were the major sources of social control. The punishment for serious rule breaking was physical and, to our eyes, often horrific. Before the seventeenth century, centralized states either did not exist or were not strong enough to sponsor the institutions of formal social control that predominate in modern societies. With the growth of market-based economies and industrialization—and the accompanying growth of a working class—state-based formal social controls emerged. The most obvious example of these formal controls is the confinement institution—prisons, asylums, poorhouses, and so forth—that emerged in the seventeenth century. These were places of residence and work where people who were unable or unwilling to work or conform to other rules were isolated from the outside world, closely watched, and continuously regimented by impersonal agents of control. Punishment based on physical pain shifted to punishment based on deprivation and discipline.

Confinement institutions remain one of the favoured responses to deviance and crime in Canada today and in most other industrialized nations. But throughout the twentieth century, these institutions were criticized for their inefficiency, costliness, repressiveness, and failure to rehabilitate. The 1960s and 1970s saw growing support for alternative methods of control through decentralization, deinstitutionalization, and decriminalization. The goal was to shift control to local governments and community agencies, close down large-scale institutions, and eliminate criminal sanctions for victimless crimes, such as sodomy and public drunkenness. This move reflected the growing popularity of the **medical model of deviance** and a therapeutic approach to social control. During the twentieth century, many forms of deviance and crime were medicalized—in

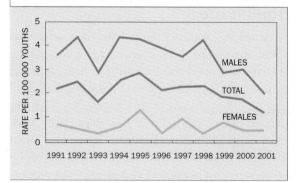

FIGURE 19.3 YOUTHS (12–17 YEARS) ACCUSED OF HOMICIDE, 1991–2001

SOURCE: *Jursitat*, Homicide Survey, Policing Services Program, Canadian Centre for Justice Statistics, Statistics Canada, September 2002.

other words, defined as illnesses in need of treatment rather than sins in need of punishment. Professional groups—psychiatrists, social workers, and psychologists—urged this redefinition of deviance and its solution through psychological adjustment and community-based care, rather than through physical discipline and confinement. Whether therapeutic social controls are less coercive and repressive, as their advocates claim, has been the subject of much debate. In addition, some argue that therapeutic controls have not so much replaced older, more punitive forms of social control, as they have added to them, widening the social control net to capture people who might otherwise have avoided formal social controls (Cohen, 1985).

RECENT TRENDS IN CRIMINAL JUSTICE IN CANADA

The kind of deviance that the public worries most about—criminal behaviour—continues to be dealt with primarily by legal forms of social control through the criminal justice system. Two competing perspectives influence the Canadian criminal justice system—the **crime control model** and the **due-process model**. While the primary goal of the crime-control model is to reduce crime and to protect society by granting legal officials broad powers, the due-process model emphasizes the protection of the legal rights of the accused to ensure justice. Historically, Canada has favoured the crime-control model, but with the introduction of the Canadian Charter of Rights and Freedoms in 1982, this emphasis has shifted. During the 1980s and 1990s, courts and legislatures expanded the due-process rights of those accused of crime—for example, by prohibiting unreasonable searches and seizures and by guaranteeing the right to legal counsel (Roach, 1999). This does not mean that the concerns of the crime-control model have been overshadowed. Rather, it has been quite the opposite. At the same time that due process rights were expanding, more people were ending up in jail. Between 1981 and 1994, the number of adults serving sentences in federal and provincial jails and prisons grew by 50 percent and the number of juvenile offenders in custody grew by 26 percent. After a decade of growth, however, prison admissions began to decline in the mid-1990s, in part, because of decreasing crime rates and

the introduction of legislation designed to encourage the use of alternatives to incarceration. In 1999–2000, about 31 600 adults were imprisoned in federal or provincial institutions, a decrease of 2 percent from the previous year (Lonmo, 2001). Despite this decline, Canada remains a leader in imprisonment among Western nations with an overall incarceration rate of 118 per 100 000 population (see Figure 19.4).

Why, until recently, was imprisonment growing when due-process concerns were on the rise? One important reason is the emergence of the victims' rights movement, which "enabled and legitimated the criminal sanction" (Roach, 1999: 4). Increased reliance on imprisonment may also reflect public attitudes toward criminal offenders, which appear to have hardened over time—at least at first glance. In the 1970s, for example, public opinion polls found that almost two-thirds of Canadians felt sentences were not harsh enough. In the mid-1990s, similar polls found that close to 85 percent of Canadians believed the justice system was "too soft" on those convicted of crime (Roberts, 2000). If we look in more depth at people's views about criminal justice, however, we see that they are more complex than these polls suggest. For example, according to the 1999 General Social Survey, Canadians support the use of community-based, noncustodial sanctions in certain situations (Tufts, 2001). Specifically, probation, fines, and community work are preferred for first-time offenders convicted of break-and-enter or minor assault, and for young, repeat offenders. And in a 1997 survey of Ontario residents, less than a third of respondents thought that lengthening prison sentences was the best way of preventing crime (Doob et al., 1998).

So, while many Canadians appear to lean toward being "tough on crime," they also seem willing to consider alternatives to traditional punitive responses for some types of crimes and criminals. Both of these views are reflected in the Youth Criminal Justice Act, which was to come into force in 2003, replacing the Young Offenders Act. The new act allows an adult sentence for any youth 14 and older convicted of a serious crime, increases the scope of cases for which youths can presumptively receive an adult sentence, lowers the age (from 16 to 14) at which youths found guilty of certain serious offences will presumptively be sentenced as adults, and permits judges to consider allowing the publication of names of some youths found guilty of serious violent offences even if they

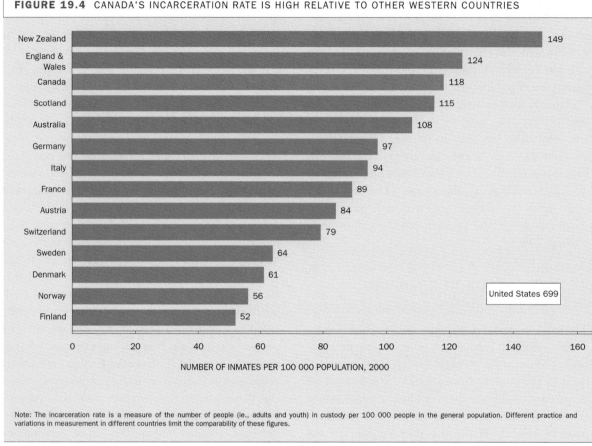

FIGURE 19.4 CANADA'S INCARCERATION RATE IS HIGH RELATIVE TO OTHER WESTERN COUNTRIES

Note: The incarceration rate is a measure of the number of people (ie., adults and youth) in custody per 100 000 people in the general population. Different practice and variations in measurement in different countries limit the comparability of these figures.

SOURCE: © Her Majesty the Queen in Right of Canada. All rights reserved. *Corrections and Conditional Release Statistical Overview*, p. 5, Solicitor General Canada, November 2001. Reproduced with the permission of the Minister of Public Works and Government Services, 2003.

were not given an adult sentence (Doob and Sprott, in press). At the same time, unlike the Young Offenders Act, the new legislation also explicitly encourages the use of community-based alternatives and forbids the use of custodial sentences in the majority of less serious cases that come before the courts. Efforts to develop alternatives to incarceration, in part, reflect the fact that, contrary to public perceptions, the incarceration rate for young offenders in Canada is among the highest of any developed nation, higher even than in the United States for many types of offences.

A willingness to consider alternatives to prison-based sanctions can also be seen in the innovative approaches to criminal justice that have gained popularity in recent years, for both adult and young offenders. For instance, conditional sentences are now available to some convicted offenders who, traditionally subject to provincial jail terms of two years less a

day, may now serve their sentences in the community under certain conditions. In addition, several provincial correctional systems have begun using electronic monitoring programs that involve placing an offender under house arrest rather than in an institution, using electronic equipment to ensure that the conditions of confinement are fulfilled. Probably the approach that has garnered the most attention in recent years, however, is the **restorative justice** movement. Restorative justice is based on a social rather than a legal view that criminal acts not only injure a victim, but affect communities and offenders and, thus, solutions need to involve all three parties (Griffiths and Cunningham, 2000). The most common types of restorative justice are victim–offender reconciliation, circle sentencing, and family group conferencing. Another recent criminal justice initiative has been the development and implementation of specialized courts to deal with chronic social and legal problems that appear to defy

Contrary to the belief of many people, crime rates in Canada are declining. Nonetheless, Canada has one of the highest incarceration rates in the Western world.
SOURCE: Photodisc.

conventional criminal justice responses or solutions. Specialized drug courts, mental health courts, and domestic violence courts are expanding at a rapid rate throughout North America. One component of these courts is the diversion of some types of cases out of the criminal justice system into treatment programs that target what are perceived to be the broader social needs of both victims and offenders.

Why the concern with finding alternatives to confinement? Those who work in the criminal justice system as well as those who study it recognize that imprisonment is not an effective way of either rehabilitating people or deterring them from subsequent offending (Doob et al., 1995). In addition, the public is becoming more aware of the high cost of imprisonment. Canada spends well over $2 billion on adult and youth corrections. For example, in 1999–2000, it cost $183.66 per day or about $67 000 a year to keep one person in federal prison in Canada (Lonmo, 2001). As governments search for ways to cut public spending, they are likely to rely more on less costly modes of social control, such as electronic moni-

toring of convicted criminals, and to experiment with privately run prisons and other types of correctional facilities. The privatization of jails and prisons has been growing in popularity in the United States, Britain, and Australia (Griffiths and Cunningham, 2000). For example, several thousand prisoners in the United States are held in jails and prisons operated by private companies and some states now administer capital punishment through private contractors. In contrast, in Canada, no federal facilities have been privatized; however, Nova Scotia has privatized at least one of its provincial jails and Ontario has contracted with private industry to operate a strict-discipline program in one of its facilities for young offenders. The increasing reliance on privatization for social control is apparent at other stages of formal social control, however. The amount of policing done through private security may now be as much as or more than the amount done through public law enforcement in many countries, including Canada.

Some observers see private entrepreneurs joining with the state to extend social control through new, technically sophisticated and more discreet techniques. Gary Marx (1995), for example, describes a **maximum-security society** characterized by "softer" social control processes where the role of human agents is reduced and control is achieved at a distance. In this maximum-security society, the goal will be to engineer away deviance and crime by controlling the physical environment, rather than people. Think of subways with graffiti-resistant metals, malls playing classical music to discourage congregations of teenagers, remote surveillance cameras, and anti-carjacking mannequins that drivers can place in the passenger seats of their cars. Whether these new techniques of control will replace or merely add another layer to existing formal controls is unclear. Some fear that the new strategies will create an Orwellian future of more powerful and intrusive state control over our lives, whereas others see technological advances as providing control that is less discriminatory, more effective, and more accountable.

In the wake of the September 11, 2001, attacks on the World Trade Center in New York City and the Pentagon in Washington, concerns over expanding governmental controls and legal powers have taken on new meaning in and outside of Canada. The passage in January 2002 of Bill C-36, Canada's anti-terrorism legislation, which gives law enforcement authorities new powers of detection, investigation, and surveillance, was accompanied by debates over how to balance needs for safety and security against protection of civil rights and citizen privacy (see Box 19.2). International debates over the very definition of the attacks—were they crimes or acts of war?—and how persons accused of terrorist activities ought to be dealt with highlight, once again, how struggles over defining deviance and deviants are inevitable and critical elements of life in a global age.

BOX 19.2 HIGH-PRICED SECURITY

Faced with a new terrorism threat, Canada's government has enacted a far-reaching law that gives authorities extraordinary power to curtail the civil rights of Canadian citizens. Under the law, police are able to: arrest people who have committed no crime but are suspected of planning to do so; keep evidence secret, even from the accused; deny the right to remain silent and not give testimony that might lead to one's own conviction. The bill also allows for the freezing and seizure of the assets of terrorists and their supporters, as well as the establishment of a list of terrorist organizations and individuals.

The Canadian Bar Association (CBA), which represents 37,000 lawyers across the country, thought the bill should expire in three years unless it is specifically extended by a vote of Parliament. "When governments seek to impose such restraints on fundamental rights and freedoms, particularly with limited time available for study and debate, those restraints must be limited in durations," said a CBA brief presented to a government justice committee. The association also raised concerns about possible discrimination against minority groups who, under the provision for preventive arrests, could be unjustly detained as suspected terrorists for up to 72 hours without a warrant. Others expressed concern about the criminalization of peaceful protests. This was an issue long before the anti-terrorism bill, looking back to the treatment of even peaceful protesters at the Summit of the Americas in Quebec City in April 2001 and the APEC summit in Vancouver in 1997.

Alan Gold, president of the Ontario Criminal Lawyers Association, was also critical of the bill, saying it violates fundamental freedoms with no real increase in security. "It strikes me as bizarre to defend liberty by giving up liberty," he said, commenting that the new measures threaten to turn Canada into a police state. Doesn't placing such curbs on our civil liberties mean that the terrorists have already won? The government doesn't think so: it takes the view that Canada is not a free and democratic society if its citizens live in fear, and maintains that the bill respects the Charter of Rights and Freedoms.

SOURCE: "High-Priced Security: Bill C-36, Canada's New Anti-Terrorism Legislation." *Canada and the World Backgrounder*, v. 67 (4), Jan. 2002, pp. 24–27.

SUMMARY

1. Deviance and crime are defined by the social reactions to them. Both what is defined as deviance and the way people react to deviance depend on social circumstances. Even what you may consider to be serious deviance is subject to conflicting opinions and changing social reactions.

2. Crime is a special case of deviance and is defined by social norms that are formalized in criminal law. The response to crime is through formal social control—such as the criminal justice and correctional systems—whereas the response to noncriminal deviance is through informal social control—such as gossip, avoidance, and other forms of disapproval. There tends to be wide—though certainly not complete—agreement that crime is wrong, but much less agreement that noncriminal forms of deviance are wrong.

3. Deviance is defined through a political process that typically involves struggles between competing groups over status, resources, knowledge, and power. While there is often some relationship between the harm that a behaviour causes and the likelihood that the behaviour is defined as deviance, many harmful behaviours are not defined as deviant and some behaviours defined as deviant are not harmful.

4. Sociological explanations of deviant behaviour can be grouped into two types: those that emphasize the social factors that motivate or allow people to engage in deviance, and those that emphasize the political processes and power relations that result in some people and behaviours being defined and treated as deviant while others are not.

5. Rates of crimes have decreased in Canada in recent years. Canadians are less likely to be victims of serious violent crime than people in the United States, but face higher risks of homicide than citizens of other developed democracies. Aboriginal Canadians are at particularly high risk of involvement in criminal homicide—both as victims and as offenders. They are also overrepresented among those incarcerated in Canadian prisons and jails. This has been attributed in part to systemic racism in the criminal justice system.

6. Crime rates are often affected by major social changes. For example, rapidly changing technologies have created new opportunities for both personal and property crime and the globalization of the world's economy has been accompanied by the globalization of corporate and organized crime. Changes in gender inequalities, on the other hand, have not reduced the gender gap in criminal offences. Men still greatly outnumber women among offenders.

7. Canada has traditionally favoured the crime-control model of the criminal process and, consistent with that model, relies heavily on incarceration. More recently, however, this emphasis has shifted. With the introduction of the Charter of Rights and Freedoms, the due-process model has gained ground. And while Canada continues to incarcerate offenders at higher rates than most other Western democracies, Canadian incarceration rates have declined in recent years as the criminal justice system explores alternatives to imprisonment.

QUESTIONS TO CONSIDER

1. Think of a behaviour that, during your lifetime, has gone from being considered deviant to nondeviant, or vice versa. What explains this changing definition? Have any individuals, lobby groups, or professions been involved in changing the definition of the behaviour?

2. Many people engage in actions that violate the law at some time in their lives. How would the different explanations of deviance discussed in this chapter explain your rule-violating behaviour? Which explanation appears most consistent with your experience and why?

3. Where do you get your information about crime? How do you think these sources of information shape your view of what crime is and what should be done about it?

GLOSSARY

Anomie, according to Merton, is a social condition in which there is a gap between the cultural goals people are taught to aspire to and the social structural means available to achieve those goals.

Control theories of deviance are explanations that emphasize the factors that prevent people from acting on deviant impulses.

The **crime-control model** is a model of the criminal process that emphasizes reducing crime and protecting society by granting legal officials broad powers.

Differential association is the process by which people learn deviance through exposure to more definitions favourable to deviance than definitions unfavourable to deviance.

The **due-process model** is a model of the criminal process that emphasizes the protection of the legal rights of the accused to ensure that justice is done.

Innovation is Merton's term for the type of adaptation to strain that involves seeking illegitimate means to achieve legitimate goals; it encompasses most types of money-making crimes.

The **labelling perspective** is a perspective on deviance that argues that rule making and rule enforcement—in other words, the definitions of and reactions to deviance—are often important causes of deviance.

Learning theories of deviance are explanations that emphasize that deviance is learned in the same fashion that conformity is learned—that is, by exposure to values, norms, and beliefs that, in the case of deviance, support unconventional behaviour.

Master status is a status that stands out above all others. Deviance is often a master status, overshadowing other statuses in the eyes of people who interact with the deviant.

A **maximum-security society** is a society characterized by growing importance of softer processes of social control that control at a distance, with technology, and with less human contact.

The **medical model of deviance** is the view that many forms of deviance are indications of physical or mental illness and therefore deserve treatment rather than punishment.

A **moral crusade** is an organized campaign to discredit an activity or group of people so that it becomes viewed as deviant and deserving of stigma.

Motivational theories of deviance are explanations that emphasize the factors that push or encourage people toward deviant behaviour.

Opportunity theories of deviance are theories that argue that, in the absence of social control, people's choices of deviant or criminal acts will depend on the deviant opportunities available to them.

Primary deviance is deviance that occurs for any of a variety of reasons, but which does not lead one to be labelled a deviant or to see oneself as a deviant.

Restorative justice is a response to crime that views it as not just injurious to a victim, but as affecting communities and offenders, and therefore involves all three parties in dealing with a crime.

Secondary deviance is deviance that occurs after one has been labelled a deviant and starts to view oneself as a deviant.

Social control refers to the various means members of society use to encourage conformity to norms and to punish violations of norms.

The **status-conflict perspective** is a perspective that argues that definitions of deviance emerge from struggles between different interest groups that compete for status, influence, and moral authority.

Strain theory is a theory that argues that people are pressured to deviate by the incompatible demands of cultural goals and social structural opportunities.

Subcultures are groups whose beliefs, values, and norms conflict with those of the wider or dominant culture, and, as a consequence, are defined by that wider culture as deviant.

White-collar crime, a term coined by Edwin Sutherland in 1939, refers to acts committed for personal profit or gain during everyday business life by people in positions of authority, with professional status, or possessing specialized skills.

SUGGESTED READING

Garland, David. (2001). *The Culture of Control: Crime and Social Order in Contemporary Society.* Chicago: University of Chicago Press. Responses to crime and criminal justice have changed dramatically in the last 30 years: more gated communities, zero-tolerance policies, racial profiling, community policing. Garland explains how the character of modern life—not just crime—is responsible for these changes.

Goode, Erich, and Nachman Ben-Yehuda. (1995). *Moral Panics: The Social Construction of Deviance.* Oxford: Blackwell Publishers Limited. To illustrate the ways in which deviance is created through social reactions, the authors focus on moral panics and discuss how this concept applies to the Renaissance witch craze as well as to drug panics in the United States and Israel in the 1980s.

Hagan, John, and Bill McCarthy. (1998). *Mean Streets: Youth Crime and Homelessness.* Cambridge: Cambridge University Press. Based on interviews and surveys from more than 400 young people living on the streets of Toronto and Vancouver, this field study looks at why youth take to the streets, how they survive once there, their experiences of victimization and offending, and their efforts to leave the street.

Roberts, Julian V., ed. (2000). *Criminal Justice in Canada: A Reader.* Toronto: Harcourt Brace. This collection presents readings on policing, the courts, corrections, and youth justice, as well as such timely topics as discrimination in the criminal justice system, gun control, and criminal justice responses to wife battering.

Silverman, Robert A., James J. Teevan, and Vincent D. Sacco, eds. (2000). *Crime in Canadian Society.* Toronto: Harcourt Brace. An overview of Canadian criminology, with sections on defining and measuring crime, theories of crime, and recent research on patterns of crime in Canada. Current topical issues, such as collecting crime statistics by race, the battered wife defence, and crime and immigration, are covered in separate chapters.

CHAPTER TWENTY

POLITICS AND SOCIAL MOVEMENTS

In this chapter you will learn that:

- The level of democracy in a society depends on the capacity of citizens to influence the state through their support of political parties, social movements, and other groups. That capacity increases as power becomes more widely distributed in society.

- The degree to which power is widely distributed influences the success of particular kinds of parties and policies.

- People sometimes riot, strike, and take other forms of collective action to correct perceived injustices. When they do so they are participating in social movements.

- People are more inclined to rebel against the status quo when they are bound by close social ties to other people who feel similarly wronged and when they have the money and other resources needed to protest.

- In order for social movements to grow, members must make the activities, ideas, and goals of the movement congruent with the interests, beliefs, and values of potential new recruits.

- The history of democracy is a struggle for the acquisition of constantly broadening citizenship rights.

ROBERT J. BRYM

UNIVERSITY OF TORONTO

INTRODUCTION

I almost caused a small riot once. It happened in Grade 11, shortly after I learned that water combined with sulphur dioxide produces sulphurous acid. The news shocked me. To understand why, you have to know where I lived: in Saint John, New Brunswick, about 100 metres downwind of one of the larger pulp and paper mills in Canada. Acrid waves of sulphur dioxide billowed day and night from the mill's imposing smokestacks. The town's pervasive rotten-egg smell was a longstanding complaint in the area. But, for me, disgust turned to upset when I realized the fumes were toxic. Suddenly it was clear why many people I knew—especially people living near the mill—woke up in the morning with a kind of "smoker's cough." By the simple act of breathing we were causing the gas to mix with the moisture in our bodies and form an acid that our lungs tried to expunge, with only partial success.

Twenty years later, I read the results of a medical research report showing that area residents suffer from rates of lung disease, including emphysema and lung cancer, significantly above the national average. However, even in 1968 it was evident a serious problem was brewing in my hometown. I therefore hatched a plan. Our high school was about to hold its annual model parliament. The event was notoriously boring, partly because, year in, year out, virtually everyone voted for the same party, the Conservatives. But here was an issue, I thought, that could turn things around. The pulp and paper mill was owned by K.C. Irving, an industrialist so powerful that his companies were said to control 40 percent of New Brunswick's economic output. *Forbes* magazine in the United States annually ranked Irving among the wealthiest men in the world. I figured that once I told my fellow students the political implications of the fact that water combined with sulphur dioxide produces sulphurous acid, they would quickly demand the closure of the mill until Irving guaranteed a clean operation.

Was *I* naïve. As head of the tiny Liberal Party, I had to address the entire student body during assembly on election day to outline the party platform and mobilize votes. When I got to the part of my speech explaining why K.C. Irving was our enemy, the murmuring in the audience, which had been growing like the sound of a hungry animal about to pounce on its prey, erupted into loud "boos." A couple of students rushed the stage. The principal suddenly appeared from the wings and commanded the student body to settle down. He then took me by the arm and informed me that, for my own safety, my speech was finished. So, I discovered on election day, was our high school's Liberal Party. And so, it emerged, was my high school political career.

This incident troubled me for many years, less because of the embarrassment it caused me than the puzzles it presented. Why did I almost cause a small riot? Why didn't my fellow students rebel in the way I thought they would? Why did they continue to support an arrangement that was enriching one man at the cost of a community's health? Why weren't they enraged? Couldn't they see the injustice? Other people did. Nineteen sixty-eight was not just the year of my political failure at Saint John High School. It was also the year that student riots in France nearly

Karl Marx predicted that capitalism would drive business owners into bankruptcy and peasants into the cities. Marx thought that in the cities huge masses of workers would become class-conscious and solidarity would be born.

SOURCE: Diego M. Rivera, *Parade in Moscow* (1956). 135.2 x 108.3 cm. Collection Banco National de Mexico, Mexico City. Reproduced with permission of the bank.

caused the fall of the government of Charles de Gaulle. It was the year in which the suppression of student strikes by the Mexican government left dozens of students dead. It was the year in which American students at Berkeley, Michigan, and other universities fought with unprecedented vigour for free speech on their campuses, an end to American involvement in the war in Vietnam, increased civil rights for American Blacks, and an expanded role for women in public affairs.

I didn't know it at the time, but by asking why students in Paris, Mexico City, and Berkeley rebelled while my fellow-students did not, I was raising the main question that animates the sociological study of politics and social movements. Why are some groups more successful than others in formulating their demands and getting them carried out? In other words, who gets what and under what social circumstances? That is the main issue addressed by this chapter.

Group power is the ability of a group to impose its will on others, even if they resist (Weber, 1946 [1922]: 180). In the first section of this chapter, you will learn that the power of a group may be widely recognized as legitimate or valid under some circumstances. If it is, raw **power** becomes legitimate **authority** (see Box 20.1). The people who occupy the command posts of institutions are then generally seen as **authorities**. Under other circumstances, however, power flows to nonauthorities. This undermines the legitimacy of authority. In this case, nonauthorities

form **social movements**, or collective attempts to change part or all of the social order. They may riot, petition, strike, demonstrate, and establish pressure groups, unions, and **political parties** in order to achieve their aims.

The terms defined above allow us to distinguish between "normal politics" and "politics beyond the rules." Normal politics is politics as it is practised when authorities are firmly in power. Politics beyond the rules is politics as it is practised when the legitimacy of authority grows weak. Sociologists have proposed various theories to explain the two types of politics. In the second and third sections of this chapter, we evaluate these theories using Canadian, Swedish, and American data.

Finally, in the chapter's concluding section, we place our discussion in historical context. How has politics developed over the past 300 years? What developments can we reasonably expect in the near future? This section will help you better to understand your political options in coming years.

POWER FROM ABOVE: NORMAL POLITICS

In 1998, the RCMP used pepper spray to disperse Vancouver crows demonstrating against visiting Indonesian President Suharto. The incident caused a scandal because it was widely seen as excessive use of force sanctioned by the prime minister. The solicitor

---

BOX 20.1 THREE BASES OF AUTHORITY

Max Weber (1947) argued that authority can have one of three bases:

1. *Traditional authority.* Particularly in tribal and feudal societies, rulers inherit authority through family or clan ties. In such circumstances, people believe the right of a family or clan to monopolize leadership derives from God's will.
2. *Legal-rational authority.* In modern societies, authority derives from respect for the law. Laws specify how one can achieve office. People generally believe these laws are rational. If someone achieves office by following these laws, their authority is respected.
3. *Charismatic authority.* Sometimes, extraordinary, charismatic individuals challenge traditional or legal-rational authority. They claim to be inspired by God or some higher principle that transcends traditional authority, such as the principle that all people are created equal. Their claim is widely believed.

Charismatic figures often emerge during a **political revolution**, a concerted attempt by many people to overthrow political institutions and establish new ones. Political revolutions take place when widespread and successful movements of opposition clash with crumbling traditional or legal-rational authority (Skocpol, 1979).

general, who is responsible for the RCMP, was forced to resign over the incident.

This incident illustrates the use of **force** or coercive power by authorities. Paradoxically, the use of force by authorities is a sign of their weakness. For if authorities are truly in a position of strength, their rule will be widely recognized as legitimate. They will not need to use force to impose their will because most people agree with their policies. Here, politics will be routine, nonviolent, or "normal." To be sure, minor outbursts of violence occur even under normal politics. However, such events are unusual in Canada today. They rarely result in fatalities. For the most part, Canadian politics today is normal politics.

Power is exercised in all social settings, from the family to the classroom to the workplace. However, the ultimate seat of power in society is the state. The **state** is a set of institutions that formulate and carry out a country's laws, policies and binding regulations. Why is the state's power "ultimate?" Because its authority stands above all others, and if the state needs to use force to maintain order or protect its borders, most people will regard its actions as legitimate.

In democratic countries such as Canada, the government is formed by the elected members of the political party that wins most seats in a general election (see Figure 20.1). It is composed of the head of the party, who becomes prime minister, and the cabinet ministers that the prime minister selects to advise him or her. It is the job of the government to initiate policies, propose laws, and see that they are enforced. That is why the government is also called the *executive* branch of the state. Proposed laws are turned into operating statutes by the *legislature*, which consists of all the people elected to parliament. It is the responsibility of the *judiciary* or court system to interpret laws and regulations, that is, to figure out whether and how particular laws and regulations apply in disputed cases. The state's *administrative apparatus* or *bureaucracy* undertakes enforcement of laws. If laws are broken or the state's security is jeopardized, it is the role of the *coercive apparatus*—the police and military—to enforce the law and protect the state.

The state, then, is a set of institutions that exercise control over society. However, individuals in **civil society**, the private sphere of life, also exercise

FIGURE 20.1 THE INSTITUTIONS OF STATE AND CIVIL SOCIETY

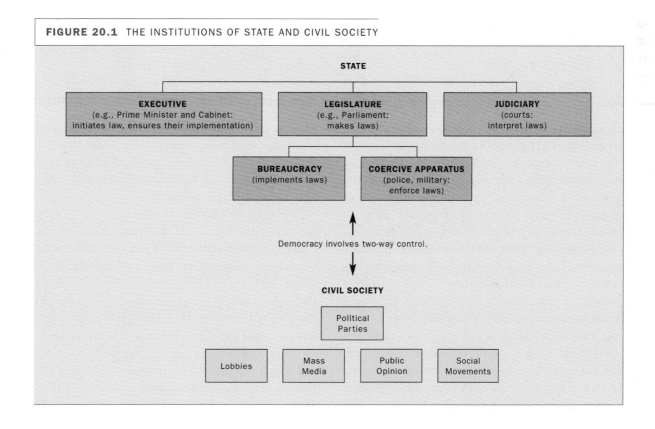

control over the state through a variety of organizations and institutions. We have already noted how social movements may influence the state. In addition, the mass media keep a watchful and critical eye on the state and help keep the public informed about the quality of government. Pressure groups or "lobbies" are formed by trade unions, manufacturers' associations, ethnic groups, and other organizations to advise politicians of their members' desires. Lobbies also remind politicians how much their members' votes and campaign contributions matter. And political parties regularly seek to mobilize voters as they compete for control of government.

But how democratic is the Canadian state? Does the interaction between state and civil society ensure that every citizen has a roughly equal say in the determination of laws and policies? Or, as George Orwell asked in *Animal Farm*, are some citizens more equal than others? Do we, as Abraham Lincoln claimed for the Americans, enjoy "government of the people, by the people, for the people?" Or is it more accurate to say, in the words of one wit, that we are subjected to "government of the people, by the lawyers, for the business owners"? These are among the chief questions asked by sociologists who study the state and its operations. It is now time to consider them in greater detail.

PLURALIST THEORY

Pluralist theory is one interpretation of the relationship between state and civil society (Polsby, 1959; Dahl, 1961). According to pluralists, we live in a heterogeneous society with many competing interests and centres of power. For example, the interests of parents with school-age children may differ from the interests of pensioners. Parents may want school budgets to grow. Pensioners may want them to shrink. Due to such heterogeneity, no one group can control politics, according to the pluralists. They argue that, over time, all voters and interest groups influence the political process almost equally. Sometimes one category of voters wins a political battle, sometimes another. Most often, however, politics involves negotiation and compromise between competing groups. According to the pluralists, because no one group of people is always able to control the political agenda or the outcome of political conflict, democracy is guaranteed.

ELITE THEORY

Elite theorists, C. Wright Mills (1956) foremost among them, sharply disagree with the pluralist account. *Elites* are small groups that occupy the command posts of a society's institutions. In the United States, the country that Mills studied, the most powerful elites are the people who run the country's two or three hundred biggest corporations, the executive branch of government, and the military. Mills wrote that the men who control these institutions (they are rarely women) make the important decisions that profoundly affect all members of society. Moreover, they do so without much regard for elections or public opinion.

Mills showed how the corporate, state, and military elites are interconnected. Personnel move from one elite to another over their careers. Their children intermarry. They maintain intimate social contacts on a day-to-day basis. They tend to be recruited from the upper-middle and upper classes. However, Mills denied that these similarities and interconnections turn the three elites into a *ruling class*, that is, a self-conscious and cohesive group of people, led by corporate executives, who act to advance their common interests. The three elites are independent of each other, Mills insisted. They may see eye-to-eye on many issues, but each has its own jealously guarded sphere of influence, and conflict between elite groups is therefore frequent (Mills, 1956: 277).

THE ELITIST CRITIQUE OF PLURALISM

Most political sociologists today question the pluralist account of democratic politics. That is because research has established the existence of large, persistent, wealth-based inequalities in political influence and political participation.

John Porter's classic, *The Vertical Mosaic* (1965), was the first in a series of Canadian studies that demonstrate the weaknesses of pluralism and corroborate some aspects of elite theory (Clement, 1975; Olsen, 1980; Brym, 1989). These studies show that a disproportionately large number of people in Canada's political and other elites come from upper- and upper-middle-class families. For example, about 40 percent of Canadian prime ministers, premiers, and cabinet ministers were born into the richest 10 percent of families in the country (Olsen, 1980: 129). In their youth, members of Canada's elites are likely to have attended expensive private schools. As adults, they tend to marry the offspring of other elite members and belong to exclusive private clubs. In the course of their careers, they often move from one elite to another. Arguably, people with this sort of background cannot act dispassionately on behalf of all Canadians, rich and poor.

Controversy persists over whether Canada's elites form a ruling class. Porter (1965), noting frequent conflict among elites, argued against the view that a ruling class controls Canada. His top students disagreed. They argued that the interests of large corporations dominate Canadian political life (Clement, 1975; Olsen, 1980). However, both Porter and his students did agree on one point: contrary to pluralist claims, Canada's well-to-do consistently exercise disproportionate influence over political life in this country.

Studies of political participation in Canada add weight to the elitist view (Blais et al., 1997; Frank, 1992; Mishler, 1979: 88–97). Many surveys show that political involvement decreases with social class. For example, the likelihood of voting falls with a person's class position. The likelihood of phoning or writing a member of Parliament, helping a candidate in an election campaign, contributing money to a political party, and running for office declines even more steeply as one moves down the class hierarchy (see Table 20.1). As intensity of political participation declines, so does political influence. Consequently, although political apathy and cynicism are high among Canadians, the poorest Canadians are the most politically apathetic and cynical. They have less interest in politics than the well-to-do, and they are more likely to think that government does not care

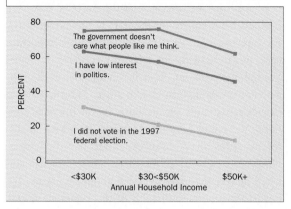

FIGURE 20.2 POLITICAL APATHY AND CYNICISM, BY ANNUAL HOUSEHOLD INCOME, CANADA, 1997

SOURCE: André Blais, Elisabeth Gidengil, Richard Nadeau, and Neil Nevitte. (1997). *1997 Canadian Election Survey*. Computer file on the World Wide Web at http://prod.library.utoronto.ca/datalib/codebooks/utm/elections/1997/ (1 December 1998).

what they think (see Figure 20.2). As one of the world's leading political sociologists writes: "The combination of a low vote and a relative lack of organization among the lower-status groups means that they will suffer from neglect by the politicians who will be receptive to the wishes of the more privileged, participating, and organized strata" (Lipset, 1981 [1960]: 226–27).

THE MARXIST CRITIQUE OF ELITE THEORY

Although compelling in some respects, elite theory has its critics, Marxists foremost among them. Some Marxists, known as "instrumentalists," deny that elites enjoy more or less equal power. Actually, they

TABLE 20.1   FEDERAL POLITICAL CONTRIBUTORS PER 10 000 TAX FILERS, BY INCOME AND REGION

ANNUAL INCOME	ATLANTIC	QUEBEC	ONTARIO	WEST	CANADA
Less than $25 000	21	17	34	80	42
$25 000–$50 000	126	73	126	253	150
$50 000–$75 000	429	242	304	467	353
$75 000+	1149	679	790	964	830

SOURCE: Based on Jeffrey Frank, "Voting and Contributing: Political Participation in Canada," *Canadian Social Trends*, Vol. 2 (Toronto: Thompson Educational Publishing, Inc., 1994), p. 337.

say, elites form a ruling class dominated by big business. From their point of view, the state, for example, is an arm (or "instrument") of the business elite. Big business gains control of the state in three main ways. First, members of wealthy families occupy important state positions in highly disproportionate numbers. Second, government officials rely mainly on the representatives of big business for advice. Third, political parties rely mainly on big business for financial support. According to some Marxists, members of different elites may disagree about specific issues. However, as a result of the three control mechanisms listed above, they always agree about one issue: the need to maintain the health of the capitalist system (Miliband, 1973 [1969]).

A second group of Marxists, known as "structuralists," offers a somewhat different interpretation of why the state in capitalist society is necessarily biased in favour of big business. For the structuralists, it is not so much the *social origins* of high government officials or the *social ties* linking them with big business that encourages the state to act with a pro-capitalist bias. Rather, they argue, the capitalist state acts as an arm of big business because it is constrained to do so by *the nature of the capitalist system itself*. For example, if the Canadian government doubled the corporate tax rate, investment would be redirected to countries with regimes that are kinder to company profits. Such a move would cost Canada jobs and prosperity. It would be highly unpopular. The government could easily fall. Fearing this outcome, governments in capitalist societies find their field of action restricted to policies that ensure the well-being of big business. According to the structuralists, it is the very fact that the state is embedded in a capitalist system that forces it to act in this way (Poulantzas, 1975 [1968]).

It follows from both the instrumentalist and structuralist positions that ordinary citizens, and especially members of the working class, rarely have much influence over state policy. According to Marxists, true democracy can emerge only if members of the working class and their supporters overthrow capitalism and establish a socialist system marked in which economic differences between people are eliminated or at least substantially reduced.

POWER-BALANCE THEORY

Pluralists assume that all major groups in society enjoy approximately equal power. Elitists assume that members of the upper class enjoy most power. Both approaches, however, assume that the distribution of power in society does not change much over time.

In contrast, **power-balance theorists** argue that the distribution of power in society does change, sometimes massively. They admit that power is usually concentrated in the hands of the wealthy. However, they also note that other classes sometimes gain power. This has big implications for political life. Among other things, the distribution of power determines how democratic a society is.

To make their case, power-balance theorists first measure variations in the social distribution of power. They then show how those variations are reflected in the successes and failures of different political parties and the rejection and adoption of different state policies. Along with the pluralists, they recognize that society is truly democratic only when power is widely distributed. Along with the elitists, they recognize that society is not very democratic when power is highly concentrated in the hands of a few wealthy citizens. However, by treating the distribution of power as a variable, they improve our understanding of the relationship between power and democracy.

We can better understand power-balance theory by examining Canadian politics in comparative perspective. We first note that a group's power is partly determined by the degree to which it forms organizations to further its interests. For example, unionized blue-collar and white-collar workers are more powerful than their non-unionized counterparts. That is because unions allow workers to speak with one voice. Unions enable workers to effectively bargain with employers and governments for improved wages, working conditions, and social policies. Moreover, if bargaining fails, they can go out on strike to force the issue.

If level of unionization increases working-class power, this should be reflected in the political behaviour of citizens and the policies adopted by governments. And, in fact, it is. Compare Sweden and Canada, for example (Casper, McLanahan and

The peak year of strike activity in Canada was 1919. In that year, 17.3 strikes took place for every 100 000 non-agricultural workers in the country. This photo was taken on "Bloody Saturday," June 21, 1919, during the Winnipeg General Strike. It shows a violent confrontation between rioters and Mounties and special police.

SOURCE: David Miller Collection/National Archives of Canada/C-33392.

Garfinkle, 1994; Korpi, 1983; Myles, 1989 [1984]; O'Connor, 1996; O'Connor and Brym, 1988; O'Connor and Olsen, 1998; Olsen and Brym, 1996; Olsen, 2002). In Sweden, over three-quarters of blue- and white-collar workers are union members. In Canada, only about a third of workers are members of unions. Several consequences follow:

- About 85 percent of Swedish citizens vote in federal elections, compared to about 65 percent in Canada. That is mainly because working-class Swedes are more likely to vote than working-class Canadians.
- The Swedish socialist party has formed the government almost continuously since World War II. In contrast, Canada's socialist party, the NDP, has never formed the federal government or even

had a representative in the federal cabinet. The parties that have formed Canada's federal governments (Liberals and Progressive Conservatives) are those that are most strongly supported by business (see Figure 20.3).

- Swedish governments have acted more vigorously than Canadian governments to eradicate poverty and equalize incomes. Thus, fewer than 4 percent of Swedes are classified as living below the poverty line. The comparable figure for Canadians is about 15 percent. In Sweden, about 20 percent of all income goes to the top 10 percent of income earners. The comparable figure for Canada is about 30 percent. And in Sweden, a broader range of retired people receive more generous pensions and more frequent cost-of-living adjustments than pensioners in Canada.

- Since women are disproportionately concentrated in low-income, low-status jobs (see Chapter 9), they benefit more than men where the working class is more powerful. As a result, the ratio of women's to men's earnings is about 80 percent in Sweden and 67 percent in Canada. Moreover, in Sweden, the ratio of women to men who live below the poverty line is just above 90 percent, while in Canada the comparable figure is nearly 130 percent. Finally, parental benefits are superior in Sweden and child-care facilities are more widely available and affordable.

We thus see that elections matter a great deal in the lives of ordinary people. Elections determine the types of parties that get elected. Elected parties, in turn, shape government policies. The outcome of any *particular* election depends on the appeal of party leaders, their effectiveness in presenting issues to the public, and myriad other short-term factors (Clarke et al., 1996; see Figure 20.4). But considering the *types* of parties that get elected *over several decades*, as we did above, we see that the distribution of power between classes and other groups shapes the character of politics in a country.

The preceding analysis also implies that Sweden is more democratic than Canada. True, citizens of both countries are legally free to vote and influence their governments. But because the working class is more powerful in Sweden, Swedes' legal right to vote and influence governments has been turned into real political influence on a wider scale. In general, only if more citizens wield more clout can society become more democratic (see Box 20.2).

STATE-CENTRED THEORY

Power-balance theory suggests that democratic politics is a contest among various classes and other groups to control the state for their own advantage. When power is substantially redistributed—when, for example, a major class gets better organized while another major class becomes less socially organized— old ruling parties usually fall and new ones take office.

Note, however, that a winner-take-all strategy would be nothing short of foolish. If winning parties monopolized the spoils of office, passing laws that benefit only their supporters, they might cause massive outrage and even violent opposition. Yet allowing opponents to become angry, organized, and resolute would be counterproductive. After all, winners want more than just a moment of glory. They want to be able to enjoy the spoils of office in a stable political environment over the long haul. To achieve such stability, it is crucial that people who *lose* elections are given a say in government. To a degree, the party in

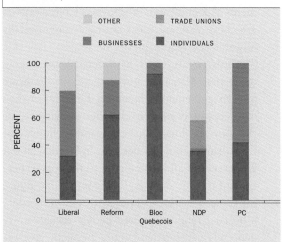

FIGURE 20.3 CONTRIBUTIONS TO FEDERAL POLITICAL PARTIES, 1997, BY SOURCE (IN PERCENT)

SOURCE: Elections Canada On-Line (2000). "Registered Political Parties' Fiscal Period Returns for 1997." On the World Wide Web at http://www.elections.ca/content.asp?section=fin&document=table03&dir=fis&lang=e&textonly=false (30 July 2002).

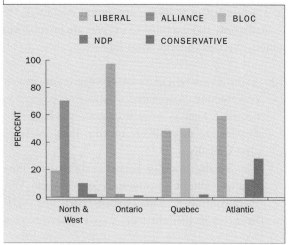

FIGURE 20.4 RESULTS OF CANADIAN FEDERAL ELECTION, 2000, BY REGION (IN PERCENT)

SOURCE: "The Federal Election" (2000).

BOX 20.2 ELECTRONIC DEMOCRACY

Recently, some analysts have proposed a technical means for making democracy more widespread. They say that computers linked to the World Wide Web could allow citizens to debate issues and vote on them directly. This would give politicians mass feedback and clear signals on how they should conduct public policy. Accordingly, in an era of low and declining political participation, computers can reinvigorate and even save democracy, making public opinion the law of the land (Westen, 1998).

The evidence does not support these claims. Already by the mid-1980s, more than a dozen experiments had been conducted on electronic public meetings. In a comprehensive review of those experiments, one researcher showed that even in the most successful of them, participation was extremely low. He concluded that, even if the technology needed for such meetings were universally available, citizen interest is so limited that no more than a third of the population would participate (Arterton, 1987).

Subsequent experience with the World Wide Web bears out this conclusion and allows us to qualify it. The people who are most likely to take advantage of electronic democracy are those who have access to large computer networks. Such people form a privileged and politically involved group that is far from representative of the adult population. That is apparent from Table 20.2, which contains data from the most respected ongoing survey of World Wide Web users. The results show that, compared to the general population, Web users are younger, better educated, wealthier, and contain a higher proportion of men, whites, and people in occupations requiring substantial computer use. Thus, if electronic democracy becomes widespread, it will probably reinforce the same inequalities in political participation that plague democracy today. It is less likely to reinvigorate democracy than it is to help form a digital divide.

TABLE 20.2 THE DIGITAL DIVIDE: SOCIAL CHARACTERISTICS OF WORLD WIDE WEB USERS, CANADA AND INTERNATIONALLY, 1998

	PERCENT OF HOUSEHOLDS
Canada (N = 38 030 Households)	
Percent of households in top income quartile with Internet access at home	45.1
Percent of households in bottom income quartile with Internet access at home	7.1
Percent of households in top income quartile with Internet access at work	50.4
Percent of households in bottom income quartile with Internet access at work	4.1
Percent of households with Internet access at home, head of household with university degree	46.7
Percent of households with Internet access at home, head of household without high school diploma	6.6
Percent of households in Canada's 15 largest Census Metropolitan Areas with Internet access at home	40.4
Percent of households outside Canada's 15 largest Census Metropolitan Areas with Internet access at home	30.1
Percent of households with head of household age 35–54 regularly using Internet	30.1
Percent of households with head of household age 65+ regularly using Internet	5.3
International (N = 5 022 Individuals)	
Under 41 years old	59.6
Completed college or higher	70.2
Annual household income CAD$75 000+	46.9

Note: The Canadian data come from a survey of a representative sample of households conducted by Statistics Canada (Dickinson and Ellison, 1999). A 2000 survey found that 42 percent of Canadians had never used the Internet and another 10 percent used it rarely. These 52 percent of Canadians tend to be elderly, have low incomes, and have no postsecondary education (Crompton, Ellison and Stevenson, 2002). The international data come from an online survey of Web users ("GVU's...," 1999). In the latter, about 4 percent of respondents were from Canada, 7 percent from Europe, and 85 percent from the U.S. People learned about the survey on the Web and volunteered to participate in it. This produces sample bias. Respondents tend to be experienced and skilled Web users. However, comparing these results with survey results based on random samples suggests that the international figures reported here are accurate (Hoffman and Novak, 1998: 390–91).

power must attend to the wants of losing minorities. That way, even determined opponents are likely to recognize the legitimacy of the government, its right to rule. Pluralists thus make a good point when they say that democratic politics is about accommodation and compromise; they only lose sight of the fact that accommodation and compromise typically give more advantages to some than others, as both elite theorists and power-balance theorists stress.

However, there is more to the story of politics than conflict between classes and other groups. Theda Skocpol and other **state-centred theorists** have shown how the state itself can structure political life independently of the way power is distributed among classes and other groups at a given point in time (Block, 1979; Skocpol, 1979; Evans, Rueschemeyer, and Skocpol, 1985). Their argument is a valuable supplement to power-balance theory.

To illustrate how state structures shape politics, consider the problem of nonvoting in the United States. Below 55 percent of American citizens have voted in recent presidential elections. With the exception of Switzerland, the United States has the lowest voter turnout of any democracy in the world (Piven and Cloward, 1989 [1988]: 5). How can we explain this?

The high rate of nonvoting is largely a product of voter registration law—a feature of the American political structure, not of the current distribution of power. In every democracy, laws specify voter registration procedures. In some countries, such as France, citizens are registered to vote automatically once they receive state-issued identity cards at the age of 18. In other countries, such as Canada, state-employed canvassers go door-to-door before each election to register voters. Only in the United States do individual citizens have to take the initiative to go out and register themselves in voter registration centres. Yet many American citizens are unable or unwilling to register. As a result, the U.S. has a proportionately smaller pool of eligible voters than the other democracies. Only about 65 percent of American citizens are registered to vote (Piven and Cloward, 1989 [1988]: 256–59).

Apart from shrinking the pool of eligible voters, American voter registration law has a second important consequence. Because some *types* of people are less able and inclined than others to register, a strong bias is introduced into the political system. Specifically, the poor are less likely to register than the better-off. People without much formal education are less likely to register than the better educated. Members of disadvantaged racial minority groups, especially African Americans, are less likely to register than whites. Thus, American voter registration law is a pathway to democracy for some, but a barrier to democracy for others. In short, the American political system is less responsive than other rich democracies to the needs of the disadvantaged. That is partly because, as state-centred theory suggests, the law requires citizen-initiated voter registration. As a result, many disadvantaged people are effectively disenfranchised.[1]

Big shocks sometimes rock state structures. In general, however, they are resistant to change. The foundations of state structures are anchored by constitutions, which can be altered only by large majorities of federally elected representatives and state- or provincial-level legislatures. Their upper stories are girded by laws, regulations, and policies, some of which help to keep potentially disruptive social forces at bay.[2] American voter registration law is a case in point. And then there are the many ideological reinforcements. All states create anthems, flags, ceremonies, celebrations, sporting events, and school curricula that stimulate patriotism and serve in part to justify existing political arrangements.

In sum, each of the schools of thought reviewed above makes a useful contribution to our appreciation of normal democratic politics (see Table 20.3). Pluralists teach us that normal democratic politics is about compromise and the accommodation of all group interests. Elite theorists teach us that, despite compromise and accommodation, power is concentrated in the hands of higher-status groups, whose interests the political system therefore serves best. Power-balance theorists teach us that, despite the concentration of power in society, substantial shifts in the distribution of power do occur, and they have discernible effects on voting patterns and public policies. And state-centred theorists teach us that, despite the influence of the distribution of power on political life, state structures exert an important independent effect on politics too.

TABLE 20.3 FIVE SOCIOLOGICAL THEORIES OF DEMOCRACY COMPARED

	PLURALIST	ELITE	MARXIST	POWER-BALANCE	STATE-CENTRED
How is power distributed?	dispersed	concentrated	concentrated	concentrated	concentrated
Who are the main power holders?	various groups	elites	ruling class	upper class	state officials
On what is their power based?	holding political office	controlling major institutions	owning substantial capital	owning substantial capital	holding political office
What is the main basis of public policy?	the will of all citizens	the interests of major elites	capitalist interests	the balance of power between classes, etc.	the influence of state structures
Do lower classes have much influence on politics?	yes	no	rarely	sometimes	sometimes

POWER FROM BELOW: POLITICS BEYOND THE RULES

RELATIVE-DEPRIVATION THEORY

All five theories of democracy reviewed above focus on normal politics. However, we know that sometimes politics is anything but normal. Routine political processes can break down. Social movements can form. Large-scale political violence can erupt. As Vladimir Lenin, the leader of the Russian revolution of 1917, said, people sometimes "vote with their feet."

Until about 1970, many sociologists argued that social movements tend to emerge when people experience **relative deprivation**. People feel relatively deprived when they experience an intolerable gap between the social rewards they think they deserve and the social rewards they expect to receive. Social rewards are widely valued goods, including money, education, security, prestige, and so on. Accordingly, people are most likely to rebel against authority when rising expectations (brought on by, say, rapid economic growth and migration) are met by a sudden decline in social rewards (due to, say, economic recession or war) (Davies, 1969). In addition, until about 1970, many sociologists held that the people who lead and first join social movements are likely to be "outsiders" who lack strong social ties to their communities.

A large body of research has now discredited these ideas. For example, we now know that the leaders and early joiners of social movements are usually well-integrated members of their communities, not socially marginal newcomers. Thus, in the 1930s, Saskatchewan farmers and workers formed the Cooperative Commonwealth Federation (CCF) to protest federal government policy toward the West in general and Western agriculture in particular. The movement's leaders and early recruits were not outsiders. The workers were mainly local trade union activists. The farmers had been involved in the establishment of community-owned retail stores, credit unions, and marketing cooperatives (Lipset, 1971 [1951]).

Much research also calls into question the idea that relative deprivation leads to the formation of social movements. For example, sociologists have compared measures of relative deprivation with the frequency of demonstrations, strikes, and acts of collective violence in France, Italy, Germany, and England. They have found that, in general, outbreaks of collective unrest do not increase with mounting relative deprivation (Lodhi and Tilly, 1973; Snyder and Tilly, 1972; Tilly, 1979a; Tilly, Tilly, and Tilly, 1975).

RESOURCE-MOBILIZATION THEORY

Because of the inadequacies of relative-deprivation theory noted above, an alternative approach to the study of social movements has gained popularity over the past 30 years. **Resource-mobilization theory** is based on the idea that social movements can emerge only when disadvantaged people can marshal the means necessary to challenge authority (Jenkins, 1983; McCarthy and Zald, 1977; Obserschall, 1973; Tilly, 1978). Foremost among the resources they need to challenge authority is the capacity to forge strong social ties among themselves. Other important resources that allow disadvantaged people to challenge authority include jobs, money, arms, and access to means of spreading their ideas.

You can appreciate the significance of resource mobilization theory by considering patterns of strike activity in Canada. When blue-collar and white-collar workers go out on strike, they are withholding their labour to extract concessions from employers or governments in the form of higher wages and improved social welfare benefits. When are workers most inclined to challenge the authority of employers and governments in this way? Research shows that in Canada since World War II, strike activity has been high when (a) unemployment is low, (b) union membership is high, and (c) governments have shown themselves to be generous in their provision of social welfare benefits. Low unemployment indicates a strong economy. Workers are inclined to strike when business activity is robust because they know employers and governments can afford to make concessions. (Employers make bigger profits and governments collect more taxes during economic booms.) A high level of unionization is also conducive to more strike activity because unions provide workers with leadership, strike funds, and coordination. Thus, as resource mobilization theory predicts, strong social ties among workers (as indicated by a high level of

unionization) and access to jobs and money (as indicated by a booming economy) increase challenges to authority (as indicated by strikes).[3]

Figure 20.5 shows the pattern of strike activity in post-World War II Canada. It supports the arguments of resource mobilization theory. Thus, until 1974, the trend in strike activity was upward. (In the 1970s, Canada was in fact the most strike-prone country in the world.) This was a period of growing prosperity, low unemployment, expanding state benefits, and increasing unionization. With access to increasing organizational and material resources, workers challenged authority increasingly more often in the three decades after World War II. In 1973, however, economic crisis struck. Oil prices tripled, and then tripled again at the end of the decade. Inflation increased and unemployment rose. Soon, the government was strapped for funds and had to borrow heavily to maintain social welfare programs. Eventually, the debt burden was so heavy that the government felt obliged to cut various social welfare programs. Unionization reached a peak in 1978, stabilized, and then began to fall (see Figure 20.6). Thus, in the post-1973, climate, the organizational and material resources of workers fell. As a result, strike activity plummeted. In 1974, nearly 16 strikes took place for every 100 000 Canadian workers. By 2000, that figure had fallen to 3 (Brym, 2003).

FRAMING DISCONTENT

As you have seen, resource mobilization theory is a useful approach to the study of social movements. Even so, the emergence of a social movement sometimes takes sociologists by surprise. In addition, the failure of an aggrieved group to press its claim is sometimes equally unexpected. And movements that do emerge are successful to varying degrees. It seems, therefore, that something lies between (a) the capacity of disadvantaged people to mobilize resources for collective action and (b) the recruitment of a substantial number of movement members. Sociologists call that "something" **frame alignment** (Goffman, 1974; Snow et al., 1986). Frame alignment is the process by which individual interests, beliefs, and values either become congruent and complementary with the activities, ideas, and goals of the movement or fail to do so. Thanks to the efforts of scholars operating mainly in the symbolic interactionist tradition (see Chapters 1

FIGURE 20.5 WEIGHTED FREQUENCY OF STRIKES CANADA, 1946–2000

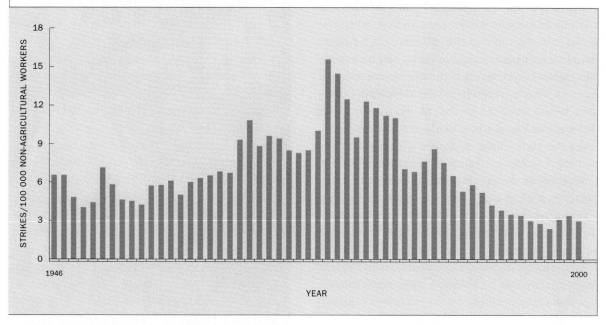

SOURCES: Strikes and Lockouts in Canada 1968 (1970: 12–13); Strikes and Lockouts in Canada 1985 (1985: 9); Workplace Information Directorate (1996); Labour Organizations…(1973: xxii–xxiii); 1994–1995 Directory…(1995: 15); "Chronological Perspective…" (1999; 2001a; 2001b).

and 4), frame alignment has recently become the subject of sustained sociological investigation.

Frame alignment can be encouraged in several ways. Social movement leaders can reach out to other organizations that, they believe, contain people who may be sympathetic to the social movement's cause. For example, an anti-nuclear movement may use the mass media, telephone campaigns, and direct mail to

FIGURE 20.6 PERCENT OF NON-AGRICULTURAL WORKERS UNIONIZED, CANADA, 1945–2000

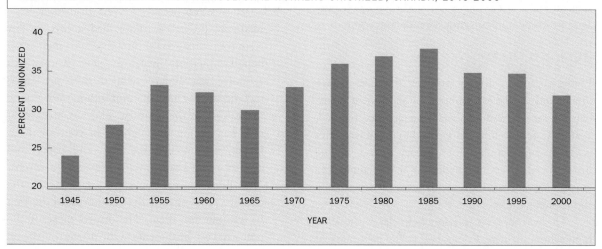

SOURCES: Calculated from *Labour Organizations…* (1973: xxii–xxiii); *1994–1995 Directory…* (1995: xiii); *1998 Directory…* (1998: 15); "Union Membership in Canada—2000" (2000); U.S. Bureau of Labor Statistics (1998, 1999, 2001).

appeal to feminist, anti-racist, and environmental organizations on the assumption they are likely to have members who would agree at least in general terms with the anti-nuclear platform. In addition, social movements can idealize values that have so far not featured prominently in the thinking of potential recruits. They can also elevate the importance of positive beliefs about the movement and what it stands for. For example, in trying to win new recruits, movement members might emphasize the seriousness of the social movement's purpose. They might analyze the causes of the problem the movement is trying solve in a clear and convincing manner. Or they might stress the likelihood of the movement's success. By doing so they might increase the movement's appeal to the potential recruit and win him or her over to the cause. Social movements can also stretch their objectives and activities to win recruits who are not initially sympathetic to the movement's original aims. This may involve a "watering down" of the movement's ideals. Alternatively, movement leaders may decide to take action calculated to appeal to non-sympathizers on grounds that have little or nothing to do with the movement's purpose. When rock, punk, or reggae bands play at nuclear disarmament rallies or gay liberation festivals, it is not necessarily because the music is relevant to the movement's goals. Nor do bands play just because movement members want to be entertained. The purpose is also to attract nonmembers. Once attracted by the music, however, nonmembers may make friends and acquaintances in the movement and then be encouraged to attend a more serious-minded meeting.

REFRAIN: BACK TO 1968

Frame-alignment theory stresses the face-to-face interaction strategies employed by movement members to recruit nonmembers who are like-minded, apathetic, or even initially opposed to the movement's goals. Resource-mobilization theory focuses on the broad social-structural conditions that facilitate the emergence of social movements. One theory usefully supplements the other.

The two theories certainly help clarify the 1968 high school incident I described at the beginning of this chapter. It now seems clear that two main factors prevented me from influencing my classmates in New Brunswick when I spoke to them about the dangers of industrial pollution:

The Assembly of First Nations, which represents 633 Native groups, demands that Aboriginal Canadians have the right to formulate their own laws and reject some Canadian laws. Here, Aboriginal people protest certain taxes outside a government office.
SOURCE: Dick Hemingway.

1. Disadvantaged people in New Brunswick were relatively powerless. They had access to few resources they could mobilize on their own behalf. That is because New Brunswick's economy was underdeveloped. Both per capita income and the level of unionization were among the lowest in the country. The unemployment rate was among the highest. In contrast, K.C. Irving, who owned the pulp and paper mill against which I railed, was so powerful that most New Brunswickers could not even conceive the need to rebel against the conditions of life that he created for them. He owned most of the industrial establishments in the province—the oil refinery and its network of gas stations, the dry docks, the pulp mills, and the mines, the logging operations. Every daily newspaper, most of the weeklies, all of the TV stations, and most of the

radio stations were his too. Little wonder one rarely heard a critical word about his operations. Many people also believed that Irving could make or break provincial governments single-handedly. Should one therefore be surprised that mere high school students refused to take him on? In their conservatism, my fellow students were only mimicking their parents, who, on the whole, were as powerless as Irving was mighty (Brym, 1979).

2. Many of my classmates did not share my sense of injustice. Most of them regarded K.C. Irving as the great provider. They thought his pulp and paper mill, as well as his myriad other industrial establishments, gave many New Brunswickers jobs. They regarded that fact as more important for their lives and the lives of their families than the pollution problem I raised. Frame-alignment theory suggests I needed to figure out ways of building bridges between their understanding and mine. I did not. I therefore received an unsympathetic hearing.

THE HISTORY AND FUTURE OF SOCIAL MOVEMENTS

I. THE RICH COUNTRIES

Three hundred years ago, social movements were typically small, localized, and violent affairs. In Europe, poor residents of a particular city might riot against public officials in reaction to a rise in bread prices or taxes. Peasants on a particular estate might burn their landowner's barns (or their landowner) in response to his demand for a larger share of the crop. But then the reach of the state grew, soon encompassing most aspects of life. The state taxed nearly all of its citizens at higher and higher rates as government services expanded. It imposed a uniform language and often a common curriculum in a compulsory education system. It drafted most young men for army service. It instilled in its citizens all the ideological trappings of modern nationalism, from anthems to flags to historical myths. And in the process, social movements changed. They became national in scope, typically directing themselves against central governments rather than local targets. They grew in size, partly because potential recruits were now literate and could communicate using the

printed word, partly because big new social settings—factories, offices, densely populated urban neighbourhoods—could serve as recruitment bases. And, in most cases, social movements became less violent. That is, their size and organization often allowed them to stabilize, bureaucratize, and become sufficiently powerful to get their way without frequent resort to extreme measures (Tilly, 1978, 1979a, 1979b; Tilly, Tilly, and Tilly, 1975).

Social movements often used their power to expand the rights of citizens. We may identify four stages in this process. In Britain, for example, rich property owners struggled against the king in the eighteenth century for **civil citizenship**: the right to free speech, freedom of religion, and justice before the law. The male middle class and the more prosperous strata of the working class struggled against rich property owners in the nineteenth century for **political citizenship**: the right to vote and run for office. In early-twentieth-century Britain, women and poorer workers succeeded in achieving these same rights despite the opposition of well-to-do men in particular. During the remainder of the century, blue- and white-collar workers struggled against the well-to-do for **social citizenship**: the right to a certain level of economic security and full participation in the social life of the country by means of the creation of the modern welfare state (Marshall, 1965).

In the last third of the twentieth century, the struggle to broaden citizenship rights entered a new phase, which we now examine in greater detail. The broadening of the struggle for citizenship rights was signalled by the emergence of so-called **new social movements** in the 1960s and 1970s (Melucci, 1980, 1995). What is new about new social movements is the breadth of their goals, the kinds of people they attract, and their potential for going global. Let us consider each of these issues in turn.

Goals

Some new social movements, such as the peace movement, the environmental movement, and the human rights movement, promote the rights not of specific groups but of humanity as a whole to peace, security, and a clean environment. Other new social movements, such as the women's movement and the gay rights movement, promote the rights of particular groups that have been excluded from full social participation. Accordingly, gay rights groups have fought for laws that eliminate all forms of discrimination based on sexual orientation. They have also fought for the repeal of laws that discriminate on the basis of sexual orientation, such as anti-sodomy laws and laws that negatively affect parental custody of children (Adam, Duyvendak, and Krouwel, 1999). Since the 1960s, the women's movement has succeeded in getting admission practices altered in professional schools, winning more freedom of reproductive choice for women, and opening up opportunities for women in the political, religious, military, educational, medical, and business systems (Adamson, Briskin, and McPhail, 1988; see Box 20.3). The emergence of the peace, environmental, human rights, gay rights, and women's movements marked the beginning of a fourth stage in the history of social movements. This fourth stage involves the promotion of **universal citizenship**, or the extension of citizenship rights to all adult members of society and to society as a whole (Roche, 1995; Turner, 1986: 85–105).

Membership

New social movements are also novel in that they attract a disproportionately large number of highly educated, well-to-do people from the social, educational, and cultural fields: teachers, college professors, journalists, social workers, artists, actors, writers, and student apprentices to these occupations. Such people are predisposed to participate in new social movements for several reasons. Their higher education exposes them to radical ideas and makes those ideas appealing. They tend to hold jobs outside the business community, which often opposes their values. And they often get personally involved in the problems of their clients and audiences, sometimes even becoming their advocates (Brint, 1984; Rootes, 1995).

Globalization Potential

Finally, new social movements are new in that they possess more potential for globalization than old social movements did. In the 1960s, social movements were typically *national* in scope. That is why, for example, the intensity and frequency of urban race riots in the United States in the 1960s did not depend on such local conditions as the degree of Black–white inequality in a given city (Spilerman, 1970, 1976). Instead, congressional and presidential action (and lack of action) on civil rights issues, national TV coverage of race issues, and growing Black consciousness

and solidarity helped to create the view among African Americans that racial problems are nationwide and can be solved only by the federal government. Many new social movements that gained force in the 1970s increased the scope of protest still further. For example, members of the nuclear disarmament and environmental movements viewed federal legislation as a necessary but insufficient solution to the issues that troubled them. Once they recognized that, say, the condition of the Brazilian rain forest affects climactic conditions worldwide, and that the spread of weapons of mass destruction can easily destroy all of humanity, movement activists pressed for international agreements binding all countries to stop environmental destruction and nuclear proliferation. Social movements went global.

The globalization of social movements was facilitated by the ease with which people in various national movements could travel and communicate with like-minded activists from other countries. In the age of CNN, inexpensive jet transportation, fax machines, and e-mail, it was possible not only to see the connection between apparently local problems and their global sources. It was also possible and, increasingly, desirable to act both locally and globally. Greenpeace, for instance, is a highly successful environmental movement that originated in Vancouver in the mid-1970s and now has offices in 41 countries, with its international office in Amsterdam ("Greenpeace…," 1999). Among many other initiatives, it has mounted a campaign to eliminate the international transportation and dumping of toxic wastes. Its representatives visited local environmental groups in African and other developing countries, supplied them with organizing kits to help them tie their local concerns to global political efforts, and published a newsletter to keep activists up-to-date about legal issues. Thus, Greenpeace coordinated a global campaign that enabled weak environmental organizations in developing countries to act more effectively, and raised the costs of continuing the international trade in toxic waste. Greenpeace is hardly alone on its efforts to go global. In 1953, there were 110 international social movement organizations. By 1993, there were 631. About a quarter were human rights organizations and about a seventh were environmental organizations, the latter representing by far the fastest-growing organizational type (Smith, 1998: 97).

BOX 20.3   THE WOMEN'S MOVEMENT

The women's movement was the first new social movement. It originated in the late nineteenth century. A century ago, women began to play a smaller role in domestic and farm work and started to enter the paid labour force in significant numbers. Owning more of their own economic resources, they became more independent-minded. They began to realize they might free themselves of oppressive authority in the home. They also started to understand there was nothing inevitable about their receiving less pay and working in worse conditions than men with comparable jobs (Strong-Boag, 1986: 179).

Formulating a program for social change requires such resources as time, money, and education. Not surprisingly, therefore, the "first wave" of the women's movement was composed of highly educated professionals. A group of women with just that social profile established the Canadian Woman Suffrage Association in Toronto in 1883. By means of demonstrating, petitioning, and gaining the support of influential liberal-minded men, women won the right to vote federally in 1918, in all provinces but Quebec by 1925, and in Quebec in 1940.

Along with the right to vote, women won the right to run for public office. They immediately exercised that right, running mainly on the CCF and Liberal Party tickets. A woman was first elected to provincial office in Alberta in 1917 and to the federal parliament in 1921.

In provincial legislatures and the federal parliament women sought institutional reform through government action. Specifically, they pursued more equitable pay for women, easier access to higher education, protection from domestic violence, and a fair share of family assets and child support in case of divorce or desertion. But progress was slow on all these fronts. That was partly because women's representation in the country's legislatures remained meagre. Even as late as the federal election in 1997, women composed just 19.6 percent of federal MPs. Some female MPs were hardly advocates of women's rights (Bashevkin, 1986; "Women—Federal Political Representation," 1999).

Because of this slow progress, feminists developed a strategy in the 1960s and 1970s that was less oriented toward established political institutions and more oriented toward grassroots action. The new strategy sought to achieve change not just "from above," by means of party politics, but also "from below," by creating a whole network of new organizations such as study groups, consciousness-raising circles, women's book stores, rape crisis centres, abortion clinics, shelters for battered women, and opportunities to publicize the importance of feminist aims, such as International Women's Day marches.

It was not only slow progress on the established political front that led women to create this network of new organizations. Many "second-wave" feminists were deeply involved in the student movement of the 1960s and 1970s. They were appalled to discover that, despite much rhetoric about liberation and equality, men controlled the student movement and men often refused to allow feminist issues to become part of their agenda. To pursue their aims they felt it was necessary to create new organizations run by women.

Today, then, the women's movement operates at both the grassroots level and within established political organizations to achieve its aims. It contains internal divisions. *Liberal feminists* believe that women can participate fully in society if they achieve equality of opportunity with men. They therefore advocate policies aimed at pay equity and the elimination of gender discrimination in the workplace. *Radical feminists* hold that male domination is rooted in the family. They champion free and safe contraception and abortion, an equitable division of domestic labour, and the like. *Socialist feminists* maintain that legal equality is not enough to ensure that women can participate fully in society. In addition, they argue, the state should provide affordable and accessible daycare facilities and other services. These services, they say, could alleviate the economic burdens that prevent most women, especially those from the working class, from taking full advantage of available opportunities for education and employment. Thus, despite their different emphases, all three types of feminism share a strong desire to see members of a previously marginal group expand their citizenship rights and become full participants in society.

The globalization of social movements can be further illustrated by coming full circle and returning to the anecdote with which I began this chapter. In 1991, I visited my hometown. I had not been back in years. As I entered the city, I vaguely sensed that something was different. I could not define the change precisely until I reached the Irving pulp and paper mill. Suddenly, it became obvious: the rotten-egg smell was virtually gone. I subsequently discovered that in the 1970s a local woman whose son developed a serious case of asthma took legal action against the mill and eventually won. The mill owner was required by law to install a "scrubber" in the main smokestack to remove most of the sulphur dioxide emissions. Soon, the federal government was putting pressure on the mill owner to purify the polluted water that poured out of the plant and into the local river system. Apparently, local citizens and the environmental movement had caused a change in the climate of opinion, influencing the government to force the mill owner to spend many millions of dollars on a cleanup. It took decades, but what was political heresy in 1968 became established practice by 1991 because environmental concerns had been amplified by the voice of a movement that had grown to global proportions. In general, as this case illustrates, globalization helps to ensure that many new social movements transcend local and national boundaries and that many of them—but, as you will now learn, not all—promote universalistic goals.

II: THE OTHER 80 PERCENT

With variations, the pattern of social movement evolution sketched above applies to the 20 or so rich countries of North America, Western Europe, Australia, New Zealand, and Japan. As we have seen, social movements in these rich countries typically sought to broaden democracy through the expansion of citizenship rights. In contrast, social movements in the other 80 percent of the world developed differently. They focused less on broadening the bases of democracy than on ensuring more elemental human rights, notably freedom from colonial rule and freedom to create the conditions for independent economic growth.

The "other 80 percent" of the world is weak economically, politically, and militarily because it began substantial industrialization only after World War I and in some cases after World War II. This circumstance allowed the early industrializers (Britain,

Anti-globalization street protests are now expected at meetings of international trade and finance organizations such as the World Trade Organization. The anti-globalization movement is a globalized movement too.
SOURCE: CP Picture Archive/Kevin Frayer.

France, Japan, Russia, etc.) to carve up most of Asia, Africa, and South America into colonies, protectorates, mandates, spheres of influence, and other administrative forms of subjugation. The nineteenth century was the age of imperialism. The early industrializers used the rest of the world as a captive market for their manufactured goods and a source of inexpensive raw materials and labour. They enriched themselves even as they limited economic growth and welfare in what is now often called the "Third World."

Events in the Muslim countries were in many respects typical and may therefore illustrate the problem (Hourani, 1991: 265–349). Already by the 1830s the armed forces of France had taken control of part of Algeria, those of Britain had taken control of part of the Arabian peninsula, and those of Russia had taken over the Muslim lands of the Caucasus. A century later, almost the entire Middle East and North Africa were under British and French control. Egyptian cotton fed the looms of Lancashire. Iraqi oil supplied half of France's needs. British and French ships brought European machinery and textiles to the region. British and French financiers profited handsomely from their control of local banking. Some indigenous merchants and landowners benefited from the new economic relations. However, the growing number of peasants and urban workers remained poor and powerless.

In the world's rich countries, a strong bourgeoisie—an affluent and politically powerful class of merchants, industrialists, and financiers—did much to promote the growth of democracy in its early stages (Moore, 1967). In contrast, in the Muslim countries and the rest of the Third World, the bourgeoisie was small, weak, and dependent on imperial interests. As a result, democratic ideals had little chance to sink deep roots. Instead, European and (after World War II) American domination of the Third World bred resentment, resistance, and revolt. Peasants, urban workers, intellectuals, and military officers were increasingly attracted to anti-imperialist independence movements based on various forms and mixes of socialism and nationalism (Brym, 1980: 50–53; Wolf, 1999 [1969]).

In the Muslim world, Islam was an additional source of anti-imperialist sentiment. In 1928, a movement known as the Society of the Muslim Brothers was formed in Egypt ("Muslim Brotherhood Movement …," 2002). It served as a prototype for many similar groups in the Muslim world. The Muslim Brothers argued against Western values and imperialist domination. They called for a return to the teaching of the Qur'an and demanded that Egypt become an Islamic state based on religious law (*shari'a*). This type of Islamic fundamentalism became popular in Egypt and throughout the Muslim world in the twentieth century, gaining impetus especially in Iran from the 1960s on and then spreading to Algeria and as far afield as Afghanistan and Sudan by the end of the century. There is a clear line of intellectual influence and development leading from the early Muslim Brothers to the assassins of Egypt's President Anwar Sadat in 1981 after he made peace with Israel to Osama bin Laden today (Worth, 2001). Bin Laden's chief aims are to remove all Western (especially American) influence from countries and regions with Muslim majorities, create in their place societies based on a fundamentalist interpretation of Islamic law, and destroy Israel as a Jewish state.

It is important to note that, however much al Qaeda is influenced by ideas dating back 70 years, it is every inch a global movement that relies on modern technology for its successes. Al Qaeda has placed operatives in as many as 60 countries. It finances itself through a complex international network of legitimate businesses, charitable and relief organizations, private donors, and opium trafficking operations (Shahar, 2001). Bin Laden communicated with his operatives via satellite telephone until U.S. law enforcement authorities inexplicably revealed they were tapping calls from his base in Afghanistan. Once he learned of these taps, he increased his use of another, more effective means of global communication: sending messages that are easily encrypted but difficult to decode via the Internet (Kelley, 2001; McCullogh, 2000). Some analysts think such messages were used to help plan and coordinate the complex, virtually simultaneous jet hijackings that resulted in the crash of an airliner in Pennsylvania and the destruction of the World Trade Center and part of the Pentagon on September 11, 2001, killing some 3000 people.

Al Qaeda is an extremist movement with few like it. However, it is also one in a whole range of reactions against Western power and influence that grips much of the Third World. In its extreme forms, this anti-Western reaction has little or no respect for minority rights, multiculturalism, elections, relatively open markets, and many of the other freedoms we enjoy and often take for granted in the West. Yet the anti-Western reaction is everywhere, even in its most extreme forms, based on the desire of people to restore the independence and dignity they lost when the industrialized world showed up on their doorstep uninvited. One of the great tasks the West faces in the twenty-first century is to defend itself against violence while doing its utmost to remove the ultimate source of that violence: the gap between rich and poor countries that opened up at the time of the Industrial Revolution and that has widened ever since. Whether we are up to the task is anyone's guess.

SUMMARY

1. Democracy involves a two-way process of control between the state (the set of institutions that formulate and carry out a country's law, policies, and binding regulations) and civil society (the private sphere, consisting of social movements, political parties, etc.).

2. The level of democracy in a society depends on the capacity of civil society to influence the state through citizen support of social movements, political parties, and other groups. That capacity increases as power becomes more widely distributed in society.

3. While pluralists are correct to note that democratic politics is about negotiation and compromise, they fail to appreciate how advantaged groups tend to have more political influence.

4. While elite theorists are correct to note that power is concentrated in the hands of advantaged groups, they fail to appreciate how variations in the distribution of power influence political behaviour and public policy.

5. While power-balance theorists focus on the effect of changes in the distribution of power in society, they fail to appreciate what state-centred theorists emphasize—that state institutions and laws also affect political behaviour and public policy.

6. The degree to which power is widely distributed influences the success of particular kinds of parties and policies. Widely distributed power is associated with the success of labour parties and policies that redistribute wealth.

7. Research does not support the view that social movements emerge when relative deprivation spreads.

8. Research does suggest that people are more inclined to rebel against the status quo when they are bound by close social ties to many other people who feel similarly wronged and when they have the money and other resources needed to protest.

9. In order for social movements to grow, members must engage in frame alignment, making the activities, goals, and ideology of the movement congruent with the interests, beliefs, and values of potential new recruits.

10. The history of democracy is a struggle for the acquisition of constantly broadening citizenship rights—first the right to free speech, freedom of religion, and justice before the law, then the right to vote and run for office, then the right to a certain level of economic security and full participation in the life of society, and finally the right of marginal groups to full citizenship and the right of humanity as a whole to peace and security.

11. In the Third World, social movements have focused less on broadening the bases of democracy than on ensuring more elemental human rights, notably freedom from colonial rule and freedom to create the conditions for independent economic growth. In some cases these movements have taken extreme, anti-democratic forms.

QUESTIONS TO CONSIDER

1. Have you ever participated in a social movement or been actively involved in a political party? If so, explain how your political choices (e.g., which party you joined, your level of participation, the timing of your recruitment, etc.) were influenced by the sociological factors discussed in this chapter. If not, explain how the sociological factors discussed in this chapter influence you to remain politically inactive.

2. How would you achieve a political goal? Map out a detailed strategy for reaching a clearly defined aim, such as a reduction in income tax or an increase in university funding. Who would you try to recruit to help you achieve your goal? Why? What collective actions do you think would be most successful? Why? To whose attention would these actions be directed? Why? Write a manifesto that frames your argument in a way that is culturally appealing to potential recruits.

3. Do you think that social movements will be more or less widespread in the twenty-first century than they were in the twentieth? Why or why not? What kinds of social movements are likely to predominate?

4. Do you think that the twenty-first century will be more or less democratic than the twentieth? Why or why not?

GLOSSARY

Authority is power that is widely viewed as legitimate.

Authorities are people who occupy the command posts of legitimized power structures.

Civil citizenship recognizes the right to free speech, freedom of religion, and justice before the law.

Civil society is the private (non-state) sphere of social life.

Elite theory maintains that well-to-do people consistently have much more political influence than people who are less well-to-do, and that society is therefore not as democratic as it is often portrayed.

Force is coercive power.

Frame alignment is the process by which individual interests, beliefs, and values either become congruent and complementary with the activities, goals, and ideology of the movement or fail to do so.

Group power is determined by a group's size, level of social organization and access to scarce resources.

New social movements are post-1950s movements that attract a disproportionately large number of highly educated people in the social, educational, and cultural fields, fight their battles mainly inside established political parties or outside the political system, have an uneasy relationship with older social movements, and universalize the struggle for citizenship.

Pluralist theory holds that there are many competing interests and centres of power in society and that no one interest or power centre predominates in the long run.

Political citizenship recognizes the right to run for office and vote.

Political parties are organizations that seek to control state power.

A **political revolution** is a concerted attempt on the part of many people to overthrow existing political institutions and establish new ones. Political revolutions take place when widespread and successful movements of opposition clash with crumbling traditional or legal-rational authority.

Power is the ability of an individual or a group to impose his, her, or its will on other individuals or groups.

Power-balance theory suggests that social movement formation and success depend on how powerful authorities are compared to partisans of change. It also holds that societies with widely distributed power are more democratic and more egalitarian than societies with narrowly held power.

Relative deprivation is an intolerable gap between the social rewards people feel they deserve and the social rewards they expect to receive.

Resource-mobilization theory holds that social movements crystallize and succeed in achieving their goals to the degree that they have access to scarce resources such as money and effective communication facilities.

Social citizenship recognizes the right to a certain level of economic welfare security and full participation in the social life of the country.

Social movements are enduring collective attempts to change part or all of the social order by means of rioting, petitioning, striking, demonstrating, and establishing pressure groups, unions, and political parties.

The **state** is a set of institutions that formulate and implement a country's laws, policies, and binding regulations. It consists of an executive branch (which initiates laws), a legislative branch (which makes laws), a judicial branch (which interprets laws), and an administrative and coercive apparatus (which enforces laws and protects state security).

The **state-centred theory** shows how the state structures political life independently of the way power is distributed among classes and other groups at a given time.

Universal citizenship recognizes the right of marginal groups to full citizenship and the rights of humanity as a whole.

SUGGESTED READING

Baer, Doug. ed. (2002). *Political Sociology: Canadian Perspectives*. Toronto: Oxford University Press. A useful compendium of Canadian materials covering major issues and debates.

Tarrow, Sidney. (1998 [1994]). *Power in Movement: Social Movements, Collective Action and Politics*, 2nd ed. Cambridge, UK: Cambridge University Press. Synthesizes resource-mobilization and framing theories and underlines the importance of political structures in shaping discontent.

Wolf, Eric. (1999 [1969]). *Peasant Wars of the 20th Century*. Norman, OK: Oklahoma University Press. The best introduction to Third World social movements.

NOTES

1. In addition, only about 14 percent of the American working class is unionized, making it the least organized working class in any of the world's rich countries.

2. For example, in the 1890s, a coalition of white and Black southern farmers threatened the established American political parties. It was precisely for this reason that American electoral laws were made more restrictive at that time.

3. Some of these generalizations do not apply to countries with a long tradition of labour governments. For example, since World War II, Sweden has experienced high levels of unionization and *low* strike rates. That is because Swedish workers and their representatives are involved in government policy-making. Decisions about wages and benefits tend to be made in negotiations between unions, employer associations, and governments rather than on the picket line.

REFERENCES

CHAPTER 1

Allen, Robert C. (1999). *Education and Technological Revolutions: The Role of the Social Sciences and the Humanities in the Knowledge Based Economy*. Ottawa: Social Sciences and Humanities Research Council of Canada. On the World Wide Web at http://www.sshrc.ca/english/resnews/researchresults/allen99.pdf (8 May 2001).

Babbie, Earl. (2000 [1973]). *The Practice of Social Research*, 9th ed. Belmont CA: Wadsworth Publishing Co.

Bell, Daniel. (1976). *The Coming of Post-Industrial Society: A Venture in Social Forecasting* New York: Basic Books.

Brym, Robert J. with Bonnie J. Fox. (1989). *From Culture to Power: The Sociology of English Canada*. Toronto: Oxford University Press.

Brym, Robert J. (2002). "Canadian Sociology: An Introduction to the Upper Thirteen." *The American Sociologist 33*, 5–11.

Brym, Robert J. and Céline Saint-Pierre. (1997). "Canadian Sociology." *Contemporary Sociology 26* (4), 543–46.

Clark, S.D. (1968 [1962]). *The Developing Canadian Community*, 2nd ed. Toronto: University of Toronto Press.

Coleman, James S. (1961). *The Adolescent Society*. New York: Free Press.

Comte, Auguste. (1975). *Auguste Comte: The Foundation of Sociology*. Ed. Kenneth Thompson. New York: Wiley.

Douglas, Jack D. (1967). *The Social Meanings of Suicide*. Princeton, NJ: Princeton University Press.

Durkheim, Émile. (1951 [1897]). *Suicide: A Study in Sociology*. Ed. G. Simpson; trans J. Spaulding and G. Simpson. New York: Free Press.

Edel, Abraham. (1965). "Social Science and Value: A study in Interrelations." In Irving Louis Horowitz, ed., *The New Sociology: Essays in Social Science and Social Theory in Honor of C. Wright Mills* (pp. 218–38). New York: Oxford University Press.

Eichler, Margrit. (1987). *Nonsexist Research Methods*. Boston: Allen & Unwin.

Eichler, Margrit. (1988 [1983]). *Families in Canada Today*, 2nd ed. Toronto: Gage.

Garfinkel, Harold. (1967). *Studies in Ethnomethodology*. Englewood Cliffs NJ: Prentice-Hall.

Giddens, Anthony. (1982). *Sociology: A Brief but Critical Introduction*. New York: Harcourt, Brace Jovanovich.

Goffman, Erving. (1959). *The Presentation of Self in Everyday Life*. Garden City NY: Anchor.

Granovetter, Mark. (1973). "The Strength of Weak Ties." *American Sociological Review 78* (6), 1360–80.

Guppy, Neil, and R. Alan Hedley. (1993). *Opportunities in Sociology*. Montreal: Canadian Sociology and Anthropology Association.

Hersch, Patricia. (1998). *A Tribe Apart: A Journey into the Heart of American Adolescence*. New York: Ballantine Books.

Hiller, Harry ed. (2001). "Legacy for a New Millennium." Special issue of *The Canadian Journal of Sociology 26* (3).

Hochschild, Arlie, with Anne Machung. (1989). *The Second Shift: Working Parents and the Revolution at Home*. New York: Viking.

Kuhn, Thomas. (1970 [1962]). *The Structure of Scientific Revolutions*, 2nd ed. Chicago, University of Chicago Press.

Martineau, Harriet. (1985). *Harriet Martineau on Women*. Ed. Gayle Graham Yates. New Brunswick NJ: Rutgers University Press.

Marx, Karl. (1904 [1859]). *A Contribution to the Critique of Political Economy*. Trans. N. Stone. Chicago: Charles H. Kerr.

Marx, Karl, and Friedrich Engels. (1972 [1848]). "Manifesto of the Communist Party." In R. Tucker, ed. *The Marx-Engels Reader* (pp. 331–62). New York: Norton.

Merton, Robert K. (1968 [1949]). *Social Theory and Social Structure*. New York: Free Press.

Mills, C. Wright. (1959). *The Sociological Imagination*. New York: Oxford University Press.

Ornstein, Michael D. (1983). "The Development of Class in Canada." In J. Paul Grayson, ed. *Introduction to Sociology: An Alternate Approach* (pp. 224–66). Toronto: Gage.

Parsons, T. (1951). *The Social System*. Glencoe, IL: Free Press.

Porter, John. (1965). *The Vertical Mosaic: An Analysis of Social Class and Power in Canada*. Toronto: University of Toronto Press.

Russett, Cynthia Eagle. (1966). *The Concept of Equilibrium in American Social Thought*. New Haven, CT: Yale University Press.

Simon, Julian. (1998). "The Five Greatest Years for Humanity." *Wired 6* (1), 66–68.

Statistics Canada. (1999). *Mortality—Summary List of Causes, 1997: Shelf Tables*. Ottawa: Health Statistics Division. Catalogue no. 84F0209XIB. On the World Wide Web at http://www.statcan.ca:80/english/freepub/84F0209XIB/0009784F0209XIB.pdf (9 July 2002).

Tierney, John. (1997). "Our Oldest Computer, Upgraded." *New York Times Magazine*, September 28, pp. 46–49, 97, 100, 104–05.

Tillyard, E.M.W. (1943). *The Elizabethan World Picture*. London: Chatto and Windus.

Toffler, Alvin. (1990). *Powershift: Knowledge, Wealth, and Violence at the Edge of the 21st Century*. New York: Bantam.

Wallerstein, Immanuel, ed. (1998). "The Heritage of Sociology and the Future of the Social Sciences in the 21st Century." *Current Sociology 46* (2).

Weber, Max. (1946). *From Max Weber: Essays in Sociology*. Eds. and trans. Hans Gerth and C. Wright Mills. New York: Oxford University Press.

Weber, Max. (1958 [1904–05]). *The Protestant Ethic and the Spirit of Capitalism*. New York: Scribner.

World Bank. (1999a). "Aid Dependency." On the World Wide Web at http://www.worldbank.org/data/wdi/pdfs/tab6_10.pdf (8 July).

World Bank. (1999b). *Global Development Finance 1999*. On the World Wide Web at http://www.worldbank.org/prospects/gdf99/tables.pdf (8 July).

World Bank. (2001a). "4.16 External Debt." *2001 World Development Indicators*. On the World Wide Web at http://www.worldbank.org/data/wdi2001/pdfs/tab4_16.pdf (9 July 2002).

World Bank. (2001b). "6.10 Aid Dependency." *2001 World Development Indicators*. On the World Wide Web at http://www.worldbank.org/data/wdi2001/pdfs/tab6_10.pdf (9 July 2002).

CHAPTER 2

Brym, R. (1986). "Incorporation versus Power Models of Working Class Radicalism with Special Reference to North America." *Canadian Journal of Sociology, 11,* 227–51.

Brym, R., and Lenton, R. (2001). *Love Online: A Report on Digital Dating in Canada*. Toronto: MSN.CA

Burt, S. (1990). "Canadian Women's Groups in the 1980s: Organizational Development and Policy Influence." *Canadian Public Policy, 16* (1), 17–28.

Creese, G. (1988). "The Politics of Dependence: Women, Work, and Unemployment in the Vancouver Labour Movement before World War II." *Canadian Journal of Sociology, 13,* 121–42.

Creese, G. (1999). *Contracting Masculinity: Gender, Class and Race in a White-Collar Union, 1944–1994*. Toronto: Oxford University Press.

Cresswell, J.W. (1998). *Qualitative Inquiry and Research Design: Choosing among Five Traditions*. Thousand Oaks, CA: Sage

Davies, S. (2003). "Stubborn Disparities: Explaining Class Inequalities in Schooling." In James Curtis, Edward Grabb, and Neil Guppy, eds., *Social Inequality in Canada: Patterns, Problems, and Policies*, 4th ed. (Chapter 13). Toronto: Prentice Hall.

Douglas, J. (1970). "Understanding Everyday Life." In J. Douglas, ed., *Understanding Everyday Life* (pp. 3–44). Chicago: Aldine.

Fisher, R.A. (1966). "Has Mendel's Work Been Rediscovered?" In C. Stern and E. Sherwood, eds., *Origin of Genetics; A Mendel Sourcebook* (pp. 139–72). San Francisco: W.H. Freeman. (Original work published 1936)

Foddy, W.H. (1993). *Constructing Questions for Interviews and Questionnaires. Theory and Practice in Social Research*. Cambridge: Cambridge University Press.

Foschi, M. and Buchan, S. (1990). "Ethnicity, Gender, and Perceptions of Task Competence." *Canadian Journal of Sociology, 15,* 1–18.

Giddens, A. (1984). *The Constitution of Society*. Berkeley, CA: University of California Press.

Ginsberg, E., and Henry, F. (1985). *Who Gets the Work?* Toronto: Urban Alliance on Race Relations and the Social Planning Council of Toronto.

Goffman, E. (1961). *Asylums: Essays on the Social Situations of Mental Patients and Other Inmates*. New York: Doubleday/Anchor.

Gold, A.D. (1998, May). "President's Report." *Criminal Lawyers Newsletter, 19* (2). On the World Wide Web at http://www.criminallawyers.ca/newslett/19-2/gold.html (3 November 2000).

Gray, G., and Guppy, N. (2003). *Successful Surveys*. Toronto: Nelson.

Guppy, N., and Davies, S. (1998). *Education in Canada*. Ottawa: Statistics Canada, Minister of Industry.

Henry, F. (1999). *The Colour of Democracy: Racism in Canadian Society*. Toronto: Harcourt Brace.

Hooper, J. (2002). *Of Moths and Men: An Evolutionary Tale*. New York: Norton.

Kaufman, F.C.M., Q.C.(1998). *Report of the Kaufman Commission on Proceedings Involving Guy Paul Morin*. (Morin Inquiry Executive Summary Report)(Conclusion 1). On the World Wide Web at http://www.attorneygeneral.jus.gov.on.ca/html/MORIN/exesumrec/morin_concl.pdf (17 July 2000).

Kleppner, D., and Jackiw, R. (2000, August). "One Hundred Years of Quantum Physics." *Science, 289,* 893–98. On the World Wide Web at http://vega.bac.pku.edu.cn/~rxxu/teach/qp100.htm (September 2000).

Kuhn, T.S. (1962). *The Structure of Scientific Revolutions*. Chicago: University of Chicago Press.

Laxer, G. (1989). *Open for Business: The Roots of Foreign Ownership in Canada*. Toronto: Oxford University Press.

Lenton, R. (1990). "Techniques of Child Discipline and Abuse by Parents." *Canadian Review of Sociology and Anthropology, 27,* 157–85.

Maybin, F. (1993). *Gender Discrimination and the Recruitment Process: Matching People and Jobs*. Unpublished M.A. thesis. University of British Columbia.

McMullan, J., and Swan, P. (1989). "Social Economy and Arson in Nova Scotia." *Canadian Journal of Criminology,* 281–308.

Orel, Vitezslav. (1996). *Gregor Mendel: The First Geneticist*. Trans. Stephen Finn. Oxford: Oxford University Press.

Park, R. (2000). *Voodoo Science: The Road from Foolishness to Fraud*. New York: Oxford University Press.

Pineo, P., and Porter, J. (1967). "Occupational Prestige in Canada." *Canadian Review of Anthropology and Sociology, 4,* 24–40.

Reitz, J. (1993). "Statistics on Racial Discrimination in Canada." *Policy Options, 14,* 32–36.

Roethlisberger, F.J., and Dickson W. (1939). *Management and the Worker*. Cambridge, MA: Harvard University Press.

Scarce, R. (2000). *Fishy Business: Salmon, Biology, and the Social Construction of Nature*. Philadelphia: Temple University Press.

Statistics Canada. (1997). *1997 Survey of Consumer Finances*. Cat. No. 13M0001XDB. Ottawa: Public Works and Government Services.

Wannell, T., and Caron, N. (1995). "Male–Female Earnings Gap among Recent Postsecondary Graduates." *Educational Quarterly Review, 2,* 20–34.

Weber, M. (1949[1904/1905/1917]). *The Methodology of the Social Sciences*. Glencoe, IL: Free Press.

Wilson, B. (2002). "The Canadian Rave Scene and Five Theses on Youth Resistance." *Canadian Journal of Sociology, 27,* 373–412.

CHAPTER 3

Adams, Michael. (1997). *Sex in the Snow: Canadian Social Values at the End of the Millennium*. Toronto: Penguin.

Albas, Daniel, and Cheryl Albas. (1989). "Modern Magic: The Case of Examinations." *The Sociological Quarterly, 30,* 603–13.

Baudrillard, Jean. (1988 [1986]). *America*. Trans. Chris Turner. London: Verso.

Bibby, Reginald W. (1987). *Fragmented Gods: The Poverty and Potential of Religion in Canada*. Toronto: Irwin.

Bissoondath, Neil. (2002 [1997]). *Selling Illusions: The Cult of Multiculturalism in Canada*. Toronto: Penguin.

Bronowski, J. (1965 [1956]). *Science and Human Values*, revised ed. New York: Harper & Row.

Brym, Robert J. (2001). "Hip-Hop from Dissent to Commodity: A Note on Consumer Culture." In R. Brym, ed., *New Society: Sociology for the 21st Century*, 3rd ed. (pp. 78–81). Toronto: Harcourt Brace Canada

Brym, Robert J., with Bonnie J. Fox. (1989). *From Culture to Power: The Sociology of English Canada*. Toronto: Oxford University Press.

"Canada: Parliamentary Elections." (2000). On the World Wide Web at http://www.idea.int/Voter_turnout/northamerica/canada.html (29 November).

Clarke, Harold D., Jane Jenson, Lawrence LeDuc, and Jon H. Pammett. (1996 [1984]). *Absent Mandate: Canadian Electoral Politics In an Era of Restructuring*, 3rd ed. Toronto: Gage.

Delmos, Monika. (2002). "Mangled Words Divide Generations in Japan." *Globe and Mail*, 24 August, A14.

Durkheim, Émile. (1976 [1915]). *The Elementary Forms of the Religious Life*. Trans. Joseph Ward Swain. New York: Free Press.

Fleras, Augie, and Jean Leonard Elliott. (2002). *Engaging Diversity: Multiculturalism in Canada*. Toronto: Nelson.

Frank, Thomas and Matt Weiland, eds. (1997). *Commodify Your Dissent: Salvos from the Baffler*. New York: W.W. Norton.

"Gap." (1999). On the World Wide Web at http://www.gap.com/onlinestore/gap/advertising/khakitv.asp (14 September).

"Garciaparra Explains his Superstitions." (1999). On the World Wide Web at http://www.geocities.com/Colosseum/Track/4242/nomar3.wav (21 June).

Gleick, James. (2000 [1999]). *Faster: The Acceleration of Just About Everything*. New York: Vintage.

"Global 1000." (1999, 12 July). *Business Week Online*. On the World Wide Web at http://www.businessweek.com/ (15 July).

Griswold, Wendy. (1992). "The Sociology of Culture: Four Good Arguments (and One Bad One)." *Acta Sociologica*, 35, 322–28.

Gunderson, Edna, Bill Keveney, and Ann Oldenburg. (2002). "'The Osbournes' Find a Home in America's Living Rooms." *USA Today*, April 19, 1A–2A.

Hall, Edward, (1959). *The Silent Language*. New York: Doubleday.

Hanke, Robert. (1998). "'Yo Quiero Mi MTV!' Making Music Television for Latin America." In Thomas Swiss, Andrew Herman, and John M. Sloop, eds., *Mapping the Beat: Popular Music and Contemporary Theory* (pp. 219–45). Oxford UK: Blackwell.

Harris, Marvin. (1974). *Cows, Pigs, Wars and Witches: The Riddles of Culture*. New York, Random House.

Henry, Frances, Carol Tabor, Winston Mattis, and Tim Ress. (1999). "The Victimization of Racial Minorities in Canada." In Robert J. Brym, ed., *Society in Question: Sociological Readings for the 21st Century*, 3rd ed. (pp. 145–70). Toronto: Harcourt Brace Canada.

Hobsbawm, Eric. (1994). *Age of Extremes: The Short Twentieth Century, 1914–1991*. London: Abacus.

Ignatieff, Michael. (2000). *The Rights Revolution*. Toronto: Anansi.

Klein, Naomi. (2000). *No Logo: Taking Aim at the Brand Bullies*. Toronto: Vintage Canada.

Kristof, Nicholas D. (1997). "With Stateside Lingo, Valley Girl Goes Japanese." *New York Times*, 19 October, Section 1, 3.

Lipset, Seymour Martin. (1963). "Value Differences, Absolute or Relative: The English-Speaking Democracies." In *The First New Nation: The United States in Historical Perspective* (pp. 248–73). New York: Basic Books.

Lowe, Graham S. (2001). "Quality of Work—Quality of Life." Keynote talk at the Work/Life Balance and Employee Wellness Strategies Conference. Edmonton: 14 May. On the World Wide Web at http://www.cprn.com/work/files/pzqwq_e.pdf (25 August 2002).

"Mad About Hockey: Superstitions." (2002). On the World Wide Web at http://www.mcg.org/societe/hockey/pages/aasuperstitions_2.html (20 June 2002).

McClaren, Leah. (2002). "Aging Punks Jump on the Jubilee Bandwagon." *Globe and Mail*, June 1, R8.

McCrum, Robert, William Cran, and Robert MacNeil. (1992). *The Story of English*, new and revised edition. London: Faber and Faber.

McDonald's Corporation. (1999). "McDonald's Nutrition Facts." On the World Wide Web at http://www.mcdonalds.com/food/nutrition/index.html (27 June).

"McDonald's Testing E-Burgers." (1999). *Wall Street Journal Interactive Edition*. 11 August. On the World Wide Web at http://www.zdnet.com/zdnn/stories/news/0,4586,2312611,00.html (29 September).

McLuhan, Marshall. (1964). *Understanding Media: The Extensions of Man*. New York: McGraw-Hill.

Naumetz, Tim. (2000). "Snow, Easy Call Kept Voters Away, Chrétien Says." *National Post*, 29 November, A8.

Nevitte, Neil. (1996). *The Decline of Deference: Canadian Value Change in Cross-National Perspective*. Peterborough ON: Broadview Press.

Pinker, Steven. (1994). "Apes—Lost for Words." *New Statesman and Society*, 15 April, 30–31.

Pool, Robert. (1997). *Beyond Engineering: How Society Shapes Technology*. New York: Oxford University Press.

Postel, Sandra. (1994). "Carrying Capacity: Earth's Bottom Line." In Linda Starke, ed. *State of the World 1994* (pp. 3–21). New York: W. W. Norton.

Postman, Neil. (1992). *Technopoly: The Surrender of Culture to Technology*. New York: Vintage.

Rifkin, Jeremy. (1998). *The Biotech Century: Harnessing the Gene and Remaking the World*. New York: Jeremy P. Tarcher/Putnam.

Ritzer, George. (1993). *The McDonaldization of Society: An Investigation into the Changing Character of Contemporary Social Life*. Thousand Oaks, CA: Pine Forge Press.

Ritzer, George. (1996). "The McDonaldization Thesis: Is Expansion Inevitable?" *International Sociology*, 11, 291–308.

Rural Advancement Foundation International. (1999). "The Gene Giants: Masters of the Universe?" On the World Wide Web at http://www.rafi.org/communique/fltxt/19992.html (29 June).

Schlosser, Eric. (2002 [2001]). *Fast Food Nation: The Dark Side of the All-American Meal*. New York: Perennial.

Schor, Juliet B. (1992). *The Overworked American: The Unexpected Decline of Leisure*. New York: Basic Books.

Scott, James C. (1998). *Seeing Like a State: How Certain Schemes to Improve the Human Condition Have Failed*. New Haven CT: Yale University Press.

Statistical Abstract of the United States. (1998). Washington DC: US Department of Commerce.

Statistics Canada. (1999). "Top 10 Places of Birth for Total Immigrants, Immigrants Arriving Before 1961 and Recent Immigrants for Canada, 1996 Census—20% Sample Data." On the World Wide Web at http://www.statcan.ca/english/census96/nov4/table1.htm (22 June).

Thompson, E. P. (1967). "Time, Work Discipline, and Industrial Capitalism." *Past and Present* 38: 59–67.

United Nations. (1998). "Universal Declaration of Human Rights." On the World Wide Web at http://www.un.org/Overview/rights.html (29 August 2002).

Weber, Max. (1946 [1922]). "Bureaucracy." In H. Gerth and C. Mills, eds. and trans., *From Max Weber: Essays in Sociology* (pp. 196–264). New York: Oxford University Press.

World Values Survey, 1990–1993. (1994). Ann Arbor MI: Inter-University Consortium for Political and Social Research.

World Values Survey, 2000. (2001). Machine readable file. (Not publicly accessible as of this writing.)

CHAPTER 4

Adler, P.A., and P. Adler. (1998). *Peer Power: Preadolescent Culture and Identity*. New Brunswick, NJ: Rutgers University Press.

Aries, Philippe. (1981). *The Hour of Our Death*. New York: Knopf.

Atchley, R.C. (1994). *Social Forces and Aging*, 7th ed. Belmont, CA: Wadsworth.

Baker, Maureen. (1985). *What Will Tomorrow Bring? A Study of the Aspirations of Adolescent Women*. Ottawa: Canadian Advisory Council on the Status of Women.

Baker, Maureen, ed. (1989). *Families: Changing Trends in Canada*, 2nd ed. Toronto: McGraw-Hill Ryerson.

Ballantine, Jeanne. (1997). *The Sociology of Education: A Systematic Analysis*, 4th ed. Englewood Cliffs, NJ: Prentice-Hall.

Barber, K., and K. Allen. (1992). *Women and Families: Feminist Reconstructions*. New York: Guilford Press.

Becker, Howard S., Blanche Geer, Everett C. Hughes, and Anselm L. Strauss. (1961). *Boys in White: Student Culture in Medical School*. Chicago: University of Chicago Press.

Begley, S. (1995). "Gray Matters." *Newsweek*, November 7, pp. 48–54.

Benokraitis, Nijole V. (1993). *Marriages and Families: Changes, Choices, and Constraints*. Englewood Cliffs, NJ: Prentice-Hall.

Berger, Peter L. (1970). "Identity as a Problem in the Sociology of Knowledge." In J. Curtis and J. Petras, eds., *The Sociology of Knowledge* (pp. 373–84). New York: Praeger.

Best, Raphaela. (1983). *We've All Got Scars: What Boys and Girls Learn in Elementary School*. Bloomington: Indiana University Press.

Blau, F., and M. Ferber. (1992). *The Economics of Women, Men, and Work*. Englewood Cliffs, NJ: Prentice Hall.

Brim, Orville G., Jr. (1968). "Socialization through the Life Cycle." In Orville G. Brim, Jr., and Stanton Wheeler, eds., *Socialization after Childhood: Two Essays* (pp. 3–49). New York: John Wiley.

Burgess, R.L., and R.A. Richardson. (1984). "Child Abuse during Adolescence." In R.M. Lerner and N.L. Galambos, eds., *Experiencing Adolescents: A Sourcebook for Parents, Teachers and Teens* (pp. 119–52). New York: Garland.

Clausen, John A. (1986). *The Life Course*. Englewood Cliffs, NJ: Prentice Hall.

Coleman, John C., and Leo Hendry. (1990). *The Nature of Adolescence*, 2nd ed. New York: Routledge, Chapman, and Hall.

Cooley, Charles Horton. (1902). *Human Nature and the Social Order*. New York: Scribner's.

Corsaro, William A. (1992). "Interpretive Reproduction in Children's Peer Cultures." *Social Psychology Quarterly*, 55, 160–77.

Duffy, Jim, Kelly Warren, and Margaret Walsh. (2001–2002). "Classroom Interactions: Gender of Teacher, Gender of Student, and Classroom Subject." *Sex Roles*, 45, 579.

Erikson, Erik H. (1982). *The Life Cycle Completed*. New York: Norton.

Freedman, Jonathan L. (2002). *Media Violence and Its Effect on Aggression: Assessing the Scientific Evidence*. Toronto: University of Toronto Press.

Fox, Bonnie. (1998). "Motherhood, Changing Relationships and the Reproduction of Gender Inequality." In S. Abbey and A. O'Reilly, eds., *Redefining Motherhood*. Toronto: Second Story Press.

Fox, Bonnie, ed. (2001). *Family Patters, Gender Relations*, 2nd ed. Toronto: Oxford University Press.

Fussel, James. A. (2003). "Violent Video Game Has Parents, Experts Concerned." *The Hamilton Spectator*, March 1, D16.

Garbarino, J. (1999). *Lost Boys: Why Our Sons Turn Violent and How We Can Save Them*. New York: The Free Press.

Giordano, Peggy C., Stephen A. Cernkovich, and Alfred DeMaris. (1993). "The Family and Peer Relations of Black Adolescents." *Journal of Marriage and the Family*, 55 (May), 277–87.

Glaser, Barney, and Anselm L. Strauss. (1967). *The Discovery of Grounded Theory: Strategies for Qualitative Research*. Chicago: Aldine.

Goffman, Erving. (1959). *The Presentation of Self in Everyday Life*. New York: Anchor Doubleday.

Goffman, Erving. (1961). *Asylums*. New York: Anchor Books.

Goffman, Erving. (1963). *Behavior in Public Places*. New York: Free Press.

Goffman, Erving. (1971). *Relations in Public*. New York: Basic Books.

Goffman, Erving. (1979). *Gender Advertisements*. New York: Harper.

Gooden, Angela M., and Mark A. Gooden. (2001). "Gender Representation in Notable Children's Picture Books: 1995–1999." *Sex Roles* 45, 89–101.

Gould, Stephen J. (1996). *The Mismeasure of Man*. New York: Norton.

Haas, Jack, and William Shaffir. (1987). *Becoming Doctors: The Adoption of a Cloak of Competence*. Greenwich, CT: JAI Press.

Handel, Gerald. (1990). "Revising Socialization Theory." *American Sociological Review, 55,* 463–66.

Hebdige, Dick. (1979). *Subculture: The Meaning of Style*. London: Methuen.

Hendricks, Jon, and C. Davis Hendricks. (1986). *Aging in Mass Society: Myths and Realities*, 3rd ed. Boston: Little, Brown.

Herrnstein, Richard J., and Charles Murray. (1994). *The Bell Curve*. New York: Free Press.

Hogan, Dennis P., and Nan Marie Astone. (1986). "Transition to Adulthood." *Annual Review of Sociology, 12,* 109–30.

Hooyman, N.R., and H.A. Kiyak. (1993). *Social Gerontology*, 3rd ed. Boston: Allyn and Bacon.

Hopf, D., and C.H. Hatzichristou. (1999). "Teacher Gender-Related Influences in Greek Schools." *British Journal of Educational Psychology, 69,* 1–18.

Huston, A.C. (1983). "Sex-typing." In Paul H. Mussen, ed., *Handbook of Child Psychology*. Vol. 4, 4th ed. (pp. 387–467). New York: John Wiley.

Kohn, Melvin L., Atsushi Naoi, Carmi Schooler, and Kazimiercz M. Slomczynski. (1990). "Position in the Class Structure and Psychological Functioning in the United States, Japan, and Poland." *American Journal of Sociology, 95,* 964–1008.

Kortenhaus, C.M., and J. Demarest. (1993). "Gender Role Stereotyping in Children's Literature: An Update." *Sex Roles, 28,* 219–32.

Lareau, A. (1987). "Social Class Differences in Family-School Relationships." *Sociology of Education, 60,* 63–72.

Lawson, David. (1996). "The Brave New World of Work." *The Silhouette*, November 7.

Leming, M.R., and G.E. Dickinson. (1990). *Understanding Dying, Death, and Bereavement*, 2nd ed. New York: Holt, Rinehart & Winston.

Light, Donald L., Jr. (1980). *Becoming Psychiatrists: The Professional Transformation of Self*. New York: W.W. Norton.

Lofland, John. (1966). *Doomsday Cult*. New York: Prentice-Hall.

Luster, Tom, Kelly Rhoades, and Bruce Haas. (1989). "The Relation between Parental Values and Parenting Behavior: A Test of the Kohn Hypothesis." *Journal of Marriage and the Family, 51* (February), 139–47.

Lytton, Hugh, and David Romney. 1991. "Parents' Differential Socialization of Boys and Girls: A Meta-Analysis." *Psychological Bulletin, 109,* 267–296.

Mackie, Marlene. (1991). *Gender Relations in Canada: Further Explorations*. Toronto: Butterworths Canada Ltd.

Mead, George H. (1934). *Mind, Self and Society*. Chicago: University of Chicago Press.

Narahara, M. (1998). *Gender Stereotypes in Children's Picture Books*. East Lansing, MI: National Center for Research on Teacher Learning (ERIC Document Reproduction Service No. ED 419248).

Oakes, Jeannie. (1985). *Keeping Track: How Schools Structure Inequality*. New Haven, CT: Yale University Press.

Piaget, Jean. (1950). *The Psychology of Intelligence*. Boston: Routledge and Kegan Paul.

Richer, Stephen. (1988). "Equality to Benefit from Schooling: The Issue of Educational Opportunity." In D. Forcese and S.

Richer, eds., *Social Issues: Sociological Views of Canada* (pp. 262–86). Toronto: Prentice Hall.

Rosenthal, Robert, and Lenore Jacobson. (1968). *Pygmalion and the Classroom*. New York: Holt, Rinehart and Winston.

Rubin, J., F. Provenzano, and Z. Luria. (1974). "The Eye of the Beholder: Parents' Views on Sex of Newborns." *American Journal of Orthopsychiatry, 44,* 512–19.

Russell, Rachael and Melissa Tyler. (2002). "Thank Heaven for Little Girls: 'Girl Haven' and the Commercial Context of Feminine Childhood." *Sociology, 36,* 619–37.

Sebald, H. (1992). *Adolescence: A Social Psychological Analysis*. Englewood Cliffs, NJ: Prentice Hall.

Shaffir, William. (1974). *Life in a Religious Community*. Toronto: Holt.

Shanas, Ethel, Peter Townsend, Dorothy Wedderburn, Henning Friis, Paul Milhøj, and Jan Stehouwer. (1972). *Old People in Three Industrial Societies*. New York: Atherton.

Shepard, Jon M. (1993). *Sociology*, 5th ed. New York: West.

Skolnick, Arlene. (1991). *Embattled Paradise: The American Family in an Age of Uncertainty*. New York: Basic Books.

Solomon, Yvette, Jo Warin, Charlie Lewis, and Wendy Langford. (2002). "Intimate Talk Between Parents and Their Teenage Children: Democratic Openness or Covert Control?" *Sociology, 36,* 965–83.

South, S., and S. Spitze. (1994). "Housework in Marital and Nonmarital Households." *American Sociological Review, 59,* 327–47.

Spitz, Rene A. (1945). "Hospitalism: An Inquiry into the Genesis of Psychiatric Conditions in Early Childhood." *The Psychoanalytic Study of the Child, 1,* 53–74.

Stebbins, Robert A. (1990). *Sociology: The Study of Society*, 2nd ed. New York: Harper and Row.

Stockard, Jean, and Miriam M. Johnson. (1992). *Sex and Gender in Society*, 2nd ed. Englewood Cliffs, NJ: Prentice-Hall.

Stryker, Sheldon. (1980). *Symbolic Interactionism*. Menlo Park, CA: Benjamin/Cummings.

Thorne, B. (1993). *Gender Play: Girls and Boys in School*. New Brunswick, NJ: Rutgers University Press.

White, L., and D. Brinkerhoff. (1981). "The Sexual Division of Labor: Evidence from Childhood." *Social Forces, 60,* 170–81.

Wolff, Michael. (1973). "Notes on the Behavior of Pedestrians." In A. Birenbaum and E. Sagarin (eds.), *People in Places: The Sociology of the Familiar*. New York: Praeger.

Wuthnow, Robert. (1998). *Loose Connections*. Cambridge, Mass.: Harvard University Press.

CHAPTER 5

Adherents.com. (2001). "Religion Statistics: Predominant Religions." On the World Wide Web at http://www.adherents.com/adh_predom.html (November 30, 2001).

Averett, Susan, and Sanders Korenman. (1996). "The Economic Reality of the Beauty Myth." *The Journal of Human Resources, 31,* 2, 304–330.

Bagley, Christopher, and Kathleen King. (1990). *Child Sexual Abuse: The Search for Healing*. London: Tavistock/Routledge.

Berch, D.B., and B.G. Bender. (1987). "Margins of Sexuality." *Psychology Today* (December), 54–57.

Bergen, D.J., and J.E. Williams. (1991). "Sex Stereotypes in the United States Revisited: 1972–1988." *Sex Roles, 24,* 413–23.

Bibby, Reginald W. (1995). *The Bibby Report: Social Trends Canadian Style.* Toronto: Stoddart.

Bleier, Ruth. (1984). *Science and Gender: A Critique of Biology and Its Theories on Women.* New York: Pergamon.

Blum, Deborah. (1997). *Sex on the Brain: The Biological Differences between Men and Women.* New York: Penguin Books.

Broverman, I.K., S.R. Vogel, D.M. Broverman, F.E. Clarkson, and P.S. Rosenkratz. (1972). "Sex-Role Stereotypes: A Current Appraisal." *Journal of Social Issues, 28,* 59–78.

Buss, D.M. (1994). *The Evolution of Desire.* New York: Basic Books.

Buss, D.M. (1995a). "Evolutionary Psychology: A New Paradigm for Psychological Science." *Psychological Inquiry, 6,* 1–30.

Buss, D.M. (1995b). "Psychological Sex Differences: Origins through Sexual Selection." *American Psychologist, 50,* 164–68.

Buss, D.M. (1998). "The Psychology of Human Mate Selection: Exploring the Complexity of the Strategic Repertoire." In C. Crawford and D.L. Krebs, eds., *Handbook of Evolutionary Psychology: Ideas, Issues, and Applications* (pp. 405–29). Mahwah, NJ: Erlbaum.

Buss, D.M., et al. (1990). "International Perspectives in Selecting Mates: A Study of 37 Cultures." *Journal of Cross-Cultural Psychology, 21,* 5–47.

Caplan, Paula J., and Jeremy B. Caplan. (1999 [1994]). *Thinking Critically about Research on Sex and Gender.* New York: Longman.

Colapinto, John. (1997). "The True Story of John/Joan." *Rolling Stone,* December 11, pp. 54–73, 92–97.

Colapinto, John. (2001 [2000]). *As Nature Made Him: The Boy Who Was Raised as a Girl.* New York: Perennial.

Condry, J., and S. Condry. (1976). "Sex Differences: A Study of the Eye of the Beholder." *Child Development, 47,* 812–19.

Coontz, Stephanie, and Peta Henderson, eds. (1986). *Women's Work, Men's Property: The Origins of Gender and Class.* London: Verso.

Creighton, Sarah, and Catherine Minto. (2001). "Managing Intersex." *British Medical Journal, 323* (7324), 1264–65.

Davis, Simon. (1990). "Men as Success Objects and Women as Sex Objects: A Study of Personal Advertisements." *Sex Roles, 23,* 43–50.

Davis, T., G. Peck, and J. Stormant. (1993). "Acquaintance Rape and the High School Student." *Journal of Adolescent Health, 14,* 220–24.

Dawkins, Richard. (1976). *The Selfish Gene.* London: Oxford University Press.

DeKeseredy, Walter S., and M.D. Schwartz. (1998). *Woman Abuse on Campus: Results from the Canadian National Survey.* Thousand Oaks, CA: Sage.

Duffy, Ann. (1998). "The Feminist Challenge: Knowing and Ending the Violence." In Nancy Mandell, ed., *Feminist Issues: Race, Class and Sexuality* (pp. 132–59). Scarborough, ON: Prentice Hall Allyn and Bacon Canada.

Durex. (2001). *Global Survey 2001: Global Survey into Sexual Attitudes and Behaviour.* On the World Wide Web at http://www.durex.com/index.html (5 September 2002).

Dworkin, Andrea. (1981). *Pornography: Men Possessing Women.* New York: Penguin.

Eagley, Alice H., and Wendy Wood. (1999). "The Origins of Sex Differences in Human Behaviour. Evolved Dispositions versus Social Roles." *American Psychologist, 54,* 408–23.

Eccles, J.S., J.E. Jacobs, and R.D. Harold. (1990). "Gender-role Stereotypes, Expectancy Effects and Parents' Socialization of Gender Differences." *Journal of Social Issues, 46,* 183–201.

Eichler, Margrit. (1980). *The Double Standard.* London: Croom Helm.

Eisler, Riane. (1995 [1987]). *The Chalice and the Blade.* New York: HarperCollins.

Elkin, F., and G. Handel. (1989). *The Child and Society: The Process of Socialization,* 5th ed. New York: Random House.

Feiring, C., and M. Lewis. (1979). "Sex and Age Differences in Young Children's Reactions to Frustration: A Further Look at the Goldberg and Lewis Subjects." *Child Development, 50,* 848–53.

Fitzgerald, Louise F. (1993). "Sexual Harassment against Women in the Workplace." *American Psychologist, 48,* 1070–76.

Freud, Sigmund. (1977 [1905]). *On Sexuality.* Trans. James Strachey; comp. and ed. Angela Richards. Vol. 7 of the Pelican Freud Library. Harmondsworth, UK: Penguin Books.

Gadd, Jane. (1997). "More Boys Physically Abused Than Girls." *The Globe and Mail,* July 9, A1, A6.

Garner, David M. (1997). "The 1997 Body Image Survey Results." *Psychology Today, 30* (January–February), 30–44, 74–80, 84.

Goldberg, S., and M. Lewis. (1969). "Play Behaviour in the Year-old Infant: Early Sex Differences." *Child Development, 40,* 21–31.

Grescoe, P. (1996). *The Merchants of Venus: Inside Harlequin and the Empire of Romance.* Vancouver: Raincoast.

Gruber, J.E. (1997). "An Epidemiology of Sexual Harassment: Evidence from North America and Europe." In W. O'Donohue, ed., *Sexual Harassment: Theory, Research and Treatment* (pp. 84–98). Boston: Allyn and Bacon.

Hamer, D., and P.F. Copeland. (1996). *The Science of Desire: The Search for the Gay Gene and the Biology of Behaviour.* New York: Touchstone Books.

Hatfield, Elaine. (1995). "What Do Women and Men Want from Love and Sex?" In E.D. Nelson and B.W. Robinson, eds., *Gender in the 1990s: Images, Realities, and Issues* (pp. 257–75). Toronto: Nelson Canada.

Hesse-Biber, Sharlene. (1996). *Am I Thin Enough Yet? The Cult of Thinness and the Commercialization of Identity.* New York: Oxford University Press.

Hobart, Charles. (1996). "Intimacy and Family Life: Sexuality, Cohabitation, and Marriage." In Maureen Baker, ed., *Families: Changing Trends in Canada* (pp. 143–73). Toronto: McGraw-Hill Ryerson.

"Homosexuality and Bisexuality." (2000). Report #5 to the *Toronto Sun* in the Third Annual Sun/COMPAS Sex Survey. On the World Wide Web at http://www.compas.ca/html/archivesdocument.asp?compasSection=Sun+Media+Sex+Poll&GO=GO&compasID=61 (9 August 2002).

Hughes, Fergus P. (1995 [1991]). *Children, Play and Development,* 2nd ed. Boston: Allyn and Bacon.

Human Rights Watch. (1995). *The Human Rights Watch Global Report on Women's Human Rights*. New York: Human Rights Watch.

Jeffreys, Sheila. (1990). "Heterosexuality and the Desire for Gender." In Diane Richardson, ed., *Theorising Heterosexuality* (pp. 75–90). Buckingham, UK: Open University Press.

Jensen, Margaret Ann. (1984). *Love's Sweet Return: The Harlequin Story*. Toronto: Women's Press.

Kerig, Patricia K., Philip A. Cowan, and Carolyn Pape Cowan. (1993). "Marital Quality and Gender Differences in Parent–Child Interaction." *Developmental Psychology, 29*, 931–39.

Kitzinger, Celia, and Sue Wilkinson. (1994). "Problematizing Pleasure: Radical Feminist Deconstructions of Sexuality and Power." In H.L. Radtke and H.J. Stam, eds., *Power/Gender: Social Relations in Theory and Practice*. London: Sage.

Koff, Elissa, and Amy Benavage. (1998). "Breast Size Perception and Satisfaction, Body Image, and Psychological Functioning in Caucasian and Asian American College Women." *Sex Roles, 38* (7/8), 655–73.

Koss, Mary P., L.A. Goodman, A. Browne, L.F. Fitzgerald, G.P. Keita, and N.F. Russo. (1994). *No Safe Haven: Male Violence against Women at Home, at Work, and in the Community*. Washington, DC: American Psychological Association.

Laumann, Edward O., John H. Gagnon, Robert T. Michael, and Stuart Michaels. (1994). *The Social Organization of Sexuality: Sexual Practices in the United States*. Chicago: University of Chicago Press.

Lenton, Rhonda, Michael D. Smith, John Fox, and Norman Morra. (1999). "Sexual Harassment in Public Places: Experiences of Canadian Women." *Canadian Review of Sociology and Anthropology, 36*, 517–40.

Lightfoot-Klein, Hanny, Cheryl Chase, Tim Hammond and Ronald Goldman. (2000). "Genital Surgery on Children Below the Age of Consent." In Lenore T. Szuchman and Frank Muscarella, eds., *Psychological Perspectives on Human Sexuality* (pp. 440–49). New York: John Wiley and Sons.

Lips, H.M. (1993). *Sex and Gender: An Introduction*, 2nd ed. Mountain View, CA: Mayfield.

Lisak, David. (1992). "Sexual Aggression, Masculinity, and Fathers." *Signs, 16*, 238–62.

MacDonald, K., and R.D. Parke. (1986). "Parent–Child Physical Play: The Effects of Sex and Age on Children and Parents." *Sex Roles, 15*, 367–78.

Mackay, Judith. 2000. *The Penguin Atlas of Human Sexual Behaviour*. New York: Penguin.

MacKinnon, C.A. (1987). *Feminism Unmodified: Discourses on Life and Law*. Cambridge, MA: Harvard University Press.

Masters, W.H., and V.E. Johnson. (1966). *Human Sexual Response*. Boston: Little, Brown.

Matrix, C., ed. (1996). *Tales for the Clit*. Edinburgh: AK Press.

Mead, Margaret. (1935). *Sex and Temperament in Three Primitive Societies*. New York: Dell.

Michael, Robert T., John H. Gagnon, Edward O. Laumann, and Gina Kolata. (1994). *Sex in America: A Definitive Survey*. Boston: Little, Brown.

Nelson, E.D., and Barrie W. Robinson. (1999). *Gender in Canada*. Scarborough, ON: Prentice Hall Allyn and Bacon Canada.

Nolen, Stephanie. (1999). "Gender: The Third Way." *The Globe and Mail*, September 25, D1, D4.

Peele, Stanton, and Richard De Grandpre. (1995). "My Genes Made Me Do It." *Psychology Today, 28*, 50–68.

Pipher, M. (1994). *Reviving Ophelia: Saving the Selves of Adolescent Girls*. New York: Ballantine.

Pryor, John B., J.L. Giedd, and K.B. Williams. (1995). "A Social Psychological Model for Predicting Sexual Harassment." *Journal of Social Issues, 51*, 69–84.

Raag, Tarja, and Christine L. Rackliff. (1998). "Preschoolers' Awareness of Social Expectations of Gender: Relationships to Toy Choices." *Sex Roles, 38*, 685–700.

Reiss, I. (1986). *Journey into Sexuality: An Exploratory Voyage*. Englewood Cliffs, NJ: Prentice Hall.

Rich, Adrienne. (1996 [1980]). "Compulsory Heterosexuality and Lesbian Existence." In Stevi Jackson and Sue Scott, eds., *Feminism and Sexuality: A Reader* (pp. 130–43). New York: Columbia University Press.

Rosenkrantz, P., S.R. Vogel, H. Bee, I.K. Broverman, and D.M. Broverman. (1968). "Sex-role Stereotypes and Self Concepts in College Students." *Journal of Consulting and Clinical Psychology, 32*, 287–95.

Rubin, J.Z., F.J. Provenzano, and Z. Lurra. (1974). "The Eye of the Beholder." *American Journal of Orthpsychiatry, 44*, 512–19.

Ryan, Kathryn M., and Jeanne Kanjorski. (1998). "The Enjoyment of Sexist Humor, Rape Attitudes, and Relationship Aggression in College Students." *Sex Roles, 38*, 743–56.

"Same-Sex Marriages and Civil Unions." (2002). On the World Wide Web at http://www.religioustolerance.org/ hom_marr.htm#menu (12 September).

Sanday, Peggy. (1981). *Female Power and Male Dominance*. Cambridge, UK: Cambridge University Press.

Saxton, Lloyd. (1990 [1968]). *The Individual, Marriage and the Family*, 7th ed. Belmont, CA: Wadsworth.

Shorter, Edward. (1997). *A History of Psychiatry*. New York: John Wiley and Sons.

Statistics Canada. (1994). *Violence against Women Survey*. Microdata File. Ottawa.

Steinem, G. (1994). *Moving beyond Words*. New York: Simon and Schuster.

Straus, Murray. (1995). "Trends in Cultural Norms and Rates of Partner Violence." In Sandra M. Stith and Murray A. Straus, eds., *Understanding Partner Violence: Prevalence, Causes, Consequences, and Solutions* (pp. 30–33). Minneapolis, MN: National Council on Family Relations.

Tavris, Carol. (1992). *The Mismeasure of Woman: Why Women Are Not the Better Sex, the Inferior Sex, or the Opposite Sex*. New York: Touchstone.

Thompson, Linda. (1991). "Family Work: Women's Sense of Fairness." *Journal of Family Issues, 12*, 181–96.

Twenge, Jean M. (1997). "Changes in Masculine and Feminine Traits over Time: A Meta-analysis." *Sex Roles, 36*, 305–25.

Udry, J.R. (1971). *The Social Context of Marriage*, 2nd ed. Philadelphia: J.B. Lippincott.

Walters, Vivienne. (1992). "Women's Views of Their Main Health Problems." *Canadian Journal of Public Health, 83* (5), 371–74.

Weeks, Jeffrey. (1986). *Sexuality*. London: Routledge.

Welsh, Sandy, and A. Nierobisz. (1997). "How Prevalent Is Sexual Harassment? A Research Note on Measuring Sexual Harassment in Canada." *Canadian Journal of Sociology, 22,* 505–22.

Welsh, Sandy. (1999). "Gender and Sexual Harassment." *Annual Review of Sociology, 25,* 169–90.

Williams, J.E., and D.L. Best. (1982). *Measuring Sex Stereotypes: A Thirty-Nation Study.* Beverley Hills, CA: Sage.

Williams, J.E., and S.M. Bennett. (1975). "The Definition of Sex Stereotypes via the Adjective Check List." *Sex Roles, 1,* 327–37.

Wilson, Edward. (1975). *Sociobiology.* Cambridge, MA: Harvard University Press.

Wilson, Edward. (1978). *On Human Nature.* Cambridge, MA: Harvard University Press.

Wilson, Margo, and Martin Daly. (1994). "Lethal and Nonlethal Violence against Wives and the Evolutionary Psychology of Male Sexual Proprietariness." In R. Emerson Dobash and Russell P. Dobash, eds., *Rethinking Violence Against Women* (199–230). Thousand Oaks, CA: Sage.

Wolf, Naomi. (1991). *The Beauty Myth.* Toronto: Vintage Books.

CHAPTER 6

Attewell, P. (2001). "The First and Second Digital Divides." *Sociology of Education, 74* (July), 252–59.

Baym, N. (2000). *Tune In, Log On: Soaps, Fandom, and Online Community.* Thousand Oaks and London: SAGE Publications.

Buckingham, D. (1998). "Children and Television: A Critical Overview of Research." In R. Dickinson, R. Harindranath, and O. Linné, eds., *Approaches to Audiences: A Reader* (pp. 131–145). London: Arnold.

Candussi, D. and J. Winters. (1988). "Monopoly and Content in Winnipeg." In R. Picard et al., eds., *Press Concentration and Monopoly: New Perspectives on Newspaper Ownership and Operation* (pp. 139–45). Norwood, NJ: Ablex.

Carroll, W., and R. Ratner. (1999). "Media Strategies and Political Projects: A Comparative Study of Social Movements." *Canadian Journal of Sociology, 24* (1), 1–34.

Carter, C., and M. Durand. (2000). "Market Opportunities: International Trade of Culture Goods and Services." Statistics Canada. *Focus on Culture, 12* (4), 1–15.

Cherny, L. (1999). *Conversation and Community: Chat in a Virtual World.* Stanford: CSLI Publications.

Collins, R. (1990). *Culture, Communication and National Identity: The Case of Canadian Television.* Toronto: University of Toronto Press.

Cooper, B. (1994). *Sins of Omission: Shaping the News at CBC TV.* Toronto: University of Toronto Press.

Cultural Access Group. (2001). *Ethnicity in the Electronic Age: Looking at the Internet Through Multicultural Lens.* On the World Wide Web at http://www.accesscag.com/internet%20report%20v.pdf.

Cuneo, C. (2002). "Globalized and Localized Digital Divides Along the Information Highway: A Fragile Synthesis Across Bridges, Ramps, Cloverleaves, and Ladders." Hamilton, ON Institute for Globalization and the Human Condition Working Paper Series.

Dickinson, P. and J. Ellison. (2000). "Plugging In: the Increase of Household Internet Use Continues into 1999." Ottawa: Ministry of Industry, Connectedness Series. Statistics Canada Catalogue No. 56F0004MIE, No. 1. November.

DiMaggio, P., et al. (2001). "Social Implications of the Internet." *Annual Review of Sociology, 27,* 307–336.

Doyle, A., B. Elliott, and D. Tindall. (1997). "Framing the Forests: Corporations, the B.C. Forest Alliance, and the Media." In W. Carroll, ed., *Organizing Dissent: Contemporary Social Movements in Theory and Practice* (pp. 240–68). Toronto: Garamond Press.

Ellis, D. (1992). *Split Screens: Home Entertainment and the New Technologies.* Toronto: Friends of Canadian Broadcasting.

Ericson, R., P. Baranek , and J. Chan. (1989). *Negotiating Control: A Study of News Sources.* Toronto: University of Toronto Press.

Felson, R. (1996). "Mass Media Effects on Violent Behaviour." In R. Hagen and K. Cook, eds., *Annual Review of Sociology, 22,* 103–28

Fiske, J. (1987). *Television Culture.* London: Methuen.

Forman, H. (1933). *Our Movie-Made Children.* New York: Macmillan.

Freedman, J. (1984). "Effect of Television Violence on Aggressiveness." *Psychological Bulletin, 96* (2), 227–46.

Friedrich-Cofer, L. and A. Huston. (1986). "Television Violence and Aggression: The Debate Continues." *Psychological Bulletin, 100* (3), 364–71.

Gauntlett, D. (1998). "Ten Things Wrong with the 'Effects' Model." In R. Dickinson, R. Harindranath, and O. Linné, eds., *Approaches to Audiences: A Reader* (pp. 120–30). London: Arnold.

Geen, R., and S. Thomas. (1986). "The Immediate Effects of Media Violence on Behaviour." *Journal of Social Issues, 42* (3), 7–27.

Gerbner, G. et al. (1994). "Growing Up With Television: The Cultivation Perspective." In J. Bryant and D. Zillmann, eds., *Media Effects: Advances in Theory and Research* (pp. 17–41). Hillsdale, NJ: Lawrence Erlbaum Associates.

Gillespie, M. (1995). *Television, Ethnicity and Cultural Change.* London and New York: Routledge.

Gitlin, T. (1980). *The Whole World Is Watching.* Berkeley: University of California Press.

Goffman, E. (1974). *Frame Analysis.* Philadelphia: University of Pennsylvania Press.

Gosselin, A. et al. (1997). "Violence on Canadian Television and Some of Its Cognitive Effects." *Canadian Journal of Communication, 22,* 143–60.

Granovetter, M. (1973). "The Strength of Weak Ties." *American Journal of Sociology, 78* (6), 1360–80.

Gunter, B. (1995). *Television and Gender Representation.* London: John Libbey and Company.

Hackett, R. (1991). *News and Dissent: The Press and the Politics of Peace in Canada.* Norwood, NJ: Ablex.

Hall, S. (1980). "Encoding/Decoding." In S. Hall et al., eds., *Culture, Media, Language* (pp. 128–38). London: Hutchinson.

Herman, E. and N. Chomsky. (1988). *Manufacturing Consent: The Political Economy of the Mass Media.* New York: Pantheon.

Hobson, D. (1982). *Crossroads: The Drama of a Soap Opera.* London: Methuen.

Hodge, R., and D. Tripp. (1986). *Children and Television: A Semiotic Approach*. Cambridge: Polity Press.

Horkheimer, M., and T. Adorno. (1982 [1947]). *Dialectic of Enlightenment*. New York: Continuum Books.

Huesmann, L., and N. Malamuth. (1986). "Media Violence and Anti-Social Behaviour: An Overview." *Journal of Social Issues*, *42* (3), 1–6.

Innis, H. (1951). *The Bias of Communication*. Toronto: University of Toronto Press.

Jupiter Media Metrix. (2001). "In Search of Love Online: Men Outnumber Women on Personals Sites." On the World Wide Web at www.jmm.com/xp/jmm/press/2001/pr_020801c.xml.

Klapper, J. (1960). *The Effects of Mass Communication*. Glencoe: Free Press.

Knight, G. (1982). "News and Ideology." *Canadian Journal of Communication*, *8* (4), 15–41.

Knight, G. (1998). "Hegemony, the Media, and New Right Politics: Ontario in the Late 1990s." *Critical Sociology*, *24* (1/2), 105–29.

Knight, G., and J. O'Connor. (1995). "Social Democracy Meets the Press: Media Coverage of Industrial Relations Legislation." *Research in Political Sociology*, 7, 183–206.

Kraut, R. et al. (1998). "Internet Paradox: A Social Technology that Reduces Social Involvement and Psychological Well-Being?" *American Psychologist*, *53* (9), 1017–1032.

Kraut, R. et al. (2002). "Internet Paradox Revisited." *Journal of social Issues*, *58* (1), 49–74.

McCombs, M. (1988). "Concentration, Monopoly, and Content." In R. Picard et al., eds., *Press Concentration and Monopoly: New Perspectives on Newspaper Ownership and Operation* (pp. 129–37). Norwood, NJ: Ablex.

McCormack, T. (1994). "Codes, Ratings and Rights." *Institute for Social Research Newsletter*. Toronto: York University, 9 (1): n.p.

McLuhan, M. (1964). *Understanding Media: The Extensions of Man*. New York: Mentor Books.

Miller, D. and D. Slater. (2000). *The Internet: An Ethnographic Approach*. Oxford and New York: Berg.

Morley, D. (1986). *Family Television: Cultural Power and Domestic Leisure*. London: Comedia.

Morley, D. (2000). *Home Territories: Media, Mobility and Identity*. London and New York: Routledge.

National Media Archive. (1993). "Immigration I: The Human Interest Story." *On Balance*, *6* (3), 1–8. Vancouver: The Fraser Institute.

NUA. (2002). "How Many Online?" On the World Wide Web at http://www.nua.ie/surveys/how_many_online/.

Perse, E.M. (2001). *Media Effects and Society*. Mahwah, NJ, and London: Lawrence Erlbaum Associates, Publishers.

Postman, N. (1992). *Technopoly: The Surrender of Culture to Technology*. New York: Knopf.

Press, A. (1991). *Women Watching Television: Gender, Class and Generation in the American Television Experience*. Philadelphia: University of Pennsylvania Press.

Reid, E. (1999). "Hierarchy and Power: Social Control in Cyberspace." In M. A. Smith and P. Kollock, eds., *Communities in Cyberspace* (pp. 107–33). London and New York: Routledge.

Schutz, A. (1970). *Reflections on the Problem of Relevance*. R.M. Zaner, ed., New Haven, CN: Yale University Press.

Statistics Canada. (1997). *Canada's Culture, Heritage, and Identity: A Statistical Perspective*. Ottawa: Minister of Industry.

Statistics Canada. (2001a). "The Internet: Who's Connected—Who's Shopping." *Focus on Culture*, *13* (2), 10–13.

Statistics Canada. (2001b). "Radio Listening, Fall 2000. Television Viewing, Fall 2000." *Focus on Culture*, *13* (2), 14–15.

Taras, D. (1990). *The Newsmakers: The Media's Influence on Canadian Politics*. Scarborough: Nelson.

Tomlinson, J. (1997). "Cultural Globalization and Cultural Imperialism." In A. Mohammadi, ed., *International Communication and Globalization* (pp. 170–90). London: SAGE Publications.

Trim, K., with G. Pizante and J. Yaraskavitch. (1983). "The Effect of Monopoly on the News: A Before and After Study of Two Canadian One Newspaper Towns." *Canadian Journal of Communication*, *9* (3), 33–56.

Watson, N. (1997). "Why We Argue About Virtual Community: A Case Study of the Phish.Net Fan Community." In S.G. Jones, ed., *Virtual Culture: Identity and Community in Cyberspace* (pp. 102–32). London and Thousand Oaks: SAGE Publications.

Wellman, B., and M. Gulia. (1999). "Virtual Communities as Communities: Net Surfers Don't Ride Alone." In M.A. Smith and P. Kollock, eds., *Communities in Cyberspace* (pp. 167–94). London and New York: Routledge.

Williams, T. M. et al. (1986). *The Impact of Television: A Natural Experiment in Three Communities*. Orlando: Academic Press.

Wober, J. M. (1998). "Cultural Indicators: European Reflections on a Research Paradigm." In R. Dickinson, R. Harindranath, and O. Linné, eds., *Approaches to Audiences: A Reader* (pp. 61–73). London: Arnold.

Znaimer, M. (1996). "TVTV Talks Back: A Rebuttal." *Canadian Journal of Communication*, *21* (1), 67–73.

CHAPTER 7

Bellah, Robert. (1967). "Civil Religion in America." *Daedalus*, *96*, 1–21.

Berger, Peter. (1961). *The Noise of Solemn Assemblies*. New York: Doubleday.

Bergin, Allan E. (1983). "Religiosity and Mental Health: A Critical Reevaluation and Meta-analysis." *Professional Psychology: Research and Practice*, *14*, 170–84.

Beyer, Peter. (1993). "Roman Catholicism in Contemporary Quebec." In W.E. Hewitt, ed., *The Sociology of Religion: A Canadian Focus* (pp. 133–55). Toronto: Butterworths.

Beyer, Peter. (1997). "Religious Vitality in Canada: The Complementarity of Religious Market and Secularization Perspectives." *Journal for the Scientific Study of Religion*, *36*, 272–88.

Bibby, Reginald W. (1987). *Fragmented Gods: The Poverty and Potential of Religion in Canada*. Toronto: Stoddart.

Bibby, Reginald W. (1993). *Unknown Gods: The Ongoing Story of Religion in Canada*. Toronto: Stoddart.

Bibby, Reginald W. (1994). *Unitrends*. Toronto: United Church of Canada, Department of Stewardship Services.

Bibby, Reginald W. (1995). *The Bibby Report: Social Trends Canadian Style*. Toronto: Stoddart.

Bibby, Reginald W. (1996). *Project Canada Consultation on Research and Ministry*. Lethbridge, AB: The University of Lethbridge.

Bibby, Reginald W. (1997). "Going, Going, Gone: The Impact of Geographical Mobility on Religious Involvement." *Review of Religious Research*, 38, 289–307.

Bibby, Reginald W. (2002). *Restless Gods: The Renaissance of Religion in Canada*. Toronto: Stoddart.

Bibby, Reginald W., and Merlin B. Brinkerhoff. (1973). "The Circulation of the Saints: A Study of People Who Join Conservative Churches." *Journal for the Scientific Study of Religion*, 12, 273–83.

Bibby, Reginald W., and Merlin B. Brinkerhoff. (1983). "Circulation of the Saints Revisited: A Longitudinal Look at Conservative Church Growth." *Journal for the Scientific Study of Religion*, 22, 253–62.

Bibby, Reginald W., and Merlin B. Brinkerhoff. (1994). "Circulation of the Saints: 1966–1990: New Data, New Reflections." *Journal for the Scientific Study of Religion*, 33, 273–80.

Brady, Diane. (1991). "Saving the Boomers." *Maclean's*, June 3, 50–51.

Brannon, Robert. (1971). "Organizational Vulnerability in Modern Religious Organizations." *Journal for the Scientific Study of Religion*, 10, 27–32.

Campbell, Robert A., and James E. Curtis. (1994). "Religious Involvement across Societies." *Journal for the Scientific Study of Religion*, 33, 215–29.

Chang, Patricia M.Y., and Viviana Bompadre. (1999). "Crowded Pulpits: Observations and Explanations of the Clergy Oversupply in the Protestant Churches, 1950–1993." *Journal for the Scientific Study of Religion*, 38, 398–410.

Clark, S.D. (1948). *Church and Sect in Canada*. Toronto: University of Toronto Press.

Cogley, John. (1968). *Religion in a Secular Age*. New York: New American Library.

Crysdale, Stewart. (1961). *The Industrial Struggle and Protestant Ethics in Canada*. Toronto: Ryerson Press.

Davies, Alan, and Marilyn F. Nefsky. (1997). *How Silent Were the Churches? Canadian Protestantism and the Jewish Plight during the Nazi Era*. Waterloo, ON: Wilfrid Laurier University Press.

Demerath, N.J., III, and Phillip E. Hammond. (1969). *Religion in Social Context*. New York: Random House.

Dobbelaere, Karel. (1981). "Secularization: A Multi-Dimensional Concept." *Current Sociology*, 29, 201–16.

Durkheim, Émile. (1965 [1912]). *The Elementary Forms of the Religious Life*. New York: Free Press.

Fallding, Harold. (1978). "Mainline Protestantism in Canada and the United States: An Overview." *Canadian Journal of Sociology*, 2, 141–60.

Finke, Roger, and Rodney Stark. (1992). *The Churching of America, 1776–1990*. New Brunswick, NJ: Rutgers University Press.

Fledderus, Bill. (1997). "Evangelicals More Similar to Catholics, American Cousins than to Each Other: Angus Reid Poll." *Faith Today* (January–February), 18–19.

Frankel, B., Gail, and W.E. Hewitt. (1994). "Religion and Well-Being among Canadian University Students." *Journal for the Scientific Study of Religion*, 33, 62–73.

Freud, Sigmund. (1962 [1928]). *The Future of an Illusion*. New York: Doubleday.

Gee, Ellen M., and Jean E. Veevers. (1990). "Religious Involvement and Life Satisfaction in Canada." *Sociological Analysis*, 51, 387–94.

Geertz, Clifford. (1968). "Religion as a Cultural System." In Donald Cutler, ed., *The Religious Situation* (pp. 1–46). Boston: Beacon Press.

Gerth, H., and C. Wright Mills. (1958). *From Max Weber: Essays in Sociology*. New York: Oxford University Press.

Glock, Charles, Benjamin Ringer, and Earl Babbie. (1967). *To Comfort and to Challenge*. Berkeley, CA: University of California Press.

Glock, Charles Y., and Rodney Stark. (1965). *Religion and Society in Tension*. Chicago: Rand-McNally.

Gorsuch, Richard L. (1988). "Psychology of Religion." *Annual Review of Psychology*, 39, 201–21.

Gorsuch, Richard, and Daniel Aleshire. (1974). "Christian Faith and Ethnic Prejudice: A Review and Interpretation of Research." *Journal for the Scientific Study of Religion*, 13, 281–307.

Hadden, Jeffrey. (1969). *The Gathering Storm in the Churches*. Garden City, NJ: Doubleday.

Herberg, Will. (1960). *Protestant, Catholic, Jew*, rev. ed. New York: Doubleday.

Hewitt, W.E. (1992). "The Social Justice Program of the Canadian Catholic Church: An International Case-Comparative Analysis." *Sociological Analysis*, 53, 141–58.

Hobart, Charles. (1974). "Church Involvement and the Comfort Thesis." *Journal for the Scientific Study of Religion*, 13, 463–70.

Hunsberger, Bruce. (1980). "A Reexamination of the Antecedents of Apostasy." *Review of Religious Research*, 21, 158–70.

Hunsberger, Bruce, and L.B. Brown. (1984). "Religious Socialization, Apostasy, and the Impact of Family Background." *Journal for the Scientific Study of Religion*, 23, 239–51.

Kanagy, Conrad L., and Leo Driedger. (1996). "Changing Mennonite Values." *Review of Religious Research*, 37, 342–53.

Kelley, Dean. (1972). *Why Conservative Churches Are Growing*. New York: Harper and Row.

Kirkpatrick, Clifford. (1949). "Religion and Humanitarianism: A Study of Institutional Implications." *Psychological Monographs*, 63 (9).

Lee, Gary, and Robert Clyde. (1974). "Religion, Socioeconomic Status, and Anomie." *Journal for the Scientific Study of Religion*, 13, 35–47.

Lewis, David L. (1993). "Canada's Native Peoples and the Churches." In W.E. Hewitt, ed., *The Sociology of Religion: A Canadian Focus* (pp. 235–51). Toronto: Butterworths.

Luidens, Donald A., and Roger J. Nemeth. (1989). "After the Storm: Closing the Clergy–Laity Gap." *Review of Religious Research*, 31, 183–95.

Marx, Karl. (1970 [1843]). *Critique of Hegel's "Philosophy of Right."* Trans. Annette Jolin and Joseph O'Malley. Cambridge, MA: Harvard University Press.

Marx, Karl, and Friedrich Engels. (1964). *On Religion.* New York: Schocken Books.

Metz, Donald. (1967). *New Congregations: Security and Mission in Conflict.* Philadelphia: Westminster Press.

Mitchell, Robert. (1966). "Polity, Church Attractiveness, and Ministers' Careers." *Journal for the Scientific Study of Religion, 5,* 241–58.

Monahan, Susanne C. (1999). "Who Controls Church Work? Organizational Effects on Jurisdictional Boundaries and Disputes in Churches." *Journal for the Scientific Study of Religion, 38,* 370–85.

Nemeth, Mary. (1993). "God Is Alive: The Religion Poll." *Maclean's,* April 12, 32–37.

O'Toole, Roger, Douglas F. Campbell, John A. Hannigan, Peter Beyer, and John H. Simpson. (1993). "The United Church in Crisis." In W.E. Hewitt, ed., *The Sociology of Religion: A Canadian Focus* (pp. 273–87). Toronto: Butterworths.

Poloma, Margaret M. (1997). "The 'Toronto Blessing': Charisma, Institutionalization and Revival." *Journal for the Scientific Study of Religion, 36,* 257–71.

Poloma, Margaret M., and Lynette F. Hoelter. (1998). "The 'Toronto Blessing": A Holistic Model of Healing." *Journal for the Scientific Study of Religion, 37,* 257–72.

Rokeach, Milton. (1965). *Paradoxes of Religious Belief.* Information Service, National Council of Churches, February 13, 1–2.

Rokeach, Milton. (1969). "Religious Values and Social Compassion." *Review of Religious Research, 11,* 3–23.

Roof, Wade Clark, and Dean R. Hoge. (1980). "Church Involvement in America: Social Factors Affecting Membership and Participation." *Review of Religious Research, 21,* 405–26.

Roozen, David A., William McKinney, and Wayne Thompson. (1990). "The 'Big Chill' Generation Warms to Worship." *Review of Religious Research, 31,* 314–22.

Rouleau, Jean-Paul. (1977). "Religion in Quebec: Present and Future." Pro Mundi Vita: Dossiers, November–December, No. 3.

Smith, Tom W. (1999). "The Religious Right and Anti-Semitism." *Review of Religious Research, 99,* 244–58.

Srole, Leo. (1956). "Social Integration and Certain Corollaries." *American Sociological Review, 21,* 709–16.

Stahl, William. (1986). "The Land That God Gave Cain: Nature and Civil Religion in Canada." Presented at the annual meeting of the Society for the Scientific Study of Religion, Washington, DC, November.

Stark, Rodney, and William Sims Bainbridge. (1985). *The Future of Religion.* Berkeley, CA: University of California Press.

Stark, Rodney, and Charles Y. Glock. (1968). *American Piety.* Berkeley, CA: University of California Press.

Statistics Canada. (1993). *Religions in Canada.* 1991 Census of Canada. Cat. no. 93-319. Ottawa: Industry, Science and Technology Canada.

Stiller, Brian. (1997). *From the Tower of Babel to Parliament Hill.* Toronto: HarperCollins.

Weber, Max. (1958 [1904–1905]). *The Protestant Ethic and the Spirit of Capitalism.* New York: Scribner's.

Weber, Max. (1963). *Sociology of Religion.* Boston: Beacon Press.

Whyte, Donald. (1966). "Religion and the Rural Church." In M.A. Tremblay and W.J. Anderson, eds., *Rural Canada in Transition* (pp. 79–92). Ottawa: Agricultural Economics Research Council of Canada.

Wilcox, W. Bradford. (1998). "Conservative Protestant Childrearing: Authoritarian or Authoritative?" *American Sociological Review, 63,* 796–809.

Wilson, Bryan. (1975). "The Secularization Debate." *Encounter, 45,* 77–83.

Wimberley, Ronald C. (1971). "Mobility in Ministerial Career Patterns: An Exploration." *Journal for the Scientific Study of Religion, 10,* 249–53.

CHAPTER 8

Antoniou, Andreas, and Robin Rowley. (1986). "The Ownership Structure of the Largest Canadian Corporations, 1979." *Canadian Journal of Sociology, 11,* 253–68.

Belford, Terrance. (2002). "Lawyers Take Defensive Over Land-Claims Mess." *Globe and Mail,* October 21, B1.

Black, Don, and John Myles. (1986). "Dependent Industrialization and the Canadian Class Structure: A Comparative Analysis." *The Canadian Review of Anthropology and Sociology, 23,* 157–81.

Boothby, Daniel. (1993). "Schooling, Literacy and the Labour Market: Towards a 'Literacy Shortage'?" *Canadian Public Policy, 19,* 29–35.

Brym, Robert J. (1979). "Political Conservatism in Atlantic Canada." In Robert J. Brym and R. James Sacouman, eds., *Underdevelopment and Social Movements in Atlantic Canada* (pp. 59–79). Toronto: New Hogtown Press.

Calliste, Agnes. (1987). "Sleeping Car Porters in Canada: An Ethnically Submerged Split Labour Market." *Canadian Ethnic Studies, 19,* 1–20.

Canadian Council on Social Development. (2002). "Free Statistics." On the World Wide Web at http://www.ccsd.ca/facts.html (23 June 2003).

Clark, Terry Nichols, and Seymour Martin Lipset. (1991). "Are Social Classes Dying?" *International Sociology, 6,* 397–410.

Corak, Miles. (1998). "Does Your Parents' Income Count?" *Canadian Social Trends* (Summer), 6–10.

Creese, Gillian, Neil Guppy, and Martin Meissner. (1991). *Ups and Downs on the Ladder of Success: Social Mobility in Canada.* General Social Survey Analysis Series 5. Cat. no. 11–612E, no. 5. Ottawa: Statistics Canada.

Davis, Kingsley, and Wilbert E. Moore. (1945). "Some Principles of Stratification." *American Sociological Review, 10,* 242–49.

Economic Council of Canada. (1992). *The New Face of Poverty: Income Security Needs of Canadian Families.* Cat. no. EC22-186/1992E. Ottawa: Supply and Services Canada.

Edmonton Journal. (2002). "Kodak To Crop up to 1,700 Jobs After Slump." October 25, F8.

Edmonton Journal. (2002). "Wendy's Earnings up 16 Per Cent." October 25, F8.

Esping-Andersen, Gøsta. (1990). *Three Worlds of Welfare Capitalism*. Princeton, NJ: Princeton University Press.

Forcese, Dennis. (1997). *The Canadian Class Structure*, 4th ed. Toronto: McGraw-Hill Ryerson.

Gee, Marcus. (2002). "Texan Could Become Only Black U.S. Senator." *Globe and Mail*, October 24, A12.

Grabb, Edward G. 2002. *Theories of Social Inequality*. 4th ed. Toronto: Harcourt Canada.

Hughes, Karen. (1995). "Women in Non-traditional Occupations." *Perspectives on Labour and Income*, 7 (Autumn), 14–19.

Kelly, Karen, Linda Howatson-Leo, and Warren Clark. (1997). "I Feel Overqualified for My Job…" *Canadian Social Trends* (Winter), 11–16.

Krahn, Harvey. (1995). "Non-standard Work on the Rise." *Perspectives on Labour and Income*, 7 (Winter), 35–42.

Krahn, Harvey, and Graham S. Lowe. (1999). "Literacy in the Workplace." *Perspectives on Labour and Income*, 11 (Summer), 38–44.

Krahn, Harvey, and Graham S. Lowe. (2002). *Work, Industry and Canadian Society*. 4th ed. Toronto, ON: Nelson.

Krugman, Paul. (1994). "Long-Term Riches, Short-Term Pain." *The New York Times*, September 25, p. F9.

Jeffs, Allyson. (2002). "More People Homeless in High-Rent Economy." *Edmonton Journal*, October 25, B6.

Lenski, Gerhard. (1966). *Power and Privilege: A Theory of Social Stratification*. New York: McGraw-Hill.

Li, Peter. (1982). "Chinese Immigrants on the Canadian Prairie, 1919–47." *Canadian Review of Sociology and Anthropology*, 19, 527–40.

Longman, Phillip. (1985). "Justice between Generations." *Atlantic Monthly* (June) 73–81.

Love, Roger, and Susan Poulin. (1991). "Family Income Inequality in the 1980s." *Perspectives on Labour and Income*, 3 (Autumn), 51–57.

Mahoney, Jill. (2002). "Edmonton Eatery Buys $22,000 Bottle of Scotch Whiskey." *Globe and Mail*, October 25, A9.

Morissette, René. (2002). "Families on the financial edge." *Perspectives on Labour and Income* (Autumn): 9–20.

Morissette, René, John Myles, and Garnett Picot. (1994). "Earnings Inequality and the Distribution of Working Time in Canada." *Canadian Business Economics*, 2 (3), 3–16.

Morissette, René, and Xuelin Zhang. (2001). "Experiencing Low Income for Several Years." *Perspectives on Labour and Income* (Summer), 25–35.

Morissette, René, Xuelin Zhang, and Marie Drolet. (2002). "Wealth inequality." *Perspectives on Labour and Income* (Spring), 15–22.

Myles, John. (1996). "Public Policy in a World of Market Failure." *Policy Options*, 17 (6), 14–19.

Myles, John, and Adnan Turegun. (1994). "Comparative Studies in Class Structure." *Annual Review of Sociology*, 20, 103–24.

National Council of Welfare. (2001–02). *The Cost of Poverty*. Ottawa: Minister of Public Works and Government Services Canada. Cat. no. H68-53/2002E.

National Council of Welfare. (2002a). *Welfare Incomes, 2000 and 2001*. Ottawa: Minister of Public Works and Government Services Canada. Cat. no. H68-27/2001E.

National Council of Welfare. (2002b). *Poverty Profile 1999*. Ottawa: Minister of Public Works and Government Services Canada. Cat. no. H67-1/4-1999E.

Palmer, Bryan. (1986). *The Character of Class Struggle: Essays in Canadian Working Class History, 1850–1985*. Toronto: McClelland and Stewart.

Parkin, Frank. (1972). *Class, Inequality and Political Order*. London: Paladin.

Parkin, Frank. (1979). *Marxism and Class Theory: A Bourgeois Critique*. London: Tavistock.

Pentland, H. Clare. (1981). *Labour and Capital in Canada: 1650–1860*. Toronto: Lorimer.

Porter, John. (1968). "The Future of Upward Mobility." *American Sociological Review*, 33, 5–19.

Richardson, R. Jack. (1990). "Economic Concentration and Social Power in Contemporary Canada." In J. Curtis and L. Tepperman, eds., *Images of Canada: The Sociological Tradition* (pp. 341–51). Scarborough, ON: Prentice Hall.

Ryscavage, Paul. (1995). "A Surge in Growing Income Inequality?" *Monthly Labor Review*, August, pp. 51–61.

Statistics Canada. (1984). *Charting Canadian Incomes, 1951–1981*. Cat. no. 13-581E. Ottawa: Supply and Services Canada.

Statistics Canada. (1998). *The Daily*. Cat. No. 11-001E.

Statistics Canada. (1999). *Income Distributions by Size in Canada, 1997*. Cat. No. 13-207. Ottawa: Statistics Canada.

Statistics Canada. (2001). *Income in Canada*. Cat. No. 75-202-XPE. Ottawa: Minister of Industry.

Suntanu, Dalal. (2002). "Coat Campaign Eases Winter's Chill for Needy." *Edmonton Journal*, October 19, B2.

Swanson, Jean. 2001. *Poor-Bashing: The Politics of Exclusion*. Toronto. Between the Lines.

Tanner, Julian, Harvey Krahn, and Timothy F. Hartnagel. (1995). *Fractured Transitions from School to Work: Revisiting the Dropout Problem*. Toronto: Oxford University Press.

Townson, Monica. (1999). *Health and Welfare: How Social and Economic Factors Affect Our Well-Being*. Ottawa and Toronto: The Canadian Centre for Policy Alternatives and Lorimer.

Wanner, Richard A. (1993). "Patterns and Trends in Occupational Mobility." In J. Curtis, E. Grabb, and N. Guppy, eds., *Social Inequality in Canada: Patterns, Problems, Policies*, 2nd ed. (pp. 153–78). Scarborough, ON: Prentice Hall.

Weber, Max. (1948 [1922]). From *Max Weber: Essays in Sociology*. Eds. and trans. H.H. Gerth and C.W. Mills. London: Routledge and Kegan Paul.

Westergaard, John. (1995). *Who Gets What? The Hardening of Class Inequality in the Late Twentieth Century*. Cambridge, UK: Polity Press.

Wilkinson, R.G. (1992). "Income Distributions and Life Expectancy." *British Medical Journal*, 304, 165–68.

Wolff, Edward N. (1991). "The Distribution of Household Wealth: Methodological Issues, Time Trends, and Cross-sectional Comparisons." In Lars Osberg, ed., *Economic Inequality and Poverty: International Perspectives* (pp. 92–133). Armonk, NY: M.E. Sharpe.

Wright, Erik Olin. (1985). *Classes*. London: Verso.

Wright, Erik Olin, and Bill Martin. (1987). "The Transformation of the American Class Structure, 1960–1980." *American Journal of Sociology, 93*, 1–29.

Yakabuski, Konrad. (2001). "The Extended Family." *Report on Business Magazine* (July): 55–56.

Yalnizyan, Armine. (1998). *The Growing Gap: A Report on Growing Inequality between the Rich and Poor in Canada*. Toronto: The Centre for Social Justice.

Zeitlin, Irving M., with Robert J. Brym. (1991). *The Social Condition of Humanity*, Cdn. ed. Toronto: Oxford University Press.

CHAPTER 9

Agocs, Carol, and Monica Boyd. (1993). "The Canadian Ethnic Mosaic Recast for the 1990s." In James Curtis, Edward Grabb, and Neil Guppy, eds., *Social Inequality in Canada: Patterns, Problems and Policies* (pp. 330–52). Scarborough, ON: Prentice Hall.

Agocs, Carol, Catherine Burr, and Felicity Somerset. (1992). *Employment Equity: Cooperative Strategies for Organizational Change*. Toronto: Prentice Hall Canada.

Armstrong, Pat, and Hugh Armstrong. (1994). *The Double Ghetto: Canadian Women and Their Segregated Work*, 3rd ed. Toronto: McClelland and Stewart.

Arscott, Jane, and Linda Trimble. (1997). "Introduction—In the Presence of Women: Representation and Political Power." In Jane Arscott and Linda Trimble, eds., *In the Presence of Women: Representation in Canadian Governments* (pp. 1–17). Toronto: Harcourt Brace and Company, Canada.

Bashevkin, Sylvia B. (1991). "Women's Participation in Political Parties." In Kathy Megyery, ed., *Women in Canadian Politics: Toward Equity in Representation* (pp. 61–79). Toronto: Dundurn Press.

Bashevkin, Sylvia B. (1993). *Toeing the Lines: Women and Party Politics in English Canada*, 2nd ed. Toronto: Oxford University Press.

Best, Pamela. (1995). "Women, Men and Work." *Canadian Social Trends, 36* (1), 30–33.

Boyd, Monica, Brenda Hughes, and Jamie Miller. (1997). "Power at Work: Women and Men in Management, Supervision and Workplace Planning." Unpublished paper. Department of Sociology, Florida State University.

Boyd, Monica, Maryann Mulvihill, and John Myles. (1991). "Gender, Power and Postindustrialism." *Canadian Review of Sociology and Anthropology, 28*, 407–36.

Boyd, Monica. (1990). "Sex Differences in Occupational Skill: Canada, 1961–1986." *Canadian Review of Sociology and Anthropology, 27*, 285–315.

Boyd, Monica. (1999). "Integrating Gender, Language and Visible Minority Groups." In Shiva S. Halli and Leo Driedger, eds., *Immigrant Canada: Demographic, Economic and Social Challenges* (pp. 282–306). Toronto: University of Toronto Press.

Brodie, Janine, ed. (1996). *Women and Canadian Public Policy*. Toronto: Harcourt Brace and Company, Canada.

Brodie, Janine. (1991). "Women and the Electoral Process in Canada." In Kathy Megyery, ed., *Women in Canadian Politics: Toward Equity in Representation* (pp. 3–59). Toronto: Dundurn Press.

Broverman, I., S.R. Vogel, S.M. Broverman, F.E. Clarkson, and P.S. Rosenkranz. (1972). "Sex Role Stereotypes: A Current Appraisal." *Journal of Social Issues, 28* (2), 59–78.

Burt, Sandra. (1993). "The Changing Patterns of Public Policy." In Sandra Burt, Lorraine Code, and Lindsay Dorney, eds., *Changing Patterns: Women in Canada*, 2nd ed. (pp. 212–37). Toronto: McClelland and Stewart.

Canada. (1958). Department of Labour. Women's Bureau. *Women at Work in Canada*. Ottawa: Supply and Services Canada.

Canada. (1995). Laws. Statutes of Canada. Employment Equity Act. 43–44 Elizabeth II, Vol. II, Chapter 44.

Chafetz, Janet Saltzman. (1999). "The Varieties of Gender Theory in Sociology" Janet Saltzman Chafetz, ed., *The Handbook of the Sociology of Gender* (pp. 3–23). New York: Kluwer Academic/Plenum Publishers.

Connelly, Patricia. (1978). *Last Hired, First Fired: Women and the Canadian Work Force*. Toronto: Women's Press.

Cranswick, Kelly. (1997). "Canada's Caregivers." *Canadian Social Trends*, No. 48 (Winter): 2–6.

Crompton, Susan, and Leslie Geran. (1995). "Women as Main Wage-Earners." *Canadian Perspectives on Labour and Income, 7* (4), 26–29.

Das Gupta, Tania. (1996). *Racism and Paid Work*. Toronto: Garamond Press.

Devereaux, Mary Sue. (1993). "Time Use of Canadians in 1992." *Canadian Social Trends, 8* (3), 13–16.

Duffy, Ann, and Norene Pupo. (1992). *Part-time Paradox: Connecting Gender, Work and Family*. Toronto: McClelland and Stewart.

Duffy, Ann. (1986). "Reformulating Power for Women." *Canadian Review of Sociology and Anthropology, 23*, 22–46.

Economic Council of Canada. (1991). *Employment in the Service Economy*. Ottawa: Supply and Services Canada.

England, Paula. (1993). *Comparable Worth: Theories and Evidence*. New York: Aldine de Gruyter.

Erickson, Lynda. (1991). "Women Candidates for the House of Commons." In Kathy Megyery, ed., *Women in Canadian Politics: Toward Equity in Representation* (pp. 101–25). Toronto: Dundurn Press.

Erickson, Lynda. (1998). "Entry to the Commons: Parties, Recruitment and the Election of Women in 1993." In Manon Tremblay and Caroline Andrew, eds., *Women and Political Representation in Canada* (pp. 219–58). Ottawa: University of Ottawa Press.

Frederick, Judith A. and Janet E. Fast. (1999). "Eldercare in Canada: Who Does How Much?" *Canadian Social Trends*, No. 54 (Autumn): 26–30.

Gagne, Patricia, and Richard Tewksbury. (1998). "Rethinking Binary Conceptions and Social Constructions: Transgender Experiences of Gender and Sexuality." *Advances in Gender Research*, series ed. Marcia Texler Segal and Vasilikie Demos. Vol. 3, 73–102.

Gaskell, Jane. (1986). "Conceptions of Skill and the Work of Women: Some Historical and Political Issues." In Roberta Hamilton and Michele Barrett, eds., *The Politics of Diversity: Feminism, Marxism and Nationalism* (pp. 361–80). London: Verso.

Gaskell, Jane. (1991). "What Counts as Skill? Reflections on Pay Equity." In Judy Fudge and Patricia McDermott, eds., *Just*

Wages: A Feminist Assessment of Pay Equity (pp. 141–59). Toronto: University of Toronto Press.

Ghalam, Nancy Zukewich. (1993). *Women in the Workplace*, 2nd ed. Statistics Canada. Cat. no. 71-534E. Ottawa: Industry, Science and Technology Canada.

Jackson, Chris. (1996). "Measuring and Valuing Households' Unpaid Work." *Canadian Social Trends, 42* (4), 25–29.

Jaggar, Alison M. (1983). *Feminist Politics and Human Nature.* New York: Rowman and Allanheld Publishers.

Krahn, Harvey. (1995). "Non-standard Work on the Rise." *Perspectives on Labour and Income, 7* (4), 35–42.

Looker, E. Dianne, and Victor Thiessen. (1999). "Images of Work: Women's Work, Men's Work, Housework." *Canadian Journal of Sociology, 24* (2) (Spring), 225–54.

Lorber, Judith. (1998). *Gender Inequality: Feminist Theories and Politics.* Los Angeles: Roxbury Publishing Company.

Lowe, Graham. (1987). *Women in the Administrative Revolution: The Feminization of Clerical Work.* Cambridge, UK: Polity Press.

Luxton, Meg, and Leah F. Vosko. (1998). "Where Women's Efforts Count: The 1996 Census Campaign and 'Family Politics' in Canada." *Studies in Political Economy, 56* (Summer), 49–81.

Mackie, Marlene. (1980). "The Impact of Sex Stereotypes upon Adult Self-Imagery." *Social Psychology Quarterly, 43,* 121–25.

Maille, Chantal. (1990). *Primed for Power: Women in Canadian Politics.* Ottawa: Canadian Advisory Council on the Status of Women.

McCormack, Thelma. (1975). "Toward a Nonsexist Perspective on Social and Political Change." In Marcia Millman and Rosabeth Moss Kanter, eds., *Another Voice: Feminist Perspectives on Social Life and Social Science* (pp. 1–33). Garden City, NY: Anchor Books.

McDonald, Marci. (1994). "Rebel with a Cause: After Nine Years on the Attack, Sheila Copps Is Learning the Lessons of Power." *Maclean's,* April 4, 16–22.

Myles, John, and Gail Fawcett. (1990). *Job Skills and the Service Economy.* Working Paper no. 4. Ottawa: Economic Council of Canada.

Pal, Leslie. (1989). *Public Policy Analysis.* Toronto: Nelson Canada.

Pendakur, Krishna, and Ravi Pendakur. (1998). "The Colour of Money: Earnings Differentials among Ethnic Groups in Canada." *Canadian Journal of Economics, 31* (3), 518–47.

Phillips, Paul, and Erin Phillips. (1983). *Women and Work.* Toronto: Lorimer.

Pierson, Ruth. (1977). "Women's Emancipation and the Recruitment of Women into the Labour Force in World War II." In Susan Mann Trofimenkoff and Alison Prentice, eds., *The Neglected Majority* (pp. 125–45). Toronto: McClelland and Stewart.

Prentice, Alison. (1977). "The Feminization of Teaching." In Susan Mann Trofimenkoff and Alison Prentice, eds., *The Neglected Majority* (pp. 49–65). Toronto: McClelland and Stewart.

Robinson, Gertrude J., and Armande Saint-Jean, with the assistance of Christine Rioux. (1991). "Women Politicians and Their Media Coverage: A Generational Analysis." In Kathy Megyery, ed., *Women in Canadian Politics: Toward Equity in Representation* (pp. 127–69). Toronto: Dundurn Press.

Segal, Edwin S. (1998). "Male Genders: Cross Cultural Perspectives." *Advances in Gender Research*, series eds. Marcia Texler Segal and Vasilikie Demos. Vol. 3, 37–77.

Séguin, Rhéal. (1996). "Quebec Puts Brakes on Pay Equity." *The Globe and Mail*, November 8, p. A7.

Ship, Susan Judith. (1998). "Problematizing Ethnicity and 'Race' in Feminist Scholarship on Women and Politics." In Manon Tremblay and Caroline Andrew, eds., *Women and Political Representation in Canada* (pp. 311–40). Ottawa: University of Ottawa Press.

Statistics Canada. (1998a). *The Daily.* Tuesday, March 17. Cat. no. 11-001E.

Statistics Canada. (1998b). *The Daily.* Tuesday, May 12. Cat. no. 11-001E.

Statistics Canada (Household Surveys Division). (1998c). *Labour Force Update: A New Perspective on Wages, 2* (3) (Summer), Cat. no. 71-005XPB.

Statistics Canada. (1999). "General Social Survey: Time Use." *The Daily*, November 9, pp. 2–5.

Statistics Canada. 2001. *Women in Canada: Work Chapter Updates.* (Target Groups Project). Catalogue 89F0133XIE. August.

Steinberg, Ronnie J. (1990). "Social Construction of Skill." *Work and Occupations, 17,* 449–82.

Tremblay, Manon, and Caroline Andrew, eds. (1998). *Women and Political Representation in Canada.* Women's Studies Series. Ottawa: University of Ottawa Press.

Ursel, Jane. (1992). *Private Lives, Public Policy: 100 Years of State Intervention in the Family.* Toronto: Women's Press.

Vickers, Jill. (1997). "Toward a Feminist Understanding of Representation." In Jane Arscott and Linda Trimble, eds., *In the Presence of Women: Representation in Canadian Governments* (pp. 20–46). Toronto: Harcourt Brace.

Weiner, Nan, and Morley Gunderson. (1990). *Pay Equity: Issues, Options and Experiences.* Toronto: Butterworths.

West, Candace, and Sarah Fenstermaker. (1993). "Power, Inequality and the Accomplishment of Gender: An Ethnomethodological View." In Paula England, ed., *Theory on Gender/Feminism on Theory* (pp. 151–74). New York: Aldine de Gruyter.

Yanz, Lynda, Deena Ladd, Joan Atlin, and Maquila Solidarity Network. (1999). *Policy Options to Improve Standards for Garment Workers in Canada and Internationally.* Ottawa: Status of Women Canada.

Young, Lisa. (1997). "Fulfilling the Mandate of Difference: Women in the Canadian House of Commons." In Jane Arscott and Linda Trimble, eds., *In the Presence of Women: Representation in Canadian Governments* (pp. 82–103). Toronto: Harcourt Brace.

Young, Lisa. (1998). "The Canadian Women's Movement and Political Parties, 1970–1993." In Manon Tremblay and Caroline Andrew, eds., *Women and Political Representation in Canada* (pp. 195–218). Ottawa: University of Ottawa Press.

Zinn, Maxine Baca. (1997). "Theorizing Difference from Multiracial Feminism" in Maxine Baca Zinn, Pierrette Hondagneu-Sotelo, and Michael A. Messner, eds., *Through the Prism of Difference: Readings on Sex and Gender* (pp. 23–29). Boston: Allyn and Bacon.

CHAPTER 10

Abella, Irving, and Harold Troper. (1982). *None Is Too Many: Canada and the Jews of Europe, 1933–1948*. Toronto: Lester & Orpen Dennys.

Anderson, Benedict. (1983). *Imagined Communities: Reflections on the Origin and Spread of Nationalism*. London: Verso.

Angus Reid Group. (1991). *Multiculturalism and Canadians: National Attitude Study 1991*. Ottawa: Multiculturalism and Citizenship Canada.

Avery, Donald. (1995). *Reluctant Host: Canada's Response to Immigrant Workers*. Toronto: McClelland and Stewart.

Badets, Jane. (1993). "Canada's Immigrants: Recent Trends." *Canadian Social Trends*. Cat. no. 11-008E. Ottawa: Statistics Canada.

Balthazar, Louis. (1993). "The Faces of Quebec Nationalism." In Alain-G. Gagnon, ed., *Quebec: State and Society*, 2nd ed. (pp. 2–17). Scarborough, ON: Nelson.

Barkan, Elazar. (1992). *The Retreat of Scientific Racism*. Cambridge, UK: Cambridge University Press.

Barker, Martin. (1981). *The New Racism: Conservatives and the Ideology of the Tribe*. London: Junction Books.

Basran, Gurcharn, and Li Zong. (1998). "Devaluation of Foreign Credentials as Perceived by Non-white Professional Immigrants." *Canadian Ethnic Studies, 30*, 6–23.

Bissoondath, Neil. (1994). *Selling Illusions: The Cult of Multiculturalism*. Toronto: Stoddart.

Bolaria, B. Singh, and Peter Li. (1988). *Racial Oppression in Canada*. Toronto: Garamond.

Boldt, Menno. (1993). *Surviving as Indians: The Challenge of Self-Government*. Toronto: University of Toronto Press.

Bonacich, Edna. (1972). "A Theory of Ethnic Antagonism: The Split Labor Market." *American Sociological Review, 37*, 547–59.

Bonacich, Edna. (1979). "The Past, Present and Future of Split Labor Market Theory." *Research in Race and Ethnic Relations, 1*, 17–64.

Bonacich, Edna. (1980). "Class Approaches to Ethnicity and Race." Insurgent Sociologist, 10, 9–23.

Bourgeault, Ron. (1988). "The South African Connection." *Canadian Dimension, 21*, 6–10.

Boyd, Monica. (1992). "Gender, Visible Minority and Immigrant Earnings Inequality: Reassessing an Employment Equity Premise." In Vic Satzewich, ed., *Deconstructing a Nation: Immigration, Multiculturalism and Racism in '90s Canada* (pp. 279–321). Halifax: Fernwood.

Brym, Robert. (1999). *Canadian Society and the 1996 Census*. Toronto: Harcourt Canada.

Brym, Robert, with Bonnie Fox. (1989). *From Culture to Power: The Sociology of English Canada*. Toronto: Oxford University Press.

Brym, Robert, and Rhonda Lenton. (1993). "The Distribution of Anti-Semitism in Canada in 1984." In Robert Brym, William Shaffir, and Morton Weinfeld, eds., *The Jews in Canada* (pp. 112–19). Toronto: Oxford University Press.

Cannon, Margaret. (1995). *The Invisible Empire: Racism in Canada*. Toronto: Random House.

Castles, Stephen, and Godula Kosack. (1984). *Immigrant Workers and Class Structure in Western Europe*. London: Oxford University Press.

Citizenship and Immigration Canada. (1996). *You Asked About ... Immigration and Citizenship*. Ottawa: Supply and Services Canada.

Citizenship and Immigration Canada. (2002). "Who Is Eligible for Selection?" On the World Wide Web at http://www.cic.gc.ca/english/refugees/resettle-2.html.

Clement, Wallace. (1975). *The Canadian Corporate Elite*. Toronto: McClelland and Stewart.

Cole, Douglas, and Ira Chaikin. (1990). *An Iron Hand upon the People: The Law against the Potlatch on the Northwest Coast*. Vancouver: Douglas & McIntyre.

Collins, Jock. (1988). *Migrant Hands in a Distant Land: Australia's Post-war Immigration*. Sydney: Pluto Press.

Daenzer, Pat. (1993). *Regulating Class Privilege*. Toronto: Canadian Scholars Press.

Darroch, Gordon. (1979). "Another Look at Ethnicity, Stratification and Social Mobility in Canada." *Canadian Journal of Sociology, 4*, 1–25.

Doob, Christopher. (1996). *Racism: An American Cauldron*. New York: HarperCollins.

Economic Council of Canada. (1991). *Economic and Social Impacts of Immigration*. Ottawa: Supply and Services Canada.

Fiske, Jo-Anne. (1996). "The Womb Is to the Nation as the Heart Is to the Body: Ethnopolitical Discourses of the Canadian Indigenous Women's Movement." *Studies in Political Economy, 51*, 65–96.

Fleras, Augie, and Jean Elliot. (1996). *Unequal Relations: An Introduction to Race, Ethnic and Aboriginal Dynamics in Canada*. Scarborough, ON: Prentice Hall.

Fournier, Marcel, Michael Rosenberg, and Deena White. (1997). *Quebec Society: Critical Issues*. Scarborough, ON: Prentice Hall.

Frideres, James, and Rene René Gadacz. (2001). *Aboriginal People in Canada: Contemporary Conflicts*. Toronto: Prentice-Hall.

Gerber, Linda. (1990). "Multiple Jeopardy: A Socio-economic Comparison of Men and Women among the Indian, Métis and Inuit Peoples of Canada." *Canadian Ethnic Studies, 22*, 69–84.

Geschwender, James. (1994). "Married Women's Wage Labor and Racial/Ethnic Stratification in Canada." *Canadian Ethnic Studies, 26*, 53–73.

Gibbins, Roger, and J. Rick Ponting. (1986). "Historical Background and Overview." In J. Rick Ponting, ed., *Arduous Journey* (pp. 18–56). Toronto: McClelland and Stewart.

GRES. (1997). "Immigration and Ethnic Relations in Quebec: Pluralism in the Making." In Marcel Fournier, Michael Rosenberg, and Deena White, eds., *Quebec Society: Critical Issues* (pp. 95–112). Scarborough, ON: Prentice Hall.

Ha, Tu Thanh. (1995). "The PQ's Narrow Ethnic Vision." *The Globe and Mail*, November 11, p. D1.

Hawkins, Freda. (1989). *Critical Years in Immigration: Canada and Australia Compared*. Montreal and Kingston, ON: McGill-Queen's University Press.

Henry, Frances. (1989). "Who Gets the Work in 1989?" Background Paper. Ottawa: Economic Council of Canada.

Henry, Frances, and Effie Ginsberg. (1985). *Who Gets the Work: A Test of Racial Discrimination in Employment*. Toronto: Urban Alliance on Race Relations and the Social Planning Directorate.

Henry, Frances, Carol Tator, Winston Mattis, and Tim Rees. (2000). *The Colour of Democracy: Racism in Canadian Society*, 2nd ed. Toronto: Harcourt Brace.

Herberg, Edward. (1990). "The Ethno-racial Socioeconomic Hierarchy in Canada: Theory and Analysis in the New Vertical Mosaic." *International Journal of Comparative Sociology*, *31*, 206–21.

Holton, Robert, and Michael Lanphier. (1994). "Public Opinion, Immigration and Refugees." In Howard Adelman, Allan Borowski, Meyer Burstein, and Lois Foster, eds., Immigration and Refugee Policy: Australia and Canada Compared, vol. 1. Toronto: University of Toronto Press.

Hou, Feng, and T.R. Balakrishnan. (1996). "The Integration of Visible Minorities in Contemporary Canadian Society." *Canadian Journal of Sociology*, *21*, 307–26.

Howard, Rhoda. (1998). "Being Canadian: Citizenship in Canada." *Citizenship Studies*, *2*, 133–52.

Howard-Hassmann, Rhoda. (1999). "Canadian as an Ethnic Category: Implications for Multiculturalism and National Unity." *Canadian Public Policy*, *25* (4), 523–37.

Iacovetta, Franca. (1992). *Such Hardworking People: Italian Immigrants in Postwar Toronto*. Montreal and Kingston, ON: McGill-Queen's University Press.

Isajiw, Wsevolod. (1999). *Understanding Diversity: Ethnicity and Race in the Canadian Context*. Toronto: Thompson Educational Publishing.

Jenson, Jane. (1993). "Naming Nations: Making Nationalist Claims in Canadian Public Discourse." *Canadian Review of Sociology and Anthropology*, *30*, 337–58.

Kazemipur, Abdolmohammad, and Shiva Halli. (2000). *The New Poverty in Canada*. Toronto: Thompson Educational Publishers.

Krosenbrink-Gelissen, Ernestine. (1994). "The Native Women's Association of Canada." In James Frideres, ed., *Native Peoples in Canada* (pp. 335–64). Scarborough, ON: Prentice Hall.

Latouche, Daniel. (1993). "'Quebec: See Under Canada': Quebec Nationalism in the New Global Age." In Alain-G. Gagnon, ed., *Quebec: State and Society*, 2nd ed. (pp. 40–51). Scarborough, ON: Nelson.

Lewis, Oscar. (1961). *The Children of Sanchez*. New York: Random House.

Li, Peter. (1988). *The Chinese in Canada*. Toronto: Oxford University Press.

Li, Peter. (1996). *The Making of Post-war Canada*. Toronto: Oxford University Press.

Li, Peter. (2000). "Earnings Disparities between Immigrants and Native-Born Canadians." *Canadian Review of Sociology and Anthropology*, *37* (3), 289–311.

Li, Peter. (2001). "The Racial Subtext in Canada's Immigration Discourse." *Journal of International Migration and Integration, 2* (1), 77–97.

Lian, Jason and David Ralph Mathhews. (1995). "Does the Vertical Mosaic Still Exist?: Ethnicity and Income in Canada, 1991." Paper presented at the Canadian Ethnic Studies Association Biennial Meetings, Gimli, Manitoba.

Lieberson, Stanley. (1991). "A New Ethnic Group in the United States." In Norman Yetman, ed., *Majority and Minority* (pp. 444–56). New York: Allyn and Bacon.

Macmillan, David. (1985). "Scottish Enterprise and Influences in Canada, 1620–1900." In R.A. Cage, ed., *The Scots Abroad: Labour, Capital and Enterprise, 1750–1914* (pp. 46–79). London: Croom Helm.

Marger, Martin. (1997). *Race and Ethnic Relations: American and Global Perspectives*, 4th ed. New York: Wadsworth.

Marx, Karl. (1967 [1867]). *Capital*, vol. 1. New York: International Publishers.

McMillan, Alan. (1988). *Native Peoples and Cultures of Canada*. Vancouver: Douglas & McIntyre.

Métis National Council. (1983). *A Brief to the Standing Committee on Legal and Constitutional Affairs*. Ottawa, September 8.

Miles, Robert. (1982). *Racism and Migrant Labour*. London: Routledge.

Miles, Robert. (1989). *Racism*. London: Routledge.

Milner, Henry, and Sheilagh Hodgins Milner. (1973). *The Decolonization of Quebec*. Toronto: McClelland and Stewart.

Mitchell, Marybelle. (1996). *From Talking Chiefs to a Native Corporate Elite*. Montreal and Kingston, ON: McGill-Queen's University Press.

Montagu, Ashley. (1972). *Statement on Race*. London: Oxford University Press.

Nagler, Mark. (1972). "Minority Values and Economic Achievement: The Case of the North American Indian." In Mark Nagler, ed., *Perspectives on the North American Indian* (pp. 131–42). Toronto: McClelland and Stewart.

Nikolinakos, Marios. (1973). "Notes towards an Economic Theory of Racism." *Race, 14*, 365–81.

Omi, Michael, and Howard Winant. (1986). *Racial Formation in the United States: From the 1960s to the 1980s*. New York: Routledge and Kegan Paul.

Pentland, H. Clare. (1981). *Labour and Capital in Canada, 1650–1860*. Toronto: Lorimer.

Pettipas, Katherine. (1995). *Severing the Ties That Bind*. Winnipeg: University of Manitoba Press.

Pineo, Peter, and John Porter. (1985). "Ethnic Origin and Occupational Attainment." In Monica Boyd, John Goyder, Frank Jones, Hugh McRoberts, Peter Pineo, and John Porter, eds., *Ascription and Achievement: Studies in Mobility and Status Attainment in Canada* (pp. 357–93). Ottawa: Carleton University Press.

Porter, John. (1965). *The Vertical Mosaic*. Toronto: University of Toronto Press.

Ramirez, Bruno. (1991). *On the Move: French-Canadian and Italian Migrants in the North Atlantic Economy 1860–1914*. Toronto: McClelland and Stewart.

Reitz, Jeffrey, and Raymond Breton. (1994). *The Illusion of Difference: Realities of Ethnicity in Canada and the United States*. Toronto: C.D. Howe Institute.

Rex, John, and David Mason, eds. (1986). *Theories of Race and Ethnic Relations*. Cambridge: Cambridge University Press.

Roy, Patricia. (1989). *A White Man's Province*. Vancouver: University of British Columbia Press.

Royal Commission on Aboriginal Peoples. (1996). *Report*. Ottawa: Supply and Services Canada.

Satzewich, Vic. (1991). *Racism and the Incorporation of Foreign Labour*. London: Routledge.

Satzewich, Vic. (1998). *Racism and Social Inequality in Canada: Concepts, Controversies and Strategies of Resistance.* Toronto: Thompson Educational Publishing.

Satzewich, Vic, and Linda Mahood. (1994). "Indian Affairs and Band Governance: Deposing Indian Chiefs in Western Canada, 1896–1911." *Canadian Ethnic Studies, 26,* 40–58.

Satzewich, Vic, and Lloyd Wong. (2002). "Immigration, Ethnicity and Race: The Transformation of Transnationalism, Localism and Identities." In Wallace Clement and Leah Vosko, eds., *Changing Canada: Political Economy as Transformation.* Montreal and Kingston: McGill-Queen's University Press.

Satzewich, Vic, and Terry Wotherspoon. (2000). *First Nations: Race, Class and Gender Relations.* Regina: Canadian Plains Research Centre.

Scott, George. (1990). "A Resynthesis of the Primordial and Circumstantial Approaches to Ethnic Group Solidarity: Towards an Explanatory Model." *Ethnic and Racial Studies, 13,* 147–71.

Special Committee on the Participation of Visible Minorities in Canadian Society. (1984). *Equality Now!* Ottawa: Supply and Services Canada.

Steinberg, Steven. (1981). *The Ethnic Myth.* Boston: Beacon Press.

Thomas, W.I., and Florian Znaniecki. (1918). *The Polish Peasant in Europe and America.* New York: Knopf.

Titley, Brian. (1986). *A Narrow Vision: Duncan Campbell Scott and the Administration of Indian Affairs in Canada.* Vancouver: University of British Columbia Press.

van den Berghe, Pierre. (1986). "Ethnicity and the Sociobiology Debate." In John Rex and David Mason, eds., *Theories of Race and Ethnic Relations* (pp. 246–63). Cambridge, UK: Cambridge University Press.

Whitaker, Reginald. (1987). *Double Standard: The Secret History of Canadian Immigration.* Toronto: Lester & Orpen Dennys.

Whitaker, Reginald. (1993). "From the Quebec Cauldron to the Canadian Cauldron." In Alain-G. Gagnon, ed., *Quebec: State and Society,* 2nd ed. (pp. 18–39). Scarborough, ON: Nelson.

White, Pamela. (1992). "Challenges in Measuring Canada's Ethnic Diversity." In Stella Hryniuk, ed., *20 Years of Multiculturalism: Success and Failure* (pp. 163–82). Winnipeg: St. John's College Press.

Wiley, Norbert. (1967). "Ethnic Mobility and Stratification Theory." *Social Problems, 15,* 147–59.

Williams, Eric. (1964). *Capitalism and Slavery.* London: Andre Deutsch.

Wilson, Edward. (1978). *On Human Nature.* New York: Vintage.

Woodsworth, J.S. (1972). *Strangers within Our Gates.* Toronto: University of Toronto Press.

York, Geoffrey. (1989). *The Dispossessed.* Toronto: Lester & Orpen Dennys.

Zong, Li. (1994). "Structural and Psychological Dimensions of Racism: Towards an Alternative Perspective." *Canadian Ethnic Studies, 26,* 122–34.

CHAPTER 11

Adams, Patricia. (1991). *Odious Debts: Loose Lending, Corruption, and the Third World's Environmental Legacy.* Toronto: Earthscan.

AFL-CIO. (2002). "Runaway CEO Pay: What's Happening and What You Can Do about It." On the World Wide Web at http://www.aflcio.org/paywatch/ceopay.htm.

Angeles, Gracia. (1993). "Building a Women's Union in the Philippines: Fighting for Women's Rights." Interview. *Multinational Monitor,* June, 16–20.

Armer, J. Michael, and John Katsillis. (1992). *Encyclopedia of Sociology.* New York: Macmillan.

Arrighi, Giovanni. (1993). "World Income Inequalities and the Future of Socialism." *Socialism of the Future, 1* (2), 195–208.

Bairoch, Paul. (1982). "International Industrialization Levels from 1750 to 1980." *Journal of European Economic History, 11* (2), 270–71.

Baran, Paul A. (1957). *The Political Economy of Growth.* New York: Monthly Review Press.

Barnet, Richard, and Richard Muller. (1974). *Global Reach: The Power of the Multinational Corporations.* New York: Simon and Schuster.

Bello, Walden. (2002). *Deglobalization: Ideas for a New World Economy.* London: Zed Books.

Block, Fred L. (1977). *The Origins of International Economic Disorder.* Berkeley, CA: University of California Press.

Bullard, Nicola, et al. (1998). "Taming the Tigers: The IMF and the Asian Crisis." In K.S. Jomo, ed., *Tigers in Trouble: Financial Governance, Liberalisation and Crises in East Asia* (pp. 85–136). London: Zed Books.

Cardoso, Fernando, and Enzo Faletto. (1979). *Dependency and Development in Latin America.* Berkeley, CA: University of California Press.

Castaneda, Jorge. (1993). "Can NAFTA Change Mexico?" *Foreign Affairs, 72* (4), 66–80.

Cobb, Clifford, et al. (1995). "If the GDP Is Up, Why Is America Down?" *Atlantic Monthly* (October), 59–78.

Crotty, James, and Gary Dymski. (1999). "The Korean Struggle: Aftermath of the IMF Takeover." In Dean Collinwood, ed., *Japan and the Pacific Rim,* 5th ed. (pp. 194–97). Guilford, CT: McGraw-Hill.

Deane, Phyllis. (1979). *The First Industrial Revolution.* Cambridge, UK: Cambridge University Press.

Delage, Denys. (1993). *Bitter Feast: Amerindians and Europeans in Northeastern North America, 1600–64.* Vancouver: University of British Columbia Press.

Dunning, John H. (1993). *Multinational Enterprises and the Global Economy.* Wokingham, UK: Addison-Wesley.

Ecumenical Coalition for Economic Justice (ECEJ). (1990). *Recolonization or Liberation: The Bonds of Structural Adjustment and Struggles for Emancipation.* Toronto: Our Times.

Ehrensaft, Philip, and Warwick Armstrong. (1981). "The Formation of Dominion Capitalism: Economic Truncation and Class Structure." In Allan Moscovitch, ed., *Inequality: Essays on the Political Economy of Social Welfare.* Toronto: University of Toronto Press.

Esping-Andersen, Gøsta. (1985). *Politics against Markets: The Social Democratic Road to Power.* Princeton, NJ: Princeton University Press.

Evans, Peter. (1985). "After Dependency: Recent Studies of Class, State, and Industrialization." *Latin American Research Review, 20,* 149–60.

Evans, Peter. (1987). "Foreign Capital and the Third World State." In Myron Weiner and Samuel Huntington, eds., *Understanding Political Development* (pp. 319–52). Boston: Little, Brown.

Forbes Magazine. (1999). "The Richest People in America." On the World Wide Web at http://www.forbes.com (October 11).

Forbes Magazine. (2002). "World's Richest People." On The World Wide Web at http://www.forbes.com/2002/02/29/billionaires.html.

Foster-Carter, Aidan. (1989). "The Myth of South Korea." *Far Eastern Economic Review*, *145* (31), 46–47.

Franke, Richard W., and Barbara H. Chasin. (2000). "Is The Kerala Model Sustainable? Lessons From the Past, Prospects for the Future." In Parayil, Govindar, ed., *Kerala: The Development Experience. Reflections on Sustainability and Replicability*. London: Zed Books.

Franke, Richard W., and Barbara Chasin. (1991). "Kerala State, India: Radical Reform as Development." *Monthly Review*, *42* (8), 1–39.

Gasslander, Olle. (1962). *History of Stockholms Enskilda Bank to 1914*. Stockholm: Stockholms Enskilda Banken.

Gerschenkron, Alexander. (1962). *Economical Backwardness in Historical Perspective*. Cambridge, MA: Harvard University Press.

Goldthorpe, J.E. (1984 [1975]). *The Sociology of the Third World*, 2nd ed. Cambridge, UK: Cambridge University Press.

Govindan, Parayil. (1996). "The 'Kerala Model' of Development: Development and Sustainability in the Third World." *Third World Quarterly*, *17*, (5), 941–57.

Gupta, Surinder Nath. (1979). *British: The Magnificent Exploiters of India*. New Delhi: S. Chand and Co.

Harrison, Paul. (1993). *Inside the Third World: The Anatomy of Poverty*, 3rd ed. Harmondsworth, UK: Penguin.

Herman, Edward S., and Noam Chomsky. (1988). *Manufacturing Consent*. New York: Pantheon.

Hobsbawm, Eric. (1968). *Industry and Empire*. Harmondsworth, UK: Penguin.

Hobsbawm, Eric. (1990). *Nations and Nationalism since 1780: Programme, Myth, Reality*. Cambridge, UK: Cambridge University Press.

Hoogvelt, Ankie M.M. (1982). *The Third World in Global Development*. London: Macmillan.

Hoogvelt, Ankie M.M. (1997). *Globalization and the Postcolonial World. The New Political Economy of Development*. Baltimore: Johns Hopkins University Press.

Howe, Gary, and David Goodman. (1992). *Small Holders and Structural Change in the Brazilian Economy: Opportunities in Rural Poverty Alleviation*. San José, Costa Rica: International Fund for Agricultural Development.

Jubilee Action UK. (2000). "Brazilian Street Children." On The World Wide Web at http://www.jubileeaction.co.uk/reports/brazil.htm.

Landes, David. (1969). *The Unbound Prometheus: Technological Change and Industrial Development in Western Europe from 1750 to the Present*. Cambridge, UK: Cambridge University Press.

Love, Joseph L. (1980). "Raúl Prebisch and the Origins of the Doctrine of Unequal Exchange." *Latin American Research Review*, *15* (3), 52–56.

MacLean, Brian, et al. (1998). "Understanding the Asian Crisis and Its Implications for Regional Economic Integration." Paper prepared for inclusion in Gavin Boyd and Alan Rugman, eds., *Deepening Integration in the Pacific*. London: Edward Elgar.

Marchak, Patricia. (1991). *The Integrated Circus: The New Right and the Restructuring of Global Markets*. Montreal and Kingston, ON: McGill-Queen's University Press.

Mardon, Russell. (1990). "The State and the Effective Control of Foreign Capital: The Case of South Korea." *World Politics*, *43* (1), 111–38.

Marx, Karl, and Friedrich Engels. (1986 [1848]). *The Communist Manifesto*. Moscow: Progress Publishers.

Meek, Ronald. (1976). *Social Science and the Ignoble Savage*. Cambridge, UK: Cambridge University Press.

Morissette, René, Xuelin Zhang, and Marie Drolet. (2002). "Wealth Inequality." *Perspectives*. Spring 2002. Ottawa: Statistics Canada. Catalogue no. 75-001-XPE.

Nelson, Joan M., ed. (1990). *Economic Crisis and Policy Choice: The Politics of Adjustment in the Third World*. Princeton, NJ: Princeton University Press.

Nordlund, Sven. (1989). *Upptackten Av Sverige [Foreign Investment in Sweden]*. Umea, Sweden: Umea University.

O'Brien, Philip. (1976). "Was the United States Responsible for the Chilean Coup?" In P. O'Brien, ed., *Allende's Chile* (pp. 217–43). New York: Praeger.

OXFAM. (2001). "Where's the Money? G8 Promises, G8 Failures." On the World Wide Web at http://www.oxfam.org.

Palma, Gabriel. (1981). "Dependency and Development: A Critical Overview." In D. Seers, ed., *Dependency Theory: A Critical Reassessment* (pp. 20–78). London: Frances Pinter.

Pastor, Manuel, Jr., and Gary Dymski. (1991). "Debt Crisis and Class Conflict in Latin America." *Capital and Class*, *43*, 203–31.

Rostow, W.W. (1965). *The Stages of Economic Growth*. Cambridge, UK: Cambridge University Press.

Sampson, Anthony. (1973). *The Sovereign State of ITT*. New York: Stein and Day.

Sassen, Saskia. (1998). "America's Immigration Problem." In Saskia Sassen, ed., *Globalization and Its Discontents: Essays on the New Mobility of People and Money*. New York: New Press.

Seers, Dudley, ed. (1981). *Dependency Theory: A Critical Reassessment*. London: Frances Pinter.

Sen, Amartya. (2001). "The Many Faces of Gender Inequality." *New Republic*, *225* (12), 35–40.

Smith, Adam. (1976 [1776]). *An Inquiry into the Nature and Causes of the Wealth of Nations*. Chicago: University of Chicago Press.

Stern, Paul C., Thomas Dietz, Vernon W. Ruttan, Robert H. Socolow, and James L. Sweeney, eds., 1997. *Environmentally Significant Consumption*. Washington, DC: National Academy Press.

Summers, Lawrence. (1996). "America's Role in Global Economic Integration." *Treasury News*, January 6.

Swedish Institute, The. (1992). "Sweden's Foreign Trade." *Fact Sheets on Sweden*. Stockholm, November.

UNICEF (United Nations International Children's Emergency Fund). (1999). "UNICEF: Will the Six Billionth Child Survive?" *Information Newsline*. On the World Wide Web at http://www.unicef.org/newsline/99pr43.htm (October 12).

United Nations Conference On Trade And Development (UNCTAD). (2001). *World Investment Report 2001—Summary.* On the World Wide Web at http://www.unctad.org/wir/contents/wir01content.en.htm.

United Nations Educational, Scientific and Cultural Organization (UNESCO). (2000a). *Education for All 2000 Assessment: Statistical Document. Executive Summary.* Paris: UNESCO Institute for Statistics. On the World Wide Web at http://uis.unesco.org/en/pub/pub0.htm.

United Nations Educational, Scientific and Cultural Organization (UNESCO). (2000b). *Facts and Figures 2000.* Paris: UNESCO Institute for Statistics. On the World Wide Web at http://www.uis.unesco.org/en/pub/pub0.htm.

United Nations. (1999). *Human Development Report 1999.* New York: Oxford University Press.

United Nations. (2000). *Human Development Report 2000.* New York: Oxford University Press.

United Nations. (2001a). *Human Development Report 2001.* On the World Wide Web at http://www.undp.org/hdr01/.

United Nations. (2001b). "Vital LDC Statistics." *Report on the 3rd United Nations Conference on the Least Developed Countries.* Brussels: United Nations Department Of Public Information.

United States (The President of). (2002). "The National Security Strategy of the United States of America." September 2002. Office of the President of the United States.

Wade, Robert. (1999). "National Power, Coercive Liberalism and 'Global' Finance." In Robert Art and Robert Jervis, eds., *International Politics: Enduring Concepts and Contemporary Issues*, p. 4.

Walker, Stuart. (1993). "This Passing Show." *Alternatives, 19* (2), 46–49.

Williamson, John. (1994). "In Search of a Manual for Technopols." In John Williamson, ed., *The Political Economy of Policy Reform.* Washington: Institute for Economic Research.

Wolf, Eric R. (1982). *Europe and the People without History.* Berkeley, CA: University of California Press.

Women's International Network News. (2003). "State of the World Population 2002—People, Poverty And Possibilities." *Women's International Network News, 29* (1).

World Bank. (2000). *Selected World Development Indicators.* On the World Wide Web at http://www.worldbank.org.

World Hunger Education Services. (2002). *World Hunger Facts 2002.* On The World Wide Web at http://worldhunger.org/articles/learn/world%hunger%202002.htm.

CHAPTER 12

Anderson, M. (1971). *Family Structure in Nineteenth-Century Lancashire.* Cambridge, UK: Cambridge University Press.

Arat-Koc, S. (1993). "The Politics of Family and Immigration in the Subordination of Domestic Workers in Canada." In B. Fox, ed., *Family Patterns, Gender Relations* (pp. 278–97). Toronto: Oxford University Press.

Baker, M. (1995). *Canadian Family Policies.* Toronto: University of Toronto Press.

Barnett, Rosalind, and Caryl Rivers. (1996). *She Works/He Works.* San Francisco: Harper.

Beach, J., J. Bertrand, and G. Cleveland. (1998). *Our Child Care Workforce: From Recognition to Remuneration.* Main Report for the Child Care Sector Study Steering Committee. Ottawa: HRDC.

Beaujot, R., E.M. Gee, F. Rajulton, and Z.R. Ravanera. (1995). *Family Over the Life Course: Current Demographic Analysis*, cat. no. 91-543. Ottawa: Industry Canada.

Bernard, J. (1972). *The Future of Marriage.* New Haven, CT: Yale University Press.

Blumenstein, P., and P. Schwartz. (1983). *American Couples.* New York: William Morrow.

Bradbury, B. (1982). "The Fragmented Family: Family Strategies in the Face of Death, Illness and Poverty, Montreal, 1860–1885." In J. Parr, ed., *Childhood and Family* (pp. 109–29). Toronto: McClelland and Stewart.

Calliste, A. (2001). "Black Families in Canada: Exploring the Interconnections of Race, Class, and Gender." In B. Fox, ed., *Family Patterns, Gender Relations*, 2nd ed. Toronto: Oxford University Press.

Clarke-Stewart, A. (1982). *Daycare.* Cambridge, MA: Harvard University Press.

Coontz, Stephanie. (1992). *The Way We Never Were: American Families and the Nostalgia Trap.* New York: Basic Books.

Cott, N. (1977). *Bonds of Womanhood: "Women's Sphere" in New England, 1780–1835.* New Haven, CT: Yale University Press.

Davidoff, L., and C. Hall. (1987). *Family Fortunes: Men and Women in the English Middle Class, 1780–1850.* Chicago: University of Chicago Press.

Edholm, F. (1982). "The Unnatural Family." In E. Whitelegg, M. Arnot, E. Bartels, V. Beechey, L. Birke, S. Himmelweit, D. Leonard, S. Ruehl, and M. Speakman, eds., *The Changing Experience of Women.* London: The Open University.

Eyer, D. (1996). *Motherguilt: How Our Culture Blames Mothers for What's Wrong with Society.* New York: Random House.

Finnie, R. (1993). "Women, Men and the Economic Consequences of Divorce: Evidence from Canadian Longitudinal Data." *Canadian Review of Sociology and Anthropology, 30* (2), 205–41.

Flandrin, J. (1979). *Families in Former Times: Kinship, Household and Sexuality.* Cambridge, UK: Cambridge University Press.

Fox, B. (1997). "Reproducing Difference: Changes in the Lives of Partners Becoming Parents." In M. Luxton, ed., *Feminism and Families.* Halifax: Fernwood.

Fox, B., and D. Worts. (1999). "Revisiting the Critique of Medicalized Childbirth." *Gender and Society, 13* (3), 326–47.

Furstenberg, F., and A. Cherlin. (1991). *Divided Families: What Happens to Children When Parents Part.* Cambridge: Harvard University Press.

Gartner, R., M. Dawson, and M. Crawford. (1998–99). "Woman Killing: Intimate Femicide in Ontario, 1974–1994." *Resources for Feminist Research*, 3 and 4, 151–73.

Gaskell, J. (1983). "The Reproduction of Family Life: Perspectives of Male and Female Adolescents." In J. Veevers, ed., *Continuity and Change in Marriage and Family* (pp. 219–34). Toronto: Holt, Rinehart and Winston.

Gerson, K. (1985). *Hard Choices: How Women Decide about Work, Career and Motherhood.* Berkeley, CA: University of California Press.

Gottlieb, B. (1993). *The Family in the Western World*. New York: Oxford University Press.

Graham, H. (1987). "Being Poor: Perceptions and Coping Strategies of Lone Mothers." In J. Brannen and G. Wilson, eds., *Give and Take in Families: Studies in Resource Distribution* (pp. 56–74) London: Allen and Unwin.

Greven, P. (1973). "Family Structure in Seventeenth-Century Andover, Massachusetts." In M. Gordon, ed., *The American Family in Social-Historical Perspective* (pp. 77–100). New York: St. Martin's Press.

Hanawalt, B. (1986). *The Ties That Bound: Peasant Families in Medieval England*. New York: Oxford University Press.

Hareven, T. (1982). *Family Time and Industrial Time: The Relationship between Family and Work in a New England Industrial Community*. Cambridge, UK: Cambridge University Press.

Hertz, R. (1986). *More Equal than Others: Women and Men in Dual-Career Marriages*. Berkeley, CA: University of California Press.

Hochschild, A. (1989). *The Second Shift: Working Parents and the Revolution at Home*. New York: Viking.

Iacovetta, F. (1992). *Such Hardworking People: Italian Immigrants in Postwar Toronto*. Montreal and Kingston, ON: McGill-Queen's University Press.

Jenson, Jane. (2002). "Against the Current: Child Care and Family Policy in Quebec." In S. Michel and R. Mahon, eds., *Child Care Policy at the Crossroads: Gender and Welfare State Restructuring*. New York: Routledge.

Kibria, N. (1993). *Family Tightrope: The Changing Lives of Vietnamese Americans*. Princeton, NJ: Princeton University Press.

Kurz, D. (1995). *For Richer, For Poorer: Mothers Confront Divorce*. New York: Routledge.

Lasch, C. (1977). *Haven in a Heartless World: The Family Besieged*. New York: Basic Books.

Laslett, B., and J. Brenner. (1989). "Gender and Social Reproduction: Historical Perspectives." *Annual Review of Sociology*, *15*, 381–404.

Leacock, E.B. (1981). *Myths of Male Dominance: Collected Articles on Women Cross-Culturally*. New York: Monthly Review Press.

Lee, R.B. (1979). *The !Kung San: Men, Women and Work in a Foraging Society*. Cambridge, UK: Cambridge University Press.

Lewontin, R.C., S. Rose, and L. Kamin. (1984). *Not in Our Genes: Biology, Ideology and Human Nature*. New York: Pantheon.

Luxton, M. (1980). *More than a Labour of Love: Three Generations of Women's Work in the Home*. Toronto: Women's Press.

Mahon, R., and S. Phillips. (2002). "Dual-Earner Families Caught in a Liberal Welfare Regime? The Politics of Child Care Policy in Canada." In S. Michel and R. Mahon, eds., *Child Care Policy at the Crossroads: Gender and Welfare State Restructuring*. New York: Routledge.

McMahon, Martha. (1995). *Engendering Motherhood: Identity and Self-Transformation in Women's Lives*. New York: The Guilford Press.

Marcil-Gratton, N. (1993). "Growing Up with a Single Parent: A Transitional Experience? Some Demographic Measurements." In J. Hudson and B. Galaway, eds., *Single Parent Families: Perspectives on Research and Policy* (pp. 73–90). Toronto: Thompson Educational Publishing.

Marshall, C. (1994). "Household Chores." In *Canadian Social Trends*. Vol. 2 (pp. 197–200) Toronto: Thompson Educational Publishing.

May, E. (1988). *Homeward Bound: American Families in the Cold War Era*. New York: Basic Books.

May, M. (1985). "Bread before Roses: American Workingmen, Labor Unions and the Family Wage." In R. Milkman, ed., *Women, Work and Protest: A Century of U.S. Women's Labor History* (pp. 1–22). Boston: Routledge and Kegan Paul.

McKie, C. (1993). "An Overview of Lone Parenthood in Canada." In J. Hudson and B. Galaway, eds., *Single Parent Families: Perspectives on Research and Policy* (pp. 53–72). Toronto: Thompson Educational Publishing.

McLanahan, S. (1985). "Family Structure and the Reproduction of Poverty." *American Journal of Sociology*, *90* (4), 873–901.

McLanahan, S., and L. Bumpass. (1988). "Intergenerational Consequences of Family Disruption." *American Journal of Sociology*, *94* (1), 130–52.

Mitterauer, M., and R. Sieder. (1982). *The European Family: Patriarchy to Partnership from the Middle Ages to the Present*. Oxford: Basil Blackwell.

Morton, M. (1988). "Dividing the Wealth, Sharing the Poverty: The (Re)formation of 'Family' in Law in Ontario." *Canadian Review of Sociology and Anthropology*, *25* (2), 254–76.

National Council of Welfare. (1998). *Poverty Profile 1996*. Ottawa: Supply and Services Canada.

Parsons, T., and R. Bales. (1955). *Family, Socialization and Interaction Process*. New York: Free Press.

Patterson, C. (1995). "Lesbian Mothers, Gay Fathers, and Their Children." In A.R. D'Augelli and C.J. Patterson, eds., *Lesbian, Gay and Bisexual Identities over the Lifespan: Psychological Perspectives*. New York: Oxford University Press.

Presser, H. (1994). "Employment Schedules, Gender and Household Labor." *American Sociological Review*, *59* (3), 348–64.

Rapp, R., and E. Ross. (1986). "The 1920s: Feminism, Consumerism and Political Backlash in the U.S." In J. Friedlander, B. Cook, A. Kessler-Harris, and C. Smith-Rosenberg, eds., *Women in Culture and Politics* (pp. 52–62). Bloomington, IN: Indiana University Press.

Rosenberg, H. (1987). "Motherwork, Stress and Depression: The Costs of Privatized Social Reproduction." In H.J. Maroney and M. Luxton, eds., *Feminism and Political Economy: Women's Work, Women's Struggles* (pp. 181–97). Toronto: Methuen.

Rubin, L. (1990). *Erotic Wards: What Happened to the Sexual Revolution?* New York: Farrar, Straus & Giroux.

Ryan, M. (1981). *Cradle of the Middle Class: The Family in Oneida County, 1790–1865*. Cambridge: Cambridge University Press.

Schwartz, P., and V. Rutter. (1998). *The Gender of Sexuality*. Thousand Oaks: Pine Forge Press.

Singh, S., and J. Lindsay. (1996). "Money in Heterosexual Relationships." *Australia and New Zealand Journal of Sociology*, *32* (4), 56–69.

Smith-Rosenberg, C. (1975). "The Female World of Love and Ritual: Relations between Women in Nineteenth-Century America." *Signs*, *1* (1), 1–31.

Stacey, J., and T. Biblarz. (2001). "(How) Does the Sexual Orientation of Parents Matter?" *American Sociological Review*, *66* (2) 159–83.

Stack, C. (1974). *All Our Kin: Strategies for Survival in a Black Community*. New York: Harper and Row.

Stansell, C. (1987). *City of Women: Sex and Class in New York, 1789–1860*. Urbana, IL: University of Illinois Press.

Statistics Canada. (1992a). Families: Number, Type and Structure. *1991 Census of Canada*. Cat. no. 93-312, Table 3. Ottawa: Industry, Science and Technology Canada.

Statistics Canada. (1992b). *Lone Parent Families in Canada*. Cat. no. 89-522E, Occasional. Ottawa: Industry, Science and Technology Canada.

Statistics Canada. (1993a). *A Portrait of Families in Canada*. Cat. no. 89-523E, Occasional, Table 1.4. Ottawa: Industry, Science and Technology Canada.

Statistics Canada. (1993b). *Labour Force Activity of Women by Presence of Children. 1991 Census of Canada*. Cat. no. 93-325, Table 1. Ottawa: Industry, Science and Technology Canada.

Statistics Canada. (1999). "Census Families in Private Households by Family Structure, Showing Number of Families, Average Family Size and Number of Never-Married Sons and Daughters at Home, for Canada, Provinces and Territories, 1991 and 1996 Censuses—20% Sample Data." Cat. no. 93F0022XDB96008, October 14, 1999. On the World Wide Web at http://www.statcan.ca/english/census96/oct14/fam1.htm.

Tarvis, C. (1992). *The Mismeasure of Woman*. New York: A Touchstone Book.

Tilly, L., and J.W. Scott. (1978). *Women, Work and Family*. New York: Holt, Rinehart and Winston.

Turnbull, C. (1961). *The Forest People*. New York: Doubleday.

Weston, K. (1991). *Families We Choose: Lesbians, Gays, Kinship*. New York: Columbia University Press.

CHAPTER 13

Adams, Tracey L. 2000. *A Gentleman and a Dentist: Gender and the Rise of Dentistry in Ontario*. Toronto: University of Toronto Press.

Althauser, Robert. (1989). "Internal Labor Markets." *Annual Review of Sociology*, 15, 143–61.

Andrew, Caroline, Céline Coderre, and Ann Denis. (1994). "Women in Management: The Canadian Experience." In Nancy J. Adler and Dafna N. Izraeli, eds., *Competitive Frontiers: Women Managers in a Global Economy* (pp. 377–87). Cambridge, MA: Oxford University Press.

Becker, Gary S. (1975). *Human Capital: A Theoretical and Empirical Analysis with Special Reference to Education*, 3rd ed. Chicago: University of Chicago Press.

Bell, Daniel. (1976). *The Coming of Post-industrial Society*. New York: Basic Books.

Bendix, Reinhard. (1974). *Work and Authority in Industry*. Berkeley, CA: University of California Press.

Blauner, Robert. (1964). *Alienation and Freedom*. Chicago: University of Chicago Press.

Boase, Sharon. 1998. "Discontented Youth Empower Labour." *Ottawa Citizen*, January 31, p. J2.

Braverman, Harry. (1974). *Labor and Monopoly Capital: The Degradation of Work in the Twentieth Century*. New York: Monthly Review Press.

Bridges, William. (1994). *Job Shift: How to Prosper in a Workplace without Jobs*. Don Mills, ON: Addison-Wesley.

Burawoy, Michael. (1979). *Manufacturing Consent: Changes in the Labour Process under Monopoly Capitalism*. Chicago: University of Chicago Press.

Calliste, Agnes. (1993). "Sleeping Car Porters in Canada: An Ethnically Submerged Split Labour Market." In Graham S. Lowe and Harvey Krahn, eds., *Work in Canada: Readings in the Sociology of Work and Industry* (pp. 139–53). Scarborough, ON: Nelson.

Campell, Andrew. (1996). "From Shop Floor to Computer Room." *The Globe and Mail*, December 30, pp. A1, A8.

Canadian Labour Congress. (1993). "Two Years under Free Trade: An Assessment." In Graham S. Lowe and Harvey Krahn, eds., *Work in Canada: Readings in the Sociology of Work and Industry* (pp. 115–19). Scarborough, ON: Nelson.

Canadian Press/Leger Marketing. 2001. *How Much Importance Canadian Place on their Work*. Montreal.

Carey, Alex. (1967). "The Hawthorne Studies: A Radical Criticism." *American Sociological Review, 32*, 403–16.

Chamberlain, Art. (1996). "Surprise! We're Happy in Our Work, Poll Shows." *The Toronto Sun*, October 8, p. A1.

Dassbach, Carl H.A. (1996). "Lean Production, Labor Control, and Post-Fordism in the Japanese Automobile Industry." In William C. Green and Ernest J. Yanarella, eds., *North American Auto Unions in Crisis: Lean Production as Contested Terrain* (pp. 19–40). Albany, NY: SUNY Press.

David, Paul A. (1990). "The Dynamo and the Computer: An Historical Perspective on the Modern Productivity Paradox." *American Economic Review, 80* (May), 355–61.

Eaton, Jonathan. (1998). "Wake up Little Suzy: Women Retail Workers Organize." *Our Times* 17(2): 23–29.

Economic Council of Canada. (1991). *Good Jobs, Bad Jobs: Employment in the Service Economy*. Ottawa: Supply and Services Canada.

Edwards, P.K., and Hugh Scullion. (1982). *The Social Organization of Industrial Conflict*. Oxford: Blackwell.

Edwards, Richard. (1979). *Contested Terrain: The Transformation of the Workplace in the Twentieth Century*. New York: Basic Books.

Friedson, Eliot. (1970). The Profession of Medicine: A Study in the Sociology of Applied Knowledge. New York: Harper and Row.

Galarneau, Diane. (1996). "Unionized Workers." *Perspectives on Labour and Income* (Spring), 42–52.

Hall, Marny. (1993). "Private Experiences in the Public Domain: Lesbians in Organizations." In Jeffrey Hearn, Deborah L. Sheppard, Peta Tancred-Sheriff, and Gibson Burrell, eds., *The Sexuality of Organization* (pp. 125–38). Berkeley, CA: Sage.

Henson, Kevin D. (1996). *Just a Temp*. Philadelphia: Temple University Press.

Hodson, Randy, and Teresa Sullivan. (1985). "Totem or Tyrant? Monopoly, Regional and Local Sector Effects on Worker Commitment." *Social Forces, 63* (3), 716–31.

Hodson, Randy, and Teresa Sullivan. (1990). *The Social Organization of Work*. Belmont, CA: Wadsworth.

Hodson, Randy. (1991). "The Active Worker: Compliance and Autonomy at the Workplace." *Contemporary Ethnography, 20* (April), 271–90.

Jones, Frank E. (1996). *Understanding Organizations: A Sociological Perspective*. Cooksville, ON: Copp Clark.

Kanter, Rosabeth Moss. (1977). *Men and Women of the Corporation*. New York: Basic Books.

Krahn, Harvey J. (1992). *Quality of Work in the Service Economy. General Social Survey Analysis Series 6*. Cat. no. 11-612E, no. 6. Ottawa: Statistics Canada.

Krahn, Harvey J., and Graham S. Lowe. (1998). *Work, Industry and Canadian Society*, 3rd ed. Scarborough, ON: ITP Nelson.

Laxer, Gordon. (1989). *Open for Business: The Roots of Foreign Ownership in Canada*. Don Mills, ON: Oxford University Press.

Lehr, Bill, and Frank Lichtenberg. (1999). "Information Technology and Its Impact on Productivity: Firm-level Evidence from Government and Private Data Sources, 1977–1993." *Canadian Journal of Economics, 32* (2), 335–62.

Livingstone, D.W. (1993). "Conclusion: Aging Dinosaurs or All-Round Workers?" In June Corman, Meg Luxton, D.W. Livingstone, and Wally Secombe, eds., *Recasting Steel Labour: The Stelco Story* (pp. 145–55). Halifax: Fernwood.

Lowe, Graham S. (1987). *Women in the Administrative Revolution: The Feminization of Clerical Work*. Toronto: University of Toronto Press.

Martinsons, Maris G., and Patrick K.C. Chong. (1999). "The Influence of Human Factors and Specialist Involvement on Information Systems Success." *Human Relations 52* (1), 123–52.

McKay, Shona. (1993). "Willing and Able." In Graham S. Lowe and Harvey Krahn, eds., *Work in Canada: Readings in the Sociology of Work and Industry* (pp. 166–71). Scarborough, ON: Nelson.

McKenzie, Donald. (2001). "90% Satisfied with Their Jobs: Poll: 70% Happy with Salary." *Financial Post*, December 31, p. FP3.

McLaughlin, D.B. (1983). "Electronics and the Future of Work: The Impact on Pink and White Collar Workers." *Annals of the American Academy of Political and Social Science, 470*, 152–62.

Mighty, E. Joy. (1997). "Triple Jeopardy: Immigrant Women of Colour in the Labour Force." In P. Prasad, A.J. Mills, M. Elmes, and A. Prasad, eds., *Managing the Organizational Melting Pot: Dilemmas of Workplace Diversity* (pp. 312–39). Thousand Oaks, CA: Sage.

Mills, Albert J., and Tony Simmons. (1999). *Reading Organization Theory: A Critical Approach to the Study of Organizational Behaviour and Structure*. Toronto: Garamond Press.

Morissette, René. (1991). "Are Jobs in Large Firms Better?" *Perspectives on Labour and Income* (Autumn), 40–50.

Myles, John. (1988). "The Expanding Middle: Some Canadian Evidence on the Deskilling Debate." *Canadian Review of Sociology and Anthropology, 25* (3), 335–64.

Myles, John. (1991). "Post-industrialism and the Service Economy." In Graham S. Lowe and Harvey Krahn, eds., *Work in Canada: Readings in the Sociology of Work and Industry* (pp. 124–34). Scarborough, ON: Nelson.

Noreau, N. (1994). "Involuntary Part-Timers." *Perspectives on Labour and Income, 6* (3), 25–30.

Osterman, Paul. (1995). "The Transformation of Work in the United States: What the Evidence Shows." In Bryan Downie and Mary Lou Coates, eds., *Managing Human Resources in the 1990s and Beyond* (pp. 71–92). Kingston, ON: Industrial Relations Centre Press.

"Paradox Lost." (1996). *The Economist, 340*, September 28, p. S13.

Pescocolido, Bernice, Steven Tuch and Jack Martin. 2001. "The Profession of Medicine and The Public: Examining American's Changing Confidence in Physician Authority from the Beginning of the 'Health Care Crisis' to the Era of Health Care Reform. *Journal of Health and Social Behavior, 42* (March), 1–16.

Polanyi, Karl. (1957). *The Great Transformation*. Boston: Beacon Press.

Powell, Gary. (1990). "One More Time: Do Female and Male Managers Differ?" *Academy of Management Executive, 4* (August), 68–75.

Prasad, P., and Albert J. Mills. (1997). "Managing the Organizational Melting Pot: Dilemmas of Diversity at the Workplace." In P. Prasad, A.J. Mills, M. Elmes, and A. Prasad, eds., *Managing the Organizational Melting Pot: Dilemmas of Workplace Diversity* (pp. 3–27). Thousand Oaks, CA: Sage.

"Productivity: Lost in Cyberspace." (1997). *The Economist, 344*, September 13, p. 72.

Rifkin, Jeremy. (1995). *The End of Work: The Decline of the Global Labor Force and the Dawn of the Post Market Era*. New York: G.P. Putnam.

Rinehart, James, David Robertson, Chris Huxley, and Jeff Wareham. (1994). "Reunifying Conception and Execution of Work under Japanese Production Management? A Canadian Case Study." In Tony Elger and Chris Smith, eds., *Global Japanization? The Transnational Transformation of the Labour Process* (pp. 152–74). London: Routledge.

Rinehart, James. (1978). "Contradictions of Work-Related Attitudes and Behaviour: An Interpretation." *Canadian Review of Sociology and Anthropology, 15*, 1–15.

Rinehart, James. (1996). *The Tyranny of Work: Alienation and the Labour Process*, 3rd ed. Toronto: Harcourt Brace.

Robertson, David, and Jeff Wareham. (1990). *Technological Change: Air Canada Customer Sales and Service*. North York, ON: CAW Research.

Robertson, David, James Rinehart, Christopher Huxley, Jeff Wareham, Herman Rosenfeld, Alan McGough, and Steve Benedict. (1993). *The CAMI Report: Lean Production in a Unionized Auto Plant*. North York, ON: CAW Research.

Rogers, Jackie Krasas. (1995). "Just a Temp: Experience and Structure of Alienation in Temporary Clerical Employment." *Work and Occupations, 22* (2), 137–66.

Rosener, Judy B. (1990). "Ways Women Lead." *Harvard Business Review*, November/December, 119–25.

Rosenthal, Patricia, Stephen Hill, and Riccardo Peccei. (1997). "Checking Out Service: Evaluating Excellence, HRM and TQM in Retailing." *Work, Employment & Society, 11* (3), 481–503.

Schmitt, R., and T.E. Moody. (1994). *Alienation and Social Criticism*. Atlantic Highlands, NJ: Humanities Press.

Shain, Alan. (1995). "Employment of People with Disabilities." *Canadian Social Trends* (Autumn), 8–13.

Sheppard, Deborah L. (1993). "Women Managers' Perceptions of Gender and Organizational Life." In Jeffrey Hearn, Deborah L. Sheppard, Peta Tancred-Sheriff, and Gibson Burrell, eds., *The Sexuality of Organization* (pp. 151–66). Berkeley, CA: Sage.

Smith, Vicki. 2001. *Crossing the Great Divide: Worker Risk and Opportunity in the New Economy*. Ithaca and Cornell: IRL Press.

Solow, Robert. (1987). "We'd Better Watch Out." *New York Times Book Review*, July 12.

Spenner, Kenneth. (1983). "Deciphering Prometheus: Temporal Change in the Skill Level of Work." *American Sociological Review*, 48 (6), 824–37.

Toffler, Alvin. (1980). *The Third Wave*. New York: Bantam.

Triplett, Jack E. (1999). "The Solow Productivity Paradox: What Do Computers Do to Productivity?" *Canadian Journal of Economics*, 32 (2) 309–34.

Tyre, Marcie J., and Wanda J. Orlikowski. (1994). "Windows of Opportunity: Temporal Patterns of Technological Adaptation in Organizations." *Organization Science*, 5, 98–118.

Wallace, Michael. (1989). "Brave New Workplace: Technology and Work in the New Economy." *Work and Occupations*, 16 (4), 393–415.

White, Julie. (1993). "Patterns of Unionization." In Linda Briskin and Patricia McDermott, eds., *Women Challenging Unions: Feminism, Democracy and Militancy* (pp. 191–206). Toronto: University of Toronto Press.

Womack, J., D. Jones, and D. Roos. (1990). *The Machine That Changed the World*. New York: Rawson and Associates.

Zuboff, Shoshana. (1988). *In the Age of the Smart Machine: The Future of Work and Power*. New York: Basic Books.

CHAPTER 14

Adler, P.A., S.J. Kless, and P. Adler. (1992). "Socialization to Gender Roles: Popularity among Elementary School Boys and Girls." *Sociology of Education*, 65, 169–87.

Ballantine, J. (2001). *The Sociology of Education: A Systematic Analysis*, 5th ed. Englewood Cliffs, NJ: Prentice-Hall.

Barr, R., and R. Dreeben. (1983). *How Schools Work*. Chicago: University of Chicago Press.

Bernstein, B. (1977). *Class, Codes, and Control*, 2nd ed. London: Routledge and Kegan Paul.

Blair, S.L. and M.C. Legazpi. (1999). "Racial/Ethnic Differences in High School Students' Academic Performance: Understanding the Interweave of Social Class and Ethnicity in the Family Context." *Journal of Comparative Family Studies*, 30, 539–55.

Boocock, S.S. (1980). *Sociology of Education*, 2nd ed. Boston: Houghton Mifflin.

Bourdieu, P. (1973). "Cultural Reproduction and Social Reproduction." In R. Brown, ed., *Knowledge, Education, and Cultural Change* (pp. 71–112). London: Tavistock.

Bowles, S., and H. Gintis. (1976). *Schooling in Capitalist America: Educational Reform and the Contradictions of Economic Life*. New York: Basic Books.

Braun, C. (1976). "Teacher Expectations: Sociopsychological Dynamics." *Review of Educational Research*, 46, 185–213.

Breton, R. (1972). *Social and Academic Factors in the Career Decisions of Canadian Youth*. Ottawa: Information Canada.

Collins, R. (1977). "Functional and Conflict Theories of Educational Stratification." In J. Karabel and A.H. Halsey, eds., *Power and Ideology in Education* (pp. 118–36). Cambridge: Oxford University Press.

Collins, R. (1979). *The Credential Society*. New York: Academic Press.

Dar, Y., and N. Resh. (1986). "Classroom Intellectual Composition and Academic Achievement." *American Educational Research Journal*, 23, 357–74.

Davies, S. (1999). "Stubborn Disparities: Explaining Class Inequalities in Schooling." in James Curtis, Edward Grabb, and Neil Guppy (eds.). *Social Inequality in Canada: Patterns, Problems, and Policies*, 3rd ed. (pp. 138–50). Toronto: Prentice Hall.

Davies, S., and N. Guppy. (1998). "Race and Canadian Education." In Vic Satzewich, ed., *Racism and Social Inequality in Canada: Concepts, Controversies and Strategies of Resistance*. Toronto: Thompson Educational Publishing Inc.

Demaine, Jack. (2001). *Sociology of Education Today*. New York: Palgrave.

Dimaggio, P. (1982). "Cultural Capital and School Success: The Impact of Status Culture Participation on the Grades of U.S. High School Students." *American Sociological Review*, 47, 189–201.

Dimaggio, P., and J. Mohr. (1985). "Cultural Capital, Educational Attainment, and Marital Selection." *American Journal of Sociology*, 90, 1231–61.

Eder, D. (198 1). "Ability Grouping as a Self-Fulfilling Prophecy: A Micro Analysis of Teacher-Student Interaction." *Sociology of Education*, 54, 151–61.

Felmlee, D., and D. Eder. (1983). "Contextual Effects in the Classroom: The Impact of Ability Groups on Student Attention." *Sociology of Education*, 56, 77–86.

Finlay, M.K. (1984). "Teachers and Tracking in a Comprehensive High School." *Sociology of Education*, 57, 233–42.

Gardner, D.P. (1983). *A Nation at Risk: The Imperative for Educational Reform*. Washington, DC: U.S. Government Printing Office.

Gardner, H. (1983). *Frames of Mind: The Theory of Multiple Intelligences*. New York: Basic Books.

Gilbert, S., and A. Pomfret. (1991). *Gender Tracking in University Programs: An Analysis of Gender Patterns in Canada Scholarships Program (CSP) Disciplines and Non-CSP University Disciplines*. Ottawa: Industry, Science, and Technology Canada.

Gomme, I.M. (2002). *The Shadow Line: Deviance and Crime in Canada*. Toronto: Nelson.

Guppy, N., and S. Davies. (1998). *Education in Canada: Recent Trends and Future Challenges*. Ottawa: Statistics Canada

Guppy, N., and S. Davies. (1999). "Understanding Canadians' Declining Confidence in Public Education." *Canadian Journal of Education*, 24 (3), 265–80.

Guppy, N., S. Davies, and A. Ludditt. (1999). "A New Twist in Education Reform: Bringing the Market to Schools." In James Curtis, Edward Grabb, and Neil Guppy, eds., *Social Inequality in Canada: Patterns, Problems, and Policies*, 3rd ed. (pp. 151–58). Toronto: Prentice Hall.

Hallinan, M.T. (2001). "Sociological Perspectives on Black–White Inequalities in American Schooling." *Sociology of Education Extra Issue*, 50–70.

Hallinan, M.T., and A.B. Sorenson. (1986). "Student Characteristics and Assignment to Ability Groups: Two Conceptual Formulations." *Sociological Quarterly*, 27, 1–13.

Herberg, E. R. (1990). "The Ethno-racial Socioeconomic Hierarchy in Canada: Theory and Analysis of the New Vertical

Mosaic" *International Journal of Comparative Sociology, 31*, 206–21.

Holland, D.C., and M. Eisenhart. (1990). *Educated in Romance: Women, Achievement, and College Culture.* Chicago: University of Chicago Press.

Horwitz, R.A. (1979). "Psychological Effects of the Open Classroom." *Review of Educational Research, 49,* 71–86.

Jackson, P.W. (1968). *Life in Classrooms.* New York: Holt, Rinehart and Winston.

Kingston, P.W. (2001). "The Unfulfilled Promise of Cultural Capital Theory." *Sociology of Education Extra Issue,* 88–99.

Kerckhoff, A.C. (1986). "Effects of Ability Grouping in British Secondary Schools." *American Sociological Review, 51,* 842–58.

Kerckhoff, A.C. (2001). "Education and Social Stratification Processes in Comparative Perspective." *Sociology of Education Extra Issue,* 3–18.

Li, P. (1988). *Ethnicity in Canada.* Toronto: Wall and Thompson.

Livingstone, D.W., D. Hart, and L.E. Davie. (2001). *Public Attitudes toward Education in Ontario: The 13th OISE/UT Survey.* Toronto: OISE.

Oakes, J. (1982). "Classroom Social Relationships: Exploring the Bowles and Gintis Hypothesis." *Sociology of Education, 55,* 197–212.

Oakes, J., (1985). *Keeping Track.* New Haven, CT: Yale University Press.

Oakes, J. and G. Guiton. (1995). "Matchmaking: The Dynamics of High School Tracking Decisions." *American Education Research Journal, 32,* 3–33.

Parsons, T. (1951). *The Social System.* Glencoe, IL: Free Press.

Porter, J. (1965). *The Vertical Mosaic: An Analysis of Social Class and Power in Canada.* Toronto: University of Toronto Press.

Porter, J. (1979). *The Measure of Canadian Society.* Toronto: Gage.

Porter, J., M. Porter, and B. Blishen. (1982). *Stations and Callings: Making It through the School System.* Toronto: Methuen.

Richer, S. (1988). "Equality to Benefit from Schooling: The Issue of Educational Opportunity." In D. Forcese and S. Richer, eds., *Social Issues: Sociological Views of Canada* (pp. 262–86). Toronto: Prentice Hall.

Ritzer, G., and D. Walczak. (1986). *Working: Conflict and Change.* Englewood Cliffs: Prentice Hall.

Rosenthal, R., and L. Jacobson. (1968). *Pygmalion in the Classroom.* New York: Holt, Rinehart and Winston.

Rowan, B., and A.W. Mirade. (1983). "Systems of Ability Grouping and the Stratification of Achievement in Elementary Schools." *Sociology of Education, 56,* 133–44.

Schafer, W.E., C. Olexa, and K. Polk. (1970). "Programmed for Social Class: Tracking in High School." *Transaction,* 7 (12), 39–46.

Schmid, C.L. (2001). "Educational Achievement, Language-Minority Students, and the New Second Generation." *Sociology of Education Extra Issue,* 71–87.

Shavit, Y. (1984). "Tracking and Ethnicity in Israeli Secondary Education." *American Sociological Review, 49,* 210–20.

Shavit, Y., and D.L. Featherman. (1988). "Schooling, Tracking, and Teenage Intelligence." *Sociology of Education, 61,* 42–51.

Statham, S. (1986). *Daughters and Sons: Experiences in Non-Sexist Childrearing.* New York: Basil Blackwell.

Statistics Canada. (2001a). *The Daily.* "Participation in Postsecondary Education and Family Income." Friday, December 7.

Statistics Canada. (2001b). *Education in Canada, 2000.* Ottawa: Ministry of Industry.

Taillon, J., and M. Paju. (1999). *The Class of '95: the Report of the 1997 National Survey of 1995 Graduates.* Ottawa: Minister of Public Works and Government Service of Canada.

Travers, E.F. (1983). "The Role of the School in Political Socialization Reconsidered: Evidence from 1970 and 1979." *Youth and Society, 14,* 475–500.

Washburn, P. (1985). "The Public School as an Agent of Political Socialization." *Quarterly Journal of Ideology, 10,* 25–34.

Wells, A.S., and J. Oakes. (1996). "Potential Pitfalls of Systemic Reform: Early Lessons from Research on Detracking." *Sociology of Education Extra Issue,* 135–44.

Willis, P. (1977). *Learning to Labour.* Farnborough: Saxon House, Teakfield.

CHAPTER 15

Abu-Lughod, Janet L. (1991). *Changing Cities: Urban Sociology.* New York: HarperCollins.

Bell, Wendell. (1968). "The City, the Suburbs and a Theory of Social Choice." In Scott Greer, Dennis McElrath, David W. Minar, and Peter Orleans, eds., *The New Urbanization* (pp. 132–68). New York: St. Martin's Press.

Berger, Bennett. (1960). *Working Class Suburb.* Berkeley, CA: University of California Press.

Brym, Robert J. (1986). "An Introduction to the Regional Question in Canada." In Robert J. Brym, ed., *Regionalism in Canada* (pp. 1–45). Toronto: Irwin.

Burgess, Ernest W. (1961). "The Growth of the City: An Introduction to a Research Project." In George A. Theodorson, ed., *Studies in Human Ecology* (pp. 37–44). Evanston, IL: Row, Peterson.

Castells, Manuel. (1989). *The Informational City: Information, Technology, Economic Restructuring and the Urban–Regional Process.* Oxford and Cambridge, MA: Blackwell.

Chandler, Tertius, and Gerald Fox. (1974). *3000 Years of Urban Growth.* New York and London: Academic Press.

Clark, David. (1996). *Urban World, Global City.* London and New York: Routledge.

Davis, Mike. (1990). *City of Quartz: Excavating the Future in Los Angeles.* London and New York: Verso.

De Oliviera, Orlandino, and Bryan Roberts. (1996). "Urban Development and Social Inequality in Latin America." In J. Gugler, ed., *The Urban Transformation of the Developing World* (pp. 250–314). Oxford: Oxford University Press.

Drakakis-Smith, David. (1988). "Third World Cities: Sustainable Urban Development II—Population, Labour and Poverty." In R. Paddison and B. Lever, eds., *International Perspectives in Urban Studies 5* (pp. 70–101). London and Bristol, PA: Jessica Kingsley Publishers.

Driedger, Leo. (1991). *The Urban Factor: Sociology of Canadian Cities.* Toronto: Oxford University Press.

Egan, Timothy. (1995). "The Serene Fortress: Many Seek Security behind Walls and Guards of Private Communities." *New York Times*, September 3, pp. 1, 10.

Epp, Roger., and Dave. Whitson. (2001). "Writing Off Rural Communities." In R. Epp and D. Whitson, eds., *Writing Off the Rural West* (pp. xii–xxxv). Edmonton, AB: The University of Alberta Press/Parkland Institute.

Fava, Sylvia Fleis. (1956). "Suburbanism as a Way of Life." *American Sociological Review*, *21*, 34–37.

Filion, Pierre. (1991). "The Gentrification–Social Structure Dialectic: A Toronto Case Study." *International Journal of Urban and Regional Research*, *15*, 553–74.

Firey, Walter. (1947). *Land Use in Central Boston*. Cambridge, MA: Harvard University Press.

Fishman, Robert. (1987). *Bourgeois Utopias: The Rise and Fall of Suburbia*. New York: Basic Books.

Fishman, Robert. (1990). "Megalopolis Unbound." *The Wilson Quarterly* (Winter), 25–45.

Flanagan, William G. (1995). *Urban Sociology: Images and Structure*. Boston: Allyn and Bacon.

Florence, Elinor. (1997). "A Happy Hoofer Gets On with Life." *The Globe and Mail*, January 7, p. A18.

Fowler, Edmund P. (1992). *Building Cities That Work*. Montreal and Kingston, ON: McGill-Queen's University Press.

Frieden, Bernard J., and Lynne B. Sagalyn. (1989). *Downtown, Inc.: How America Rebuilds Cities*. Cambridge, MA: The MIT Press.

Garreau, Joel. (1991). *Edge City: Life on the New Frontier*. New York: Doubleday.

Ginsburg, N., B. Koppel, and T.G. McGee, eds. (1991). *The Extended Metropolis: Settlement Transition in Asia*. Honolulu: University of Hawaii Press.

Goldberger, Paul. (1996). "The Rise of the Private City." In Julia Vitullo Martin, ed., *Breaking Away: The Future of Cities* (pp. 135–47). New York: The Twentieth Century Fund Press.

Golden, Hilda H. (1981). *Urbanization and Cities*. Lexington, MA: D.C. Heath.

Goldsmith, Charles. (1996). "Prefab Irish Pubs Sell Pints World-Wide." *Wall Street Journal*, October 25, pp. B1 and B5.

Gordon, Ian, and Saskia Sassen. (1992). "Restructuring the Urban Labor Markets." In Susan S. Fainstein, Ian Gordon, and Michael Harloe, eds., *Divided Cities: New York and London in the Contemporary World* (pp. 105–28). Oxford and Cambridge, MA: Blackwell.

Gugler, Josef. (1996). "Preface." In J. Gugler, ed., *The Urban Transformation of the Developing World*. Oxford: Oxford University Press.

Hannigan, John A. (1995). "The Postmodern City: A New Urbanization?" *Current Sociology*, *43* (1), 152–217.

Harris, Chauncey, and Edward Ullman. (1945). "The Nature of Cities." *Annals of the American Academy of Political and Social Science*, *242* (November), 7–17.

Hauser, Philip M. (1965). "Urbanization: An Overview." In Philip M. Hauser and Leo F. Schnore, eds., *The Study of Urbanization*. New York: Wiley.

Hoyt, Homer. (1939). *The Structure and Growth of Residential Neighborhoods in American Cities*. Washington, DC: Federal Housing Authority.

Jackson, Kenneth T. (1985). *Crabgrass Frontier: The Suburbanization of the United States*. New York: Oxford University Press.

Kleniewski, Nancy. (1997). *Cities, Change and Conflict: A Political Economy of Urban Life*. Belmont, CA: Wadsworth.

Leinberger, Christopher B., and Charles Lockwood. (1986). "How Business Is Reshaping America." *The Atlantic Monthly, 258* (October), pp. 43–52.

Ley, David. (1991). "Gentrification." In Kent Gerecke, ed., *The Canadian City* (pp. 181–96). Montreal: Black Rose Books.

Little, Bruce. (1999). "Tale of Three Canadian Cities: What Makes Them Grow So Big." *The Globe and Mail*, September 20, p. A20.

Lofchie, Michael F. (1997). "The Rise and Demise of Urban-biased Developmental Policies in Africa." In Josef Gugler, ed., *Cities in the Developing World: Issues, Theory and Policy* (pp. 23–39). Oxford: Oxford University Press.

Logan, John R., and Harvey L. Molotch. (1987). *Urban Fortunes: The Political Economy of Place*. Berkeley, CA: University of California Press.

Lorimer, James. (1978). *The Developers*. Toronto: Lorimer.

Lorinc, John. (1996). "Trespassers Will Be Prosecuted." *Toronto Life*, September, pp. 47–52.

McGahan, Peter. (1995). *Urban Sociology in Canada*, 3rd ed. Toronto: Harcourt Brace.

McGee, T.G. (1991). "The Emergence of Deschata Regions in Asia." In N. Ginsberg, B. Koppel and T.G. McGee, eds., *The Extended Metropolis* (pp. 3–25). Honolulu: University of Hawaii Press.

McKenzie, Evan. (1989). "Morning in Privatopia." *Dissent, 36* (Spring), 257–60.

Michelson, William D. (1973). *Environmental Change*. Research Paper No. 60, Centre for Urban and Community Studies, University of Toronto.

Nader, George A. (1975). *Cities of Canada, Volume One: Theoretical, Historical and Planning Perspectives*. Toronto: Macmillan.

Palen, J. John. (1995). *The Suburbs*. New York: McGraw-Hill.

Reid, Barton. (1991). "A Primer on the Corporate City." In Kent Gerecke, ed., *The Canadian City* (pp. 63–78). Montreal: Black Rose.

Reynolds, Malvina. (1964). *Little Boxes and Other Handmade Songs*. New York: Oak.

Rose, D. (1984). "Rethinking Gentrification: Beyond the Uneven Development of Marxist Urban Theory." *Environment and Planning D: Society and Space, 2* (1), 47–74.

Seeley, R.A. Sim, and E.W. Loosley. (1956). *Crestwood Heights: A Study of the Culture of Suburban Life*. New York: Wiley.

Sewell, John. (1993). *The Shape of the City: Toronto Struggles with Modern Planning*. Toronto: University of Toronto Press.

Simmel, Georg. (1950). "The Metropolis and Mental Life." In Kurt H. Wolff, ed. and trans., *The Sociology of Georg Simmel* (pp. 409–24). Glencoe, IL: The Free Press.

Smith, David A. (1996). *Third World Cities in Global Perspective: The Political Economy of Uneven Urbanization*. Boulder, CO: Westview Press.

Smith, Neil. (1979). "Towards a Theory of Gentrification." *Journal of the American Planning Association, 45*, 538–48.

Smith, Neil, and Michael LeFaivre. (1984). "A Class Analysis of Gentrification." In John J. Palen and Brian London, eds., *Gentrification, Displacement and Neighborhood Revitalization* (pp. 43–64). Albany, NY: SUNY Press.

Sorkin, Michael. (1992). "Introduction: Variations on a Theme Park." In Michael Sorkin, ed., *Variations on a Theme Park: The New American City and the End of Public Space* (pp. xi–xv). New York: The Noonday Press.

Stone, Leroy O. (1967). *Urban Development in Canada*. Ottawa: Dominion Bureau of Statistics.

Stren, R. and M. Halfari. (2001). "The Cities of Sub-Saharan Africa: From Dependency to Marginality." In Ronan Paddison, ed., *Handbook of Urban Studies* (pp. 466–85). London: Sage.

Thomas, William I., and Florian Znaniecki. (1918–20). *The Polish Peasant in Europe and America*, 5 vols. Chicago: University of Chicago Press.

Tönnies, Ferdinand. (1957 [1887]). *Community and Society*. Trans. Charles Loomis. East Lansing, MI: Michigan State University Press.

Warde, Alan. (1991). "Gentrification as Consumption: Issues of Class and Gender." *Environment and Planning D: Society and Space, 9* (2), 223–32.

Weber, A.F. (1963 [1899]). *The Growth of Cities in the Nineteenth Century*. Ithaca, NY: Cornell University Press.

Whyte, William H. (1956). *The Organization Man*. New York: Simon and Schuster.

Wilson, Elizabeth. (1991). *The Sphinx in the City: Urban Life, the Control of Disorder, and Women*. London: Virago Press.

Wirth, Louis. (1938). "Urbanism as a Way of Life." *American Journal of Sociology, 44*, 1–24.

Wittberg, Patricia. (1992). "Perspectives on Gentrification: A Comparative Review of the Literature." *Research in Urban Sociology, 2*, 17–46.

Zorbaugh, Harvey. (1929). *The Gold Coast and the Slum*. Chicago: University of Chicago Press.

CHAPTER 16

Adams, W.M. (1990). *Green Development: Environment and Sustainability in the Third World*. New York: Oxford University Press.

Blowers, A., D. Lowry, and B.D. Solomon. (1991). *The International Politics of Nuclear Waste*. London: Macmillan.

Bullard, R.D. (1990). *Dumping in Dixie: Race, Class and Environmental Quality*. Boulder, CO: Westview Press.

Buttel, F.H. (1975). "The Environmental Movement: Consensus, Conflict and Change." *Journal of Environmental Education, 7*, 53–63.

Buttel, F.H. (1987). "New Directions in Environmental Sociology." *Annual Review of Sociology, 13*, 465–88.

Cable, S., and M. Benson. (1993). "Acting Locally: Environmental Injustice and the Emergence of Grassroots Environmental Organizations." *Social Problems, 40*, 464–77.

Capek, S.M. (1993). "The Environmental Justice Frame: A Conceptual Discussion and an Application." *Social Problems, 40*, 5–24.

Clarke, L., and J.F. Short, Jr. (1993). "Social Organization and Risk: Some Current Controversies." *Annual Review of Sociology, 19*, 375–99.

Cotgrove, S. (1982). *Catastrophe or Cornucopia: The Environment, Politics, and the Future*. Chichester, UK: Wiley.

Cotgrove, S., and A. Duff. (1981). "Environmentalism, Values and Social Change." *British Journal of Sociology, 32*, 92–110.

Cylke, F.K., Jr. (1993). *The Environment*. New York: HarperCollins College.

d'Eaubonne, F. (1974). *La Feminisme ou la Mort*. Paris: P. Horay.

Denq, F., D.H. Constance and S. Joung. (2000). "The Role of Class, Status, and Power in the Distribution of Toxic Superfund Sites in Texas and Louisiana." *Journal of Poverty, 4*, 81–100.

Derksen, L., and J. Gartrell. (1993). "The Social Context of Recycling." *American Sociological Review, 58*, 434–42.

Devall, B., and G. Sessions. (1985). *Deep Ecology: Living As If Nature Mattered*. Salt Lake City, UT: Peregrine Smith Books.

Downs, A. (1972). "Up and Down with Ecology: The 'Issue-Attention Cycle.'" *The Public Interest, 28*, 38–55.

Dunlap, R.E., and W.R. Catton, Jr. (1979). "Environmental Sociology." *Annual Review of Sociology, 5*, 243–73.

Dunlap, R.E., and W.R. Catton Jr. (1983). "What Environmental Sociologists Have in Common (Whether Concerned with 'Built' or 'Natural' Environments)." *Sociological Inquiry, 53*, 113–35.

Dunlap, R.E., and K.D. Van Liere. (1978). "The New Environmental Paradigm: A Proposed Measuring Instrument and Preliminary Results." *Journal of Environmental Education, 9*, 10–19.

Dwyer, A. (1992). "The Trouble at Great Whale." *Equinox* (January/February), 28–41.

"End War in Woods, Poll Says" (2000). *Sustainability Update: A Quarterly Publication of the Forest Alliance of British Columbia* (Spring), 5.

Eyerman, R., and A. Jamison. (1989). "Environmental Knowledge as an Organizational Weapon: The Case of Greenpeace." *Social Science Information, 28*, 99–119.

Fields, D.M. (1993). "We Can't Grow on Like This (Review of Beyond the Limits)." *The Futurist* (January–February), 40–41.

Foster, J. (1978). *Working for Wildlife*. Toronto: University of Toronto Press.

Fowlkes, M., and P. Miller. (1987). "Chemicals and Community at Love Canal." In B.B. Johnson and V.T. Covello, eds., *The Social and Cultural Construction of Risk* (pp. 55–78). Dordrecht, Holland: D. Reidel.

Freudenburg, W.R. (1991). "Rural–Urban Differences in Environmental Concern: A Closer Look." *Sociological Inquiry, 61*, 167–98.

Freudenburg, W.R. (1993). "Risk and Recreancy: Weber, the Division of Labour and the Rationality of Risk Perceptions." *Social Forces, 71*, 909–32.

Gale, R.P. (1983). "The Environmental Movement and the Left: Antagonists or Allies?" *Sociological Inquiry, 53*, 179–99.

Gallopin, G.C., P. Gutman, and H. Maletta. (1989). "Global Impoverishment, Sustainable Development and the

Environment: A Conceptual Approach." *International Social Science Journal, 41*, 375–97.

Gerhards, J., and D. Rucht. (1992). "Mesomobilization: Organizing and Framing in Two Protest Campaigns in West Germany." *American Journal of Sociology, 98*, 555–95.

Gidengil, E. (1990). "Centres and Peripheries: The Potential Culture of Dependencies." *Canadian Review of Sociology and Anthropology, 27*, 23–48.

Greenbaum, A. (1995). "Taking Stock of Two Decades of Research on the Social Bases of Environmental Concern." In Michael D. Mehta and Eric Ouellet, eds., *Environmental Sociology: Theory and Practice* (pp. 125–52). North York, ON: Captus Press.

Grossman, G.M., and H.R. Potter. (1977). "A Trend Analysis of Competing Models of Environmental Attitudes." Working Paper no. 127. Department of Sociology and Anthropology, Purdue University, West Lafayette, IN.

Hallman, W.K., and A. Wandersman. (1992). "Attribution of Responsibility and Individual and Collective Coping with Environmental Threats." *Journal of Social Issues, 48*, 101–18.

Hannigan, J. A. (1995). *Environmental Sociology: A Social Constructionist Perspective.* London and New York: Routledge.

Harrison, K., and G. Hoberg. (1991). "Setting the Environmental Agendas in Canada and the United States: The Cases of Dioxin and Radon." *Canadian Journal of Political Science, 24*, 3–27.

Hays, S. (1959). *Conservation and the Gospel of Efficiency: The Progressive Conservation Movement.* Cambridge, MA: Harvard University Press.

Jones, R., and R.E. Dunlap. (1992). "The Social Bases of Environmental Concern: Have They Changed over Time?" *Rural Sociology, 57*, 28–47.

Koppes, C. (1988). "Efficiency, Equity, Esthetics: Shifting Themes in American Conservation." In D. Worster, ed., *The Ends of the Earth: Perspectives on Modern Environmental History* (pp. 230–51). Cambridge, UK: Cambridge University Press.

Kriesi, H. (1989). "New Social Movements and the New Class in the Netherlands." *American Journal of Sociology, 94*, 1078–1116.

Ladd, A.E., and S. Laska. (1991). "Opposition to Solid Waste Incineration: Pre-Implementation Anxieties Surrounding a New Environmental Controversy." *Sociological Inquiry, 61*, 299–313.

Lovelock. J. (1987). *Gaia: A New Look at Life on Earth.* Oxford: Oxford University Press.

Macdonald, D. (1991). *The Politics of Pollution: Why Canadians Are Failing Their Environment.* Toronto: McClelland and Stewart.

Maloney, M., and M. Ward. (1973). "Ecology: Let's Hear from the People: An Objective Scale for the Measurement of Ecological Attitudes and Knowledge." *American Psychologist, 28*, 583–86.

Meadows, D.H., D.L. Meadows, and J. Randers. (1992). *Beyond the Limits: Confronting Global Collapse, Envisioning a Sustainable Future.* Post Mills, VT: Chelsea Green.

Meadows, D.H., D.L. Meadows, J. Randers, and W.W. Behrens. (1972). *The Limits to Growth.* New York: Universe Books.

Milbrath, L.W. (1984). *Environmentalists: Vanguard for a New Society.* Albany, NY: SUNY Press.

Naess, A. (1973). "The Shallow and Deep Long-range Ecology Movement." *Inquiry, 16*, 95–100.

Novek, J., and K. Kampen. (1992). "Sustainable or Unsustainable Development? An Analysis of an Environmental Controversy." *Canadian Journal of Sociology, 17*, 249–73.

Perron, B., J.G. Vaillancourt, and C. Durand. (2001). "A Global Problem for a Global Movement? An Exploratory Study of Climate Change Perception by Green Groups' Leaders from Québec (Canada) and Costa Rica." *Society and Natural Resources, 14*, 837–55.

Perrow, C. (1984). *Normal Accidents.* New York: Basic Books.

Roberts, J.T. (2001). "Global Inequality and Climate Change." *Society and Natural Resources, 14*, 501–09.

Schnaiberg, A. (1980). *The Environment: From Surplus to Scarcity.* New York: Oxford University Press.

Schumacher, E.F. (1973). *Small Is Beautiful.* New York: Harper.

Séguin, C., L.G. Pelletier, and J. Hunsley. (1998). "Toward a Model of Environmental Activism." *Environment and Behavior, 30* (5), 628–52.

Shrivastava, P. (1987). *Bhopal: Anatomy of a Crisis.* Cambridge, MA: Ballinger.

Silvertown, J. (1989). "A Silent Spring in China." *New Scientist* (July), 55–58.

Smith, C. (1992). *Media and Apocalypse: News Coverage of the Yellowstone Forest Fires, Exxon Valdez Oil Spill, and Loma Prieta Earthquake.* Westport, CT: Greenwood Press.

Stein, I.P. (1988). *Cities under Siege.* Toronto: Atlantic Press.

Theodori, G.L. , and A.E. Luloff. (2002). "Position on Environmental Issues and Engagement in Pro-Environmental Behaviors." *Society and Natural Resources, 15*, 471–82.

Tindall, D.B. (1994). "Collective Action in the Rainforest: Personal Networks, Collective Identity, and Participation in the Vancouver Island Wilderness Preservation Movement." Ph.D. thesis, Department of Sociology, University of Toronto.

Turner, J.H. (1981). *Sociology: Studying the Human System*, 2nd ed. Santa Monica, CA: Goodyear.

Ungar, S. (1992). "The Rise and (Relative) Decline of Global Warming as a Social Problem." *Sociological Quarterly, 33*, 483–501.

Uusitalo, L. (1990). "Are Environmental Attitudes and Behavior Inconsistent? Findings from a Finnish Study." *Scandinavian Political Studies, 13*, 211–26.

Van Liere, K.D., and R.E. Dunlap. (1980). "The Social Bases of Environmental Concern: A Review of Hypotheses, Explanations and Empirical Evidence." *Public Opinion Quarterly, 44*, 181–97.

Warren, K.J. (1990). "The Power and Promise of Ecological Feminism." *Environmental Ethics, 12*, 125–46.

Williams, G. (1992). "Greening the New Canadian Political Economy." *Studies in Political Economy, 37*, 5–30.

World Commission on Environment and Development [The Brundtland Commission]. (1987). *Our Common Future: Report to the United Nations General Assembly.* New York: Oxford University Press.

Wynne, B. (1992). "Risk and Social Learning: Reification to Engagement." In S. Krimsky and D. Golding, eds., *Social Theories of Risk* (pp. 275–97). Westport, CT: Praeger.

Yearley, S. (1991). *The Green Case: A Sociology of Environmental Issues, Arguments and Politics*. London: HarperCollins Academic.

CHAPTER 17

Abella, Irving, and Harold Troper. (1982). *None Is Too Many*. Toronto: Lester & Orpen Dennys.

Armstrong, Jane. (2002). "Canada is 30 million, but will that last?" *The Globe and Mail*, 13 March 2002: A1.

Avery, Don. (1979). *Dangerous Foreigners: European Immigrant Workers and Labour Radicalism in Canada, 1896–1932*. Toronto: McClelland and Stewart.

Bah, Sulaiman, and Rajulton Fernando. (1991). "Has Canadian Mortality Entered the Fourth Stage of the Epidemiologic Transition?" *Canadian Studies in Population, 18*, (2) 18–41.

Beaujot, Roderic, and Alain Bélanger. (2001). "Perspectives on Below Replacement Fertility in Canada: Trends, Desires, and Accommodations." Paper presented at the International Union for the Scientific Study of Population Working Group on Low Fertility meeting, Tokyo, March 2001.

Beaujot, Roderic, and Judy-Lynn Richards. (1997). "Intergenerational Equity in Reforming the CPP." *Policy Options, 17* (9), 45–48.

Beaujot, Roderic, and Kevin McQuillan. (1982). *Growth and Dualism: The Demographic Development of Canadian Society*. Toronto: Gage.

Beaujot, Roderic, K.G. Basavarajappa, and Ravi Verma. (1988). *Income of Immigrants in Canada*. Statistics Canada Cat. No. 91-527. Ottawa: Supply and Services Canada.

Beaujot, Roderic. (1991). *Population Change in Canada: The Challenges of Policy Adaptation*. Toronto: Oxford University Press.

Beaujot, Roderic. (2000). *Earning and Caring in Canadian Families*. Peterborough, ON: Broadview Press.

Bélanger, Alain. (2002). *Report on the Demographic Situation in Canada 2001*. Ottawa: Statistics Canada Cat No. 91-209.

Belliveau, Jo-Anne, and Leslie Gaudette. (1995). "Changes in Cancer Incidence and Mortality." *Canadian Social Trends, 39*, 2–7.

Canada. (1996). Citizenship and Immigration. *1997 Annual Immigration Plan*. Ottawa: Supply and Services Canada.

Careless, J.M.S. (1963). *Canada: A Story of Challenge*. Toronto: Macmillan.

Charbonneau, Hubert. (1987). *Naisance d'une population*. Montreal: Presses de l'Université de Montreal.

Chard, Jennifer, and Vivianne Renaud, 1999. "Visible Minorities in Toronto, Vancouver and Montreal." *Canadian Social Trends, 54*, 20–25.

Chen, Jiajian, and Russell Wilkins. (1998). "Seniors' Needs for Health-Related Personal Assistance." *Health Reports, 10* (1), 39–50.

Chen, Jiajian, and Wayne Millar. (1998). "Age of Smoking Initiation: Implications for Quitting." *Health Reports, 9* (4), 39–46.

Coale, Ansley J. (1973). "The Demographic Transition." In *International Population Conference*. Liège: International Union for the Scientific Study of Population.

Demeny, Paul. (1988). "Social Science and Population Policy." *Population and Development Review, 14*, 451–79.

Desjardins, Bertrand. (1993). *Population Aging and the Elderly*. Statistics Canada Cat. No. 91-553. Ottawa: Supply and Services Canada.

Duchesne, Louis. (1993). "Evolution de la population au Québec et au Canada depuis un siècle et demi en l'absence de migrations." *Cahiers québécois de démographie, 22* (1), 1–22.

Dumas, Jean. (1996). *Report on the Demographic Situation in Canada, 1995*. Statistics Canada. Cat. no. 91-209. Ottawa: Supply and Services Canada.

Eberstadt, N. (2001). "The Population Implosion." *Foreign Policy*, March/April, 42–53.

Economic Council of Canada. (1991). *Economic and Social Impacts of Immigration*. No. 22-176. Ottawa: Economic Council of Canada.

Ehrlich, Paul R., and Anne H. Ehrlich. (1990). *The Population Explosion*. New York: Simon and Schuster.

Fellegi, Ivan P. (1988). "Can We Afford an Aging Society?" *Canadian Economic Observer, 1* (10), 4.1–4.34.

Foot, David, and Daniel Stoffman. (1998). *Boom, Bust and Echo 2000*. Toronto: Macfarlane Walter and Ross.

Ford, David, and François Nault. (1996). "Changing Fertility Patterns, 1974 to 1994." *Health Reports, 8* (3), 39–46.

Galambos, Nancy, and Lauree Tilton-Weaver. (1998). "Multiple Risk Behaviour in Adolescents and Young Adults." *Health Reports, 10* (2), 9–20.

Haines, Michael, and Richard Steckel. (2000). *A Population History of North America*. Cambridge: Cambridge University Press.

Hill, Gerry, et al. (1996). "Dementia among Seniors." *Health Reports, 8* (2), 7–10.

Howell, Nancy. (1979). *Demography of the Dobe !Kung*. New York: Academic Press.

Ibbitson, John. (2002). "The Long, Slow Exit of the Human Race." *The Globe and Mail*, March 2, F1.

Lesthaeghe, Ron, and C. Vanderhoeft. (1997). "Ready, Willing and Able: A Conceptualization of Transitions to New Behavioral Forms." Brussels: Interuniversity Papers in Demography, no. 1997-8.

Lesthaeghe, Ron. (1995). "The Second Demographic Transition in Western Countries: An Interpretation." In K. Oppenheim Mason and A-M. Jensen, eds., *Gender and Family Change in Industrialized Countries*. Oxford: Clarendon.

Lindsay, Colin. (1999). "Seniors: A Diverse Group Aging Well." *Canadian Social Trends, 52*, 24–26.

Livi-Bacci, Massimo. (1992). *A Concise History of World Population*. Cambridge, UK: Blackwell.

Malthus, T.R. (1798). *An Essay on the Principle of Population, as It Affects the Future Improvement of Society. With Remarks on the Speculations of Mr. Godwin, M. Condorcet and Other Writers*. London: J. Johnson.

Martel, Laurent, and Alain Bélanger. (1999). "An analysis of the change in dependence-free life expectancy in Canada between 1986 and 1996." In *Report on the Demographic Situation in Canada 1998–1999* (pp. 164–86). Ottawa: Statistics Canada Cat. No. 91-209.

Martel, Laurent, Alain Bélanger, and Jean-Marie Berthelot. (2001). "Smoking and Disability-Free Life Expectancy in

Canada." In *Report on the Demographic Situation in Canada 2001* (pp. 113–36). Ottawa: Statistics Canada Cat. No. 91-209.

McKeown, K., R.G. Brown, and R.G. Record. (1972). "An Interpretation of the Modern Rise of Population in Europe." *Population Studies, 26*, 345–82.

Meek, Ronald L., ed. (1971). *Marx and Engels on the Population Bomb: Selections from the Writings of Marx and Engels Dealing with the Theories of Thomas Robert Malthus.* Trans. Dorothea L. Meek and Ronald L. Meek. Berkeley, CA: Ramparts Press.

Merrick, Thomas W. (1986). "World Population in Transition." *Population Bulletin, 41* (2).

Michaud, Jean-Francois, M.V. George, and S. Loh. (1996). *Projections of Persons with Disabilities.* Statistics Canada Cat. no. 91-538. Ottawa: Supply and Services Canada.

Millar, Wayne, and Marie Beaudet. (1996). "Health Facts." *Canadian Social Trends, 40*, 24–27.

Millar, Wayne, and Thomas Stephens. (1992). "Social Status and Health Risks in Canadian Adults: 1985 and 1991." *Health Reports, 5* (2), 143–56.

Muhsam, Helmut V. (1979). "The Demographic Transition: from Wastage to Conservation of Human Life." In *Population Science in the Service of Mankind.* Ordina: International Union for the Scientific Study of Population.

Nathanson, Constance, and Alan Lopez. (1987). "The Future of Sex Mortality Differentials in Industrialized Countries: A Structural Hypothesis." *Population Research and Policy Review, 6* (2), 123–36.

Nault, Francois. (1997). "Narrowing Mortality Gaps." *Health Reports, 9* (1), 35–41.

Pacini, Marcello. (1992). Foreword to special issue, "The New Europe and International Migration." *International Migration Review 26* (2), 231–33.

Palmer, D.L. (1997). "Canadians' Attitudes toward Immigration: November and December 1996, and February 1997 Surveys." Report prepared for Strategic Policy, Planning and Research Branch, Citizenship and Immigration Canada.

Population Reference Bureau. (2001). *2001 World Population Date Sheet.* Washington, DC: Population Reference Bureau.

Ravanera, Zenaida. (1995). "A Portrait of the Family Life of Young Adults." In R. Beaujot, Ellen M. Gee, Fernando Rajulton, and Zenaida R. Ravanera, eds., *Family over the Life Course* (pp. 7–35). Statistics Canada Cat. no. 91-543. Ottawa: Supply and Services Canada.

Reitz, Jeffrey. (2001). "Immigrant success and changing national institutions: recent trends in Canada, a U.S. comparison, and policy options." Paper prepared for Weatherhead Centre for International Relations and Department of Sociology, Harvard University, February 2001.

Richmond, Anthony H. (1988). *Immigration and Ethnic Conflict.* New York: St. Martin's Press.

Romaniuc, Anatole. (1984). *Fertility in Canada: From Baby-boom to Baby-bust.* Statistics Canada Cat. No. 91-524. Ottawa: Supply and Services Canada.

Simon, Julian L. (1990). *Population Matters.* New Brunswick, NJ: Transition Publishers.

Sinding, Steven. (1993). Panel presentation to the Plenary Session on the contribution IUSSP to the 1994 UN International Conference on Population and Development. Paper presented at the General Conference of the IUSSP, Montreal, August.

Statistics Canada. (2001a). "How Healthy Are Canadians? 2001 Annual Report." *Health Reports, 12* (3): 9–52.

Statistics Canada. (2001b). *Population Projections for Canada and the Provinces and Territories, 2000–2026.* Ottawa: Statistics Canada Cat. No. 91-520.

Statistics Canada. (2002). *Profile of the Canadian Population by Age and Sex: Canada Ages.* Ottawa: Statistics Canada Catalogue No. 96F0030.

Statistics Canada. (1993). *Selected Birth and Fertility Statistics, Canada, 1921–1990.* Statistics Canada Cat. no. 82-553. Ottawa: Supply and Services Canada.

Statistics Canada. (1999). *Annual Demographic Statistics 1998.* Statistics Canada Cat. no. 91-213. Ottawa: Supply and Services Canada.

Tepper, Elliot L. (1987). "Demographic Change and Pluralism." *Canadian Studies in Population, 14*, 223–35.

Trovato, Frank. (1998). "Nativity, Marital Status and Mortality in Canada." *Canadian Review of Sociology and Anthropology, 35* (1), 65–91.

United Nations. (1995). *Population and Development: Programme of Action Adopted at the International Conference on Population and Development, Cairo, 5–13 September 1994.* UN ST/ESA/Ser. A/149. New York: United Nations.

United Nations. (1999). *Sex and Age Distribution of the World Population: The 1998 Revision.* UN ST/ESA/Ser A./180. New York: United Nations.

United Nations. (2001). *World Population Prospects: The 2000 Revision.* UN ST/ESA/Ser.A/198. New York: United Nations.

Van de Kaa, Dirk. (1987). "Europe's Second Demographic Transition." *Population Bulletin, 42* (1), 1–58.

Van de Walle, Étienne, and John Knodel. (1980). "Europe's Fertility Transition: New Evidence and Lessons for Today's Developing World." *Population Bulletin, 34* (6), 1–34.

Wargon, Sylvia T. (2002). *Demography in Canada in the Twentieth Century.* Vancouver: University of British Columbia Press.

Weinfeld, Morton. (1988). "Immigration and Canada's Population Future: A National Building Vision." Discussion paper, McGill University, Department of Sociology.

Wolfson, Michael. (1996). "Health-adjusted Life Expectancy." *Health Reports, 8* (1), 41–46.

Ziegler, E. (1988). "Refugee Movements and Policy in Canada." Report for Review of Demography and Its Implications for Economic and Social Policy. Ottawa: Health and Welfare Canada.

CHAPTER 18

Albrow, M. (1990). "Introduction." In M. Albrow and E. King, eds., *Globalization, Knowledge and Society* (pp. 3–13). London: Sage.

Albrow, M. (1993). "Globalization." In W. Outhwaite and T. Bottomore, eds., *The Blackwell Dictionary of Twentieth Century Social Thought* (pp. 248–49). Cambridge, MA: Blackwell.

Albrow, M. (1997). *The Global Age: State and Society Beyond Modernity.* Stanford, CA: Stanford University Press.

Albrow, M., J. Eade, N. Washbourne, and J. Dürrschmidt. (1994). "The Impact of Globalization on Sociological Concepts: Community, Culture and Milieu." *Innovation, 7*, 371–89.

American Sociological Association. (2001). "Sociologists Reflect on the Events of September 11." On the World Wide Web at http://www.asanet.org/footnotes/septoct01/fn20.html (2 December 2002).

Anderson, B. (1991). *Imagined Communities: Reflections on the Origin and Spread of Nationalism*. London: New Left Books.

Appadurai. A. (1996). *Modernity at Large: Cultural Dimensions of Globalization*. Minneapolis, MN: University of Minnesota Press.

Archer, M.S. (1991). "Sociology for One World: Unity and Diversity." *International Sociology*, 6, 131–47.

Barlow, M. (1996). "Globalization and the Dismantling of Canadian Democracy, Values and Society." PCD Forum Article No. 17. On the World Wide Web at http://members.tripod.com/savard_2/barlow.html.

Basavarajappa, K.G., R.P. Beaujot, and T.J. Samuel. (1993). *Impact of Migration in the Receiving Countries: Canada*. Geneva: International Organization for Migration.

Bauman, Z. (1991). *Intimations of Postmodernity*. London: Routledge.

Beck, U. (1992). *The Risk Society: Towards a New Modernity*. Newbury Park, CA: Sage.

Beck, U. (2000). *What Is Globalization?* Cambridge: Polity Press.

Bell, D. (1976). *The Coming of Post-Industrial Society: A Venture in Social Forecasting*. New York: Basic Books.

Bellah, R., R. Madsen, W.M. Sullivan, A. Swidler, and S.M. Tipton. (1985). *Habits of the Heart: Middle America Observed*. Berkeley, CA: University of California Press.

Best, M. (1990). *The New Competition*. Cambridge, MA: Harvard University Press.

Brown, L.R., H. Kane, and E. Ayres. (1993). *Vital Signs: The Trends That Shape Our Future*. New York: W.W. Norton.

Brym, R.J., with Bonnie J. Fox. (1989). *From Culture to Power: The Sociology of English Canada*. Toronto: Oxford University Press.

Budd, L., and S. Whimster, eds. (1992). *Global Finance and Urban Living*. New York: Routledge.

Burbach, R., and W. Robinson. (1999). "The Fin de Siècle Debate: Globalization as Epochal Shift." *Science and Society* (Spring). On the World Wide Web at http://www.igc.org/globalpolicy/globaliz/define/findesie.htm.

Cardoso, F.H., and E. Faletto. (1979). *Dependency and Development in Latin America*. Berkeley, CA: University of California Press.

Carnoy, M., M. Castells, S.S. Cohen, and F.H. Cardoso. (1993). *The New Global Economy in the Information Age: Reflections on Our Changing World*. Philadelphia: Pennsylvania State University Press.

Carroll, W.K., and M. Alexander. (1999). "Finance Capital and Capitalist Class Integration in the 1990s: Network of Interlocking Directorships in Canada and Australia." *Canadian Review of Sociology and Anthropology*, 36, 331–56.

Castells, M. (1996–98). *The Information Age: Economy, Society and Culture: Vol. 1, The Rise of the Network Society; Vol. 2, The Power of Identity; Vol. 3, End of the Millennium*. Malden, MA: Blackwell.

Castles, S., and M.J. Miller. (1993). *The Age of Migration: International Population Movements in the Modern World*. New York: St. Martin's Press.

"Council of Canadians." (2002). On the World Wide Web at http://www.canadians.org/ (2 December).

Coupland, D. (1991). *Generation X: Tales for an Accelerated Culture*. New York: St. Martin's Press.

Dahrendorf, R. (1975). *The New Liberty*. London: Routledge.

Department of Sociology, Columbia University. (2002). "Small World Research Project." On the World Wide Web at http://smallworld.sociology.columbia.edu/ (1 December).

Dicken, P. (1992). *Global Shift: The Internationalization of Economic Activity*. London: Chapman.

Dürrschmidt. J. (2000). *Everyday Lives in the Global City: The Delinking of Locale and Milieu*. London: UCL Press.

Eade, J., ed. (1997). *Living the Global City: Globalization as a Local Process*. New York: Routledge.

Ekins, P. (1992). *A New World Order: Grassroots Movements for Global Change*. New York: Routledge.

Elias, N. (1978, 1982). *The Civilizing Process. Vol. 1: The History of Manners* (1978). *Vol. 2: State and Civilization* (1982). Oxford: Blackwell.

Etzioni, A. (1994). *The Spirit of Community: The Reinvention of American Society*. New York: Touchstone.

Falk, R. (1992). *Explorations at the Edge of Time: The Prospects for World Order*. Philadelphia: Temple University Press.

Frank, A.G. (1967). *Capitalism and Under-Development in Latin America*. New York: Monthly Review Press.

Friedman, T.L. (1999). *The Lexus and the Olive Tree: Understanding Globalization*. New York: Farrar, Straus and Giroux.

Fröbel, F., J. Heinrichs, and O. Kreye. (1980). *The New International Division of Labour: Structural Unemployment in Industrialized Countries and Industrialization in Developing Countries*. Cambridge, UK: Cambridge University Press.

German Embassy, Washington DC. 2002. "QuickFacts: Society." On the World Wide Web at http://www.germany-info.org/relaunch/info/facts/society.html (2 December).

Giddens, A. (1990). *The Consequences of Modernity*. Stanford, CA: Stanford University Press.

Giddens, A. (1991). *Modernity and Self-Identity: Self and Society in the Late Modern Age*. Cambridge, UK: Polity.

Giddens, A. (1998). *The Third Way: The Renewal of Social Democracy*. Cambridge, UK: Polity.

Giddens, A. (1999). *Runaway World: How Globalization Is Reshaping Our Lives*. London: Profile Books.

Guillén, Mauro F. (2001). "Is Globalization Civilizing, Destructive or Feeble? A Critique of Five Key Debates in the Social Science Literature." *Annual Review of Sociology*, 27. On the World Wide Web at http://knowledge.wharton.upenn.edu/PDFs/938.pdf (1 December 2002).

Hall, J.A. (1985). *Power and Liberties: The Causes and Consequences of the Rise of the West*. Oxford: Blackwell.

Hall, S. (1992). "The Question of Cultural Identity." In S. Hall, D. Held, and T. McGrew, eds., *Modernity and Its Futures* (pp. 274–313). Cambridge, UK: Polity and Open University Press.

Hannerz, U. (1996). *Transnational Connections: Culture, People, Places*. London: Routledge.

Harvey, D. (1989). *The Condition of Postmodernity: An Enquiry into the Conditions of Cultural Change*. Cambridge, MA: Blackwell.

Held, D. (1995). *Democracy and the Global Order*. Cambridge, UK: Polity.

Held, D., A. McGrew, D. Goldblatt, and J. Perraton. (1999). *Global Transformations: Politics, Economics and Culture*. Cambridge, UK: Polity.

Inkeles, A. (1983). *Exploring Individual Modernity*. New York: Columbia University Press.

International Civil Aviation Organization. (2002). "World Scheduled Airlines: System Scheduled Traffic and Operations, 1929-2001E." On the World Wide Web at http://www.air-transport.org/public/industry/bin/ICAOTraffic.pdf (1 December).

"International organizations by year and type (Table 2)." (2001). *Yearbook of International Organizations*. On the World Wide Web at http://www.uia.org/uiastats/ytb299.htm (1 December 2002).

Internet Software Consortium. (2002). "Internet Domain Survey Host Count." On the World Wide Web at http://www.isc.org/ds/hosts.html (1 December).

Jameson, F. (1991). *The Cultural Logic of Late Capitalism*. New York: Verso.

Janelle, D.G. (1991). "Global Interdependence and Its Consequences." In S.D. Brunn and T.R. Leinbach, eds., *Collapsing Space and Time: Geographic Aspects of Communications and Information* (pp. 49–81). London: HarperCollins.

Kerr, C., J.T. Dunlop, F.H. Harbison, and C.A. Myers. (1960). *Industrialism and Industrial Man*. Cambridge, MA: Harvard University Press.

King, A.D. (1990). *Global Cities: Post-Imperialism and the Internationalization of London*. London: Routledge.

Laszlo, E. (1989). *The Inner Limits of Mankind*. London: Oneworld.

Latour, B. (1993). *We Have Never Been Modern*. Hemel Hempstead, UK: Harvester Wheatsheaf.

Lyotard, J.-F. (1984). *The Postmodern Condition*. Minneapolis, MN: University of Minneapolis Press.

MacCannell, D. (1976). *The Tourist: A New Theory of the Leisure Class*. New York: Schocken.

Mann, M. (1986). *The Sources of Social Power. Vol. 1: A History of Power from the Beginning to A.D. 1760*. Cambridge, UK: Cambridge University Press.

Marx, K. (1970 [1867]). *Capital*. Vol. 1. London: Lawrence and Wishart.

McLuhan, M. (1962). *The Gutenberg Galaxy*. Toronto: University of Toronto Press.

Meadows, D.H., D.L. Meadows, J. Randers, and W.W. Behrens. (1972). *The Limits to Growth*. New York: Universe Books.

Mills, C.W. (1956). *The Power Elite*. New York: Oxford University Press.

Morgan, R., ed. (1984). *Sisterhood Is Global*. New York: Anchor Press.

Oman, C. (1994). "Globalisation and Regionalisation: The Challenge for Developing Countries." *OECD Development Centre Paper*. Paris: OECD.

Perlmutter, T. (1993). "Distress Signals: A Canadian Story—An International Lesson." In T. Dowmunt, ed., *Channels of Resistance: Global Television and Local Empowerment* (pp. 16–26). London: British Film Institute Publishing.

Polanyi, Karl. (1944). *The Great Transformation*. New York: Rinehart.

"Policy Research Initiative." (2002). On the World Wide Web at http://policyresearch.gc.ca/page.asp?pagenm=root (2 December).

Porter, J. (1965). *The Vertical Mosaic: An Analysis of Social Class and Power in Canada*. Toronto: University of Toronto Press.

Putnam, T. (1993). "Beyond the Modern Home: Shifting the Parameters of Residence." In T. Bird, B. Curtis, T. Putnam, G. Robertson, and L. Tickner, eds., *Mapping the Futures: Local Cultures, Global Change* (pp. 150–68). New York: Routledge.

Ritzer, G. (1992). *The McDonaldization of Society*. Newbury Park, CA: Pine Forge.

Robertson, R. (1992). *Globalization: Social Theory and Global Culture*. Newbury Park, CA: Sage.

Sachs, W., ed. (1993). *Global Ecology: A New Arena of Political Conflict*. Halifax: Fernwood.

Sassen, S. (1991). *The Global City: New York, London, Tokyo*. Princeton, NJ: Princeton University Press.

Sieghart, P. (1985). *The Lawful Rights of Mankind*. New York: Oxford University Press.

Sklair, L. (1991). *Sociology of the Global System*. New York: Harvester Wheatsheaf.

Smith, A. (1910 [1776]). *The Wealth of Nations*. 2 vols. New York: E.P. Dutton.

Soros, George. (2002). *On Globalization*. Oxford: Public Affairs.

Statistics Canada. (2002). "Immigrant population by place of birth and period of immigration, 1996 Census, Canada." On the World Wide Web at http://www.statcan.ca/english/Pgdb/demo25a.htm (1 December).

Stehr, N. (1994). *Knowledge Societies*. Thousand Oaks, CA: Sage.

Stiglitz, Joseph, (2002). *Globalization and its Discontents*. New York: W.W. Norton.

Thoreau, H.D. (1927 [1854]). *Walden, or Life in the Woods*. London: Chapman and Hall.

Tomlinson, J. (1991). *Cultural Imperialism: A Critical Introduction*. Baltimore, MD: Johns Hopkins University Press.

Touraine, A. (1971). *The Post-Industrial Society: Tomorrow's Social History: Classes, Conflicts and Culture in the Programmed Society*. New York: Random House.

United Nations Educational, Scientific and Cultural Organization "World Culture Report 2000—Cultural Trade and Communications Trends: International Tourism." On the World Wide Web at http://www.unesco.org/culture/worldreport/html_eng/stat2/table18.pdf (5 December 2001).

United States Census Bureau. (2002). "Total Midyear Population for the World: 1950-2050." On the World Wide Web at http://blue.census.gov/ipc/www/worldpop.html (1 December).

Van der Pijl, K. (1989). "The International Level." In T. Bottomore and R.J. Brym, eds., *The Capitalist Class: An International Study* (pp. 237–66). Hemel Hempstead, UK: Harvester Wheatsheaf.

Wallerstein, I. (1974, 1980, 1989). *The Modern World-System*. 3 vols. New York and San Diego: Academic Press.

Waters, M. (1995). *Globalization*. London: Routledge.

Watson, W.G. (1998). *Globalization and the Meaning of Canadian Life*. Toronto: University of Toronto Press.

Weber, M. (1976 [1904–1905]). *The Protestant Ethic and the Spirit of Capitalism*. London: Allen and Unwin.

Willetts, P. (1982). *Pressure Groups in the Global System*. London: Pinter.

World Bank. (2002). "6.1: Integration with the World Economy." On the World Wide Web at http://www.worldbank.org/data/wdi2002/tables/table6-1.pdf (1 December 2002).

World Tourism Organization. (2002). "International Tourist Arrivals by (Sub)region." On the World Wide Web at http://www.world-tourism.org/market_research/facts&figures/latest_data/tita01_07-02.pdf (1 December 2002).

Yip, G.S. (1993). *Total Global Strategy: Managing for Worldwide Competitive Advantage*. Englewood Cliffs, NJ: Prentice Hall.

CHAPTER 19

Adam, Barry. (1995). *The Rise of a Gay and Lesbian Movement*, 2nd ed. New York: Twayne.

Anderson, Elijah. (1990). "The Police and the Black Male." In *Streetwise* (pp. 190–206). Chicago, IL: University of Chicago Press.

Becker, Howard. (1973). *Outsiders: Perspectives on Deviance*. New York: Free Press.

Becker, Howard, ed. (1964). *The Other Side*. New York: Free Press.

Bergman, Brian. (1999). "Tragedy in Taber." *Maclean's*, May 10, 1999, 20–23.

Besserer, Sandra, and Catherine Trainor. (2000). "Criminal Victimization in Canada, 1999." *Juristat*, 20, 10.

Canadian Centre for Justice Statistics. (1996). *Canadian Crime Statistics: 1995*. Ottawa: Statistics Canada.

Cawsey, R.W. (1991). *Report of the Task Force on the Criminal Justice System and Its Impact on the Indian and Métis People of Alberta*. Edmonton: Province of Alberta.

Chambliss, William. (1973). "The Saints and the Roughnecks." *Society*, 11, 24–31.

Chisholm, Patricia. (1999). "The Copycat Syndrome." *Maclean's*, May 10, 23.

Cohen, Albert K. (1955). *Delinquent Boys: The Culture of the Gang*. Glencoe, IL: Free Press.

Cohen, Lawrence E. and Marcus Felson. (1979). "Social Change and Crime Rate Trends: A Routine Activity Approach." *American Sociological Review*, 44, 588–608.

Cohen, Stanley. (1985). *Visions of Social Control*. Cambridge: Polity Press.

Commission on Systemic Racism in the Ontario Criminal Justice System. (1995). *Report of the Commission on Systemic Racism in the Ontario Criminal Justice System*. Toronto: Queen's Printer.

Committee of Concerned Journalists. (1998). "Changing Definitions of News." *Reports and Studies*. On the World Wide Web at http://www.journalism.org (March 6).

Criminal Intelligence Service Canada. (1996). *Annual Report on Organized Crime in Canada 1996*.

Dauvergne, Mia. (2002). "Homicide in Canada, 2001." *Juristat*, 22, 7.

Doob, Anthony N., and Jane B. Sprott. (In press). "Changing Models of Youth Justice in Canada." *Youth Justice Systems, A Special Issue of Criminal Justice Review of the Research*. Ed. M. Tonry. Chicago: University of Chicago Press.

Doob, Anthony N., Voula Marinos, and Kimberly N. Varma. (1995). *Youth Crime and the Youth Justice System in Canada: A Research Perspective*. Toronto: Centre of Criminology, University of Toronto.

Doob, Anthony N., Jane B. Sprott, Voula Marinos, and Kimberly N. Varma. (1998). *An Exploration of Ontario Residents' Views of Crime and the Criminal Justice System*. Toronto: Centre of Criminology, University of Toronto.

Durkheim, Émile. (1938). *The Rules of Sociological Method*. Trans. S. Solovay and J. Mueller, ed. G.E.G. Catlin). Chicago: University of Chicago Press.

Erickson, Patricia. (1996). "The Selective Control of Drugs." In B. Schissel and L. Mahood, eds., *Social Control in Canada* (pp. 59–77). Don Mills: Oxford University Press.

Eron, L.D. (1986). "Interventions to Mitigate the Psychological Effects of Media Violence on Aggressive Behavior." *Journal of Social Issues*, 42, 155–69.

Findlay, Deborah. (1996). "The Body Perfect: Appearance Norms, Medical Control, and Women." In B. Schissel and L. Mahood, eds., *Social Control in Canada* (pp. 174–200). Don Mills: Oxford University Press.

Findlay, Michael. (1999). *The Globalization of Crime*. Cambridge: Cambridge University Press.

Fine, Sean, and Brian Milner. (1999). "Medical Issue Raised in Law-Firm Affair." *Globe and Mail*, November 17, p. A2.

Foster, Cecil. 1996. *A Place Called Heaven: The Meaning of Being Black in Canada*. Toronto: HarperCollins.

Foucault, Michel. (1979). *Discipline and Punish: The Birth of the Prison*. New York: Vintage Books.

Frazier, Charles. (1976). *Theoretical Approaches to Deviance: An Evaluation*. Columbus, Ohio: Charles Merrill.

Frideres, Jim. (1996). "Native Canadian Deviance and the Social Control of Race." In B. Schissel and L. Mahood, eds., *Social Control in Canada* (pp. 288–319). Don Mills: Oxford University Press.

Gartner, Rosemary, Kathryn Baker, and Fred Pampel. (1990). "Gender Stratification and the Gender Gap in Homicide Victimization." *Social Problems*, 37, 593–612.

Gottfredson, Michael, and Travis Hirschi. (1990). *A General Theory of Crime*. Stanford: Stanford University Press.

Griffiths, Curt T., and Alison Cunningham. (2000). *Canadian Corrections*. Toronto: Nelson Thomson Learning.

Hagan, John, John Simpson, and A.R. Gillis. (1987). "Class in the Household: A Power-Control Theory of Gender and Delinquency." *American Journal of Sociology*, 92, 788–816.

Hamilton, A.C., and C.M. Sinclair. 1991. *Report of the Aboriginal Justice Inquiry of Manitoba*. Winnipeg: Government of Manitoba.

Hermer, Joe, and Janet Mosher. (2002). *Disorderly People: Law and the Politics of Exclusion in Ontario*. Halifax: Fernwood Press.

Hirschi, Travis. (1969). *Causes of Delinquency*. Berkeley: University of California Press.

Irwin, Darrell. (1999). "The Straight Edge subculture: Examining the Youths' Drug Free Ways." *Journal of Drug Issues*, 29, 365–80.

Lemert, Edwin. (1967). *Human Deviance, Social Problems, and Social Control*. Englewood Cliffs, NJ: Prentice Hall.

Lonmo, Charlene. (2001). "Adult Correctional Services in Canada, 1999–00." *Juristat*, 21, 5.

Marx, Gary. (1981). "Ironies of Social Control: Authorities as Contributors to Deviance Through Escalation, Nonenforcement, and Covert Facilitation." *Social Problems*, 28, 221–33.

Marx, Gary. (1995). "The Engineering of Social Control: The Search for the Silver Bullet." In J. Hagan and R. Peterson, eds., *Crime and Inequality* (pp. 225–46). Stanford: Stanford University Press.

Merton, Robert. (1938). "Social Structure and Anomie." *American Sociological Review*, 3, 672–82.

Merton, Robert. (1957). *Social Theory and Social Structure*. New York: Free Press.

Ontario Legislature. (1999). *Legislative Debates*. November 2.

Ouimet, Marc. (2002). "Explaining the American and Canadian Crime "Drop" in the 1990's." *Canadian Journal of Criminology* (January), 33–50.

Phillips, Andrew. (1999). "Lessons of Littleton." *Maclean's*, 3 May, 18–21.

Province of Manitoba. (1991). *Report of the Aboriginal Justice Inquiry of Manitoba*. Winnipeg: Public Inquiry into the Administration of Justice and Aboriginal People.

Quinney, Richard. (1970). *The Social Reality of Crime*. Boston: Little, Brown.

Rankin, Jim et al. (2002). "Black Crime Rates Highest: 'No One Born Violent…' What's Causing These Problems?" *Toronto Star*, 26 October, pp. A1, A14–A15.

Richards, James R. (1999). *Transnational Criminal Organizations, Cybercrime, and Money Laundering*. Boca Raton: CRC Press.

Roach, Kent. (1999). *Due Process and Victims' Rights: The New Law and Politics of Criminal Justice*. Toronto: University of Toronto Press.

Roberts, Julian. (2000). "Introduction to Criminal Justice in Canada." In Julian Roberts, ed., *Criminal Justice in Canada: A Reader*. Toronto: Harcourt Brace & Co.

Roberts, Julian V., and Anthony N. Doob. (1997). "Race, Ethnicity, and Criminal Justice in Canada." In Michael Tonry, ed., *Ethnicity, Crime, and Immigration: Comparative and Cross-National Perspectives* (pp. 469–522). Chicago: University of Chicago Press.

Rosoff, Stephen M., Henry N. Pontell, and Robert Tillman. (1998). *Profit Without Honor: White-Collar Crime and the Looting of America*. Upper Saddle River, NJ: Prentice Hall.

Satzewich, Victor. (1998). *Racism and Social Inequality in Canada: Concepts, Controversies, and Strategies of Resistance*. Toronto: Thompson.

Savoie, Josee. (2002). "Crime Statistics in Canada, 2001." *Juristat*, 22, 6.

Scott, Robert A. (1969). *The Making of Blind Men*. New York: Russell Sage.

Sutherland, Edwin. (1939). *Principles of Criminology*. Philadelphia: Lippincott.

Sutherland, Edwin. (1949). *White Collar Crime*. New York: Dryden.

Tanner, Julian. (1996). *Teenage Troubles: Youth and Deviance in Canada*. Toronto: Nelson Canada.

Tufts, Jennifer. (2001). "Public Attitudes Toward the Criminal Justice System." *Juristat*, 20, 12.

Turk, Austin. (1969). *Criminality and the Legal Order*. Chicago: Rand McNally.

United Nations. (1999). *Global Studies on Organized Crime*. Vienna: Office for Drug Control and Crime Prevention.

Vold, George. (1958). *Theoretical Criminology*. New York: Oxford University Press.

World Health Organization. (1998). *World Health Statistics Annual, 1996*. Geneva: WHO.

Wolfgang, Marvin, Robert Figlio, Paul Tracy, and Simon Singer. (1985). *The National Survey of Crime Severity*. Washington DC: U.S. Government Printing Office.

Wortley, Scot. (1996). "Justice For All? Race and Perceptions of Bias in the Ontario Criminal Justice System—A Toronto Survey." *Canadian Journal of Criminology*, 38, 439–67.

Wortley, Scot, and Andrea McCalla. (2003). "The Debate Continues: Evidence of Bias against Black People in the Ontario Criminal Justice System?" In J.V. Roberts and M. Grossman, ed., *Criminal Justice in Canada: A Reader*, 2nd ed. Toronto: Thomson Nelson.

CHAPTER 20

Adam, Barry, Jan Willem Duyvendak, and Andre Krouwel. (1999). *The Global Emergence of Gay and Lesbian Politics*. Philadelphia: Temple University Press.

Adamson, Nancy, Linda Briskin, and Margaret McPhail. (1988). *Feminist Organizing for Change: The Contemporary Women's Movement in Canada*. Toronto: Oxford University Press.

Arterton, F. Christopher. (1987). *Teledemocracy: Can Technology Protect Democracy?* Newbury Park, CA: Sage Publications.

Baer, Doug, ed. (2002). *Political Sociology: Canadian Perspectives* Toronto: Oxford University Press.

Bashevkin, Sylvia. (1986). "Independence versus Partisanship: Dilemmas in the Political History of Women in English Canada." In V. Strong-Boag and A. Fellman, eds., *Rethinking Canada: The Promise of Women's History* (pp. 246–75). Toronto: Copp Clark Pitman.

Blais, André, Elisabeth Gidengil, Richard Nadeau, and Neil Nevitte. (1997). *1997 Canadian Election Survey*. On the World Wide Web at http://prod.library.utoronto.ca/datalib/codebooks/utm/elections/1997/ (20 June 2002).

Block, Fred. (1979). "The Ruling Class Does Not Rule." In R. Quinney, ed. *Capitalist Society* (pp. 128–40). Homewood IL: Dorsey Press.

Brint, Stephen. (1984). "New Class and Cumulative Tend Explanations of the Liberal Political Attitudes of Professionals." *American Journal of Sociology*, 90, 30–71.

Brym, Robert J. (1979). "Political Conservatism in Atlantic Canada." In Robert J. Brym and R. James Sacouman, eds., *Underdevelopment and Social Movements in Atlantic Canada* (pp. 59–79). Toronto: New Hogtown Press.

Brym, Robert J. (1980). *Intellectuals and Politics*. London UK: Allen & Unwin.

Brym, Robert J. (1989). "Canada." In Tom Bottomore and Robert J. Brym, eds., *The Capitalist Class: An International Study* (pp. 177–206). New York: New York University Press.

Brym, Robert J. (2003). "Affluence, Srikes, and Power in Canada, 1973–2000." In James Curtis, Edward Grabb, and Neil Guppy, eds., *Social Inequality in Canada: Patterns, Problems, Policies*, 4th ed. Scarborough ON: Prentice-Hall Canada.

Casper, L.M., S.S. McLanahan, and I. Garfinkel. 1994. "The Gender-Poverty Gap: What Can We Learn from Other Countries?" *American Sociological Review*, 59, 594–605.

"Chronological Perspective on Work Stoppages in Canada." (1999). On the World Wide Web at http://labour.hrdc-drhc.gc.ca/doc/wid-dimt/eng/ws-at/table.cfm (30 June).

Clarke, Harold D., et al. (1996). *Absent Mandate: Canadian Electoral Politics In an Era of Restructuring*, 3rd ed. Toronto: Gage.

Clement, Wallace. (1975). *The Canadian Corporate Elite: An Analysis of Economic Power*. Toronto: McClelland and Stewart.

Crompton, Susan, Jonathan Ellison, and Kathryn Stevenson. (2002). "Better Things To Do or Dealt Out of the Game? Internet Dropouts and Infrequent Users." *Canadian Social Trends*, Summer, 2–5.

Dahl, Robert A. (1961). *Who Governs?* New Haven CT: Yale University Press.

Davies, James C. (1969). "Toward a Theory of Revolution." In Barry McLaughlin, ed. *Studies in Social Movements: A Social Psychological Perspective* (pp. 85–108). New York: Free Press.

Elections Canada On-Line. (2000). "Registered Political Parties' Fiscal Period Returns for 1997." On the World Wide Web at http://www.elections.ca/content.asp?section=fin&document=table03&dir=fis&lang=e&textonly=false (30 July 2002).

Evans, Peter B., Dietrich Rueschemeyer, and Theda Skocpol. (1985). *Bringing the State Back In*. Camdridge, UK: Cambridge University Press.

Frank, Jeffrey. (1994). "Voting and Contributing: Political Participation in Canada." In *Canadian Social Trends* (pp. 333–37). Toronto: Thompson Educational Publishers.

Goffman, Erving. (1974). *Frame Analysis*. Cambridge MA: Harvard University Press.

"Greenpeace Contacts Worldwide." (1999). On the World Wide Web at http://adam.greenpeace.org/information.shtml (29 April).

"GVU's WWW User Survey." (1999). On the World Wide Web at http://www.gvu.gatech.edu/user_surveys/survey-1998-10/graphs/graphs.html#general (23 September).

Hoffman, Donna L. and Thomas P. Novak. (1998). "Bridging the Racial Divide on the Internet." *Science*, 280, 390–91.

Hourani, Albert. (1991). *A History of the Arab Peoples*. New York: Warner Books.

Jenkins, J. Craig. (1983). "Resource Mobilization Theory and the Study of Social Movements." *Annual Review of Sociology*, 9, 527–53.

Kelley, Jack. (2001). "Terror Groups Hide Behind Web Encryption." *USA Today* (June 19). On the World Wide Web at http://www.usatoday.com/life/cyber/tech/2001-02-05-binladen.htm (13 September).

Korpi, Walter. (1983). *The Democratic Class Struggle*. London UK: Routledge & Kegan Paul.

Labour Organizations in Canada 1972. (1973). Ottawa: Economics and Research Branch, Canada Department of Labour. Cat. No. L2-2-1972.

Lipset, Seymour Martin. (1971 [1951]). *Agrarian Socialism: The Cooperative Commonwealth Federation in Saskatchewan*, revised ed. Berkeley CA: University of California Press.

Lipset, Seymour Martin. ([1960] 1981). *Political Man: The Social Bases of Politics*, 2nd ed. Baltimore: Johns Hopkins University Press.

Lodhi, Abdul Qaiyum, and Charles Tilly. (1973). "Urbanization, Crime, and Collective Violence in 19th Century France." *American Journal of Sociology*, 79, 296–318.

Marshall, T. H. (1965). "Citizenship and Social Class." In T. H. Marshall, ed., *Class, Citizenship, and Social Development: Essays by T. H. Marshall* (pp. 71–134). Garden City, NY: Anchor.

McCarthy, John D., and Mayer N. Zald. (1977). "Resource Mobilization and Social Movements: A Partial Theory." *American Journal of Sociology*, 82, 1212–41.

McCullogh, Declan. (2000). "Bin Laden: Steganography Master?" *Wired*, February 7. On the World Wide Web at http://www.wired.com/news/print/0.1294.41658.00.html (13 September 2001).

Melucci, Alberto. (1980). "The New Social Movements: A Theoretical Approach." *Social Science Information*, *19*, 199–226.

Melucci, Alberto. (1995). "The New Social Movements Revisited: Reflections on a Sociological Misunderstanding." In Louis Maheu, ed., *Social Classes and Social Movements: The Future of Collective Action* (pp. 107–19). London: Sage.

Miliband, Ralph. (1973 [1969]). *The State in Capitalist Society*. London: Fontana.

Mills, C. Wright. (1956). *The Power Elite*. New York: Oxford University Press.

Mishler, William. (1979). *Political Participation in Canada: Prospects for Democratic Citizenship*. Toronto: Macmillan.

Moore, Barrington, Jr. (1967). *Social Origins of Dictatorship and Democracy: Lord and Peasant in the Making of the Modern World*. Boston: Beacon.

"Muslim Brotherhood Movement Homepage." (2002). On the World Wide Web at http://www.ummah.org.uk/ikhwan/ (7 May).

Myles, John. (1989 [1984]). *Old Age in the Welfare State: The Political Economy of Public Pensions*, revised ed. Lawrence KS: University Press of Kansas.

1994–1995 Directory of Labour Organizations in Canada. (1995). Ottawa: Minister of Supply and Services Canada. Cat. No. L2-2-1995.

1998 Directory of Labour Organizations in Canada. (1998). Ottawa: Workplace Information Directorate.

Oberschall, Anthony. (1973). *Social Conflict and Social Movements*. Englewood Cliffs NJ: Prentice-Hall.

O'Connor, Julia S. (1996). "From Women in the Welfare State to Gendering Welfare State Regimes." *Current Sociology*, *44* (2), 1–130.

O'Connor, Julia S., and Robert J. Brym. (1988). "Public Welfare Expenditure in OECD Countries: Towards a Reconciliation of Inconsistent Findings." *British Journal of Sociology*, 39, 47–68.

O'Connor, Julia S. and Gregg M. Olsen, eds. (1998). *Power Resources Theory and the Welfare State: A Critical Approach*. Toronto: University of Toronto Press.

Olsen, Gregg. (2002). *The Politics of the Welfare State: Canada, Sweden, and the United States*. Toronto: Oxford University Press.

Olsen, Gregg, and Robert J. Brym. (1996). "Between American Exceptionalism and Swedish Social Democracy: Public and Private Pensions in Canada." In Michael Shalev, ed., *The Privatization of Social Policy? Occupational Welfare and the Welfare State in America, Scandinavia and Japan* (pp. 261–79). London: Macmillan.

Olsen, Dennis. (1980). *The State Elite*. Toronto: McClelland and Stewart.

Piven, Frances Fox, and Richard A. Cloward. (1989 [1988]). *Why Americans Don't Vote*. New York: Pantheon.

Polsby, Nelson W. (1959). "Three Problems in the Analysis of Community Power." *American Sociological Review*, 24, 796–803.

Porter, John. (1965). *The Vertical Mosaic: An Analysis of Social Class and Power in Canada*. Toronto: University of Toronto Press.

Poulantzas, Nicos. (1975 [1968]). *Political Power and Social Classes*. T. O'Hagan, trans. London: New Left Books.

Roche, Maurice. (1995). "Rethinking Citizenship and Social Movements: Themes in Contemporary Sociology and Neoconservative Ideology." In Louis Maheu, ed. *Social Classes and Social Movements: The Future of Collective Action* (pp. 186–219). London: Sage.

Rootes, Chris. (1995). "A New Class? The Higher Educated and the New Politics." In Louis Maheu, ed., *Social Classes and Social Movements: The Future of Collective Action* (pp. 220–35). London: Sage.

Shahar, Yael. (2001). "Tracing bin Laden's Money: Easier Said than Done." International Policy Institute for Counter-Terrorism. On the World Wide Web at http://www.ict.org.il/articles/articledet.cfm?articleid=387 (30 July 2002).

Skocpol, Theda. (1979). *States and Revolutions: A Comparative Analysis of France, Russia, and China*. Cambridge, UK: Cambridge University Press.

Smith, Jackie. (1998). "Global Civil Society? Transnational Social Movement Organizations and Social Capital." *American Behavioral Scientist*, 42, 93–107.

Snow, David A. et al. (1986). "Frame Alignment Processes, Micromobilization, and Movement Participation." *American Sociological Review*, 51, 464–81.

Snyder, David, and Charles Tilly. (1972). "Hardship and Collective Violence in France, 1830–1960." *American Sociological Review*, 37, 520–32.

Spilerman, Seymour. (1970). "The Causes of Racial Disturbances: A Comparison of Alternative Explanations." *American Sociological Review*, 35, 627–49.

Spilerman, Seymour. (1976). "Structural Characteristics of Cities and the Severity of Racial Disorders." *American Sociological Review*, 41, 771–93.

Strikes and Lockouts in Canada 1968. (1970). Ottawa: Economic and Research Branch, Canada Department of Labour. Cat. No. L2-1/1968.

Strikes and Lockouts in Canada 1985. (1985). Ottawa: Minister of Supply and Services Canada. Cat. No. L160-2999/85B.

Strong-Boag, Veronica. (1986). "Ever a Crusader: Nellie McClung, First-Wave Feminist." In V. Strong-Boag and A. Fellman, eds., *Rethinking Canada: The Promise of Women's History* (pp. 178–90). Toronto: Copp Clark Pitman.

Tarrow, Sidney. (1998 [1994]). *Power in Movement: Social Movements, Collective Action and Politics*, 2nd ed. Cambridge, UK: Cambridge University Press.

Tilly, Charles. (1978). *From Mobilization to Revolution*. Reading MA: Addison-Wesley.

Tilly, Charles. (1979a). "Collective Violence in European Perspective." In H. Graham and T. Gurr, eds., *Violence in America: Historical and Comparative Perspective*, 2nd ed. (pp. 83–118). Beverly Hills: Sage.

Tilly, Charles. (1979b). "Repertoires of Contention in America and Britain, 1750–1830." In Mayer N. Zald and John D. McCarthy, eds., *The Dynamics of Social Movements: Resource Mobilization, Social Control, and Tactics* (pp. 126–55). Cambridge, MA: Winthrop Publishers.

Tilly, Charles, Louise Tilly, and Richard Tilly. (1975). *The Rebellious Century, 1830–1930*. Cambridge, MA: Harvard University Press.

Turner, Bryan S. (1986). *Citizenship and Capitalism: The Debate over Reformism*. London, UK: Allen & Unwin.

"Union Membership in Canada—2000." (2000). *Workplace Gazette: An Industrial Relations Quarterly, 3* (3) 68–75.

Weber, Max. (1946 [1922]). "Class, Status, Party." In H. H. Gerth and C. Wright Mills, eds. and trans., *From Max Weber: Essays in Sociology* (pp. 180–95). New York: Oxford University Press.

Weber, Max. (1947). *The Theory of Social and Economic Organization*, T. Parsons, ed., A.M. Henderson and T. Parsons, trans. New York: Free Press.

Westen, Tracy. (1998). "Can Technology Save Democracy?" *National Civic Review*, 87, 47–56.

Wolf, Eric. (1999 [1969]). *Peasant Wars of the 20th Century*. Norman OK: Oklahoma University Press.

"Women—Federal Political Representation." (1999). On the World Wide Web at http://www.parl.gc.ca/36/rcfmat/library/womenrep-e.htm (23 September).

Workplace Information Directorate. (1996). Special Tabulation of Strikes Statistics for 1986–95. Ottawa: Human Resources Development Canada.

Worth, Robert. (2001). "The Deep Intellectual Roots of Islamic Terror." *The New York Times on the Web*. On the World Wide Web at http://www.nytimes.com (13 October).

NAME INDEX

SUBJECT INDEX

scientific practices, application of, 30
and social stratification, 184–185
Sociology of Religion (Weber), 157
Source Country Class refugees, 263
South Korea, 294–295
Soviet-style societies, and the environment, 422
space-biased media, 129, 153
spirituality
in Canada, 176
increase in, 155
needs, 169
split labour-market theory, 252–254, 269
sponsor effect, 143, 153
spurious connections, 33
spuriousness, 54
"squeegee kids," 393, 497
standard of living, increase in, 202
standard work, 228, 242
state, 521, 540
state-centred theory, 526–528, 540
Statistics Canada, 40, 48, 137, 203, 246, 334
statistical discrimination, 229, 243
statistical techniques, 51
status
achieved status, 185, 212
ascribed status. *See* ascribed status
defined, 89, 102, 185, 213
and education, 360
and family, 94
health status, 458–459
master status, 499
meritocracy, 186
occupational status attainment, 199
status-conflict perspective, 497–498, 516
status Indian, as term, 254
stereotypes
Aboriginal people, 257
defined, 269
the elderly, 92
elimination of, 89
and ethnicity, 261–262
gender-role, 89
gender stereotypes, 216–217, 224, 236
immigration and, 261–262
perpetuation by media, 97
and race, 261–262
strain theories, 500–501, 516
stratification. *See* social stratification
stratification theory. *See* social stratification theories
streaming, 372–374
structural adjustment programs (SAPs)
in Africa, 292
defined, 299
failure of, 284

imposition of, on Third World countries, 284
and neoliberal principles, 271
Western recolonization, 284
structural functionalism
criticisms of, 191
defined, 213, 329
emergence as alternative theoretical approach, 191
families, 307
problems with, 307
and social stratification, 190–191
structural mobility, 199, 213
structure-centred explanations of religious commitment, 167–169
The Structure of Scientific Revolutions (Kuhn), 31
subculture
and consumerism, 74
defined, 78, 82, 102, 516
deviance and, 499
youth subculture in Canada, 43
subjective social facts, 17
subjectivity, 30
suburbanism
class and life-cycle interpretation, 396
Don Mills model, 395, 396
dry-martini culture, 395
familism, 396
myth of suburbia, 396
vs. postmodern urban lifestyle, 399
selective migration, 396
structural interpretation, 396
urban-growth machine, 396–397
Suharto, 520
suicide
adolescents, 504
altruistic suicide, 24
anomic suicide, 24
in Canada today, 6–7
Durkheim's theory, 5–6
gender differences, 5, 6
guns, availability of, 503
married adults and, 6
and psychological disorders, rates of, 6
and social solidarity, degree of, 6, 7
sociological explanation, 5–6
statistics, 5
subjective social fact, 17
and symbolic interactionism, 17
and youth, 6–7
superstitions, 60
supranational institutions, 277, 299
surplus value, 188–189, 213
Survey of Consumer Finance (1997), 48
Survey of Labour and Income Dynamics, 203, 369

survey research
assumptions to avoid, 41–42
different units of observations, 42
and Internet, 38
interviews, 38
language, ambiguity of, 41
measurements, 38
random-digit-dialling, 40
reliability, 38
samples, 39–40
sampling frame, 40
self-administered questionnaire, 38, 40
telephone interviews, 40
usefulness of, 38
validity, 38
sustainable development, 412–413, 429
Sweden
development, 295–296
family support policies, 325
unions in, 524–526
Sydney tar ponds (Nova Scotia), 426
symbolic economy, 402, 406
symbolic interactionism
ability grouping, 372–374
cultural capital, 376
defined, 25, 102, 380
described, 16–17, 371
dramaturgical approach, 87–88
and education, 371–378
Goffman's approach, 87–88
language, 374–376
Mead, and foundation of, 85
microlevel framework, 363
self, definition of, 371
self-fulfilling prophecy, 372
society, definition of, 371–372
streaming, 372–374
teacher expectations, 372
tracking, 372–374
symbols, 60, 78, 85, 102
systemic discrimination, 251

T

Taber, Alberta shootings, 96, 500–503
taking the role of the other, 34–35, 86, 103
Taylorism, 344–345, 358
teacher expectations, 372
technological convergence, 135–136, 153
technological determinist, 129
technological perspective on media, 129
technology
as agent of socialization, 96–97
computers, and productivity, 343–344
detrimental effects on work, 341
as element of culture, 60
productivity paradox, 343–344
and rationalization of science, 64
and service industry, 341–344